EARLY MIDDLE ENGLISH
VERSE AND PROSE

EARLY MIDDLE ENGLISH VERSE AND PROSE

EDITED BY

J. A. W. BENNETT

AND

G. V. SMITHERS

WITH A GLOSSARY BY

NORMAN DAVIS

SECOND EDITION

OXFORD
AT THE CLARENDON PRESS

Oxford University Press, Ely House, London W. 1

GLASGOW NEW YORK TORONTO MELBOURNE WELLINGTON
CAPE TOWN IBADAN NAIROBI DAR ES SALAAM LUSAKA ADDIS ABABA
DELHI BOMBAY CALCUTTA MADRAS KARACHI LAHORE DACCA
KUALA LUMPUR SINGAPORE HONG KONG TOKYO

ISBN 0 19 811493 1

First published 1966
Second Edition 1968
Reprinted with corrections 1974

Printed in Great Britain
at the University Press, Oxford
by Vivian Ridler
Printer to the University

CONTENTS

EDITORIAL NOTE

THE texts contained in this volume, and the individual introductions and sections of Commentary for each, were divided between the two editors as follows:

I, VIII s–y, X–XIII, XVI, XIX: J. A. W. Bennett
II–VII, VIII a–r, IX, XIV–XV, XVII–XVIII: G. V. Smithers

The general Introduction is by the former; the section *Early Middle English*, and those on the *Orthography*, *Language*, *Vocabulary*, and *Provenance* (in the Commentary) of all the texts, are by the latter.

The editors wish to express their thanks for help given by Mr. C. J. E. Ball, Professor F. W. Baxter, Mr. R. W. Burchfield, Dr. A. I. Doyle, Mr. D. Gray, Mr. C. A. Ladd, and Professor M. L. Samuels, and for the generosity of the Librarian of the University of Edinburgh in lending microfilms, and of the Research Fund Committee of the University of Durham in assisting one of the editors.

Note to second edition, *ab erroribus olim commissis purgatior* (1968):

The editors wish to thank Mrs. A. S. C. Ross, Mr. J. A. Burrow, Professor S. R. T. O. d'Ardenne, Professor E. J. Dobson, Professor A. McIntosh, and Professor R. M. Wilson for corrections and suggestions, and Mr. S. J. Arthur of the British Museum for help given with one or two difficult readings.

Further corrections and some new findings (see, e.g., p. 246, n. 1) are incorporated in the present reprint (1974).

ABBREVIATIONS

1. *Key to Abbreviated Titles of Periodicals and some other Works*

Archiv	*Archiv für das Studium der neueren Sprachen*
Arch. Ling.	*Archivum Linguisticum*
C.T.	*Canterbury Tales*
Class. Phil.	*Classical Philology*
E. and S.	*Essays and Studies by Members of the English Association*
E.E.T.S.	*Early English Text Society* (OS = Original Series; ES = Extra Series)
E.G.S.	*English and Germanic Studies* (now named *English Philological Studies*)
F.E.W.	*Französisches etymologisches Wörterbuch*, ed. W. von Wartburg
Hav.	*Havelok the Dane*, ed. W. W. Skeat and revised by K. Sisam
Hist. Eccles.	Bede, *Historia Ecclesiastica*
J.E.G.P.	*Journal of English and Germanic Philology*
L.S.E.	*Leeds Studies in English*
M.Æ.	*Medium Ævum*
M.E.D.	*Middle English Dictionary*, ed. H. Kurath, S. M. Kuhn, and J. Reidy.
Migne, *P.L.*	*Patrologia Latina*, ed. Migne
M.L.N.	*Modern Language Notes*
M.L.R.	*Modern Language Review*
Mod. Phil.	*Modern Philology*
Mon. Germ. Hist.	*Monumenta Germaniae Historica*
N. & Q.	*Notes and Queries*
N.T.	*New Testament*
O. & N.	*The Owl and the Nightingale*
O.E.D.	*Oxford English Dictionary*
O.T.	*Old Testament*
P.L.	see Migne, *P.L.*
PMLA	*Publications of the Modern Language Association*

R. de Ren.	*Roman de Renart*
R.E.S.	*The Review of English Studies*
S.A.T.F.	*Société des Anciens Textes Français*
Trans. Phil. Soc.	*Transactions of the Philological Society*
Trans. Roy. Hist. Soc.	*Transactions of the Royal Historical Society*

2. *Other Abbreviations*

Angl.	Anglian (variety of Old English)
AN	Anglo-Norman
Bodl.	Bodleian Library
C.C.C.C.	Corpus Christi College, Cambridge
Du	Dutch
EMidl	East Midland(s)
edd.	editors
Gmc	Germanic
Gl	Glossary
Kt	Kentish
(L)OE	(Late) Old English
L	Latin
(L)G	(Low) German
Merc	Mercian (variety of Old English)
MDu	Middle Dutch
MKt	Middle Kentish
MLG	Middle Low German
ModE	Modern English
NEMidl	North-East Midland(s)
NMidl	North Midland(s)
North	Northern
Nb	Northumbrian (variety of Old English)
OE	Old English
OF	Old French
OHG	Old High German
OIcel	Old Icelandic
OEN	Old East Norse
OIr	Old Irish
OKt	Old Kentish (variety of Old English)
ON	Old Norse
ONb	Old Northumbrian (variety of Old English)
OWN	Old West Norse

SE	South-East(ern)
SW	South-West(ern)
SWMidl	South-West Midland(s)
VPs	Vespasian Psalter
WMerc	West Mercian (variety of Old English)
WMidl	West Midland(s)
WS	West Saxon (variety of Old English)

<	from, deriving from
>	became, becomes
*	hypothetical etymon or form not actually recorded

c.	Latin *circa*
cf.	Latin *confer*
ead.	Latin *eadem*
ibid.	Latin *ibidem*
loc. cit.	Latin *loco citato*
n. (commonly in conjunction with a line reference)	note (e.g. in commentary here)
ob.	Latin *obiit*
s.a.	Latin *sub anno*
s.v.	Latin *sub voce*
v.	(i) Latin *vide* (ii) *verb*

INTRODUCTION

T HE growth of literature in these islands has been affected in a decisive way by two battles: Hastings and Flodden Field. It could be argued that of the two Flodden was the more disastrous, since long before the Conquest English culture and institutions of learning had become conservative if not sterile;[1] that many of the changes often attributed to William's victory would have occurred in any case as the Norman orbit widened;[2] and that the sheer need to communicate preserved certain media as links between conquerors and conquered.[3] It is clear that in at least two areas some literary traditions remained unbroken. At Worcester the saintly Saxon Wulfstan was left on his episcopal throne, and under his aegis, as for long afterwards, the recopying or modernizing of the classical Old English homilies continued, presumably in response to demand; whilst his biography (now lost) was perhaps the first to be written in the vernacular. At Peterborough, cut off as it was from the main life of the Midlands by the fens in which Hereward made his last stubborn resistance, 'the good abbot Martin', though a Norman (see p. 209 below), did not object to his abbey's annals being preserved in English: had his successor been as satisfactory

---

[1] Surviving pre-conquest manuscripts from Christ Church, Canterbury, include not a single volume of basic patristic theology and show not the slightest interest in the new scholastic disciplines that were stimulating scholastic activity in France. Those manuscripts in late OE or glossed in OE reveal a low standard of Latin and an insularity of taste: R. W. Southern, *Saint Anselm and his Biographer* (1963), p. 243.

[2] Edward the Confessor had already introduced French-speaking courtiers (and collated Norfolk villages to the Abbey of S. Riquier).

[3] William evidently took over the chancery in its entirety, and he continued to issue vernacular writs: R. R. Darlington, *The Norman Conquest* (1963), p. 5.

an abbot, the record might have continued much longer. At Rochester, too, Anglo-Saxon texts were still being used, and altered, in the twelfth century,[1] and entries were made in English in a Winchester chronicle as late as 1183. A little earlier, at Christ Church, Canterbury, English glosses were inserted into that masterpiece of native art, the Psalter of Eadwine; they stand alongside a French gloss (providing the earliest of French psalters) and a Latin marginal gloss that typifies the impact of twelfth-century continental learning.[2]

Yet such evidence, and such arguments, hardly impugn the traditional view that the reigns of William and his sons mark an hiatus in our literature and in the widespread literary use of the vernacular that is such a distinctive feature of Anglo-Saxon culture. William not only brought Norman soldiers and Norman monks, Norman civilization and Norman feudalism to English soil: he made England part of Normandy. One result was the creation of a new dialect and a new literature—Anglo-Norman.[3] Another was to make writers in England far more susceptible to literary influences from northern France than they might otherwise have been. Before the end of the twelfth century Latin writers like Reginald of Canterbury and Geoffrey of

[1] When interesting linguistic alterations were made in the Textus Roffensis and in the Ælfrician MSS. Bodley 340, 342; from Rochester may come C.C.C.C. 303, a copy of these manuscripts. A Latin sermon by Ralph d'Escures, a Bishop of Rochester who became Archbishop of Canterbury in 1114, was translated into English: see N. R. Ker, *Catalogue of MSS. containing Anglo-Saxon* (1957), p. 275. Dr. Ker notes that the Augustinian priory of Southwick (Hants) founded in 1133 owned several OE manuscripts: op. cit., pp. 234, 280, 361.

[2] See the facsimile edition by M. R. James, 1935. Eadwine evidently wrote a work in English that is now lost (ibid., p. 1). The English part of the Canterbury monastic community survived as a distinct element till *c.* 1150 and a twelfth-century Canterbury manuscript like Cotton Caligula A.xv preserves the miscellaneous interests and even physical appearance of pre-conquest books: Ker, op. cit., pp. 275–6.

[3] See M. Dominica Legge, *Anglo-Norman Literature and its Background* (1963).

Winchester bear, it is said, the impress of the new Latin poetry emanating from the valley of the Loire.[1] As Latin became the dominant literary medium the prestige of native verse and prose declined; and England was now cut off from Scandinavian influences that might have encouraged the growth of a native saga-prose. For such prose—indeed for vernacular prose of any sort—neither Normandy nor France could provide models or inspiration. On the other hand, the new and strong ties with the Continent meant that England was to be touched by every important religious movement, from the Cistercian to the Franciscan, with effects clearly recognizable in literature and thought. Eventually there resulted a fused 'Channel' culture in which English, Norman, and French contributions, whether in style or stained glass, in the architecture of cathedrals or the construction of romances, are often indistinguishable. Typical of the interwoven character of this culture is the history of St. Edmund's *Speculum Ecclesie* (see p. 333): written in French by an archbishop born at Abingdon and acquainted with English devotional poetry, it was dedicated to the monks of Pontigny; it was soon translated into Latin, and ultimately into English, and thus came to influence the contemplatives of whom Richard Rolle was chief.

How the fusion of cultures proceeded we can also see from the career of Wace, the clerical author of the French verse *Brut*. Born in Jersey about the year 1100, he went first to Caen, thence to the Île de France, thence again to Caen. The Abbey of Caen possessed lands in Dorset, and several local allusions in his *Brut* (which was dedicated to Eleanor, wife of Henry II) suggest that Wace knew more of southern England than did Geoffrey of Monmouth, author of the *Historia Regum Britanniae*, his chief source. Yet Wace would not need to come to England to find a

---

[1] C. H. Haskins, *The Renaissance of the Twelfth Century* (1927, repr. 1957), p. 28.

copy of the *Historia* since Henry of Huntingdon came upon one in the abbey of Bec about 1139—a few years after its composition.[1] Again, the first French historian, Gaimar, evidently knew enough English to draw on two versions of the Anglo-Saxon Chronicle whilst preparing his verse *Estorie des Engleis*. In what language wrote the nun of Norman birth 'inclyta versificatione' who was buried at Wilton in 1133 we cannot say. But there is no reason to doubt the word of the first French poetess Marie de France who, writing some sixty years later, tells us that she was born in France (possibly meaning the Île de France) and translated her Fables from English into French ('de l'engleis en romanz'). It seems probable that she lived and wrote in England; the only complete manuscript of her *lais* is in Anglo-Norman; and we owe to her the knowledge that the *fable* existed in England—in oral, if not written form—at If these English fables were, like hers, in verse, it wou the appearance in the twelfth century of such an accomp vernacular poem as *The Owl and the Nightingale* a t surprising. The writer of the Anglo-Norman romance likewise avouches an English source; and in the thirteenth tury even a work of *courtoisie*, the *débat Blancheflour et Flo* claims to have a similar origin:

> Banastre en engleis le fist
> E Brykhulle cest escrit
> En franceois translata.[2]

[1] It was about this time that the Cistercian migration to Yorkshire which was to have such important cultural and economic consequences aroused St. Bernard's interest in England: in one of his letters pleads the cause of the Crusade with Englishmen and in part English merchants (*Letters*, ed. and trans. B. Scott James (1 no. 391).

[2] For comment on these lines and the identification of 'Brykhulle' with a canon of Hereford see Legge, op. cit., p. 334. The theme of *courtoisie* in AN literature has been studied by C. B. West in a *Medium Ævum* monograph (1938).

Though works in Anglo-Norman or Anglo-French (they included an early massbook for the laity, now lost) lie outside the scope of this book, it must never be forgotten that inasmuch as they were written for use in England they form part of the English literary heritage. A twelfth-century dramatic masterpiece, *Le Jeu d'Adam*, is certainly earlier than any surviving play in French. By the end of the century religious plays were being performed regularly in London, and fifty years later Bishop Grosseteste found them dangerously popular.[1] Whether the *Interludium de Clerico et Puella* should be called a play has been reasonably doubted; but here it is enough to note that this lively entertainment bears no trace of foreign origins.[2] That by the end of the thirteenth century England was exercising an influence on French religious literature is suggested by recent research into the numerous French versions of the Miracles of the Virgin, the earliest of which may well have been made from an English original.[3] Again, the English contribution to verse and prose, secular and religious, was never more marked than in the two centuries after the Conquest, one of the chief effects of which was to increase the clerkly element in the population. Two of the ablest theologians in twelfth-century Paris were Englishmen: Stephen Langton and Robert of Melun;[4] and English, despite his name, was Geoffroi de

---

[1] It was a Norman clerk at St. Albans who prepared a 'ludus de Sancta Katarina' for performance at Dunstable *c.* 1100: see E. K. Chambers, *The Medieval Stage* (1903), ii. 366 (and ibid. i. 91 for Grosseteste). For *Le Jeu d'Adam* see Grace Frank, *The Medieval French Drama* (1954), pp. 76–84.

[2] For a dramatic fragment that may be earlier see *MLN* lxv (1950), 70. For the later 'Shrewsbury fragments' of religious plays in which some Latin speeches have English renderings, see Hardin Craig, *English Religious Drama of the Middle Ages* (1955), pp. 97–98, and *Non-Cycle Plays and Fragments*, ed. N. Davis, E.E.T.S., s.s. 1 (1970).

[3] See R. W. Southern, *Medieval and Renaissance Studies*, iv (1958), 176–216.

[4] See R. W. Hunt, *Trans. Roy. Hist. Soc.* (1936), pp. 23–24.

Vinsauf whose treatise on rhetoric (*Nova Poetria*) was still influential in Chaucer's day.

The very copiousness of clerkly and monastic Latin prose may have hindered the development of vernacular equivalents. But in macaronic hymn and song Latin, French, and English lie happily side by side. Such verse was a favourite form of the *clerici vagantes*, amongst whom English clerks certainly figured; and that by the end of the twelfth century English professional minstrels were known for their wide repertoire is suggested by an incident in the Provençal *Flamença*: a character acting the part of an English jongleur says, 'I know good Breton lays of Merlin and Noton, King Arthur and Tristan, Marie's Chevrefoil and the Voyage of St Brendan'. Twelfth-century love-lyrics in English are hard to find; but the refrain of one of them survives in a revealing story told by Giraldus Cambrensis: a Worcestershire priest having listened all night to people singing a love-song in his churchyard so far forgot himself at mass next morning as to intone, instead of *Dominus vobiscum*, the refrain 'swete lamman dhin are' (*þin ore*). A sermon written late in the following century begins with a quotation from a song sung during a ring-dance, or carole:

> Atte wrastlinge my lemman I ches
> And atte ston-kasting I him forles.[1]

If we identify the song that William of Malmesbury heard at the crossroads in the mid-twelfth century with the ballad of Sir Aldingar[2] then we can trace the native ballad further back than the native carol. When in 1296 the Lowlanders of Berwick drove off Edward I and burnt some of his ships they sang their

[1] See R. L. Greene, *The Early English Carols* (1935), pp. xxxv, cxvii, and *Secular Lyrics of the XIVth and XVth Centuries*, ed. R. H. Robbins (2nd edn., 1954), p. xxxix. See also p. 321 below. [The date given by Greene is corrected by E. J. Dobson, *The English Text of the Ancrene Riwle* (E.E.T.S., 267, 1970), p. cxlvii, n. 3.]

[2] See W. J. Entwistle, *Saga Book of the Viking Society*, XIII. ii (1947–8), 97–112. A more intelligible version is found in C.U.L. MS. Ii. 3. 8, f. 87.

triumph in verses such as this one preserved in Fabyan's Chronicle:

> What wenys Kynge Edward with longe shankys
> To have wonne Berwyk all our onthankys?
> > Gaas pykes him,
> > And when hath it
> > Gaas dykeis him.[1]

And scattered in other chronicles are earlier fragments of speech and song that give us more of the pith of native speech than do formal writings—like the 'Schort red, god red, slea ye the bischop' cited by Roger of Wendover as the cry of the murderers of the Bishop of Durham at Gateshead in 1080.[2]

It is still commonly suggested that the most distinctive features of Anglo-Saxon literature—the elaborate, formulaic verse and the alliterative measure—disappeared with the Conquest, not to be revived till the fourteenth century (thereafter alliterative verse flourished in the north till the disaster of Flodden itself). Certainly there was no longer any place for this polished and courtly verse in its traditional setting of royal palace or noble hall. Certainly, too, the alliterative verse found in Laȝamon's *Brut* at the beginning of the thirteenth century is markedly different from the verse of *Beowulf* and of Cynewulf. But there are indications that a looser, simpler, and more 'popular' alliterative line had begun to develop in the late Old English period; and this kind of verse might well have become in a different cultural context a serious rival to the 'classical'. A few fragments composed after the Conquest, and of little merit, survive in a late twelfth-century manuscript at Worcester. It was from Worcestershire that Laȝamon came, and he probably

[1] Edward is said to have helped at digging during the siege. For other versions of the rhyme see Legge, op. cit., pp. 352–3.

[2] See *Flores Historiarum* (1841), ii. 17; but *slea we* (Matthew Paris, *Hist. Angl.*) is a better reading. R. M. Wilson has collected several such fragments in *The Lost Literature of Medieval England* (2nd edn., 1970), c. 9.

knew verse of this kind, either as written or recited. His *Brut* was probably over 13,000 lines long when complete, and a scribe must have been sure of an audience, if only a clerkly one, before he undertook such a labour. The writers of the four-teenth-century poems on *Alexander* and the *Destruction of Troy* are far more regular in rhythm and alliteration than Laȝamon; but it may well have been his example that prompted them to turn pseudo-historical works into English alliterative verse.

One other kind of alliterative writing survived the Conquest —the loose alliterative prose employed so effectively by Ælfric in his Saints' Lives. It is in the Lives of the Saints Margaret, Katherine and Juliana, written for 'alle leawede men þe under-stonden ne muhen latines ledene' that this poetic prose reappears with the alliteration increased till it becomes tedious. But it also had its influence on works more restrained in style—the *Ancrene Wisse* and the *Sawles Warde*, notably in the passages on the beatific vision, a theme traditionally treated in this poetic fashion.

When and where English returned to the pulpit cannot be said with precision. Samson, Abbot of Bury St. Edmunds from 1185 to 1211, the hero of Carlyle's *Past and Present*, could read the scriptures aloud in English 'most attractively', says his bio-grapher—leaving us to guess that he translated extempore from the Vulgate—'and was wont to preach [to the monks?] in the Norfolk dialect'. Grosseteste, from 1235 to 1253 Bishop of Lin-coln (a vast diocese in the Middle Ages), taking to heart the pre-scriptions of the Lateran Council of 1215, encouraged all his clergy to preach in English, just as John Peckham, Archbishop of Canterbury from 1279 to 1292, enjoined that a priest should instruct his parishioners in the vulgar tongue. The incident described by Robert of Gloucester (see p. 161, below) shows how ill it fared in the reign of Henry III with a French bishop who did not speak English. English was evidently the language normally used by the well-born anchoresses to whom the *Ancrene Riwle* was addressed. Yet the existence of a version of this Rule in French suggests that others were more at ease in that language; and the nuns of Lacock Abbey still read their rule in 'Old' French up to the time of the Dissolution.

A student of literature should bear in mind that it was not only the English language but also the English landscape that in the two centuries after the Conquest began to take on its present aspect. This book opens with a nightingale singing 'in one hurne of one breche'. The line should remind us not merely of the delight in nature that characterizes early English song but also of the conquest of the forest that had been going on ever since the Normans came. With the clearing of the forest came new settlements, new parishes, new churches—the towns, parishes, and churches that for the most part still survive, however deformed or transformed, peopled still by the descendants of those men and women for whose benefit and whose delight the texts presented here were first composed. In reading them we should also remember that they were written down under conditions that by modern standards were unbearably austere: in stuffy rooms or cold cloisters. Parchment was dear, pens needed constant mending. Every scribe would have sympathized with friar Osbern Bokenham, fifteenth-century versifier of Saints' Legends:

> . . . My penne also gynnyth make obstacle
> And lyst no lengere on paper to renne,
> For I so ofte haue maad to grenne
> Hys snowte vpon my thombys ende
> That he ful ny is waxyn vnthende.[1]

[1] *Legendys of Hooly Wummen* (EETS, o.s. 206 (1938), p. 25, ll. 898–902) [*unthende* = poor, of bad quality].

ADDENDA

p. xxxvi, l. 12, after 'pronoun':

'; though *-es* was used in all persons if the verb was separated from the pronoun (e.g. in an adjectival or co-ordinate clause).'

p. 324, *Studies*: R. Woolf, 'The Construction of In a Fryht as I con fare fremede', *M.Æ.* xxxviii (1969), pp. 55–9.

p. 369, l. **109**:

The equivalent of l. 109 in the Latin *Legende* in the copy of MS. Gg. 4. 25 ff. of the Cambridge University Library (printed by Miss B. Hill, *M.Æ.* xxxiv (1965), p. 213, para. 3), reads: *ad Cherubin in Paradiso qui custodit atrium ligni vite.* Thus *ward* here is not, as in l. 256, the second element of a noun-compound *yateward*, but the 3 pr. sg. indic. of the verb *warde(n)* 'to guard'. The uninflected form is paralleled in *breid* XVIII. 175, *vind* V. 253, *ifind* XVIII. 541, 599, and *stand* p. 369, l. 107, of C. Horstmann, *Altenglische Legenden* (Neue Folge, 1881). Each example is a verb whose root ends in the voiced dental plosive *d*.

p. 405, ll. **46–47**:

þine leoueste freond: a genitive, in apposition to *þi*, as the OF versions represent it (Tr. 21, 2; H 164, 1). This is an example of a syntactic idiom common from ME until recent times, in which a second possessive form in apposition (or similar relation) to a previous one is unmarked. Cf. *The Miller's Tale C.T.* A 3257–8:

> But of *hir* song, it was as loude and yerne
> As *any swalwe* sittynge on a berne

and *Macbeth*, II. i. 34:

> *his* soldiership
> is twice *the other twain*

and see O. Jespersen, *Progress in Language* (1894), paras. 234–6.

EARLY MIDDLE ENGLISH

THE question 'What marks off Middle English from Old English?', which sounds a reasonable and proper one, proves to be unanswerable in that form. The changes that go really deep in the language up to 1400 (in both the written and the spoken form), and whose effects go really deep in English since 1400, are changes in accidence. As a result of the drastic simplification of the system of endings,[1] grammatical gender was eliminated, and case ceased to be expressed by endings. It is these things that one commonly thinks of as the distinctive characteristics of 'Middle' English; and what one commonly forgets is that they occur in a well-developed stage in the Northumbrian 'Old' English of the Lindisfarne Gospels in the late tenth century.

This last fact should not surprise us: it means merely that, even when the same linguistic changes are at work in more than one speech-community using the same language, the rate of change may vary considerably.[2] But it does show that the question posed above must be re-formulated: 'What marks off any given form of Middle English from the antecedent form of Old English?' It exposes as a fallacy the implicit or half-conscious assumption that there is such a thing as 'Middle English', isolable as such from 'Old English'—each being implied to be a single and invariable form of the English language. In fact,

---

[1] The ultimate effect of this (after final -e had been discarded, soon after 1400) was that double consonants were virtually eliminated from the language (since, for example, *dogge* > *dog*) and the number of monosyllables thereby greatly increased in post-medieval English.

[2] Another possible example of this is the retention of grammatical gender in the South-East (e.g. in the *Ayenbite of Inwyt*, as in XVII here) till over 200 years after it had been discarded in the East Midlands (in the *Peterborough Chronicle*).

the term 'Middle English', as normally used, is a summary and loose mode of reference to a conglomeration of widely differing *written* versions of English, spread over a large area and at least three centuries in time (1100–1400).

The example of the Lindisfarne Gospels is a warning that the date of the Norman Conquest may have no essential bearing on the emergence of 'Middle' English. And since all the materials for our knowledge of ME are written records, it follows that to speak of the 'dialect' (without further definition) of a ME document is likewise loose and misleading. If every ME work of substantial length were extant in precisely the form in which the author had set it down, it might (in some circumstances) faithfully reproduce the accidence and the phonology of a spoken form of ME. But it would inevitably be (*a*) a more formal variety of the language than the spoken one, and (*b*) the English of one man rather than of a community, i.e. an 'idiolect'.

The scope of the first of these two factors naturally varies with the character of the work in question, the literary and intellectual cultivation of the author, and so on. Someone translating a didactic treatise, or even simply-written sermons, from Old French would inevitably introduce from his source some words or syntactic features not previously used in English (and some of these not destined to get into general use in speech or even in literature). On the other hand, the *Ancrene Wisse*, with its relaxed tone and intermittently conversational style, gives us scraps of colloquial idiom and syntax that are not matched in the more formal writing of Orm. And its vocabulary is relatively rich in 'ideophonic' formations[1]—which are words that belong first and foremost to spoken usage.

So far as the second factor is concerned, we cannot hope to

---

[1] On the nature of these, see 'Some English Ideophones', *Archivum Linguisticum*, vi (1954), 73–111.

know at all points what is individual and what is the usage of the community in a given ME work. But the margin of ignorance can be reduced. If it turns out that the phonology and the accidence of a post-Conquest document are closely matched in others of the same period, and especially in those of an OE work, and if it is clear that their form of English is not a literary 'standard' (which in the nature of things might spread far beyond the area of its origin), the language in question is likely to be a substantially accurate version of the phonology and accidence of a local variety of spoken ME.

To distinguish and characterize the local varieties of English (spoken or written) is not the be-all and end-all of ME studies. It is more important to ascertain the major structural characteristics of the main varieties of ME, and to understand how and why these characteristics came into being. The issues formulated above bear on both these tasks. The one other essential preliminary is to understand what constitutes admissible evidence for both. The ideal ME document for this purpose is an extensive work extant in an autograph (or author's) manuscript, and placed in space and time by an explicit statement of the author or by equally valid external or internal evidence. The only one that meets these requirements is the *Ayenbite of Inwyt*, which its author tells us he composed in Canterbury in 1340. The only others that come near to doing so are the *Ancrene Wisse* (along with certain works in MS. Bodley 34)[1] and the *Ormulum*: the former appears to be in a language maximally consistent and minimally remote from the author's, and the latter survives in an autograph manuscript, though neither is localized or dated for us. These three groups of material, and only these, must be the basis for a valid conception of regional or other varieties of ME,[2] as of individual

[1] Viz. *Sawles Warde*, *St. Juliene*, *St. Margarete*, *St. Katherine* and *Hali Meiðhad*, which are composed in the same form of ME.

[2] Though the forthcoming study of unpublished material by Prof.

systems of accidence, stressed vowels and diphthongs, and vocabulary as they actually existed and functioned. The information they yield is an indispensable control for the critical analysis of works in the extant form of which the author's language is blurred or covered by strata of scribal forms that differ from his own.

Late OE manuscripts, copied *c.* A.D. 1000 onwards, are sprinkled with spellings in which either back vowel (*a* or *u*, the latter being commonly spelt *o* in later OE) in an unstressed final syllable may be written for the other, and *e* for either of them (or either for *e*). This can mean only one thing: all these vowels had merged in pronunciation into a single one, whatever its phonetic value (e.g. [e] or [ə]).

It also means that many of the grammatical endings of OE were now unserviceable—since most of the endings of nouns, for example, had consisted solely of one of these vowels, and were therefore now no longer differentiated from other endings. For instance, in the OE system of inflexions there had been six ways of marking plurality in the subject and object cases of nouns: *-as*, *-u* or zero (in short- or long-stemmed neuters), *-e*, *-a*, *-an*, and *i*-mutation of the root-vowel or diphthong, as in *dagas*, *scipu/word*, *giefe*, *suna*, *guman*, and *bec*. After the reduction of all the vowels in question to [ə], spelt *-e* in final unstressed syllables, only *-es* and *-en* were still distinctive (because of the consonant) and therefore efficient as endings; in the nature of things, they alone could effectively survive.

In what followed, in all forms of ME, endings which were still distinctive were generalized, and replaced those which were now ineffective. Thus *-es* and *-en* in some varieties of ME became the main or the only signs marking plurality in nouns—

A. McIntosh and Prof. M. L. Samuels is likely to enlarge the stock of precisely localizable documents of first-class evidential value.

i.e. they were substituted for the -*e* which in many classes of nouns was the historically regular form in the subject and object cases and the genitive (OE -*a* or -*ena*), and (by processes explained below) they were adopted in functions proper to the old dative. In the most economical type of system, -*es* was virtually the sole sign marking plurality and the genitive singular. Hence, in most varieties of ME, the inflexion of nouns (other than a few mutated ones) had been reduced to two simple patterns, if not one, which derive (A) from the masculine *o*-declension, and (B) from the feminine *a*-declension and weak nouns:

		A	B		
Sg.	N.	kyng	sunne		
	A.	kyng	sunne		
	G.	kynges	sunne		
	D.	kyng	sunne		
Pl.	N.	kynges	*Either* (i) sunnen	*or*	(ii) sunnes
	A.	kynges	sunnen		sunnes
	G.	kynges	sunnen		sunnes
	D.	kynges	sunnen		sunnes

In the process by which the number of endings (and hence of distinct cases) in nouns was drastically reduced, the details are obscure. A main point is that the old dat. sg. and pl. became identical in form with the subject and object case of sg. and pl. respectively, in which latter pairs both members were already identical in some noun-classes of OE. Thus, in nouns of the type *kyng*, this form replaced *kynge* (OE *cyninge*) in functions proper to the old dative; and in the *sunne* type, *synne* (the form of all the oblique cases in OE) replaced *synn* as a subject form—no doubt because nouns of the *synn* class with short root-syllable had -*e* in the subject case by normal phonetic development (OE *giefu*) as well as in the oblique ones.

Both these two major examples of 'syncretism' (i.e. merging of two cases under one ending) are consistently displayed in the

language of the *Ancrene Wisse*; and in addition, examples of
final -*e* other than those in the second category are historically
regular (e.g. from the -*en* < OE -*an* of old weak nouns):

   (i) *of (ed) ure Lauerd* XVIII. 34, 58, *of þin ahne deað* 16,
     in hare hus 54, *to þet þing* 27.

   (ii) *þurh Godes ʒeoue* 73, *to þe sawle* 96, *þurh sunne* 121 (all
     synn-class), and *on eorðe* 134, *i þe heorte* 39 (old weak
     nouns).

A different and specially important development of these
old dat. sg. forms is illustrated in the *Ormulum*. Old mono-
syllabic masculines and neuters of this class actually have two
forms, with and without -*e* respectively, in functions corresponding to those of the old dative, and therefore also in the
subject and object case: *dæþ, dæþe; king, kinge; lac, lake; land,
lande*, &c. In one instance, a further step is represented in the
use, in all three types of function, of an endingless form as well
as one with -*e* in a noun in which only the latter is historically
regular: *le(o)m, le(o)me* (< OE *leoma*, oblique *leoman*). The
momentous implications of this material from the *Ormulum*
are explained below (pp. xxviii–xxx).

In some varieties of ME in which -*en* was retained as a
plural ending of nouns, it is historically regular in the functions of the old dative as well as in the subject and the object
case, since -*an* had begun to replace -*um* in the dat. pl. in OE.
The signs are that this was not a phonetic change (of final -*m*
to -*n*),[1] but an analogical process (with OE -*an* levelled into
the dat. pl. from the nom. and accus. pl., first in weak nouns
and adjectives, and thence in other classes of nouns).[2] The

----

[1] Notwithstanding S. Moore, 'Earliest Morphological Changes in
Middle English' (*Language*, iv (1928), 238–66), p. 248 and n. 18.

[2] It is highly significant that, as Luick has pointed out (*Historische
Grammatik der englischen Sprache*, § 697 and n.), already in Alfredian
prose there are a number of forms in -*an* for the dat. pl. of the weak

normal phonetic development of OE *-an* in the *Ormulum* is to
-en (*biforenn, sippenn, wipputenn,* &c.); while unstressed final
-um of OE is intact in at least one example, *aðum* 'son-in-law'
(even if one discounts the dat. pl. *-malum* in *wukemalum* 'at
intervals of a week' as being an adoption from ON).

Next, the *Ormulum* establishes that:

(*a*) In this language (and hence in varieties of ME with the
same type of accidence), in the A declension *-es* was
levelled into the gen. pl. not from the subject and object
cases but from the gen. sg. Orm uses *freondess, ӡeress,
menness, shepess* as genitives of the plural; and since his
forms of the subject and object cases in the plural are
the historically regular *freond, ӡer, menn, shep,* the former
must derive from the gen. sg. (which in OE was *-es* in
all four).

(*b*) This came about through the very common occurrence
of the genitive (sg. and pl.) in what became in ME
a virtually adjectival function. This new function turned
on the fact that in OE a dependent genitive preceded the
word that governed it (*heofona cyning,* &c.). When vowel
endings had all been reduced to [ə], spelt *-e,* the first
element in this type of collocation might end in *-e* (< OE
gen. pl. *-a* or gen. sg. *-e, -a*), *-es* (< OE gen. sg. *-es*), or
-ene (< OE gen. pl. *-ena*). All these were felt as equivalents in ME, and (because of the word-order) as primarily
adjectival in function. One of the symptoms of this is
that both *-es* and *-e* are used in the singular and in the
plural (occasionally even in the same word) in the
Ormulum: *off ure* (*ӡure*) *sawle nede* beside *off ure* (*ӡure*)
sawless nede, and (*ӡe*) *neddre streon* 'generation of vipers'

adjective (in which *-an* was the ending of nearly all the other cases of
the plural and nearly all those of the singular), while there are fewer
such in the strong adjective inflexion.

beside *neddress streon*. In examples of this sort (which are common in ME), number is no longer strongly felt as an element in the meaning of the genitival *-es* and *-e*. And since this *-es* is the only differentiated form in the singular of the main types of noun paradigm, it is clear that case is no longer marked by endings in nouns. In fact, it is, though convenient, somewhat misleading to set out those endings in paradigms of the traditional type.

The inflexion of adjectives is most profitably studied in the *Ormulum*, the rigid syllable-counting metre of which makes it possible to prove that a final *-e* cannot have been pronounced in given instances. In this work (i) the subject case is the sole form used for all 'cases'; (ii) the OE distinction between 'strong' and 'weak' inflexion has left a solitary but important trace. The subject case (*a*) is normally endingless or ends in *-e* (according as the OE antecedent was endingless or ended in a vowel) after the indefinite article; as the sole attribute word; or as predicate—*god* beside *clene*; (*b*) ends in *-e* in attribute use after the definite article, demonstratives, and possessives: *þe alde mann*, &c.; (iii) *-e* is used to mark the plural in both types of flexion.

In all these points the language of the *Ancrene Wisse* in its extant form is substantially the same, though this work is so much more conservative than the *Ormulum* in other areas of the accidence, and though the use of final *-e* in prose texts might normally be expected to be disastrously blurred by scribes.

A point of the utmost importance is that, in both types of flexion specified under (ii), a few words have both the endingless and the *-e* form in identical conditions. In the two instances of the half-line *god heorrte annd aȝȝ god wille* (3383 and 3929), *gode* was originally written for the second *god*; but it was corrected to *god*, and *aჳჳ* was inserted to give the extra syllable needed. The same was done in lines 3955 and 3969:

> annd habbenn aჳჳ god wille
> þat hafeþþ aჳჳ god wille

and it was clearly by an oversight that l. 3967 still reads *þat hafeþþ gode wille*.

What all this means is that:

(i) when the text was written, *god* and *gode* were fully equivalent forms of the object case in conditions corresponding to the OE strong inflexion. In the abundant other examples of this in the *Ormulum*, it is clear that the choice between the two was made purely on rhythmic and not on grammatical grounds, as for *leme* and *lem* above. And it was a matter of speech rhythm, not merely of verse rhythm: two successive full stresses were avoided. In other words, -*e* was here not (as in nouns) a grammatical ending at all (though it still serves as one in marking the plural of adjectives)

(ii) within Orm's lifetime, the need for the -*e* was no longer felt, and it had already begun to be discarded.

Till these facts were observed and nearly all correctly interpreted ten years ago,[1] the nature and use of final -*e* were not understood. Because of its origins, one inevitably supposes it to have been a grammatical sign, used, for example, in nouns, adjectives, and adverbs. One is then faced with a baffling inconsistency: why, in various types of thirteenth-century English, as in the *Ormulum* (and even 150 years later, in the language of Chaucer), were forms with and without -*e* used indifferently in words belonging to the same grammatical category (such as the same grammatical case in nouns of a given class), and even

[1] See M. Lehnert, *Sprachform und Sprachfunktion im 'Orrmulum' (um 1200)* (Berlin 1953).

in one and the same word? But there can be 'inconsistency' in the use of final -*e* only if it is regarded as a grammatical ending. And since the *Ormulum* shows that this conception of it is mistaken, the problem of final -*e* turns out (at least if formulated in such terms) to be a pseudo-problem.

One major stage in the total process that transformed the functions of this linguistic element has likewise been illuminated by Lehnert's study of the *Ormulum*. According to the entrenched view, the reduction of OE back vowels in unstressed final syllables to -*e* was first and last a sound-change, brought about by a progressively heavier stressing of the root syllable. It was the resulting loss of effective distinctions in the case-endings that led speakers to find other means for marking the differences of grammatical meaning in question—notably prepositions, and a fixed word-order.

The objections to this view need not be stated here, since Lehnert has made an overwhelming case for thinking that it puts the cart before the horse: the reduction of final unstressed vowels was an effect, not a cause, of the shifting to prepositions of the functions so far borne primarily by inflexions. From the earliest stage in English, prepositions had been abundantly used in conjunction with endings, and must have shared in implying the grammatical notion of case. Lehnert points out that, already in Latin, prepositions used in this way had duplicated the meaning of endings (e.g. *Romam ire* and *ad Romam ire*); that this is in origin an emphatic and therefore 'affective' device; and that Romance philologists have for half a century regarded it as the main factor in reducing the inflexion of nouns in Latin to the system used in Old French. This last step is comparable, in kind and degree, with the simplification carried out in noun inflexions in some types of English by *c.* 1100.

Certain major axioms may be deduced from these processes.

If a linguistic form ceases to be needed, it may be discarded: the loss of function makes possible a loss of the form. This view, if difficult to prove up to the hilt, does explain why final -*e* was quite soon totally discarded (viz. after 1400). It is in any case undeniable that there was in the Middle English period a great pruning of repeated and therefore superfluous marking of grammatical meanings. One main example happens to be an incidental result of the changes in the inflexion of nouns. When the majority of noun-endings were reduced to a single one (-*e*), differences of gender were wiped out along with differences of case. But grammatical gender is essentially a matter of purely formal patterning of the type known as 'concord'; and in OE the concord extended only to the inflexion of the adjective and above all of the definite and indefinite articles and the demonstratives. The different forms taken by this concord depended on the form of nouns. Once noun-endings had been reduced to near-uniformity, differences of gender could no longer be known, and therefore could no longer be expressed in the form of articles, &c. (since the forms of the latter traditionally proper to individual nouns would soon fade from memory).

It is therefore usual to say that, as between synthesis and analysis as means of expressing grammatical meaning (e.g. in Latin *dabo* and Zulu *ngizomshaya* on the one hand, and the English equivalents 'I shall give' and 'I shall hit him' on the other), the balance was tilted towards the latter in English after the Conquest. It is also usual, in saying this, to have in mind the increased use of prepositions to express case, and of auxiliary verbs to express tense: the conversion of the old preterite-present verbs *sculan* 'to be under a necessity, obligation, &c.' and *willan* 'to wish' into auxiliaries of the future tense is first clearly discernible after the Conquest. But there is another example as important as any (though hitherto imperfectly understood in its historical aspects, where English is concerned, and hence unregarded in this connexion).

One of the most idiomatic, productive, and characteristic elements in the vocabulary of English is its wealth of 'phrasal verbs', which consist of a verb plus adverb or preposition, such as *draw up*, *lay out*, *run over*, *take up*, *stand by*. Though many of these are in varying degrees late formations, they are made on an ancient pattern: *stand by*, in uses such as 'He will stand by us to the bitter end', is the lineal descendant of OE *bistandan*. The relevant OE and ME examples of this pattern (which is one common to all the early Gmc languages) were *separable compounds*.

Alongside these verbs, there was another group, represented, for example, by *understand*, *withdraw*, which were and still are inseparable compounds (as also in German, Dutch, and Afrikaans). On both types there were corresponding noun formations with the same distinctive word-order but with the stress on the prefix. The original pattern is handily fossilized in (and hence, apart from copious verb-noun pairs in Gothic, German, &c., sufficiently vouched for by) OE *bihátan* v. beside *bēot* n. 'boast' < *bíhāt*, in which latter the reduction of the second syllable was possible only because the stress was on *bi-*.

The nouns, even when formed on separable verbs, remained inseparable compounds and preserved their original word-order and stress. Many ancient ones survived (*insight*, *thorough-fare*, *upshot*), and many new ones have been coined (*bypass*, *offshoot*, *output*). The same applies to the cognate agent-nouns (*bystander*, *onlooker*, &c.). The type *passer-by*, *stander-by* is a product of reformation on the new separated form of the verb: this type first emerges in ME (as in Chaucer's *hoolder up*), and is therefore a symptom that the verb-pattern in *hoolde up* is itself an innovation in medieval English.

The verbs are very clearly revealed as separable compounds

in modern German, Dutch, and Afrikaans, because they have not in these languages evolved beyond a stage at which, in some of their forms, the prefix and the verb are separated (and the word-order of the two elements changed), and in others not. The forms concerned, among simple tenses and in main clauses, are respectively (*a*) the present indicative, the past participle, and the preterites, and (*b*) the infinitive; though in subordinate clauses the two elements are not separated. Thus G *ging(en) aus*, Du *ging(en) uit* 'went out' and G *ausgegangen*, Du *uitgegaan* are the preterite and the past participle of a compound verb the infinitive of which is G *ausgehen*, Du *uitgaan*.

The stage illustrated in modern German, Dutch, and Afrikaans was evidently beginning in late OE, but is first clearly traceable soon after the Conquest. Cf. 2 pres. sg. *miʒt over* I. 64 with the 3 pres. sg. *ofermæg* of late OE and (in a subordinate clause) the ME 3 pres. pl. *ouermai*[1] (which is shown to be an ancient compound by the OE noun *ofermægen* and the MDu verb *overmogen*); *scawe fore* XVI. 61 with OE *foresceawian*; *drou up* pret. sg. IV. 4 beside *opdrowe* pret. pl. V. 287 (where the second of two co-ordinate main clauses has—as in OE—the word-order proper to a subordinate clause and therefore the unseparated form); *drowen ut* pret. pl. IV. 264 beside *vt drow* pret. sg. IV. 221 (again, in the second of two co-ordinate main clauses). The pret. *ouermyhte* XVI. 195 (in a subordinate clause) is historically orthodox; but it is mere chance and the rarity of the verb that have denied us an example of the separated form of the preterite (subjunctive) till 1400:

> Ful foule schulde þi foos be fesid
> If þou *myʒte ouer* hem as Y *ouer þee may*.[2]

[1] *Vices and Virtues* (ed. F. Holthausen, E.E.T.S. 89 (1888), p. 13, l. 13).

[2] *Christ's Complaint* 471 (ed. F. J. Furnivall, *Political, Religious, and Love Poems* (1866), p. 198).

The momentous further step by which the separated form of all such verbs came to be the only possible one in English appears to be substantially complete by the time of Shakespeare. It is remarkable that an advanced stage had already been reached in Old Icelandic, the following being representative examples (in the notation of which the acute accent denotes length, not stress):

áhlaup n. 'attack'	*hlaupa á* v. 'assault'
atburðr n. 'chance; event'	*bera at* v. 'happen'
upphaf n. 'beginning; cause'	*hefja upp* v. 'begin, etc.'
útlausn n. 'redemption from captivity; ransom'	*leysa út* v. 'redeem, bail out, etc.'

For purposes of the next stage in our discussion, the main regional types in which early ME literature is recorded must be set out here, along with similar antecedent types in OE:

	OE			ME
I	Anglian	(a) Northumbrian	I	Northern
		(b) Mercian	II(a)	East Midland
			II(b)	West Midland
II	Kentish		III	South-Eastern
[III	*East Saxon]		IV	Essex/London
IV	West Saxon		V	South-Western

The correspondences are restricted partly by the fact that there are no extant OE documents to represent either the eastern part of the Mercian area or Essex/London. The Essex/London type of ME combines with its distinctive features, such as -ă- in words like *fan, han* 'fen, hen' and -ā- in, for example, *dāde, strāt* 'deed, street', some which are identical with features of West-Saxon derivation, such as -ă- implying an antecedent OE -æ̆- in *fader* 'father', &c., and the absence of smoothing (on which see 6, p. xli below).

So far as the inflexion of verbs is concerned, the varieties of early ME can be grouped in three main types, according to the endings used at focal points in the system of accidence. These varieties are regional ones, as shown in the following table (in which the type of noun plural inflexion associated with each is included):

	A (South, WMidl, and SE)	*B* (EMidl)	*C* (North)
1. 3 pres. sg.	-*eþ*	-*eþ*	-*es*
2. 3 pres. pl.	-*eþ*; -*ieþ* or -*īþ* in wk. II, -*en* in pret.-pres.	-*en*	-*es* and -(*e*)
3. Imper. pl.	-*eþ*	-*eþ*	-*es*
4. Pres. part.	-*inde*‡	-*ende*	-*ande*
5. Past part.	*y*+verb-root+-*e*	-*en*	-(*e*)*n*
6. Wk. verbs of Class II	-*i*- suffix preserved*	not differen- tiated	not differen- tiated
7. Noun pl.	-*es* and -*en*	-*es*	-*es*

‡ -*ynge* in some areas, by 1200.

* The -*i*- survived intact in verbs with short root-syllables, and coalesced with the following vowel of the ending to produce -*ī*- in verbs with polysyllabic or long roots (*lŏuien*, but *lōkīn*).

Certain forms here, in relation to their OE antecedents, make it clear that the endings are first and foremost units in a system of distinctions or 'oppositions', and that in some degree the inherited endings are retained or replaced according as they serve the needs of such a system by marking differences unambiguously. In type B, represented, for example, in the *Ormulum*, -*eþ* as the ending of the 3 pres. pl. (< OE -*að*) was evidently discarded because it did not distinguish the plural from the singular. This is clear from its retention in the imper. pl., where no ambiguity in relation to the imper. sg. was in question (since the singular was endingless or ended in -*e*, < OE endingless forms and -*e* or -*a* respectively). The -*en* was adopted, we must assume, from the preterite-present verbs (OE -*on*), since in them alone did it mark the combined grammatical meanings of present tense, plural number, and indicative mood.

In type A, however (represented, for example, in *Ancrene Wisse* and *Kentish Sermons*, and later the *Ayenbite*), -*eþ* has nevertheless been retained in the pres. pl.: this type of ambiguity could be tolerated for a time, presumably because it was not an absolute one (since many contexts would contain a pronoun as subject of the verb). In type C, in which -*es* was the ending (inherited from ONorthumbrian) of the 3 (as well as the 2) pres. sg. and the pl., an -*e* ending or an endless form (a reduction of -*e*) was used when the subject of the verb was a pronoun. This is clearly because the plural of the personal pronoun was felt to be an adequate sign of plurality in the verb; and it is a striking example of the natural trend to 'economy' by the pruning of superfluous marking of grammatical meanings.

In the present participle, -*ende* is the inherited form (OE -*ende*); -*inde* a modification of it, by a ME tendency to raise *ĕ* before *n*+a consonant;[1] and -*ande* is usually explained as an adoption of the ON form (-*andi*). In the past participle, it is hardly accidental that -*en* is retained as the sole sign in those systems in which it is discarded as a plural ending in nouns, and that on the other hand -*n* is discarded in systems in which -*en* marks the plural of nouns.

The most important point in the ME inflexion of pronouns is the emergence of new forms in the pronoun of the third person. The result is a distinctive set of local types, as follows:

	SE	WMidl	EMidl	North
Nom. sg. fem.	*hye*	(i) *ha* (ii) *ho* *s(c)ho*	*scæ* *ʒho*	*s(c)ho*
Nom. pl. (all genders)	*hi*	(i) *ha* (ii) *þei*	*þei*	*þei*

[1] On the problems raised by -*yng(e)*, see T. F. Mustanoja, *A Middle English Syntax* I (Helsinki 1960), 547–8 and 567–73.

The two WMidl types represent respectively the Southern part of the area *c.* 1200 (*Katherine* Group) and a more Northerly one *c.* 1350 (*Gawain* group). The EMidl *ʒho* (Orm) is evidently an antecedent stage of the types *sho*, *she* (of which latter *scæ* in the *Peterborough Chronicle* is a spelling): see *infra*. Wherever OE *ēo* > ME tense *ē* (as in the WMidl in the fourteenth century, the EMidl, and the North), *hē* 'she' < OE *hēo* was identical with the masculine form and therefore had to be replaced by an unambiguous one.

Speakers of a language virtually never create anything out of a void, but either evolve a new form on an existing pattern or use an existing form in a new function. The means used here was a variant, with stress shifted from the first to the second element of the diphthong, of the inherited form: OE *hjǒ* instead of *hěo*. In such contexts as *was hjǒ*, the sequence *-s+* the unique *hj-* 'might naturally (in speech) have developed into [ʃ], to produce *sho*. Some believe[1] that this was through the voiceless palatal fricative [ç] < *hj-*. But the form *yo* (see XV, 47 and 49), which directly attests the variant with rising diphthong by shift of stress, indicates that [ʃ] may well have arisen immediately from the sequence *-s+j-* (with elimination of the unstable breathing that is written *h*). And Orm's *ʒho* (the only word in which he writes *ʒh*, as against *ȝ* for the back fricative [ɣ] in, for example, *aȝenn* 'own'), can be interpreted as *hjo* no less than [ço:] (as it is improbably explained in the other view quoted above).

A phonetic development of *sho* from *-s+yo* would be most likely to have taken place in those varieties of ME in which the 3 pr. sg. indic. of all verbs normally ended in *-(e)s*, i.e. in NMidl or Northern—which are the types in which *sho* in fact occurs. But *she* cannot be explained in these terms: it is

[1] See K. Luick, *Historische Grammatik der englischen Sprache* § 705; and C. Clark, *The Peterborough Chronicle* (Oxford, 2nd edn., 1970), pp. lxvi–lxvii, for references to other discussions.

recorded well before *sho*, viz. from 1140, and in texts in which the 3 pr. sg. ends in *-eþ*. The tense *ē* implies either a remodelling of *hjō* after *hē* 'he', or an antecedent *hjē* < the OE acc. fem. sg. *hie* used as a nom. And the [ʃ] in *she* is a *substitute* for [ç]—which occurred in no other ME word—rather than a product of normal sound-change. This last process (as well as the emergence of *sho*) has been explained as an example of a tendency to discard a phoneme which is put to very little use.[1] And if a substitute for the voiceless palatal fricative [ç] had to be found, the voiceless palato-alveolar fricative [ʃ] (produced very near it in the mouth) is in purely phonetic terms an obvious and natural one.

Ha 'she' of the *Katherine* Group arose by an analogical process which set in already in OE, when the gen. pl. *þeara* 'of the' of the Vespasian Psalter (by back-mutation < *þæra* by the 'Second Fronting' < *þăra* as an unstressed and therefore shortened form of *þāra*) produced a gen. pl. *heara* 'their'. This process produced the plural paradigm *ha, hare, ham* of the *Katherine* Group on the model of *þa, þare, þam*, and hence (because of the original identity of the OE fem. acc. sg. with nom. and acc. pl., *þa* and *hie*) *ha* as acc. sg. fem. and thence nom. sg. fem. The plural type *þei, þeire, þeim* is a straightforward adoption from ON.

Other main points under this head are:

(i) The development of an uninflected definite article *þe*, already in some forms of OE by levelling of the initial consonant of oblique forms of the pronoun *se, seo, þæt* into the nom. sg. masc. and fem., and in ME at rates that varied, in individual systems, according to the rate at which inflexions in general were simplified.

---

[1] See J. Vachek, 'Notes on the Phonological Development of the NE Pronoun *she*', *Sborník Prací Filosofické Fakulty Brněnské University*, iii (1954), 3, 67–80; and *Brno Studies in English*, iv (1964), 21–29.

(ii) The eventual elimination of the inherited relative *þe* in favour of *þat* (which in the last part of the *Peterborough Chronicle* had been used only with an inanimate antecedent, while *þe* was used with an animate one[1]).

One other form of analogical process which has wrought great changes in the accidence of English (though it cannot be gone into here), and which got under way in ME, concerns the principal parts of strong and weak verbs. In most of these changes the principle of 'rhyme-association'[2] is at work: if one of the principal parts of any verb develops a historically irregular form, this is because it was remodelled on other verbs (sometimes specifically on one) with which it rhymed and was therefore closely associated in the minds of speakers. Clear examples may be found in the Glossary s.v. *lete, steo, straf*. Less clearly, *speu* IV. 246 has replaced OE *spāw*, perhaps by association of the weak verb *spēowan* (for *spīwan* of strong class I) with some such verb of class II as *cēowan*. The uninflected *bet* IV. 343 is a weak-type pp. (common in early modern English) for *bēten* < OE *bēaten*; but the specific model is uncertain, as for the pp. *lopen* IV. 323 of cl. II type replacing OE *hlēapen*, and the pt. sg. *lop* V. 78, as well as *belæf, beleaf* XVI. 69 and 70.

The main phonological differences between the major types of ME arose in OE by the following processes of phonetic change in stressed syllables:

1. *ǣ* was early raised to *ē* in OKt and WMerc (represented by the V.Ps and Hymns): and *ă* was in WMerc fronted to *ǣ* except before *l* (e.g. *hwalas*). Thus WS and Northumbrian

---

[1] See A. McIntosh, 'The Relative Pronouns *þe* and *þat* in Early Middle English', *E.G.S.* i (1947–8), 73–90; and Addenda, p. xx.

[2] See S. R. T. O. d'Ardenne, *Seinte Iuliene* (1936) §102.

dăg, OKt and WMerc *dĕg*; WS, Northumbrian, Kt *dŏgas*, WMerc *dăgas*.

2. OE *ǣ* was of two different origins, and is therefore denoted *ǣ*[1] if it represents primitive Gmc *ǣ*, and *ǣ*[2] when derived from Gmc *ai* (which developed into OE *ā*) by *i*-mutation (see 5 below). The non-WS equivalents were:

WS	*Angl*	*Kt*
ǣ[1] (*dǣd*)	*ē* (*dēd*)	*ē* (*dēd*)
ǣ[2] (*lǣran*)	*ǣ* (*lǣran*)	*ē* (*lēran*)

ME evidence shows that in Essex and its environs both *ǣ*[1] and *ǣ*[2] were retracted to *ā*: *dād*, *strāt*, *tāchen* 'teach'.

3. By the process termed 'Breaking', *h*, *l*, or *r* plus consonant, and single *h* or *w*, when preceded by a front vowel threw off a back glide (thus being evidently back consonants), which combined with the vowel to produce a diphthong:

ắ > *ĕa*: *sĕah*, *ĕald*, *nēah*;

ĕ > *ĕo*: *fĕoh*; Angl-Kt *nēoh, > Angl *nēh* (see 6), Kt *nīoh (see under *ĭ*);

ĭ > *ĭo* (> *ĕo* by *c.* 900, except that in Kt *ĭo* remained and *ēo* > *ĭo*): *mĭox*, later *mĕox*; *betwĭoh > WS *betwēoh*, Angl *betwīh* (see 6).

In Angl, *ắ* was not 'broken' before *l*-groups, and was retracted to *ă*: WS, Kt *hĕaldan*, Angl *hăldan*.

4. In WS, and in some degree in Nb, each of the palatal consonants written *c*, *g*, or *sc* (i.e. [ʃ], as in 'sheep') threw off a front glide before the front vowels *ắ*, *ĕ*, which combined with it to form the diphthongs *ĕa*, *ĭe* respectively:

WS	*Kt and Merc*
*cĕali (> *cĭele*, see 5)	*cĕle*
gĕaf	*gĕf* (see 1)
scĕal	*scĕl*

WS	Kt and Merc
gĭefan	*gĕfan*
gēar (with *ǣ*[1])	*gēr* (2 above)
scēap	*scēp*

5. By the process of *i*-mutation:

(*a*) *ǣ* before *l*-groups (= WS, Kt *ĕa*; see 3) is represented by (i) *ǣ* in the V.Ps, (ii) *ĕ* elsewhere in Angl: *wælle* 'spring'/*welle*.

(*b*) *ǣ* before nasal, or nasal plus consonant, normally became *ĕ*, but remained *ǣ* in an area which on ME evidence is identifiable as Essex-London: *fæn* 'fen', *mænn* pl. 'men'.

(*c*) *ĕa* > *ĭe* in WS, but *ĕ* in non-WS: *fĭellan* 'to fell' (cf. *feallan* 'to fall'), non-WS *fĕllan*; *cĭele*/*cĕle*; *hĭeran*/*hēran*.

(*d*) *ĕo* > *ĭe* in WS, *ĭo* in Kt but elsewhere is represented by *ĕo*.

6. By the process of 'smoothing', the diphthongs *ĕa*, *ēa*, *ĕo*, and *ēo* (of all origins, including 'Breaking') were in Angl reduced to *ǣ* (later *ĕ* when followed by *r*), tense *ē*, *ĕ*, and tense *ē* respectively before any of the consonants *c*, *g*, *h* either standing alone or preceded by *l* or *r*. Thus *sĕah* > *sǣh*; *bēag* > Angl *bēg*, *ēac* > *ēc*; *weorc* > *werc*.

7. By 'back-mutation', the front vowels *ǣ*, *ĕ*, *ĭ*, if a following syllable contained an *ă*, *ŏ*, or *ŭ*, developed into diphthongs with a second element of back quality: *fearan* 'to go'; *heofon*; *hiora* 'their'. In WS this occurred only before a liquid (*l*, *r*) or a labial stop or fricative: *tiolode*, *cliopode*, *liofað* (and *ĭo* later > *ĕo*). Only in Kt did it operate before the velar consonants *c* and *g*.

Back-mutation of *ǣ* was possible only in WMerc (see 1). The product *ĕa* is still traceable in the ME *Katherine* Group (see XVIII, *Language*) in the traditional spelling *ea*, though there reduced to a vowel (which was probably [ɛ], since the graph *ea* is intermittently used as a spelling for OF *ĕ*, as in *leattres*, or OE *ĕ* as in *hweat*).

8. OE *y̆* (the product of *i*-mutation of *ŭ*) > *ĕ* in Kt by *c.* 900: *pytt* > *pett*, *mȳs* > *mēs*.

9. By *c.* 900, the diphthongs *ĭe* in WS > the rounded vowels written *y̆*, and (in unknown conditions) to some extent the unrounded vowels written *ĭ*: *fyllan* 'to fell', *hȳran* 'to hear'.

10. In the earliest OE the stops [k] and [g] had become front or 'palatal' consonants:

   (a) in initial position before a primary front vowel (i.e. other than those produced by *i*-mutation), or a front glide or vowel as the first element of a diphthong: *ċeæf* 'chaff', *ċēald* (> early ME *chęld*, beside *cǫld* < Angl *cāld*); *ġefan*, *ġēotan*;

   (b) in medial position before an original (Gmc) *i* or *j*, or between front vowels: *bycgan*, *tǣċan* 'to teach'; *bæċe* dat. sg. 'back', *slæġen* p.p. 'slain';

   (c) in final position after front vowels: *iċ* (ME *ich*) 'I', *bæċ* 'back', *dīċ* 'ditch', *dæġ*, *weġ*.

11. By *c.* 900 the front ('palatal') *ġ* > [j], and *ċ*, *ġġ* (written *cg*) were assibilated to [tʃ], [dʒ]. This latter point is deduced from the OE spellings *orceard* and *feccan* for earlier *ortgeard* and *fetian*, in both of which [tj] is shown to have become [tʃ]. But if the front *ċ* and *ġġ* were originally followed in Gmc by *j* (which was regularly eliminated in prehistoric OE) and were thus later brought into immediate contact with a back vowel that originally followed the *j*, they lost their front quality. This is why unassibilated forms (i.e. with [k] and [g]) occur in ME, in such words as *þenke* 'to think' < **þankjan*, and (on the evidence of modern dialects) *brig(g)*, *rigg* < OE *brycg*, *hrycg* (in the gen. and dat. pl. of which the Gmc *j* was followed

by a back vowel), as well as in present English pairs such as *dyke* (< OE *dícas*) beside *ditch* (< *dić* nom. sg., &c.).

12. In the later OE period short vowels and diphthongs in disyllabic words were lengthened before any consonant group consisting of liquid or nasal (*l, r*; *m, n*) plus homorganic voiced stop (*mb, nd, ng, ld, rd*), or *r* plus the voiced fricatives *s* or *ð*: WS, Kt *hēaldan*, Angl *hāldan*.

13. In late WS and Kt *ĕa* were reduced to *ĕ* before *c, g, h*: *seh* (Angl *sæh*, 6 above), **hēh* 'high'.

The main further developments were as follows:

14. By c. A.D. 1000:
(i) *ea* and *ēa* developed (by progressive reduction of the second element) into the front vowels *æ* and *ǣ* respectively;
(ii) *æ* and *ǣ*, of whatever origin, then > ME *a* (a back vowel) and slack *ę̄* respectively: *ealle* > *alle*, *hearm* > *harm*, *fæder* > *fader*, *sæt* > *sat*; *dēaþ* > *dę̄þ*, *hlēapan* > *lę̄pen*, *dǣl* > *dę̄l*, *slǣpan* > *slę̄pen*.

Note. The hitherto unexplained development of *ēa* in MKt is not (as it is commonly believed to be) a divergent one: here, as elsewhere, the unconditioned development in stressed syllables is slack *ę̄* (spelt *e* or *ea*)—and this is clearly the normal type of process for ME at large, since, for example, the passage of OE *eo* and *ēo* to *ĕ* and tense *ē* implies that in OE diphthongs the stress was on the first element. The graphs *ia, ya* of XVII (*q.v.*) represent a contextual variant, viz. a rising diphthong *i̯a*, which developed especially after a dental consonant, as in *dyaþ*. In the graph *yea*, used in the *Ayenbite of Inwyt* mostly in words beginning with slack *ę̄*, or with *ē* preceded (in the written form of the word) by *h*, the *y* evidently expresses a front glide *i̯* developed (in speech) before the normal slack *ę̄* < Œ *ēa* or *ǣ* when the previous word ended in a front vowel. Sequences like *þe ealde* would otherwise have produced hiatus (the arrest by the chest muscles of one vowel, followed by the release of the next, with a cessation of sound between them: see R.-M. S. Heffner, *General Phonetics* (1952), 182–8). The glide was in fact, then as now, a device to avoid hiatus. It occurs in the *Ayenbite* in words with initial *h* because the latter (as a mere breathing) is unstable, and would often have been eliminated in some contexts. Thus the first syllable of *healden* 'to hold' would have been in some contexts identical with that in *ealde* 'old', and would equally have been pronounced with the initial front glide (written *y* in *yea-*) when preceded by a word ending in a vowel.

15. OE short and long *eo* > respectively short and long [ø] by the late twelfth century, which were unrounded to *ĕ* and tense *ē* respectively by *c.* 1200: *heorte*, *beoden* v. The [ø] stage is clearly attested in texts which use the graph *eo* both for OE *ēo* and for the OF [ø] of, for example, *pueple*, and is fossilized in the *Ormulum* (see XIII, *Commentary*, under *Orthography*).

16. By *c.* 1200, [eị] > [aị]: members of the class of words represented by *wei* < OE *wĕg* now rhymed on those of the class represented by *dai* < OE *dǽg*.

17. OE *ā* was rounded to slack *ō* soon after 1200, except in the North and parts of the NMidl, where it was unchanged: *bǭn*, *stǭn*. The demarcation of the *ō* and *ā* areas has been worked out[1] from the ME forms of place-names. The *ā*-area includes North Lancs., the northern West Riding and the North Riding, and North Lincs., and is bounded approximately by the Ribble and the Humber.

18. OE short and long [y], spelt *y*,

   (i) were unrounded to short and long [i] respectively in the EMidl and the North;

   (ii) survived as rounded vowels, spelt with the OF graph

[1] By E. Ekwall, 'The Middle English *ā/ō* boundary', *English Studies*, xx (1938), 147–68.

u, in the WMidl and the SW, and were not unrounded
in these areas till after 1200;

(iii) were represented in the SE by the short and long [e]
which already in OKt had developed from [y] spelt *y*:
pett 'pit', *fēr* 'fire'.

19. (i) Soon after 1200, the short vowels written *a, e, o* were
lengthened in disyllabic forms with open root-
syllable: *nāme, tāle; mēte, stēlen; hōpe, nōse*. Since
the *ē* and *ō* can be proved to have been slack, it
is clear that the inherited *ĕ* and *ŏ* (which can be
shown to have been tense in OE) had undergone
lowering before the lengthening.

(ii) The vowels written *i* and *u* were lengthened in the
same kind of phonetic context (though a little later,
and only in northern areas) to tense *ē* and tense *ō*
respectively (which imply a lowered variety of *ĭ* and *ŭ*
as the starting-point): 3 pr. sg. *gēves* beside inf. *gif*;
3 pr. sg. *cōmes* beside inf. *cum*.

20. One of the most important features of ME is the
emergence by *c.* 1200 of new diphthongs, of a type previously
unknown, in which the second element was by origin either
a front or a back glide, written *y* (or *ȝ*) and *w* or *u* respectively.
The spelling system of Orm (see XIII, *Language*) shows that in
words like OE *ege, clawu* the medial consonants *i̯* and *w* (which
originally belonged to the second syllable) had been drawn into
the first. This was probably by the emergence before each of a
glide of a character corresponding to it (front or back), which
was an anticipation of it: *ei̯e > ei̯-i̯e*, and later *ei̯i̯-e*. Thus
Orm writes *eȝȝe* and *clawwess*, in which the medial consonant
could not have been doubled (in his system) unless it belonged
to the same syllable as the preceding vowel.

In OE there were a great many words in which a variety
of vowels and diphthongs occurred before medial *i̯* or *w*. The

Ormulum shows that long vowels coalesced with following *i̯*
or *w* later than short vowels did: Orm still writes *cnawenn* (OE
cnāwan), *flowenn* (OE *flōwan*), *shæwenn* (OE *scēawian*). When
the coalescence did take place, the long vowels were reduced
to short ones as first elements of the new diphthongs.

21. Between the voiceless fricative /x/, written *h*, and a
preceding vowel, a glide emerged which was of front or back
quality according to that of the vowel and was spelt *i* or *y* and
u or *w* respectively: *seiȝ* < OE *sĕh* (see 13 above) beside *sauȝ*
< OE *sǽh* (6 above).

22. (i) In OE words, a *-g-* which was preceded by a front
vowel but followed by a back vowel had the quality
of the following vowel (since it belonged to the
second syllable) and was a back fricative ([ɣ]). The
reduction of back vowels to something like [ə] or
[e] by *c.* 1000 having eliminated the back quality of
its environment, the back fricative became a front
one: [plɛɣə] 'play' > [plɛjə], [stiːɣən] 'to climb' >
[stiːjən]. This happened later than the processes
described in 20 (in, for example, the *Ormulum* the
back fricative was still intact, *c.* 1200).

(ii) In words in which it had stood between back vowels
in OE, or between a liquid (*l* or *r*) and a vowel, and
was therefore a voiced back fricative, *-g-* > ME *w*:
OE *dagas* > ME *dawes*; *morgen* > *morwe* (perhaps
through a stage in which a parasitic vowel developed
between the liquid and [ɣ]). The back fricative was
still intact in MKt even till 1340 in the *Ayenbite of
Inwyt*.

The result of both (i) and (ii) was to produce more diphthongs
of the type described in 20. In the sequences tense *ē* plus *i̯* and
tense *ō* plus *u̯*, in which the vowel was raised (by assimilation

to the following consonant), the result *c*. 1300 was $\ddot{\underset{\circ}{u}} > \bar{\imath}$ and $u\underset{\circ}{u} > \bar{u}$: OE *wrēgan* > ME *wrēȝe* > *wrē̆ie* > *wrī̆ie* > *wrīe*; OE *bōgas* 'boughs' > ME *bōȝes* > *bo̤wes) bṳṳes* > *būes*.

The effect of these processes was to produce something like the following system of vowels in stressed syllables:

I. *Up to 1200*

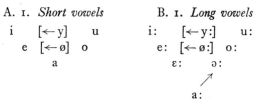

A. 1. *Short vowels*			B. 1. *Long vowels*		
i	[← y]	u	i:	[← y:]	u:
e	[← ø]	o	e:	[← ø:]	o:
	a		ɛ:		ɔ:
				a:	

The bracketed vowels came to be merged with those towards which the arrow points in each case. In B. 1, the movement of [a:] towards slack *ō* ([ɔ:]) applies only to non-Northern varieties of ME.

In unstressed final syllables there was a vowel which probably varied, according to the quality of the preceding consonant, between [ə] and [i] (cf. Chaucerian rhymes such as *onis* : *is* and *wyvis* : *is*, *Wife of Bath's Prologue* 9 and 39).

II. *After c. 1200*

A. 2. *Short vowels*		B. 2. *Long vowels*	
i	u	i:	u:
		e:	o:
ɛ	ɔ	ɛ:	ɔ:
	a		a:

In B. 2 the [a:] is the product of lengthening of *a* in disyllabic forms with open root-syllables, as in *ape* 'ape'; and since it moved into the series of front vowels in the ModE period, it is usually believed to have been different in quality from the original *ā* which became slack *ō*. No account is taken here of the probability that the [ɔ:] produced by the lengthening of [ɔ] in disyllabic forms with open root-syllables was, for a time at least and in some areas, distinct from the [ɔ:] < [a:].[1] The shift of [a:] to slack ō is likely to have been due to an unconscious impulse in speakers to restore symmetry to the system of long vowels by filling the empty place in the back series. For one source of [ɛ:] and [ɔ:] see 19 (i).

The following sets of diphthongs existed in ME up to *c.* 1200:

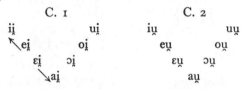

C. 1   C. 2

This system was reduced by the development of *ei̯* to *ai̯* (see 16 above) and, in the fourteenth century, of *ou̯* (< ō plus *w*) to *ɔu̯*. In C. 1, *ui̯*, *oi̯*, and *ɔi̯* occurred only in foreign words (apart from *ɔi̯* in the p.p. *broyden*, which was apparently a blend of the past participial form of the root (with *o*) with the *i̯* proper to the infinitive and pret. sg.).

The example of Icelandic, German, Dutch, and Afrikaans shows that the conversion of the separable compound verbs in English from a synthetic into an analytical form was entirely in accord with the 'drift' (or unconscious prevailing direction of change) of the Germanic languages. Equally, the fundamental changes in the inflexion of nouns, adjectives, and pronouns, since they were under way before the Conquest (p. xxi), were the outcome of internal processes likely to operate in any language with a moderately ample system of accidence. The main changes in the endings of verbs, being due to the need for

[1] See E. J. Dobson, 'Middle English Lengthening in Open Syllables', *Transactions of the Philological Society*, 1962, 124–48.

unambiguous expression of grammatical meaning, are likewise
the product of purely internal factors. And though the causes
of unconditioned (i.e. 'isolative') phonetic change are complex
and notoriously hard to determine, it is clear that, for example,
the reduction of OE diphthongs to what was in effect their
first element had set in before the Conquest.

Thus the impact of an alien language spoken by a new ruling
class did not substantially affect or modify the structure of
English. A comparative analysis of ME and OF syntax might
uncover a somewhat more substantial Gallic imprint. But it
would be a matter of individual syntactic usages (such as the
mode of expression of the gerund), rather than of a systemic
revolution (e.g. in the structure and articulation of sentences
and clauses). Thus it is curious, and perhaps not by an independent development, that in both ME and OF the gerund is
identical in form with the present participle. In OF this is the
outcome of regular phonetic change: both L *cantando* and
L *cantantem* > *chantant*. As the endings of the other two Latin
conjugations were discarded and that of the verbs in *-are* was
used in their place, in both gerund and present participle, the
outcome was the same as in those forms of ME which had very
early adopted *-yng(e)* as the ending of the present participle.
But in ME the present participle in *-ynge* (which was in OE
the suffix of nouns of action formed on verbs, and was therefore a more serviceable gerund than the unhandy gerundial
infinitive, OE *to ridenne* 'for riding', &c.) had replaced the
historically regular type in *-inde*, *-ende*. This has not been fully
explained in terms of internal processes. Locutions like *tojanes
þo sunne risindde* (XVII. 7), in which the ME present participle
is used in the function of a gerund (evidently because the OF
forms of both were identical), do suggest that the ME present
participle in *-ynge* has been evolved on the model of OF *-ant*.

From what has been said above, it should be clear that the

structure and organization of a language and its characteristic trends of change are what matter. It is the vocabulary that lies nearest the surface, and is therefore most easily touched by an alien tongue; it is the vocabulary of ME (and hence of present English) that has been affected by OF. It is a common fallacy to imagine that the French contribution to the vocabulary of ME is a matter of the number of words adopted. The resources of a vocabulary depend less on the sheer numbers of words in the lexicon than, for example, on the means it offers of forming new words by compounding or derivation, and hence on the suffixes and prefixes available. One can make a list of those adopted from OF (and Latin), and another of the native ones discarded after the Conquest. But a mere count, of affixes as of words, leaves out a great deal. The 'yield' of an affix—the range of its applicability, and its expressive range—matters profoundly; and these qualities are not easily measured or computed.

A count of words, moreover, leaves out the mass of phrases which were reproduced partly or wholly by ME equivalents, as in *do* (someone) *a service, hold dear* (*tenir chier*), or *put to death* (*metre a mort*). Many of these are highly idiomatic. And among them are many of one particular type which has evidently proliferated in new native formations, and which consists of verb plus noun-object:

> *avoir* (someone's) *acointance, paor; faire homage, honor, justise, merveille(s), servise(s).*

These are verb-equivalents, in which the verb actually used is one such as *do, give, have, make, take*:

> *do battle, penance; give offence, thought, way; have mercy, pity, speech* (*with*); *make peace, a start; take care, heed, notice, pains, part* (*in*).

The pattern existed in OE, for example in *niman andan* (or

graman) 'take offence', *niman geme* 'take heed', *niman ware* 'take care'. But the corresponding OF usage seems to have encouraged the massive increase in such locutions after the Conquest. It is, for example, striking how often in Chaucerian examples the noun used is French:

> *do correccioun, diligence, execucioun, offence, oppression, servyse*; *have* (someone's) *acquaintance, a blame, (no) doute, gerdon, in gouvernaunce, jurisdiccioun*; *make avow, a maistrie, rehersaille, stryf.*

It was by exploiting this device, along with 'phrasal verbs', that Ogden and Richards were able to reduce the number of 'operators' (i.e. verbs) in Basic English to only eighteen. It must therefore be of central importance in the structure of English, since it would not otherwise have the requisite 'yield'.

Another relevant fact that a word-count leaves out is that the opportunity or occasion to use OF words must have varied greatly, with the nature of the subject, the work, and the literary genre in question—and this variation likewise cannot be measured. Yet, as a glance at some of the pieces in this book will show, this cannot wholly explain the startling differences between individual works (and therefore in some sense their authors) in regard to the number of French words they use. At one end of the scale is the extract from *Kyng Alisaunder*, with at least 40 (not counting recurrences) in *c.* 200 lines. At the other is the *Ormulum*, with none at all in 288 lines; then come *The Fox and the Wolf*, with only 21 in 295 lines, and *Dame Sirith* with 43 in 450.

It is easy to show that the author of *Kyng Alisaunder* had a command of OF or AN idiom possible only for someone bilingual. Yet the same manifestly applies to the author of *Ancrene Wisse*, who in this extract of 677 lines used *c.* 107 or (in proportion to the 40 in *Kyng Alisaunder*) *c.* 15. And why and how it is that the Augustinian canon Orm does without French altogether in this extract?

A point commonly overlooked in attempts to assess the contribution of French to the vocabulary of English is the crucial difference in this regard between colloquial and other forms of English. It is a curious and impressive fact that one can compose a piece of English conversation without using a single French word; and one can often hear or take part in conversations containing very few. This is often a matter of 'register' rather than social differences: even the talk of the highly educated, which is sometimes more bookish than that of others, commonly contains far fewer French words than their letters might. This may well be true of English just after the Conquest: the talk of Pandarus with his niece in *Troilus and Criseyde* contains noticeably fewer OF words than the sections of narrative. The manner and the vocabulary of conversation would be altogether apt in a tale from beast epic, such as *The Fox and the Wolf*, or a *fabliau*.

It is hardly conceivable, however, that Orm (consciously or otherwise) refrained from using French words solely because—in Biblical exegesis aimed at the unlettered—he set himself to use a homely diction and tone throughout. It was probably not only an author's audience, but also his own background, endowments, and tastes that determined the number of adoptions from OF that he used. This is one of the reasons why the first record of a French word in ME should not necessarily be assumed (as is commonly done) to imply that it was, or even soon became, generally current in the 'language'. In fact, so long as we are dealing with any one ME work, the influence of the French vocabulary on the 'language' is an abstraction: such a notion applies only to words which are found, on analysis of many works, to recur in several of them.

There are ample words of this class in early ME: *beastes,*

blame, destruet, entente, fame, gref, manere, pece, poure (adj.) are
among many in the extract here from *Ancrene Wisse*. Of these,
all but *entente* are among the most familiar and serviceable
words of present English; they have, moreover, ousted native
words of similar meaning,[1] except that *deer* survives in a
restricted application, and *wise* as a poetic and archaic synonym
of *manner*, and *sorrow* along with *grief*. Words of this type serve
to prevent our being blinded by the undeniable if banal fact
that OF provided a new terminology of the religious life, the
law, administration, feudal institutions and warfare, and aristocratic social life and its ethical values. This was indeed a
contribution of incalculable importance. Our extract from
Ancrene Wisse naturally abounds in French words relating to
various aspects of the religious life, including the fundamental
terms *deciples, deuociun* 'a prayer', *grace, lesceun, mearci,
miracle, passiun, patriarches, prophetes, saluatiun, temptatiun,*
and (from the monastic life) *cloistre, meditatiuns, ordre, priur,
religiun, riwle.*

But the work done by such words sometimes goes beyond
their functions as technical terms. Since they belong to a special
vocabulary evolved by one or another social group (for an
activity shared by its members), they may pass back into the
general vocabulary, and in that case commonly undergo changes
of meaning. Specific applications (natural in the special vocabulary) are often replaced by general ones; and the result is
therefore again a highly serviceable word. Two important legal
expressions occur in an unexpected setting in this book (both
in relation to Alexander of Macedon). *By atturne* II. 14 and
þe kynges person II. 22 constitute a pair of notions which are a
standing contrast in juridical use, though not recorded by the
O.E.D. till Shakespeare:

[1] Cf. OE *dēor; witan; awierdan; geþōht; mǣrðu, hrēð; sorg; wise;
wǣdlig.*

> Then *in* mine own *person* I die.
> *Rosal.* No, faith—die *by attorney*.
>   (*As You Like It*, iv. i. 94.)

The phrase *crieȝ* (*hire*) *merci* (III. 263), used with a pronominal object, is from the vocabulary of the religious life (in application to private prayers), but is here already applied within a different sphere (viz. of social relations) in a use which survives into Shakespeare's English.

The period *c.* 1050 to *c.* 1400 begins with the end of one form of standard written English and ends with the emergence of another. It is a truism that the extant OE literature has been transmitted to us in 'West Saxon'. It is not so widely realized that this form of written OE lived on into the early ME period, till *c.* 1150, and was used not merely in centres such as Worcester and Canterbury, but in other areas much more remote from the West Saxon kingdom from which it was diffused. It occurs after the Conquest not only, for example, in the *Peterborough Chronicle* (in the annals for 1070 to 1121, made from an earlier copy), but in three Yorkshire documents of *c.* 1050,[1] and a Northumbrian code of laws for priests,[2] and has left distinct traces in a charter from Durham.[3] But the evidence of ME writings leaves no doubt that the spoken language in these areas had a strongly marked local character: it follows that the vestigial use of the old WS written standard had no relation to spoken usage in early ME.

Whatever the reasons, there was no immediate successor to this version of the WS written standard (so far as extant documents show). The English of Chaucer's writings, however, is

[1] W. H. Stevenson, 'Yorkshire Surveys and Other Eleventh-Century Documents in the York Gospels', *English Historical Review*, xxvii (1912), 1 ff.

[2] F. Liebermann, *Die Gesetze der Angelsachsen*, i. 380 ff.

[3] F. Liebermann, 'Drei nordhumbrische Urkunden um 1100', Herrig's *Archiv*, cxi (1903), 275–84.

clearly near to having this status, since in its basic features it
corresponds closely to the language of the state documents
written in London from 1430 onwards. In the view of Professor
M. L. Samuels[1] it is the language of these latter ('Chancery
Standard') that is the standard written form of late ME, rather
than that represented by Chaucer's writings and the earlier
London documents which (apart from a handful in early ME)
begin in 1384. A selective sample of the differences between
these two groups is available on p. 9, n. 10, in his paper.

What concerns us here is that none of these varieties of ME
could originally have been proper to London. The general
character of the earlier (i.e. those of Chaucer and the London
documents of 1384 onwards) is Anglian-derived; but it is clear
that at least *c.* 1300 the literary language of London was a very
different one, of strongly marked non-Anglian derivation (see
p. liv below). In fact, the written ME of Chaucer corresponds,
in certain main features of its accidence and phonology, with
that of the *Ormulum* (*c.* 1200) and of the 'Final Continuation'
(1132–54) of the *Peterborough Chronicle*.[2] They agree in having:

(*a*) virtually only one ending for the pl. and for the possessive sg. of nouns, viz. *-es*;

(*b*) the analogical *-en* (or a reduction of it to *-e* or zero, in
Chaucer's case, the difference being merely between
successive stages in the development of one and the
same feature) as the ending of the pres. indic. pl. of all
verbs, in place of the historically regular *-eþ*;

(*c*) *-eþ* in the imper. pl. (though it does not happen to occur
in the very restricted material of the *Peterborough
Chronicle*);

[1] 'Some Aspects of Middle English Dialectology', *English Studies*,
xliv (1963), 1–14.

[2] For which see C. Clark, *The Peterborough Chronicle* (2nd edn.,
1970), pp. xlv–lxxiv.

(*d*) certain Anglian-derived phonological features, such as *cālde*, *hālde* or the *cǭlde*, *hǭlde* later developed from those south of the Humber (as against SE—including earlier London English *c.* 1300—and SW *chę̄lde*, *hę̄lde*); and 'smoothed' forms such as *werk* (non-Anglian *work*).

There are of course differences, such as the sporadic survival in Chaucer's written English of the earlier London *ě* for OKt *ě* (*ў̆* otherwise in OE). But they are details that do not substantially modify the general picture. There are great differences in vocabulary, such as the very strong Scandinavian element and the minimal French element in that of Orm, and the opposite relationship in Chaucer's. But vocabulary, considered in terms of individual words, is hardly more than top-hamper.

It is thus clear that the later fourteenth-century written English of London must, as an Anglian-derived type, be in some sense an intrusion there. The personal names preserved in London documents of the ME period have lately been used[1] to show how this happened. They are commonly of the form *William de Hackeforde* (1309–10), or *Alan de Scarnyngge* (1348), in which the second element is a place-name (normally identifiable); and the occupations of their bearers are also given. Ekwall has therefore been able to establish that, out of 2,900 odd such names, *c.* 1,970 attest EMidl origin for the persons concerned, as against *c.* 350 from the North, and 380 from the WMidl. He has thus solved a major problem in the history of London (and therefore standard) English, since these figures led him to deduce that the displacement of an antecedent type of London ME by an EMidl one was due to the immigration of merchants, &c., from the EMidl who became well-to-do and thereby gave their form of English a prestige that caused its adoption as an upper-class one in London.

[1] By E. Ekwall, *Studies on the Population of Medieval London* (Stockholm, 1956).

It has only lately been fully demonstrated[1] that an extensive body of London English from before the time of Chaucer is available, viz. in the romances *Kyng Alisaunder* and *Arthour and Merlin* (composed *c.* 1300). If this form of ME had survived in London and duly developed into standard English, the classes of words represented by *pit, deed, clean, fen,* and *cold/wold* would now have a form corresponding to that of *pet, dade, clane, fan,* and *cheald/weald* respectively. These features of pronunciation are named here because they also happen to be characteristic of those ME forms of place-names and street-names in Essex and London that occur in Latin documents of the twelfth and thirteenth centuries.[2] Thus in those features, at least, the language of *Kyng Alisaunder* and *Arthour and Merlin* probably reflects actual spoken usage.

The touchstone for a written standard is that it be extensively used by persons whose spoken usage is that of a different area, or to record works composed in a different area. By this criterion the London English of *c.* 1300 was evidently already (or was on the way to becoming) a written standard. A large part of the Auchinleck MS.,[3] which contains works composed far from London, such as the NMidl *Legend of Gregory* and the Northern *Sir Tristrem*, exhibits features of that type of London ME (i.e. in rhymes in which the author's forms have been replaced by the scribes and thereby corrupted, or in forms within the line that diverge from the author's).

[1] Ekwall (op. cit., p. xvii, ll. 7–9) is not aware of the strength and the significance of the evidence. See *Kyng Alisaunder*, ii (E.E.T.S. 237, 1957), 40–55.

[2] See W. Heuser, *Altlondon* (1914); Ekwall, op. cit. xviii–xix, besides *Early London Personal Names* (1947), 180 ff.

[3] The parts written by scribes 1 and 3. See Samuels, op. cit., p. 7, n. 7; and pp. 652–3 of A. J. Bliss, 'Notes on the Auchinleck MS.', *Speculum*, xxvi (1951), 652–8.

SPELLING

The following are the graphies commonly used in early ME for (I) vowels and (II) consonants;

I. *Vowels*   *Graphy*

  1. [a]   *a, ea*: *sat, feallen*
  2. [ɛ]   *e*: *beren*
  3. [i]   *i, y* (before a letter consisting of minims), *j* (in initial position, and especially before minims): *þis, kyn, jn*
  4. [ɔ]   *o*: *þolen*
  5. [u]   *u, o* (next to minims), *v* (in initial position, and especially before minims): *full, loue, vnder*
  6. [y]   *u*: *kunne*
  7. [aː]   *a*: *stan*
  8. [ɛː]   *æ* (early), *ea, e*: *dæþ, deaþ, deþ*
  9. [eː]   *e*: *fet*
 10. [iː]   *i, y*: *tid, hyden*
 11. [ɔː]   *o*, and (for [ɔː] < OE *ā*:) *oa*: *ston, boan, before*
 12. [oː]   *o*: *fot*
 13. [uː]   *u* (early), *ou, ow*: *ful, hous, now*
 14. [yː]   *u, ui, uy*: *fur, huyden*

II. *Consonants*   *Graphy*

  1. [k]   *k*: *kyng.* When geminated, *kk, ck*: *þikke, þycke*
  2. [x]   *h, ȝ, ȝh, gh*: *myhte, nyȝt, þouȝhte, ought*
  3. [ɣ]   *ȝ, ȝh, gh,* and occasionally (as in *Ancrene Wisse*) *h*: *daȝes,* &c., *mahen*
  4. [s]   *s*: *senden*
  5. [z]   *s*: *chesen*
  6. [θ]   *þ, ð*: *þenken, ðolen*
  7. [ð]   *þ, ð*: *oþer, baðe* 'both'
  8. [v]   *u,* and (in initial position) *v*: *uermin, louen*; *verray*
  9. [ʃ]   *sh, sch, s(s)*: *s(c)hip, fis(s)*
 10. [tʃ]   *ch*: *child.* When geminated, *cch*: *fecchen*
 11. [dʒ]   *i, j, g*: *iewes, jugen, gentil.* When geminated, *gg*: *biggen* 'buy'
 12. [j]   *i* (early), *ȝ, y*: *iaf, ȝelden, yelden*

13. [w]   þ (up to *c.* 1200), *u, uu, w*: *þolde, uylle, uuolle,*
             wenden

The spellings for [f] [p], [b], [d], [t], [g], [l], [r], [m], [n],
and [ŋ] are omitted from this list, because identical with those
used today.

Though the foregoing is a conglomerate (of all the common
symbols, wherever used), many things in it occur in any individual system used in an individual ME manuscript. A main
practical necessity is to notice the cases of *ambiguity* and
redundancy which will be found in most ME systems. Ordinary
systems of spelling never embody a uniformly one-to-one
correspondence with the phonemes of the language concerned,
since (like everything else associated with the use of language)
they cannot be maximally consistent or economical. They
reflect changes of pronunciation or grammar by changing the
spellings concerned; but they do not always or immediately
shed those that have been superseded or have lost their function. They may also be exposed to external influences, such as
new factors in the social or cultural setting of the community.

Thus, where ME is concerned, the inherited apparatus of OE
(which was based on that of Latin) was modified (*a*) by internal
changes in the spoken variety of ME in question, and (*b*) by
the historical accident of the Conquest, which furnished
another apparatus from which individual symbols were necessarily adopted along with the French words in which they were
used.

ME spelling systems are in fact less orderly than those of
OE: but there are few major cases of ambiguity. The letter
'yogh' (ȝ) was in origin a form of symbol for the velar fricative
[ɣ], but already in late OE the latter had become a voiced stop
in initial position, and front varieties of *g* had become the
palatal fricative [j]. In ME it also came to be extensively used
for the voiceless palatal and velar fricatives [ç, x] (as in the

Scots *dreich* and *loch*); it is therefore used in three different values, in, for example, ȝelden 'pay', aȝen a. 'own', and nyȝt. And its similarity to the (foreign) letter *z* led to its use in a few manuscripts for [z], for example, in endings: soneȝ 'sons', biddeȝ 'asks'. On the other hand, ȝ is also involved in redundancies, since *h*, ȝh, and *gh* are all possible as symbols for [ç, x]. In other systems, ȝelden might be represented by *yelden*. This relieves ambiguity at one point, but adds it at another: since *y* is by a historical process also a symbol for a vowel, spellings such as *byyete* or *yyeuen* are possible.

J and *v*, being by origin variant forms of *i* and *u* respectively, were used to represent both the consonants [dʒ] and [v] and the vowels [i] and [u], just as *i* and *u* were. *J* and *v* were preferred as symbols for a vowel in initial position, especially when followed by a letter consisting of minims such as *i, u, n, m* (*jn, vnder*).

The use of *ea* for [a] or [ɛ:] and of *eo* for [e] or [e:] is the result of English sound-changes (see pp. xl–xli, 14–15). In each instance, the product of the change happened to be identical with an existing vowel. The inherited symbol for the diphthong could therefore be used for the vowel, whatever the origin of the latter. Because, for example, OE ēa > ME slack ē, ME slack ē of any origin could be spelt *ea*. Since OE ǣ also happened to have become ME slack ē, it was thus often spelt *ea* (*eani* < ǣnig): this is the phenomenon known as an 'inverted spelling'.

The more important graphies adopted from OF are as follows:

    (i) *u* for short and long [y]: L ū had developed into [y] in OF (apart from certain Northern French areas);

    (ii) *ou* for [u:]: in the Western area (the speech of which was the main variety of OF introduced into England) L ō and ŭ, having become the diphthong *ou* as elsewhere, did not then develop into *eu*, but remained *ou*—whence *flour*, the antecedent of E *flower*, instead of *fleur* < L *flōre-*. Already in early OF *ou* > *u* in the West; hence such spellings as *sulement*, XVIII. 294.

(iii) *ch*, in which *h* is a diacritic, for [tʃ]. ME *sh*, *sch* for [ʃ] are believed to have been modelled on *ch*.

(iv) *qu*, used as well as the native *cw*, for [kw].

As distinct from these generally used and handy devices, certain graphies in some manuscripts are the work of AN-speaking scribes who represent certain sounds (in ME texts which they were copying) by alien spellings. Since OF *s* before a consonant passed through the pronunciation [ç] before becoming silent, the very common ME consonant-group [çt] is by them written *st* (which is thus an inverted spelling).[1] ME [ç] also, by being imperfectly distinguished from ME [θ], came to be written *þ* before *t* (*miþte*): while ME [θ] might even be written *z* (as in the name *Siriz* in VI. 161, and *wiz* VI. 162 and *seiz* VI. 179).

[1] See M. K. Pope, *From Latin to Modern French* (Manchester, 1934), §§ 378 (ii), 1178 (ii).

THE OWL AND THE NIGHTINGALE

THE appearance of this witty and sophisticated poem as early as the twelfth century has been described as miraculous. It reflects, to be sure, the humanism of the age of Walter Map and John of Salisbury; but it also reveals a masterly skill in naturalizing French metre, and presents us with a self-portrait of a poet such as we do not find outside Chaucer and Dunbar. Everything favours the supposition that this poet is the Master Nicholas of Guildford who is twice referred to in the poem: its humanity and tolerance are themselves the best proof that he is 'ripe an fastrede', a man of mature wisdom who 'wot insiȝt in eche songe'. The humorous hyperbole of the assertion that he has spread sweetness and light all over England makes it easy to accept the self-advertisement involved in the closing plea for advancement, flavoured as this is with blunt comments on the bishops and nobles whose patronage he sought. But who this Nicholas was, how he earned the title of 'Master' (v. 147n.), and when he went to live at Portisham, we cannot say. He was clearly familiar with the life of woods and fields, yet equally familiar with the Anglo-Norman culture of the court—a culture epitomized in the *Fables* of Marie de France, which he appears to have drawn on. His potential patrons would be more familiar with French or Latin verse than with the obsolescent native alliterative metre; and much of his art consists in naturalizing, apparently without help from any models, the French octosyllabic couplet with its easy rhythm and colloquial flavour.

The poem survives in two composite manuscripts: Cotton Caligula A. ix and Jesus Coll., Oxford, 29: the portion containing the poem in each manuscript was probably copied after 1250. The two texts share some two hundred common errors or peculiarities, pointing to alteration in an exemplar which

cannot have been the original manuscript and may have been
a copy of a copy; and each scribe has independently made
further changes. The Cotton MS. (C) is the basis of the
present text; but the readings of the Jesus MS. (J) are not
always inferior. Many features of the language of both versions
are associated with the south-eastern region, but both also
show a south-west-midland colouring: a copy of the original
evidently found its way westwards, perhaps via London to the
scriptorium of one of the larger western abbeys (? Worcester or
Gloucester).

A reference to 'Þe king Henri'—'Jesus his soule do merci':
ll. 1091–2 of the complete text—provides a *terminus a quo* for
the date of the poem, and is usually taken to indicate the recent
death of Henry II (died 1189). At ll. 1015 ff. there is reference
to the northern journey of a certain 'god man' from Rome—
evidently Cardinal Vivian, who in 1176 was given legatine
authority in 'Ireland, Scotland, Norway, and other adjacent
islands'. It is unlikely that his legation would be remembered
for more than a quarter of a century; and equally unlikely that
ll. 1730 ff. (688 ff. below) would be written in the troublesome
reign of King John (1199–1216). Thus the poem probably
belongs to the reign of Richard I.

f. 233ʳ 1

ICH was in one sumere dale,
In one suþe diȝele hale;
Iherde Ich holde grete tale
An hule and one niȝtingale.
Þat plait was stif an starc an strong,   5
Sumwile softe an lud among;
An eiþer aȝen oþer sval
An let þat vuele mod ut al;
An eiþer seide of oþeres custe
Þat alreworste þat hi wuste;   10
An hure an hure of oþeres songe

7 eiþer] *marginal correction* (*in later hand*) *of* asþer   8 vuele J]
wole C, *marked for correction*   11 oþeres] oþere C oþres J

Hi holde plaiding suþe stronge.
  Þe niȝtingale bigon þe speche
In one hurne of one breche,
An sat up one vaire boȝe   15
Þar were abute blosme inoȝe,
In ore waste þicke hegge
Imeind mid spire an grene segge.
Ho was þe gladur uor þe rise
An song a uele cunne wise.   20
Bet þuȝte þe dreim þat he were
Of harpe an pipe þan he nere;
Bet þuȝte þat he were ishote
Of harpe an pipe þan of þrote.
  Þo stod on old stoc þarbiside,   25
Þar þo vle song hire tide,
An was mid iui al bigrowe:
Hit was þare hule earding-stowe.
  Þe niȝtingale hi iseȝ
An hi bihold an ouerseȝ,   30
An þuȝte wel wl of þare hule,
For me hi halt lodlich an fule.
'Vnwiȝt,' ho sede, 'awei þu flo.
Me is þe wrs þat Ich þe so:
Iwis, for þine wle lete   35 f. 233ʳ 2
Wel oft Ich mine song forlete;
Min horte atfliþ, an falt mi tonge,
Wonne þu art to me iþrunge;
Me luste bet speten þane singe
Of þine fule ȝoȝelinge'.   40
  Þos hule abod fort hit was eve—
Ho ne miȝte no leng bileue:

17 waste C] vaste J   21 Bet J] Het C, *marked for correction*
31 wl C] ful J

Vor hire horte was so gret
þat welneȝ hire fnast atschet—
An warp a word þarafter longe: 45
'Hu þincþe nu bi mine songe?
Wenst þu þat Ich ne cunne singe,
Þeȝ Ich ne cunne of writelinge?
Ilome þu dest me grame
An seist me boþe tone an schame.   50
Ȝif Ich þe holde on mine uote
(So hit bitide þat Ich mote!)
An þu were vt of þine rise,
Þu sholdest singe anoþer wise.'

      Þe niȝtingale ȝaf answare: 55
'Ȝif Ich me loki wit þe bare
An me schilde wit þe blete,
Ne reche Ich noȝt of þine þrete;
Ȝif Ich me holde in mine hegge,
Ne recche Ich neuer what þu segge.   60
Ich wot þat þu art unmilde
Wiþ hom þat ne muȝe from þe schilde;
An þu tukest wroþe an vuele,
Whar þu miȝt over, smale fuȝele.
Vorþi þu art loþ al fuel-kunne,   65
An alle ho þe driueþ honne
An þe bischricheþ an bigredet
An wel narewe þe biledet;
An ek forþe þe sulue mose,
Hire þonkes, wolde þe totose.   70
Þu art lodlich to biholde,
An þu art loþ in monie volde:
Þi bodi is short, þi swore is smal:

51 uote] note C vote 𝒥   54 wise 𝒥] wse C   62 þe 𝒥] se C
64 over (ouer 𝒥) ?miswritten for oþer, as at l. 1524 of MS.

Grettere is þin heued þan þu al;
Þin eȝene boþ colblake an brode,   75
Riȝt swo ho weren ipeint mid wode.
Þu starest so þu wille abiten
Al þat þu mist mid cliure smiten.
Þi bile is stif an scharp an hoked,
Riȝt so an owel þat is croked;   80
Þarmid þu clackes oft an longe
An þat is on of þine songe.
Ac þu þretest to mine flesche,
Mid þine cliures woldest me meshe:
Þe were icundur to one frogge   85
Þat sit at mulne vnder cogge;
Snailes, mus, an fule wiȝte
Boþ þine cunde an þine riȝte.
Þu sittest adai an fliȝst aniȝt:
Þu cuþest þat þu art on vnwiȝt.   90
Þu art lodlich an unclene;
Bi þine neste Ich hit mene
An eke bi þine fule brode:
Þu fedest on hom a wel ful fode.

        .   .   .   .   .   .   ᾽

   Þos word aȝaf þe niȝtingale;   95 [139] f. 234ʳ 1
An after þare longe tale
He song so lude an so scharpe
Riȝt so me grulde schille harpe.
Þos hule luste þiderward
An hold hire eȝe noþerward,   100
An sat tosvolle an ibolwe,
Also ho hadde one frogge isuolȝe:
For ho wel wiste an was iwar

81 clechest euer among 𝒥   86 *supplied from* 𝒥   89 fliȝst]
fliȝt C flyhst 𝒥   100 noþerward] noþerwad C neþerward 𝒥

Þat ho song hire abisemar.

An noþeles ho ȝaf andsuare: 105

'Whi neltu flon into þe bare

An sewi weþer unker bo

Of briȝter howe, of uairur blo?'

'No! Þu hauest wel scharpe clawe;

Ne kepich noȝt þat þu me clawe.   110

Þu hauest cliuers suþe stronge;

Þu tuengst þarmid so doþ a tonge.

Þu þoȝtest, so doþ þine ilike,

Mid faire worde me biswike.

Ich nolde don þat þu me raddest—   115

Ich wiste wel þat þu me misraddest.

Schamie þe for þin unrede.

Vnwroȝen is þi svikelhede.

Schild þin svikedom vram þe liȝte

An hud þat woȝe among þe riȝte;   120

Þane þu wilt þin unriȝt spene,

Loke þat hit ne bo isene:

Vor svikedom haueð schome an hete

Ȝif hit is ope an underȝete.

Ne speddestu noȝt mid þine unwrenche: 125

For Ich am war an can wel blenche;

Ne helpþ noȝt þat þu bo to þriste;

f. 234ʳ 2   Ich wolde viȝte bet mid liste

Þan þu mid al þine strengþe;

Ich habbe on brede an eck on lengþe   130

Castel god on mine rise.

"Wel fiȝt þat wel fliȝt," seiþ þe wise.

Ac lete we awei þos cheste,

---

107 weþer] þare C (*marked for correction*) hweþer Ɉ   119 svikel- C
120 among Ɉ] amon C   123 haveð] haued C (*uncrossed ð not
henceforth noted*)

Vor suiche wordes boþ vnwreste;
An fo we on mid riȝte dome,   135
Mid faire worde an mid ysome.
Þeȝ we ne bo at one acorde,
We muȝe bet mid fayre worde,
Witute cheste an bute fiȝte,
Plaidi mid foȝe an mid riȝte   140
An mai hure eiþer wat hi wile
Mid riȝte segge an mid sckile.'
   Þo quaþ þe hule: 'Wo schal us seme,
Þat kunne an wille riȝt us deme?'
'Ich wot wel,' quaþ þe niȝtingale,   145
'Ne þaref þarof bo no tale:
Maister Nichole of Guldeforde.
He is wis an war of worde;
He is of dome suþe gleu,
An him is loþ eurich unþeu.   150
He wot insiȝt in eche songe,
Wo singet wel, wo singet wronge;
An he can schede vrom þe riȝte
Þat woȝe, þat þuster from þe liȝte.'
   Þo hule one wile hi biþoȝte,   155
And after þan þis word up broȝte:
'Ich granti wel þat he us deme:
Vor þeȝ he were wile breme,
An lof him were niȝtingale
An oþer wiȝte gente an smale,   160
Ich wot he is nu suþe acoled.
Nis he vor þe noȝt afoled,   f. 234ᵛ 1
Þat he for þine olde luue
Me adun legge an þe buue;
Ne schaltu neure so him queme   165

134 vnwrest 𝒥] unwerste C   143 Wo] þu C hwo 𝒥

Þat he for þe fals dom deme;
He is him ripe an fastrede,
Ne lust him nu to none unrede.
Nu him ne lust namore pleie;
He wile gon a riȝte weie.'   170

  Þe niȝtingale was al ȝare;
Ho hadde ilorned wel aiware:
'Hule,' ho seide, 'seie me soþ:
Wi dostu þat unwiȝtis doþ?
Þu singist aniȝt an noȝt adai,   175
An al þi song is "wailawai".
Þu miȝt mid þine song afere
Alle þat ihereþ þine ibere;
Þu schrichest an ȝollest to þine fere,
Þat hit is grislich to ihere;   180
Hit þincheþ boþe wise an snepe
Noȝt þat þu singe, ac þat þu wepe.
Þu fliȝst aniȝt an noȝt adai,
Þarof Ich wndri an wel mai:
Vor eurich þing þat schuniet riȝt   185
Hit luueþ þuster and hatiet liȝt;
An eurich þing þat is lof misdede
Hit luueþ þuster to his dede.'

      ·   ·   ·   ·   ·   ·

f. 234ᵛ 2   Þos hule luste suþe longe   [253
An was oftoned suþe stronge.   190
Ho quaþ: 'Þu hattest niȝtingale;
Þu miȝtest bet hoten galegale,
Vor þu hauest to monie tale.
Lat þine tunge habbe spale!

---

167 is nv ripe *J*   179 schrichest] schirchest *C* (*marked for correction*)   181 þincheþ *J*] þinchest *C*   191 Ho quaþ *marked for correction* (*? to* Quaþ ho)

Þu wenest þat þes dai bo þin oȝe. 195
Lat me nu habbe mine þroȝe.
Bo nu stille an lat me speke,
Ich wille bon of þe awreke.
An lust hu Ich con me bitelle
Mid riȝte soþe, witute spelle. 200
Þu seist þat Ich me hude adai:
Þarto ne segge Ich nich ne nai;
An lust, Ich telle þe wareuore—
Al wi hit is an wareuore:
Ich habbe bile stif an stronge 205
An gode cliuers scharp an longe,
So hit bicumeþ to hauekes cunne;
Hit is mine hiȝte, hit is mi wunne
Þat Ich me draȝe to mine cunde;
Ne mai me noman þareuore schende. 210
On me hit is wel isene:
Vor riȝte cunde Ich am so kene.
   'Vorþi Ich am loþ smale foȝle
Þat floþ bi grunde an bi þuuele.
Hi me bichermet an bigredeþ 215
An hore flockes to me ledeþ.
Me is lof to habbe reste
An sitte stille in mine neste.

  .   .   .   .   .   .

Wenestu þat haueck bo þe worse [303
Þoȝ crowe bigrede him bi þe mershe 220
An goþ to him mid hore chirme
Riȝt so hi wille wit him schirme?
Þe hauec folȝeþ gode rede,
An fliȝt his wei an lat hi grede. f. 235ʳ 2

208 wunne] wune (*with init.* wynn) C ynne Ɉ   210 me Ɉ] *om.* C
224 hi *altered in* C *to* hem (?) hi Ɉ

'ȝet þu me seist of oþer þinge,   225
An telst þat Ich ne can noȝt singe,
Ac al mi rorde is woning
An to ihire grislich þing.
Þat nis noȝt soþ: Ich singe efne,
Mid fulle dreme an lude stefne.   230
Þu wenist þat ech song bo grislich
Þat þinc pipinge nis ilich:
Mi stefne is bold an noȝt unorne;
Ho is ilich one grete horne;
An þin is ilich one pipe   235
Of one smale wode unripe.
Ich singe bet þan þu dest;
Þu chaterest so doþ on Irish prest.
Ich singe an eue a riȝte time,
An soþþe won hit is bedtime;   240
Þe þridde siþe ad middelniȝte;
An so Ich mine songe adiȝte
Wone Ich iso arise vorre
Oþer dairim oþer daisterre.
Ich do god mid mine þrote   245
An warni men to hore note.
Ac þu singest alle longe niȝt
From eue fort hit is dailiȝt,
An eure lesteþ þin o song
So longe so þe niȝt is long,   250
An eure croweþ þi wrecche crei
Þat he ne swikeþ niȝt ne dai.
Mid þine pipinge þu adunest
Þas monnes earen þar þu wunest,

---

233 bold *Ʒ*] blod *C*   236 wode, *with* e *inserted above between* o
and d *C* weode *Ʒ*   238 prest *Ʒ*] prost, *with* e *inserted above* o *C*
249 lesteþ *Ʒ*] leist *?altered from* seist *C*

An makest þine song so unwrþ   255
Þat me ne telþ of þar noȝt wrþ.
Eurich murȝþe mai so longe ileste
Þat ho shal liki wel unwreste: f. 235ᵛ 1
Vor harpe an pipe an fuȝeles song
Mislikeþ ȝif hit is to long,   260
Ne bo þe song neuer so murie
Þat he ne shal þinche wel unmurie
Ȝef he ilesteþ ouer unwille.
So þu miȝt þine song aspille:
Vor hit is soþ—Alured hit seide,   265
An me hit mai ine boke rede:
"Eurich þing mai losen his godhede
Mid unmeþe an mid ouerdede."
  .   .   .   .   .   .   '

  Þe niȝtingale in hire þoȝte   [391] f. 235ᵛ 2
Athold al þis, an longe þoȝte   270
Wat ho þarafter miȝte segge:
Vor ho ne miȝte noȝt alegge
Þat þe hule hadde hire ised,
Vor he spac boþe riȝt an red;
An hire ofþuȝte þat ho hadde   275
Þe speche so for uorþ iladde,
An was oferd þat hire answare
Ne wrþe noȝt ariȝt ifare.
Ac noþeles he spac boldeliche:
Vor he is wis þat hardeliche   280
Wiþ is uo berþ grete ilete,
Þat he uor areȝeþe hit ne forlete:
Vor suich worþ bold ȝif þu fliȝst
Þat wle flo ȝif þu vicst;

255 unwrþ] vnwiht *Ĵ*   256 of þe nowiht *Ĵ*   259 song *Ĵ*] songe *C*
283 fliȝst] fliȝste *C* flyhst *Ĵ*   284 isvicst *C* (is *cancelled*)] swykst *Ĵ*

Ʒif he isiþ þat nart areʒ,   285
He wile of bore wrchen bareʒ.
An forþi, þeʒ þe niʒtingale

Were aferd, ho spac bolde tale:
    'Hule,' ho seide, 'Wi dostu so?
Þu singest a winter "wolawo";   290
Þu singest so doþ hen a snowe;
Al þat ho singeþ hit is for wowe;
A wintere þu singest wroþe an ʒomere,
An eure þu art dumb a sumere.
Hit is for þine fule niþe   295
Þat þu ne miʒt mid us bo bliþe:
Vor þu forbernest welneʒ for onde
Wane ure blisse cumeþ to londe.
Þu farest so doþ þe ille:
Evrich blisse him is unwille;   300
Grucching an luring him boþ rade
Ʒif he isoþ þat men boþ glade;
He wolde þat he iseʒe
Teres in evrich monnes eʒe;
Ne roʒte he þeʒ flockes were   305
Imeind bi toppes an bi here.
Also þu dost on þire side:
Vor wanne snov liþ þicke an wide
An alle wiʒtes habbeþ sorʒe,
Þu singest from eue fort amorʒe.   310
Ac Ich blisse mid me bringe;
Ech wiʒt is glad for mine þinge,
An blisseþ hit wanne Ich cume
An hiʒteþ aʒen mine kume.
Þe blostme ginneþ springe an sprede,   315
Boþe ine tro an ek on mede.

296 bo *with stroke through* o C] be *J*   313 blisseþ] blesseþ *J*

þe lilie mid hire faire wlite
Wolcumeþ me, þat þu hit wite;
Bid me mid hire faire blo
Þat Ich shulle to hire flo;   320
þe rose also mid hire rude

Þat cumeþ ut of þe þorne-wode
Bit me þat Ich shulle singe
Vor hire luue one skentinge.

.   .   .   .   .   .   ,

    Þos hule luste an leide an hord   325 [467
Al þis mot, word after word;
An after þoȝte hu he miȝte
Ansvere uinde best mid riȝte:
Vor he mot hine ful wel biþenche
Þat is aferd of plaites wrenche.   330
    'Þv aishest me', þe hule sede,
'Wi Ich a winter singe an grede.
Hit is gode monne iwone
An was from þe worlde frome,
Þat ech god man his frond icnowe   335

An blisse mid hom sume þrowe
In his huse at his borde,
Mid faire speche an faire worde;
An hure an hure to Cristesmasse,
Þane riche an poure, more an lasse,   340
Singeþ cundut niȝt an dai.
Ich hom helpe what Ich mai.

.   .   .   .   .   .

An ek Ich frouri uele wiȝte   [535] f. 236ᵛ 2
Þat mid hom nabbeð none miȝte.
Hi boþ hoȝfule an uel arme,   345

318 wite] wte C þeyh þu hit wite J   319 Bid apparently altered
from bit by scribe; Bid J (but Bit J 323)

An secheþ ȝorne to þe warme.
Oft Ich singe uor hom þe more,
For lutli sum of hore sore.
Hu þincþ þe? Artu ȝut inume?
Artu mid riȝte ouercume?'   350
    'Nay, nay,' sede þe niȝtingale;
'Þu shalt ihere anoþer tale.
Ȝet nis þos speche ibroȝt to dome.

Ac bo wel stille an lust nu tome:
Ich shal mid one bare worde   355
Do þat þi speche wrth forworþe.'
    'Þat nere noht riȝt,' þe hule sede;
'Þu hauest bicloped also þu bede,
An Ich þe habbe iȝiue ansuare.
Ac ar we to unker dome fare   360
Ich wille speke toward þe
Also þu speke toward me,
An þu me ansuare ȝif þu miȝt.
Seie me nu, þu wrecche wiȝt,
Is in þe eni oþer note   365
Bute þu hauest schille þrote?
Þu nart noȝt to non oþer þinge
Bute þu canst of chateringe:
Vor þu art lutel an unstrong,
An nis þi reȝel noþing long.   370
Wat dostu godes among monne?
Namo þe deþ a wrecche wranne!
Of þe ne cumeþ non oþer god
Bute þu gredest suich þu bo wod;
An, bo þi piping ouergo,   375
Ne boþ on þe craftes namo.

356 wrth] wrht C wrþ J   363 ansuare, e above second a in
different ink   372 wrecche J] wercche C

. . . . . .

3et þu atuitest me mine mete,   [597] f. 237ʳ 2
An seist þat Ich fule wi3tes ete.
Ac wat etestu, þat þu ne li3e,
Bute attercoppe an fule uli3e?   380
An wormes, 3if þu mi3te finde
Among þe uolde of harde rinde?
3et Ich can do wel gode wike,
Vor Ich can loki manne wike;
An mine wike boþ wel gode   385
Vor Ich helpe to manne uode:
Ich can nimen mus at berne
An eke at chirche ine þe derne:
Vor me is lof to Cristes huse
To clansi hit wiþ fule muse;   390
Ne schal þar neure come to
Ful wi3t, 3if Ich hit mai iuo.
An 3if me lust one mi skentinge
To wernen oþer wnienge,   f. 237ᵛ 1
Ich habbe at wude tron wel grete,   395
Mit þicke bo3e noþing blete,
Mid iui grene al bigrowe,
Þat eure stont iliche iblowe
An his hou neure ne uorlost
Wan hit sniuþ ne wan hit frost.   400
Þarin Ich habbe god ihold,
A winter warm, a sumere cold;
Wane min hus stont bri3t an grene,
Of þine nis noþing isene.

. . . . . . '

Þe ni3tingale at þisse worde   405 [659] f. 237ᵛ 2
Was welne3 ut of rede iworþe,

    400 sniuþ] sniuw C snywe J

An þoȝte ȝorne on hire mode
Ȝif ho oȝt elles understode—
Ȝif ho kuþe oȝt, bute singe,
Þat miȝte helpe to oþer þinge.   410
Herto ho moste andswere uinde
Oþer mid alle bon bihinde.
An hit is suþe strong to fiȝte
Aȝen soþe an aȝen riȝte.
He mot gon to al mid ginne   415
Wan þe horte biþ ouerþinne;
An þe man mot onoþer segge,
He mot bihemmen an bilegge,
Ȝif muþ wiþute mai biwro
Þat me þe horte noȝt n'iso.   420
An sone mai a word misreke
Þar muþ shal aȝen horte speke;
An sone mai a word misstorte
Þar muþ shal speken aȝen horte.
Ac noþeles ȝut upe þon   425
Her is to red, wo hine kon:
Vor neuer nis wit so kene

So þane red him is awene;
Þanne erest kumeð his ȝephede
Wone hit is alremest on drede: 430
For Aluered seide of olde quide,
An ȝut hit nis of horte islide:
'Wone þe bale is alrehecst,
Þonne is þe bote alrenecst':
Vor wit west among his sore   435
An for his sore hit is þe more.
Vorþi nis neuere mon redles
Ar his horte bo witles;

416 ouer-] on *C, J*   428 So þane] So hwanne *J*

Ac ȝif þat he forlost his wit,
Þonne is his red-purs al toslit: 440
Ȝif he ne kon his wit atholde
Ne uint he red in one uolde:
Vor Alured seide, þat wel kuþe—
Eure he spac mid soþe muþe:
'Wone þe bale is alrehecst,   445
Þanne is þe bote alrenest.'

    Þe niȝtingale al hire hoȝe
Mid rede hadde wel bitöȝe;
Among þe harde, among þe toȝte,
Ful wel mid rede hire biþoȝte;   450
An hadde andsuere gode ifunde
Among al hire harde stunde:
    'Hule, þu axest me,' ho seide,
'Ȝif Ich kon eni oþer dede
Bute singen in sume tide   455
An bringe blisse for an wide.
Wi axestu of craftes mine?
Betere is mine on þan alle þine;
Betere is o song of mine muþe
Þan al þat eure þi kun kuþe.   460
An lust, Ich telle þe wareuore:
Wostu to wan man was ibore?   f. 238ʳ 2
To þare blisse of houeneriche
Þar euer is song an murȝþe iliche;
Þider fundeþ eurich man   465
Þat eniþing of gode kan.
Vorþi me singþ in holi chirche,
An clerkes ginneþ songes wirche,
Þat man iþenche bi þe songe
Wider he shal, an þar bon longe: 470

442 inone] in none ȝ   443 Alured ȝ] Aluid C

Þat he þe murȝþe ne forȝete,
Ac þarof þenche an biȝete
An nime ȝeme of chirche steuene,
Hu murie is þe blisse of houene.
Clerkes, munekes, an kanunes,   475
Þar boþ þos gode wicke-tunes,
Ariseþ up to midelniȝte
An singeþ of þe houene-liȝte;
An prostes upe londe singeþ
Wane þe liȝt of daie springeþ   480
An Ich hom helpe wat I mai:
Ich singe mid hom niȝt an dai;
An ho boþ alle for me þe gladdere,
An to þe songe boþ þe raddere.
Ich warni men to here gode   485
Þat hi bon bliþe on hore mode
An bidde þat hi moten iseche
Þan ilke song þat euer is eche.
Nu þu miȝt, hule, sitte an clinge.
Heramong nis no chateringe;   490
Ich graunti þat we go to dome
Tofore þe sulfe pope of Rome.
Ac abid ȝete noþeles—
Þu shalt ihere anoþer þes;
Ne shaltu for Engelonde   495
At þisse worde me atstonde.

.   .   .   .   .   .’

'Abid, abid,' þe ule seide;   [837
'Þu gest al to mid swikelede;
Alle þine wordes þu bileist,
Þat hit þincþ soþ al þat þu seist;   500

f. 238ᵛ 1

f. 239ʳ 1

492 þe sulve pope Ĵ] þe sulfe þe pope C   494 þes or wes C]
abyde on oþer bles Ĵ (bles in later hand)

Alle þine wordes boþ isliked
An so bisemed an biliked
Þat alle þo þat hi auoþ
Hi weneþ þat þu segge soþ.
Abid, abid. Me schal þe ȝene,   505
Nu hit shal wrþe wel isene
Þat þu hauest muchel iloȝe,
Wone þi lesing boþ unwroȝe.
Þu seist þat þu singist mankunne
An techest hom þat hi fundieþ honne   510
Vp to þe songe þat eure ilest.
Ac hit is alre wnder mest
Þat þu darst liȝe so opeliche.
Wenest þu hi bringe so liȝtliche   f. 239ʳ 2
To Godes riche al singinde?   515
Nai, Nai, hi shulle wel auinde
Þat hi mid longe wope mote
Of hore sunnen bidde bote
Ar hi mote euer kume þare.

'Ich rede þi þat men bo ȝare   520
An more wepe þane singe,
Þat fundeþ to þan houen-kinge:
Vor nis no man witute sunne.
Vorþi he mot, ar he wende honne,
Mid teres an mid wope bete   525
Þat him bo sur þat er was swete.
Þarto Ich helpe, God hit wot,
Ne singe Ich hom no foliot.

.   .   .   .   .   .

Al þu forlost þe murȝþe of houene,   [897] f. 239ᵛ 1
For þarto neuestu none steuene.   530
Al þat þu singst is of golnesse,

506 Nu *J*] þu *C*   515 singinde *J*] singinge *C*   528 Ich *J*] ih *C*

For nis on þe non holinesse.
Ne weneð na man for þi pipinge
Þat eni preost in chirche singe.
ʒet I þe wulle anoðer segge   535
ʒif þu hit const ariht bilegge:
Wi nultu singe an oðer þeode
Þar hit is muchele more neode?
Þu neauer ne singst in Irlonde,
Ne þu ne cumest noʒt in Scotlonde.   540
Hwi nultu fare to Noreweie,
An singin men of Galeweie?
Þar beoð men þat lutel kunne
Of songe þat is bineoðe þe sunne.
Wi nultu þare preoste singe   545
An teche of þire writelinge,
An wisi hom mid þire steuene
Hu engeles singeð in heouene?
Þu farest so doð an ydel wel
Þat springeþ bi burne þat is snel,   550
An let fordrue þe dune
An flowþ on idel þar adune.
Ac Ich fare boþe norþ an souþ;

f. 239ᵛ 2   In eauereuch londe Ich am cuuþ;
East an west, feor an neor,   555
I do wel faire mi meoster,
An warni men mid mine bere
Þat þi dweole-song heo ne forlere.

                .   .   .   .   .   ,

f. 242ʳ 2   Þe niʒtingale sat an siʒte,   [1291
An hohful was—an ful wel miʒte—   560

534 chirche ʒ] chircce C   550 þat . . . þat ʒ] þar . . . þar C
551 fordrue] fordruye ʒ   552 flowþ] flohþ ʒ floh C   553 souþ ʒ]
soþ C

For þe hule swo ispeke hadde
An hire speche swo iladde;   f. 242ᵛ 1
Heo was hohful an erede
Hwat heo þarafter hire sede.
Ah neoþeles heo hire understod: 565
'Wat!' heo seide, 'hule, artu wod?
Þu ȝeolpest of seolliche wisdome,
Þu nustest wanene he þe come
Bute hit of wicchecrefte were.
Þarof þu, wrecche, moste þe skere   570
Ȝif þu wult among manne beo;
Oþer þu most of londe fleo:
For alle þeo þat þerof cuþe,
Heo uere ifurn of prestes muþe
Amanset; swuch þu art ȝette: 575
Þu wiecchecrafte neauer ne lete.
Ich þe seide nu lutel ere
An þu askedest ȝef Ich were
—Abisemere—to preost ihoded.
Ah þe mansing is so ibroded,   580
Þah no preost a londe nere
A wrecche neoþeles þu were:
For eauereuch child þe cleopeþ fule,
An eauereuch man a wrecche hule.
Ich habbe iherd—an soþ hit is—   585
Þe mon mot beo wel storre-wis
An wite inoh of wucche þinge kume,
So þu seist þat is iwune.
Hwat canstu, wrecche þing, of storre
Bute þat þu bihaltest hi feorre?   590

563 hohful] hoþful *C* houhful *J*   571 beo *J*] boe *C*
583 child] d *in later hand*   587 inoh *J*] innoþ *C*   590 bihaltest]
bihaitest *CJ*

Alswo deþ mani dor an man
Þeo of swucche nawiht ne con.
On ape mai a boc bihalde
An leues wenden an eft folde:
Ac he ne con þe bet þaruore   595

f. 242ᵛ 2

Of clerkes lore top ne more.
Þah þu iseo þe steorre alswa
Nartu þe wisure neauer þe mo.'

.   .   .   .   .   .

f. 245ʳ 1

'Þu ȝulpest þat þu art manne loþ   [1641
An euereuch wiht is wið þe wroþ,   600
An mid ȝulinge an mid igrede
Þu anst wel þat þu art unlede.
Þu seist þat gromes þe ifoð
An heie on rodde þe anhoð
An þe totwichet an toschakeð   605
An summe of þe schawles makeð.
Me þunch þat þu forleost þat game.
Þu ȝulpest of þire oȝe schame;
Me þunch þat þu me gest an honde;
Þu ȝulpest of þire oȝene schonde.'   610
Þo heo hadde þeos word icwede,
Heo sat in one faire stude,
An þarafter hire steuene dihte
An song so schille an so brihte
Þat feor an ner me hit iherde.   615
Þaruore anan to hire cherde
Þrusche an þrostle an wudewale
An fuheles boþe grete an smale.

592 swucche] hswucche *C*   599 ȝulpest] ȝeilpest, *possibly
changed to* ȝulpest *C*   600 wroþ *J*] worþ *C*   602 anst] wanst *C*
þinchst *J*   607 þunch] þinkþ *J*   þu *J*] þir *C*   609 þunch]
þinkþ *J*   610 schonde *J*] schomme *C*

For þan heom þuhte þat heo hadde
Þe houle ouercome, uor þan heo gradde   620
An sungen alswa uale wise,
An blisse was among þe rise,
Riȝt swa me gred þe manne a schame
Þat taueleþ an forleost þat gome.

Þeos hule, þo heo þis iherde,   625
'Hauestu,' heo seide, 'ibanned ferde?   f. 245ʳ 2
An wultu, wreche, wið me fiȝte?
Nai, nai, nauestu none miȝte.
Hwat gredeþ þeo þat hider come?
Me þuncþ þu ledest ferde tome.   630
Ȝe schule wite ar ȝe fleo heonne
Hwuch is þe strenþe of mine kunne:
For þeo þe haueþ bile ihoked
An cliures scharpe an wel icroked,
Alle heo beoþ of mine kunrede   635
An walde come ȝif Ich bede.
Þe seolfe coc, þat wel can fiȝte,
He mot mid me holde mid riȝte:
For boþe we habbeþ steuene briȝte
An sitteþ under weolcne bi nihte.   640
Schille Ich an utest uppen ow grede,
Ich schal swo stronge ferde lede
Þat ower proude schal aualle;
A tort ne ȝiue Ich for ow alle!
Ne schal, ar hit beo fulliche eue,   645
A wreche feþer on ow bileaue.
Ah hit was unker uoreward
Þo we come hiderward

630 þuncþ] þᵗ *altered from* h?   634 scharpe *Ɉ*] charpe *C*
639 habbeþ] hableþ *C*   640 weolcne] weoline *C* welkne *Ɉ*
643 ower] oþer *C* oure *Ɉ*   proude] prude *Ɉ*

Þat we þarto holde scholde
Þar riht dom us ȝiue wolde.   650
Wultu nu breke foreward?
Ich wene dom þe þincþ to hard.
For þu ne darst domes abide
Þu wult nu, wreche, fiȝte an chide.
Ȝut Ich ow alle wolde rede,   655
Ar Ich utheste uppon ow grede:
Þat ower fihtlac leteþ beo
An ginneþ raþe awei fleo:

For, bi þe cliures þat Ich bere,
Ȝef ȝe abideþ mine here,   660
Ȝe schule onoþer wise singe
An acursi alle fiȝtinge:
Vor nis of ow non so kene
Þat durre abide mine onsene.'
Þeos hule spac wel baldeliche: 665
For, þah heo nadde swo hwatliche
Ifare after hire here,
Heo walde neoþeles ȝefe answere
Þe niȝtegale mid swucche worde:
For moni man mid speres orde   670
Haueþ lutle strencþe, an mid his schelde,
Ah neoþeles in one felde
Þurh belde worde an mid ilete
Deþ his iuo for arehþe swete.
Þe wranne, for heo cuþe singe,   675
Þar com in þare moreȝeninge
To helpe þare niȝtegale:
For, þah heo hadde steuene smale,

652 þincþ J] þing C   655 Ȝut] ȝot C yet J   656 Ar ich J]
Ariht C   671 schelde] chelde C   676 moreȝeninge]
moreȝennge C   679 þrote J] þorte C

Heo hadde gode þrote an schille
An fale manne song awille.   680
Þe wranne was wel wis iholde:
Vor, þeg heo were ibred a wolde,
Ho was itoȝen among mankenne
An hire wisdom brohte þenne;
Heo miȝte speke hwar heo walde,   685
Touore þe king þah heo scholde.
'Lusteþ', heo cwaþ, 'lateþ me speke:
Hwat! Wulle ȝe þis pes tobreke
An do þan kinge swuch schame?
Ȝe, nis he nouþer ded ne lame.   690
Hunke schal itide harme an schonde
Ȝef ȝe doþ griþbruche on his londe.
Lateþ beo, an beoþ isome.   f. 245ᵛ 2
An fareþ riht to ower dome,
An lateþ dom þis plaid tobreke   695
Alswo hit was erur bispeke.'
    'Ich an wel,' cwað þe niȝtegale;
'Ah, wranne, nawt for þire tale
Ah do for mine lahfulnesse:
Ich nolde þat unrihtfulnesse   700
Me at þen ende ouerkome;
Ich nam ofdrad of none dome.
Bihote Ich habbe, soþ hit is,
Þat Maister Nichole, þat is wis,
Bituxen vs deme schulle;   705
An ȝet Ich wene þat he wulle.
Ah war mihte we hine finde?'
Þe wranne sat in ore linde:

---

682 þeg] g *doubtful*; þeih *Ʒ*   were] nere *CƷ*   683 mankunne *Ʒ*]
mannenne *C*   689 þan] þanne *CƷ; Edd. ins.* kinge   705 schulle *Ʒ*]
schulde *C*   706 yet *Ʒ*] ȝef *C*   wulle *Ʒ*] wule *C*   709 Nuste]
nuȝte *or* miȝte *C*   mihte *Ʒ*

'Hwat! Nuste ȝe,' cwaþ heo, 'his hom?
He wuneþ at Porteshom,   710
At one tune ine Dorsete,
Bi þare see in ore utlete;
Þar he demeþ manie riȝte dom
An diht an writ mani wisdom;
An þurh his muþe an þurh his honde   715
Hit is þe betere into Scotlonde.
To seche hine is lihtlich þing.
He naueþ bute one woning—
Þat is bischopen muchel schame `
An alle þan þat of his nome   720
Habbeþ ihert, an of his dede.
Hwi nulleþ hi nimen heom to rede
Þat he were mid heom ilome
For teche heom of his wisdome,
An ȝiue him rente a uale stude   725
Þat he miȝte heom ilome be mide?'

f. 246ʳ 1   'Certes,' quaþ þe hule, 'þat is soð.
Þeos riche men wel much misdoð
Þat leteþ þane gode mon
Þat of so feole þinge con,   730
An ȝiueþ rente wel misliche
An of him leteþ wel lihtliche.
Wið heore cunne heo beoþ wel mildre
An ȝeueþ rente litle childre.
Swo heore wit hi demþ adwole   735
Þat euer abid Maistre Nichole.
Ah ute we þah to him fare,
For þar is unker dom al ȝare.'
     'Do we,' þe niȝtegale seide,
'Ah wa schal unker speche rede   740

An telle touore unker deme?'
  'Þarof Ich schal þe wel icweme,'
Cwaþ þe houle, 'for al, ende of orde,
Telle Ich con, word after worde;
An ȝef þe þincþ þat Ich misrempe,   745
Þu stond aȝein an do me crempe.'
Mid þisse worde forþ hi ferde,
Al bute here an bute uerde,
To Portesham þat heo bicome.
Ah hu heo spedde of heore dome   750
Ne can Ich eu namore telle.
Her nis namore of þis spelle.

747 ferden *CJ*   751 can *J*] chan *C*

II

KYNG ALISAUNDER

THE legend (as distinct from the history) of Alexander the Great first appears in a systematic literary form in the late Greek romance known to scholars as the *Pseudo-Callisthenes* after its *soi-disant* author, and now believed to have been composed some time after A.D. 200.[1] The material in it was made available to Western Europe in the Middle Ages by the translations of Julius Valerius (*Res Gestae Alexandri Macedonis, c.* A.D. 300) and the Archpriest Leo (*Historia de Preliis,* composed between 951 and 969). The latter, in one or other of the expanded versions now called the I[1], I[2], and I[3] recensions, was a main source of the Alexander-books in medieval vernacular literature. The former was reduced to a bald summary called the *Epitome*, which provided the nucleus for the extended treatment by Thomas of Kent in the twelfth-century Anglo-Norman *Roman de toute cheualerie,* on which *Kyng Alisaunder* is principally based.

Given the exploits of a great military leader as an ostensible subject, it is inevitably the world of medieval epic and its ideals that are depicted in *Kyng Alisaunder,* as in the *Roman de toute cheualerie.* Heroic and romantic interests are reasonably distinct in the genres of epic and romance in Old French, from which literature Middle English poets learned the art of narration in verse. But a time-lag of 100 to 150 years in the effective imitation of the foreign models had blurred the distinction for most English writers. The excerpt below shows how, even in writing a work of predominantly heroic sympathies, two English storytellers of the late twelfth and the early fourteenth centuries found an opportunity to deck out an amorous episode with the spirit and the trappings of courtly love.

[1] The oldest recension has been edited by W. Kroll under the title of *Historia Alexandri Magni* (1958).

In scale, apart from anything else, *Kyng Alisaunder* is a more ambitious work than the technically assured but brief thirteenth-century English romances such as *Havelok* and *Floris and Blauncheflour*. Though not better organized than these, it is a stronger and technically a more sophisticated performance, and implies a broader literary culture in the author. The visual descriptions of his nature-introductions show a freshness of fancy, and their gnomic and sententious axioms a spontaneous ease, that raise him above most writers of Middle English romances. And his forceful and lively verse is much superior to the toneless alexandrines of his Anglo-Norman source.

> ON a day sone after þan   f. 61ᵛ 1
> Com Candulek, a gentil man—   (7446 ff.)
> Candaces son, kyng of Brye—
> Wiþ wel faire chyualrye,
> And wolde wiþ Alisaunder speke,   5
> Forto ben þorouȝ hym awreke
> Of a prynce þat by striif
> Had bynomen hym his wiif.
> Ac Alisaunder had a wone:
> Þeiȝ to court com kyng oiþer his sone,   10
> Prynce, oiþer duk, oiþer gret caiser,
> Kniȝth, oiþer sweyn, oiþer messagere,
> He ne shulde nouȝth þe kyng ysee
> Bot it were by atturne.
> Now is hym tolde þat wiþ hym speke   15
> Wolde þe kyng Canduleke.
> Tholomew, þat is nexte þe kyng,
> So hym seiþ þis tydyng,
> And Alisaunder makeþ a stille cry
> Þat non ne be so hardy   20
> To ben aknowe to Candaces son
> Who be þe kynges person,

1 On a day] n a *conjectural—obscured by patch in MS.*   12 *MS.* oiþer gret messagere

Ac þat hii shulden euerychon
Clepen þe kyng Antygon.
He dude on Tholomew, verrayment,   25
Quiclich his vestement,
And sette hym in þe kynges deys,
And he took Tholomeus herneys,
And made hym in heiӡ mester
Þe kynges first conseiler.   30
Hii clepen and siggen Canduleke
He shulde wiþ þe kyng speke.
He comeþ quyk on boþe his knewes
And kneleþ tofore Tholomewes,
Ac for he was a gentyl gome   35
He was sone vp ynome.
His pleynte he telleþ in þe manere
Als ӡee mowen now yhere:

'Alisaunder, riche caysere,
Þou ne haste on erþe no pere!   40
Many is þe riche londe
Þou hast ywonne to þine honde.
On þee hii ben wel bysett,
For þou art ful of þewes pett.
Þou batest wronge, þou hauntest riӡttes;   45
Þou art fader of alle kniӡttes.
Þou louest alle gentil manne
And abatest alle tyranne.
Þou art caiser of þis londe—
Ich me ӡelde to þine honde,   50
And amendyng I bidde þee to
Of vnriӡth þat is me do!'
'Telle on þi wronge,' quoþ Tholomay,
'We shulle þe helpe ӡif we may.'

'Sir, graunt mercy! Þerwhiles I was fare   f. 61ᵛ 2
On pilgrimages to Ierusalem and Yndare,   56
Þe duk Hirtan, a tyraunt of Brye,
Com wiþ grete chyualrie,
Robbed my make Blasfame
Also fair as was Dyane.   60
She is my quene—Ich hire chalenge.
Of þis despyt helpe me avenge!'
'Hou fele kniȝttes, as þou wenes,
Miȝtten awreken þine tenes?'
'Of foure þousande Ich had ynowe   65
To awreken myne wowe.'
Tholomeus gynneþ grade onon:
'What seistou here-of, Antigon?'
Alisaunder seide: 'For þat þis gome
Is to vs from fer ycome   70
And to ȝoure frenderede trest,
I rede ȝou þe conseil best,
Þat ȝe lene to his socoure
Swich folk þat ben to ȝoure honoure,
And faileþ hym nouȝth at þis nede.'   75
'Nay,' quoþ Tholomeu, 'so God me fede!
Wende wiþ hym,' he seide, 'Antigon,
And hym wreke on his fon,
For þou art wiȝth, hardy, and stronge—
Not Ich better vs amonge.   80
I þee biteche þe bayllye
My folk wiþ hym to conduye.'
Alisaunder hem fawe afongeþ.
Ne wolde he bileue longe—
Ygreiþed ben his foure þousynde   85
Quyklich and on hors wende.

82 folk] MS. self

Wiþ Canduleke he wendeþ swiþe.
His kniȝttes maden chere bliþe,
For her lorde in tapynage
Was ywent in þat veiage.   90
So he rideþ dales and doune
Þat he seeþ þat cite-toune
Where hym heldeþ þe duk Hirtan,
Þat haþ Canduleke lemman.
Canduleke seiþ: 'Sir Antygon,   95
Hou shullen we now taken on?'
Bote quoþ Alisaunder: 'Here and þere
Tofore vs sette al on fyre,
Forto hii comen to vs a felde,
Oiþer þat lefdy to vs ȝelde.'   100
Hii setten a fyre, wiþouten pyte,
Al þe londe to þe cite,
And bysetten it aboute
Þat hii ne miȝtten in ne oute.
Þe burgeys seiȝ her wynes barne—   105
Eueryche oþer harme gan warne,
And seiden wel her was þe gylt
To ben forbarnd, to ben forswelt,
Þat suffreden þe duk Hirtan

Haue in demayne oþere womman.   110
Alle þe burgeis of þe toun
Duden by on red commune—
To þe palays hii wenten alle
And quyk beten doune þe walle,
In cuntek and slouȝen Hirtan,   115
And ȝulden to Candulek his womman.
Þus comen þise burgeis,

---

94 Canduleke] *MS.* Candulek, *with abbreviation for* us *after* k *by a corrector on erasure of one letter*   116 Candulek] *MS.* Candulelek

And han of her werre peis.
After soiour of fourtene niȝth,
To kynges court hii done hem riȝth   120
And fynden Tholomeu, als he was bede,
Sette in Alisaunders stede.
Candulek on knowe hym sett,
And þe kyng oft he grett,
And þanked hym of his socour,   125
Þorouȝ whiche he had his honour
Yconquered and his quen.
He was vptaken of gentil men,
And ysette on heiȝe benche,
And wyne and pyement gynneþ shenche,   130
And wyne clarre and wyne Greek,
And þoo seide Tholomeu to Candulek:
'Sir,' he seide, 'men tellen me
Þou hast a moder fair and fre.
She is yhote dame Candace;   135
Fair and briȝth is hir face—
Nis in þis werlde so fair quene.
Fayn Ich wolde hir ysene,
Her castels and ek her toures,
Ȝif hii weren to myne honoures.'   140
Quoþ Candulek: 'Leue sire,
Also mychel she ȝou desireþ—
Ich ȝou sigge, by Goddes ore,
She desireþ noþing more
Þan to ben to ȝou aqueinte.   145
Ne habbeþ now none herte feinte—
Now is tyme it to done.
Ich wil ȝou brynge þider sone.
Ne be it ȝou for my broþer looþ,
Þeiȝ he be wiþ ȝou wrooþ   150

For ȝee duden Porus of lyue,
Whas douȝtter he haþ to wyue.
For on honde Ich wil hym take
Þat he shal don ȝou no wrake.'
Tholomeus ȝaf ansueryng   155
In þe name of þe kyng,
And seide: 'I nyl nouȝth comen hir ner,
Bot by a speciale messager
I wil hir sende loue-drurye,
And her estres ek aspye',   160
And cleped Alisaunder 'Antygon',
And bad hym wende wiþ hym onon,
And rouned wiþ hym a grete while.
Ac al þat was for gyle!

After þis queynt rounyng,   165
Alisaunder spedde in þis doyng.
Quyk on hors went wiþ hym ek
Þoo þat he had myd Candulek.

Candulek was wel bliþe—
Quyk he ladde hem and swiþe.   170
Whan hii into Saba come,
To þe paleys waie hii nome.
Þe lefdy wandreþ in a plas,
And syngeþ of Dido and Eneas,
Hou loue hem ladde by strange bride.   175
Comeþ Candulek tofore ride,
And seiþ: 'Ma dame, beeþ redy,
And welcomeþ here myne amy,
Kyng Alisaunder messagere,
Noble kniȝth of gent manere.   180
He haþ ȝolden me my wyf,
And duk Hirtan brouȝth of lyf.

Kyng Alisaunder ne haþ to gye
Non foller of chyualerye.'
Ar her tale were at þe ende   185
Kyng Alisaunder com hem hende.
Quyk hii ben of horses aliȝth—
Þe lefdy comeþ ononriȝth,
And clippeþ hym in armes tueye,
And he hir, wiþ grete joye.   190
She hym þankeþ of Candulek,
And of his gentil wyue ek,
And he hire bryngeþ many gretyng
On Alisaunder halue þe kyng.
'Do way!' quoþ þe quene Candace,   195
'Ich vnderstonde by þi face
Þat þou Alisaunder be.
Ne hele þou nouȝth, sir, for me!'
'Nay', he seide 'by Goddes ore!
Alisaunder is wel more,   200
Redder man on visage,
And sumdel more of age,
And þou shalt certeyn ben,
Sum day whan þou shalt hym sen!'
'Depart Dieux!' quoþ þe quene,   205
'Go we now myne estres sene.
Oure mete shal þerbituene
Ygreiþed and redy bene.'
She led hym to chaumbres of nobleys—
Þere he dude of his herneys.   210
Of Troye was þere-inne al þe story,
Hou Gregeis hadden þe victory.

184 foller] *MS.* feller, *with* el *altered by corrector from* oo *or* eo
198 þou] *MS.* þe, *with* e *altered by corrector* (*possibly from original* o)
209 nobleys] *MS.* nobeys

Þe bemes þere-inne weren of bras.
Þe wyndewes of riche glas.
Þe pynnes weren of yuory.　　　　　　　215
Þe kyng went wiþ þe lefdy,
Hymself al one from boure to boure,
And seiȝ wel mychel tresoure,
Gold, and siluer, and preciouse stones,

Baudekyns made for þe nones,　　　　　　220
Mantles, robes, and pauylouns,
Of gold and siluer grete foysouns.
And she hym asked, par amour,
Ȝif he seiȝ euer swiche tresour;
And he seide in his contreye　　　　　　225
Tresour he wist of swiche nobleye.
She þouȝth more þan she seide,
And ledde hym to anoþer stede,
To hire owen chaumbre þat was—
In al þis werlde fairer non nas.　　　　　　230
Þe atyre was þere-inne so riche
In al þis werlde was non it liche.
She led hym to one stage,
And shewed hym an ymage,
And seide: 'Alisaunder, yleue me!　　　　235
Þis ymage is made after þee.
I dude it an ymageoure
Casten after þi vigoure,
Þis oþere ȝer þoo þou nolde
To me come for loue ne golde.　　　　　　240
It is þee als liche, my leue broþer,
Als any peny is anoþer.
O, Alisaunder, of grete renoun!
Þou art ytake in my prisoun!

　　　　234 ymage] e *by corrector*

Al þi strengþe ne gayneþ þe nauȝth, 245
For a womman þee haþ ycauȝth.
A womman þee haþ in her laas!'
'O!' quoþ Alisaunder, 'allas,
Þat I nere y-armed wel,
And had my swerd of broun steel! 250
Many an heued wolde I claue
Ar I wolde in prisoun laue.
Ac noman ne may hym waite
From þise wymmens dissaite.'
'Alisaunder,' she seide, 'þou seis sooþ. 255
Ne be nouȝth adradde ne þerfore wrooþ—
Myne tale þou miȝth yleue.
Adam was biswike þorouȝ Eue,
And Sampson also, þe stronge,
Dalida hym dude wronge. 260
And Dauid was brouȝth in exyl
Þorouȝ his wiif Abygayl.
And Salomon, for wommans loue,
Forlete his Lorde þat is aboue.
And þou art fallen in hondes myne, 265
Þee to solas and to no pyne,
For here, vnder þis couertoure,
Ich wil haue þine amoure,
To my baundon, leue sire!
Longe it haþ ben my desire. 270
Ne shaltou haue oþer skaþe,
Bot me to baundon late and raþe.'
Þoo Alisaunder gan ysee
Þat it most so nedes be,
He dude al þe lefdyes wille 275 f. 62ᵛ 2

248 r *in* Alisaunder *and* s *in* allas *in lighter ink; the latter by corrector*
250 broun] *MS.* boun

Vnder couertoure stille.
Many niȝth and many day
Þus hii duden her play—
In halle at table he sat hire by,
In chaumbre gest, in bed amy.   280
Antygon he hiȝth in halle,
And Alisaunder vnder palle.

Longe hii han þus ypleiede.
On a day it was yseide
To Candidus by on stodmere,   285
Candaces son þe ȝongere,
Þat had Porus douȝtter to spouse,
A fair lady and delitouse,
Þat Alisaunder sat at his boord,
Þat had yslawe Porus his lord,   290
And dude hym clepen Antigon.
To þe quene he stirte onon,
And seide: 'Ma dame, þou hast wrong
Þou heldest here Alisaunder so long.
He haþ yslawȝe my lorde Pore—   295
Myne honde ne skapeþ he neuermore!'
'Pes!' quoþ Candace, 'þou congeoun!
It is Antigon, a gent baroun,
Þat is ycome to message.
Ne bede þou hym non outrage!   30c
Ȝif þou doost, by God aboue,
Þou shalt forlese myne loue!'
'Dame, whom so Ich euere serue,
Of myne honde he shal sterue.
Alisaunder hymseluen it is,   305
And haþ ychaunged name his.'
'Nartou so hardy', quoþ Candace,

'More to seen Candulekes face!
And þou dude hym ouȝth bot good,
He wolde sen þine herte blood,   310
And Ich myself, for þat wronge,
Heiȝe wolde þee don anhonge.
For messagere to me ysent
Ne shal here fynde encumbrement.'
Candidus wrooþ went away,   315
And com aȝein nouȝth many a day.
Þo þe table was ydrawe
Þe wayte gan 'A choger!' blawe.
Alisaunder and Candace
To chaumber token her trace,   320
And, als we fynden on þe book,
Þat niȝth þe kyng his leue took,
And went to Ynde to his barouns,
By wodes, by dales, and by douns.
Leue he had wiþ mournyng,   325
And went forþ in a daweyng
By an heiȝe waie þat he knew,
Forto he com to Tolomew.

III

FLORIS AND BLAUNCHEFLOUR

THIS romance is a translation, with substantial 'cutting', of
what is known as the 'aristocratic' version of the story in OF
(the 'popular' one being nearer to the world of the OF epic).
The story-material of the former OF version is an 'idyllic
romance'—a genre which is believed to derive ultimately from
certain Greek works such as Longus's *Daphnis and Chloe* (composed between the second and the fifth centuries A.D.).[1]

Two children, born on the same day, are reared together and
very early become devoted to each other. The boy's royal father
attempts to destroy the attachment by selling the girl to visiting
merchants while his son is absent, and builds a sumptuous tomb
to support the lie that she is dead. But Floris discovers the truth,
and sets off in search of Blauncheflour, suitably equipped by his
repentant father, and taking with him the gold cup which was
part of the price paid for her. Blauncheflour has, in the meantime, been sold to the Emir of Babylon and lodged in 'The
Tower of Maidens' in his impregnable city. After the clandes-
tine reunion of the lovers (in the episode printed below), Floris
is discovered by the emir in bed with Blauncheflour; and they
both face the punishment of death. But they are finally pardoned,
and thenceforward lead the happy life together which had been
denied them.

In the French and the English version alike, the emir's para-
disal garden contains a Tree of Love, the function of which is
to choose a wife for him every year; yet, if he happens to favour
any one of the assembled maidens in advance, the flower is made
to fall on her by magic.[2] This unnecessary duplication may be a

[1] See G. Cohen, *Le Roman courtois au XIIe siècle* (Les Cours de
Sorbonne, Paris, n.d.), 5–21.
[2] *Floire et Blancheflor*, 1836–43 and 1848–51; ll. 57 ff. in the ME
below.

symptom of imperfect integration of one or the other device into an existing story. In the ME (Auchinleck MS.), the detail by which the loss of virginity in any of the girls is revealed is curiously pointless in the context: the washing of hands is not called for here (45 ff.), and has evidently been transferred from another point in the story (see *Floire et Blancheflor*, 1656–66, and Taylor's edition of *Floris and Blancheflour*, 645–54).

For some of the distinctive elements in the story there are arresting parallels in the literature of the Orient. The ruse by which the lover gains access to his beloved in the Tower of Maidens is matched in a comparable story-structure in the Indian *Jātakas*, a collection of *exempla* composed in the early fifth century. The hero's choice of disguise (as a merchant) is a plebeian touch alien to the chivalric milieu of OF romance, and likely to be of foreign origin; the Tower of Maidens is a highly exotic one, and is reminiscent of a harem; the armed eunuchs who stand guard, and the odalisques who each have a room of their own—all these (and various other motifs) have been equated by Huet with elements in Arabian stories contained in *The Thousand and One Nights*.

Huet's theory that the story is ultimately of Eastern and specifically Arabian origin has not been generally accepted. The parallels that he has produced are undeniable, even though they are not combined in a single and demonstrably earlier Arabian story that could be equated in whole or in part with *Floire et Blancheflor*. What is really at issue is whether the features concerned are integral or merely incidental in the story: the former seems more likely, even though none of his analogues contains the common *enfances*. The names of the two lovers allude to and imply the hero's concealment in a basket of flowers, and were therefore probably suggested by it. It follows that the basket of flowers (which is used at a crucial point, and is an integral part of the action) must have been contained in the story when these names were devised—and there is no French form of the story with any other names. A theory of Oriental origin in general, if not demonstrable, is credible. Reinhold, however, sees the story as a synthesis of individual motifs from diverse sources, and actually believes that the ruse of the basket was suggested by the use of the wooden horse in the story of Troy.

What is beyond doubt is that most of the story-material is

highly unusual in medieval romance, and that the telling of the
story has unusual virtues. Each stage in the action directly depends on the previous one. The reunion of the lovers in the
episode printed below leads to the discovery of Floris by the
emir. In this final crisis the lovers are saved from death by
the irresistible power of love itself. Each attempts to force on the
other a ring of Blauncheflour's which has the power to preserve
life; but the assembled onlookers are so overcome by the touch-
ing evidences of their love that the emir can do nothing but
pardon them. The crisis is dissolved not by the crude intrusion
of some extraneous agency, but by a force contained within it.
There could be no more consistent affirmation of the primacy
and the power of romantic love.

f. 101ʳ 2
(661 ff).

'Nou beþ þer inne þat riche toure
Four and twenty maidenes boure.
So wel were þat ilke man
Þat miȝte wonen in þat an—
Now þourt him neuere, ful iwis,   5
Willen after more blisse!
Nou beþ þer seriaunts in þe stage
To seruen þe maidens of parage;
Ne mai no seriaunt be þerinne
Þat in his brech bereþ þe ginne,   10

f. 101ᵛ 1

Neiþer bi dai ne bi niȝt,
But he be ase capoun diȝt,
And at þe gate is a gateward—
He nis no fol ne no coward!
Ȝif þer comeȝ ani man   15
Wiȝinne þat ilche barbican,
But hit be bi his leue,
He wille him boþe bete and reue.
Þe porter is proud wiȝalle—
Euerich dai he goþ in palle.   20

7 *and* 15 þer] *MS.* þe

And þe amerail is so wonder a gome
Þat euerich ȝer hit is his wone
To chesen him a newe wif
(Þei he loueþ his queene as his lyf!)
And whan he a newe wif vnderfo   25
Yknaweȝ hou hit schal be do:
Þanne scholle men fechche doun of þe stage
Alle þe maidenes of parage
An brenge hem into on orchard
(Þe fairest of al middelhard).   30
Þer is mirie foulen song—
Men miȝte libben þeramong.
Aboute þe orchard goþ a wal:
Þe werste ston is cristal.
Þer man mai sen on þe ston   35
Mochel of þis werldes wisdom.
And a welle þer springeȝ inne
Þat is wrowt wiȝ mochel ginne.
Þe welle is of mochel pris:
Þe strem com fram Paradis,   40
Þe grauel in þe grounde of preciouse stone
(And of vertu, iwis, echone)—
Of saphires and of sardoines,
Of onecles and of calsidoines.
Nou is þe walle of so mochel eye,   45
Ȝif þer comeȝ ani maiden þat is forleie,
And hi bowe to þe grounde
Forto waschen here honde,
Þe water wille ȝelle als hit ware wod

---

24 *Not in Auchinleck; supplied from Trentham MS.*   26 Yknaw-
eȝ] *MS.* He knaweȝ   31 mirie] *not in MS.; Taylor* merie
42 echone] *MS.* ethone   44 onecles] *MS.* onethes   45 walle]
MS. waie; *C* wal   46 þer] *MS.* þe

And bicome on hire so red so blod.   50
Wich maiden þe water fareȝ on so,
Hi schal sone be fordo.
And þilke þat beþ maidenes clene
Þai mai hem wassche of þe rene:
Þe water wille erne stille and cler—   55
Nelle hit hem make no daunger.
At þe welle-heued þer stant a tre—
Þe fairest þat mai in erthe be.
Hit is icleped "Þe Tre of Loue";
For floures and blosmes beþ euer aboue,   60
And þilke þat clene maidenes be,
Men schal hem bringe vnder þat tre,
And wich so falleȝ on þat flour,
He schal ben chosen quen wiȝ honur.
And ȝif þer ani maiden is   65
Þat þamerail halt of mest pris,
Þe flour schal on here be went
Þourh art and þourgh enchantement.
Þous he cheseþ þourȝ þe flour,
And euere we herkneȝ when hit be Blaunche-   70
   flour.'
Þre sithes Florice swouned nouþe
Er he miȝte speke wiȝ mouþe.
Sone he awok and speke miȝt,
Sore he wep and sore he siȝt.
'Darie,' he saide, 'Ich worht ded   75
But Ich haue of þe help and red.'
'Leue child, ful wel I se
Þat þou wilt to deþe te.
Þe beste red þat I can
(Oþer red I ne can):   80

Wende tomorewe to þe tour
Ase þou were a god ginour,
And nim in þin hond squir and scantiloun
Als þai þou were a masoun.
Bihold þe tour vp and doun.   85
Þe porter is coluard and feloun:
Wel sone he wil come to þe
And aske what mister man þou be,
And ber vpon þe felonie,
And saie þou art comen þe tour aspie.   90
Þou schalt answeren him swetelich,
And speke to him wel mildelich,
And sai þou art a ginour
To biheld þat ilche tour,
And forto lerne and forto fonde   95
To make anoþer in þi londe.
Wel sone he wil come þe ner
And bidde þe plaien at þe scheker—
To plaien he wil be wel fous
And to winnen of þin wel coueitous.   100 f. 102ʳ 1
When þou art to þe scheker brouȝt,
Wiȝouten pans ne plai þou nowt:
Þou schalt haue redi mitte
Þritti mark vnder þi slitte.
And ȝif he winne ouȝt al þin,   105
Al leue þou hit wiȝ him;
And ȝif þou winne ouȝt of his,
Þou lete þerof ful litel pris.
Wel ȝerne he wille þe bidde and praie
Þat þou come amorewe and plaie.   110
Þou schalt sigge þou wilt so,
And nim wiȝ þe amorewe swich two;

92 mildelich] *MS.* delich *preceded by four minims* (**undotted**)

And euer þou schalt in þin owen wolde
Þi gode cop wiȝ þe atholde
(Þat ilke self coppe of golde   115
Þat was for Blauncheflour iȝolde).
Þe þridde dai bere wiȝ þe an hondred pond
And þi coppe al hol and sond.
Ȝif him markes and pans fale—
Of þi mone tel þou no tale.   120
Wel ȝerne he þe wille bidde and praie
Þat þou legge þi coupe to plaie.
Þou schalt answeren him ate first:
No lenger plaie þou ne list.
Wel moche he wil for þi coupe bede,   125
Ȝif he miȝte þe better spede.
Þou schalt bleþeliche ȝiuen hit him,
Þai hit be gold pur and fin,
And sai: "Me þinkeȝ hit wel bisemeȝ te,
Þai hit were worȝ swiche þre."   130
Sai also þe ne faille non
Gold ne seluer ne riche won,
And he wil þanne so mochel loue þe,
Þat þou hit schalt boþe ihere and see
Þat he wil falle to þi fot   135
And bicome þi man, ȝif he mot.
His manred þou schalt afonge
And þe trewþe of his honde.
Ȝif þou miȝt þous his loue winne,
He mai þe help wiȝ som ginne.'   140
Nou also Florice haþ iwrowt
Also Darie him haþ itawt,
Þat þourgh his gold and his garsome
f. 102ʳ 2   Þe porter is his man bicome.

114 þe] *MS.* he   117 hondred] h *altered from* d

'Nou', quaþ Florice, 'þou art mi man, 145
And al mi trest is þe vpan:
Nou þou miȝt wel eþe
Arede me fram þe deþe.'
And euerich word he haþ him told
Hou Blauncheflour was fram him sold, 150
And hou he was of Spaine a kynges sone,
And for hire loue þider icome
To fonde wiȝ som ginne
Þe maiden aȝen to him winne.
Þe porter þat herde and sore siȝte: 155
'Ich am bitraied þourȝ riȝte—
Þourȝ þi catel Ich am bitraid,
And of mi lif Ich am desmaid.
Nou Ich wot, child, hou hit geþ:
For þe Ich drede to þolie deþ. 160
And naþeles Ich ne schal þe neuere faile mo
Þerwhiles I mai ride or go.
Þi foreward Ich wil helden alle,
What so wille bitide or falle.
Wende þou hom into þin in, 165
Whiles I þink of som ginne.
Bitwene þis and þe þridde dai
Don Ich wille þat I mai.'
Florice spak and wep among:
Þat ilche terme him þouȝte wel long. 170
Þe porter þouȝte what to rede.
He let floures gaderen in þe mede
(He wiste hit was þe maidenes wille);
Two coupen he let of floures fille.
Þat was þe rede þat he þouȝt þo— 175
Florice in þat o coupe do.

159 Ich] *MS.* ith 175 *MS.* he þouȝt he þout þo

Tweie gegges þe coupe bere;
So hem charged þat wroþ þai were.
Þai bad God ȝif him euel fin
Þat so mani floures dede þerin.   180
Þider þat þai weren ibede
Ne were þai nowt ariȝt birede,
Acc þai turned in hire left hond
Blaunchefloures bour an hond—
To Clarice bour þe coupe þai bere,   185
Wiȝ þe floures þat þerinne were.
Þere þe couppe þai sette adoun,
And ȝaf him here malisoun
Þat so fele floures em brouȝte on honde;
Þai wenten forht and leten þe coppe stonde.   190

Clarice to þe coppe com and wolde
Þe floures handlen and biholde.
Florisse wende hit hadde ben his swet wiȝt—
In þe coupe he stod vpriȝt,
And þe maide al for drede   195
Bigan to schrichen an to grede.
Þo he seghȝ hit nas nowth ȝhe,
Into þe coupe he stirte aȝe
And held him bitraied al clene—
Of his deȝ he ne ȝaf nowt a bene.   200
Þer come to Clarice maidenes lepe
Bi ten, be twenti, in one hepe,
And askede what here were
Þat hi makede so loude bere.
Clarice hire vnderstod anonriȝt   205
Þat hit was Blauncheflour swete wiȝt

f. 102ᵛ 1

192 handlen] *MS.* handleden   197 he] *MS.* ȝhe   ȝhe] *MS.* he
201 maidenes] i *suprascript*   206 *MS.* Blaunceflour þat swete

(For here boures neȝ were,
And selden þat þai neren ifere,
And aiþer of oþer counseil þai wiste
And michel aiþer to oþer triste).   210
Hii ȝaf hire maidenes answere anon
Þat into boure þai sscholden gon:
'To þis coupe Ich cam and wolde
Þe floures handli and biholde,
Ac er Ich hit euer wiste   215
A boterfleȝe toȝain me fluste!
Ich was sor adrad of þan,
Þat sschrichen and greden I bigan.'
Þe maidenes hadde þerof gle
And turnede aȝen and let Clarisse be.   220
So sone so þe madenes weren agon,
To Blauncheflours bour Clarice wente anon
And saide leyende to Blauncheflour:
'Wiltou sen a ful fair flour
(Swiche a flour þat þe schal like,   225
Haue þou sen hit a lite)?'
'Auoy, dameisele!' quaþ Blauncheflour,
'To scorne me is litel honur.
Ich ihere, Clarice, wiȝoute gabbe,
Þe ameral wil me to wiue habbe.   230
Ac þilke dai schal neuer be
Þat men schal atwite me   f. 102ᵛ 2
Þat I schal ben of loue vntrewe,
Ne chaungi loue for non newe,
For no loue ne for non eie,   235
So doþ Floris in his contreie.
Now I schal swete Florice misse,

Schal non oþer of me haue blisse.'
Clarice stant and bihalt þat reuþe
And þe treunesse of þis treuþe.   240
Leiȝande sche saide to Blaunch
eflour:
'Com nou, se þat ilche flour!'—
To þe coupe þai ȝeden þo.
Wel blisful was Florisse þo
For he had iherd al þis: 245
Out of þe coupe he stirte, iwis.
Blaunchefl
our chaungede hewe—
Wel sone aiþer oþer knewe.
Wiȝouten speche togidere þai lepe:
Þai clepte and keste and eke wepe.   250
Hire cussing laste a mile,
And þat hem þouȝte litel while.
Clarice bihalt al þis,
Here contenaunce and here bliss,
And leiȝende saide to Blaunchefl
our: 255
'Felawe, knouestou ouȝt þis flour?
Litel er noldest þou hit se,
And nou þou ne miȝt hit lete fro þe!
He moste conne wel mochel of art
Þat þou woldest ȝif þerof ani part!'   260
Boþe þise swete þinges for blis
Falleȝ doun here fet to kis,
And crieȝ hire merci al weping,
Þat ȝhe hem biwraie nowt to þe king—
To þe king þat ȝhe hem nowt biwreie   265
(Wherþourgh þai were siker to deye).
Þo spak Clarice to Blaunchefl
our
Wordes ful of fin amour:

240 treunesse] *MS.* treuuesse   250 þai] *MS.* Þat   264 biwraie]
MS. briwaie   266 deye] *MS.* deþe

'Ne doute ȝou nammore wiȝalle
Þan to miself hit hadde bifalle: 270
White ȝhe wel witerli
Þat hele Ich wille ȝoure boþer druri.'
To on bedde ȝhe haþ hem ibrowt
Þat was of silk and sendal wrouȝt.
Þai sette hem þere wel softe adoun,   275
And Clarice drowȝ þe courtyn roum;   f. 103ʳ 1
Þo bigan þai to clippe and kisse,
And made joie and mochele blisse.
Florice ferst speke bigan,
And saide, 'Louerd þat madest man,   280
Þe I þanke, Godes sone!
Nou al mi care Ich haue ouercome
And nou Ich haue mi lef ifounde,
Of al mi kare Ich am vnbounde.'
Nou haþ aiþer oþer itold   285
Of mani a car foul cold,
And of mani pine stronge,
Þat þai han ben a two so longe.
Clarice hem seruede al to wille,
Boþe dernelich and stille;   290
But so ne miȝte ȝhe hem longe iwite
Þat hit ne sscholde ben vnderȝete.

276 roum] *MS. has* ro *followed by three minims (undotted) and* n

IV

HAVELOK

THE tale of *Havelok* was of such interest to Geoffrey Gaimar that he used it to introduce his *Estoire des Engleis*. His version is now thought to have been the model for the *Lai d'Haveloc*, the one other account earlier than the Middle English romance, which is nevertheless independent of both. The extant material therefore offers unusual opportunities for comparison of the interests and the talents of writers dealing in English and French (or Anglo-Norman) with romantic stories.

Extract A below is represented only in a rudimentary form in Gaimar's account (442–53), and the vivid episode of ll. 56–192 not at all; while the *Lai* merely has Grim advise Havelok to go and make his fortune in Lincoln (159–89). The content of extract B is told in not more than forty lines by Gaimar (531 ff.), and in seventy-odd in the *Lai* (679 ff.). The English version is in fact on a larger scale, better shaped, and much more imaginative than either; and some, at least, of the elaborations or inventions of individual scenes are likely to have been evolved in this rather than an antecedent version. But all three of the early versions contain, on the one hand, features preserved in one of the other two and therefore likely to be ancient, and on the other, inconsistencies such as imply recasting of the received story.

Havelok is an example of a well-known type of popular story about a dispossessed king's son who rises from a menial condition to win a princess. But the hero bears the name of a historically attested person: the Viking Ánlaf Sigtryggson, whose by-name Cuaran is preserved in Gaimar's version and the *Lai* (though misunderstood in the latter), was known in Irish as Amhlaibh, and the Welsh form of this (*Abloec*) is the name used in all three early versions. Some believe that a Welsh intermediary version (thought to be implied by the name *Havelok*) is reflected in a part of the thirteenth-century *Historia Meria-duci*; but this alleged analogue is signally unlike the story of *Havelok* in essentials. The popular tale of the king's son has (for unknown reasons) been hitched on to Ánlaf Sigtryggson (Olaf Cuaran). The latter's own history has hardly anything in common with it. But Deutschbein's ingenious suggestion that the 'history' in the tale of *Havelok* is that of Ánlaf's uncle Rœgnald (died 921) is vulnerable.[1] In fact, virtually nothing is discoverable in precise terms of the genesis of our story.

A

In Humber Grim bigan to lende,   f. 208ʳ 1
In Lindeseye, rith at þe north ende.   (733 ff.)
Þer sat is ship upon þe sond;
But Grim it drou up to þe lond,
And þere he made a litel cote   5
To him and to hise flote.
Bigan he, þere forto erþe,
A litel hus to maken of erþe,
So þat he wel þore were
Of here herboru herborwed þere;   10
And for þat Grim þat place aute
Þe stede of Grim þe name laute,
So þat Grimesbi calleth alle
Þat þeroffe speken alle.
And so shulen men callen it ay   15
Bituene þis and Domesday.

Grim was fishere swiþe god
And mikel couþe on þe flod.
Mani god fish þerinne he tok,
Boþe with neth and with hok.   20
He tok þe sturgiun, and þe qual,

[1] See Laura Hibbard, *Mediæval Romance in England*, 109–11.

And þe turbut, and lax withal.
He tok þe sele, and þe hwel—
He spedde ofte swiþe wel.
Keling he tok, and tumberel,   25
Hering, and þe makerel,
Þe butte, þe schulle, þe þornebake.
Gode paniers dede he make—
On til him, and oþer þrinne
Til hise sones, to beren fish inne   30
Vp o londe to selle and fonge.
Forbar he neyþer tun ne gronge,
Þat he ne to yede with his ware.
Kam he neuere hom handbare,

Þat he ne broucte bred and sowel   35
In his shirte or in his couel,
In his poke benes and korn—
Hise swink ne hauede he nowt forlorn.
And hwan he tok þe grete laumprei,
Ful wel he couþe þe rithe wei   40
To Lincolne, þe gode boru:
Ofte he yede it þoru and þoru,
Til he hauede wol wel sold
And þerfore þe penies told.
Þanne he com þenne he were bliþe,   45
For hom he brouthe fele siþe
Wastels, simenels with þe horn,
Hise pokes fulle of mele an korn,
Netes flesh, shepes, and swines,
And hemp to maken of gode lines,   50
And stronge ropes to hise netes
(In þe se-weres he ofte setes).

32 neyþer] *MS.* neyþe   40 wel] *MS.* we   52 se-weres]
MS. se werē

Þusgate Grim him fayre ledde—
Him and his genge wel he fedde
Wel twelf winter oþer more.   55
Hauelok was war þat Grim swank sore
For his mete, and he lay at hom—
Þouthe, 'Ich am nou no grom:
Ich am wel waxen, and wel may eten
More þan euere Grim may geten.   60
Ich ete more, bi God on liue,
Þan Grim an hise children fiue!
It ne may nouth ben þus longe—
Goddot, Y wile with þe gange
Forto leren sum god to gete.   65
Swinken Ich wolde for mi mete—
It is no shame forto swinken!
Þe man þat may wel eten and drinken
Þat nouth ne haue but on swink long.
To liggen at hom it is ful strong.   70
God yelde him, þer I ne may,
Þat haueth me fed to þis day!
Gladlike I wile þe paniers bere;
Ich woth ne shal it me nouth dere
Þey þer be inne a birþene gret   75
Also heui als a neth.
Shal Ich neuere lengere dwelle—
Tomorwen shal Ich forth pelle!'

On þe morwen, hwan it was day,
He stirt up sone and nouth ne lay,   80 f. 208ᵛ 1
And cast a panier on his bac
With fish giueled als a stac.
Also michel he bar him one
So he foure, bi mine mone!

Wel he it bar and solde it wel.   85
Þe siluer he brouthe hom il del
Al þat he þerfore tok—
Withheld he nouth a ferþinges nok.
So yede he forth ilke day
Þat he neuere at home lay—   90
So wolde he his mester lere.
Bifel it so a strong dere
Bigan to rise, of korn of bred,
Þat Grim ne couþe no god red
Hw he sholde hise meine fede.   95
Of Hauelok hauede he michel drede,
For he was strong and wel mouthe ete
More þanne heuere mouthe be gete;
Ne he ne mouthe on þe se take
Neyþer lenge ne þornbake,   100
Ne non oþer fish þat douthe
His meyne feden with he mouthe.
Of Hauelok he hauede kare
Hwilgat þat he micthe fare.
Of his children was him nouth;   105
On Hauelok was al hise þouth,
And seyde, 'Hauelok, dere sone,
I wene þat we deye mone
For hunger—þis dere is so strong,
And hure mete is uten long.   110
Betere is þat þu henne gonge
Þan þu here dwelle longe;
Heþen þou mayt gangen to late!
Þou canst ful wel þe ricthe gate
To Lincolne, þe gode borw—   115
Þou hauest it gon ful ofte þoru.
Of me ne is me nouth a slo.

Betere is þat þu þider go,
For þer is mani god man inne—
Þer þou mayt þi mete winne.   120
But wo is me þou art so naked:
Of mi seyl Y wolde þe were maked
A cloth þou mithest inne gongen,
Sone, no cold þat þu ne fonge.'

He tok þe sheres of þe nayl   125 f. 208ᵛ 2
And made him a couel of þe sayl,
And Hauelok dide it sone on;
Hauede neyþer hosen ne shon,
Ne none kines oþer wede—
To Lincolne barfot he yede.   130
Hwan he kam þer he was ful wil—
Ne hauede he no frend to gangen til.
Two dayes þer fastinde he yede,
Þat non for his werk wolde him fede.
Þe þridde day herde he calle: 135
'Bermen, bermen, hider forth alle!'

.   .   .   .   .   .

Sprongen forth so sparke on glede.
Hauelok shof dun nyne or ten
Rith amidewarde þe fen,
And stirte forth to þe kok.   140

.   .   .   .   .   .

Þat he bouthe at þe brigge;
Þe bermen let he alle ligge
And bar þe mete to þe castel,
And gat him þere a ferþing wastel.

Þet oþer day kepte he ok   145

125 sheres] *MS.* shres   129 oþer] *MS.* oþe   131 þer] *MS.* þe

Swiþe yerne þe erles kok,
Til þat he say him on þe brigge
And bi him mani fishes ligge.
Þe herles mete hauede he bouth
Of Cornwalie, and kalde oft: 150
'Bermen, bermen, hider swiþe!'
Hauelok it herde and was ful bliþe
Þat he herde 'Bermen!' calle.
Alle made he hem dun falle
Þat in his gate yeden and stode—   155
Wel sixtene laddes gode.
Als he lep þe kok til
He shof hem alle upon an hyl,
Astirte til him with his rippe,
And bigan þe fish to kippe.   160
He bar up wel a carte-lode
Of segges, laxes, of playces brode,
Of grete laumprees, and of eles.
Sparede he neyþer tos ne heles
Til þat he to þe castel cam,   165
Þat men fro him his birþene nam.
Þan men haueden holpen him doun
With þe birþene of his croun,
Þe kok stod and on him low

f. 208ᵛ 2   And þoute him stalworþe man ynow,   170
And seyde, 'Wiltu ben wit me?
Gladlike wile Ich feden þe.
Wel is set þe mete þu etes,
And þe hire þat þu getes!'
'Goddot,' quoth he, 'leue sire,   175
Bidde Ich you non oþer hire.

147 brigge] *MS.* bigge   175 Goddot] *MS.* Soddot   176 you]
MS. þou

But yeueþ me inow to ete,
Fir and water Y wile you fete,
Þe fir blowe an ful wel maken.
Stickes kan Ich breken and kraken   180
And kindlen ful wel a fyr,
And maken it to brennen shir.
Ful wel kan Ich cleuen shides,
Eles toturuen of here hides;
Ful wel kan Ich dishes swilen   185
And don al þat ye euere wilen.'
Quoth þe kok, 'Wile I no more—
Go þu yunder and sit þore,
And Y shal yeue þe ful fair bred,
And make þe broys in þe led.   190
Sit now doun and et ful yerne—
Daþeit hwo þe mete werne!'

B

Also he seten and sholde soupe,   f. 212ᵛ 2
So comes a ladde in a ioupe   (1766 ff)
And with him sixti oþer stronge,   195
With swerdes drawen and kniues longe,
Ilkan in hande a ful god gleiue,
And seyde, 'Undo, Bernard þe greyue!
Vndo swiþe and lat us in,
Or þu art ded, bi Seint Austin!'   200
Bernard stirt up, þat was ful big,
And caste a brinie upon his rig,
And grop an ax þat was ful god—
Lep to þe dore so he wore wod,
And seyde, 'Hwat are ye þat are þeroute,   205
Þat þus biginnen forto stroute?

203 ax] *MS.* ar

Goth henne swiþe, fule þeues!
For, bi þe Louerd þat man on leues,
Shol Ich casten þe dore open,
Summe of you shal Ich drepen,   210
And þe oþre shal Ich kesten
In feteres and ful faste festen!'
'Hwat haue ye seid?' quoth a ladde,
'Wenestu þat we ben adradde?
We shole at þis dore gonge   215
Maugre þin, carl, or outh longe!'
He gripen sone a bulder-ston
And let it fleye ful god won
Agen þe dore, þat it torof.
Auelok it saw and þider drof,   220
And þe barre sone vt drow
Þat was unride and gret ynow,
And caste þe dore open wide
And seide, 'Her shal Y now abide.
Comes swiþe vnto me—   225
Daþeyt hwo you henne fle!'
'No!' quodh on, 'Þat shaltou coupe!'
And bigan til him to loupe,
In his hond his swerd ut drawe.
Hauelok he wende þore haue slawe,   230
And with him comen oþer two
Þat him wolde of liue haue do.
Hauelok lifte up þe dore-tre
And at a dint he slow hem þre—
Was non of hem þat hise hernes   235
Ne lay þerute ageyn þe sternes.
Þe ferþe þat he siþen mette,
Wit þe barre so he him grette

f. 213ʳ 1

231 him] *not in MS.*

Bifor þe heued þat þe rith eye
Vt of þe hole made he fleye, 240
And siþe clapte him on þe crune
So þat he standed fel þor dune.
Þe fifte þat he ouertok
Gaf he a ful sor dint ok
Bitwen þe sholdres þer he stod, 245
Þat he speu his herte blod.
Þe sixte wende for to fle,
And he clapte him with þe tre
Rith in þe fule necke so
Þat he smot hise necke on to. 250
Þanne þe sixe weren doun feld,
Þe seuenþe brayd ut his swerd
And wolde Hauelok riht in þe eye,
And Hauelok let þe barre fleye
And smot him sone ageyn þe brest 255
Þat hauede he neuere schrifte of prest,
For he was ded on lesse hwile
Þan men mouthe renne a mile.
Alle þe oþere weren ful kene:
A red þei taken hem bitwene 260
Þat he sholde him bihalue
And brisen so þat wit no salue
Ne sholde him helen leche non.
Þey drowen ut swerdes, ful god won,
And shoten on him so don on bere 265
Dogges þat wolden him totere,
Þanne men doth þe bere beyte.
Þe laddes were kaske and teyte
And vmbiyeden him ilkon;

254 Hauelok let þe] *MS*. haue le   256 schrifte] *MS*. schifte
269 vmbiyeden] *MS*. vn bi yeden

Sum smot with tre and sum wit ston;   270
Summe putten with gleyue in bac̄ and side
And yeuen wundes longe and wide
In twenti stedes and wel mo,
Fro þe croune til þe to.
Hwan he saw þat, he was wod,   275
And was it ferlik hw he stod;

f. 213ʳ 2

For þe blod ran of his sides
So water þat fro þe welle glides.
But þanne bigan he forto mowe
With þe barre, and let hem shewe   280
Hw he cowþe sore smite;
For was þer non, long ne lite,
Þat he mouthe ouertake
Þat he ne garte his croune krake,
So þat on a litel stund   285
Felde he twenti to þe grund.

Þo bigan gret dine to rise,
For þe laddes on ilke wise
Him asayleden wit grete dintes.
Fro fer he stonden him with flintes   290
And gleyues schoten him fro ferne,
For drepen him he wolden yerne;
But dursten he newhen him no more
Þanne he bor or leun wore.
Huwe Rauen þat dine herde   295
And þowthe wel þat men misferde
With his louerd for his wif,
And grop an ore and a long knif
And þider drof also an hert,
And cham þer on a litel stert   300

290 stonden] *MS.* stoden   299 drof] *MS.* dorof

And saw how þe laddes wode
Hauelok his louerd umbistode,
And beten on him so doth þe smith
With þe hamer on þe stith.
'Allas,' hwat Hwe, 'þat Y was boren,   305
Þat euere et Ich bred of koren,
Þat Ich here þis sorwe se!
Roberd, Willam, hware ar ye?
Gripeth eþer unker a god tre,
And late we nouth þise doges fle   310
Til ure louerd wreke be.
Cometh swiþe and folwes me—
Ich haue in honde a ful god ore.
Daþeit wo ne smite sore!'
'Ya, leue, ya!' quod Roberd sone,   315
'We hauen ful god lith of þe mone.'
Roberd grop a staf strong and gret
Þat mouthe ful wel bere a net,
And William Wendut grop a tre,
Mikel grettere þan his þre,   320
And Bernard held his ax ful faste
(I seye was he nouth þe laste),   f. 213ᵛ 1
And lopen forth so he weren wode
To þe laddes þer he stode,
And yaf hem wundes swiþe grete.   325
Þer mithe men wel se boyes bete,
And ribbes in here sides breke,
And Hauelok on hem wel wreke!
He broken armes, he broken knes,
He broken shankes, he broken thes.   330
He dide þe blod þere renne dune
To þe fet rith fro þe crune,

            311 be] *not in MS*.

For was þer spared heued non—
He leyden on heuedes ful god won
And made croune breke and crake   335
Of þe broune and of þe blake.
He maden here backes also bloute
Als here wombes, and made hem rowte
Als he weren kradel-barnes,
So dos þe child þat moder þarnes.   340
Daþeit þe recke! for he it seruede—
Hwat dide he þore? wéren he werewed!
So longe haueden he but and bet,
With neues under hernes set,
Þat of þo sixti men and on   345
Ne wente þer awey lyues non.

338 here] *MS.* he

V

THE FOX AND THE WOLF

The Fox and the Wolf tells a story which was also available to Englishmen in summary form in the Latin prose fables of Odo of Cheriton (*c.* 1219) and John of Sheppey (*ob.* 1360), and in the AN *Contes moralisées* of Nicholas Bozon (first half of the fourteenth century). These last three versions are lineal descendants of Æsopian beast-fable, though Odo's use of the names *Ysengrimus*, *Reynard*, and *Berengarius* for the wolf, the fox, and the ass implies knowledge of the medieval beast-epic in its fully cyclic form. On the other hand, Odo and John contributed the *moralitee* (which is proper only to derivates of beast-fable) to Chaucer's *Nun's Priest's Tale*, which is from medieval beast-epic.

The earliest extended treatment of animal stories is the *Ecbasis Captivi*, composed in the early tenth century, and itself relatively unimportant, though mainly concerned with the centrally important and ancient fable of the Lion's illness, the fox's prescription for it, and the wolf's loss of his skin. In it the animals still have only generic names. The earliest evidence of individual names is an anecdote of Guibert of Nogent, dated 1112, which cites *Ysengrimus* as the name for the wolf, but gives no clear indication of a story or a literary form associated with the name. The first cyclic treatment of the material is the Latin *Ysengrimus* (composed 1148) of Nivard of Ghent, which was the main source of the OF *Roman de Renart*. The latter is a composite built up by several authors. Its earlier 'branches', or sections, composed *c.* 1175–90, in turn provided the model for both the MHG *Reinhart Fuchs* (*c.* 1180) of Henry Glichezære and the MDu *Van den vos Reinaerde* (*c.* 1250).

The episode of the fox and the wolf in the well, as told in the *Roman de Renart*, is an ingenious elaboration of some such form of story as is represented in item *xxiii* of the *Disciplina Clericalis* (a collection of *exempla* assembled by the converted Spanish Jew Petrus Alfonsus between 1109 and 1114), and possibly of this latter version itself. The *exemplum* embodies the cardinal device of the buckets, and motivates the wolf's descent into the well by the reflection of the moon in the water (which the fox dupes the wolf into thinking a cheese). It derives from the version[1] (containing both these features) of Rabbi Raschi (1040–1105), in his commentary on the Talmud; and this in turn goes back to a second-century collection of Rabbi Meir.

Certain details of expression show that *The Fox and the Wolf* was directly based either on the corresponding episode in the *Roman de Renart* or on something very like it. But the ME version is at two points simpler in structure. In the *Roman*, the fox, like the wolf, sees his own reflection in the water and mistakes it for his wife; this provides an extra motive for the fox's descent, and an occasion for jealousy on the wolf's part (because the fox is already in the well), but is otiose. A variant OF version[2] agrees with the ME on this point. The comic possibilities of the wolf's confession are much more effectively realized in the ME version. In the *Roman*, the seduction of the wolf's wife by the fox falls outside the actual framework of the story (since the wolf is told of it by one of his whelps immediately after his escape); the ending is consequently much less direct and telling than in the ME. In the latter, the seduction is the more pointedly outrageous for being reported in the wolf's confession, which is given dramatic effect by being addressed to the fox and by the wolf's naïve repudiation of the evidence of his own eyes. In the *Roman*, the wolf merely reports that he has made his confession to an old hare and to dame Hersent the goat (3567–9).

The Scriptural notion of the 'ravening wolf' was the central idea which Nivard combined with beast-fables to make an allegory in which the wolf was a monk and the central figure. The professional entertainers of the Middle Ages, inheriting this allegory of the cloister, created from it the miraculously

---

[1] Translated by J. Derenbourg, *Johannis de Capua Directorium vitae humanae*, Bibliothèque de l'École des Hautes Études, lxxii (1887–9), p. viii, n. 1.

[2] ed. Chabaille, in the *Supplément* (1835) to Méon, *Le Roman de Renart* (1826), 111–21.

original animal comedy of the vernacular beast-epic, the main
interest of which was concentrated in the fox. *The Fox and the
Wolf* fittingly represents the final stage of this process, in which
the ethical values implicit in allegory have given place to un-
inhibited relish for the scandalous triumphs of a brazen repro-
bate. The anthropomorphism of beast-epic is evident in the
allusively introduced cuckolding of the wolf, and the morality
of beast-fable in the fox's sententious comment on his own folly
(96 ff.). The authentic flavour of beast-epic is achieved *inter
alia* by the ironic metaphor (40 and 45) on which the fox founds
his blandly insolent claim to have done Chantecler's hens good,
as by the unusual ironic metaphors of ll. 255–6.

A vox gon out of þe wode go,   f. 138ᵛ 2
Afingret so þat him wes wo—
He nes neuere in none wise
Afingret erour half so swiþe.
He ne hoeld nouþer wey ne strete,   5
For him wes loþ men to mete;
Him were leuere meten one hen
Þen half an oundred wimmen!
He strok swiþe oueral
So þat he ofsei ane wal.   10
Wiþinne þe walle wes on hous:
The wox wes þider swiþe wous,
For he þohute his hounger aquenche,
Oþer mid mete oþer mid drunche.
Abouten he biheld wel ȝerne.   15
Þo eroust bigon þe vox to erne
Al fort he come to one walle;
And som þerof wes afalle,
And wes þe wal oueral tobroke,
And on ȝat þer wes iloke.   20
At þe furmeste bruche þat he fond
He lep in, and ouer he wond.

Þo he wes inne, smere he lou
And þerof he hadde gome inou
(For he com in wiþouten leue   25
Boþen of haiward and of reue!)

On hous þer wes: þe dore wes ope.
Hennen weren þerinne icrope
Fiue (þat makeþ anne flok),
And mið hem sat on kok.   30
Þe kok him wes flowen on hey,
And two hennen him seten ney.
'Wox!' quad þe kok, 'wat dest þou þare?
Go hom! Crist þe ȝeue kare:
Houre hennen þou dest ofte shome.'   35
'Be stille, Ich hote, a Godes nome!'
Quaþ þe wox, 'Sire Chauntecler,
Þou fle adoun and com me ner.
I nabbe don her nout bote goed—
I have leten þine hennen blod.   40
Hy weren seke ounder þe ribe,
Þat hy ne miȝtte non lengour libe
Bote here heddre were itake.
Þat I do for almes sake—
Ich haue hem leten eddre-blod.   45
And þe, Chauntecler, hit wolde don goed
(Þou hauest þat ilke ounder þe splen—
Þou nestes neuere daies ten);
For þine lif-dayes beþ al ago
Bote þou bi mine rede do.   50
I do þe lete blod ounder þe brest,
Oþer sone axe after þe prest.'
'Go wei!' quod þe kok, 'wo þe bigo!
Þou hauest don oure kunne wo—

Go mid þan þat þou hauest nouþe.   55
Acoursed be þou of Godes mouþe!
For were I adoun, bi Godes nome
Ich miȝte ben siker of oþre shome.
Ac weste hit houre cellerer
Þat þou were icomen her,   60
He wolde sone after þe ȝonge
Mid pikes and stones and staues stronge.
Alle þine bones he wolde tobreke—
Þene we weren wel awreke!'

He wes stille ne spak namore,   65 f. 138ᵛ 2
Ac he werþ aþurst wel sore:
Þe þurst him dede more wo
Þen heuede raþer his hounger do.
Oueral he ede and sohvte:
On auenture, his wiit him brohute   70
To one putte wes water inne,
Þat wes imaked mid grete ginne.
Tuo boketes þer he founde:
Þat oþer wende to þe grounde,
Þat wen me shulde þat on opwinde   75
Þat oþer wolde adoun winde.
He ne hounderstod nout of þe ginne:
He nom þat boket and lop þerinne,
For he hopede inou to drinke.
Þis boket biginneþ to sinke: 80
To late þe vox wes biþout
Þo he wes in þe ginne ibrout.
Inou he gon him biþenche,
Ac hit ne halp mid none wrenche:
Adoun he moste, he wes þerinne—   85

59, 66 Ac] *MS*. At

Ikaut he wes mid swikele ginne.
Hit miȝte han iben wel his wille
To lete þat boket hongi stille.
Wat mið serewe and mid drede,
Al his þurst him ouer-hede.   90
Al þus he com to þe grounde,
And water inou þer he founde.
Þo he fond water, ȝerne he dronk
(Him þoute þat water þere stonk,
For hit wes toȝeines his wille!)   95
'Wo worþe', quaþ þe vox, 'lust and wille,
Þat ne con meþ to his mete!

ȝef Ich neuede to muchel i-ete,
Þis ilke shome neddi nouþe,
Nedde lust iben of mine mouþe.   100
Him is wo, in euche londe,
Þat is þef mid his honde.
Ich am ikaut mid swikele ginne
Oþer soum deuel me broute herinne.
I was woned to ben wiis,   105
Ac nou of me idon hit hiis!'

Þe vox wep and reuliche bigan.
Þer com a wolf gon, after þan,
Out of þe depe wode bliue,
For he wes afingret swiþe.   110
Noþing he ne founde, in al þe niȝte,
Wermide his honger aquenche miȝtte.
He com to þe putte, þene vox iherde:
He him kneu wel bi his rerde,
For hit wes his neiȝebore   115
And his gossip, of children bore.

106 Ac] MS. At

Adoun bi þe putte he sat.
Quod þe wolf: 'Wat may ben þat
Þat Ich in þe putte ihere?
Hertou Cristine oþer mi fere?   120
Say me soþ—ne gabbe þou me nout:
Wo haueþ þe in þe putte ibrout?'
Þe vox hine ikneu wel for his kun,
And þo eroust kom wiit to him;
For he þoute, mid sommne ginne,   125
Himself houpbringe, þene wolf þerinne.
Quod þe vox: 'Wo is nou þere?
Ich wene hit is Sigrim þat Ich here.'
'Þat is soþ,' þe wolf sede,
'Ac wat art þou, so God þe rede?'   130

'A!' quod þe vox, 'Ich wille þe telle—   f. 139ʳ 2
On alpi word Ich lie nelle.
Ich am Reneuard, þi frend;
And ʒif Ich þine come heuede iwend,
Ich hedde so ibede for þe   135
Þat þou sholdest comen to me.'
'Mid þe?' quod þe wolf, 'warto?
Wat shulde Ich ine þe putte do?'
Quod þe vox: 'Þou art ounwiis!
Her is þe blisse of Paradiis—   140
Her Ich mai euere wel fare,
Wiþouten pine, wiþouten kare.
Her is mete, her is drinke;
Her is blisse wiþouten swinke.
Her nis hounger neuermo,   145
Ne non oþer kunnes wo—
Of alle gode her is inou!'

121 Say] *MS*. May   130 Ac] *MS*. At

Mid þilke wordes þe volf lou.
'Art þou ded, so God þe rede,
Oþer of þe worlde?' þe wolf sede.   150
Quod þe wolf: 'Wenne storue þou,
And wat dest þou þere nou?
Ne beþ nout ȝet þre daies ago
Þat þou, and þi wif also,
And þine children, smale and grete,   155
Alle togedere mid me hete!'
'Þat is soþ,' quod þe vox,
'Gode þonk, nou hit is þus
Þat Ihc am to Criste vend!
Not hit non of mine frend;   160
I nolde, for al þe worldes goed,
Ben ine þe worlde, þer Ich hem fond.
Wat shuld Ich ine þe worlde go

f. 139ᵛ 1

Þer nis bote kare and wo,
And liuie in fulþe and in sunne?   165
Ac her beþ ioies fele cunne—
Her beþ boþe shep and get.'
Þe wolf haueþ hounger swiþe gret,
For he nedde ȝare i-ete;
And þo he herde speken of mete,   170
He wolde bleþeliche ben þare.
'A!' quod þe wolf, 'gode ifere,
Moni goed mel þou hauest me binome!
Let me adoun to þe kome,
And al Ich wole þe forȝeue.'   175
'Ȝe!' quod þe vox, 'were þou isriue,
And sunnen heuedest al forsake,
And to klene lif itake,
Ich wolde so bidde for þe

166 Ac] *MS.* At

Þat þou sholdest comen to me.'   180
'To wom shuld Ich', þe wolf seide,
'Ben iknowe of mine misdede?
Her nis noþing aliue
Þat me kouþe her nou sriue.
Þou hauest ben ofte min ifere—   185
Woltou nou mi srift ihere,
And al mi liif I shal þe telle?'
'Nay!' quod þe vox, 'I nelle.'
'Neltou?' quod þe wolf, 'þin ore!
Ich am afingret swiþe sore—   190
Ich wot, toniȝt Ich worþe ded,
Bote þou do me somne reed.
For Cristes loue, be mi prest!'
Þe wolf bey adoun his brest
And gon to siken harde and stronge.   195
'Woltou', quod þe vox, 'srift ounderfonge?
Tel þine sunnen, on and on,   f 139ᵛ 2
Þat þer bileue neuer on.'

'Sone,' quad þe wolf, 'wel ifaie!
Ich habbe ben qued al mi lif-daie: 200
Ich habbe widewene kors—
Þerfore Ich fare þe wors.
A þousent shep Ich habbe abiten
And mo, ȝef hy weren iwriten;
Ac hit me ofþinkeþ sore.   205
Maister, shal I tellen more?'
'Ȝe!' quad þe vox, 'al þou most sugge,
Oþer elleswer þou most abugge.'
'Gossip!' quod þe wolf, '(forȝef hit me)
Ich habbe ofte sehid qued bi þe.   210

          199 ifaie] *MS*. jfare

Men seide þat þou on þine liue
Misferdest mid mine wiue.
Ich þe aperseiuede one stounde,
And in bedde togedere ou founde:
Ich wes ofte ou ful ney   215
And in bedde togedere ou sey.
Ich wende, also oþre doþ,
Þat Ich iseie were soþ,
And þerfore þou were me loþ—
Gode gossip, ne be þou nohut wroþ!'   220
'Vuolf!' quad þe vox him þo,
'Al þat þou hauest herbifore ido,
In þohut, in speche, and in dede,
In euch oþeres kunnes quede,
Ich þe forȝeue at þisse nede.'   225
'Crist þe forȝelde!' þe wolf seide,
'Nou Ich am in clene liue,
Ne recche Ich of childe ne of wiue!
Ac sei me wat I shal do

f. 140ʳ 1 And ou Ich may comen þe to.'   230
Ðo quod þe vox: 'Ich wille þe lere.
Isiist þou a boket hongi þere?
Þer is a bruche of heuene blisse!
Lep þerinne, mid iwisse,
And þou shalt comen to me sone.'   235
Quod þe wolf: 'Þat is liȝt to done!'
He lep in and way sumdel
(Þat weste þe vox ful wel!)
Þe wolf gon sinke, þe vox arise—
Þo gon þe wolf sore agrise!   240
Þo he com amidde þe putte,
Þe wolf þene vox opward mette.

229 Ac] MS. At

'Gossip,' quod þe wolf, 'wat nou?
Wat hauest þou imunt—weder wolt þou?'
'Weder Ich wille?' þe vox sede,   245
'Ich wille oup, so God me rede!
And nou go doun wiþ þi meel—
Þi biȝete worþ wel smal!
Ac Ich am þerof glad and bliþe
Þat þou art nomen in clene liue.   250
Þi soule-cnul Ich wile do ringe,
And masse for þine soule singe!'
Þe wrecche bineþe noþing ne vind,
Bote cold water and hounger him bind.
To colde gistninge he wes ibede—   255
Wroggen haueþ his dou iknede!

Þe wolf in þe putte stod,
Afingret so þat he ves wod.
Inou he cursede þat þider him broute!
Þe vox þerof luitel route.   260
Þe put him wes þe house ney
Þer freren woneden, swiþe sley.
Þo þat hit com to þe time   f. 140ʳ 2
Þat hoe shulden arisen ine,
Forto suggen here houssong,   265
O frere þer wes among
Of here slep hem shulde awecche.
Wen hoe shulden þidere recche,
He seide: 'Ariseþ, on and on,
And komeþ to houssong heuereuchon!'   270
Þis ilke frere heyte Ailmer—

---

249 Ac] MS. At   253 vind] *altered from* vint   264 ine]
*MS. .jne or .jme. The e is written on a third minim, which the scribe
probably meant to cancel.*

He wes hoere maister curtiler.
He wes hofþurst swiþe stronge:
Riȝt amidward here houssonge
Al hone to þe putte he hede,   275
For he wende bete his nede.
He com to þe putte and drou,
And þe wolf wes heui inou.
Þe frere mid al his maine tey,
So longe þat he þene wolf isey.   280
For he sei þene wolf þer sitte,
He gradde: 'þe deuel is in þe putte!'

To þe putte hy gonnen gon,
Alle mid pikes and staues and ston—
Euch mon mid þat he hedde   285
(Wo wes him þat wepne nedde!)
Hy comen to þe putte, þene wolf opdrowe:
Þo hede þe wreche fomen inowe
Þat weren egre him to slete
Mid grete houndes, and to bete!   290
Wel and wroþe he wes iswonge—
Mid staues and speres he wes istounge.
Þe wox bicharde him, mid iwisse,
For he ne fond nones kunnes blisse
Ne hof dintes forȝeuenesse.   *Explicit.*

283 gonnen] *MS.* gonnnen   293 bicharde] *MS. possibly* bicherde
(*fifth letter altered, and difficult to read*)

VI

DAME SIRITH

Dame Sirith is a fabliau, and its main point a cunning stratagem: so much we are plainly told in the Anglo-Norman heading.
It is typical of the genre in awarding success to a disreputable
person and discomfiture to a virtuous and innocent one, and in
its comic purpose. The female go-between is also the central
figure in the OF *fabliau D'Auberee la vielle maquerelle* and in
Richeut (still best regarded as a *fabliau*; composed *c.* 1170, and
hence the oldest extant). The medieval literature of entertainment (which was especially needed as a counterpart to a mas-
sively entrenched literature of edification) inevitably provided
for relaxations of conscience. There is thus a kind of justice in
the fact that the other early Western versions of this widely
diffused tale are short prose anecdotes embodied in collections
of stories which were meant to be edifying. But there may be
historical reasons for this: according to the view favoured in
three recent works, the origin of the *fabliau* as a kind is to be
sought in the fable,[1] or the fable and the *exemplum*.[2]

As transmitted in the unique manuscript, *Dame Sirith* has
at least four features which in conjunction raise an interesting
question: (i) the marked preponderance of dialogue over narration, transitions, and explanations (which, apart from the
opening ll. 1–24, are limited to five short passages[3]); (ii) the
unmarked transition in ll. 279–80, where Dame Sirith addresses
Wilekin and her dog respectively; (iii) the mixing of metres
(four-beat lines in tail-rhyme stanzas;[4] four-beat lines in rhymed
couplets;[5] three-beat lines in tail-rhyme stanzas[6]); (iv) the

[1] Johnston and Owen, *Fabliaux* (1957), xiii–xviii; T. B. W. Reid,
Twelve Fabliaux (1958), ix–xi.

[2] P. Nykrog, *Les Fabliaux* (1957), 242–62.

[3] 149–60, 297–302, 331–2, 406–8, 417–22.

[4] 1–132, 149–92, 237–84, 379–408, 417–22, 433–5.

[5] 133–48, 193–236, 285–378. 409–16, 423–6.   [6] 427–32, 436–50.

marginal letters which identify the interlocutors and distinguish narration from dialogue (see note on line 1).

On the one hand, *Dame Sirith* is evidently not a full-blown drama: the dialogue lacks the very brief replies appropriate to a play. But in combination the above peculiarities suggest that the work was meant to be declaimed with due differentiation of the three characters concerned. This would have been done not by three actors, but by a single minstrel who spoke all three parts, and by means of changes in the voice and dress and of appropriate gestures. The practice of miming of this kind is directly attested by the epitaph composed (some time between the ninth and the twelfth centuries) by one Vitalis for himself;[1] and it accounts for the form of certain short OF pieces of a comic (mostly satiric) kind,[2] which are convincingly classified as dramatic monologues. Among these, *Le Privilege aux Bretons*, ii, and Rutebeuf's *Dit de la Herberie* are written in a mixture of octosyllabic couplets or series of couplets with strophes comparable to the tail-rhyme type.[3] It is therefore likely that in *Dame Sirith* the mixture (so rare in ME) of metres was due to OF models, and not (as Schröder has concluded in the most recent substantial study) to reworking of some passages by a redactor.

The marginal initials identifying interlocutors in *Dame Sirith* are paralleled in some manuscripts of the twelfth-century Latin works styled 'elegiac comedies' (e.g. *Geta*, *Babio*, and *De Nuncio Sagaci*). The marked affinities in subject and tone of these pieces

[1]   Fingebam vultus, habitus, ac verba loquentum,
          Ut plures uno crederes ore loqui.
          (Riese, *Anthologia latina*, ii. 143)
[2] See E. Faral, *Mimes français du XIII⁰ siècle* (1910) and *Les Jongleurs en France au moyen âge* (1910), 231–46, for the evidence and arguments on which this theory is based.
[3] *Courtois d'Arras*, which is either a dramatic monologue or one of the earliest secular plays, uses a tail-rhyme stanza (1–90), rhymed octosyllabic couplets (91–426, 447–652), and five monorhymed stanzas of four 12-syllable lines (427–46). *Le Garçon et l'aveugle*, which is the oldest OF farce (*c.* 1275), uses a stanza (1–8, 83–90) as well as rhymed octosyllabic couplets; and *Pirame et Tisbe* uses tail-rhyme stanzas exclusively in six long passages which are laments by the lovers, but otherwise rhymed octosyllabic couplets.

with the OF *fabliaux* have led Faral to class them as Latin
fabliaux, i.e. as stories which were never acted.[1] But the form of
all three pieces named above is such that they might in any case
have been mimed.[2] And it seems curious that two of the Latin
'comedies' (*Geta* and *Aulularia*) are by Vitalis of Blois, i.e. a
namesake of and therefore perhaps identical with the man who,
on his own testimony, practised the kind of miming in question.
In *Dame Sirith*, it is precisely the rarity of anything explicitly
marking a change of speaker that gives point to the marginal
indications and is explained by them: no signals would have been
needed in the text if the piece had been written for some kind of
semi-dramatic presentation. And, given mimed performance of
Dame Sirith by a minstrel, it would have been a short and easy
step to compose the *Interludium de Clerico et Puella* (see XV) on
the same subject, and possibly with *Dame Sirith* as its specific
source (see XV, Introduction).

Dame Sirith is one of the very few medieval stories which
are probably of Indian origin: it meets Bédier's test[3] of being
preserved in independent form as well as in the comprehensive
medieval translations of Oriental story-collections. The only
other works of which this can be said are six OF *fabliaux* (out
of some 140 extant), two other short stories in OF, and five
exempla.[4] Among the latter Bédier ranges the other European
versions of *Dame Sirith*, since they are contained in the *Disciplina Clericalis*[5] and the *Exempla* of Jacques de Vitry.[6] Neither of
the Latin *exempla* can be the immediate source of *Dame Sirith*.
For instance, Petrus Alfonsus does not say who transformed
the go-between's daughter into a dog, and Jacques de Vitry says
nothing about the husband and his temporary absence; but
Dame Sirith agrees on the first point with Jacques de Vitry and
on the second with Petrus. It is clear that many OF *fabliaux*
are re-creations in the vernacular of stories that circulated orally

---

[1] 'Le fabliau latin au moyen âge', *Romania*, l (1924), 321–85.
[2] See M. Cohen and others, *La 'Comédie' latine en France au XII*
siècle (1931), i. 17–20; 67–69 and 71; ii. 115 ff.
[3] *Les Fabliaux* (1893), 101.
[4] Ibid. 111.
[5] Ed. A. Hilka and W. Söderhjelm (1911), 18–19.
[6] Ed. T. F. Crane (1890), no. ccv.

in briefer (i.e. anecdotal) form; and *Dame Sirith* in its extant
form may well have been affected by details from oral tradition,
though it is substantially of literary origin.

Ci comence le fablel e la cointise de dame Siriz

f. 165ʳ 1

As I com bi an waie,   T
Hof on Ich herde saie—
    Ful modi mon and proud.
Wis he wes of lore,
And gouþlich vnder gore,   5
    And cloþed in fair sroud.

To louien he bigon
On wedded wimmon;
    Þerof he heuede wrong!
His herte hire wes al on,   10
Þat reste neuede he non—
    Þe loue wes so strong.

Wel ȝerne he him biþoute
Hou he hire gete moute
    In ani cunnes wise.   15
Þat befel on an day
Þe louerd wend away
    Hon his marchaundise.

He wente him to þen inne
Þer hoe wonede inne   20
    (Þat wes riche won!)
And com into þen halle,
Þer hoe wes srud wiþ palle,
    And þus he bigon: C

'God almiȝtten be herinne!' 25
'Welcome, so Ich euer bide wenne!'
    Quod þis wif. V
'His hit þi wille, com and site,
And wat is þi wille let me wite,
    Mi leue lif.· 30

Bi houre Louerd, heuene-king,
If I mai don aniþing
    Þat þe is lef,
Þou miȝtt finden me ful fre: f. 165ʳ 2
Fol bleþeli will I don for þe, 35
    Wiþhouten gref.'

'Dame, God þe forȝelde! C
Bote on þat þou me nout bimelde
    Ne make þe wroþ,
Min hernde will I to þe bede. 40
Bote wraþþen þe for ani dede
    Were me loþ.'

'Nai, iwis, Wilekin! V
For noþing þat euer is min,
    Þau þou hit ȝirne, 45
Houncurteis ne will I be.
Ne con I nout on vilte,
    Ne nout I nelle lerne.

Þou mait saien al þine wille,
And I shal herknen and sitten stille 50
    Þat þou haue told.
And if þat þou me tellest skil,
I shal don after þi wil—
    Þat be þou bold.

And þau þou saie me ani same,   55
Ne shal I þe nouiȝt blame
    For þi sawe.'
'Nou Ich haue wonne leue,
Ȝif þat I me shulde greue
    Hit were hounlawe.   60

Certes, dame, þou seist as hende,   C
And I shal setten spel on ende,
    And tellen þe al—
Wat Ich wolde, and wi Ich com.
Ne con Ich saien non falsdom,   65
    Ne non I ne shal.

f. 165ᵛ 1

Ich habbe iloued þe moni ȝer,
Þau Ich nabbe nout ben her
    Mi loue to schowe.
Wile þi louerd is in toune,   70
Ne mai no mon wiþ þe holden roune
    Wiþ no þewe.

Ȝurstendai Ich herde saie,
As Ich wende bi þe waie,
    Of oure sire: 75
Me tolde me þat he was gon
To þe feire of Botolfston
    In Lincolneschire.

And for Ich weste þat he ves houte,
Þarfore Ich am igon aboute   80
    To speken wiþ þe.

Him burþ to liken wel his lif
Þat miȝtte welde secc a vif
    In priuite.

Dame, if hit is þi wille,   85
Boþ dernelike and stille,
    Ich wille þe loue.'
'Þat wold I don for non þing,   V
Bi houre Louerd, heuene-king,
    Þat ous is boue!   90

Ich habe mi louerd þat is mi spouse,
Þat maiden broute me to house
    Mid menske inou.
He loueþ me and Ich him wel;
Oure loue is also trewe as stel,   95
    Wiþhouten wou.

Þau he be from hom on his hernde,
Ich were ounseli if Ich lernede
    To ben on hore.
Þat ne shal neuere be   100   f. 165ᵛ 2
Þat I shal don selk falsete,
    On bedde ne on flore.

Neuermore his lif-wile,
Þau he were on hondred mile
    Biȝende Rome,   105
For noþing ne shuld I take
Mon on erþe to ben mi make
    Ar his hom-come.'

        88 þing] *MS.* þin

'Dame, dame, torn þi mod!   C
þi curteisi wes euer god,   110
    And ȝet shal be:
For þe Louerd þat ous haueþ wrout,
Amend þi mod, and torn þi þout,
    And rew on me!'

'We, we! oldest þou me a fol?   V 115
So Ich euer mote biden ȝol,
    þou art ounwis!
Mi þout ne shalt þou never wende.
Mi louerd is curteis mon and hende,
    And mon of pris,   120

And Ich am wif boþe god and trewe.
Trewer womon ne mai no mon cnowe
    þen Ich am—
þilke time ne shal neuer bitide
þat món for wouing ne þoru prude   125
    Shal do me scham.'

'Swete lemmon, merci!   C
Same ne vilani
    Ne bede I þe non;
Bote derne loue I þe bede,   130
As mon þat wolde of loue spede,
    And finde won.'

f. 166ʳ 1

'So bide Ich euere mete oþer drinke,   V
Her þou lesest al þi swinke.
þou miȝt gon hom, leue broþer,   135
For wille Ich þe loue ne non oþer,

127 lemmon] *MS*. lenmon   132 finde] *MS*. fide

Bote mi wedde houssebonde—
To tellen hit þe ne wille Ich wonde.'
'Certes, dame, þat me forþinkeþ!
An wo is þe mon þat muchel swinkeþ   140
And at þe laste leseþ his sped!
To maken menis his him ned.
Bi me I saie, ful iwis,
Þat loue þe loue þat I shal mis.
An dame, haue nou godnedai!   145
And þilke Louerd þat al welde mai
Leue þat þi þout so tourne
Þat Ihc for þe no leng ne mourne.'

Drerimod he wente awai,   T
And þoute boþe niȝt and dai   150
     Hire al forto wende.
A frend him radde forto fare
(And leuen al his muchele kare)
     To dame Siriz þe hende.

Þider he wente him anon   155
So suiþe so he miȝtte gon
     (No mon he n'imette);
Ful he wes of tene and treie.
Mid wordes milde and eke sleie
     Faire he hire grette.   160

'God þe iblessi, dame Siriz!   C
Ich am icom to speken þe wiz,
     For ful muchele nede.
And Ich mai haue help of þe,
Þou shalt haue, þat þou shalt se,   165
     Ful riche mede.'   f. 166ʳ 2

140 þat] *MS.* þa   142 menis] *MS.* menig

'Welcomen art þou, leue sone!   F
And if Ich mai oþer cone
In eni wise for þe do,
I shal strengþen me þerto.   170
Forþi, leue sone, tel þou me
Wat þou woldest I dude for þe.'
'Bote, leue nelde! ful euele I fare—   C
I lede mi lif wiþ tene and kare.

Wiþ muchel hounsele Ich lede mi lif,   175
And þat is for on suete wif
        Þat heiȝtte Margeri.
Ich haue iloued hire moni dai,
And of hire loue hoe seiz me nai;
        Hider Ich com forþi.   180

Bote if hoe wende hire mod,
For serewe mon Ich wakese wod
        Oþer miselue quelle.
Ich heuede iþout miself to slo;
Forþ þen radde a frend me go—   185
        To þe mi sereue telle.

He saide me, wiþhouten faille,
Þat þou me couþest helpe and uaile,
        And bringen me of wo
Þoru þine crafftes and þine dedes.   190
And Ich wile ȝeue þe riche mede,
        Wiþ þat hit be so.'

'Benedicite be herinne!   F
Her hauest þou, sone, mikel senne.
Louerd, for his suete nome,   195
        185 Forþ] *MS*. For

Lete þe þerfore hauen no shome!
Þou seruest affter Godes grome
Wen þou seist on me silk blame.
For Ich am old, and sek, and lame—   f. 166ᵛ 1
Seknesse haueþ maked me ful tame.   200
Blesse þe, blesse þe, leue knaue!
Leste þou mesauenter haue,
For þis lesing þat is founden
Oppon me, þat am harde ibonden.
Ich am on holi wimon;   205
On wicchecrafft nout I ne con,
Bote wiþ gode men almesdede
Ilke dai mi lif I fede,
And bidde mi paternoster and mi crede,
Þat Goed hem helpe at hore nede   210
Þat helpen me mi lif to lede,
And leue þat hem mote wel spede
(His lif and his soule worþe ishend
Þat þe to me þis hernde haueþ send!)
And leue me to ben iwreken   215
On him þis shome me haueþ speken.'

'Leue nelde, bilef al þis!   C
Me þinkeþ þat þou art onwis.
Þe mon þat me to þe taute,
He weste þat þou hous couþest saute.   220
Help, dame Siriþ, if þou maut.
To make me wiþ þe sueting saut;
And Ich wille geue þe gift ful stark
(Moni a pound and moni a mark,
Warme pilche and warme shon)   225
Wiþ þat min hernde be wel don.

218 þat] *MS.* þa

Of muchel godlec miȝt þou ȝelpe,
If hit be so þat þou me helpe.'
'Liȝ me nout, Wilekin, bi þi leute: F
Is hit þin hernest þou tellest me?   230
Louest þou wel dame Margeri?'

f. 166ᵛ 2   'Ȝe, nelde, witerli—
Ich hire loue! Hit mot me spille
Bote Ich gete hire to mi wille.'
'Wat God, Wilekin, me reweþ þi scaþe—   F 235
Houre Louerd sende þe help raþe!

Weste Hic hit miȝtte ben forholen,
Me wolde þunche wel folen
      Þi wille forto fullen.
Make me siker wiþ word on honde   240
Þat þou wolt helen, and I wile fonde
      If Ich mai hire tellen.

For al þe world ne wold I nout
Þat Ich were to chapitre ibrout
      For none selke werkes.   245
Mi iugement were sone igiuen
To ben wiþ shome somer-driuen
      Wiþ prestes and wiþ clarkes.'

'Iwis, nelde, ne wold I   C
Þat þou heuedest uilani   250
      Ne shame for mi goed.
Her I þe mi trouþe pliȝtte:
Ich shal helen bi mi miȝtte,
      Bi þe holi roed!'

238 folen] *Mätzner and McKnight* solen; *but there is unquestionably a thin hairline in the MS. that is almost certainly intended to represent the cross-stroke of an f.*

'Welcome, Wilekin, hiderward!   F 255
Her hauest imaked a foreward
        Þat þe mai ful wel like.
Þou maiȝt blesse þilke siþ,
For þou maiȝt make þe ful bliþ—
        Ðar þou namore sike!   260

To goder-hele euer come þou hider,
For sone will I gange þider
        And maken hire hounderstonde.
I shal kenne hire sulke a lore
Þat hoe shal louien þe mikel more   265 f. 167ʳ 1
        Þen ani mon in londe.'

'Al so haui Godes griþ,   C
Wel hauest þou said, dame Siriþ,
        And goder-hele shal ben þin!
Haue her twenti shiling: 270
Þis Ich ȝeue þe to meding,
        To buggen þe sep and swin.'

'So Ich euere brouke hous oþer flet,   F
Neren neuer pones beter biset
        Þen þes shulen ben!   275
For I shal don a iuperti
And a ferli maistri,
        Þat þou shalt ful wel sen.

Pepir nou shalt þou eten;
Þis mustart shal ben þi mete,   280
        And gar þin eien to rene.

        279 Pepir] *MS.* Pepis

I shal make a lesing
Of þin heie renning—
    Ich wot wel wer and wenne.'

'Wat! nou const þou no god!   285
Me þinkeþ þat þou art wod—
Ʒeuest þou þe welpe mustard?'
'Be stille, boinard!
I shal mit þis ilke gin
Gar hire loue to ben al þin.   290
Ne shal Ich neuer haue reste ne ro
Til Ich haue told hou þou shalt do.
Abid me her til min hom-come.'
'Ʒus, bi þe somer blome!
Heþen null I ben binomen   295
Til þou be aʒein comen.'
Dame Siriþ bigon to go

f. 167ʳ 2

As a wrecche þat is wo,
Þat hoe com hire to þen inne
Þer þis gode wif wes inne.   300
Þo hoe to þe dore com,
Swiþe reuliche hoe bigon:
'Louerd,' hoe seiþ, 'wo is holde wiues,
Þat in pouerte ledeþ ay liues!
Not no mon so muchel of pine   305
As poure wif þat falleþ in nausine.
Þat mai ilke mon bi me wite,
For mai I nouþer gange ne site—
Ded wold I ben ful fain.
Hounger and þurst me haueþ nei slain;   310

287 þou] *MS.* þo   306 nausine] *MS.* ausine; *Mätzner and McKnight* ansine

Ich ne mai mine limes onwold
For mikel hounger and þurst and cold.
Warto liueþ selke a wrecche?
Wi nul Goed mi soule fecche?'

'Seli wif, God þe hounbinde!   315
Todai wille I þe mete finde
    For loue of Goed.
Ich haue reuþe of þi wo,
For euele icloþed I se þe go
    And euele ishoed.   320

Com herin—Ich wile þe fede.'
'Goed almiʒtten do þe mede
And þe Louerd þat wes on rode idon,
And faste fourti daiis to non,
And heuene and erþe haueþ to welde—   325
As þilke Louerd þe forʒelde!'
'Haue her fles and eke bred,
And make þe glad—hit is mi red!
And haue her þe coppe wiþ þe drinke—
Goed do þe mede for þi swinke!'   330
Þenne spac þat holde wif   f. 167ᵛ 1
(Crist awarie hire lif!):
'Alas, Alas, þat euer I liue!
Al þe sunne Ich wolde forgiue
Þe mon þat smite of min heued—   335
Ich wolde mi lif me were bireued!'
'Seli wif, what eilleþ þe?'
'Bote eþe mai I sori be!
Ich heuede a douter feir and fre—
Feiror ne miʒtte no mon se.   340

Hoe heuede a curteis hossebonde—
Freour mon miȝtte no mon fonde.
Mi douter louede him al to wel;
Forþi mak I sori del.
Oppon a dai he was out wend, 345
And þarþoru wes mi douter shend.
He hede on ernde out of toune,
And com a modi clarc wiþ croune—
To mi douter his loue beed,
And hoe nolde nout folewe his red. 350
He ne miȝtte his wille haue,
For noþing he miȝtte craue.
Þenne bigon þe clerc to wiche,
And shop mi douter til a biche.
Þis is mi douter þat Ich of speke: 355
For del of hire min herte brekeþ.
Loke hou hire heien greten;
On hire cheken þe teres meten.
Forþi, dame, were hit no wonder
Þau min herte burste assunder. 360
A, wose euer is ȝong houssewif,
Ha loueþ ful luitel hire lif,
And eni clerc of loue hire bede,
Bote hoe grante and lete him spede!'
'A! Louerd Crist, wat mai I þenne do! 365
Þis enderdai com a clarc me to
And bed me loue on his manere,
And Ich him nolde nout ihere.
Ich trouue he wolle me forsape.
Hou troustu, nelde, Ich moue ascape?' 370
'God almiȝtten be þin help
Þat þou ne be nouþer bicche ne welp!

f. 167ᵛ 2

356 brekeþ] *MS.* breke   365 I] *not in MS.*

Leue dame, if eni clerc
Bedeþ þe þat loue-werc,
Ich rede þat þou grante his bone   375
And bicom his lefmon sone.
And if þat þou so ne dost,
A worse red þou ounderfost.'

'Louerd Crist, þat me is wo,
Þat þe clarc me hede fro   380
 Ar he me heuede biwonne!
Me were leuere þen ani fe
That he heuede enes leien bi me,
 And efftsones bigunne.

Euermore, nelde, Ich wille be þin,   385
Wiþ þat þou feche me Willekin,
 Þe clarc of wam I telle.
Giftes will I geue þe
Þat þou maiȝt euer þe betere be,
 Bi Godes houne belle!'   390

'Soþliche, mi swete dame,
And if I mai wiþhoute blame,
 Fain Ich wille fonde,
And if Ich mai wiþ him mete
Bi eni wei oþer bi strete;   395
 Nout ne will I wonde.

Haue goddai, dame! forþ will I go.'   f. 168ʳ 1
'Allegate loke þat þou do so
 As Ich þe bad.
Bote þat þou me Wilekin bringe,   400
Ne mai I neuer lawe ne singe
 Ne be glad.'

  401 I] *not in MS.*

'Iwis, dame, if I mai,
Ich wille bringen him ȝet todai,
   Bi mine miȝtte.'   405
Hoe wente hire to hire inne:
Þer hoe founde Wilekinne,
   Bi houre Driȝtte!

'Swete Wilekin, be þou nout dred,
For of þin hernde Ich haue wel sped.   410
Swiþe com forþ þider wiþ me,
For hoe haueþ send affter þe.
Iwis nou maiȝt þou ben aboue,
For þou hauest grantise of hire loue!'
'God þe forȝelde, leue nelde,   415
Þat heuene and erþe haueþ to welde!'

Þis modi mon bigon to gon
Wiþ Siriz to his leuemon
   In þilke stounde.
Dame Siriz bigon to telle   420
And swor bi Godes ouene belle
   Hoe heuede him founde.

'Dame, so haue Ich Wilekin sout,
For nou haue Ich him ibrout.'
'Welcome, Wilekin, swete þing!   425
Þou art welcomore þen þe king.

Wilekin þe swete,
Mi loue I þe bihete,
   To don al þine wille!

410 hernde] *MS.* herde   411 forþ] *MS.* for

Turnd Ich haue mi þout, 430 f. 168ʳ 2
For I ne wolde nout
    Þat þou þe shuldest spille.'

'Dame, so Ich euere bide noen,
And Ich am redi and iboen
    To don al þat þou saie. 435
Nelde, par ma fai!
Þou most gange awai,
    Wile Ich and hoe shulen plaie.'

'Goddot, so I wille;
And loke þat þou hire tille 440
    And strek out hire þes.
God ȝeue þe muchel kare
Ȝeif þat þou hire spare,
    Þe wile þou mid hire bes.

And wose is onwis 445
And for non pris
    Ne con geten his leuemon,
I shal, for mi mede,
Garen him to spede,
    For ful wel I con.' 450

VII

SAINT KENELM

THE Middle English *Life* of St. Kenelm has a special claim to notice among the saints' legends of the thirteenth-century collection known as *The Southern English Legendary*. Unlike the pre-Conquest legend of St. Edmund (which is comparable, because concerned with a native saint), it is not founded on facts verifiable in historical sources of the saint's own time; indeed, Kenelm is not even mentioned in the *A.S. Chronicle* at the appropriate point (819). But it has all the marks of being rooted in local (and in their inception oral) traditions. Apart from the entertaining contest between the men of Gloucestershire and the men of Worcestershire for the possession of Kenelm's body, the miracles in the latter part of the twelfth-century Latin *Vita* (the source of ours, though the latter does not include any miracles) contain references to the area near Winchcombe. This *Vita* is the work of a monk of Worcester, named Wulfwine (in MS. Bodl. 285 Wulfwine Winnoc), who was a pupil of St. Oswald (Archbishop of York 971–92). Moreover, the *Winchcombe Annals* of MS. Tiberius E. iv give a summary of Kenelm's story, in phrasing identical with that of the *Vita*, and by naming the evil sister *Quendritha* and the murderer *Ascebert* imply detailed knowledge of the legend in the author.

The story has one unusual appendage of great interest. The saint's legend, and the summaries of it in Latin chronicles, have alike fossilized a couplet of alliterative verse:

> In Clent Cubeche Kenelm cunebearn
> lith under haȝeþorn, haudes bereafed.

This couplet evidently circulated independently of the legend, for it is separately recorded, for example, on the first leaf of MS. Pembroke College (Cambridge) 82, by about 1207. It is probably a commemorative snatch, complete in itself, and is not necessarily the debris of an early form of the legend. But the alliterative verse of the couplet is that of the Old rather than the Middle English period: the metrical form is in fact consistent with composition in late OE. Moreover, the application to Kenelm of the noun-compound *cunebearn* (which in O.E. is used mainly in verse) recurs in the entry *ðonne resteð Sancte Kenelm cynebearn on Wincelescumbe* in an OE *Martyrology* begun before 995 and completed between 1013 and 1030.[1] Since the alliterative snatch is likely to be of comparable antiquity, this entry may well imply the existence of the legend in a complete (if briefer) form by 1030.

The story of Kenelm never developed such literary ramifications as that of Edmund did. But it was widely known in England in the thirteenth and fourteenth centuries; and it caught the fancy of Chaucer, who airs his knowledge of it with delectable self-satisfaction in *The Nonnes Preestes Tale* (3,120 ff.). And to this day the visitor to the parish church of Winchcombe may there inspect a very large leaden coffin, which is among the things that have come to be attached to the name of the boy saint.

Þᴇ kyng þat was of þe March, ase Ich telle bigan,
Kenulf kyng he was icleoped, swiþe holi and guod man.
Seint Kenelm was is sone and is eir also;
Borewenild and Quendrith weren is douȝtrene two.
In þe foure and twentiþe ȝere of is kynedom   5
Þe kyng Kenulf deide, and to þe ioie of heuene he com;
Hit was afftur þat ore Louerd in his moder aliȝte
Eiȝte hundret ȝer and nyntene, bi acountes riȝte.

Seint Kenelm, is ȝonge sone, in is seuenþe ȝere
Kyng was imad aftur him, alþei he ȝong child were.   10
His soster Borewenild louede him inouȝ
And in eche manere to alle guodnesse heo drouȝ.
Quendrith þe oþur soster of hire maneres nas nouȝt,
For heo tornede to feolonie and to quede hire þouȝt.

f. 150ʳ
(75 ff.)

---

[1] Ed. F. Liebermann, *Die Heiligen Englands* (1889), 17–18.

Heo isaiȝ þat hire ȝungue broþer, þat nas nouȝt of seue ȝer,
Kyng was imad of al þat lond þat heore fader hadde er.   16
To him heo hadde gret onde þat he scholde so riche beo,
And eir of hire fader lond, and of more power þane heo:
Heo þouȝte ȝif heo miȝte bringue þis child of liif-dawe,
Þat heo wolde of is heritage beo quene with lawe.   20
Al hire þouȝt was, niȝt and day, to biþenche sum outrage,
Þat þis child were ibrouȝt of dawe, forto habbe is heritage.
Heo porueide hire riȝt feolonliche a poysun, strong inouȝ,
f. 150ᵛ Forto ȝiue þis ȝongue child, to slen him with wouȝ.
Þo þat poysun him was iȝiue þat so strong and luþer was,   25
Ore Louerdes miȝte was so muche þat no þe worse him nas.
Þo þe luþere quene þat isai þat hit was al for nouȝt,
Þat no poysun ne miȝte him sle, heo þouȝte anoþur þouȝt.
Þis ȝongue child ane maister hadde, þat his wardein was;
Askebert he was icleoped (a strong trichour, alas!   30
For noman ne may to oþur sonere tricherie do
Þane þilke þat is him euere neiȝ and þat he trist mest to).
Þis luþere quene biþouȝte hire of one false wrenche
(Men seith þat feolonie nas neuere non þat womman ne can
   biþenche!)
With þis Askebert heo spac þis child to slen and spille: 35
Heo bihet him mede and guod inovȝ, and of eche þing don
   is wille,
So þat þis to luþere þingues weren at one rede,
And bispeken hou huy miȝten best don þe luþere dede.
Þe ȝwyle huy bispeken boþe þis ȝongue child to quelle,
Þis swete sweuene þis child matte þat Ich ov wolle nouþe   40
   telle.

Him þouȝte þat þare stod a treo riȝt bifore is bedde,
Þat anon to þe steorrene it tilde, and swyþe wide it spradde.

36 him] *altered from* hem, *probably by the scribe*

Þis treo was fair and noble inov3 and schon wel bri3te and
   wide,
Ful of blostmene and of fruyt and mani a riche bou3 biside,
Berninde wex and laumpes also þicke brenninde and li3te; 45
So noble treo nas neuere isei3e, ne non þat schon so bri3te.
Him þou3te he cam op on þat treo to þ'exte bowe an hei3
And biheold aboute into al þe world and aperteliche isei3.
Þe 3wyle he stod opon þis treo and biheold aboute so,
Him þou3te þat on of is nexte frend, and þat he truste mest
   to, 50
On þe grounde stod bineþe and smot ato þis treo
Þat it feol adoun to grounde, þat deol it was to seo.
'To a luyte foul Ich bicam (non fairore ne mi3te beo)
And bigan with joye inov3 ri3t into heouene fleo.'
Þo þis child þou3te so, at Wynchecombe he lay; 55
He awok and in grete þou3te was boþe ni3t and day.
He nuste 3wat tockninge it was—wel þe more was his þou3t;
Are he þarof sumþing wuste bliþe nas he nou3t.
His norice, þat him hadde ifed and with hire milk forth
   ibrou3t,
Þat child heo louede euere muche with dedes and with þou3t.
To hire þat child triste mest (Woluene hire name was)— 61
Þis child tolde hire priueliche of is metingue al is cas.
Þo þis norice hadde iheord þe sweuene, þat was so guod,
Heo bigan to siche sore and in grete þou3te stod:
'Alas', heo seide, 'þat Ich scholde euere þis day abide— 65
Þat mi child, mi swete heorte, swych cas schal bitide!
Alas, mi child, mi swete fode, þat Ich habbe forth ibrou3t,
Þi soster, þat bispekez þi deth, to quelle þe heo hath iþou3t.

47 þou3tc] o *altered from a letter not now identifiable*   53 *MS.*
mi3te non beo   56 in *not in MS.*   57 his] *Horstmann;*
MS. hire   59 him] m *conjectural, for writing that has been rubbed*
or erased; space for about three minims in this scribe's hand

f. 151ʳ Ake þe foul, þat þou bicome to and to heuene gan iwende,
Þat was þi soule, þat þudere schal aftur þi liues ende.'   70
Þis metyngue bicam soth inou3: þat he fond at þe laste,
For is soster and Askebert bispeken is deth wel faste.

Askebert seide a day þat þis child scholde wende
An hontingue to plei3en him bi þe wodes ende,
And he with him, ase hit was ri3t, to witien him bi þe wei3e.
He wende to þe wode of Clent, ase it were heom forto pleie.   76
Ase huy wenden aboute þe wode, ase ore Louerd 3af þe
     grace,
Grete wille þat child hadde þare to slepen in one place;
Adoun he lai wel soffteliche and gan to slepe anon.
Askebert ne þou3te nou3t þat he scholde þannes gon: 80
Biside in one derne stude he gan to deluen faste
Ane put, 3wane þat child were ded þare-inne him to caste.
Þat child bigan awakien sone, ase þei it were bi cas;
After is maister he biheold and ne sai3 nou3t 3ware he was.
Ake ore Louerd him 3af þe grace, þei he nuste nou3t of is dede,
Þat he spac to his maister and þeos wordes sede: 86
'Þou tr auailest' he seide, 'aboute nou3t, and þine 3wyle þou
     dost spille;
For in ane oþure stude I schal deie, 3ware hit is Godes wille.
And þoru3 tokningue of þis 3eorde þou schal wel iseo
Þare al þi wille þou mi3t do þat Ich imartred beo.'   90
Forth wende þis luþere man and þis child also;
Huy comen to on oþur stude, þare þe dede was ido.
Þis maister nam þe 3eorde and sette hire on þe grounde;
And heo bigan to leui þare in wel luyte stounde
And a swyþe gret asch bicam sethþe, and 3eot stant in   95
     þulke place,
To schewi þe mi3te of Seint Kenelm and ore Louerdes grace.
Þes luþere man nam þis child in þe wode of Klent

And ladde him, ase men doth a þeof to afongue is jugge-
    ment—
He ladde him into a priue stude al out of þe weiȝe,
Bitwene hulles heiȝe into a deop ualeie.   100
Þis child, þoruȝ þe Holi Gost, þei þe oþur it nolde him telle,
Wuste wel is luþere þouȝt—þat he him wolde aquelle.
And þo he targede a luyte þis luþere dede to done,
Þat child seide wel mildeliche: 'Ȝwy ne dost þou sone?'
He bigan ane saume þat men singuth in holie churche aday 105
(Þat was *Te Deum laudamus*) are þat he adoun lay.
Riȝt ase he seide an holi vers þat þare-inne was and is
(A Latyn iwrite, as alle þe oþure; and þe Englisch so is þis:
'Þe faire compaygnie of martyrs, Louerd, herieth þe')—
Riȝt ase he hadde þat fers iseid, as þe boc tellez me,   110
Þe luþere man smot of is heued onder an hawȝþorn treo,
Þare ase Godes wille was þat he imartred scholde beo.
A coluere ȝwiȝt so eni milk out of him gan teo,
And riȝt euene heo was iseiȝe into heouene fleo.   f. 151ᵛ
Onneþe he was seue ȝer old are he imartred were—   115
Al to soth is sweuene was, ase men miȝten iseo þere!

Þis luþere man þat him aslovȝ bigan to delue faste,
And made ane put, deop inouȝ, and þare-inne þis child
    caste.
He burede hit þare faste inou þat he ifounde nere,
And wende hom aȝein in is wei and liet him ligge þere.   120
To Quendrith, his luþere soster, anonriȝt he gan iwende
And tolde al þis luþere ded, hou he was ibrouȝt to ende.
Þeos womman was þo glad inouȝ—aboute heo sende anon
Forto saisi alle his londes to hire, and þe maneres euerechon,
And liet hire makien quiene of þe Marche, ase hire broþur
    was king.   125

    116 men] *not in MS.; supplied by Horstmann*

A schrewe lauedi heo was inouȝ, and wicke þoruȝ alle þing!
Heo wende aboute ope al hire lond and nam hire manrede,
And bicam stuyrne and biladde hire men harde with muche
   wrechhede.
Heo liet hote into al þat lond þat no man so wod nere
To nemmen hire broþer name, for loue ne for fere;   130
And ȝif man miȝte ani iwite þat nadde it nouȝt bileued,
Þat he were sone inome and ismiten of is heued.
Þus fierde þis luþere womman and sturede hire wel faste,
Þat no man ne dorste hire broþur bimene—huy weren so
   sore agaste.
And euere lai þis holie bodi ibured swiþe stille,   135
Þat no man ne dorste of him speke aȝein þe quiene wille,
So longue, þat he was al forȝite þo men ne moste of him
   speke.
Ake hit nas nouȝt þat at þe laste ore Louerd him nolde awreke.

Þane no man nolde þat witti was of him þenchen ene,
Ore Louerd nolde nouȝt þat he were allingues forȝite so
   clene.   140
Ȝwane no man þat witti was of him ne hadde muynde,
A doumb best, þat is withoute witte, hadde aȝein kuynde.
For a wydewe hadde ane ȝwite kov þat wonede þarebiside,
Þat ȝeode adai to fetten hire mete in þe wode wel wide,
Þo Seint Kenelm was ibured in þe valeie þare doune.   145
Þis kou wolde eche daye (ȝwane heo come fram toune
To gaderi hire mete, with oþure kuyn)—heo wolde gon al
   one
Fer adoun into þis valeie, and hire felawes bileue echone,
And sitte bi þis holie bodi al þe longue dai,
Ase it were forto honouri him for hit so one lay.   150

127 manrede] *MS.* manrade, *possibly altered to* manrede   142
doumb] *MS.* toumb

And so heo sat withoute mete al þe day to þen ende,
And ȝwane hit at þe eue was hamward heo wolde wende.
Ȝwane heo cam hom at eue fair and round heo was,
And swyþe mielch also—þat was a wonder cas!
For þare ne was no oþur kov þat half so muche milk ȝeoue: 155
Heo ne ȝaf amorewe no þe lasse þei heo were imilked an eue!
Folk þat þis wonder isaiȝ guode ȝeme alle huy nome,
And awaiteden wel a dai ȝware þe kou bicome.
Heo seien hire sitte al þe day in þe valeie þare doune,   f. 152ʳ
Stille in one stude, meteles, forto heo eode an eue to toune. 160
Ake ȝwi heo sete þare so heo ne miȝten iwite noþing,
Bote in heore heorte huy onderstoden þat it was sum tokning.
For þis kov wonede so þere and adai drouȝ hire þareto,
Þe ualeye men cleopeden 'Koubache', and ȝeot men doth
    also.
In Kovbache þat holie bodi lai wel mani a ȝer,   165
Þat men nusten of him noþing, ase Ich ov seide er;
For is soster, þat was so forth in grete pruyte ibrouȝt,
So gret þretningue for him heo made þat men ne dorsten
    him nemme nouȝt.

Þo þis bodi ne moste beo ifounde in Engelonde,
Ore Louerd, þat wot alle þing, to him he sende is sonde. 170
Ase þe pope stod at Rome in his masse a day
At Seint Peteres weouede, ase muche folk þat isai,
A coluere ȝwiȝt so ani snov cam fram heouene fleo,
And leide on þe weuede a luyte writ, and sethþe aȝen gan
    steo—
He flevȝ op into heouene an heiȝ, ase ore Louerd it wolde. 175
Þat writ was ȝwiit and schon wel briȝte—þe lettres weren of
    golde.
Þe pope þonkede Iesu Crist, and þat folk dude also.
He nam þe lettre on his hond, and þo heo was ondo,

He nuste ʒwat it was to segge, ne non insiʒt he ne couþe
    iwite;
For he ne couþe Englisch non, and on Englis it was iwrite.   180
He liet cleopie eche manere men of eche diuerse londe,
ʒif any covþe of þis holie writ aniþing onderstonde.
Þo weren þare men of Engelonde þat wusten ʒwat it sede,
And onderstoden wel þat writ þo heo iheorden it rede.
Þat writ was puyr on Englisch iwrite, ase men it radden þere;
And forto tellen withoute ryme þeos wordes it were: 186
'In Klent Covbache Kenelm kyngues sone
Liith onder haweþorne, is heued him bireued.'
Þis writ was wel nobleliche iwust and up ido,
And iholde for gret relike, and ʒeot it is also—   190
Þe nobleste relike it is on þarof þat is in þe churche of Rome.
So it ouʒte wel, hoso it understode fram ʒwanne þat it come;
For ʒwane it out of heouene cam fram ore Louerdes honde,
ʒwat noblere relike miʒte beo? I ne can non onderstonde.
Þarefore Seint Kenelmes day, ase þe pope makede is heste,   195
At Rome huy holdez heiʒliche and makiez wel heiʒ feste.

Þe pope, þo he þe soþe wuste (þat it was swuch tockningue),
His messagers into Engelonde he sende wit þis tiþingue:
To þe Erchebischope of Kaunterburi (Wolfred þat was þo)
His lettre he sende, þat he scholde of swuche þingue ondergo
And seche after þe wode of Klent ʒif ani man miʒte iwite,   201
And seche ane þorn in Kovbache, ase it was in þe write,
And forto seche þat holie bodi þat derneliche lay þere,
And nimen it up with gret honour þat hit ischrined were.
f. 152ᵛ Þo þe lettre fram þe pope to þe Erchebischope cam,   205
Of bischopes and of clerkus conseil þarof he nam,
So þat in þe wode of Klent, þat in Wyricestreschire is,
He liet seche þat holie bodi and fond it out, iwis,

188 haweþorne] *MS.* ane þorne

Onder þe þorne at Covbache, ase þat writ seide of Rome,
For þe contreiemen biside manie þudere huy come— 210
Þo men of þarebiside onderȝeten þat cas,
Ortreweden wel ȝware it lay, for þe miracle so fair was.
Anon so þat bodi was op inome, þe ȝwile þat folk þare stod,
Þere sprong a welle þare he lay þat ȝeot is fair and guod.
A welle þare is cler inouȝ and euer eft hath ibeo, 215
In þe stude þare he lai on, ase man mai þare iseo,
Men cleopieth 'Seint Kenelmes Welle', þat mani man hath
    isouȝt;
And manie þoruȝ þe watere of grete anguisse beoth ibrouȝt.

Of þe cite of Wynchecumbe and of þe contreie þarebiside
Þe men weren þat souȝten so þat holie bodi so wide; 220
And þe bischopes hadden er iloked þat it scholde to Winche-
    cumbe beo ibore
And ischrined, þare is fader lai, þat arerde þat hous bifore.
Þis men nomen up þat holie bodi þat of Gloucestreschire were,
And nobleliche toward Wynchecumbe with procession it bere.
Þat folk of Wyricestreschire þat woneden þarebiside 225
Nomen heom to rede manie to maken þat bodi abide,
And sworen þat huy it wolden habbe and noman ne scholde
    it heom bireue,
For in þe schire þare it ifounde was (huy seiden) it scholde bileue.
Bi þe watere of Pireford þis two schirene hem mette,
And conteckeden for þis holie bodi, and faste togadere sette,
So þat huy nomen ane fourme of pays to don bi Godes grace,
Ȝif God heom wolde is wille schewen are huy wenden fram
    þat place. 232
Feor huy weren itrauailed and sore so þat heom luste slepe
    echon:
Huy maden ane fourme þat huy scholden alle ligge slepe anon,

232 schewen] *MS.* schwen

And ȝweþur of þis twei schires miȝten sonore awake   235
Huy scholden sauf inovȝ wenden forth and þat bodi with hem
　　take.
Stille huy leiȝen slepe faste, þis schirene boþe to,
And resten heom of hore werienesse, for ore Louerd it wolde
　　so,
Þat huy of Gloucestreschire awoken sone echon
At one tyme alle, ase God it wolde, and of Wyricestreschire
　　nouȝt on.   240
In pais huy wenden forth heore wey and þis bodi with heom
　　toke;
Wel fif mile wei huy weren iwende are þe oþere awoke.
Þis oþere iseiȝen heom bigylede anon so huy bigounne awake,
And siweden þis oþere swiþe faste, ake huy ne miȝten heom
　　nouȝt oftake.
Þis men toward Wynchecombe þat holie bodi huy bere.   245
Are heo miȝten it þudere bringue swyþe werie huy were,
So þat huy comen into one wode a luyte bi este þe toune,
And resten heom, þo huy weren so neiȝ, opon ane heiȝe doune.
Aþurst huy weren for werienesse so þat it nas non ende;
f. 153ʳ Huy beden ore Louerd for Seint Kenelmes loue þat he scholde
　　heom drinke sende—   250
A fair welle þare sprong op an heiȝ opon þe doune
Þat ȝuyt is þare, cler and cold, half a mile fram toune.
Heo is nouþe wel faire iheoled with freo ston, ase riȝt is,
Iredi ech man to drinken of þat cometh þareforth, iwis.
Þe monekes of Wynchecombe arerd habbez þarebiside   255
A fair chapele of Seint Kenelm þat men sechez ful wide.

Quendrith, þe luþere womman, at Wynchecumbe þo was;
Bote heo nuste nouȝt hire broþer so neiȝ ne nowiȝt of þat cas.

236 hem] *Horstmann; MS.* him   245 Wynchecombe] *MS.*
Wychecombe

In Seint Peteres churche heo sat, biside þe Abbeie ȝate,
In a soler in þe est side, and lokede out þare-ate.   260
Heo isaiȝ al þis grete folk come adoneward of þe doune heiȝe
Toward Wynchecumbe a luyte fram Suydleiȝe.
Heo axede ȝwat men it weren and ȝwat huy þouȝten þere;
Men seiden þat huy to churche wolden and þat huy hire broþer
  bere.
Þo was þis quiene sori inovȝ! In grete deole and fere   265
Hire sauter heo nam on honde ase þei heo witles were.
Of þe sauter þe laste saume bifore þe Euesongus, iwis
(Of corsingue and of luþere men and of mansingue imaked
  heo is)
Deus laudem is icleoped: þis saume þe Quiene radde,
For to acorsi hire broþur bodi and alle þat him þudere ladde.
Þo heo cam to þe ninteoþe vers, ase þe mansingue endez, iwis,
Þat *hoc opus eorum* a Latin icleoped it is   272
(Þat seit what men it beo scholden þat duden þat ilke dede),
Opon hire owene heued it cam ase heo þat vers gan rede.
For riȝt ase heo þat vers radde, out borsten boþe hire eiȝe   275
And fullen adoun opon hire sauter, ase manie men iseiȝe.
Þe sauter is ȝuyt at Wynchecombe, and hoso come wole þareto,
Aperteliche man may þare ise ȝware þe dede was ido.
Þis holie bodi was forth ibore with gret honour ate fine,   279
And in þe Abbeie, þare he liith ȝuyt, idon in wel noble schrine.
Þis luþere quiene deide sethþe in schrewedenesse inouȝ;
Þat bodi, ase a corsede wrechche, into ane diche man it drovȝ,
Into þe fouleste þat was þare-aboute, and þare-inne man it
  slong.
Bote hire endingue sunful were, me þinchez elles it hadde ibeo
  wrong!
Nov God for þe loue of Seint Kenelm is swete grace vs sende,
Þat we moten to þulke joie þare he is inne iwiende. Amen.   286

  273 what] *MS.* þat   285 vs] *Horstmann; MS.* it

VIII

LYRICS

PIECE A is an example of the genre known as the *reverdie*, or spring-song. It differs from the simplest type of love-lyric (represented by *Lenten is come wiþ loue to toun* and B and C below) only in having no reference to the joy or the grief of a human being who is a lover. The music to which it is set clearly shows that the words were composed to fit the tune (though this was not necessarily a previously existing tune). In a series of nine two-bar phrases composed in six-eight rhythm (i.e. with six quavers to the bar), the three syllables of l. 5 are each allotted a dotted crotchet. Each thus has the same time-duration as any unit consisting of stressed + unstressed syllable (e.g. *cú-mĕn* or *Á-wĕe*), and each must accordingly have a full stress in the verse. This is so unusual, in M.E. verse composed in alternating stressed and unstressed syllables, that it must be due to a special factor—here, that the words were composed to fit the music.

The explicit directions given in the manuscript (in Latin) for the performance of the song (there called a *rota*), show that it was a four-part canon, accompanied by two voices singing what the manuscript calls the *pes*. A cross in the musical notation marks the entry of the second upper voice at the word *Lhude* (line 2). The text of a religious poem in Latin (see Commentary) which is written underneath the English words has usually been thought not to be the words originally composed for the music. The musicologist who has discussed the matter most recently thinks otherwise,[1] having discovered that the music of the *pes* is identical with the first five notes of *Regina coeli*, the Mary-antiphon of the Easter season. But the stresses in l. 5 (which have not so far been taken into account), the fact that the English text is written first in the manuscript, and the absence of any

[1] F. L. Harrison, *Music in Medieval Britain* (1958), 142–4.

Latin text for the *pes* seem to be not altogether negligible objections.

B and C are remarkable examples of the assimilation and the creative use of a common literary convention in Western Europe by English lyrists. The nature-introduction which is one of the peculiar glories of the medieval love-lyric of western Europe is here reduced to a brevity which would make it unintelligible for a later age but for the abundance of explicit examples in OF, Old Provençal, and medieval Latin poetry. In B, lines 5 and 6 (like line 4 of C) express stereotyped details of the medieval love-plaint. In C, the use of external nature as a background (here in contrast) to the feelings of the lover is beautifully reduced to a mere hint. In B the parallelism of external and internal desolation is another of the standard patterns.

Pieces D to N, which are all from the collection of poems in MS. Harley 2253, are with one exception love-lyrics representing two standard types learnt from OF and Anglo-Norman poets. D, G, K, M, and probably E and H, are examples of the *chanson* or love-song, which embody as standard elements a description extolling the charms of the beloved, a statement of the ravages wrought in the lover by longing or the lack of his lady's favour, and commonly a complaint and a plea. F is a *pastourelle*, and the intermittently cryptic L something of essentially the same kind. N is a light-hearted and fanciful treatment of a widely attested piece of popular superstition.

Pieces O, P, and Q are refrains of dance-songs, which have evidently been detached from their original setting—no doubt because of the natural prominence of a refrain within a love-lyric, and because they lent themselves to illustrative quotation within a sermon (to which circumstance we owe the survival of O and P). Many such refrains have survived in OF.[1] R is a fierce and direct statement of passion; the tone of vengeful resolve in the lover is unusual.

The music for A, B, and C alone among these pieces has survived. The musical setting of B is one of the few extant examples of English monody. That of C is an early example of the two-part writing with a marked tendency to parallel thirds or sixths

[1] See A. Jeanroy, *Les Origines de la poésie lyrique en France au moyen âge* (1925), 102–26.

which is known by the fifteenth-century name of *gymel* (<
(*cantus*) *gymellus* 'twin (song)'). In its earlier stages in Provence
and France, the lyric was literally a song; but by the time the
Harleian collection was composed a musical setting was probably no longer felt to be essential for some types of love-lyric.
The courtly personifications used in K and L imply a stage of
some literary sophistication or even artificiality; and the refrain
of K may originally have had no connexion with it.

The religious lyrics here printed (S–Y) represent the chief
themes of the century's outpourings of devotional verse. Several
reflect the devotion to the Virgin that was to prove such a fecund
source of later lyric, and the accents of *Swete Iesu, king of blisse*
are heard again in the fourteenth century, in the writings of
Richard Rolle and his followers.

A

f. 11ᵛ

SVMER is icumen in—
Lhude sing, cuccu!
Groweþ sed and bloweþ med
And springþ þe wde nu.
Sing, cuccu!   5

Awe bleteþ after lomb,
Lhouþ after calue cu,
Bulluc sterteþ, bucke uerteþ.
Murie sing, cuccu!
Cuccu, cuccu,   10
Wel singes þu, cuccu!
Ne swik þu nauer nu!

Pes {Sing, cuccu, nu! Sing, cuccu!
     {Sing, cuccu! Sing, cuccu, nu!

B

Mirie it is while sumer ilast   f. 1ᵛ
    Wið fugheles song;
Oc nu necheð windes blast
    And weder strong.
Ei, ei! What þis nicht is long!   5
And Ich wið wel michel wrong
    Soregh and murne and fast.

C

Foweles in þe frith,   f. 5ʳ
Þe fisses in þe flod—
And I mon waxe wod!
Mulch sorw I walke with,
For beste of bon and blod.   5

D

Wiþ longyng Y am lad,   f. 63ᵛ
On molde Y waxe mad—
    A maide marreþ me.
Y grede, Y grone vnglad,
For selden Y am sad   5
    Þat semly forte se.
    Leuedi, þou rewe me!
To rouþe þou hauest me rad—
    Be bote of þat Y bad!
    My lyf is long on þe.   10

B 1 Mirie] *M no longer visible*   2 Wið] *no longer fully legible,*
because partly rubbed   4 weder] *w partly obliterated, as first* e *is*
completely, by a small hole in MS.   5 is] *not now visible*   fast]
not visible

Leuedy of alle londe,
Les me out of bonde!
  Broht Ich am in wo.
Haue resting on honde,
Ant sent þou me þi sonde   15
  Sone, er þou me slo;
  My reste is wiþ þe ro.
Þah men to me han onde,
To loue nul Y noht wonde
  Ne lete for non of þo.   20

Leuedi, wiþ al my miht
My loue is on þe liht,
  To menske when Y may.
Þou rew ant red me ryht!
To deþe þou hauest me diht—   25
  Y deȝe longe er my day.
  Þou leue vpon mi lay!
Treuþe Ichaue þe plyht,
To don þat Ich haue hyht
  Whil mi lif leste may.   30

Lylie-whyt hue is,
Hire rode so rose on rys,
  Þat reueþ me mi rest.
Wymmon war ant wys,
Of prude hue bereþ þe pris,   35
  Burde on of þe best.
  Þis wommon woneþ by west,
Brihtest vnder bys;
Heuene Y tolde al his
  Þat o nyht were hire gest!   40

E

Mosti ryden by Rybbesdale,   f. 66ᵛ
Wilde wymmen forte wale
  Ant welde wuch Ich wolde,
Founde were þe feyrest on
Þat euer wes mad of blod ant bon,   5
  In boure best wiþ bolde.
Ase sonnebem hire bleo ys briht—
In vche londe heo leomeþ liht,
  Þourh tale as mon me tolde,
Þe lylie-lossum is ant long,   10
Wiþ riche rose ant rode among,
  A fyldor fax to folde.

Hire hed when Ich biholde apon,
Þe sonnebeem aboute noon
  Me þohte þat Y seȝe.
Hyre eyȝen aren grete ant gray ynoh;   15
Þat lussom, when heo on me loh,
  Ybend wax eyþer breȝe.
Þe mone wiþ hire muchele maht
Ne leneþ non such lyht anaht   20
  Þat is in heouene heȝe,
Ase hire forhed doþ in day
For wham þus muchel Y mourne may—
  For duel to deþ Y dreyȝe!

Heo haþ browes bend an heh,   25
Whyt bytuene ant nout to neh.
  Lussum lyf heo ledes.

12 *MS.* fyld or   17 þat] *MS.* þ

Hire neose ys set as hit wel semeþ.
Y deȝe for deþ þat me demeþ.
   Hire speche as spices spredes—   30
Hire lockes lefly aren ant longe—
For sone he mihte hire murþes monge
   Wiþ blisse when hit bredes.
Hire chyn ys chosen ant eyþer cheke
Whit ynoh ant rode on eke,   35
   Ase roser when hit redes.

Heo haþ a mury mouht to mele,
Wiþ lefly rede lippes lele,
   Romaunz forte rede.
Hire teht aren white ase bon of whal,   40
Euene set ant atled al,
   Ase hende mowe taken hede—
Swannes swyre swyþe wel ysette,
A sponne lengore þen y mette,
   Þat freoly ys to fede.   45
Me were leuere kepe hire come
Þen beon pope ant ryde in Rome,
   Styþest vpon stede.

When Y byholde vpon hire hond,
Þe lylie-white, lef in lond,   50
   Best heo mihte beo.
Eyþer arm an elne long,
Baloygne mengeþ al bymong.
   Ase baum ys hire bleo;
Fyngres heo haþ feir to folde.   55
Myhte Ich hire haue ant holde,
   In world wel were me.

30 spredes] *MS*. spredeþ   48 Styþest] *MS*. styþes

Hyre tyttes aren anvnder bis
As apples tuo of Parays—
   Ouself ȝe mowen seo. 60

Hire gurdel of bete gold is al,
Vmben hire middel smal,
   Þat trikeþ to þe to,
Al wiþ rubies on a rowe
Wiþinne coruen, craft to knowe 65
   Ant emeraudes mo.
Þe bocle is al of whalles bon.
Þerwiþinne stont a ston
   Þat warneþ men from wo:
Þe water þat hit wetes yn 70
Ywis, hit worþeþ al to wyn—
   Þat seȝen, seyden so.

Heo haþ a mete myddel smal,
Body ant brest wel mad al,
   Ase feynes wiþoute fere; 75
Eyþer side soft ase sylk,
Whittore þen þe moren-mylk,
   Wiþ leofly lit on lere.
Al þat Ich ou nempne noht
Hit is wonder wel ywroht, 80
   Ant elles wonder were.
He myhte sayen þat Crist hym seȝe
Þat myhte nyhtes neh hyre leȝe—
   Heuene he heuede here.

64 wiþ] *MS.* whiþ

F

In a fryht as Y con fare fremede,
Y founde a wel feyr fenge to fere—
Heo glystnede ase gold when hit glemede.
Nes ner gome so gladly on gere:
Y wolde wyte in world who hire kenede,   5
Þis burde bryht, ȝef hire wil were.
Heo me bed go my gates, lest hire gremede:
Ne kepte heo non henyng here.

'Yhere þou me nou, hendest in helde—
Nauy þe none harmes to heþe!   10
Casten Y wol þe from cares ant kelde;
Comeliche Y wol þe nou cleþe.'

'Cloþes Y haue on forte caste
Such as Y may weore wiþ wynne.
Betere is were þunne boute laste   15
Þen syde robes ant synke into synne.
Haue ȝe or wyl, ȝe waxeþ vnwraste;
Afterward or þonk beþ þynne.
Betre is make forewardes faste
Þen afterward to mene ant mynne.'   20

'Of munnyng ne munte þou namore;
Of menske þou were wurþe, by my myht.
Y take an hond to holde, þat Y hore,
Of al þat Y þe haue byhyht.
Why ys þe loþ to leuen on my lore   25
Lengore þen my loue were on þe lyht?
Anoþer myhte ȝerne þe so ȝore
Þat nolde þe noht rede so ryht.'

18 beþ] *MS.* be   23 Y hore] *MS.* yhore

'Such reed me myhte spaclyche reowe
When al my ro were me atraht;   30
Sone þou woldest vachen an newe,
Ant take anoþer wiþinne nyȝe naht.
Þenne miht I hongren on heowe,
In vch an hyrd ben hated ant forhaht,
Ant ben ycayred from alle þat Y kneowe,   35
Ant bede cleuyen þer Y hade claht.

Beter is taken a comeliche ycloþed
In armes to cusse ant to cluppe
Þen a wrecche Y wedded so wroþe—
Þah he me slowe ne myht I him asluppe.   40
Þe beste red þat Y con to vs boþe:
Þat þou me take ant Y þe toward huppe.
Þah Y swore by treuþe ant oþe,
Þat God haþ shaped mey non atluppe.

Mid shupping ne mey hit me ashunche.   45
Nes Y neuer wycche ne wyle.
Ych am a maide—þat me ofþuncheþ!
Luef me were gome boute gyle.'

G

A wayle whyt ase whalles bon,   f. 67^r
A grein in golde þat godly shon,
A tortle þat min herte is on,
      In tounes trewe—
Hire gladshipe nes neuer gon   5
      Whil Y may glewe.

F 31 þou] *MS.* þo   33 hongren] *MS.* hengren   37 ycloþed]
MS. ycloþe   39 Y wedded] *MS.* ywedded   46 Nes] *MS.* nos
47 ofþuncheþ] *MS.* ofþunche

When heo is glad,
Of al þis world namore Y bad
Þen beo wiþ hire myn one bistad,
    Wiþoute strif.   10
Þe care þat Ich am yn ybrad
    Y wyte a wyf.

A wyf nis non so worly wroht—
When heo ys blyþe to bedde ybroht,
Wel were him þat wiste hire þoht,   15
    Þat þryuen ant þro!
Wel Y wot heo nul me noht;
    Myn herte is wo.

Hou shal þat lefly syng
Þat þus is marred in mournyng?   20
Heo me wol to deþe bryng
    Longe er my day.
Gret hire wel, þat swete þing
    Wiþ eȝenen gray!

Hyre heȝe haueþ wounded me, ywisse,   25
Hire bende browen, þat bringeþ blisse.
Hire comely mouth þat mihte cusse
    In muche murþe he were—
Y wolde chaunge myn for his
    Þat is here fere.   30

Wolde hyre fere beo so freo
Ant wurþes were þat so myhte beo,
Al for on Y wolde ȝeue þreo,
    Wiþoute chep.

From helle to heuene ant sonne to see   35
    Nys non se ȝeep
Ne half so freo.
Wose wole of loue be trewe, do lystne me.

Herkneþ me! Y ou telle—
In such wondryng for wo Y welle.   40
Nys no fur so hot in helle
    Al to mon
Þat loueþ derne ant dar nout telle
    Whet him ys on.

Ich vnne hire wel ant heo me wo;   45
Ych am hire frend ant heo my fo.
Me þuncheþ min herte wol breke atwo
    For sorewe ant syke.
In Godes greting mote heo go,
    Þat wayle whyte.   50

Ich wolde Ich were a þrestelcok,
A bountyng oþer a lauercok,
    Swete bryd!
Bituene hire curtel ant hire smok
    Y wolde ben hyd.   55

H

In May hit murgeþ when hit dawes   f. 71ᵛ 2
In dounes wiþ þis dueres plawes,
    Ant lef is lyht on lynde.
Blosmes bredeþ on þe bowes;
Al þis wylde wyhtes wowes,   5
    So wel Ych vnderfynde.

Y not non so freoli flour
Ase ledies þat beþ bryht in bour,
   Wiþ loue who mihte hem bynde.
So worly wymmen are by west—   10
One of hem Ich herie best
From Irlond into Ynde.

Wymmen were þe beste þing
Þat shup oure heȝe heuene-kyng,
   Ȝef feole false nere: 15
Heo beoþ to rad vpon huere red
To loue þer me hem lastes bed,
   When heo shule fenge fere.
Lut in londe are to leue,
Þah me hem trewe trouþe ȝeue,   20
   For tricherie to ȝere:
When trichour haþ is trouþe yplyht,
Byswyken he haþ þat suete wyht,
   Þah he hire oþes swere.

Wymmon, war þe wiþ þe swyke   25
Þat feir ant freoly ys to fyke—
   Ys fare is o to founde.
So wyde in world ys huere won,
In vch a toune vntrewe is on
   From Leycestre to Lounde.   30
Of treuþe nis þe trichour noht,
Bote he habbe is wille ywroht
   At steuenyng vmbe stounde.
Ah, feyre leuedis, be onwar!
To late comeþ þe ȝeyn-char,   35
   When loue ou haþ ybounde.

Wymmen bueþ so feyr on hewe, f. 72^r 1
Ne trow Y none þat nere trewe
   Ʒef trichour hem ne tahte.
Ah, feyre þinges, freoly bore! 40
When me ou woweþ, beþ war bifore
   Whuch is worldes ahte.
Al to late is send aʒeyn
When þe ledy liht byleyn,
   Ant lyueþ by þat he lahte. 45
Ah, wolde lylie-leor in lyn
Yhere leuely lores myn,
   Wiþ selþe we weren sahte!

K

   Blow, northerne wynd, f. 72^v 1
   Sent þou me my suetyng!
   Blow, norþerne wynd,
   Blou, blou, blou!

Ichot a burde in boure bryht 5
Þat sully semly is on syht—
Menskful maiden of myht,
   Feir ant fre to fonde.
In al þis wurhliche won,
A burde of blod ant of bon 10
Neuer ʒete Y nuste non
   Lussomore in londe.
     Blow, *etc*.

Wiþ lokkes lefliche ant longe,
Wiþ frount ant face feir to fonde,
Wiþ murþes monie mote heo monge, 15
   Þat brid so breme in boure,

Wiþ lossom eye grete ant gode,
Wiþ browen blysfol vnder hode.
He þat reste Him on þe rode
    Þat leflich lyf honoure!   20
      Blou, *etc*.

Hire lure lumes liht
Ase a launterne anyht;
Hire bleo blykyeþ so bryht—
    So feyr heo is ant fyn.
A suetly suyre heo haþ to holde,   25
Wiþ armes, shuldre ase mon wolde,
Ant fyngres feyre forte folde.
    God wolde hue were myn!
      [Blow, *etc*.]

Middel heo haþ menskful, smal,
Hire loueliche chere as cristal;   30
Þeȝes, legges, fet, ant al
    Ywraht wes of þe beste.
A lussum ledy lasteles
Þat sweting is ant euer wes;
A betere burde neuer nes,   35
    Yheryed wiþ þe heste.
      [Blow, *etc*.]

Heo is dereworþe in day,
Graciouse, stout, ant gay,
Gentil, iolyf so þe jay,
    Worhliche when heo wakeþ,   40

28 Blow, etc.] *not in MS. Also after 36, 44, 52, etc.*

Maiden murgest of mouþ—
Bi est, bi west, by norþ ant souþ
Þer nis fiele ne crouþ
    Þat such murþes makeþ.
      [Blow, *etc.*]

Heo is coral of godnesse,   **45**
Heo is rubie of ryhtfulnesse,
Heo is cristal of clannesse,
    Ant baner of bealte;
Heo is lilie of largesse,
Heo is paruenke of prouesse,   50
Heo is solsecle of suetnesse,
    Ant ledy of lealte.
      [Blow, *etc.*]

To Loue, þat leflich is in londe,
Y tolde him as Ych vnderstonde—
Hou þis hende haþ hent in honde   55
    On huerte þat myn wes.
Ant hire knyhtes me han so soht,
Sykyng, Sorewyng, ant Þoht—
Þo þre me han in bale broht
    Aȝeyn þe poer of Pees.   60
      [Blow, *etc.*]

To Loue Y putte pleyntes mo: f. 73^r 1
Hou Sykyng me haþ siwed so,
Ant eke Þoht me þrat to slo
    Wiþ maistry ȝef he myhte,

Ant Serewe sore in balful bende   65
Þat he wolde, for þis hende,
Me lede to my lyues ende
        Vnlahfulliche in lyhte.
        [Blow, *etc.*]

Hire Loue me lustnede vch word
Ant beh him to me ouer bord,   70
Ant bed me hente þat hord
        Of myne huerte hele—

f. 73ʳ 2

'Ant bisecheþ þat swete ant swote,
Er þen þou falle ase fen of fote,
Þat heo wiþ þe wolle of bote   75
        Dereworþliche dele.'
        [Blow, *etc.*]

For hire loue Y carke ant care,
For hire loue Y droupne ant dare,
For hire loue my blisse is bare,
        Ant al Ich waxe won.   80
For hire loue in slep Y slake,
For hire loue al nyht Ich wake,
For hire loue mournyng Y make
        More þen eny mon.
        [Blow, *etc.*]

L

f. 80ᵛ 'My deþ Y loue, my lyf Ich hate, for a leuedy shene.
Heo is brith so daies liht; þat is on me wel sene—
Al Y falewe so doþ þe lef in somer when hit is grene.
Ʒef mi þoht helpeþ me noht, to wham shal Y me mene?

Sorewe ant Syke ant Drery Mod byndeþ me so faste   5
Þat Y wene to walke wod ȝef hit me lengore laste.
My serewe, my care, al wiþ a word he myhte awey caste.
"Whet helpeþ þe, my suete lemmon, my lyf þus forte gaste?"'

'Do wey, þou clerc, þou art a fol! Wiþ þe bydde Y noht chyde.
Shalt þou neuer lyue þat day mi loue þat þou shalt byde.   10
Ȝef þou in my boure art take, shame þe may bityde!
Þe is bettere on fote gon, þen wycked hors to ryde.'

'Weylawei! Whi seist þou so? Þou rewe on me, þy man!
Þou art euer in my þoht in londe wher Ich am.
Ȝef Y deȝe for þi loue, hit is þe mykel sham;   15
Þou lete me lyue ant be þi luef, ant þou my suete lemman!'

'Be stille, þou fol! Y calle þe riht—cost þou neuer blynne?
Þou art wayted day ant nyht wiþ fader ant al my kynne.
Be þou in mi bour ytake, lete þey for no synne
Me to holde ant þe to slon—þe deþ so þou maht wynne.'   20

'Suete ledy, þou wend þi mod! Sorewe þou wolt me kyþe:
Ich am also sory mon so Ich was whylen blyþe.
In a wyndou þer we stod we custe vs fyfty syþe—
Feir biheste makeþ mony mon al is serewes mythe.'

'Weylawey! Whi seist þou so? Mi serewe þou makest newe.
Y louede a clerk al par amours; of loue he wes ful trewe.   26
He nes nout blyþe neuer a day bote he me sone seȝe;
Ich louede him betere þen my lyf—whet bote is hit to leȝe?'

'Whil Y wes a clerc in scole, wel muchel Y couþe of lore.
Ych haue þoled for þy loue woundes fele sore,   30
Fer from þe ant eke from men, vnder þe wode-gore.
Suete ledy, þou rewe of me! Nou may Y no more.'

17 riht] *MS.* riþt   31 þe] *not in MS.; Böddeker* hom, *Brown*
bour

'Þou semest wel to ben a clerc, for þou spekest so stille!
Shalt þou neuer for mi loue woundes þole grylle.
Fader, moder, ant al my kun ne shal me holde so stille   35
Þat Y nam þyn, ant þou art myn, to don al þi wille!'

M

'. 80ᵛ When þe nyhtegale singes þe wodes waxen grene.
Lef ant gras ant blosme springes in Aueryl, Y wene,
Ant loue is to myn herte gon wiþ one spere so kene—
Nyht ant day my blod hit drynkes; myn herte deþ me tene.

f. 81ʳ Ich haue loued al þis ʒer, þat Y may loue namore!   5
Ich haue siked moni syk, lemmon, for þin ore—
Me nis loue neuer þe ner, ant þat me reweþ sore.
Suete lemmon, þench on me! Ich haue loued þe ʒore.

Suete lemmon, Y preye þe of loue one speche!
Whil Y lyue in world so wyde oþer nulle Y seche.   10
Wiþ þy loue, my suete leof, mi blis þou mihtes eche:
A suete cos of þy mouþ mihte be my leche.

Suete lemmon, Y preʒe þe of a loue-bene:
ʒef þou me louest ase men says, lemmon, as Y wene,
Ant ʒef hit þi wille be, þou loke þat hit be sene!   15
So muchel Y þenke vpon þe þat al Y waxe grene.

Bituene Lyncolne ant Lyndeseye, Norhamptoun ant Lounde,
Ne wot Y non so fayr a may as Y go fore ybounde.
Suete lemmon, Y preʒe þe þou louie me a stounde!
     Y wole mone my song   20
     On wham þat hit ys on ylong.

M 11 eche] *MS.* ethe   12 þy] *MS.* þy—— (*across part of a
patch*). *There is one stroke immediately before* mouþ (*the other side of
the patch*) *which is very difficult to interpret—most like* i. *And the
abbreviation for* er *is written above* u *in* mouþ

N

f. 114ᵛ

Mon in þe mone stond ant strit;
On is bot-forke is burþen he bereþ.
Hit is muche wonder þat he n'adoun slyt—
For doute leste he valle he shoddreþ ant shereþ!
When þe forst freseþ, muche chele he byd.   5
Þe þornes beþ kene—is hattren totereþ.
Nis no wyþt in þe world þat wot wen he syt,
Ne (bote hit bue þe hegge) whet wedes he wereþ.

f. 115ʳ

Whider troweþ þis mon ha þe wey take?
He haþ set is o fot is oþer toforen.   10
For non hiþte þat he haþ ne syþt me hym ner shake—
He is þe sloweste mon þat euer wes yboren.
Wher he were o þe feld pycchynde stake,
For hope of ys þornes to dutten is doren,
He mot myd is twybyl oþer trous make,   15
Oþer al is dayes werk þer were yloren.

Þis ilke mon vpon heh when er he were,
Wher he were y þe mone boren ant yfed,
He leneþ on is forke ase a grey frere.
Þis crokede caynard sore he is adred!   20
Hit is mony day go þat he was here.
Ichot of is ernde he naþ nout ysped:
He haþ hewe sumwher a burþen of brere—
Þarefore sum hayward haþ taken ys wed.

'Ʒef þy wed ys ytake, bring hom þe trous!   25
Sete forþ þyn oþer fot, stryd ouer sty!
We shule preye þe haywart hom to vr hous
Ant maken hym at heyse for þe maystry—

9 troweþ] *MS.* trowe

Drynke to hym deorly of fol god bous,
Ant oure dame Douse shal sitten hym by.   30
When þat he is dronke ase a dreynt mous,
Þenne we schule borewe þe wed ate bayly.'

Þis mon hereþ me nout, þah Ich to hym crye;
Ichot þe cherl is def—þe del hym todrawe!
Þah Ich ʒeʒe vpon heþ nulle nout hye—   35
Þe lostlase ladde con nout o lawe.
Hupe forþ, Hubert, hosede pye!
Ichot þart amarscled into þe mawe.
Þah me teone wiþ hym þat myn teh mye,
Þe cherld nul nout adoun er þe day dawe.   40

O

f. 146ᵛ 2   A gurdul of gile—
Ich wolde go a mile
To see þe mordaunt.

P

f. 148ᵛ 1   Ianekyn of Londone—
Is loue is al myn.

Q

f. 8   I ne may cume to mi lef bute by þe watere.
Wanne me lust slepen, þanne moti wakie—
Wnder is þat Hi liuie.

R

f. 46ʳ 2   Ne saltou neuer, leuedi,
Tuynklen wyt þin eyen.
Hic abbe ydon al myn youth
Ofte, ofte, ant ofte,

Q 1 I ne] *MS*. He

Longe yloued ant yerne ybeden—   5
  Ful dere it his about.
Dore, go þou stille,
  Go þou stille, stille,
Þat Hic abbe in þe boure
  Ydon al myn uylle, uylle.   10

            S
                                      f. 55ᵛ
Nou goth sonne vnder wod
Me reweth, Marie, þi faire rode;
Nou goþ sonne vnder tre
Me reweþ, Marie, þi sone and þe.

            T
                                      f. 2ʳ
  Of on þat is so fayr and briȝt
  velud maris stella,
  Briȝter þan þe dayis liȝt
  parens et puella,
  Ic crie to þe, þou se to me,   5
  Leuedy, preye þi sone for me,
  tam pia,
  Þat Ic mote come to þe,
  Maria.

  Of kare conseil þou ert best,   10
  felix fecundata;
  Of alle wery þou ert rest,
  mater honorata.
  Bisek him wit milde mod
  Þat for ous alle sad is blod   15
  in cruce,
  Þat we moten komen til him
  in luce.

R 8 stille, stille: *MS.* stille e   9 þat] *MS.* yat   10 uylle,
uylle] *MS.* uyllee, *followed by* dix   Robs seynte mar[y] clericus
811493   N

Al þis world was forlore
Eua peccatrice
Tyl our Lord was ybore
de te genitrice;
With *Aue* it went away
Þuster nith, and comet þe day
salutis;   25
Þe welle springet hut of þe
uirtutis.

Leuedi, flour of alle þing,
rosa sine spina,
Þu bere Iesu, heuene-king,   30
gratia diuina.
Of alle þu berst þe pris,
Leuedi, quene of Parays
electa,
Mayde milde moder is   35
effecta.

Wel he wot he is þi sone
uentre quem portasti;
He wyl nout werne þe þi bone
paruum quem lactasti.   40
So hende and so god he his,
He hauet brout ous to blis
superni,
Þat hauet hidut þe foule put
inferni.   45

Explicit cantus iste

24 comet] *MS.* comȝ   35 is] *MS.* es *underlined*

U

Swete Iesu, king of blisse,   f. 134ᵛ
Min herte loue, min herte lisse,   (col. 1)
Þou art swete mid iwisse;
Wo is him þat þe shal misse.

Swete Iesu, min herte liȝt,   5
Þou art dai wiþhouten niȝt;
Þou ȝeue me strengþe and eke miȝt
Forto louien þe al riȝt.

Swete Iesu, mi soule bote,
In min herte þou sette a rote   10
Of þi loue þat is so swote,
And wite hit þat hit springe mote.

V

Exemplum de Beata Virgine et gaudiis eius

Nu þis fules singet hand maket hure blisse   f. 81ᵛ
And þat gres up þringet and leued þe ris;
Of on Ic wille singen þat is makeles,
Þe king of halle kinges to moder he hire ches.

Heo his wituten sunne and wituten hore,   5
Icumen of kinges cunne, of Gesses more;
Þe louerd of monkinne of hire was ybore
To bringen us hut of sunne, elles wue weren forlore.

Gabriel hire grette, and saide hire 'Aue.
Marie ful of grace, vre Louerd be uit þe,   10
Þe frut of þire wombe ibleset mot id be.
Þu sal go wit childe, forsout Ic suget þe.'

V 4 king] *MS.* kind   7 ybore] *MS.* yboren   10 Louerd]
MS. lover   12 childe] *MS.* chide

And þare gretinke þat angle hauede ibrout
He gon to biþenchen and meinde hire þout.
He saide to þen angle, 'Hu may tiden þis?   15
Of monnes ymone nout Y nout iuis.'

Mayden heo was uid childe and maiden herbiforen,
And maiden ar sothent hire child was iboren;
Maiden and moder nas neuer non wimon boten he;
Wel mitte he berigge of Godes sune be.   20

Iblessed beo þat suete child and þe moder ec,
And þe suete broste þat hire sone sec;
Ihered ibe þe time þat such child uas ibore,
Þat lesed al of pine þat arre was forlore.

W

Nv Yh she blostme sprynge,
Hic herde a fuheles song.
A swete longinge
Myn herte þureþhut sprong,
Þat is of luue newe,   5
Þat is so swete and trewe
Hyt gladiet al my song;
Hic wot mid ywisse
My lyf an heke my blysse
Is al þarhon ylong.   10

Of Iesu Crist Hi synge
Þat is so fayr and fre,
Swetest of alle þynge;
His oþwe hic oȝe wel boe.

V 15 Hu] *MS.* þu   18, 23 child] *MS.* chid   20 he] *MS.* þe
23 ibore] *MS.* iboren   W 7 song] *MS.* þong

Wl fer he me soþte,   15
Myd hard he me boþte
Wyþ wnde to and þree;
Wel sore he was yswnge
And for me myd spere istunge,
Ynayled to þe tree.   20

Wan Hic myself stond
And myd herte ysee
Yþerled fetd and onde
Wyt grete neyles þree—
Blody was hys eved,   25
Of hym nas novt byleved
Þet of pyne were vre—
Wel oþte myn herte
Al for hys lvue smerte,
Syc and sory be.   30

A way, þat Hy ne can
To hym tvrne al my þovt
And makien hym my lefman
Þat þvs me haued hybovt
Wyt pine and sorewhe longe,   35
Wyt wnde depe and stronge—
Of luue ne can Hy novt.
Hys blod fel to þe grvnde
Hut of ys swete wnde,
Þat of pyne hvs hauet hybrovt.   40

Iesu, lefman suete,
Þv hyef me strenghte and myþt,
Longinge sore and ofte
To servi þe aryþt,

A lene me pine drye   45
Al for þe, swete Marie
Þat art so fayr and bryþt
[Mayden and moder mylde,
For loue of þine childe
Ernde vs heuene lyht.]   50

Iesu, lefman swete,
Ih sende þe þis songe
And wel ofte Ih þe grete
And bydde þe among.
Hyf me sone lete   55
And myne sennes bete,
Þah Ih haue do þe wrong.
At myne lyues hende,
Wan Ih shal henne wende,
Iesu, me hvnderfonge! Amen.   60

X

f. 15ʳ

No more ne willi wiked be;
Forsake Ich wille þis worldis fe,
Þis wildis wedis, þis folen gle;
Ich wul be mild of chere;
Of cnottis scal mi girdil be,   5
Becomen Ich wil frere.

Frer menur I wil me make,
And lecherie I wille asakė;
To Iesu Crist Ich wil me take
And serue in holi churche,   10
Al in mi ouris forto wake,
Goddis wille to wurche.

W 45 lene me pine] *MS.* lene pine 48–50 *supplied from MS. Harley 2253*

Wurche I wille þis workes gode
For him þat boyht us in þe rode;
Fram his side ran þe blode,   15
So dere he gan vs bie.
Forsothe I tel him mor þan wode
Þat hantit licherie.

Y

Wen þe turuf is þi tuur,   f. 47ᵛ
And þi put is þi bour,
Þi wel and þi wite þrote
Ssulen wormes to note.
Wat helpit þe þenne   5
Al þe worilde wnne?

THE LAND OF COKAYGNE

THE Cloud-Cuckoo-Land of sensual bliss depicted here is a comic counterpart of the Earthly Paradise of European literary tradition and the spiritual one of medieval Christianity. The author's comparison of the two gives him an opening for his impudently reasoned rejection of the Christian *Paradis* (5-9, 9-12, 15-16, 47-48). But the naturalness of the framework afforded by this equation is somewhat diminished when the hitherto distinct equivalents are fused, and the cloister of lines 65 ff. is depicted in the terms proper to accounts of the Earthly Paradise (67-100). In consequence, the birds ready roasted for eating (102-10)—a traditional amenity of the Paradise of Sloth and Sensuality—are here out of key.

The poem nevertheless has incomparably more force than the OF analogue misnamed *Le Fabliau de Coquaigne*, which makes no explicit use either of Paradise or of an abbey or nunnery, and whose only component deriving from either the Earthly or the spiritual Paradise is a Fountain of Youth. The OF piece is otherwise entirely concerned with the delights of sloth, food, drink, money, and clothes in abundance, and sexual freedom; it has the typical reference to houses made of things to eat (as here in lines 54-59), and to the fat geese which fly through the air turning on the spit. The MDu analogue corresponds closely in content to the OF one; and the eight or nine constituents of each actually occur in almost entirely the same order.

If an OF work like these was known to our author, it can have suggested to him no more than the main topic and some stock motifs for his own. In any case, the dominant theme of the monks and the nuns and their relations is almost certainly an invention at the ME stage, if the evidence for local Irish connexions means anything (see 52 n.). Sexual freedom, and the indulgence in sleep as a condition of merit, both of which are fixed elements in the conception of Cokaygne, have been shifted and imputed to the monks, because this author's Cokaygne is a monks' Paradise. In fact, the ME piece reads like a goliard's notion of it, the OF one like a minstrel's.

The Land of Cokaygne is first and foremost not, as it is commonly called in handbooks and elsewhere, a satire or (still less) a *fabliau*, but a parody. A main reason for thinking this is that the author was evidently aware of an imaginative correspondence with the Christian Paradise, since he has made it explicit by comparing the two (a happy touch not matched in the OF or the MDu piece). Another is that the cornerstone of the work is an extremely ancient comic device, which has had a vigorous life of its own in (*inter alia*) folk-tales for centuries. A humorously conceived land of milk and honey (or at any rate cheese) is briefly depicted by Lucian in the second century A.D. (see 45–46 n.). And he next describes at some length an 'Isle of the Blest'—in a work in which he himself declares everything to be a parody[1] of similar accounts by older writers of remote places—in which, apart from other characteristics of a sensual Utopia, all men have their wives in common without jealousy. In the fifth century B.C., Athenaeus quotes other such accounts[2] by authors of Attic comedy (Teleclides, Crates, and Cratinus in reference to the golden age under Kronos; Pherecrates in reference to the under-world, in the Μεταλλῆς, and in reference to a remote land in the Πέρσαι).

This sort of conception, seen as a comic anti-type of Paradise, has been further elaborated in *The Land of Cokaygne* into a more topical comic fantasy. The last stage in its growth probably, in the first instance, vents the urge (inevitable in men and writers living under extreme restraints) to kick over the traces and play the fool from time to time. The same impulse might go far to account for the introduction of human beings under a monastic rule (even if the author was one of them) as a natural vehicle for this kind of humour. He is more likely to have been a goliardic cleric; indeed, the author of the next piece in the manuscript calls himself a clerk. And it is significant that one of

[1] οὐκ ἀκωμῳδήτως ἤνικται . . ., *A True Story*, i. 1–4 (Loeb Library; ed. A. M. Harmon, vol. i).

[2] Δειπνοσοφίσται, vi. 268 ff. (Loeb Library; ed. Gulick, vol. iii).

the Latin drinking-songs of the early thirteenth century *Carmina Burana* introduces an 'abbot of Cokaygne' (*abbas Cucaniensis*); and that the Latin poems in the manuscript containing our sole copy of *The Land of Cokaygne* include a 'Tipplers' Mass' (*Missa de Potatoribus*) and other pieces of a goliardic character.

It is conceivable, but it does not necessarily follow, that a goliard clerk (if the author was such) was, in writing *The Land of Cokaygne*, being deliberately hurtful to those religious with whom he was not in sympathy (perhaps as inmates of an abbey actually known to him). The AN *L'Ordre de Bel Eyse*,[1] which ridicules various orders of monks, friars, and regular canons, and which likewise imputes sexual licence to men and women (in this instance, living in adjacent quarters) in one of the forms of the religious life, is more clearly censorious and malicious. The *abbas Cucaniensis*, whom a poet of the *Carmina Burana* identifies with his fictive self, occurs in a context too brief to show whether he is satirically conceived or not. But *The Land of Cokaygne* has not the edge or the intensity of tone of a work designed to castigate and reform the vices of real life: it is banter, in a strain outrageous rather than bitter.

The Land of Cokaygne was evidently composed in Ireland. The word *russin* (l. 20) is a link with the evidence for Irish origin of several other pieces in the manuscript, such as the *Hymn* composed by 'Frere Michel Kyldare (i.e. of Kildare)'; the poem on the death of Pers of Birmingham, who died in 1308 and was buried in the Grey Abbey in Kildare; the *Satire* which mentions Drogheda; an OF poem that concerns New Ross; and the Proverbs (in OF) of a 'Count Desmond'.

f. 3ʳ

> F UR in see bi west Spayngne
> Is a lond ihote Cokaygne.
> Þer nis lond vnder heuenriche
> Of wel, of godnis, hit iliche.
> Þoȝ Paradis be miri and briȝt,   5
> Cokaygn is of fairir siȝt.
> What is þer in Paradis
> Bot grasse and flure and grene ris?

---

[1] Ed. T. Wright, *Political Songs of England* (1884), ii. 64–77.

Þoʒ þer be ioi and gret dute,
Þer nis met bote frute;   10
Þer nis halle, bure, no bench,
Bot watir manis þurst to quench.
Beþ þer no men bot two—
Hely and Enok also;
Elinglich mai hi go   15
Whar þer woniþ men no mo.
In Cokaigne is met and drink
Wiþvte care, how, and swink;
Þe met is trie, þe drink is clere,
To none, russin, and sopper.   20
I sigge forsoþ, boute were,
Þer nis lond on erþe is pere;
Vnder heuen nis lond, iwisse,
Of so mochil ioi and blisse.
Þer is mani swete siʒte;   25 f. 3ᵛ
Al is dai, nis þer no niʒte.
Þer nis baret noþer strif,
Nis þer no deþ, ac euer lif;
Þer nis lac of met no cloþ,
Þer nis man no womman wroþ,   30
Þer nis serpent, wolf, no fox,
Hors no capil, kowe no ox,
Þer nis schepe no swine no gote,
No non horwʒ, la, God it wote,
Noþer harace noþer stode—   35
Þe lond is ful of oþer gode.
Nis þer flei, fle, no lowse
In cloþ, in toune, bed, no house;
Þer nis dunnir, slete, no hawle,
No non vile worme no snawile,   40

12 þurst to] *MS.* þursto

No non storme, rein, no winde.
Þer nis man no womman blinde,
Ok al is game, joi, and gle.
Wel is him þat þer mai be!
Þer beþ riuers gret and fine   45
Of oile, melk, honi, and wine;
Watir seruiþ þer to noþing
Bot to siȝt and to waiissing.
Þer is mani maner frute—
Al is solas and dedute.   50

f. 4ʳ   Þer is a wel fair abbei
Of white monkes and of grei.
Þer beþ bowris and halles:
Al of pasteiis beþ þe walles,
Of fleis, of fisse, and rich met,   55
Þe likfullist þat man mai et.
Fluren cakes beþ þe schingles alle
Of cherch, cloister, boure, and halle.
Þe pinnes beþ fat podinges—
Rich met to princeȝ and kinges.   60
Man mai þerof et inoȝ,
Al wiþ riȝt and noȝt wiþ woȝ.
Al is commune to ȝung and old,
To stoute and sterne, mek and bold.
Þer is a cloister, fair and liȝt,   65
Brod and lang, of sembli siȝt;
Þe pilers of þat cloister alle
Beþ iturned of cristale,
Wiþ har bas and capitale
Of grene jaspe and rede corale.   70
In þe praer is a tre

49 mani] *not in MS.*   69 bas] *MS.* las

Swiþe likful forto se:
Þe rote is gingeuir and galingale,
Þe siouns beþ al sedwale,
Trie maces beþ þe flure,   75
Þe rind canel of swet odur,
Þe frute gilofre of gode smakke.   f. 4ᵛ
Of cucubes þer nis no lakke.
Þer beþ rosis of rede ble
And lilie likful forto se;   80
Þai faloweþ neuer dai no niȝt.
Þis aȝt be a swet siȝt!
Þer beþ .iiij. willis in þe abbei
Of triacle, and halwei,
Of baum, and ek piement,   85
Euer ernend to riȝt rent—
Of þai stremis al þe molde—
Stonis preciuse, and golde.
Þer is saphir and vniune,
Carbuncle and astiune,   90
Smaragde, lugre, and prassiune,
Beril, onix, topasiune,
Ametist and crisolite,
Calcedun and epetite.
Þer beþ briddes mani and fale: 95
Þrostil, þruisse, and niȝtingale,
Chalandre, and wodwale,
And oþer briddes wiþout tale,
Þat stinteþ neuer bi har miȝt
Miri to sing dai and niȝt.   100

Ȝite I do ȝow mo to witte: f. 5ʳ
Þe gees irostid on þe spitte

89 and] *MS.* a

Fleeȝ to þat abbai, God hit wot,
And grediþ: 'Gees, al hote, al hot!'
Hi bringeþ garlek, gret plente,   105
Þe best idiȝt þat man mai se.
Þe leuerokes, þat beþ cuþ,
Liȝtiþ adun to manis muþ
Idiȝt in stu ful swiþe wel,
Pudrid wiþ gilofre and canel.   110
Nis no spech of no drink,
Ak take inoȝ wiþvte swink.
Whan þe monkes gooþ to masse,
Al þe fenestres þat beþ of glasse
Turneþ into cristal briȝt   115
To ȝiue monkes more liȝt.
Whan þe masses beþ iseiid
And þe bokes up ileiid,
Þe cristal turniþ into glasse
In state þat hit raþer wasse.   120
Þe ȝung monkes euch dai
Aftir met goþ to plai:
Nis þer hauk no fule so swifte
Bettir fleing bi þe lifte
Þan þe monkes, heiȝ of mode,   125
Wiþ har sleuis and har hode.
Whan þe abbot seeþ ham flee,
Þat he holt for moch glee;
Ak naþeles, al þeramang,
He biddiþ ham liȝt to euesang.   130
Þe monkes liȝtiþ noȝt adun,
Ac furre fleeþ in o randun.
Whan þe abbot him iseeþ
Þat is monkes fram him fleeþ,

113 gooþ] *MS.* geeþ

f. 5ᵛ

He takeþ maidin of þe route 135
And turniþ vp hir white toute,
And betiþ þe taburs wiþ is hond
To make is monkes liȝt to lond.
Whan is monkes þat iseeþ,
To þe maid dun hi fleeþ 140
And goþ þe wench al abute,
And þakkeþ al hir white toute,
And siþ aftir her swinke
Wendiþ meklich hom to drink,
And goþ to har collacione 145
A wel fair processione.

Anoþer abbei is þerbi—
Forsoþ, a gret fair nunnerie,
Vp a riuer of swet milke, f. 6ʳ
Whar is gret plente of silk. 150
Whan þe someris dai is hote,
Þe ȝung nunnes takiþ a bote
And doþ ham forþ in þat riuer,
Boþe wiþ oris and wiþ stere.
Whan hi beþ fur fram þe abbei, 155
Hi makiþ ham nakid forto plei,
And lepiþ dune into þe brimme
And doþ ham sleilich forto swimme.
Þe ȝung monkes þat hi seeþ:
Hi doþ ham vp and forþ hi fleeþ, 160
And commiþ to þe nunnes anon,
And euch monke him takeþ on,
And snellich beriþ forþ har prei
To þe mochil grei abbei,

141, 145 goþ] *MS.* geþ   159 monkes] *MS.* monkeþ

And techiþ þe nunnes an oreisun   165
Wiþ iambleue vp and dun.
Þe monke þat wol be stalun gode
And kan set ariȝt is hode,
He schal hab wiþoute danger
xij. wiues euch ȝere,   170
Al þroȝ riȝt and noȝt þroȝ grace,
Forto do himsilf solace,

And þilk monke þat slepiþ best,
And doþ his likam al to rest,
Of him is hoppe, God hit wote,   175
To be sone uadir abbot.
Whose wl com þat lond to,
Ful grete penance he mot do:
Seue ȝere in swineis dritte
He mote wade, wol ȝe iwitte,   180
Al anon vp to þe chynne—
So he schal þe lond winne.

Lordinges gode and hend,
Mot ȝe neuer of world wend
Fort ȝe stond to ȝure cheance   185
And fulfille þat penance,
Þat ȝe mote þat lond ise
And neuermore turne aȝe,
Prey we God so mote hit be!
Amen, pur seint charite.   190

X

LAƷAMON

ALL that we know of LaƷamon is contained in the earlier version of his *historia Brutonum*, or *Brut*:[1]

> An preost wes on leoden, LaƷamon wes ihoten.
> He wes Leouenaðes sone—liðe him beo Drihten.
> He wonede at ErnleƷe at æðelen are chirechen
> Vppen Seuarne staþe; sel þar him þuhte;
> Onfest Radestone; þer he bock radde.
> Hit com him on mode and on his mern þonke
> Þet he wolde of Engle þa æðelæn tellen:
> Wat heo ihoten weoren and wonene heo comen
> Þa Englene londe ærest ahten . . .

That is, he was a priest at King's Areley in Worcestershire (twenty miles from Wenlock, the site of a shrine of the Mildburga mentioned by LaƷamon at l. 31008) who applied himself to books and decided to write a history of the English people; to do this he acquired 'the English book that St. Bede made', a Latin book by 'St Albin and the fair Austin' (presumably Bede's Latin *Historia*, though LaƷamon uses it hardly more than does his predecessor Geoffrey of Monmouth, who makes similar brief references to Bede and a certain *vetustissimus liber*); and a book by 'a French clerk' called Wace.[2] It is on this Norman-French rhymed version (in 15,000 couplets) of Geoffrey's History that LaƷamon's *Brut* (32,241 half ll.) is largely based. But he is much more than a translator: he omits, expands—and regularly (as at l. 91 *infra*) substitutes vivid direct speech for Wace's para-phrase. To him we owe the first telling of the Arthurian story—as well as the Lear story—in English, and the first glimpses of its glamour.

[1] For the origin and meaning of this term see *O.E.D.*, s.v., and G. Gordon, 'The Trojans in Britain', *E. and S.* ix. [2] See p. xi.

O

Wace completed his 15,000 couplets in the year 1155, and
Laƺamon, in speaking of Wace's presentation of it to Eleanor
'þe wes Henries quene' (l. 23), seems to suggest that Henry II
(*ob.* 1189) was dead by the time that the English *Brut* was finished.
The linguistic evidence is inconclusive, but gives some support
to a late twelfth-century date (cf. l. 323 n.). The two extant
manuscripts, Cott. Cal. A. IX (*v.* p. 1 above) and Otho C. XIII,
belong to the period 1250–1300. The Otho text is shorter by
about one-sixth; in the narrative here printed it is defective at
several points, whilst elsewhere it sometimes preserves details
not found in C but which were doubtless in the common original
of both manuscripts (parts of which Hall attempted to recon-
struct in his *Selections* of 1924). The reasons for O's changes are
often obscure; but v. *M.Æ.* xxix for some suggestions. The
language of C is closely related to that of other texts from the
West Midlands.

Laƺamon was clearly familiar with the traditional alliterative
measure, particularly in its late and 'popular' form. Many of his
half-lines preserve the old stress patterns, but in some rhyme
and (more often) assonance and imperfect rhyme appear, and
sometimes syllabic rhythm has completely displaced the older
technique. He uses little of the older poetic vocabulary and
formulae, but has his own supply of similes, stock phrases, and
terse comment, his own devices of repetition.

f. 164ᵛ 2 ÞA com þer in are tiden an oht mon riden,
And brohte tidinge Arðure þan kinge
From Moddrede his suster sune; Arðure he wes wilcume:
For he wende þat he brohte boden swiðe gode.
Arður lai alle longe niht and spac wið þene ƺeonge cniht,   5
Swa nauer nulde he him sugge soð hu hit ferde.
Þa hit wes dæi a marƺen and duƺeðe gon sturien,
Arður þa up aras, and strehte his ærmes.
He aras up and adun sat, swulc he weore swiðe seoc.
Þa axede hine an uæir cniht: 'Lauerd, hu hauest þu iuaren
toniht?'   10
Arður þa andswarede, a mode him wes uneðe:

'Toniht a mine slepe, þer Ich læi on bure,
Me imætte a sweuen; þeruore Ich ful sari æm.
Me imette þat mon me hof uppen are halle,
Þa halle Ich gon bistriden swulc Ich wolde riden.   15
Alle þa lond þa Ich ah, alle Ich þer ouersah;
And Walwain sat biuoren me; mi sweord he bar an honde.
Þa com Moddred faren þere mid unimete uolke;   f. 165ʳ 1
He bar an his honde ane wi-ax stronge.
He bigon to hewene hardliche swiðe,   20
And þa postes forheou alle þa heolden up þa halle.
Þer Ich iseh Wenheuer eke, wimmonnen leofuest me;
Al þere muche halle rof mid hire honden heo todroh.
Þa halle gon to hælden and Ich hæld to grunden,
Þat mi riht ærm tobrac. Þa seide Modred: "Haue þat!"   25
Adun ueol þa halle, and Walwain gon to ualle,
And feol a þere eorðe; his ærmes breken beine.
And Ich igrap mi sweord leofe mid mire leoft honde
And smæt of Modred is hafd þat hit wond a þene ueld.
And þa quene Ich al tosnaðde mid deore mine sweorede   30
And seoððen Ich heo adun sette in ane swarte putte.
And al mi uolc riche sette to fleme,
Þat nuste Ich under Criste whar heo bicumen weoren.
Buten miseolf Ich gon atstonden uppen ane wolden,
And Ich þer wondrien agon wide 3eond þan moren.   35
Þer Ich isah gripes and grisliche fu3eles.   f. 165ʳ 2
Þa com an guldene leo liðen ouer dune,
Deoren swiðe hende þa ure Drihten makede.
Þa leo me orn foren to and iueng me bi þan midle
And forð hire gun 3eongen and to þere sæ wende.   40
And Ich isæh þæ vðen i þere sæ driuen

23 honden] *MS.* hondeden   27 breken] *MS.* brekeen
31 seoððen] *MS.* seodðen [*uncrossed* ð *is not noted henceforth*]   adun]
MS. adum   34 gon] *MS.* gond   38 makede] *MS.* make

And þe leo i þan ulode iwende wið me seolue.
Þa wit i sæ comen, þa vðen me hire binomen.
Com þer an fisc liðe and fereden me to londe.
Þa wes al Ich wet and weri of sorƷen and seoc.   45
Þa gon Ich iwakien, swiðe Ich gon to quakien.
Þa gon Ich to biuien swulc Ich al furburne,
And swa Ich habbe al niht of mine sweuene swiðe iþoht.
For Ich wat to iwisse agan is al mi blisse.
For a to mine liue sorƷen Ich mot driƷe.   50
Wale þat Ich nabbe here Wenhauer mine quene!'
Þa andswarede þe cniht: 'Lauerd, þu hauest unriht;
Ne sculde me nauere sweuen mid sorƷen arecchen.
Þu ært þe riccheste mon þa rixleoð on londen
f. 165ᵛ 1 And þe alrewiseste þe wuneð under weolcne.   55
Ʒif hit weore ilumpe—swa nulle hit ure Drihte—
Þat Modred þire suster sune hafde þine quene inume
And al þi kineliche lond isæt an his aƷere hond,
Þe þu him bitahtest þa þu to Rome þohtest,
And he hafde al þus ido mid his swikedome;   60
Þe Ʒet þu mihtest þe awreken wurðliche mid wepnen
And æft þi lond halden and þine leoden walden
And þine feond fallen þe þe ufel unnen,
And slæn heom alle clane, þet þer no bilauen nane.'
Arður þa andswarede, aðelest alre kinge: 65
'Longe bið æuere þat no wene Ich nauere
Þat æuere Moddred mæi mi þat man is me leouest
Wolde me biswiken for alle mine richen,
No Wenhauer mi quene wakien on þonke;
Nulleð hit biginne for nane weorld-monne.'   70
Æfne þan worde forðriht þa andswarede þe cniht:

45 al Ich] O ich al   48 sweuene] MS. sweuenene   49 wat]
MS. what   56 MS. ilunþe   62b MS. walden þine leoden
67b missing in MS. O þat man is me leouest   70 O worle þinge

'Ich sugge þe soð, leofe king, for Ich æm þin vnderling.
Þus hafeð Modred idon: þine quene he hafeð ifon,
And þi wunliche lond isæt an his a3ere hond.
He is king and heo is quene, of þine kume nis na wene: 75 f. 165ᵛ 2
For no weneð heo nauere to soðe þat þu cumen a3ain from
    Rome.
Ich æm þin a3en mon, and iseh þisne swikedom,
And Ich æm icumen to þe seoluen soð þe to suggen.
Min hafued beo to wedde þat isæid Ich þe habbe
Soð buten lese of leofen þire quene   80
And of Modrede þire suster sune, hu he hafueð Brutlond þe
    binume.'
Þa sæt hit al stille in Arðures halle.
Þa wes þer særinæsse mid sele þan kinge.
Þa weoren Bruttisce men swiðe vnbalde uor þæn.
Þa umbe stunde stefne þer sturede: 85
Wide me mihte iheren Brutten iberen,
And gunne to tellen a feole cunne spellen,
Hu heo wolden fordeme Modred and þa quene
And al þat moncun fordon þe mid Modred heolden.
Arður þa cleopede, hendest alre Brutte: 90
'Sitteð adun stille, cnihtes inne halle,
And Ich eou telle wulle spelles vncuðe:
Nu tomær3e þenne hit dæi bið—and Drihten hine sende—
Forð Ich wulle bu3e in toward Bruttaine,
And Moddred Ich wulle slæn and þa quen forberne   95 f. 166ʳ 1
And alle Ich wulle fordon þa biluueden þen swikedom;
And her Ich bileofuen wulle me leofuest monne:
Howel, minne leofue mæi, hexst of mine cunne,
And half mine uerde Ich bilæfuen a þissen ærde,
To halden al þis kine-lond þa Ich habbe a mire hond;   100
And þenne þas þing beoð alle idone a3an Ich wulle to Rome

    75 quene] MS. que   95 slæn] MS. scaln O slean

And mi wunliche lond bitæche Walwaine mine mæie
And iuorþe mi beot seoððe, bi mine bare life!
Scullen alle mine feond wæi-sið makeȝe.'
Þa stod him up Walwain, þat wes Arðures maei,   105
And þas word saide—þe eorl wes abolȝe:
'Ældrihten Godd, domes waldend,
Al middelærdes mund, whi is hit iwurðen
Þat mi broðer Modred þis morð hafueð itimbred?
Ah todæi Ich atsake hine here biuoren þissere duȝeðe, 110
And Ich hine fordemen wulle mid Drihtenes wille.
Miseolf Ich wulle hine anhon haxst alre warien;
f. 166ʳ 2 Þa quene Ich wulle mid Goddes laȝe al mid horsen to-
  draȝe:
For ne beo Ich nauere bliðe þa wile a beoð aliue,
And þat Ich habbe minne æm awræke mid þan bezste.' 115
Bruttes þa andswarede, mid baldere stefne:
'Al ure wepnen sunden ȝarewe; nu tomarȝen we scullen
  uaren.'
A marȝen, þat hit dæi wes and Drihten hine senden,
Arður uorð him wende mid aðelen his folke.
Half he hit bilæfde, and half hit forð ladde.   120
Forð he wende þurh þat lond þat he com to Whitsond.
Scipen he hæfde sone, monie and wel idone;
Ah feowertene niht fulle þere læi þa uerde,
Þeos wederes abiden, windes bidelde.
Nu was sum forcuð kempe in Arðures ferde;   125
Anæn swa he demen iherde of Modredes dede,
He nom his swein aneouste and sende to þissen londe,
And sende word Wenhaueren heou hit was iwurðen,
And hu Arður wes on uore mid muclere ferde,
And hu he wolde taken on and al hu he wolde don. 130

---

  102 bitæche] *MS.* bitatæche *O* bitak 110 atsake hine] *O* hine
asake 119 Arður] *MS.* Arðu 126 dede] *MS.* ðeðe

Þa quene com to Modred, þat wæs hire leofuest monnes,   f. 166ᵛ 1
And talde him tidende of Arður þan kinge—
Hu he wolde taken an, and al hu he wolde don.
Modræd nom his sonde and sende to Sexlond
After Childriche, þe king wes swiðe riche,   135
And bæd hine cume to Brutaine—þerof he bruke sculde.
Modræd bad Childriche, þene stronge and þene riche,
Weide senden sonde a feouwer half Sexlonde
And beoden þa cnihtes alle þat heo biȝeten mihte
Þat heo comen sone to þissen kinedome,   140
And he wolde Childriche ȝeouen of his riche
Al biȝeonde þere Humbre, for he him scolde helpe
To fihten wið his æme Arðuren kinge.
Childrich beh sone into Brutlonde.
Þa Modred hafde his ferde isomned of monnen,   145
Þa weoren þere italde sixti þusende
Here-kempen harde of heðene uolke,
Þa heo weoren icumen hidere for Arðures hærme,
Modred to helpen, forcuðest monnen.
Þa þe uerde wes isome of ælche moncunne,   150
Þa heo weoren þer on hepe an hundred þusende,   f. 166ᵛ 2
Heðene and cristene, mid Modrede kinge.
Arður lai at Whitsond, feouwertene niht him þuhte to long,
And al Modred wuste wat Arður þær wolde:
Ælche dæi him comen sonde from þas kinges hirede.   155
Þa ilomp hit an one time muchel rein him gon rine,
And þæ wind him gon wende, and stod of þan æst ende,
And Arður to scipe fusde mid alle his uerde
And hehte þat his scipmen brohten hine to Romerel,
Þer he þohte up wende into þissen londe.   160
Þæ he to þere hauene com, Moddred him wes auornon.

135 þe king wes] ? l. þe wes   140 kinedome] MS. kinedone
142 þere] MS. þerere   151 hundred] MS. hund dred

Ase þe dæi gon lihte, heo bigunnen to fihten
Alle þene longe dæi—moni mon þer ded læi.
Summe hi fuhten a londe, summe bi þan stronde,
Summe heo letten ut of scipen scerpe garen scriþen.   165
Walwain biforen wende and þene wæi rumde
And sloh þer aneuste þeines elleouene.
He sloh Childriches sune, þe was þer mid his fader icume.

f. 167ʳ 1 To reste eode þe sunne; wæ wes þa monnen.
Þer wes Walwain aslæƷe and idon of life-daƷe   170
Þurh an eorl Sexisne—særi wurðe his saule!
Þa wes 'Arður særi and sorhful an heorte forþi,
And þas word bodede, ricchest alre Brutte:
'Nu Ich ileosed habbe mine sweines leofe.
Ich wuste bi mine sweuene whæt sorƷen me weoren Ʒeueðe.
IslaƷen is Angel þe king, þe wes min aƷen deorling,   176
And Walwaine mi suster sune. Wa is me þat ich was mon
    iboren.
Up nu, of scipen biliue, mine beornes ohte!'
Æfne þæ worde wenden to fihte
Sixti þusend anon selere kempen   180
And breken Modredes trume, and welneh himseolue wes
    inome.
Modred bigon to fleon and his folc after teon;
FluƷen ueondliche, feldes beoueden eke,
Ʒurnen þa stanes mid þan blodstremes.
Þer weore al þat fiht idon, ah þat niht to raðe com;   185
Ʒif þa niht neore, islaƷen hi weoren alle.
Þe niht heom todelde Ʒeond slades and Ʒeond dunen,

f. 167ʳ 2 And Modred swa vorð com þat he wes at Lundene.
Iherden þa burhweren hu hit was al ifaren
And warnden him inƷeong, and alle his folke.   190
Modred þeone wende toward Winchastre,

184 Ʒurnen] MS. Ʒurren   187 Ʒeond dunen] MS. Ʒeon dunen

And heo hine underuengen mid alle his monnen;
And Arður after wende mid alle his mahte
Þat he com to Winchestre mid muchelre uerde
And þa burh al biræd, and Modred þerinne abeod.   195
Þa Modred isæh þat Arður him wes swa neh,
Ofte he hine beþohte wæt he don mahte.
Þa a þere ilke niht he hehte his cnihtes alle
Mid alle heore iwepnen ut of burhȝe wenden
And sæide þat he weolde mid fihte þer atstonden.   200
He bihehte þere burȝewere auermare freo laȝe
Wið þan þa heo him heolpen at heȝere neoden.
Þa hit wes dæiliht, ȝaru þa wes heore fiht.
Arður þat bihedde; þe king wes abolȝe,
He lette bemen blawen and beonnen men to fihten;   205
He hehte alle his þeines and aðele his cnihte   f. 167ᵛ 1
Fon somed to fihten and his ueond auallen,
And þe burh alle fordon and þat burh-folc ahon.
Heo togadere stopen and sturnliche fuhten.
Modred þa þohte what he don mihte;   210
And he dude þere alse he dude elleswhare—
Swikedom mid þan mæste, for auere he dude unwraste.
He biswac his iueren biuoren Winchestren,
And lette him to cleopien his leofeste cnihtes anan,
And his leoueste freond alle of allen his folke,   215
And bistal from þan fihte—þe feond hine aȝe!—
And þat folc gode lette al þer forwurðe.
Fuhten alle dæi, wenden þat here lauerd þer læi
And weore heom aneouste at muchelere neode.
Þa heold he þene wai þat touward Hamtone lai,   220
And heolde touward hauene, forcuðest hæleðe,
And nom alle þa scipen þa þer oht weore,
And þa steormen alle to þan scipen neodde,

207 ueond] *MS*. ueod *O* feondes

And ferden into Cornwalen, forcuðest kingen a þan daȝen;
And Arður Winchestre þa burh bilai wel faste,   225
f. 167ᵛ 2 And al þe moncun ofsloh—þer wes sorȝen inoh—
Þa ȝeonge and þa alde, alle he aqualde.
Þa þat folc wes al ded, þa burh al forswelde,
Þa lette he mid alle tobreken þa walles alle.
Þa wes hit itimed þere þat Merlin seide while: 230
'Ærm wurðest þu, Winchæstre, þæ eorðe þe scal forswalȝe.'
Swa Merlin sæide, þe witeȝe wes mære.
Þa quene læi inne Eouwerwic, næs heo næuere swa sarlic—
Þat wes Wenhauer þa quene, særȝest wimmonne.
Heo iherde suggen soððere worden,   235
Hu ofte Modred flah and hu Arður hine bibah.
Wa wes hire þere while þat heo wes on life.
Ut of Eouerwike bi nihte heo iwende
And touward Karliun tuhte swa swiðe swa heo mahte.
Þider heo brohten bi nihte of hire cnihten tweiȝe,   240
And me hire hafd biwefde mid ane hali rifte,
And heo wes þer munechene, karefullest wife.
Þa nusten men of þere quene war heo bicumen weore,
No feole ȝere seoððe nuste hit mon to soðe
f. 168ʳ 1 Whaðer heo weore on deðe . . .   245
Þa heo hireseolf weore isunken in þe watere.
Modred wes i Cornwale and somnede cnihtes feole:
To Irlonde he sende aneoste his sonde;
To Sexlonde he sende aneouste his sonde;
To Scotlonde he sende aneouste his sonde;   250
He hehten heom to cume alle anan þat wolde lond habben
Oðer seoluer oðer gold, oðer ahte oðer lond.
On ælchere wisen he warnede hine seoluen;
Swa deð ælc witer mon þa neode cumeð uuenan.
Arður þat iherde, wraðest kinge,   255

          245 *A half-line is missing. O has no exact parallel*

Þat Modred wæs i Cornwale mid muchele mon-weorede
And þer wolde abiden þat Arður come riden.
Arður sende sonde 3eond al his kine-londe,
And to cumen alle hehte þat quic wes on londe,
Þa to uihte oht weoren, wepnen to beren;   260
And whaswa hit forsete þat þe king hete
Þe king hine wolde a folden quic al forbernen.
Hit læc toward hirede folc vnimete,
Ridinde and ganninde swa þe rim falleð adune.
Arður for to Cornwale mid unimete ferde.   265
Modred þat iherde and him to3eines heolde   f. 168ʳ 2
Mid vnimete folke; þer weore monie uæie.
Uppen þere Tambre heo tuhten togadere.
Þe stude hatte Camelford; euermare ilast þat ilke weorde.
And at Camelforde wes isomned sixti þusend,   270
And ma þusend þerto; Modred wes heore ælder.
Þa þiderward gon ride Arður þe riche
Mid unimete folke, uæie þah hit weore.
Uppe þere Tambre heo tuhte tosomne,
Heuen here-marken, halden togadere,   275
Luken sweord longe, leiden o þe helmen.
Fur ut sprengen, speren brastlien,
Sceldes gonnen scanen, scaftes tobreken;
Þer faht al tosomne folc vnimete.
Tambre wes on flode mid vnimete blode;   280
Mon i þan fihte non þer ne mihte ikenne nenne kempe,
No wha dude wurse no wha bet, swa þat wiðer wes imenged:
For ælc sloh adunriht, weore he swein weore he cniht.
Þer wes Modred ofsla3e and idon of lif-da3e,
And alle his cnihtes isla3e in þan fihte.   285

261 *MS.* wah swa   262 quic] *MS.* quid *O* slean   265 unimete]
MS. unilte   282 wiðer] *MS.* wiðe   285 And . . . isla3e
supplied from O

Þer weoren ofslaȝe alle þa snelle
Arðures heredmen, hehȝe and lowe,
And þa Bruttes alle of Arðures borde,
f. 168ᵛ 1 And alle his fosterlinges of feole kineriches,
And Arður forwunded mid wal-spere brade.   290
Fiftene he hafde feondliche wunden:
Mon mihte i þare laste twa glouen iþraste.
Þa nas þer namare i þan fehte to laue
Of twa hundred þusend monnen þa þer leien tohauwen
Buten Arður þe king ane, and of his cnihtes tweien.   295
Arður wes forwunded wunder ane swiðe.
Þer to him com a cnaue þe wes of his cunne:
He wes Cadores sune, þe eorles of Cornwaile.
Constantin hehte þe cnaue, he wes þan kinge deore.
Arður him lokede on, þer he lai on folden,   300
And þas word seide mid sorhfulle heorte:
'Costæntin, þu art wilcume; þu weore Cadores sone.
Ich þe bitache here mine kineriche,
And wite mine Bruttes a to þines lifes,
And hald heom alle þa laȝen þa habbeoð istonden a mine daȝen
And alle þa laȝen gode þa bi Uðeres daȝen stode.   306
And Ich wulle uaren to Aualun, to uairest alre maidene,
To Argante þere quene, aluen swiðe sceone,
And heo scal mine wunden makien alle isunde,
f. 168ᵛ 2 Al hal me makien mid haleweiȝe drenchen.   310
And seoðe Ich cumen wulle to mine kineriche
And wunien mid Brutten mid muchelere wunne.'
Æfne þan worden þer com of se wenden
þet wes an sceort bat liðen, sceouen mid uðen,
And twa wimmen þerinne wunderliche idihte,   315
And heo nomen Arður anan and aneouste hine uereden,

287 and lowe *supplied from* O   298 Cornwaile] *MS.* Corwaile
309 scal] *MS.* slal

And softe hine adun leiden and forð gunnen hine liðen.
Þa wes hit iwurðen þat Merlin seide whilen:
Þat weore unimete care of Arðures forðfare.
Bruttes ileueð 3ete þat he bon on liue   320
And wunnien in Aualun mid fairest alre aluen;
And lokieð euere Bruttes 3ete whan Arður cumen liðe.
Nis nauer þe man iboren of nauer nane burde icoren,
Þe cunne of þan soðe of Arðure sugen mare.
Bute while wes an wite3e Mærlin ihate;   325
He bodede mid worde, his quiðes weoren soðe,
Þat an Arður sculde 3ete cum Anglen to fulste.

'ROBERT OF GLOUCESTER'

'ANTIQUARIES (amongst whom Mr. *Selden*) more value him for his *History* than *Poetry*, his lines being neither *strong* nor *smooth*, but sometimes *sharp* . . . .' Thus writes Fuller of the chronicler who refers to himself as Robert and who since the sixteenth century has been assumed to be a monk of Gloucester. The use made of the chronicle by Stow, Weever, Wood, and Hearne bears out part of Fuller's comment, and the rest of it may fairly be tested by this excerpt. The writer's couplets may be loose but his sense of incident is lively. 'Colours of rhetoric' and the Arthurian glamour are not for him; but he has a relish for authentic detail. His description of events at Gloucester in 1263 is clearly based on first-hand information; and if he had been a student at Oxford before he became a monk of St. Peter's Abbey (the connexion of which with the university may well go back beyond 1283: *v.* l. 25 n.) it would be easy for him to visualize the town and gown riot of 1264.

In his plain and unpretentious style the writer is no unworthy successor to the Peterborough chronicler. If he follows French fashion by writing in verse, he shows a certain independence in using the vernacular at a time when 'bot a man conne Frenss me tellþ of him lute'. In the west midlands, to be sure, English never lost its self-respect. But his patriotism is neither local nor chauvinistic; and his play with 'asoyne' (97) shows that he had the saving grace of a dry humour.

The long chronicle that goes under Robert's name exists in two recensions which have the opening section (covering events to 1135) in common. It is probable that more than one author was concerned in the work. The name Robert occurs only once (in connexion with portents preceding the Battle of Evesham, 1265), and the association with Gloucester must be regarded as unproved. There is no clear evidence that the work was

finished much before about 1325, the date proposed for the
Caligula MS.

IN þis manere þe barons bigonne hor vrning: f. 156ʳ
A Freinss kniȝt was at Gloucetre, þe sserreue þoru þe king,
Sir Maci de Besile, and constable also.
Þe barons it bispeke þat it nas noȝt wel ido,
Ac aȝe þe pourueance, vor hii nolde Frenss man non.   5
An oþer sserreue hii made þoru commun conseil echon,
A kniȝt of þe contreie, Sir Willam Traci,
And of þulke poer clene pulte out Sir Maci.
As Sir Willam ssire huld in a Monenday
Sir Maci com iarmed, as mani man isay,   10
Wiþ poer isend fram þe court, iarmed wel inou,
And, euene as þe ssire sat, to þe tounes ende him drou.
Hii aliȝte wiþ drawe suerd, wiþ macis mani on,
And wiþ mani an hard stroc rumede hor wey anon
Vort hii come vp to þe deis, and þe sserreue vaste   15
Bi þe top hii hente anon and to þe grounde him caste,
And harlede him vorþ villiche wiþ mani stroc among.
In a foul plodde in þe stret suþþe me him slong,
And orne on him mid hor hors and defoulede him vaste,
And bihinde a squier suþþe villiche hii him caste,   20
And to þe castel him ledde þoru out þe toun,
Þat reuþe it was vorto se, and caste him in prison.
Þo þe tiþinge herof com to þe baronie
Hii þoȝte in time amendi suich vileinie:
So þat Sir Roger de Clifford and Sir Ion Giffard nome   25 f. 156ᵛ
Gret poer in somer and to Gloucetre come.
Hii sende to Sir Maci þat he þun castel ȝolde
To hom and to þe baronie, oþer hii him nime wolde.

9 As] *MS.* Ac   17 *MS.* williche

Sir Maci hom sende aȝen þat þe king him tok biuore
Þun castel him to loki, mid trewe oþ isuore,   30
Ne þat he nolde traitour be ne þen castel neuere ȝelde
Bote þe king oþer is sone, þe wule he him miȝte welde.
He adde wiþinne lute folk þun castel to defende.
Arblastes sone, and ginnes, wiþoute me bende,
And ssote inward vaste inou; atte laste hii ssende   35
Al þe brutaske wiþoute, and þe brugge brende,
Vor he was al of tre; and Sir Maci and his
Flowe in to þe tour an hey þo hii seye þis,
And defendede hom vaste þe wule hii miȝte, iwis.
Ac vor defaute of helpe mani man issend is.   40
Wiþ an quarel on wiþinne an squier þeroute slou;
Sir Ion Giffard uor is deþ made deol inou.
And þo Sir Maci was inome, and hii wiþinne come.
An carpenter, þat hii sede þat sset þe ssute, hii nome,
And ladde him vpe þe tour an hei, and made him huppe to
    grounde.   45
He hupte and debrusede, and deide in an stounde.
And Sir Roger of Clifford þo þe castel in warde hadde,
And hii nome Sir Maci, and into Marc him ladde,
And Sir Ion Giffard nom to him is quic eiȝte echon,
And al þat he fond of is, and nameliche at Sserston.   50
A Freinss bissop þer was at Hereforde þo,
Sir Peris de Egeblaunche, þat hii dude also wo:
Hii come vorto nime him, i-armed mani on;
Þe godeman vor drede to churche wende anon
And reuestede him bi þe auter; ac Sir Roger ne Sir Ion,   55
Vor honour of holichurche, nolde wiþinne gon.
Ac Sir Tomas Torbeuille and oþer ssrewen mo
Wende vp, and wiþ strengþe made him out go.

34 *MS.* faste me   35 ssote] *MS.* sote · ssende] *MS.* sende
48 Marc] *MS.* þe march

Þo he sei þat he ne moste habbe churche peis,
'Par Crist,' he sede, 'Sir Tomas, tu es maveis; 60
Meint ben te ay fet': vor he adde muche god
Þerbiuore him ido—and he it vuele vnderstod.
Hii harlede him out of churche, þat lute pite adde,
And is god nome vaste inou, and to Erdesleye him ladde,
And him and Sir Maci ek in god warde dude þere 65 f. 157ʳ
In þe castel of Erdesleye, uorte it betere were.
    So it ferde oueral ware me Freinsse fond;
Me harlede hom villiche about into al þe lond.
And þe kinges men robbede hom þat aȝen hom were,
And þe barons ek hor fon þat aȝen hom armes bere. 70
Atte biginninge þer hulde wiþ þe king vewe wel
Bote Sir Robert Walrond and Sir Ion Mauncel;
Ac suþþe, þo Sir Edward so wel armes ber,
He drou to him mani on þat wiþ þe barons were er.
Þe Marcheis he adde sone—as Sir Roger þe Mortimer, 75
And Sir Warin of Bassingbourne, and of Clifford Sir Roger,
Sir Gemes de Audele, Sir Haumond þe Strange also,
Sir Roger of Leibourne, and mani oþer þerto.
Þo was þe castel of Gloucetre and þe toun also
Þoru Sir Roger of Clifford in þe kinges hond ido; 80
And he astorede þe castel wiþ poer inou,
And to is castel of Brumesfeld Sir Ion Giffard vaste drou,
And astorede him wel inou; and goinde adde is route
To driue and to gaderi þuder god of neiȝebores aboute.
Þe stalwardeste men þat me fond to him vaste he drou, 85
And of porchas of neiȝebores ssipede hom wel inou.
Bituene þe castel of Gloucetre and Brumefeld also
Þer was ofte biker gret and much harm ido.
Ac þe constable of Gloucetre, as mid þe kinges poer,

61 vor he] *MS.* vor he uor he   74 He drou] *MS.* þo drou
85 me] *MS.* he   86 ssipede hom] *MS.* hom sondede

Helde ofte in þe kinges name courtes ver and ner,   90
So þat at Quedesle, wiþoute þe toun to mile,
He let someni an hundred, and þer he hent an gile:
Vor as he huld þis hundred, mid gret folk and onour,
—And Adam of Arderne was is chef countour—
Hii clupede Sir Ion Giffard, þat siwte ssolde þerto,   95
To come, oþer he ssolde in þe merci be ido.
He com bi asoyne: vor is men inowe
Come out of Brumsfeld, and i-armed to hom drowe,
And asoynede hor louerd, and to grounde slowe.
Glad he was þat miȝte fle ar þat suerd is nekk gnowe.   100
Manie flowe to churche, and þe constable vnneþe
Atarnde aliue, and mani were ibroȝte to deþe.
Þis luþer bailifs, þat pouere men so gret wo doþ ilome,
Suich Giffardes asoyne, Icholde hom ofte come!

f. 157ᵛ   Wel a ȝer and an half þus it ferde aboute,   105
Þat ech heiman dude is fon ssame mid is route.
Atte laste, þo winter towarde ende drou,
At Candelmasse ech of hom gret ost nom inou;
And Sir Roger of Clifford Gloucetre wuste also,
And at ech ȝat of þe toun god warde let do.   110
Sir Ion Giffard com a day, and Sir Ion de Balun þere,
Ride vpe tueye wolpakces, chapmen as hii were,
To the west ȝate, ouer þe brugge, and þe porters bede
To late in tueie wolmongers, hor chaffare in to lede;
Biweued hii were boþe mid Welsse mantles tueie.   115
Þo þe ȝates were vndo, hii hupte adoun beye
Of hor hors, and caste hor mantles awei anon,
And þo stode hii iarmed fram heued to þe ton.
Þo were þe porters agrise sore of þulke siȝte,
And caste hom þe keyen, vawe þat hii miȝte.   120
Poer þer was inou atte brugge ende;
Þo þe ȝates were vndo, hii gonne þuder wende—

Sir Simondes sone de Monfort, Sir Henri þe hende,
And mani god bodi ek, as God þuder sende.
Þo þe barons adde þe toun, and þe castel þe king, 125
Þer was ofte bituene hom gret bikering.

Sir Edward, þat was bi este þo, mid poer gret inou,
Sone, toward Leinte, toward þe March he drou.
Is wei he nom bi Oxenford; ac þe borgeis anon
Þe ȝates made [uaste] aȝen him of þe toun echon. 130
He wende, and lai wiþoute toun, atte Kinges Halle,
And wende vorþ amorwe mid is men alle.
Þe ȝates, þo he was iwend, were alle vp ibroȝt
Sone, bote Smiþe gate, ac þat nas vndo nouȝt.
Þe clerkes adde þerþoru muche solas ilore 135
To pleye toward Beumond; anuid hii were þeruore.
Þe bailifs hii bede ofte to graunti hor solas
To pleie, and vndo þut ȝat; ac vor noȝt it was;
So þat an vewe wilde hinen a liȝt red þerof nome,
And a dai after mete wiþ axes þuder come 140
And þat ȝat tohewe and todasste þere,
And suþþe þoru Beumond to Harewelle it bere,
And *subvenite sancti* vaste gonne singe,
As me deþ wan a ded man me wole to putte bringe.
Willam þe Spicer and Geffray of Hencsei, þat þo were 145
Portreuen, and Nicole of Kingestone, þat was mere, f. 158ʳ
Nome of þis clerkes, and in prison caste,
And nolde hom nouȝt deliueri, ȝut þe chaunceler bed vaste.
Þe clerkes were þo wroþe, þe burgeis were þo bolde,
And þretnede to nime mo, and of hor wraþþe lute tolde. 150
Þe verste þorsdai in Lente, þe burgeis were wel fers,
And, þe wule men were atte mete, arerde tueie baners,
And wende hom vorþ iarmed mid al hor poer þere

127 þat] *MS.* þ 137 bailifs] *MS.* bailif; *v.*145 n. 141 todasste]
MS. to dasse

To defouli alle þe clerkes ar hii iwar were.
As hii come aȝen Alle Halwen mid poer so strong,   155
At Seinte Marie churche a clerc þe commun belle rong.
Þis clerkes vp fram hor mete, and to Godes grace truste,
And seie þat hii were issend, bote hii þe bet hom wuste.
Hii mette wiþ þis burgeis, and bigonne to ssete vaste.
Iwounded þer was mani on; ac þe borgeis atte laste   160
Hii bigonne to fle vaste, hom poȝte longe er,
So þat þe clerkes adde þe stretes sone iler.
Þe bowiares ssoppe hii breke, and þe bowes nome echon,
Suþþe þe portereues house hii sette a fure anon
In þe souþhalf of þe toune, and suþþe þe spicerie   165
Hii breke fram ende to oþer, and dude al to robberie.
Vor þe mere was viniter, hii breke þe viniterie,
And alle oþere in þe toun, and þat was lute maistrie.
Hii caste awei þe dosils, þat win orn abrod, so
Þat it was pite gret of so muche harm ido.   170
Þeruore, þo þe king com, and wuste suich trespas,
Alle þe clerkes out of þe toun he drof vor þut cas,
Ne, vort after Misselmasse, hii ne come namore þer.

XII

THE BESTIARY

No student of medieval art or thought can afford to neglect the
bestiaries, reflecting as they do the characteristic medieval view
that, in St. Bonaventure's words, 'the creatures of this sensible
world signify the invisible things of God; in part because God is
the source, exemplar, and end of every creature; in part through
their proper likeness; in part from their prophetic prefiguring
. . .'. Everything is a symbol, and the Bible and Nature explain
each other. Symbolic interpretation of beasts and birds came
easily to writers nurtured on allegorical interpretations of the
scriptures, who could cite Job xii. 7: 'Ask now the beasts, and
they shall teach thee . . .'; and the classic justification of the
method is to be found in St. Augustine's comment on Ps. cii. 5
(Vulgate), concluding: 'Nos quidquid illud significat faciemus
et quam sit verum non laboremus.' The fact that Sir Thomas
Browne understood this point of view gives special value to
his *Pseudodoxia Epidemica* as a commentary on bestiary lore.

The oddly named *Physiologus* ('one learned in natural history'),
the Latin basis of all vernacular bestiaries, probably goes back
to a fourth-century compilation of Hellenistic and Oriental
matter. This was christianized by being attached to animals,
plants, and stones mentioned in scripture (pelican, unicorn,
eagle, lion, &c.); notable qualities were transferred from the
animals possessing them to Christ or the devil; conflict between
animals was interpreted as a struggle between good and evil;
and the symbolism of numbers was exploited to the full. In the
eleventh century the Latin text was versified by a mysterious
Thetbaldus, possibly abbot of Monte Cassino, and in the
twelfth century it was greatly expanded, in England, by the
addition of material from Greek and patristic sources, while
versions in French and OHG began to appear. Hugh of St.
Victor's commentary on this enlarged text[1] is a notable example

[1] Migne, *P.L.* 177. 14 ff.

of the theological treatment of Bestiary matter, whilst much of
the natural history becomes embodied in later medieval encyclo-
paedias (e.g. Albert the Great's *De Naturalibus*). The poems in
the Exeter Book on the panther, whale, and (?) peacock testify
to English knowledge of the *Physiologus* in pre-Conquest times;
and the appearance of numerous illuminated manuscripts of it is
a feature of twelfth-century English art. But the only surviving
text in M.E. is that in B.M. MS. Arundel 292, a late thirteenth-
century miscellany, from which the following extracts are taken.
Its corrupt state suggests that it has passed through several stages
of copying: the English versifier generally follows Thetbaldus,
but was doubtless familiar with bestiary material in other versions (as Chaucer would be: cf. *C.T.* B 4460–2).

Thetbaldus uses five different metres, ranging from sapphics
to leonine hexameters (i.e. with rhyme or assonance). Philippe de
Thaon's Anglo-Norman Bestiary (early twelfth century) is in
six-syllabled rhyming couplets for the greater part, but then
suddenly changes to eight syllables 'pur ma raisun mielz
ordener'. Similarly the English version uses a mixture of the
long alliterative line (sometimes with rhyme) and syllabic verse
(cf. ll. 1–9 below).

Natura aquile

KIÐEN I wille ðe ernes kinde,
Also Ic it o boke rede:
Wu he neweð his guðhede,
Hu he cumeð ut of elde,
Siðen hise limes arn unwelde,   5
Siðen his bec is alto wrong,
Siðen his fligt is al unstrong,
f. 4ᵛ   And his egen dimme.
Hereð wu he neweð him:
A welle he sekeð ðat springeð ai,   10
Boðe bi nigt and bi dai;

8 *MS. 7 is expanded as* and *passim*

Ðerouer he flegeð, and up he teð
Til ðat he ðe heuene seð—
Ðurg skies sexe and seuene,
Til he cumeð to heuene.   15
So rigt so he cunne
He houeð in ðe sunne.
Ðe sunne swideð al his fligt,
And oc it makeð his egen brigt.
His feðres fallen for ðe hete,   20
And he dun mide to ðe wete;
Falleð in ðat welle-grund
Ðer he wurdeð heil and sund,
And cumeð ut al newe,
Ne were his bec untrewe: 25
His bec is get biforn wrong,
Ðog hise limes senden strong;
Ne maig he tilen him non fode
Himself to none gode.
Ðanne goð he to a ston   30
And he billeð ðeron,
Billeð til his bec biforn
Haueð ðe wrengðe forloren;
Siðen wið his rigte bile
Takeð mete ðat he wile.   35

Significacio

Al is man so is tis ern   36
    —Wulde ge nu listen—
Old in hise sinnes dern
    Or he bicumeð Cristen.
And tus he neweð him ðis man,   40
    Ðanne he nimeð to kirke.

Or he it biðenken can
  His egen weren mirke.
Forsaket ðore Satanas
  And ilk sinful dede;   45
Takeð him to Iesu Crist,
  For he sal ben his mede;
Leueð on ure Louerd Crist,
  And lereð prestes lore.
Of his egen wereð ðe mist   50
  Wiles he drecceð ðore—
His hope is al to Gode ward,
  And of his luue he lereð:
Ðat is te sunne sikerlike,
  Ðus his sigte he beteð.   55
Naked falleð in ðe funt-fat,
  And cumeð ut al newe;
Buten a litel wat is tat
  His muð is get untrewe:
His muð is get wel unkuð   60
  Wið paternoster and crede.
Fare he norð er fare he suð,
  Leren he sal his nede;
Bidden bone to Gode,
  And tus his muð rigten;   65
Tilen him so ðe sowles fode

f. 5ʳ   Ðurg grace off ure Drigtin.

Natura formice

f. 5ᵛ   Ðe mire is magti; mikel ge swinkeð
In sumer and in softe weder, so we ofte sen hauen.
In ðe heruest hardilike gangeð,   70

48 Louerd] *MS.* loued

And renneð rapelike, and resteð hire seldum,
And fecheð hire fode ðer ge it mai finden.
Gaddreð ilkines sed,
Boðen of wude and of wed,
Of corn and of gres,   75
Ðat hire to hauen es.
Haleð to hire hole ðat siðen hire helpeð,
Ðar ge wile ben
Winter agen: f. 6ʳ
Caue ge haueð to crepen in, ðat winter hire ne derie;
Mete in hire hule ðat ge muge bi liuen.   81
Ðus ge tileð ðar wiles ge time haueð
—So it her telleð.
Oc finde ge ðe wete, corn ðat hire qwemeð
Al ge forleteð ðis oðer sed ðat Ic er seide,   85
Ne bit ge nowt ðe barlic beren abuten,
Oc suneð it and sakeð forð so it same were.
Get is wunder of ðis wirm more ðanne man weneð:
Ðe corn ðat ge to caue bereð al get bit otwinne,
Ðat it ne forwurðe, ne waxe hire fro,   90
Er ge it eten wille.

Significacio

Ðe mire muneð us mete to tilen—
Long liuenoðe ðis little wile
Ðe we on ðis werld wunen.
For ðanne we of wenden, ðanne is ure winter.   95
We sulen hunger hauen, and harde sures,
Buten we ben war here.
Do we forði so doð ðis der —ðanne be we derue,
On ðat dai ðat dom sal ben, ðat it ne us harde rewe.
Seke we ure liues fod, ðat we ben siker ðere,   100

76 hire] *MS.* Ire   81 hule ðat ge] *MS.* hule ðat ðat ge

So ðis wirm in winter is, ðan ge ne tileð nummore.
Ðe mire suneð ðe barlic ðanne ge fint te wete:
Ðe olde lage we ogen to sunen, ðe newe we hauen moten.
Ðe corn ðat ge to caue bereð, all ge it bit otwinne:
Ðe lage us lereð to don god, and forbedeð us sinne.   105
It bet us eröliche bodes and bekneð euelike.
It fet ðe licham and te gost, oc nowt o geuelike.
Vre Louerd Crist it lene us ðat his lage us fede
Nu and o Domesdei and tanne we hauen nede.

Natura cerui ii^a

f. 6ᵛ   Ðe hertes hauen anoðer kinde   110
Ðat us og alle to ben minde.
Alle he arn off one mode;
For if he fer fecchen fode,
And he ouer water ten,
Wile non at nede oðer flen;   115
Oc on swimmeð biforn
And alle ðe oðre folegen,
Weðer so he swimmeð er he wadeð.
Is non at nede ðat oðer lateð,
Oc leigeð his skinbon   120
On oðres lendbon.
Gef him ðat biforn teð bilimpes forto tirgen,
Alle ðe oðre cumen mide, and helpen him forto herien.
Beren him of ðat water-grund
Up to ðe lond al heil and sund,   125
And forðen here nede.
Ðis wune he hauen hem bitwen,
Ðog he an hundred togiddre ben.

106 bet us eröliche] *MS.* ben us ebriche   bekneð] *MS.* bekned

Significacio ii^a

Ðe hertes costes we ogen to munen:
Ne og ur non oðer to sunen,   130
Oc eurilc luuen oðer
Also he were his broder,
Wurðen stedefast his wine,   f. 7^r
Ligten him of his birdene,
Helpen him at his nede;   135
God giueð ðerfore mede:
We sulen hauen heuenriche
Gef we bitwixen us ben briche.
Ðus is ure Louerdes lage luuelike to fillen;
Herof haue we mikel ned ðat we ðarwið ne dillen.   140

Natura cetegrandie

Cethegrande is a fis
Ðe moste ðat in water is,
Ðat ðu wuldes seien get,   f. 8^r
Gef ðu it soge wan it flet,
Ðat it were a neilond   145
Ðat sete one ðe se-sond.
Ðis fis ðat is vnride,
Ðanne him hungreð he gapeð wide;
Vt of his ðrote it smit an onde,
Ðe swetteste ðing ðat is o londe.   150
Ðerfore oðre fisses to him dragen.
Wan he it felen he aren fagen;
He cumen and houen in his muð;
Of his swike he arn uncuð.
Ðis cete ðanne his chaueles lukeð,   155
Ðise fisses alle in sukeð.

138 bitwixen] *MS.* ben twixen

Ðe smale he wile ðus biswiken;
Ðe grete maig he nogt bigripen.
Ðis fis wuneð wið ðe se-grund,
And liueð ðer eure heil and sund   160
Til it cumeð ðe time
Ðat storm stireð al ðe se:
Ðanne sumer and winter winnen
Ne mai it wunen ðerinne;
So droui is te sees grund   165
Ne mai he wunen ðer ðat stund,
Oc stireð up and houeð stille
Wiles ðat weder is so ille.
Ðe sipes ðat arn on se fordriuen,
Loð hem is ded and lef to liuen;   170
Biloken hem, and sen ðis fis,
A neilond he wenen it is.
Ðerof he aren swiðe fagen,
And mid here migt ðarto he dragen,
Sipes on festen   175
And alle up gangen,
Of ston mid stel in ðe tunder
Wel to brennen one ðis wunder;
Warmen hem wel, and heten and drinken.
Ðe fir he feleð, and doð hem sinken: 180
For sone he diueð dun to grunde.
He drepeð hem alle wiðuten wunde.

Significacio

Ðis deuel is mikel wið wil and magt,
So witches hauen in here craft.
He doð men hungren and hauen ðrist,   185
And mani oðer sinful list;

Tolleð men to him wið his onde.
Woso him folegeð he findeð sonde:
Ðo arn ðe little, in leue lage.
Ðe mikle ne maig he to him dragen: 190
Ðe mikle I mene ðe stedefast
In rigte leue mid fles and gast.
Woso listneð deueles lore
On lengðe it sal him rewen sore.
Woso festeð hope on him   195
He sal him folgen to helle dim.

XIII

ORMULUM

'THE Ormulum. A manuscript of metrical English sermons composed and phonetically written by a priest named Orm in the East Midlands late in the 12th century.' So runs the notice accompanying MS. Junius 1 when it is displayed in the Bodleian library; and the modern editor accepts this as an accurate statement of present knowledge and conjecture about this singularly ugly and untidy narrow folio. Except for some corrections it appears to be an autograph. Its 20,000 lines probably represent about one-eighth of the work as planned. Its literary merits are few: tedious repetitions (cf. ll. 50–60), cumbersome conjunctions and otiose adverbs characterize Orm's style, and the monotony of the language is equalled by the regularity of the verse line, which, as Orm says in the dedication to his brother Walter, an Augustinian canon, is often padded:

> Shollde Icc well offte nede
> Amang Goddspelless wordess don
> Min word, min ferrs to fillenn.

Yet his motives were unexceptionable: to set forth Christian teaching as found in the Gospels of the Mass throughout the year, so that all English folk should understand it. Freakish as his text looks at first sight, his purpose is not essentially different from that of Ælfric in his *Catholic Homilies*. There was surely a place for such a compilation, and even for Orm's strict phonetic spelling principles. The regular stress rhythm suggests that he may have intended the work to be intoned.

'þiss boc iss nemmnedd Orrmulum Forrþi þatt Orrm itt wrohhte' is the first line of the Preface. Orm is a Scandinavian name found in the old Danelaw area and as far west as Staffordshire. The name of the book is probably modelled on *Speculum* (*Ecclesiae*, &c.)—a form of title that came into vogue in the twelfth century. Henry Bradley suggested that the writer may have been an Augustinian monk at Elsham Priory in north Lincolnshire. The large Scandinavian element in the vocabulary would support a location of the text in that area—though it also

contains 'a surprisingly large number of words that are otherwise
nearly peculiar to western texts'.

¶ An Romanisshe kaserr-kinᵹ   f. 32ᵛ
    Wass Auᵹusstuss ᵹehatenn,   (col. 83)
  Annd he wass wurrþenn kaserr-kinᵹ
    Off all mannkinn onn erþe,
  Annd he ᵹann þennkenn off himmsellf,   5
    Annd off hiss miccle riche.
  Annd he biᵹann to þennkenn þa,
    Swa summ þe ᵹoddspell kiþeþþ,
  Off þatt he wollde witenn wel
    Hu mikell fehh himm come,   10
  ᵹiff himm off all hiss kinedom   col. 84
    Illc mann an peninnᵹ ᵹæfe.
  Annd he badd settenn upp o writt,
    All mannkinn forr to lokenn,
  Hu mikell fehh he mihhte swa   15
    Off all þe werelld sammnenn,
  Þurrh þatt himm shollde off illc an mann
    An peninᵹ wurrþenn reccnedd.
¶ Annd ta wass sett tatt iwhillc mann,
    Whær summ he wære o lande,   20
  Ham shollde wendenn to þatt tun
    Þatt he wass borenn inne,
  Annd tatt he shollde þær forr himm
    Hiss hæfedd-peninnᵹ reccnenn,
  Swa þatt he ᵹæn þe kaserr-kinᵹ   25
    Ne felle nohht i wíte.
¶ Annd i þatt illke time wass
    Iosæp wiþþ Sannte Marᵹe
  I ᵹalilew, annd i þatt tun
    Þatt Nazaræþ wass nemmnedd.   30

    3 *MS.* 7 *is expanded as* annd *passim*

Annd ta ðeȝȝ baþe forenn ham
   Till þeȝȝre baþre kinde;
Inntill þe land off Ȝerrsalæm
   Þeȝȝ forenn samenn baþe,
Annd comenn inn till Beþþleæm,   35
   Till þeȝȝre baþre birde—
Þær wass hemm baþe birde to,
   Forr þatt teȝȝ baþe wærenn
Off Dauiþþ kinȝess kinnessmenn,
   Swa summ þe ȝoddspell kiþeþþ.   40
Annd Dauiþþ kinȝess birde wass
   I Beþþleæmess chesstre;
Annd hemm wass baþe birde þær
   Þurrh Dauiþþ kinȝess birde;
Forr þatt teȝȝ baþe wærenn off   45
   Dauiþess kinn annd sibbe.
¶ Annd Sannte Marȝess time wass
   Þatt ȝho þa shollde childenn,
Annd tær ȝho barr Allmahhtiȝ Ȝodd
   Ðatt all þiss werelld wrohhte,   50
Annd wand himm sone i winnde-clũt,
   Annd leȝȝde himm inn an cribbe;
Forr þi þatt ȝho ne wisste whær
   Ȝho mihhte himm don i bure.
¶ Annd tohh þatt Ȝodd wass borenn þær   55
   Swa dærnelike onn erþe,
Annd wundenn þær swa wreccheliȝ
   Wiþþ clutess inn an cribbe,
Ne wollde he nohht forrholenn ben
   Þohhwheþþre i þeȝȝre clutess,   60
Acc wollde shæwenn whatt he wass
   Þurrh hefennlike takenn.

46 kinn] *MS*. kin   62 hefennlike] *MS*. hefenlike

¶ Forr sone anan affterr þatt he
  Wass borenn þær to manne,
Þær-onnfasst i þatt illke land   65
  Wass seȝhenn mikell takenn.
¶ An ennȝell comm off heffness ærd,
  Inn aness weress hewe,
Till hirdess þær þær þeȝȝ þatt nihht
  Biwokenn þeȝȝre faldess.   70
Þatt ennȝell comm annd stod hemm bi
  Wiþþ heffness lihht annd leme.
Annd forrþrihht summ þeȝȝ sæȝhenn himm,
  Þeȝȝ wurrdenn swiðe offdredde;
Annd Ȝodess ennȝell hemm biȝann   75
  To frofrenn annd to beldenn,
Annd seȝȝde hemm þuss o Ȝodess hallf
  Wiþþ swiþe milde spæche:
'Ne be ȝe nohht forrdredde off me,
  Acc be ȝe swiþe bliþe,   80
Forr Icc amm sennd off heffness ærd
  To kiþenn Ȝodess wille,
To kiþenn ȝuw þatt all follc iss
  Nu cumenn mikell blisse.
Forr ȝuw iss borenn nu todaȝȝ   85
  Hælennde off ȝure sinness,
An wennchell þatt iss Iesu Crist,
  Þatt wïte ȝe to soþe.
Annd her-onnfasst he borenn iss
  I Dauiþþ kinȝess chesstre,   90
Þatt iss ȝehatenn Beþþleæm
  I þiss Iudisskenn birde.
¶ Annd her Icc wile shæwenn ȝuw
  Summ þing to witerr tákenn:
Ȝe shulenn findenn ænne child   95

I winnde-clutess wundenn,
    Annd itt iss inn a cribbe leȝȝd,
      Annd tær ȝët muȝhenn findenn.'
¶ Annd sone anan se þiss wass seȝȝd
    Þurrh an off Ȝodess enngless,   100
A mikell hĕre off enngle-þed
    Wass cumenn ŭt off heffne,
Annd all þatt hirde-flocc hemm sahh
    Annd herrde whatt teȝȝ sunȝenn.

Þeȝȝ alle sunȝenn ænne sang   105
    Drihhtin to lofe annd wurrþe,
Annd tuss þeȝȝ sunȝenn alle imæn,
    Swa summ þe ȝoddspell kiþeþþ:
'Si Drihhtin upp inn heffness ærd
    Wurrþminnt annd loff annd wullderr,   110
Annd upponn erþe ȝriþþ annd friþþ,
    Þurrh Ȝodess mildherrtnesse,
Till iwhillc mann þatt habbenn shall
    Ȝod herrte annd aȝȝ ȝod wille.'
¶ Annd sone anan se þiss wass þær   115
    Þurrh Ȝodess enngless awwnedd,
Þeȝȝ wenndenn fra þa wăke-menn
    All ŭt off þeȝȝre sihhþe.

Þa hirdess tokenn sone þuss
    To spekenn hemm bitwenenn: 120
'Ȝa we nu till þatt illke tun
    Þatt Beþþleæm iss nemmnedd,
Annd loke we þatt illke word
    Þatt iss nu wrohht onn erþe,
Þatt Drihhtin Ȝodd uss hafeþþ wrohht   125
    Annd awwnedd þurrh hiss are.'
Annd sone anan ðeȝȝ ȝedenn forþ

Till Beþþleæmess chesstre,
Annd fundenn Sannte Marȝe þær
   Annd Iosæp hire macche, 130
Annd ec þeȝȝ fundenn þær þe child
   Þær itt wass leȝȝd i cribbe.
Annd ta þeȝȝ unnderrstodenn wel
   Þatt word tatt Ȝodess ennȝless
Hemm haffdenn awwnedd off þatt child 135
   Þatt teȝȝ þær haffdenn fundenn.
Annd ta þeȝȝ wenndenn hemm onnȝæn
   Wiþþ rihhte læfe o Criste,
Annd tokenn innwarrdlike Ȝodd
   To lofenn annd to þannkenn 140
All þatt teȝȝ haffdenn herrd off himm,
   Annd seȝhenn þurrh hiss are.
Annd sone anan þeȝȝ kiddenn forþ
   Amang Iudisskenn þede
All þatt teȝȝ haffdenn herrd off Crist, 145
   Annd seȝhenn wel wiþþ eȝhne.
Annd iwhillc mann þatt herrde itt ohht
   Forrwunndredd wass þæroffe.
¶ Annd ure laffdiȝ Marȝe toc
   All þatt ȝho sahh annd herrde, 150
Annd all ȝhŏt held inn hire þohht,
   Swa summ þe ȝoddspell kiþeþþ,
Annd leȝȝde itt all to-samenn aȝȝ
   I swiþe þohhtfull herrte,
All þatt ȝho sahh annd herrde off Crist, 155
   Whas moderr ȝho wass wurrþenn.

Annd o þatt illke nahht tatt Crist
   Wass borenn her to manne,
Wass he ȝĕt, alls hiss wille wass,

Awwnedd onn oþerr wise.   160

He sette a sterrne upp o þe lifft
  Full brad, annd brihht, annd shene,
Onn æsthallf off þiss middellærd,
  Swa summ þe ȝoddspell kiþeþþ,
Amang þatt follc þatt cann innsihht   165
  Off maniȝ þing þurrh sterrness.
Amang þe Calldewisshe þed
  Þatt cann innsihht o sterrness.

¶ Annd tatt þed wass hæþene þed
  Þatt Crist ȝaff þa swillc tákenn;   170
Forr þi þatt he þeȝȝm wollde þa
  To rihhte læfe wendenn.

¶ Annd son se þeȝȝ þatt sterrne-lem
  Þær sæȝhenn upp o liffte,
Þre kingess off þatt illke land   175
  Full wel itt unnderrstodenn,
Annd wisstenn witerrliȝ þærþurrh
  Ðatt swillc new king wass awwnedd,
Þatt wass soþ ȝodd annd soþ mann ec,
  An had off twinne kinde.   180
All þiss þeȝȝ unnderrstodenn wel
  Forr þatt itt ȝodd hemm úþe,

f. 33ᵛ
(col. 87)

Annd cómenn samenn alle þre,
  Annd settenn hemm bitwenenn,
Þatt illc an shollde þrinne lac   185
  Habbenn wiþþ himm o lade,
Annd tatt teȝȝ sholldenn farenn forþ
  To leȝȝtenn annd to sekenn
Þatt newe king þatt borenn wass
  Amanȝ Iudisskenn þede.   190
Annd sone anan þeȝȝ forenn forþ
  Illc an wiþþ þrinne lakess,

Forr þatt ta lakess sholldenn uss
  Well mikell Ᵹod bitacnenn.
Annd teᴣᴣre sterrne wass wiþþ hemm.   195
  To ledenn hemm þe weᴣᴣe,
Forr aᴣᴣ itt flǽt upp i þe lifft
  Biforenn hemm a litell,
To tæchenn hemm þatt weᴣᴣe rihht
  Þatt ledde hemm towarrd Criste.   200
Acc fra þatt Kalldewisshe land
  Þatt teᴣᴣ þa comenn offe,
Wass mikell weᴣᴣe till þatt land
  Ðatt Crist wass borenn inne.
Annd forr þi wass hemm ned to don   205
  Ᵹod þraᴣhe to þatt weᴣᴣe,
Forr rihht onn hiss þrittende daᴣᴣ
  Þeᴣᴣ comenn till þatt chesstre
Þær ure Laferrd Iesu Crist
  Wass borenn her to manne.   210
¶ Þuss wass þe Laferrd Iesu Crist
  Awwnedd o twinne wise
Forrþrihht anan, i þatt tatt he
  Wass borenn her to manne,
Forr þatt menn sholldenn cnawenn himm   215
  Annd lofenn himm annd wurrþenn,
Annd cumenn till þe Crisstenndom
  Annd till þe rihhte læfe,
Annd winnenn swa to cumenn upp
  Till hefennrichess blisse.   220

¶ Her endenn twa ᵹoddspelless þuss,
  Annd uss birrþ hemm þurrhsekenn
To lokenn whatt teᴣᴣ lærenn uss
  Off ure sawle nede.

Forrþrihht anan se time comm   225
  Þatt ure Drihhtin wollde
Ben borenn i þiss middellærd
  Forr all mannkinne nede,
He chæs himm sone kinnessmenn
  All swillke summ he wollde,   230
Annd whær he wollde borenn ben
  He chæs all att hiss wille.
Annd alls hiss lefe wille wass,
  Hiss moderr Sannte Márȝe
Comm rihht inntill þatt illke tun   235
  Annd till þatt illke bottle
Þatt he wollde inne borenn ben
  Annd awwnedd her onn erþe.

col. 88
Annd forr þi þatt maȝȝþhadess lif
  Iss heȝhesst allre life,   240
Forr þi chæs ure Laferrd Crist
  An maȝȝdenn himm to moderr,
Forr þatt he lufeþþ alle þa
  Þatt soþ clænnesse follȝhenn.

¶ Annd forr þatt he wass borenn her   245
  Sahhtnesse annd griþþ to settenn
Bitwenenn Drihhtin, heffness king,
  Annd mannkinn her onn erþe,
Forr þi chæs he to wurrþenn mann
  O þatt keȝȝseress time   250
Þatt held wiþþ mikell griþþ annd friþþ
  Hiss kinedom onn erþe.

¶ Annd forr þatt he wass wurrþenn mann
  To ȝifenn menn onn erþe
Hiss aȝhenn hallȝhe flæsh annd blod,   255
  Soþ bræd to þeȝȝre sawle,
Forr þi chæs he þatt illke tun

To wurrþenn borenn inne
Þatt wass ȝehatenn Beþþleæm,
    Forr þi þatt itt bitacneþþ   260
Þatt hus þatt bræd iss inne don,
    Annd tatt iss Cristess kirrke.
Forr Cristess flæsh annd Cristess blod
    Iss hallȝhedd inn hiss kirrke,
Forr þær to wurrþenn lifess bræd   265
    Till alle Cristess þewwess.
Annd all allswa se þa wass sett
    Þurrh þatt kaseress hæse
Þatt illc mann shollde cumenn ham
    Inn till hiss aȝhenn birde,   270
Forr þær to reccnenn till þe kinȝ
    An peninȝ forr himm sellfenn,
Annd tatt mann shollde hiss name þær
    Att hame o wrïte settenn,
All allswa biddeþþ ure kinȝ,   275
    Þe Laferrd Crist off heffne,
Þatt illc mann shule cumenn ham
    Inn till hiss aȝhenn birde,
Þatt iss inn till rihht Crisstenndom,
    Annd inn till rihhte læfe,   280
Inn till þatt soþfasstnessess ham
    Þatt mann wass shapenn inne,
Annd reccnenn himm þatt peninȝ þær
    Þatt tacneþþ rihhtwisnesse.
Annd he shall wrïtenn alle þa   285
    Þatt cwemmdenn himm o life
Onn eche lifess bokess writt
    To brukenn heffness blisse.

       281 Inn] *MS.* In

XIV

CURSOR MUNDI

THE work from which the extract below is taken is a monumental treatment (in 30,000 lines) of the spiritual history of man, from the Creation to the Day of Judgement. As the author says of the book:

> Cursur o werld man aght it call,
> For almast it ouer-rennes all.
>
> (267–8)

The history of the wood from which the Cross was made was presented in two main forms (here called A and B) in the middle ages. A is represented in ME by a homily in the collection (mostly post-Conquest transcriptions of OE homilies) in MS. Bodl. 343, and by versions in Latin, OF, MDu, and in *Cursor Mundi*.[1] B is embodied in the M.E. *History of the Rood-tree*, the *Canticum de Creatione*, a version in *The South English Legendary*, and others in German, Swedish, Icelandic, Italian, Cornish, and Irish. A similar distinction applies to the medieval Latin works from which both these groups derive (immediately or otherwise): they are known as the *Historia* and the *Legend* respectively. But the early history of the wood of the Cross, beginning with Seth's expedition to Paradise, has been interpolated into some works of the A group (including *Cursor Mundi*) either from the Latin *Legend* or from the Latin *Vita Adae et Euae* (composed before 700). In whichever main form, the comprehensive story of the Cross had its growth between the twelfth and the fourteenth centuries, except that the ME *History of the Rood-tree* is likely to derive from an eleventh-century OE antecedent.

In the oldest A version, the tree (the history of which here

[1] Ll. 1237–1432 (the section B printed below); 6301–68, 6659–66, 6937–46, 7973–8978, 15961 ff., 16543 ff., 16861 ff., and 21347 ff.

begins with Solomon) has three leaves (a symbolic reference to the Trinity). An interpolation in the Windberg MS. of Honorius' *De Imagine Mundi* adds two important points, that (*a*) the wood of the Cross came from Paradise, and (*b*) the angel of God placed a seed of the forbidden tree in Adam's mouth just before his burial. The origin of the latter statement is unknown.

Next, according to Jean Beleth, in an account of *c.* 1170,[1] Adam sent his son (unnamed) to Paradise, and the latter brought back a branch, given him by an angel, which grew into a great tree from which eventually the Cross was made. This is based on the *Vita Adae et Euae*, in which Adam sends Seth to Paradise to fetch the oil of mercy and alleviate his sufferings.

Finally, *c.* 1180, Godfrey of Viterbo, elaborating on the *Historia* or A group, recounts in his *Pantheon* xiv[2] that Ionitus, one of the sons of Noah, goes to Paradise and brings back three plants (fir, palm, and cypress), which grow together with one bark and a triple form of leaves.

These are the elements which were combined in the framework of the Seth episode in the Latin *Legend*, which is faithfully reproduced in the ME version below. But four of the most effective features of the story are not traceable earlier, and are therefore probably innovations characterizing the *Legend* (and the B group after it): they are the withered tracks left by Adam and Eve on their departure from Paradise, and the three visions of Seth. The 'oil of mercy' derives immediately from the Latin *Vita Adae et Euae*, and goes back to a very ancient treatment of the story of Adam, which was probably composed by a Jew in pre-Christian times.[3]

A

MAN yhernes rimes forto here   **f.** 2ʳ 1
And romans red on manere sere—

---

[1] *De exaltatione sanctae crucis*, in his *Rationale divinorum officiorum* (Migne, *P.L.* ccii).

[2] Ed. Pistorius and Struve, *Germanicorum Scriptorum Tomus Alter*, 346.

[3] See W. Meyer, *Vita Adae et Evae* (*Abhandlungen der philosophisch-philologischen Classe der königlich bayerischen Akademie der Wissenschaften*, xiv, iii (München 1878), 202–28).

Of Alisaundur þe conquerour,
Of Iuly Cesar þe emparour;
O Grece and Troy þe strang striif,   5
Þere many thosand lesis þer liif;
O Brut, þat bern bald of hand,
Þe first conquerour of Ingland;
O Kyng Arthour þat was so rike,
Quam non in hys tim was like,   10
O ferlys þat hys knythes fell,
Þat aunters sere I here of tell,
Als Wawan, Cai and oþer stabell,
Forto were þe Ronde Tabell;
How Charles kyng and Rauland faght—   15
Wit Sarazins wald þai na saght;
O Tristrem and hys leif, Ysote,
How he for here becom a sote;
O Ioneck and of Ysambrase,
O Ydoine and of Amadase;   20
Storis als o serekin thinges—
O princes, prelates, and o kynges;
Sanges sere of selcuth rime,
Inglis, Frankys, and Latine.
To rede and here ilkon is prest   25
Þe thynges þat þam likes best.
Þe wisman wil o wisdom here—
Þe foul hym draghus to foly nere.
Þe wrang to here o right is lath,
And pride wyt buxsumnes is wrath.   30
O chastite has lichur leth;
On charite ai werrais wreth.

---

14 For] F *illegible*   15 How] H *illegible*   16 Wit] *illegible*
17 O] *illegible*   18 How] Ho *illegible*   21 serekin] *MS.*
ferekin

Bot be the fruit may scilwis se
O quat vertu is ilka tre:
Of alkyn fruit þat man schal fynd 35
He fettes fro þe rote his kynd.
O gode per-tre coms god peres—
Wers tre, vers fruit it beres.
Þat I speke o þis ilke tre
Bytakens, man, both me and þe. 40
Þis fruit bitakens alle our dedis—
Both gode and ille, qua rightly redis.
Ovr dedis fro vr hert tas rote,
Quedur þai be worth or bale or bote;
For be þe thyng man drawes till 45 f. 2ʳ 2
Men schal him knaw for god or ill.
A saumpul her be þaem I say
Þat rages in þare riot ay—
In riot and in rigolage
Of all þere liif spend þai þe stage. 50
For now is halden non in curs
Bot qua þat luue can par amurs;
Þat foly luue, þat uanite—
Þam likes now nan oþer gle.
Hit ne ys bot fantum forto say: 55
Today it is, tomoru away.
Wyt chaunce of ded, or chaunce of hert,
Þat soft began has endyng smart;
For wen þow traistest wenis at be,
Fro hir schalt þou, or scho fro þe. 60
He þat tiithest wenis at stand,
Warre hym! his fall is nexst his hand.

---

42 Both gode and] *illegible*   qua] *illegible*   43 Ovr dedis] Ovr
de *illegible*   vr] *illegible; perhaps* þe   44 Quedur] Que *illegible*
second or] *illegible*   46 knaw] *MS.* kaw   59 traistest] *MS.* traistes

Ar he sua brathly don be broght,
Wydur to wende ne wat he noght,
Bytuixand his luf haf hym ledd　　　　　　65
To sli mede als he him forwit. . . .
(For þan sal mede witoten mer
Be mette for dede, or bettur or wer.)
Forþi blisce I þat paramour
Quen I haue nede me dos socure,　　　　　70
Þat saues me first in herth fra syn
And heuen-blys me helps to wyn.
For þof I quilum haf ben untrew,
Hir luue is ay ilik new;
Hir luue sco haldes lele ilike　　　　　　75
Þat suetter es þan hony o bike.
Suilk in herth es fundun nan,
For scho es modur and maiden—
Modur, and maiden neuer þe lesse;
Forþi of hir tok Crist his flesse.　　　　　80
Qua truly loues þis lemman,
Þis es þe loue bes neuer gan;
For in þis loue scho failes neuer,
And in þat toþer scho lastes euer.
Of suilk an suld ȝe mater take,　　　　　85
Crafty þat can rimes make,
Of hir to mak bath rim and sang
And luue hir suette sun amang!
Quat bote is to sette traueil
On thyng þat may not auail,　　　　　　90

f. 3ʳ 1

Þat es bot fantum o þis warld,
Als ȝe haue sene inogh and herd?

---

66 forwit] it *illegible*　　　　69 I] *MS.* ⁊ (*abbreviation for* and)
78 maiden] *penultimate letter smudged and illegible*　　　84 euer]
illegible　　　85 mater] *illegible*

Mater fynd ȝe large and brade,
Þof rimes fele of hir be made.
Quasa will of hyr fayrnes spell,   95
Find he sal inogh to tell.
Of hir godnes and hir treuthede
Men may fynd euermar to rede;
O reut, o luue, and charite
Was neuer hir mak, ne neuer sal be.   100

B

Adam had pasid nine hundret yere—   f. 8ᵛ 1
Nai selcut þof he wex vnfere!
Forwroght wit his hak and spad,   f. 8ᵛ 2
Of himself he wex al sad.
He lened him þan apon his hak--   105
Wit Seth his sun þusgat he spak:
'Sun,' he said, 'þou most now ga
To Paradis, þat I com fra,
Til Cherubin, þat þe yate ward.'
'Yai, sir, wist I wyderward   110
Þat tat vncuth contre ware—
Þou wat þat I was neuer þare!'
Þus he said: 'I sal þe sai
Howgate þou sal tak þe wai.
Toward þe est end of þis dale   115
Find a grene gate þou sale.
In þat way sal þou find, forsoth,
Þi moders and mine (our bather) slogh,
Foluand thoru þat gresse gren
Þat euer has siþen ben gren   120

95 *MS.* hy farnes

Þat we com wendand als vnwis
Quen we war put o Paradis—
Vnto þis wretched warld slade—
Þar I first me self was made.
Thoru þe gretnes of our sin   125
Moght na gres groue siþen þarin;
Þe falau slogh sal be þi gate
O Paradis right to þe yate.'
'Fader,' he said, 'sai me þi will:
Quat sal I sai þat angel till?'   130
'Þou sal him tell I am vnfere,
For I haue liued so mani a yere
Ai in striif and soruuing stad
Þat o mi liif I am al sad.
Þou prai him þat he word me send   135
Quen I sal o þis werld wend.
Anoþer erand sal þar be—
Þat he wald send me word wit þe
Quedir þat I sal haue it in hii
Þe oile me was hight o merci,   140
Þe tim þat I lest Paradis.
Well I knau now mi foliis:
Again Godds wil haue I wroght.
And þat sumdel haue I now boght—
Mi soru has ai siþen ben neu;   145
Nou war it time o me to reu.'

Seth went him forth witouten nai
To Paradis þat ilk way.
Þe slogth he fand þat him gan wiss
Tilward þe ȝate of Paradis.   150
Quen he þarof son had a sight

f. 9ʳ 1

133 soruuing] *MS.* soruning   151 he] *not in MS.*

Al was he gloppend for þat light:
Þe mikel light þat he sagh þar
A brennand fire he wend it ware.
He senid him, als his fader badd,   155
And ȝode forth and was noght raidd.
Þis angel at þe ȝatte he fand
And asked him of his errand.
Seth þen sette him spell o nend
And tald him warfor þat he was send—   160
Tald him of his fader care
(Als he him taght, sum yee herd are),
To send him word wen he suld dei
(To liue moght he na langar drei)
And wen þat Drightin had him tight   165
To send him þe oile þat he him hight.
Quen Cherubin þis errand herd
Mikelik he him answard:
'Ga to þe ȝatte,' he said, 'and lote—
Þi hed inwar, þi self witoutte—   170
And tent to thinges at þi might
Þat sal be sceud vnto þi sight.'
Quen Seth a quil had loked in,
He sagh sua mikel welth and win
It es in erth na tung may tell   175
Þat flour, þat frutte, þat suette smell—
O blis and ioy sua mani thing.
Inmiddes þe land he sagh a spring
Of a well þat es vtenemes,
Þat oute of ran four gret stremmes: 180
Gyson, Fison, Tigre, Eufrate—
Þis four mas al þis erth wate.

155 senid] *MS.* seuid   156 raidd] *or* raadd   165 Drightin]
MS. drightim

Out-ouer þat well þan lokes he
And sagh þar stand a mikel tre
Wit braunches fel, o bark al bare—   185
Was þar na leue on, less na mare.
Seth bigan to thinc for qui
Þat þis tre bicom sua dri;
O þe steppes vmthoght he þan
Þat welud war for sin of man.   190
Þat ilk schil did him to min
Þis tre was dri for Adam sin.

He com þan to þat angel scene
And sceud him al þat he had sene;
Quen he his sight al had him tald,   195
He badd him eft ga to behald.
He loked in eft and stod þeroute
And sagh þe thing þat gart him doute:
Þis tre, þat I of forwit said,
A neddur hit hade al vmbilaid.   200

Cherubin, þat angel blyth,
Bad him ga lok þe thrid syth.
Þis tre was of a mikel heght:
Him thoght þan, at þe thrid sight,
Þat to þe sky it raght þe toppe.   205
A newborn barn lay in þe croppe
Bondon wit a sueþelband—
Þar (him thoght) it lay sueland.
He was al ferd wen he þat sei,
And to þe rotte he kest his he: 210
Him thoght it raght fra erth til hell,
Quare-vnder he sagh his broþer Abell.

190 þat] *MS.* þeit *or* þert   208 *MS.* suelland, *with second* l
subpuncted

In his saul he sagh him þare
Þat Caim slogh forwit ful o care.
He went agayn þan forto scau   215
To Cherubin al þat he sau.
Cherubin, wit chere sa milde,
Bigan to tel him o þat child.
'Þis barn,' he said, 'þat þou has sene
Is Goddes sun, witouten wene.   220
Þi fader sin now wepes he
Þat he sal clens sum time sal be,
Quen þe plenteʒ sal cum o time:
Þis is þe oile þat was hight him—
Til him and til his progeni—   225
Wit pite sal sceu his merci.'
Quen Seth had vnderstanden wele
Þat angel said him ilk dele,
His leue wald tak at Cherubin.
Pepins þen he gaue him thrin,   230
Þe quilk a þe appel-tre he nam
Þat his fader ete of, Adam.
'Þi fader', he said, 'þan sal þou say
Þat he sal dei þe thrid day
Efter þat þou be commun ham,   235
And als he was turn into lam.
Bot þou sal tak þis pepins thre
Þat I toke o þat appel-tre,
And do þam vnder his tong-rote.
Þai sal til mani man be bote: 240
Þai sal be cedre, ciprese, and pine—   f. 9ᵛ 1
O þam sal man haue medicen.
Þe fader in cedre þou sal take—
A tre of heght þat has na make.

240 til] il *illegible;* o *in different ink above it*

And cipres, be þe suete sauur,   245
Bitakens ur suete sauueur—
Þe mikel suetnes þat es þe Sun.
Þe pine to bere a frut es won:
Mani kirnels of a tre mast—
Gain gifes o þe Holi Gast.   250

Seth was of his errand fain
And sune com til his fader again.
'Sun,' he said, 'has þou sped oght,
Or has þou ani merci broght?'
'Sir, Cherubin, þe hali angel   255
Þat es yateward, þe gretes wel—
Sais it sal negh þe warlds end
Ar þat oile þe may be send,
Thoro birth of a blisful child
Þat sal fra harm þe werld schild.   260
O þi ded he bad me sai
Sal be todai þe thrid dai.'
Adam was for þis tiþand blith—
Sua glad was he neuer his sith.
Quen he herd he suld liue namare,   265
Þan he logh, bot neuer are,
And þus on Godd began to cri:
'Lauerd, inogh now liued haue I:
Þou tak mi saul out of þe flexs
And do it ware þi wils es.'   270
Quat of þis werld he was ful sad
Þat neuer a dai þarin was glad!—
Þat liued nine hundret yeir and mare,
And al his liue in site and care,

272 þat] *MS.* þare

And leuer was siþen to lenge in hell   275
Þan langer in þis liue to duell.

Adam, als him was tald beforn,
Was ded apon þe thrid morn;
Doluen he was thoru Seth his sun
In þe dale þat hat Ebron.   280
Þe pipins war don vnder his tung:
Þar ras o þam thre wandes yong.
Son of a nellen heght þai ware:
Þai stod þan still and wex namare,
Ful many yeir ilike grene.   285
Halines was o þam sene.
Stil ai stod þai wandes thre   f. 9ᵛ 2
Fra Adam tim until Noe;
Fra Noe, quen þe flod ras,
Til Abraham þat haly was;   290
Fra Abraham ai stil stod þai
Til Moyses, þat gaf þe lai.
Euer stod þai still in an,
Witouten wax, witouten wain.

275 lenge] *MS.* leng*er*   277 als] *MS.* al

XV

INTERLUDIUM DE CLERICO ET PUELLA

THIS fragment is the oldest secular play extant in English and the first specimen of the interlude. Since the terms *interludium* and *interlude* are in the medieval period attested only in England, the nature and the origin of the kind must be deduced from English evidence in the first instance. The subject-matter of our piece is the same as that of *Dame Sirith* (see VI, Introduction). It follows that the interlude was, at the earliest stage of its history, a dramatic form, the action of which was restricted to two or three stages of a single episode, and which was comic in spirit and intention. The same may be said of the earliest secular play in OF, *Le Garçon et l'aveugle*, which is classified as a farce. The other early French specimens of the latter genre confirm the impression that the interlude is the English equivalent of the medieval French farce: indeed, no other OF kind is comparable.

In spirit our piece clearly belongs to the world of the *jongleur* or minstrel, who (among other things) was the performer of the dramatic monologues or 'mimes' of which *Dame Sirith* is probably an English example. Indeed, Fabyan speaks in his *Chronicle* (1494)[1] of a minstrel who performed 'interludes and songs': the interlude itself, evidently, might be mimed by a single performer just as the older dramatic monologues in OF were. But the authors of both kinds are likely to have included clerics, who as a class are known to have been the authors of *fabliaux* as of the Latin 'comedies' of the twelfth century. Audiences were not restricted to any single class: the two other early references to interludes, in *Sir Gawayne and the Green Knight*, 472, and *Handlyng Synne*, 8993, place them in a courtly and a popular setting respectively. Both passages associate the performance of interludes with that of carols; the implications

[1] VI. clxxii. 167.

of this are not clear. But it is significant that in *Sir Gawayne* interludes are performed at a time when feasting is going on. Gavin Douglas also vouches for this:

> Greit was the preis, the feist royall to sene;
> At eis thay eit, with interludis betwene.
>
> (*The Palice of Honour*, ed. Small, *The Poetical Works of Gavin Douglas*, i, p. 45)

Medwall's interlude *Fulgens and Lucres* tells us precisely what is meant: internal evidence in this work shows that in Tudor times the interlude was performed between the courses of a banquet. This evidently also applies to the medieval interlude as presented in courtly society.

There are remarkable verbal correspondences between this piece and *Dame Sirith*,[1] and even identical rhymes at certain points. Correspondences between *Dame Sirith* and other versions (notably the fact that the woman is married) show that *Dame Sirith* cannot derive from the *Interludium*. The converse cannot be ruled out: an alteration of the names, as of the virtuous wife Margery to the maiden whose name implies easy virtue, would not have been impossible. In fact, the rhymes and the expression in ll. 63–71, 84 of the *Interludium* sound like a rewriting of VI. 193, 196 ff. The only other possibility is descent of both works from a common antecedent version (which must have contained rhyme-sequences used in both parts of the extant *Dame Sirith*, and was thus perhaps itself composed in a mixture of tail-rhyme stanzas and four-beat couplets).

Hic incipit interludium de clerico et puella

'Damishel, reste wel!'	*Clericus*	
'Sir, welcum, by Saynt Michel!'	*Puella*	
'Wer es ty sire, wer es ty dame?'	*Clericus*	
'By Gode, es noþer her at hame.'	*Puella*	
'Wel wor suilc a man to life	*Clericus*	5
Þat suilc a may mithe haue to wyfe!'		

[1] See XV, Commentary.

---

4 noþer] *MS.* nouer

'Do way! By Crist and Leonard,   *Puella*
No wil Y lufe na clerc fayllard,
Ne kep I herbherg clerc in huse no y flore,
Bot his hers ly wituten dore.   10
Go forth þi way, god sire,
For her hastu losyt al þi wile!'
'Nu, nu! By Crist and by Sant Ihon,   *Clericus*
In al þis land ne . . . Hi none,
Mayden, þat Hi luf mor þan þe,   15
Hif me micht euer þe bether be!
For þe Hy sorw nicht and day—
Y may say 'Hay, wayleuay!'
Y luf þe mar þan mi lif;
Þu hates me mar þan gayt dos chnief!   20
Þat es nouct for mysgilt—
Certhes, for þi luf ham Hi spilt.
A! suythe mayden, reu of me
Þat es ty luf hand ay sal be!
For þe luf of þe moder of efne,   25
Þu mend þi mode and her my steuene!'
'By Crist of heuene and Sant Ione,   *Puella*
Clerc of scole ne kep I non,
For many god wymman haf þai don scam.
By Crist, þu michtis haf ben at hame!'   30
'Synt it noþir-gat may be,   *Clericus*
Iesu Crist bytech Y þe,
And send neulic bot þarinne,
Þat Yi be lesit of al my pyne.'

---

10 hers] s *illegible*   ly] y *illegible*   11 way] y *illegible*
13 *second* by] *illegible*   14 þis] *MS.* y.s (i *illegible*)   . . .] *illegible*
16 micht] *MS.* michc   þe] *MS.* ye   17 sorw] *MS.* sory
19 mi] m *illegible*   20 mar] r *illegible*   þan] *MS.* .an (þ *illegible*)
gayt] g *illegible*   21 for mysgilt] or m *illegible*   25 *second* þe]
no e *in MS.*   28 Clerc] erc *illegible*   32 bytech] *MS.* by teth

'Go nu, truan! go nu, go!   *Puella*   35
For mikel canstu of sorw and wo.'
'God te blis, mome Helwis!'   *Clericus*
'Son, welcum, by San Dinis!'   *Mome Elwis*
'Hic am comin to þe, mome: *Clericus*
þu hel me noth, þu say me sone.   40
Hic am a clerc þat hauntes scole.
Y lydy my lif wyt mikel dole:
Me wor leuer to be dedh
þan led þe lif þat Hyc ledh!
For ay mayden, with and schen,   45
Fayrer ho lond haw Y non syen.
Yo hat mayden Malkyn, Y wene:
Nu þu wost quam Y mene.
Yo wonys at the tounes ende,
þat suyt lif so fayr and hende.   50
Bot if yo wil hir mod amende,
Neuly Crist my ded me send!
Men kend me hyder, vytvten fayle,
To haf þi help an ty cunsayle:
þarfor am Y cummen here   55
þat þu salt be my herand-bere,
To mac me and þat mayden sayct,
And Hi sal gef þe of my nayct,
So þat heuer, al þi lyf,
Saltu be þe better, wyf!   60
So help me Crist—and Hy may spede,
Riclic saltu haf þi mede.'
'A, son! vat saystu? Benedicite!   *Mome Elwis*
Lift hup þi hand and blis þe!

---

36 canstu] *MS.* yu canstu   sorw] *MS.* sory   41 hauntes]
MS. haū t . s (*with hole between* t *and* s)   56 den *written above*
and *in* herand-bere

For it es boyt syn and scam   65
Þat þu on me hafs layt thys blam,
For Hic am an ald quyne and a lam.
Y led my lyf wit Godis loue;
Wit my roc Y me fede.
Can I do non oþir dede   70
Bot my pater noster and my crede
To say Crist for missedede,
And myn Auy Mary
(For my scynnes Hic am sory),
And my *De profundis*   75
For al þat yn sin lys.
For can I me non oþir þink—
Þat wot Crist, of heuene kync.
Iesu Crist, of heuene hey,
Gef þat þay may heng hey,   80
And gef þat Hy may se
Þat þay be henged on a tre
Þat þis ley as leyit me on
For aly wyman am I on.'

65 boyt *third letter undotted*   76 yn] *MS.* y   80 þay] *MS.*
Hay   82 henged] *MS.* heng'   83 me on] *MS.* onne me

XVI

PETERBOROUGH CHRONICLE

THE manuscript from which the following extracts are taken
(Bodl. Laud Misc. 636) is very properly called the Peterborough
Chronicle, though the work itself bears no such title, and cannot
be identified in any medieval list of Peterborough books (unless
it is the *Elfredi regis liber anglicus* listed in MS. Bodl. 163—an
identification which assumes that the compiler of that list knew of
the relation of this chronicle to that sponsored by Ælfred). The
contents clearly indicate that it was composed in the Benedictine
monastery of Peterborough; marginalia show that the manuscript was there in the Middle Ages; the hand of the first section
—ending at 1121—resembles that of two manuscripts certainly
from Peterborough (cf. *M.Æ.* xxiii), and the hand of the rest resembles that of two other Peterborough books; whilst the Anglo-
Norman Chronicle, or *Brut*, written on the margins of the last
four folios is closely related to that in a manuscript certainly
from Peterborough (C.C.C.C. 53, ff. 180ᵇ–184ᵃ).

The annals begin with events prior to 449, and close at the
foot of a verso (91) with the election of an abbot in 1155.
Those prior to 1121 represent a copy of an older chronicle, perhaps one borrowed after the fire of 1116 from St. Augustine's,
Canterbury,[1] but into this copy have been inserted entries for
various years (beginning at 654), and pseudo-charters, distinguished by their language as belonging to the twelfth century,
and by their content as inserted at Peterborough.[2] From the

---

[1] For evidence of a connexion between the two abbeys see W.
Levison, *England and the Continent in the Eighth Century* (1947),
pp. 200 ff.

[2] For these passages see p. 31 of Professor D. Whitelock's Introduction to the complete facsimile, and C. Clark, *The Peterborough
Chronicle* (1958); *s.a.* 654 the original foundation of the monastery
(then called Medeshamstede) is described, and *s.a.* 870 its destruction
by the Danes.

annal 1080 onwards the Peterborough Chronicle is the sole remaining record in English. The entry from 1132 to the end was apparently made all at one time, and in this section the annalistic form almost disappears (e.g. the martyrdom of William of Norwich in 1144 is described before the battle of the Standard in 1138; the death of Archbishop William is mis-dated by four years); which lends colour to Hall's suggestion that it represents the dictated recollections of an old monk. At the same time the chronicle takes on a warmth of tone rarely found in the earlier annals, and its phrases seem to reflect personal knowledge or experience of famine and oppression. This section has been familiar to historians and others from the time that Dr. Johnson reprinted it from Edmund Gibson's edition of the Chronicle (Oxford, 1692) in the History of the English Language prefixed to his *Dictionary*. Its vividness has led many writers to treat the 'nineteen long winters' as a period of unrelieved misery; it must be remembered that they are here described by a provincial chronicler writing in a part of the country that suffered more than the rest from the depredations of such men as Geoffrey de Mandeville, and that ecclesiastical architecture, and historiography, flourished during Stephen's reign. Other chroniclers vary in their estimates of Stephen: all agree that he was a brave and skilful soldier, but only the anonymous author of the *Gesta Stephani* is consistently favourable to him. The writer of the Peterborough account of his reign had possibly himself seen the king, who is known to have visited the abbey, presumably on his way to or from Stamford (*v.* 278). For the relation of this chronicle to the Latin chronicle of Hugo Candidus, subprior of Peterborough in Stephen's reign (ed. W. T. Mellows, 1949), see D. Whitelock, ed. cit., p. 33 (and cf. n. to 125 below): Hugo probably used the chronicle, but also the other annals or documents on which the *Chronicon Petroburgense* (ed. T. Stapleton, Camden Soc., 1849) was likewise based: this commences in 1122, continuing the story of the abbey and its abbot till 1295.

f. 85^r **M^{o}c^{o}xxvii^o**: Ðis gear heald se kyng Heanri his hird æt Cristesmæsse on Windlesoure. Þær wæs se Scotte kyng Dauid and eall ða heaued, læred and læuued, þet wæs on Engleland; and þær he let sweren ercebiscopes and biscopes and abbotes

and eorles and ealle þa ðeines ða þær wæron his dohter Æðelic 5
Englaland and Normandi to hande æfter his dæi, þe ær wæs
ðes caseres wif of Sexlande. . . . Ðes ilce gæres he gæf þone f. 85ᵛ
abbotrice of Burch an abbot, Heanri wæs gehaten, of Peitowe,
se hæfde his abbotrice Sancte Iohannis of Angeli on hande;
and ealle þa ærcebiscopes and biscopes seidon þet hit wæs 10
togeanes riht and þet he ne mihte hafen twa abbotrices on
hande. Oc se ilce Heanri dide þone king to understandene þet
he hæfde læten his abbotrice for þet micele unsibbe þet wæs
on þet land, and þet he dide ðurh þes papes ræd and leue of
Rome and ðurh þes abbotes of Clunni and þurh þæt he wæs 15
legat of ðone Romescott; oc hit ne wæs naðema eall swa, oc
he wolde hauen baðe on hande, and swa hafde swa lange swa
Godes wille wæs. He wæs on his clærchade biscop on Scess-
scuns; siððan warð he munec on Clunni, and siððon prior on
þone seolue minstre; and siððon he wærð prior on Sauenni. 20
Þaræftor, þurh·þet he wæs ðes kynges mæi of Engleland and
þes eorles of Peitowe, þa geaf se eorl him þone abbotrice of
Sancte Iohannis minstre of Angeli. Siððon, þurh his micele
wrences, ða beiæt he þone ærcebiscoprice of Besencun, and
hæfde hit þa on hande þre dagas; þa forlæs he þet mid rihte 25
forþi þet he hit hæfde æror beieten mid unrihte. Siððon þa
beiet he þone biscoprice of Seintes, þet wæs fif mile fram his
abbotrice; þet he hæfde ful neah seoueniht on hande; þenon
brohte se abbot him of Clunni, swa swa he æror dide of
Besencun. Þa beþohte he him þet gif he mihte ben rotfest on f. 86ʳ
Engleland þet he mihte habben eal his wille; besohte þa ðone 31
kyng and sæide him þet he wæs eald man and forbroken man,
and þet he ne mihte ðolen þa micele unrihte and þa micele
unsibbe ða wæron on here land, and iærnde þa þurh him and
ðurh ealle his freond namcuðlice þone abbotrice of Burhc; 35
and se kyng hit him iætte, forði þet he wæs his mæi and forþi
þet he wæs an hæfod ða að to swerene and witnesse to berene

þær ða eorles sunu of Normandi and þes eorles dohter of
Angeow wæron totwemde for sibreden. Þus earmlice wæs
40 þone abbotrice gifen betwix Cristesmesse and Candelmesse
at Lundene. And swa he ferde mid þe cyng to Wincestre and
þanon he com to Burch, and þær he wunede eall riht swa drane
doð on hiue: eall þet þa beon dragen toward, swa frett þa drane
and dragað fraward—swa dide he. Eall þet he mihte tacen
45 wiðinnen and wiðuten, of læred and of læwed, swa he sende
ouer sæ; and na god þær ne dide, ne na god ðær ne læuede. Ne
þince man na sellice þet we soð seggen: for hit wæs ful cuð
ofer eall land þet swa radlice swa he þær com (þet wæs þes
Sunendæies þet man singað *Exurge, quare obdormis, Domine?*)
50 þa son þæræfter þa sægon and herdon fela men feole huntes
hunten. Ða huntes wæron swarte and micele and ladlice, and
here hundes ealle swarte and brad-egede and ladlice, and
hi ridone on swarte hors and on swarte bucces. Þis wæs
segon on þe selue derfald in þa tune on Burch and on ealle
55 þa wudes ða wæron fram þa selua tune to Stanforde; and þa
muneces herdon ða horn blawen þet hi blewen on nihtes.
Soðfeste men heom kepten on nihtes; sæidon, þes þe heom
þuhte, þet þær mihte wel ben abuton twenti oðer þritti horn-
blaweres. Þis wæs sægon and herd fram þet he þider com eall
f. 86ᵛ 60 þet Lenten-tid onan to Eastren. Þis was his ingang; of his
utgang ne cunne we iett noht seggon. God scawe fore! . . .

f. 88ʳ **Mcxxxi** Ðis gear, æfter Cristesmesse on an Moneniht æt þe
forme slæp, wæs se heouene o ðe norðhalf eall swilc hit wære
bærnende fir, swa þet ealle ðe hit sægon wæron swa offæred
65 swa hi næfre ær ne wæron: þet wæs on iii Idus Ianuarii. Ðes
ilces geares wæs swa micel orfcwalm swa hit næfre ær ne wæs
on manne gemynd ofer eall Engleland. Þet wæs on næt and
on swin swa þet on þa tun þa wæs tenn ploges oðer twelfe
gangende, ne belæf þær noht an; and se man þa heafde twa

60 Lenten] *MS.* lented

hundred oðþe ðre hundred swin, ne beleaf him noht an. Þær- 70
æfter swulten þa hennefugeles. Þa scyrte ða flescmete and
se ceose and se butere. God hit bete þa his wille beð! And se
kyng Heanri com ham to Engleland toforen heruest æfter
Sancte Petres messe þe firrer.

Ðes ilces geares for se abbot Heanri toforen Eastren fram 75
Burch ofer sæ to Normandi, and þær spreac mid þone kyng,
and sæide him þet se abbot of Clunni heafde him beboden þet
he scolde cumen to him and betæcen him þone abbotrice of
Angeli, and siðþen he wolde cumen ham be his læfe; and swa
he ferde ham to his agen mynstre and þær wunode eall to 80
Midsumer Dæi. And ðes oðer dæies æfter Sancte Iohannis
messedæi cusen þa muneces abbot of hemself and brohten
him into cyrce mid processionem; sungen *Te Deum laudamus*,
ringden þa belle, setten him on þes abbotes settle, diden him
ealle hersumnesse swa swa hi scolden don here abbot; and se 85
eorl and ealle þa heafedmenn and þa muneces of þa mynstre
flemden se oðer abbot Heanri ut of þa mynstre. Hi scolden
nedes: on fif and twenti wintre ne biden hi næfre an god dæi.
Her him trucode ealle his mycele cræftes; nu him behofed þet
he crape in his mycele codde in ælc hyrne, gif þær wære hure 90
an unwreste wrenc þet he mihte get beswicen anes Crist and
eall Cristene folc. Þa ferde he into Clunni, and þær man him
held þet he ne mihte na east na west. Sæide se abbot of Clunni f. 88ᵛ
þet hi heafdon forloron Sancte Iohannis mynstre þurh him and
þurh his mycele sotscipe. Þa ne cuþe he him na betre bote 95
bute behet hem and aðes swor on halidom þet, gif he moste
Engleland secen, þet he scolde begeton hem ðone mynstre of
Burch, swa þet he scolde setten þær prior of Clunni and circeweard and hordere and reilþein, and ealle þa ðing þa wæron
wiðinne mynstre and wiðuten, eall he scolde hem betæcen. 100
Þus he ferde into France, and þær wunode eall þet gear. Crist
ræde for þa wrecce muneces of Burch and for þet wrecce

stede! Nu hem behofeð Cristes helpe and eall Cristenes
folces.

¹⁰⁵ **Mcxxxii** Ðis gear com Henri king to þis land. Þa com Henri
abbot and uureide þe muneces of Burch to þe king forþi ðat
he uuolde underþeden ðat mynstre to Clunie; sua ðat te king
was wel neh bepaht, and sende efter þe muneces; and þurh
Godes milce and þurh þe biscop of Seresbyri and te biscop of
¹¹⁰ Lincol and te oþre rice men þe þer wæron þa wiste þe king
ðat he feorde mid suicdom. Þa he nammor ne mihte, þa uuolde
he ðat his nefe sculde ben abbot in Burch, oc Crist it ne uuolde.
Was it noht suithe lang þerefter þat te king sende efter him,
and dide him gyuen up ðat abbotrice of Burch and faren ut
¹¹⁵ of lande; and te king iaf ðat abbotrice an prior of Sancte Neod,
Martin was gehaten. He com on Sancte Petres messedei mid
micel wurscipe into the minstre.

Mcxxxv On þis gære for se king Henri ouer sæ æt te Lammasse. And ðat oþer dei, þa he lai an slep in scip, þa þestrede
¹²⁰ þe dæi ouer al landes, and uuard þe sunne suilc als it uuare
thre niht ald mone, an sterres abuten him at middæi. Wurþen
men suiðe ofuundred and ofdred, and sæden ðat micel þing
sculde cumen herefter. Sua dide: for þat ilc gær warth þe
king ded ðat oþer dæi efter Sancte Andreas massedæi, on
¹²⁵ Normandi. Þa þestreden sona þas landes, for æuric man sone
ræuede oþer þe mihte. Þa namen his sune and his frend and
brohten his lic to Englelande, and bebirieden in Redinge.
God man he wes, and micel æie wes of him: durste nan man
misdon wið oðer on his time. Pais he makede men and dær.
¹³⁰ Wuasua bare his byrthen gold and sylure, durste nan man sei
to him naht bute god.

f. 89ʳ   Enmang þis was his nefe cumen to Englelande, Stephne
de Blais, and com to Lundene; and te Lundenisce folc him

111 nammor] *MS.* nãmor   125 þestreden] *MS.* þestre
127 bebirieden] *MS.* bebiriend   130 nan man] *MS.* nãman

underfeng, and senden efter þe ærcebiscop Willelm Curbuil;
and halechede him to kinge on Midewintre Dæi. On þis kinges 135
time wes al unfrið and yfel and ræflac, for agenes him risen
sona þa rice men þe wæron swikes: alre fyrst Balduin de
Reduers, and held Execestre agenes him; and te king it besæt,
and siððan Balduin acordede. Þa tocan þa oðre and helden her
castles agenes him. And Dauid king of Scotland toc to uuerrien 140
him; þa, þohuuethere þat, here sandes feorden betwyx heom,
and hi togædere comen and wurðe sæhte, þoþ it litel forstode.
Mcxxxvii Ðis gære for þe king Stephne ofer sæ to Normandi,
and ther wes underfangen forþi ðat hi uuenden ðat he sculde
ben alsuic alse the eom wes, and for he hadde get his tresor; 145
ac he todeld it and scatered sotlice. Micel hadde Henri king
gadered gold and syluer, and na god ne dide me for his saule
tharof.

Þa þe king Stephne to Englalande com, þa macod he his
gadering æt Oxeneford; and þar he nam þe biscop Roger of 150
Serebyri, and Alexander biscop of Lincol, and te canceler
Roger—hise neues—and dide ælle in prisun til hi iafen up here
castles. Þa the suikes undergæton ðat he milde man was, and
softe and god, and na iustise ne dide, þa diden hi alle wunder.
Hi hadden him manred maked and athes suoren, ac hi nan 155
treuthe ne heolden. Alle he wæron forsworen and here treothes
forloren. For æuric rice man his castles makede and agænes
him heolden, and fylden þe land ful of castles. Hi suencten
suyðe þe uurecce men of þe land mid castel-weorces. Þa þe
castles uuaren maked, þa fylden hi mid deoules and yuele 160
men. Þa namen hi þa men þe hi wenden ðat ani god hefden—
bathe be nihtes and be dæies, carlmen and wimmen—and
diden heom in prisun, and pined heom efter gold and syluer
untellendlice pining: for ne uuæren næure nan martyrs swa
pined alse hi wæron. Me henged up bi the fet and smoked 165
heom mid ful smoke. Me henged bi the þumbes other bi the

hefed, and hengen bryniges on her fet. Me dide cnotted
f. 89ᵛ strenges abuton here hæued, and uurythen it ðat it gæde to þe
hærnes. Hi diden heom in quarterne þar nadres and snakes
170 and pades wæron inne, and drapen heom swa. Sume hi diden
in crucethur, ðat is, in an ceste þat was scort and nareu and
undep; and dide scærpe stanes þerinne, and þrengde þe man
þærinne, ðat him bræcon alle þe limes. In mani of þe castles
wæron lof and grin, ðat wæron rachenteges ðat twa oþer thre
175 men hadden onoh to bæron onne. Þat was sua maced ðat is
fæstned to an beom, and diden an scærp iren abuton þa
mannes throte and his hals, ðat he ne myhte nowiderwardes,
ne sitten ne lien ne slepen, oc bæron al ðat iren. Mani þusen
hi drapen mid hungær. I ne can ne I ne mai tellen alle þe
180 wunder ne alle þe pines ðat hi diden wrecce men on þis land;
and ðat lastede þa xix wintre wile Stephne was king, and
æure it was uuerse and uuerse. Hi læiden gæildes on the tunes
æure umwile, and clepeden it 'tenserie'. Þa þe uurecce men ne
hadden nammore to gyuen, þa ræueden hi and brendon alle
185 the tunes, ðat wel þu myhtes faren al a dæis fare, sculdest thu
neure finden man in tune sittende, ne land tiled. Þa was corn
dære, and flec and cæse and butere, for nan ne wæs o þe land.
Wrecce men sturuen of hungær. Sume ieden on ælmes þe
waren sum wile rice men; sume flugen ut of lande. Wes næure
190 gæt mare wreccehed on land, ne næure hethen men werse ne
diden þan hi diden. For ouersithon ne forbaren hi nouther
circe ne cyrceiærd, oc namen al þe god ðat þarinne was, and
brenden sythen þe cyrce and al tegædere. Ne hi ne forbaren
biscopes land ne abbotes ne preostes, ac ræueden munekes and
195 clerekes, and æuric man other þe ouermyhte. Gif twa men oþer
iii coman ridend to an tun, al þe tunscipe flugæn for heom,
wenden ðat hi wæron ræueres. Þe biscopes and lered men heom
cursede æure, oc was heom naht þarof, for hi uueron al forcursæd and forsuoren and forloren. War sæ me tilede, þe erthe

ne bar nan corn, for þe land was al fordon mid suilce dædes, 200
and hi sæden openlice ðat Crist slep, and his halechen. Suilc,
and mare þanne we cunnen sæin, we þoleden xix wintre for
ure sinnes.

On al þis yuele time heold Martin abbot his abbotrice xx f. 90ʳ
wintre and half gær and viii dæis, mid micel suinc, and fand 205
þe munekes and te gestes al þat heom behoued, and heold
mycel carited in the hus, and þoþwethere wrohte on þe circe,
and sette þarto landes and rentes, and goded it suythe, and læt
it refen, and brohte heom into þe neuuæ mynstre on Sancte
Petres mæssedæi mid micel wurtscipe; ðat was *anno ab in-* 210
carnatione domini mcxl, a combustione loci xxiii. And he for to
Rome, and þær wæs wæl underfangen fram þe pape Eugenie,
and begæt thare priuilegies—an of alle þe landes of þabbotrice,
and an oþer of þe landes þe lien to þe circewican; and gif he
leng moste liuen alse he mint to don of þe horderwycan. And 215
he begæt in landes þat rice men hefden mid strengthe. Of
Willelm Malduit, þe heold Rogingham þæ castel, he wan
Cotingham and Estun; and of Hugo of Walteruile he uuan
Hyrtlingbyri and Stanewig, and lx solidos of Aldewingle ælc
gær. And he makede manie munekes, and plantede winiærd, 220
and makede mani weorkes, and wende þe tun betere þan it
ær wæs; and wæs god munec and god man, and forþi him
luueden God and gode men.

Nu we willen sægen sumdel wat belamp on Stephnes kinges
time. On his time þe Iudeus of Noruuic bohton an Cristen 225
cild beforen Estren, and pineden him alle þe ilce pining ðat
ure Drihten was pined, and on Lang Fridæi him on rode
hengen for ure Drihtines luue, and sythen byrieden him.
Wenden ðat it sculde ben forholen, oc ure Dryhtin atywede
ðat he was hali martyr; and to munekes him namen, and be- 230
byried him heglice in þe minstre, and he maket þurh ure

202 þoleden] *MS.* þolenden   231 þurh] *MS.* þur

Drihtin wunderlice and manifældlice miracles; and hatte he Sanct Willelm.

Mcxxxviii On þis gær com Dauid king of Scotland mid or-
235 mete færd to þis land; wolde winnan þis land. And him com togænes Willelm eorl of Albamar, þe þe king adde beteht Euorwic—and to other æuez men—mid fæu men, and fuhten wid heom, and flemden þe king æt te Standard, and sloghen suithe micel of his genge.

f. 90ᵛ **Mcxl** On þis gær wolde þe king Stephne tæcen Rodbert eorl
241 of Gloucestre, þe kinges sune Henries, ac he ne myhte, for he wart it war. Þerefter in þe lengten þestrede þe sunne and te dæi abuton non-tid dæies, þa men eten, ðat me lihtede candles to æten bi, and þat was xiii kalendarum Aprilis. Wæron men
245 suythe ofwundred. Þerefter fordfeorde Willelm ærcebiscop of Cantwarbyri, and te king makede Teodbald ærcebiscop, þe was abbot in the Bec. Þerefter wæx suythe micel uuerre betuyx þe king and Randolf eorl of Cæstre; noht forþi ðat he ne iaf him al ðat he cuthe axen him, alse he dide alle othre, oc
250 æfre þe mare he iaf heom þe wærse hi wæron him. Þe eorl heold Lincol agænes þe king, and benam him al ðat he ahte to hauen; and te king for þider, and besætte him and his brother Willelm de Romare in þe castel. And te æorl stæl ut and ferde efter Rodbert eorl of Gloucestre, and brohte him
255 þider mid micel ferd, and fuhten suythe on Candelmasse dæi agenes heore lauerd, and namen him, for his men him suyken and flugæn; and læd him to Bristowe and diden þar in prisun and in feteres. Þa was al Engleland styred mar þan ær wæs, and al yuel wæs in lande. Þerefter com þe kinges dohter
260 Henries, þe hefde ben emperice in Alamanie and nu wæs cuntesse in Angou, and com to Lundene; and te Lundenissce folc hire wolde tæcen, and scæ fleh, and forles þar micel. Þerefter þe biscop of Wincestre, Henri þe kinges brother

242 in þe] *MS.* hi þe

Stephnes, spac wid Rodbert eorl and wyd þemperice, and suor
heom athas ðat he neure ma mid te king his brother wolde 265
halden, and cursede alle þe men þe mid him heoldon, and sæde
heom ðat he uuolde iiuen heom up Wincestre, and dide heom
cumen þider. Þa hi þærinne wæren, þa com þe kinges cuen
mid al hire strengthe, and besæt heom, ðat þer wæs inne micel
hungær. Þa hi ne leng ne muhten þolen, þa stalen hi ut and 270
flugen; and hi wurthen war widuten, and folecheden heom, and
namen Rodbert eorl of Gloucestre and ledden him to Rouecestre
and diden him þare in prisun; and te emperice fleh into an
minstre.

Þa feorden þe wise men betwyx þe kinges freond and te f. 91ʳ
eorles freond and sahtlede sua ðat me sculde leten ut þe king of 276
prisun for þe eorl, and te eorl for þe king, and sua diden.
Sithen þerefter sathleden þe king and Randolf eorl at Stanford,
and athes suoren and treuthes fæston ðat her nouþer sculde
besuyken other. And it ne forstod naht: for þe king him sithen 280
nam in Hamtun, þurhc wicci ræd, and dide him in prisun, and
efsones he let him ut, þurhc wærse red, to ðat forewarde ðat
he suor on halidom and gysles fand þat he alle his castles sculde
iiuen up. Sume he iaf up, and sume ne iaf he noht; and dide
þanne wærse þanne he hær sculde. Þa was Engleland suythe 285
todeled: sume helden mid te king, and sume mid þemperice.
For, þa þe king was in prisun, þa wenden þe eorles and te
rice men þat he neure mare sculde cumen ut, and sæhtleden
wyd þemperice, and brohten hire into Oxenford, and iauen
hire þe burch. Þa þe king was ute, þa herde ðat sægen, and toc 290
his feord and besæt hire in þe tur, and me læt hire dun on
niht of þe tur mid rapes, and stal ut, and scæ fleh and iæde
on fote to Walingford. Þærefter scæ ferde ouer sæ, and hi of
Normandi wenden alle fra þe king to þe eorl of Angæu (sume
here þankes and sume here unþankes) for he besæt heom til hi 295

270 stalen] *MS.* stali   278 sathleden] *? l.* sahtleden: *cf. 288*

aiauen up here castles, and hi nan helpe ne hæfden of þe king.

Þa ferde Eustace þe kinges sune to France and nam þe kinges suster of France to wife; wende to bigæton Normandi þærþurh; oc he spedde litel—and be gode rihte, for he was an yuel man: for ware se he com he dide mare yuel þanne god. He reuede þe landes and læide micele gæildes on. He brohte his wif to Engleland and dide hire in þe castel in Cantebyri. God wimman scæ wæs, oc scæ hedde litel blisse mid him; and Crist ne wolde ðat he sculde lange rixan; and wærd ded, and his moder beien. And te eorl of Angæu wærd ded, and his sune Henri toc to þe rice. And te cuen of France todælde fra þe king, and scæ com to þe iunge eorl Henri, and he toc hire to wiue and al Peitou mid hire. Þa ferde he mid micel færd into Engleland, and wan castles; and te king ferde agenes him mid micel mare ferd; and þoþwæthere fuhtten hi noht, oc ferden þe ærcebiscop and te wise men betwyx heom and makede ðat sa
hte ðat te king sculde ben lauerd and king wile he liuede and æfter his dæi ware Henri king; and he helde him for fader, and he him for sune, and sib and sæhte sculde ben betwyx heom, and on al Engleland. Þis and te othre foruuardes þet hi makeden suoren to halden þe king and te eorl and te biscopes and te eorles and rice men alle. Þa was þe eorl underfangen æt Wincestre and æt Lundene mid micel wurtscipe, and alle diden him manred, and suoren þe pais to halden; and hit ward sone suythe god pais, sua ðat neure was here. Þa was þe king strengere þanne he æuert her was. And te eorl ferde ouer sæ and al folc him luuede, for he dide god iustise and makede pais.

301–3 *A hole in the leaf makes a few letters at this point conjectural, but there is little doubt what they were*

322 here. *Mrs. Clark reads* herere under ultra-violet light, and interprets as *æror*, 'before'.

XVII

KENTISH SERMONS

MAURICE DE SULLY, Bishop of Paris, composed between 1168 and 1175 a cycle of sixty-seven homilies in French on the Gospel lessons for the year. A ME translation of five of these is preserved in a thirteenth-century manuscript, which also contains an Anglo-Norman version of Maurice's sermon 1, and sermons 7–22, ii, and 23–36 (partly in Latin, partly in Anglo-Norman) of Maurice's series. Both the English and the Anglo-Norman sets may be the work of one man, a bilingual Englishman of the thirteenth century.

Maurice's exegetical method is usually tripartite treatment of the Gospel text for the day, according to the 'literal', the 'allegorical', and the 'moral' sense of Scripture—i.e. the normal form of his sermons is an historical account of the events mentioned in the text, an exposition of its spiritual meaning, and an exhortation. This form of structure is worked out with the utmost economy. It is represented in all but one of the English versions printed here: the third lacks the spiritual interpretation. Maurice's prose has an exquisite simplicity of style, of which somewhat is preserved in the close and rather stiff English rendering.

Sermo in die Epiphanie

C V M natus esset Iesus in Betleem Iude in diebus Herodis regis, f. 128ᵛ 1
*ecce magi ab oriente uenerunt Ierosolimam, dicentes: 'Vbi est
qui natus est rex Iudeorum?'* We redeth i þo holi godespelle of tedai ase ure Louerd God Almichti ibore was of ure
Lauedi Seinte Marie i þe cite of Bethleem, þet si sterre was 5
seauinge of his beringe swo apierede te þo þrie kinges of

heþenesse tojanes þo sunne risindde. And alswo hi biknewe
f. 128ᵛ 2 his beringe bi þo sterre, swo hi nomen conseil betuene hem
þet hi wolden gon forto hyne anuri, and þet hi wolden offri
10 him gold, and stor, and mirre.

And alswo hi hedden aparailed here offrendes, swo kam si
sterre þet yede tofor hem into Ierusalem. Þere hi speken to
Herodes, and hym askede wer was se king of Gyus þet was
ibore. And Herodes iherde þet o king was ibore þet solde bi
15 king of Geus, swo was michel anud, and alle hise men, for þet
he was ofdred forto liese his kingriche of Ierusalem. Þo dede
he somoni alle þo wyse clerekes þet kuþe þe laghe and hem
askede wer Crist solde bien ibore. Hi answerden þet ine
Ierusalem; for hit was swo iseid and behote hwilen bi þo pro-
20 fetes. And alswo Herodes iherde þis, swo spac te þo þrie
kinges, and hem seide: 'Goþ' ha seide 'into Bethleem and
secheȝ þet child; and wanne ye hit habbeth hifunde, swo
anuret hit. And efter þet cometh to me, and Hic wille go and
anuri hit.'

f. 129ʳ1   Þet ne seide he nocht, Herodes, for þet he hit wolde onuri,
26 ac for þet he hit wolde slon, yef he hit michte finde. Þo kinges
hem wenten, and hi seghen þo sterre þet yede bifore hem,
alwat hi kam over þo huse war ure Louerd was; and alswo hi
hedden ifonden ure Louerd, swo hin anurede and him offrede
30 hire offrendes—gold, and stor, and mirre. Þo nicht efter þet
aperede an ongel of heuene in here slepe ine metinge, and hem
seide and het þet hi ne solde ayen-wende be Herodes, ac be anoþer weye wende into hire londes.

Lordinges and leuedis, þis is si glorius miracle and si glorius
35 seywinge of ure Lordes beringe þet us telþ þet holi godespel
of teday. And ye muee wel understonde be þo speche of þe
godspelle þet me sal todai mor makie offrinke þan anoþren
dai; and þerof us yeft ensample þo þrie kinges of heþenesse,
f. 129ʳ 2 þet comen fram verrene londes ure Louerd to seche and him

makie offrinke. And be þet hi offrede gold, þet is cuuenable 40
yeftte to kinge, seawede þet he was sothfast kink; and be þet
hi offrede stor, þet me offrede wylem be þo ialde laghe to here
godes sacrefise, seawede þet he was verray prest; and be þet
hi offrede mirre, þet is biter þing, signefieth þet hi hedde beliaue þet he was diadlich þet diath solde suffri for manken. 45

Nu ihiereth wet signefieth þet gold, þet stor, þet mirre; and
offre we gostliche to ure Lorde þet hi offrede flesliche. Þet
gold, þet is bricht and glareth ine þo brichtnesse of þo sunne,
signefieth þe gode beleaue þet is bricht ine þe gode Cristenemannes herte: si gode beleaue licht and is bricht ine þo herte 50
of þo gode manne ase gold. Offre we þanne God Almichti god
gold: beleue we stedefastliche þet Fader and Sune and Holy
Gost is onlepi God. Woso hath beleaue ine Gode swo offreth
him god gold. Þet stor signefied gode werkes; for ase se f. 129ᵛ 1
smech of þe store wanne hit is ido into þe ueree and goth 55
upward to þo heuene and to Gode ward, swo amuntet si gode
biddinge to Gode of þo herte of þo gode Cristenemanne. Swo
we mowe sigge þet stor signefieth þe herte, and se smech luue
of Gode. Bi þet mirre þat is biter, and be þo biternesse defendet
þet cors þet is mide ismered, þet no werm nel come ihende, 60
signefiet þo gode werkes þet is biter to þo yemernesse of ure
flesce. Si mirre signefiet uastinge, for þo luue of Gode wakie,
go ine pelrimage, uisiti þe poure and to sike, and to do alle þe
gode þet me may do for Godes luue; þo ilke þinges so bieth
bitere to þo wrichede flessce. Ac also si mirre loket þet bodi 65
þet no werm ne may þer-ihende come, so us defendet þo ileke
þinges fram senne, and fram þe amonestement of þo dieule,
þet ha ne may us misdo.

40 *First* þet] t *suprascript (with caret) in red*   offrede] *MS.* offrēde
43 godes] *suprascript (with caret) in red*   þet] *MS.* þe   47 þet
hi] *MS.* þe i, *with* t *suprascript (with caret) in red*   52 he is
suprascript (with caret) in red between þet *and* Fader   59 Bi] *MS.*
Li; þet *suprascript, in same ink*   60 come] *MS.* cōme

69   Lordinges, nu ye habbet iherd þo signefiance of þo offringes
f. 129ᵛ 2   þet maden þo þrie kinges of heþenesse to Gode; ye habbet to
Gode i-offred of yure selure and of yure erþliche godes. Ne ne
offreth him nacht onlepiliche today, ac alle þo daies i þo yere,
gostliche gold, and stor, and mirre, ase Hic habbe itold—gold,
fore gode belaue; stor, for holy urisun; mirre, for gode werkes.
75   Þet bieth þo offringes þet ure Louerd besekeþ aueriche daye
þo Cristenemanne, and werefore se Cristenman, yef has deþ,
ofseruet þo blisce of heuene. And Iesu Crist, þet for us wolde
an erþe bi bore and anured of þo þrie kinges of painime, he
yeue us his grace of þo Holi Gost in ure hertes, werbi we moue
80   hatie þo ileke þinges þet he hatedh, and lete þo ileke þinges þat
he forbiet, and luuie þo ilek þinkes þat he luued, and do þo
ilek þinges þat he hoot, ine him so bileue and bidde and serui
þet we mowe habbe þo blisce of heueriche. *Quod uobis pre-*
stare dignetur per [*Iesum Christum dominum nostrum*].

DOMINI[CA] SECUNDA POST OCTAVAM EPIPHANIE

Sermo Euan[gelicus]

f. 130ʳ 1   *Nuptie facte sunt in Chana Galilee, et erat mater Iesu ibi;*
86 *vocatus est autem Iesus ad nuptias et discipuli eius.* Þet holi
godspel of today us telþ þet a bredale was imaked ine þo londe
of Ierusalem, in ane cite þat was icleped Cane, in þa time þat
Godes sune yede in erþe flesliche. To þa bredale was ure Leuedi
90   Seinte Marie, and ure Louerd Iesus Crist and hise deciples.
So iuel auenture þet wyn failede at þise bredale; þo seide ure
Leuedi Seinte Marie to here sune: 'Hi ne habbet no wyn.' And
ure Louerd answerde and sede to hire: 'Wat belongeth hit to
me oþer to þe, wyman?' Nu ne dorste hi namore sigge, ure

70 ye] *MS.* hye   79 yeue us] *MS.* yeuus   89 At *suprascript,*
in same ink, before To

Lauedi; hac hye spac to þo serganz þet seruede of þo wyne, and 95
hem seyde: 'Al þet he hot yu do, so doþ.'

And ure Louerd clepede þe serganz and seyde to hem:
'Folvellet', ha seyde, 'þos ydres [þet is to sigge þos croos, oþer
þos faten] of watere.' For þer were vi ydres of stone þet ware
iclepede baþieres, wer þo Gius hem wesse for clenesse and for 100
religiun, ase þe custome was ine þo time. Þo serganz uuluelden f. 130ᵣ 2
þo faten of watere, and hasteliche was iwent into wyne, bie
þo wille of ure Louerde. Þo seide ure Lord to þo serganz:
'Moveth togidere and bereth to Architriclin [þat was se þet
ferst was iserued].' And also hedde idrunke of þise wyne þet 105
ure Louerd hedde imaked of þe watere (ha niste nocht þe
miracle, ac þo serganz wel hit wiste þet hedde þet water
ibrocht), þo seide Architriclin to þo bredgume: 'Oþer men',
seyde he, 'doþ forþ þet beste wyn þet hi habbeþ ferst at here
bredale; and þu hest ido þe contrarie, þet þu hest ihialde þet 110
beste wyn wath nu!' Þis was þe commencement of þo miracles
of ure Louerde þet he made flesliche in erþe; and þo beleuede
on him his deciples. I ne sigge nacht þet hi ne hedden þerbefore
ine him beliaue; ac fore þe miracle þet hi seghe was here
beliaue þe more istrengþed.   •   115

Nu ye habbeþ iherd þe miracle; nu ihereþ þe signefiance.
Þet water bitockned se euele Cristeneman. For also þet f. 130ᵥ 1
water is natureliche schald, and akelþ alle þo þet hit drinkeþ,
so is se euele Cristeman chald of þo luue of Gode, for þo
euele werkes þet hi doþ; ase so is lecherie, spusbreche, roberie, 120
manslechtes, husberners, bakbiteres, and alle oþre euele deden,
þurch wyche þinkes man ofserueth þet fer of helle, ase Godes
oghe mudh hit seid. And alle þo signefied þet water, þet
þurch yemere werkes oþer þurch yemer iwil liesed þo blisce
of heuene. Þet wyn, þat is naturelliche hot ine himselue, and 125

112 Louerde] *MS.* loruerde   þo] *suprascript in red*   114 þe]
suprascript in red

anhet alle þo þet hit drinked, betokned alle þo þet bied anheet
of þe luue of ure Lorde.

Nu, lordinges, ure Lord God Almichti, þat hwylem in one
stede and ine one time flesliche makede of watere wyn, yet ha
130 deþ mani time maked of watere wyn gostliche, wanne þurch
his grace maked of þo euele manne good man, of þe orgeilus
f. 130ᵛ 2 umble, of þe lechur chaste, of þe niþinge large; and of alle
oþre folies, so ha maket of þo watere wyn. Þis his si signefiance
of þe miracle. Nu loke euerich man toward himseluen, yef he
135 is win, þet is to siggen yef he is anheet of þo luue of Gode, oþer
yef he is water, þet is yef þu art chold of Godes luue. Yef þu
art euel man, besech ure Lorde þet he do ine þe his uertu, þet
ha þe wende of euele into gode, and þet he do þe do swiche
werkes þet þu mote habbe þo blisce of heuene. *Quod uobis*
140 *prestare dignetur.*

Dominica quarta post octavam Epiphanie

f. 131ʳ 2 *Ascendente Iesu in nauiculam, secuti sunt eum discipuli*
eius. Et ecce motus factus est magnus in mari, ita ut nauicula
f. 131ᵛ 1 *operiretur fluctibus; erat autem illis uentus contrarius.* We
redeth i þe holi godspelle of todai þat ure Lord Iesu Crist
145 yede one time into ane ssipe, and ise deciples mid him, into
þe see. And so hi were in þo ssipe, so aros a great tempeste
of winde; and ure Lord was ileid him don to slepe ine þo
ssipe, er þane þis tempeste aroos. Hise deciples hedde gret
drede of þise tempeste, so awakede hine and seiden to him:
150 'Lord, saue us, for we perisset.' And ha wiste wel þet hi ne
hadde nocht gode beleaue ine him; þo seide to hem: 'Wat dret
yw, folk of litle beliaue?' Þo aros up ure Lord and tok þane
wynd and to see; and also raþe hit was stille. And alse þo

134–5 he is] *MS.* he heis

men þet weren in þo ssipe hedde iseghe þo miracle, so awondrede hem michel. 155

Þis is si vaire miracle þet þet godspel of teday us telþ; þerefore sal hure beliaue bie þe betere astrengþed ine swiche lorde
þet siche miracle mai do and doþ wanne he wile. Ac hit is us
nyede þet se þet sucurede hem ine þa peril, þet us sucuri ine
ure niedes—þet we clepie to him þet ha us helpe. And he hit f. 131ᵛ 2
wille do bleþeliche yef we him bisecheth merci mid good iwille; 161
also himseluen seith bi þe Holi Writes: *Salus populi ego sum,
et cetera*—'Hic am', ha seiþ, 'helere of þe folke. Wanne hi to
me clepiedh ine hire sorghen and ine hire niedes, Hic hi sucuri
and beneme hem al here euel withute ende.' Grede we to him 165
merci sikerliche, yef se deuel us wille acumbri þurch senne,
þurch prede, oþer þurch anvie, oþer þurh wreþe, oþer þurch
oþer manere of diadliche senne. Grede we to him merci, and
sigge we him: 'Lord, sauue us þet we ne perissi', and þet he us
deliuri of alle eueles, and þet ha yef us swiche werkes to done 170
in þise wordle þet þo saulen of us mote bien isauued a Domesdai and gon to þo blisce of heuene. *Quod ipse prestare dignetur.*

Dominica in sexagesima Sermo

*Simile est regnum celorum homini patrifamilias, qui exiit
primo mane conducere operarios in uineam suam.* Hure Lord f. 132ʳ 1
God Almichti to us spekeþ ine þo holi godespelle of teday, and 175
us seaweth one forbisne þet yef we uilleth don his seruise, þet
we sollen habbe þo mede wel griat ine heuene. For so seyth
ure Lord ine þo godspelle of todai þet on goodman was, þat
ferst uutyede bi þe moreghen forto here werkmen into his
winyarde, for ane peny of forewerde. And also he hedde imad 180
þise forewerde, so ha sente hi into his wynyarde; so ha dede at
undren, and at midday also.

176 þet] *MS.* þe, *with t suprascript (and caret) in red*

Þo þat hit was ayen þan euen, so ha kam into þe marcatte, so he fond werkmen þet were idel; þo seyde he to hem: 'Wee

185 bie ye idel?' And hie answerden and seyde: 'Lord, for we ne fonden tedai þet us herde.' 'Goþ nu', ha seide, se godeman, 'into mine wynyarde, and Hic þat richt is yu sal yeue.' Þos yede into þise wynyarde mid þo oþre. Þo þet hiwel euen, þo seide þe lord to his sergant: 'Clepe þo werkmen and yeld hem here

190 trauail. And agyn to hem þat comen last, and go al to þo ferste;

f. 132ʳ 2 yef eueriche of hem ane peny.' Se sergant dede þes lordes commandement—so paide þo werkmen and yaf euerich ane peny. And so hi seghen, þo þet bi þe morghen waren icomen, þet hi þet waren last icume hedden here euerich ane peny, þo

195 wenden hi more habbe. Þo gruchchede hi amenges hem and seyden: 'Þos laste on ure habbeþ itravailed, and þu his makest velaghes to us, þet habbeth al deai ibye ine þine wynyarde, and habbetþ iþoled þe berdene of þo pine and of þo hete of al þo daie.' Þo ansuerede se godeman to on of hem: 'Frend,' ha

200 seide, 'I ne do þe noon unricht. Wat forþingketh þat Hic do min iwil?' And also ure Lord hedde itold þise forbisne, so he seide efterward: 'So sulle þo uerste bie last, and þo laste ferst. Fele bieþ iclepede, ac feaue bieþ icornee.'

Nu ihereþ þe signefiance. Þes godeman betockneþ God

205 Almichti ure Lord; se winyard betockneþ þe seruise of ure Lorde; þe werkmen betockneþ alle þo þet doþ Cristes seruise;

f. 132ᵛ 1 þo tides of þo daie betokneþ þe time of þis world. Bie þe morghen iherde ure Lord werkmen into his winyarde, þo ha sente þe patriarches ate begininge of þis wordl ine is seruise,

210 þet þurch gode beleauee him seruede, and seden his techinge to alle þo þet hi hedden hit to siggen. Also at undren and at midday iherede he werkmen into is winyarde, þo ha sente be þo time þet Moyses was and Aaron, and i þe time of his pro-phetes dede he mani god man into his seruise, þet þurch

185 ne] *suprascript (with caret) in red*

griate luue to him helden and deden his seruise. Toyenes þan 215
euen God Almichti ihierde werkmen into his winyarde, þo þat
he alast of þis wordle naam fles and blod ine þe maidene Seinte
Marie, and seauede ine þis world. Þo fond he men þet al
day hedden ibe idel, fore he fond þet heþen folk þet be þo
time þet was igo hedden ibe ut of Godes beliaue, and of his 220
luue, and of his seruise (hi ne hedden nocht ibe idel forto done f. 132ᵛ 2
þo deueles werkes!). Ac þerefore seith þet godspel þet hedden
ibe idel, þo þet hi nedden bileued ane God Almichti, ne him
louie ne him serui, for al þat is ine þis wordle, þet man is, bote
yef ha luuie God Almichti and him serui, al hit him may þenche 225
forlore and idelnesse.

Þo aresunede ure Lord þe paens be ise apostles werefore hi
hedden ibe so longe idel, þo þet hi ne hedden ibe in his seruise.
Þo answerden þe paens þet non ne hedden iherd hii—þet is to
sigge, þet hi ne hedden neuerte iheed prophete, ne apostle, ne 230
prechur, þet hem seaude ne hem tachte hu i solden ine Gode
beleue ne him serui. 'Goþ', a seide, ure Lord, 'inte mine winyarde' (þet is, inte mine beleaue), 'and Hic yw sal yeue yure
peni' (þet is, heueriche blisce). Þo heþen men yeden be þa
daghen into Cristes seruise. And we þet of hem bieþ icume, and 235
habbeþ Cristendom underfonge, bieþ i-entred into Cristes
seruise; þerefore we sollen habbe ure peni (þet is, þe blisce of
heuene) alŝo wel ase þo þet comen bi þe morghen, for also we f. 133ʳ 1
hopieþ forte habbe heueriche blisce ase þo patriarches, and þo
prophetes, and þo apostles, and þo gode men þet hwilem ine 240
þis world God Almichti serueden.

So as we habeþ iseid, of diuers wordles, þet God Almichti
dede werkmen into his winyarde, so we mowe sigge of þe elde
of eueriche men. For God Almichti deþ werkmen into his winyarde bi þe morghen, wanne ha clepeþ of swiche þer bieþ into 245
his seruise ine here childhede, wanne hi of þis world wendeþ,

219 fore] *MS.* werefore   227 werefore] *MS.* vre fore

be swo þet hi ne be ine no diadlich senne. At undren ha sent
men into his winyarde þet a turneþ into his seruise of age of
man. At middai, wanne þo dai is alþerhotestd, betokned þo
250 men of xxxti wyntre oþer of furti; for þe nature of man is of
greater strengþe and of greater hete ine þo age. Se euen bitockneþ elde of man, þet is se ende of þe liue. Vre Lord deþ werk-
f. 133ʳ 2 men into his winyarde agenes þo euen wanne fele ine here
elde wendeþ ut of here senne into Cristes seruise; also solle
255 hi habbe þo blisce of heuene ase þo þet ferst comen into þe
winyarde. Nocht for þan for þise griate bunte þet ure Lord
yefþ, ne solde noman targi forto wende to God Almichti ne
him to serui; for also seid þet Holi Writ þet non ne wot þane
dai of his diaþe, for 'Man mai longe liues wene, and ofte him
260 legheþ se wrench'.

Nu, gode men, ye habbeþ iherd þet godspel and þe forbisne:
nu lokeþ yef ye bieþ withinne þo winyarde— þet is þet yef ye
bieþ ine Godes seruise, yef ye bieþ withute diadliche senne,
yef ye hatied þat he hateþ, yef ye luuieþ þet he luueþ, and
265 doþ þet he hot; and bute ye do, ye bieþ hut of his winyarde, þet is, ut of his seruise. And ye doþ þet ure Lord hoot,
so ye ofserueþ þane peni, þet is, heueriche blisce—ye ofserueþ
þet good þet noon herte ne may iþenche, ne noon yare ihere ne
f. 133ᵛ 1 tunge telle, þo blisce þet God halt alle þo þet hine luuieþ. Þider
270 Lord granti us to cumene. *Quod ipse prestare dignetur per
Iesum Christum dominum nostrum.*

254 al] *MS*. As, *with* l *squeezed in after* A *or over it, in the same ink*
264 *first* he] *MS*. he he   266 *first* þet] *MS*. þe   267 is] *suprascript in red* (*with caret*)

XVIII

ANCRENE WISSE

Ancrene Wisse is the contemporary title in MS. Corpus Christi Cambridge 402 of the work which, as preserved without a title in the other manuscripts, has been named *Ancrene Riwle* by modern scholars. It is a manual, specially composed for the guidance (*Wisse*) of three sisters of noble birth who had become recluses. For this class of religious there was no codified 'Rule'; and they differed further from monks and nuns in being (for the most part) committed to a solitary life, and from hermits in being literally 'enclosed' (since they were ceremonially immured in their anchorages and were not free to leave them). The anchor-cell in some instances (including this one) was built on to the wall of a church; and in such cases its occupant followed the service through a window in this wall.

The anonymous author of the *Ancrene Riwle*, who is thought to have been probably a secular priest or regular canon,[1] has earned just praise for his humanity and good sense, his emphasis on the inner life and his slight regard for the details of external conduct. But the true glory of his achievement is his prose style, the nature and the genesis of which have not been accurately understood in modern times (with one recent exception). Profuse imagery makes it signally vivid and rich: metaphors (often drawn out into miniature allegories), illustrations, and comparisons are for him a natural mode of discourse. They charm the inner eye and the fancy; but for the author they were a means to frame an argument and to persuade—and a part only of the means that he brought to bear. His style as a whole is in fact nothing other than a technique of exegesis and instruction; and it was not of his own making.

[1] See C. H. Talbot, 'Some Notes on the Dating of the *Ancrene Riwle*', *Neophilologus*, xxx (1956), 38–50.

Twice, before 1400, masterpieces of English prose were made possible by the methods of Scriptural exegesis evolved by the Fathers and their medieval successors, on the one hand, and of preaching to the unlettered on the other. But the ornamented exuberance of the *Ancrene Riwle* and the dazzling clarity, polish, and urbanity of Ælfric's *Catholic Homilies* belong to different worlds. The exegetical apparatus available to Ælfric was necessarily a much simpler one. What had happened in the meantime was the birth of the universities in the early twelfth century; the intensified study of logic; and the public exercise of the two main forms of exegetical activity by the same person, since the master of theology who lectured on his subject also preached sermons to university audiences. The result was a virtually new technique of preaching, and a much more elaborate and schematized one. That we owe the main elements in the style of the *Ancrene Riwle* to these two forms of Biblical exegesis seems probable, though it has not yet been demonstrated in detail.[1]

The dogma that the *Ancrene Riwle* is a main example of the 'continuity' of Old and Middle English prose is thus a major error of literary history. The author's warm, intimate, easy tone and his conversational syntax are as novel in our prose as his apparatus of style. If he cannot match the music of Ælfric, he speaks in his loftier passages with an affecting eloquence that gives him a secure place among our masters of prose.

·

A

f. 65ᵣ　A3ein alle temptatiuns, ant nomeliche a3ein fleschliche, saluen beoð ant bote under Godes grace—halie meditatiuns, inwarde ant meadlese ant angoisuse bonen, hardi bileaue, redunge, veasten, wecchen, ant licomliche swinkes, oþres
5 froure forte speoke toward i þe ilke stunde þet hire stont stronge. Eadmodnesse, freolec of heorte, ant alle gode þeawes beoð armes i þis feht; ant anrednesse of luue ouer alle þe oþre. Þe his wepnen warpeð awei, him luste beon iwundet.

Interlinear glosses: remedies (beside "saluen beoð"); continually (above "meadlese"); anxious prayers (above "angoisuse bonen"); reading fasting vigils (above "redunge, veasten, wecchen"); bodily works (above "licomliche swinkes"); others (above "oþres"); comfort (above "froure"); with (above "toward"); Humility (above "Eadmodnesse"); Constancy (above "anrednesse"); He who (above "Þe his"); throws (above "warpeð")

---

[1] For some evidence see the note on lines 25, 33.

Hali meditatiuns beoð bicluppet in a uers þet wes ȝare itaht
ow, mine leoue sustren: 10

> Mors tua, mors Cristi, nota culpe, gaudia celi,
> Iudicii terror, figantur mente fideli—

þet is:

þench ofte wið sar of þine sunnen;
þench of helle wa, of heouueriches wunnen; 15
þench of þin ahne deað, of Godes deað o rode;
þe grimme dom of Domesdei munneð ofte ofte i mode;
þench hu fals is þe worlt, hwucche beoð hire meden;
þench hwet tu ahest Godd for his goddeden.

Euchan of þeose word walde a long hwile forte beo wel i- 20
openet; ah ȝef Ich hihi forðward, demeori ȝe þe lengre. A word
Ich segge. Efter ower sunnen, hwen se ȝe þencheð of helle wa
ant of heouueriches wunnen, understondeð þet Godd walde o
sum wise schawin ham to men i þis world bi worltliche pinen
ant worltliche wunnen, ant schaweð ham forð as schadewe; f. 65ᵛ
for na lickre ne beoð ha to þe wunne of heouene ne to þe wa 26
of helle þen is schadewe to þet þing þet hit is of schadewe. Ȝe
beoð ouer þis worldes sea upo þe brugge of heouene: lokið
þet ȝe ne beon nawt þe hors eschif iliche, þe schuncheð for
a schadewe ant falleð adun i þe weater of þe hehe brugge. To 30
childene ha beoð þe fleoð a peinture þe puncheð ham grislich
ant grureful to bihalden: wa ant wunne i þis world—al nis
bute peintunge, al nis bute schadewe.

Nawt ahe hali meditatiuns (as of ure Lauerd, ant of alle his
werkes, ant of alle his wordes, of þe deore Leafdi, ant of alle 35
hali halhen), ah oþre þohtes sum-chearre i meadlese fondunges
habbeð iholpen. Fowr cunne nomeliche, to þeo þe beoð of
flesches fondunges meadlese asailet—dredfule, wunderfule,
gleadfule, ant sorhfule, willes wiðute neod arearet i þe heorte;
as, þenchen hwet tu waldest don ȝef þu sehe openliche stonde 40

biuore þe ant ӡeoniende wide upo þe þen deouel of helle, as
he deð dearnliche i þe fondunge; ӡef me ӡeide 'Fur! fur!', þet
te chirche bearnde; ӡef þu herdest burgurs breoke þine wahes
—þeos ant oþre þulliche dredfule þohtes. Wunderfule ant
45 gleadfule, as ӡef þu sehe Iesu Crist ant herdest him easki þe
hwet te were leouest (efter þi saluatiun ant þine leoueste
freond) of þing o þisse liue ant beode þe cheosen, wiþ þet tu
wiðstode; ӡef þu sehe al witerliche heouene-ware ant helle-
ware i þe temptatiun bihalde þe ane; ӡef me come ant talde þe
50 þet mon þet te is leouest þurh sum miracle (as þurh steuene of
heouene) were icoren as pape; ant alle oþre swucche wunder-
f. 66r fule ant sorhfule, as ӡef þu herdest seggen þet mon þet te is
leouest were ferliche adrenct, oþer imurðret, þet tine
sustren weren in hare hus forbearnde.

55 Þulliche þohtes ofte i fleschliche sawlen wrencheð ut sonre
fleschliche temptatiuns þen sum of þe oþre earre. Inwarde ant
meadlese ant ancrefule bonen biwinneð sone sucurs ant help
ed ure Lauerd aӡeines flesches fondunges: ne beon ha neauer
se ancrefule ne se fulitohene, þe deouel of helle duteð ham
60 swiðe. For teke þet ha draheð adun sucurs aӡein him ant Godes
hond of heouene, ha doð him twa hearmes—bindeð him, ant
bearneð. Lo her preoue of baðe. Publius, an hali mon, wes in
his bonen, ant com þe feond fleonninde bi þe lufte, ant
schulde al on hihðe toward te west-half of þe worlt, þurh
65 Iulienes heast þe empereur; ant warð ibunden heteueste wið
þe hali monne bonen, þe oftoken him as ha fluhen uppard
toward heouene, þet he ne mahte hider ne þider ten dahes
fulle. Nabbe ӡe alswa of Ruffin þe deouel, Beliales broðer, in
ower Englische boc of Seinte Margarete? Of þet oðer me redeð
70 þet he gredde lude to Sein Bartholomew, þe muchel wes i
benen: *Incendunt me orationes tue*—'Bartholomew, wa me! þine
beoden forbearneð me.'

64 hihðe] *not in MS*.

Hwase mei þurh Godes ӡeoue i beoden habbe teares, ha
mei don wið Godd al þet ha eauer wule; for swa we redeð:
Oratio lenit, lacrima cogit; hec ungit, illa pungit. Eadi bone 75
softeð ant paieð ure Lauerd; ah teares doð him strengðe.
Beoden smirieð him wið softe olhnunge, ah teares prikieð him,
ne ne ӡeoueð him neauer pes, ear þen he ӡetti ham al þet ha
easkið. Hwen me asaileð burhes oðer castel, þeo wiðinnen f. 66ᵛ
healdeð scaldinde weater ut ant werieð swa þe walles. Ant ӡe 80
don alswa, as ofte as þe feond asaileð ower castel ant te sawle
burh: wið inwarde bonen warpeð ut upon him scaldinde
teares, þet Dauið segge bi þe: *Contribulasti capita draconum in
aquis*—'þu hauest forscaldet te drake heaueð wið wallinde
weater', þet is, wið hate teares. Þear as þis weater is, sikerliche 85
þe feond flið, leste he beo forscaldet. Eft anoþer: castel þe
haueð dich abuten, ant weater beo i þe dich þe castel is wel
carles aӡeines his unwines. Castel is euch god man þet te
deouel weorreð. Ah habbe ӡe deop dich of deop eadmodnesse
ant wete teares þerto, ӡe beoð strong castel; þe weorrur of helle 90
mei longe asailin ow ant leosen his hwile.

Eft me seið, ant soð hit is, þet a muche wind alið wið a lute
rein, ant te sunne þrefter schineð þe schenre. Alswa a muche
temptatiun, þet is þe feondes bleas, afealleð wið a softe rein of
ane lut wordes teares, ant soðe sunne schineð þrefter schenre 95
to þe sawle. Þus beoð teares gode wið inwarde bonen; ant ӡef
ӡe understondeð, Ich habbe iseid of ham her fowr muchele
efficaces for hwi ha beoð to luuien. In alle ower neoden sendeð
cwicliche anan þes sonde toward houene; for, as Salomon seið,
Oratio humiliantis se penetrat nubes et c.—þet is, þe eadmodies 100
bone þurleð þe weolcne. Ant ter seið Seint Austin: *Magna est
uirtus pure conscientie que ad deum intrat et mandata peragit
ubi caro peruenire nequit.* O, muchel is þe mihte of schir ant
cleane bone þe flið up ant kimeð in biuoren Almihti Godd, ant f. 67ʳ
deð þe ernde se wel þet Godd haueð o liues boc iwriten al þet 105

ha seið (as Sein Beornard witneð), edhalt hire wið himseolf,
ant sent adun his engel to don al þet ha easkeð! Nule Ich her
of bone segge namare.

Hardi bileaue bringeð þe deouel o fluht ananrihtes. Þet
110 witneð Sein Iame: *Resistite diabolo et fugiet a uobis*—edstont
ane þe feond ant he deð him o fluhte. Edstond þurh hwet
strengðe? Seinte Peter teacheð: *Cui resistite fortes in fide.*
Stondeð aȝein him wið stronge bileaue, beoð hardi of Godes
help, ant witeð hu he is wac þe na strengðe naueð on us, bute
115 of us seoluen. Ne mei he bute schawin forð sumhwet of his eape-
ware, ant olhnin oðer þreatin þet me bugge þrof. Hweðer se
he deð, scarnið him: lahheð þe alde eape lude to bismere þurh
treowe bileaue, ant he halt him ischent ant deð him o fluht
swiðe. *Sancti per fidem uicerunt regna*—þet is, þe hali halhen
120 alle ouercomen þurh bileaue þe deofles rixlunge, þet nis bute
sunne; for ne rixleð he i nan bute þurh sunne ane. Neomeð nu
gode ȝeme hu alle þe seouene deadliche sunnen muhen beon
afleiet þurh treowe bileaue. On earst nu of prude.

Hwa halt him muchel, as þe prude deð, hwen he bihalt hu
125 lutel þe muchele Lauerd makede him inwið a poure meidenes
breoste? Hwa is ontful þe bihalt wið ehnen of bileaue hu Iesu
Godd, nawt for his god, ah for oþres god, dude ant seide ant
þolede al þet he þolede? Þe ontfule ne kepte nawt þet eani
dealde of his god; ant Godd Almihti ȝet, efter al þet oþer,
f. 67ᵛ lihte dun to helle forte sechen feolahes ant to deale wið ham
131 þe god þet he hefde. Lo nu, hu frommard beoð ontfule ure
Lauerd! Þe ancre þe wearnde anoþer a cwaer to lane, for ha
hefde heoneward hire bileaue ehe.

Hwa halt wreaððe þe bihalt þet Godd lihte on eorðe to
135 makien profal sahte—bitweone mon ant mon, bitweone Godd
ant mon, bitweone mon ant engel? Ant efter his ariste, þa
he com ant schawde him, þis wes his gretunge to his deore

119 halhen] *MS.* halhen alhen

deciples: *Pax uobis*—'sahtnesse beo bitweonen ow'. Neomeð
nu ȝeorne ȝeme: hwen leof freond went from oþer, þe leaste
wordes þet he seið, þeo schulen beo best edhalden. Vre 140
Lauerdes leaste wordes, þa he steah to heouene ant leafde his
leoue freond in uncuðe þeode, weren of swote luue ant of
sahtnesse: *Pacem relinquo uobis: pacem meam do uobis*—þet
is, 'sahtnesse Ich do imong ow; sahtnesse Ich leaue wið ow'.
Þis wes his druerie þet he leafde ant ȝef ham in his departunge. 145
*In hoc cognoscetis quoð dicipuli mei sitis, si dilectionem adinuicem
habueritis.* Lokið nu ȝeorne, for his deorewurðe luue, hwuch a
mearke he leide upon his icorene þa he steah to heouene: *In
hoc cognoscetis quoð et c.* 'Bi þet ȝe schulen icnawen', quoð he,
'þet ȝe beoð mine deciples, ȝef swete luue ant sahtnesse is eauer 150
ow bitweonen.' Godd hit wite ant he hit wat, me were leouere
þet ȝe weren alle o þe spitel-uuel þen ȝe weren ontfule oðer
feol-iheortet; for Iesu is al luue, ant i luue he resteð him ant
haueð his wununge: *In pace factus est locus eius. Ibi confregit
potencias, arcum, scutum, gladium, et bellum*—þet is, i sahtnesse 155
is Godes stude; ant hwer se sahte is ant luue, þear he bringeð
to nawt al þes deofles strengðe, þer he brekeð his bohe, hit f. 68ʳ
seið (þet beoð dearne fondunges þet he scheot of feor), ant his
sweord baðe (þet beoð temptatiuns keoruinde of neh ant kene).
Neomeð nu ȝeorne ȝeme bi moni forbisne hu god is anred- 160
nesse of luue ant annesse of heorte; for nis þing under sunne
þet me is leouere ne se leof þet ȝe habben. Nute ȝe, þer men
fehteð i þes stronge ferdes, þe ilke þe haldeð ham feaste
togederes ne muhe beo descumfit o neauer nane wise? Alswa
hit is in gastelich feht aȝeines þe deouel: al his entente is forte 165
tweamen heorten, forte bineomen luue þet halt men togederes.
For hwen luue alið, þenne beoð ha isundret, ant te deouel deð
him bitweonen ananriht ant sleað on euche halue. Dumbe
beastes habbeð þis ilke warschipe, þet hwen ha beoð asailet of
wulf oðer of liun, ha þrungeð togederes—al þe floc—feste, 170

ant makieð scheld of hamseolf, euch of heom to oþer, ant
beoð þe hwile sikere; ȝef eani unseli went ut, hit is sone awuriet.
Þe þridde: þer an geað him ane in a slubbri wei, he slit ant
falleð sone. Þer monie gað togederes ant euch halt oþres hond,
175 ȝef eani feo to sliden, þe oðer hine breid up ear he ful falle;
ȝef ha wergið, euchan halt him bi oþer. Fondunge is sliddrunge; þurh wergunge beoð bitacnet þe unþeawes under
slawðe þe beoð inempnet þruppe. Þis is þet Sein Gregoire seið:
Cum nos nobis per orationis opem coniungimus per lubricum
180 *incedentes, quasi adinuicem manus teneamus, vt tanto quisque*
amplius roboretur quanto alteri innititur. Alswa i strong wind
ant swifte weattres þe me mot ouerwaden, of monie euch halt
oðer; þe isundrede is iswipt forð ant forfeareð eauer. To wel
we witen hu þe wei of þis world is slubbri, hu þe wind ant te
185 stream of fondunge aren stronge: muche neod is þet euch halde
wið bisie bonen ant wið luue oþres honden. For, as Salomon
seið: *Ve soli, quia cum ceciderit non habet subleuantem*—'Wa
eauer þe ane, for hwen he falleð, naueð he hwa him areare.'
Nan nis ane þe haueð Godd to fere; ant þet is euch þet soð
190 luue haueð in his heorte.

Þe seoueðe forbisne is þis, ȝef ȝe riht telleð: dust ant greot,
as ȝe seoð, for hit is isundret ant nan ne halt to oþer, a lutel
windes puf todriueð hit al to nawt; þear hit is in a clot ilimet
togederes, hit lið al stille. An hondful of ȝerden beoð earueð to
195 breoken hwil ha beoð togederes; euchan itweamet lihtliche
bersteð. A treo þe wule fallen, undersete hit wið anoþer ant
hit stont feste; tweam ham, ant ba falleð. Nu ȝe habbeð
nihene: þus i þinges utewið neomeð forbisne hu god is annesse
of luue ant sometreadnesse, þet halt þe gode somet þet nan
200 ne mei forwurðen. Ant þis wule iwiss habben þe rihte bileaue.

Bihald ȝeorne ant understont Iesu Cristes deorewurðe
wordes ant werkes, þe i luue weren alle ant i swetnesse. Ouer

178 inempnet] *MS.* itemptet

alle þing Ich walde þet ancren leorneden wel þis lesceunes
lare. For monie (mare hearm is!) beoð Samsones foxes, þe
hefden þe neb euchan iwend frommard oþer, ant weren bi þe 205
teiles iteiet togederes, as Iudicum teleð, ant in euchanes teil
a blease bearninde. Of þeose foxes Ich spec feor þruppe, ah
nawt o þisse wise. Neomeð gode ȝeme hwet þis beo to seggen:
me turneð þe neb bliðeliche towart þing þet me luueð ant f. 69ʳ
frommard þing þet me heateð. Þeo þenne habbeð þe nebbes 210
wrong-wende euch frommard oðer hwen nan ne luueð oþer;
ah bi þe teiles ha beoð somet ant beoreð þes deofles bleasen, þe
brune of galnesse. On anoðer wise, teil bitacneð ende: in hare
ende ha schulen beon ibunden togederes, as weren Samsones
foxes bi þe teiles, ant iset bleasen þrin (þet is þet fur of helle). 215

Al þis is iseid, mine leoue sustren, þet ower leoue nebbes
beon euer iwent somet wið luueful semblant ant wið swote
chere, þet ȝe beon aa wið annesse of an heorte ant of a wil
ilimet togederes, as hit iwriten is bi ure Lauerdes deore
deciples: *Multitudinis credentium erat cor unum et anima una;* 220
pax uobis. Þis wes Godes gretunge to his deore deciples: 'Grið
beo bimong ow'. Ȝe beoð, þe ancren of Englond, swa feole
togederes—twenti nuðe oðer ma. Godd i god ow mutli þet
meast grið is among, meast annesse, ant anrednesse, ant sometreadnesse of anred lif, efter a riwle, swa þet alle teoð an, alle 225
iturnt answeis ant nan frommard oðer. Efter þet word is,
forþi ȝe gað wel forð ant spedeð in ower wei, for euch is wiðward oþer in a manere of liflade, as þah ȝe weren an cuuent of
Lundene ant of Oxnefort, of Schreobsburi, oðer of Chester.
Þear as alle beoð an wið an imeane manere ant wiðuten singu- 230
larite—þet is anful frommardschipe, lah þing i religiun, for hit
towarpeð annesse ant manere imeane þet ah to beon in ordre—
þis nu þenne þet ȝe beoð alle as an cuuent is ower hehe fame,
þis is Godd icweme, þis is nunan wide cuð, swa þet ower
cuuent biginneð to spreaden toward Englondes ende. Ȝe beoð 235

as þe moder hus þet heo beoð of istreonet. ȝe beoð ase wealle:
ȝef þe wealle woreð, þe strunden worið alswa. A, weila! ȝef
ȝe worið, ne bide Ich hit neauer. Ȝef ei is imong ow þe geað
i singularite ant ne folheð nawt þe cuuent, ah went ut of þe
floc (þet is as in a cloistre þet Iesu Crist is heh priur ouer),
went ut as a teoþi schep ant meapeð hire ane into breres teilac,
into wulues muð, toward te þrote of helle—ȝef ei swuch is
imong ow, Godd turne hire into floc, wende hire into cuuent,
ant leue ow þe beoð þrin swa halden ow þrin þet Godd, þe
hehe priur, neome ow on ende þeonne up into þe cloistre of
heouene.

Hwil ȝe haldeð ow in an, offearen ow mei þe feond, ȝef he
haueð leaue, ah hearmin nawt mid alle. Þet he wat ful wel, ant
is forþi umben deies ant nihtes to unlimin ow wið wreaððe
oðer wið luðer onde, ant sent mon oþer wummon þe telle
an bi þe oþer sum suhinde sahe þet suster ne schulde nawt
segge bi suster. Ower nan (Ich forbeode ow) ne leue þe
deofles sondesmon; ah lokið þet euch of ow icnawe wel hwen
he spekeð i þe vuele monnes tunge, ant segge ananrihtes: 'Vre
meistre haueð iwriten us, as in heast to halden, þet we tellen
him al þet euch of oþer hereð. Ant forþi loke þe þet tu na þing
ne telle me þet Ich ne muhe him tellen, þe mei don þe amendement ant con swaliches don hit, þet Ich ant tu baðe, ȝef we
beoð i þe soð, schule beon unblamet.'

Euch noðele warni oþer, þurh ful siker sondesmon, swete-
liche ant luueliche, as hire leoue suster, of þing þet ha misnimeð,
ȝef ha hit wat to soðe; ant makie hwase bereð þet word recordin
hit ofte biuoren hire, ear ha ga, hu ha wule seggen, þet ha ne
segge hit oðerweis ne cluti þerto mare (for a lute clut mei
ladlechin swiðe a muchel hal pece). Þeo þe ed hire suster þis
luue-salue underueð, þoncki hire ȝeorne ant segge wið þe
salmwruhte: *Corripiet me iustus in misericordia et increpabit me;*

240 Crist] *not in MS.*   241 teoþi] *MS.* teowi

oleum autem peccatoris non inpinguet caput meum; ant þrefter
wið Salomon: *Meliora sunt uulnera corripientis quam oscula
blandientis*—'ʒef ha ne luuede me, nalde ha nawt warni me i 270
misericorde; leouere me beoð preagendes wunden þen fikiende
cosses.' Þus ondswerie eauer. Ant ʒef hit is oðerweis þen þe
oðer understont, sende hire word aʒein prof luueliche ant
softe; ant te oþer leue ananriht.

  For þet Ich chulle alswa, þet euch of ow luue oþer as hire- 275
seoluen. Ʒef þe feond bitweonen ow toblaweð eani wreaððe
oþer great heorte (þet Iesu Crist forbeode!), ear ha beo iset
wel, nawt ane to neomen Godes flesch ant his blod ne wurðe
nan se witles; ah ʒet (þet is leasse) þet ha eanes ne bihalde
þeron, ne loki i ful wreaððe toward him þe lihte to mon in 280
eorðe of heouene to makien preouald sahte, as is iseid þruppe.
Sende eiðer þenne oþer word þet ha haueð imaket hire, as þah
ha were biuoren hire, eadmodliche venie. Ant þeo þe ear
ofdraheð þus luue of hire suster, ant ofgeap sahte, ant nimeð
þe gult toward hire þah þe oþer hit habbe mare, ha schal beo 285
mi deorewurðe ant mi deore dohter; for ha is Godes dohter
he himseolf hit seið: *Beati pacifici quoniam filii dei uocabuntur.*
Þus prude, ant onde, ant wreaððe beoð ihwer afleiet hwer se
soð luue is ant treowe bileaue to Godes milde werkes ant
luuefule wordes. 290

B

Ondes salue, Ich seide, wes feolahlich luue, ant god unnunge, f. 77ʳ
ant god wil þer mihte of dede wonteð. Swa muchel strengðe
haueð luue ant god wil þet hit makeð oþres god ure god, ase
wel as his þet hit wurcheð. Sulement luue is god. Beo wilcweme ant glead prof: þus þu turnest hit to þe ant makest hit 295
þin ahne. Sein Gregoire hit witneð: *aliena bona si diligis, tua*

271 þreagendes] *in margin, in light ink and different hand; MS.* hire
(*before* wunden) *marked for deletion in same ink*

facis. Ȝef þu hauest onde of oþres god, þu attrest te wið healewi ant wundest te wið salue. Þi salue hit is, ȝef þu hit luuest, aȝein sawle hurtes; ant ti strengðe aȝein þe feond is al
300 þe god þet oðer deð, ȝef þu hit wel unnest.

Witerliche, Ich leue, ne schulen flesches fondunges, namare þen gasteliche, meistrin þe neauere, ȝef þu art swote-iheortet, eadmod, ant milde, ant luuest se inwardliche alle men ant wummen (ant nomeliche ancres, þine leoue sustren) þet tu art
305 sari of hare uuel ant of hare god glead as of þin ahne. Vnnen þet al þe luueð þe luuede ham ase þe, ant dude ham froure as þe; ȝef þu hauest cnif, oðer claðe, oðer mete, oþer drunch, scrowe, oðer cwaer, hali monne froure, oðer ei oþer þing þet ham walde freamien, vnnen þet tu hefdest wonte þe seolf þrof,
310 wið þon þet heo hit hefden—ȝef eani is þe naueð nawt þe heorte þus afeitet, wið sorhfule sikes ba bi dei ant þi niht grede on ure Lauerd, ne neauer grið ne ȝeoue him ðet he þurh his grace habbe hire swuch aturnet.

Salue of wreaððe, Ich seide, is þolemodnesse þet haueð þreo
315 steiren—heh, ant herre, ant alre hest ant nest te hehe heouene. Heh is þe steire, ȝef þu þolest for þi gult; herre, ȝef þu nauest gult; alre hest, ȝef þu þolest for þi goddede. 'Nai!' seið sum ameaset þing, 'ȝef Ich hefde gult þerto, nalde Ich neauer meanen.' Art tu þet swa seist ut of þe seoluen? Is þe leouere
320 to beon Iudase feolahe þen Iesu Cristes fere? Ba weren anhonget; ah Iudas for his gult—Iesu wiðute gult for his muchele godlec wes ahon o rode. Hweðeres fere wult tu beon? Wið hweðer wult tu þolien?

Of þis is þruppe iwriten muchel, hu he is þi file þe misseið
325 oðer misdeð þe; 'lime' is þe Frensch of file. Nis hit or acurset þe iwurðeð swartre ant ruhre se hit is ifilet mare, ant rusteð þe swiðere þet me hit scureð hearde? Gold, seoluer, stel, irn—al is or. Gold ant seoluer cleansið ham of hare dros i þe fur; ȝef þu gederest dros þrin, þet is aȝein cunde. Þe chaliz þe wes þerin

imealt ant strongliche iweallet, ant seoððen þurh se moni dunt 330
ant frotunge to Godes neƀ se swiðe feire afeitet—walde he, ȝef
he cuðe speoken, awearien his cleansing fur ant his wruhte
honden? *Argentum reprobum uocate eos.* Al þis world is Godes
smiððe to smeoðien his icorene: wult tu þet Godd nabbe na
fur in his smiððe, ne bealies, ne homeres? Fur is scheome ant 335
pine; þine bealies beoð þe þe misseggeð, þine homeres þe þe
hearmið. Þench of þis essample.

Hwen dei of riht is iset, ne deð he scheome þe deme þe a þis
half þe isette dei brekeð þe triws ant wrekeð him o þe oðer 339
on himseoluen? *Augustinus: quid gloriatur impius si de ipso* f. 78ʳ
flagellum faciat pater meus? Ant hwa nat þet Domesdei nis þe
dei iset to don riht alle men? Hald þe triws þe hwiles. Hwet
woh se me deð þe, ne do þu nawt him scheome (forhohie
wrake of his dom ant neomen to þin ahne). Twa þinges beoð
þet Godd haueð edhalden to himseoluen; þet beoð wurðscipe 345
ant wrake, as Hali Writ witneð: *Gloriam meam alteri non dabo.*
Item: michi vindictam; ego retribuam. Hwase euer on himseolf
takeð owðer of þeos twa, he robbeð Godd ant reaueð. Deale,
art tu se wrað wið mon oþer wið wummon, þet tu wult, forte wreoke þe, reauin Godd mid strengðe? 350

Accidies salue is gastelich gleadscipe ant froure of gleadful
hope, þurh redunge, þurh hali þoht, oðer of monnes muðe.
Ofte, leoue sustren, ȝe schulen uri leasse, forte reden mare.
Redunge is god bone: redunge teacheð hu ant hwet me bidde,
ant beode biȝet hit efter. Amidde þe redunge, hwen þe heorte 355
likeð, kimeð up a deuotiun þet is wurð monie benen. Forþi
seið Sein Ierome: [*Ieronimus*]. *Semper in manu tua sacra sit*
lectio; tenenti tibi librum sompnus subripiat, et cadentem faciem
pagina sancta suscipiat—'Hali redunge beo eauer i þine honden;
slep ga upo þe as þu lokest þron, ant te hali pagne ikepe þi 360

334 smiððe] *MS.* smið   341 *faciat*] *MS.* fatiat

fallinde neb'. Swa þu schalt reden ȝeornliche ant longe. Euch
þing þah me mei ouerdon; best is eauer mete. . . . .

Forþi, mi leoue suster, sone se þu eauer underȝetest þet tes
dogge of helle cume snakerinde wið his blodi flehen of stinkinde
365 þohtes, ne li þu nawt stille, ne ne site nowðer, to lokin hwet he
wule don ne hu feor he wule gan. Ne sei þu nawt slepinde 'Ame
dogge, ga herut! Hwet wult tu nu herinne?'—þis tolleð him
inward; ah him anan þe rode-steaf mid nempnunge i þi muð,
mid te mearke i þin hond, mid þoht i þin heorte, ant hat him
370 ut heterliche, þe fule cur-dogge, ant liðere to him luðerliche
mid te hali rode-steaf stronge bacduntes. Þet is, rung up;
sture þe; hald up ehnen on heh ant honden toward heouene;
gred efter sucurs—*Deus in adiutorium meum intende. Domine
ad adiuuandum. Veni creator spiritus. Exurgat Deus et dissipentur*
375 *inimici eius. Deus in nomine tuo saluum me fac. Domine, quid
multiplicati sunt. Ad te, Domine, leuaui animam meam. Ad te
leuaui oculos meos. Leuaui oculos meos in montes.* Ȝef þe ne
kimeð sone help, gred luddre wið hat heorte: *Vsque quo,
Domine, obliuisceris me in finem? usque auerteris faciem tuam
380 a me?*—ant swa al þe salm ouer, *Pater noster, Credo, Aue Maria.*
Wið halsinde bonen o þin ahne ledene, smit smeortliche adun
þe cheon to þer eorðe ant breid up þe rode-steaf ant sweng him
o fowr half aȝein, helle-dogge—þet nis nawt elles bute blesce
þe al abuten wið þe eadi rode-taken, spite him amid te beard to
385 hoker ant to scarne þe flikereð swa wið þe ant fikeð dogge-
fahenunge. Hwen he for se liht wurð, for þe licunge of a lust
ane hwile stucche chapeð þi sawle, Godes deore bune þet he
bohte mid his blod ant mid his deorewurðe deað o þe deore
rode, aa bihald hire wurð þet he paide for hire ant dem prefter
390 hire pris ant beo on hire þe deorre. Ne sule þu neauer se eðeliche
his fa ant þin eiðer his deorewurðe spuse þet costnede him se
deore: makie deofles hore of hire is reowðe ouer reowðe. To
unwreast mid alle ha is þe mei wið to heouen up hire þreo

fingres ouercumen hire fa, ant ne luste for slawðe. Hef forþi
wið treowe ant hardi bileaue up þine þreo fingres, ant wið þe 395
hali rode-steaf, þet him is laðest cuggel, lei o þe dogge deouel—
nempne ofte Iesu, cleope his passiunes help, halse bi his pine,
bi his deorewurðe blod, bi his deað o rode. Flih to his wunden:
muchel he luuede us þe lette makien swucche þurles in him for
te huden us in. Creop in ham wið þi þoht; ne beoð ha al opene? 400

C

Seinte Pawel witneð þet alle uttre heardschipes, alle flesches f. 104ʳ
pinsunges ant licomliche swinkes, al is ase nawt aȝeines luue,
þe schireð ant brihteð þe heorte. *Exercitio corporis ad modicum
ualet: pietas autem ualet ad omnia.* Þet is, licomlich bisischipe
is to lutel wurð; ah swote ant schir heorte is god to alle þinges. 405
*Si linguis hominum loquar et angelorum et c.; si tradidero corpus
meum ita ut ardeam et c.; si distribuero omnes facultates meas in
cibos pauperum, caritatem autem non habeam, nichil michi prodest.*
'Þah Ich cuðe', he seið, 'monne ledene ant englene, þah Ich dude
o mi bodi alle pine ant passiun þet bodi mahte þolien, þah 410
Ich ȝeue poure al þet Ich hefde—ȝef Ich nefde luue þerwið
to Godd, ant to alle men in him ant for him, al were ispillet.'
For, as þe hali abbat Moyses seide, al þet wa ant al þet
heard þet we þolieþ o flesch, ant al þet god þet we eauer doð,
alle swucche þinges ne beoð nawt bute as lomen to tilie wið 415
þe heorte. Ȝef þe axe ne kurue, ne spitelsteaf ne dulue, ne þe
sulh ne erede, hwa kepte ham to halden? Alswa as na mon ne
luueð lomen for hamseolf, ah deð for þe þinges þet me wurcheð
wið ham, alswa na flesches derf nis to luuien bute forþi þet
Godd te reaðere þiderward loki mid his grace, ant makeð þe 420
heorte schir ant of briht sihðe, þet nan ne mei habben wið
monglunge of unþeawes ne wið eorðlich luue of worltliche
þinges; for þis mong woreð swa þe ehnen of þe heorte þet ha

ne mei cnawen Godd ne gleadien of his sihðe. Schir heorte, as
425 Seint Bernard seið, makieð twa þinges—þet tu, al þet tu dest,
do hit oðer for luue ande of Godd, oðer for oþres god ant for
his biheue. Haue in al þet tu dest an of þes twa ententes, oðer
ba togederes; for þe leatere falleð into þe earre. Haue eauer
schir heorte þus, ant do al þet tu wult; haue wori heorte—al
430 þe sit uuele. *Omnia munda mundis, coinquinatis uero nichil est
mundum. Apostolus. Item Augustinus: Habe caritatem, et fac
quicquid uis, uoluntate uidelicet rationis.*

Forþi, mine leoue sustren, ouer alle þing beoð bisie to habben schir heorte. Hwet is schir heorte? Ich hit habbe iseid ear:
435 þet is, þet ʒe na þing ne wilnin ne ne luuien bute Godd ane,
ant te ilke þinges, for Godd, þe helpeð ow toward him. For
Godd, Ich segge, luuien ham, ant nawt for hamseoluen, as is
mete, oðer clað, mon oðer wummon þe ʒe beoð of iʒodet. For,
ase seið Seint Austin, ant spekeð þus to ure Lauerd: *Minus te
440 amat qui preter te aliquid amat quod non propter te amat.* Þet is,
'Lauerd, leasse ha luuieð þe þe luuieð eawt bute þe, bute ha
luuien hit for þe.' Schirnesse of heorte is Godes luue ane. I þis
is al þe strengðe of alle religiuns, þe ende of alle ordres.
Plenitudo legis est dilectio. 'Luue fulleð þe lahe' seið Seinte
445 Pawel. *Quicquid precipitur, in sola caritate solidatur.* Alle
Godes heastes, as Sein Gregoire seið, beoð i luue irotet. Luue
ane schal beon ileid i Seinte Mihales weie. Þeo þe meast
luuieð schulen beo meast iblisset, nawt þeo þe leadeð heardest
lif; for luue hit ouerweieð. Luue is heouene stiward, for hire
450 muchele freolec. For heo ne edhalt naþing, ah, ʒeueð al þet ha
haueð, ant ec hireseoluen; elles ne kepte Godd nawt of þet
hiren were.

Godd haueð ofgan ure luue on alle cunne wise: he haueð
muchel idon us, ant mare bihaten. Muchel ʒeoue ofdraheð
luue. Me al þe world he ʒef us in Adam, ure alde-feader;
456 ant al þet is i þe world he weorp under ure fet—beastes ant

fuheles—ear we weren forgulte. *Omnia subiecisti sub pedibus
eius, oues et boues uniuersas, insuper et pecora campi, uolucres
celi, et pisces maris qui perambulant semitas maris.* Ant ȝet al
þet is, as is þruppe iseid, serueð þe gode to sawle biheue; ȝet
te uuele seruið eorðe, sea, ant sunne. He dude ȝet mare—ȝef us
nawt ane of his, ah dude al himseoluen. Se heh ȝeoue nes
neauer iȝeuen to se lahe wrecches. *Apostolus: Cristus dilexit
ecclesiam et dedit semet ipsum pro ea.* Crist (seið Seinte Pawel)
luuede swa his leofmon þet he ȝef for hire þe pris of himseoluen.
Neomeð nu gode ȝeme, mine leoue sustren, for hwi me ah him
to luuien: earst, as a mon þe woheð—as a king þet luuede a
gentil poure leafdi of feorrene londe. He sende his sonden
biuoren (þet weren þe patriarches ant te prophetes of þe Alde
Testament) wið leattres isealet. On ende he com himseoluen,
ant brohte þe Godspel as leattres i-openet, ant wrat wið his
ahne blod saluz to his leofmon, luue-gretunge forte wohin hire
wið ant hire luue wealden. Herto falleð a tale, a wrihe forbisne.

A leafdi wes mid hire fan biset al abuten, hire lond al
destruet, ant heo al poure, inwið an eorðene castel. A mihti
kinges luue wes þah biturnd upon hire, swa unimete swiðe þet
he for wohlech sende hire his sonden, an efter oðer, ofte somet
monie; sende hire beawbelez baðe feole ant feire, sucurs of
liueneð, help of his hehe hird to halden hire castel. Heo underfeng al as on unrecheles, ant swa wes heard-iheortet þet hire
luue ne mahte he neauer beo þe neorre. Hwet wult tu mare?
He com himseolf on ende; schawde hire his feire neb, as þe þe
wes of alle men feherest to bihalden; spec se swiðe swoteliche,
ant wordes se murie, þet ha mahten deade arearen to liue; f. 105ᵛ
wrahte feole wundres ant dude muchele meistries biuoren hire
ehsihðe; schawde hire his mihte; talde hire of his kinedom;
bead to makien hire cwen of al þet he ahte.

463 wrecches] *MS.* wrecch|ces *divided at line end*   469 prophetes]
MS. prophes

Al þis ne heold nawt. Nes þis hoker wunder? For heo nes
neauer wurðe forte beon his þuften. Ah swa, þurh his de-
490 boneirte, luue hefde ouercumen him þet he seide on ende;
'Dame, þu art iweorret, ant þine van beoð se stronge þet tu
ne maht nanesweis wiðute mi sucurs edfleon hare honden, þet
ha ne don þe to scheome deað efter al þi weane. Ich chulle, for
þe luue of þe, neome þet feht upo me ant arudde þe of ham þe
495 þi deað secheð. Ich wat þah to soðe þet Ich schal bituhen ham
neomen deaðes wunde; ant Ich hit wulle heorteliche, forte
ofgan þin heorte. Nu þenne biseche Ich þe, for þe luue þet
Ich cuðe þe, þet tu luuie me, lanhure efter þe ilke dede dead
hwen þu naldest liues.' Þes king dude al þus—arudde hire of
500 alle hire van, ant wes himseolf to wundre ituket ant islein on
ende, þurh miracle aras þah from deaðe to liue. Nere þeos ilke
leafdi of uueles cunnes kunde, ȝef ha ouer alle þing ne luuede
him herefter?

Þes king is Iesu, Godes sune, þet al o þise wise wohede ure
505 sawle þe deoflen hefden biset. Ant he, as noble wohere, efter
monie messagers ant feole goddeden, com to pruuien his luue,
ant schawde þurh cnihtschipe þet he wes luuewurðe; as weren
sumhwile cnihtes iwunet to donne, dude him i turneiment ant
hefde for his leoues luue his scheld i feht as kene cniht on euche
510 half iþurlet. His scheld þe wreah his goddhead wes his leoue
licome þet wes ispread o rode—brad as scheld buuen in his
istrahte earmes, nearow bineoðen as þe an fot (efter monies
wene, set upo þe oðer). Þet þis scheld naueð siden, is for
bitacnunge þet his deciples, þe schulden stonden bi him ant
515 habben ibeon his siden, fluhen alle from him ant leafden him
as fremede, as þe Godspel seið: *Relicto eo omnes fugerunt.* Þis
scheld is iȝeuen us aȝein alle temptatiuns, as Ieremie witneð:
Dabis scutum cordis laborem tuum. Nawt ane þis scheld ne
schilt us from alle uueles, ah deð ȝet mare—cruneð us in
520 heouene *scuto bone uoluntatis.* 'Lauerd', he seið, Dauið, 'wið þe

scheld of þi gode wil þu hauest us icrunet'—scheld, he seið,
of god wil, for willes he þolede al þet he þolede. *Ysaias:*
Oblatus est quia uoluit.

'Me, Lauerd!' þu seist, 'hwerto? Ne mahte he wið leasse
gref habben arud us?' Ʒeoi, iwiss, ful lihtliche; ah he nalde. 525
For hwi? Forte bineomen us euch bitellunge aʒein him of ure
luue þet he se deore bohte. Me buð lihtliche þing þet me luueð
lutel. He bohte us wið his heorte blod—deorre pris nes neauer
—forte ofdrahen of us ure luue toward him, þet costnede him
se sare. I scheld beoð þreo þinges—þe treo, ant te leðer, ant 530
te litunge. Alswa wes i þis scheld—þe treo of þe rode, þet leðer
of Godes licome, þe litunge of þe reade blod þet heowede hire
se feire. Eft þe þridde reisun: efter kene cnihtes deað me
hongeð hehe i chirche his scheld on his mungunge. Alswa is
þis scheld, þet is þe crucifix, i chirche iset i swuch stude þer 535
me hit sonest seo, forte þenchen þerbi o Iesu Cristes cnihtschipe þet he dude o rode. His leofmon bihalde þron hu he
bohte hire luue—lette þurlin his scheld, openin his side to
schawin hire his heorte, to schawin hire openliche hu inward- f. 106ᵛ
liche he luuede hire, ant to ofdrahen hire heorte.

Fowr heaued-luuen me ifind i þis world: bitweone gode 541
iferen, bitweone mon ant wummon, bitweone wif ant hire
child, bitweone licome ant sawle. Þe luue þet Iesu Crist
haueð to his deore leofmon ouergeað þeos fowre, passeð ham
alle. Ne teleð me him god fere þe leið his wed i Giwerie to 545
acwitin ut his fere? Godd Almihti leide himseolf for us
i Giwerie, ant dude his deorewurðe bodi to acwitin ut his
leofmon of Giwene honden. Neauer fere ne dude swuch fordede for his fere.

Muche luue is ofte bitweone mon ant wummon. Ah þah ha 550
were iweddet him, ha mahte iwurðen se unwreast, ant swa
longe ha mahte forhorin hire wið oþre men, þet þah ha walde

542 *second* bitweone] *MS.* bi

aȝein cumen, he ne kepte hire nawt. Forþi Crist luueð mare.
For þah þe sawle (his spuse) forhori hire wið þe feond under
555 heaued-sunne feole ȝeres ant dahes, his mearci is hire eauer
ȝarow hwen ha wule cumen ham ant leten þen deouel. Al þis
he seið himseolf þurh Ieremie: *Si dimiserit uir uxorem suam
et c. Tu autem fornicata es cum multis amatoribus: tamen
reuertere ad me, dicit Dominus.* Ȝet he ȝeiȝeð al dei: 'þu þet
560 hauest se unwreaste idon, biturn þe ant cum aȝein; welcume
schalt tu beo me.' *Immo et occurrit prodigo uenienti.* Ȝet he
eorneð (hit seið) aȝein hire ȝein-cume, ant warpeð earmes anan
abuten hire swire. Hweat is mare milce? Ȝet her gleadfulre
wunder. Ne beo neauer his leof forhoret mid se monie deadliche
565 sunnen, sone se ha kimeð to him aȝein, he makeð hire neowe
meiden. For, as Seint Austin seið, swa muchel is bitweonen
Godes neoleachunge ant monnes to wummon, þet monnes
neoleachunge makeð of meiden wif, ant Godd makeð of wif
meiden. *Restituit, inquit Job, in integrum.* Gode werkes ant
570 treowe bileaue—þeose twa þinges beoð meiðhad i sawle.

Nu of þe þridde luue. Child þet hefde swuch uuel þet him
bihofde beað of blod ear hit were ihealet, muchel þe moder
luuede hit þe walde þis beað him makien. Þis dude ure Lauerd
us, þe weren se seke of sunne ant swa isulet þerwið þet naþing
575 ne mahte healen us ne cleansin us bute his blod ane; for swa
he hit walde. His luue makeð us beað þrof: iblescet beo he
eaure! þreo beaðes he greiðede to his deore leofmon, forte
weschen hire in ham se hwit ant se feier þet ha were wurðe
to his cleane cluppunges. Þe earste beað is fulluht; þe oðer
580 beoð teares inre oðer uttre, efter þe forme beað, ȝef ha hire
suleð; þe þridde is Iesu Cristes blod, þet halheð ba þe oþre,
as Sein Iuhan seið i þe Apocalipse: *Qui dilexit nos et lauit nos
in sanguine suo.* Þet he luueð us mare þen eani moder hire child,
he hit seið himseoluen þurh Ysaie. *Nunquid potest mater*

566 bitweonen] *MS.* bitweonen bituhhen

obliuisci filii uteri sui? Etsi illa obliuiscatur, ego non obliui- 585
scar tui. 'Mei moder', he seið, 'forȝeoten hire child? Ant þah
heo do, Ich ne mei þe forȝeoten neauer.' Ant seið þe resun
efter: *In manibus meis descripsi te.* 'Ich habbe', he seið, 'depeint te
i mine honden': swa he dude, mid read blode upo þe rode. Me
cnut his gurdel to habben þoht of a þing; ah ure Lauerd, for 590
he nalde neauer forȝeoten us, dude mearke of þurlunge, in ure
munegunge, i ba twa his honden.

Nv þe feorðe luue. Þe sawle luueð þe licome swiðe mid alle,
ant þet is etscene i þe twinnunge; for leoue freond beoð sari
hwen ha schulen twinnin. Ah ure Lauerd willeliche totweamde 595
his sawle from his bodi for te veien ure baðe togederes, world
buten ende, i þe blisse of heouene. Þus, lo, Iesu Cristes luue f. 107ᵛ
toward his deore spuse, þet is Hali Chirche, oðer cleane sawle,
passeð alle ant ouerkimeð þe fowr measte luuen þet me ifind
on eorðe. Wið al þis luue, ȝetten he woheð hire o þis wise: 600
'Þi luue', he seið, 'oðer hit is forte ȝeouen allunge, oðer hit
is to sullen, oðer hit is to reauin ant to neomen wið strengðe.
Ȝef hit is forte ȝeouen, hwer maht tu biteon hit betere þen
upo me? Nam Ich þinge feherest? Nam Ich kinge richest? Nam
Ich hest icunnet? Nam Ich weolie wisest? Nam Ich monne 605
hendest? Nam Ich þinge freoest? For swa me seið, bi large
mon þe ne con nawt edhalden, þet he haueð þe honden—as
mine beoð—iþurlet. Nam Ich alre þinge swotest ant swetest?
Þus alle þe reisuns hwi me ah to ȝeoue luue þu maht ifinden
in me, nomeliche ȝef þu luuest chaste cleannesse; for nan ne 610
mei luuie me bute ha hire halde. Ah ha is þreouald—i widewe-
had, i spus-had, i meidenhad (þe heste). Ȝef þi luue nis nawt
to ȝeouene, ah wult þet me bugge hire—buggen hire hu? Oðer
wið oðer luue, oðer wið sumhweat elles? Me suleð wel luue for
luue; ant swa me ah to sulle luue, ant for naþing elles. Ȝef þin 615
is swa to sullen, Ich habbe iboht hire wið luue ouer alle oþre;

613 hu] *not in MS.* 614–15 for luue] *not in MS.*

for, of þe fowr measte luuen, Ich habbe icud toward te þe
measte of ham alle. Ȝef þu seist þu nult nawt leote þron se
liht chap, ah wult ȝette mare: nempne hweat hit schule beon—
620 sete feor o þi luue. Þu ne schalt seggen se muchel þet Ich nule
ȝeoue mare. Wult tu castles, kinedomes? Wult tu wealden al
þe world? Ich chulle do þe betere—makie þe, wið al þis, cwen
of heoueriche. Þu schalt te seolf beo seoueuald brihtre þen þe
f. 108ʳ sunne; nan uuel ne schal nahhi þe, na wunne ne schal wonti
625 þe; al þi wil schal beon iwraht in heouene ant ec in eorðe—ȝe,
ant ȝet in helle. Ne schal neauer heorte þenchen hwuch selhðe
þet Ich nule ȝeouen for þi luue unmeteliche, vneuenliche,
unendeliche mare. Al Creatuse weole, þe wes kinge richest;
Absalones schene wlite, þe as ofte as me euesede him salde his
630 euesunge (þe her þet he kearf of) for twa hundret sicles of
seoluer iweiet; Asaeles swiftschipe, þe straf wið heortes of-urn;
Samsones strengðe, þe sloh a þusent of his fan al ed a time ant
ane bute fere; Cesares freolec; Alixandres hereword; Moysese
heale—nalde a mon, for an of þeos, ȝeouen al þet he ahte?
635 Ant alle somet aȝein mi bodi ne beoð nawt wurð a nelde. Ȝef
þu art se swiðe anewil, ant swa ut of þi wit, þet tu, þurh nawt
to leosen, forsakest swuch biȝete, wið alles cunnes selhðe—lo,
Ich halde her heatel sweord upo þin heaued, to dealen lif ant
640 sawle ant bisenchen ham ba into þe fur of helle, to beon
deofles hore schentfulliche ant sorhfulliche, world a buten
ende! Ondswere nu ant were þe, ȝef þu const, aȝein me; oðer
ȝette me þi luue þe Ich ȝirne se swiðe, nawt for min, ah for þin
ahne, muchele biheue.

Lo, þus ure Lauerd woheð: nis ha to heard-iheortet þet a
645 þulli wohere ne mei to his luue turnen?—ȝef ha wel þencheð
þeose þreo þinges: hwet he is, ant hwet heo is, ant hu muchel
is þe luue of se heh as he is toward se lah as heo is. Forþi

628 weole] MS. wule, with o suprascript as correction of u corrected to e

seið þe salmwruhte *Non est qui se abscondat a calore eius*—nis
nan þet mahe edlutien þet ha ne mot him luuien. Þe soðe
sunne i þe under-tid wes forþi istihen on heh o þe hehe rode, 650
forte spreaden oueral hate luue-gleames. Þus neodful he wes,
ant is aþet tes dei, to ontenden his luue in his leoues heorte, ant
seið i þe Godspel: *Ignem ueni mittere in terram; et quid uolo* f. 108ᵛ
nisi ut ardeat? 'Ich com to bringen', he seið, 'fur into eorðe
(þet is, bearninde luue into eorðlich heorte); ant hwet ȝirne
Ich elles bute þet hit bleasie?' Wlech luue is him lað, as he 656
seið þurh Sein Iuhan i þe Apocalipse: *vtinam frigidus esses aut
calidus! Set quia tepidus es, incipiam te euomere de ore meo.* 'Ich
walde', he seið to his leofmon, 'þet tu were i mi luue oðer
allunge cald, oðer hat mid alle! Ah forþi þet tu art ase wlech 660
bitweone twa, nowðer hat ne cald, þu makest me to wleatien,
ant Ich wulle speowe þe ut, bute þu wurðe hattre.'

Nu ȝe habbeð iherd, mine leoue sustren, hu ant for hwi
Godd is swiðe to luuien. Forte ontenden ow wel, gederið wude
þerto, wið þe poure wummon of Sarepte—þe burh þe spealeþ 665
ontendunge. '*En*', *inquit*, '*colligo duo ligna.*' *Regum iii.* 'Lauerd',
quoð ha to Helye, þe hali prophete, 'lo, Ich gederi twa treon.'
Þeos twa treon bitacnið þet a treo þet stod upriht ant þet oþer
þe eode þwertouer o þe deore rode; of þeos twa treon ȝe
schulen ontende fur of luue inwið ower heorte. Biseoð ofte 670
towart ham; þencheð ȝef ȝe ne ahen eaðe to luuien þe king of
blisse þe tospreat swa his earmes toward ow, ant buheð (as to
beoden cos) duneward his heaued. Sikerliche Ich segge hit:
ȝef þe soðe Helye (þet is Godd Almihti) ifint ow þeose twa
treon bisiliche gederin, he wule gestnin wið ow ant monifalden 675
in ow his deorewurðe grace, as Helie dude hire liueneð ant
gestnede wið hire þet he ifond þe twa treon gederin i Sarepte.

652 in] *MS.* ꝗ, *i.e.* ant

XIX

SAWLES WARDE

THIS text is found in three manuscripts, which also include
Lives of Saints Katherine, Margaret, and Juliana, and *Hali Meiðhad*—works that all appear to have been written in the same area,
and towards the end of the twelfth century, and that have close
affinities with *Ancrene Wisse* (see XVIII). Like the Saints' Lives,
it derives from a Latin original, being based on ch. xiii–xv of
Book IV of *De Anima*, a work ascribed to Hugh, Abbot of St.
Victor (ob. 1141/6),[1] to whom this monastery of Augustinian
Canons, founded in 1108, owed much of its fame. Hugh's
magnum opus, *De sacramentis Christianae fidei*, is an attempt to
set forth a symbolical interpretation of scripture and the whole
of creation. It signalizes *inter alia* a new use of allegory to express
the mystical experience of the vision of God, which is likewise
found in *De Anima*, and which St. Bonaventure was to develop.
The allegory of the body as the habitation of the soul is also
found in St. Bonaventure (*Itinerarium mentis in Deum*, c. 2) and
striking use was later made of it in *Piers Plowman* (B. IX); the
five senses figure as wards of the heart in *Ancrene Wisse* (Morton's ed. pp. 48 ff.: cf. E.E.T.S. 225, pp. 21 ff., and 232 *passim*).
The allegory of the Four Daughters of God (see 39 ff. below),
which had been used by several writers before St. Hugh (e.g.
Alcuin, *Liber de virtutibus et vitiis*), is found also in Grosseteste's
Chasteau d'Amour, *Piers Plowman* (B. XVIII), and elsewhere.

[1] These chapters have now been recognized as an independent work,
De custodia interioris hominis, which circulated widely in the Middle
Ages under the name of St. Anselm. It is edited from English and
French MSS. in *Memorials of St. Anselm*, ed. R. W. Southern and
F. S. Schmitt, o.s.b. (1969), pp. 355–60.

About 1170 Abbot Simon of St. Albans wrote to Richard of St. Victor
asking for leave to copy all the works of St. Hugh, not already in the
St. Albans library; Henry of Blois (see p. 387) gave copies of the works
to Glastonbury (Knowles, *Monastic Order*, pp. 265, 526); and copies
from Durham (xii cent.) and Llanthony (xiii cent.) survive.

The rhythmic, alliterative patterns into which the text often falls are doubtless related to those of late Old English homilies as Prof. D. Bethurum has indicated in her study (see p. 417); but it should be noted that rhythm was a distinctive feature of the Victorine writers, and that *De Anima* itself uses alliteration effectively. On the other hand, the general pattern of *Sawles Warde* is more markedly homiletic than its original, and differs from it in many details: thus the description of the messenger of death is entirely new, the account of hell is much elaborated, the entry of 'Liues Luue' (*Amor vitae eternae*) is made more dramatic, if more domestic; in the English description of the beatific vision the nine orders are specified, the references to *monachi* are omitted, whilst the section devoted to the virgins is much enlarged; various scriptural allusions are given a new context, and new ones are added; and the effective conclusion, linking with the opening parable, has no parallel in the Latin. The effective use of words of limited local currency (e.g. *nurð*, *dosc*, *etlunge*) is another fresh feature.

The text here printed is from MS. Bodley 34, with variants from MSS. Royal 17 A. XXVI and Cotton Titus D. XVIII (all early thirteenth century). All three manuscripts are of almost pocket size (less than $6\frac{1}{2}$ by 5 in.); but on the top margin of f. 75^v of the Bodleian manuscript a later scribbler has found room to write 'ly þow me ner lemmon in þy narmus' (probably fourteenth century).

Her bigineð Sawles Warde: f. 72^r

Si sciret paterfamilias qua hora fur uenturus esset, vigilaret utique et non sineret perfodi domum suam.

Ure Lauerd i þe godspel teacheð us þurh a bisne hu we ahen wearliche to biwiten us seoluen wið þe unwiht of helle ant 5 wið his wernches. 'ʒef þes lauerd wiste', he seið, 'hwenne ant hwuch time þe þeof walde cume to his hus, he walde wakien, ne nalde he nawt þolien þe þeof forte breoken hire.' Þis hus þe ure Lauerd spekeð of is seolf þe mon; inwið, þe monnes wit i þis hus is þe huse-lauerd, ant te fulitohe wif mei beon Wil 10

Headline partially restored 9 Lauerd] *MS.* lauerð: *all such miswritings of* ð *for* d, *and vice versa, are henceforth corrected silently*

ihaten; þet ga þe hus efter hire, ha diht hit al to wundre, bute
Wit ase lauerd chasti hire þe betere, ant bineome hire muchel
of þet ha walde; ant tah walde al hire hird folhin hire oueral,
ȝef Wit ne forbude ham, for alle hit beoð untohene ant reche-
15 lese hinen, bute ȝef he ham rihte. Ant hwucche beoð þeos
hinen? Summe beoð wiðvten ant summe wiðinnen. Þeo wiþvten
beoð þe monnes fif wittes—sihðe ant herunge, smechunge ant
smeallunge, ant euch limes felunge. Þeos beoð hinen vnder
Wit, as under huse-lauerd, ant hwer se he is ȝemeles, nis hare
20 nan þe ne feareð ofte untoheliche ant gulteð ilome, oðer i fol
semblant oder in vuel dede. Inwið beoð his hinen in se moni
mislich þonc to cwemen wel þe husewif aȝein Godes wille,
f. 72ᵛ ant swerieð sometreadliche þet efter hire hit schal gan. Þah
we hit ne here nawt, we mahen felen hare nurð ant hare untohe
25 bere, aþet Wit cume forð ant ba wið eie ant wið luue tuhte
ham þe betere. Ne bið neauer his hus for þeos hinen wel iwist,
for hwon þet he slepe oðer ohwider fare from hame—þet is
hwen mon forȝet his wit ant let ham iwurðen. Ah ne bihoueð
hit nawt þet tis hus beo irobbet, for þer is inne þe tre[sor]
30 þet Godd ȝef himseolf fore—þet is monnes sawle. Forte
breoke þis hus efter þis tresor þet Godd bohte mid his deað
ant lette lif o rode is moni þeof abuten, ba bi dei ant bi niht:
vnseheliche gasttes wið alle unwreaste þeawes; ant aȝein euch
god þeaw þe biwiteð i þis hus Godes deore chatel vnder Wittes
35 wissunge þet is huse-lauerd is eauer hire unþeaw forte sechen
inȝong abute þe wahes, to amurðrin hire þrinne. Þet heaued
þrof is þe feont, þe meistreð ham alle. Aȝeines him ant his keis
þe husebonde, þet is Wit, warneð his hus þus: vre Lauerd
haueð ileanett him fowre of his dehtren, þet beoð to vnder-

14 ȝef] *MS.* gef   24 felen *R*] fele *C*   nurð] *MS.* nurþð: nurð
R murð *C*   25 Wit *RC*] *MS.* hit   27 fare] *supplied from R*:
fares *C*   29 tresor] sor *om. in MS.*   34 chatel *R*] castel *MS.*, *C*
39 fowre *R*] froure *MS.*, *C*

stonden þe fowr heaued-þeawes. Þe earste is Warschipe 40
icleopet, ant te oðer is ihaten Gastelich Strengðe, ant te þridde
is Meað; Rihtwisnesse þe feorðe.

Wit þe husbonde, Godes cunestable, cleopeð Warschipe forð f. 73ʳ
ant makið hire durewart, þe warliche loki hwam ha leote in
ant ut, ant of feor bihalde alle þe cuminde—hwuche beo 45
wurðe inȝong to habben, oðer beon bisteken þrute. Strengðe
stont nest hire, þet ȝef ei wule in Warschipes vnþonkes warni
Strengðe fore, þet is hire suster, ant heo hit ut warpe. Þe
þridde suster, þet is Meað, hire he makeð meistre ouer his
willesfule hird þet we ear of speken, þet ha leare ham mete, 50
þet me meosure hat, þe middel of twa uueles (for þet is þeaw
in euch stude, ant tuht forte halden) ant hateð ham alle þet
nan of ham aȝein hire nohwer wið vnmeað ne ga ouer mete.
Þe feorðe suster, Rihtwisnesse, sit on hest as deme, ant
beateð þeo þe agulteð, ant cruneð þeo þe wel doð, ant demeð 55
euchan his dom efter his rihte. For dret of hire nimeð his hird,
euch efter þet he is, warde to witene: þe ehnen hare, þe muð
his, þe earen hare, þe honden hare, ant euch alswa of þe oþre
wit, þet onont him ne schal nan unþeaw cumen in.

As þis is ido þus, ant is al stille þrinne, Warschipe þet aa is 60
waker, is offearet lest sum fortruste him, ant feole o slepe ant
forȝeme his warde, ant sent ham in a sonde þet ha wel cnaweð,
of feorren icumen, forte offearen þeo þe beoð ouerhardi, ant f. 73ᵛ
þeo þe ȝemelese beoð halden ham wakere. He is underuon in
ant swiðe bihalden of ham alle, for lonc he is ant leane, ant his 65
leor deaðlich ant blac ant elheowet, ant euch her þuncheð þet
stont in his heaued up. Warschipe hat him tellen biuoren hwet
he beo ant hweonene he comme ant hwet he þer seche. 'Ne
mei Ich,' he seið, 'nohwer speoken bute Ich habbe god lust.
Lustnið me þenne: Fearlac Ich hatte, ant am Deaðes sonde ant 70

55 agulteð RC] aȝulteð MS.   56 his hird] þis hird RC

Deaðes munegunge ant am icumen biuore hire to warnin ow
of hire cume.' Warschipe, þet best con bisetten hire wordes
ant ec hire werkes, spekeð for ham alle, ant freineð hweonene
ha cume ant hwuch hird ha leade. Fearlac hire ontswereð:
75 'Ich nat nawt þe time, for ha ne seide hit me nawt; ah eauer
lokið hwenne, for hire wune is to cumen bi stale ferliche ant
unmundlunge hwen me least weneð. Of hire hird þet tu easkest,
Ich þe ondswerie: ha lihteð hwer se ha eauer kimeð wið a
þusent deoflen, ant euchan bereð a gret boc al of sunnen
80 iwriten wið swarte smeale leattres, ant an unrude raketehe
gledread of fure, forte binden ant to drahen into inwarde helle
hwuch se he mei preouin þurh his boc, þet is on euch sunne
f. 74ʳ enbreuet þet he wið wil oðer wið word oðer wið werc wrahtte
in al his lif-siðe, bute þet he haueð ibet earþon wið soð schrift
85 ant wið deadbote.' Ant Warschipe hire askeð: 'Hweonene
cumest tu, Fearlac, Deaðes munegunge?' 'Ich cume,' he seið,
'of helle.' 'Of helle?' ha seið, Warschipe, 'ant hauest tu isehen
helle?' 'Ʒe,' seið Fearlac, 'witerliche, ofte ant ilome.' 'Nu,' seið
þenne Warschipe, 'for þi trowðe treoweliche tele us hwuch is
90 helle ant hwet tu hauest isehen þrin.' 'Ant Ich,' he seið,
Fearlac, 'o mi trowðe bluðeliche, nawt tah efter þet hit is—for
þet ne mei na tunge tellen—ah efter þet Ich mei ant con, þertowart Ich chulle reodien.

'Helle is wid wiðute met ant deop wiðute grunde; ful of
95 brune uneuenlich, for ne mei nan eorðlich fur euenin þertowart; ful of stench unþolelich, for ne mahte in eorðe na
cwic þing hit þolien; ful of sorhe untalelich, for ne mei na
muð for wrecchedom ne for wa rikenin hit ne tellen. Se þicke
is þrinne þe þosternesse þet me hire mei grapin. For þet fur
100 ne ʒeueð na liht, ah blent ham þe ehnen þe þer beoð wið a
smorðrinde smoke, smeche forcuðest, ant tah i þet ilke swarte

74 ha] *MS.* he   94 wid] *supplied from C*   101 smoke] *MS.* smeke
or smoke: smoke *RC*

þeosternesse swarte þinges ha iseoð, as deoflen þet ham meallið
ant derueð aa ant dreccheð wið alles cunnes pinen, ant iteilede
draken grisliche ase deoflen þe forswolheð ham ihal ant
speoweð ham eft ut biuoren ant bihinden, oðer-hwile torendeð f. 74ᵛ
ham ant tocheoweð ham euch greot, ant heo eft iwurðeð hal 106
to a swuch bale bute bote as ha ear weren. Ant ful wel ha
iseoð, ham to grisle ant to grure ant to echen hare pine, þe
laðe helle-wurmes, tadden ant froggen, þe freoteð ham ut te
ehnen ant te nease-gristles, ant snikeð in ant ut neddren ant 110
eauroskes, nawt ilich þeose her ah hundret siðe grisluker, et
muð ant et earen, ed ehnen ant ed neauele, ant ed te breoste-
holke as meaðen i forrotet flesch, eauerȝete þickest. Þer is
remunge i þe brune ant toðes hechelunge i þe snawi weattres.
Ferliche ha flutteð from þe heate into þe chele, ne neauer nuten 115
ha of þeos twa hweðer ham þuncheð wurse, for eiðer is unþolelich. Ant i þis ferliche mong þe leatere þurh þe earre derueð
þe mare. Þet fur ham forbearneð al to colen calde, þet pich
ham forwalleð aðet ha beon formealte, ant eft acwikieð anan to
drehen al þet ilke ant muchedeale wurse a wiðuten ende. Ant 120
tis ilke unhope is ham meast pine, þet nan naueð neauermare
hope of nan acouerunge, ah aren sikere of euch uuel to þurhleasten i wa from worlde into worlde aa on echnesse. Euch
aþrusmeð oðer, ant euch is oðres pine, ant euchan heateð oðer
ant him seoluen as þe blake deouel; ant eauer se ha i þis world f. 75ʳ
luueden ham mare, se ha þer heatieð ham swiðere; ant eiðer curseð 126
oðer ant fret of þe oðres earen, ant te nease alswa. Ich habbe
bigunne to tellen of þing þet Ich ne mahte nawt bringe to eni
ende, þah Ich hefde a þusent tungen of stele ant talde aðet ha
weren alle forwerede. Ah þencheð nu herþurh hwuch þe 130
measte pine beo: for þe leaste pine is se heard þet hefde a mon
islein ba mi feader ant mi moder ant al þe ende of mi cun, ant
ido me seoluen al þe scheome ant te hearm þet cwic mon mahte
þolien, ant Ich isehe þes mon i þe ilke leaste pine þet Ich iseh

135 in helle, Ich walde, ȝef hit mahte beon, þolien a þusent deaðes to
arudden him ut þrof, swa is þe sihðe grislich ant reowðful to
bihalden. For þah neauer nere nan oðer pine bute to iseon
eauer þe unseli gastes ant hare grisliche schape, biseon on hare
grimfule ant grurefule nebbes, ant heren hare rarunge, ant hu
140 ha wið hokeres edwiteð ant upbreideð euchan his sunnen, þis
schendlac ant te grure of ham were unimete pine—ant hure
þolien ant abeoren hare unirude duntes wið mealles istelet,
ant wið hare eawles gledreade hare dustlunges as þah hit were
a pilche-clut euchan towart oðer i misliche pinen. O helle,
145 deaðes hus, wununge of wanunge, of grure ant of granunge,
f. 75ᵛ heatel ham ant heard wan of alle wontreaðes, buri of bale ant
bold of euereuch bitternesse, þu laðest lont of alle, þu dorc
stude ifullet of alle dreorinesses, Ich cwakie of grisle ant of
grure, ant euch ban schekeð me ant euch her me rueð up of
150 þi munegunge, for nis þer na steuene bituhhe þe fordemde bute
"wumme", ant "wa is me" ant "wa beo þe" and "wa beo þe".
"Wa" ha ȝeieð ant wa ha habbeð, ne of al þet eauer wa is ne
schal ham neauer wontin. Þe swuch wununge ofearneð for ei
hwilinde blisse her o þisse worlde, wel were him ȝef þet he
155 neauer ibore nere. Bi þis ȝe mahen sumdel witen hwuch is
helle, for iwis Ich habbe þrin isehen a þusent siðe wurse; ant
from þeonne kimeð Deað wið a þusent deoflen hiderwart, as
Ich seide, ant Ich com þus,' quoð Fearlac, 'forte warnin ow
fore, ant tellen ow þeos tidinges.'

160   'Nu, Lauerd Godd,' quoð Warschipe, 'wardi us ant werie,
ant rihte us ant reade hwet us beo to donne, ant we beon þe
warre ant wakere to witen us on euch half under Godes wengen.
Ȝef we wel werieð ant witeð ure hus ant Godes deore tresor þet
he haueð bitaht us, cume deað hwen he wulle, ne þurue we
165 nowðer beon ofdred for hire ne for helle, for ure deað bið
deore Godd, ant inȝong into heouene. Of þeos fikelinde world

149 rueð] runeð RC

ne of hire false blisse ne neome we neauer ȝeme, for al þet is
on eorðe nis bute as a schadewe, for al wurðeð to noht bute þet f. 76ʳ
deore tresor, Godes deorewurðe feh þet is us bitaht to witene.
Ich habbe þeruore sar care, for Ich iseo,' seið Warschipe, 'hu 170
þe unwhiht wið his ferd ase liun iburst geað abuten ure hus,
sechinde ȝeornliche hu he hit forswolhe. Ant tis Ich mei', seið
Warschipe, 'warnin ow of his lað ant for his wrenches; ah Ich
ne mei nawt aȝeines his strengðe.'

'Do nu', quoð Strengðe, Warschipe suster, 'þet te limpet to 175
þe, ant warne us of his wiheles, for of al his strengðe ne drede
we nawiht: for nis his strengðe noht wurð bute hwer se he
ifindeð eðeliche ant wake, unwarnede of treowe bileaue. Þe
apostle seið: "Etstont þen feont, ant he flið ananriht." Schulde
we þenne fleon him? Ȝe, nis Godd ure scheld? and alle beoð 180
ure wepnen of his deore grace, ant Godd is on ure half ant
stont bi us i fehte. Ȝef he schute towart me wið weole ant
wunne of þe world, wið este of flesches lustes, of þulliche nesche
wepnen Ich mahte carien summes weis, ah ne mei me na þing
heardes offearen, ne nowcin ne na wone falsi min heorte ne 185
wursi mi bileaue towart him þet ȝeueð me alle mine strengðen.'

'For ba me ah,' quoð Meað, 'ant for heart of nowcin ant for
wone of wunne, dreden ant carien. For moni for to muchel
heard of wa þet he dreheð forȝet ure Lauerd, ant ma þah for
nesche ant for flesches licunge forȝemeð ham ofte. Bituhhen f. 76ᵛ
heard ant nesche, bituhhe wa of þis world ant to muche 191
wunne, bituhhe muchel and lutel is in euch worldlich þing þe
middel wei guldene. Ȝef we hire haldeð, þenne ga we sikerliche, ne þerf us nowðer for deað ne for deouel dreden. Hwet
se beo of heardes, ne drede Ich nawiht nesches, for ne mei na 195
wunne ne na flesches licunge ne licomlich este bringe me ouer
þe midel of mesure ant of mete.'

Rihtwissnesse spekeð nu. 'Mi suster,' ha seið, 'Warschipe,
þe haueð wit ant schad bituhhe god ant uuel, ant wat hwet is in

200 euch þing to cheosen ant to schunien, readeð us ant leareð
forte ȝeme lutel alle fallinde þing ant witen warliche þeo þe
schulen a lesten. Ant seið as ha soð seið, þet þurh unweotenesse
ne mei ha nawt sunegin, ant tah nis nawt siker of þe unwihtes
strengðe, as þeo þe halt hire wac, þah ha beo muche wurð to
205 ure alre ehnen, ant demeð hire unmihti onont hireseoluen to
etstonden wið his turnes, ant deð ase þe wise. Mi suster
Strengðe is swiðe bald, ant seið þet nawiht heardes ne mei hire
offearen, ah þah ha ne trust nawt on hire ahne wepnen, ah deð
o Godes grace, ant þet Ich demi riht ant wisdom to donne. Mi
210 þridde suster, Meað, spekeð of þe middel sti bituhhe riht ant
f. 77ʳ luft, þet lut cunnen halden, ant seið i nesche ha is bald, ant
heard mei hire offearen, ant forþi ne ȝelpeð ha of na sikernesse,
ant deð as þe wise. Mi meoster is to do riht ant riht forto demen,
ant Ich deme me seolf þet Ich þurh me ne do hit nawt: for al
215 þet god is of Godd þet we her habbeð. Nu is riht þenne þet
we demen us seolf eauer unmihtie to werien ant to witen us
oðer ei god to halden wiðute Godes helpe. Þe rihtwise Godd
wule þet we demen us seolf eðeliche ant lahe, ne beo we neauer
swucche, for þenne demeð he us muche wurð, ant gode, ant
220 halt for his dehtren. For þah mi forme suster war beo of euch
uuel, ant min oðer strong beo toȝeines euch nowcin, ant mi
þridde meaðful in alles cunnes estes, ant Ich do riht and deme,
bute we wið al þis milde beon ant meoke, ant halden us wake,
Godd mei mid rihte fordemen us of al þis þurh ure prude; ant
225 forþi is riht dom þet we al ure god þonkin him ane.'

Wit þe husebonde, Godes cunestable, hereð alle hare sahen
and þonkeð God ȝeorne wið swiðe glead heorte of se riche lane
as beoð þeos sustren, his fowr dehtren þet he haueð ileanet
him on helpe forte wite wel ant werien his castel, ant Godes

204–5 to . . . demeð *R*] ant ure alre ehnen demeð *MS.*: ant ure alre
ehnen ant demeð *C*   213 ant riht] *supplied from C*: ant riht fon ant *R*
226 Wit] *MS.* Wjit

deorewurðe feh þet is biloke þrinne. Þe willesfule husewif 230
halt hire al stille, ant al þet hird þet ha wes iwunet to dreaien
efter hire turneð ham treowliche to Wit hare lauerd ant to þeos f. 77ᵛ
fowr sustren. Vmben ane stunde spekeð eft Warschipe ant
seið: 'Ich iseo a sonde cumen, swiðe glead-icheret, feier ant
freolich ant leofliche aturnet.' 'Let him in,' seið Wit, 'ʒef Godd 235
wule, he bringeð us gleade tidinges, ant þet us were muche
neod, for Fearlac, Deaðes sonde, haueð wið his offearet us
swiðe mid alle.' Warschipe let him in, ant he gret Wit, þen
lauerd, ant al þet hird seoðen wið lahhinde chere, ant ha ʒeldeð
him his gretunge, ant beoð alle ilihtet, ant igleadet ham 240
þuncheð of his onsihðe, for al þet hus schineð ant schimmeð
of his leome. He easkeð ham ʒef ham biluueð to heren him
ane hwile. 'ʒe,' quoð ha, Rihtwisnesse, 'wel us biluueð hit, ant
wel is riht þet we þe liðeliche lustnin.'

'Hercnið nu þenne,' he seið, 'ant ʒeornliche understondeð. 245
Ich am Murðes sonde, ant munegunge of eche lif, ant Liues
Luue ihaten, ant cume riht from heouene, þet Ich habbe isehen
nu ant ofte ear þe blisse þet na monnes tunge ne mei of tellen.
Þe iblescede Godd iseh ow offruhte ant sumdel drupnin of þet
Fearlac talde of deað ant of helle, ant sende me to gleadien ow, 250
nawt forþi þet hit ne beo al soð þet he seide, ant þet schulen
alle uuele fondin ant ifinden. Ah ʒe, wið þe fulst of Godd, ne
þurue na þing dreden, for he sit on heh þet is ow on helpe, f. 78ʳ
ant is alwealdent þet haueð ow to witene.'

'A,' seið Warschipe, 'welcume, Liues Luue, ant for þe luue 255
of Godd seolf, ʒef þu eauer sehe him tele us sumhwet of him
ant of his eche blisse.' 'ʒe, i seoð,' quoð Liues Luue, Murhðes
sonde, 'Ich habbe isehen him ofte, nawt tah alswa as he is—for
aʒein þe brihtnesse ant te liht of his leor þe sunne-gleam is
dosc ant þuncheð a schadewe; ant forþi ne mahte Ich nawt 260
aʒein þe leome of his wlite lokin ne bihalden, bute þurh a

234 glead] MS. gledd (?)   246 Ich] I om. in MS.

schene schawere bituhhe me ant him þet schilde mine ehnen;
Swa Ich habbe ofte isehen þe hali þrumnesse, Feader ant Sune
ant Hali Gast, þreo an untodealet. Ah lutle hwile Ich mahte
265 þolie þe leome, ah summes weis Ich mahte bihalden ure Lauerd
Iesu Crist Godes sune, þet bohte us o rode, hu he sit blisful
on his Feader riht half þet is alwealdent, rixleð i þet eche lif
bute linnunge, se unimete feier þet te engles ne beoð neauer ful
on him to bihalden. Ant ȝet Ich iseh etscene þe studen of his
270 wunden, ant hu he schaweð ham his feader to cuðen hu he
luuede us ant hu he wes buhsum to him þe sende him swa to
alesen us, ant bisecheð him a for moncunnes heale.

'Efter him Ich iseh on heh ouer alle heouenliche wordes þe
f. 78ᵛ eadi meiden his moder, Marie inempnet, sitten in a trone se
275 swiðe briht wið ȝimmes istirret, ant hire wlite se weoleful þet
euch eorðlich liht is þeoster þera ȝeines. Þear Ich iseh as ha bit
hire deorewurðe sune se ȝeornliche ant se inwardliche for þeo
þet hire seruið, ant he hire ȝetteð bliðeliche al þet ha bisecheð.

'Þet liht þa Ich ne mahte lengre þolien, Ich biseh to þe
280 engles ant to þe archangles ant to þe oðre þe beoð buuen ham,
iblescede gastes þe beoð a biuore Godd ant seruið him eauer,
ant singeð a unwerget. Nihe wordes þer beoð, ah hu ha beoð
i-ordret ant sunderliche isette, þe an buue þe oðre, ant euchanes
meoster, were long to tellen. Se muche murhðe Ich hefde on
285 hare onsihðe þet ne mahte Ich longe hwile elleshwider lokin.

'Efter ham Ich iseh towart te patriarches ant te prophetes þe
makieð swuch murhðe þet ha aren nuðe i þet ilke loi ᵗ of blisse
þet ha hefden of feor igret ear on eorðe, ant seoð ᵑu al þet
isoðet þet ha hefden longe ear icwiddet of ure Lauerd, as he
290 hefde ischawed hom i gastelich sihðe. Ich iseh þe apostles,
poure ant lah on eorðe, ifullet ant bigoten al of unimete blisse,
sitten i trones, ant al under hare uet þet heh is i þe worlde,

---

273 wordes] *om. MS.* Cf. *De Anima*: super omnes ordines
276 þera ȝeines] þe a ȝeines *MS.*: þer- *RC*

ȝarowe for te demen i þe dei of dome kinges ant keiseres ant
alle cunreadnes of alles cunnes ledenes.   f. 79ʳ

Ich biheolt te martyrs ant hare unimete murhðe þe þoleden 295
her pinen ant deað for ure Lauerd, ant lihtliche talden to alles
cunnes neowcins ant eorðliche tintreohen aȝeines þe blisse þet
Godd in hare heorte schawede ham to cumene.

Efter ham Ich beheolt þe cunfessurs hird þe liueden i god
lif ant hal[il]iche deiden, þe schineð as doð steorren i þe eche 300
blissen, ant seoð Godd in his wlite þet haueð alle teares iwipet
of hare ehnen.

Ich iseh þet schene ant þet brihte ferreden of þe eadi
meidnes ilikest towart engles, ant feolahlukest wið ham blissin
ant gleadien þe, libbinde i flesche, ouergað flesches lahe ant 305
ouercumeð cunde, þe leadeð heouenlich lif in eorðe as ha
wunieð. Hare murhðe ant hare blisse, þe feierleac of hare wlite,
þe swetnesse of hare song, ne mei na tunge tellen. Alle ha
singeð þe þer beoð, ah hare song ne mahe nane buten heo
singen. Se swote smeal ham folheð hwider se ha wendeð, þet 310
me mahte libben aa bi þe swotnesse. Hwamse heo bisecheð
fore is sikerliche iborhen, for aȝein hare bisocnen Godd himseolf ariseð þet alle þe oðre halhen sittende ihereð.'

'Swiðe wel,' quoð Warschipe, 'likeð us þet tu seist. Ah nu þu
hauest se wel iseid of euch a setnesse of þe seli sunderlepes, 315
sumhwet sei us nu hwuch blisse is to alle iliche meane.' And
Liues Luue hire ondswereð: 'Þe imeane blisse is seouenfald, f. 79ᵛ
lengðe of lif, wit, ant luue, ant of þe luue a gleadunge wiðute
met, murie loft-song ant lihtschipe, ant sikernesse is þe
seoueðe.' 'Þah Ich þis,' seið Warschipe, 'sumdel understonde, 320
þu most unwreo þis witerluker ant openin to þeos oðre.' 'Ant
hit schal beon,' seið Liues Luue, 'Warschipe, as þu wilnest.'

'Ha liuieð a in a wlite þet is brihtre seoueuald ant schenre
þen þe sunne, ant eauer in a strengðe to don buten euch swinc
al þet ha wulleð, ant eauermare in a steal in al þet eauer god 325

is wiðute wonunge, wiðuten euch þing þet mahe hearmin oðer
eilin, in al þet eauer is softe oðer swote; ant hare lif is Godes
sihðe ant Godes cnawlechunge, as ure Lauerd seide: "Þet is,"
quoð he, "eche lif, to seon ant cnawen soð Godd ant him þet
330 he sende, Iesu Crist ure Lauerd, to ure alesnesse"; ant beoð
forþi ilich him i þe ilke wlite þet he is, for ha seoð him as he is,
nebbe to nebbe. Ha beoð se wise þet ha witen alle Godes
reades, his runes, ant his domes þe derne beoð, ant deopre
þen eni sea-dingle. Ha seoð i Godd alle þing, ant witen of al
335 þet is ant wes ant eauer schal iwurðen, hwet it beo, hwi, ant
hwerto, ant hwerof hit bigunne.

Ha luuieð God wiðute met, for þet ha understondeð hu he
haueð bi ham idon þurh his muchele godlec ant hwet ha ahen
his deorewurðe milce to ȝelden, ant euchan luueð oðer ase
340 muchel as himseoluen.

f. 80ʳ   Se gleade ha beoð of Godd þet al is hare blisse se muchel þet
ne mei hit munne na muð ne spealie na speche. Forþi þet euchan luueð oðer as himseoluen, euchan haueð of oðres god ase
muche murhðe as of his ahne. Bi þis ȝe mahen seon ant witen
345 þet euchan haueð sunderlepes ase feole gleadschipes as ha beoð
monie alle, ant euch of þe ilke gleadschipes is to eauereuchan
ase muche gleadunge as his ahne sunderliche. Ȝet ouer al þis,
hwen euchan luueð Godd mare þen himseoluen ant þen alle
þe oðre, mare he gleadeð of Godd wiðuten ei etlunge þen of his
350 ahne gleadunge ant of alle þe oðres. Neomeð nu þenne ȝeme:
ȝef neauer anes heorte ne mei in hire underuon hire ahne
gleadunge sunderliche—se unimete muchel is þe anlepi blisse
—hu nimeð in hire þus monie ant þus muchele? Forþi seide
ure Lauerd to þeo þe him hefden icwemet: *Intra in gaudium*
355 etc. "Ga," quoð he, "into þi Lauerdes blisse. Þu most al gan

333 *MS*. derne *or* derue
*f. 80 is badly stained; some words and letters are wholly invisible and
have been supplied from C and R*   353 hu] *MS*. þet ha

þrin, ant al beon bigotten þrin, for in þe ne mei hit nanesweis neomen in." Herof ha herieð Godd ant singeð a unwerget eauer iliche lusti in his loft-songes, as hit iwriten is: *Beati qui habitant* etc: Eadi beoð þeo, Lauerd, þe i þin hus wunieð; ha schulen herien þe from worlde into worlde. 360

Ha beoð alle ase lihte ant ase swifte ase sunne-gleam þe scheot fram est into west as tin ehlid tuneð ant openeð: for f. 80ᵛ hwer se eauer þe gast wule, þe bodi is ananriht wiðute lettunge. For ne mei ham naþing aȝeines etstonden, for euchan is almihti to don al þet he wule, ȝe, makie to cwakien heouene ba ant 365 eorðe wiþ his an finger.

Sikere ha beoð of al þis, of þulli lif, of þulli wit, of þulli luue ant gleadunge þrof, ant of þulli blisse, þet hit ne mei neauermare lutlin ne wursin, ne neome nan ende. Þis lutle ich habbe iseid of þet ich iseh in heouene, ah nower neh ne 370 seh ich al, ne þet ȝet þet ich seh ne con ich half tellen.'

'Witerliche,' quoð Warschipe, 'wel we understondeð þet tu hauest ibeo þear ant soð hauest iseid trof efter þi sihðe. Ant wel is him þet is war ant bisið him hu he mahe beast halden his hus þet Godes tresor is in aȝeines Godes unwine þe weorreð 375 þertowart a wið unþeawes: for þet schal bringen him þider as he schal al þis þet tu hauest ispeken of, an hundret siðe mare, of blisse buten euch bale fondin ant ifinden.' Quoð Strengðe: 'Hwen hit swa is, hwet mei tweamen us from Godd ant halden us þeonne? Ich am siker ine Godd þat ne schal lif ne deað ne 380 wa ne wunne nowðer todealen us ant his luue þat al þis us haueð iȝarcket ȝef we as treowe tresurers witeð wel his tresor þet is bitaht us to halden as we schulen ful wel under his wengen.'

'Varpeð ut,' quoð Warschipe, 'Farlac ure fa. Nis nawt riht 385

358 his C] MS. þis R þis loftsong   371 seh¹ C] MS., R neh
376 as] C þer   378 fondin] C fonden MS. folhin R folhen
381 nothing legible after nowðer; remainder of text largely from R

þet an hus halde þeos tweien: for þer as murðes sonde is and
soð luue of eche lif, farlac is fleme.' 'Nu ut!' quoð Strenðe,
'Farlac, ne schaltu na lengere leuen in ure ende.' 'Nu,' quoð he,
'Ich seide for god al þet ich seide; and þah it muri nere nes na
390 lessere mi tale þen wes Murhðes sondes ne unbihefre to ow,
þah it ne beo so licwurðe ne icweme'. 'Eiðer of ow* haueð his
stunde to speokene, ne nis incker noðres tale to schunien in
his time. Þu warnest of wa, he telleð of wunne. Muche neod
is þet me ow ba ȝeornliche hercni. Flute nu, Farlac, þah, hwil
395 Liues Luue is herinne, and þole wið efne heorte þe dom
of Rihtwisnesse: for þu schal ful bliðeliche beon underfon in
as ofte as Liues Luue stutteð forto spekene.'

Nu is Wil þet husewif al stille þet er wes so willesful, al
ituht efter Wittes wissunge þet is husebonde; ant al þet hird
400 halt him stille þet wes iwunet to beon fulitohen ant don efter
Wil, hare lefdi, ant nawt efter Wit; lustneð nu his lare
ant fondeð eauereuchan efter þet him limpeð to þurh þeos
twa sonden þet ha iherd habbeð ant þet fowr sustren lerden
þruppe: for euch unþeawes inȝong his warde te witene and te
405 warden treowliche.

Þus ah mon te þenchen ofte ant ilome ant wið þulliche þohtes
awecchen his heorte, þe i slep of ȝemeles forȝet hire sawle
heale, efter þeos twa sonden; from helle sihðe biseon to þe
blisse of heouene; to habben farlac of þet an, luue toward þet
410 oðer, ant leaden him ant his hinen, þet beoð his limen, alle nawt
efter þat his Wil, þe untohe lefdi, and his lust leareð, ah efter þet
Wit wule þet is husebonde, tuhten ant teachen þet Wit ga
euer biuore ant teache Wil efter him to al þet he dihteð ant
demeð to donne ant wið þe fowr sustren þerfore, þe fowr
415 heued-þeawes—Warschipe, Strencðe in Godd, ant Með and

391 * C quoð Með   407 hire] C his   410 his hinen C; R om.
his   410–11 nawt . . . leareð] C, with efter for C's after; R nawt
efter Wil, etc.   413 teache] C drahe   414 R inserts þerfore
after sustren

Rihtwisnesse—witen Godes treosor þet is his ahne sawle i þe hus of þe bodi from þe þeof of helle. Þulli þoht makeð mon te fleon alle unþeawes ant ontent his heorte toward þe blisse of heouene. Þet ure Lauerd ȝeue us þurh his hali milce, þet wið þe Feder ant e Sune ant e Hali Gast rixleð in þreohad a buten 420 ende. Amen.

Par seinte charite biddeð a paternoster for Iohan þet þeos boc wrat.

> Hwase þis writ haueð ired
> Ant Crist him haueð swa isped, 425
> Ich bidde par seinte charite
> Þat ȝe bidden ofte for me
> Aa paternoster ant Aue Marie,
> Þet Ich mote þet lif her drehen
> Ant ure Lauerd wel icwemen 430
> I mi ȝuheðe ant in min elde
> Þet Ich mote Iesu Crist mi sawle ȝelde. Amen.

432 ȝelde] MS. ȝelden. *The scribe's verses are found in R only*

COMMENTARY

I

MS.: Cotton Caligula A. ix, British Museum. The folios containing the poem were reproduced in facsimile for the E.E.T.S. (O.S. 251, 1963) with introduction by N. R. Ker.

Editions: J. E. Wells, *The Owl and the Nightingale* (Boston and London 1907). [Parallel texts.]

W. Gadow, *Das mittelenglische Streitgedicht Eule und Nachtigall* (Palaestra LXV, 1909).

J. W. H. Atkins, *The Owl and the Nightingale* (Cambridge 1922). [Parallel texts.]

J. H. G. Grattan and G. F. H. Sykes, *The Owl and the Nightingale* (E.E.T.S., E.S. 119, 1935). [Diplomatic edition of both MSS.]

E. G. Stanley, *The Owl and the Nightingale* (London, 1960). [Revised E. J. Dobson, *N. & Q.* (1961).]

Studies: H. Walther, *Das Streitgedicht in der lateinischen Literatur des Mittelalters* (Quellen und Untersuchungen zur lateinischen Philologie des Mittelalters, V. 2, 1920).

C. T. Onions, 'An Experiment in Textual Reconstruction', *E. & S.* xxii (1936), 86–102.

B. Sundby, *The Dialect and Provenance of the Middle English Poem 'The Owl and the Nightingale'* (Lund Studies in English, ed. O. Arngart, xviii, 1950).

S. R. T. O. d'Ardenne, 'The Editing of Middle English Texts', *English Studies Today* (ed. C. L. Wrenn and G. Bullough, Oxford 1951), pp. 74–84.

Language

1. The reflex of OE *ǣ* (OKt, WMerc *ē*) rhymes on *ē* in *iwar* 103: *abisemar* (with etymologically required *e*).
2. The reflex of Gmc *ǎ* before *ng* rhymes: (*a*) normally only on itself (*longe* 81: *songe* etc.), and (*b*) once (though not in this extract) on *ǔ* in *songe* 1072: *tunge*.
3. The reflex of OE *ǣ*, *ē* < Gmc *ǎ*+nasal+consonant+*i*, *j* rhymes:
   (*a*) on *ē* in *schende* 210: *cunde* (see 4, below).

(*b*) probably on *ă* in *wranne* 372: *monne* prep. pl. (if the latter is regularly derived from OE *monnum*).

4. The reflex of OE *ў* (OKt *ĕ*) rhymes on *ĕ* in *cunde* 209: *schende*; *kunne* 65, 509, 632: *honne, mankenne* 683: *þenne*; *sunne* 523: *honne*; *worse* 219: *mershe*.

5. The reflex of OE *ǣ*¹ rhymes:

(*a*) on *ǣ*² in *bere* 557: *forlere*; *-dede* 268: *godhede*; *drede* 430: *ӡephede*; *eve* 41: *bileue*; *mede* 316: *sprede*.

(*b*) on tense *ē* in *iseӡe* 303: *eӡe*; *snepe* 181: *wepe*; *were* 569: *skere*.

(*c*) on [a] < OE *ĕa* in *aiware* 172: *ӡare*; *þare* 519: *ӡare*.

6. The reflex of OE *ǣ*² rhymes:

(*a*) on slack *ē* < OE *ēa* in *vnwreste* 134: *cheste*.

(*b*) when shortened, on the reflex of OE *ǣ*/*ĕ* in *iladde* 276, 562: *hadde*.

7. OE *ĕo* have been unrounded to *ĕ* and tense *ē* respectively in:

(*a*) *honne* 66: *kunne* (see 4, above); *houene* 474, 529, 548: *steuene*.

(*b*) *prest* 238: *dest*.

8. There was no diphthongization of front vowels by preceding palatal consonants in the antecedent type of OE: *underӡete* 124: *hete*.

9. The products of *i*-mutation in the antecedent type of OE were:

(*a*) *ĕ* < early OE *ǣ*+*ll* in *wel* n. 549: *snel*.

(*b*) *e* < Gmc *ă*+*r*+consonant in *derne* 388: *berne*; *cherde* 616: *iherde*; *cherme* 221: *scherme* (MS. *chirme*: *schirme*).

(*c*) *ēo* < *īo* < *ĕo*+[ç]+vowel in *isene* 404: *grene*; 211,664: *kene*.

10. ME [ọu] < OE *ā*+*w* rhymes on ME [ou] < OE (tense) *ō*+*w* in *iblowe* 398: *bigrowe*, implying either [ọu] or [au] derived from it (cf. *traw(e)* in *Ayenbite of Inwyt* < *trou* < *triow*).

11. OE *g* had been absorbed between a short vowel and *d* or *n*, with lengthening of the preceding vowel:

(*a*) *ised* 273: *red*; *sede* 357: *bede*; *seide* 453: *dede*, 564: *erede*, 265: *rede*.

(*b*) *ӡene* 505: *isene*.

12. OE [ʃ] has become [s] in *mershe* 220: *worse* (see 4, above).

13. The 3 pres. sg. indic. of verbs ends in *-eþ* in *springeþ* 480: *singeþ* pl. (see 14, below).

14. The pres. pl. indic. of verbs ends:
    (a) in *-þ* in *auoþ* 503: *soþ*; *doþ* 174, 728: *soþ*.
    (b) and therefore in *-eþ* in *singeþ* 479: *springeþ* (sg.).
15. The pres. part. ends in *-inde*: *singinde* 515: *auinde*.
16. Disyllabic verbs of weak class II with short root-syllables have preserved the *-i-*, since it is established by the metre in the verbal noun *wnienge* 394: *skentinge*.

Provenance

The type of rhyme illustrated in 2 (*b*), which implies an [u] in *stronge*, is usually claimed to be Western in ME:[1] it occurs in *Pearl* 470 ff., 529 ff., and in the writings of Mirk and Audelay, both of whom are known to have lived in Shropshire. But if *The Owl and the Nightingale* substantially and consistently represents a spoken form of ME, either this type of rhyme cannot have been restricted to the West,[2] or the example recorded here is not an exact rhyme, since other evidence in the poem decisively excludes Western provenance.

The WMidl is excluded by 4 and 7; 11 is Southern; 9 (*a*), (*b*), and (*c*) exclude the SW (as an area corresponding to WS in OE); 12 is SE and EMidl; and 4 is specifically SE (an area with which, among others, 8 is compatible). Closer localization is hardly possible: the evidence of 5 and 6 is inconsistent.

The SE word *fort* 41 (corrupted in the Jesus MS., as in the other examples in 248 and 310) probably goes back to the author himself. On the other hand, the exclusively SE *wnienge* 394 is likely to be a scribe's form, in view of the rhyme on *skentinge*.

1–4. The first of several examples of a single rhyme in two successive couplets (cf. e.g. 191–4), sometimes with an effect of speed or emphasis.

1. If *sumere* is < *sumre* (dat. sg. fem. of *sum* 'a certain'), it is tautologous after *one* ('a') and fails to agree in gender with *dale* if that had remained neut. as in OE. We should perhaps read *sumer* and recognize an attributive use evidenced in OE

---

[1] Jordan, *Handbuch der mittelenglischen Grammatik*, § 31; but see M. S. Serjeantson, *R.E.S.* vii (1931), 450–2.

[2] Cf. the discussion by B. Sundby, op. cit., pp. 129–30.

(*sumorselde* 'summer house') and later ME: cf. *O.E.D.* s.v. *summer* sb.⁴. Professor d'Ardenne, *R.E.S.* N.S. ix (1958), 342, suggests that the original reading was *Ich was one* ('alone') and that the transposition was helped by the pattern of the following line.

2. *hale*: Hall regards this as a reference to a valley near Portisham (see 710); but the context in 710 requires the imagined scene of the debate to be at some distance from that village.

8. *wole* (C) is probably due to a misreading of *uule* (=*fule*); so in 31 *uuel* was perhaps read as *wel*, and *wl* (=*uul*, 'foul') then inserted to improve sense and metre.

14. *one hurne of one breche*: established as the correct reading by the phrase *breches hurne* in a thirteenth-century Oxfordshire cartulary; see C. T. Onions, *A Grammatical Miscellany offered to Otto Jespersen* (1930), pp. 105–8. *Breche* ('piece broken off from the edge of a forest; a clearing') was evidently a word of limited range; but J's *beche* may be due simply to the accidental omission of *r*.

16. *Þar . . . abute*: 'around which'.

17. *waste*: 'deserted, solitary', may be thought inferior in sense to J's *vaste* ('secure, safe'); but the choice is difficult.

33. *unwiht*: 'miscreant'. In this compound *un*- retains the pejorative force that it has in some OE words, e.g. *unræd*: cf. XIX, 5 n.

41. The owl, of course, cannot speak till nightfall. The debate lasts the whole night, ending when dawn wakes the other birds (610–11).

45. *warp a word*: a phrase probably belonging to the common Germanic poetic stock: cf. ON *varpa orði*. It occurs in *St. Katherine* and in later alliterative poetry: cf. *O.E.D. warp* v. 11, and *Piers Plowman* A. IV. 142.

þarafter longe: i.e. it took the owl a long time to find words to answer the nightingale's provocative remarks.

54. *anoþer wise*: cf. *Confessio Amantis*, ii. 3012: 'Now schalt thou singe another song.' C evidently interpreted the phrase in his exemplar as meaning 'in a different fashion'.

62. The line is overlong. *Wiþ* may be a later insertion to re-inforce the dat. *hom*; but the cause of the corruption may lie elsewhere—one would expect a reflexive pron. with *schilde*.

63–64. Onions regards *vuele* as a corruption of *fule* ('foully'); but it is doubtful whether *fuȝel* (64) became a monosyllable before the xiii c. For the assonance of the voiced fricatives [ɣ] and [v] cf. 213–14. [See, however, E. J. Dobson, *N. & Q.* (1961), p. 377.]

miȝte over is apparently a transitive form of the verb *ouermyhte* found in XVI. 195, where it is used absolutely. Later *over* in this unit came to be felt as a preposition: see the fuller discussion on p. xxxiii; and see also the note in Stanley's edition.

66. The owl attacked by small birds is a common subject of medieval art, e.g. on misericords at Norwich and Beverley.

73. The owl's neck is in fact quite slender.

85. *þe . . . to* (governing dat. *one frogge*) probably results from a fusion of two constructions: 'your natural bent is to the frog' and 'a frog would be more appropriate for you'. Cf. 389–90.

[95–138: *the nightingale concludes with an* exemplum *about an owl who defiled a falcon's nest by laying eggs therein; the falcon detected the young bird with the big head, and threw it out: 'þeȝ appel trendli from þon trowe, he cuþ wel whonene he is icume.*']

107. *þare* (C), an obvious error, is corrected by most editors to *ware* 'whether'; but metre requires an unelided form, which occurs in *O. & N.* as *weþer* (991) or *waþer* (1064).

116. *Me* is probably repeated accidentally from 115.

132. *þe wise*: OE *se wīsa*, 'the wise man'. The proverb is found in OF and in the thirteenth-century *Proverbs of Hending*, and alluded to in *Hali Meiðhad*: 'þu most turne þe rug ȝef þu wult ouercomen & wið fluht fehten' (ed. Colborn, p. 16, l. 236).

147. *Maister Nichole*. In the twelfth century the title *magister* was applied not only to members of the two universities who had incepted as M.A.s or Doctors, but by courtesy to all those admitted in one of the higher faculties. It is interesting to find a cleric 'Nicholas de Guldeforde' appearing at Oxford in 1322 (Emden, *Register of the University of Oxford*, ii. 769).

160. *gente an smale*: epithets regularly applied to women in lyrics and romances.

163. *þine olde luue*: 'his former love for thee'.

166. *fals dom*: (? read *domes, metri causa*): 'the complaint of "false judgment" was the method by which a judgment given by an inferior court could be questioned [in the King's court]' (Atkins, p. 21).

167. *him*: the 'ethic' dat. is rare with the verb *to be*: hence '*nu*' (J) may be the better reading. Either word could be an erroneous anticipation of 168.

179. If the general reference at 175 ff. is to monastic chant, this will allude to antiphonal singing in choir.

181. *wise an snepe*: 'all and sundry'. Such inclusive formulae are a feature of ME: Cf. e.g. *blak or reed, C.T.* A. 294, and XII. 62.

187. *þat*: here used as an indecl. rel. = 'to whom'.

207–8. *wune* (C) ('custom') is intelligible but gives a poor rhyme with *cunne*. C's exemplar probably had *wnne* (= *wunne*, 'delight', cf. 34 n.); *ynne* (J) must derive from a MS. in which *w* was written *þ* [*wynn*], which J misread as *y* (as he did thrice elsewhere).

212. *Vor riȝte cunde*: 'because of my proper (*or* essential) nature'; hence 'by Nature's laws' (Atkins).

217–18. G. G. Coulton (*M.L.R.* xvii (1922), 71) saw here a reference to the contemplative monastic life.

[283–302: *the owl goes on to explain why she does not reply to the small birds 'mid chauling and mid chatere': 'one should not yawn against an oven.'*]

225. It is doubtful if *of*, here in unstressed position, can govern *me*, and *þinge* would be unusual as an acc. pl. form. Translate: 'Thou speakest to me of other things.'

238. *on Irish prest*: the Irish clergy were notoriously lax and illiterate: cf. *Piers Plowman* B. XX. 220 ff., where a 'mansed [i.e. excommunicate] preest of the marche of Yrlonde' is represented as avaricious and regardless of Conscience. *chaterest* may refer to the brogue, or to a rapid way of saying mass.

239. *a riʒte time*: i.e. not all night long, like the nightingale, but only at the times when religious should perform the duty (*note*, 246) of singing their night hours—Vespers (*an eue*), Compline (*bedtime*), Matins (*ad middelniʒte*), Lauds (243–4). In the *South English Legendary* (E.E.T.S. o.s. 235, 1956), i. 187, the birds in the *foulen parais* visited by St. Brendan are represented as singing the day hours: 'eche tyde songe of þe daye, as Cristene men ssolde don.'

256. *of þar*: = ? *þarof*. J rationalizes to *of þe*, inappropriately (J's *unwiht* 255 can scarcely = 'monstrous', *pace* Wells). The sense 'so that nothing of it is accounted worth anything' is barely possible, and the original reading remains doubtful; it may have been *of þan/þen* (OE *þam*, *þæm*, sg.)

260. *hit*: neut. in generalized reference to music.

261. *ne bo ... neuer*: *ne*, with the verb, is idiomatically necessary with *neuer*—though in modern usage both negatives have disappeared. To accord with 262, this line must be translated 'the song can never be so pleasing'; the construction is possibly influenced by that of 257–8.

263. *ouer unwille*: historically an adverbial use of the dat. sg. of the noun *unwilla*, qualified by the poss. pron. (OE *urum*). Cf. *Ure gast biÞ swiÞe wide farende urum unwillum* (OE *Boethius*, ed. Sedgefield, p. 93, l. 7), MDu *mijns onwillen*, 'against my wishes', and ON *at úvilja* with gen. Onions suggests that the original reading here was *ure unwille*.

265. *Alured*: twelve proverbs cited in the poem are attributed to Alfred (one being said to be written, another to be extant 'in books'); only one of them appears in the extant *Proverbs of Alfred*, but there were several collections carrying his name current in the twelfth century. Marie de France attributed to him (perhaps for political reasons) the original of her *Ysopet* (a book of fables). For the present apophthegm cf. *C.T.* F. 400 ff.

[351–90: *the owl goes on to answer the taunt that she is weak-sighted: she does not go about by day, it is true; but neither does the hare—yet it knows how to escape the hounds well enough.*]

278. *wrþe . . . ifare*: *noþeles* (279) suggests that the reference is to an answer about to be given: hence render: 'would not [prove to] have fared aright.'

282. *hit*: 'his position' rather than 'his case' (Hall). The hypermetrical *ne* of the MSS. is probably due to a wrong identification of *he* with the *he* of 280.

283–4. The context requires a negative. *nesuicst* or *nisuicst* ('if thou dost not fail') was probably the original reading; one copyist must have omitted *ne-/ni-*, and a later one added *i-* (from OE *ge-*); the corrector of C could interpret the resultant *isvicst* only by treating it as a form of 'fightest' with an erroneous prefix.

286. *wrchen bareʒ*: 'make a barrow' (castrated pig)—i.e. turn his fierceness into timidity; but the original may have had *wurthen/wurþen*, 'become'.

296. *þat . . .*: the clause is the subject of *is* (295).

305–6. 'He would not care though whole companies [of men] were mingled together [pulling each other] by heads and by hair' (thus Skeat, in effect): cf. colloquial American 'to mix it' (=fight). Atkins's interpretation of *flockes* as 'flocks of wool' (cf. *M.E.D.*), and of the whole sentence as referring to impurities which made the combing process necessary, is inappropriate to the context. [Cf. also Chambers and Daunt, *London English* (1931), p. 28, l. 170: '. . I wot wel eueri man sholde haue be in others top'.]

318. *þat þu hit wite*: 'take note of that.' For a similar construction with imperative force cf. *Piers Plowman* B. VI. 11 ('þat ʒe han silke and sendal to sowe') and *O. & N.* 122 ('þat his necke him toberste') and ? 379 below. J evidently misunderstood *wite* as < *witen* 'to blame'.

341. For 'coundutes' (*conducti*, Latin part-songs) at Christmas cf. *Sir Gawain and the Green Knight*, 1654–5.

[447–66: *the nightingale explains that she goes away in high summer, lest men be sated with joy.* 485–534: *the owl reproaches the nightingale for its lecherous song, which is over 'wane þi lust is ago'; whereas the owl sings, and solaces men, on hard winter nights.*]

348. For *lutli*: '(in order) to lessen'. Cf. *for teche*, 724.

353–4. For the rhyme cf. *C.T.* A. 671–2 (*Rome, to me*); the stress would be on *to*. Cf. 629–30 and III. 103 n. below.

355. *bare worde*: 'nude parole', *simplex dictum*—as Atkins says, the legal terms for a mere assertion on the part of a plaintiff unsupported by witnesses.

358. *bicloped*: 'made your charge' (OE *bicleopian*, 'to summon, sue at law'): cf. examples cited by Atkins, and *M.E.D.* s.v. *biclepen* (1).

367–8. 'You are of no use for anything, except that you are skilled in twittering.'

370. *long* may be due to the exigencies of rhyme, and a reference to the owl's ample feathers; but possibly it is a deliberate allusion to the 'long clothes' (cf. *Piers Plowman* C. VI. 41) of the religious, with whom the owl identifies itself *passim*.

375. 'Once your piping is finished.'

[570–96: *moreover, the nightingale is a dim and dirty-coloured bird who shuns clean places.*]

389. *to Cristes huse*: the exact force of *to* is uncertain. It suggests a confusion of two constructions similar to those cited at 85 n.

394. *oþer wnienge*: ? sc. 'than the [hollow] trees' (of 395 ff.); but some edd. emend *wernen* to *ȝernen* (sc. 'other than barns or churches').

400. MS. *sniuþ*: evidently miswritten for *sniu(w)þ*; it is doubtful whether J's *snywe* is intended as a subj. form.

[625–58: *you say my nest isn't clean—but young birds, like young children, can't help themselves; it's very roomy and soft, and has a privy-arrangement, just like men's houses . . . 'Hong up þin ax'.*]

415. *He*: indef.,=*þe man* (417).

426. *wo hine kon*: 'for anyone who knows himself', i.e. his own powers and limitations' (or ? 'for anyone who knows it' [= *red*]).

428. 'as when a plan is in doubt for Wit'—i.e. as when Wit is perplexed, in extremity.

430. *hit is*: 'things are . . . .'

431. *Aluered*: 432–3 are not in the extant *Proverbs*, but the sentiment is common (cf. *Oxford Dictionary of English Proverbs*, 2nd ed., p. 21) and a variant occurs in the *Proverbs of Hending*. The repetition at 444–5 is the poet's characteristic way of closing a paragraph.

435. *west*: 'waxes, increases'; probably a variant phonetic development of the heavy consonantal grop *hst* in *wehst*, the [ç] being assimilated to the following *-s-*.

449. *þe toʒte*: 'strained situation(s)'. The general sense appears to be: 'She had bethought herself in this crisis, and managed to find a good answer, though in dire straits.'

455. *in sume tide* (CJ): 'at certain seasons'; but *sume* is possibly a misreading of *sum̄e* (= *sumere*).

474. Most of the hymns sung at matins mention heaven.

476. *wicke-tunes* appears to cover both monasteries and foundations of canons. In the OE metrical version of the Psalms *wictunas* translates *atria*. Alcuin (*De Luxuria* 15–20), Neckam (*De Naturis Rerum*, i. 51), Odo of Cheriton (*Les fabulistes latins*, iv. 241), Dunbar (*The Merle and the Nightingale*) all associate the nightingale's song with the praises of God.

480 ff. The nightingale (in contrast to the owl: see 239 ff.) seems to identify itself with seculars, who would say or sing matins along with lauds or prime before mass. *mid hom* (482) is perhaps in contrast with the Owl's emphasis on *its* warning note (246).

492. The papal curia was the ultimate court of appeal for any cleric (cf. E. Stanley, *E.G.S.* vi. 37), and the reference makes it clear that the author (doubtless himself in orders) envisaged the contestants as representing two types of monk or priest.

494. *þes*: it is almost certain that the initial letter is a dot-less *þ*, not *p* [*wynn*]. Gadow's explanation of *þes* as an archaic gen. of respect (OE *þæs*) is supported by the recurrence of the word in the same sense and rhyme at *O. & N.* 882. C. L. Wrenn (*M.Æ.* i. 151) interpreted *þes* as a form of OE *þys*, 'storm', a cognate of ON *þyss*, 'uproar, tumult'; alternatively, an adoption of the latter in ME is conceivable; 352 would offer a parallel in phrasing.

[751–836: *the nightingale goes on to produce examples of the superiority of skill to strength, concluding with the cat who by means of the only trick he knows saves his skin when the nimble fox loses his.*]

498. *al*: apparently 'entirely', though we should expect it to follow *to*.

509–11. Coulton found here 'one of the many medieval echoes' of St. Jerome's *monachus non docentis sed plangentis habet officium*; another occurs in Richard of Bury's *Philobiblon* (ed. M. Maclagan (Oxford 1960), p. 54).

514–15. 'Do you expect to bring them all singing to God's kingdom so easily?' [Metre suggests the reading *alle*, with elision.]

528. *foliot*: Atkins's suggestion that this is an allusion to the learned (and austere) Gilbert Foliot, Bishop of London (1163–88), is implausible and supererogatory: *foliot* is well evidenced in OF in the sense 'a device to catch larks'; cf. *E.G.S.* vi. 46.

530. 'You have no voice for that' or 'you have no song proper for that place'.

539–42. The nightingale is not found in Ireland, Scotland, or Scandinavia. The inhabitants of Galloway (an independent principality in the twelfth century) had a reputation for wildness and 'bestiality'. In 1186 they rose against William the Lion, who invoked Henry II's aid.

[927–1290: *the nightingale replies that Norway is a 'grislich' land where men drink milk and live like beasts; it is useless to sing to such people. The owl angrily retorts with an* exemplum *about a lady tempted by a nightingale to unlawful love; the nightingale then offers its own interpretation of that story, following it with a denunciation of the owl as a detested bird of evil augury. 'Although you can certainly* curse *well enough', flings back the owl, 'I doubt whether you're an ordained priest; as to my knowledge of the future, I use it to give helpful warning to man.'*]

565. *hire understod*: 'made a plan' or 'knew how to behave' (though the latter sense is not evidenced till much later).

568. *he*=*wisdome* (m.) 567; *hit* (568) includes the notion of its coming.

579. *abisemere* must be taken with *askedest* (578): 'artu ihoded?' the owl had asked sneeringly at 1177.

586 ff. The passage may be corrupt, but the sense is clear: 'how can a miserable owl know the future, when even a man cannot, unless he is an expert astrologer?' *þe mon* (586) seems to require a defining rel. clause, which could be provided by emending *An* to *Þat*. It is tempting to insert *þe* after *þat* (588), which may, indeed, represent a *þe* (dat.) in the exemplar, mistaken for a rel. pron. [For a fuller discussion see Dobson, *N. & Q.* (1961), pp. 445–6.]

It has been suggested that *An* may represent an earlier *And*, used by the poet in the sense 'if' (cf. ON *enda*) first found in Laȝamon.

590. *bihaltest*: *bihaitest*, CJ. For confusion of *l* with a minim cf. e.g. *freuch* for *frelich*, *Pearl* 1086.

[*1331–164c. It is true, continues the nightingale, that I sing of love; but I should not therefore be blamed if a woman practises 'derne luue'. In any case, are sins of the flesh worse than those of the spirit? My song reminds girls that love 'nis bute a litel breþ'; and I'm astonished that a man should ever entice away another man's wife. The owl then speaks on behalf of married women, describes their trials and the complaints they make to it, and how it sings at night to solace the lonely wife; it admits that men attack it and use it as a scarecrow; but even its death does some good—men use it as a decoy, and so obtain food.*

599 ff. *are part of the nightingale's reply.*]

609. *gest an honde*: 'surrenderest'; in many ME expressions 'hand' implies control, power, or possession: cf. Gl. s.v. *hond(e)*.

617. *wudewale*: in a fourteenth-century glossary the word glosses *l'oriol*, i.e. the golden oriole—'which has a loud, flute-like whistle': by the sixteenth-century (? or earlier) it had come to be used for the woodpecker—which has a distinctive laughing cry rather than a song.

621. *alswa uale wise*: 'in so many strains' (sc. as there were birds).

623. *gred þe manne a schame*: 'cries shame on the man.'

645. *fulliche eue*: viz. the evening of the day that has now dawned.

658. *ginneþ*: here used as an auxiliary of the ingressive present: 'take flight'.

680. 'and sang to the pleasure of many men': *manne* is presumably a partitive gen. dependent on *fale*; but it could also be construed as a dat. of advantage.

681. Atkins suggests that the respect accorded to the wren, and the part it plays at this point are due to the widespread tradition that the wren is king of birds (cf. OF *roitelet*, &c.).

683. *mankenne*: C's omission of -*k*- may well be accidental. But Grattan held that the scribe did not recognize [SE] -*kenne* in this compound, though he knew it when it stood alone (and then altered to *kunne*, as at 632).

688–9. *þis pes*: variously interpreted as referring to (1) Hubert Walter's peaceful administration as justiciar (1194–8); (2) the Edictum Regis (1193) of Richard I, designed to preserve the peace; (3) Richard's treaty with Scotland (Dec. 1189). But it may simply allude to *pax regis* (OE *cyninges griþ*) in general: see *O.E.D.* s.v. *Peace* 9a.

kinge is supplied by all edd. as a necessary antecedent for *he* (690); *þanne* is probably a result of reading *þan* (dem.) as 'then'; *swuche* (agreeing with *schame*) would further improve rhythm and grammar.

691. *Hunke* (CJ) should represent 1st dual *unc*, 'to me and to thee'; J reads *we* at 696; but unless arbitrarily interpreted as 'any birds' *we* is impossible: the wren is not involved in any breach of the peace. Probably *hunke* (not a unique form) is a miswriting, or due to a misunderstanding, of a 2nd dual *ȝunk(e)* (OE *inc*).

709. J's *mihte*, taken with the C form, suggests that the common exemplar had a form that could be misread as *miȝ-* or *mih-*: hence, presumably, Wells's reading *nuȝte* (pl. pres.); but it is hard to relate this to OE *nyton*. Onions improves on Stratmann's *nute ȝe* by proposing *nete ȝit*.

710. *Porteshom*: a village in S. Dorset (*hom < hamme*, 'water meadow'), two or three miles from the Swannery, the outlet of a stream running through Abbotsbury, the site of a monastery to which the village belonged. It was in the diocese of Salisbury, with which Guildford was connected (see *V.C.H.*, *Surrey*, iii. 41, 570).

713. *manie riȝte dom*: 'he may have been the bailiff of the hundred court, or steward of a manor, or commissary for the neighbouring Abbotsbury' (Hall). For literary evidence that parish priests engaged in such activities see *Piers Plowman* B, Prol. 96.

716. *into Scotlonde*: 'from here right up to Scotland'. The construction is modelled on OF phrases like *desqua Rome*; cf. *Havelok* 64 and the note in the Skeat–Sisam ed. of that poem.

718. i.e. he lacks pluralities—on which advancement depended. Since pluralism helped poor students and promising men, it was not always regarded as an evil: cf. Powicke, *The Thirteenth Century*, pp. 459, 487.

733. The appointment of well-connected boys was a familiar abuse; Atkins gives instances mentioned by Grosseteste, Hall cites Odo of Cheriton. St. Bernard remonstrated with a bishop who conferred an archidiaconate on a mere child, 'who cannot rule himself' (*Letters*, ed. B. S. James, p. 342); in the fourteenth century one Philip Beauchamp had a canonry before he was six and fourteen preferments by the time he was as many years old (Workman, *Wiclif*, ii. 112).

735–6. 'Their own common sense convicts them of error inasmuch as Master Nicholas is kept continually waiting' [for preferment].

II

MS.: Laud Misc. 622, Bodleian Library.

Editions: H. Weber, in *Metrical Romances* (1810), i. 3–327.
    G. V. Smithers, *Kyng Alisaunder*, E.E.T.S., o.s. 227 (1952) and 237 (1957).

Source: *Le Roman de Toute Chevalerie* (unpublished).

Studies: M. D. Legge, *Anglo-Norman in the Cloisters* (Edinburgh 1950), pp. 35–43.

Ead., *Anglo-Norman Literature and its Background* (Oxford 1963), pp. 105–7.

Language

1. The reflex of OE *ĕ* (SE *ǣ* in late OE) < Gmc *ă*+nasal+ consonant+*i, j* rhymes on (i) tense *ē* and *ĕ* in *men* 128: *quen*; *ysent* 313: *encumbrement* respectively (ii) AN *a* in *manne* 47: *tyranne*.

2. The reflex of OE *ĕ*+*ġ* rhymes on that of OE *ǣ* (OKt and OWMerc *ĕ*)+*ġ* in *away* 315: *day*; *play* 278: *day*.

3. The reflex of OE *ȳ* (OKt *ĕ*) rhymes on *e* in *gylt* 107: *forswelt*; *pett* 44: *bysett*.

4. The reflex of OE *ā* rhymes on AN *o* (of uncertain quality, in *Antigon*) in *euerychon* 23, *fon* 78, *onon* 67.

5. The reflex of OE *ȳ* (OKt *ē*) rhymes on an *ē* which may be either slack or tense (according to the variety of ME in question) in *fyre* 98: *þere*.

6. Breaking of primitive OE *ǽ* before *rh* is possible in *mere* 6115 (with either ME slack *ē*, < OE *ēa* by lengthening after the elimination of [ç], or ME *ĕ* by shortening of slack *ē*): *bere* n. OE *mearh* is likelier here than OE *mĕre* 'mare'.

7. There was no diphthongization of a front vowel preceded by a palatal consonant in the antecedent type of OE: *ʒelde* 100: *felde* n.

8. The product of the OE *i*-mutation of *ēa* rhymes on tense *ē* in *nede* 75: *fede* v.

9. In the antecedent form of OE, *g* had been absorbed between a short vowel and *d* or *n*, with lengthening of the preceding vowel, in *seide* 227: *stede*. But the variant development in which it was unaffected is attested in *yseide* 284: *ypleiede*.

10. ME [ai] rhymes on OF *oi* in *tueye* 189: *joye*—a rare type of rhyme, the phonological interpretation of which is doubtful (see *Kyng Alisaunder*, ii. 52–55).

11. OE [ɣ] has become [u̯] in *ydrawe* 317: *blawe* inf.

12. The plural of nouns rhymes on (i) *-es* in *tenes* 64: *wenes*; (ii) *-(e)* in *doune* 91: *cite-toune*; (iii) *-n* when the root ends in a vowel, in *fon* 78: *Antigon*.

13. The 2 pres. sg. ends in -*es* in *wenes* 63: *tenes*.
14. The 3 pres. sg. (i) ends in -*eþ* in *afongeþ* 83: *longe, desireþ* 142: *sire*; (ii) if the root ends with a dental, is of the old type with syncope of the vowel of the ending and assimilation of the -*þ* in *trest* 71: *best*. See *Note*, below.
15. The infinitive (i) has no final -*n* in *ride* 176: *bride* n.; *speke* 15, 32: *Canduleke*; *sterue* 304: *serue*; (ii) ends in -*n(e)* when the root ends in a vowel, in *bene* 208: *bituene*; *sene* 206: *quene*.
16. The past part. of strong verbs (i) has no final -*n* in *bede* 121: *stede* n.; *do* 52: *to*; *fare* 55: *Yndare*; (ii) retains the prefix *y*- in *ynome* 36 (where it is metrically necessary).

Note. The rhymes do not prove that -*eþ*, rather than -*es*, was the ending of the 3 pres. sg., or that -*es* has been adopted as the plural of old weak nouns, since the author's practice included the rhyming of final -*e* on final -*e* plus consonant (*Kyng Alisaunder*, ii., n. on ll. 149–50, and p. 50, 17). The same applies to *wende* 86 as 3 pres. pl. (: *þousynde*), which might have been *wendeþ, wenden,* or *wend(e)* in the author's language.

Provenance

South-Eastern (almost certainly London). The SE is indicated by 3 and 5; 7 is consistent with an antecedent Kentish type in OE; 9 is Southern, and excludes Anglian as an antecedent OE type, and therefore Midland and Northern as the ME one; and 1 (ii) is Essex–London. Evidence in the work as a whole establishes the SE origin beyond doubt and points to London (*Kyng Alisaunder*, ii. 40–55). Forms within the line do not materially diverge from the type of ME implied by the rhymes. The ON element in the vocabulary is limited (*casten* 238, *gest* 280, *skaþe* 271, *sweyn* 12, *taken* 96, *wyndewes* 214, *wrong* 53, *ygreiped* 208), the OF so rich and recondite as to imply an author who was bilingual.

———

14. *atturne*: this sense is attested in OF ('someone else representing him'). The word is by origin the past part. of OF *atorner* 'put in order, arrange, etc.', and therefore means 'one who has been assigned to a particular function'. Its later history illustrates and is due to the role of social groups in a community as a leading factor in semantic change: a technical application in the juridical vocabulary has come to be virtually the only sense surviving in English.

22. (*kynges*) *person*: most of what matters in the semantic development of this word took place in L *persōna*. 'Mask worn by an actor in a drama' (which did not get into French or English) > 'the character represented in the play' (since the mask expressed a dominant quality in the character) > 'the essential feature of any human being' > 'the human being himself', whence 'individual human being'. By the fifth century the sense 'bodily or visible presence' had emerged; and in ecclesiastical Latin the occasion to designate socially important members of a community produced *persona regis·* (echoed here in *Kyng Alisaunder*) and the like. The same milieu contributed the sense 'ecclesiastical dignitary', the origin of the English use in the phonetic variant *parson*. The semantic development of the word has thus been determined by its use in the specialized vocabulary of at least two social groups.

33. *on boþe his knewes*: to be construed with *And kneleþ* 34. The 'inverted *and*' construction is well attested in *Kyng Alisaunder*, as in 86 (rephrased in 87), 115 below; and cf. 2226, ed. cit. Though rare in ME, it also occurs in *Confessio Amantis*, e.g. i. 433, 1190, 2320, 2454.

40. *ne . . . no*: this type of repeated negation is inherited from OE, and occurs in many languages at their earliest stage. The negation was originally expressed by *ne*, and reinforced by the addition of *ne* elsewhere (OE *nan* < *ne an*). The repetition is due to a desire for emphasis (which is sometimes affective), and is therefore clearly in origin a matter of spoken and especially colloquial usage. Its disappearance from standard English after 1600 coincides with and is evidently due to the substitution of the phonetically more substantial negative *not* for *ne*.

51. *þee to*: 'from you, of you'; a survival of a common semi-adverbial use of OE prepositions.

61. *chalenge*: the semantic history of OF *chalengier* is essentially that of L *calumnia* (< *calu(i)o* 'to practise deception'), which was determined by the application of the noun in classical times in a juridical sense as 'false charge', whence in med. L 'objection to a (legal) judgment', besides 'demand for something to which one professes a claim'. The last two senses are attested for the verb in early English; 'to invite, summon (to fight, &c.)' is first recorded in the sixteenth century.

65. *Of*: the *on* of the Lincoln's Inn MS. (see ed. cit.) is shown to be the correct reading here by *en* in the corresponding passage of the AN source: *En quantz auez assez?* (Durham Cathedral MS. 10640).

82. *folk*: established by the source (10652): *Oueque ly an alez, mes homes conduiez.* A scribe misread *f* in his exemplar as a long *s* and *o* as *e* (both of which are standard palæographical errors in ME MSS.).

83–84. Rhymes involving a discrepancy in a final unstressed syllable (and especially within the series -*e*: -*ed*, -*el*, -*en*, -*er*, -*es*, -*eþ*) are common in *Kyng Alisaunder* and the *Kyng Alisaunder* group (*Arthour and Merlin*, *The Seven Sages of Rome*, and *Richard Cœur de Lion*). Cf. 141–2 here, and 149–50 in the E.E.T.S. edition. Cf. also *Sir Orfeo* 341–2:

> þe selue way Ichil streche—
> Of liif no deþ me no reche

where *recheþ* is prescribed by the impersonal construction; and VI. 356 and VIII. F 47 below.

89. *in tapynage*: a calque on OF *en tapinage*.

91. The use of *ride* as 'ride over', without a preposition, is idiomatically unorthodox in ME. A parallel usage is not uncommon in ON, as in *Gylfaginning*, ch. 49: *hann reið niú nætr døkkva dala ok djúpa* (*Edda Snorra Sturlusonar*, ed. Finnur Jónsson, p. 90). For other examples see M. Nygaard, *Norrøn Syntax* (1906), § 96 (*b*).

94. *Canduleke*: cf. *Kyng Alisaunder* 179, *Alisaunder* 194; these uninflected forms of gen. sg. are on the model of the declension of nouns in OF.

106. *harme gan warne*: nothing quite like this construction with a double accusative (of the person warned and the thing warned about) is traceable in the recorded uses of *warn*.

110. *oþere*: this is curious, since *oþeres* (gen. sg.) might have been expected. It is confirmed by *oþir* of the Lincoln's Inn MS. (though this and the Laud MS. derive from a common antecedent, and might both be reproducing an error from it).

126. *honour*: 'honours', in the technical use of feudalism, viz. 'fiefs, domains; seigniory' (see *O.E.D.* s.v. 7). The pl. without ending—and the complementary phenomenon of a sg. in *-s*, as in *honoures* 140 and *foysouns* 222—directly reproduce the inflectional pattern which is one of the main systems in the OF declension of nouns:

	Sg.	*Pl.*
Nom.	murs	mur
Obl.	mur	murs

130. *gynneþ*: pl.; the subject is understood from *gentil men* 128, in accordance with a syntactic idiom that is attested from OE into Shakespeare's time. Cf. e.g. *Beowulf* 30–31 (where the object of *ahte* is implied in *Scyldinga*); and *A Winter's Tale* IV. iv. 159:

> They call him Doricles, and boasts himself
> To have a worthy feeding.

Thus a word, once used in any grammatical case in a sentence, may be understood (i.e. without being expressed) in any other grammatical case in a later clause of the sentence.

140. *honoures*: see 126 n.

159. *(loue-)drurye*: formed on OF *dru* 'lover', with the suffix *-erie* < L *-aria*. The earliest occurrence of the root represented in *dru* is in the med. L verb *indruticāre* 'flaunt, behave wantonly' in Aldhelm's *De Virginitate*, xvii (ed. Ehwald, *Mon. Germ. Hist.*, *Auctorum Antiquissimorum*, xv 246, l. 16); and there are a mass of derivatives in the Romance languages. Its origin is a Celtic **drutō-* 'strong' (OIr *drúth* 'mad', Welsh *drud* 'valiant'); see von Wartburg, *F.E.W.*, **drūto-*, and J. Jud, 'Zur Geschichte und Herkunft von frz. *dru*', *Archivum Romanicum*, vi (1922), 313–39.

165. *queynt*: the welter of recorded senses (all but one attested already in ME) is reducible to two main groups: subjective ('having knowledge of one sort or another') and objective ('a quality which is the product of knowledge or ingenuity'). Only the first is represented in the OF adj.—the second, however, in OF *cointie* and *cointise* 'dress'. The L etymon *cognitus* belongs to a class of past participles which were by origin adjectives (in IE *-to-*); these expressed a state (as in *potus* 'having drunk', *tacitus* 'one who is silent'), and acquired a passive force only by a later development. The subjective group of senses is thus the more ancient type.

175. A courtly metaphor (like that of 247) of a type not commonly to be found in ME before the time of Chaucer. Cf. *Anelida and Arcite* 183-4, *Troilus and Criseyde* i. 953.

197. *be*: this use of the subjunctive in a noun-clause governed by a verb meaning 'comprehend' is inherited from OE, in which it occurs both in statements regarded as probable but not assured, and in statements regarded as assured fact. The latter type is believed to have been evolved on the analogy of the former.

211. *was þere-inne*: i.e. was the theme of painted scenes on the walls and the ceiling. References such as this to pictorial decoration in interiors, and on objects of costly workmanship, are common in medieval romance. They have a more specific point than might be thought: they are applications of the rhetorical colour *descriptio*, which was not restricted to personal descriptions. An example in the OF *Roman de Thèbes* 2933 ff. concerns the tent or pavilion of a military leader. In the ME *Le Bone Florence* 322 ff., the description of a palace interior mentions that the seven deadly sins were painted in the hall or on the pillars in it; and in 384-93 an emperor's tent is described as being painted with animals and fish.

In *Floris and Blancheflour* 163-81 a goblet is said to be adorned with a representation of Paris's abduction of Helen and of their love. The material for painted decorations of interiors was commonly drawn from the medieval system of knowledge synthesized in various encyclopædic works. A Latin poem (composed between 1099 and 1102) of Baudry de Bourgueil[1] describes a bedroom containing tapestries on which were represented

[1] Ed. P. Abrahams, *Les Œuvres poétiques de Baudri de Bourgueil* (Paris 1926), CXCVI, pp. 197-253.

the story of Creation, scenes from the Old Testament, and the siege of Troy (93–206); on the ceiling were depicted the heavens and the signs of the zodiac (583–676); and on the floor was a *mappa mundi* (719–82).

222. *foysouns*: see 126 n.

247. *laas*: another courtly metaphor; cf. *C.T.* A. 1815–17, 1951.

258–64. This list of *exempla* is a commonplace in medieval literature. The most interesting ME parallel is in *Sir Gawain and the Green Knight* 2416 ff. (omitting *Abygayl*): as in *Kyng Alisaunder*, the *exempla* are invoked not merely as an anti-feminist gesture, but to salve the wounded pride of a man who has been outwitted by a woman.

269. *to my baundon*: a calque on an OF phrase *a (mon*, &c.) *bandon* 'at (my, &c.) disposal'.

310. An idiom in ME; cf. *Sir Tristrem* 1578–9, *Ipomedon* 1963, *Amis and Amiloun* 1116, and *Troilus and Criseyde* ii. 445.

318. 'The attendant sounded on his trumpet the signal that it was time to retire for the night.' *A choger* is an AN phrase (OF **a coucher*) containing OF *a* 'to' < L *ad* and the infinitive represented in OF as *coucher* < L *collocāre*. The scribes of the Lincoln's Inn and Auchinleck MSS. were baffled by it and substituted *a pipe* and *a flegel* respectively (i.e. by a contextual guess that *choger* was the name of a musical instrument).

III

MS.: W 4 1, National Library of Scotland ('Auchinleck' MS.).

Editions: A. B. Taylor, *Floris and Blancheflour* (Oxford 1927).
   G. H. McKnight, *King Horn, Floriz and Blauncheflur, The Assumption of Our Lady*, E.E.T.S., o.s. 14 (1901) (MSS. Cambridge Cg. 4. 27. 2, Trentham (now B.M. Egerton 2862), and Cotton Vitellius D iii).

Source: *Floire et Blancheflor*, ed. M. Pelan (Publications de la Faculté des Lettres de l'Université de Strasbourg. Textes d'étude 7, 1937, revised ed. 1956).

Studies: L. A. Hibbard, *Mediæval Romance in England* (New York 1960), pp. 184–94.

G. Huet, 'Sur l'origine de *Floire et Blanchefleur*', *Romania*, xxviiii (1899), 348–59.

Id., 'Encore *Floire et Blanchefleur*', *Romania*, xxxv (1906), 95–100.

J. Reinhold, *Floire et Blancheflor* (Paris, 1906).

M. Lot-Borodine, *Le Roman idyllique au moyen âge* (Paris 1913), ch. i.

J. W. Spargo, 'The Basket Incident in *Floire et Blanceflor*', *Neuphilologische Mitteilungen*, 28 (1927), 69–75.

Language

The following account is based only on rhymes which are corroborated by one or more of the other MSS.

1. The reflex of OE $\breve{a}$, $\breve{o}$ (i) before a single nasal rhymes on $\breve{o}$ in *man* 145: *vpan*, and (ii) before nasal+consonant (constituting a lengthening group) on OE *u* in *honde* 48: *grounde*.

2. The reflex of Gmc $\breve{a}$+nasal when subject to *i*-mutation rhymes on $\breve{e}$ in *went* 67: *enchantement*.

3. The reflex of OE $\breve{y}$ (OKt $\breve{e}$) rhymes on [i] in *kisse* 277: *blisse*.

4. The reflex of OE $\bar{a}$ rhymes on (i) tense $\bar{o}$ in *so* 51: *fordo*, *þo* 175: *do*, and (ii) OE *a, o* in *an* 4: *man*.

5. The reflex of Gmc $\bar{æ}$ rhymes on slack $\bar{e}$ < OE $\bar{e}a$ in *red* n. 76: *ded* a.

6. The reflex of Gmc *ai* when *i*-mutated rhymes on slack $\bar{e}$ < OE $\bar{e}a$ in *geþ* 159: *deþ*; *clene* 199: *bene*.

7. The reflex of OE $\bar{e}o$ rhymes on tense $\bar{e}$ in *be* 88: *þe*, 231: *me*; *bede* 125: *spede*; *se* 257: *þe*.

8. Breaking of early OE $\breve{æ}$ before *ld* either did not take place in the antecedent type, or has been set aside by the spread of ME forms derived from unbroken ones, in *biholde* 192: *wolde*.

9. Diphthongization of front vowels by preceding front consonants in the OE antecedent type is not necessarily attested in *vnderȝete* 292: *iwite*, since the form *wete* (like pret. *weste*) is well attested in Southern texts.

10. The reflex of primitive OE *iu* when *i*-mutated rhymes on tense *ē* < OE *ēo* in *newe* 234: *vntrewe* a., *hewe* 'hue' 247: *knewe*.

11. ME *ǫu* and *au* before *ht* rhyme in *iwrowt* 141: *itawt*.

12. The plural of an OE neuter noun with long root-syllable is still uninflected in *boure* 2: *toure*.

13. The ending of the 3 pres. sg. indic. is *-þ* (implying *-eþ* in uncontracted verbs) in *geþ* 159: *deþ* n.

14. The 3 pres. pl. indic. is endingless in *be* 61: *tre*. This necessarily implies an antecedent ME stage with *-en*, which alone can be reduced in this way.

15. The past part. of strong verbs has no *-n* (*forleie* 46, *icome* 152, *bifalle* 270), except when the root of the verb ends in a vowel (*agon* 221, beside *fordo* 52).

Provenance

The North is excluded by 4 and 15, Kent by 7, 8, and 14, Essex–London by 2, as the West probably is by 7, and the SW by 7 and 10. Items 4, 8, and 14 are consistent with an EMidl provenance; and this is what the evidence as a whole suggests, so far as it goes. The rhyme cited in 1 (i) is not conclusive, since both words concerned would often occur with reduced stress or without stress; and it is therefore not admissible as evidence of Western origin.

———

3. *wel were þat ilke man*: shown to be an impersonal construction by such examples as VIII. E 57 and G 15. *þat ilke man* is thus historically a dative, though the ME loss of final *-e* has made the form identical with the nominative.

7. *þe*: perhaps a corruption either of *þer* (as in the Trentham and Cambridge MSS., and in 15), or possibly of *þre*. The OF version reads *Trois en a en chaucun estage* 1709. Since in the latter there are three *estages*, there were nine attendants in all; but this has been bungled or misunderstood by the English author.

26. *Yknaweʒ*: Taylor's emendation to *knaweþ* (imperative pl.) is attractive, since in the OF version the following words (perhaps corresponding to this line) are addressed to Floris (1744–5):

> Or devez du vergier oir
> Et pourquoi les i fet venir.

Yknawe3 is preferred here (as an equivalent, i.e. an imperative) merely because, being more like MS *he knawe3*, it comes nearer to accounting for the corruption.

35–36. There is nothing in the OF version to explain this cryptic statement. The defective Cotton MS. has *Iwrite muchel of þe*: either the author or a scribe took it that something was inscribed on the wall.

40. *fram Paradis*: the OF adds *Eüfrates est apelez* (1768), which shows that its author was familiar with the legend of the Earthly Paradise. The latter was founded on Gen. ii. 8 ff. and enriched with Oriental elements; see IX below, 26–27 n., 45–46 n., and 71–100 n. (Cf. A. Graf, *Il Mito del Paradiso Terrestre*, in *Miti, Leggende e Superstizioni del medio Evo* (1925), pp. 1–175; E. Faral, *Recherches sur les sources latines des contes et romans courtois du moyen âge* (1913), pp. 369–72). O. M. Johnston, 'The Description of the Emir's Orchard in *Floire et Blancheflor*', *Zeitschrift für romanische Philologie*, xxxii (1908), 705–10, merely identifies the orchard with other descriptions of the Other World in medieval literature, and makes no distinction between the Christian Earthly Paradise and the Irish Other World.

42. *vertu*: a technical term for the properties and the curative or magical powers attributed to precious stones in the Middle Ages, as expounded in the medieval Lapidaries. The latter are represented in Latin by Book XVI, 4, of Isidore of Seville's *Etymologiae* (seventh century; ed. W. M. Lindsay), and Marbodus's *De Gemmis* (late eleventh century; *P.L.* 171. 1738 ff.); and there are not less than thirteen in AN.

49. *3elle* is also the reading of the Trentham MS., and must therefore be retained (though there is no certainty that it derives from the author). The Cambridge MS. has *bulmeþ* (for *wulmeþ* 'gushes, springs, wells (up)'). The OF version reads *L'eve est tretoute conmeüe* (1833).

In the French account, the test of chastity operates when a woman crosses a channel leading from the fountain; for the ME equivalent, see Introduction to the excerpt printed here. See further Faral, op. cit. 370 n. 2, and F. Liebrecht, *Des Gervasius von Tilbury Otia Imperialia* (1856), p. 146 n. 63.

56. *daunger*: on the semantic development (L *dominiarium*) see C. S. Lewis, *The Allegory of Love* (1936), pp. 364–6.

63. *on*: governs *which* (*so*); cf. 67.

88. *what mister man*: this phrase (in which *mister man* originally meant 'man with a craft, occupation') was destined to catch the fancy of Spenser, and to produce (with the substitution of the synonymous *wight* for *man*) one of the more blatant and clumsy archaisms of Pope:

> Right well mine eyes arede *the myster wight*
> (*Dunciad* iii. 187)

and Scott:

> Sometimes *this mister wight* held his hands clasped over his head (*Waverley* ix),

neither of whom understood *mister*. On the nature of the process see *O.E.D.* s.v. 5, and cf. native expressions such as *ech(es) kynn(es) men*.

98. *scheker*: an extended medieval description of the game of chess, and of the type of move proper to the six pieces (*roy, roc, chevalier, alphin, fierge*, and *peon*), is preserved in the fourteenth-century *La Vieille* of Jean Lefevre (ed. H. Cocheris, 1861, pp. 77–79), which is a translation of Richard of Furnival's *De Vetula*. Another informative one has been made available by F. Lecoy, 'Le Jeu des échecs d'Engreban d'Arras', *Mélanges de philologie romane et de littérature médiévale offerts à E. Hœpffner* (Paris 1949), pp. 307–12. Other illustrative passages are cited in F. Strohmeyer's collection of material in 'Das Schachspiel im Altfranzösischen', *Abhandlungen A. Tobler* (Halle 1895), pp. 381–403.

103. *mitte*: for this type of stressing in rhyme cf. *dome: to me* in *O. & N.* 545–6 (I. 353–4), and *come: to me*, ibid. 1671–2.

123–4. *list: first* is a phonetically significant rhyme, which attests the elimination of *r* (by assimilation) before an alveolar consonant. Cf. *Kyng Alisaunder* 5089 and n.

136–8. An echo of the institution of 'homage'. This depended on the swearing of an oath, according to a fixed ceremonial in which the man concerned had to place his hands between those of his lord. Homage properly accompanied a tenure of land (which is not in question here). See Jolliffe, *The Constitutional History of Medieval England* (1948), pp. 153–5 and 162 n. 2; G. J. Turner and H. E. Salter, *The Register of St. Augustine's, Canterbury*, part ii (Records of the Social and Economic History of England and Wales (British Academy), iii (1924), 426; D. C. Douglas, 'A Charter of Enfeoffment under William the Conqueror', *English Historical Review*, xlii (1927), 245–7; Pollock and Maitland, *History of English Law* (1911), i. 296–307.

178. *hem*: the strictly palæographical evidence slightly supports this reading rather than Taylor's *heui*, though the scribe does sometimes leave his minims undotted (and Taylor's reading of one of these three as an *i* is therefore not impossible). And *hem* (with a pronominal subject unexpressed but implied in *coupe* 177) is also slightly preferable in terms of ME syntax, since a past part. *charged* (which the reading *heui* requires) referring either to *coupe* or to *gegges* would be suspiciously modern.

182–4. The OF versions runs (2113–15):

> Mes a la chambre failli ont;
> La Blancheflor lessent a destre,
> En une autre entrent a senestre.

An hond may be either a spelling of *anond*, or a phrase containing the preposition *on* and the noun *hond* in the sense 'side' (as in 183). In the former interpretation, the *h* might be either inorganic (as in *middelhard* 30), or an early example of the spelling (which is recorded from the later thirteenth century). The latter spelling may well be etymologically significant in *anond*, *anent*, since the sense 'side' in *hond* is recorded here in 183: this would account for the problematic *h* (OE *on emn* > *onend*, *onent*, *anent*).

The OF version admits equally of the interpretation 'alongside' or 'opposite, confronting' for *an hond*; and both are attested for *anent*.

206. The emendation is contextually necessary, and is supported by the OF version (2138–40):

> Cele se fu raseüree
> Et de Blancheflor porpensee.
> Ce fu ses amis, bien le sot.

Blauncheflour: the gen. sg. of personal names is commonly uninflected in OF (see the quotation in 182–4 n.), and hence sometimes in ME adoptions of them.

276. *roum*: on Taylor's reading *rouin* (which he emends to *roun* and treats as an adverb and an aphetic form of *aroun*, a calque on OF *en rond* 'around') in relation to the scribe's mode of writing *i*, see 178 n. It must be added that the scribe does sometimes write *u* for *n* and vice versa. But *roum* is slightly preferable to *rouin* as a strictly palæographic interpretation of the word as written in the MS.

What is vulnerable in Taylor's treatment, even on the solely palæographic level, is the emendation to *roun*; and as a matter of textual criticism, corruption of a rhyming word to an assonating one is unlikely. The OF runs:

> En un lit envols de cortine
> De soie gisoit la meschine.
> Sus ont assis priveement.   (2246–8)

The other ME MSS. read:

> And drouȝ hemself al a room (Trentham 824)
> . . . wende aroum (Cotton)
> An hure self wende hem fram (Cambridge 538).

IV

MS.: Laud Misc. 108, Bodleian Library.

Editions: W. W. Skeat, *Havelok the Dane* (E.E.T.S., E.S. 4, 1868).

   Id., revised K. Sisam, *The Lay of Havelok the Dane* (Oxford 1950).

   F. Holthausen, *Havelok* (Alt- und mittelenglische Texte ed. L. Morsbach I), 3rd ed., 1928.

Studies: H. Le Sourd Creek, 'The Author of "Havelok the Dane" ', *Englische Studien*, 48 (1915), 193–212.

   J. II. Kern, 'De taalvormen van 't middelengelse gedicht *Havelok*', *Mededeelingen der koninklijke akademie van wetenschappen*, afd. Letterkunde, 55, serie A, no. 2, Amsterdam 1923.

Other Versions: A. Bell, ed., '*Le Lai d'Havelof*' and *Gaimar's Haveloc Episode* (Manchester 1925).

Studies: H. E. Heyman, *Studies on the Havelok-Tale* (Inaugural Diss., Uppsala 1903).

C. T. Onions, 'Comments and Speculations on the text of *Havelok*' (Philologica: *The Malone Anniversary Studies*, ed. T. A. Kirby and H. B. Woolf, Baltimore 1949), pp. 154–63.

Language

1. The reflex of OE *ĕ+g* rhymes on that of OE *ǣ+g* in *sayl* 126: *nayl*.

2. The reflex of OE *ǣ¹* rhymes:
   (a) on slack *ē* < OE *ēa* in *red* 94: *bred*.
   (b) on tense *ē* in *drede* 96: *fede*.
   (c) on OE *ĕ* (or possibly slack *ē* by lengthening in a disyllable with an open root-syllable in *wele*: cf. Scots *weel*) in *del* 86: *wel*.
   (d) when shortened, on the reflex of shortened *ǣ²* in *adradde* 214: *ladde*.

3. The reflex of OE *ǣ²* rhymes:
   (a) when shortened, on *e* < OE [e:] shortened in *ledde* 53: *fedde*.
   (b) when shortened, on the reflex of shortened *ǣ¹* in *ladde* 213: *adradde*.

4. OE *ȳ* has been unrounded to *ī* in *fyr* 181: *shir*; *hides* 184: *shides*; *hire* 176: *sire*.

5. OE *ēo* has been reduced to a long vowel that rhymes on tense *ē* in *be* 311: *me*; *se* 307: *ye*; *þeues* 207: *leues*.

6. The product of i-mutation:
   (a) of OE *ĕa* rhymes on *ĕ* in *werne* 192: *yerne*.
   (b) of OE *ēa* rhymes on tense *ē* in *leues* 208: *þeues*.

7. The reflex of OE *-gg-* is unassibilated in *rig* 202: *big*, and that of OE *-kk-* in *recke* 341 (within the line).

8. The pl. of nouns ends:
   (a) in *-es*: *kradel-barnes* 339, *sides* 277, *þeues* 207.
   (b) in *-n* if the root ends in a vowel, in *shon* 128.
   (c) in *-e*: *siþe* 46 (which is not really an exception to (a) above: cf. p. 363, 18(c) on *kinde* 180).

9. The dual of the pronoun of the first person survives in the possessive *unker* (309) (within the line).

10. The accus. pl. of the pronoun of the 3rd person is *-es* (agglutinated) in *setes* 52, and possibly *his* in 320 (within the line).

11. The infin. has no final -*n* (*fare* 104, *go* 118, *ligge* 142, *take* 99), except in *drepen* 210.

12. The 3 pres. sg. indic. ends in -*es*: *glides* 278, *leues* 208, *þarnes* 340.

13. The past part. of strong verbs ends in:

(*a*) -*en* in *boren* 305: *koren*, if -*re*- in the latter represents a syllabic *r* in the author's speech.

(*b*) -*n* in *forlorn* 38: *korn*.

But both examples, since they both rhyme on the same word, probably represent a single form, whether it be -*en* or -*n*.

14. Disyllabic verbs of weak class II with an open root-syllable have no -*i*-: *dere* 74: *bere*; *swilen* 185: *wilen*.

Vocabulary

There are many adoptions from ON (some of them rare):

ay 15, *beyte* 267, *bloute* 337, *gar* 284, *gate* 114, *genge* 54, *geten* 60, *kippe* 160, *knif* 298, *loupe* 228, *mone* (auxiliary) 108, *ok* 145, *rippe* 159, -*rof* 219, *stac* 82, *sternes* 236, *stith* 304, *tok* 19, *þrinne* 29, *wil* 131, *won* 218 (all in rhyme); and within the line, *brennen* 182, *brinie* 202, *carl* 216, *caste* 202, *hernes* 344 (the only example in English), *kaske* 268, *neues* 344.

The following are significantly restricted in distribution:

coupe 227 (mentioned by Ray (1691) as a North-country word; and recorded later only in Scots and Northern dialect).

greyue 198 (also in *Ormulum* and *Boke of Curtasie*, NEMidl and NMidl respectively, and the unlocalized *Medulla grammatice*, and Middle Scots; and, as an 'occupational' surname, in Yorks., Lincs., Lancs., Norf., and Suff. It occurs later in parts of Lincs. and Yorks. as a name for an administrative official in a township).

rowte 338 (otherwise in ME only in Rolle and the *Catholicon Anglicum*, the former being a Yorkshireman). Mentioned by Ray as a North-country word; and after ME recorded only in Northern and Scots.

teyte 268 (otherwise only in the *Gawain*-group and *Wynnere and Wastoure*, and fifteenth- and sixteenth-century Scots).

þarne 340 (only EMidl, NMidl, Northern, and Middle Scots).

Provenance

4 and 5 point to the EMidl or the North. The 3 pres. sg.

ending -*es*, in conjunction with -*e* as the uniform ending of the pl. (which by chance does not occur in our extracts), excludes both the southern EMidl (which would have a sg. in -*eþ*) and the North (where -*es* would occur in the pl. as well as the sg.).

The evidence of the vocabulary as a whole; the great similarity of the language as a whole to that of Robert Mannyng (of Bourne, in South Lincs.); and the localization of the story in Grimsby—these point to an area densely settled by Scandinavians, and specifically Lincolnshire.

---

7. *erþe*: possibly a scribal alteration of *erde* 'dwell' < OE *eardian*, made for the sake of a formally exact rhyme. But [rð] and [rd] do not commonly assonate in ME texts, and *erþe* may therefore be due to the tendency (active from ME times into the seventeenth century, at least) for the stop [d] to be opened to the homorganic fricative [ð] before or after a liquid or a nasal.

11–12. Cf. the suggestively similar phrasing and the identical rhyme-words in Robt. Mannyng's *Chronicle of England* 4117–18 (which may therefore be a reminiscence of this):

> He yt made, & he yt aughte—
> Lodgate for hym þe name laughte.

13. *Grimesbi*: on the naming of places in the Danelaw by composition of -*by* with the name of a minor leader, see Stenton, *Anglo-Saxon England*, pp. 516–18. -*By* is not a secure philological criterion of settlement by Danes rather than Norwegians (Ekwall, *Scandinavians and Celts in the North-West of England* (*Lunds Universitets Årsskrift*, N.F. Avd. 1, vol. 14, Nr. 27, 1918), p. 8, n. 1).

The *Lai d'Haveloc* (131–2, 143–4, 795–6) also asserts that Grimsby was named after Grim (though Gaimar does not). But this personal name also appears in *Grimsthorpe* (Lincs.) and other place-names in other counties; and the connexion with Grimsby (and presumably the name of Grim) may have entered the story at a late stage (cf. M. Deutschbein, *Studien zur Sagengeschichte Englands* I (1906), pp. 138–9).

13–14. The duplication of *alle* is probably a symptom of corruption. Skeat's emendation of *calleth alle* to *it calle* requires the assumption that *it calle* was inverted to *calle it* and that a scribe added *alle* to patch the rhyme. But *calleth* may be interpreted as an AN spelling (with *th* for *t*, as in *woth* 213, *leth* 252) of *callet* (for *calle it*; cf. *bihetet* 677, *hauedet* 714). It follows that the corruption would be in *alle* 14.

18. *coupe on*: a native idiom (OE *cunnan on*) meaning 'be versed in, be at home with'; cf. Laȝamon's *Brut* (ed. Brook), ll. 3639, 7202, and *Cursor Mundi* 740.

21. *qual*: usually interpreted 'whale' (*O.E.D.* s.v. *whale*; Skeat–Sisam), with the Northern-type spelling used in *Quan(ne)*, *Hav.* 134, 204, &c., *qui* 1650. But a whale seems out of place in the company of sturgeon, turbot, and salmon; and the whale is almost certainly mentioned in 23 (where it *is* appropriate). *Qual* is best interpreted as an early example of the Gmc word represented in Du *kwal* 'jelly-fish', mod. G and LG *Qualle* 'basket-fish' (a star-fish with five rays).

23. *hwel*: the usual emendation to *el* 'eel' is palæographically improbable and must be rejected. This form cannot represent OE *hwæl*, which in the EMidl language of *Hav.* would necessarily have been *hwal*; it may be referred to an OE **hwele*, which would be the normal form of the *-es* stem attested in Gmc by OHG *wels* (< **walis*).

31. *vp o londe*: occurs in virtually identical form in Henryson's *Taill of the vponlandis Mous and the burges Mous* (*c.* 1480), 4: *The uther wynnit vponland, weill neir* (ed. C. Elliott (1963), p. 6, l. 165). See *O.E.D. up* prep. 5, *uponland*, and *upland* sb[1].

31–32. The rhyme of $n+g$ on $n+$ [dž] is a type of assonance.

40. *þe rithe wei*: a semantic borrowing of OF *la dreite uoie*; *rithe* thus means 'direct'.

43. *wol wel*: an emphatic reduplication, which occurs also in *Kyng Alisaunder* 1747; *Arthour and Merlin* 5079; *The Seuen Sages of Rome* 2456; and *English Lyrics of the Thirteenth Century* (ed. Carleton Brown), p. 112, l. 19; cf. *ofte ofte*, XVIII. 17. An absolute use of *selle* 'sell' is attested from 1200.

50. *to maken of*: 'from which to make'; cf. *to æten bi*, XVI. 244.

52. *se-weres*: the existence of a late OE *sæwære* (though it is recorded only once) suggests that this is a compound of *were* 'enclosure for catching fish'. Many examples of the latter in the conjunction with nets (l. 51) are available from the thirteenth century onwards. See J. Strachey, J. Pridden, and E. Upham, *Index to the Rolls of Parliament* (1832), s.v. *wears*; R. W. Chambers and M. Daunt, *A Book of London English 1384–1425*, p. 257, note on l. 326; O.E.D. *weir-nets*, s.v. *weir*.

setes: i.e. *sette es* 'placed them'. *Es, is* (*ys* in *Hav.* 1174), *hes, his, hise* are first recorded in England *c.* 1200, as the acc. pl. or fem. sg. of the pronoun of the third person, and (apart from 'Robt. of Gloucester's' *Chronicle*) are restricted to SE or EMidl texts. This pronoun is best explained as an adoption of the comparable MDu pronoun *se*, which is likewise used enclitically in the reduced form -*s*; for a pronoun (as an essential and prominent element in the grammatical machinery of a language) would hardly have escaped record till 1200 if it had been a native word.

53. *him ledde*: a calque on OF *se mener*.

58. *þouthe*: with absorption (in speech and hence in the written form) of a following *he*, as in *hauede* 128.

69. *on swink long*: 'in proportion to his work; by working for it'; see C. T. Onions in *Philologica* (1949, p. 160). This is a native idiom (OE *gelong æt* 'depending on, in accordance with') which survives today in the non-standard *long of*. In the latter, *on* must have been early reduced to *o*, and this was erroneously expanded to *of* (since *o* might represent either *on* or *of* in late ME and early mod. E).

Þat need not be emended to *þar* (as by Skeat–Sisam), if *nouht* is interpreted as *n'ouht* for *ne ouht*.

82. *giueled*: a ἅπαξ λεγόμενον that is usually referred to a northern F form (with [g]) of OF *javeler* 'lay in heaps'. But there are traces of -*i*- in the first syllable of this and related words only in mod. F dialects, and very rarely at that (see von Wartburg, *F.E.W.*, s.v. *gabella). Since *gavel* n. 'heap' and v. 'gather in heaps' are recorded in English (from *c.* 1440 in the *Prompt. Parv.*), it seems likely that *giuelen* v. is a nonce-formation of ideophonic type on *gauel* (i.e. an apophonic variant, like *higgle* on *haggle*); see 'Some English Ideophones', *Arch. Ling.* vi (1954), 88–91.

110. *uten*: cannot represent OE *utan*, since *-an* in OE adverbs normally expresses 'direction from (which)'. But ON *úti* is recorded in the sense 'exhausted, finished' in application to food or drink; and *uten* may therefore be an adoption of it (with a non-etymological *-n*)—though the titulus over the *e* in the MS. is regarded as an error by C. T. Onions (loc. cit.). *Out* a. does not occur till Shakespeare's time in the sense prescribed by the context here.

124. *fonge*: probably a preterite, and in that case comparable with *underfong* in *Hav.* 115.

128. *hauede*: see 58 n.

149–50. *þe herles mete* ... *Cornewaille*: 'the earl of Cornwall's food'. This variety of the ME split genitive (i.e. with a prepositional adjunct containing *of*) probably derives from an OE antecedent type with a dependent genitive, as in *þæs* ... *Mercna cyninges Pendan* (Bede, *Hist. Eccles.*, ed. T. Miller, p. 234, l. 19): *of* has replaced the inflected genitive, on the model of the OF use of *de*. For another variety see XVIII. 65. See E. Ekwall, *Studies on the Genitive of Groups in English* (Lund 1943), pp. 6–8, 68–69; O. Jespersen, *Progress in Language* (1894), pp. 293–6, and *A Modern English Grammar*, vi. 286–8; Tauno Mustanoja, *A Middle English Syntax*, i (1960), 78–79.

bouth/oft: Kern's proposal, op. cit., pp. 15–16 (reported by Holthausen, *Anglia Beiblatt*, 35 (1924), 35), to read *keft* and *eft* is ingenious: *keft* 'bought' (OSw *köft*) occurs in *Hav.* 2005; *eft* 'again' might refer to the earlier episode in 136 above. But the rhyme as transmitted in the MS. is in fact a standard and common type of assonance (in which any voiceless fricative may rhyme with any other) and must therefore be retained.

162. *segges*: there is no need for doubts about identifying this with OF *sèche* 'cuttle-fish'. The *-gg-* might be explained as an inverted spelling implying the Picard unvoicing of [dž] (see Gossen, *Petite Grammaire de l'ancien Picard*, pp. 73, 83). But it more probably represents a native tendency to voice [tʃ], as in *choger* II. 318 and *grudge* beside *grutch* (OF *gruchier*).

173. *wel is set*: essentially the same idiom as in I. 43; cf. OF *bien emploié* in the same sense.

209–10. *open/drepen*: a rare type of rhyme on the second syllable of disyllabic words, as in *lokeþ/spekeþ* in *O. & N.* 1555–6.

218. *won*: the principal senses in ME are (i) 'hope, expectation' (the central sense, as in the etymon ON *ván*, cognate with OE *wēn*); (ii) 'expedient; remedy; course of action'; (iii) 'resources; abundance'; (iv) 'wealth, riches'. Senses (ii), (iii), and (iv) are evidently individual applications of 'that which is hoped for'.

246. *speu*: see Introduction, p. xxxvi.

251–2. *feld/swerd*: there is no need to assume corruption, since *l* and *r* assonate in ME rhyme-technique (e.g. *þole/bifore*, *Floris and Blancheflour* 1217; *dole/sore*, *King Horn* 1092–3, *damysele/palmere*, ibid. 1208–9).

253. *riht*: if the line is not corrupt, the main verb can be represented only in *wolde* or *riht*; but the former will not do, since no known word of that form will fit here. A verb *riȝten* 'aim at (to strike)' is attested in *Kyng Alisaunder* 3900 and 3905, there possibly an adoption of MDu *rechten, richten* id. The emendations proposed by E. J. Dobson (*E.G.S.* i (1947–8), 58–59) are not idiomatically or palæographically probable.

280. *shewe*: evidently substituted by a scribe for *showe*, of which it is a phonetic variant.

290–2. See *E.G.S.* iii (1949–50), 68–69. *Him* in 291 is a dative of disadvantage.

320. *his þre*: 'three of him (i.e. of his own size)'. This extraordinary expression is not precisely matched by any known ME idiom. It is perhaps analogically formed on the common pattern of such phrases as *hire þre* 'three of them' (< OE *hiora þreo*), possibly by misinterpretation of the genitive in the latter as a possessive. It is less likely that *his* is the pronoun 'them', used in apposition to the numeral as commonly in OE and ME, e.g. *of him þrim* 'by the three of them', *Anglia*, xi (1888), 2, l. 45, since this pronoun occurs only twice in *Hav.* (see 52 n.), and both times in agglutinated forms. In any case, the palæographically dubious emendation of Skeat–Sisam to *þe* 'thigh' (which Skeat defends on the assumption that *-r-* has intruded from *tre* 319) must be rejected.

323. *lopen*: see Introduction, p. xxxvi.

326. *Boy* does not appear in English before the thirteenth century. In *M.Æ.* ix (1940), 121–54, xii (1943), 71–76, E. J. Dobson has constructed an etymological explanation founded on pronunciations attested by the early modern English orthoepists Hart ([bwɛ] or [bwe:]), Butler ([bwoe]), Gill ([buoi]), and Cooper ([buɔi]), whose works appeared in 1569, 1633, 1619, and 1685 respectively. His etymon is an aphetic form of the AN past participle *embuié* 'fettered', formed on OF *boie* < L *boia* 'fetter'; on the semantic side, a hypothetical 'slave' (i.e. 'some-one fettered') is implied as the starting-point for the recorded series 'low fellow; servant; young male servant; male child'.

341. *seruede/werewed*: since there is no means of accounting for a rhyme of [v] on [w], Dr. Sisam suggests that this (like those in *Hav.* 949–50, 2676–7) implies a phonetic change of [ɣ] (in *werged*, replaced by a scribe's *wer(e)wed* with [w] < [ɣ]) to [v], parallel to the known change of the corresponding voiceless [x] to [f]. But this theory conflicts with the evidence that in texts from the NEMidl a little later than *Hav.* *a*+[ɣ] in ME > [au]; see O. Boerner, *Die Sprache Roberd Mannyngs of Brunne* (1904), pp. 169–71, 211, 17 and 18, and Luick, *Unter-suchungen zur englischen Lautgeschichte* (1896), § 39. And the rhyme of *lowe* (< *hlāw*) on *awe* (< *āgan*) in *Hav.* 1291–2 shows that early ME [ɣ] had become [w] in the author's language. See also E. J. Dobson, *E.G.S.* i (1947–8), 56–57.

343. *bet*: see Introduction, p. xxxvi.

344. A remarkable example of a calque on and combination of two foreign phrasal idioms. ON *setja hnefann* (*við*) 'to strike with the fist' is represented in *Hav.* 2405–6:

> With þe neue he Robert sette
> Biforn þe teth a dint ful strong.

An OF expression *desuz l'oie* 'under the ear' (*oie* < **audita*, lit. 'hearing') is used in connexion with blows (with the fist), and is imitated in ME:

> And he went vp anon his *fest*
> And buffeyt hir *vnder þe lest*
>
> (*Arthour and Merlin* 8437–8)

In 346 here the OF idiom has been blended with the ON expression illustrated in the prose *Edda* (ed. F. Jónsson, p. 56,

l. 17): 'En þórr reiddi til *hnefann* ok *setr við eyra* Hymi.' In both passages in *Hav.* ON *við* 'against' (governing the accusative) has been erroneously reproduced by the native *with* in its usual function of expressing instrumentality; and ON *eyra* has been replaced by the synonymous ON *heyrn*. See *R.E.S.* xiii (1937), 458–62.

V

MS.: Digby 86, Bodleian Library.

Edition: G. H. McKnight, *Middle English Humorous Tales in Verse* (Boston 1913).

Source: *Le Roman de Renart*, Branche II (ed. M. Roques, Classiques Français du Moyen Âge, 79, Paris 1951).

Studies: G. Paris, in *Mélanges de littérature française du moyen âge*, ed. M. Roques, ii (Paris 1912), 337–423.

 L. Foulet, *Le Roman de Renard* (Bibliothèque de l'École des Hautes Études, Paris 1914).

 R. Bossuat, *Le Roman de Renard* (Connaissance des Lettres, 49, Paris 1957).

 L. Flinn, *Le Roman de Renart dans la littérature française et dans les littératures étrangères au moyen âge* (Paris 1963).

Language

1. The reflex of Gmc *ă*+nasal+*i, j* rhymes on slack *ē* or *ĕ* in *iwend* 134: *frend* (ON *frǽndi* rather than OE *freond*, in either of which a short vowel would be possible as a paradigmatic variant of the long one).

2. The reflex of OE *ȳ* (OKt *ē*) rhymes on (i) *ĕ* in *putte* 241: *mette*; (ii) *ĭ* in *putte* 282: *sitte*.

3. OE *ā* must have undergone rounding to slack *ō*, since it rhymes on tense *ō* in *ago* 49: *do*; *þo* 221: *ido*; *wo* 67: *do*.

4. The reflex of OE *ǽ¹* rhymes on (i) slack *ē* < OE *ēa* in *dede* 223: *quede*; *hete* pt. pl. 156: *grete* a.; *reed* n. 192: *ded* a.; (ii) tense *ē* in *strete* 5: *mete* v.; *þere* 127: *here* v., *ifere* 172; (iii) the reflex of OE *ǽ²* in *þere* 232: *lere* v., *drede* 89: -*hede*.
 Þare 33: *kare* is best interpreted as implying a short vowel developed under reduced stress, since there is otherwise no trace of Essex–London *ā* for OE *ǽ*.

5. The reflex of OE *ǽ²* rhymes on (i) slack *ē* < OE *ēa* in *slete* 289: *bete* v.; *get* 167: *gret* a.; (ii) the reflex of OE *ǽ¹*: see 4 (iii).

6. The reflex of OE *ēa* rhymes on (i) tense *ē* in *leue* 25: *reue* n.; (ii) see 4 (i) and 5 (i).

If the pronunciation of *leue* 25 was historically regular (i.e. with slack *ē*), the rhyme is qualitatively inexact. The same necessarily applies to those in either 4 (i) or 4 (ii), unless we posit variant pronunciations of one and the same phoneme without any traceable cause (which would be hazardous).

7. OE *ĕo* must have become long vowels (by reduction of the second element), since one or the other of them rhymes on *ĕ* in *rerde* n. 114: *iherde*.

8. Breaking of *ǽ* before [ç] is attested for the antecedent type of OE in (*i*)*sey* pt. sg. 216: *ney*, 280: *tey* (if not an analogical form after pl. *seye* < *sǽgon*).

9. Diphthongization of front vowels by preceding palatal consonants in the antecedent type of OE is implied in *forȝeue* 175: *isriue* (if not a form with the stem of the 2 and 3 pres. sg. levelled into the infinitive).

10. In the antecedent form of OE, *g* had been absorbed between a short vowel and *d* or *n*, with lengthening of the preceding vowel, in *seide* 181: *misdede*; 129, 150: *rede*; 226: *nede*.

11. Final [ç] has been eliminated in *ney* 261: *sley* pl.

12. The 3 pres. sg. *vind* 253 (for *vint*) implies an OE antecedent with syncope of the vowel in the ending and assimilation of the *-þ* (i.e. a non-Anglian type) in roots ending in a dental, if *bind* 254 is a singular (see n.).

13. The 3 pres. pl. ends in *-þ* in *doþ* 217: *soþ*.

14. The infinitive has no final *n* in *go* 1: *wo*; *mete* 6: *strete*; *aquenche* 13: *drunche*, &c.

15. The past participle of strong verbs has no *-n* in *afalle* 18: *walle*; *ago* 49: *do*; *do* 68: *wo*, &c.

The rhyme *meel* 247: *smal* a. is consistent either with a SE or WMidl *smĕl*, or with a *māl* adopted from ON (in either case, with a rhyme of a long on a short vowel, as in *hiis* 106: *wiis*). But the WMidl is excluded for other reasons (see *Provenance*).

Provenance

Probably Southern; the text does not yield evidence for any more specific localization. The North is excluded by 3, the

North and the EMidl by 13, and the whole of the Midlands by 9 if this is a straightforwardly valid rhyme. 10 is Southern. The unique example of SE *e* in 2 (i) would necessarily imply the SE but for the discrepant non-SE type in (ii), and probably does so in any case: the language used by the author may be either a literary (and therefore dialectally 'mixed') one, or may represent an area where the spoken language admitted of these two variants —both of which possibilities point to London.

The virtual absence of ON words (see *gistninge* 255; note on *meel* supra, and 133 n.) and the specifically Southern *al fort* 17 and *mid iwisse* 234, 293 are incompatible with Midland or Northern origin. Forms within the line do not materially diverge. *Sugge* 207 (within the line 265) is specifically SW or SWMidl. But the frequent *u* for OE *y* (marring the rhyme in 123, 241, 282) is consistent with London (see W. Heuser, *Altlondon*, pp. 50–52); and the occasional voicing of initial *f* is Southern.

The hand of a bilingual scribe is shown in the frequent use of an inorganic initial *h* in words beginning with a vowel, and the use of *w* for *v* and *v* for *w*, as of *s* for OE *sc*, all of which are (in this text) of AN type.

---

26. *haiward*: see VIII N 24, n.

29. *flok*: this sense 'a group of five' is attested for the ON cognate in legal terminology: *þat heitir flokkr er fimm menn eru saman* (Keyser and Munch, *Norges Gamle Love*, i. 61). Since this meaning is not recorded in any of the dictionaries of English, *flok* is here probably an adoption of ON *flokkr*, rather than an independent survival of a Gmc conception common to early English and Norse.

31. *him*: 'for his part'; an ethic dative, common in OE and ME.

32. *two*: the fox's ironic claim in 39–40 suggests that either the author or a scribe has omitted (between 30 and 31) an account of the killing of three hens. This is also implied in 55 and in 68 (where it is clear that his recent hunger has been assuaged). And in fact, in the *R. de Ren.* (3381–94), the fox captures and kills three hens, of which he eats two (at once) and carries away with him the third.

51. If this is the correct form of the text, *do* is an idiomatic use (as in OE) of a present tense-form as a future: 'I will cause you to be bled.' In that case, *oþer* does not introduce an alternative that is co-ordinate with *lete blod*, but merely amounts to 'failing that'.

59. *cellerer*: in the *R. de Ren.* (3627) it is the 'cellarer' who appears as the main agent of the wolf's punishment at the end of the story, where the *maister curtiler* figures in the ME version (less appropriately, since he is the official in charge of the garden). The weapons named in 62 exactly correspond to those actually used later (287): the earlier reference is evidently an anticipation of the later. And since the *R. de Ren.* does not mention Chauntecler or his exchanges with the fox (33–64), it follows that the whole Chauntecler episode is here an intrusion, and hence that its presence implies derivation of *The Fox and the Wolf* from the beast-epic in its cyclic form (i.e. in OF).

72. *ginne*: this aphetic form of *engin* is ultimately < L *ingenium* 'that which is inborn' (*gignere, genitus*), whence 'ability; skill'. The semantic history of *engin* and *gin* is a matter of individual applications of the sense 'that which requires skill in the making', as in the uses of 77 and 86 ('a contrivance').

78. *lop*: see Introduction, p. xxxix.

81. *wes biþout*: 'took thought'.

107. *reuliche bigan*: cf. VI. 302, and *Trinity Homilies*, 2nd series, ed. Morris (E.E.T.S., o.s. 53, 1873), p. 181, l. 3:

> ac shrikeð and *reuliche biginneð* and is welneih dead

and p. 183, l. 5:

> wo beð þe sowle þanne hie him shal forleten, and
> *rewliche biginneð*, and þus to him seið.

The occurrence of these four examples shows the phrase to be an idiom (though a rare one, not recorded in any dictionaries); and the first and third show that the verb means something like 'to go on, behave'.

115–16. This corresponds to *R. de Ren.* 3492–3, where the fox says to the wolf:

> Ja sui ge vostre bon *voisin*,
> Qui fu jadis vostre *conpere*.

The wolf addresses him as *conpere* (< med. L *compater*) again in 3516, and terms Hersent (the wife of the wolf) Renart's *comere* (< med. L *commater*) in 3474. *Gossip* here (as in 209, 220, and 243) is thus clearly meant to render *conpere*. All three words originally denoted 'a sponsor in baptism (of one's own child)'. Cf. further *R. de Ren.* 4464, 4467, and 4475–7. Most of this is paralleled in *Ysengrimus*, where a father and a god-father call each other *compater* (the wolf and the goat IV. 164; the fox and the cock IV. 929).

When Sigrim recognizes the fox as *his kun* (123), this is an authentic detail ultimately derived from the beast-epic: in the *Ysengrimus* (e.g. I. 112), the wolf is the fox's uncle, while in the *Ecbasis Captivi* (ed. E. Voigt, 1875), 496, he is his godfather (*patrinus*). Many of the other creatures in *Ysengrimus* are repre-sented as kindred in this kind (uncle/aunt and nephew/niece); and the terms for 'baptismal sponsor' are also applied to these kindred, because this relationship, as the spiritual counterpart of the other, is identified with it (see E. Voigt, *Ysengrimus*, lxxviii–lxxix). Thus the wolf calls the older and the younger sows respectively *matrinis et neptibus* VII. 83.

On this basis, however, the terms *conperes* and *gossip* are not strictly applicable to the fox by the wolf (or *comere* to Hersent by Renart), if he is understood to be the nephew of the wolf. Presumably, no specific form of kinship was in the minds of the French and the English poet.

128. *Sigrim*: a phonologically difficult form (*Ysengrin(s)* of the *R. de Ren.*), and evidently a specifically English one, to judge by the near-equivalent *Sigrinus* of Lydgate's *The Order of Fools* 148 (Additional and Harley MSS.) beside *Isigrinus* of MS. Laud Misc. 683 (*Minor Poems* ii, ed. H. N. McCracken, E.E.T.S., O.S. 192 (1934), p. 454).

133. *Reneuard*: a form matched by the AN Nicholas Bozon's *Reneward* (*Les Contes Moralisés*, ed. L. T. Smith and P. Meyer (S.A.T.F. 1889), no. 30, p. 48), and evidently an English one. It is probably a reformation of OF *Renart* (< **Raginhard-*, with the Gmc suffix *-hard* adopted in OF from Frankish personal names), as if *Renouart (with the Gmc suffix *-ward* of the same type). Cf. *Renaud* in *Sir Gawain and the Green Knight* 1898,

and the surname *Reynolds*, as if $<$ **Raginwald-*, with a Gmc
suffix of the same origin and type as *-hard*.

frend: cf. the evidence cited *supra* (115–16 n.), and especially
his kun 123. Since 'kinsman' is not one of the early senses of OE
frēond, it may be here a semantic borrowing from ON (*frændi*),
or the word may be an adoption of the ON one. Cf. *Hav.* 326.

150. There is no need to posit a lacuna after this line: the repetition in *Quod þe wolf* is stylistically admissible in ME verse, and
the question in 151 is not wholly incompatible with 149–50.

157–8. In the relatively regular rhyming technique of *The Fox
and the Wolf*, this rhyme is extraordinary; it is not a well-
attested type in ME practice as a whole.

158. The existence of *Gode þonc* (as already in OE) shows that
thank in *thank God!* (of which it is the antecedent) is a noun,
and *God* an ancient dative. Cf. the equivalent OF *Dieu merci*.

161. The rhyme is not of a type admissible in ME, and must
therefore be corrupt. But the corruption may lie anywhere within
the couplet, and emendation is not advisable.

211–16. The gist of this occurs as a distinct episode in *Ysengrimus* (V. 705–820), which does not contain the episode of the
well; but Petrus Alfonsus' version of the latter makes no mention of it. Clearly, it is an intrusion in *The Fox and the Wolf*
and the corresponding tale in the *R. de Ren.*: in the latter
and the MDu *Reinaert*, it is the gravamen of the wolf's formal
indictment of the fox before the assembled 'parliament' presided over by the lion as the king of beasts. *The Fox and the
Wolf* therefore necessarily derives either from the episode of the
well in the *R. de Ren.* or from a cognate version of this which
also belonged to the beast-epic in its cyclic form.

233. *bruche*: a contextually inappropriate use, because a reminiscence of 21, where a 'gap' or 'opening' in the wall *is* appropriate.

237. *way*: not 'weighed' (which would be weak). The sense is
near to that recorded in *O.E.D. weigh* v.[1] 19; the equivalent
in the following closely similar passage of the *R. de Ren.* is the
third line, rather than the second (3597–9):

> Il jont les piez, si sailli enz.
> Isengrin fu li plus pesenz,
> Si s'en avale contre val.

247. *wiþ þi meel*: the sense of *wiþ* ('towards') is established by the exclusive use of *mid* in this text to express accompanying circumstances (30, 62, 89, 148, 234), comitative function (55, 156, 212), and instrumentality (14, 72, 84, 86, 102, 103, 125). The meaning of *meel* is established by 167–71 and 173.

253–4. The syntax is ambiguous: *Bot colde water* is either the object of *vind*, or the subject (along with *hounger*) of *bind*. In the first view, both verbs are irregularly spelt, for *vint* and *bint*. In the second, either sg. *bint* (which would be admissible with a composite subject) or pl. *bind(e)* is likely to be concerned.

264. *ine* (MS. *jne*): the reading *prime* by Dickins and Wilson is unsupported by other examples of the abbreviation (for *pr*) which they believe to be represented in the dot in the MS. before the *j*. Their suggestion that *prime* is here used loosely as 'very early' posits a sense unlikely in a context referring to a specific time. An initial *j* is normally used in this text for the prefix *i-* <OE *ge-*, and is marked off by a raised dot before and after it; but this difficulty must be accepted for the present.

VI

MS.: Digby 86, Bodleian Library.

Editions: E. Mätzner, *Altenglische Sprachproben*, I. i (Berlin 1867), 103–13.

    G. H. McKnight, *Middle English Humorous Tales in Verse* (Boston 1913).

    A. S. Cook, *A Literary Middle English Reader* (Boston &c. 1915, 1943).

Studies: W. Heuser, 'Das Interludium de Clerico et Puella und das Fabliau von Dame Siriz', *Anglia*, xxx (1907), 306–19.

    E. Schröder, 'Dame Sirith', *Nachrichten von der Gesellschaft der Wissenschaften zu Göttingen*, Phil.-hist. Klasse. Fachgruppe IV, N.F. Nr. 8 I (1936), pp. 179–202.

Language

  1. The reflex of Gmc *ă* before a single nasal in an originally disyllabic word rhymes:

    (*a*) on [a] in *sham* 126: *am*.

    (*b*) on OF/AN. *â* (< *as*+consonant) in *grome* 197· *blame*.

2. The reflex of Gmc *ă* before *nd* rhymes on ON *ó* in *wonde* 138: *houssebonde*; *fonde* 342: *hossebonde*.

3. OE *ȳ* has been unrounded in *wenne* 26: *-inne*, *senne* 194: *-inne* (where the SE *-e-* spellings are due to a scribe).

4. The products of OE *-ǣg* and OE *-ĕg* rhyme in *day* 16, 150: *away*.

5. ON *á* is shown by 1 (*a*) and (*b*) (where *ō* is excluded) to have remained unrounded in *won* 21: *bigon*; the same must therefore have applied to the reflex of OE *ā* in the author's form of ME.

6. The reflex of OE *ǣ*[1] rhymes:
   (*a*) on slack *ē* < OE *ēa* in *red* 328: *bred*, 350: *beed*.
   (*b*) on tense *ē* in *dede* 41: *bede*, 207: *fede*, *dedes* 190: *mede*.
   (*c*) when shortened, on *ĕ* < tense *ē* in *dred* 409: *sped*, and on *ĕ* < *ĕo* in *hernde* 97: *lernede*.

   ȝer 67: *her* either derives from a non-WS antecedent form of OE (with tense *ē* for WGmc *ā*, and without diphthongization of front vowels by preceding palatal consonants), or implies a qualitatively inexact rhyme of slack *ē* (< *ēa* < *ǣ*[1]) on tense *ē* in *her*.

7. The reflex of OE *ǣ*[2] rhymes on tense *ē* in *lede* 211: *spede*.

8. The reflex of OE *ēa* rhymes:
   (*a*) on the reflex of OE *ǣ*[1] in *bred* 327: *red*.
   (*b*) on tense *ē* in *leue* 58: *greue*.

9. The reflex of OE *ēo* rhymes only on tense *ē* in *fe* 382: *me*; *fre* 34: *þe*; *lef* 33: *gref*.

10. There was no diphthongization of front vowels by preceding palatal consonants in the antecedent type of OE: *-ȝelde* 37: *bimelde*, 326: *welde*; *ȝelpe* 227: *helpe*; *ȝirne* 45: *lerne*.

11. Smoothing is attested for the antecedent OE type in *werc* 374: *clerc*, *werkes* 245: *clarkes*.

12. The plural of nouns ends in:
    (*a*) *-s* in *þes* 441: *bes*.
    (*b*) *-n* in a noun ending in a vowel in *shon* 225: *don*.

13. The infinitive:
    (*a*) ends in *-n* in *gon* 156: *anon*.
    (*b*) commonly has no *-n*: *fare* 152: *kare*; *saie* 2: *waie*; *se* 165: *þe*; *spede* 449: *mede*.

14. The 2 pres. sg. ends in *-s* in *bes* 444: *þes*.
15. The past part. of strong verbs:
    (*a*) ends in *-n* in *idon* 323: *non*; *slain* 310: *fain*.
    (*b*) has no *-n* in *founde* 422: *stounde*.

Vocabulary

The ON element is not negligible; but it is made up of every-day words: *allegate* 398, *ay* 304, *blome* 294, *bone* 375, *come* 108, 293, *fro* 380, *gar* 290, *gete* 14, *gift* 223, *godlec* 227, *heþen* 295, *iboen* 434, *kenne* 264, *menske* 93, *mis* 144, *nai* 43, *nausine* 306*, *rene* 281, *ro* 291, *saut(e)* 220, 222, *scaþe* 235, *skil* 52, *sleie* 159, *take* 106, *til* 293, *witerli* 232, *won* 21, 132, *wrong* 9, and possibly *forgiue* 334 and *igiuen* 246. Pre-Conquest adoptions are *griþ* 267, *hounlawe* 60, and *houssebonde* 137.

Setten spel 62 (see n.) and *selk* 101, 245 (see 101 n.) are pretty certainly adoptions from MDu; and *Wilekin* (43 n.) is an as-sured example of a Flemish personal name.

Orm's frequent use of *come* n. at the end of his 3-beat line (where he uses disyllables of the type *inne*, or *swelltenn*, or *tælenn*, with short vowel in a closed root-syllable, or with long vowel in whatever sort of syllable, but never with short vowel in an open root-syllable) shows that in his idiolect it must have had a long vowel. And since OE *ŭ* (and the other short vowels) had clearly not been lengthened in disyllables with open root-syllable, *come* must have been an adoption of ON *kváma*, later *koma*. This explains the rhymes of *come* on *ō* in *Rome* 105, *blome* 294.

Provenance

At least one SE stage in the copying of the text is implied by the spellings *biȝende* 105 (a specifically MKt form of the root), *senne* 194, *wenne* 26 (with which the *-u-* of *prude* is compatible[1]). *Nome*, *shome*, and *grome* 195–7 imply a Western scribal stratum.

The reference to Boston in Lincs. (77) does not necessarily establish the provenance of *Dame Sirith*, since it might have been taken over from an antecedent version of the story. But 5 (Northern or NMidl); 1 (which excludes the WMidl); 9 (not WMidl or SE); the lack of exclusively Northern features—in combination, these indicate the EMidl. This is pointedly cor-roborated by *iboen* 434, as an adoption of an OEN form (*bōin* =

[1] See W. Heuser, *Altlondon* (1914), pp. 50–52.

OWN *búinn*), since it necessarily implies an area of Danish and not Norwegian settlement, and therefore the East and not the West Midlands (cf. *o-bon* < OENse *ofbōin* in *Hav.* 2355, 2505, 2571).

———

1. The *T* in the margin recurs only at 149, which opens another narrative passage (the only other such passage being 417–22). The other capital letters written in the margin of the MS. refer to the three characters in the story, and mark the beginning of passages of direct speech attributed to each. *C* clearly represents *Clericus*, *V* (applied to the wife) probably *Vxor* (a suggestion which I owe to my wife), and *F* (applied to Dame Siriþ) perhaps *Femina*. The interpretation of these as the initials of Latin words is confirmed by the example of the related piece XV, where the names of the interlocutors are written in full in the margin of the MS; *T* presumably designates the narrator. The other initials are distributed thus:

C 24, 37, 61, 109, 127, 161, 173, 217, 249, 267.
V 27, 43, 88, 115, 133.
F 167, 193, 229, 235, 255, 273.

9. *heuede wrong*: probably a semantic borrowing of OF *avoir tort*.

10. *hire*: object case of the personal pronoun, in an idiom occasionally attested in ME, e.g. *The Harley Lyrics* 9. 3: *A tortle þat min herte is on*, and *Festivall* (W. de Worde 1515): *Suche thynges as mannes herte is moost on.*

21. *won*: see IV. 218 n.

38. *Bote* (*on*) *þat*: a calque (reinforced by *on* 'only') on a corresponding use of OF *mais que*. Cf. *Hav.* 388, 505.

43. *Wilekin*: cf. *Ianekyn*, VIII. P 1. The MDu diminutive suffix *-kin* (also MLG *-kin*; MHG *-chin*) evidently first found its way into English from Flanders in personal names (by *c.* 1216); but it appears in other words by 1300 (e.g. *maidekin* in *Arthour and Merlin* 671). The native equivalent is represented in OE by *-cen* in *tyncen* 'small cask', *þyrncen* 'a little thorn'.

47. *con on*: cf. 206, and IV. 18 n.

62. *setten spel on ende*: otherwise recorded only in *Cursor Mundi* 1295 (XIV. 159 n.) and *An Alphabet of Tales*, i. 84, which are both Northern. *O.E.D.* takes *spel* as 'speech' (*spell* sb. 1 b, *end* sb. 17)—partly, no doubt, because of the variant reading *tale* 'speech' for *spell* in *C.M.*—and glosses the phrase 'to begin to speak, to begin a discourse', evidently because in all three examples there follows a statement that someone discourses. But *tale* may be a scribe's misunderstanding, not a true synonym, of *spell* (as variant readings of the less common words in the Cotton MS. of *C.M.* usually are); and the total absence of OE examples of the idiom suggests foreign origin.

The phrase is in fact likely to be a metaphor from the vocabulary of chess. There is an amply attested MDu *sette* (*dat, haer, sijn*) *spel* 'set out in readiness or move (the, her, his) pieces on a chessboard or draughtboard', in which *spel* 'game' is used in a transferred sense. But the ME idiom as a whole probably owes something to the OF phrase *metre a point* 'to place in due order, reduce to a desired state of affairs', which is applied in OF to the game of chess (or the chessmen) in a late thirteenth-century treatise explaining it:

> Quant *li jus* est *mis a point*
> Et cascuns des escies a point

> (Engreban d'Arras, *Li Jus des Esques*, ed.
F. Lecoy, *Mélanges . . . E. Hœpffner* (1949), p. 309, ll. 85–6).

'when the game has (the chessmen have) been duly laid out in readiness and each of the pieces occupies a space on the board'.

On ende is probably a calque on *a point*, through the use of OF *point* n., and hence of ME *point* (*O.E.D.* sb. 29), as 'culmination'. There is a noteworthy occurrence (once) in MHG of an *endèspil* n., which is clearly from the vocabulary of chess (cf. mod. Du *eindspeel*, E *end-game*), and which is already, like the ME idiom, used in a transferred sense:

> . . . daz erz ane der guoten danc
> braht uf ein endespil

> (Hartmann's *Gregorius*, ed. H. Paul (1912),
> 394–5)

'. . . brought the matter to a head, conclusion.'

If this interpretation is correct, *setten spel* must be an adoption of the MDu phrase, since there is no noun *spel* 'game' recorded in English. On the evidence as a whole, the ME idiom means something like 'brought the matter to a head, came to the point'.

77. *feire*: the earliest English example. The only explicit reference to a fair before the Conquest is in a charter (the word used being *gearmarkett*) dated between 1053 and 1055 (H. E. Salter, *The Cartulary of the Abbey of Eynsham*, i. 29 (Oxford Historical Society, xlix (1906–7))), and it happens to relate to Stow St. Mary, which—like Boston—is in Lincolnshire. On the origin of the fair as an institution, see F. E. Harmer, '*Chipping* and *Market*: a Lexicographical Investigation', in *The Early Cultures of North-West Europe* (ed. Sir Cyril Fox and Bruce Dickins (1950)), and especially pp. 355 ff.

Botolfston: according to the *Anglo-Saxon Chronicle* St. Botolf began the building of a monastery at *Icanhoh* in 654; and according to the *Life* of Abbot Ceolfriδ of Wearmouth (ed. Plummer, *Venerabilis Baedae Opera Historica*, i. 389), it was located in the territory of the East Angles. Since Botolf's name is preserved in *Boston*, some modern scholars have identified the latter with *Icanhoh*; but there is no direct evidence for this.

82. *his lif*: subject of *burþ*; for the syntax of the construction *liken his lif*, see *Sir Gawain and the Green Knight* 87.

101. *selk*: again 245. This remarkable form is not recorded in any other text, and is therefore virtually certain to be an adoption of MDu *selc* (a phonetic variant of *sulc*, &c.). Though *secc* 83 might be a phonetic variant of the native *seche* (a fourteenth-century NMidl type), it may be a reduction of *selk*. Both are paralleled in Old Frisian (*selk*, *sek*).

135. *leue broþer*: a colloquial form of address; cf. *Kyng Alisaunder* 7686, and *The Hous of Fame* 816.

142. *menis*: since *mening* 'lamentation' would be feeble in this context, the palæographically probable emendation of MS. *menig* to *menīg* (for *mening*) can be ruled out. *Make means* is an idiom attested from 1400 onwards, in the sense 'get someone to intercede for one' (lit. 'employ as intermediary'), and is clearly what is required here. In this scribe's hand (and hence possibly in the antecedent MS.) *g* and *s* are very similar.

144. Cf. *The Harley Lyrics* (ed. Brook), p. 72, l. 14:

> Wo is him þat loueþ þe loue
>   þat he ne may ner ywynne.

170. *strengþen me*: the *O.E.D.*'s only example of this reflexive use is from the late fifteenth century. It is evidently a calque on OF *s'afforcer* 'exert oneself', or a synonymous variant of the ME adoption of the latter (in reflexive use) as *afforce* (1297 onwards).

173. *nelde*: usually explained as the noun *elde* 'old age' (< non-WS *eldu*), which is recorded twice in late OE in the sense 'old people'. The latter are slightly different in being used with the definite article (*seo yldu*). But there is no difficulty in the implied metanalysis (common in ME) of the final consonant of a preceding word such as (*min*) *elde*; cf. *my nayct* XV. 58.

Schröder (op. cit., p. 185) has cited MLG *nelle* 'procuress' as a possible etymon; and adoption from LG is intrinsically likely in this text (see 43 n., 62 n., and 101 n.). But the intrusion of inorganic *d* after final *l* (e.g. *vilde* 'vile') is normally traceable only from the sixteenth century onwards). And the rhyme on *welde* (< OAnglian *wēldan*, weak class I) supports the first explanation.

206. *on . . . con*: cf. 47 n.

230. *þin hernest*: an isolated early example of an idiom (with the possessive adjective) that is otherwise recorded only in Milton's 'this caitiff, never worth my earnest' (*Colasterion*, in *The Works of John Milton*, Columbia U.P., iv. 267).

238. *folen*: the metre shows that an unstressed element has dropped out before this word; the author may well have written *bifolen*, in some such sense as that of *wel biset* 274 (a standard ME phrase) and *wel set* in IV. 173, which is probably a calque on OF (*bien*) *emploié* '(well) applied, bestowed'.

244. *chapitre*: for a convincing explanation of the remarkable semantic development see *O.E.D. chapter* sb. 4 (*aliter* von Wartburg, *F.E.W.* s.v. *capitulum*).

The 'chapter' here is shown to be an ecclesiastical court by *iugement* 246; and 248 probably modifies *were . . . igiuen* 246 rather than *ben . . . somer-driuen* 247. The court was presided over either by the archbishop of the diocese or the archdeacon. Valuable contemporary evidence for this, as for the kinds of offence that fell within the jurisdiction of ecclesiastical courts, is available in the opening of *The Friar's Tale* (*C.T.* 1301–21) D.

which specifies both witchcraft and *bauderye* (the activity of pimps and procuresses) as well as fornication. It is on the score of 'bawdry' that Dame Siriþ is so apprehensive, notwithstanding her reference to witchcraft in 206: Chaucer's Summoner (perhaps at the instance of his archdeacon) had a special interest in *bauderye* and fornication. (See A. L. Poole, *From Domesday Book to Magna Carta*, pp. 200–19; F. M. Powicke, *The Thirteenth Century*, pp. 452–69, 475–85; H. W. C. Davis, *England under the Normans and Angevins*, pp. 206–18.)

279–84. Addressed to the dog; cf. 287.

288. *boinard*: OF *buisnart*, used as a proper name for the buzzard in the *Roman de Renart*, is formed on *buse* 'buzzard' < L *buteo*. The contemptuous application here to a human being is rooted in the notion that the buzzard (which is a type of falcon) was sluggish and dull by nature; whence the OF proverb *L'en ne puet faire de buisart espervier* (J. Morawski, *Proverbes français antérieurs au XVe siècle* (1925), 1514; cf. 965 and 96).

298. *þat is wo*: originally an impersonal construction (as 379 shows); cf. V. 2.

299. *hire*: ethic dative.

302. *reuliche . . . bigon*: cf. V. 107.

303–4. These lines are both hypermetrical: the normal pattern requires only four main stresses in each. In 303, *hoe seiþ* is the kind of otiose addition commonly made by scribes, and is probably spurious. *Ledeþ ay liues* 304 is not idiomatic; and *ledeþ ay lif*, rhyming on the sg. *wif*, would be no better. In fact, *ledeþ* may have been inserted by a scribe who failed to recognize *liues* as a pres. pl. form of the verb (because it was not the one current in his own form of ME).

306. Again hypermetrical; the spurious element may be the otiose *poure*. The emendation implies that in the sequence *in nausine* two successive *n*'s have been reduced to one (a process which might be either purely graphic or a fact of living speech). *Ansine*, representing OE *onsīen* 'lack', seems unlikely, in the absence of other post-Conquest examples.

324. *faste . . . to non*: the meaning of this is established by the exact parallel in the ME version of *The Rule of St. Benedict* (ed. Kock, E.E.T.S., o.s. 120 (1902), p. 95):

> In somer, fro Witsunday be past,
> Wedinsday and Friday sal þai fast,
> Bot if þai oþer swink or swete
> In hay or corn with travel grete.
> And if þai non slike travel done,
> On þos days sal þai *fast to none*.

Thus *to* means 'until'; and it is clear from what precedes and follows this passage that *non* is 'the ninth hour', i.e. 3 p.m.:

> Fro Pas right unto Witsunnday,
> At þe sext our ete sal þai,
> þe whilk es midday for to mene,
> And sine sal þai soupe bedene. . . .
>
> And on oþer days, als I air saide,
> At mydday sal þer mete be graide.

See further D. Knowles, *The Monastic Order in England* (1950), pp. 449 and 456, and B. Miller, *M.Æ.* xxviii (1959), 180.

326. The use of ME *as* to introduce a wish is relatively rare, and is so far unexplained. The comparable OF use of the otherwise synonymous *que* may have been the model (since it does not appear in OE).

356. MS. *breke* can hardly be a preterite here, among the series of presents in 355–8. It is a patching by a scribe who was not familiar with rhymes involving a discrepancy in a final unstressed syllable (see II. 83–84 n.).

390. *Godes houne belle*: also 421. The expletive *by Seint Poules belle* in *The Nonne Preestes Tale* (*C.T.* B. 3970) concerns the bell of St. Paul's Church. But the reference here is probably to the use of a bell in the Mass, and specifically at the elevation of the Host (see *O.E.D. sacring-bell* 1, and B. Miller, loc. cit., pp. 183–8).

418. The spelling *Siriz* cannot be satisfactorily etymologized, and must therefore be an inexact one (as in 154 and 420). It is due to the uncertainty of Anglo-Norman scribes regarding the use of the graph þ and its phonetic value.

433. 'As I hope to live to see the ninth hour'. The point of this expletive is that in monasteries *non(e)* was the time of the first meal of the day in winter and on certain days in summer (see *supra*, 324 n.). Since the monastic day began at 2 a.m. in winter and at 5 a.m. in summer (see Knowles, op. cit., pp. 448–58), the arrival of *none* must have been welcome. The expletive here used (if not meant to show the monastery-trained cleric Wilekin speaking in character) suggests that the author of *Dame Siriþ* may himself have been an inmate of a monastery.

VII

MS.: Laud 108, Bodleian Library.

Editions: C. Horstmann, *The Early South-English Legendary*, E.E.T.S., o.s. 87 (1887): MS. Laud.

C. D'Evelyn and A. J. Mill, *The South English Legendary*, E.E.T.S., o.s. 235, 236, 245 i (1956), ii (1956), iii (1959): MSS. Corpus Christi College, Cambridge 145 and Harley 2277.

Source: Latin *Vita* in MSS. Douce 368 (f. 80 r 2–83 v 2), Bodleian Library, and Bodley 285 (f. 80 r 2–83 v 1).

Studies: E. S. Hartland, 'The Legend of St. Kenelm', *Transactions of the Bristol and Gloucestershire Archæological Society*, xxxix (1916), 13–65.

E. Rickert, 'The Old English Offa Saga', *Modern Philology*, ii (1904–5), 13–48, 321–76 (on Kenelm, pp. 9–10, 335–7).

Language

1. The reflex of OE *ǽ* (WMidl, OKt *ě*) rhymes on *ǎ* in *was* 61, 84, 153, 212, 257: *cas*.
2. The reflex of OE *ā* when *i*-mutated (WS *ǽ²*) rhymes (i) on slack *ē* < OE *ēa* in *bileue* 228: *bireue*, and (ii) when shortened before two consonants on *ě* in *spradde* 42: *bedde*.
3. *g* is eliminated before *d*, with lengthening of the preceding vowel, in *sede* pt. 86: *dede*, 183: *rede*.

Provenance

1 excludes both the SE and the WMidl; and the rhyme cited

under 2 (i), if exact, would exclude the SE, the Midlands, and the North. Since 3 is conclusively Southern, the work seems (so far as this scanty evidence goes) to have been composed in the SW.

———

3. *Seint Kenelm*: see W. Levison, *England and the Continent in the Eighth Century* (1946), pp. 249–51.

4. *Quendrith* is attested in historical documents as a daughter of Cenwulf. She became abbess of *Suthmynstre* (Minster) in Kent, and was probably abbess also of Winchcombe (see Levison, op. cit., pp. 251–2, 257).

8. As in the *Vita* in MS. Douce 368 (f. 80 v 1); the actual period of Cenwulf's reign was 796–821.

31–32. Proverbial; cf. the OF axiom *On ne se puet garder de privé larron* (J. Morawski, *Proverbes français antérieurs au XVe siècle* (1925), no. 1526).

40 ff. Dreams in medieval literature are commonly constructed so as to be obviously prophetic. Cf. *King Horn* (MS. L) 657 ff., *Hav.* 1285 ff.

51. *on . . . smot*: according to the *Vita*, however, *quidam . . . succiderunt*.

53. *luyte*: possibly a corruption of *whyte* (*candida* in the *Vita*).

89–90. Not altogether clear, because the author has altered the functioning of the twig as a proof of Kenelm's prophetic insight. MS. Douce 368 reads (f. 81 r 1):
'Vnde tibi certum dabit signum hec uirga (nam uirgam manu gestabat et terre affixerat), si modo plantata frondeat.' Hec eo pronuntiante, statim radicata uirga cepit frondescere; unde adhuc ingens fraxinus ostenditur que in memoriam beati Kenelmi celebris habetur. Hinc seuissimus carnifex, percussus et uoce ueridica et dira conscientia longius puerum abducit, obturata fouea.

98. *ase . . . juggement*: not in the *Vita*.

117–20. Then follows in MS. C.C.C.C. 367 (f. 47 v):
Sed qui solo teste est iugulatus, celo teste per columpnam lucis ex diuina bonitate postmodum est reuelatus.

MS. Douce 368 says more specifically (f. 81 r 2):

Denique qui celo teste erat martyrizatus, celo teste est declaratus, quatinus fulgida lucis columna ab ethereis arcibus sepe uideretur super eum effusa.

151. *withoute mete*, 160 *meteles*: the *Vita* says:

tam salubri circa sanctam glebam pascebatur herba et gramina. Miroque modo quod uesperi detonsum erat recrescente uirore mane habundantius inueniebat (MS. Douce 368, f. 81 r 2).

171. *þe pope*: *Leo papa iunior* (Leo III, 795–816) in MSS. Douce 368 (f. 81 v 1) and C.C.C.C. 367 (f. 48 r) of the *Vita*, but *Siluester* (999–1003) according to MS. Bodl. 285. The similar discrepancy, noted by Levison, op. cit., p. 250 n. 6, between Henry of Huntingdon's account (Silvester: Rolls Series, 1879, p. xxvi) and Tynemouth's abbreviated *Legend* (Leo: C. Horstmann, *Nova Legenda Anglie*, ii. p. 111, l. 29) is thus genuinely ancient.

Though the legend of Kenelm in its full form is likely to be fiction, the compiler of it has taken the trouble to introduce personages who are chronologically appropriate and authentic, as well as accurate topographical details. For the former, cf. the other instance of Wolfred, archbishop of Canterbury, 199 and n.; and for the latter, see 229 n. and 247–56 n.

189–96. Not represented in the *Vita*.

199. Wolfred held the see from 805 to 832; cf. 171 n.

214–17. *Seint Kenelmes Welle*: the facts are briefly reported in the *Vita*, but without any indication that the 'holy spring' (*fons sacer*) was named and known after the saint. The stream cannot now be seen, as the water was diverted in the mid-nineteenth century. There is still a church, at the reputed scene of Kenelm's martyrdom, near Halesowen, which is dedicated to him. For a description and a line drawing of the church see R. C. S. Walters, *The Ancient Wells, Springs, and Holy Wells of Gloucestershire* (Bristol 1928), pp. 13–14.

225–54. Not in MS. C.C.C.C. 367 of the *Vita*, though represented in MS. Douce 368.

229. *Pireford*: a new example of a lost *Perryford* 'ford by the pear-tree', which Mawer and Stenton (*The Place-names of Worcestershire*, p. 120) cite only from an OE charter of 972 and a document of 1536. On the evidence of the two passages concerned, Perryford is located by Mawer and Stenton on the Avon, at a point 'on the common bounds of Cropthorne and Bricklehampton where they meet the Avon'.

247–56. St. Kenelm's Well and Chapel are located on the Ordnance Survey map (Sheet SP 02) about 2,000 yards east of Winchcombe, at a level of *c*. 600 feet on Sudeley Hill, which rises to *c*. 1,000 feet. The phrases *a luyte bi este þe toune* 247, *opon ane heiȝe doune* 248 (*opon þe doune* 251), and *of þe doune heiȝe . . . a luyte fram Suydleiȝe* 261–2 are topographically accurate, even if *half a mile* 252 underestimates the distance by a half.

The reason for an approach to Winchcombe from the east (as Professor F. W. Baxter has kindly suggested) is probably that the party would have followed the course of the old saltway which (hereabouts) ran along Salter's Lane in Hailes, Salt Way in Pinnock, and between Sevenhampton and Hawling. This is confirmed by the fact that the *Pireford* of 229 is traceable to a point on this very saltway; and Salter's Hill, which the saltway passes, and which clearly owes its name to it, is one mile east of Winchcombe. See Mawer and Stenton, op. cit., pp. 4–9, and A. H. Smith, *The Place-names of Gloucestershire*, i. 19–21, for this and the other saltways. Those in Gloucestershire are extensions of the Worcestershire ones, which are centred on Droitwich; the latter area was the only one where salt was made in the Middle Ages.

St. Kenelm's Chapel is not thus named in the *Vita*, nor indeed mentioned. See Hartland, op. cit., pp. 63–64: the stream is now used to supply Winchcombe with water, and the chapel no longer exists. For a description and a photograph of the wellhouse see Walters, op. cit., pp. 9–11 and Fig. 4.

There are not less than eight existing churches dedicated to Kenelm, viz. Little Hinton in Dorset, Minster Lovell and Enstone in Oxfordshire, Sapperton and Alderley in Gloucestershire, Upton Snodsbury and Clifton-on-Teme in Worcestershire, and Rockfield in Monmouthshire (see F. Arnold-Forster, *Studies in Church Dedications* (London 1899), i. 174–5 and iii. 388).

260. *est*: but *occidentalis* in the *Vita* (MS. Douce 368, f. 82 r 1).

262. *fram Suydleiȝe*: not mentioned in the *Vita*.

267. *centesimum octauum psalmum* (MS. Douce 368).

278. Unclearly put; the *Vita* says:

Adhuc autem ipsum psalterium argento paratum huius correptionis prebet indicium, in eadem serie lapsorum orbium cruore maculatum (MS. Douce 368, f. 82 r 1).

282. The *Vita* says somewhat cryptically:

quam ferunt . . . quendam infantem lucidissimum apparentem cuidem iussisseque in quodam profundo semoto proici (MS. Douce 368, f. 82 r 1).

VIII

Note. The language and provenance of the following pieces are either not clear, or not ascertainable, from the philological evidence:

B, D, O, P, Q, R, S, X.

Those for which a stray clue either whittles the possibilities down somewhat or is in itself enough to indicate a particular area are as follows:

A: the metrically essential prefix *i-* in the past part. *icumen* 1 excludes the EMidl and the North.

B: *Oc* 3, if the author's form, would imply an area of very strong Scandinavian influence. It is recorded in the *First* and *Final Continuations* of the *Peterborough Chronicle*, both of which were composed in the EMidl.

C: *mon* 3 is a word restricted to NMidl and Northern texts up to the mid-fifteenth century; and if not due to a scribe, it implies composition within those areas.

E: *breȝe* 18, established by the rhyme on *heȝe*, implies composition in the Midlands or the North, since the OE antecedent *brēg* is specifically Anglian (non-Angl. *brǣw*, ME *brę̄w*).

F: *heþe* 10 (established by rhyme) is restricted to the North and the NMidl.

T: the lengthening of $\breve{u}$ to tense $\bar{o}$ in a disyllable with open root-syllable in *sone* 37 (: *bone*) indicates the NMidl or the North. The Northern *es* 35 has probably been substituted for *is*, which is also used in the NMidl.

U, W: the SMidl or the South is indicated by the phrase *mid iwisse* 3 and 8 respectively (established by rhyme).

V: the tense $\bar{e}$ (implying OE $\bar{e}o$) in *be* 11 (: *Aue*, *þe*) excludes the SE and possibly the WMidl.

Y: the SE is indicated by *e* in *wnne* 6 (: *þenne*), implying OKt -$\breve{e}$- in *wynn*.

The language and provenance of H, K, L, M, N are discussed in the Commentary below.

A

MS.: Harley 978, British Museum.

Editions: Carleton Brown, *English Lyrics of the Thirteenth Century* (1932), p. 13.
Dickins and Wilson, *Early Middle English Texts* (1951), p. 118.

Facsimile of Music: H. E. Wooldridge, *Early English Harmony*, i (1897), plate 22.

Transcription: *Oxford History of Music*, i (ed. H. E. Wooldridge, 2nd ed., 1929), p. 185.

Recording: *The History of Music in Sound*, ii, side 15.

Studies: M. F. Bukofzer, 'Sumer is icumen in, A revision', *University of California Publications in Music*, ii (1944), 79–114.

N. Perrotta, 'On the Problem of "Sumer is icumen in" ', *Musica Disciplina*, ii (1948), 205–16.

B. Schofield, 'The Provenance and Date of *Sumer is Icumen in*', *Music Review*, ix (1948), 81–86.

J. Handschin, 'The Summer Canon and its Background', *Musica Disciplina*, iii (1949), 55–94.

A. Hughes, *Early Medieval Music up to 1300* (New Oxford History of Music, ii (1954)), pp. 402–4.

F. L. Harrison, *Music in Medieval Britain* (1958), pp. 142–4.

Provenance

The MS. is shown by internal evidence to be connected with the Abbey of Reading. Immediately after the music of the *rota*, on f. 11 v, there is a calendar recording obits of officials and bene-factors of the abbey. Moreover, on ff. 160b and 161 a table of contents of a collection (now lost) of books names *W. de Wint-[onia]* (possibly the owner), *R. de Bur.*, and *W. de Wic.* All have been identified by Schofield (op. cit., pp. 83–84) as respectively: (i) a monk who is traceable at Leominster Priory (a cell of Read-ing) from 1276 to *c.* 1281, and later at Reading; (ii) *Richard de Burgate*, Abbot of Reading 1286–90; (iii) a monk of Reading who spent four years at Leominster.

The following Latin hymn[1] is written below the ME poem in the MS., and was also intended to be sung to the music: for a transcription with the words distributed in the various parts see F. L. Harrison, op. cit., p. 143, Ex. 14:

> Perspice Christicola
> que dignacio
> celicus agricola
> pro uitis uicio
> Filio
> non parcens exposuit
> mortis exicio
> qui captiuos
> semiuiuos
> a supplicio
> vite donat
> et secum coronat
> in celi solio.

B

MS.: Rawlinson G 22, Bodleian Library.

Editions: Carleton Brown, op. cit., p. 14.
Dickins and Wilson, op. cit., p. 118.

Facsimile of Music: J. F. R. and C. Stainer, *Early Bodleian Music*, i (1901), plate 3.

[1] For which see U. Chevalier, *Repertorium Hymnologicum* (1892 ff.), 14854.

Transcription: Stainer, op. cit. ii (1901), p. 5.

This piece has been transmitted with a musical setting, on the verso of a leaf which is otherwise occupied by AN love-lyrics. Among the latter, the following verses are also accompanied by a musical setting:

A	*B*
ch . . . ai entendu	[M]ult s'aprisme li termines
Icele mun sanc remue	Kar rancunes e ba . . . es
Dunt ieo fremis e tressu	M . . . rrunt de pres ueisines
A li dunt ai peine e delit	Quant les dames e m[e]schines
Cri merci, qu'ele ne m'ublit.	E cuntesses palaines
	Unt les queors f. . . .

A is immediately followed by other verses constructed on one of the two rhymes used in *A*:

> Afublee ne uestue
> Unc si bele rien ne fu
> Sun simple semblant me tue
> Si que n'ai sen ne uertu
> De la dulcur qu'ai sentue
> Sui ieo maz murnes . . .
> S'ele ne m'auertue
> . . . m'ad amur deceu &c. &c.

C

MS: Douce 139, Bodleian Library.

Editions: Carleton Brown, op. cit., p. 14.
  Dickins and Wilson, op. cit., p. 119.

Facsimile of Music: H. E. Wooldridge, *Early English Harmony*, i, plate 7.
  Stainer, *Early Bodleian Music*, i, plate 6.

Transcription: A. Hughes, *Early Medieval Music up to 1300* (1954), p. 343.

Studies: G. Reese, *Music in the Middle Ages* (New York 1940), pp. 338–40.
  A. Hughes, op. cit., pp. 341–3.

5. The meaning of this is made clear by the more explicit form of expression in E 4–5.

D

MS.: Harley 2253, British Museum

Facsimile: E.E.T.S., o.s. 255 (1965) with introduction by N. R. Ker.

Editions: Carleton Brown, op. cit., p. 139.

  G. L. Brook, *The Harley Lyrics* (Manchester, 2nd ed. 1956), p. 34.

  K. Böddeker, *Altenglische Dichtungen des MS. Harl.* 2253 (Berlin 1878), pp. 149–50.

Studies: T. Stemmler, *Die englischen Liebesgedichte des MS. Harley* 2253 (Bonn 1962), pp. 119–21.

Vocabulary

  Burde 36 is found almost exclusively in alliterative poetry. Adoptions from ON are *gest* 40, *menske* 23, *slo* 16.

---

10. Cf. M 21 below, and IV. 69 and n.

15. *sonde*: the diverse senses of this word in ME are comprehensible if regarded as individual applications of the sense 'that which is sent'.

17. Lines 33 and 14 show that this is a roundabout way of putting the stock comparison represented, e.g. in *The Harley Lyrics* (ed. Brook), p. 43, l. 50.

20. *þo*: the envious ones of 18.

23. *to menske*: with an object *þe*, understood from 22.

36. *burde*: on the etymology, see J. R. R. Tolkien, 'Some Contributions to Middle-English Lexicography', *R.E.S.* i (1925), 210–12.

38. *Brihtest vnder bys*: this phrasal pattern (foreshadowed in OE *heard under helme*) became a stereotyped element of style in all ME poetry in which alliteration was used, whether organically as in alliterative verse, or for ornament, as in some tail-rhyme romances. The first element regularly names a personal quality, and the second a part of the dress or the like, as in *Pearl* 775: *comly onvunder cambe*. See J. P. Oakden, *Alliterative Poetry in Middle English*, ii (1935), pp. 292, 321; and VI. 5.

E

MS.: Harley 2253.

Editions: Brook, op. cit., pp. 37–39.
    Böddeker, op. cit., pp. 155–8.

Studies: Stemmler, op. cit., pp. 176–91.

Provenance

Since the parallels to K listed in 31 n. below probably indicate common authorship, the word *crouþ* in K 43 suggests that E was also composed by someone living near the Welsh border.

2. *Wilde wymmen*: as in the introductory reference in a ME sermon to the precious fragment which is evidently the refrain of a lost dancing-song:

> Atte wrastlinge my lemman I ches,
> And atte ston-kasting I him forles.

. . . Mi leue frend, wilde wimmen and goliue [MS. gólme] i mi contreie, wan he gon o þe ring . . . (ed. Förster, *Anglia*, xlii (1918), 152–4). Cf. p. xvi, n. 2.

The collocation with *goliue* 'lascivious' establishes the sense 'wanton' for *wilde*.

10. *lylie*: '(the) lily-flower' will not make sense if interpreted literally. *Rose* and *rode* in 11 and *long* in 10 show that the poet is referring to the lady's complexion (as in *bleo* 7) or face. *Lylie* (if the word 'lily') must therefore be a comparable reference to the whiteness of her complexion; cf. 35 and D 31–32. This might be explained as an early example of a consociation (containing *lily* and *rose* sb. in reference to the mistress whom a poet celebrates) which helped to produce the semantic change of *lily* to 'lady' (see *O.E.D.* s.v. 3), and which may be represented in the line:

> The lily, the rose, the rose I lay!

(Chambers and Sidgwick, *Early English Lyrics*, p. 82).

But this interpretation would be strained; and a more natural one is suggested by the remarkably similar collocation of words in *The Harley Lyrics*, p. 31, ll. 11–12:

> Hire *rode* is ase *rose* þat red is on rys;
> Wiþ *lilye*-white leres *lossum* he is.

This indicates a compound adj. *lylie-lossum*, and in *þe* an instance (admittedly exceptional in MS. Harl. 2253) of the relative, referring back to *heo* 8 or *bleo* 7. Line 11 refers to *bleo*.

24. Professor Brook's interpretation of *dreyȝe* as < OE *drēogan* is formally possible; *dreyȝe duel* 'suffer sorrow' occurs as a collocation, e.g. in *The Sege of Melayne* 1055, and *to deþ* as 'to the point of death' is amply attested. In that view, *for* is a preposition—as in the analysis adopted here, in which *dreyȝe* is the mainly Western and Northern variant of *drawe* v., and 24 is a main clause. This is contextually natural and is in keeping with what is known of the provenance of this poem.

31. The contextual conjunction of this line with the collocation *murþes monge* 32 is matched by that of K 13 and K 15. An echo as close as this suggests common authorship of the two pieces rather than an imitation or reminiscence in one of them. Moreover, if one disregards correspondences that might have been common form in this sort of poetry, others remain that add up to a considerable similarity in expression and style between these two poems. Thus the comparisons respectively with the moon at night (E 19–20) and a lantern (K 22) are by no means obvious ones in medieval poetry. The conjunction of *hire bleo ys briht* and *leomeþ liht* E 7–8 is matched in K 21 and 23 (though *The Harley Lyrics* 3. 3 and 3. 17 are faintly similar). *A mury mouht* E 37, *murgest of mouþ* K 41 and *eye(n) grete* E 16, K 17 are collocations not used elsewhere in *The Harley Lyrics*. And *fyngres feir to folde* E 55 and K 27 are paralleled only by *may no fynger folde* in 13. 21 (which is not a love-lyric), in a quite different context.

32. *murþes monge*: the other example of this collocation in K 15 (see n. ad loc.), though straightforward, does not explain the transitive use here, which may be compared with that of *mengan* (in a synonymous phrase) in the OE *Rhyming Poem* 11:

> Giestas gengdon,   gerscype mengdon.

Here *mengan* might mean either 'stir up, set on foot', or 'exchange', as in *Solomon and Saturn* 424: *meðelcwidas mengdon*. *Gerscype mengdon* (if the ἅπαξ λεγόμενον *ger* = OIcel *gár* 'fun') thus means 'talked entertainingly' or 'conversed lightheartedly'.

Similarly, *murþes monge* evidently amounts to 'indulge in (*or* exchange) innocent pleasantries'.

33. *Hit* is best referred to *blisse* (less probably *speche* 30): Professor Brook's treatment of it as referring collectively to hair (in *lockes* 31) is implausible. The line apparently means: 'in the midst of any social gaiety that may be afoot.'

35. *eke*: not (as Brook) the adverb 'also', but a noun governed by *on* in a unique phrase which is a synonymous variant of *to eken*, *to echen* (< OE *tō ēacan*), for which cf. XVIII. 60.

50. *lef*: not (as Brook) 'leaf of a book', but the adj. *lēf* (< OE *lēof*), here used substantively. Thus: 'When I gaze on her hand, the lily-white (one), she might well seem the best mistress in the land.'

57. *wel were me*: cf. III. 3.

59. *of Parays*: i.e. from the tree of knowledge, like the fatal apple of Eve—an unusual and ingenious conceit which may, however, have been prompted by the latent simile that is expressed in the fifteenth-century poem beginning *When the son the laumpe of heuen ful lyght* 384–6:

> Hyr appul brestys . . .
> So lyte, so white, so hard, so rounde
> (ed. E. P. Hammond, *Mod. Phil.* xxi (1924), p. 393).

61. *bete gold*: see *Kyng Alisaunder*, ii (E.E.T.S., o.s. 237, 1957), 1032 n.

69–71. A reference to the magical properties or 'virtues' of precious stones; see III. 41–42, and n.

82. *seȝe*: probably a semantic borrowing of the OF use of *veeir* 'to see' as 'to watch over, provide for' in such expressions as *Deus te voie!* 'may God protect you!'

F

MS.: Harley 2253.

Editions: Brook, op. cit., pp. 39–40.
   Böddeker, op. cit., pp. 158–60.

Studies: Stemmler, op. cit., pp. 147–54; R. Woolf, *M.Æ.* xxxviii (1969), 55–9.

Vocabulary

Adoptions from ON are *casten* 11, *gates* 7, *heþe* 10, *ycayred* 35, *laste* 15, *menske* 22, *mynne* 20, *ro* 30, *spac-* 29.

---

4. Since *gome* is used solely of men, it must here imply a reference to the narrator, rather than the maiden. *Gere* is thus best interpreted, not as 'clothing' < ON *gervi* (as Brook), but as the quite distinct word 'feelings, mood (here of fleshly desire)' < MDu *gere* '(carnal) desire'.

9. *helde*: Brook's identification with OE *hyldo* 'favour' requires an idiomatically dubious use of *in*, and is phonologically inadmissible in this poem: a SE *helde* (OKt **heldo*) cannot be harmonized with *faste* 19, which cannot here rhyme in the SE form *feste* on the noun *laste* (prim. ON **last-*).

10. *þe*: dative of disadvantage, to be construed with *to heþe*.

23. *þat*: a reduction of OE *oð þæt*.

31. *vachen*: best interpreted by reference to OE *fatian*, which occurs once in the collocation with *wif* rendering *uxorem ducere*, and which, though rare, is amply supported by the cognate ON *fata* (*veg sinn*) 'find (one's way)', OHG *sih fazzon* 'climb'. These represent a Gmc verb of weak class II formed on the strong one attested by OE *fetan* 'fall', OHG *fezzan* 'fall', ON *feta* 'step'. They are distinct from the Gmc weak verb attested by OFris *fatia* 'take', OHG *fazzon* 'ride in a cart', formed on the noun seen in OHG *fazza* 'load', ON *fot* pl. 'baggage'. See W. Wissmann, *Nomina Postverbalia*, i (1932), 11–12.

Vachen here must be a blend of *fatian* with *feččan* < *fetian* (weak class III), since the assibilation to -*čč*- depends on the sequence -*tĭ*-, and the -*i*- in *fatian* is a vowel.

34. *forhaht*: otherwise recorded only in *forheccheð* in *Hali Meiðhad* (ed. A. F. Colborn, p. 36, l. 611; v.l. *forhoheð* 'despises'). *O.E.D.* acknowledges that the root is obscure; and Professor Brook's identification with the word 'hatch', as literally 'misbegotten' and thence 'despised', implies a semantic development that is not credible. The ME forms (if of native origin) imply an OE *forhæccan, *forheccan, a causative of weak class I, which might be referred to the base *hak- 'be pointed', on which are also formed the ideophonic OE ahaccian 'peck out' and ofhæccan 'cut off' (as also the noun hak in XIV. 105 below). *Forhæccan might therefore have meant originally 'drive away' and hence 'reject scornfully'; cf. the figurative use 'be hostile' registered in O.E.D. for the simplex hack v. under 8 b.

36. Brook's 'and beg the man whom I had embraced to remain faithful to me' depends on the interpretation of bede as the infinitive < OE bēodan (see his Glossary). But it is best taken as the past part. of bidde (OE beden), with ben understood from the previous line. Thus: 'and be enjoined to stick to him on whom I had laid hold.'

39. 'Than that I should marry a wretch given to anger (i.e. because he is jealous).'

45. ashunche: in the absence of an assured OE antecedent, the simplex shunche (which occurs three times, in texts of the Katherine Group) has been explained as a blend of schuhten 'turn aside (trans.); blench, shy' with schunien and schunten (S. T. R. O. d'Ardenne, S. Iuliene, p. 164). Either a transitive use 'frighten off' or an intrans. 'evade' is possible here; but the obscure context of 45–46 does not show which was intended.

   Shupping may mean either 'devising (counter-) measures' (OED shape v. II), or 'taking (another) shape, shape-shifting' (cf. OE scypian 'take shape'). Somewhat similarly P. Dronke, M.Æ. xxxii (1963), 150, who is however mistaken in taking me as 'me': the syntactically parallel non in 44 indicates me 'one' < OE man.

47. ofþuncheþ: for the emendation, cf. II. 83–84 n.

G

MS.: Harley 2253.

Editions: Brook, op. cit., pp. 40–41.
   Böddeker, op. cit., pp. 161–3.

Studies: St. H. L. Degginger, ' "A Wayle Whyt ase Whalles Bon" Reconstructed', J.E.G.P. liii (1954), 84 ff.
   Stemmler, op. cit., pp. 121–6.

Language

1. OE *ȳ* has been unrounded in *cusse* 27: *ywisse, blisse, his.*
2. The reflex of OE *ēo* is a long vowel rhyming on tense *ē* in *freo* 37, 31, *beo* 32, *þreo* 33, *see* 35: *me* 38. But 37–38, which alone in the poem imply this development, are under suspicion of being corrupt (see n.).

Vocabulary

Adoptions from ON are *þryuen* 16, and probably *wayle* 1; *wondryng* 40 is a reformation of ON *vandræði* with a native suffix.

Provenance

1 excludes the SE; otherwise obscure.

8. *bad*: a preterite subjunctive is idiomatically required here ('I would never ask more . . .'). Thus the poet probably wrote *bēde* (< OE *bǣde*): rhyming of a long and a short vowel is admitted in ME verse (cf. 2–3). An *ě* in *gled* would necessarily imply SE or SWMidl origin; the former is excluded by the rhymes of 26–27.

9. *myn one*: a historically irregular development of OE *mē ānum*, in an idiom in which any personal pronoun may be combined with *ān* in the sense 'alone', agreeing with it in number, case, and gender. *Hire* in OE *hire ānum* came to be erroneously analysed as the gen. (instead of the dat.); whence in ME gen. *myn* (< OE *mīnum*) instead of dat. *mē*.

19. *þat lefly*: subject of *syng*.

29. *myn, his*: referring either to *murþe* or to 'lady' understood.

32. 'And if there were measurable values, so that it could be done.'

37–38. These two lines go beyond the number used in all the other stanzas except the last (which might occasionally in a lyric be different in structure), and may therefore be corrupt. Degginger suggests that 38 was properly the opening line of the poem (because of its demand for the audience's attention), and that the next stanza followed it at the beginning of the piece.

38. *do*: a polite softening or a reinforcement of an imperative, exactly paralleled in OF *faites* and L *age*.

H

MS.: Harley 2253.

Editions: Carleton Brown, op. cit., pp. 146–7.
   Brook, op. cit., pp. 44–45.
   Böddeker, op. cit., pp. 166–7.

Studies: Stemmler, op. cit., pp. 140–4.

Language

1. The 3 pres. sg. ends in *-es* is *dawes* 1 : *plawes*.
2. The 3 pres. pl. ends (*a*) in *-es* in *wowes* 5 : *bowes* (*b*) is ending-less (which implies reduction from *-en*) in *bed* 17 (: *red*), if the subject *me* is the well-attested reduction of the pl. of the impersonal pronoun (< *men*). But *me* can equally well represent the sg. *man*, and *bed* the sg. *bedeþ*.

Vocabulary

Adoptions from ON are *lastes* 17, *sahte* 48, *won* 28.

Provenance

   1 implies an area not further south than the NMidl, and 2 (*a*) one at least north of Lincs. at this date (by comparison with *Havelok*). The phrase *by west* 10, which also occurs in D 37, is unlikely to refer to the author's own area, since *Lounde*[1] 30 may well (in view of 1 and 2 above) be Lound in Lincs. or Notts.; one reason for this identification is the sort of context in which it recurs in M 17.

----

15. *false*: i.e. men.

43. 'It is much too late [for her] to send to [him] (i.e. demanding back the *worldes ahte* of 42) when . . . he is living off what he has taken from her.' The subject of *lyueþ* 45 is *he* (understood from *trichour* 39).

[1] On this name see A. H. Smith, 'Old Scandinavian "Lundr" ', *L.S.E.* ii (1933), 72–75.

K

MS.: Harley 2253.

Editions: Carleton Brown, op. cit., pp. 148–50.
Dickins and Wilson, op. cit., pp. 119–21.
Brook, op. cit., pp. 48–50.
Böddeker, op. cit., pp. 168–71.

Studies: Stemmler, op. cit., pp. 168–75.

Language

1. The reflex of Gmc *ă* is (*a*) *ĕ* in *wes* 34: *lasteles*, : *Pees* 56; (*b*) *ă* in *smal* 29, *al* 31: *cristal*.
2. The reflex of prim. OE *ǣ* before *ld* derives from the unbroken and retracted type, in *holde* 25, *folde* 27: *wolde*.

Vocabulary

Adoptions from ON are *droupne* 78, *-lah-* 68, *lasteles* 33, *legges* 31, *menskful* 7, *slo* 63, *won* 9.

Provenance

2 is consistent with the North and the Midlands. The Welsh word *crouþ* 43 is a strong argument for localization near the Welsh border and therefore in the WMidl. 1 (*a*), since it involves the word *wes*, evidently represents a development in reduced stress; and 1 (*b*) thus reflects the normal development in stressed syllables. It follows that the *ă* of 1 (*b*) has displaced the *ĕ* which was proper to the WMidl *c*. 1200, as had happened in the *Gawain* group by *c*. 1350.

––––––––––

13. See E 31 n.

15. The meaning of *Wiþ murþes monge* (which has so far been generally misunderstood) is easily established, once it is recognized that *monge* is a variant (formed directly on *mong* sb. in ME) of *menge* < OE *mengan*. The phrase is thus clearly a variant of *wiþ murþ(es) menge* 'to cheer (trans.)', which occurs in *Sir Perceval* 1327 and *Towneley Plays*, xvi. 1. In the latter *menge* means literally 'stir up', as in the comparable expression in *Cursor Mundi* 27770: *And sua he mengges him wit ire*. Thus *monie* is the grammatical object (acc. pl.); and the line means 'she is capable of gladdening many people'.

65. *sore*: glossed by Brook as adj. 'grievous'. But interpretation of it as a verb is prescribed by stylistic criteria, since *Sykyng* and *Þoht*, in the same sentence, are each associated with an alliterating verb. The elimination of the labial consonant *w* before the lip-rounded vowels ǭ or ọ̄ is amply attested in the sixteenth century in various words, including the preterite and past part. of *swere* 'to swear' (see E. J. Dobson, *English Pronunciation 1500–1700*, ii. 980–3). But it must have set in sporadically in ME: the present pronunciation of *two, who* presupposes a raising of slack ō̧ to tense ō̄ after *w* by 1400, since it was tense ō̄ that was raised to /uː/ by the Vowel Shift.

L

MS.: Harley 2253.

Editions: Carleton Brown, op. cit., pp. 152–4.
  Dickins and Wilson, op. cit., pp. 121–2.
  Brook, op. cit., pp. 62–63.
  Böddeker, op. cit., pp. 172–3.

Studies: Stemmler, op. cit., pp. 154–7.

Language

1. The reflex of Gmc ă before a single nasal is ă in *sham* 15: *am* (since *a* is invariable in this latter word).
2. OE ȳ̆ has been unrounded in *kynne, synne* 18–19: *blynne, kyþe* 21: *syþe, mythe*.

Vocabulary

Serewe 25 is a Midland word. Adoptions from ON are *caste* 7, *slon* 20, *weylawei* 13, *wyndou* 23.

Provenance

2 excludes the SE, and 1 the WMidl. A Northern text might be expected to contain a less commonplace and a larger ON element; and *serewe* may well be the author's own form. The scanty evidence suggests the EMidl.

---

9. *bydde*: this idiom (as in *Hav.* 1733 and 2530) is a calque on an OF one in which the synonymous *rouvoir* (< L *rogāre*) 'ask' is used in the sense 'wish'. See XII. 86 n., and 'A Middle English Idiom and its Antecedents', *E.G.S.* i (1947–8), 101–13.

23. *custe vs*: a rare reciprocal use.

26. *par amours*: the semantic development represented in current English *paramour* directly depends on the existence of the code of courtly love in the Middle Ages, since the latter fostered adulterous love.

M

MS.: Harley 2253.

Editions: Carleton Brown, op. cit., p. 154.
　Dickins and Wilson, op. cit., p. 123.
　Brook, op. cit., p. 63.
　Böddeker, op. cit., p. 174.

Studies: Stemmler, op. cit., pp. 138–40.

Provenance
　The references in 17 are the sole evidence. The use of no less than four, all to places that can be identified within the NEMidl, is so specific as to be significant. They suggest that the *Lounde* of H 30 is the same as in 17 here; and this is corroborated by the linguistic evidence of NEMidl provenance for H.

---

3. A stock image in medieval love-poetry. Cf. the similar expression of the troubadour Folquet de Marseille: *E·l dieus d'amor a.m nafrat de tal lansa* . . . 'And the God of love has wounded me with a spear of such a kind . . .' (ed. S. Stronski, p. 33, l. 23).

12. *leche*: another commonplace of medieval love-poetry.

21. *on ylong*: cf. IV. 69 and n.

N

MS.: Harley 2253.

Editions: Carleton Brown, op. cit., pp. 160–1.
　Dickins and Wilson, op. cit., pp. 123–4.
　Brook, op. cit., pp. 69–70.
　Böddeker, op. cit., pp. 176–7.

Studies: R. J. Menner, 'The Man in the Moon and Hedging', *J.E.G.P.* xlviii (1949), 1–14.

Language

1. *-en* is the pl. ending of an old strong noun (with a root that ended in a vowel in the subject case) in *doren* 14: *yboren*, *yloren*.
2. The 3 pres. sg. in verbs with roots ending in a dental has the syncopated and assimilated form in *strit*, *slyt*, *byd* 1, 3, 5: *syt*.
3. The *y*-prefix is metrically essential in the past parts. *yboren* 12: *doren* and *yfed* 18, *ysped* 22.

Provenance

1 and 3 exclude the EMidl and the North. It follows that the verb-forms in the 3 pres. sg. *bereþ* 2, *shereþ* 4, *wereþ* 8: *totereþ* pl. cannot be scribal substitutions for the Northern forms *-es*, but are the author's own. Like 1 and 3 they indicate that the SE, the SW, or the southern part of the WMidl, are all possible.

---

8. Menner explains this as implying that the man's clothes are regarded as rags picked off the hedgerows.

13–16. Menner has shown that this is a reference to the process of hedging, in which brushwood or thorns (*trous*) were laid over the live cuttings (used to fill up gaps in the hedges, 14) to protect them. The *oþer trous* refers to the former.

24. I.e. he has been caught in the act of stealing wood. Alexander Neckam quotes a saying which reflects this belief about the Man in the Moon:

Nonne novisti quid vulgus vocet rusticum in luna portantem spinas? Unde quidam vulgariter loquens ait:

> Rusticus in luna, quem sarcina deprimit una,
> Monstrat per spinas nulli prodesse rapinas
> (*De Naturis Rerum*, ed. T. Wright (Rolls Series
> 34, 1863), i, 14; p. 54).

In popular superstition the Man in the Moon is still commonly believed to be a human being who was caught red-handed, in the light of the moon, at some illicit activity. See Bächtold–Stäubli, *Handwörterbuch des deutschen Aberglaubens*, vi. 510–14.

35. *nulle*: a reduction (probably in speech rather than purely graphic) of *nulle he*.

36. *con nout o lawe*: in Brook's interpretation 'does not know anything about law', *con o* is identified with the idiom *cunnen on* 'be versed in' (for which see IV. 18 n.). The interpretation adopted here has the advantage of providing something that is rephrased in 40 and is above all apposite: the sinister power of the moon has made the man a prisoner (cf. 38 n.).

38. *amarscled*: the *O.E.D.*'s interpretation 'stuffed full' (followed by Brook) is a contextual gloss without any etymological basis. Menner identifies the root with OF *mascle* 'spot' < L *macula*; but his explanation of the *-r-* in *amarscled* as due to blending of OF *mascle* with OF *merler* < OF *mesler* 'mix' is hazardous and highly improbable. The interpretation 'bemused'; (?) 'enchanted' is clinched by the fact (not mentioned in the original formulation of it in *E.G.S.* ii (1948–9), 64–67) that popular conceptions of the Man in the Moon express a belief in the power of the moon to affect human beings balefully (see Bächtold-Stäubli, loc. cit.).

O

MS.: Merton College (Oxford), 248.

Editions: Hitherto unpublished.

P

MS.: Merton College (Oxford), 248.

Editions: Hitherto unpublished.

---

1. *Ianekyn*: this name, with the MDu diminutive suffix *-kijn*, as in *Wilekin* VI. 43, occurs in another dance-refrain, in MS. Rawlinson 913, the text of which is only partly legible:

> Al gold Ionet is þin her
> [al gold] Ionet is þin her
> þin Iankyn   Iankyn leman
>   (ed. W. Heuser, *Anglia*, xxx (1907), 176).

A fuller text (read under an ultraviolet lamp) is offered by P. Dronke, *N. & Q.* ccvi (1961), 246.

Q

MS.: Worcester Cathedral Chapter Library F. 64.

Editions: J. K. Floyer and S. G. Hamilton, *Catalogue of the Manuscripts in the Chapter Library of Worcester Cathedral* (Worcestershire Historical Society 1906), pp. 30–31.

    B. Dickins, 'Two Worcester Fragments of Middle English Secular Lyric', *L.S.E.* iv (1935), 44–46.

R

MS.: Worcester Cathedral Chapter Library Q. 50.

Edition: B. Dickins, op. cit.

1–3. The metrical structure here (and therefore in the piece as a whole) is not clear. The absence of rhyme within the three lines points to corruption or the loss of a line or two (before or after ll. 1–2). See C. Sisam, *N. & Q.* ccx (1965), 245–6.

S

MS.: Arch. Selden supra 74, Bodleian Library.

Edition: Carleton Brown, op. cit., p. 1.

Studies: S. Manning *M.L.N.* lxxiv (1959), 578–81; *The Explicator*, iv. 7, xi. 25.

This quatrain is found at the end of a passage on the sorrows of the Virgin in St. Edmund of Abingdon's *Speculum Ecclesie* (ed. Helen P. Forshaw (1973), p. 73; for the French version, made *c.* 1240, see M. Dominica Legge, *Anglo-Norman in the Cloisters* (1950), pp. 91 ff.). It follows a version of *Cant.* i. 5, a verse traditionally applied to the Virgin and alluded to in 2 (cf. *quia sol decoloravit me*). Carleton Brown (op. cit., p. 166) suggests that the quatrain was written by Archbishop Edmund himself, but this is doubtful. It is remarkable for its compression of feeling and allusion: the reference to the eclipse of the sun suggests both the figure of Christ as *sol justitiae* and the sorrow of the natural world at the death of its creator. Cf. Donne, *Good Friday*, l. 11.

In the Selden MS. the quatrain is introduced thus:

Cele reson dit ele en le chaunson de amor. Ne vous ameruey-

lez si ie suy brunecte e haule qar le solayl me ad tote des-
coloures e pur ceo dit vn engleis en tel manere de pite. . .

1. *Nou*: for *nou* as a conjunction, see C. T. Onions, *M.Æ.*
xvii (1948), 32–33.

T

MS.: Egerton 613, British Museum.

Edition: Carleton Brown, op. cit., p. 26 (for stanza form see
p. 178).

---

2. The comparison (like that of 29) is traditional. Cf.

Stella maris comprobans
Claritatis radiis

(Mone, Lateinische Hymnen des Mittelalters, no. 586)

or the well-known hymn *Ave Maris Stella*.

4. *parens et puella*: a traditional (and common) paradox.

20. The antithesis of Eva and the Ave of Gabriel at the An-
nunciation is common. Cf. the *Ave Maris Stella*:

Sumens illud Ave
Gabrielus ore,
Funda nos in pace,
Mutans Evae nomen.

35. *es*: the MS. suggests that the scribe treated a Northern *es*
as a Latin verb connected with *effecta*; but a version of the
poem in MS. Trinity Coll. Camb. 323 reads *ec*.

U

MS.: Digby 86, Bodleian Library (cf. V and VI above).

Edition: Carleton Brown, op. cit., p. 91.

The lyric shows the same intensity of personal feeling that
receives fuller expression in the *Iesu dulcis memoria*. For a later,
expanded version, see Carleton Brown, *Religious Lyrics of the
Fourteenth Century*, no. 7.

V

MS.: Trinity College, Cambridge, 323.

Edition: Carleton Brown, op. cit., p. 55

For the metre, see Carleton Brown, op. cit., p. 192. Ll. 3–4 reappear as the opening and conclusion of the fifteenth-century song, *I syng of a m[a]yden þat is makeles* (MS. Sloane 2593, printed by Carleton Brown, *Religious Lyrics of the Fifteenth Century*, no. 81).

W

MS.: Royal 2 F viii, British Museum.

Edition: Carleton Brown, op. cit., p. 120.

A version differing in a few phrases is found in MS. Harley 2253, from which 48–50 are supplied here. For the conception of Christ as the 'lover' (*lefman*) of the sinner, see the note on XVIII. 474 ff.

X

MS.: Digby 2, Bodleian Library.

Edition: Carleton Brown, op. cit., p. 126.

MS. Digby 2 is a small book containing two other English lyrics. It includes a table dated 1282 and a Kalendarium in which St. Francis is specially mentioned (under 4 October), and possibly came from the library of the Grey Friars in Oxford (Carleton Brown, op. cit., pp. xxvii–xxviii). For the part played by the Franciscans in the development of the medieval English religious lyric, see R. H. Robbins, 'The Authors of the Middle English Religious Lyrics', *J.E.G.P.* xxxix (1940), 230 and 'The Earliest Carols and the Franciscans', *M.L.N.* liii (1938), 239 and R. L. Greene, *The Early English Carols* (Oxford 1935), pp. cxxi–cxxxii, and *A Selection of English Carols* (Oxford 1962), pp. 12 ff.

Y

MS.: Trinity College, Cambridge, 323.

Edition: Carleton Brown, op. cit., p. 54.

In the MS. the English verse is prefaced by its Latin original:

> Cum sit gleba tibi turris
> Tuus puteus conclauis.
> Pellis et guttur album
> Erit cibus vermium.

Quid habent tunc de proprio
Hii monarchie lucro?

IX

MS.: Harley 913, British Museum.

Editions: E. Mätzner, *Altenglische Sprachproben*, I. i. 147 ff.

    W. Heuser, *Die Kildare-Gedichte* (Bonner Beiträge zur Anglistik xiv, 1904), pp. 141–50.

    R. H. Robbins, *Historical Poems of the XIVth and XVth Centuries* (1959), pp. 121 ff.

Analogues: V. Väänänen, 'Le "fabliau" de Cocagne', *Neuphilologische Mitteilungen*, xlviii (1947), 3–36. (Includes the text of both the OF and the MDu piece, and a good summary discussion of the conception of *Cokaygne*.)

Studies: Heuser, op. cit., pp. 141–5.

    J. Poeschel, 'Das Märchen vom Schlaraffenlande', Paul and Braune's *Beiträge zur Geschichte der deutschen Sprache und Literatur*, V (1878), 389–427.

    A. Graf, *Miti, Leggende, e Superstizioni del Medio Evo* (1925), pp. 169–75.

    H. R. Patch, *The Other World* (1950), pp. 7–22, 134–74.

Language

1. OE *ȳ* has been unrounded, since it rhymes on *ī* in *lifte* n. 124: *swifte*.

2. OE *ēo* has been monophthonged to tense *ē*, since it rhymes on OF tense *e* in *se* 106: *plente, stere* 154: *riuer*, &c.

3. OE *ĕ+g* rhymes on OE *ǽ+g* in *plai* 122: *dai*.

4. The 3 pres. pl. indic. evidently ended in -*eþ*. The rhyme of *fleeþ* pl. 134: *iseeþ* sg. is admittedly compatible with original (i.e. author's) forms in -*es* in both. But as a plural ending this latter would be specifically Northern; and in the absence of other Northern features, these two words are best interpreted as being the original forms.

5. -*es* has evidently been adopted as the plural ending of all classes of noun, since it occurs in the old strong fem. *halles* 53 (OE *healle* n.a. pl.): *wallès*. The apparently aberrant *hode* 126: *mode* sg. might be a scribal patching of a rhyme *hodes*: *mode*, of a type (-*e*: -*e*+consonant) which was admissible in ME (see *Kyng Alisaunder*, ii. 149–50 n.).

Vocabulary

Fale 95 (: *niȝtingale*) is, so far as is known, otherwise restricted to documents of SW origin.

Provenance

An unusual point which emerges from the admittedly scanty evidence of the rhymes is that the language fails to conform to any single local type of ME: 2 and 3, which are otherwise EMidl/Northern, conflict with 4, which is Southern and southern WMidl. The varied evidence for Irish origin both of the MS. and of several pieces in it is probably sufficient to localize *The Land of Cokaygne* in Ireland. Provenance in an area cut off from the ME of England might be the sort of special factor that would account for a conjunction of linguistic features which does not match any normal type of ME.

—————

4. See XIV. 244 n.

14. *Hely and Enok*: on their association with the Earthly Paradise, see M. M. Lascelles, 'Alexander and the Earthly Paradise in Mediæval English Writings', *M.Æ.* v (1936), especially pp. 32–46, 100–3. They were to be overcome and slain by Antichrist, and after three days would be resurrected. See K. Strecker, *Moralisch-Satirische Gedichte Walters von Chatillon* (1929), p. 137. 21 and 145. 28; Douglas Hyde, 'Mediaeval Account of Antichrist', in *Medieval Studies in Memory of Gertrude Schoepperle Loomis* (1927), pp. 391–8. On the coming of Antichrist, and also on Enoch and Elias, see Adso, *De ortu et tempore Antichristi*, ed. E. Sackur, *Sibyllinische Texte und Forschungen* (1898), p. 112.

20. *russin*: this (= Ir. *ruisin*), and *corrin* (= Ir. *cuirin*) in the *Satire* in the same MS. (Heuser, *Kildare-Gedichte*, p. 155. 8, l. 1), corroborate the evidence for the Irish origin of several of the poems in this MS. See the Introduction to our text here.

26–27 and **30.** These two points also occur in immediate succession in an account of the Earthly Paradise in the *De iudicio domini* (*P.L.* ii. 1095):

> Nox ibi nulla, suas defendunt astra tenebras;
> Iraeque insidiaeque absunt . . . .

The darkness of night has likewise no place in Lucian's Isle of the Blest: οὐ μὴν οὐδὲ νὺξ παρ' αὐτοῖς γίνεται, οὐδὲ ἡμέρα πάνυ λαμπρά—'among them there is neither night nor altogether brilliant daylight' (*A True Story* ii. 12).

The second point is matched in the MDu analogue (ed. Väänänen, op. cit., p. 35) 70: *draecht men hat noch nijt.*

31–35, 37–38, 40. These advantages are not established elements in accounts of any type of Paradise.

45–46. Patch (*The Other World*, pp. 13–14) cites examples of four rivers of honey, milk, oil, and wine from the Slavonic *Book of the Secrets of Enoch* (ed. R. H. Charles, 1896), viii. 5 ff. In Lucian's Isle of the Blest there are springs of water, honey, myrrh, milk, and wine (*A True Story*, 11, 13). In the *Visio Sancti Pauli*, the four rivers of the Earthly Paradise are represented in similar terms: Phison is a river of honey, Euphrates of milk, Geon of oil, Tigris of wine (M. R. James, *Apocrypha Anecdota* (1893), § 23, in *Texts and Studies*, ed. J. A. Robinson, ii. 3, pp. 1–42). But these four rivers in *The Land of Cokaygne* are historically, at least, distinct from the four rivers of 83 ff.: the context here shows that they derive from a Lucianesque Utopia.

51–52. See 164 n.

54–60. For the same device, worked out with different details, in the OF version see Väänänen, op. cit., p. 22, ll. 31–38, and in the MDu ibid., pp. 33–34, ll. 22–25, 31–40.

69. *bas*: this emendation of Mätzner's (*Altenglische Sprachproben*, I. i. 150) is made certain here by the application of the word to pillars in a contextual association with 'capitals'. For both these, cf. *The Pilgrimage of the Soul*, iv. 38. 82 a; for the former, cf. *The Destruction of Troy* 1652 and *The Buke of John Maundeuill* (ed. G. F. Warner, Roxburghe Club 1889), p. 47, l. 9. In this last example, *þe base of þe piler* is represented in the OF version (ibid., l. 34) by *le pie de la columpne.*

71–100. Among the components of this passage, all but the aromatic root, shoots, blossom, bark, and fruit of the tree are stock elements of the innumerable descriptions of Paradise in medieval (especially Latin) literature. When only one tree is mentioned in such accounts, it is normally the tree of life (Gen. ii. 9), as in Theodulfus' *De Paradiso* (*c.* 800):

> Arbor in immensum spaciatur nomine vitae
> Helisii medio e vertice surgit eri

(ed. E. Duemmler, *Poetae Latini aevi Carolini, i* (1880–1), 573).

The tree here derives from the latter, though it has been conflated with the herbs which were properly distinct from it, as they are in Bernardus Sylvestris, *De Mundi Universitate*, I. iii. 323–6 (ed. Barach and Wrobel):

> Surgit ea *gingiber* humo surgitque *galanga*
> Longior, et socio baccare dulce *thymum.*
> Perpetui quem floris honor commendat *acanthus*
> Grataque conficiens unguina *nardus* olet.

The flowers that never fade; the four rivers (see 83 n.); the birds; and the precious stones, are all stereotyped elements of Paradise, as may be gathered from the comprehensive material in Patch, op. cit. (see Index, s.v. Tree of Life, &c.). The precious stones were originally and properly situated in the river-beds, as in Godfrey of Viterbo's *Pantheon*, part i:

> Civibus angelicis meruit locus ille beari,
> Fluminibus variis varia statione rigari
>   *Gemmas* mirificas *alveus* ille *parit.*
> Flumina bis bina Paradisus habere notatur;
> Tigris et Euphrates Phisonque Gehonque vocatur,
>   *Aurum cum gemmis* fluminis unda vehit
>   (ed. Pistorius and Struve, *Germanicorum Scriptores*, ii
>   (1726), 29).

83. *.iiij. willis*: the four rivers of Paradise (see 45–46 n. and 71–100 n.).

87. *þai*: used also (in the same MS.) in *Sarmun* 186 and *Song on the Times* 4. 2 and 16. 7, and thus an authentic form here.

The clue to the meaning of this line likewise is to be found in one of the recurrent details in descriptions of the Earthly Paradise:

(*a*) Quattuor inde *rigant* partitas flumina terras
           (Tertullian, *De Judicio Domini*, ch. viii)

(b) Fægrum flodwylmum *foldan leccaþ*
wæter wynsumu of þæs wuda midle . . .
. . . . . *bearo ealne* geondfarað

(*The Phoenix*, 64–67)

(loosely rendering:
fons . . . dulcibus uber aquis . . . *inrigat omne nemus*)

(c) Physon, Gyon, Tygris, Effrates
Die meenich lant ende meneghe stat
Verversschen ende *maken nat*

(Jan Deckers, *Der leken spieghel*, 1. i, ch. 21)

It reappears in XIV. 174–82, below (*þis four mas al þis erth
wate*), just as in the OIcel version of Seth's journey (*þessar
fjórar ár fylla vatni heim allan*).[1]

The link of *ealne*, *al*, and *allan* in three of these examples with
al (*þe molde*) 87 suggests that *stremis* is a verb, here meaning
'overflow with moisture (intrans.), be drenched' (cf. *O.E.D.*
s.v. 5). *Molde* is not recorded in the sense 'gravel; river-bed';
88 therefore cannot be the object of *stremis*, and must be a
resumption of 83–86 (i.e. as a delayed additional subject of *beþ*
83). *Molde* here is more likely to mean 'earth, ground (in that
spot)' than 'the earth (as the habitation of men)'; the other
passages quoted above vary on this point.

90. *astiune*: probably not (as it is not recorded elsewhere)
an authentic form, but a corruption, of *astrium* (a rare word in
English, but recorded in AN). See Isidore of Seville, *Etymologiae* (ed. W. M. Lindsay), XVI. xiii. 7, whose etymological analysis happens to be correct (Gk. ἀστέριος 'starry').

102–10. Cf. the MDu analogue 72–75; and the OF 39–42:

Par les rues vont rostissant
Les crasses oies et tornant
Tout par eles, et tout ades
Les siut la blanche aillie apres.

145. *collacione*: by etymology 'a bringing together'; in the
language of the monastic life, a gathering of the monks to hear
a reading before Compline, at which a drink was taken, and
on certain days a light meal. In this 'consociation' the word

[1] Ed. Th. Möbius, *Analecta Norrœna* (1877), p. 205, l. 20.

was naturally transferred to the meal itself, and then passed into the general vocabulary in that sense.

147–8. See 164 n.

160. This surprising power of flight is presumably due to an equation of the monks of Cokaygne with angels in Paradise.

164. *þe mochil grei abbei*: Heuser's seductive argument identifying this with the Franciscan foundation attested for this period in Kildare and named Gray Abbey (op. cit., pp. 14–15 and 142) depends on the assumptions that (i) the 'white' and 'grey' monks of 52 are Carmelites and Franciscans respectively, and (ii) the sentence there (despite the singular *abbei*) therefore refers to two abbeys. But it is weakened by the following facts: (*a*) the piece consistently speaks of 'monks' and never of 'friars' (as would be appropriate for Carmelites and Franciscans), (*b*) the two nouns are strictly distinguished in English at this time, and (*c*) the Cistercians were known both as 'white' and as 'grey' monks in English *c.* 1300 (*O.E.D. grey* a. 2). Thus 52 must surely refer to Cistercians, and 51 to one abbey; Heuser himself mentions the interesting fact (p. 142) that the only other 'Gray Abbey' in Ireland at this time was a Cistercian foundation in Co. Down.

It follows that Heuser's identification of the *nunnerie* of 148 with the nunnery founded by St. Brigid at Kildare, which was part of an ancient abbey also housing Carmelites and Franciscans (op. cit., pp. 15 and 142), is unlikely to be valid.

X

MS.: Cotton Caligula A ix, British Museum.

Editions: F. Madden, *Layamon's Brut* (London 1847) [both MSS.].

    J. Hall, *Layamon's Brut* (Oxford 1924): v. pp. 43–45, for part of the extract printed here.

    G. L. Brook and R. F. Leslie, E.E.T.S. 250 (1961) [Vol. I of text].

    G. L. Brook, *Selections from Laȝamon's Brut* (1963); see pp. 109–18 for the extract printed here.

Source: Wace's *Le Roman de Brut*, ed. I. Arnold (Société des Anciens Textes Français, Paris 1938–40).

Studies: J. S. P. Tatlock, 'Epic Formulas, especially in Laȝa-
    mon', *PMLA* xxxviii (1923), 494–529.
Id., 'Laȝamon's Poetic Style and its Relations', *Manly
    Anniversary Studies* (Chicago 1923), pp. 3–11.
Id., *The Legendary History of Britain* (Berkeley 1950), c. xxi.
H. C. Wyld, 'Studies in the Diction of Laȝamon's *Brut*',
    Language, vi (1930), 1–24, ix (1933), 47–71, 171–91, x
    (1934), 149–201, xiii (1937), 29–59.
Id., 'Laȝamon as an English Poet', *R.E.S.* vi (1930), 1–30.
F. L. Gillespy, *Layamon's Brut* (University of California
    Publications in Modern Philology, iii (1916), 361–510).
D. Everett, 'Laȝamon and the Earliest Middle English
    Alliterative Verse', *Essays on Middle English Literature*
    (Oxford 1955), pp. 28–45.
R. S. Loomis, 'Laȝamon's *Brut*', *Arthurian Literature in the
    Middle Ages* (Oxford 1959), pp. 104–11.
H. S. Davies, 'Laȝamon's Similes', *R.E.S.* N.S. xi. (1960),
    129–42.
W. J. Keith, 'Laȝamon's *Brut . . .*' *M.Æ.* xxix (1960), 161–72.
C. S. Lewis, Introduction to Brook's *Selections* (see above).
E. G. Stanley, 'Laȝamon's Antiquarian Sentiments', *M.Æ.*
    xxxviii (1969), 23–37.

Language

Since Laȝamon does not regularly use exact rhymes, and
the MS. is not an autograph, it is not possible to establish
the features of his language, but only to analyse the language
of the MS. Moreover, the ambiguous use of the graph *æ* for
the reflexes both of OE *ǽ* and of OE *ě* (as well as that of OE
ea, as in *ærmès*, and of *ǽ²*, as in *sæ*) prevents valid conclusions
at certain points (see e.g. 7). The language of the Caligula
MS. is, however, surprisingly consistent; it is in essentials much
like one known homogeneous form of written ME; and it
may preserve many of the main features of Laȝamon's English.

  1. The reflex of Gmc *ă* (*a*) when not followed in OE by a back
     vowel in the next syllable is *a*, in *aðele* 206, *bistal* 216, &c.,
     but is also spelt (traditionally) *æ* in *bæd* 136, *hæfde* 122, *hæleðe*
     221, &c.; (*b*) before a single nasal is *o* in e.g. (*a*)*gon* 34, 35.
  2. The reflexes of OE *ȳ* are shown by the graph *u* to be still
     rounded vowels (*cunne* 98, *dude* 211; *fur* 277), except
     when *ȳ* was unrounded in OE before a palatal consonant
     (*Drihte* 56, *kine-* 311, *kinge* 299).

3. OE *ā* has not been rounded to slack *ō*: *agan* 49, *aras* 8, *bat* 314, *wat* 49.

4. The reflexes of OE *ĕo* are spelt *eo*, probably with value [ø(ː)]: *heorte* 301, *leofe* 72.

5. The reflex of prim. OE *ǣ+ld* derives from the unbroken and retracted OE type: *alde* 227, *aqualde* 227, *halden* 62.

6. The evidence of forms which must display either smoothing or the absence of it in OE is ambiguous: *seoc* 9, 45, *Sexlond(e)* 134, 138, *iseh* 22, beside *isæh* 41, *isah* 36.

7. The product of *i*-mutation of Gmc *ā* before *l*-groups is (*a*) *a* in *auallen* 207, *fallen* 63; (*b*) *æ* in *ælder* 271.

8. The sporadic OE unrounding of *ŏ* after a labial consonant is attested in *marʒen* 117, 118.

9. In the plural of nouns, (*a*) *-en* has been adopted as the ending of the nom. and acc. of many words that were not of the OE weak declension: *laʒen* 305, *scipen* 122, *wunden* 291; (*b*) *-en* (< the OE dat. pl. *-an*) is the ending of the prepositional case, even in nouns with *-es* in the nom. and acc.: *cnihten* 240 (acc. *cnihtes* 214), *daʒen* 306, *helmen* 276, *londen* 54, *spellen* 87 (acc. *spelles* 92).

10. The old inflexions of the strong adjective declension and the pronouns are well preserved in:

   (*a*) the dat. sg. fem. *ælchere* 253, *aʒere* 58, *muchelere* 312.

   (*b*) the pronoun 'that' (used also as def. article):

	Masc.	*Fem.*
Acc.	*þen(e)*	
Gen.		*þere*
Dat.	*þan*	*þere*
Prep.	*þan*	*þere*

   (*c*) the nom. sg. fem. *heo* 243, 245; acc. sg. fem. *heo* 31; nom. pl. *heo* 33.

   (*d*) the dual nom. *wit* 43.

11. The 3 pres. sg. indic. ends in *-eð*: *falleð* 264, *hafeð* 73, *rixleoð* 54.

12. The 3 pres. pl. ends in *-eð* (*habbeoð* 305), and therefore likewise the imper. pl. (*sitteð* 91).

13. All verbs of the OE weak class II preserve the *-i-* element: *biuien* 47, *cleopien* 214, *lokieþ* 322, *quakien* 46.

Provenance

8 and 10 (*c*) are specifically Western, and as a whole the language is close to that of *Ancrene Wisse* and *Sawles Warde* (XVIII and XIX); the only notable differences are 1 (*a*) and 6. The SE is excluded by 1, 2, 5, and 7; the EMidl by 2, 9 (*a*), 12, 13; the North by 2, 9 (*a*), 13; and 5 and 7 are decisively 'non-Saxon' in terms of OE antecedents. In fact, the language of the MS. is that of an area in or near the WMidl.

[*The passage follows an account of Arthur's victories in Burgundy over the Roman Emperor Lucius; he had left Modred and Guenevere in charge of Britain*]

ll. 1–109 are, as Madden said, 'one of the most striking instances of amplification in the whole poem'. Wace covers the news of Modred's treason, Arthur's division of his army, and his decision to return to Britain, in 34 lines. Other noteworthy additions to or expansions of Wace are 125–36, 155–9, 168–70, 208–15, 232–8, 268–72, 291–5.

1. com . . . riden: in such combinations *com* is practically an auxiliary verb: cf. *com liðen* 37.

6. swa: 'in such a way that' ('with such reserve on the part of the young knight that': Hall). Otho MS.: *ac no weis he. . .*

10. The question appears to be part of courtly custom: cf. *Beowulf* 1319–20, where Beowulf 'frægn gif him [Hroþgar] wære æfter neodlaðum niht getæse'.

13 ff. The dream recalls the Icelandic belief that the 'undead' could *ríða húsum* ('ride on the housetop'); cf. *Eyrbyggjasaga*, c. 34 and the story of Glám in *Grettissaga*, c. 78 and c. 83. Tatlock (p. 491 n. 24) thinks that it is suggested by his earlier dream before his Roman campaign (Madden III. 13–16) where Laȝamon is following Wace or Geoffrey of Monmouth.

17. Walwain. For this form of the Celtic name Gawain cf. William of Malmesbury's *Walwen* and Geoffrey of Monmouth's *Walwanus* (Cambridge MS.)

[See also R. S. Loomis, *Wales and the Arthurian Legend* (1956), pp. 208–9, and *Sir Gawain and the Green Knight*, ed. Tolkien and Gordon, p. 83. The form perhaps survives as *Walwyn* as late as the seventeenth century. For a criticism of the usual etymology see *Oxford Dictionary of Christian Names*, s.v.]

19. *wi-ax*: the compound is found only in Laȝamon.

30. *deore mine sweorede*: the order adj.+possv. is common in Laȝamon: cf. 119.

38. *Deoren*: if treated as a gen. pl. requires to be followed by a superlative: hence Hall reads *alre hendest þe*.

40. *hire*: reflexive dat., frequent with verbs of motion.

45. Hall emends to: *and weri and of sorȝen seoc*.

47. Hall, evidently regarding *fur* as a form of 'fire', used erroneously, emends to *forburne*.

53. *mid sorȝen arecchen*: 'give a sinister meaning to'.

56. *swa nulle hit ure Drihte*: 'may the Lord not so will it' = 'which God forbid'.

59. *to Rome þohtest*: 'didst decide (*or* plan) to go to Rome'.

66. *longe bið æuere*: cf. *swa long swa beoð auere, Brut* 22614, *longe bið auere, na iseo ȝe me eft næuere*, 32160–1. The phrase can hardly be translated literally; here it has a strongly intensive effect (and is perhaps a reduced form of the phrase in 22614). The proverbial 'Never is a long day [or word]' has a different force. For the consuetudinal use of *bið* cf. XIX. 26 and n.

70. 'She will refuse to take such a course for the sake of any man in the whole world'.

76. Hall emends to *cumen from Rome æuere*.

79. *min hafued beo to wedde*: 'let my head be for a pledge' = 'on my life'.

95. Burning at the stake as a punishment (for *inter alia* petty treason) was inflicted on women rather than men: cf. Pollock and Maitland, *History of English Law*, ii. 511, and Malory, *Morte D'Arthur*, xx (*Works*, ed. Vinaver (1947), p. 1176).

92. *Howel*. Geoffrey of Monmouth (*Historia Brittonum* ix. 2) described him as Arthur's nephew and king of Brittany, and as sent by Arthur at the present juncture to restore peace in the Gaulish regions.

107. *domes waldend*: cf. OE *eorðan/engla waldend* (also of God) and *worldes wealdent* in texts of the *Ancrene Wisse* group.

114. *a*: Madden proposed to emend to *heo*; but *beoð* is plural, and *a* either a miswriting or a genuine variant of *ha* (pl.): so translate: 'I shall (*or* may I) never be happy while they are alive and until I have avenged my uncle in the most fitting way.'

121. *Whitsond*: Wissant (Wace, *Witsant*, 13049). Geoffrey gives no details of the journey until he describes the battle on Arthur's arrival at Richborough haven. Medieval sailing ships could not go much to windward.

133. *taken an*: Laȝamon is the first to use this expression in the sense 'act, proceed': later found in *Piers Plowman* A. III. 76, and elsewhere. Cf. the development of *biginne*, V 107 n.

137. *Childriche*: an old enemy of Arthur, whose expulsion from Britain Laȝamon has vividly described in 20541–905.

142. Geoffrey (xi. 1) followed by Wace (13063) adds that Modred also promised him 'whatsoever Horsus and Hengist had possessed in Kent'.

146. 60,000 is Wace's estimate of the combined forces. Geoffrey says 800,000.

159. *Romerel* (Romenel in Wace) = Romney; see R. Blenner-Hassett, *A Study of the Place-Names in Lawman's Brut* (1950), s.v. *Romelan*. Geoffrey says that Arthur landed *in Rutupi portum* (= Richborough), which Wace probably did not identify with a particular port. The Welsh text (see Griscom's ed. of Geoffrey, p. 199) refers to Southampton, which makes the flight to Winchester (Geoffrey does not mention London) feasible. Some MSS. of Wace read *Sandwiz*.

Laȝamon's account of the battle resembles Geoffrey's rather than Wace's: Wace says that though Modred fiercely opposed the landing, his forces fled as soon as Arthur reached the shore, being unaccustomed to warfare.

176. *Angel*: King of Scotland. The form in Wace is *Angusel*, and in Geoffrey *Anguselus*.

201. *freo laȝe*: there is no mention of this promise of franchise in Geoffrey or Wace.

231. The prediction is part of Merlin's long prophecy as recorded by Geoffrey (vii. 3, 4): the relevant section begins: 'Hither, Wales, and bringing Cornwall at thy side, say to Winchester: "The earth shall swallow thee. Bring the see of the shepherd hither where ships come to haven and let the rest of the members follow the head. For the day is at hand wherein thy citizens shall perish for thy crimes of perjury. Woe to the perjured race for because of them shall the renowned city fall into ruin".' This is not in Wace nor in any other French text known to Laȝamon.

239. *Karliun*: Caerleon on Usk. The Roman remains were still impressive in the twelfth century (see Giraldus Cambrensis, *Opera* (1886) vi. 55), and so easily suggested that the town had a place in the Arthurian story.

247 ff. Geoffrey does not mention this further summons to Modred's allies; Wace (13226–8) says that he sent for 'pagans, Christians, Irish, Norwegians, Saxons and Danes'.

264. The simile is Laȝamon's.

267. *þer weore monie uæie*: an OE poetic formula found in *Andreas* 1532.

268. *Uppen þere Tambre* (MS. *Tanbre*). In the earliest source (*Annales Cambriae*) the name is given as *Camlann*; hence Geoffrey's *Cambla*, *Cablanus*, by which he evidently intended the R. Camel (cf. 276). Wace (13253) has 'Juste Camble/Cambre/Tambre', *c-* and *t-* being easily confused in medieval script. For further discussion see E. Faral, *La Légende arthurienne*, ii. 295, n. 2, and A. L. Brown, *Folklore* lxxii (1961), 612 ff.

273. *hit*: 'þe folk', 'army, troop', as at 120.

288. *borde*: Laȝamon's name for the round table, the making of which he has described earlier.

295. *tweien*: the detail is Laȝamon's, but is found also in the prose *Mort Arthur* and in Malory (xxi. 4). A Welsh triad (v. *Trioedd Ynys Prydein*, ed. Rachel Bromwich, Cardiff, 1961, pp. xcii, 161) names three survivors.

298. *Cador* of Cornwall figures in earlier battles with the Saxons and the Romans.

307. *Avalun*: *Insula Avallonis* in Geoffrey and in *Draco Nor-mannicus* (cf. Tatlock, p. 78); *insula pomorum* in Geoffrey's metrical *Vita Merlini* (908): a translation depending on the derivation of the word from Welsh *Afalxon* (apples) or *Afallon* (apple-trees).

308 ff. The story of the barge is not found in Geoffrey or Wace. Later OF texts (the *Didot Perceval* and the Vulgate *Mort Artu*) ascribe Arthur's healing in Avalon to his sister Morgan (le Fay), of whose name 'Argante' is perhaps a corruption. Giraldus Cambrensis in his *Speculum Ecclesie* (*c*. 1216) states that Morgan brought the king's body to Avalon, and the metrical *Vita Merlini* describes her as learned in the virtues of all herbs. For the relevant passages see E. K. Chambers, *Arthur of Britain* (1927), pp. 252, 272, and *R.E.S.* x (1934), 81. In the OIr *Táin bo Fráic* women carry the wounded hero into a fairy hill, and in the *Táin bo Cuailnge* fairy plants and herbs are brought for Cuchulain's healing by his supernatural father (T. P. Cross, *Manly Anniversary Studies* (1929), pp. 289 f.). [For a hitherto unknown story of Arthur's departure see N. R. Ker, *Medieval Manuscripts in British Libraries*, i (1969), pp. 435–7.]

323 ff. Cf. Wace, 13282–7:

> Maistre Wace, ki fist cest livre,
> Ne volt plus dire de sa fin
> Qu'en dist li prophetes Merlin;
> Merlin dist d'Arthur, si ot dreit,
> Que sa mort dutuse serreit.
> Li prophetes dist verité

—following Geoffrey (vii. 3) who simply attributes to Merlin (whom he is the first to name) the prophecy 'tremebit Romulea domus saevitiam ipsius et exitus ejus dubius erit'. Since Arthur is traditionally associated with the *British* (cf. the interpolation in William of Malmesbury, cit. *M.Æ.* xii (1943), 28 n. 4) Tatlock (p. 504) sees in 327 an allusion to Arthur of Brittany (*ob.* 1203)— so named to please his Breton subjects—whom Richard I declared to be his heir in default of any children of his own.

For the association of Merlin (Myrddin) with such prophecies see Parry, *History of Welsh Literature* (trans. I. Bell, 1955), pp. 26 ff., and *Speculum*, ix (1934), 136–8.

XI

MS.: Cotton Caligula A. xi, British Museum.

Edition: W. A. Wright, *The Metrical Chronicle of Robert of Gloucester* (Rolls Series, 1887).

Studies: J. H. P. Pafford, 'University of London Library MS. 278, Robert of Gloucester's Chronicle' in *Studies presented to Sir Hilary Jenkinson* (1957), pp. 308–19.

Language

1. The reflex of OE ǽ (OKt, WM ĕ) rhymes on [a] in *was* 138: *solas*.
2. OE *ā* has been rounded to slack *ō* in (*al*)*so* 3, 79, 87: *ido*, 77: *þerto*.
3. The reflex of OE *ǽ²* when shortened rhymes on the reflex of OE ǽ (OKt WM ĕ) in *ladde* 48, 64: *hadde*, and must therefore have been [a] (see 1).
4. The past part. of strong verbs (*a*) has no -*n* in *go* 58: *mo*, *ido* 80, 88: *also*, 96: *þerto*; (*b*) has a metrically essential *i*- in *ido* 96: *þerto*.

Provenance

Must be SW, since the North is excluded by 2; the WMidl by 1, and the SE by 1 and 3; and the EMidl by 4 (*a*) and (*b*) in combination.

The first part of the passage describes the rising in 1262–3 of those barons who supported Simon de Montfort against Henry III's French relatives and other supporters: F. M. Powicke, *The Thirteenth Century*, c. v, and E. F. Jacob, *Oxford Studies in Social and Legal History*, viii (1925), p. 74. The account resembles that in the *Calendar of Patent Rolls, 1258–66*, p. 220 (6 July 1262):

Whereas certain contentions had arisen between the king and certain of his barons, and they without the king's assent

and of their own will committed certain counties to certain
persons who bare themselves as sheriffs thereof, and William
de Tracy on behalf of the barons, came to the county of
Gloucester where Matthias Bezill was holding the shrievalty
of that county, as was customary, wishing to expel him from
the said office; the said Matthias took the said William as a
transgressor of the king's mandates and an invader of the
king's right, and caused him to be kept in prison, until he
should receive further orders from the king; the king, therefore, avowing this deed, wills and orders that the said Matthias
be saved harmless in this behalf.

3. *Sire Maci de Besile*: elsewhere called Sire Mathi, or Matthew,
de Besilles.

7. *Sir William Traci*: presumably kin to the William Traci who
was one of the murderers of St. Thomas Becket.

25. *Sir Roger*: of Clifford on the Wye.
  Sir Ion Giffard: his castle, at Brimpsfield (see 82) stood on the
road between Gloucester and Cirencester. On his career see
Helen Cam, *Liberties and Communities in Medieval England*
(Oxford 1944), pp. 138–41. (In December 1263 Clifford and
he were made wardens of Gloucester, Worcester, and Hereford.)
In 1283 he helped to establish at Oxford a small house under the
ægis of St. Peter's Abbey, Gloucester, which later became
Gloucester College (Snappe's *Formulary*, ed. H. E. Salter (1923),
p. 383; Knowles, *Religious Orders*, i. 26–27).

32. *is sone* (dat.) i.e. the Lord Edward, the future Edward I.

52. *Sir Peris*: Peter of Aigueblanche was a 'turbulent and ambitious Savoyard' who had been made Bishop of Hereford by
Court favour in 1240; it was by his advice that all church
preferments had been given to foreigners. He himself knew
no English, cf. 60–61.

57. *Sir Tomas Torbeuille*: the Turbevilles of Coety were a
prominent Marcher family. Thomas later became a notorious
traitor.

59. *churche peis*: protection from violence within the precincts
of a church; the *cyric-griþ* of OE law.

66. *Erdesleye*: Eardisley (W. Herefordshire). At this date the castle was held by Walter de Baskerville (F. M. Powicke, *Henry III and the Lord Edward* (Oxford 1947), p. 538 n.).

72. *Sir Robert Walrond*: Walerand was one of Henry's most trusted counsellors, and at this time castellan of Bristol, Marlborough, and Ludgershall.

Sir Ion Mauncel: the king's chaplain, and provost of Beverley, has been described as 'the Wolsey of the thirteenth century'. He organized the opposition to Earl Simon in France.

75. *Sir Roger þe Mortimer* (1231 ?–82): Lord of Wigmore, &c. In December 1263 he and four other leading Marchers were made military wardens of Shropshire and Staffs.

77. Sir James of Audley had been a member of the baronial party since 1258 when he attached his seal to the famous letter to the Pope defending the confederates' actions. By the 'counsel of the nobles', Hamo l'estrange succeeded him as sheriff of Salop and Staffs. in August 1263 (*C.P.R.*, p. 272).

78. *Roger of Leibourne*: his career as leader of the young Marcher barons is outlined by Powicke, op. cit., p. 436. Like Clifford, Bassingburn, and Hamo Lestrange, he had been associated with Edward as early as 1259.

91. *Quedesle*: Quedgeley, a small parish two miles south of Gloucester. Arderne (94) is presumably the Forest of Arden (Warw.).

111. *Ion de Balun*: of Marcle (Heref.).

123. *Sir Simondes sone de Monfort*: for the construction cf. XVI. 241. Henry de Montfort was Simon's eldest son; he and his brother had been ravaging Roger Mortimer's lordship of Radnor.

127. *bi este*: the Lord Edward had been at Amiens when, on 23 January 1264, Louis IX had declared the Provisions of Oxford (1258) invalid. He succeeded in getting into the castle of Gloucester by 5 March, and made a truce with Henry under the terms of which the latter withdrew from the town.

131. *atte Kinges Halle*: the royal hall or manor house (often miscalled 'palace') of Beaumont, on the site of the present Gloucester Green and Beaumont St.; it was later given to the Carmelite Friars (hence 'Friars Entry', opposite St. Mary Magdalen Church).

134. *Smiþe gate*: the 'gate of the smiths' in the city wall on the North, where Catte St. now joins Broad St. According to Walter of Hemmingbank (311) the students were in general pro-Montfort, and some of them later joined the younger Simon's army at Northampton.

136. *Beumond*: 'Bellus Mons' was the name applied (? if ironically) to the flat open arable North of the city wall, partly in the parish of St. Giles, partly in Holywell. In 1288 the king's bailiff vigorously denied the university's rights in the area.

142. *Harewelle*: this cannot be identified, though Wood (who interpreted it as 'hore, ancient well') took it to be the Walton Well that gives its name to a modern street. The variant reading *Charewelle* (in Brit. Mus. Add. 19677) makes acceptable sense.

M. Gelling, *Place-Names of Oxfordshire* (Cambridge 1953), p. xxiv, makes unnecessary difficulties by translating 'suþþe' (142) as 'south'.

143. *Subvenite sancti* [*Dei, occurrite angeli Domini, suscipientes animam eius, offerentes eam in conspectu altissimi*]; the antiphon sung as a corpse is carried to church for burial.

145. *Willam þe Spicer*: the High St. between St. Mary's and All Saints' was occupied by the *apotecaria* and the spicery, where 'spices seeds and certaine rootes were sold' (Wood, *City of Oxford*, i. 494). William's 'seld', or shop, is mentioned in the inquisition rolls of 1278.

Hencsei (*Hengestes ieg*): either North (Ferry) or South Hinksey, probably the former: the Oxford city boundary has included part of this parish (which is in Berks.) from early times.

The portreeves were the two bailiffs of the town, whose duty was to keep order. The office goes back to Saxon times.

146. *Kingestone*: the village of this name nearest to Oxford is Kingston Bagpuize; but there was once a tenement or hall called Kingston in West Oxford (Wood, op. cit. i. 160 and Index), which may have been a royal *tun* or manor attached to Beaumont, if not Beaumont itself. In *C.P.R.*, cit. *supra*, p. 264 (22 October 1264), Nicholas is described as 'of Stocwell': Stockwell was on the present site of Worcester College, i.e. adjacent to Beaumont.

148. *þe chaunceler*: the chancellor of the university at this time was John de Wynton, *juris canonici professor*.

156. *Seinte Marie churche*: (*Marie* represents the Latin genitive); the church of St. Mary the Virgin in the High St., a little to the East of All Saints'. Its bell still summons the university to Congregation. For the ringing of the rival bells of St. Mary's and St. Martin's in the town-and-gown riots of St. Scholastica's Day, 1355, see H. Rashdall, *Universities of Europe in the Middle Ages* (rev. ed. 1936), iii. 97.

163. The bowyers are not elsewhere mentioned except in an account of a later riot (1298) when the Scholars again broke up 'the fletchery' (south-east of Carfax) and the spicery.

167. The only other reference to the *forum vinarium* locates it in the parish of St. Martin's (on the west side of St. Aldate's).

171. The king heard of the affray from two Dominicans at Rochester and in letters of 28 February 1264 asked to be informed of the decisions of the arbitrators who had been agreed on with the town (*C.P.R.*, cit. *supra*, p. 383). He arrived at Oxford on 8 March, lodging with the Dominicans in their house outside the south-west wall. On 12 March he wrote to the chancellor and scholars ordering them to disperse on the grounds that his feudal host, which he had summoned to meet him at Oxford, might be too savage to restrain (ibid., p. 307). For a discussion of the motives for the dispersion see Powicke, op. cit., App. F.

XII

MS.: Arundel 292, British Museum.

Editions: R. Morris, *An Old English Miscellany* (E.E.T.S., o.s. 49 (1872), 1–25.

J. Hall, *Selections from Early Middle English* (Oxford 1920),
i. 176–96.

Source: A version, or versions, of the Latin *Physiologus*, for
which cf.:

Thetbaldus, *Liber Fisiologus*, ed. Morris, op. cit., pp. 201–9.

A. W. Rendell, *Physiologus: A Metrical Bestiary . . . by Bishop
Theobald* (London 1928).

F. J. Carmody, *Physiologus Latinus*, Versio B (Paris 1939);
Versio Y, Univ. Calif. Pubns. in *Class. Phil.* xii (1941);
T. H. White, *Book of Beasts* (London 1954).

The Epic of the Beast (Broadway Translations, n.d.).

M. R. James, *The Bestiary* (Roxburghe Club 1928).

Studies: see Bibliography in Florence McCulloch, *Medieval
Latin and French Bestiaries* (Chapel Hill 1960); to which
add:

B. White, 'Medieval Animal Lore', *Anglia*, lxxii (1954), 21–30.

Language

1. The reflex of OE $\breve{æ}$ (OKt, WM $\breve{e}$) rhymes on [a:] (< OE
   $\bar{a}$) in *stedefast* 191: *gast*.
2. OE $\breve{y}$ have been unrounded in *briche* 138: *heuenriche*;
   fligt 18: *brigt*; *listen* 37: *cristen*.
3. OE $\bar{a}$ has been rounded to slack $\bar{o}$ in *ston* 30: *þeron*.
4. The reflex of OE $\bar{æ}^1$ rhymes on (*a*) tense $\bar{e}$ in *dede* 45:
   mede; (*b*) the reflex of OE $\bar{æ}^2$ in *rede* 2: *-hede*.
5. There was no diphthongization, in the antecedent OE
   type, of a front vowel by a preceding palatal consonant in
   get 143: *flet*.
6. Smoothing in OE of $\breve{e}a$ before *ht* is attested in *magt* 183:
   craft, since the root-vowel in the latter is shown by 1 to
   have been [a].
7. The product of *i*-mutation of (*a*) prim. OE *æ* before *r* +
   consonant rhymes on slack $\bar{e}$ < $\bar{e}a$ < $\breve{e}a$ in *dern* 38: *ern*;
   (*b*) OE $\bar{e}a$ rhymes on tense $\bar{e}$ in *nede* 109: *fede*.
8. The reflex of OE [ʃ] is [s] in *fis* 141, 171: *is*.
9. The 3 pres. sg. indic. (*a*) of a verb with a root ending in a
   dental here has the syncopated and assimilated form in
   flet 144: *get*; (*b*) of the verb *ben* is (i) *es* 76: *gres*, (ii) *is* 142,
   172: *fis*.

10. The 3 pres. pl. ends in (a) -en in *dragen* 151, 174: *fagen*; (b) -en or -e (< -en) in *winnen* 163: *inne*.

11. The infin. ends in (a) -en in *listen* 37: *Cristen*, *rigten* 65: *Drigtin*; (b) possibly -e in *dragen* 190: *lage*.

[For the scribe's 'hookless' *g* functioning as a *yogh* in, e.g., *guðhede* 3, *Drigtin* 67, see now *M.Æ.* xl (1971), 56–7.]

Vocabulary

Adoptions from ON are *ai* 10, *derue* 98, *es* 76, *gres* 75, *ille* 168, *kirke* 41, *lage* 189, *lateð* 119, *mirke* 43, *wrong* 6. In addition, most or all of the numerous and important examples within the line almost certainly reflect the usage of the author rather than a scribe: *bone* 64, *brennen* 178, *costes* 129, *festeþ* 195, *heil* 23, *lage* 105, *oc* 19, *rape(like)* 71, *skies* 14, *swideð* 18, *takeð* 46, *(o)twinne* 89, *ðog* 128. This material implies dense settlement by Scandinavians in the area concerned.

Provenance

The North is eliminated by 3, 9(a), and 10; the SW and the SE by 2 and 6; and the WMidl by 2 and 8. This leaves only the EMidl, which is also clearly indicated by the correspondence with the *Ormulum* in respect of 1, 2, 5, 6, 7, and 9 and 10 in combination.

———

Natura aquile: Spenser (*Faerie Queene*, 1. xi. 34) and Milton (*Areopagitica*) made notable use of this fable, in which O.T. references to the eagle and the sun of righteousness (Mal. iv. 2) are given a Christian application. Bartholomaeus Anglicus gives a similar account in his *De proprietatibus rerum* (*c.* 1250, translated into English by John Trevisa, 1397).

2. *o boke*: i.e. in *Physiologus*; for *o[n]* in the sense 'in' cf. 'romanz reding on þe bok' (*Hav.* 2327).

3. *neweð*: this verb is last recorded in *O.E.D. s.a.* 1555; but 'muing [his mighty youth]' in *Areopagitica* is perhaps a printer's corruption of *newing*: cf. Ps. cii. 5 (Vulg.), and *R.E.S.* xix (1943), 61–66, xxi (1945), 44–46.

7. Hall compares Hugh of St. Victor: *Solet dici de aquila dum senectute premitur . . . rostrum illius aduncetur et incurvetur, ita ut sumere cibum nequeat et macie languescat.*

10. The ultimate source is Isa. lviii. 11: *fons aquarum, cuius non deficient aquæ.*

14. Hall translates: 'he flies through seven to the highest (eighth) heaven.' But that would take him *above* the sun, which was placed in the fourth 'heaven'. *Phys.* has: *nubes transcendit solisque incendia sentit*; and *skyes* regularly means 'clouds'. *sex and seuene* is probably a mere tag: cf. *Troilus and Criseyde*, iv. 622, the first instance of the phrase recorded in *O.E.D.*: it is probably a variation on 'cinque et six', the highest throw at dice, from which it derives the association of chance. Hence translate: 'through whatever clouds may chance to come his way'.

23. *heil*: the Scand. doublet (see Gl and cf. 125) has replaced *hol* (OE *hāl*) in the phrase *hol and isunde*.

29. *himself to none gode*: '. . . with any benefit to himself.'

38. *dern*: 'secret, concealed', i.e. innate, inherited: *ab origine matris* (*Phys.*). Cf. Ps. l. 7. The medieval gloss printed with *Phys.* at Cologne (1492) has: *vetus homo* [cf. Col. iii. 9] *per peccatum*.

42–43. 'His eyes were blind (because of sin) even (?) before he began to think about it': 'bethink', *pace* Hall, does not occur in the sense 'repent' before the seventeenth century. The interpretation is probably derived from St. John ix. 1–14—the story of the man blind from birth who was told to wash in the pool of Siloam; cf. also Ps. cxlv. 8. *can* appears to be an early example of the Northern pa. t. auxiliary, possibly altered from *gan* in a late recension 'not much earlier than the date of the manuscript' (N. Davis, *M.Æ.* xix (1950), 57).

44–45. At baptism the child, in the person of his sponsor, renounces *Sathanee et omnibus operibus eius*.

47. *mede*: possibly an allusion to the reward of Gen. xv. 1 or Matt. v. 12.

49. *prestes lore*: i.e. Paternoster and creed; cf. 61.

50. *wereð*: *O.E.D.*, following Morris, derives from OE *werian* 'to defend', and translates 'From his eyes he keeps off the mist'. But *Phys.* has: *Tunc quoque caligo consumitur igne propinquo*. Thus we may translate 'The mist wears off his eyes' or ? 'the mist of his eyes fades away'.

54. *ðat*: i.e., God.

62. *fare he norð er fare he suð* . . .: an example of a common type of tag in which opposites are used to include all possibilities 'wherever he goes, whatever he does, he will have to learn that he lacks something [or, what is necessary for him], namely that he must pray'.

64. *bidden bone*: an alliterative phrase first found in ME but probably of common Gmc stock: cf. ON *biðja bónar*.

65. *Phys.*: *Obterit obliquum per verba precancia rostrum.*

67. Cf. the gloss on *Phys.*: *post hoc valeat capere cibum .i. graciam dei.*

Natura formice: the Biblical source is Prov. vi. 6, xxx. 25. See also Browne, *Pseud. Ep.* iii. 27. A procession of ants is delightfully drawn in a Bodleian MS. of the Latin Bestiary, Ashmole 1511, f. 36ᵛ.

76. Literally 'that is to be had for her', i.e. that she can get.

83. *So it her telleð*: 'So the Physiologus says at this point.'

84. *finde ge*: 'if she finds. . . .'

86. *Ne bit ge nawt ðe barlic beren abuten*: 'She has no wish to go on carrying barley.' For this use of *bidde* see VIII. L 9 n.

89. *get*: an elision of *ge + it*.

90. *fro*: in emphatic post-position bears alliteration, as in OE. Browne knew that ants could arrest the germination of seeds, but it was not proved in modern times till 1873.

98. *derue* ['bold'?]: Hall emends to *glewe* ('prudent') on grounds of sense (cf. Prov. vi. 6) and rhyme.

103. *ðe olde lage*: i.e. the legalism of the Old Testament. The remainder of the *significacio* appears to depend on an exegesis of 2 Tim. ii. 15: 'rightly dividing [*tractantem*] the word of truth'. Cf. Hugh of St. Victor: (col. 75) *Et tu, homo Dei, scripturae veteris* [Ashmole 1511 adds *et novi*] *testamenti divide in duas partes, hoc est secundum historiam et secundum spiritualem intellectum. Divide veritatem a figura. Separa corporalia a spiritualibus et* *spiritualia a corporibus. Transcende a littera occidente ad spiritum vivificantem, ne littera germinante in die hiemis, id est in die judicii, fame pereas.* Cf. also St. Augustine, *De Doctrina Christiana,* xi. Thetbaldus has

> Hoc est quod binas lex habet una vias
> Quae terrena sonat, simul et celestia monstrat.
> Nunc mentem pascit, et modo corpus alit;

where *terrena* supports Mätzner's emendation to *erŏliche* in 106. The scribe's *ebriche* ('hebrew') is perhaps due to a reminiscence of the Latin [*res spirituales, Quas*] *Judaeus non amat.* Hall's interpretation of *lex* as 'the facts of natural history' is forced and unnecessary.

For the general conception as represented on a capital at Vézelay see E. Mâle, *Revue de l'Art ancien et moderne* (1914), p. 117.

Natura cerui 11ª. The first part (omitted here) describes how the stag quenches the poison of adders by drinking water— symbolic of the 'living water' of Christ.

111. *minde*: dat.: 'which ought to be present in thought to us all.'

115. *oðer flen*: 'flee the other', i.e. go ahead without the others.

120. *skinbon*: the Cologne *Physiologus* (see 38 n.) has *mentum* ('chin') and Hugh of St. Victor *capita clunibus precedentium superponunt*; hence Hall emends to *chinbon*. Conceivably OE *cin-* had in this dialect early developed the pronunciation represented in the spelling *schynne* of a fifteenth-century gloss; in this text [ʃ] would be represented by *s*; thus the original reading may have been *sinbon*, which was erroneously corrected by a transcriber (for spgs. *shyne, schyn* see *M.E.D.* s.v. *chin*).

123. N. Davis's proposed *ferien* (*M.Æ.* xix (1950), 57–58) is now withdrawn. The translator has evidently misunderstood *Phys.*:

> Set qui precedit fessus ad ima redit,
> Sic se vertentes cuncti mutuoque ferentes
> Numquam deficiunt atque viam peragunt.

124. *of ðat water-grund*: the phrase is due to a misunderstanding of *Phys. ad ima redit* 'he proceeds to the rear'; *ima* could mean 'bottom' *or* 'rear'.

126. *forðen here nede*: Hall takes as equivalent to *numquam deficiunt* and translates 'supply their necessity'. The absence of any equivalent to *viam peragunt* suggests that some words may have been omitted.

129 ff. The English writer has introduced a note of *charitas* in this *significacio*, and appears to have blended the thought of the verse text and of the gloss, which cites Gal. vi. 2; cf. 134.

138. 'if we are serviceable to one another'.

145 ff. Cf. *Paradise Lost*, i. 203 ff. Bestiary illuminations (e.g. in the Dyson Perrins MS. and Ashmole 1511) show a fishlike whale simultaneously swallowing small fishes and diving with fire and sailors on his back.

146. *Ðat sete one ðe se-sond*: *in oceano insula sit medio* (*Phys.*). 'Herbs and small trees and bushes grow thereon, so that that great fish seemeth an island', says Bartholomaeus; and the bushes are depicted in Bestiary illustrations, e.g. B.M. Harl. MS. 4751, f. 69. The image is as old as St. Ambrose, who describes the whale as resembling a vast bank of sand—*innare insulas putes*; for other references see A. Schultze, 'Zur Brendanlegende', *Zeitschrift für romanische Philologie* xxx (1906), 264.

163. i.e. at the equinoctial gales: cf. *Gawain and the Green Knight* 504, and, for a similar metaphor, *Beowulf* 1132. *Phys.* has merely *cum vadit vel venit æstas*.

178. *wel*: Hall proposed to read *welm*, but this word does not occur in the sense '(blazing) fire', which he favoured; *walm*, which he cites from Laȝamon's *Brut* 22123, is probably a variant of *qualm* 'killing'. N. Davis's proposal, *bel* (< OE *bæl* 'bonfire'), has the virtue of yielding an alliterative phrase which may well have been suggested by *Accendunt vigilem quem navis portitat ignem* (*Phys.*); cf. *M.Æ.* xix. 59. But the detail of 177 is not found in *Phys.*

185 ff. *Mentes . . . Esurit atque sitit, quosque potest perimit* (*Phys.*). The entrance to hell was often represented as the mouth of a whale: cf. *Patience* 252, 306.

189. *in leve lage*: *modicos fidei* (*Phys.*) (glossed *parvos in fide*).

XIII

MS.: Junius I, Bodleian Library.

Edition: R. M. White (1852), revised R. Holt (Oxford 1878).

Studies: H. M. Flasdieck, 'Die sprachliche Einheitlichkeit des Orrmulums', *Anglia* xlvii (1923), 289–331.

J. E. Turville-Petre, 'Studies in the Ormulum MS.', *J.E.G.P.* xlvi (1947), 1–27.

K. Sisam, 'MSS. Bodley 340 and 342: Ælfric's Catholic Homilies', *R.E.S.* vii (1931), 7 ff.; viii (1932), 51 ff.; ix (1933) 1 ff. (reprinted in *Studies in the History of Old English Literature* (Oxford 1953), pp. 148–98 (see especially 188 ff.)).

M. Lehnert, 'Sprachform und Sprachfunktion im "Orrmulum"' (*Zeitschrift für Anglistik und Amerikanistik*, Beiheft I (1953)).

R. W. Burchfield, 'The Language and Orthography of the Ormulum MS.', *Trans. Phil. Soc.* (1956), pp. 56–87.

Orthography

Orm writes a double consonant after a short vowel or diphthong in words like *full, wollde, aʒʒ, leʒʒtenn, þewwess*, but never in *sune* 'son' or the like. It is thus clear that he doubled a consonant only if it belonged to the same syllable as a preceding short vowel or diphthong, i.e. only in a closed syllable; and that in the sequence $V+C+V$ the consonant belonged to the second syllable, and the root-syllable was therefore open. One corollary of his practice is that a single consonant in a closed syllable implies length of the preceding vowel or diphthong; and the *Ormulum* therefore provides a mass of material to illustrate the late OE lengthening of a short vowel or diphthong before any of the consonant-groups *ld, nd, rd, mb, ng, rð*.

Moreover, at the end of the three-beat lines Orm uses disyllables of the type *inne*, *swelltenn*, or *tælenn*, with short vowel in a closed root-syllable, or long vowel in whatever sort of syllable, but never disyllables such as *sune*, with short vowel in an open root-syllable. This clearly implies that in the first two of these categories the root-syllables were long; and it is direct evidence that the ME lengthening of short vowels in disyllables with open root-syllable had not yet taken place in his idiolect. It also follows that Orm's intermittent use of an acute accent on the root-vowels of the latter words has no bearing on this lengthening. In any case, he normally intends it, like his intermittent breve, to distinguish homographs, e.g. *wīte* 88 and *wĭte* n: 26 (< OE *wīte*); *tăkenn* n. 94 (< OE *tācn*), implying that *takenn* inf. and past part. had a short vowel.

Orm's spelling of *ĕo* as *e* after *c*. 13,000 lines, when he had used both *eo* and *e* up to that point, provides our best evidence for dating the change of OE *ĕo* to early ME *ĕ* in his speech (since on palæographical evidence the MS. is dated *c*. 1200). Other invaluable information is given by (*a*) his use (not represented in our extract) of a separate symbol for the assibilated [dʒ], which would otherwise not be distinguished from the stop [g]— itself represented by a distinctive letter-form, and (*b*) such spellings as *faȝȝerr* (< OE *fæger*), which show that in OE sequences of vowel or diphthong + [i] or [u] new ME diphthongs were beginning to develop.

Language

1. The reflex of Gmc *ă* (*a*) when fronted to OE *ǽ* (OKt, VPs *ĕ*) is spelt *a*: *barr* 49; (*b*) before nasals is a non-rounded vowel: *sammnenn* 16, *þannkenn* 140.
2. OE *ȳ* have been unrounded and are spelt *i*: *birrþ* 222, *-kinn* 4, *sinness* 86; *kinde* 32, *kiþeþþ* 40.
3. OE *ā* has not been rounded to slack *ō*: *brad* 162, *had* 180, *lac* 185, *lade* 186.
4. The reflex of OE *ǽ*¹ is spelt (*a*) *æ* (denoting a long vowel): *ȝæfe* 12, *sæȝhenn* 73, *wære* 20; (*b*) *e* when shortened before two consonants: *forrdredde* 79, *offdredde* 74.
5. The reflex of OE *ǽ*² is spelt (*a*) *æ* in *ænne* 95, *clænnesse* 244, *Hælennde* 86, *lærenn* 223, but (*b*) *e* in *ledenn* 196, and (*c*) *e* when shortened before two consonants: *ledde* 200.

6. OE *ēa* has become a long front vowel: *ærd* 67, *læfe* 138, *shæwenn* 61.

7. OE *ĕo* have been reduced to a long and short front vowel respectively: *hewe* 68, *leme* 72, *erþe* 4, *þed* 101; *heffness* 81.

8. Diphthongization of front vowels by preceding palatal consonants at the OE stage had not taken place in Orm's idiolect, but is exceptionally represented in *ʒiff* 11. *Chesstre* 42, 90, 128, 208, the root-vowel of which in prim. OE was -*æ*-, is best explained as a form with raising of an undiphthongized OE -*ǣ*- to -*ĕ*- between palatal consonants. *ʒifenn* 254 is ambiguous, since the -*i*- may have been analogically levelled from the 2 and 3 pres. sg. into the 1 sg. and thence the infin. at an earlier stage.

9. The reflex of prim. OE *ǣ*+*ld* shows that there was no breaking at the antecedent OE stage (though there are no examples in our extract): *ald(e)* 'old' Holt-White 746, 745.

10. *i*-mutation in OE of (*a*) *æ* before *l*-groups had produced *e*: *beldenn* 76; (*b*) *ĭ* before *r*-groups followed at the Gmc stage by *i* or *j* had lapsed in *hirde(ss)* 69, 103, 119.

11. Smoothing of *ĕa* in OE is attested in *sahh* 103, 150 (since WS and Kt *sĕah* > late OE *sĕh*), *heʒhesst* 240, *ec* 179.

12. Tense *ō* has been raised to *ū* in *ʒuw* 85, *ʒure* 86.

13. [k] has been extensively levelled into forms in which assibilated [tʃ] would have been historically regular, from others in which it was followed by a back vowel: *Icc* 81, *Illc* 12, *iwhillc* 19, *mikell* 10, *sekenn* 188, 222, *swillc* 170, 178.

14. The velar fricative [ɣ] has not yet become [w]: *muʒhenn* 98, *sæʒhenn* 73.

15. The prepositional sg. of nouns is (*a*) commonly identical with the nom. sg., and hence in many words endingless: *off all mannkinn* 4, *to* (*i*) *þatt tun* 21, 29; (*b*) sometimes still inflected even when the nom. sg. is endingless: *o lande* 20, *i bure* 54.

16. The dat. sg. is endingless (in a noun with endingless nom.) in *all follc* 83; but the object case has -*e* in *weʒʒe* 199.

17. The gen. sg. normally ends in -*ess* in all classes of nouns, though represented here only in the old strong feminine *bokess* 287 and *soþfasstnessess* 281 (apart from strong masculines and neuters, in which it was historically regular: *heffness* 72, *kingess* 39, *lifess* 265, *maʒʒþhadess* 239).

18. The ending of the plural of virtually all nouns is *-ess*:
    (*a*) in the nominative, even in old endingless neuters (*lakess* 192) and strong feminines (*sinness*, as implied by the prep. pl. *sinness* 86).
    (*b*) in the genitive (not represented in our extract), except that a historically regular vowel-ending is fossilized in a few nouns used as adjectival genitives: *all mannkinne* (*nede*) 228, *ure sawle* (*nede*) 224.
    (*c*) in the prepositional: *enngless* 100, *lakess* 192, *sinness* 86. *eʒhne* 146 is an isolated example of *-ne* as a pl. ending (used by Orm also in other cases of this word, contrasting with his sg. *eʒhe* in all cases). The starting-point for it would have been the LOE gen. pl. *ēgenan*: this is established by the ME pl. *eʒnen*, Northern *eghen*.[1] *kinde* 180 is not a true plural but an indeterminate form, the plurality being expressed by the preceding numeral.

19. In adjectives, (*a*) final *-e* is normal in forms which would have been inflected weak in OE: *þatt illke land* (*tun*) 175, 235; *þe rihhte læfe* 218; but (*b*) in conditions requiring strong inflexion in OE, one and the same word may have final *-e* or be endingless, solely according to the stress pattern within the phrase: *inn till rihht Crisstenndom* 279 beside *inn till rihhte læfe* 280; (*c*) the old inflexion of the gen. pl. survives in one or two words (*allre* 240, *baþre* 32) in which it was probably analysed as adjectival.

20. The loss of grammatical gender is established by the use of (*a*) *þe* as the sg. form of the definite article equally with the old neuters (acc. *child* 131, prep. *land* 33), feminines (prep. *þed* 167), and masculines (prep. *king* 271); (*b*) the old mutated masc. acc. sg. of the indefinite article (*ænne*) equally with an old masc. (*sang* 105) and a neuter (*child* 95)—but clearly as a fossil, alongside *an* 12 without inflexion.

21. In the pronoun of the 3rd person (*a*) the nom. sg. fem. is *ʒho* 48, 49; (*b*) the pl. includes three forms of ON origin: nom. *þeʒʒ* 34; acc. *þeʒʒm* 171, *hemm* 75, 222; gen. *þeʒʒre* 32; dat. *hemm* 37, 77, 182.

[1] K. Luick, *Studien zur englischen Lautgeschichte* (Vienna 1903), p. 154.

22. The 3 pres. indic. ends (*a*) in the sg. in -*eþþ: biddeþþ* 275, *bitacneþþ* 260, *kiþeþþ* 8; (*b*) in the pl. in -*enn: follȝhenn* 244.

23. The infin. ends in -*enn: sammnenn* 16, *wurrþenn* 18.

24. Weak verbs of OE class II have no -*i*- element: *lofenn* 140, *lokenn* 14.

25. The past part. (*a*) of strong verbs ends in -*enn*, and (*b*) in all verbs has discarded the prefix (OE *ge-*), with the sole exception of *ȝehatenn* 259 (cf. *iwhillc* 19, 113).

Vocabulary

Adoptions from ON are *aȝȝ* 114, *fra* 201, *griþþ* 248, *keȝȝseress* 250, *leȝȝten* 188, *sahhtnesse* 246, *sterrne* 161, *summ* 8, 20, *twinne*, 180, 212, *toc* 149, *token* 119, *þohh-* 60, *þrinne* 185, 192, *witerrliȝ* 177, possibly *till* 113.

Provenance

A specifically Anglian antecedent type in OE is established by 9, 10 (*b*), and 11. But the North is excluded by 22; and 3 therefore merely implies an early date of composition (i.e. before *c.* 1200). And the WMidl is excluded by 1, 2, and 22 (*b*). The only remaining possibility is the EMidl; and this fully accords with the strong ON element in the vocabulary, and especially with the adoption of grammatically basic words such as the conjunctions *summ*, *þohh-*, and the numerals *twinne*, *þrinne*.

---

5. *himmsellf*. Hand 'A' uses -*sellf* or -*sellfenn* indifferently for nom. and obl. forms. Hand 'B', at some point after the completion of 9993, attempted to regularize, but omitted to do so here.

8. *þe goddspell*: Luke ii. 157–220 render Matt. ii. 1–12: cf. 221.

9. *Off*: 'how'; but it is almost otiose, as elsewhere in Orm, e.g. 3265 '[Nu wile icc here shæwenn ȝuw . . .] off hu ȝho barr þe laferrd Crist.' *wel*: Orm uses *wel* and *well*, *metri causa*.

10. *come*: pret. subj.: '[he began to consider that he would like to know exactly] how much money he would get if each man were to give him a penny.'

33. *Ȝerrsalæm*: for the trisyllabic form cf. L *Ȝersolimis* and *C.T.* A 463.

61. *Acc* retains the strongly adversative force that it has after negatives in OE: 'On the contrary.'

64. *borenn to manne*: for the idiom cf. *Kyng Alisaunder* 2688: 'An hore þee to man bare', and *Piers Plowman* B. 1. 82. Hall (*Early Middle English*, xv. 30 n.) cites OE parallels.

67. *heffness ærd*: 'the region of heaven'; evidently modelled on *middelærd*.

68. *Inn aness weress hewe*: for this type of phrase see Lehnert.

71. *hemm bi*: as in OE verse, *bi* in post-position bears stress.

76. *to frofrenn annd to beldenn*: a frequent combination in Orm: cf., e.g., *Dedication*, p. 237.

110. N.T. has *Gloria* simply; but similar combinations appear in (e.g.) Apoc. v. 13 (*benedictio et gloria et potestas*).

111. *griþþ annd friþþ*: adopted from OWN *grið ok frið*: cf. Orm, *Preface*, 87. *Griþ* orig. meant the royal protection given to certain persons. The phrase is found in LOE and elsewhere in ME with the sense 'peace and prosperity'.

148. (*þær*)*offe*: such extended forms are common in this position.

153. *leȝȝde itt all to-samenn* = Vulg. *conferens in corde suo* (Luke ii. 19).

175. The Biblical Magi became the three kings as early as Tertullian; cf. H. Kehrer, *Die hl. drei könige in literatur und kunst* (Leipzig. 1919). But they are not usually represented as each bearing *three* gifts—as in 185 ff.

179–80. Orm inserts traditional exegetical phrases into his paraphrase: cf., e.g., St. Leo on the Nativity: 'true God and true man are welded into the unity of One Lord' (trans. in *Sunday Sermons of the Great Fathers*, ed. M. F. Toal (1957), i. 119).

238–52. The exposition follows Bede on Luke c. ii (trans. in *Sunday Sermons*, loc. cit., pp. 100 ff.).

260. Cf. St. Gregory, *Hom. VIII in Evang.* (*P.L.* 76. 1103): 'Bethlehem was formerly called the house of bread because it was there He was to appear in the nature of our flesh who would fulfil the heart of the faithful with inward satiety.' A similar interpretation is to be found in St. Jerome (*P.L.* 22. 885, 25. 197) and St. Isidore (*Etymologiæ*, xv. 1), &c.

275 ff. Cf. Bede (loc. cit.): 'so now in the reign of Christ . . . we must enroll ourselves unto justice.'

285. Cf. St. Gregory (loc. cit.): 'He then appeared in the flesh who should enroll his elect for all eternity.'

XIV

MS.: Cotton Vespasian A. iii, British Museum.

Edition: R. Morris, E.E.T.S. o.s. 57, 59, 62, 66, 68, 99, 101 (1874–93).

Studies: W. Meyer, *Die Geschichte des Kreuzholzes vor Christus*, Abhandlungen der philosophisch-philologischen Classe der königlich bayerischen Akademie der Wissenschaften xvi, ii (Munich 1882), 101–66 [includes the text of the Latin *Legend*].

   A. S. Napier, *History of the Holy Rood-Tree*, E.E.T.S. o.s. 103 (1894), Introduction.

   M. Lazar, 'La Légende de "l'Arbre de Paradis" ou "bois de la croix" ', *Zeitschrift für romanische Philologie*, lxxvi (1960), 34–63.

   E. C. Quinn, *The Quest of Seth for the Oil of Life* (Chicago 1962).

   B. Hill, 'The Fifteenth-century Prose *Legend of the Cross before Christ*', *M.Æ.* xxxiv (1965), 203–22.

   O. Strandberg, *The Rime-Vowels of Cursor Mundi* (1919).

   R. Kaiser, *Zur Geographie des mittelenglischen Wortschatzes* (Palæstra 205, 1937), especially pp. 5–14.

Language

   1. The reflex of OE *ȳ* rhymes on [i] in *sin* 192 : *min*, 71 : *wyn*; *win* 174 : *in*.
   2. The reflex of OE *ā* had evidently not undergone rounding, since it rhymes on (i) *ā* in *brade* 93 : *made*, and probably in *an* 293 : *wain*, *are* 162 : *care*, *mare* 273 : *care* (with OE *ă* lengthened to *ā*—see 4); (ii) *ă* in *ras* 289 : *was*.

3. OE *ēo* had become a long vowel by reduction of its second element, since it rhymes on tense *ē* in *be* 100: *charite*, 222: *he*; *tre* 184: *he*, 39: *þe*.

4. Lengthening of *ă* and *ĕ* in disyllabic forms with open root-syllables is implied (if the rhymes are exact) in *bare* 185: *mare*; *care* 161: *are*; *wele* 227: *dele*.

5. The reflex of OE *sc* was evidently [s] in *flesse* 80: *lesse*, *flexs* 269: *es*.

6. OE *werold* is represented by *werd* 91 (: *herd*, MS. *warld*).

7. *-es* had evidently been adopted as the plural ending of all classes of nouns, since it appears (i) in an endingless neuter of OE in *thinges* 21: *kynges*; (ii) in an OE fem. *i*-stem in *dedis* 41: *redis*.

8. The 2 pres. sg. of the preterite-present verb 'shall' (OE *scealt*) has been replaced by the form of the 1 and 3 person in *sale* 116: *dale*.

9. The 3 pres. sg. (i) ends in *-s* in *beres* 38: *peres*; *redis* 42: *dedis*; (ii) of the verb 'to be' is *es* 270: *flexs*.

10. The pres. part. ends in *-and* in *sueland* 208: *suepelband*.

Vocabulary

The numerous adoptions from ON (which total *c.* 33) imply an area densely settled by Scandinavian invaders: *ai* 32, *bark* 185, *brathly* 63, *brennand* 154, *fra* 108, *gain* 250, *gart* 198, *-gat* 106, *gloppend* 152, *gresse* 119, *ille* 42, *kest* 210, *min* 191, *nai* 147, *raidd* 156, *rote* 43, *saght* 16, *scilwis* 33, *sere* 2, *site* 274, *sli* 66, *slogh* 118 (v.l. *slop*), 127, *stad* 133, *sum* 162, *thrin* 230, *tiþand* 263, *traist-* 59, *þof* 73, *vnfere* 102, *vtenemes* 179 (with ON *-næmr*), *wandes* 282, *wer* 68, *wrang* 29.

Provenance

In general, the language clearly is of either the EMidl or the Northern type (e.g. 3 and 7). Since a work from the northern part of the EMidl might exhibit (in rhyme) both slack *ō* and *ā* for OE *ā*, the total absence of the former from *Cursor Mundi* as a whole indicates an area north of the Humber. And it is worth noting that the vocabulary of *Cursor Mundi* as a whole contains something like fifty words otherwise recorded only in Scottish texts.

1–20. A valuable contemporary catalogue of romances and epics in ME and OF. For other lists of subjects of romances, see *Sir Thopas* 898–900 (*C.T.* B. 2088–90), and *Richard Cœur de Lion* (ed. K. Brunner, 1913), ll. 7–20.

3. The only extant version (in verse) composed by this time in English was *Kyng Alisaunder* (see II). During the fourteenth century *Alexander A* and *Alexander B*, and at its end *The Wars of Alexander*, were composed in alliterative verse.

5. The main ME examples are *The Laud Troy-Book*, the alliterative *Destruction of Troy*, and *Troilus and Criseyde*; and in OF, the twelfth-century *Roman de Troie*, one of the earliest French specimens of the romance as a genre.

7. *Brut*: mentioned after 5–6 because he is the main figure in the legend of the Trojan descent of the Britons. This latter notion was modelled on the similar one regarding the Franks, itself suggested by the descent of the Romans from Aeneas. Its incorporation into medieval traditions of Britain began in the *Historia Britonum* (composed in 800 or 801), ch. ii: this states that Brutus, a brother of Remus and Romulus and a grandson of Aeneas, occupied Britain, and that the Britons got their name from him. For the genesis and evolution of the legend see E. Faral, *La Légende arthurienne* (1929) i. 81–86, 170–4, 181–4, 192–8, 262–93.

15. Perhaps a reference specifically to the *Chanson de Roland*, which is one of the earliest extant OF epics, rather than to some other poem of the Charlemagne cycle (for ME examples of which see Wells, *Manual of the Writings in Middle English*, pp. 82–94).

17. The only ME version is *Sir Tristrem* (*c.* 1300); for those in OF and their relationship see F. Whitehead, in R. S. Loomis, *Arthurian Literature in the Middle Ages* (1959), pp. 134–44.

18. An episode treated in the two OF poems *La Folie Tristan* (of Oxford and Berne respectively, so called after the extant MSS. of both), in which Tristan visits the court of Mark disguised as a court fool.

19. *Ioneck*: known only as the leading figure in Marie de France's *Yonec*, which is among those of her lays that deal in story-materials of specifically Celtic origin (see 'Story-Patterns in some Breton Lays', *M.Æ.* xxii (1953), 61–92).

Ysambrase: an edifying tale of a knight who, because he forgot God, was afflicted along with his family by sore trials, but duly emerged from them.

20. The only extant version is the OF romance *Amadas et Ydoine*, the two protagonists of which are mentioned in *Emare* 122 ff. as notable examples of true lovers, along with Tristan and Iseult, and Floris and Blancheflour (for whom see III).

66. The lost rhyme-word cannot be reconstructed from the versions of the other MSS.: Fairfax reads *To suche mede as he before dede*; Göttingen *To suilk mede as he him forbedd*; Trinity *To take suche mede shal he be sted.*

104. But L § 3 *fatigatus de exstirpatione ueprum.* Cf. 134, which renders L § 4 *me tedere uitae meae.*

109. See p. xx, Addenda.

118. *slogh*: L § 4 *passus marcidos quae sunt uestigia mea et matris tuae.* Cf. 127.

126. *þarin*: L § 4 *ubi pedes nostri calcauerunt.*

140. *o merci*: to be construed with *oile.* According to the *Vita*, § 36: *forsitan . . . transmittet angelum suum ad arborem misericordiae suae, de qua currit oleum vitae.* In the *Recognitiones Clementis Romani*, i. 45, Christ is said to have been anointed by the oil *quod ex ligno vitae fuerat sumtum* (Meyer, *Vita Adae et Euae*, p. 203).

152. *þat light*: L § 5 *splendorem.*

158. The subject of *asked* is understood from the accusative case (*þis angel*) 157. Cf. XVII. 102 and n.

159. *sette spell o nend*: L § 5 *respondit.* See VI. 62 n.

163. Not in L.

169–70. L § 5 *intromisso solummodo capite.*

208. *sueland*: not in L.

E e

213. *In his saul*: but L § 8 *ubi recognouit animam fratris sui Abel.*

226. Qualifying *oile* 224: 'which will compassionately reveal his mercy'. L. § 9: *qui et faciet parentibus tuis et posteritatibus eorum misericordiam; et haec pietas dilectionis uera.*

240 and 242. Not in L.

243. *take*: L § 10 *intelligimus.*

244. *Of heght*: modifying *make*, with the same word-order as in the use of the synonymous *iliche* in IX. 4.

249. L § 10 *quae multos nucleos generat.*

250. L § 10 *dona spiritus sancti praedicat.*

253–62. Not in direct speech in L.

264. *his sith*: cf. 266 n.

266. *bot neuer are*: L § 11 *risit et laetatus est semel in tota uita sua.*

271–6. Not in L.

284 and 294. L (MS. Royal 8 E 17) § 12 *nunquam crescentes nec decrescentes.*

288–92. A reference to the first three of the six (or seven) ages into which the history of the world was divided in medieval exegesis. The next were from Moses to David, from David to Christ, and from Christ to the end of the world. See *M.Æ.* xxvi (1957), 144 and notes 20 and 22; and M. Förster, 'Die Weltzeitalter bei den Angelsachsen', *Neusprachliche Studien* (*Festgabe Luick; Die neueren Sprachen*, 6 Beiheft, 1925), 183–203.

XV

MS.: Additional 23986, British Museum.

Editions: W. Heuser, 'Das Interludium De Clerico et Puella und das Fabliau von Dame Siriz', *Anglia*, xxx (1907), 306–19.

    G. H. McKnight, *Middle English Humorous Tales in Verse* (Boston 1913), pp. 21–24.

Studies: Allardyce Nicoll, *Masks Mimes and Miracles* (London 1931), pp. 171–5.

C. M. Gayley, *Representative English Comedies* (1903), 1. xvii.

F. E. Richardson, 'Notes on the Text and Language of Interludium de Clerico et Puella', *N. & Q.* ccvii (1962), 133–4.

B. D. H. Miller, 'Further Notes on "Interludium de Clerico et Puella" ', *N. & Q.* ccviii (1963), 248–9.

Language

1. The reflex of OE *ā* has not undergone rounding in *hame* 4: *dame*, 30: *scam*; *sory* 74: *Mary*. In 27–28 the author probably wrote *Iohan*: *nan*.

2. The reflex of OE *ǣ¹* rhymes on tense *ē* in *dede* 70: *fede* v.

3. The reflex of OE *ǣ²* rhymes on slack *ē* in *ledh* 44: *dedh* a.

4. ME *ŭ* has undergone the NMidl and Northern lengthening to tense *ō* (in disyllabic words with open root-syllable) in *dore* 10: *flore*.

5. The 3 pres. pl. ends in *-s* in *lys* 76: *profundis*.

6. The infinitive has no final *-n* in *be* 16, 31: *þe*, 24: *me*; *amende* 51: *send*.

Orthography

There are some features of AN type—the erratic treatment of *þ* and *t* (*wituten* 10, *bether* 16, *certhes* 22, *wyt* 42, *boyt* 65); the abundant use of inorganic initial *h* in words beginning with a vowel (*Hi* passim, *hers* 10, *ham* 22, *hup* 64) and the suppression of etymological initial *h* (*aly* 84, *efne* 25); and possibly *sh* for *s* (*damisheŀ* 1), *ch* for *c* (*chnief* 20), *dh* for *d* (*dedh*, *ledh* 43–44), and *sc* for *s* (*scynnes* 74).

Provenance

Clearly Northerly (1 and 5). Forms within the line accord with those in rhyme: the 3 pres. sg. *es* 3, 4, etc. (EMidl, NMidl, and Northern), *dos* 20; the unambiguously NMidl and Northern 1 pres. sg. *es* 24 and *-s* in *as* 83; the pronoun *yo* 'she' 47, 49, 51 (comparable with *ȝho* of the *Ormulum*); and the elimination of final *-e* with unvoicing of the final consonant in *gef* 58, *haf* 54. The high proportion of ON words is in keeping: *es* 3, &c., *-gat* 31, *heng* 80, 82, possibly *kend* 53, *gayt* 20, and possibly *roc* 69 (*sayct* 57 was taken over from the corresponding passage in *Dame Siriþ* or a common source).

The correspondences with *Dame Siriþ* (see VI, Introduction) are as follows:

Interludium	*Dame Siriþ*
5–6	82–83 (the same rhyme-words)
25–26	112–13 (different rhyme-words)
39	162 (different rhyme-words)
42	175
54 and 62	164–6, 188, 191 (one rhyme-word in common)
57–58	222–3 (one rhyme-word in common)
63–64	193 (different rhyme) and 201 (different rhyme)
65–68 and 69–72 (rhyme-sequences only)	196, 198–9, 207–11
83–84	203 (different rhyme-word) and 208.

2. *Saynt Michel*: there seems to be no very specific point in this invocation. One of the aspects in which the archangel Michael was most familiar in the Middle Ages was that of the *psychopompos* who appeared at the Last Judgement and is depicted with a balance in sculptured representations of it. See E. Mâle, *L'Art religieux du XIIIᵉ siècle en France* (1925), pp. 380–3; K. Künstle, *Ikonographie der christlichen Kunst*, I (1928), 247–50.

5. *Wel . . . to life*: the sole ME parallel to, and an early antecedent of, Shakespeare's idiom *well to live* (*A Winter's Tale*, III. iii. 124 and *Merchant of Venice*, II. ii. 55), which is synonymous with *well-to-do* and *well-to-pass* and is constructed on the same syntactic pattern. This pattern is clearly in origin a calque on an OF idiom: the OF inf. *a faire* is used (as a noun) in the roughly comparable phrase *de buen afaire* 'well off'.

7. St. Leonard lived in the sixth century as a hermit at Noblac, near Limoges. He was the patron saint of captives; and his day is the 6th of November. The historical basis for the legend of

St. Leonard is beyond recovery from the inventions of the early eleventh-century *Life* (ed. B. Krusch, *Mon. Germ. Hist.*, *Scriptores rerum Merovingicarum*, iii. 394–9).

37. *mome* is shown by OHG *muoma* 'maternal aunt', MHG *muome* (mod. G *Muhme*), to be authentic and ancient. Since it is otherwise recorded in English once only (*Promptorium Parvulorum* 292), and there are no other Gmc cognates, it is likely to be an adoption from German.

38. *San Dinis*: the first Bishop of Paris, who was sent to Gaul from Rome in the middle of the sixth century; his day is the 9th of November. See *Passio Sanctorum Martyrum Dionisii, Rustici et Eleutherii* (ed. B. Krusch, *Mon. Germ. Hist., Auctorum Antiquissimorum*, iv. 2. 101 ff.); Gregory of Tours, *Historia Francorum*, i. 48, l. 9 (ed. Arndt and Krusch, *Mon. Germ. Hist., Scriptores rerum Merovingicarum*, i).

47. *Malkyn*: although *O.E.D.* does not recognize the sense 'slut, drab; lewd woman' till nearly 1600, several of the ME contexts quoted s.v. have contemptuous implications that seem near to it.

67–68. Either one of the rhyme-words is corrupt, or there is a lacuna of at least two lines (which would have contained words rhyming on *lam* and *loue*). Schröder's ingenious reading *Wit Godis loue my lyf Y lede*, which is based on the correspondence noted above apropos of 63–64, leaves us with an odd number of rhymes in 65–67 and 68–72.

75. *De profundis*: Ps. 130, used in the Office of the dead.

76. i.e. in purgatory.

79 ff. The rhyme-words here show that a line has been omitted, and the contextual inadequacy of 80 that it was after this line.

XVI

MS.: Laud Misc. 636, Bodleian Library (reproduced in facsimile in *The Peterborough Chronicle*, ed. Dorothy Whitelock (Copenhagen 1954)).

Editions: C. Plummer and J. Earle, *Two of the Saxon Chronicles Parallel* (Oxford 1892, 1899).

Cecily Clark, *The Peterborough Chronicle 1070–1154* (Oxford 1958, 2nd edition, 1970).

(Selections in several Readers.)

Translations include those by G. N. Garmonsway (Everyman's Library, 1953), and D. C. Douglas, Susie Tucker [and Dorothy Whitelock] (1961).

Contemporary chronicles: Hugo Candidus, *The Peterborough Chronicle*, ed. W. T. Mellows and A. Bell (Oxford 1949).

Chronicon Petroburgense, ed. T. Stapleton (Camden Society, 1849).

Gesta Stephani, ed. K. R. Potter (Nelson's Medieval Texts, 1955).

William of Malmesbury, *Historia Novella*, ed. K. R. Potter (Nelson's Medieval Texts, 1955).

See also: A. L. Poole, *From Domesday Book to Magna Carta* (Oxford 1951), ch. v.

B. Mitchell, 'Syntax and Word-Order in "The Peterborough Chronicle" 1122–1154', *Neuphilologische Mitteilungen*, lxv (1964), 113–44.

Language

The extracts are contained in the 'First Continuation' (1122–31) and the 'Final Continuation' (1132–54), which, on the evidence of the content in conjunction with changes of handwriting at 1122 and 1132, are believed to have been composed and written at Peterborough. Their philological value is reduced by a slight admixture, not of scribal divergences from an 'author's' form of ME (since they are virtually of autograph status), but of forms from the standard written language of late OE, which was WS (see 6 (*a*) and 7), and by a disordered system of spelling.

Ĕa have both manifestly become slack *ē* and *ă* respectively: *cæse* 187, *forles* 262, *hæfod* 37, *læfe* 79, *næt* 67, and *wærd* 305, 306 (cf. *heafde* 'had' 69, 77, *spreac* 'spoke' 76, both of which can only be inverted spellings implying that OE *ĕa* had become a vowel). Forms like *beiæt* 24 might therefore represent either OE *begeat* or *begæt*, and do not show whether in such cases there had been diphthongization in OE of the front vowel by the preceding palatal consonant. Similarly, *fleh* 273, 292, *heglice* 231 might imply either OE *flæh*, *hæh-* with smoothing, or unsmoothed *fleah*, *heah-*; though *weorces* 159 (*weorkes* 221) looks like an unsmoothed form.

But the following features do emerge:

1. The reflex of OE *ȳ* is spelt *i* in *circe* 192, *sinnes* 203, beside *y* in *cyrce* 193, *hyrne* 90, and *fir* 64 beside *gemynd* 67.

2. OE *ā* has not been rounded to slack *ō*: *að* 37, *ham* 73.

3. The reflex of OE *ǣ¹* is spelt (*a*) *æ* in *læten* 13, *ræd* 14, *sægon* 50, *wæron* 34, &c., beside (*b*) *e* in *eten* 243, *red* 282, &c.

4. The reflex of OE *ǣ²* is spelt (*a*) usually *æ*, in *ær* 66, *betæcen* 78, 100, *sæ* 118, beside (*b*) *e* in *hethen* 190, &c.

5. OE *ēo* had been reduced to a long vowel, since it is spelt (*a*) commonly *e* (*blewen* 56, *frend* 126, *held* 93, 138), beside (*b*) *eo* (*freond* 275, 276).

6. Breaking, at the OE stage, (*a*) of *ǽ*+*ld* had lapsed in *ald* 121, *halden* 321, beside the type with breaking in *eald* 32; (*b*) had occurred before *h* in *neah* 28.

7. -*g*- had been eliminated at the OE stage before *d* in *sæde* 266, with lengthening of the preceding vowel.

8. The prepositional singular of many endingless nouns is identical with the nominative: *mid þe cyng* 41, *on land* 190, *to þis land* 105 (beside *of lande* 189), *in scip* 119.

9. In the plural of nouns:
   (*a*) -*es* has been adopted as the ending of OE feminines (prep. *sinnes* 203), many weak nouns (prep. *bucces* 53, acc. *huntes* 50, nom. *neues* 152, *rachenteges* 174, *sterres* 121), and endingless neuters (acc. *weorkes* 221, prep. -*weorces* 159), though
   (*b*) some endingless forms of OE survive intact (*frēond* 35, *hors* 53, *ðing* 99, *wunder* 154); and
   (*c*) the weak -*n* may be retained in nouns with roots ending in a vowel: *beon* 43 (*halechen* 201 was originally a substantivized adj., and tended to be fossilized in formulae, as Shakespeare's *All-hallond* (< ME *halwen*) *Eve* shows).

10. In the personal pronoun, (*a*) the nom. sg. fem. is the new type *scæ* 262, 292, 293, and (*b*) the pl. forms are of the native type: nom. *hi*, acc. *heom*, gen. *here*, dat. *heom*, prep. *heom*.

11. In the definite article, (a) grammatical gender no longer functions: acc. sg. masc. *se* 87; acc. sg. *þone abbotrice* 22, but *ðat abbotrice* 114, 115; *ðat oþer dæi* 124 (*dæi* having been masculine in OE), and (b) the singular of the old masculine is uninflected except in the gen. *þes* (e.g. prep. *to þe iunge eorl* 308, *of þe king* 296).

12. In the 3 pres. indic., (a) the sg. ends in *-eð*: *behofeð* 103 (and *frett* 43, *dragað* 44 both imply that the main type was *-eð*), and (b) the pl. ends in *-en*: *dragen* 43, *lien* 214, *seggen* 47.

13. Weak verbs of the old class II have no *-i-* element: *axen* 249, *hunten* 51, *ðolen* 33, 270.

Vocabulary

Adoptions from ON are *bryniges* 167, *carlmen* 162, *drapen* 179, *hærnes* 169, *iætte* 36, *oc* 12, 16, 112, *sahte* 313, *tacen* 44, *þoh-* 141, and possibly *þrengde* 172.

Provenance

The WMidl, the SW, and the SE are excluded by 1, 9, 10 (a), 12 (b), and 13; and the North by 12 (a) and (b); and this leaves only the EMidl. 3 (a) is almost certainly not a vestigial feature of the late OE literary standard language, but an EMidl (and specifically Northamptonshire) one, since place-names in this county show that OE *æ* had not become tense *ē* in that area.[1] 7 and the forms with OE breaking in 6 (a) and (b), and stray forms like *atywede* 229, are therefore to be explained as survivals of the old written standard language. The ON element, and especially the adoption of words with a primarily grammatical function, such as *drapen*, *oc*, *þoh-*, amount to a strong Scandinavian influence that accords with this localization.

---

1. *Ðis gear*. The formula is modern in its form and lack of inflexion. In the earlier annals a new entry is usually prefaced by *her* alone, with reference to the column of years prepared by the scribe; it occurs thus as late as 1121, and, combined with *eall þis gear* s.a. 1118. But the usual twelfth-century formula is *on þis gear*. The inflected dat. *geare* does not appear after 1123. *þis gear* is probably a reduced form of the dat. (*on*) *þissum geare*,

---
[1] Pointed out by C. Clark, op. cit., pp. xlvi–xlviii.

influenced by the acc. of extent found, e.g. *s.a.* 1119: *þis gear eall.*

5. *Æðelic*, i.e. Adeliza, generally known as Matilda; she had married the Emperor Henry V in 1114, but he had died in 1125.

8. *Burch.* This name began to replace *Medeshamstede* after the destruction of the earlier monastery by the Danes in 870. As at Bury St. Edmunds (originally *Beadurices worþ*), the town grew up round the monastery, on land owned by the monks: hence the abbot's power to alter the site (cf. 221, and see also D. Knowles, *The Monastic Order in England* (1950), p. 445, n. 3). The monastery was dedicated to St. Peter, but the present form of the name is rare before the thirteenth century.

an abbot, Heanri wæs gehaten. This colloquial paratactic construction with *hatan* is confined to names of persons and places. Cf. Laȝamon's *Brut* 1, cit. p. 145 *supra.*

Henry is mentioned *s.a.* 1123 as a papal legate, appointed to collect the *Romescott* (see Gl.). St. Jean d'Angeli was a daughter-house of Cluny, an abbey founded by William of Aquitaine in 1090 (?) and at this period at the height of its power. The Pope having granted the Cluniac order exemption from episcopal control, all its houses were directly subject to the Abbot of Cluny; hence the opposition described *s.a.* 1132 below.

17. *swa lange swa Godes wille wæs*: suggesting that this annal was not written until Henry had ceased to hold St. Jean d'Angeli (1131); on the other hand, the expression in 61 indicates that these passages were composed before his departure from England in 1132 [see C. Clark, *English Hist. Review*, lxxxiv (1969), 548–60].

27. *fif mile.* Plummer notes that the distance between Saintes and St. Jean d'Angeli is in fact about 15 miles. Miss Clark suggests that there was confusion between 'mile' and *leuca.*

39. *sibreden.* William Clito, younger (?) son of Robert Duke of Normandy, had married Sybilla, second daughter of Fulk Count (= 'earl') of Anjou, but Henry I had procured the annulment of the marriage in 1124 on grounds of consanguinity.

43. *swa frett þa drane*: *swa* here, as in 45, has pronominal function: see E. E. Ericson, *J.E.G.P.* xxx (1931), 6–20; *drane*

is probably sg. (rather than archaic pl.) and *frett* a syncopated
sg.: cf. Clark, p. xliii³, and W. F. Bryan, *Mod. Phil.* xviii (1921),
122–3.

49. *ex*[*s*]*urge, quare obdormis, Domine*: the introit, from Ps. xliii.
23, for Sexagesima Sunday, which in 1127 fell on 6 February.

50. *huntes*: allusions to *la mesnie Hellequin* (hell-rout) or *pha-
langes noctivagae* are found in several French and English
writers of about this period, e.g. Ordericus Vitalis, *Historia
Ecclesiastica* (*c.* 1122–30), and Gervase of Tilbury, who in *Otia
Imperialia* (*c.* 1211), writes:

> . . . in sylvis Britanniae majoris aut minoris consimilia
> contigisse referuntur, narrantibus nemorum custodibus . . .
> se alternis diebus circa horam meridianam et in primo noctium
> conticinio, sub plena luna lucente, saepissime videre militum
> copiam venantium et canum et cornuum strepitum, qui
> sciscitantibus se de societate et familia Arturi sese affirmant.

Cf. also John of Salisbury, *Policraticus* (ed. C. C. J. Webb,
1909), p. 100 and n.; *Mum and the Sothsegger* (ed. Day and
Steele, E.E.T.S. o.s. 199 (1934)), l. 90 and n.; *Sir Orfeo*,
281 ff., and the passage cited by G. R. Owst in *Studies presented
to Sir Hilary Jenkinson* (1957), p. 278. For further discussion see
E. K. Chambers, *Arthur of Britain* (1927), pp. 227–8; H. Flasdieck, 'Herlekin', *Anglia*, lxi (1937), 225–338; Scott's *Min-
strelsy of the Scottish Border* (2nd ed.), ii. 194; G. Cohen, *La
Grande Clarté du m.-âge* (1943), p. 48; and *O.E.D.* s.v.
Hurlewayn. Paulus Diaconus describes similar happenings in
sixth-century Italy (*Historia Langobardorum*, Bk. II, c. 4). See
also Clark², p. 102.

66. *orfcwalm*: thus described by William of Malmesbury,
Historia Novella, § 456:

> plene porcorum are subito vacuabantur; integra boum pre-
> sepia repente destituebantur. Duravit sequentibus annis ea-
> dem pestis, ut nulla omnino totius regni villa, huius miserie
> immunis, alterius incommoda ridere posset.

74. *Sancte Petres messe þe firrer*: the feast of SS. Peter and Paul
(29 June) as distinct from St. Peter *ad vincula* (1 August).

81. *Sancte Johannis messedæi*: 24 June. From this point until 117 the wording of the chronicle for the most part closely resembles that of Hugo Candidus (or 'Albus') (ed. cit., pp. 102–4), though Hugo has no equivalent to some of the more memorable phrases (e.g. 'he crape in his mycle codde . . .').

85. *se eorl*: i.e. William Count of Poitou, who as chief patron of the abbey expelled Henry's successor: see Clark[2], p. 104.

93. *se abbot of Clunni*: Peter the venerable, whose visit to Peterborough (sanctioned by the king) is mentioned *s.a.* 1130.

101. *he ferde into France*: i.e. from Cluny, in Burgundy. Hugo says merely *sicque per hoc pactum exivit, et ad Angliam venit*.

105. *Henri King*: for the word order cf. e.g. 'Ælfred cyning' at the beginning of the OE *Pastoralis*. Henry spent much of his time in Normandy. He had himself a special devotion to Cluny, which he had helped to rebuild; and his own foundation at Reading was begun with the help of Cluniacs; but to allow Peterborough to become a daughter-house of Cluny would have been to forfeit the royal power of appointing to the abbey, or at least of confirming the monks' choice (see Poole, pp. 181 ff.). The Bishop of Lincoln would be equally concerned, since Peterborough lay within his diocese.

111. *feorde mid suicdom*: an adaptation of the ON idiom *fara með* 'to deal in'; for later examples see Clark[2], p. 104.

þa he . . . þa uuolde he: this construction, with inversion after the second 'þa', is a survival of OE usage: cf. Laȝamon, *Brut* 7793 (Calig. MS.):

      þa þa Mærling wes ilad, þa wes Dinabus ful glad.

114. *ut of lande*: Hugo (ed. cit., p. 104) says that he recovered the abbacy of St. Jean d'Angeli, *et ideo sicut dictum est bonum finem fecit. Nam non diu postquam ibi venit vixit.*

115. *Sancte Neod*: a 'cell', or dependent monastery, of the Norman abbey of Bec, near Eynesbury (Hunts.), the burial place of the Saxon saint Neot.

Martin was appropriately inducted on the day on which the dedication of the monastery would be commemorated. For an account of such an induction 'cum debito honore et etiam processione' see the *Chronicle of Jocelin of Brakelond* (ed. H. E. Butler, 1949), §. 24.

118. *Lammasse*: the chronicler uses the English designation of 1 August, Hugo, *festivitas sancti Petri que dicitur ad vincula*. 2 August 1133 is the correct date for the eclipse, *pace* some chroniclers: cf. Lord Cooper of Culross, *Selected Papers*, 1957, p. 312. Henry set sail, according to the *Historia Novella* (ed. cit., p. 11, § 457), on 5 August.

125. *þestreden*: the emendation (see Bradley, *M.L.R.* xii (1917), 72 ff., 492; Ker, *M.Æ.* iii (1934), 136–7) is confirmed by the corresponding passage in Hugo (ed. cit., p. 104): *Tunc contenebrata est terra, quia pax et veritas et iusticia de terra ablate sunt*: an allusion to the eclipse of 2 August, when *celi contenebrati sunt* (cf. 120). Thus the sense is 'Then things did indeed grow black in these parts'. For a similar stylistic turn cf. Walter Map, *De Nugis Curialium*, i. xv: 'This year 1187 must be called a nubilous year [L. *nobis est nubileus a nubilo dicendus*] alike from the cloudiness of the weather and the gloom of misfortune'; and for similar portents cf. *Gesta Stephani*, ed. cit., pp. 33–35.

126. *his sune and his frend*: other sources indicate that among those present were Henry's natural son Robert of Gloucester, his son-in-law Rotrow of Mortagu, Count Waleran, and his brother, Robert Earl of Leicester. He died on 1 December at St. Denis-le-Ferment, *c*. 40 m. from Rouen 'from eating too heartily of eels'. His body was taken to Caen, and thence to Reading Abbey, the eastern arm of which had by now been finished, so that he was able to be buried before the High Altar.

The chronicler justly praises Henry's achievement in giving England thirty years of peace: cf. the letter of the Archbishop of Rouen cited *Hist. Nov.* (§ 458 [p. 14, ed. cit.]): *pacem det ei Deus, quia pacem dilexit*. The peace he gave to beasts was that he provided by making more forests in which only authorized persons could kill them: *Gesta Stephani*, c. 1 [p. 2, ed. cit.], notes that in Stephen's reign, on the other hand, they were 'fearlessly struck down by all', so that whole herds were exterminated.

127. *bebirieden*: the MS. form in *-end-* is possibly genuine: cf. MS. *þolenden* 202.

130. *Wuasua bare his byrthen*, &c.: a traditional formula for describing a peaceful kingdom: cf. *Pet. Chron. s.a.* 1087 (ed. Clark, p. 12, l. 90) *Hav.* 45–50, *Guy of Warwick* 137 ff. and Laȝamon, *Brut* (Calig. MS. 18486–9):

He sette suiþe god griþ þat ech man mihte faren wiþ
fram londe to londe þeh he bere golde an honde.

132. *Enmang þis*: i.e. whilst Henry's body was being brought to Reading, which took over a month (according to *Hist. Nov.* § 462); Stephen was present at the burial. Stephen's claim to be recognized as king rested as much on the fact that he filled a vacuum as that he was the grandson of the Conqueror. The chronicler omits to mention that Dover and Canterbury, held by adherents of Robert of Gloucester (see below) refused him admittance; that he went to Winchester, the pre-conquest capital and still the seat of the royal treasury, before being crowned; and that the archbishop had some scruples about consecrating him, in view of the oath Henry had extorted from his barons that they would recognize his daughter Matilda as his successor (note that 'Willelm' is the subject of 'halechede': cf. the absence of a pron. before 'stal' in 292).

138. *Execestre*: the castle as distinct from the town, the citizens of which, according to *Gesta Stephani* (cc. 16–20), received the king gladly. His clemency on this occasion was interpreted as weakness.

141. According to *Hist. Nov.* § 462, Stephen went to Northumbria to meet David 'a little before Lent' (1136), i.e. *before* the siege of Exeter.

144. *sculde*: a survival of the OE use of *sculan* in reported speech.

147. *gold and syluer*: the amassing, and dispersal, of part of Henry's treasure is referred to in *Hist. Nov.* (§ 463) and the *Liber* of Abbot Suger of St. Denis (ed. Panofsky, 1946, p. 59). Henry's soul is said not to have benefited therefrom since it was not used for pious purposes; cf. the account *s.a.* 1086 for 1087 of William Rufus's disposal of his father's treasure at Winchester:

'dælde þa gersuman for his fæder saule to ælcen mynstre þe wes innan Englelande . . . in to ælcere scire man seonde hundred punda feos to dælanne earme mannan for his saule'. According to *Hist. Nov.* § 458, Henry wished to make similar provision for the poor.

150. *Oxeneford*: the meeting of the great council referred to in fact took place in June 1139. Roger, Bishop of Salisbury, had been Henry I's justiciar; 'his neves' refers to Alexander and Roger, Bishop Roger's illegitimate son (described in *Hist. Nov.* § 469 as *nepos, vel plusquam nepos*). Stephen evidently had some justification for taking action against these men: Bishop Roger had fortified Sarum, Sherborne, Devizes, and Malmesbury, and Alexander a building at Newark ('niwe werke')— not far from the royal castle of Lincoln (on the forms and origin of this place-name see *Oxford Dictionary of English Place-Names*, s.v.). But to imprison them was to impugn the right of the clergy to be judged by canon law; and even the *Gesta* agrees that in this case Stephen yielded to *stultissimo, immo et insano consilio* (c. 34, ed. cit., p. 50). *Hist. Nov.* § 469 states that he took Bishop Roger in chains to Devizes, where Nigel, Bishop of Ely, was holding out.

With the mention of castles the chronicler returns to his earlier theme of the nobles' treachery: he doubtless had specially in mind Geoffrey de Mandeville, who converted Ramsey Abbey (near Peterborough) into a fortress (for details of his career see the monograph by J. H. Round).

153. *milde . . . and softe.* Cf. *manna mildust, Beowulf* 3181, AS *Chron.* (C) *s.a.* 1065 (St. Edward the Confessor is praised as *clæne and milde*), and (E) *s.a.* 1114 (the worthy Abbot Ernulf is *god and softe*). *Gesta*, c. 12, uses the epithets *benignus* and *mansuetus*. For *iustise* see Gl.

154. *hi alle*, 'all of them'; cf. *hi nan*, 155.

164. *untellendlice pining*, &c.: the account is very similar to that in *Hist. Nov.* § 483. But the chronicler was possibly influenced by accounts of the sufferings of early martyrs: e.g. Eusebius describes a punishment in which they were 'smoaked and suffocated to death' as in 165–6 (cited by T. Jackson, *The True Evangelical Temper* (1641), p. 44).

167. *bryniges*: Miss Clark compares *collo atque pedibus immensis loricarum sive saxorum ponderibus alligatis* (Symeon of Durham, *Opera*, ed. T. Arnold (Rolls Series, 1882), i. 153).

170. *pades*: thought to be venomous: cf. *As You Like It*, II. i. 13 and *Macbeth*, IV. i. 6 ff.

171. *crucethur*: former edd., *crucethus*. J. Gerritsen (*English Studies*, xlii (1961), 300–1) pointed out the correct reading.

174. *lof and grin*: MS. *grī*. OE *lof* usually glosses *redimicula*, a string, fillet, or fetter; *grin* is found in the sense 'halter, snare', as late as the 1611 text of the English Bible (Ps. cxl. 5). See B. Dickins, *R.E.S.* ii (1926), 34. Evidently a single device is here signified; cf. *ðat . . . onne* below—'one of which it took two or three men all their time to carry'. F. P. Magoun (*M.L.N.* xl, (1925), 411–22) translates the phrase 'headband and noose which were of chains'.

185. *wel þu myhtes faren*, &c. Cf. *Gesta*, c. 78: 'Pars hominum, ubique provinciarum, famis praevalente angustia tabescens cateruatim mori, pars, cum omni familia, spontaneum lugubriter subiens exilium, exterminari. Videres famosissimi nominis villas, defunctis totius sexus et aetatis colonis, solitarias stare'; and *Hist. Nov.* § 483: 'Milites castellorum abducebant ab agris et pecora et pecudes, nec ecclesiis nec cimiteriis parcentes.'

191. *ouersithon*: C. Sisam (*R.E.S.* N.S. xiii (1962), 386) suggests that this is a scribal error for *ofsithon*, a form of *oftsithen* 'often', noting a similar omission of *t* in *efsones* 288; but see Gl.

195. *æuric man other þe ouermyhte*: possibly an echo of Isa. xix. 2, which is cited in *Gesta*, c. 1. in the form: *vir immisericorditer in virum, unusquisque irruere in proximum suum.*

198. *forcursæd*, &c.: cf. Wulfstan 'mænige synd forsworene and swyþe forlogene . . .' (Sweet, *A.-S. Reader* (ed. of 1967), XVI, l. 93, *Homilies* ed. D. Bethurum, p. 271, l. 96).

201. *Crist slep*: In allusion to Matt. viii. 24 ff., &c. (see XVIII. 148 f.). Cf. John of Salisbury, *Metalogicon, ad fin.*: *velud in navi dormiens, fidelium precibus excitandus est, ut procellam com-*

ponat Ecclesiæ naufragantis (ed. C. C. J. Webb, p. 219). Emerson (*M.E. Reader*) gives a similar illustration from *M.E. Metrical Homilies*, ed. J. Small (1862), p. 35.

206. *gestes*: the medieval monastery often served as an inn and had a considerable guest house; the Benedictine Rule requiring monks to accept all comers, especially the poor, 'in whom Christ is received the more'.

207. *carited*: see Gl., and du Cange (*Glossarium Mediae et Infimae Latinitatis*), s.v. *caritas*, where the definitions include (1) *convivium quo amici vel etiam pauperes excipiuntur*, and (2) *quævis extraordinaria refectio, maxime illa quæ fiebat extra prandium et cœnam in monasteriis* (cf. the *poculum caritatis* still drunk in some colleges). The *Liber Niger* of Peterborough explicitly mentions gifts given to the abbey for the *caritas* of St. Peter, i.e. 29 June (Camden Soc. vol. xlvii (1849), 158).

wrohte on þe circe, &c.: cf. Hugo, op. cit.: *Et in omnibus tribulacionibus bene operatus est in ecclesia, et in officinis, et villam mutavit et in illa operatus est, et presbiterium ecclesie perfecit . . . .* The abbey church and buildings had been wholly destroyed in the fire of 1116. Some rebuilding had taken place in 1118–25 but it was not resumed until Martin became abbot; it had probably proceeded as far as the transepts and eastern bays of the nave by the time of his death.

212. *Eugenie*: Pope Eugenius III (1145–63), a Cistercian. The first of the *privilegia* (printed in Stevens's Appendix to Dugdale's *Monasticon* (1722), II, no. cxli, and, with the second, in Hugo, ed. cit., pp. 109 ff.) refers to Martin's visit, and is dated 16 Kal. Jan. 1146; it mentions all the places here listed in the Chronicle. The effect of such documents was to ensure for the abbey a large number of inalienable lands and properties such as mills, and to prevent the king from appropriating the revenue from them during a vacancy: cf. D. Knowles, *The Monastic Order in England*, pp. 433–6, 614, and the *Chronicle of Jocelin of Brakelond*, ed. cit., pp. 56, 60.

214. *circewican*: the sacrist was sometimes responsible for building operations and repairs and even for the town: cf. *Brakelond*, ed. cit. xxvii.

215. *horderwycan*: the office of cellarer, or steward, whose duties, according to the Benedictine Rule, c. 31, included the care of all the utensils of the monastery, purchase of food, clothes, and agricultural materials, and provision of better bread on feast days.

220. *winiærd*: a building in the minster precincts is still called 'The Vineyard'. The vine was extensively cultivated on monastic lands, e.g. at Thorney, Winchester, and the Vale of Gloucester. Henry VI often stayed at Bury St. Edmunds *propter vineæ odorem delectabilem.*

221. *mani weorkes,* &c.: according to Hugo (p. 122) *portam monasterii et mercatum et portum navium et villam multo melius mutavit, et multa emendavit.*

223. *God and gode men*: an old alliterative phrase found (as C. T. Onions noted, *T.L.S.* 13 August 1931, p. 621) in the ON lawbook *Grágás*: 'guðs vingan oc góðra manna'. Cf. *South English Legendary* (E.E.T.S., o.s. 235, p. 9, l. 26); *Ormulum*, 5268, 8975; *Piers Plowman* C. vi. 67, B. xvi. 9; *Richard II*, I. i. 114, &c. For examples from OWN religious prose see E. S. Olszewska in *English and Medieval Studies presented to J. R. R. Tolkien* (1962), p. 125. 'God and good people' is a 17c variant.

225–6. *an Cristen cild,* &c.: *Chron. Petroburg.* assigns this event to 1144. For the charge of ritual murder brought against the Jews (of which this is the first record) in England see A. Jessup and M. R. James, *Life and Miracles of St. William of Norwich* (1896), the introduction to the Prioress's Tale in F. N. Robinson's ed. of Chaucer (1957, p. 734), and *Brakelond*, p. 16 and n. C. Roth has noted that in 1144 the Jewish feast of Purim, when the effigy of Haman was burnt and excitement ran high, fell in Holy Week, and that the attack on the child may have been connected with this celebration (*Speculum*, viii (1933), 520–6). But the incident probably also reflects the increasing scope of Jewish financial operations. The Sheriff of Norwich, and some of the clergy, scouted the charge: see M. D. Anderson, *A Saint at Stake* (1964). An unnoticed variant of the story occurs in *Middle English Sermons*, ed. W. O. Ross (E.E.T.S., o.s. 209, 1940), pp. 63–6. St. William's day is 24 March. Cf. Clark², p. 209.

227. *Lang Fridæi*: Easter Friday; apparently an adoption of ON 'langi frjádagr' (where 'langi' evidently refers to the length of the fast: cf. ON 'langafasti' (Lent), and MScots 'lang lenten').

230. *to munekes*: *to* is probably a reduced form of *þā*: cf. *to other*, 237; the context hardly allows the interpretation 'two'.

234. *On þis gær*: the Scots first crossed the Tweed on 10 January, but withdrew. They reappeared in April, reaching Clitheroe *c.* 22 July with an army of marauding Galwegians. Resistance was largely organized by Thurstan, Archbishop of York. The standards from which the battle (or rather rout) took its name were the banners of St. John of Beverley, St. Peter of York, and St. Wilfrith of Ripon, which were carried on a wagon. Another English account is extant in the works of Aelred (Rolls Ser. lxxxii. 186), who lived near by at Rievaulx Abbey which had been founded by Walter Lespec, a leader of the English forces.

240. *Rodbert*: natural son of Henry I, who had created him Earl of Gloucester *c.* 1122; he had given conditional homage to Stephen in 1136, but withdrawn it two years later. Some MSS. of Geoffrey of Monmouth's *Historia* bear a dedication to him: see Griscom's ed., c. vi, *passim*.

243. *abuton non-tid dæies*, &c.: the date was 20 March 1140: cf. *Hist. Nov.* § 484: ... *fuit eclipsis per totam Angliam ut accepi. Apud nos certe, et apud omnes vicinos nostros, ita notabiliter solis deliquium fuit ut homines, quod tunc fere ubique accidit, erat enim Quadragesima, mensis assidentes, antiquum chaos timerent.* The eclipse took place *c.* 2. 54 p.m. and was total in the Midlands: cf. Cooper, loc. cit. at 118 n.

244. *to æten bi*: cf. IV. 50 n.

245. *Willelm*: the death of William of Corbeil actually took place in November 1136, and a monastic chronicler might be expected to record it more accurately. *þerefter* is perhaps used very loosely, or altered from *Efter*, which may originally have introduced a sentence of slightly different construction.

246. *Teodbald*: the appointment was delayed for political reasons, and he was not consecrated till 8 January 1139. His famous predecessors, Lanfranc and Anselm, had also come from Bec,

the intellectual capital of Normandy, where in 1034 Herlouin had
established a monastery that was intended to recapture the
simplicity and austerity of the religious life: see Porée, *Histoire
de l'Abbaye du Bec* (1901), and, for an estimate of its influence in
England, Knowles, op. cit., p. 96. Theobald was a monk there
before he became abbot; his life has been written by Avrom
Saltman (1956).

248. *Randolf*: the second Earl of Chester of that name. He had
married Robert Earl of Gloucester's daughter, and William of
Roumare, Earl of Lincoln, was his half-brother. The honour
of Chester included important Lincolnshire fiefs; and J. H.
Round suggested that Randolf wished to reign at Lincoln as he
reigned at Chester and to unite these strongholds by a chain of
fortresses (*English Historical Review*, x (1895), 87 ff.). The details
of his rupture with Stephen are not clear (the account in *Transactions of the Royal Historical Society*, 4th ser. xx (1937), 114–16,
does not refer to that in the Chronicle). He seized the keep of
Lincoln (a royal castle) by a stratagem in December 1140, and
made exorbitant demands on the city and neighbourhood.
Stephen answered the appeal of the citizens by hurrying to besiege the castle, from which Randolph slipped away—to return
with *Walensium gravi et intolerabili multitudine* (*Gesta*, c. 54).
In the subsequent battle (2 February 1141) Stephen himself
fought bravely, but was deserted by his Flemish mercenaries.
Earl Robert took the king to Bristol; and *tota Anglia concussa
obstupuit* (*Gesta*, c. 57: cf. 258).

260. *emperice*: Matilda had first (1114) married Henry V,
Emperor of Germany, and in 1129 Geoffrey of Anjou; she was
crowned by the anti-pope Gregory VIII in 1118, and was never
given the title of empress in any official documents. Everything
suggests that she was her own worst enemy. In September
1139 she landed at Arundel, where Stephen had the opportunity of capturing her but with characteristic leniency allowed
her to join Robert. Early in 1140 she began negotiations with
Stephen's versatile brother, Henry of Blois, Bishop of Winchester, who in April 1141 proclaimed her *Angliæ Normanniæque
domina* and pronounced the excommunication of l. 266. She
was received by the London citizenry in June, but refused their
demand for 'the laws of the Conqueror' and was soon forced to

flee to Winchester, though by this time Bishop Henry had lost sympathy with her (the invitation referred to in 267 would appear to be one given much earlier in the year, when Matilda had certainly visited the city).[1] At Winchester she and Earl Robert were besieged by Stephen's queen Matilda, a woman of some spirit and military ability. On 14 September 1141 she fled to Gloucester Abbey. Robert's capture led in 1142 to the exchange and reconciliation at Stamford—a meeting not recorded elsewhere; Stamford had become important in the tenth century as one of the 'five boroughs' founded by Æþelflæd, and a Peterborough monk would be likely to have authentic information about events there.

275. *þe wise men*: the same phrase is used in a similar context, *s.a.* 1052 (ed. Earle and Plummer i. 181) and below, l. 312.

279. *her nouþer sculde besuyken other*: 'The question at issue between them (at Lincoln) was a feudal question, the King and the Earl each, in effect, alleging a breach on the part of the other of their feudal relationship . . .' (J. H. Round, *Geoffrey de Mandeville*, p. 120).

281. *Hamtun*: whilst the king was holding court at Northampton in 1146 Randolph appeared, asking for assistance against Welsh incursions. Suspecting a plot, the king's advisers insisted that if the earl did not give hostages and surrender certain castles (including Lincoln) he should be arrested as a traitor. Soon after he attacked the king, though unsuccessfully, at Lincoln.

285. *hær sculde*: 'ever ought to have done': *ær* as a form of 'ever' is not elsewhere found before Laȝamon (14320); C. Sisam (loc. cit.) would take *hær* as a form of *ær* 'before' and *sculde* in the sense 'is said to'; but this sense seems attested only when an infinitive follows.

290. *burch*: Oxford was delivered up to the empress by Robert d'Oilly, who not only was governor of the castle but had bought the shrievalty of the town in 1130.

ute: usually interpreted as 'out of prison', though Stephen had been out of prison since September 1141 and by June

[1] For Henry's part in the sacking of the city (and of Hyde Abbey) see E. Bishop, *Liturgica Historica* (Oxford 1918), pp. 394–5.

1142 was campaigning with his army. In the annals 894A, 1006E, *ute* is used precisely in regard to a *fierd* (cf. *feord*, 291) on a campaign, and that sense possibly survived along with the *fierd* organization.

After capturing Cirencester, Stephen followed the upper Thames, taking Radcot and Bampton; then, leaving the road that led via Cumnor to the castle, approached Oxford from Abingdon, across the ford where Folly Bridge now stands.

291 ff. *þe tur*: i.e. the stone tower that still stands. The manner of escape is not elsewhere mentioned; Robert d'Oilly held Craneford in fee from Peterborough, and it is conceivable that messengers of his carried the information.

Wallingford, eight miles down the Thames, was held by Matilda's cousin and adherent Brian Fitzcount; she did not leave England until 1147/8. Robert of Gloucester had gone to Normandy five years earlier, and helped Geoffrey of Anjou to conquer it. Rouen had surrendered in 1144 and in that year Louis VII invested Geoffrey with the duchy. Eustace's attempt to regain it (see 299) did not take place till 1151. His betrothal to Constance, Louis's sister, had occurred in 1140. Her confinement in Canterbury is not elsewhere mentioned though William of Newburgh (44. 5) credits Geoffrey de Mandeville with imprisoning her in the Tower *c*. 1140.

295. *here þankes*: see Gl., Sweet, *A.-S. Reader*, VIII, l. 155 n., and (for later developments) *Hali Meiðhad*, ed. Colborn, 709 n.

305. *rixan*: the verb is evidently used because Stephen wished to follow the French custom (cf. *Hist. Nov.* § 455) of crowning or consecrating a future king: this the English prelates refused to do. Eustace died (mad) in August 1153, his mother in May 1152.

307. *þe rice*: the 'earldom' of Anjou. Geoffrey had handed over Normandy to Henry his son (*æt*. 17) in 1150, after the return of the latter from an abortive visit to England.

te cuen of France: Eleanor of Aquitaine, whose divorce from Louis VII was eventually sanctioned on grounds of consanguinity; Walter Map (*De Nugis Curialium*, Dist. V, c. vi) censures her action as 'unchaste' and 'iniquitous'. Henry married her two months later (May 1152), and thus doubled his dominions. He landed in England in January 1153 with some 3,000 men and met Stephen at Winchester, where the negotiations were carried on by the great council: Stephen declared Henry his successor 'jure hereditario'; and it was agreed that all castles built during his reign should be destroyed.

The last entry in the Chronicle (*s.a.* 1154) records Stephen's death, the consecration of Henry as king, the death of Abbot Martin, and the election of William de Walteuile as his successor. The MS. being defaced, it is not printed here.

XVII

MS.: Laud Misc. 471, Bodleian Library.

Editions: R. Morris, *An Old English Miscellany*, E.E.T.S., o.s. 49 (1872), pp. 26–36.

J. Hall, *Early Middle English* (Oxford 1920), i. 214–22.

Source: Sermons 2, 3, 5, and 6 of Maurice of Sully, ed. C. A. Robson, *Maurice of Sully and the Medieval Vernacular Homily* (Oxford 1952), pp. 88 ff.

Language

1. The reflex of OE ǽ (OKt, WMerc ě) is:
   (a) e (*efterward* 202, *hedden* 222, *hest* 110), beside
   (b) frequent a (*faten* 102, *spac* 20, *uastinge* 62, *watere* 99).
2. The reflex of Gmc ǎ before nasal+consonant constituting an OE lengthening group is spelt o: *fond* 219, *londes* 33; similarly (with OF a) *ongel* 31.
3. OE ā has been rounded to slack ō: *gon* 9, *gostliche* 47, *hoot* 82, *slon* 26. See also 17, below.
4. The reflex of OE ǽ¹ (non-WS ē) is spelt:
   (a) e (*drede* 149, *euen* 183, *slepe* 31).
   (b) when shortened before two consonants in OE., e (*dret* 151, *ofdred* 16).
5. The reflex of OE ǽ² (OAngl ǣ, OKt ē) is spelt:
   (a) e (*anhet* 126, *hete* 251).
   (b) when shortened in trisyllabic forms usually e (*clenesse* 100, *flesliche* 47, *hepenesse* 38), and exceptionally a in *aueriche* 75.
6. The reflexes of OE ȳ (OKt ě) are spelt e: *senne* 67, *werm* 66; *bredale* 87, *fer* 122.

7. The reflex of OE *ēa* is spelt:
   (a) *ea* in *beleaue* 50, 53, *feaue* 203, *seawede* 41.
   (b) *ia* in *beliaue* 44, 152, 157; *diaþ(e)* 45, 259; *griat(e)* 177, 215; *ialde* 42, *ihialde* 110.
   (c) *ya* initially in *yare* 268.
8. The reflex of OE *ēo* (OKt *īo*) is:
   (a) *ie* (*forbiet* 81, *liese* 16, *niedes* 160).
   (b) *i* in final position (*bi* 14; confirmed by the inverted spelling in *bie* 102).
9. Breaking of *ǽ* before *ld* in the antecedent OE type is attested in *ialde* 42, *chald* 119 (a non-rounded and therefore evidently unlengthened form—see 3, above—beside the type which was lengthened and (in ME) rounded in *chold* 136, and therefore presumably in *itold* 73).
10. Front vowels preceded by a palatal consonant had not been diphthongized in the antecedent OE type: *yeftte* 41, *yeld* 189, *yeue* 79.
11. The product of *i*-mutation in OE of:
    (a) *ǽ* before *ld* is *e* (*elde* 243).
    (b) *ĕa* before an *h*-group is *e* (*manslechtes* 121).
    (c) *ēa* is *e* (*bileue* 232, *iherde* 20).
12. Back-mutation of *ĭ* before a nasal in an antecedent OE type is attested in *beneme* 165.
13. In the antecedent OE type *g* had been absorbed before *d* or *n*, with the lengthening of the preceding vowel: *sede(n)* 93, 210; *ayen-wende* 32, *tojanes* 7.
14. ME *ĕ* is sporadically raised to *ĭ* before a palatal consonant: *wrichede* 65.
15. The reflexes of OE *ǽ+g* and *ĕ+g* are distinguished in spelling, and evidently in pronunciation (as [ai] and [ei] respectively): *mai* 158, *todai* 178, *weye* 33.
16. Tense *ō* has been raised to *ū* by preceding [i̯] in the diphthong [i̯ō] developed by shift of stress in *ĕo* before *w*: *furti* 250, *yu* 96, 187, *yure* 71.
17. The reflex of OE *ā* before *w* is spelt *au*, with ME unrounding of slack *ō* (see 3, above): *saulen* 171.
18. No ME glide has developed between a vowel and the voiceless fricative [x]: *tachte* 231.
19. The OE voiced fricative [ɣ] is preserved: *daghen* 235, *laghe* 17, *seghen* 27.

20. Initial *f* is occasionally voiced: *uastinge* 62, *verrene* 39.
21. The reflex of OE *sc* is spelt *s* or *ss*: *seauinge* 6, *ssipe* 148, *wesse* 100.
22. Both in medial and in final position the graph *ng* is sporadically replaced by *nk*, which may either reflect an unvoicing of *g* (originally in final position) or be an inverted spelling, implying that [ŋk] had become [ŋg] in medial position (as in the *OKt Glosses* and the *Ayenbite*): *kink* 41, *offrinke* 37, 40, *þinkes* 81, 122. In *forþingketh* 200, *ng* is an occasional spelling for the velar nasal [ŋ].
23. In the plural of nouns:
    (*a*) *-es* has been adopted for all grammatical cases in endingless neuters of OE (nom. *þinges* 64, acc. *werkes* 61, prep. *eueles* 170, *londes* 33), and in old weak nouns (prep. *hertes* 79).
    (*b*) *-en* has been adopted for all grammatical cases in strong nouns which in OE ended in a vowel in the nom. and acc. pl. (nom. *deden* 121, prep. *sorghen* 164; acc. *faten* 99).
24. Grammatical gender is substantially preserved: *se king* 13, *þane dai* 258, *si sterre* 11, *þet child* 22. But *þo* (< OE *þa*) is used as acc. and prep. form with nouns of all genders.
25. The pronoun of the third person includes the following forms:

	Masc.	*Fem.*
	Masc.	*Fem.*
Nom.	*ha*	*hi, hye*
Acc.	*hyne, him*	
Gen.	*his*	
Dat.	*him*	
Prep.		*hire*

	Pl.
Nom.	*hi*
Acc.	*hi, his, -es* (in *has* 76), *hem*
Gen.	*here, hire*
Dat.	*hem*
Prep.	*hem*

26. The 3 pres. sg. ends in:
    (*a*) *-(e)þ*: *akelþ* 118, *besekeþ* 75, *telþ* 35. An old variant of this, with syncope and assimilation of the *-þ* to a dental ending the root, is retained in *dret* 151, *halt* 269, *licht*

50, *sent* 247. In *yeft* 38 the *-t* may be due to dissimilation of the voiceless fricative immediately after another one (cf., however, *yefþ* 257).

(b) *-et*: *amuntet* 56, *defendet* 59, *loket* 65, *signefiet* 61 (cf. 27 (b)). This is probably a spelling variant used by a scribe familiar with AN.

27. The pres. pl. ends in:

    (a) *-(e)ð*: *betockneþ* 205, *bieth* 64, *doþ* 109, *habbeþ* 109.

    (b) Occasionally *-et*: *habbet* 69, 92, *perisset* 150.

    (c) *-e(n)* in old preterite-present verbs: *sollen* 177.

28. The imper. pl. ends in *-(e)ð* or the equivalent: *cometh* 23, *folvellet* 98, *goþ* 21.

29. The ending *-inde* is implied for the pres. part. by the gerund *risindde* 7.

30. The past part. of uncompounded verbs normally has the prefix *i-*, and ends mostly in *-e* (*ibye* 197, *ibore* 4, *idrunke* 105), but occasionally *-n* < *-en* (*icornee* 203).

31. Weak verbs of class II in OE with short root-syllables are still distinguished from those with long or polysyllabic root-syllables: *hatie* 80, *louie* 224, *wakie* 62; *lokeþ* 262, *serui* 224.

Vocabulary

Adoptions from ON are very few, and all pre-Conquest: *laghe* 17, 42, *niþinge* 132, *velaghes* 197. *Alwat* (cf. *wath* 111) 28 is Southern and overwhelmingly SE in distribution.

Provenance

1 (a) and 27 (a) and (b) exclude the EMidl and the North, and 6 and 9 the WMidl. The SE is clearly indicated by 4 and 5 in conjunction, 6, and 8. There is a slight admixture of forms that (historically or by comparison with the fourteenth-century *Ayenbite of Inwyt*) are non-Kentish and may be scribal: 1 (b), and the Anglian-derived form *werkes* 120, 170, 222 and *werkmen* 192. But the correspondence with the language of the *Ayenbite* (localized in Canterbury by the author's own statement) is remarkable, as e.g. in regard to 7, and such details as the form *yemer(nesse)* 61, 124, which is a specifically Kentish one in ME, and the SE *wordl(e)* 171, 209; and *slon* 26 matches the *ofslanne* of the OKt Glosses 829.

---

1. *Cum natus esset* . . .: Matt. ii. 1–2.

4. *ase*: *que quant* M 2, 5.

5. *was seauinge*: renders a relative clause (*qui estoit demostrance* M 2, 6).

6. *swo*: though not represented in M, is best interpreted as the gallicism illustrated in 11, 15, and 22 (*swo kam*; *swo was michel anud*; *swo anuret*), where it renders OF *si* (< L *sic*), an almost meaningless co-ordinating conjunction. This use of *so* is exceptional in ME.

7. *þo sunne risindde*: a not uncommon ME calque on an OF idiom which it here directly translates (*soleil levant*). The ME form, with a present participle, is syntactically irrational: it is due to a mistaken interpretation of the OF *-ant* form as a present participle, though it is in fact a gerund (as both L *-antem*, *-entem* on the one hand, and *-andum*, *-endum* on the other produced OF *-ant*).

9. *forto hyne anuri*: un-English word-order, by a literal rendering of *por lui aorer* M 2, 9.

15. *swo was*: the absence of the pronominal subject is here due to the OF original (*si fu* M 2, 14), as in 29 (*swo hin*).

18. *þet*: not in M (2, 17).

25. *Þet ne . . .*: introduced in M (2, 21) by *Expositio*: *Segnor. He . . . Herodes*: not in M; cf. *hi . . . Ure Lauedi* 94–95. This is a usage common in OF (there in its various forms styled 'reprise' by modern grammarians) and also current in this form (with repetition of a grammatical subject) in OE, and used by Shakespeare (e.g. *Cymbeline*, I. i. 40). In origin it is probably colloquial and therefore essentially affective.

27. *seghen* is probably corrupt: M 2, 24 reads *sivirent* ('followed').

41. *seawede*: but M 2, 37 with expressed subject (*demostrerent il*).

44. *þet is biter þing*: but M 2, 41 *de coi l'on oignoit les cors que vers nes maignascent*.

46. *Nu ihiereth*: M introduces this section with *Expositio*: *Segnor*.

54. *werkes*: not obviously consistent with *biddinge* 57; and M 2, 51 has *proiere*.

55. *ueree*: *feu de l'encensier* M 2, 52.

59. MS. *Li* before *þet* (which is suprascript) is here interpreted as reproducing (by an error of the translator or a scribe) the OF definite article *Li*, with which the sentence begins in the exemplar (M 2, 59). But a miswriting of *Bi*, in a construction roughly like that of 40–41 (*be þet . . . seawede*), is also conceivable.

61. *yemernesse*: M 2, 59 *malvaiste*; cf. 124 n.

63. First *to*: probably the definite article (OE *þā*). There is no equivalent in M (2, 61).

65. *loket*: M 2, 63 *deffent*, literally 'prevents'.

74. *for(e)*: in all three instances M has *par* 'by'.

82. *bidde*: M 2, 79 *amer*.

85. *Nuptie . . .*: John ii. 1.

89. *To*: a literal rendering of *A* 'at' in M 3, 6.

94. *hi*: not represented in M (3, 11); cf. 25 n.

95. *of þo wyne*: M 3, 12 *del vin* (a partitive use).

96. *so*: again renders *si*, M 3, 13 (cf. 6 n.).

100. *baþieres*: recorded nowhere else, and obviously a nonce-formation directly prompted by OF *baignoires* 'bath-tub', which it renders here (M 3, 15). The OF suffix *-oire*, the fem. form of *-oir* (< L *-ōria*), which latter denotes the locality or the instrument of an action, designates only an instrument. OF *-iere*, the fem. form of *-ier* < *-ārium*, designates, among other things, a receptacle or an instrument. Substitution of one for the other in ME (and in AN) would therefore have been natural.

102. The absence of an expressed pronominal subject was not suggested by M (3, 17); similarly 131 (M 3, 44). See 41 n., and cf. 20.

104. *Moveth togidere*: but M 3, 19 *Puisies* 'pour out'.

105. *ferst was iserued*: but M 3, 20 *avoit en garde le cose a l'espous*.
    hedde: the subject is *he*, implied in *Architriclin* (cf. *ha* 'he' 21).

110. *ihialde*: M 3, 25 *estuie* 'reserved'.

117. *bitockned*: present tense.

121. *manslechtes, husberners*: not in M (3, 35).

124. *yemer(e)*: *male* M 3, 37–38.

128. *Nu*: introduced in M 3, 41 by *Expositio*.

130. *maked*: not in M (3, 43); evidently ('to be) made'.

131. *maked*: see 102 n.

132. *þe niþinge*: M 3, 45 *l'aver* 'the miser'.

146. First *so*: M 5, 5 *com*.
    Second *so*: M 5, 6 *si* (cf. 6 n.).

149. *so*: M 5, 8 *si*.

150. *wiste wel*: but *les blasma* M 5, 9.

151. *ine him*: not in M (5, 10).

152. *tok*: M 5, 11 *acoisa* 'calmed, quietened'.

154. *awondrede hem*: reflexive, with subject understood from *þo men* (M 5, 13 *si s'esmerveillierent*).

159. *þet us*: M 5, 18 *qu'il nos*.

164. *clepiedh . . . sucuri*: these are uses of the present as a future (*apeleront . . . socorrai* M 5, 20–21).

171. *þo saulen of us*: directly suggested by M (*les anmes de nos* 5, 27).

176. *seruise*: followed in M 6, 4 by *en terre*.

179. *bi*: here a *gallicism* (M 6, 7 *par*).

182. *undren*: representing *tierce* M 6, 9.

183–4. *so . . . so*: M 6, 10 *si . . . si*.

186. *þet*: M 6, 12 *qui*.
  ha: not represented in M (6, 12); cf. 25 n.

190. *to*: idiomatically irregular, because a literal rendering of OF *a* in M 6, 16.

193. *so*: M 6, 18 *quant*.

195. *habbe*: then in M (6, 20–21) *mais quant li serjans vint a els, si ne dona a cascun c'un denier.*

211. *hedden hit to siggen*: M 6, 36 *l'avoient a dire.*

219. *fore*: M 6, 42 *quar* 'for'; Hall's *werefore* will not do, because not attested in the required sense.

223. *þo þet hi*: *qu'il* M 6, 46 'that they' (i.e. 'because they').

224. *louie . . . serui*: these are not corruptions of two past participles, but exact equivalents of the OF version, which has the infinitives *amer . . . seruir*. The translator had altered the construction in M (*s'estoient de rien entremis de Deu croire ne de lui amer* 6, 46) by using the past part. *bileued*, but by an oversight reverted to it here.
  al þat is ine þis wordle, þet man is: this is likely to be corrupt, since it is not really congruous with what is said of the subject *hit* in the main clause. And M's version is convincing (6, 48): *quanqu'on fait en cest siecle des qu'on n'aime Deu, ne ne sert.*

227. MS. *vre* may be a miswriting (possibly in an earlier copy, and here misunderstood) of *vore* as a form of *fore*.

232. *a*: not represented in M (6, 55); cf. 25 n.

236. *bieþ i-entred*: M 6, 57 *i entrames par baptesme.*

242. *wordles*: 'epochs'; M 6, 63 *divers tens de cest siecle.*

243. *of þe elde*: not in M.

252. *elde of man*: *la vieillece* M 6, 69.

259–60. *for 'Man . . . wrench'*: not in M.

269. *halt*: M 6, 87 *estuie* (cf. 110 n.).

XVIII

MS.: Corpus Christi College, Cambridge, 402.

Editions: J. Morton, *The Ancren Riwle* (Camden Society, 1852). Corpus MS. pts. vi–vii in G. Shepherd, *Ancrene Wisse* (1959).

    M. Day, *The English Text of the Ancrene Riwle* (MS. Cotton Nero A. xiv) E.E.T.S., o.s. 225 (1952).

    R. M. Wilson, *The English Text of the Ancrene Riwle* (Gonville and Caius College, Cambridge, MS. 234/120), E.E.T.S., o.s. 229 (1954).

    A. C. Baugh, *The English Text of the Ancrene Riwle* (MS. Royal 8 C. I), E.E.T.S., o.s. 232 (1956).

    J. R. R. Tolkien, *Ancrene Wisse* (Corpus Christi College, Cambridge, MS. 402), E.E.T.S., o.s. 249 (1962).

    F. M. Mack, *The English Text of the Ancrene Riwle* (MS. Cotton Titus D. xviii), E.E.T.S., o.s. 252 (1963).

    E. J. Dobson, *The English Text of the Ancrene Riwle* (MS. Cotton Cleopatra C. vi) E.E.T.S., o.s. 267 (1972).

Studies: D. Dymes, 'The Original Language of the *Ancren Riwle*', *Essays and Studies*, ix (1924), 31–49.

    R. W. Chambers, 'Recent Research upon the *Ancren Riwle*', *Review of English Studies*, i (1925), 4–23.

    J. R. R. Tolkien, '*Ancrene Wisse* and *Hali Meiðhad*', *Essays and Studies*, xiv (1929), 104–26.

    M. L. Samuels, '*Ancrene Riwle* Studies', *Medium Ævum*, xxii (1953), 1–9.

    Dom Gerard Sitwell, in M. B. Salu's translation, *The Ancrene Riwle* (London 1955), pp. vii–xxii and 193–6.

    C. H. Talbot, 'Some Notes on the Dating of the *Ancrene Riwle*', *Neophilologus*, xxx (1956), 38–50.

Parallel Versions: C. D'Evelyn, *The Latin Text of the Ancrene Riwle*, E.E.T.S., o.s. 216 (1944).

    J. A. Herbert, *The French Text of the Ancrene Riwle* (MS. Cotton Vitellius F. vii), E.E.T.S., o.s. 219 (1944).

    W. H. Trethewey, *The French Text of the Ancrene Riwle* (Trinity College, Cambridge, MS. R. 14. 7), E.E.T.S., o.s. 240 (1958).

The following abbreviations are used throughout the Commentary for the various texts (ME, OF, and Latin):

N   MS. Cotton Nero A. xiv.
C   MS. Cotton Cleopatra C. vi.
T   MS. Cotton Titus D. xviii.
V   MS. Vernon, Bodleian Library (unpublished).
Tr.   OF version, MS.Trinity College Cambridge R. 14. 7.
H   OF version, MS. Cotton Vitellius F. vii.

Language

1. The reflex of Gmc *ă* is:
    (a) *ĕ* in root-syllables not followed by a back vowel in OE: *ʒef* 461, *neþ* 331, *spec* 207. *Beað* 573, *glead* 305, *steaf* 368 all have OE -*ĕa*- levelled into the nom. and accus. sg. from oblique cases with back-mutation: see 11 (a), and cf. *beaðes* 577.
    (b) *ă* in root-syllables followed by a back vowel in OE: *bac-* 371, *dahes* 67, *haueð* 314, 345.
    (c) *ŏ* before single nasals and *ŏ* or *ō* before nasal + consonant: *lomen* 415, *nomeliche* 1; *onde* 288, *þoncki* 266.

2. The reflexes of OE *ȳ* are spelt *u*, which must be an OF graph and implies that they were both still rounded vowels: *fluht* 109, *gult* 321; *fur* 42, *huden* 400. *Kimeð* 104, &c., is probably due to rhyme-association with *nimeð* through the preterites (*nom, nomen; com, comen*).

3. OE *ā* has not been rounded: *halie* 2, *sari* 305.

4. The reflex of OE *ǣ*[1] (non-WS *ē*) is spelt *e*: *dede* 292, *slepinde* 366.

5. The reflex of OE *ǣ*[2] (OKt *ē*) is spelt *ea*, which represents a slack *ē* (see 6): *arearet* 39, *cleane* 579, *eauer* 74, *sea* 28.

6. OE *ēa*, the reflex of which is spelt *ea*, is shown to have been reduced to a long vowel by the use of *ea* as an inverted spelling in the forms cited in 5, and to have been a slack *ē* by the processes of the Vowel Shift (*c.* 1400–1550): *deadliche* 122, *heaueð* 84, *teares* 90.

7. The reflexes of OE *ĕo* are spelt *eo* (which is also used for [ø] in adoptions from OF, and must therefore imply long and short [ø] respectively): *heorte* 6, *leof* 162.

8. (a) The product of breaking of OE *ǣ* before *ld* is *a*, which implies an unbroken and retracted vowel (later lengthened

by the consonant group) in OE: *bihalden* 32, and notably *cald* 660 (in which the absence of assibilation to [tʃ] shows that breaking could not have taken place).

(*b*) The reflex of Gmc *ă* before other *l*-groups is spelt *a*: *alle* 7, *half* 64, *halse* 397, *walles* 80.

(*c*) Breaking of *ĭ* before *r*-groups + Gmc *i* or *j* had not taken place in the antecedent OE type: *swire* 563.

9. There was no diphthongization of front vowels by preceding palatal *c*, *g*, or *sc* in the antecedent OE type: *biʒete* 637, *vnderʒetest* 363.

10. In the antecedent OE type there had been smoothing of
(*a*) *ĕa*: *maht* 603, *nahhi* 624; *ehe* 133, *hehe* 233, *teke* 60.
(*b*) *ĕo*: *feht* 165, *werkes* 289; *seke* 574. In *neoleachunge* 567, 568 the voiceless fricative *h* had been eliminated before *l* before smoothing took place.

11. The product of *i*-mutation in OE of:
(*a*) *ǽ* before *l*-groups is spelt *ea*, which is shown by the occurrence of *e* as a variant graph (though not in our extract) to represent [e]: *afealleð* 94, *imealt* 330, *iweallet* 330, *wealle* 236, and (with vowel lengthened by *ld*) *healdeð* 80, *wealden* 473.
(*b*) *ēa* is spelt *e*: *afleiet* 123, *leue* 274.

12. In the antecedent OE type, *ĕa* and *ĕo* had developed by back-mutation of respectively:
(*a*) *ǽ* (which was possible before back vowels only by the 'Second fronting'): *eape* 117, *heateð* 210. In *freamien* 309, the OE *æ* is probably from the cognate noun **fræmu*, later OE *fremu*, as the product of *i*-mutation of *a* before the Gmc abstract-forming suffix *-in* (see Flasdieck, *Beiblatt zur Anglia*, 41 (1930), 283–5).
(*b*) *ĭ* and *ĕ* before dentals, nasals, and the voiced labio-dental fricative: *ʒeouen* 603, *neomeð* 160, *smeoðien* 334.
Apparent exceptions to the OE lapse of back-mutation of *e* before [k] and [g] are all strong verbs, and therefore clearly due to the analogy of other verbs with a root ending in a different consonant: *breoke* 43, *speoke* 5, *wreoke* 350.

13. *ĕ* has been sporadically rounded to [ø] by a preceding labial: *feol-iheortet* 153, *weolcne* 101.

14. In the antecedent OE type, *ŏ* had been sporadically unrounded after a labial consonant: *iwraht* 625, *wrahte* 485,

and (if not from a different IE grade of vowel) *naldest*
499, *walde* 309.

15. In the antecedent OE type there had been no syncope of
unstressed *i* between intervocalic [ç] and *-st* or *-þ*, and the
normal elimination of the voiceless fricative between vowels
had taken place: *flið* 86, 104; *hest* 315, 317.

16. In the plural of nouns, the ending:
   (*a*) *-es* has been extended to OE neuters in *-u* or without
   ending, and to strong feminines in *-ung*: acc. *þinges*
   646, prep. *weattres* 182, nom. *wordes* 141, prep. 35;
   prep. *fondunges* 36.
   (*b*) *-en* has been extended to OE strong feminines having
   -e in all or most of the oblique cases of the sg. and
   a vowel ending in the nom. acc. pl., and to an endingless nom. acc. pl. of a neuter: acc. *honden* 186, prep.
   sawlen 55, prep. *sunnen* 22; acc. *wepnen* 8.

17. The normal forms:
   (*a*) of the pronoun of the 3 person include nom. sg. fem.
   ha; nom. pl. *ha*, acc. pl. *ham*, gen. *hare*, dat. *ham*,
   prep. *ham*.
   (*b*) of the demonstrative 'that' include the nom. sg. fem.
   þeo, nom. pl. *þeo*, prep. pl. *þeo*.
   (*c*) of the fem. possessive include sg. *hiren* 452 (used dis-
   ˘ junctively).

18. The 3 pres. sg. indic.:
   (*a*) ends in *-(e)ð* (*ʒeueð* 450, *luueð* 418, *spekeð* 254), and
   (*b*) in verbs with roots ending in a dental is the old type
   with syncope and assimilation: *biʒet* 355, *halt* 118,
   ifint 674, *scheot* 158, *sit* 430, *slit* 173, *stont* 197.

19. The pres. pl. indic. ends in:
   (*a*) *-eð* in strong verbs and in weak verbs of OE class I
   and III (*-ð* in contract verbs): *bindeð* 61, *þencheð* 22,
   habbeð 37.
   (*b*) *-ieð* and *-ið* in weak verbs of OE class II with respectively short root-syllable and long or polysyllabic roots:
   prikieð 77, *easkið* 79.
   (*c*) *-en* in old preterite–present verbs: *muhen* 122, *schulen*
   140, *witen* 184.

20. The imperative pl. ends in:
   (*a*) *-eð* (*lahheð* 117, *neomeð* 121).

G g

(b) *-ieð* or *-ið* in verbs etymologically or by adoption belonging to OE class II, according to the structure of the
root (see 19): *lokið* 28, *scarnið* 117.
21. The present part. ends in:
    (a) *-inde* (*suhinde* 251).
    (b) *-iende* in weak verbs of OE class II with short root-
    syllable: *fikiende* 271.

Vocabulary

The following are ideophonic formations: *cur* 370, *flikereð*
385, *meapeð* 241, *puf* 193, *slubbri* 184, *snakerinde* 364. The adoptions from ON are *bonen* 3, *feolahe* 320, *gestnede* 677, *greiðede*
577, *grið* 221, *ʒetti* 78, *lah* 231, *lane* 132, *lit(unge)* 531,
sahte 135, *takeð* 348, *twinnunge* 594, *wei(la)* 237, *witer(liche)* 48,
witneð 106, *wonte* 309, *wonteð* 292.

Provenance

The antecedent type of OE is shown to have been Anglian
by the important features 4 and 5 in combination, 8 (a) and
(c), 10, and 15. Northern origin is excluded by 16 (b), 17,
19 (a) and (b), 21. The WMidl alone remain.

The close correspondence of the language as a whole, and the
remarkable agreement in unusual details, with that of the OE
Gloss to the Vespasian Psalter and Hymns show that the *Ancrene
Wisse* derives from a form of OE almost identical with it.
1 (a) and 12 (a) in conjunction depend on an OE sound-change
peculiar to WMercian. The process represented in *freamien*
(see 12 (a)) is attested only in the Vespasian Psalter (*freamsum*
134, 3; *deanum* 103, 10). An OE starting-point for the cross-
analogies that produced the forms of 17 (a) and (b) is attested
only in the Vespasian Psalter, which already has not only
ðeara (< *ðæ̈ra* < *ðǎra* < *ðāra*), but *heara* modelled on it.

There is strong circumstantial evidence for a connexion of the
Ancrene Wisse (and therefore of the *Ancrene Riwle*) with Wigmore in Herefordshire. According to a thirteenth-century in-
scription in the MS., this copy was presented to the Abbey
of Wigmore. An *Anglo-Norman History of the Foundation of
Wigmore Abbey* is extant[1] which describes how Oliver de Merle-

---

[1] Dugdale, *Monasticon Anglicanum* (1830), vi. 344–8. See J. C.
Dickinson, 'English Regular Canons and the Continent in the 12th

mond, the steward of Hugh of Mortimer, after building a stone church at Shobdon (some time before *c.* 1140), launched a monastic community there by inviting over two canons of St. Victor in Paris.

This community was the earliest house of St. Victor in England, and was in unbroken contact with the Abbey of St. Victor. It drew thence not only some of its canons but the eminent Master of Divinity, Andrew of St. Victor, as its abbot during two periods (*c.* 1149–55, and from 1162).[1] But quarrels between Oliver and his lord denied it a settled abode till *c.* 1172, when Hugh of Mortimer laid the first stone of a new monastic church at *Beodune* (near Wigmore), which was dedicated in 1179 and became the Abbey of Wigmore.

Moreover, the Anglo-Norman *History* says that before Oliver built his stone church at Shobdon there had been only a wooden chapel of 'Saincte Juliane', subject to the church of Aymestrey.[2] It may therefore be significant that the subject of one of the four Saints' Lives composed in the same variety of ME as the *Ancrene Wisse* (and included in what is now termed the 'Katherine Group') was Juliana. Finally, it should be remembered that *Sawles Warde* (which also belongs to the 'Katherine Group') is a translation of the *De Anima* ascribed to Hugh of St. Victor. In view of the close ties between Wigmore and St. Victor, this may be a further indication of a connexion of the Katherine Group with Wigmore Abbey.

---

2. *beoð* is in the same position as the equivalent in the Tr. text of the OF, which therefore confirms the punctuation adopted here after *grace*: *medecines sunt e saunte* (19. 18–19). The other OF text places *sunt* before *seintes meditacions* (H 161. 24–25).

4–5. *opres . . . toward*: apparently 'comfort from another person who is available to confide in'—*confort de autre a ki homme puet*

Century', *Transactions of the Royal Historical Society*, 5th ser., i (1951), 73–76.

[1] On his life (including the probable dates for the main events in it) and his works see B. Smalley, 'Andrew of St. Victor, Abbot of Wigmore: A Twelfth Century Hebraist', *Recherches de théologie ancienne et médiévale*, x (1938), 358–73.   [2] Between Shobdon and Wigmore.

parler (Tr. 19. 21). V reads *also oþer maner cumfort* (f. 383 r 2), in which *maner* is evidently a corruption of *mannes*.

11. *nota culpe*: refers to a 'mark of guilt' such as is even now worn on the forehead on Ash Wednesday.

14. The metrically defective second half of the line scans perfectly in V (f. 383 r 2), which is therefore probably the correct version: *of þyne schome synne*.

14–19. Another version of the first four lines occurs in *St. Marherete* 34. 18–21 (ed. F. M. Mack, E.E.T.S., o.s. 193 (1934)). Dr. Mack thinks that the author of the *A.R.* owed the idea of using these verses to the example of *St. Marherete*, though 'the converse is not impossible'. But her argument from the two renderings of the first line seems inconclusive.

Both the Latin verses and the ME translation (in the version of the *A.R.*) also occur on f. 76ᵇ of MS. Arundel 507, copied *c.* 1400 (ed. Horstman, *Yorkshire Writers*, i. 156).

17. *ofte ofte*: the metre indicates that the word may have been wrongly repeated by a scribe; and this is confirmed by V, which has *mung ofte in moode* (f. 383 r 2). But for a genuine idiom of this type cf. IV. 43 and n. The occasional ME examples of reiteration of an adverb are shown to be authentic idiom by Elizabethan practice, as in Shakespeare's *too too*.

24. *bi*: 'by means of' (Tr. 20.9 *par*).

25, 33. *schadewe*: this is remarkable as a semantic borrowing (first recorded in the *Ancrene Riwle*) of L *umbra* and the equivalent Gk σκιά as a technical term in the vocabulary of Christian typology (which deals especially with situations and events of the Old Testament as foreshadowings of others in the New Testament). It is a use illustrated in Heb. x. 1 and Col. ii. 17.

Like *peinture* 31 and *peintunge* 33, *schadewe* is the equivalent of one among the set of Latin and Greek words used in Christian exegesis to designate the individual levels of a three-tiered structure which is formulated as follows by Hugh of St. Victor in a commentary on Col. ii. 17:

Aliud est *umbra*, aliud *corpus*, aliud *spiritus*: quae tria aliis nominibus dicuntur *figura*, *res*, *veritas*, ut idem sit *umbra* et *figura*; idem *corpus* et *res*; idem *spiritus* et *veritas*. Legales caeremoniae *umbra*, et *figura* futurorum dicebantur. Sacramenta gratiae *corpus*, sive res illarum *umbrarum* vel *figurarum* sunt: *spiritus* vel *veritas* dicitur gratia spiritalis scilicet quam conferunt sacramenta Novi Testamenti, et significant; sacramenta vero Veteris Testamenti, tantum gratiam spiritualem significant, et non conferunt (*P.L.* 175. 584).

This hierarchy of three stages corresponds to the theory of knowledge expressed in Plato's doctrine of 'ideas', in which the same terms are used. See G. V. Smithers, 'Two Typological Terms in the *Ancrene Riwle*', *M.Æ.* xxxiv (1965), 126–8.

For typology in various aspects see R. P. C. Hanson, *Allegory and Event* (1959), e.g. p. 22; K. J. Woollcombe, 'The Biblical Origins and Patristic Development of Typology', in G. W. H. Lampe and K. J. Woollcombe, *Essays on Typology* (1957); J. Danielou, *Sacramentum Futuri* (1950).

27. *þet . . . of*: 'of which'.

28. *þis worldes sea*: the allegorical interpretation of the sea as the world (for the Christian who has to traverse it, in the ship which is the Church, to reach his spiritual home in Heaven) is a stock element in Scriptural exegesis from the earliest times. See 'The Meaning of *The Seafarer* and *The Wanderer*', *M.Æ.* xxvi (1957), 150–2, xxviii (1959), 1–7. The addition of a bridge to the basic figure is not altogether happy.

46–47. See p. xx, Addenda.

55. *i fleschliche sawlen*: V also *in fleschliche soulen* (f. 383 r 2). It seems a little surprising that the author should (by implication) think of anchoresses as having *fleschliche sawlen*. And the OF of Tr. 21. 9, if we include a *varia lectio*, has two small but important differences which give much smoother sense: . . . *de charneus amis en chacent* '(often such thoughts) of friends in the flesh dispel (temptations of the flesh)'. The discrepancy is hardly intelligible except as due to a misreading of *ames* as *amis* or vice versa (according as English or French was the language in which the original was composed).

62–68. A Latin version of this *exemplum* is contained in the *Vitae Patrum*, which was one of the great medieval sourcebooks for edifying stories (ed. Migne, *P.L.* 73. 1003). Another early ME version occurs in the homilies of MS. Bodl. 343, which are post-Conquest transcripts of OE homilies (ed. A. O. Belfour, *Twelfth-Century Homilies*, E.E.T.S., o.s. 137 (1909), 16–18; see N. R. Ker, *Catalogue of Manuscripts containing Anglo-Saxon* (1957), pp. 368–9).

These two accounts agree with that of *Ancrene Wisse* in naming Julian the Apostate, and in specifying a delay of ten days; they differ in describing Publius as a monk. The outline in *A.W.* clearly derives from the *Vitae Patrum*, since it preserves two details of the latter version in 64 (*ut velocius vadens in Occidentem*); and one of these is blurred in the homily (*to sume londe* for *in Occidentem*).

65. *Iulienes heast þe empereur*: Julian the Apostate (*Julianus þe wiðersacæ*, Belfour, op. cit. 16. 27). This construction (with one of two genitives uninflected) derives from an antecedent OE type in which two nouns used in apposition in the genitive were separated by the noun governing the genitive, as in *Apollines dohtor Iobes suna* 'the daughter of Apollo the son of Jove'. For another variety see IV. 149–50 n.

68. *Ruffin*: the demon who assailed the heroine in the form of a dragon in the saint's legend of St. Margaret. See *St. Marherete*, p. 28, ll. 1–3 and p. 30, ll. 21–22, where the identity of the dragon is revealed to St. Margaret bӯ his brother, another demon who had sent Ruffin to attack her. She was enabled to slay the dragon by the power of the Cross, and overcame the other fiend by her prayers. The cryptic allusion of *A.W.* is clarified by the information in *St. Marherete*, and thus not only shows the latter to have been composed before *A.W.*, but constitutes the kind of link between the two that would support a case for common authorship.

Beliales: not named in *St. Marherete*.

69. *Of þet oðer me redeð*: i.e. Ruffin's brother. Tr. states: *E de vn autre dyable lisom nus en la uie de seint bartholomeu* (p. 21, ll. 24–25).

69–72. Also narrated in *The Abbey of the Holy Ghost*,[1] which cites *The Lyfe of Saynte Barthilmewe* as its source (cf. 69 n.,

---

[1] Ed. G. Perry, *Religious Pieces in Prose and Verse*, E.E.T.S., o.s. 26 (1914), p. 55, l. 28.

above). This claim is correct: the saint's life of Bartholomew in *The South English Legendary*[1] says of a demon, who had entered into a man and made him demented, that on being confronted in a temple by the saint:

> Wel loude he gradde: 'Sein Bartelmeu, ich biseche þe
> þin orisons me brenneþ al—haue merci of me!'

74. *we redeð*: Tr. 21. 30 *lisom nus ke seint Gregorie dit.*

83. *Contribulasti*: . . . .: Ps. lxxiii. 13.

92. *þet . . . rein*: a common proverb. Cf. *Kyng Alisaunder* 1309, and the OF equivalent *petite plue abat grant vent* (J. Morawski, *Proverbes français antérieurs au XVᵉ siècle*, 1924), and the Middle Flemish one cited by Ives, *M.L.R.* xxix (1934), 264.

95. *wordes*: not represented in Nero, p. 110, l. 9, Vernon (f. 383 v 1), or either OF version.

98. *efficaces*: Tr. 22. 23 *quatre grant efficaces ceo sunt quatre uertuz* . . . .

100. *Oratio* . . .: Ecclus. xxxv. 21.

102. *conscientie*: but Tr. 23. 1 *oracionis* (which is in accord with *bone* here in 104).

110. *Sein Iame*: Jas. iv. 7.

112. *Seinte Peter*: 1 Pet. v. 9.

115. *sumwhet of his eape-ware*: Tr. 23. 10 *aucune sotie ou aucun pecche*. And this OF version reads *le* for *þe alde eape* 117, and omits *þet me bugge þrof* 116. But V confirms the *A.W.* reading at all three points.

117. *(lahheð . . .) to bismere*: the meaning is established by Tr. 23, 13 *riez le a escharn.*

119. Miss Salu compares Heb. xi. 33.

132-3. 'The anchoress who refused another a small book as a loan would have her eye of faith [cf. 126] far from here.' *For* must represent *feor* 'far', with the AN graph *o* for ME [ø] <

---

[1] Ed. D'Evelyn and Mill (E.E.T.S., o.s. 236, 1956), ii. 376, ll. 87–88.

OE *ĕo*. The author's intention is not in doubt, since the only alternative interpretation (with *for* as conjunction 'because') would produce a quite unjustifiable anacoluthon. It is remarkable that V also has the spelling *for* (f. 383 v 1): this probably implies a common antecedent MS. at least at this point. The passage is not represented in Tr.; but H 168. 33 has *loinz* as the equivalent of *for*, and clinches the matter.

143. John xiv. 27.

146. Miss Salu compares John xiii. 35.

151. *Godd hit wite*: see C. T. Onions, *R.E.S.* iv (1928), 334–7.

152. *o þe spitel-uuel*: Tr. 24. 20 *leprus*.

153. *feol-iheortet*: the meaning is established by Tr. 24. 21 *de feloun quer*, H 169. 38–170. 1 *de felon queor*.

154. *In pace . . .*: Ps. lxxv. 3–4.

175. *ful falle*: Tr. 25. 21 *i chece en la bouue*, probably implying that *ful* was interpreted as *fūl*. But the author meant 'completely': cf. *feð to sliden* 175, and V's reading *fulliche* (f. 383 v 2).

178. *inempnet* (MS. *itemptet*): Nero 112. 34 *inemmed*; V f. 383 v 2 *inempnet*; H 171. 17 *auant nomez* (not represented in Tr.).

187. *Ve soli . . .*: Eccles. iv. 10.

191. *seoueðe*: in fact the fifth; and Tr. 26. 13 has *quint*. But Nero 113. 13 reads *seoueðe*, V f. 383 v 2 *seueþe*, and H 172. 7 *septime*.

198. *nihene*: sc. *forbisnen* (cf. 191); but in fact only seven have been given.

200. *þis*: sc. 'love'; Tr. 26. 26 *icest amur*.

206. *Iudicum*: Judges xv. 4.

207. *feor þruppe*: Corpus MS. (ed. Tolkien) f. 35a, 4–22.

215. 'And brands (i.e. the flames of hell) will be placed in it'— *schulen beon* understood from 214, and *ham* (a dative of disadvantage) from *ha* 214.

222–46. Not in Tr. (27. 22), H (174. 1), Nero (114. 6–7), Caius (67. 20–21), Titus (87. 15), or V. This remarkable passage is thus evidently an addition to the original work. The only available *terminus ad quem* is the date of the MS., viz. (on palæographical evidence) the thirteenth century.

222. For records of anchoresses (many of whom are known by name) in the thirteenth, fourteenth, and fifteenth centuries, see F. Darwin, *The Medieval English Recluse* (n.d.), pp. 60–70.

223. *mutli*: examples of this form are restricted to the 'Katherine Group'. Cf. *mutleð* in *Ancrene Wisse* f. 81ᵃ. 4; *mutli* in *St. Juliene* 174; and *muclin* in *St. Marherete* 34. 28 (both the latter in MS. Bodl. 34). It is evidently a form of *mucli, much(e)lin*. However, it is probably not the product of the standard palæographical error of writing *t* for *c* (or vice versa), but a phonetically significant spelling and an early example of the tendency for [k] to become [t] before *l* or *n* (for which see E. J. Dobson, *English Pronunciation*, ii, § 378).

227–9. Apparently meaning that when this passage was written, there really were separate anchor-holds specifically at the places named.

241. *teoþi*: MS. *teowi* defies etymological analysis, and is otherwise unknown. *Teoþi* is formally congruous with ME *tethee* 'peevish', later *teethy*, and with *teety, tetty* 'fractious', &c., both of unknown etymology.

meapeð: no word of this form is recorded in the dictionaries of English. In the language of *A.W.* -ea- might represent either a short vowel < OE *ĕa* (in this instance by the back-mutation—restricted to the Vespasian Psalter—of *ǣ* in a weak verb of class II **mĕapað < *mǣpað < *mǎpað*) or a slack *ē* < OE *ēa*, in a root of the form *mēap-* in OE. The latter is believed to be attested in the two place-names Meopham (OE *Meapaham* 788) and Mepal (twelfth-century *Mepahala*), with a first element conjectured to be an OE personal name *Mēapa*. But the meaning of the name (or the root) is not ascertainable from the name. There is, however, a ME pres. part. *mepyng* (likewise not recorded in our dictionaries) attested in the early fifteenth-century *St. Editha* 3616–17:

> & in to þat chirche he come sone þo
> & fonde þe goldsmethus *mepyng* vp & downe in þat same plase.
> (ed. C. Horstmann, 1883)

In this text an OE *măpað would necessarily be *mapeð; the -*e*- in *mepyng* must therefore in this instance represent slack *ē*, in a ME verb *mēpen*, and *meapeð* of *A.W.* is likely to be a form of the same word, rather than a distinct *mĕapien < OE *mĕapian.

The meaning of *mepyng* is clearly indicated by a synonymous variant in *St. Editha* 3565–71 (applied to the goldsmiths):

> Bot þey myȝt no fote þer-wiþ go þ[e]nne . . .
> & so þey *walkede* in þat chirche vp & doune.

The sense here is 'move (aimlessly), wander'; and since the sense 'wander, stray' is prescribed by the context in AW for *meapeð*, the latter is virtually certain to be a form of the same verb as *mepyng* is.

For the ultimate etymology of *meapeð*, see A. Zettersten, 'Middle English Word Studies', *Lunds Universitets Årsskrift*, N.F. Avd. I, Bd. 56, Nr. I (1964), 32–34. The extra example of the verb in *St. Editha* invalidates his translation of *meapeð* as 'mopes' in *Studies in the Dialect and Vocabulary of the Ancrene Riwle* (Lund Studies in English 34, 1965), p. 242.

teilac: see Zettersten, *Studies in the Dialect etc.* p. 203.

295. *þrof*: referring (as also *hit* 295) to *oþres god* 293.

305–7. 'To be willing that everyone who loves you should love them and do them solace as he does you.'

332. *wruhte*: an 'adjectival genitive'; see p. xxvii, (*b*).

333 ff. This striking image occurs in a partially equivalent application in the so-called 'O.E. *Honorius*' (ed. R. D.-N. Warner, *Early English Homilies*, E.E.T.S., O.S. 152 (1917)), p. 141. 27–32.

343. *forhohie* . . . : not surprisingly, the syntax has caused some difficulty to scribes making other copies. Caius 81. 29 alone has exactly the same reading. Nero 128. 25 has a mild rewriting: *so ðet tu uorhowie*, and V f. 385 r 2 an extensive one: *for to wreke þe ar his doom be*. Tr. 8. 30 uses a gerund: *en pernant ueniance* *deuant soen iugement*; and H 199. 33 a participle: *despisant la vengance* . . . .

347. *mihi vindictam*, etc.: for the reading *vindictam* for Vulg. *vindicta* (Rom. xii. 19) see Skeat's note on *Piers Plowman*, B vi. 228.

348. *Deale*: recorded by *O.E.D.* only from *A.R.* and Mannyng's *Chronicle.* Another example is to be found in *The South English Legendary*, ii (E.E.T.S., o.s. 236 (1956)), p. 490. 212. Tr. 9. 9–10 reads *Maleure irrus este vus* . . .; H 200. 7–8 *Qe dele estes vous* . . . .

363. The reference is to Ps. xxi. 21, which is cited in the part omitted.

364. *snakerinde*: otherwise recorded only in *A.R.* The final voiceless stop of the root and the iterative suffix *-r-* are clear signs of an ideophonic formation. *O.E.D.*'s reference to *snake* v.[2] will not do, as the latter is not recorded till the nineteenth century. A Gmc **snak-* is attested in ON *snaka* 'go snuffing or sneaking about', MDu *snaken* 'snap at greedily' (of a dog). *Snakeren* is a formation either on an unrecorded OE cognate of these or on a post-Conquest adoption of one of them. For the group to which they belong see W. Wissmann, *Nomina postverbalia in den altgermanischen Sprachen*, i (1932), 187.

366. *Ame*: also Caius 83. 29 and Nero 130. 22; but V f. 383 v 1 has *A*. Tr. 14. 17 reads *A vus*; H 203. 17 has no equivalent.

370. *liðere*: see d'Ardenne, *St. Iuliene*, pp. 161–2.

413. *þe hali abbat Moyses*: a desert father of this name is mentioned in the *Collations* 1 and 2 of John Cassian (*c.* 360–435). See G. Shepherd, op. cit. 19. 15 n.

428. *falleð into*: Tr. 139. 28 *partient a.*

452. *hiren*: this unusual form occurs in the *Ayenbite*, along with *þinen*—both always in disjunctive use and after a preposition. Adjectives in the *Ayenbite* also have *-en* in comparable conditions (after a preposition and in substantival use), this being the orthodox replacement of the OE dat. pl. *-um. Hiren* and *þinen* are therefore probably analogical forms modelled on them (both sets of words being felt to have the same function).

455. *Me*: Tr. 141. 6 *Mes*, the AN form of OF *mais*, with the usual monophthonging to *ē* before dental consonants. *Mes* is further reduced in AN (in reduced stress) to *me*, thus actually spelt in the Durham MS. of the *Roman de toute Chevalerie*, e.g. 10161:

> Chastiez lur folie, me pas ne les tuez.

alde-feader: as in OE *ealdfæder*, OS *ald-fader*, and OHG *alt-fater* (the latter applied to Adam, like the ME word here).

457. Ps. viii. 8–9.

463. Eph. v. 25–26.

467. On the history of this allegory see Shepherd, *Ancrene Wisse*, 21. 1 ff. n.

470. *leattres isealet*: actually sealed up, i.e. 'closed', because a private communication (in contrast to the 'open' letters of 471, which also had a seal attached).

471. *leattres i-openet*: a semantic borrowing of either OF *patentes lettres* or med. L *litterae patentes*. But the remarkable thing is that the OF phrase is not recorded before 1307 (though it occurs in AN by 1291), nor the med. L one (which is an adoption of the OF form) before 1201. The 'open' or public letters were issued, normally by a king, to authorize the grant of a privilege, right, title, or office, or to bestow one. See the quotation in *O.E.D. patent* a. 1, i *s.a.* 1891.

wrat wið his ahne blod: an allusion to the medieval conceit according to which Christ made a 'charter' or deed bestowing on man his own 'heritage' of life in Heaven, in the manner of a legal document. There are Latin treatments in verse (fourteenth century) and prose (fifteenth century). The ME *Short Charter* is edited by M. Förster, *Anglia*, xlii (1918), 192–7, and the *Long Charter* by F. J. Furnivall, *Minor Poems of the Vernon MS.* ii (E.E.T.S., o.s. 117 (1901), pp. 637–57), and both by M. C. Spalding, *The Middle English Charters of Christ* (Bryn Mawr 1914). According to the *Long Charter*, the parchment for the Charter was Christ's skin (51–54); the ink was the spittle of the Jews (83–84); the pen was the scourges with which he was beaten (85–86); the writing consisted of the 5,460 wounds inflicted on him (87–90); the seals were the spear and the nails (135–42); the sealing-wax was his heart's blood (143–6).

474 ff. No specific source of this allegory of Christ the Lover-knight has been discovered. A dozen other examples in Latin sermons, in an OF poem by Nicolas Bozon, and in various ME works are known; but all are later or no earlier than the *Ancrene Riwle*. Those which refer, like the latter, to Christ's battle on behalf of mankind or the human soul in terms of a tournament or jousting are the well-known one in *Piers Plowman* B. XVIII. 11–28, and *The Towneley Plays* p. 261, 89–94, 101–18 (ed. G. England, E.E.T.S., E.S. 71 (1897)). See W. Gaffney, 'The Allegory of the Christ-Knight in *Piers Plowman*', *P.M.L.A.* xlvi (1931), 155–68; R. Woolf, 'The Theme of Christ the Lover-knight in Medieval English Literature', *R.E.S.*, N.S. xiii (1962), 1–16.

478. *beawbelez*: Tr. 142. 7 *ioeaus*; H 283. 36 *beaubelez*.

480. *unrecheles*: Tr. 142. 9 *nonchalereuse*. The *un-* is a rare intensive prefix, restricted in ME to the Katherine Group, but recorded occasionally in OE. Cf. *unforht* in *The Dream of the Rood* (ed. Dickins and Ross) 117 and n., and *unhar* in *Beowulf* 357.

482. *þe þe*: replacing earlier OE *se þe*. The analogical forms *þe* for *se* and *þeo* for *seo* emerged already in late OE.

488. *heold*: H 284. 18 (*Tout cest rien ne*) *valut*; apparently misunderstood in Tr. 142. 19 *tot ceo ne tint ele a rien*. For this use, cf. *forheol[d]* in *The Peterborough Chronicle* (ed. C. Clark, 1958), *s.a.* 1114. 25 and n., and *M.Æ.* xxiii (1954), 74–75.

500. *to wundre*: adverbial; representing the OE tendency to use a noun in the dative, governed by *to*, as an adverb-equivalent, e.g. *to soðe*. Cf. XIX. 11.

507. *cnihtschipe*: evidently a translation of OF *chevalerie*; and an indication (cf. 533 and n.) that the author's reading included courtly romance in OF.

507–8. *as weren sumhwile cnihtes iwunet to donne*: it is odd that the author should refer to jousting in the service of romantic love as if it belonged to a bygone age. According to Shepherd (op. cit., note on 22. 8), he must have been thinking of Geoffrey

of Monmouth's notable account of the festivities at Arthur's
coronation, which alludes to the presence of ladies as spectators
at a joust, and which Shepherd regards as an idealization:

> *Mox milites, simulacrum proelii facientes, equestrem ludum
> componunt; mulieres* in edito murorum aspicientes *in furiales
> amoris flammas more joci irritant* ... (*Historia Regum Britan-
> niae*, ed. E. Faral, *La Légende arthurienne*, iii (1929), ch. 157,
> p. 246. 45–73).

But it is not exactly clear that Geoffrey's account (composed
between 1135 and 1138) is remote from reality—notwithstanding
William of Newburgh's statement[1] that the tournament was
introduced into England by Richard I (who issued a writ in
1194 licensing tournaments).[2] The first mention of tournaments
in general in England is in one of the *Consuetudines* of William
the Conqueror (K. G. T. Webster and R. S. Loomis, *Ulrich
von Zatzikhoven, 'Lanzelet'* (1951), pp. 187–8; see C. H.
Haskins, *English Historical Review*, xxiii (1908), 50). The presence
of ladies as spectators at a tournament is attested in France in
the later twelfth century in the episode of *Li Contes del Graal*
in which Gawain jousts on behalf of a small girl and sends her
one of the horses forfeited by defeated adversaries. Moreover, it
is described in much the same terms as by Geoffrey:

> Armé fors de la vile amassent,
> Et les dameiseles resont
> *Montees sor les murs amont*
> Et les dames del chastel totes.

(ed. A. Hilka 5498–5501)

For the history of the tournament in France, see Joan Evans,
Life in Medieval France (1957), pp. 19–20; and in England,
N. Denholm-Young, 'The Tournament in the Thirteenth
Century', in *Studies in Medieval History presented to F. M.
Powicke* (1948), pp. 240–68.

510–13. Shepherd quotes from St. Bernard, *Sermon* V on Ps.
xc. 5 the same statement, there, however, referring to 'the grace
of the divine protection' (*P.L.* 183, 196).

---

[1] *s.a.* 1194, *Historia rerum Anglicarum*, ed. R. Howlett in *Chronicles
of the Reigns of Stephen*, &c. (1884–5), ii, p. 422.

[2] See Roger de Hoveden, *Chronica*, iii. 268 (ed. W. Stubbs, 1868–
71); Rymer's *Foedera*, i. 9.

512–13. *efter monies wene*: reflects a change *c.* 1200 in the representation of Christ's feet on the crucifix, from the earlier mode in which they were affixed separately. For twelfth-century examples of the latter, see the miniature from the *Hortus Deliciarum* in É. Mâle, *L'Art religieux du XIIIe siècle* (1948), p. 193, and another from the Floreffe Bible (MS. Additional 17738, f. 187) in *Early Medieval Art* (British Museum, 1940), pl. 43.

516. Matt. xxvi. 56.

518. Lam. iii. 65.

520. Ps. v. 13.

523. Isa. liii. 7.

526. *bitellunge*: H 286. 24–26 *Pur tolir nous chescune de[fense] et surdit encontre li de nostre amour.* Tr. 143. 32–144. 1 is quite different and probably corrupt.

533–4. Lancelot's action in *La Mort le Roi Artu*, before he goes into exile abroad from which he does not expect to return, is similar:

'Pren mon escu en cele chambre et t'en va droit a Kamaalot, et si le porte en la mestre eglise de Saint Estienne et le lesse en tel leu ou il puisse remanoir et ou il soit bien veuz, si que tuit cil qui des ore mes le verront aient en remenbrance les merveilles que ge ai fetes en ceste terre. Et sez tu por quoi ge faz a cel leu ceste enneur? por ce que ge i reçui primes l'ordre de chevalerie; si en aing plus la cité que nule autre; et por ce voil je que mes escuz i soit en leu de moi, car je ne sai se james aventure m'i amenra' (ed. J. Frappier (1936), ch. 120, p. 137. 2–10).

557. Jer. iii. 1.

567. Shepherd calls attention to the roughly similar passages in *De Civitate Dei*, i. xviii, and *Vices and Virtues*, i. 131. 9–14 (ed. F. Holthausen, E.E.T.S., o.s. 89 (1888)).

569. Job xii. 23.

582. Rev. i. 5.

584. Isa. xlix. 15.

586–92. Shepherd cites a strikingly similar passage from Peter of Blois, *De XII Utilitatibus Tribulationis* (*P.L.* 207. 996).

588. Isa. xlix. 16.

605. *weolie*: also Nero 181. 13. Both Miss Day and Tolkien take this as a corruption of *weore* 'of men' (< OE *weora*, Tolkien). Neither OF version has anything corresponding to either word (Tr. 148. 5; H 291. 7–8).

620. The identity and the meaning of *feor* are established by Tr. 148. 24 *certein foer*.

628–34. This catalogue of qualities is not arbitrary, but corresponds to the beatitudes enjoyed by the saints in bliss, especially as formulated by Anselm of Canterbury and his followers, as in his *Proslogion*, ch. xxv (*Opera*, ed. F. S. Schmitt (1938), i. 118–20) and *De Beatitudine cælestis patriæ* (*P.L.* 159. 587–606). The list of *exempla* derives ultimately from Honorius' *Elucidarium*, Bk. iii (*P.L.* 172. 1169); Crœsus is added to it in Richard of St. Victor's *De timore Dei* (*P.L.* 177. 920). See G. Shepherd, 'All the Wealth of Crœsus', *M.L.R.* li (1956), 161–7.

631. 2 Sam. ii, 18: porro Asael cursor velocissimus fuit, quasi unus de capreis quæ morantur in silvis.

636–7. *þurh nawt to leosen*: obscure. Nero 182. 11 reads *þuruh nout to uorleosen*; H 292. 36–37 *pur nule rien perdre*; Tr. 149. 14 *pur nule chose perdre*.

648. Ps. xviii. 7.

653–4. Luke xii. 49.

657–8. Rev. iii. 16–17.

665–77. Shepherd traces this form of interpretation to St. Augustine (*P.L.* 38. 97–99), and cites Hugh of St. Victor (*P.L.* 175. 709), Baldwin of Ford (*P.L.* 204. 523), and Peter of Blois (*P.L.* 207. 574); but Baldwin's use is different.

666. 1 Kings xvii. 12.

XIX

MS.: Bodley 34.

Facsimile: *Facsimile of MS. Bodley 34*, E.E.T.S., o.s. 247 (1959).

Editions: R. Morris, *Old English Homilies*, i, E.E.T.S., o.s. 34 (1868), 245–67.
  J. Hall, *Early Middle English* (Oxford 1920), pp. 117–28.
  R. M. Wilson, *Sawles Warde* (Leeds School of English Language Texts and Monographs, iii, 1938).

Source: Hugh of St. Victor (?), *De Anima* (*Patrologia Latina*, clxxvii. 185 ff.).

Studies: D. Bethurum, 'The Connection of the Katherine Group with Old English Prose', *J.E.G.P.*, xxxiv (1935), 553–64.
  R. Furuskog, 'A Collation of the *Katherine Group* (MS. Bodley 34)', *Studia Neophilologica*, xix (1946/7), 119–66. [See the critical comments on this, ibid. xx. 65–72.]
  See also S. R. T. O. d'Ardenne, *Þe Liflade ant te Passiun of Seinte Iuliene*, 1936, repr. E.E.T.S., o.s. 248 (1961).

Language

The sounds and accidence so closely match those of XVIII that no separate account of them is given here: points 1–21 in the analysis of *Ancrene Wisse* all apply equally to *Sawles Warde*, except that no forms of 21 (*b*) occur. The following are not represented in XVIII:

10. *Meoke* 223 is not a true exception to smoothing, since it is an adoption from ON (i.e. long after smoothing had taken place in OE).

22. *Wumme* 151 is an example of a rare sporadic raising to tense ō (and then shortening) of slack ō before a nasal, as in *num-more* < *nǭ mōre* in XII. 101; and these are comparable with the -*ǔ*- (< tense ō) in *ʒomere*: *sumere* in I. 293–4 and *An God Oreisun of ure Leuedi* 39–40.

23. *Rikenin* 98 has undergone a sporadic ME raising of ĕ to ĭ before a palatal consonant.

24. *Incker* 392 is an example of a rare survival of the old dual form of the genitive of the second person.

Vocabulary

The following are adoptions from ON: (*huse*)*bonde* 412, *drupnin* 249, *etlunge* 349, *flutteð* 115, *ʒetteð* 278, *lane* 227, *meoke* 223, *munne* 342, *nowcin* 185, *stutteð* 397, *wengen* 162, *wontin* 153, *wontreaðes* 146. *Keis* 37 is a spectacular example of adoption from Welsh (which is extremely rare in ME).

Provenance

As for XVIII. The ἅπαξ λεγόμενον *keis* 37 points unmistakably to composition of the work in an area near to the Welsh border.

———

4. *þe godspel* Matt. xxiv. 43–51. *De Anima* describes the parable as told *ad insinuandam interioris hominis custodiam*.

5. *unwiht*: v. I. 33 n. Here and elsewhere in this group of texts used specifically of the Devil. The form is not found in OE and is perhaps anglicized from ON *úvættr*: a transference possibly helped by such expressions as *wiht unhælo*, used of Grendel, *Beowulf* 120; similarly LOE *unwine* (likewise applied to the Devil in this group of texts) was anglicized from ON *úvinr*.

6. *wernches*: a metathesized form of, or scribal error for, *wrenches*.

8. *hire*: the fem. pronoun doubtless reflects the gender of *domus* in the Latin (OE *hus* being neut.). Similarly *amor* (masc.) influences the gender of (*liues*) *luue* (OE fem.) below. *Deað* varies in gender between masc. (cf. OE) and fem. (Latin).

9. *inwið . . . .*: 'Inside, Reason is master in this house'. Interpretation of this passage will differ according to the punctuation adopted: RC supply a stop before *inwið*; the somewhat otiose use of *inwið* is found elsewhere in this group: cf. *O.E.D.*, s.v. Since *De Anima* has *Pater iste familias animus potest intelligi*, Hall reconstructs the original as '. . . is seolf þe monnes inwit; wit i þis hus is þe huselauerd'. *Piers Plowman* B. IX. 1–24 (where Anima is a lady living in the castle of the body, of which Inwit is constable) suggests that the allegory had several variants. 'Wil', the careless mistress of the house (10), has no

equivalent in the *De Anima*; but cf. the *De Similitudinibus* (for which see now Southern and Schmitt, *Memorials*, p. 247 n. 1), c. ii: *Similitudo inter Voluntatem et Mulierem* (*P.L.* 159. 606). [*De custodia* reads *animus rationalis*.]

For the various aspects of *Anima* cf. *Piers Plowman* B. xv. 39 and Skeat's note; and for the five senses as subordinates of (*In*)-*wit*, ibid. ix. 2 ff.

10. *huse-lauerd*: see Introduction, p. xxiv. Cf. *Ancrene Wisse* (Corpus MS., ed. Tolkien), p. 29, l. 5.

11. *þet . . . hire . . .*: 'Who, if the household is guided by her (she) brings it entirely to ruin': for the construction cf. XVIII. 500 and *Hali Meiðhad* (ed. Colborn, l. 218).

20. *fol semblant*: the emphasis is on the appearance of evil, in contrast to *vuel dede*: the phrase occurs only once again in English (in *A.R.*), though *semblant* is a common word in the Katherine Group.

24. *felen*: a word has been inserted after *mahen* in Bodl. 34 in a different ink, and only the second letter *p* (*wynn*) and the last two letters are clear; Tolkien and d'Ardenne (*English Studies*, xxviii (1947), 168–70) read *rw?len*; but 'rule' is unacceptable in this context, whereas *felen* occurs elsewhere in the meaning 'to sense'.

nurð: a word peculiar to the Katherine Group: Titus substitutes *mur(h)ð* here and in *Hali Meiðhad* (ed. cit., l. 453). The context here suggests the meaning 'unpleasant noise', which is borne out by the fact that it corresponds to *noise* in the OF version of *A.W.* and to *sonus* in the Latin source of *St. Katherine*: see *E.G.S.* iii. 73, for a proposed connexion with MDu *norren* 'to wrangle', MLG *nurren* 'to grumble, grunt, growl'. *Norne, nurne* (*Sir Gawain and the Green Knight*, 1661, 1669) is a formation on the same root.

25. *bere*: the meaning 'outcry' is evidenced as early as the Parker Chronicle, *s.a.* 755 ('þæs wifes gebærum') and is common in M Scots.

26. *bið*: the Katherine Group preserves the OE use of *bið* (not *is*) in gnomic or consuetudinal statements: Professor d'Ardenne observes that this distinction is lost, as in WS, in the plural.

28. *let ham iwurðen*: 'lets them be, lets them alone': a calque (common in ME) on OF *laissier ester*, in which *ester* represents *stare* 'to stand' but was interpreted as 'to be' by English speakers owing to the confusion in OF between *estre* (< * *essere* < L *esse*) and *ester* (< *stare*): cf. J. Orr, *Words and Sounds in English and French* (Oxford 1953), p. 37 and n. 1.

34. *chatel* (R): '. . . who guards God's precious property within this house'. Cf. *De Anima*: *Domus est conscientia, in qua pater iste habitans thesauros virtutum congregat, propter quos ne domus effodiatur, summopere vigilatur. Castel* (see *var. ll.*) probably reflects the scribe's familiarity with the allegory of 226 ff.

35. *hire unþeaw*: 'the opposite vice': *hire* referring elliptically to *euch god þeaw*, with agreement in gender *ad sensum*. Cf. *De Anima: singulis virtutibus singula vitia insidiantur.*

37. *keis*: an adoption of med. W. *keys, cais* 'sergeant of the peace', the earliest example of which found by Miss Joy Russell-Smith (*M.Æ.* xxii (1953), 104) is in a S. Wales charter *a.* 1241, where it occurs alongside *ballivus*; but elsewhere these officers are referred to as *satellites* (the word used at this point in *De Anima*); the equivalent passage in *Ayenbite* has *kachereles*, a word which evidently suffered a similar degradation of meaning, since *cacherellus* was originally the name of an officer: cf. Spelman, *Glossarium Archaiologicum*, s.v. *Furca*.

Miss Russell-Smith cites a thirteenth-century Welsh verse text in which the compound *keisseid* occurs in a context very similar to the present passage: '. . . may you throw into confusion the devilish *keisseid*. . . . May you completely guide the body and its five senses. Set up bars of spears in the bosom and place there faithful door-keepers.'

39. *fowre*: cf. MS. *froure* with a similar error in *Ancrene Wisse* (ed. Tolkien, E.E.T.S., o.s. 247, p. 59).

42. *Meað*: cf. *Memorials*, p. 356, l. 11: *Porro temperantia familiæ intime præesse debet, ut eius coherceat et cohibeat turpes appetitus*: see 49–50 below. *heaued* H (40) represents L *cardinalis*, which is not found anglicized till *Cursor Mundi*: cf. *Ancrene Wisse*, *heauedsunnes* (and Ælfric's *heafodleahtras*).

43. *Godes cunestable*: similarly in *Piers Plowman*, B. ix, 'Sir Inwit' is constable of the castle. In both instances (as in *Hav.* 2366) the sense 'governor of a (royal) fortress' is perhaps more appropriate than 'chief officer of a household' (*O.E.D.* s.v. 1) and perhaps more likely to be in the mind of a WMidl writer at a time when royal castles were being built on the Welsh border.

44. *þe warliche loki*: 'who may watch carefully', i.e. 'that she may . . .': cf. *De Anima, quæ discernat.*

50. *mete, þet me meosure hat*: 'Temperance, another name for which is Measure'. For the linking of the French and English synonyms by alliteration cf. 197 and *milce* (OE) *and merci* (OF) in *Ancrene Wisse*; the habit is found in LOE, e.g. *læth* (ON *láþ*) *and land; sib and sæhte* (ON *sátt*).

51. *for þet is þeaw . . .*: Hall paraphrases: 'for the observance of that moderation is under all circumstances virtuous conduct': R, C have a punctum after *stude*, suggesting the variant: 'for measure is in all circumstances virtue, and the right course to follow'. 'Measure' is a commonplace of the ascetical writers: see, e.g., *S. Columbani Regulae*, xiii (*Opera*, 1957, p. 136): *Igitur inter parvum et nimium rationabilis est in medio mesura, revocans semper ab omni utrimque superfluo . . .*; cf. also *Legend of Good Women*, F 165.

61. *lest sum fortruste him*: the watch may fall asleep through over-confidence. *De Anima* has simply *ne somnus peccati subrepat* (slightly expanded in the Anselmean text).

66. *elheowet*: 'eerie-looking': also in R (C *ille heowet*): the word occurs again in *Ancrene Wisse* (ed. cit. p. 187, l. 6) with variants *helhewet, eliheowed, vuele iheowed*. C's form is probably a misreading of, or a substitute for, a rare word (in which *el-* = 'foreign'). ON *illr* begins to replace E *vuele* in the late twelfth century; but as it does not certainly occur in other parasynthetic compounds before the fourteenth century, C's reading may not be intended for it.

70–1. *Ego sum timor et memoria mortis*: *Memorials*, p. 356, l. 20.

74. *hwuch hird ha leade*: 'what sort of company Death leads'. In *De Anima* Prudentia speaks in *oratio recta*.

81. *gledread*: 'glowing': an accommodation of ON *glóðrauðr* 'red as fiery embers'. Cf. *dedebondes, Hav.* 332 < ON *dauðabǫnd*, with similar phonetic changes.

84–85. *wið soð schrift ant wið deadbote*: the phrase recurs in *Hali Meiðhad* (ed. Colborn, 179).

87. *ha seið, Warschipe*: the expansion of the pronoun by means of a noun following the verb is common in the Katherine Group. Hall compares *Bestiary* 504, 602.

88. *ofte ant ilome*: a traditional homiletic phrase found in Wulfstan (*Homilies*, ed. Bethurum, p. 262, l. 64), Lambeth Homilies, *Poema Morale*, &c.

Nu . . . þenne; perhaps to be taken as part of Warschipe's speech, the two words regularly introducing a request or command in the Katherine Group; but at 215 it has illative force ('Now, this being the case, it follows that . . .').

91. *bluðeliche*: a much-discussed abnormality, the usual AB form in this group of texts being *bliðeliche*; -*u*- forms are also found in *Lambeth Homilies* and Laȝamon (with comp. *bloðelocor* in the Otho MS.); *Ayenbite* and other Eastern texts have *bleðelice*, which suggests OE forms in -*y*-; the present form may be (1) western development of OE **blȳþelīce* or (2) *blīþelīce*, with shortening of *i* and rounding > *u* through influence of preceding labials and following *ð*. The development of OE *circe* > 'church' is perhaps analogous.

94. *wid*: the C reading is justified by *De Anima*: *Infernus latus est*. The following description closely resembles that in the SE *Vices and Virtues, c.* 1200 (ed. Holthausen, E.E.T.S. o.s. 89, pp. 17–19).

99. *me hire mei grapin*: the phrase—one of the many details added by the English writer—is derived from Exod. x. 21.

108. *ham to grisle ant to grure . . .*: equivalent to a Latin 'double dative' construction (cf. *M.L.R.* xxxv (1940), 382): 'They see all too well, to their horror and dismay, and in aggravation of their torments, the horrible reptiles of hell.'

114. *toðes hechelunge i þe snawi weattres*: *De Anima* quotes Matt. xxiv. 51 and continues: *ibi transitur a frigore nivium ad calorem* *ignium et utrumque intolerabile*—alluding to Job xxiv. 19 (cf. OE *Genesis B* 69–71): thus supplying some suggestion that the *stridor dentium* is to be regarded as a result of physical conditions.

123. *from worlde into worlde aa on echnesse* (*In sæcula sæculorum semper in æternum*): the phrase recurs in *Hali Meiðhad* 404.

129. *þah Ich hefde a þusent tungen of stele*: cf. *Aeneid* vi. 625–7:

> non, mihi si linguæ centum sint oraque centum,
> ferrea vox, omnis scelerum comprendere formas,
> omnia pœnarum percurrere nomina possim.

which is quoted by St. Jerome, *Ep.* lx. 5 (*P.L.* xxii. 641). The phrase found its way into vernacular homiletic literature. It occurs, e.g. in *Three ME Sermons, from the Worcester Chapter MS. F. 10*, ed. D. M. Grisdale (1939), p. 14, ll. 148 ff.: 'The grete clerk Virgilius, 6to eneydos, seith þat þowth a man had an red of hund mowþes & eueri mouth an hundrid of tunges & euery tonge wer maad of bras, ȝit he were nawth suffisaunt, he seith þis clerk, for to telle plenerlich þe peynus þat ben in helle.'

132. *al þe ende of mi cun*: the first example of a phrase recorded some five times in ME. A. McI. Trounce, *Athelston* (1933), p. 106, suggests that *ende* may have developed the required meaning 'members, persons' from such collocations as 'mycelne ende þes folces' ('a large section of the people': *Peterborough Chron., s.a.* 1052).

141–4. *ant . . . pinen*. In its present awkward position this passage is an anti-climax. It may have been omitted in an early copy after *pinen* (103) because of the like ending *pinen*, then inserted in the margin and wrongly introduced into the text by a later copyist after *pine* (141).

143. *eawles* (OE *awul*, distinct from *æl*, '*subula*'): curved pronged hooks of the kind regularly shown being wielded by devils in illustrations of the torments of hell: e.g. MS. Junius 11, ff. 17, 20.

dustlunges: a unique form, though a related verb occurs in *Ancrene Wisse . . .* 'þe deoflen schulen pleien wið him mid hare scharpe eawles . . . ant dusten ase pilche clut euch toward oðer' (Corpus MS., ed. Tolkien, p. 110.)

151. *þe . . . þe*: deictic: first one of the damned is pointed to, then another.

161. *reade hwet us beo to donne . . .*: 'counsel us what there is for us to do, and (thus) we may be the more wary . . .'.

165–6. *for ure deað bið deore Godd*: cf. Ps. cxv. 15.

187 f. *For ba me ah . . .* 'It behoves one to be afraid and concerned', said Measure, 'on account of these two things—the vigour of adversity and the lack of joy': an early instance of *ah* (OE *āgan* 'have') in the sense of 'have to, ought': cf. *O.E.D.* s.v. *owe*.

203 ff. *ant tah nis nawt siker . . .*: 'and yet she is not self-confident as regards the strength of the Devil, being one who regards herself as weak (though in the eyes of us all she is of great merit) and judges herself not strong enough, in her own strength, to withstand his wiles'. The scribe appears to have misplaced *ant*.

208. *deð*: i.e. 'trusts'—this vicarious use is common in *Ancrene Wisse* and other early texts: cf. d'Ardenne, Gloss. s.v. *don* (4).

213. C's reading is supported by 'Ich do riht ant deme' (222 below).

233. *Vmben ane stunde*: see Gl.; the phrase is also found in Laȝamon, e.g. xi. 87 above. R. W. Burchfield (*M.L.R.* 1 (1955), 485) compares *Beow.* 219: 'ymb an tid' (usually printed *ymb antid*), and Wilson cites OE *ymbe stunde*, and the form *emban*, alongside *embe*.

246. *Ich am Murðes sonde . . .*: L *Ego sum Amor Vitæ æternæ et Desiderium cælestis patriæ.*

247. *þet* occurs in the sense 'in which' (of time or place) in *St. Marherete* (ed. Mack) p. 38, 24, p. 40, 35, and *St. Juliene* 332.

260. *dosc*: used of light (or sight) elsewhere in the Katherine Group (cf. *doskin*, *Hali Meiðhad* 515, and Colborn's note thereto).

263–4. *þe hali þrumnesse . . . þreo an untodealet*: L *illam ineffabilem individuæ trinitatis maiestatem.*

268–9. *ful . . . to bihalden*: Hall notes several examples in EME of dat. inf. with genitival force, and compares the translation of Bede's *tanta dicendi peritia* as 'swa mycel getydnes and gelærednes to sprecanne'.

282. For the orders of angels see Skeat's note to *Piers Plowman* B. i. 105.

284–5. *on hare onsihðe*: the only other occurrence of *onsihðe* yet recorded is in *Ancrene Wisse* (Corpus MS., ed. Tolkien, p. 215 mid.) where the reference is to the propriety of women veiling their heads *propter angelos* 'leste uuel þoht arise þurh hire onsihðe'—'lest evil intent should arise through the sight of her': apparently a fusion of OE *onsīen* and *sihð*; perhaps implying steadfast gazing.

288. *þet ha hefden of feor igret . . .*: L *quam olim a longe salutaverant patriam*: cf. Isa. xxxiii. 17 (*Regem in decore suo videbunt oculi eius, cernent terram de longe*) the first clause of which is cited, in the form in which it occurs in Rev. xxi. 7, a little later in the *De Anima* (cf. 265); R's *igreiðet*, *pace* Wilson, does not give 'quite good sense'.

293. *kinges ant keiseres*: in this alliterative formula (cf. e.g. *Seafarer* 82, Wulfstan, *Homilies*, ed. Napier (1883) p. 148, l. 19), OE *cāsere* has been replaced by a form of ON *keisari*.

299. *cunfessurs*: L specifies *viri apostolici, et doctores . . .* and *monachi, qui pro claustris et cellis angustis immensa et sole clariora palatia possidentes, pro asperis tunicis nive candidiores*. Its account of the *chorus virginum* is briefer, and has no equivalent to 306–8.

301. Cf. Rev. vii. 17, xxi. 4, and 288 n.

323–4. *brihtre seouefald . . . þen þe sunne*: the comparison (not in the Latin) owes something to Isa. xx. 26 and is found elsewhere, e.g. *Château d'Amour* (ed. Sajavaara (1967), l. 158), and xviii. 623.

328–9. *Þet is . . . eche lif. De Anima* cites John xvii. 3.

332. *nebbe to nebbe*: a rendering of *facie ad faciem* 1 Cor. xiii. 12. There is no equivalent in *De Anima*; but the phrase is in contrast to *þurh a schene schawere* (261) which represents *per speculum et in ænigmate* in *De Anima* (cited from the same verse).

332–3. *ha witen alle Godes reades* . . . : . . . *Sapiunt consilia atque judicia Dei, quæ sunt abyssus multa* (cf. Ps. xxxv. 7).

For the (customary) reading *derne* see fn. *St. Marherete* has *þine domes dearne beon* (18/25) and *ha dearne beon ant derue, þine domes* (46/18); *Ancrene Riwle*: *Godes derne runes and his derue domes* (cit. Mack, p. 78, q.v.).

349. *wiðuten ei etlunge*: also in *Hali Meiðhad* (591, ed. cit.).

353. *hu*: Hall's emendation; cf. L *Si ergo cor uniuscuiusque vix capit suum gaudium, quomodo capit tot et tanta gaudia?*

378. *fondin*: As Hall points out, this verb, which gives better sense than 'follow' (see *var. ll.*), is found elsewhere in combination with *finden*, e.g. *St. Juliene* 243 and *Surtees Psalter* xvi. 4.

379–81. *hwet mei tweamen us* . . . : Latin cites Rom. viii. 35, 38–39. The following clauses have no equivalent in *De Anima*.

385. *Warschipe*: C has *rihtwisnesse*, translating L *Justitia*. There are several other variations from the original at this point; and 'will' and 'wit' are introduced by the English writer of his own accord.

408–16. *biseon, to habben, leaden, tuhten ant teachen, witen*, are, as Hall points out, all dependent on *ah mon* (355).

420. *ant e Sune*: the author (or more probably the scribe) has ignored the fact that he has previously mentioned the second person of the Trinity. The same slip is made in *Middle English Sermons from MS. Roy. 18 B. xxiii* (ed. W. D. Ross, E.E.T.S. 208 (1938), p. 187, l. 9.

GLOSSARY

T HE Glossary attempts to record every form of every word that occurs in the texts in this book, with a selection of references sufficient to illustrate each form and suggest something of its distribution among the texts, and to exemplify the principal senses and uses of each word. The very numerous words which appear in variant forms and spellings are generally given under that which is most extensively used in these texts, but this may sometimes be disturbed by the overriding rule that words subject to inflexion are set out according to a fixed order. This affects mostly verbs, which are given under the infinitive if it is recorded, followed by the present tense, indicative, in order of person in the singular, then the plural, the subjunctive, and so on; theoretical headwords are not used. Cross-references are given as fully as possible. Brackets enclose letters which may appear either as optionally alternative spellings or as part of certain inflexions. Final -e originally stressed in words from French is marked by an acute accent: thus *moné* is distinguished from *mone*. Forms of nouns and adjectives ending in -e are not usually separately parsed as dative, plural, &c., because in some of the texts the significance of this spelling is uncertain; but in a few cases, where the distinction is clear, the abbreviation *dat.* is to be understood historically, as including use after prepositions. The sign ～ represents the headword in any of its forms.

Within entries the order of alternatives sometimes departs from alphabetical arrangement to bring commoner forms before isolated or eccentric spellings. Generally senses are shown close to the forms they gloss, but with some common verbs variation of spelling crosses the range of senses to such an extent that this is impracticable. In such entries the various senses, usually numbered, are given together after the forms of the infinitive, and all other inflexions are brought together later. Where a series of variant spellings is given together the order of the references, if it can conveniently do so, follows that of the forms.

Etymologies. Each etymon is given in the dialectal form that best accounts for the form in the texts, but 'dictionary' forms of nouns and verbs are given if the derivation of particular inflexions is obvious. In native words stable long vowels are shown by the usual macron, as in *āh*; those which were, or might have been, shortened in the Old English period as in *ắhte*; those which were, or might have been, lengthened as in *áld*. Old Norse words are quoted in the usual normalized spelling, so that long vowels are shown as in *ár*. When the prefix *ge-* was usual in a word in Old English but lost in Middle English it is separated by a hyphen as *ge-mǽdd*; when it was variable it is bracketed as *(ge)maca*; but in past participles it is generally ignored. An asterisk denotes a form theoretically reconstructed. The sign + shows that a compound or derivative is first recorded in Middle English. Words in bold type refer to entries in this Glossary; 'from' is used when the word glossed either has suffixes, &c., not present in the etymon or is derived by a change of function; 'cf.' indicates uncertain or indirect relation. When the spelling of an etymon does not differ from that in the texts it is not repeated. For words in extracts XVIII and XIX reference is often made to *Iuliene*, that is the edition of *Þe Liflade ant te Passiun of Seinte Iuliene* by S. R. T. O. d'Ardenne (Liége 1936; reissued as E.E.T.S. no. 248, 1961).

Order. æ has the place of *ae.* ʒ has a separate place after *g*, and *þ, ð, th* a separate place after *t*. *i* and *y* when they represent a vowel are treated as the same letter and take the order of *i*. *i* representing a consonant, modern *j*, is taken (together with *j*) after *i/y* representing a vowel; but initial *y* representing a consonant has its usual place after *w*. *u* and *v* are alternative forms of the same letter and are treated in the same way as *i/j*— when representing a vowel they come in the position of modern *u*, when a consonant in that of *v*; the few words beginning with *uu*, equivalent to *w*, are at the end of *v*. The same principles are observed for medial *u*, so that for example *about* precedes *aboue*.

References are to number of extract and line.

ABBREVIATIONS

absol.	absolute	adv.	adverb, -ial
acc.	accusative	app.	apparently
act.	active	art.	article
adj.	adjective	assim.	assimilated

attrib.	attributive	num.	numeral
auxil.	auxiliary	obj.	object, -ive
cl.	clause; with numeral, class	obl.	oblique
		occas.	occasional
coll.	collective	*OED*	*The Oxford English Dictionary*
comp.	comparative		
compd.	compound	orig.	originally
condit.	conditional	part.	partitive
conj.	conjunction	pass.	passive
cons.	consonant	pa. t.	past tense
contr.	contracted	perf.	perfect
correl.	correlative	perh.	perhaps
corresp.	corresponding	pers.	person, -al
dat.	dative	phr.	(in) phrase(s)
decl.	declined	pl.	plural
def.	definite	pos.	positive
demons.	demonstrative	poss.	possessive
deriv.	derivative	pp.	past participle
dial.	dialect, -al	pr.	present
fem.	feminine	prec.	preceding (word)
fold.	followed	predic.	predicative
fut.	future	pref.	prefix
gen.	genitive	prep.	preposition
imit.	imitative	prob.	probably
imper.	imperative	pron.	pronoun
impers.	impersonal	pr. p.	present participle
indecl.	indeclinable	recip.	reciprocal
indef.	indefinite	refl.	reflexive
infin.	infinitive	rel.	relative, related
infl.	influenced	sg.	singular
infl. infin.	inflected infinitive	sim.	similarly
inst.	instrumental	subj.	subjunctive
interj.	interjection	suff.	suffix
intr.	intransitive	sup.	superlative
introd.	introducing; introduction	tr.	transitive
		ult.	ultimately
masc.	masculine	uninfl.	uninflected
MED	*Middle English Dictionary* (Michigan)	usu.	usually
		v., vb.	verb
mod.	modern	var.	variant
n.	noun	vbl. n.	verbal noun
neg.	negative	voc.	vocative
neut.	neuter	wk.	weak
nom.	nominative	=	corresponding to

Languages and dialects

A	Anglian dialects of Old English	MW	Medieval Welsh
AN	Anglo-Norman	Nb	Northumbrian
Arab	Arabic	NFris	North Frisian
CF	Central (Old) French	Norw	Norwegian
Du	Dutch	nWS	non-West Saxon
Gmc	Germanic	OA	as A
		ODan	Old Danish
		OE	Old English
Gr	Greek	OEN	Old East Norse
Heb	Hebrew	OF	Old French
I	Icelandic	OHG	Old High German
Ir	Irish	OI	Old Icelandic
K	Kentish	OK	Old Kentish
L	Latin	ON	Old Norse
LL	Late Latin	ONb	Old Northumbrian
LOE	Late Old English	ONF	Northern dialects of Old French
LWS	Late West Saxon		
M	Mercian	OS	Old Saxon
MDu	Middle Dutch	OSw	Old Swedish
ME	Middle English	Scand	Scandinavian
MHG	Middle High German	Sw	Swedish
ML	Medieval Latin	W	Welsh
MLG	Middle Low German	WS	West Saxon
MSw	Middle Swedish		

GLOSSARY

a *adv.* always, for ever 10.50, 304, 19.202; **aa** 18.218, 389, 19.60; **o** 8H.27. [OE *ā*]

a *interj.* ah 5.131, 6.361, 8W.31, 15.23, 18.237, 19.255; **ah** 8H.34.

a *prep.* on 1.170, 2.99, 10.27, 17.171; ~ *fyre, fure* see **fir(e)**; in 1.20, 581, 725, 7.108, 10.7, 11; ~ *Godes nome* in God's name 5.36; into 10.138; (of time) at 1.239. **an** (before vowel or *h*) 1.239, 325, 537, 609, 8F.23, 10.17, 58, 17.78; see **hei3(e)**; ~ *hontingue* hunting 7.74; (of time) in 7.156; (before cons.) ~ *slep* asleep 16.119. [weakened form of **on**] Cf. **abrod, adai, alast, aliue, aneouste, ani3t, ari3t, atwo, awai, awene, awille.**

a(n) *indef. art.* a, an (generally as in modern use) 1.4, 45, 5.1, 8, 16.8, 17.31; wrongly divided in *a neilond* 12.145, *a nellen* 14.283; **aa** 19.428; **ay** 15.45 **an** before cons.: 6.1, 8F.31, 10.10, 11.41, 13.1, 16.62. **ane** 5.10, 7.29, 82, 105, 10.19, 34, 17.88, 18.95. **one** 4.234; *a day* one day 7.73, 158, 171, 11.111, 140; *on an day* 6.16. *acc. masc.* **anne** 5.29; **ænne** 13.95 (with *child*, OE neut.), 105. *gen.* **aness** 13.68. *dat. fem.* **are** 10.1, 14. [variant of **on(e)**, partly reduced]. See **fele.**

a. See **he**; **hi(i)**; **of**; **on(e)** *adj.*

abatest *pr. 2 sg.* bring low, humble 2.48. [OF *abatre*]

abbai, *n.* abbey 9.103; **abbei(e)** 7.280, 9.51; *attrib.* 7.259. [OF *abbaïe*]

abbat; **abbe.** See **abbot**; **habbe(n).**

abbot *n.* abbot 9.127, 16.8 (*dat.*), 29; **abbat** 18.413. *gen. sg.* **abbotes** 16.194. *pl.* **abbotes** 16.4. [OE *abbod* re-formed after ML *abbat-*]

abbotrice *n.* abbacy 16.8; (with prefixed art.) **þabbotrice** 16.213. *pl.* **-rices** 16.11. [prec.+ OE *rīce*]

abeod. See **abide(n).**

abeoren *v.* endure, put up with 19.142. [OM *abeoran*; see **ber**]

abide(n) *v. intr.* stay, remain, wait 4.224, 7.226, 10.257. *tr.* wait for 1.653 (with gen.), 10.124 (perh. *pa. t. pl.*); endure 1.664; live to see, experience 7.65. *pr. 3 sg.* **abid** 1.736. *pl.* **abideþ** 1.660. *imper. sg.* **abid** 1.493, 6.293. *pa. t. sg.* **abod** 1.41; **abeod** 10.195. [OE *abīdan*; see **byde**]

abisemar *prep.* (with dat., postponed) in mockery of 1.104. [**a** prep.+**bismere**]

abisemere *adv.* sneeringly 1.579. [as prec.]

abiten *v.* bite to death, slaughter 1.77. *pp.* (i) 5.203. [OE *abītan*, pp. *-biten*] See **bit.**

abod. See **abide(n).**

abol3e *pp. adj.* enraged 10.106, 204. [OE *abolgen* from *-belgan*] See **ibolwe.**

about. See **abugge.**

aboute(n) *adv.* about, around 2.103, 5.15, 7.48, 11.84, **about** 11.68; **abuten** 12.86, 18.87; **abuton** 16.58. *al* ~ on all sides 18.474; *is* ~ busies himself, strives 19.32; *igon* ~ taken steps 6.80. [OE *abūtan*]

aboute *prep.* about, around 3.33,

7.77, 8E.14; **abute(n)** 16.121, 18.563, 19.36, 171, (postponed) 9.141; **abuton** 16.168. ~ *nou3t* to no purpose 7.87; *þar* .. ~ 1.16 see **þer(e)**. [as prec.]

aboue *adv.* above, in heaven 2.264, 301; on (it) 3.60. *ben* ~ succeed 6.413. [OE *abufan*] Cf. **buue(n)**.

abrod *adv.* in all directions 11. 169. [a prep.+**brod(e)**]

abugge *v.* pay for, atone for 5.208. *pp.* **about** 8R.6. [OE *abycgan*; see **buggen**]

abute(n), **-on.** See **aboute(n)**.

ac(c) *conj.* but (on the contrary) 1.83, 2.9, 3.183, 5.59, 11.5; **ak(e)** 7.85, 9.112; **hac** 17.95; **ah** 1.565, 10.123, 18.21, 19.111; and 7.69, 11.134; **oc, ok** 8B.3, 9.43, 12.84, 116, 16.12, 16, 112. [OE *ac*; cf. ON *ok* and]

accidies, *n. gen.* of sloth 18.351. [ONF *accidie*]

a choger *interj.* to bed! (a trumpet call) 2.318 (note). [AN = OF **a coucher*]

acoled *pp.* grown cool, become less ardent 1.161. [OE *acōlian*]

acorde *n.* agreement: *at one* ~ of one mind 1.137. [OF]

acordede *pa. t. sg.* came to terms 16.139. [OF *acorder*]

acorsi. See **acursi.**

acountes *n. pl.* calculations 7.8. [AN *ac(o)unte*]

acoursed. See **acursi.**

acouerunge *n.* recovery 19.122. [from OE *acofrian*]

acumbri *v.* burden, harass 17. 166 [cf. OF *encombrer*; prefix altered]

acursi *v.* curse 1.662; **acorsi** pronounce a formal curse upon 7.270. *pp.* **acoursed** accursed 5.56; **acurset** 18.325. [pref. *a-* +OE *cursian*; see **curseð**]

acwikieð *pr. pl.* come to life, revive 19.119. [OE *acwician*]

acwitin *v.* release: ~ *ut* buy out 18.546. [OF *aquiter*]

ad. See **at.**

adai, aday *adv.* in the daytime 1.89, 175; daily 7.144, 105. [OE *on dæge*] Cf. **ani3t.**

adde. See **habbe(n).**

adi3te *pr. 1 sg.* order, dispose 1.242. [pref. *a-*+OE *dihtan*]

adoneward *adv.* down 7.261. [OE *adūnweard*]

adoun *adv.* down 3.187, 5.38, 57, 7.52, 8N.40, 11.116; **adun(e)** 1.552, 9.108, 10.9, 264, 18.30; below 1.164; (with prefixed neg.) **n'adoun** 8N.3, see **ne.** [OE *adūne*, *of-dūne*] See **doun(e), doune.**

adrad(de) *pp. adj.* afraid 2.256, 3.217, 4.214; **adred** 8N.20. [OE *ofdrǣdd*, *-drědd*; see **ofdrad**]

adrenct *pp.* drowned 18.53. [OE *adrencan*]

adun(e). See **adoun.**

adunest *pr. 2 sg.* assail with noise 1.253. [pref. *a-*+*dunen*, rel. to OE *dynian* make noise]

adunriht *adv.* straight down, strongly 10.283. [**adoun**+**ri3t** adv.]

adwole *adv.* in error 1.735. [OE *on dwolan*]

æfne; æfre; æft; æfter; æie; ælc(he). See **euene; euer(e); eft; after; eie; ech(e).**

ælder *n.* leader 10.271. [OE *ealdor*]

ældrihten *adj.* almighty 10.107. [OE *æl-*+*dryhten* adj.]

ælle; ælmes. See **al** *adj.*; **almes.**

æm(e) *n.* uncle 10.115, 143. [OE *ēam*]

æm; ænne; æorl; ær. See **am; a(n); eorl; er(e).**

ærcebiscop *n.* archbishop 16. 134, 245; **erchebischope** 7.199, 205. *pl.* **ærcebiscopes** 16.10; **erce-** 16.4. [OE *ærce-, ercebiscop*]

ærcebiscoprice *n.* archbishop-
ric 16.24. [OE *ærcebiscoprīce*]
ærd(e) *n.* land, region 10.99, 13.
67, 109. [OE *éard*]
ærm; æror; ært; æst; æt;
æten. See arme; er(e); art;
est; at; et.
æsthallf *n.* eastern part 13.163.
[OE *éasth(e)alf*] See est, half.
æðelæn *n.* origin, descent 10.in-
trod. [OE *æþelu*]
æuere. See euer(e).
æuert *adv.* ever (hitherto) 16.
322. [euer(e)+to] Cf.
neuerte.
æuez *adj.* trustworthy 16.237.
[OE *ǣ-fæst* upright]
æure; æuric. See euer(e);
euerich(e) *adj.*
afalle, afealleð. See aualle.
afeitet *pp. adj.* disposed 18.311;
fashioned 18.331. [OF *afaitier*]
afere *v.* frighten 1.177. *pp. adj.*
aferd 1.288, 330. [OE *afǣran*]
Cf. offearen.
afingret *pp. adj.* hungry 5.2, 110.
[OE *ofhyngred*, pp. of *ofhyngrian*]
Cf. aþurst.
afleiet *pp.* driven away 18.123,
288. [OA *aflēgan*]
afoled *pp.* made a fool of 1.162.
[OF *afoler*]
afonge *v.* accept, receive 3.137;
afongue 7.98. *pr. 3 sg.* afongeþ
2.83. *pl.* auoþ hear 1.503. [OE
afōn; see fon]
after *adv.* after, behind 10.182;
afterwards, then 1.327; efter
18.355. [OE *æfter*, M *efter*]
after *prep.* 1.96, 2.119, 3.6, 5.52;
affter(r) 6.412, 13.63; aftir 9.
122; af(f)tur 7.7, 10; æfter 16.
6, 314; efter 14.235, 16.108,
17.23, 18.22. (of time) after
1.96, 2.119, 7.10, 11.140, 16.6,
18.22. (of place) after, in pur-
suit of 5.61; through 7.201. (of
an object sought, &c.) for: see
axen, biholde, fare(n), ferde,
grede(n), send, willen; sim.

seruest, and 8A.6, 7; in order
to get 16.163, 19.31. (of con-
gruence) according to 6.53, 18.
512, 19.23, 56; in imitation of
2.236. ~ þan after that, then
(see þat pron.) 1.156, 2.1, 5.108;
~ þat(t) (*conj.*) after 7.7, 13.63,
14.235; according as 19.57, 91,
411. [as prec., and *æfter þǣm*]
afterward *adv.* afterwards, later
8F.18; efterward 17.202. [OE
æfterweard, efter-]
agænes. See agenes.
again, agayn *adv.* back 14.215,
252. [as aȝein, with *g* after ON
i gegn]
again *prep.* against 14.143; agen
4.219; (postponed) to meet
(winter) 12.79; ageyn full in
4.255; exposed to, under (the
stars) 4.236. [as prec.]
agan. See ago(n).
agaste *pp. adj.* afraid 7.134.
[pref. *a-*+pp. of OE *gǣstan*
frighten]
age *n.* age; *more of* ~ older 2.202;
of ~ *of man* in manhood 17.248.
[OF *ēage, aage*]
ageyn; agen. See again;
owen(e).
agenes *prep.* against 16.136, 310;
towards 17.253; agænes 16.
157. [again or aȝein+adv. *-es*]
See aȝeines.
aght. See ah.
agyn *imper. sg.* begin 17.190.
pa. t. sg. agon 10.35. [OE
onginnan, -gonn] Cf. biginne.
ago(n) *pp.* gone away 3.221;
passed 5.153; gone, past 5.49;
agan departed 10.49. [OE
agān; see go(n)]
agon. See agyn.
agrise *v.* be afraid 5.240. *pp.* (i)
afraid 11.119. [OE *agrīsan*, pp.
-grisen]
agulteð *pr. pl.* are guilty, offend
19.55. [OE *agyltan*; see gul-
teð]
aȝaf *pa. t. sg.* gave back, retorted

1.95. *pl.* **aiauen** gave (up), surrendered 16.296. [OA *agæf* from *-gefan*; see **ʒeue**]

aʒein, aʒeyn *adv.* back, back again 2.316, 6.296, 18.273, 8H. 43; **aʒain** 10.76; **aʒen** 3.154, 220, 7.174, 11.29; **aʒan** 10.101; **aʒe** 3.198, 9.188; **onnʒæn** 13. 137. *stond* ~ protest, object 1. 746. [OE *ongegn, -gēn, -gēan*]

aʒein, aʒeyn *prep.* 7.136, 8K.60, 18.1, 19.22; **aʒen** 1.7, 11.69; **ayen** 17.183; **aʒe** 11.5. against 1.7, 7.136, 11.69, 18.299, (postponed) 383; contrary to 7.142, 8K.60; opposite 11.155; towards 17.183, 18.526, 19.261; at 1.314; to meet, to receive 18.562, 19. 312; compared with 18.635, 19. 259. [as prec.]

aʒeines *prep.* against 18.58, 88, 19.37, (postponed) 364; compared with 18.402, 19.297. [prec.+adv. *-es*] See **aʒenes**.

aʒen, aʒere, aʒhenn; aʒʒ; aʒt. See **owen(e); ai; ah.**

ah *pr. 1 sg.* own, have 10.16; **oʒe** am bound to, ought to 8W.14. *2 sg.* **ahest** owe 18.19. *3 sg.* **ah** ought 18.232, 466, 19.187; **oʒ** 12.130, (impers. with dat.) 111. *pl.* **ahen** 18.671, 19.4, 338; **oʒen** 12.103, 129. *subj. sg* **aʒe** in *þe feond hine* ~ the Devil take him 10.216. *pa. t. sg.* **ahte** owned 18.487, 634, ought 16.251; **aute** owned 4.11; **aʒht** ought to 14. introd.; **aʒt** must 9.82; **ouʒte** ought (to be) 7.192; **oþte** (= *oʒte*) 8W.28. *pl.* **ahten** possessed 10. introd. [OE *āh, āgon; ǽhte*]

ah; ahne. See a *interj.*, **ac(c); owen(e).**

ahon *v.* hang 10.208. *pp.* 18.322. [OE *ahōn*, pp. *-hángen*]

ahte *n.* goods, possessions, wealth 8H.42, 10.252; **eiʒte** 11. 49 (see **quic**); **nayct** in *my* ~ for *myn ayct* 15.58. [OE *ǽht*]

ai, ay *adv.* always 12.10, 14.32,

6.304, 15.24; **aʒʒ** 13.114, continuously 197. [ON *ei*]

ay; aiauen; ayen. See **a(n); aʒaf; aʒein** *prep.*

ayen-wende *v.* return 17.32. [**aʒein**+**wend**]

aishest. See **aske.**

aiþer *pron.* either, each (of two, persons or things, often assoc. with **oþer**) 3.209, 248; **eiþer, eiðer** 1.7, 9, 141, 18.282, 19.116; **eþer** 4.309. [OE *ǽʒþer* both, *ā(w)þer* either]

aiware *adv.* everywhere 1.172. [OE *ǽghwǽr*]

ak(e). See **ac(c).**

akelþ *pr. 3 sg.* cools 17.118. [OE *acēlan*]

aknowe *pp.* in *ben* ~ admit, reveal 2.21. [OE *oncnāwen*, pp. of *-cnāwan*; see **knowe, icnawen**]

al(le) *n.* all, everything 1.78, 743, 2.98, 6.63, 146, 8E.53, 79, K.31, 16.136, 193; **eall** 16.43; all the time 9.26; everyone 10.259, 18. 306. *mid alle* completely 1.412, 10.229, 18. 248, 660; *swiðe mid alle* very greatly 18.593, 19.238. [OE *eal(l)*, A *al(l)*; *mid (e)alle*] See **oueral, withal.**

al *adj.* all, the whole of 1.8, 74, 2.164, 3.106, 4.87, 7.16, 8G.33, 18.559 (see **dai(e)**); **all** 12.104, 13.50; **alle** 5.147, 7.12, 10.5; **eal(l)** 16.31, 3, 48; **ealle** complete 16.85. *gen.* **alles**, see **kinn.** *dat.* **allen** 10.215. *pl.* **alle** 1.499, 635, 2.46, 3.28, 4.142, 8D.11, 17.269 (*dat.*); *hi* ~ all of them 16.154; **halle** 8v.4; **ealle** 16.5, 10; **al** 1.515, 8L.24. as *n.* **alle** 1.178, 4.13, 7.270, 8F.35; **ealle, ælle** 16.64, 152; **al** 15.76. *gen.* **alre** 1.512, 10.65, 16.137, 18.315, 608; *ure* ~ of all of us 19.205; **allre** 13.240. [OE *(e)all*, gen. pl. *(e)alra*] See **alkyn**, and superlatives intensified by **alre-**.

al *adv.* entirely, fully, quite, just, right, 1.27, 498 (note), 3.118,

5.17, 49, 6.10, 12.7, 19.11; **all**
13.267; **eall** 16.16, 42; ~ *one*
see **on(e)**; altogether 19.341;
all (too) 6.343, 7.116, 8H.43; (as
mere intensive) 3.263, 8G.42,
X.11, 9.104. [prec.] See **als,
also.**

alas *interj.* alas! 6.333, 7.30, 65;
allas 2.248, 4.305. [OF (*h*)*a
las*]

alast *adv.* in ~ *of þis wordle* in
this last age 17.217. [*a* prep.+
last, see **leatere**]

ald(e). See **old(e).**

alde-feader *n.* first father 18.
455. [OE *ealdfæder* ancestor,
M. *aldfeder; see **fader**]

alegge *v.* refute 1.272. [OE
alecgan]

alesen *v.* deliver 19.272. [OA
alēsan] Cf. **les.**

alesnesse *n.* deliverance 19.330.
[from prec.]

aly. See **holi(e).**

aliȝte *pa. t. sg.* alighted, came to
earth 7.7; dismounted 11.13.
pp. **aliȝth** 2.187. [OE *alīhtan*]
Cf. **liȝt** *v.*

aliö *pr. 3 sg.* subsides, is laid 18.
92; ceases, fails 18.167. [OE
alīþ from -*licgan*; see **ligge(n)**]

aliue *adj.* living, alive 5.183, 10.
114, 11.102. [OE *on līfe*; see **on,
lif**]

alkyn *adj.* of every kind 14.35.
[OA *alra cynna; see **kinn**]

allas. See **alas.**

allegate *adv.* in every way, by all
means 6.398. [cf. ON *alla gǫtu*
throughout, always; see **gate**
n.²]

allingues *adv.* altogether, entirely 7.140. [OA *allinga*+adv.
-*es*]

allmahhtiȝ; allswa. See **almichti; also** *adv.*

allunge *adv.* entirely 18.601,
660. [OA *allunge*]

almast *adv.* almost 14. introd.
[al *adv.*+ONb *māst*, see **more**]

almes *n.* charity; *gen.* in *for* ~
sake for the sake of charity 5.44;
ælmes in *on* ~ begging 16.188.
[OE *ælmesse*]

almesdede *n.* almsgiving, charity
6.207. [prec.+**ded(e)**]

almichti *adj.* almighty 17.4, 51;
almihti 18.104, 129, 19.364;
allmahhtiȝ 13.49. [OE *ælmihtig, ælmeahtig*]

almiȝtten *adj.* almighty 6.25,
322, 371. [prec., with suff. after
dryhten; see **Drihten**]

alpi; alre. See **onlepi; al**
adj.

alrehecst *adj. sup.* most acute of
all 1.433. [OA *alra hēhst*; see **al**
adj. and **heiȝ(e)**]

alremest *adv. sup.* most of all
1.430. [as prec., with OE *mǣst*;
see **mor(e)**]

alrenecst, -nest *adv. sup.* nearest of all 1.434, 446. [as prec.;
see **ner(e)**]

alrewiseste *adj. sup.* wisest of
all 10.55. [as prec., see **wis(e)**]

alreworste *adj. sup.* worst possible 1.10. [as prec.; see
wors(e)]

als *adv. rel., conj.* as 2.38, 121,
4.157, 14.236; such as 14.13;
like 4.82, 14.121; **alls** 13.159.
~.. ~, *also* .. ~ as .. as 2.241-
2, 4.76; rel. after **sli** 14.66. as
if (with subj.) 3.49, 4.339, 16.
120; ~ *þai*, see **þei**. [reduced
form of **also**] See **as, so.**

also *adv. demons.* 2.259, 3.131,
7.3; **alse** 16.215; **als** 14.21;
alswa 1.597, 18.68; **allswa** 13.
267; **alswo** 1.591. (1) also, as
well 1.621, 2.259, 3.131, 14.21,
17.182, 18.68. (2) so, just so, the
same 1.591, 7.164, 16.215, in the
same way 1.597. ~ .. *als, as, so*
as .. as 4.76, 6.95, 8L.22; *also* ..
~, *alswa se, alswa as* .. ~ just
as .. so 3.141, 13.275, 18.419.
~ *raþe*, see **raþe**. [OA *al swā*]
Cf. **als, so, swa.**

also *adv. rel., conj.* 4.192, 299; **alse** 10.211, 16.249; **alswo** 1. 696, 17.7. as, like 1.696, 4.299, 5.217, 12.2; when 4.192; as soon as 17.7, 11, 105. as, so (in adjurátion, cf. **as(e), so)** 6.267. rel. with **alsuic**, as 16.145. correl. (see prec.) ~ .. *also, so* just as .. so 3.142, 17.65, 117. as if (with subj.) 1.102, 12.132. [as prec.]

alsuic *adj.* just such 16.145. [OA *al swilc*; see **swich(e)**]

alto *adv.* completely 12.6. [al adv.+**to**-]

alþei *conj.* (with subj.) although 7.10. [al adv.+**þei**]

alþerhotestd *adj. sup.* hottest of all 17.249. [pref. devel. from *alre-*; see **alrehecst**, &c., and **hot(e)**]

aluen *n.* supernatural being, 'elf' 10.308. *pl. gen.* 10.321. [OA *ælfen* nymph, supernatural woman]

alwat *conj.* until 17.28. [al adv. +**what**]

alwealdent *adj.* all-powerful 19. 254. [OA *alwáldend* infl. by *wáldan*; see **welde** *v.*]

am *pr. 1 sg.* am 1.126, 4.58, 5. 133, 8D.13, 14.131, 17.163; **æm** 10.13, 72. *auxil.* (forming pass.) 3.156, 5.103, 6.204, 8D.1, **amm** 13.81, **ham** 15.22; (forming perf. of intr. vbs.) have 5.159, 6.80, 10.78, 15.39, 19.71. [OA *(e)am*] See **be(n)** and other parts.

amang. See **among(e).**

amanset *pp.* excommunicated 1.575. [OE *amǎnsod* from *amǎns(um)ian*]

amarȝen. See **amorȝe.**

amarscled *pp. adj.* bewildered, bemused (?) 8N.38. [pref. *a-*+ pp. of OE **malscrian* bewilder, implied in n. *malscrung*; note]

ame *interj.* (addressed to a dog) come! 18.366. [app. an invented gesture-word; but perh. rel. to me conj.]

ameaset *pp. adj.* confused, foolish 18.318. [OM **ameasian* = WS *amasian*]

amen *interj.* amen 8w.60, 9.190, 19.421. [L, ult. Heb]

amende *v.* change for the better, soften 15.51; **amendi** correct, redress 11.24. *imper. sg.* amend 6.113. [OF *amender*]

amendement *n.* remedy, redress, in *don þe* ~ put the matter right 18.257. [OF]

amendyng *n.* redress 2.51. [from **amende**]

amenges *prep.* among 17.195. [as **among(e)**, but infl. by OE *mengan* (see **mengeþ**)+adv.-*es*]

amera(i)l *n.* emir 3.21, 230; (with prefixed art.) **þamerail** 3.66. [OF *ameral* from Arab]

ametist *n.* amethyst 9.93. [OF *amatiste*]

amy *n.* friend 2.178, lover 280. [OF *ami*]

amid(de) *prep.* in the middle of, half-way down 5.241; in the course of 18.355; in 18.384. [OE *onmiddan*]

amidewarde *prep.* in the middle of 4.139; **amidward** 5.274. [prec.+OE -*weard*]

amonestement *n.* incitement, temptation 17.67 [OF]

among *adv.* at times, by turns 1.6, 3.169, 8w.54, 11.17; mingled 8E.11; among them 5. 266; **amang** at the same time 14.88. [OE *on(ge)máng, -móng*]

among(e) *prep.* among 1.120, 371, 18.224; in the midst of 1. 435; (postponed) 2.80: **amang** 13.144; **imong** 18.144, 238. [as prec.]

amoreȝ *adv.* (on) the next day 1.310; **amor(e)we** 3.110, 7. 156, 11.132; **amarȝen** 10.7, 118. [OE *on morgene*] See **moreghen, tomorewe.**

amour(e) *n.* love 2.268, 3.268. [OF *amo(u)r*]. See **par amour.**

amuntet *pr. 3 sg.* ascends 17.56. [AN *amunter*]

amurðrin *v.* murder 19.36. [OE *amyrþrian*]

an; anæn, anan(-); anaht. See a *prep.*, a(n), and, on(e), vnnen; anon(-); ani3t.

ananrihtes *adv.* immediately 18.109, 254. [anonri3t+adv. *-es*]

ancre *n.* anchoress 18.132. *pl.* ancren 18.203, 222, ancres 304. *gen.* ancrene 18. title. [OE *ancre*]

ancrefule *adj.* anxious 18.57. [ON *angr* anxiety+-ful]

and *conj.* and 1.4, 2.5, 3.2, 4.5; annd 13.3; hand 8v.1, 15.24; ant 8D.15, H.45, 18.1, 2, 19.5; an 1.5, 8w.9, 15.54, 16.121, 19.377. if (?) 1.587 (note), 2.309, 6.164, 363, 15.61, 17.266, 18.87; ~ *if* if 6.168, 392; ~ .. ~ both .. and 19.187. [OE *and, ond*]

andsuare; andswar-. See answere; answeren.

ane *adv.* only 18.34, 111, 278; uniquely, in *wunder* ~ 10.296, see **wonder** *adv.* [OE *āna, āne*] See **one.**

ane *prep.* in 17.223. [OE *on* (see **a** prep.) with *-e* after *in, inne*]

ane. See a(n); one *adj.*

aneouste *adv.* quickly 10.127, 316, aneoste, aneuste 248, 167. *prep.* near (postponed) 10.219. [OE *on* *oefeste in haste, *on nēaweste* in the neighbourhood]

anes *adv.* once, in *get* ~ once again 16.91. [OE *ānes,* adv. gen.] See **on(e).**

anesweis *adv.* in one direction 18.226. [OE **ānes weges,* adv. gen.] See **wai(e).**

anewil *adj.* obstinate 18.636. [Cf. OE *ānwille*]

anful *adj.* individual, personal 18.231. [OE *ān*+-ful]

angel *n.* angel 14.130; angle 8v.13, 15; ongel 17.31. [OF *angele*] Cf. **engel.**

Anglen *n. pl. dat.* the English 10.327. [OE *Angle*]

angoisuse *adj.* anxious 18.3. [OF *angoissous*]

anguisse *n.* suffering 7.218. [OF]

anhet *pr. 3 sg.* warms 17.126. *pp.* anheet 17.126, 135. [OE *onhǣtan*]

anhon *v.* hang 10.112; anhonge 2.312. *pr. pl.* anhoð 1.604. *pp.* anhonget 18.321. [variant of **ahon** with altered pref.; OE pp. *-hángen*]

ani, any *adj.* any 3.15, 6.15 (see **kinn**), 7.173, 14.254, 16.161, 2.242; eni, eny 1.365, 6.169, 7.113, 19.128, 8K.84; eani 18.172, 276. [OE *ǣnig,* vowel shortened in trisyllabic forms]

ani *pron.* anyone 7.131; eani 18.128. [prec.]

ani3t *adv.* at, by night 1.89, 175; anyht 8K.22; anaht 8E.20. [OE *on niht*; see **ni3t(e)**] Cf. **adai.**

aniþing *n.* anything 6.32, 7.182; eni- 1.466. [ani+þing(e)]

anlepi; anne. See onlepi; a(n).

annesse *n.* unity 18.161, 198. [OE *ānnes(se)*]

anon *adv.* at once, immediately 3.211, 6.155, 7.79, 9.161, 10.180; anan 1.616, 10.214, 13.63, 18.99, 19.119; onon 2.67, 162. all the way, right 7.42, 9.181; onan 16.60. ~ **so** *conj.* as soon as 7.213, 243; anæn swa 10.126. [OE *on ān*]

anonri3t *adv.* at once 3.205, 7.121; ananriht 18.168, 274, 19.179, 363; ononri3th 2.188. [prec.+ri3t *adv.*]

anoþer, -ur, anoðer *adj.* another, a different 1.54, 352, 2.228, 14.137, 7.28, 12.110. *dat.* anoþren 17.37. [a(n)+oþer(e)] anoþer *pron.* another 2.242, 3.96, 8F.27, 32. another thing, something else 18.86; **anoðer**, **onoþer** 1.535, 417. [as prec.]

anred *adj.* constant 18.225. [OE *ānrǣd*]

anrednesse *n.* steadfastness, constancy 18.7, 160. [OE *ānrǣdnes(se)*]

anst; ansuar-, -svere. See vnnen; answere, answeren.

ansueryng *n.* answer 2.155. [from answeren]

answere *n.* answer 1.668, 3.211; ansvere, andswere, -suere 1.328, 411, 451; answare, -suare, andsuare 1.55, 277, 359, 105. [OE *andswaru, -swere*]

answeren *v.* answer 3.91, 123. *pr. 1 sg.* ondswerie 19.78. *3 sg.* ondswereð, ont- 19.317, 74. *subj. sg.* ondswerie 18.272. *imper. sg.* ansuare 1.363; ondswere 18.641. *pa. t. sg.* answard 14.168; andswarede 10.11, 52, 65; answerde, ansuerede 17.93, 199. *pl.* andswarede 10.116; answerden, ansuerden 17.18, 229. [OE *andswarian, ond-, -swerian*]

ant. See and.

anuid *pp.* annoyed, displeased 11.136; anud 17.15. [pp. of *anuen,* OF *anuier*]

anvnder *prep.* under 8E.58 (see bis). [OE *on under*]

anuri *v.* do homage to, worship 17.9, 24; onuri 17.25. *imper. pl.* anuret 17.23. *pa. t. pl.* anurede 17.29. *pp.* anured 17.78. [AN *anurer,* blend of *onurer* honour and *aorer* adore]

anvie *n.* envy 17.167. [OF *envie*]

aparailed *pp.* prepared 17.11. [OF *apareillier*]

ape *n.* ape 1.593; eape 18.117. [OE *apa,* M **eapa*]

aperede *pa. t. sg.* appeared 17.31; apierede 17.6. [OF *aper-,* accented stem of *apareir*]

aperseiuede *pa. t. sg.* observed, noticed 5. 213. [OF *aperceiv-,* accented stem of *aperceveir*]

aperteliche *adv.* clearly 7.48, 278. [OF *apert+-liche*]

apierede. See aperede.

Apocalipse *n.* the Book of Revelation 18.582, 657. [L. *apocalypsis*]

apon. See upon.

apostle *n.* apostle 17.230, 19. 179. *pl.* apostles 17.227, 19. 290. [OE *apostol,* OF *apostle*]

appel *n.* apple 1, note to 95. *pl.* apples 8E.59(note). [OE *æppel*]

appel-tre *n.* apple-tree 14.231. [prec.+tre(e)]

aqualde. See aquelle.

aqueinte *pp.* adj. personally known, acquainted (with *to*) 2. 145. [OF *acoint*]

aquelle *v.* kill 7.102. *pa. t. sg.* aqualde 10.227. [OE *acwellan,* pa. t. (A) -*cwálde;* see quelle]

aquenche *v.* assuage, satisfy 5. 13, 112. [OE *acwencan;* see quench]

ar(e) *pr. pl.* are 4.205, 308, 8H. 10; aren 8E.16, 12.152, 173, 18.185, 19.122; arn 12.5, 112. [ONb *aron,* M *earun*] See be(n) and other parts.

ar; aras. See er(e) *conj.,* euer(e); arise(n).

arblastes *n. pl.* cross-bows 11. 34. [OF *arbaleste*]

archangles *n. pl.* archangels 19. 280. [OF *archangel(e)*]

Architriclin *n.* the master of the feast 17.104. [OF]

are. See a(n); er(e); ore *n.¹*

arearen *v.* raise, lift up 18.484. *pr. subj. sg.* areare 18.188. *pa. t. sg.* arerde built 7.222. *pl.* 11. 152. *pp.* arerd 7.255; arearet arising 18.39. [OE *arǣran*]

arecchen *v.* interpret 10.53 (note). [OE *areccan*]

arede *v.* save, rescue 3.148. [OE *ahreddan*]

are3 *adj.* cowardly 1.285. [OE *earh*]

are3eþe *n.* cowardice 1.282; **arehþe** 1.674. [from prec.; cf. OE *ierhþu*]

arer-. See **arearen.**

aresunede *pa. t. sg.* called to account 17.227. [AN *aresun-*, stem of *araisnier* arraign]

ari3t *adv.* rightly, correctly, properly 1.278, 3.182, 9.168; **ariht** 1.536; **aryþt** (= *ary3t*) 8w.44. [OE *on riht, ariht*]

arise(n) *v.* rise, arise 1.243, 5. 239; (from bed) 5.264. *pr. 3 sg.* **arise∂** stands up 19.313. *pl.* **ariseþ** 1.477. *imper. pl.* **ariseþ** 5.269. *pa. t. sg.* **aras** 10.8, 18. 501; **aro(o)s** 17.146, 148. [OE *arīsan*; see **rise**]

ariste *n.* resurrection 18.136. [OM *ērist*, LOE *arist* re-formed on prec.]

arm *n.*[1] arm 8E.52; **ærm** 10.25. *pl.* **armes** 2.189, 4.329, 8F.38, K.26; **ærmes** 10.8; **earmes** 18.512, 562. [OE *earm*]

arme *adj.* wretched, unhappy 1. 345; **ærm** 10.231. [OE *earm*]

armes *n.*[2] *pl.* weapons 18.7; ~ *ber(e)* fought 11.70, 73. [OF *armes*]

arn; aro(o)s; arre. See **ar(e); arise(n); er(e).**

art *n.* artifice 3.68; cunning, in *conne .. mochel of* ~ be very astute 3.259. [OF]

art *pr. 2 sg.* art, are 1.38, 2.46, 3.93, 4.121; **ært** 10.54; **ert** 8T.10; (with suffixed pron.) **artu** 1.349, 566; **hertou** 5.120; (with prefixed pron.) **þart** 8N. 38. *auxil.* (forming pass.) 1.349, 2.244; (forming perf. of intr. vbs.) hast, have 2.265, 3.90. [OE *eart*] See **be(n)** and other parts.

arudde(n) *v.* deliver, rescue 18. 494, 19.136. *pa. t. sg.* **arudde** 18.499. *pp.* **arud** 18.525. [pref.

a-+OE (*h*)*ryddan* strip, sense infl. by *hreddan* save; see **arede**]

as(e) *conj.* as, like 2.63, 3.12, 6. 298, 7.1, 18.236; (introd. adjuration) 6.326; as, while 6.1, 7.77, 19.306; when 10.162, 17.4; how 19.276; such as 18.40. ~ *so* as 17.120; ~ .. ~, *also* .. ~ as .. as 18.81, 19.397, 2.60. ~ *hende* as one who is gracious, graciously 6.61; ~ *mon þat wolde* wishing 6.131. as if (with subj.) 3.82, 7.76, 150, 11.89, 112; ~ *þah,* see **þah**; forming conj. with adv., see **þer(e), þider(e)**. [further reduced from **als**] See **so**.

as. See **habbe(n)**.

asailin *v.* attack 18.91. *pr. 3 sg.* **asaile∂** 18.81; **asale∂** 18.79. *pa. t. pl.* **asayleden** 4.289. *pp.* **asailet** 18.38, 169. [OF *asaillier, asalir*]

asake *v.* renounce 8x.8. [OE *onsacan* refuse, deny; cf. **atsake**]

ascape *v.* escape 6.370. [AN *escaper, ascaper*]

asch *n.* ash (tree) 7.95. [OE *æsc*]

ashunche *v.* frighten (?) 8F.45 (note). [obscure; see **schunche∂**]

aske *v.* ask (a question) 3.88; **easki** 18.45. *pr. 2 sg.* **aishest** 1.331; **easkest** ask about 19.77. *3 sg.* **easke∂** 19.85, 242; asks for 18.107. *pl.* **easki∂** 18.79. *pa. t. 2 sg.* **askedest** 1.578. *3 sg.* **asked(e)** 2.223, 14.158; 17.13. *pl.* **askede** 3.203. [OE *ascian, æscan*; see *Iuliene* pp. 149–50] See **axen**.

aslov3 *pa. t. sg.* killed 7.117. *pp.* **aslæ3e** 10.170. [OE *aslōh, -slægen* from *aslēan* strike; see **sle(n)**]

asluppe *v.* slip away, escape from (with dat. of pers.) 8F.40. [cf. OE *aslūpan,* MDu *ontslip-pen*]

asoyne *n.* excuse for non-appearance at court 11.104; *bi* ~ by proxy 11.97. [OF *essoi(g)ne*]

asoynede *pa. t. pl.* made excuse (for non-attendance) for 11.99. [from prec.]

aspie, aspye *v.* find out about 2.160; spy on 3.90. [cf. OF *espier*]

aspille *v.* spoil 1.264. [OE *aspillan*]

assunder *adv.* apart, to pieces 6.360. [OE *on sundran*]

astirte *pa. t. sg.* sprang, leapt 4.159. [pref. *a-*+OE *styrtan*; see **sterteþ**]

astiune *n.* astrion, a kind of precious stone 9.90 (note). [L from Gr *astēr* star]

astorede *pa. t. sg.* provided, fitted out 11.81. [cf. OF *estorer*]

astrengþed *pp.* fortified 17.157. [pref. *a-*+**strengþen**]

at *prep.* 1.86, 2.75, 3.13, 4.57, 5.21; **att** 13.232; **ad** 1.241; **æt** 16.1; **et** 19.111; **ed** 18.58, 19.112. (of place) at 1.86, 3.13, 4.141, 16.150, 19.112, ~ *hom* 4.57; in 1.395; at the hands of, from 14.229, 18.58, 265. (of time) at 1.241, 16.1, 18.632. in phrs. with certain nouns: according to (*wille*) 13.232, (*might*) 14.171; of (*one acorde*) 1.137, (*one rede*) 7.37; in (*nede*) 2.75, 5.225, 6.210, 10.202, 12.115, 135; (after *plaien*) at 3.98; (introd. infin.) to 14.59, 61. **ate** = *at þe* 7.279, 8N.32, 17.209; **atte** 11.35, 71. [OE *æt*, M *et*; with infin., ON *at*]

atarnde *pa. t. sg.* escaped 11.102. [OE *ætarn* from *-irnan* (see **erne**)+wk. ending]

atfliþ. See **edfleon**.

atholde *v.* keep, retain, hold back 1.441, 3.114; **edhalden** 18.607. *pr. 3 sg.* **edhalt** 18.106, 450. *pa. t. sg.* **athold** took heed of 1.270. *pp.* **edhalden** reserved 18.345; kept in mind 18.140. [OA *æt-*, *et-háldan; see **holde(n)** and cf. **atwite**]

atyre *n.* furnishing 2.231. [OF *atir*]

atywede *pa. t. sg.* showed 16.229. [OE *ætȳwan*]

atled *pp.* arranged, placed 8E.41. [ON *ætla* think] Cf. **etlunge**.

atluppe *v.* escape 8F.44. [prob. rel. to OE *æt-hlēapan*]

ato. See **atwo**.

atraht *pp.* taken away (with dat. of pers.) 8F.30. [OE *æt-*+*ræ̆ht*, *ráht* from *ræcan*]

atsake *pr. 1 sg.* disown, reject 10.110. [OE *ætsacan*]

atschet *pa. t. sg.* departed, left (her) 1.44. [OE *æt-*+*scēat* from *scēotan*; see **ssete**]

atstonde(n) *v. intr.* take up a position, stand 10.34; make a stand 10.200; *tr.* withstand, resist 1.496; **etstonden** *wið*, *aȝeines* resist 19.206, 364. *imper. sg. tr.* **edstond, ed-, etstont** 18.111, 110, 19.179. [OE *ætstóndan*, M *et-*]

atte. See **at**.

attercoppe *n. pl.* spiders 1.380. [OE *attorcoppe*]

attrest *pr. 2 sg.* poison 18.297. [OE *ǣttrian*]

atturné *n.* proxy 2.14. [AN *aturné*]

aturnet *pp.* transformed into 18.313; arrayed 19.235. [AN *aturner*]

atwite *v.* reproach 3.232. *pr. 2 sg.* **atuitest** (with dat. of pers. and direct obj. of the matter of reproach) 1.377. *pl.* **edwiteð** 19.140. [OE *ætwítan* and *edwítan*; *ed-* and M *et-* confused in ME]

atwo *adv.* in two 8G.47; apart 3.288; **ato** 7.51. [OE *on twā*]

aðele *adj.* noble 10.206. *dat.* **æðelen**, a- 10.introd., 119. *sup.* **aðelest** 10.65. [OE *æþele*]

að(es), ath-. See **oþ(e)**.

aþet *conj.* until 19.25; **aðet** 18.312, 19.119, 129. [OM *oþ þet*]

aþet *prep.* until 18.652. [*prec.*]

aþrusmeð *pr. 3 sg.* smothers 19.124. [OE *aþrysmian*]

aþurst *pp. adj.* thirsty 5.66, 7. 249. [OE *ofþyrst*, pp. of *ofþyrstan*] See **hofþurst** and cf. **afingret**.

aunters *n. pl.* adventures 14.12. [popular form of **auenture**]

aute. See **ah**.

auter *n.* altar 11.55 [AN]

auail *v.* be of value, do good 14. 90. [prob. formed in AN on *vaill-*; see **uaile**]

aualle *v.* fall, be brought low 1.643. *pr. 3 sg.* **afealleð** subsides 18.94. *pp.* **afalle** fallen down 5.18. [OE *afeallan*, A *-fallan*]

auallen *v.* fell, kill 10.207. [OA *afællan*]

Aue Marie *n.* the prayer 'Hail Mary' 19.428; **Auy Mary** 15. 73; **Aue** 8т.23. [L *Ave Maria*]

avenge *v.* avenge (with *of*) 2.62. [OF *avengier*]

auenture *n.* chance, accident 17. 91; *on* ~ by chance 5.70. [OF *aventure*] See **aunters**.

auere· **aueriche**. See **euer(e)**; **euerich(e)** *adj.*

Aueryl *n.* April 8м.2. [OF *avril*]

auermare; **Auy Mary**. See **euermar(e)**; **Aue Marie**.

auinde *v.* find, learn 1.516. [pref. *a-*+**find(e)**]

auoy *interj.* fie! 3.227. [OF]

auornon *prep.* in front of, facing (postponed) 10.161. [OE *on foran*+on]

auoþ. See **afonge**.

awai, away *adv.* away 6.149, 2.315, 6.17; **awei, awey** 1.33, 11.117, 18.8, 4.346; *lete* ~ see **lete(n)**. [OE *on weg*; see **wai(e)**]

awaiteden *pa. t. pl.* kept watch 7.158. [ONF *awaitier*]

awake *v. intr.* awake, wake up 7.235, 243; **awakien** 7.83. *pa. t. sg.* **awok** 7.56; came to his senses 3.73. *pl.* **awoke(n)** 7. 239, 242. *tr., pa. t. pl.* **awakede** woke 17.149. [OE *awacian*, pa.

t. *awacode*, and *awōc* from *awæcnan*; both intr.] Cf. **awecche(n)**.

awarie. See **awearien**.

awe *n.* ewe 8a.6. [OE *eowu*]

awearien *v.* curse, damn 18.332. *pr. subj. sg.* **awarie** 6.332. [OM *awergan, -wærgan*]

awecche(n) *v. tr.* wake, rouse 5.267, 19.407. [OE *aweccan*] Cf. **awake**.

awei, awey. See **awai**.

awene *adv.* in doubt 1.428. [a prep.+**wene**]

awille *prep.* to the pleasure of (postponed) 1.680. [OE *on willan*; see **wil** *n.*[1]]

awok(en). See **awake**.

awondrede *pa. t. pl. refl.* marvelled 17.154. [OE *awundrian*] Cf. **wndri**.

awreke(n) *v.* avenge 2.64, 66 (app. with dat.), 7.138, 10.61. *pp.* **awræke** 10.115; **awreke** (*of*) avenged (upon) 1.198, 2.6, 5.64. [OE *awrecan*; see **wreoke**]

awuriet *pp.* torn to death 18.172. [OE *awyrgan*]

awwnedd *pp.* shown, made known 13.116, 178. [ON, rel. to Norw dial. *öygna*; cf. OE *æt-ȳwan*]

ax(e) *n.* axe 4.203, 321, 18.416. *pl.* **axes** 11.140. [OE *æx*]

axen *v.* ask, request 16.249; *pr. 2 sg.* **axest** 1.453; (with suffixed pron.) **axestu** 1.457. *imper. sg.* (with *after*, for) **axe** 5.52. *pa. t. sg.* **axede** 7.263, 10.10. [OE *axian*, var. of *ascian*] See **aske**.

ba *pron.* both 18.197, 320, 19. 187; *attrib.* 18.581, 639, 19.394; ~ **twa** 18.592. *adv.* ~ .. *ant* 18.311, 19.25, 132. [OE *bā*, neut. and fem.] See **beye**.

bac *n.* back 4.81, 271. *pl.* **backes** 4.337. [OE *bæc*]

bacduntes *n. pl.* blows on the back 18.371. [prec.+**dint**]

bad(d), bæd ; bærnende ; bæron. See **bidde(n); berninde; ber.**

bayly *n.* bailiff, estate steward 8N.32. *pl.* **bailifs** 11.103. [OF *baillif*, later *bailli*]

bayllye *n.* charge, authority 2.81. [OF *baillie*]

bakbiteres *n. pl.* backbiters 17. 121. [bac+OE *bītere*]

bald ; baldeliche. See **bold(e); boldeliche.**

bale *n.* pain, misery 1.433, 8K.59; torment, punishment 14.44, 19. 107, 146. [OE *b(e)alu*]

balful *adj.* pernicious, grievous 8K.65. [OE *bealoful*]

baloygne *n.* whalebone 8E.53. [OF]

ban. See **bon.**

baner *n.* banner, standard 8K.48. *pl.* **baners** 11.152. [OF *banere*]

bar(r). See **ber.**

barbican *n.* fortification, esp. a double tower over a gate 3.16. [OF *barbacane*]

bare *adj.* bare, stripped (*o*, of) 14.185; poor, beggarly 8K.79; plain, unsupported 1.355 (note); very, in *bi mine ~ life* or die in the attempt 10.103. as *n.* in *þe ~* the open 1.56, 106. [OE *bær*]

bare. See **ber.**

bareȝ *n.* barrow (castrated boar) 1.286. [OE *bearh*]

baret *n.* conflict, contention 9.27. [OF *barat*]

barfot *adj.* barefoot 4.130. [OE *bærfōt*]

bark *n.* bark 14.185. [ON; cf. OI *bǫrk-r* from **barku-*]

barlic *n.* barley 12.86,102. [OE *bærlic*]

barn *n.* child 14.206, 219. [OE *béarn*]

barne *v. intr.* burn 2.105. *pa. t. sg.* **bearnde** was burning 18.43. *tr., pr. pl.* **bearneð** 18.62. [OE *bærnan*, tr.] Cf. **berninde, brennen, forberne(n).**

baronie *n.* barons, nobility 11 23. [OF]

baroun *n.* baron, nobleman 2. 298. *pl.* **barouns** 2.323; **barons** 11.1, 4. [OF *barun*, *baron* (nom. *ber*)]

barre *n.* bar (of door) 4.221, 238. [OF]

bas *n.* base 9.69. [OF *base*]

bat. See **bote.**

batest *pr. 2 sg.* redress 2.45. [MDu *baten*]

baþ-, baðe, bath-. See **boþ(e), boþe.**

baþieres *n. pl.* bath-tubs 17.100 (note). [from OE *baþian*]

baudekyns *n. pl.* rich stuffs of silk and gold thread 2.220. [OF *baudequin*]

baum *n.* balsam, a fragrant resin 8E.54; balm, aromatic ointment 9.85. [OF *baume*]

baundon *n.* control, authority: *to my ~, me to ~* at my disposal 2.269, 272. [AN *baundun*]

be(n) *v.* 2.6, 3.9, 4.63, 98, 5.58, 8M.12, 9.44, 16.30; **bene** 2.208; **beo(n)** 1.571, 7.17, 8E.47, 51, 18.8, 19.10; **bo(n)** 1.146, 198; **bi** 17.14, 78; **bie(n)** 17.18, 157. be 1.146, 2.20, 3.9, 4.63, 5.58; stay, live 1.571, 4.171; see **lete(n);** pr. with fut. sense 8F. 18, 12.98, 14.82, 16.72. *auxil.* (forming pass.) 1.198, 2.6, 3.26, 4.98, 8F.34, 18.8, 19.10; (forming perf. of intr. vbs.) have 5. 153, 6.296, 14.235. *pr. 2 sg.* **bes** 6.444. *3 sg.* **beþ, beð** 8F.18, 16.72; **biþ, bið** 1.416, 10.66 (note), 93, 19.26; **boþ** 1.508; **bes** 14.82. *pl.* **be(n)** 2.43, 3.61, 4.214, 12.98; **beþ** 3.1, 5.49, 8H.8, 9.13; **beoþ, beoð, beoth** 8H.16, 1.543, 10.101, 18.2, 7. 218; **boþ** 1.75, 88; **bueþ** 8H.37; **bie** (before *ye*) 17.185; **bieþ, bieth, bied** 17.203, 64, 126. *subj. sg.* **be** 2.20, 197, 3.12, 4.75, 5.56, 6.25, 296; **beo** 7.90, 8v.21,

10.79, 114, 18.86, 19.29; **bo**
1.107, 127, 375; **bon** 10.320;
bue 8N.8. *pl.* be(n) 12.97, 14.
44, 15.82, 17.247; beo(n) 18.
29, 19.45, 161: *ne ~ we neauer
swucche* even if we are by no
means so 19.218; **bo(n)** 1.137,
486. *imper. sg.* be 2.256, 5.36,
6.54, 8D.9; beo 18.390; **bo** 1.
197, 354. *pl.* be 8H.34, 13.79;
be(e)þ 2.177, 8H.41; beoþ,
beoð 1.693, 18.433. *pp.* ben
2.270, 3.193, 5.185, 14.73, 15.30,
16.260; ibe(n) 5.87, 100, 17.
219; ibeo(n) 7.215, 18.515, 19.
373; ibye 17.197. [OE *bēon*,
biþ, &c.] See **am, ar(e), art,
es, is, nas, nis, senden, was.**
be-. See also **bi-.**
be; bead. See **bi; bede.**
bealies *n. pl.* bellows 18.335.
[OA *bælg*]
bealté *n.* beauty 8K.48. [OF]
beard *n.* beard 18.384. [OE
béard]
**bearnde, -eð; bearninde;
beastes; beateð.** See **barne;
berninde; best; bete** *v.*[1]
beað *n.* bath 18.572. *pl.* beaðes
18.577. [OM *beð*, pl. *beaðu*]
beawbelez *n. pl.* jewels 18.478.
[OF *beaubelet*]
bebirieden *pa. t. pl.* buried 16.
127 (note); **bebyried** 16.230.
[OE *bebyrgan*]
beboden *pp.* ordered 16.77.
[OE *beboden* from *-bēodan*; see
bede]
bec *n.* beak 12.6, 25. [OF]
becom(en); bed. See **bicome;
bede.**
bed(de) *n.* bed 2.280, 3.273, 6.
102, 7.41, 9.38; *in ~* 5.214, 216.
[OE *bedd*]
bede *v.* 3.125, 6.40; **beode(n)**
10.139, 18.47, 673. (1) offer 2.
300, 3.125, 6.129, 349, 12.106,
18.673. (2) announce 6.40.
(3) order, command 8F.7, K.71,
11.148, 18.47. (4) summon 10.

139. (5) ask (*of*, for) 6.363. *pr. 1
sg.* bede 6.129. *3 sg.* bedeþ
6.374; bet 12.106. *subj. sg.* bede
6.363. *imper. sg.* bede 2.300.
pa. t. sg. bed 6.367, 8F.7, H.17,
K.71, 11.148; **beed** 6.349; **bead**
18.487. [OE *bēodan, bēad*] See
bidde(n).
bede(n). See **bidde(n).**
bedtime *n.* bedtime 1.240.
**beed; befel; before(n), -forn ;
begæt; began, -ǵininge;
beh; behald; behet; behofeð ;
behote; bey; beiæt, -iet(en).**
See **bede; bifel; bifor(e);
bifore; biȝeten; biginne,
-inge; buȝe; biholde; bi-
hete; bihoueð; bihete; buȝe;
biȝeten.**
beye *adj.* both 11.116; **beine** 10.
27; **beien** also 16.306. [OE
bēgen masc.] See **ba.**
beyte *v.* bait, set dogs to worry
4.267. [ON *beita*]
bekneð *pr. 3 sg.* shows, points to
12.106. [OE *bē(a)cnian*]
belæf *pa. t. sg.* remained 16.69;
beleaf 16.70. [OE *belāf* from
-līfan; vowel after *belǣfan*,
wk.]
belamp; belde. See **bilimpes ;
bold(e).**
beldenn *v.* encourage 13.76.
[OA *béldan*]
beleaf. See **belæf.**
beleaue *n.* belief, faith 17.49;
beleauee 17.210; **beliaue** 17.
45, 114; **belaue** 17.74; **bileaue**
18.3, 109, 19.178, *gen.* 18.133.
[Cf. OE *ge-lēafa*]
beleue, bi- *v.* believe (with *in*)
17.232, 82. *pr. subj. 1 pl.* let (us)
believe 17.52. *pa. t. pl.* beleuede
(with *on*, in) 17.112. *pp.* bileued
(with *ane*) 17.223. [LOE *belē-
fan*; see **leue(n)** *v.*[3]]
belle *n.* bell 11.156; *Godes
(h)ou(e)ne ~* (rung during mass)
6.390, 421. *pl.* 16.84. [OE
belle, pl. *bellan*]

belongeth *pr. 3 sg.* (with *to*) concerns 17.93. [OE *be-+longen* from long adj.[1]]

bemen *n. pl.* trumpets 10.205. [OA *bēme*]

bemes; benam. See beom; bineomen.

bench(e) *n.* bench, seat 2.129, 9.11. [OE *benc*]

bende *n.* (? *pl.*) bonds, captivity 8K.65. [OE *bénd*, pl. *bénda*]

bende *pa. t. sg.* bent, drew 11.34. *pp. adj.* bend(e) curved, arched 8E.25, G.26; ybend E.18. [OE *béndan*]

bene *n.*[1] bean; *of his deȝ he ne ȝaf nowt a ~* he thought his life not worth a straw 3.200. *pl.* benes 4.37. [OE *bēan*]

benedicite *interj.* bless (me) 15. 63; *~ be herinne* God bless us! 6.193. [L imper. pl.]

beneme. See bineomen.

benen *n.*[2] *pl.* prayers 18.356; *muchel i ~* assiduous in praying 18.71. [OE *bēn*]

beo(n). See be(n).

beode *n.* prayer 18.355. *pl.* beoden 18.72. [OM *ge-bed*, pl. *-beodu*]

beode(n). See bede.

beom *n.* beam 16.176. *pl.* bemes 2.213. [OE *bēam*]

beon *n. pl.* bees 16.43. [OE *bēo*, pl. *bēon*]

beonnen *v.* summon 10.205. [OE *bannan*, vowel infl. by pa. t. *bēonn*]

beoreð; beornes. See ber; bern.

beot *n.* vow, threat 10.103. [OE *bēot*]

beoueden. See biuien.

bepaht *pp.* deceived 16.108. [OE *bepǽht* from *-pǽcan*]

ber, bere(n) *v.* 3.89, 4.73, 30, 10.260, 12.86, 14.248; bæron 16.175, 178. (1) carry, wear, take 1.659, 3.10, 4.30, 7.224, 8N.2, 9.163, 17.104; *armes,*

wepnen ~ take up arms, fight 11.70, 73, 10.260; *~ grete ilete* put on a bold front 1.281; carry off, win (a prize) 8D.35, T.32; *~ vpon* lay to (one's) charge 3.89. *infl. infin.* to berene (*witnesse*) give (evidence) 16.37. (2) bear (the weight of) 4.318. (3) bear (fruit, &c.) 14.38, 248, 16.200. (4) give birth to 8T.30, 13.49, and most cases of pp. *pr. 1 sg.* bere 1.659. *2 sg.* berst 8T.32. *3 sg.* bereþ, -ð 3.10, 8D.35, 12.89, 18.262, 19.79; berþ 1.281; beres 14.38. *pl.* beren 12.124; beriþ 9.163; beoreð 18.212. *imper. sg.* bere 3.117. *pl.* bereth 17.104. *pa. t. 2 sg.* bere 8T.30. *3 sg.* bar 4.83, 10.17, 16.200; barr 13.49; ber 11.73. *pl.* bere 3.177, 7.224, 264, 11.70. *subj. sg.* bare 16. 130. *pp.* carried: ibore 7.221, 279; born: bore 5.116, 8H.40, 17.78; boren(n) 4.305, 8N.18, 13.22; ibore, y- 1.462, 8v.23, 17.4, 19.155, 8T.21, v.7; iboren, y- 10.177, 323, 8v.18, N.12. [OE *beran*, M *beoran*; *bær*, *bǽron*; *boren*]

berdene. See birdene.

bere *n.*[1] bear 4.265. [OE *bera*]

bere *n.*[2] outcry, clamour 1.557, 3.204, 19.25. [OE *ge-bǽru*; see ibere]

bereafed. See bireue.

berigge *n.* mother 8v.20. [ber + OE fem. suff. *-icge*]

beril *n.* beryl 9.92. [OF]

beringe *n.* birth 17.6, 35. [from ber]

bermen *n. pl.* porters 4.136, 142. [OE *bǽrmann*]

bern *n.* warrior, hero 14.7. *pl.* beornes 10.178. [OE *béorn*]

berne *n.* barn 1.387. [OE *ber(er)n*]

berninde *pr. p. adj.* burning 7. 45; bærnende 16.64; bearninde 18.207, (fig.) 655. [OE *béornende, bǽrnende*] See **for-berne(n), barne, brennen.**

bersteð *pr. 3 sg. intr.* bursts, breaks 18.196. *pa. t. pl.* **borsten** 7.275. *subj. sg.* **burste** 6.360. [OE *berstan, burston*]

besæt *pa. t. sg.* besieged 16.138, 269. [OE *besǽt* from *-sittan*; see **site**]

besætte; besech, -sekeþ, -sohte. See **bisetten; biseche.**

best *n.* animal 7.142. *pl.* **beastes** 18.169, 456. [OF *beste*]

best(e); besuyken, -swicen. See **beter(e), betere; biswike(n).**

bet *adv. comp.* better 1.128, 138, 10.282, 11.158; rather 1.21, 39. [OE *bet*] See **beter(e).**

bet; betæcen, -teht. See **bede; bitæche.**

bete *v.*[1] beat, strike 3.18, 5.290; strike blows 4.326. *pr. 3 sg.* **beateð** 19.55; **betiþ** 9.137. *pa. t. pl.* **beten** 2.114, 4.303. *pp.* **bet(e)** 4.343, (*adj.*) 8E.61. [OE *béaten, béoton, béaten*]

bete *v.*[2] make amends, atone 1.525; atone for 8w.56; satisfy, assuage 5.276. *pr. 3 sg.* **beteð** restores 12.55. *subj. sg.* **bete** remedy, amend 16.72. *pp.* **ibet** atoned for 19.84. [OE *bétan*]

betere, better(e) *adj. comp.* better 1.458, 2.80, 4.111, 8F.15, K.35, L.12, 11.66, 16.221; better off 6.389, 15.60; **bether** 15.16; **bettur** 14.68; **betre** 8F.19, 16.95. *sup.* **best** best 2.72, 8D. 36, E.51, T.10, 18.362; (*þe*) **beste** 3.79, 8F.41, H.13, 17.109; **bezste** 10.115; ~ *of* **bon** and **blod** the most beautiful 8c.5; *of þe* ~ in the finest way, to perfection 8K.32; *mid þan* ~ in the most fitting way 10.115. [OE *betera, bet(t)ra; bet(e)st, betsta*] See **god(e).**

beter(e), better *adv. comp.* bet-ter 6.274, 8L.28, 17.157, 18.603, 3.126; **bettir** 9.124. *sup.* **best** best, most 1.328, 7.38, 8H.11, 14.26, 18.140, 19.72; **beast** 19. 374. [prec., and OE *betst*] See **wel.**

betockneþ, -tokned; betuene. See **bitacnenn; bitwen(e).**

betwix, -twyx, -tuyx *prep.* between 16.40, 141, 248. [OE *betwix*]

beþohte; bezste. See **biþenche(n); betere.**

bi, by *prep.* 1.306, 2.7, 3.17, 4.61, 5.57; **be** 3.202, 14.33, 16.162, 17.32; **bie** 17.102. (of place) near, beside 1.214, 4.148, 5.117, 7.74, 19.182, 3.279; with, see **ligge(n)**; by way of, over, through (the land of) 2.324, 8E.1, Q.1, 17.32; through (the air) 9.124, 18.63; along 6.1, 10.164; on, in 6.395; ~ *þe weiȝe* on the way 7.75; (forming adv. or prep. of direction) ~ **est, norþ, souþ, west,** see the nouns. (of time) at 17. 212; in 10.306, 17.179, 207; in the course of, in ~ *dai, niȝt*, &c. 3.11, 10.238, 16.162, 18.311, 19. 32. (of means) by, through 2.7, 5.114, 10.175, 14.33, 17.162, (following *infin.*) 16.244; be-cause of 1.469; (with *live*) on 8H.45, 12.81, 19.311; (of *leave*) by, with 3.17, 16.79; (defining a part of the body held, &c.) 1.306, 10.39, 16.165; (with numeral) in groups of 3.202; ~ *me* by my example 6.307. (of agent) by 17.19, 227. (in oaths, &c.) 1.659, 2.143, 4.61, 5.57, 15.2. (of reference) of, about, concerning 1.46, 5.210, 6.143, 14.47, 18.83, 19.338; with re-spect to 1.92; according to 2. 112, 5.50, 7.8, 231, 17.42; ~ *(mi, har) miȝt(te)* as well as (I, they) can 6.253, 8F.22, 9.99. ~ *þet* by the fact that, inasmuch

as 17.40; ~ *swa þet* see **swa**. [OE *be, bī*]
bi. See **be(n)**.
bibah *pa. t. sg.* pursued 10.236. [OE·*bebēah* from *bebūgan* surround]
bicam. See **bicome**.
bic(c)he *n.* bitch 6.354, 372. [OE *bicce*]
bicharde *pa. t. sg.* deceived, tricked 5.293. [OA *becerran*, *-*cærran*; cf. **cherde**]
bichermet *pr. pl.* scream at 1.215. [OA *be-*+*cerman* = WS *cirman*]
bicloped *pp.* made a charge 1.358. [OA *becleopian*]
bicluppet *pp.* embraced, contained 18.9. [OE *beclyppan*]
bicome *v.* 3.50, 136; **becomen** 8x.6. (1) come 1.749; (with *where*) go 7.158, 10.33, 243. (2) become 3.50, 6.376, 8x.6, 14.18; ~ *to* turn into 7.53; ~ *soth* come true 7.71. (3) suit, be fitting (impers., subject *hit*) 1.207. *pr. 3 sg.* **bicumeþ**, -**ð** 1.207, 12.39. *subj. sg.* **bicom** 6.376. *pa. t. 1, 3 sg.* **bicam** 7.53, 95, **bicom**, **be-** 14.188, 18. *2 sg.* **bicome** 7.69. *pl.* **bicome** 1.749. *pp.* **bicome** 3.144; **bicumen** 10.33. [OE *becuman*; see **com**]
bidde(n) *v.* 1.518, 3.98, 109, 5.179, 12.64, 17.82. (1) ask (for), request, beg 1.323, 358, 518, 2.51, 3.98, 109, 4.176, 8D.9, G.8, 11.113, 19.425; invite 1.319, 5.255, 10.136; implore 8R.5. (2) pray 1.487, 3.179, 5.135, 7.250, 8W.54, 17.82; say (a prayer) 6.209, 12.64, 19.421. (3) order, command 2.121, 3.181, 8F.36, 9.130, 13.13, 275, 14.155, 202. (4) wish 8L.9 (note), 12.86. *pr. 1 sg.* **bidde, bydde** 1.487, 2.51, 6.209, 8L.9, W.54. *3 sg.* **biddiþ** 9.130; **biddeþþ** 13.275; **bid** 1.319; **bit** 1.323, 12.86, 19.276. *subj. sg.* **bidde**

18.354. *pl.* **bidden** 19.427. *imper. pl.* **biddeð** 19.422. *pa. t. 1, 3 sg.* **bad** 8D.9, 14.202; **badd** 13.13, 14.155; **bæd** 10.136. *2 sg.* **bede** 1.358. *pl.* **bede(n)** 7.250, 11.113, 137; **bad** 3.179. *subj. sg.* **bede** 1.636; **bad** 8G.8. *pp.* **bede** 2.121, 8F.36 (note); **ibede** 3.181, 5.135, 255; **ybeden** 8R.5. [OE *biddan*; *bæd, bǣdon*; *beden*; senses confused already in OE with *bēodan*, see **bede**]
biddinge *n.* prayer 17.57. [from **bidde(n)**]
byde, biden *v.* expect, experience, live to see 8L.10, 6.116. *pr. 1 sg.* (fut. sense) **bide** will endure 18.238. *3 sg.* **byd** suffers 8N.5. *subj. sg.* **bide** (in asseverations) may experience, enjoy 6.26, 133, 433. *pa. t. pl.* **biden** enjoyed 16.88. [OE *bīdan*, *bidon*]
bidelde *pp.* (*pl.*) deprived (with gen. of object withheld) 10.124. [OE *bedǣled*]
bie; bien. See **be(n), bi, buggen; be(n)**.
bifel *pa. t. sg.* befell, happened 4.92; **befel** 6.16. *pp.* **bifalle** 3.270. [OA *befēoll, -fallen*; see **falle(n)**]
bifore *adv.* 7.222, 8H.41; **bifor(e)n** 10.166, 12.26; **beforn** 14.277; **biuore(n)** 18.469, 19. 67, 413. (of time) before, earlier 7.222, 14.277; beforehand, first 8H.41, 19.67. (of place) in front 10.166, 12.26, 116, 19.105, 413; ahead 18.469. [OE *beforan*]
bifor(e) *prep.* 4.239, 7.41, 17.27; **biforenn** 13.198; **beforen** 16. 226; **biuore(n)** 10.17, 18.41, 19.71. (of time) before 7.267, 16.226. (of place) in front of 7.41, 10.17, 18.41, 485; ahead of 19.71; in the presence of 10.110; ~ *þe heued* in the face 4.239. [OE *beforan*]

big *adj.* strong, sturdy 4.201. [obscure]

bigan, **-ʒann**; **bigæton,** **-ʒeton.** See **biginne**; **biʒeten.**

bigylede *pp.* deceived 7.243. [OE *be-*+OF *guiler*]

biginne *v.* begin, set about, undertake, do (with pron. obj.) 10. 70. *pr. 3 sg.* **biginneþ, -ð** (with *to+*infin.) 5.80, 18.235; **bigineð** *intr.* 19.1. *pl.* **biginnen** (*forto*) 4.206. *pa. t. sg.* **bigan** (*to*) 3.196, 4.7, 93, 7.64; **biʒann** 13.7; **bigon** 5.16, 6.7, 10.20; (with plain infin.) 3.218, 279; (with n. obj.) 7.105, 1.13; **began** *intr.* 14.58; began to complain, 'took on' 5.107, 6.302; as mere auxil. forming with infin. equivalent of pa. t., as **gan**: (with *to*) 4.1, 14.218, 6.297, 417; (without *to*) 7.1, 54, 83. *pl.* **bigan** 3.277; **bigounne** (*auxil.*) 7.243; **bigonne** 11.1, 159; **bigunnen** 10.162. *subj. sg.* **bigunne** 19.336. *pp.* **bigunne** 6.384, 19.128. [OE *beginnan*; see **ginneþ**]

biginninge *n.* beginning 11.71; **begininge** 17.209. [from prec.]

bigo *pr. subj. sg.* betide, come upon 5.53. [OE *begān*]

bigon(ne). See **biginne.**

bigot(t)en *pp.* infused 19.291, soaked 356. [OE *begoten* from *-gēotan*]

bigounne. See **biginne.**

bigredet, -þ *pr. pl.* cry out at, scold 1.67, 215. *subj. pl.* **bigrede** 1.220. [OE *be-+grede(n)*]

bigripen *v.* seize, grasp 12.158. [OE *begrīpan*]

bigrowe *pp.* overgrown 1.27, 397. [OE *be-+grōwen* from *grōwan*]

bigunne(n). See **biginne.**

biʒende *prep.* beyond 6.105; **biʒeonde** 10.142. [OE *begéondan, geóndan*]

biʒete *n.* gain, profit 5.248, 18. 637. [from next]

biʒeten *v.* get, find 10.139; **bigæton, -ʒeton** acquire, obtain 16.299, 97. *pr. 3 sg.* **biʒet** 18.355. *subj. sg.* **biʒete** attain 1.472. *pa. t. sg.* **beiæt, -ʒæt** 16.24, 213; ~ *in* recovered 16. 216; **beiet** 16.27. *pp.* **beieten** 16.26. [OA *begetan, -ʒæt, -ʒeten*] Cf. **ʒete(n).**

bihalde(n), -halt. See **biholde.**

bihalue *v.* surround 4.261. [from OE *be-+half*]

bihaten. See **bihete.**

bihedde *pa. t. sg.* observed 10. 204. [OE *be-+hēdan*]

bihehte; biheld. See **bihete; biholde.**

bihemmen *v.* hem round, add trimmings 1.418. [from OE *be-+hem* border]

biheold, -t. See **biholde.**

biheste *n.* promise 8L.24. [OE *behǣs*; see **heste**]

bihete *pr. 1 sg.* promise 6.428. *pa. t. sg.* **bihet, be-** 7.36, 16.96; **bihehte** 10.201. *pp.* **bihote, be-** 1.703, 17.19; **bihaten** 18. 454; **byhyht** 8F.24. [OE *behātan*; see **hote(n)**]

biheue *n.* advantage 18.427, 460. [OE *behōf* re-formed on *behēfe* adj.]

byhyht. See **bihete.**

bihinde(n) *adv.* behind 1.412, 19.105. [OE *behindan*]

bihinde *prep.* behind 11.20. [prec.]

biholde *v.* look (at), examine, observe 1.71, 3.192, 214; **bihalde(n)** 1.593, 18.32, 49, 19.137, 261; **behald** 14.196; **biheld** 3.94. *pr. 1 sg.* **biholde, by-** look (with *upon*) 8E.13, 49. *2 sg.* **bihaltest** 1.590. *3 sg.* **bihalt** 3.239, 253, 18.124. *subj. sg.* **bihalde** 18.279, 537 (with *on*), 19.45. *imper. sg.* **bihold** 3.85;

bihald 18.201. *pa. t. sg.* biheld 5.15; biheold 7.48, 84 (with *after*); biheolt, be- 19.295, 299; bihold 1.30. *pp.* bihalden 19.65. [OA *behaldan*, WS *-héaldan*; see holde(n)]

bihote. See bihete.

bihoueð *pr. 3 sg.* is fitting (with impers. subject *hit*) 19.28; behofeð is necessary 16.103. *pa. t. sg.* bihofde 18.572; behofed 16.89; behoued 16.206. [OE *behófian*]

bike *n.* wild bees' nest 14.76. [obscure]

biker *n.* skirmishing 11.88. [cf. MDu *bicken* thrust]

bikering *n.* skirmishing 11.126. [from vb. assoc. with prec.]

biknewe *pa.t.pl.* recognized 17.7. [OE *becnéowon* from *-cnáwan*; see knowe]

biladde; bilæf-. See biledet; bileue.

bilai *pa. t. sg.* besieged 10.225. *pp.* byleyn deflowered 8H.44. [OE *belæg*, *-legen* from *-licgan*; see ligge(n)]

bilauen. See bileue.

bile *n.* bill 1.79, 205, 12.34. [OE *bile*]

bileaue. See beleaue; bileue.

biledet *pr. pl.* in *narewe ~* harass 1.68. *pa. t. sg.* biladde (with *harde*) treated 7.128. [OE *belǽdan*; see led(e)]

bilegge *v.* embroider, embellish (deceitfully) 1.418, interpret 536. *pr. 2 sg.* bileist colour 1.499. [OE *belecgan*, *-legst*]

byleyn. See bilai.

bileue *v.*[1] *tr.* leave, abandon 7.148; bileofuen leave behind 10.97. *intr.* remain, stay 2.84, 7.228, keep silent 1.42; bileaue 1.646. *pr. 1 sg.* bilæfuen leave 10.99. *subj. sg.* bileue remain 5.198. *pl.* bilauen 10.64. *imper. sg.* bilef leave off 6.217. *pa. t. sg.*

bilæfde left 10.120. *pp.* bileued ceased, given up 7.131; byleved left, remaining 8w.26. [OE *belǽfan*]. See leue(n) *v.*[1]

bileue *v.*[2] See beleue.

biliked *pp.* made pleasing 1.502. [OE *be-+lícian*; see like(n)]

bilimpes *pr. 3 sg.* (impers. with dat. of person) it happens 12.122. *pa. t. sg.* belamp happened 16.224. [OE *belimpan*; cf. ilomp]

biliue *adv.* quickly 10.178; bliue 5.109. [OE **be lífe*]

billeð *pr. 3 sg.* strikes 12.31. [from OE *bil*, cutting weapon]

biloke *pp.* locked up 19.230. [OE *belocen* from *-lúcan*; see lukeð]

biloken *pr. pl. refl.* look about 12.171. [OE *be-+lócian*; see lok]

biluueð *pr. 3 sg.* it pleases (impers.) 19.242, (with subject *hit*) 243. *pa. t. pl.* biluueden favoured 10.96. [OE *be-+lufian*; see loue *v.*]

bimelde *pr. subj. sg.* inform against 6.38. [OE *beméldian*]

bimene *v.* lament, grieve for 7.134. [OE *bemǽnan*]

bimong, bymong *prep.* among 18.222; (postponed) 8E.53. [OE *be-+-móng* as in among]

bynde, binden *v.* bind, tie, fetter 8H.9, 19.81. *pr. pl.* bindeð, byndeþ 18.61, 8L.5; bind make helpless 5.254 (note). *pp.* bondon wrapped 14.207; ibonden in *harc'e ~* hard pressed, in difficul ies 6.204; ybounde 8H.36, ii bondage M.18; ibunden 18.65, 214. OE *bindan*, *búnden*]

bineomen *v.* take away (from), deprive of (with dat. of person deprived) 18.166, 526. *pr. 1 sg.* beneme 17.165. *pr. subj. sg.* bineome 19.12. *pa. t. sg.* benam 16.251. *pl.* binomen 10.43. *pp.* binome(n), bynomen 2.8, 5.173; taken away,

removed 6.295; **binume** 10.81.
[OE *beniman*, see **nim**; also
benæman wk.]
bineoðe *prep.* under 1.544 (see
sunne). [OE *beneoðan*]
bineþe *adv.* below, underneath
5.253; 7.51; **bineoðen** 18.512.
[OE *beneoðan*]
binome(n), by-, binume. See
bineomen.
biræd *pa. t. sg.* surrounded 10.
195. [cf. OE *berād* from *-rīdan*;
see **ride(n)**]
birde *n.* family, tribe 13.36, 270,
people 92. [OE *ge-bȳrd(u)*]
birdene *n.* burden, load 12.134;
berdene 17.198; **birþene,**
byrthen 4.75, 166, 16.130;
burþen 8N.2, 23. [OE *bȳrþen*]
birede *pp.* informed; *ne were þai*
nowt arizt ~ they did not correctly understand 3.182. [OE
be-+red(e)]
bireue *v.* take away (from), deprive of (with dat. of person) 7.
227. *pp.* **bireued** 6.336, 7.188;
bereafed 7T.introd. [OE *berēa-*
fian; for constr. cf. **bineomen**]
byrieden. See **burede.**
birrþ *pr. 3 sg.* (impers. with dat.
of person) it behoves, befits:
uss ~ we ought 13.222; **burþ**
(*him*) 6.82. [OE *(ge)byrian*]
birth *n.* birth 14.259. [either OE
ge-bird infl. by nouns in *-þu,* or
Scand, as OSw *byrþ*]
byrthen, birþene. See **bir-**
dene.
bis, bys *n.* fine linen: *(an)vnder*
~ tag of little meaning 8E.58,
(intensifying sup.) wearing fine
clothes, among ladies 8D.38
(note; cf. **gore**). [OF *bysse*]
bischricheþ *pr. pl.* screech at
1.67. [*be-+*ME *schrichen*, imit.]
biscop *n.* bishop 16.18, 109;
bissop 11.51. *gen.* **biscopes**
16.194. *pl.* **bischopes** 7.206,
221; **biscopes** 16.4, 10; *dat.*
bischopen 1.719. [OE *biscop*]

biscoprice *n.* bishopric 16.27.
[OE]
biseche *pr. 1 sg.* beg, entreat 18.
497. *3 sg.* **bisecheð** 19.272; ask
for 19.278; **besekeþ** (with dat.
of person asked) 17.75. *pl.*
bischeð, -th 19.311, 17.161.
imper. sg. **besech** 17.137; **bisek**
8T.14. *pl.* **bischeþ** 8K.73. *pa.*
t. sg. **besohte** appealed to 16.31.
[OE *besēcan*; see **seche(n)**]
biseh. See **biseon.**
bisemezh(= *-þ*) *pr. 3 sg.* befits,
suits 3.129. *pp.* **bisemed** made
agreeable 1.502. [OE *be-+*ME
semen, see **semest**]
bisenchen *v.* plunge 18.639.
[OE *besencan*]
biseon *v.* look, gaze 19.138, (with
to, towards, upon) 408. *pr.*
3 sg. refl. **bisið** (*him*) is on his
guard 19.374. *imper. pl.* **biseoð**
18.670. *pa. t. sg.* **biseh** 19.279.
[OE *besēon,* A *pr.* 3 *sg. -sið*; see
se]
bisetten *v.* (1) apply, employ
19.72. *pp.* **biset** 6.274; **bysett**
bestowed 2.43. (2) surround,
besiege: *pr. pl.* **bysetten** 2.103.
pa. t. sg. **besætte** 16.252. *pp.*
biset 18.474, 505. [OE *besettan*;
see **set**] Cf. **besæt.**
biside *adv.* besides 7.44; near by
7.81, 210. [OE *be sīdan* at the
side]
biside *prep.* beside 7.259. [prec.]
bisie *adj.* assiduous 18.186, 433.
[OE *bisig*]
bisiliche *adv.* diligently 18.675.
[prec.+*-liche*]
bisischipe *n.* exertion 18.404.
[OE *bisig+-schipe*]
bisið. See **biseon.**
bismere *n.* scorn, mockery, in
phr. *to* ~ (with dat. of person)
in mockery of, 'to scorn' (see **to**)
18.117. [OE *bismer*] See **abise-**
mar.
bisne *n.* example, parable 19.4.
[OE *bisen*]

bisocnen *n. pl.* petitions 19.312. [cf. OE *sōcn* question, and **biseche**]

bispekez (= -*þ*) *pr. 3 sg.* is planning 7.68. *pa. t. pl.* **bispeke(n)** plotted 7.38, 72; spoke against, opposed 11.4. *pp.* **bispeke** agreed 1.696. [OE *besprecan*; see **speke(n)**]

bissop. See **biscop.**

bistad *pp.* placed, set 8G.9. [OE *be-*+ON *stadd-r* pp. of *steðja* place]

bistal *pa. t. sg.* went stealthily 10.216. [OE *bestæl* from -*stelan*]

bisteken *pp.* shut, locked 19.46. [OE *be-*+*stecan*]

bistriden *v.* bestride 10.15. [OE *bestrīdan*]

biswike(n) *v.* deceive, betray 1.114, 10.68, 12.157; **beswicen besuyken** 16.91, 280. *pa. t. sg.* **biswac** 10.213. *pp.* **biswike, byswyken** 2.258, 8H.23. [OE *beswīcan, -swāc, -swicen*] Cf. **swikeþ, swyke.**

bit *pr. 3 sg.* bites 12.89, 104. [OE *bītt* from *bītan*]

bit; bitache. See **bidde(n); bitæche.**

bitacnenn *v.* signify, symbolize 13.194. *pr. 3 sg.* **bitacneþþ** means 13.260; **bitacneð** symbolizes 18.213; **bitakens, by-** 14.41, 246, 40; **be-, bitockneþ, -d** 17.204, 251, 117; **betokned** 17.126, 249; *pl.* **bitacnið** 18.668; **beto(c)kneþ** 17.206, 207. *pp.* **bitacnet** 18.177. [OE *be-*+*tācnian*] Cf. **tacneþþ.**

bitacnunge *n.* symbol; *for* ~ *to* signify 18.514. [from prec.]

bitæche *v.* commit, entrust 10.102; **betæcen** hand over 16.78, 100. *pr. 1 sg.* **biteche** 2.81, **bytech** (-*y* joined in MS.) 15.32; **bitache** 10.303. *pa. t. 2 sg.* **bitahtest** 10.59. *pp.* **bitaht** 19.164; **beteht** 16.236. [OE *betæcan, -tǎhte, -tǽhte*]

bitelle *v.* speak for, justify 1.199. [OE *betellan*]

bitellunge *n.* excuse (for not offering) 18.526. [from prec.]

biteon *v.* bestow 18.603. *pp.* **bito3e** applied 1.448. [OE *betēon*; see **te**]

biter(e) *adj.* bitter 17.44, 65. [OE *bit(t)er*]

bit(t)ernesse *n.* bitterness 17.59, 19.147. [OE *bit(t)ernes(se)*]

bitide, -tyde *v.* happen 3.164; happen to, befall 7.66, 8L.11; come 6.124. *pr. subj. sg.* in *so hit* ~ *may it so happen* 1.52. [OE *be-*+*tiden*]

bitockned, -þ; bito3e. See **bitacnenn; biteon.**

bitraid, -traied *pp.* betrayed 3.157, 156. [OE *be-*+OF *trair*]

bituhen *prep.* between, among 18.495; **bituhhe(n)** 19.150, 190. [OE *betuh*+-*en* after **bitweonen**, &c.]

biturn *imper. sg. refl.* turn 18.560. *pp.* **biturnd** in ~ *upon* directed towards 18.476. [OE *betyrnan*; see **turn(e)**]

bituxen. See **bitwixen.**

bytuene *adv.* between 8E.26; **bitweonen** 18.168. [as **bitwen(e)**]

bytuixand *conj.* until, before 14.65. [see **bitwixen**]

bitwen(e) *prep.* between, among 3.167, 4.245, 7.100; **bituene** 4.16, 8G.54, M.17, 11.87; **bitwenenn** 13.184; **betuene** 17.8; **bitweone(n)** 18.135, 138; (postponed) 12.127, 13.120, 18.151; *swa muchel is* ~ there is so much difference between 18.566. [OE *betwēonan*]

bitwixen *prep.* between, among; ~ *us* to one another 12.138; **bituxen** 1.705. [cf. OE *betweoxn* and **betwix**]

biþ, bið. See **be(n).**

biþenche(n) *v.* 1.329, 5.83, 7.21, 8v.14; **biðenken** 12.42. devise, contrive 7.21, 34; consider 16. 30; think about 12.42, (with gen. obj.) 8v.14. *refl.* deliberate, reflect (with refl. acc.) 1.155, 329, (with refl. obl.) 1.450, 5.83, (fold. by *of*) think of, devise 7. 33. *pass.* take thought 5.81. *pa. t. sg.* biþoȝte, beþohte 1.155, 10.197, 16.30; biþouȝte 7.33; biþoute 6.13. *pp.* biþout 5.81. [OE *beþencan*; see þenchen]

biuien *v.* tremble, shudder 10. 47. *pa. t. pl.* beoueden 10.183. [OE *bifian, beofian*]

biuore(n). See bifor(e), bifore.

biwefde *pp.* covered, wrapped 10.241; biweued 11.115. [OE *bewæfan*]

biwinneð *pr. pl.* gain, obtain 18. 57. *pp.* biwonne got possession of 6.381. [OE *bewinnan*; see winne(n)]

biwiten *v.* defend, guard 19.5. *pr. 3 sg.* biwiteð 19.34. [OE *bewitan*]

biwokenn *pa. t. pl.* watched 13. 70. [OE *be-+wōcon*, from *wacan* (wake, spring) but in sense of *bewacian*]

biwraie, -wreie *pr. subj. sg.* betray 3.264, 265. [OE *be-+wrēgan*]

biwro *v.* cover, conceal 1.419. [OE *bewrēon*] Cf. wreah.

blac *adj.* pale 19.66. [OE *blāc*]

blake *adj.*, black 19.125; dark 4.336 (see broun(e)). [OE *blæc, blac-*]

blam(e) *n.* blame, charge, accusation 6.198; reproach 6.392; dishonour 15.66. [OF *bla(s)me*]

blame *v.* blame 6.56. [OF *bla(s)mer*]

blast *n.* blowing 8B.3. [OE *blæst*]

blawe(n). See blowe.

ble *n.* colour 9.79; bleo complexion, face 8E.7, 54, K.23; blo 1.319, appearance 108. [OE *blēo*]

bleas *n.* blowing, blast 18.94. [OE *blæs*]

blease *n.* firebrand 18.207. *pl.* bleasen 18.212. [OE *blæse*]

bleasie *pr. subj. sg.* blaze up 18. 656. [from prec.]

blenche *v.* dodge, escape 1.126. [OE *blencan* deceive]

blent *pr. 3 sg.* blinds 19.100. [OE *bléndan*]

bleo. See ble.

blesse *v.* bless 6.258. *pr. 1 sg.* blisce 14.69. *subj. sg.* blis 15.37. *imper. sg.* blesce bless with the sign of the cross, cross (yourself) 18.383; blesse 6.201; blis 15.64. *pp.* iblescede 19. 249, 281; iblescet 18.576; ibleset, iblessed 8v.11, 21. [OE *blētsian*, already infl. by *blissian*; see blissin]

blete *adj.* bare 1.396. as *n.* in þe ∼ exposure, lack of cover 1.57. [OE *blēat*]

bleteþ *pr. 3 sg.* bleats 8A.6. [OE *blætan*]

bleþeli(che); blewen. See bliðeliche; blowe.

blykyeþ *pr. 3 sg.* shines 8K.23. [OE *blician*]

blinde *adj.* blind 9.42. [OE *blind*]

blynne *v.* cease, stop 8L.17. [OE *blinnan*]

blis(ce). See blesse.

blis(s), blisse, blysse *n.* joy, happiness 3.254, 261, 8M.11, 1.298, 3.6, 5.140, 8E.33, w.9; blisce 17.77; *make (hure)* ∼ rejoice 3.278, 8v.1. *pl.* blissen 19. 301. [OE *bliss*]

blisful *adj.* glad, happy 3.244; blessed 14.259, 19.266; blysfol beautiful 8K.18. [prec.+ -ful]

blissin *v.* rejoice, be glad 19.304. *pr. 3 sg. refl.* blisseþ 1.313. *subj. sg.* blisse 1.336. *pp.* iblisset gladdened, joyful 18. 448. [OE *blissian*] bliþe, blyþe, bliðe *adj.* happy, glad 1.296, 2.88, 4.45, 8L.22, 10.114; bliþ, blith, blyth 6.259, 14.263 (with *for*), blessed 14.2ò1 [OE *blīþe*]

blyþe *adv.* gladly 8G.14. [OE *blīþe*]

bliðeliche *adv.* gladly, willingly 18.209, 19.278, 396; bleþeliche 3.127, 5.171, 17.161; bleþeli 6.35; bluðeliche 19.91 (note). [OE *blīþelīce*]

bliue; blo. See biliue; ble.

blod(e) *n.* blood 3.50, 4.246, 5.40, 10.280; blood 2.310; phr. *fles and ~* 17.217, sim. 13.255, cf. 18.278; tag *~ ant bon* body 8K.10, cf. E.5 and *bon and ~* C.5. See hert(e). [OE *blōd*]

blodi, -y *adj.* bloody 8W.25, 18.364. [OE *blōdig*]

blodstremes *n. pl.* streams of blood 10.184.   [blod(e)+strem]

blome *n. coll.* blossom, flowers 6.294. [ON *blóm(i)*]

blood. See blod(e).

blosme *n̄. coll.* blossom 8M.2; blostme 1.315, 8W.1. *pl.* blosme blossoms, flowers 1.16; blosmes 3.60, 8H.4; blostmene 7.44. [OE *blŏsma*]

bloute *adj.* soft 4.337. [ON *blaut-r*]

blowe *v.* blow *tr.* 4.179; blawe(n) sound (trumpet) 10.205, (trumpet-call) 2.318; *intr.* 16.56. *imper. sg. intr.* blow, blou 8K.1, 4. *pa. t. pl.* blewen 16.56. [OE *blāwan, blēowon*]

bloweþ *pr. 3 sg.* flowers 8A.3. *pp. adj.* iblowe in leaf 1.398. [OE *blōwan*]

bluðeliche; bo(n). See bliðeliche; be(n).

boc *n.* book 7.110, 18.69, 19.79; bock (prob. missal) 10.introd.; boke 1.266, 12.2; book 2.321. *gen.* bokess 13.287. *pl.* bokes 9.118. [OE *bōc*]

bocle *n.* buckle 8E.67. [OF *bo(u)cle*]

bodede *pa t. sg.* proclaimed, uttered 10.173; foretold 10.326. [OE *bodian*]

boden *n. pl.* messages, news 10.4; bodes teachings 12.106. [OE *bod*, pl. *bodu*]

bodi, body *n.* body 1.73, 7.135, 8E.74, 17.65, 18.410; person, man 11.124; *mi ~* me 18.635. [OE *bodig*]

boght. See buggen.

boȝe *n.* bough, branch 1.15. [OE *bōg*]

bohe *n.* bow 18.157. *pl.* bowes 11.163. [OE *boga*]

bohte, -on. See buggen.

boyes *n. pl.* fellows, ruffians 4.326. [perh. AN *(em)buié*; see note]

boyht. See buggen.

boinard *n.* fool 6.288. [OF *bui(s)nard*]

boyt; boke.   See boþ(e); boc.

boket *n.* bucket 5.78, 80. *pl.* boketes 5.73. [OF *buket* from Gmc]

bold *n.* house, dwelling 19.147. [OE *bóld*] Cf. bottle.

bold(e) *adj.* bold, brave 1.233, 288, 9.64; arrogant 11.149; bald 14.7, 19.207; belde 1.673; confident, assured: *þat be þou ~* be sure of that 6.54. *dat. fem.* baldere 10.116. as *n. pl.* bolde in *wiþ ~* in noble company 8E.6. [OA *báld*, WS *béald*]

boldeliche, balde- *adv.* boldly 1.279, 665. [OE *baldlíce*]

bon *n.* bone 8c.5, E.5, K.10 (see blod(e)); *~ of whal* 8E.40, *whalles ~* 8E.67, G.1 ivory (from walrus tusks); ban 19.149. *pl.* bones 5.63. [OE *bān*]

bonde *n.* bondage, captivity 8D.12. [ON *band*]

bondon. See bynde.

bone *n.* prayer, request 6.375,

8T.39, 12.64, 18.75. *pl.* bonen
18.3, 57. [ON *bón*]

book; boord. See boc;
bord(e).

bor(e) *n.* (wild) boar 1.286, 4.
294. [OE *bár*]

bord(e) *n.* table 1.337, 8K.70,
household 10.288; boord 2.289.
[OE *bórd*]

bore(n). See ber.

borewe *v.* redeem 8N.32. [OE
borgian be surety for]

borgeis; borsten; boru, borw.
See burgeis; bersteð; burh.

bot *adv.* only 14.91. [devel. from
bot(e) prep. used with neg.]

bot(e) *n.*[1] remedy, cure 1.434,
8D.9, 14.240, 15.33, 16.95, 18.2;
forgiveness 1.518; salvation, re-
demption 8U.9, 14.44; *of ~* as a
remedy 8K.75; *what, quat ~*
what use 8L.28, 14.89. [OE
bót]

bot(e) *conj.* 2.14, 5.43, 6.234, 7.
162, 8H.32, 15.10; but(e) 1.
366, 3.12, 4.4, 10.325, 16.96,
19.11; buten 10.34, 12.58, 19.
309. (1) except 2.272 (*to be*
understood), 4.69, 8Q.1, 14.52;
except that 1.366, 16.96. (2) unless (with subj.) 1.569, 2.14,
3.12, 5.43, 6.234, 15.10; *~ if*,
&c. unless 6.181, 15.51, 17.224,
19.15; *~ þat, þet* 6.400, 18.656;
~ on þat provided (only) that
6.38 (note). (3) but 2.97, 4.4,
6.173, 7.162, 9.12, 12.58. [OE
bútan, búte]

bot(e) *prep.* 2.309, 5.39, 6.137,
11.32; bute 1.139, 16.131, 18.
441; buten 10.80; boute 8F.
15, 9.21. (1) but, except 1.380,
9.8, 10.295, 11.32, 16.131, 19.
84; with *neg.*, only 1.718, *ne
ys, nis ~* is nothing but 14.55,
18.33, 19.168. (2) without 1.139,
8F.15, 48, 9.21, 10.80, 18.633,
19.107. [prec.]

bote *n.*[2] boat 9.152; bat 10.314.
[OE *bát*]

boterfleȝe *n.* butterfly 3.216.
[OE *buter-flēoge*]

bot-forke *n.* hay-fork 8N.2.
[MDu *bot(t)e* (whence OF *botte*)
bundle + OE *forca*]

bottle *n.* building 13.236. [OE
botl] Cf. bold.

boþ(e), boðe, both *adv., conj.*:
~ .. and both .. and 1.50, 3.18,
4.20, 5.167, 6.86, 12.11, 14.40;
boþen, boðen 5.26, 12.74;
boyt 15.65; bath(e) 14.87, 16.
162. baðe also 18.159, 258.
[next]

boþe *adj.* both 1.639, 2.33, 3.261,
7.39, 8F.41, 11.115; *~ to* 7.237;
baþe 13.31, 37 (*dat.*). *pron.*
baðe 16.17, 18.596. *gen.*
boþer: *ȝoure ~* of you both
3.272; sim. bather 14.118;
baþre 13.32. [ON *báðir* and
perh. OE *bā þā*]

boþ; boþte; boue. See be(n);
buggen; buue(n).

bouȝ *n.* bough 7.44; bowe 7.47.
pl. bowes 8H.4. [OE *bóg*]

bountyng *n.* bunting 8G.52.
[obscure]

bour(e) *n.* room, bedroom (esp.
a woman's) 2.217, 3.184, 8L.11,
R.9, Y.2, 9.58; bure 9.11, 10.12,
lodging 13.54; *into ~* to their
rooms 3.212; *in ~* (tag, of ladies)
8E.6, H.8, K.5. *pl.* boure (after
numeral, representing OE gen.)
3.2; boures 3.207; bowris
9.53. [OE *búr*]

bous *n.* liquor, drink 8N.29.
[MDu *búse* beaker, *búsen*
tipple]

boute; bouth(e); bowe;
bowes. See bot(e); buggen;
buȝe; bohe, bouȝ.

bowiares *n. gen.* bow-maker's
11.163. [OE *boga* + suff. *-yer*]

bowris; brad. See bour(e);
brod(e).

brad-eȝede *adj.* broad-eyed 16.
52. [brod(e) + eȝe + adj. suff.
OE *-ede*]

bræcon; bræd; brayd. See breke(n); bred; breid.

bras *n.* brass 2.213. [OE *bræs*]

brastlien *v. intr.* clash 10.277. [OE *brastlian*]

brathly *adv.* violently 14.63. [ON *bráðliga*]

braunches *n. pl.* branches 14.185. [AN *braunche*]

brech *n.* breeches 3.10. [OE *brēc*, pl. of *brōc*]

breche *n.* clearing (at edge of a wood) 1.14 (note). [OE *brǣc*]

bred *n.* bread 4.35, 93, 6.327; bræd 13.256. [OE *brēad*]

bredale *n.* wedding feast 17.87. [cf. WS *brȳd-ealu* 'bride-ale']

brede *n.* breadth 1.130. [OE *brǣdu*]

bredes *pr. 3 sg.* spreads out, expands 8E.33 (note). [OE *brǣdan*]

bredeþ *pr. pl., intr.* grow 8H.4. *pp.* ibred bred 1.682. [OE *brēdan,* tr.]

bredgume *n.* bridegroom 17.108. [cf. WS *brȳd-guma*]

breȝe *n.* eyebrow 8E.18. [OA *brēg*]

breid *pr. 3 sg.* pulls 18.175. *imper. sg.* lift 18.382. *pa. t. sg.* brayd drew (a sword) 4.252. [OE *bregdan, brægd*]

breke(n) *v.* break *tr.* 1.651, 4.180; breoke(n) 18.43, 195, break into 19.8, 31. *intr.* 4.335, 8G.47. *pr. 3 sg.* brekeþ, -ð *tr.* 18.157, 339; *intr.* 6.356. *pa. t. pl.* breke(n) *tr.* 10.181, broke into 11.163, wrecked 166; *intr.* 10.27; bræcon 16.173; broken *tr.* 4.329. [OE *brecan,* M 1 sg. -breocu; brǣcon, brēcon;* pp. *brocen*]

breme *adj.* excellent, splendid 8K.16; passionate 1.158. [OE *brēme* famous, ME also fierce]

brenge. See bryng(e).

brennen *v.* burn *intr.* 4.182; make a fire 12.178. *pr. p.* brennand 14.154; brenninde

7.45. *pa. t. pl. tr.* brende 11.36; brenden, -on 16.193, 184. [ON *brenna*] Cf. barne, berninde.

breoke(n); breoste. See breke(n); brest.

breoste-holke *n.* hollow of the chest 19.112. [brest+OE *holc* cavity]

brere *n. coll.* briers 8N.23. *pl. gen.* breres 18.241. [OE *brǣr,* A *brēr*]

brest *n.* breast, chest 4.255, 5.51, 194, 8E.74; breoste womb 18.126; broste breast 8V.22. [OE *brēost*]

briche *adj.* useful, serviceable 12.138. [OE *brȳce*]

bricht. See briȝt(e).

brichtnesse *n.* brightness, light 17.48; brihtnesse 19.259. [OE *be(o)rhtnes(se),* M *birht-*]

bryd *n.*[1] (small) bird 8G.53. *pl.* briddes 9.95. [OE *brid*]

brid *n.*[2] See burde.

bride *n.* bridle, rein 2.175. [OF from Gmc]

brigge *n.* bridge 4.141; brugge 11.36, 113, 18.28; *attrib.* in ~ ende head of the bridge 11.121. [OE *brycg,* or in 4 ON *bryggja*]

briȝt(e) *adj.* bright, radiant, beautiful 1.403, 639, 9.5, 115; briȝth 2.136; briht, bryht 8E.7, F.6, K.5, 19.275; brihht 13.162; bricht 17.48; brigt 12.19; brith 8L.2; bryþt (= -ȝt) 8W.47; clear 1.639, 18.421. *comp.* briȝter 1.108, 8T.3; brihtre 18.625, 19.323. *sup.* brihtest 8D.38. [OE *be(o)rht,* A *breht,* WS *-bryht*]

briȝte *adv.* bright(ly) 7.43, 176; bryht 8K.23; brihte brilliantly 1.614. [cf. OE *beorhte*]

brihteð *pr. 3 sg.* makes bright 18.403. [OA *ge-brihtan*]

brihtnesse. See bricht-.

brimme *n.* water 9.157. [OE *brim*]

bryng(e), bringe(n) *v.* 2.148,
8G.21, 1.456, 18.654, 19.128;
bringue 7.19, 246; brenge 3.
29. bring 1.311, 2.193, 6.400,
8N.25, 18.654, 19.128; rescue,
relieve 6.189, 7.218; take 2.148,
3.62; send 2.261. ~ *forth* see
forþ; ~ *up* utter 1.156, open
11.133; ~ *o fluht* put to flight
18.109; ~ *of lyf*, *(liif-) dawe* kill
2.182, 7.19, 22 (cf. do(n)); ~ *to
depe, ende* kill 8G.21, 11.102, 7.
122, ~ *to putte* bury 11.144.
pr. 1 sg. bringe 1.311. *3 sg.*
bringeð, bryngeþ 18.109, 156,
19.236, 2.193. *pl.* bringeþ 8G.
26, 9.105. *subj. sg.* bringe 6.400.
imper. sg. bring 8N.25. *pa. t. sg.*
broȝte 1.156; brohte 1.684,
10.2, 16.29, 18.471; broucte,
brouthe 4.35, 46, 86; brohute,
broute 5.70, 104, 259, 6.92. *pl.*
brohten 10.240, 16.82. *subj. pl.*
brohten 10.159. *pp.* broght
14.63, 254; broht 8D.13, K.
59; brouȝt(h) 2.182, 3.101;
brout 8T.42; ibrocht 17.108;
ibroȝt(e) 1.353, 11.102; y-
broht 8G.14; ibrouȝt 7.22,
59; ibrout 5.82, 6.244, 8V.13;
ibrowt 3.273; hybrovt 8w.40.
[OE *bringan, bröhte, (ge)bröht*]
brinie *n.* coat of mail 4.202. *pl.*
bryniges 16.167. [ON *brynja*]
brisen *v.* crush 4.262. [OE
brȳsan, OF *brisier*]
brith. See briȝt(e).
brod(e) *adj.* broad 1.75, 4.162,
9.66; brad(e) 10.290, 18.511;
large 13.162; extensive 14.93.
[OE *brād*]
brode *n.* brood 1.93. [OE *bröd*]
broder; broght, broȝte,
broht(e), brohute. See
broþer; bryng(e).
broys *n.* broth 4.190. [OF *broez*]
broken. See breke(n).
broþer, broðer, brother *n.*
brother 2.149, 10.109, 16.253;
friend 6.135; broþur 7.125;

broder 12.132. *gen.* broþer,
broþur 7.130, 270. [OE *brōþor*,
gen. unchanged]
broucte, brouȝt(h). See
bryng(e).
brouke *v.* possess, enjoy 6.273;
brukenn 13.288; bruke have
possession *(of)* 10.136. [OE
brūcan]
broun(e) *adj.* brown; fair-
haired: as *n.* in inclusive phr.
þe ~ *and þe blake* fair and dark,
one and all 4.336; (of metal)
bright, gleaming 2.250. [OE
brūn]
brout(he). See bryng(e).
browen *n. pl.* eyebrows 8G.26,
K.18; browes E.25. [OE *brū*,
pl. *brū(w)a*, gen. *brūna*]
bruche *n.* breach, opening 5.21,
233. [OE *bryce*]
brugge; bruke(nn). See
brigge; brouke.
brune *n.* fire 18.213; 19.95, 114.
[OE *bryne*]
brutaske *n.* brattice, wooden
parapet 11.36. [AN *brutesche*,
ML *brutescha*, &c.]
Bruttes *n. pl.* Britons 10.116,
288. *gen.* Brutte 10.90, 173,
Brutten 86. *dat.* Brutten 10.
312. [OE *Bryttas*]
Bruttisce *adj.* British 10.84.
[OE *Bryttisc*]
bucke *n.* buck (male deer) 8A.8.
pl. bucces he-goats 16.53. [OE
bucca]
bue(þ). See be(n).
buggen *v.* buy, purchase, pay
for 6.272, 18.613; bie redeem
8x.16. *pr. 3 sg.* buð 18.527.
subj. sg. bugge 18.116, 613.
pa. t. sg. bohte 18.388, 527, 19.
31, 266; boþte (= *boȝte*) 8w.16;
bouthe 4.141; boyht 8x.14. *pl.*
bohton 16.225. *pp.* boght paid
for 14.144; bouth 4.149; iboht
18.616; hybovt 8w.34. [OE
bycgan, pr. 3 sg. *bygþ; bohte, boht*]
buȝe *v. intr.* go 10.94. *pr. 3 sg. tr.*

buheð bends, bows 18.672. *subj. sg. intr.* **bowe** stoop 3.47. *pa. t. sg.* **bey** *tr.* 5.194; **beh** *intr.* went 10.144, *refl.* bent 8к.70. [OE *būgan, bēah*]

buhsum *adj.* obedient 19.271. [stem of prec.+OE suff. *-sum*]

bulder-ston *n.* boulder 4.217. [cf. Sw dial. *bullersten*; second element *ston(e)*]

bulluc *n.* young bull 8A.8. [OE]

bune *n.* purchase 18.387. [OE *bygen*]

bunté *n.* gift 17.256. [AN *bunté*]

burch. See **burh.**

burde *n.* lady, girl 8D.36 (note), F.6, к.5, 35, 10.323; **brid** 8к.16. [OE **byrde*, deriv. of *-byrdan* embroider, cf. *byrdestre* embroideress; sometimes confused with *bride*, OE *brȳd*]

bure. See **bour(e).**

burede *pa. t. sg.* buried 7.119. *pl.* **byrieden** 16.228. *pp.* **ibured** 7.135, 145. [OE *byrgan*]

burgeis, burgeys *n. pl.* burgesses, citizens 2.105, 111, 11.151; **borgeis** 11.129. [OF *burgeis*, sg. and pl.]

burgurs *n. pl.* burglars 18.43. [AN *burgur*]

burȝewere. See **burhweren.**

burh *n.* stronghold 18.82; city 10.195, 18.665; **burch** 16.290; **boru, borw** 4.41, 115; **burhȝe** (*dat.*) 10.199; **buri** habitation 19.146. *pl.* **burhes** strongholds 18.79. [OE *burh, burg*; dat. *byrig*]

burh-folc *n.* people of a city 10.208. [prec.+**folk(e)**]

burhweren *n. pl.* citizens, community 10.189, **burȝewere** 201. [OE *burh-, burgware*]

burne *n.* stream 1.550. [OE *burna, -e*]

burste; burþ; burþen. See **bersteð; birrþ; birdene.**

but *pp.* thrust 4.343. [AN *buter*]

but(e), buten. See **bot(e)** *conj., prep.*

butere *n.* butter 16.72, 187. [OE]

butte *n.* a flat fish, perh. halibut 4.27. [cf. MDu *butte*]

buð. See **buggen.**

buue(n) *adv.* above 1.164, 18.511. [OE *bufan*] Cf. **aboue.**

buue(n) *prep.* above, over 19.280, 283; **boue** (postponed) 6.90. [prec.]

buxsumnes *n.* obedience, humility 14.30. [from **buhsum**]

cæse. See **ceose.**

caynard *n.* idler 8N.20. [cf. F *cagnard*]

caiser, caysere *n.* emperor 2.11, 39. *gen.* **keȝȝseress** 13.250. *pl.* **keiseres** 19.293. [MDu *keiser*, ON *keisari*] Cf. **caseres.**

cakes *n. pl.* cakes, small loaves 9.57. [ON *kaka*]

calcedun *n.* chalcedony 9.94. *pl.* **calsidoines** 3.44. [OF from L *calcēdonius*]

cald(e). See **cold(e).**

Calldewisshe, K- *adj.* Chaldean 13.167, 201. [from *Kalldea*, Orm's form of *Chaldea*; only in Orm]

calle(n) *v.* shout, cry out 4.135, 153; call, name 4.15. *pr. 1 sg.* **calle** describe, call 8L.17. *pl.* (with suffixed pron.) **calleth** = *call it* 4.13 (note). *pa. t. sg.* **kalde** shouted 4.150. [LOE *ceallian* from ON *kalla*]

calsidoines. See **calcedun.**

calue *n.* (*dat.*) calf 8A.7. [OA *calf*, dat. *calfe*]

cam; can; canceler. See **com; con, conne; chaunceler.**

Candelmasse *n.* Candlemas, 2 February 11.108; ~ **dæi** 16.255; **-messe** 16.40. [OE *candelmæsse*]. See **masse.**

candles *n. pl.* candles 16.243. [OE *candel*]

canel *n.* cinnamon 9.76, 110. [OF *canele*]

cann, canst(u). See **conne.**

capil *n.* horse, nag 9.32. [cf. ON *kapall*, L *caballus*]

capitale *n.* capital 9.69. [ONF *capital*]

capoun *n.* capon 3.12 (see **diht**). [OE *capun* from L or F]

car(e), kare *n.* misery, sorrow, unhappiness 3.282, 286, 5.34, 6.153, 8G.11, L.7, T.10; anxiety 4.103, 9.18, 19.170. *pl.* **cares** 8F.11. [OA *caru*]

carbuncle *n.* carbuncle 9.90. [ONF]

carien *v.* feel anxiety, fear 19.184. *pr. 1 sg.* **care** grieve, sorrow 8K.77. [OA *carian*]

carited *n.* observance of commemorative feasts 16.207. [ONF] See **charité**.

carke *pr. 1 sg.* fret, pine 8K.77. [ONF *carkier* burden; cf. **charged**]

carl *n.* churl, serf 4.216. [ON *karl*]

carles *adj.* free from anxiety, secure 18.88. [OA *carlēas*]

carlmen *n. pl.* men 16.162. [ON *karlmenn*, pl. of *karlmaðr*]

carpenter *n.* carpenter 11.44. [AN]

carte-lode *n.* cartload 4.161. [ON *kart-r*+OE *lād* way]

cas *n.* chance; *bi* ∼ by chance 7.83; experience 7.62; fate 7.66; circumstance, event 7.154, 211, 258, 11.172. [OF]

caseres *n. gen.* emperor's 16.7; **kaseress** 13.268. [OE *cāsere*] Cf. **caiser**.

caste(n) *v.* cast, throw, fling 4.209, 7.82; cast (in metal) 2.238; set free 8F.11; *on* ∼ put on 8F.13; ∼ *awey* banish 8L.7; **kesten** 4.211. *pa. t. sg.* **cast(e)** 4.81, 202, 7.118; **kest** 14.210. *pl.* **caste** 11.16, 20. [ON *kasta* with partial substitution of OE *æ* for *a* and association with other vbs. having -*est*-; see *Iuliene* pp. 159–61]

castel *n.* castle 4.143, 11.21, 16. 253, 18.79; stronghold 1.131. *pl.* **castels** 2.139; **castles** 16. 140, 18.621. [ONF].

castel-weorces *n. pl.* the building of castles 16.159. [prec.+ **werk**]

catel *n.* goods, money 3.157. [ONF] See **chatel**.

caue *n.* cave 12.80. [OF]

cedre *n.* cedar 14.241. [OF]

cellerer *n.* cellarer, steward 5. 59. [AN *celerer*]

ceose *n.* cheese 16.72, **cæse** 187. [OA *cēse*]

certeyn *adj.* certain, sure 2.203. [OF *certain*]

certes *adv.* certainly, truly 1.727, 6.61, 139; **certhes** 15.22. [OF *certes*]

ceste *n.* chest 16.171. [OA *cest*]

cete *n.* whale 12.155. [OF *cete* fem.]

cethegrande *n.* whale 12.141. [prec.+OF *grande*]

chæs. See **cheosen.**

chaffare *n.* merchandise, goods 11.114. [OE *cēap*+*faru*, cf. ON *kaup-fǫr*] See **chep.**

chalandre *n.* calander, a species of lark 9.97. [cf. OF *calandre*]

chald. See **cold(e).**

chalenge *pr. 1 sg.* claim, demand as a right 2.61. [OF *chalengier*]

chaliz *n.* chalice 18.329. [OF]

cham ; chap. See **com ; chep.**

chapele *n.* chapel 7.256. [OF]

chapeð *pr. 3 sg.* bargains for 18. 387. [OE *cēapian*] Cf. **chapmen, chep.**

chapitre *n.* chapter, ecclesiastical court 6.244. [OF]

chapmen *n. pl.* merchants 11. 112. [OE *cēap-mann*] See **chep.**

charged *pa. t. sg.* burdened, weighed upon 3.178. [OF *charg(i)er*]

charité *n.* charity, compassion 14.32, 99; in French phr. *pur,* *par, seint(e)* ~ in the name of holy charity 9.190, 19.422, 426. [OF *charité*] Cf. **carited**.

chaste *adj.* chaste 17.132, 18. 610. [OF]

chasti *pr. subj. sg.* discipline 19. 12. [OF *chastier*]

chastité *n.* chastity 14.31. [OF *chasteté*]

chatel *n.* possession, treasure 19.34. [OF] See **catel**.

chaterest *pr. 2 sg.* chatter 1.238. [imit.]

chateringe *n.* chattering 1.368, empty words 490. [from prec.]

chaumbre *n.* room 2.229, 280, bedroom 320. *pl.* **chaumbres** 2.209. [AN *chaumbre*]

chaunce *n.* chance, accident 14. 57; **cheance** fortune, risk 9.185; see **stonde(n)**. [OF *ch(e)ance*, AN *chaunce*]

chaunceler *n.* chancellor (of the university) 11.148; **canceler** (of England) 16.151. [ONF *canceler*, OF *chancelier*]

chaunge *v.* change, exchange 8G.29; **chaungi** 3.234. *pa. t. sg.* **chaungede** 3.247. *pp.* **ychaunged** 2.306. [AN *chaunger*]

chaueles *n. pl.* jaws 12.155. [OE *ceafl*]

cheance. See **chaunce**.

chef *adj.* head 11.94. [OF]

cheke *n.* cheek 8E.34. *pl.* **cheken** 6.358. [OE *cēace*]

chele *n.* cold 8N.5, 19.115. [OA *cele*]

cheosen *v.* choose 18.47, 19.200; **chesen** 3.23. *pr. 3 sg.* **cheseþ** 3.69. *pa. t. sg.* **chæs** 13.229, 249; **ches** 8v.4. *pl.* **cusen** 16. 82. *pp.* **chosen** 3.64, beautiful 8E.34; **icornee** 17.203; **icoren** 18.51, excellent 10.323; as *adj.* (*n.*) *pl.* **icorene** chosen (ones), elect 18.148, 334. [OE *cēosan*, *cēas*, *curon*, *coren*]

chep *n.* bargaining 8G.34; **chap** value 18.619. [OE *cēap*]

cherch. See **churche**.

cherde *pa. t. pl.* went 1.616. [OA *cerran* turn]

chere *n.* face, appearance 8K.30; expression 18.218, 19.239; manner, demeanour 8x.4, 14.217; *maden* ~ *bliþe* looked happy 2. 88. [OF *chiere*, *chere*]

cherl *n.* boor 8N.34, **cherld** 40. [OE *ceorl*]

ches(en). See **cheosen**.

chesstre *n.* city, town 13.42, 128. [OE *ceaster*]

cheste *n.* quarrelling 1.133, 139. [OE *cēast*]

chide, chyde *v.* quarrel 1.654; wrangle, argue 8L.9. [OE *cīdan*]

child(e) *n.* child 1.583, 4.340, 7.10, 13.95, 18.543; **cild** 16.226; youth of noble birth (as form of address) 3.77, 159; *go wit* ~ conceive 8v.12. *pl.* **children** 4.62, 5.116. *dat.* **childre** 1.734. [OE *cíld*, pl. *cildru*]

childene *adj.* childish 18.31. [prec.+-*en* adj. suff.]

childenn *v.* give birth 13.48. [from **child(e)**]

childhede *n.* childhood 17.246. [cf. OE *cildhād* and **-hede**]

chyn(ne) *n.* chin 8E.34, 9.181. [OE *cinn*]

chirche, chirechen. See **churche**.

chirme *n.* clamour 1.221. [OE *cirm*] Cf. **bichermet**.

chyualrie, -rye, -erye *n. coll.* knights in company 2.4, 58; knightly qualities, prowess 2. 184. [ONF *chivalerie*]

chnief; choger; chold; chosen; chulle. See **knif; a choger; cold(e); cheosen; wil(e)**.

churche *n.* church 7.191, 259, 8x.10, 11.54; *attrib.* 11.59 (see **pais**); **chirche** 1.388, 18.43, 534; **chirechen** 10.introd.; **circe, cyrce** 16.192, 83; **cherch** 9.58. *gen.* **chirche** 1.473.

holi(e) ~ 1.467, 7.105, 8x.10, 11.
56. [OE *cirice, circe, cyrice*]
cild; **cyng**. See **child(e)**;
king(e).
cipres(e) *n.* cypress 14.241,
245. [OF *ciprès*]
circe, **cyrce**. See **churche**.
cyrceiærd *n.* churchyard 16.192.
[**churche**+OE *géard*]
circeweard *n.* sacristan 16.98.
[OE]
circewican *n.* (*dat.*) office of
sacrist 16.214. [**churche**+OE
wice office; see **wike** n.²]
cité *n.* city, town 2.102, 7.219,
17.5, 88. [OF]
cité-toune *n.* walled city 2.92.
[prec.+**toun(e)**]
clackes *pr. 2 sg.* chatter 1.81.
[cf. ON *klaka*]
clænnesse *n.* purity 13.244;
cleannesse 18.610; **clannesse**
8k.47; **clenesse** cleanliness 17.
100. [OE *clænnes(se)*] See
clene *adj.*
clærchade *n.* status of a secular
clerk (as opposed to monk) 16.
18. [OE *clerichād*]
claht *pp.* grasped, laid hold 8f.36
(note). [ME infin. *clechen*, app.
OE *clæcan, pp. *clǣht]
clane ; **clannesse** ; **clansi**. See
clene ; **clænnesse** ; **cleansin**.
clapte *pa. t. sg.* struck, hit 4.241,
248. [cf. ON *klappa*]
clarc, **clarkes**. See **clerc**.
clarré *adj.* (wine) flavoured with
honey and spices 2.131. [OF
claré]
claðˇ. See **cloþ**.
claue *v.* cleave, split 2.251. [OE
*clǣfan stick, crossed with
clēofan split; see **cleuen**]
clawe *n. pl.* claws 1.109. [OE
clawu, pl. *clawa*]
clawe *pr. subj. sg.* claw, tear
1.110. [OE *clawan, -ian*]
cleane ; **cleannesse**. See **clene** ;
clænnesse.
cleansin *v.* cleanse 18.575;

clansi rid (fold. by *wiþ*, of)
1.390; **clens** wash away 14.222.
pr. pl. refl. **cleansiðˇ** (*ham*) are
purified 18.328. [OE *clænsian*]
cleansing *n.* (*attrib.*) purifying
18.332. [cf. OE *clænsung*]
clene, **klene** *adj.* pure 3.53, 61;
virtuous, innocent, free from
sin 5.178, 227; **cleane** 18.104,
579. [OE *clæne*]
clene *adv.* entirely, completely
3.199, 7.140, 11.8; **clane** 10.64.
[OE *clæne*]
clenesse ; **clens**. See **clænnesse** ; **cleansin**.
clepen *v.* 2.24, 291; **cleopie(n)**
7.181, 10.214. (1) call, cry 10.
90, 17.160; invoke 18.397.
(2) name 2.24, 3.59, 7.2, 16.183,
17.88, 19.41. (3) call (by a
descriptive term) 1.583. (4)
summon 2.31, 7.181, 10.214,
11.95, 17.97, 19.43. *pr. 3 sg.*
clepeþ 17.245; **cleopeþ**, **-ðˇ**
1.583, 19.43. *pl.* **clepen** 2.31;
clepiedh 17.164; **cleopieth**
7.217. *subj. pl.* **clepie** 17.160.
imper. sg. **clepe** 17.189; **cleope**
18.397. *pa. t. sg.* **cleped(e)**
2.161, 17.97; **cleopede** 10.90.
pl. **clepeden** 16.183; **cleopeden**
7.164; **clupede** 11.95. *pp.*
icleped(e) 3.59, 17.88, 100;
icleoped, **-t** 7.2, 30, 269, 19.41.
[OE *cleopian, clipian*]
cler(e) *adj.* clear 3.55, 7.215, 9.
19 [OF *cler*]
clerc, **clerk** *n.* man in holy
orders, cleric, scholar 6.353,
363, 8l.9, 26; student 11.156,
15.8, 41; **clarc** 6.348, 366. *gen.*
clerkes 1.596. *pl.* **clerkes** 1.
468, 475; students 11.135, 147.
clerkus 7.206; **clerekes** 16.
195, 17.17; **clarkes** 6.248.
[OE *cler(i)c*; OF *clerc*]
cleþe *v.* provide with clothes
8f.12. [OE *clæþan* (Nb)]
cleuen *v.* split 4.183. [OE
clēofan]

cleuyen v. cling 8F.36. [OE *cleofian*]

clinge v. shrivel up 1.489. [OE *clingan*]

clippe v. intr. embrace 3.277; **cluppe** tr. clasp, embrace 8F.38. pr. 3 sg. tr. **clippeþ** 2.189. pa. t. pl. intr. **clepte** 3.250. [OE *clyppan*]

cliure n. claw, talon 1.78. pl. **cliuers, cliures** 1.111, 206, 84. [OE *clifer*]

cloister n. cloister 9.58, 65; **cloistre** monastery 18.240. [OF *cloistre*]

clot n. lump 18.193. [OE *clott*]

cloþ, cloth n. article of clothing, garment 4.123; clothing 9.29, 38; **cla𝄐** 18.307, 438. pl. **cloþes** clothes 8F.13. [OE *cláþ*]

cloþed pp. clothed, dressed 6.6; **icloþed** 6.319; **ycloþed** 8F.37. [OE *cláþian*]

clupede; cluppe. See **clepen; clippe.**

cluppunges n. pl. embraces 18. 579. [from OE *clyppan*; see **clippe**]

clut n. patch 18.264. pl. **clutess** swaddling clothes 13.58. [OE *clút*]

cluti pr. subj. sg. add (as a patch) 18.264. [OE *clútian*]

cnaue; cnawen(n). See **knaue; knowe** v.

cnawlechunge n. knowledge 19. 328. [OE *cnáwlǽcung* acknowledgement]

cneon; cnif; cniht. See **knes; knif; kni3t(h).**

cnihtschipe n. knightly conduct, prowess 18.507, 536. [*kni3t(h)* +-schipe]

cnotted adj. knotted 16.167. [next + suff. -ed]

cnottis n. pl. knots 8x.5. [OE *cnotta*]

cnowe. See **knowe** v.

cnut pr. 3 sg. ties a knot in 18. 590. [OE *cnyttan*]

coc n. cock 1.637; **kok** 5.30. [OE *cocc*, OF *coq*]

codde n. bag (of tricks) 16.90. [OE *codd*]

cogge n. cog-wheel 1.86. [obscure; cf. **cuggel**, and Sw *kugge* cog]

colblake adj. coal-black 1.75. [OE *col* (see **colen**) + **blake**]

cold n. cold 6.312; ~ *fon* catch cold 4.124. [OA *cáld*]

cold(e) adj. cold 5.254, 255, 7. 252; cool 1.402; painful, grievous 3.286; **cald(e)** 18.660, 19. 118; **chold** 17.136; **schald** 17. 118; **chald** (*of*) unwarmed (by) 17.119. [OE *ceáld*, A *cáld*]

colen n. pl. cinders 19.118. [OE *col*, pl. *colu*]

collacione n. light evening meal 9.145 (note). [OF *collacion*]

coluard adj. villainous 3.86. [OF *culvert* serf]

coluere n. dove 7.113, 173. [OE *culfre*]

com, come(n) v. come 9.177, 1.391, 3.87, 7.261, 8T.8, 11.96, 2.157, 5.136; **kome(n)** 5.174, 8T.17; **cum(e), cumen(n)** 10. 327, 14.223, 10.136, 19.7, 16.78, 19.234, 13.217; **kume** 1.519. arrive 4.131; descend 17.235. ~ *in(to)* go in(to) 5.25, 6.22; ~ *to* get to, reach 8Q.1, 9.161; ~ *up(þ)* go up, ascend 13.219, arise 18. 356; ~ *ut of* free oneself from 12.4; with dat. refl. pron. 6.299; fold. by infin. (mod. pr. p.): *comeþ ride* comes riding 2.176, *come lepe* came running 3.201, sim. 5.108; pa. t. as quasi-auxil. with *fleo* 7.173, *riden, faren, liðen, wenden* 10.1 (note), 257, 18, 37, 313. *infl. infin.* to **cumene** 17. 270, 19.298. pr. *1 sg.* **cume** 1.313, 19.247. *2 sg.* **cumest** 1.540, 19.86. *3 sg.* **comeþ, -th** 2.33, 8H.35, 7.254; **come3** (= -þ) 3.15; **comet** 8T.24; **comes** 4.194; **cumeþ, -ð** 1.298,

10.254, 12.4; **kumeð** 1.429;
kimeð 18.104, 19.78. *pl.* **comen**
2.99; **commiþ** 9.161; **coms**
14.37; **cumen** 12.123. *subj. sg.*
come 3.110; **cume** 18.364, 19.25;
cumen 10.76, 322. *pr. p.* **cuminde** as *n. pl.* people coming
19.45. *imper. sg.* **com** 3.242,
5.38, 6.28; **cum** 18.560. *pl.*
cometh 4.312, 17.23; **komeþ**
5.270; **comes** 4.225. *pa. t. 1,
3 sg.* **com** 1.676, 2.2, 3.40, 4.45,
5.25, 6.64; **kom** 5.124; **come**
5.17, 7.146; **comm** 13.67;
cam 3.213, 4.165, 7.47; **kam**
4.34, 17.11; **cham** 4.300.
2 sg. **come** 6.261. *pl.* **com(e)**
14.121, 1.629, 2.171, 3.201, 11.
15; **comen** 4.231, 7.92, 10.43,
16.142, 17.190; **comenn**,
cómenn 13.35, 183; **coman**
16.196. *subj. sg.* **come** 1.568,
7.192, 10.257, 18.49, would
come 11.104, 13.10; **comme**
19.68. *pl.* **comen** 10.140. *pp.*
comen 3.90, 6.296; **comin**
15.39; **commun** 14.235;
cumenn 13.84; **cummen** 15.
55; **icom(e)**, **ycome** 6.162,
3.152, 2.70; **icomen** 5.60, 17.
193; **icume** 1, note to 95, 10.
168, 17.194; **icumen** 8A.1, 10.
78, 19.63. [OE *cuman, cōm,
cōmon, cumen*]
come *n.* ˑcoming 5.134, 8E.46.
[app. ON *kváma*; see 6, note on
lang.] See **hom-come, cume.**
comely *adj.* beautiful 8G.27.
[OE *cỹmlic*, vowel altered after
bicome]
comeliche *adv.* beautifully 8F.
12, 37. [OE *cỹmlice*; see prec.]
commandement *n.* command
17.192. [OF]
commencement *n.* beginning
17.111. [OF]
commun(e) *adj.* common,
general 2.112, 11.6; public 11.
156; held in common 9.63. [OF
com(m)une]

compaygnie *n.* company 7.109.
[OF *compai(g)nie*]
con *v.*[1] *auxil. sg.* (forming with
infin. equivalent of pa. t.) did:
~ *fare* walked, was walking
8F.1; can 12.42. [var. of **gan**
(see **ginneþ**) confused with
conne]
con *v.*[2] See **conne.**
conduye *v.* lead 2.82. [OF *con-
duire*]
congeoun *n.* fool 2.297. [cf.
AN *cangiun* corresp. to OF
changon changeling, imbecile]
conne *v.* 3.259. (1) (with n. or
pron. obj.) know, be skilled in
or familiar with 1.589, 3.259,
4.40, 7.180, 8L.29, W.37, 15.77
(with dat. refl. pron.), 17.17;
know of 16.95; ~ *innsihht* have
knowledge 13.165; ~ *meþ to* use
moderation in 5.97; ~ *no god*
be unwise 6.285; ~ *red* know a
course of action, see what to do
1.426, 3.79, 80, 8F.41; ~ *of*
know about, be versed in 1.368,
573, sim. ~ *on* 4.18 (note),
6.47, 206. (2) (with infin.) be
able to, (I, &c.) can 1.126, 4.
180, 5.184, 7.179; (infin. understood) 8N.36; *I ne can ne I ne
mai* I do not know how to, nor
am I able to 16.179, sim. 6.
168, 19.92. *pr. 1 and 3 sg.* **can**
1.383, 3.79, 7.34, 14.52, 15.70;
cann 13.165; **kan** 4.180; **con**
1.199, 5.97, 6.47, 8F.41, 19.92;
cone 6.168; **kon** 1.426. *2 sg.*
canst 1.368, 4.114; (with suffixed pron.) **canstu** 1.589, 15.
36; **const** 1.536, 6.285, 18.641;
cost 8L.17. *pl.* **cunne(n)** 16.61,
202, 19.211; **kunne** 1.543; **can**
14.86. *subj. sg.* **cunne** 1.47, 10.
324, 12.16; **kunne** 1.144. *pa. t.
1, 3 sg.* **couþe, covþe, cowþe**
4.18, 7.179, 8L.29, 7.182, 4.281;
kouþe 5.184; **cuþe** 1.675, 16.
95; **kuþe** 1.443. *2 sg.* **couþest**
6.188, 220. *pl.* **cuþe** 1.573;

kuþe 17.17. *subj. sg.* **cuðe,**
cuthe 18.332, 16.249; **kuþe**
1.409. [OE *cunnan*; *cann, conn,*
cunnon; *cūþe*] See **cuþ.**

conquerour *n.* conqueror 14.3.
[AN].

conseil *n.* advice, counsel 7.206;
plan 2.72; agreement 11.6;
nomen ~ decided 17.8; adviser,
counsellor 8T.10; **counseil**
(*coll.*) matters of confidence,
secrets 3.209; **cunsayle** 15.54.
[OF *conseil*, AN *cun-*]

conseiler *n.* counsellor 2.30.
[AN *cunseiler*]

constable *n.* constable 11.3, 89;
cunestable governor of a fortress 19.43 (note), 226. [OF
conestable, AN *cun-*]

conteckeden *pa. t. pl.* contended
7.230. [cf. ONF *contekier*, but
this means 'touch'] See **cuntek.**

contenaunce *n.* (joyful) demeanour, behaviour 3.254. [OF]

contrarie *n.* contrary 17.110.
[OF]

contré *n.* country, land 14.111;
contreie, contreye (own)
country, native land 3.236,
2.225; district, region 11.7; sur-
rounding country (opposed to
town) 7.219. [OF *contrée*]

contreiemen *n. pl.* people of the
district 7.210. [prec.+OE *menn*]

cop(pe) *n.*[1] cup 3.114, 115, 6.329.
[OE *cuppe* and *copp*, OF *cope*]
coppe *n.*[2] See **coup(p)e.**

coral(e) *n.* coral 8K.45, 9.70.
[OF *coral*]

corn *n.* corn, grain 12.75, 84,
16.186, 200; **korn** 4.37, 48,
koren 306; ~ *of bred* bread-corn,
prob. wheat 4.93. [OE]

cors *n.* body 17.60. [OF]

corsede. See **cursed.**

corsingue *n.* anathema 7.268.
[cf. OE *cursung*; see **cursed**]

coruen *pp.* carved 8E.65. [OE
corfen from *ceorfan*; see **keor-**
uinde]

cos *n.* kiss 8M.12, 18.673. *pl.*
cosses 18.272. [OE *coss*]

cost. See **conne.**

costes *n. pl.* qualities, characteristics 12.129. [ONb *cost*
from ON *kost-r*]

costnede *pa. t. sg.* cost 18.391,
529. [from OF *coster*]

cote *n.* cottage 4.5. [OE *cot(e)*]

couel *n.* cloak 4.36, 126. [OE *cufel*]

counseil. See **conseil.**

countour *n.* accountant 11.94.
[AN; cf. CF *contĕor, conteur*]

coupe *n.*[1] cup 3.122, 125. [OF]

coup(p)e *n.*[2] basket 3.176, 177,
187; **coppe** 3.190, 191. *pl.*
coupen 3.174. [cf. MDu *cūpe*
prob. from L *cūpa*]

coupe *v.* pay for 4.227. [ON
kaupa buy]

court *n.* (royal) court 2.10, 120,
11.11. *pl.* **courtes** courts (of
law) 11.90. [OF]

courtyn *n.* curtain 3.276. [OF
courtine]

couþe, covþe. See **conne.**

coueitous *adj.* greedy 3.100. [OF]

couertoure *n.* coverlet, quilt 2.
267, 276. [OF *coverto(u)r*]

coward *n.* coward 3.14. [OF
couard]

cowþe. See **conne.**

craft *n.* skill, art 8E.65; magic
art, sorcery 12.184. *pl.* **craftes**
accomplishments 1.376, 457;
crafftes devices, tricks 6.190;
cræftes 16.89. [OE *cræft*]

crafty *adj.* as *n. pl.* skilful (men)
14.86. [OE *cræftig*]

crake; crape. See **krake(n);**
crepen.

craue *v.* ask, beg 6.352. [OE
crafian demand]

crede *n.* the Creed 6.209, 12.61,
15.71. [OE *crēda* from L *crēdo*]

crei *n.* crowing, croaking 1.251.
[cf. MDu(*ge*)*crei* crying, *craeyen*
to crow]

crempe *v.* check, stop 1.746.
[cf. MDu *krempen* restrain]

GLOSSARY

crepen *v.* creep 12.80. *imper. sg.*
creop 18.400. *pa. t. subj. sg.*
crape 16.90o. *pp.* icrope 5.28.
[OE *crēopan,* pp. *gecropen;* pa. t.
re-formed on cl. V]
cry *n.* exclamation 2.19. [OF *cri*]
cri *v. intr.* cry out, call (*on*) 14.
267. *pr. 1 sg.* crie (*to*) 8T.5.
subj. sg. crye shout 8N.33. *tr.,*
pr. pl. crieȝ (= *-þ*) beg (someone, dat.) for 3.263. [OF *crier*]
cribbe *n.* crib, manger 13.52.
[OE *crib*]
crisolite *n.* chrysolite, a green
gem 9.93. [OF]
cristal(e) *n.* crystal 3.34, 8K.30,
9.68. [OF *cristal*]
Cristen(e), Cristine *adj.* Christian 10.152, 12.39, 16.92, 5.120.
gen. Cristenes 16.103. [OE
cristen]
Cristendom *n.* Christianity 17.
236; Crisstenndom 13.279,
(with def. art.) 217. [OE
cristendōm]
Cristen(e)man *n.* Christian 17.
76, 117, Cristeman 119. *gen.*
Cristenemannes 17.49. *dat.*
Cristenemanne 17. 57, 76.
[Cristen(e)+man]
Cristesmasse *n.* Christmas 1.
339; -mæsse 16.2; -messe 16.
40, 62. [OE *Cristes mæsse;* see
masse]
croked(e) *adj.* crooked 1.80;
bent, deformed 8N.20. [OE *ge-*
crōcod from ON *krók-r*]
croos *n. pl.* water-pots 17.98.
[OE *crōh*]
croppe *n.* top (of a tree) 14.206.
[OE *croppa*]
croun(e) *n.* (top of the) head 4.
168, 274 (see to n.), crune 241;
tonsure 6.348. [AN *cor(o)une*]
crouþ *n.* fiddle 8K.43. [W
crwth]
crowe *n. pl.* crows 1.220. [OE
crāwe, pl. *crāwan*]
croweþ *pr. 3 sg.* sounds harshly
1.251. [OE *crāwan*]

crucethur *n.* 'torturer', torture-
box 16.171. [app. from L.
crūciātor; see note]
crucifix *n.* crucifix 18.535. [AN,
and ML *crucifixus*]
crune. See croun(e).
cruneð *pr. 3 sg.* crowns 18.519,
19.55. *pp.* icrunet 18.521.
[AN *coruner*]
cu. See kou.
cuccu *n.* cuckoo 8A.2, 5. [OF *cucu*]
cucubes *n. pl.* cubebs, a kind of
spicy berries 9.78. [OF from
Arab]
cuggel *n.* cudgel 18.396. [OE
cycgel]
cume *n.* coming 19.72; kume
1.314, 587, 10.75. [OE *cyme,*
vowel infl. by *cuman*] See
come, com.
cum(m)en; cun; cunde. See
com; kinn; kinde.
cundut *n.* part-song, carol 1.341.
[AN, = OF *condut* from ML
conductus motet]
cunebearn *n.* prince 7.introd.
[OE *cynebéarn*]
cunestable. See constable.
cunfessurs *n. pl. gen.* confessors
(witnesses to the faith who do not
suffer martyrdom) 19.299. [AN]
cunne(n); cunne(s); cunreadnes; cunsayle. See conne;
kinn; kunrede; conseil.
cuntek *n.* strife, violence 2.115.
[AN] Cf. conteckeden.
cuntesse *n.* countess 16.261.
[AN]
cur-dogge *n.* cur 18.370. [cf.
Scand dial. *kurre*+dogge]
curs *n.* course: *in ~* in the usual
order, in fashion 14.51. [OF]
curseð *pr. 3 sg.* curses 19.126.
pa. t. sg. cursede 5.259; excommunicated 16.266. *pl.* 16.
198. *pp. adj.* corsede accursed
7.282. [OE *cursian,* origin ob-
scure] Cf. kors.
curteis *adj.* well-bred, consider-
ate 6.119, 341. [AN]

curteisi *n.* graciousness, kind disposition 6.110. [AN *curteisie*]

curtel *n.* (woman's) gown 8G.54. [OE *cyrtel*]

curtiler *n.* gardener 5.272. [AN]

cusen ; cusse. See **cheosen ; kis(se).**

cussing *n.* kissing 3.251. [from OE *cyssan*; see **kis(se)**]

custe *n. pl. (dat.)* qualities, character 1.9. [OE *cyst*, pl. *cysta*]

custe. See **kis(se).**

custome *n.* custom, practice 17. 101. [OF *custume*]

cuþ, cuð *adj.* known 16.47, 18. 234; well-known, renowned 9. 107; **cuuþ** 1.554. [OE *cūþ* pp. of *cunnan*; see **conne**]

cuþ, cuþest, cuðen ; cuþe, cuthe ; cuðe. See **kyþe ; conne ; kyþe, conne.**

cuuenable *adj.* appropriate 17. 40. [AN variant of *convenable*]

cuuent *n.* community 18.228, 233. [AN]

cuen. See **quen(e).**

cwaer *n.* small book 18.132, 308. [OF *quaer*]

cwakien *v.* tremble 19.365; **quakien** 10.46. *pr. 1 sg.* **cwakie** 19.148. [OE *cwacian*]

cwaþ, cwað. See **quaþ.**

cwemen *v.* please 19.22; **queme** 1.165. *pr. 3 sg.* **quemeð** 12.84. *pa. t. pl.* **cwemmdenn** 13.286. *pp.* **icwemet** 19.354. [OE *cwēman*] Cf. **icweme(n).**

cwen ; cwic(liche). See **quen(e) ; quic ; quiclich.**

dædes ; dær ; dære ; dærnelike. See **ded(e) ; der ; dere** *adj.*; **dernelich(e).**

dai(e), day(e) *n.* day 1.195, 480, 2.1 (see **on**), 316, 3.20, 4.89, 7.65, 8L.10, 12.99, 17.38; **dæi** 10.7, 16.120; **daȝȝ** 13.207; **dei** 16.119, 18.311; **deai** 17.197. daylight 4.79, 9.26; lifetime 16.6, 314; appointed time 8D.26, G.22. *al* ~ always 18.559; *bi, in* ~ by day 3.11, 8E.22, (tag) to see 8K.37; *to þis* ~ until now 4.72; (adv.) ~ *and nyht* 8L.18, 9.100, with neg. ~ *no niȝt* 9.81; see **niȝt(e)**. *gen.* **daies, dayes, -is** 8L.2, N.16, T.3, (adv.) **dæies** 16.81, *be* ~ 16.162; **deies** in ~ *ant nihtes* day and night 18.249. *pl.* **daies, dayes** 5.48, 17.72, 4.133; **daiis** 6.324; **dæis** 16. 205; **dagas** 16.25; **dahes** 18. 555. *dat.* **daghen** days, time, in *be þa* ~ in those days 17.235; **daȝen** 10.224, 305; **dawe** life, see **bryng(e).** [OE *dæg*, pl. *dagas*]

dailiȝt *n.* daylight 1.248; **dæi-liht** 10.203. [prec.+**liȝt(e)**]

dairim *n.* daybreak 1.244. [OE *dæg-rima*]

daisterre *n.* day-star 1.244. [OE *dæg-steorra*]

dale *n.* valley 1.1, 14.115, 280. *pl.* **dales** 2.91, 324. [OE *dæl*]

dame *n.* (as title) dame, lady 2.135, 6.154, 420; (as address) madam 2.303, 6.37, 61, 18.491 (see **ma dame**); mother 15.3; mistress of a house, housewife 8N.30. [OF]

dameisele *n.* young unmarried woman (of good birth), girl; (as address) 3.227; **damishel** 15.1. [AN *dameisele*]

danger *n.* difficulty, trouble 9.169; **daunger** 3.56 (note). [OF *dangier*, AN *daunger*]

dar *pr. 3 sg.* dare(s) 8G.43. *2 sg.* **darst** 1.513, 653. *subj. sg.* **durre** 1.664. *pa. t. sg.* **dorste** 7.134, 17.94; **durste** 16.128. *pl.* **dorsten** 7.168; **dursten** 4. 293. [OE *dearr, durron*; *dorste*]

dare *pr. 1 sg.* lie dazed 8K.78. [OE *darian*]

daþeit, daþeyt *interj.* a curse on! 4.192, 226, 314. [from OF *dahait, dehait* God's displeasure]

daunger ; dawe. See **danger ; dai(e).**

daweyng *n.* daybreak 2.326. [cf. OE *dagung*]

dawes *pr. 3 sg.* (impers., subject *hit*) dawns 8H.I. *subj. sg.* **dawe** (of day) 8N.40. [OE *dagian*]

dead(e). See **ded** *adj.*

deadbote *n.* penance 19.85. [OE *dǣdbōt*]

deadliche *adj.* deadly, mortal (of sin) 18.122, 564; **diadlich(e)** 17.168, 263; subject to death 17.45. [OE *dēadlic*]

deai. See **dai(e).**

deale *interj.* (of surprise, incredulity, &c.) what! 18.348 (note). [cf. OF *dea* and OE *lā*]

deale(n) *v.* divide, separate 18.638, share 130; **dele** deal, behave 8K.76. *pa. t. subj. sg.* **dealde** (*of*) shared (in) 18.129. [OE *dǣlan*]

dearne ; dearnliche ; deað. See **dern(e)** *adj.*; **dernelich(e) ; deþ(e).**

deaðlich *adj.* deathly (pale) 19.66. [OE *dēaþlic*]

deboneirté *n.* gentleness, graciousness 18.489. [OF *debonaireté*]

debrusede *pa. t. sg. intr.* was dashed to pieces 11.46. [ONF *debrusier* break to pieces]

deciples *n. pl.* disciples 17.90, 18.137. [OF *deciple*]

ded *n.* death 12.170, 14.57, 261, 15.52. [variant, usu. northerly, of **deþ(e)**]

ded *adj.* dead 1.690, 5.149, 6.309, 10.163, 11.144; **dead** 18.498; **dedh** 15.43; *art* ~ shall die, *was* ~ died 4.200, 257, 14.278; *worht, worþe* ~ shall die, *warth, wærd* ~ died 3.75, 5.191, 16.124, 305. as *n. pl.* **deade** dead men 18.484. [OE *dēad*]

ded(e) *n.* deed, action, thing done 1.188 (? *pl.*), 454, 5.223, 6.41, 7.38, 122, 14.68 (? *pl.*), 18.292.

811493 L l

pl. **dedes, -is** 6.190, 7.60, 14.41; **dædes** 16.200; **deden** 17.121. *dat.* **dede** 1.721. [OE *dǣd*, A *dēd*, pl. *-a*, *-e*]

dede(n). See **do(n).**

dedute *n.* pleasure, enjoyment 9.50. [OF]

def *adj.* deaf 8N.34. [OE *dēaf*]

defaute *n.* lack 11.40. [OF]

defende *v.* defend, protect 11.33. *pr. 3 sg.* **defendet** 17.59. *pa. t. pl.* **defendede** 11.39. [OF *defendre*]

defouli *v.* trample under foot, crush 11.154. *pa. t. pl.* **defoulede** 11.19. [OF *defouler*]

dehtren ; dei. See **dohter ; dai(e).**

dei(e), deye *v.* die 7.88, 14.163, 3.266, 4.108. *pr. 1 sg.* **deȝe** 8D.26, E.29, L.15. *pa. t. sg.* **deide** 7.6, 281, 11.46. *pl.* **deiden** 19.300. [ON *deyja*]

deis, deys *n.* dais 11.15; a seat on this, throne 2.27. [OF *deis*]

del *n.*[1] lament, mourning, in *mak* ~ lament 6.344; sorrow, grief (*of*, over) 6.356; **deol(e)** 7.265, 11.42; a grievous thing, a pity 7.52; **dole** sorrow 15.42; **duel** 8E.24. [OF *duel, deul, del, dol*]

del(e) *n.*[2] part, in phr. *il(k)* ~ every bit, all 4.86, 14.228 (see **ilk(e)**[2]). [OE *dǣl*]

del ; dele. See **deuel ; deale(n).**

delitouse *adj.* charming 2.288. [OF *delitous*]

deliueri *v.* release, set free 11.148. *pr. subj. sg.* **deliuri** 17.170. [OF *delivrer*]

delue(n) *v.* dig 7.81, 117. *pa. t. subj. sg.* **dulue** 18.416. *pp.* **doluen** buried 14.279. [OE *delfan, dulfe, dolfen*]

demayne *n.* possession 2.110. [OF *demaine*]

deme *n.* judge 1.741, 18.338, 19.54. [OE *dēma*]

deme(n) *v. intr.* judge, give a

verdict 1.705; speak, talk (*of*)
10.126. *tr.* judge (a person)
1.157, 735, 19.293; consider,
deem 18.389, 19.209, 214, 219;
pronounce 1.166, 713, *riȝt, riht*
~ give just judgement 1.144,
19.213; decree 19.414 assign
19.55; *for deþ þat me demeþ* of
the death to which she condemns
me 8E.29. *pr. 1 sg.* deme, demi
19.214, 222, 209. *3 sg.* demeþ,
-ð 1.713, 19.55, 414; demþ
1.735. *subj. sg.* deme 1.157.
pl. demen 19.216. *imper. sg.*
dem 18.389. [OE *dēman*]
demeori *imper. pl.* stay, delay
18.21. [OF *demuer-*, accented
stem of *demorer*]
deoflen, -s; deol(e); deop;
deore(-). See deuel; del *n.*[1];
depe; dere(-).
deoren *n.* female animal 10.38.
[OE *dēor* + fem. suff. *-en*; see der]
deorly *adv.* heartily 8N.29. [OE
dēorlīce]
deorling *n.* dear friend 10.176.
[OE *dēorling*]
deorre; deouel, deoules. See
dere *adj.*; deuel.
depart Dieux *interj.* in God's
name 2.205. [OF *de par dieux*
by God]
departunge *n.* departure 18.145.
[from OF *departir*]
depe *adj.* deep 5.109, 8w.36;
deop 7.100, 18.89, 19.94. *comp.*
deopre 19.333. [OE *dēop*]
depeint *pp.* painted 18.588.
[OF, pp. of *depeindre*]
De profundis *n.* Psalm 130, one
of the seven 'penitential psalms'
15.75. [opening words]
der *n.* creature 12.98; dær
animal, beast (*dat.*) 16.129; dor
1.591. *pl.* dueres 8H.2 [OE *dēor*,
sg. and pl.]
dere *n.* dearth, scarcity 4.92, 109.
[from next]
dere *adj.* dear, beloved 4.107;
deore 18.35, 137, (with dat.)

10.299; precious 10.30, 19.163;
dære expensive 16.187. *comp.*
deorre 18.528, in *beo on hire þe*
~ have a higher regard for her
18.390. [OE *dēore*, comp. *dēorra*]
dere *adv.* dear, dearly 8R.6, x.16;
deore 18.392, 527. [OE *dēore*]
dere *v.* harm, injure 4.74. *pr.*
subj. sg. derie 12.80. [OE
derian]
dereworþe *adj.* precious, excellent 8K.37; deorewurðe 18.147,
201, 19.169, 230, beloved 19.
277. [OE *dēorwýrþe*]
dereworþliche *adv.* affection-
ately 8K.76. [OE *dēorwurþlīce*]
derf *n.* suffering 18.419. [OE
ge-deorf, prob. infl. by ON*derf,
OI *djarf-r* severe] Cf. derue.
derfald *n.* deer park 16.54. [OA
dēorfáld]
derie. See dere *v.*
dern(e) *adj.* secret, hidden 6.
130, 7.81, 19.333, innate (but
not apparent) 12.38; dearne
18.158. as *n.* dark 1.388. [OA
dérne]
derne *adv.* secretly 8G.43.
[prec.]
dernelich(e) *adv.* secretly 3.290,
7.203; dernelike 6.86; dærnelike 13.56; dearnliche 18.42.
[OA *dernlīce*]
derue *adj.* confident 12.98. [ON
derf-, OI *djarf-r*]. Cf. derf.
derueð *pr. 3 sg.* harasses, torments 19.117. *pl.* 19.103. [OA
derfan = WS *dyrfan*]
descumfit *pp.* defeated 18.164.
[AN, pp. of *descumfir*]
desire *n.* desire 2.270. [OF
desir]
desireþ *pr. 3 sg.* desires (to
know) 2.142, wishes 144. [OF
desirer]
desmaid *pp. adj.* in despair 3.
158. [prob. AN *desmaier*, cf.
OF *esmaier* perturb]
despyt *n.* injury, outrage 2.62.
[OF *despit*]

dest. See do(n).

destruet *pp.* laid waste 18.475.
[OF *destruire*]

deþ(e), deðe, deth *n.* death 3.
78, 160, 8D.25, E.24, L.1, 9.28,
11.42, 10.245, 7.68; **deȝ** (= -þ)
3.200; **deaðe** 18.16, 501, 19.
31; **diath, diaþe** 17.45, 259.
þe ~ 3.148, 8L.20. *gen.* **deaðes**
19.145, D- 70, mortal 18.496.
pl. **deaðes** 19. 135. [OE *dēaþ*]
See **ded** *n.*

deuel *n.* devil 5.104, 18.396; (the)
Devil 5.282, 12.183, 17.166; **del**
8N.34; **deouel** 18.41, 556, 19.
125; **dieule** 17.67. *gen.* **deueles**
12.193, 17.222; **deofles** 18.120,
157. *pl.* **deoflen** 18.505, 19.79;
deoules 16.160. [OE *dēofol*,
pl. *dēofol, dēoflu*]

deuotiun *n.* feeling of devotion
18.356. [AN *devociun*]

diadlich(e); diath, diaþe. See
deadliche; deþ(e).

dich(e) *n.* ditch 7.282; moat
18.87. [OE *dīc*]

dide(n); dieule. See **do(n);
deuel.**

diȝele *adj.* hidden, secluded 1.2.
[OE *dīegol*]

diht *pr. 3 sg.* prepares, composes
1.714; ~ *al to wundre* brings to
ruin 19.11 (see **wonder**); **dihteð**
arranges 19.413. *pa. t. sg.* **dihte**
tuned 1.613. *pp.* **diȝt, diht:**
ase capoun ~ castrated 3.12; *to
deþe* ~ condemned to death
8D.25; **idiȝt** dressed 9.106;
idihte arrayed 10.315. [OE
dihtan arrange]

dillen *pr. subj. pl.* should be
sluggish 12.140. [from OE
*dylle adj., rel. to *dol* stupid]

dim(me) *adj.* dim, clouded
12.8; dark 12.196. [OE *dimm*]

dine *n.* din, clamour 4.287.
[OE *dyne*]

dint *n.* blow 4.234; **dunt** 18.330.
pl. **dintes** 4.289, 5.295; **duntes**
19.142. [OE *dynt*]

dishes *n. pl.* dishes 4.185. [OE
disc]

dissaite *n.* deceitfulness, 2.254.
[AN *deceite*]

diuers(e) *adj.* different, various
7.181, 17.242. [OF *divers*]

diueð *pr. 3 sg.* dives 12.181.
[OE *dȳfan* dip]

do(n) *v.* 1.115, 356, 2.154, 3.176,
5.46, 229, 6.32, 365, 18.107,
19.213. (1) do, perform, commit 1.174, 2.52, 3.26, 4.186,
18.425; give 6.322; practise
7.31; ~ *go(e)d* do good (to),
benefit 1.245, 2.309, 5.46; ~ *her
play* take their pleasure 2.278;
warde ~ keep watch 11.110; *pp.*
made: *wel idone* 10.122, finished
8R.3, *of me idon hit hiis* it's all
up with me 5.106. (2) *intr.* act
1.289, 2.112, 6.35, 7.231, 10.
282, 16.14; *bi ham idon* behaved
towards them 19.338. (3) put,
place, set 3.176, 9.174, 13.261,
16.152, 17.137, 18.144; apply,
devote 13.205, 18.547; ~ *forþ*
put out 17.109; ~ *of* take off
2.210; ~ *on* put on 2.25, 4.127;
up ido laid up, put away 7.189;
~ *way* see **way**; ~ *of liue, lifdaȝe*
kill 2.151, 4.232, 10.170, 284 (cf.
bryng(e)); *refl.* betake oneself,
go 2.120, 9.153, 18.167, proceed
9.158, *deð him o fluhte* runs
away 18.111, *dude him i* entered
18.508. (4) cause, occasion
(with n. obj.) 5.67, 8M.4; make,
have (with obj.+infin.) 1.674,
2.237, 12.180, 14.191, ~ *to witte*
let (one) know 9.101, sim. ~ *to
understandene* 16.12; (with *þat*
clause) 1.356; (fold. by infin.
without expressed subject, corresp. to mod. passive constr.)
~ *me crempe* have me stopped
1.746, sim. 2.291, 312, 4.28,
267, 5.251, 17.16, *I do þe lete
blod* I will have you bled 5.51
(note); (with pp.) 17.130. (5) representing another verb: 1.112,

699, 2.301, 3.236, 5.68, 15.20, 16.123, 18.418, 462, 19.208. (6) *auxil.* forming periphrastic tense with infin. 7.87. (7) intensifying imper. 8G.38. *infl. infin.* to done 2.147, 5.236, 7.103, 17. 170; to donne 18.508, *hwet us beo* ~ what we should do 19.161. *pr. 1 sg.* do 1.245, 5.44, 17.200. *2 sg.* dest 1.49, 5.33, 18.425; dost 1.307, 6.377, 7.87; deost 2.301; (with suffixed pron.) dostu 1.174, 289. *3 sg.* deþ, deð 1.372, 8M.4, 10.254, 18.111; doþ, doð, doth 1.112, 8E.22, 17.158, 12.98, 16.43, 4.267; dos 4.340, 14.70, 15.20. *pl.* don(e) 2.120, 4.265; doþ, doð, doth 1.113, 5.217, 17.109, 18.61, 7. 98, 164. *subj. sg.* do 5.50, 6.398, 17.137. *pl.* do 17.265, (before *we*) 1.739, 12.98; don 18.81. *imper. sg.* do 1.746, 2.195, 8G.38, L.9. *pl.* doþ 17.96. *pa. t. sg.* did(e) 4.127, 14.191, 16.12; dede 3.180, 4.28, 5.67, 17.16; dude 2.25, 7.177, 10.211, 11. 106, 18.127. *pl.* dide(n) 4.342, 16.84; deden 17.215; dude(n) 2.112, 7.273, 11.52. *subj. sg.* dude 2.309, 6.172, 18.306. *pp.* do 2.52, 3.26, 4.232, 5.68; don 5.39, 6.226, 13.261, 14.281; ido 5.222, 7.92, 10.60, 11.4, 19.60; idon, y- 5.106, 6.323, 7.280, 18.454, 8R.3; *pl.* idone 10.101, 122. [OE *dōn*; *dyde, dede*; see Campbell, *OE Grammar* p. 348]
dogge *n.* dog 18.364, *attrib.* 396. *pl.* dogges 4.266, doges 310. [OE *docga*]
dogge-fahenunge *n.* doglike fawning 18.385. [prec.+vbl. n. from OE *fagnian*]
dohter *n.* daughter 16.5, 38, 18.286; douʒtter 2.152, 287; douter 6.339. *pl.* dehtren 19.39, 220; douʒtrene 7.4. [OE *dohtor*, dat. *dehter*, pl. *dohtru*]

doyng *n.* affair, course of action 2.166. [from do(n)]
dole; doluen. See del *n.*[1]; delue(n).
dom(e) *n.* judgement 1.149, 166, 12.99, 18.17, 19.225; trial 1.135; sentence 19.56, 395. *gen.* domes 1.653, 10.107. *pl.* domes 19.333. [OE *dōm*]
-dom *suff.* forming nouns, as Cristen-, fals-, swike-, wrecche-. [OE *-dōm*]
Domesdai, -day, -dei *n.* the Day of Judgement 4.16, 12.109, 17.171, 18.17. [OE *dōmes dæg*]
don; don(e), doost; dor. See doun(e); do(n); der.
dorc *adj.* dark 19.147. [OE *de(o)rc* perh. infl. by dosc; see *Iuliene* pp. 147–8]
dore *n.* door 4.204, 5.27, 8R.7; 15.10. *pl.* doren openings (in a hedge) 8N.14. [OE *duru*, pl. *dura*, and *dor*, pl. *doru*]
dore-tre *n.* bar of a door 4.233. [prec.+tre(e)]
dorste(n). See dar.
dosc *adj.* dark in colour 19.260. [cf. OE *dox*]
dosils *n. pl.* plugs, spigots 11. 169. [OF *dosil*]
dou *n.* dough 5.256. [OE *dāh*, *dāg*-]
douʒtter; doumb. See dohter; dumb.
doun(e) *adv.* down 2.114, 3.27, 4.167, 7.145; dun(e) 4.138, 242, 9.140, 12.21; don 14.63, 17.147. phr. *vp and* ~ see up. [see adoun]
doune *n.* hill 2.91, 7.248; dune 10.37; hillside 1.551. *pl.* dounes 8H.2; douns 2.324; dunen 10. 187. [OE *dūn*]
doute *n.* fear 8N.4. [OF]
doute *v.* fear 14.198. *pr. 3 sg.* duteð 18.59. *imper. pl. refl.* doute 3.269. [OF (*se*) *douter*]
douter. See dohter.

douthe *pa. t. sg.* was of value, was good 4.101. [OE *dohte* pa. t. of **dugan*]

dragen *v.* 12.190; drahen 19. 81; dreaien 19.231. *tr.* draw, pull, drag 3.276, 4.4, 7.282, 12.190, (without obj.) 5.277; bring 16.43; attach 11.74, 85; (of a table) clear 2.317. *refl.* make one's way, move, go 7.163, 11.12, 14.28; conform (to) 1. 209. *intr.* move, go 8E.24 (note), 11.82, 107, 12.151, 14.45; ~ *to* follow 7.12. *pr. 1 sg.* draʒe 1.209; dreyʒe 8E.24. *3 sg.* dragaðʒ 16.44; draghus 14.28; drawes 14.45. *pl.* dragen 12. 151, 174, 16.43; draheðʒ 18.60. *pa. t. sg.* drouʒ, drovʒ, drowʒ 7.12, 163, 282, 3.276; drou, drow 4.4, 5.277, 11.12, 82, 4.221. *pl.* drowe(n) 4.264, 11.98. *pp.* drawe(n) 11.13, 4.229, 196; ydrawe 2.317. [OE *dragan*; *drōg, drōh, drōgon*; *dragen*; on *dreaien* see *Iuliene* p. 245]

drahen. See dragen.

drake *n. gen.* dragon's 18.84. *pl.* draken 19.104. [OE *draca*]

drane *n.* drone 16.42. [OE *drān*]

drapen ; drawes, dreaien. See drepen ; dragen.

drecheðʒ *pr. 3 sg.* remains, stays 12.51. *pl.* afflict, torment 19. 103. [OE *dreccan* vex]

dred *pp. adj.* afraid 6.409. [see adrad(de) and dreden]

drede *n.* fear 1.430, 3.195, 5.89; concern, anxiety 4.96; dret 19.56. [from next]

dreden *v.* (1) dread, fear (with *for*, on account of) 19.188, 194. *pr. 1 sg.* drede (with infin.) 3.160, (with direct obj.) 19.195. *pl.* (before *we*) 19.176. (2) frighten: *pr. 3 sg.* dret 17.151. [LOE *drǣdan*, cf. *a-*, *on-drǣdan*, *-drēdan*]

dredfule *adj.* full of fear, fearsome 18.38, 44. [from drede]

drehen *v.* suffer, endure 19.120, lead (life) 429; drei 14.164; driʒe 10.50; drye 8w.45. *pr. 3 sg.* dreheðʒ 19.189. [OE *drēogan*]

dreyʒe. See dragen.

dreynt *pp.* drowned 8N.31. [OE *drenct* pp. of *drencan*]

dreme *n.* sound 1.230; dreim 1.21. [OE *drēam*]

drenchen *n. pl.* drinks 10.310. [OE *drenc*, pl. *-as*] Cf. drink(e).

dreorinesses *n. pl.* sorrows, woes 19.148. [OE *drēorignes(se)*]

drepen *v.* kill 4.210, 292. *pr. 3 sg.* drepeðʒ 12.182. *pa. t. pl.* drapen 16.170, 179. [OE *drepan* strike, pa. t. pl. *drǣpon*; cf. ON *drepa, drápu*]

drery *adj.* sad (see mod(e)) 8L.5. [OE *drēorig*] Cf. next.

drerimod *adj.* sad at heart 6.149. [OE *drēorigmōd*] See mod(e).

dret. See drede ; dreden.

dri *adj.* dry, dried up 14.188. [OE *drȳge*]

drye, driʒe. See drehen.

Drihten *n.* Lord 10.38, 16.227; (without art. or pron.) the Lord, God 10.93; Drihte 10.56; Driʒtte 6.408; Drihtin, Dryhtin 16.232, 229; Drihhtin 13. 226, *attrib.* 125, *dat.* 106, 109; Driʒtin 12.67; Driʒhtin 14. 165. *gen.* Drihtenes 10.111; Drihtines in *for ure* ~ *luue* because of his love for our Lord 16.228. [OE *dryhten, -in* by infl. of *ælmihtig*; see *Iuliene* p. 148]

drink(e) *n.* drink, something to drink 5.143, 6.133, 7.250, 9.17. [from next] Cf. drunch(e).

drink, drinke(n), drynke *v.* drink 9.144, 4.68, 5.79; give drink (to) 8N.29. *pr. 3 sg.* drynkes 8M.4. *pl.* drinken 12. 179; drinkeþ 17.118; drinked 17.126. *pa. t. sg.* dronk 5.93.

pp. idrunke 17.105; as *adj.*
dronke drunk 8N.31. [OE
drincan, dronc, druncen]
dritte *n.* dung 9.179. [ON *drit*]
driue(n) *v. tr.* drive 11.84; *intr.*
rush, dash 10.41. *pr. pl. tr.*
driueþ 1.66. *pa. t. sg.* drof *tr.*
11.172; *intr.* 4.220, 299. [OE
drīfan, drāf]
dronk(e). See drink.
dros *n.* dross 18.328. [OE *drōs*]
drou(ʒ), drovʒ; droupne. See
draʒen; drupnin.
droui *adj.* turbid, troubled 12.
165. [OE *drōfig*]
drow, drowe(n), drowʒ;
druerie. See draʒen; druri.
drunch(e) *n.* drink 5.14, 18.307.
[OE *drync*] Cf. drink(e).
drupnin *v.* be downcast 19.249.
pr. 1 sg. droupne languish
8K.78. [ON *drúpa* with *n*- suff.]
druri *n.* love 3.272; druerie
love-token 18.145. [OF *druerie*]
dude(n); duel; dueres. See
do(n); del *n.*[1]; der.
duʒeðe *n.* (company of) nobles,
courtiers, knights 10.7, 110.
[OE *duguþ*]
duk *n.* duke 2.11, 57. [OF *duc*]
dulue. See delue(n).
dumb(e) *adj.* dumb 1.294, 18.
168; doumb 7.142. [OE *dúmb*]
dun(e); dune. See doun(e);
doune.
duneward *adv.* down 18.673.
[see adoneward and doun(e)
adv.]
dunnir *n.* thunder 9.39. [OE
þunor with initial cons. altered;
cf. MHG *doner*]
dunt. See dint.
durewart *n.* doorkeeper 19.44.
[OE *duruweard*]
durre, durste(n). See dar.
dust *n.* dust 18.191. [OE *dūst*]
dustlunges *n. pl.* throwings,
flingings 19.143. [from **dustlin*,
frequentative of *dusten* fling,
OE **dystan*; see *Iuliene* p. 149]

dute *n.* pleasure 9.9. [from
dedute]
duteð. See doute *v.*
dutten *v.* close, stop up 8N.14.
pp. hidut 8T.44. [OE *dyttan*]
dwell(e) *v.* stay, delay 4.77, 112,
14.276. [OE *dwellan*]
dweole-song *n.* seductive song
1.558. [OE *ge-dweola* deceit+
song(e)]

e. See þe *art.*
eadi *adj.* devout 18.75; blessed
18.384, 19.274, 303. [OE *ēadig*]
eadmod *adj.* humble 18.303.
[OE *ēadmōd*]
eadmodies *adj.* as *n. gen.* of the
humble man 18.100. [prec.+
OE suff. *-ig*]
eadmodliche *adv.* humbly 18.
283. [OE *ēadmōdlīce*]
eadmodnesse *n.* humility 18.6,
89. [OE *ēadmōdnes(se)*]
eal(-); eald; eanes; eani. See
al, al(le); old(e); enes;
ani.
eape. See ape.
eape-ware *n. pl.* deceptive
goods 18.115. [prec.+ware]
ear. See er(e).
earding-stowe *n.* dwelling-
place 1.28. [cf. OE *éardung-
stōw*]
earen *n. pl.* ears 1.254, 19.58,
112. *sg.* yare 17.268. [OE
ēare, pl. *ēaran*]
earmes. See arm.
earmlice *adv.* miserably, con-
temptibly 16.39. [OE *earmlīce*]
Cf. arme.
earre *adj. comp.* former, before-
mentioned 18.56, 428; earlier
19.117. *sup.* earst first 18.579,
19.40; *on ~* in the first place
18.123. [OE *ǣrra, ǣrest(a)*; see
er(e) adv.]
earst. See er(e) *adv.*
earþon *adv.* beforehand 19.84.
[OE *ǣr þon*; see er(e) prep.]

earueð *adj.* difficult 18.194.
[OE *earfoþe*]

easki. See aske.

east *adv.* east 1.555, 16.93. [OE
ēast] See est, est(e).

Eastren *n.* Easter 16.60, 75;
Estren 16.226. [OE *Ēastran*
pl.]

eaðe; eauer(-), eauereuch;
eauereuchan. See eþe;
euer(-); euerich(e); euerechon.

eauerȝete *adv.* ever up to this
time 19.113. [euer(e)+ȝet(e)]

eauroskes *n. pl.* water-frogs 19.
111. [OE *ēa+frosc*]

eawles. See owel.

eawt *n.* anything 18.441. [OM
ǣwiht; cf. oȝt]

ec(k). See ek(e).

ech(e) *adj.* each, every 1.151,
231, 7.12, 36, 146; euch(e) 5.
101, 9.121, 18.88, 168, 19.18,
162, ~ *a* 19.315; (after *wiðuten,
buten*) any 19.326, 378; vch(e)
8E.8, K.69, ~ *a(n)*F.34, H.29; ælc
10.254, 16.90; ælche 10.150,
155. *dat. fem.* ælchere 10.253.
pron. euch everyone 18.189;
ælc 10.283. [OE *ælc, ylc*, M
oeghwelc]

eche *adj.* eternal, everlasting
1.488, 13.287, 19.246. [OE *ēce*]

eche(n) *v.* increase 8M.11, 19.
108. [OA *ēc(e)an*]

echnesse *n.* eternity: *on* ~ for
ever 19.123. [OE *ēcnes(se)*]

echon(e) *pron.* each one (person
or thing), everyone, all 3.42,
7.148, 233, 11.6, 49; euchan
18.20, 195, 19.56 (*dat.*), 348.
gen. euchanes 18.206, 19.283.
[OE *ælc ān*; see ech(e),
on(e)]

ed(-). See at; as pref., M *et* confused with *ed*-, see atwite.

eddre-blod *n.* blood in the veins
5.45. [OE *ǣd(d)re+blod(e)*]

ede. See eode.

edfleon *v.* escape 18.492. *pr. 3 sg.*

atfliþ runs away, fails 1.37.
[OE *æt-, *et-flēon*, 3 sg. *-flī(h)þ*;
see fle(n)]

edhalt. See atholde.

edlutien *v.* hide oneself 18.649.
[cf. OE *ætlūtian*]

edstonden; edwiteð. See
atstonde(n); atwite.

efficaces *n. pl.* efficacies, powers
18.98. [OF]

efftsones *adv.* immediately 6.
384; efsones 16.282. [OE *eft
sōna*+adv. *-es*]

efne *adj.* unmoved, calm 19.395.
[OE *efen*]

efne; efsones. See euene,
heuen(e); efftsones.

eft *adv.* again 1.594, 14.197, 19.
105; æft 10.62; back 14.196;
then 18.86, 533; *euer* ~ ever
since 7.215. [OE *eft*]

efter(-); egen. See after(-);
eȝe.

egre *adj.* eager 5.289. [OF]

eȝe *n.* eye 1.304; ehe 18.133;
eye 4.239; he 14.210. *pl.* eȝe
1.100; eye 8K.17; eiȝe 7.275;
egen 12.8, eien, eyen 6.281,
8R.2; eyȝen 8E.16; eȝene 1.75;
eȝhne 13.146; eȝenen 8G.24;
ehnen 18.126, 372, 19.57, 100;
heȝe 8G.25; heien 6.357. [OE
ē(a)ge, pl. *ē(a)gan*]

ehlid *n.* eyelid 19.362. [stem of
prec.+OE *hlid*]

ehsihðe *n.* sight, eyes 18.486.
[as prec.+OE *(ge)sihþ*; see
siȝt(e)]

ei *interj.* oh, alas 8B.5. [cf. L *ei*,
OF *ahi*]

ei *adj.* any 19.153. [contr. from
OE *ǣnig*; see *Iuliene* p. 151]

ei *pron.* any, anyone 18.238, 242,
19.47. [as prec.]

eie, eye *n.* fear, terror 3.45, 19.
25; *for no loue ne for non* ~ whatever happens 3.235, cf. fere *n.*[2];
æie 16.128. [OE *ege*]

eye, eien, eiȝe, eyȝen. See eȝe.

eiȝte *adj.* eight 7.8. [OE *eahta*]

ei3te. See ahte.
eilin v. intr. cause trouble or annoyance 19.327. pr. 3 sg. tr. eilleþ ails, troubles 6.337. [OE eglian]
eir n. heir 7.3, 18. [AN (h)eir]
eyþer adj. each 8E.18, 34. [see aiþer]
eiðer adv. also 18.391. [prec.; cf. boþ(e)]
eiþer, eiðer pron. See aiþer.
ek(e) adv. also 1.69, 93, 2.139, 3.250, 6.159, 8K.63; ec 8V.21, 13.131, 18.625, 19.73; eck 1.130; heke 8w.9. [OE ē(a)c]
eke n. addition: on ~ in addition, moreover 8E.35. [OE ēaca] Cf. teke.
elde n. age 17.243; old age 12.4, 17.252, 19.431. [OA éldo]
eles n. pl. eels 4.163, 184. [OA ēl]
elheowet adj. of unearthly appearance or colour 19.66. [OE el- strange (cf. el-þēod), hēow, +suff. -ed; see hewe]
elinglich adv. miserably 9.15. [OE ǣlenge tedious+-liche]
elleouene adj. eleven 10.167. [OE endleofon]
elles adv. else, otherwise 1.408, 8E.81, V.8, 18.383, 615; (otiose) 7.284. [OE elles]
elleswer adv. elsewhere, in another place 5.208; elleswhare 10.211. [OE elles hwǣr]
elleshwider adv. in any other direction 19.285. [OE elles hwider]
elne n. ell (45 in.) 8E.52. a nellen for an ellen (attrib.) 14.283. [OE eln]
em. See hi(i).
emeraudes n. pl. emeralds 8E. 66. [OF]
emparour n. emperor 14.4; empereur 18.65. [AN emperēur, obl. case]
emperice n. empress 16.260, 273, (with prefixed art.) þem-

perice 264, 286. [OF emper(er)-is]
enbreuet pp. inscribed, enrolled 19.83. [OF embrever]
enchantement n. magic 3.68. [OF]
encumbrement n. ill-treatment 2.314. [OF]
end(e) n. end 1.701, 4.2, 7.70, 8K.67, 11.107; edge, outskirts 7.74, 11.12, 15.49; boundaries 18.235; quarter 10.157; region, district 19.388; purpose 18.443; death 7.122; hende 8w.58. o nend = on end 14.159, on ~ 6.62, see spel; on ~ at last 18.245, 470, finally 18.501; at þe ~ finished 2.185; ~ of orde from beginning to end 1.743; fram ~ to oþer from end to end 11.166; withute ~ for ever 17.165; al þe ~ every part 19. 132 (note). [OE énde]
endez (= -þ) pr. 3 sg. ends 7.271. pl. endenn 13.221. [OE éndian]
enderdai n. in þis ~ the other day 6.366. [ON endr adv. formerly+dai(e)]
endyng n. end, ending 14.58; endingue death 7.284. [cf. OE éndung]
ene adv. once, ever 7.139. [OE ǣne]
enes adv. once 6.383; eanes 18.279. [prec.+adv. -es]
engel n. angel 18.107, 136; enngell 13.67. pl. engeles 1. 548; engles 19.268; enngless 13.100. gen. englene 18.409. [OE engel] Cf. angel.
Engle n. pl. the English 10. introd. [OE]
Englisch n. English 7.108, 180; Englis 7.180. [OE englisc]
Englische adj. English 18.69; Inglis 14.24. [as prec.]
eni(-). See ani(-).
enmang prep. among: ~ þis meanwhile 16.132. [OE onmáng]

enngell. See **engel.**

enngle-þed *n.* (the company of) angels 13.101. [OE *engla þēod*]

ensample *n.* example 17.38; **essample** illustration 18.337. [OF *essample*, AN also *ensample* with altered pref.]

entente *n.* endeavour 18.165. *pl.* **ententes** intentions 18.427. [OF]

eode *pa. t.* (serving as past of **go(n)**) *sg.* went 7.160, 10.169, 18.669; **ede** 5.69; **ȝeode** 7.144; **ȝode** 14.156; **ȝæde, iæde** 16. 168, 292; **ȝede** 4.33, 89, 17.12; **hede** 5.275, 6.347, 380. *pl.* **ȝeden(n)** 3.243, 13.127; **ieden, yeden** 16.188, 4.155, 17.234; **yede** 17.187. [OE *(ge)ēode*]

eom *n.* (maternal) uncle 16.145. [OE *ēam*]

eorl *n.* earl 10.298, 16.236, 240, 248; count 16.22, 86, 306; noble 10.106, 171; **æorl** 16.253. *gen.* **eorles** 10.298, 16.22, 38; **erles** 4.146; **herles** 4.149. *pl.* **eorles** 16.5, 287. [OE *éorl*, sense infl. by ON *jarl*]

eorneð; eorðe. See **erne; erþe.**

eorðene *adj.* made of earth 18. 475. [OE *eorþen*]

eorðlich; eou. See **erþliche; ȝe(e).**

epetite *n.* a kind of red precious stone 9.94. [L *hēpatītes*]

er *conj.*[1] or 12.62, 118. [reduced from OE *ǣgþer*; cf. **or** conj.[1]]

er *prep.* before 8D.26, G.22; **ar** 6.108. [OE *ǣr*]

er. See **euer(e).**

er(e) *adv.* before 1.526, 7.16, 11.74, 12.85, 19.398; before now, in *lutel* ∼ a short time ago 1.577, 3.257; **her(e)** 16.322 (2); **ear** 18.434, 19.50, first 18.283; **are** 14.162, 266; **ær** (with pa. t., forming pluperf. equivalent) 16.6, 65. *comp.* **erour** before, earlier 5.4; **erur** 1.696; **æror** 16.26; **arre** 8V.24. *sup.* **erest**

first, in *þanne* ∼ then (and not before), only then 1.429; **eroust** sim. in *þo* ∼ 5.16, 124; **earst** 18.467; **ærest** 10.introd. [OE *ǣr, ǣror, ǣrest*, Nb *ār*]

er(e) *conj.*[2] (usu. with subj.) before 3.72, 215, 8D.16, N.40, 12. 91, until 11.161; **ear** 18.175, 263, 572; **ar(e)** 1.360, 519, 2. 185, 6.381, 7.58, 11.100, 14.63, unless 1.438; ∼ *þat* 7.106. *prep.* forming *conj.* in ∼ *þane*, *þen* before 17.148, 8K.74, 18.78. [as prec.; *ar* forms from weak stress or ON *ár* early; and OE *ǣr þǣm, þon (þe)*]

erand *n.* errand, message, business 14.137; **errand** 14.158, 251; **ernde** 8N.22, 18.105; *on* ∼ on business 6.347; **hernde** 6.40, 97, 226; *þis* ∼ on this errand 6.214. [OE *ǣrende*]

erc(h)ebisc(h)op(e). See **ærcebiscop.**

erede *adj.* at a loss 1.563. [OE **ǣrǣde*, from *ǣ-* privative pref.+*rǣd*, see **red(e)** n.]

erede *pa. t. subj. sg.* ploughed 18.417. [OE *erian*]

erles. See **eorl.**

ern *n.* eagle 12.36. *gen.* **ernes** 12.1. [OE *éarn*]

ernde *imper. sg.* obtain by intercession 8w.50. [OE *ǣrendian*]

ernde. See **erand.**

erne *v.* run 3.55, 5.16. *pr. 3 sg.* **eorneð** 18.562. *pr. p.* **ernend** 9.86. *pa. t. sg.* **orn** 10.39, 11. 169. *pl.* **orne** 11.19. [OE *irnan, ýrnan*, M *éornan*; *órn, úrnon*] See **renne.**

erour, eroust; errand; ert. See **er(e); erand; art.**

erþe, erth(e) *n.* earth, the world 2.40, 6.107, 9.22, 13.4, 17.78; **herth** 14.71; **eorðe** 10.231, 18.134, 281, 19.96, ground 10.27; soil, clay (as building material) 4.8, (as cultivated ground) 16.199. *in* ∼ on earth

3.58, 14.175, 17.112, 19.96, 306. [OE *éorþe*]

erþe *v.* stay, dwell 4.7. [OE *éardian*, infl. by **erþe** n.; but see note]

erþliche, erðliche *adj.* earthly, of this world 12.106; material 17.71; **eorðlich** 18.422, 655, 19.95, 276. [OE *eorþlic*]

erur. See **er(e).**

es *pron. 3 pl. acc.* them: (suffixed to prec. verb) **setes** 4.52; (to prec. pron.) **has** = *ha es* 17.76; **his** 17.196. [origin obscure; cf. MDu *si, se*: see *OED* under *His, hise,* and note to 4.52]

es *pr. 1 sg.* am 15.24. *pr. 3 sg.* is 12.76, 14.76, 15.3. [ON *es*] See **be(n)** and other parts.

eschif *adj.* easily frightened, shy 18.29. [OF]

essample. See **ensample.**

est *adj.* east 7.260, 14.115; **æst** 10.157. [as next]

est(e) *n.* east 19.362; *bi ~* (in the) east 8K.42, 11.127, as *prep.* east of 7.247. [OE *éast* adv.; see **east**]

este *n.* pleasure, gratification 19.183, 196. *pl.* **estes** 19.222. [OE *ést*]

Estren. See **Eastren.**

estres *n. pl.* dwellings, courts 2.160, 206. [OF *estre* ('to be' used as n.)]

et, ete(n) *v.* eat 9.56, 4.59, 97, 6.279, 12.91; **æten** 16.244. *pr. 1 sg.* ete 1.378, 4.61. *2 sg.* etes 4.173; (with suffixed pron.) etestu 1.379. *pl.* heten 12.179. *imper. sg.* et 4.191. *pa. t. sg.* et(e) 4.306, 14.232. *pl.* eten 16.243; hete 5.156. *pp.* i-ete 5.98, 169. [OE *etan, ǽt, ǽton, eten*]

et. See **at.**

etlunge *n.* estimate 19.349. [from ON *ætla* think] Cf. **atled.**

etscene *adj.* easily seen, plain,

clear 18.594, 19.269. [OA **ēþ-gesēne* = WS *ȳþgesȳne*]

etstonden. See **atstonde(n).**

eþe *adv.* easily 3.147; well 6.338; **eaðe** readily 18.671. [OE *éaþe*]

eðeliche *adj.* humble 19.218. as *n. pl.* frail, weak 19.178. [OE *éaþelic*]

eðeliche *adv.* easily, readily 18.390. [OE *éaþelīce*]

eþer; eu; euch(e); euchan. See **aiþer; ȝe(e); ech(e); echon(e).**

eue, eve *n.* evening 7.152, 156, 1.239, 41; **euen** 17.183, 188. [OE *ǽfen*, A *ēfen*]

eved. See **heued.**

euel *n.* trouble 17.165; **yfel, yuel** evil, wrongdoing, harm 16.136, 259, 301; **ufel, uuel** 19.199, 221; misfortune 10.63, 18.305; suffering 19.122; disease 18.571. *pl.* **eueles** 17.170; **uueles** 18.519, 19.51. [OE *yfel*]

euel(e) *adj.* bad, evil, 3.179, 17.117; **yuel(e)** 16.160, 204, 301; **vuel(e)** malicious 1.8; wicked 18.254, 19.21; as *n. pl.* **uuele** 18.461, 19.252. [OE *yfel*] See **wors(e).**

euele *adv.* badly, miserably 6.173, 319; **uuele, vuele** 18.430, poorly 11.62, wickedly 1.63. [OE *yfele*] See **wors(e).**

euelike; euen. See **heouenlich(e); eue.**

euene *adv.* evenly, regularly 8E.41; directly, straight 7.114; exactly, just 11.12; **efne** smoothly 1.229. as *prep.* **æfne** with, immediately upon 10.71, 179, 313. [OE *efne, efen*]

euenin *v.* be equal 19.95. [OE *efnian* make equal]

euer(e) *adv.* 1.488, 2.224, 3.60, 4.60, 5.141, 14.84; **eure** 1.249, 12.160; **heuer(e)** 4.98, 15.59; **eauer** 18.74, 183, 19.78, 152; **æu(e)re, æfre** 10.66, 16.182,

250; **er** 8N.17; **hær** 16.285
(?—see note); **auere** 10.212; **ar**
8V.18. (1) always 1.488, 2.303,
3.60, 5.141, 7.32, 8K.34; all the
time 7.135; still 1.736, 8V.18, ~
ȝete 10.322; at any rate 6.261.
(2) ever, at any time 2.224, 4.60,
98, 306, 8E.5, 10.66 (note).
(3) (intensifying) at all, in any
way 3.215, 6.26, 116, 7.65;
added to indef. prons. and advs.
6.361, 18.347, 19.78, see **whose,
wher(e)**; giving indef. sense
with *when* 8N.17; generalizing
rel. clauses, as *al þat ye* ~ *wilen*
everything you wish, no matter
what 4.186, so 18.74 and sim.
6.44, 18.363, 19.327; ~ *se* .. *se*
in proportion as .. so 19.125–6
(see **so** conj.). [OE *æfre*]
euerechon, euerychon *pron.*
every one, each 7.124, 2.23;
eauereuchan 19.346, 402;
heuereuchon 5.270. [eue-
rich(e)+on(e)]
euerich(e) *adj.* every, each
3.20, 149, 17.134, 244; **eurich,
evrich** 1.150, 300; **eauereuch**
1.554, 583, 19.147; **æuric** 16.
125, 157; **aueriche** 17.75. [OE
æfre ælc, **ylc*, &c., see **ech(e)**]
euerich(e), eueryche *pron.*
each, everyone 17.191, 192;
~ *oþer* each other 2.106; **eurilc**
12.131. [prec.]
euermar(e) *adv.* for ever, always
14.98, still 10.269; **eauer-,
auer-** 19.325, 10.201; **euermore** 6.385. [euer(e)+
mor(e)]
euesang, *n.* evensong vespers
9.130. *pl.* **evesongus** 7.267.
[OE *æfensáng*]
euesede *pa. t. sg.* cut the hair of
18.629. [OE *efesian*]
euesunge *n.* trimmings 18.630.
[from prec.]
eure; eurich, evrich, eurilc.
See **euer(e); euerich(e).**
exyl *n.* exile. 2.261. [OF *exil*]

fa(n). See **fo.**
face *n.* face 2.136, 196, 8K.14.
[OF]
fader *n.* father 7.16, 8L.18, 10.
168, 14.129, 233 (*dat.*), 16.315;
feader 19.132; **Feder** 19.420;
uadir 9.176. protector, patron
2.46. *þe* ~ God 14.243; sim.
17.52, 19.263, 420. *gen.* **fader**
7.18, 14.161, 221; **Feader** 19.
267. [OE *fæder*, gen. unchanged; M *feder*, gen. *feadur*]
færd. See **ferd(e).**
fæstned *pp.* fastened 16.176.
[OE *fæstnian*]
fæston. See **festen.**
fæu *adj.* few 16.237; **vewe** 11.
139. [OE *fēawe*] See **feaue.**
fagen; faght, faht. See **fain**
adj.; **fiȝte** *v.*
fai *n.* faith, in French phr. *par
ma* ~ on my word 6.436. [AN
fei]
fayle, faille *n.* in *wiþhouten* ~
for certain 6.187, sim. 15.53.
[OF *fail(l)e*]
fail(l)e *v.* fail, be wanting, lacking (with dat. of pers.) 3.161.
pr. 3 sg. **failes** 14.83. *subj. sg.*
faille 3.131. *imper. pl.* **faileþ**
2.75. *pa. t. sg.* **failede** was exhausted 17.91. [OF *faillir*]
fayllard *adj.* good-for-nothing,
delinquent 15.8. [fail(l)e+OF
suff. *-ard*]
fain *adj.* glad, well pleased (with
of) 14.251; **fagen** 12.152, 173;
vawe in ~ *þat hii miȝte* content
that they could (in default of a
better course) 11.120. [OE
fægen, fagen]
fain, fayn *adv.* gladly 6.393, esp.
in *I(ch) wold(e)* ~ I should be
glad to 2.138, 6.309; **fawe**
2.83. [from prec.]
fair(e), fayr *adj.* fair, beautiful,
handsome, splendid 1.114, 2.4,
6.6, 7.43, 212, 8s.2, 9.51, 15.50;
noble 7.109; good, fine 4.189;
becoming, courteous 1.136, 338;

feir(e), feyr(e) 6.339, 8E.55, F.2, H.34, 18.478; favourable 8L.24; **feier** 18.578, 19.234; **vaire** 1.15, 17.156; **uæir** 10.10. phr. ~ *and fre* 2.134, 6.339, 8K.8, W.12. *comp.* **fairer, -ir, fayrer** 2.230, 9.6, 15.46; **feiror(e)** 6.340, 7.53; **uairur** 1.108. *sup.* **fairest** 3.30, 10.321; **feyrest** 8E.4; **feherest** 18.483, 604; **uairest** 10.307. [OE *fæger*, M *feger*]

faire, fayre *adv.* well 1.556, 4.53; courteously 6.160; beautifully 7.253; **feire** 18.331, 533. [OE *fægre*, M *fegre*]

fayrnes *n.* beauty 14.95. [OE *fægernes*]

falau *adj.* brown, withered 14. 127. [OE *f(e)alu, f(e)alw-*]

faldess *n. pl.* sheepfolds 13.70. [OA *fáld*]

fale. See **fele.**

falewe *pr. 1 sg.* fade, wither 8L.3. *pl.* **faloweþ** 9.81. [OE *f(e)al(u)-wian*]

fall *n.* downfall 14.62. [OA *fall*]

falle(n) *v.*[1] fall 3.135, 4.154, 18. 196; **ualle** 10.26; befall, happen 3.164. *pr. 3 sg.* **falleþ, -ð** 6.306, 10.264, 12.22, 18.30, belongs 18.473, ~ *into* is included in 18.428; **falleȝ** (= -þ) 3.63. *pl.* **fallen** 12.20; **falleð, -ȝ** 18.197, 3.262. *subj. sg.* **falle** 8K.74, 18.175; **valle** 8N.4. *pr. p. (adj.)* **fallinde** drooping 18.361, transitory 19.201. *pa. t. sg.* **fel** 4.242, 8w.38; **feol** 7.52, 10.27; **ueol** 10.26. *pl.* **fell** befell 14.11; **fullen** 7.276. *subj. sg.* **felle** 13.26. *pp.* **fallen** 2.265. [OA *fallan, fēoll, -on, fallen*]

fallen *v.*[2] fell, strike down 10.63. *pa. t. sg.* **felde** 4.286. *pp.* **feld** 4.251. [OA *fællan, fellan*]

faloweþ. See **falewe.**

fals(e) *adj.* false, deceitful 8H.15, 18.18, 19.167; treacherous 7.33;

unjust 1.166. [OE *fals* from L *falsus*]

falsdom *n.* lie 6.65. [prec.+ -dom]

falseté *n.* infidelity 6.101. [OF *falseté*]

falsi *v.* make false, lead astray 19.185. [OF *falser*]

falt. See **folde.**

fame *n.* reputation 18.233. [OF]

fand. See **find(e).**

fantum *n.* illusion 14.55, 91. [OF *fantosme*]

fare *n.* journey 16.185; behaviour, conduct 8H.27. [OE *faru*]

fare(n) *v.* 1.541, 4.104, 6.152, 10.18, 16.185; **farenn** 13.187; **uaren** 10.117, 307. (1) go, travel 1.541, 737, 2.55, 8F.1, 13.31, 16.114; march 10.18. (2) fare, do, get on 1.278, 4.104, 5.141, 6.173, 10.10. (3) behave, act 1.299, 549, 3.51, 19.20. *pr. 1 sg.* **fare** 1.553, 5.202, 6.173. *2 sg.* **farest** 1.299. *3 sg.* **fareȝ** (= -þ) 3.51; **feareð** 19.20. *subj. sg.* **fare** 12.62, 19.27. *pl.* 1.360. *imper. pl.* **fareþ** 1.694. *pa. t. sg.* **for** 10.265, 16.75. *pl.* **forenn** 13.31. *pp.* **fare** 2.55; **ifare(n)** 1.278, 667 (with *after*, for), 10.189; **iuaren** 10.10. [OE *faran*, M *fearan*; *fōr, -on, faren*] Cf. **ferde.**

farlac, F-. See **Fearlac.**

fast *pr. 1 sg.* fast, go without food 8B.7. *pr. p.* **fastinde** 4.133. *pa. t. sg.* **faste** 6.324. [OE *fæstan*] Cf. **veasten.**

faste *adj.* firm 8F.19. [OE *fæst*]

faste *adv.* fast, firmly 4.212, 321, 7.230, 8L..5, 10.225, (of sleep) 7.237; vaste 11, see below; **feaste** 18.163; **feste** 18.197, closely 170; as intensive with various verbs (esp. characteristic of the style of 7 and 11): hard, strongly, thoroughly 7.81, 117, 119, 244, 11.15, 19, 35, 39;

eagerly, earnestly 7.72, 133, 11. 143, 148; quickly 11.82. [OE *fæste, feste*]

fastrede *adj.* of steady purpose 1.167. [OE *fæst-ræd*]

fat *adj.* fat, rich 9.59. [OE *fǣtt*]

faten *n. pl.* vessels 17.99, 102. [OE *fæt*, pl. *fatu*]

fawe. See fain *adv.*

fax *n.* hair 8E.12. [OA *fæx*]

fe *n.* property, money, wealth 6.382, 8X.2; feh 19.169, 230; fehh 13.10. [OE *feoh*]

feader; feareð. See fader; fare(n).

Fearlac *n.* Fear (personified) 19. 70, 74, 237; Farlac 19.385, 394; f- fear 19.409. [fere n.² + -lac]

feaste. See faste *adv.*

feaue *pron. pl.* few 17.203; vewe 11.71. [OE *féawe*] See fæu.

fechche, fecche *v.* fetch, bring 3.27; take 6.314; vachen look for 8F.31. *pr. 3 sg.* fecheð 12. 72. *pl.* fecchen 12.113. *subj. sg.* feche 6.386. [OE *feccan, fæccan*, var. of *fetian*; see fete]

fede(n) *v.* feed, provide food for 4.95, 102; *intr.* give pleasure 8E.45. *pr. 1 sg.* fede nourish, sustain 6.208, keep 15.69. *2 sg.* fedest 1.94. *3 sg.* fet 12.107. *subj. sg.* fede 2.76, 12.108. *pa. t. sg.* fedde 4.54. *pp.* fed 4.72; ifed, y- 7.59, 8N.18. [OE *fédan*]

feder; 'feh(h); feherest; feht(e); fehten; feier. See fader; fe; fair(e); fiȝte *n., v.*; fair(e).

feierleac *n.* beauty 19.307. [OM *feger* + suff. *-lec* from ON *-leik-r*, cf. -lac; *e* here written above *a*]

feynes *n.* phoenix 8E.75. [OF *fenix*]

feinte *adj.* faint 2.146. [OF *feint*]

feir(e), feyr(-). See fair(e), faire.

feire *n.* fair 6.77. [OF]

fel; fela. See falle(n) *v.¹*, fele.

felawe *n.* companion, friend (in address) 3.256; feolahe fellow, associate 18.320. *pl.* felawes companions 7.148; feolahes 18.130; velaghes equals 17. 197. [OE *féolaga* from ON *félagi*]

feld(e) *n.* field 8N.13, (of battle) 1.672, 2.99; ueld ground 10.29. *pl.* feldes earth 10.183. [OE *feld*]

feld(e). See fallen *v.²*

fele *adj.* many 2.63, 3.189, 4.46, 8L.30, 14.94; fela 16.50; fel 14.185; feole 1.730, 8H.15, 10.244, 16.50, 18.222, *a* ~ 10. 87; fale 1.680, 3.119, 9.95; uele, uale 1.20, 343, 621, 725. [OE *fela, feola, feala*, adv., &c.]

fele *pron.* many 17.203. [as prec.]

felen *v.* perceive 19.24. *pr. 3 sg.* feleð feels 12.180. *pl.* felen smell 12.152. [OE *félan*]

fell(e). See falle(n) *v.¹*

felonie *n.* malice 3.89; feolonie wickedness 7.14; evil deed 7.34. [OF *felonie*]

feloun *adj.* fierce, ill-disposed 3.86. [AN *felun*, orig. obj. case of *fel*]

felunge *n.* feeling, (sense of) touch 19.18. [from felen]

fen *n.* mud 4.139, 8K.74. [OE *fenn*]

fenestres *n. pl.* windows 9.114. [OF]

fenge *n.* capture, prize 8F.2. [OE *féng*]

fenge; feol; feolahe. See fon; falle(n) *v.¹*; felawe.

feolahlich *adj.* comradely, friendly 18.291. [from OE *féolaga*; see felawe]

feolahlukest *adv. sup.* in the most friendly way 19.304. [as prec., with suff. -liche, OE sup. -liocost]

feole *pr. subj. sg.* enter: ~ *o slepe* fall asleep 19.61. [OE *féolan*]

feole. See fele.

feol-iheortet *adj.* cruel-hearted 18.153. [OF *fel*+OE *heorte* with adj.-forming pref. and suff.; see **feloun, hert(e)**]

feolonliche *adv.* wickedly 7.23. [OF *felon* (see **feloun**)+-**liche**]

feond *n.* enemy; *þe* ~ the Devil 10.216, 18.63; **feont** 19.37, 179. *gen.* **feondes** 18.94. *pl.* **feond, ueond** enemies 10.63, 104, 207. [OE *fēond*, sg. and pl.]

feondliche *adj.* terrible 10.291. [from prec.]

feor *n.* price 18.620. [OF *fuer*]

feor; feord; feorde(n). See **fer; ferd(e); ferde.**

feorre(n) *adv.* from afar 1.590; *of* ~ 19.63; **vorre** at a distance, far away 1.243;* **ferne** in *fro* ~ from far away 4.291. [OE *feorran*]

feorrene *adj.* distant 18.468; **verrene** 17.39. [from prec.]

feorðe; feouwer; feowertene. See **ferþe; four(e); fourtene.**

fer *adv.* far (away) 7.148, 8L.31, 12.113; ver 11.90; **feor** 1.555, a long way 7.233, 18.207; for 1.276, 18.132; **fur** 9.1, 155. ~ *uorþ* far (forward) (later treated as one word) 1.276; *fro, from, of* ~ from a long distance 4.290, 2.70, 18.158, 19.45; phrs. ~ *an ner*, ~ *an wide* 1.555, 615, 456. *comp.* **furre** 9.132. [OE *feorr*, comp. *fyrr*]

fer. See **fir(e).**

ferd *pp. adj.* afraid 14.209. [from OE *fǣran* frighten]

ferd(e) *n.* army 1.626, 10.125, 16.255, 311, 19.171; **færd** 16.235, 309; **feord** 16.291; **uerdes** 1.748, 10.99, 123. *pl.* **ferdes** 18.163. [OA *férd*]

ferde *pa. t. sg.* went, marched 16.41, 298, 309; went on, happened 11.67; ~ *aboute* went on 11.105; ~ *efter* pursued 16.254; *impers.* in *hu hit* ~ how things were going 10.6; **ferden** 10.224;

feorde in ~ *mid suicdom* was acting treacherously 16.111; **fierde** behaved 7.133. *pl.* **ferde(n)** 1.747, 16.312; **feorden** 16.141, 275. [OE *fēran*; cf. **fare(n)**, and ON *fara með* handle, deal with]

fere *n.*[1] companion, friend 5.120, 18.189, 320; equal, peer 8E.75; mate 1.179; mistress 8F.2; lover (or perhaps husband) 8G.30, 31, H.18. [OE *ge-fēra*]

fere *n.*[2] fear 7.265; *for loue ne for* ~ on any account 7.130, cf. **eie.** [OE *fǣr*, A *fēr*]

fereden *pa. t. sg.* carried 10.44. *pl.* **uereden** 10.316. [OE *ferian*]

ferli *adj.* marvellous, wonderful 6.277; **ferlik** 4.276. [app. OE *feorlic* strange (cf. **feorrene**); cf. ON *ferlig-r* monstrous]

ferliche *adj.* sudden 19.117. [OA *fērlic*]

ferliche *adv.* suddenly 18.53, 19.76, 115. [OA *fērlīce*]

ferlys *n. pl.* marvels 14.11. [from **ferli**]

ferne. See **feorre(n).**

ferreden *n.* company 19.303. [OE *ge-fēr-rǣden*, cf. **ifere** and -**rede(n)**]

fers *adj.* fierce, violent 11.151. [OF *f(i)ers*, nom. of *f(i)er*]

ferrs; ferst(e). See **uers; first.**

ferþe *adj.* fourth 4.237; **feorðe** 19.42, 54. [OE *fēorþa*]

ferþing *n.* farthing: (*attrib.*) worth a farthing 4.144. *gen.* **ferþinges** 4.88. [cf. OE *fēorþung*, ON *fjórðung-r*]

feste *n.* feast, festival 7.196. [OF]

feste. See **faste** *adv.*

festen *v.* make fast, bind 4.212. *pr. 3 sg.* **festeð** fixes, sets 12.195. *pl.* **festen** moor 12.175. *pa. t. pl.* **fæston** made firm, pledged 16.279. [OE *fæstan*, ON *festa*]

fet. See **fede(n); fot(e).**

fete *v.* fetch, get 4.178; **fetten**

7.144. *pr. 3 sg.* **fettes** derives
14.36. [OE *fetian*; see **fechche**]
feteres *n. pl.* fetters, irons 4.212,
16.258. [OE *feter*]
feð. See **fon.**
feþer *n.* feather 1.646. *pl.* **feðres**
12.20. [OE *feþer*]
fiele *n.* a stringed instrument,
viol 8K.43. [OF]
fierde. See **ferde.**
fif *adj.* five 7.242, 16.27, 19.17;
~ *and twenti* twenty-five 16.88;
fiue 4.62, 5.29. [OE *fif(e)*]
fifte *adj.* fifth 4.243. [OE *fifta*]
fiftene *adj.* fifteen 10.291. [OA
fiftēne]
fyfty *n., adj.* fifty 8L.23. [OE
fiftig]
fiȝte, fiht(e) *n.* fighting 1.139;
battle 10.179, 185; battle array
10.203; **uihte** 10.260; **feht(e)**
10.293, 18.7, 165, 19.182. [OE
feoht(e)]
fiȝte, fihten *v.* fight 1.413, 627,
10.143, 162; **viȝte** 1.128; **fehten**
1, note to 132. *pr. 2 sg.* **vicst**
1.284. *3 sg.* **fiȝt** 1.132. *pl.*
fehteð 18.163. *pa. t. sg.* **faht** 10.
279. *pl.* **faght** 14.15. **fuht(t)en**
10.164, 209, 16.237, 311. [OE
feohtan, feaht, fuhton]
fiȝtinge *n.* fighting 1.662. [from
prec.]
fihtlac *n.* fighting 1.657. [OE
feohtlāc; see **-lac**]
fyke *v.* flatter, deceive: *to* ~ in
his (deceitful) flattery 8H.27.
pr. 3 sg. offers flatteringly 18.
385. *pr. p. adj.* **fikiende** delud-
ing 18.271. [cf. OE *befician*]
fikelinde *pr. p. adj.* deceitful 19.
166. [frequentative of **fyke**]
fyldor *n.* gold thread *(attrib.)*
8E.12. [OF *fil d'or*]
file *n.* file 18.324. [OA *fil*]
fille(n) *v.* fill 3.174; observe
12.139; **fillenn** complete. 13.
introd.; **fullen** fulfil 6.239. *pr.
3 sg.* **fulleð** is the fullness of 18.
444. *pa. t. pl.* **fylden** filled

16.158. *pp.* **ifullet** filled 19.148,
291. [OE *fyllan*]
fin(e) *n.* end, death 3.179; *ate* ~
finally 7.279. [OF *fin*]
fin(e) *adj.* fine, refined 3.128;
pure, true 3.268; exquisite 8K.
24; excellent 9.45. [OF *fin*]
find(e), fynd(e), finden(n) *v.*
find 14.96, 1.707, 6.132, 17.26,
14.35, 2.314, 6.34, 12.72, 16.
186, 13.95; **uinde** 1.328, 411;
provide 6.316. *pr. 3 sg.* **findeð**
12.188; **fint** 12.102; **vind** 5.253;
uint 1.442. *pl.* **fynd(en)** 2.121,
14.93. *subj. sg.* **finde** 12.84.
pa. t. sg. **fond** 5.21, 93, 7.71,
11.50, 67, 17.184, ~ *out* discovered 7.208; **fand** 14.149,
16.283, provided 205; **founde**
5.73, 92, 6.407, 8F.2. *pl.*
fonden 17.186; **fundenn** 13.
129. *pp.* **founde** 6.422, 8E.4;
founden invented 6.203; **fundenn** 13.136; **fundun** 14.77;
ifounde 3.283, 7.119, 169;
ifonden 17.29; **ifunde** 1.451;
hifunde 17.22. [OE *findan,
fánd, fúndon, fúnden*]
finger *n.* finger 19.366. *pl.*
fingres, fyngres 18.394, 8E.55
K.27. [OE *finger*]
fir(e), fyr(e) *n.* fire 4.179, 181,
14.154, 16.64; fuel 4.178; **fur(e)**
8G.41, 18.42, 215, 19.81; sparks
10.277; **fer, ueree** 17.122, 55.
a, on ~ on fire 2.101, 98, 11.164.
[OE *fŷr*, K *fèr*]
firrer *adj. comp.* earlier 16.74.
[cf. ON *fyrri* former, corresp. to
sup. *fyrstr*]
first, fyrst *adj.* first, chief 2.30,
16.137; earliest 14.8; *ate* ~ at
first 3.123; **ferst(e)** 17.190,
202; **uerste** 17.202; **verste** 11.
151. [OE *fyrst*]
first *adv.* first, in the first place
14.71, 124; **ferst** 3.279, 17.105.
[OE *fyrst*]
fish *n.* fish 4.19, 101, *coll.* 30, 82;
fisc 10.44; **fis** 12.141, 147;

fisse *coll.* 9.55. *pl.* **fishes** 4.148; **fisses** 8c.2, 12.151. [OE *fisc*]
fishere *n.* fisherman 4.17. [OE *fiscere*]
fis(se); **fiue**; **flæsh**. See **fish**; **fif**; **flesch(e)**.
flǽt *pa. t. sg.* floated, sailed 13.197; **flet** was floating 12.144. [OE *flēat* from *flēotan*]
flah. See **fle(n)**.
fle *n.* flea 9.37. [OE *flēa*]
fle(n) *v.* 4.247, 11.100, 161, 12.115; **flee** 9.127; **fleo(n)** 1.572, 658, 7.54, 114, 10.182, 19.180, 418; **flo(n)** 1.106, 284. (1) flee, run away, escape: *intr.* 1.284, 572, 4.247, 10.182, 11.38, 100, 16.189, 271, 18.86, 398, 19.179; *tr.* run away from 4.226, 18.31, 19.180, 418; desert 12.115. (2) fly 1.33, 106, 320, 5.38, 7.54, 114, 9.103, 124, 18.63, 104. *pr. 3 sg.* **fliō** 18.86, 104, 19.179. *pl.* **fleeþ**, **-ȝ** (= -*þ*) 9.132, 103; **fleoō** 18.31; **floþ** 1.214. *subj. sg.* **fle** 4.226. *pl.* **fleo** 1.631. *pr. p.* **fleing** 9.124; **fleonninde** 18.63. *imper. sg.* **fle** 5.38; **flo** 1.33; **flih** 18.398. *pa. t. sg.* **flah** 10.236; **fleh** 16.262, 273. *pl.* **flowe** 11.38, 101; **flugen**, **flugæn** 16.189, 271, 196, 257; **fluȝen** 10.183; **fluhen** 18.66, 515. [OE *flēon* flee, *flēah*, *flugon*, *flogen*, confused with *flēogan* fly; see **fleye**]
flec; **flegeō**. See **flesch(e)**; **fleye**.
flei *n.* fly 9.37. *pl.* **flehen** 18.364; **uliȝe** 1.380. [OE *flēoge*]
fleye *v.* fly 4.218, 240. *pr. 2 sg.* **fliȝst** 1.89, 183, flee 283. *3 sg.* **flegeō** 12.12; **fliȝt** 1.224, flee 132. *pa. t. sg.* **flevȝ** 7.175. *pp.* **flowen** 5.31. [OE *flēogan*, *flēag*, pp. *flogen*; see **fle(n)**]
fleis. See **flesch(e)**.
flemden *pa. t. pl.* expelled 16.87, put to flight 238. [OA *flēman*]
fleme *n.*[1] flight 10.32. [OE *flēam*]

fleme *n.*[2] fugitive, outcast 19.387. [OA *flēma*]
fleo(n); **fleonninde**. See **fle(n)**.
flesch(e) *n.* 1.83, 18.278, 19.113; **flesh** 4.49; **flæsh** 13.255; **fles(s)ce** 17.62, 65; **fles(se)** 6.327, 12.192, 17.217, 14.80; **flec** 16.187; **fleis** 9.55; **flexs** 14.269. (1) flesh, body 1.83, 14.269, 17.62; Body 18.278; human form 14.80; *phr.* ~ *and blod* 13.255, 17.217; *o, i* ~ in the flesh, in human life 18.414, 19.305; *mid* ~ *and gast* in body and soul 12.192. (2) meat 4.49, 6.327, 9.55, 16.187, 19.113. *gen.* **flesches** of the body, carnal 18.419, 19.183, 305, esp. ~ *fondunges* 18.38, 58, 301. [OE *flǽsc*]
fleschliche *adj.* carnal 18.1, 55. [OE *flǽsclic*]
flescmete *n.* meat 16.71. [OE *flǽsc-mete*; see **met(e)** *n.*[1]]
flesliche *adv.* in the flesh, materially 17.47; while incarnate 17.89, 112. [OE *flǽsclice*]
flet *n.* floor 6.273. [OE *flett*]
flet; **flevȝ**; **flexs**. See **flǽt**; **fleye**; **flesch(e)**.
fliȝt *n.* flight, flying 12.7; wings 12.18. [OE *flyht* from *flēogan*; cf. **fluht(e)**]
fliȝst, **fliȝt**; **flih**. See **fleye**; **fle(n)**.
flikereō *pr. 3 sg.* trifles 18.385. [OE *flicorian* flutter]
flintes *n. pl.* flints, stones 4.290. [OE *flint*]
fliō, **flo(n)**. See **fle(n)**.
floc *n.* flock, herd 18.170, 240; flok group of five 5.29 (note). *pl.* **flockes** 1.216; companies, crowds 1.305. [OE *flocc*, ON *flokk-r*]
fiod(e) *n.* flood 14.289; *on* ~ flooded 10.280; sea 4.18, 8c.2; **ulode** 10.42. [OE *flōd*]

flor(e) *n.* floor 6.102; *y* ~ inside (but see *MED*) 15.9. [OE *flōr*]

flote *n.* company, household 4.6. [OE *flote*]

flour *n.* flower 3.63, 67, 8H.7, T.28; **flure** 9.8; *coll.* blossom 9.75, 14.176. *pl.* **floures** 3.60, 172. [AN *flur, flour*]

flowe; flowen. See **fle(n); fleye.**

flowþ *pr. 3 sg.* flows 1.552. [OE *flōwan*]

flugen, fluȝen, fluhen. See **fle(n).**

fluht(e) *n.* flight, running away 1, note to 132; **bringeð o** ~ puts to flight 18.109. [OE **flyht* from *flēon*; see **fle(n)** and **fliȝt**]

flure. See **flour.**

fluren *adj.* made of flour 9.57. [from **flour**; senses 'flower' and 'flour' not distinguished in spelling until 18th century]

fluste *pa. t. sg.* flew up suddenly 3.216. [from infin. *flusshen*, app. imitative]

flutteð *pr. pl.* move 19.115. *imper. sg.* **flute** go away 19.394. [ON *flytja*]

fnast *n.* breath 1.44. [OE *fnǣst*]

fo *n.* foe, enemy 8G.46; **fa** 18.391, 19.385; **uo** 1.281. *pl.* **fon** 2.78, 11.70, 106; **fan** 18.474, 632; **van** 18.491, 500. [OE *ge-fā*]

fo. See **fon.**

fod(e) *n.* food 12.28, 100; **uode** 1.386; offspring, family 1.94; child, foster-son 7.67. [OE *fōda*]

foȝe *n.* fitness, order 1.140. [OE *ge-fōg*]

foȝle. See **foul.**

foysouns *n.* (*sg.*—see note) plenty, abundance 2.222. [AN *fuisun(s)*]

fol *n.* fool 6.115, 8L.9; **foul** 14.28. *pl. gen.* **folen** 8x.3. [OF *fol*]

fol *adj.* sinful, evil 19.20. [OF *fol*]

fol; folc. See **ful(l); folk(e).**

folde *v. tr.* bind 8E.12; close 1.594; in *feir to* ~ clasp 8E.55, K.27. *intr., pr. 3 sg.* **falt** grows weak, falters 1.37. [OA *fáldan*]

folden *n.* (*dat.*) the ground, the field: *a, on* ~ 10.262, 300. [OE *fólde, on fóldan*]

folecheden, folegen. See **folewe.**

folen *pp.* applied, directed 6.238. [app. shortened or corrupted from *bifolen* from OE *befēolan*; see note]

folewe *v.* follow 6.350; **folgen** 12.196; **folhin** 19.13. *pr. 3 sg.* **folegeð** 12.188; **folȝeþ** 1.223; **folheð** 18.239, 19.310. *pl.* **folegen** 12.117; **follȝhenn** 13.244. *pr. p. intr.* **foluand** going forward 14.119. *imper. pl.* **folwes** 4.312. *pa. t. pl.* **folecheden** 16.271. [OE *folgian*]

foly *n.* folly, foolishness 14.28, 53. *pl.* **folies** 17.133; **foliis** 14.142. [OF *folie*]

foliot *n.* foolishness 1.528. [OF *foliot* snare; cf. prec.]

folk(e) *n.* 2.74, 7.157, 10.119, 11.33, 17.152; **folc** 10.182, 16.92; **follc** 13.83; **uolc, uolke** 10.32, 18, 147. *gen.* **folces** 16.104. (1) people, men 2.74, 82, 7.157, 172, 10.228, 11.33, 13.83 (*dat.*), 165, 16.92, 262, 17.152; (construed as pl. 2.74, sg. 7.172, 10.228, 13.165, mixed 7.157, 225). (2) company, crowd 7.261, 10.279; company (of retainers) 10.32, 182; army 10.18, 119, 215; assembly 11.93; nation 10.147. [OE *folc*]

foller; follȝhenn, foluand, folwes; folvellet. See **ful(le); folewe; fulfille.**

fomen *n. pl.* enemies 5.288. [OF *fāh-mann*]

fon *v.* take: ~ *to* proceed, begin 10.207 (cf. **take(n)**); **fonge** take 4.31; **fenge** 8H.18. *pr. 3 sg.*

feð 18.175. *subj. pl.* fo in ~ *we on* let us proceed 1.135. *pa. t. subj. sg.* fonge should catch 4.124. *pp.* ifon 10.73. [OE *fōn, fēþ*; pa. t. *fēng*, pp. *fángen*] Cf. iuo.

fond(en). See find(e).

fonde *v.* try 3.95, 153, 6.241, 393; look for, seek 6.342; *to* ~ (tag) to know, see 8κ.8, 14; fondin experience 19.252, 378. *pr. 3 sg.* fondeð tries 19.402. [OE *fándian, fóndian*]

fondunge *n.* temptation 18.42, 176. *pl.* fondunges 18.36, 58. [OE *fóndung*]

fonge. See fon.

for *conj.* for 1.32, 2.44, 3.60, 4.46, 5.6; fore 17.219; forr 13.63, 85; vor 1.43, 123, 11.5. because, since 1.561, 652, 2.35, 89, 5.281, 6.79, 7.150, 163, 16. 145; on consideration that 10. 142. ~ *þat*(t), *þet* because 2.69, 4.11, 13.38, 182, 17.15, 19.337; in order that 13.193, 215. [OE *for þæm* (*þe*), *for þȳ þæt*]

for *prep.* (of cause) for, because of 1.295, 2.149, 311, 3.195, 6.41, 7.168, 8c.5, ε.23, 12.20, 17.100; uor, vor 1.19, 11.172; fore (next to vb.) 8μ.18, (at end of clause) 19.30, 312; for fear of 8ʟ.19; against 19.173, 404; in spite of 8ɴ.11; in (*hope*) 8ɴ.14; of (after *die*) 4.109. (of benefit) for the sake of 1.162, 3.160, forr 13.228, ~ *almes sake* 5.44; (in oath) 6.112. (of indir. obj.) from 2.198. (of purpose) with the object of, in order to procure 4.57, 10.148; (with plain infin.) in order to 1.348, 724; (with *to* + infin.) 13.265, 271; see forto. (of equivalence) in exchange, return, for 3.116, 125, 4.134, 8ɢ.33, 16.277; representing 17. 74; ~ *noþing, noȝt*, &c., without result, in vain 6.352, 7.27, 11. 138; with neg. as intensive of refusal, as *þou nolde come for loue ne golde* 2.240, sim. 1.495, 5.161, 6.44, 106; (after vbs. of knowing, considering, &c.) as 5.123, 7.190, 9.128, 14.46. ~ *qui* why, see whi. (forming *adv.*) ~ *þan* therefore, on that account 10.84, 17.256, correl. with same phr. as *conj.* since 1.619–20. [OE *for, fore*] See maistri(e), nones.

for. See fare(n); fer.

forbar *pa. t. sg.* refrained: ~ . . *þat he ne to yede* he did not fail to go to any . . 4.32. *pl.* forbaren spared 16.191, 193. [OE *forbær* from *-beran*; see ber.]

forbarnd, -bearnde, -eð. See forberne(n).

forbeode *pr. 1 sg.* forbid 18.252. *3 sg.* forbedeð 12.105; forbiet 17.81. *subj. sg.* forbeode 18. 277. *pa. t. subj. sg.* forbude 19. 14. [OE *forbēodan*, pa. t. subj. *-bude*; see bede]

forberne(n) *v. tr.* burn (at the stake) 10.95, 262. *pr. 3 sg.* forbearneð burns up 19.118. *pl.* 18.72. *pp.* forbarnd 2.108; forbearnde 18.54. *intr.* burn up, be consumed, *pr. 2 sg.* forbernest 1.297. *pa. t. subj. sg.* furburne 10.47. [OE *forbærnan* tr., *forbéornan* intr., pa. t. subj. *-búrne*; see barne]

forbiet. See forbeode.

forbisne *n.* example 18.160; parable 17.176, 201, 261, 18. 473. [cf. OE *forebysen*; see bisne]

forbroken *pp. adj.* broken-down, decrepit 16.32. [OE *forbrocen* pp. of *-brecan*; see breke(n)]

forbude. See forbeode.

forcursæd *pp. adj.* accursed 16.198. [OE *for-* + pp. of *cursian*; see curseð]

forcuð *adj.* infamous, wicked 10.125. *sup.* forcuðest, 10.221, 149; foulest 19.101. [OE *forcūþ*]

fordede *n.* service 18.548. [for prep.+ded(e), perh. modelled on L *profectio*]

fordeme(n) *v.* condemn 10.88, 19.224; execute 10.111. *pp.* as *n. pl.* **fordemde** damned 19.150. [OE *fordēman*]

fordfeorde *pa. t. sg.* died 16.245. [OE *forþfēran*] Cf. **forðfare.**

fordon *v.* destroy, ruin 10.208; kill 10.89. *pp.* **fordo(n)** 3.52, 16.200. [OE *fordōn*; see **do(n)**]

fordriuen *pp.* driven about, storm-tossed 12.169. [OE *fordrifen* from *-drifan*; see **driue(n)**]

fordrue *v.* dry up 1.551. [OE *fordrūgian*]

fore *adv.* beforehand 19.48, 159; in *scawe* ∼ 16.61, see **schawin.** [OE *fore*]

fore. See **for.**

foren *adv.* in front, forming compound prep. ∼ *to* (postponed) in front of 10.39. [OE *foran to*]

forenn. See **fare(n).**

foreward(e) *n.* agreement, covenant 1.651, 3.163, 6.256; *to ðat* ∼ on condition 16.282; **uoreward** 1.647; **forewerde** 17.181, agreed wages 180. *pl.* **forewardes** 8F.19; **foruuardes** 16.317. [OE *foreweard*]

forfeareð, *pr. 3 sg.* perishes 18.183. [cf. OE *forfaran*; see **fare(n)**]

forgiue *v.* forgive 6.334. [OE *forgifan* infl. by Scand; see **forȝeue, ȝeue**]

forgulte *pp.* convicted of sin 18.457. [OE *forgyltan*]

forȝelde *pr. subj. sg.* repay, reward, in phr. *God (&c.) þe* ∼ 5.226, 6.37, 326, 415. [OA *forgéldan*]

forȝemeð *pr. pl. refl.* are negligent 19.190. *subj. sg. tr.* **forȝeme** neglect 19.62. [OA *forgēman*]

forȝeoten *v.* forget 18.586. *pr. 3 sg.* **forȝet** 19.28, 189. *subj. sg.* **forȝete** 1.471. *pp.* **forȝite** 7.137, 140. [OA *forgetan*, M-*geotan*; WS pp. *-giten*]

forȝeue *v.* forgive 5.175. *pr. 1 sg.* 5.225. *imper. sg.* **forȝef** 5.209. [OA *forgefan*] Cf. **forgiue.**

forȝeuenesse *n.* remission, respite 5.295. [OA *forgefenes*]

forȝite. See **forȝeoten.**

forhaht *pp.* repudiated 8F.34. [pp. of *forhecche*, origin obscure; see note]

forhed *n.* forehead, brow 8E.22. [OE *for(e)hēafod*]

forheou *pa. t. sg.* cut down 10.21. [OE *forhēow* from *-hēawan*; see **hewene**]

forhohie *v.* despise 18.343. [OE *forhogian*]

forholen *pp.* concealed, hidden 6.237, 16.229; **forrholenn** 13.59. [OE *forholen* from *-helan*; see **hele(n)**]

forhorin *v. refl.* commit adultery 18.552. *pr. subj. sg.* **forhori** 18.554. *pp.* **forhoret** prostituted 18.564. [from OE *for-*+ *hōre* whore]

forht. See **forþ.**

forke *n.* fork 8N.19. [OE *forca*]

forleie *pp. adj.* unchaste 3.46. [OE *forlegen* pp. of *forlicgan*]

forleost. See **forlese.**

forlere *pr. subj. sg.* lead astray 1.558. [OE *forlǣran*]

forlese *v.* lose (completely), forfeit 2.302. *pr. 2 sg.* (fut. sense) **forleost**, -**lost** 1.607, 529. *3 sg.* **forleost** -**lost** 1.624, 439, 399. *pa. t. sg.* **forlæs**, -**les** 16.25, 262. *pp. adj.* **forlore(n)** 8T.19, v.8, 24, 12.33, abandoned 16.156, 199; **forloron** 16.94; **forlorn** 4.38. [OE *forlēosan*; see **leosen**]

forlete *pr. 1 sg.* forsake, abandon, give up 1.36. *3 sg.* **forleteð** 12.85. *subj. sg.* **forlete** 1.282.

pa. t. sg. **forlete** 2.264. [OE *forlǽtan*; see **lete(n)**]

forlore *n.* loss 17.226. [OE *forlor*]

forlor(-), **-lost**. See **forlese**.

forme· *adj. sup.* first 16.63, 18.580, 19.220. [OE *forma*]

formealte *pp.* melted away 19.119. [OE *for-*+M *-mæltan*; see **imealt**]

forrdredde *pp. adj.* afraid 13.79. [OE *for-*+**dred**; cf. **adrad(de)**]

forrotet *pp. adj.* decayed 19.113. [OE *forrotian*]

forrþi. See **forþi**.

forrwunndredd *pp. adj.* astonished 13.148. [OE *for-*+*wundrian* be astonished] Cf. **ofuundred**, **wndri**.

forsake *v.* renounce, reject, refuse 8x.2. *pr. 2 sg.* **forsakest** 18.637. *3 sg.* **forsaket** 12.44. *pp.* **forsake** 5.177. [OE *forsacan*, *-sacen*]

forsape *v.* change the shape of, transform 6.369. [OE *forsc(i)eppan*; see **shop**]

forscaldet *pp.* scalded 18.84. [OE *for-*+ONF *escalder*]

forsete *pa. t. sg. subj.* neglected 10.261. [OE *forsǽte* from *-sittan*; see **site**]

forsoþ, forsoth(e) *adv.* certainly, indeed 9.21, 148, 8x.17, 14.117; **forsout** as truth, for a fact 8v.12. [OE *forsōþ*; see **soþ(e)**]

forst *n.* frost 8N.5. [OE]

forstod *pa. t. sg.* availed, was of use 16.280. *subj. sg.* **forstode** 16.142. [OE *forstōd* from *-stándan*; see **stonde(n)**]

forsuoren. See **forsworen**.

forswalȝe *v.* swallow up, devour 10.231. *pr. pl.* **forswolheð** 19.104. *subj. sg.* **forswolhe** 19.172. [OE *forswe(o)lgan*, *-sw(e)alg*, *-swolgen*] Cf. **isuolȝe**.

forswelde *pp.* burnt down 10.228. [OE *forswǽlan*]

forswelt *pp.* killed 2.108. [OE *forsweltan* die]

forswolhe(ð). See **forswalȝe**.

forsworen, -suoren *pp. adj.* forsworn, perjured 16.156, 199. [OE, from *forswerian*; see **sweren**]

fort *conj.* until 1.41, 248, 5.17, 9.185; **forto** 2.99, 328, 7.160; **vort, uorte** 11.15, 66. [next]

fort *prep.* until 1.310; **vort** 11.173. [**forþ**+**to**]

forto *prep.* (with infin.) in order to 2.6, 3.48, 4.7, 6.151, 7.22, 14.215, 17.9; **forrto** in *all mannkinn ~ lokenn* for all men to see 13.14; **forte** 8E.2, 18.349, 651, 19.81; **vorto** 11.22. (merely introducing infin.) to 4.67, 6.152, 8D.6, K.27, 9.72, 12.122, 14.1, 19.8; ~ *speoke* in speaking 18.5; ~ *halden* in the observance 19.52. [**for** prep.+**to**]

fortruste *pr. subj. sg. refl.* be over-confident 19.61. [OE *for-*+**trust**]

forþ, forð, forth *adv.* forth, out, away, forward, on 1.747, 2.326, 6.185, 8N.26, 13.127, 10.40, 12.87, 19.25, 4.78, 7.91, 14.156; widely 13.143; **forht** 3.190; **uorþ, uorð, vorþ** 1.276 (see **fer**), 10.119, far 188, 11.17, 132. ~ *ibrouȝt* reared 7.59, 67, far advanced 7.167. [OE *forþ*]

forþe. See **forþi**.

forðen *pr. pl.* provide for 12.126. [OE *ge-fórþian*]

forðfare *n.* death 10.319. [cf. OE *forþfōr* and *faru*]

forþi, -ði *adv.* therefore, (and) so 1.287, 6.171, 344, 12.98, 16.222, 19.212; **forrþi** 13.205; **forþe** 1.69; **vorþi** 1.65, 213; for that reason 6.180, 10.172; anticipating phrase or correl. conj.: *forþi .. for* for this reason .. (namely) because 18.227; sim. 18.650, 13.239–41. [OE *for þȳ*]

for(r)þi *conj.* because 19.251; ~ *þatt, ðat, þet* 13.53, 16.106,

26, 18.660; with the object that
18.419. [OE *for þ̄y þæt*]
forþingketh, -þinkeþ *pr. 3 sg.*
displeases, causes resentment
17.200; causes regret to: *þat
me* ~ I am sorry to hear it 6.139.
[OE pref. *for-+*þinche] Cf.
ofþinkeþ.
forðriht *adv.* at once, immediately 10.71; forrþrihht in
~ *anan* 13.213, forming conjs.
~ *anan se*, ~ *summ* as soon as
13.225, 73. [OE *forþrihte*]
forðward *adv.* onward, on 18.21.
[OE *forþweard*]
foruuardes. See foreward(e).
forwalleð *pr. 3 sg.* boils down
19.119. [OA *for-+wællan*]
forwerede *pp.* worn out 19.130.
[OE *forwered* from *-werian*]
forwit *adv.* before 14.66, 199,
214. [fore+wiþ]
forworþe. See forwurðe(n).
forwroght *pp.* overworked, exhausted 14.103. [OE *forworht*
from *-wyrcan*; see wirche]
forwunded *pp.* mortally wounded
10.290. [OE *forwúndian*]
forwurðe(n) *v.* perish, be destroyed 10.217, 18.200. *pr. subj.
sg.* forwurðe decay 12.90. *pp.
adj.* forworþe worthless 1.356.
[OE *forwurþan*; see wurðen]
fosterlinges *n. pl.* foster-chil-
dren 10.289. [OE *fóstorling*]
fot(e) *n.* foot 8K.74, 1N.26, 18.512;
uote claw 1.51. *pl.* fet 3.262,
4.332, 16.165; fetd 8w.23; uet
19.292. *dat.* fot(e) in *to þi* ~ at
your feet 3.135, *on* ~ on foot
8L.12, 16.293. [OE *fót*, pl. *fét*,
dat. *fótum*]
foul *n.* bird 7.53, 69; fule 9.123.
gen. fuȝeles, fuheles 1.259,
8w.2. *pl.* foweles 8c.1; fules
8v.1; fuȝeles, fuheles 10.36,
1.618, 18.457. *gen.* foulen 3.31;
fugheles (? *sg.*) 8B.2. *dat.*
foȝle, fuȝele 1.213, 64. [OE
fugol]

foul; foul(e). See fol *n.*; ful(l);
ful(e).
founde *v.* test: *to* ~ to be tested
8H.27. *pr. 3 sg.* fundeþ aspires,
endeavours to go 1.465. *pl.*
fundeþ, -ieþ 1.522, 510. [OE
fúndian] Cf. fonde.
founde(n). See find(e).
four(e) *adj., n.* four 2.65, 4.84,
14.180, 19.39; ~ *and twenty*
twenty-four (construed as *n.*)
3.2; (forming part of ordinal) ~
and twentiþe 7.5; fowr(e) 18.37,
97, 544, 19.40, 228; feouwer
10.138. [OE *féower*]
fourme *n.* agreement, settlement
7.231. [OF]
fourtene *adj.* fourteen 2.119;
feowertene 10.123, 153. [OE
féowertēne]
fourti *n., adj.* forty 6.324; furti
17.250. [OE *féowertig*]
fous *adj.* eager 3.99; wous eager
to go 5.12. [OE *fús*]
foweles; fowr(e). See foul;
four(e).
fox *n.* fox 9.31; vox, wox 5.1,
12, 16. *pl.* foxes 18.204. [OE *fox*]
fra; fram. See fro; from.
Frankys *adj.* French 14.24.
[OE *frencisc* infl. by n. *franca*]
Cf. Frensch.
fraward *adv.* away 16.44. [ON
frá+OE *-weard*; cf. OE *from-
weardes*]
fre. See freo.
freamien *v.* benefit, be of use to
18.309. [OM *freamian*]
freineð *pr. 3 sg.* asks 19.73. [OE
frægnian, M **fregnian*]
Freinss. See Frensch.
fremede *adj.* as a stranger 8F.1,
18.516. [OE]
frend *n.* friend 4.132, 6.152,
8G.46, 17.199; kinsman, relative
5.133; freond 18.139. *pl.* frend
friends 5.160, 7.50, kinsmen
16.126; freond 10.215, 16.35,
275, 18.47 (note), 142, 594;
frond 1.335. [OE *fréond*, pl.

friend, frēond; ON *frǽndi* kins-man]

frenderede *n.* friendship 2.71. [OE *frēondrǽden*]

Frensch *adj.* French 18.325; **Freinss, Frenss** 11.2, 51, 5. as *n. pl.* **Freinsse** Frenchmen 11.67. [OE *frencisc*] Cf. **Frankys.**

freo *adj.* free 10.201; (conventional epithet of praise) gracious, noble 8G.37; generous 8G.31; **fre** 6.34; in phr. *fair and ~*, see **fair(e)**; **vre** free (from) 8w.27. **freo ston** freestone, fine limestone 7.253. *comp.* **freour** nobler 6.342. *sup.* **freoest** most generous 18.606. [OE *frēo*]

freolec *n.* nobility, generosity 18.6, 450. [prec.+ON *-leik-r*; cf. OE *frēolāc* oblation, and *-lac*]

freoli, -ly *adj.* beautiful, fine, handsome 8E.45, H.7, 26; **freo-lich** 19.235. [OE *frēolic*]

freoly *adv.* in *~ bore* of gentle birth 8H.40. [OE *frēolīce*]

freond; freoteð. See **frend; fret(t).**

frer(e) *n.* friar 5.266, 271, 8x.6; *grey ~* 8N.19, *~ menur* 8x.7 Franciscan. *pl.* **freren** 5.262. [OF *frere*]

freseþ *pr. 3 sg.* freezes 8N.5; (impers., subject *hit*) frost 1.400. [OE *frēosan*]

fret(t) *pr. 3 sg.* devours 16.43; bites 19.127. *pl.* **freoteð** eat 19.109. [OE *fretan*, cf. M *eotan*]

Fridæi *n.* Friday: *Lang ~ Good Friday* 16.227. [OE *(Langa) Frīg(e)dæg*]

frith, fryht *n.* wood 8c.1, F.1. [OE *fyr(h)þ*]

friþþ *n.* peace, prosperity 13.111 (note), 251. [ON *frið-*, OE *friþ*]

fro *prep.* from 3.258, 4.166, 274, 14.36; (postponed) 6.380, *hire ~* so that she loses it 12.90; **fra** 13.201, 14.71, away from 13.117, 16.294. [ON *frá*]

frofrenn *v.* comfort, reassure 13.76. *pr. 1 sg.* **frouri** 1.343. [OE *frōfrian*]

frogge *n.* frog 1.85, 102. *pl.* **froggen** 19.109; **wroggen** 5.256. [OE *frogga*]

from *prep.* from 1.62, 2.70, 8F.11, 10.3, 18.139; away from 6.97; **fram** 3.40, 7.146, 8x.15, 9.134, 16.27; (of agent) by 16.212; *a luyte ~* a short distance from 7.262; **vrom, vram** 1.153, 119. (forming *conj.*) *~ þet* from the time that 16.59; see **whonene.** [OE *fram, from*]

frome *n.* beginning 1.334. [OE *fruma*]

frommard *prep.* away from 18. 205, 210. [from+OE *-weard*] Cf. **fraward.**

frommard *adj.* contrary, different (with dat.) 18.131. [OE *fromweard*]

frommardschipe *n.* independence, wilfulness 18.231. [prec. +-schipe]

frond; frost. See **frend; freseþ.**

frotunge *n.* rubbing, polishing 18.331. [from OF *froter*]

frount *n.* forehead, brow 8K.14. [AN *frunt*]

froure *n.* comfort, help 18.5, 306, 351. [OE *frōfor*]

frouri. See **frofrenn.**

fruit, fruyt *n.* fruit 7.44, 14.33; **frut(e)** 8v.11, 9.10, 14.248; **frutte** 14.176. [OF *fruit*]

fuel-kunne *n. dat.* to the race of birds 1.65. [OE *fugelcynn*; see **foul, kinn**]

fugheles, fuʒeles, fuheles; fuht(t)en. See **foul; fiʒte** *v.*

-ful *suff.* forming adjs., as **ancre-, an-, bal-, willes-.** [OE *-ful* (uncommon)]

ful(le) *adj.* full (with *of*) 2.44, 3.268, 4.48, 6.158, 7.44, 8v.10; (fold. by infin.) sated (with), weary (of) 19.268; whole 10.123,

18.68; ample 1.230. *comp.* **foller** 2.184. [OE *full*]

ful(l) *adv.* completely 16.47, 18. 175; very, quite 3.224, 4.70, 5.215, 6.3, 13.162, esp. ~ *wel* 1.450, 3.77, 4.40, ~ *iwis* 3.5, 6.143; **fol** 6.35, 8N.29; **foul** 3.286; **wl** 8w.15. [OE *full*]

ful(e) *adj.* foul, evil, dirty 1.32, 87, 4.207, 249, 16.166, 18.280, 370; **foul(e)** 8T.44, 11.18; **wl(e)** 1.31, 35. *sup.* **fouleste** 7.283. [OE *fūl*]

fule. See **foul.**

fulfille *pr. pl.* perform 9.186. *imper. pl.* **folvellet** fill up 17.98. *pa. t. pl.* **uuluelden** filled 17. 101. [OE *full-fyllan,* K *-fellan,* accomplish] Cf. **fille(n).**

fulitohe(n), -ene *adj.* ill-disci-plined 18.59, 19.10, 400. [OE *fūle* (cf. **ful(e)**)+*getogen,* pp. of *tēon* bring up; see **te**]

fullen. See **falle(n) ; fille(n).**

fulliche *adv.* fully 1.645. [OE *fullīce*]

fulluht *n.* baptism 18.579. [OE]

fulst(e) *n.* help 10.327 (see **to**), 19.252. [OE *fylst*]

fulþe *n.* uncleanness, wicked-ness 5.165. [OE *fylþ*]

fundenn, -un; fundeþ, -ieþ. See **find(e); founde.**

funt-fat *n.* font 12.56. [OE *font* infl. by AN *funz,*+*getogen, -iep.* *fæt*]

fur; fur(e); furburne; fur-cuðest. See **fer; fir(e); for-berne(n); forcuð.**

furmeste *adj. sup.* first 5.21. [OE *fyrmest*]

furre; furti. See **fer; fourti.**

fusde *pa. t. sg.* hastened 10.158. [OE *fȳsan,* tr. and refl.]

ga(n), ȝa. See **go(n).**

gabbe *n.* deceit: *wiȝoute* ~ truly 3.229. [ON *gabb;* cf. OF *gab(e)*]

gabbe *imper. sg.* lie to, deceive 5.121. [ON *gabba;* cf. OF *gaber*]

gaderen *v.* gather, accumulate 3.172; **gaderi** 7.147, 11.84; **gederin** 18.675, 677. *pr. 1 sg.* **gederi** 18.667. *2 sg.* **gederest** 18.329. *3 sg.* **gaddreð** 12.73. *imper. pl.* **gederið** 18.664. *pp.* **gadered** amassed 16.147. [OE *gad(e)rian,* infl. by *tō-gædere,* M **-gedere*]

gadering *n.* council 16.150. [cf. OE *gaderung*]

gæde ; gæf. See **eode ; ȝeue.**

gæildes *n. pl.* taxes 16.182, 302. [OA *géld*]

gær(e) ; gæt ; gaf. See **ȝer(e) ; ȝet(e) ; ȝeue.**

gay *adj.* fair, charming 8K.38. [OF *gai*]

gain *adj.* useful, profitable 14. 250. [ON *gegn* straight]

gayneþ *pr. 3 sg.* avails, serves 2.245. [ON *gegna;* cf. prec.]

gayt *n.* goat 15.20. [ON *geit-r*] Cf. **gote.**

galegale *n.* windbag 1.192. [humorous reduplication of *-gale* in **niȝtegale**]

galingale *n.* galingale, an aro-matic root 9.73. [OF *galingal* from Arab]

galnesse. See **golnesse.**

game ; gan ; gann. See **gome** *n.*[1] **go(n) ; ginneþ.**

gange(n) *v.* go, go about 4.64, 113, 6.262, 437, wade 368; **gonge(n)** 4.123, ~ *at* attack 215; **ȝeongen, ȝonge** run 10.40, 5.61. *pr. 3 sg.* **gangeð** 12.70. *pl.* **gangen** 12.176. *subj. sg.* **gonge** 4.111. *pr. p.* **gangende** 16.69; **ganninde** walking 10. 264. [OE *gángan, góngan,* Nb *geónga*]

gapeð *pr. 3 sg.* opens his mouth wide 12.148. [ON *gapa*]

gar *v.* make, cause (with *to* and infin.) 6.281, 290; **ȝaren** 6.449. *pa. t. sg.* **gart(e)** (with simple infin.) 4.284, 14.198. [ON *gøra, gera*]

garen *n. pl.* spears 10.165. [OE *gār*, pl. *-as*]

garlek *n.* garlic 9.105. [OE *gārlēac*]

garsome *n.* treasure 3.143. [LOE *gærsuma* from ON *gørsemi*]

gart(e); **gast.** See **gar**; **gost.**

gaste *v.* spoil, ruin 8L.8. [OF *gaster*]

gastelich(e); **gat.** See **gost-liche**; **gete(n).**

gate *n.*[1] gate 3.13, 11.134. [OE *gatu*, pl. of *geat, gæt*; see **3at(e)**]

gate *n.*[2] road, way, path 4.114, 155, 14.116, 127. *gen. adv.* **gates** in *go my ~* go away 8F.7. [ON *gata*]

gateward *n.* gate-keeper 3.13. [**gate**[1]+OE *weard*; see **yateward**]

gaue; **ge**; **geaf**; **gear**; **geað**; **gederi(n).** See **geue**; **3e(e)**, **3he**; **3eue**; **3er(e)**; **go(n)**; **gaderen.**

gees *n. pl.* geese 9.102. [OE *gēs*, pl. of *gōs*]

gef. See **geue**; **3ef.**

gegges *n. pl.* servants (?) 3.177. [obscure]

gehaten. See **hote(n).**

gemynd *n.* memory 16.67. [OE]

genge *n.* company, household 4.54; army 16.239. [ON *gengi*]

gent(e) *adj.* noble, well-bred 2.180, 298; elegant 1.160. [OF *gent*]

gentil, -tyl *adj.* well-born, of gentle birth, noble 2.2, 35, 47, 18.468; gracious 8K.39. [OF *gentil*]

gere *n.* dress, clothing 8F.4. [ON *gervi*; but see note]

gest *n.* guest 2.280, 8D.40. *pl.* **gestes** 16.206. [ON *gest-r*]

gest. See **go(n).**

gestnin *v.* stay, lodge 18.675. *pa. t. sg.* **gestnede** 18.677. [from **gest** + suff. *-nian*, or back-formation from *gestning*; see **gistninge**]

get 12.89 = *ge it*, see **3he, hit.**

get. See **gote**; **3et(e).**

gete(n) *v.* get, earn, acquire 4.60, 65; win (a woman) 6.14, 447. *pr. 2 sg.* **getes** 4.174. *subj. sg.* **gete** 6.234. *pa. t. sg.* **gat** 4.144. *pp.* **gete** 4.98. [ON *geta, gat, getinn*]

geþ; **Geus.** See **go(n)**; **Gius.**

geue *v.* give 6.223, 388; **gef** 15.58. *pr. 3 sg.* **giueð** 12.136. *imper. sg.* **gef** grant 15.80. *pa. t. sg.* **gaf** 4.244; issued 14.292; **gaue** 14.230. *pp.* **igiuen** 6.246. [ON *gefa, gaf, gefinn*, and ODan *give*] See **3eue.**

geuelike *adj.* equal: *o ~* on equal terms, equally 12.107. [OE *ge-efenlic*]

gye *v.* direct: *to ~* at his command 2.183. [OF *guier*]

gif; **gifen.** See **3ef**; **3eue.**

gifes *n. pl.* gifts 14.250. [OE *gifu*, infl. by **geue**]

gift *n.* gift 6.223. *pl.* **giftes** 6.388. [ON *gift*]

gile, gyle *n.* guile, cunning, deception 2.164, 8F.48, 0.1; treacherous attack 11.92. [OF *guile*]

gilofre *n.* clove 9.77, 110. [OF]

gylt *n.* desert (of punishment): *her was þe ~* they deserved 2.107; **gult** guilt 18.316, 317, blame 285. [OE *gylt*]

gin(ne) *n.* skill, ingenuity 1.415, 3.38, 5.72; stratagem 3.140, 153, 5.125; trick, contrivance 5.86, 6.289; trap 5.82; device 5.77; instrument, tool 3.10. *pl.* **ginnes** military engines, catapults 11.34. [shortened from OF *engin*]

gingeuir *n.* ginger 9.73. [OE *gingifer* from LL *gingiber*]

ginneþ, gynneþ *pr. 3 sg.* (with plain infin.) begins 1.315; (as mere auxil.) sets about, does 2.67. *pl.* (*auxil.*) 1.468, 2.130. *imper. pl.*

ginneþ 1.658. *pa. t. sg.* gan 2.106, 7.69, 8x.16, 14.149; yann 13.5; gon 5.1, 8v.14, 10.7; gun 10.40. *pl.* gonne(n) 5.283, 10. 278, 11.122; gunne(n) 10.87, 317. (1) began (with *to* and infin.) 5.195, 7.79, 8v.14, 10.24, 46 (2nd), 87; (with plain infin.) 5.83, 239, 10.7, 13.5. (2) (as auxil. forming with infin. equivalent of pa. t.) did (without *to*) 2.106, 273, 5.1, 7.69, 8x.16, 10.15, 46 (1st), 11.122, 14.149. [OE *-ginnan, -gann, -gunnon, -gunnen*; see biginne]

ginour *n.* mason, builder 3.82, 93. [shortened, with altered ending, from OF *engignĕor*; see gin(ne)]

girdil. See gurdel.

gysles *n. pl.* hostages 16.283. [OE *gīsl*]

gistninge *n.* feast 5.255. [cf. OSw *gästning*]

Gius, Gyus *n. pl.* Jews 17.13, 100; Geus 17.15. *gen.* Giwene 18.548. [OF *Giu*]

giueled *pp.* heaped up 4.82. [OF *gaveler*; see note]

gyuen; giueð. See 3eue; geue.

Giwerie *n.* Jewry: *in* ~ in pawn to Jews 18.545. [OF *Giu*+suff. *-erie*; cf. AN *Juerie*]

glad(e) *adj.* glad 5.249, 7.123, 11.100, 14.264; happy, cheerful 1.302, 6.328, 402, 8G.7, 14.272; glead(e) 18.295, 305, 19.227, 236. *comp.* gladdere, gladur 1.483, 19. [OE *glæd*, M *gled*, *gleadum*]

gladiet. See gleadien.

gladly *adj.* beautiful 8F.4. [OE *glædlic*]

gladlike *adv.* gladly 4.73, 172. [OF *glædlīce*]

gladshipe *n.* gladness, joy 8G.5; gleadschipe 18.351. *pl.* gleadschipes 19.345. [OE *glædscipe*]

glareth *pr. 3 sg.* gleams 17.48. [cf. MDu *glaren*]

glas(se) *n.* glass 2.214, 9.114. [OE *glæs*]

gle(e) *n.* entertainment, amusement, pleasure 8x.3, 9.43, 128, 14.54; *hadde* ~ were amused 3.219. [OE *glēo*]

glead(-). See glad(-).

gleadful(e) *adj.* joyful 18.39, 351. *comp.* gleadfulre 18.563. [from OM *glead-*; see glad(e)]

glead-icheret *adj.* happy-looking 19.234. [OM *glead-*+adj. from chere; cf. feol-iheortet]

gleadien *v. tr.* cheer 19.250; *intr.* rejoice 19.305, (with *of*, in) 18. 424. *pr. 3 sg. tr.* gladiet makes glad 8w.7; *intr.* gleadeð 19.349. *pp.* igleadet gladdened 19.240. [OE *gladian*, M *gleadian*]

gleadunge *n.* rejoicing, joy 19.318, 347. [from prec.]

glede *n.* a live coal 4.137. [OE *glēd*]

gledread(e) *adj.* red-hot 19.81, 143. [prec.+red(e); cf. ON *glóð-rauð-r*]

gleiue, gleyue *n.* spear 4.197, 271. *pl.* gleyues 4.291. [OF *glaive*]

glemede *pa. t. sg.* gleamed 8F.3. [from OE *glǣm*]

gleu *adj.* prudent, skilful 1.149. [OE *glēaw*]

glewe *v.* make music, play and sing 8G.6. [OE *glēowian*]

glides *pr. 3 sg.* flows 4.278. [OE *glīdan*]

glystnede *pa. t. sg.* shone 8F.3. [OE *glisnian*]

gloppend *pp. adj.* astounded 14. 152. [cf. ON *glúpna* be downcast]

glorius *adj.* glorious 17.34. [OF]

glouen *n. pl.* gloves 10.292. [OE *glōf*, pl. *glōfan*]

gnowe *pa. t. subj. sg.* bit 11.100. [OE *gnōge* from gnagan]

go(n) *v.* go, go about 1.170,

3.162, 5.1, 283, 6.135, 7.80,
8F.7, 11.56, 58, 17.9; walk 3.162,
8L.12, com .. ~ came walking
5.108 (see com); live 5.163,
8G.49, M.18, 9.15, ~ to proceed
1.415; ga(n) 14.107, 196, 18.
366, 19.355, hit schal ~ things
shall be done 19.23. pr. 2 sg.
gest 1.609, ~ to are dealing
498. 3 sg. goþ, goð, goth 3.20,
8s.3, 12.30, 8s.1, 17.55; geþ in
hou hit ~ how things stand
3.159; geað 18.173, 238, 19.171.
pl. go(o)þ 1.221, 9.113, 122;
gað 18.174, 227; ga (before we)
19.193. subj. sg. go 4.118; ga
19.11, 53, 18.263, ~ upo come
over 360. pl. go 1.491, (before
we) 2.206, ga 13.121 let us go.
pr.p. goinde 11.83. imper. sg. go
4.188, 5.34, 8R.7, 15.35; ga 14.
169. pl. goþ, goth 17.21, 4.207.
pp. go ago 8N.21; gon gone
4.116, 6.76, 8M.3; past, over
8G.5, gan 14.82; igo past 17.
220; igon 6.80 (see aboute(n)).
[OE gān, pr. 3 sg. gǣþ] See
eode.

God(e) n. God 1.527, 2.76, 3.179,
4.61, 15.4, 19.227; Godd 10.
107, 14.267, 18.19, 23, 19.30;
Ᵹodd 13.49; Goed 6.210, 314.
gen. Godes 1.515, 3.281, 5.36,
18.16, ~ beliaue belief in God
17.220; Ᵹodess 13.75; Godis
in ~ loue love of God 15.68;
Goddes 2.143, 14.220; Goddis
8x.12; Godds 14.143. dat.
Gode in ~ þonk thank God
5.158; Godd 19.166. pl. gen.
godes gods' 17.43. [OE God,
god] See wite(n).[1]

god(e) n. good, benefit 1.245,
373, 6.285 (see conne), 11.61,
16.46 (1st), 147, 18.127, 293,
19.225; goed 5.39, 6.251; good
17.268; himself to none ~ with
any benefit to him 12.29 (see to);
see do(n). that which is good
1.466, 5.147, 12.105, 16.131, 19.

199; for ~ with good intentions
19.389. goods, property, wealth
4.65, 5.161, 9.36, 11.64, 84,
16.46 (2nd), 161, 19.217; guod
7.36. gen. godes (part. in wat ~
what good) 1.371. pl. godes
goods 17.71. [OE gōd]

god(e) adj. good 1.131, 223,
3.82, 114, 4.17, 5.172, 18.160;
ᵹod 13.114; goed 5.173; good
17.131, 161; guod(e) 7.2, 157;
fine 8K.17; strong 11.65; good-
humoured, well-disposed 16.
154; ~ þraȝhe a good while
13.206. as n. pl. gode (the)
good, righteous 18.199. pl. gen.
gode 1.333. [OE gōd] See
betere.

goddai, godnedai n. good day,
farewell: haue ~ goodbye 6.145,
397. [god(e)+dai(e); godne-
from OE acc.]

goddede n. good action, doing
good 18.317. pl. goddeden
benefits 18.19, kindnesses 506.
[OE gōddǣd]

goddhead n. divinity 18.510.
[God(e)+-hede]

Goddot interj. God knows 4.64,
175, 6.439. [God(e)+wot, see
wite(n)]

ᵹoddspell. See godspel(le).

goded pa. t. sg. endowed 16.208.
pp. igodet benefited 18.438.
[OE gōdian]

godeman n. good man (as vague
term of respect) 11.54; head of
a household 17.186, 199; goodman 17.178. [god(e)+man]

goder-hele n. good fortune,
prosperity 6.269, to ~ to your
advantage 261. [OE (tō) gōdre
hǣle]

godespel(le); Godeward. See
godspel(le); toward(e).

godhede n. goodness 1.267.
[god(e)+-hede]

godlec n. goodness, kindness 18.
322, 19.338; benefit 6.227. [ON
gōðleik-r; cf. -lac]

godly *adv.* beautifully 8G.2.
[OE *gōdlīce*]
godnedai. See **goddai.**
godnes(se), -nis *n.* goodness,
virtue, excellence 8K.45, 14.97,
9.4; **guodnesse** 7.12. [OE
gōdnes(se)]
godspel(le) *n.* gospel 17.37, 87,
18.471; **godespel(le)** 17.4, 35;
goddspell 13.8, 40. *gen.* **godd-
spelless** 13.introd. *pl.* 13. 221.
[OE *godspell*]
goed ; Goed. See **god(e) ; God.**
gold(e) *n.* 2.219, 3.115, 7.176,
8E.61, F.3, 18.327. [OE *góld*]
golnesse *n.* lechery 1.531; **galnesse** 18.213. [OE *gālnes(se)*]
gome *n.*[1] game 1.624; pleasure,
enjoyment 5.24; **game** 1.607,
9.43. [OE *gamen, gomen*]
gome *n.*[2] man 2.35, 69, 3.21,
8F.48; person, anyone 8F.4. [OE
guma]
**gon, gonne(n); gonge(n);
good; goodman.** See
**ginneþ; gange(n); god(e);
godeman.**
gore *n.* gown, robe: in tag intensifying sup. *vnder* ~ wearing
clothes, among men, alive 6.5
(cf. **bis**). [OE *gāra* piece]
gossip *n.* co-sponsor (at baptism); kinsman 5.116 (note), (as
address) 209, 220. [OE *godsibb*]
gost *n.* spirit, soul 12.107; **gast**
12.192, 19.363; *þe Holi, Hali* ~
the Holy Ghost 7.101, 14.250,
17.52, 19.264, 420. *pl.* **gast(t)es**
spirits 19.33, 138, 281. [OE *gāst*]
gostliche *adj.* spiritual 17.73;
gastelich(e) 18.165, 302, 19.
41, 290. [OE *gāstlic*]
gostliche *adv.* in a spiritual way
17.47, 130. [OE *gāstlice*]
gote *n.* goat 9.33. *pl.* **get** 5.167.
[OE *gāt*, pl. *gǣt*] Cf. **gayt.**
gouþlich *adj.* handsome 6.5.
[OE *gōdlic*] Cf. **godly.**
grace *n.* grace (of God) 7.96,
8V.10, 9.171, 11.157, 12.67,

18.2; *ʒaf þe* ~ granted 7.77, 85.
[OF]
graciouse *adj.* graceful, elegant
8K.38. [OF *gracious*]
gradde, grade. See **grede(n).**
gray *adj.* grey (of eyes) 8E.16,
G.24; **grey, grei** (of Franciscan
friars) 8N.19, (of Cistercian
monks) 9.52, 164 (note). [OE
grǣg]
grame *n.* harm, wrong 1.49;
grome wrath 6.197. [OE
grama, groma]
grante, -i. See **graunti.**
grantise *n.* grant 6.414. [OF]
granunge *n.* groaning 19.145.
[OE *grānung*] See **grone.**
grapin *v.* feel, touch 19.99. [OE
grāpian]
gras(se) *n.* grass 8M.2, 9.8;
gres(se) 8v.2, 12.75, 14.119,
126. [OE *gærs, græs*, M *gers*;
OEN *gres*]
graunti *v.* allow 11.137. *pr.* *1 sg.*
granti, graunti grant, am
willing 1.157, 491. *subj. sg.*
grante 6.364, 375; **granti**
17.270. [OF *graanter*, AF
graunter]
graunt mercy *interj.* thank you
(*lit.* great thanks) 2.55. [AN
graunt merci]
grauel *n.* gravel 3.41. [OF
gravele]
great. See **gret(e).**
grede(n) *v.* cry out, shout 1.224,
3.196, 218; **grade** 2.67; *utest* ~
raise a hue and cry 1.641. *pr. 1
sg.* **grede** 1.332, 8D.4. *2 sg.*
gredest 1.374. *3 sg.* **gred**
1.623. *pl.* **gredeþ, -iþ** 1.629,
9.104. *subj. sg.* **grede** 1.656,
18.311. *pl.* **grede** cry for 17.
165, 168. *imper. sg.* **gred** (with
efter, for) 18.373. *pa. t. sg.*
gradde 5.282; **gredde** 18.70.
pl. **gradde** 1.620. [OE *grǣdan*]
Greek *adj.* Greek 2.131. [cf. OE
Grēcas, adj. *Grēcisc,* and OF *grec*]
gref *n.* pain 18.525; displeasure,

in *wiþhouten* ~ ungrudgingly 6.36. [OF]

Gregeis *n. pl.* Greeks 2.212. [AN]

grei, grey. See **gray**.

grein *n.* pearl 8G.2. [OF *grain* seed, in special sense]

greiðede *pa. t. sg.* prepared 18. 577. *pp.* **ygreiþed** 2.85, 208. [ON *greiða*]

greyue *n.* town governor, sheriff 4.198. [ON *greifi* in sense of OE *gerēfa*]

gremede *pa. t. subj. sg. impers.* angered: *lest hire* ~ lest she should get angry 8F.7. [OE *gremian* enrage]

gren(e) *adj.* green 1.18, 8L.3, M.1, 9.8, 14.116, 119. [OE *grēne*]

greot *n.*[1] grit, sand 18.191. [OE *grēot*]

greot *n.*[2] fragment, particle 19. 106. [OE *grot*, confused with prec.]

gres(se). See **gras(se).**

gret(e) *adj.* great, large, big (of physical size, and with wide fig. range) 1.234, 2.58, 4.39, 5.155, 8E.16, 12.158; 2.190, 5.72, 7.17, 9.9, 11.170; **great** 17.146, 18.277; **griat(e)** 17.177, 215. long 2.163; powerful 2.11; precious 7.190; sharp, severe 1.3, 5.168; strong, bold 1.281; swollen (with rage) 1.43, cf. **hert(e).** *comp.* **grettere** 1.74, 4.320; **greater** 17.251. [OE *grēat*, comp. (A) *grēttra*]

grete *pr. 1 sg.* greet, salute 8w.53. *3 sg.* **gret(t)** 2.124, 19.238; **gretes** 14.256. *imper. sg.* **gret** 8G.23. *pa. t. sg.* **grette** 6.160, 8v.9, attacked 4.238. *pp.* **igret** 19.288. [OE *grētan* greet, attack]

greten *pr. pl.* weep 6.357. [OE *grēotan* and *grētan*]

greting, -yng *n.* greeting, salutation 2.193; blessing 8G.49; **gretinke** 8v.13; **gretunge** 18. 137, 221, 19.240. [OE *grēting*]

gretnes *n.* enormity 14.125. [OE *grēatnes*]

grettere. See **gret(e).**

greue *v. refl.* feel unhappy, complain 6.59. [OF *grever*]

griat(e). See **gret(e).**

grylle *adj.* painful 8L.34. [cf. MDu *gril*]

grimfule *adj.* savage, fearsome 19.139. [OE *grimful*]

grimme *adj.* grim, stern 18.17. [OE *grimm*]

grin *n.* halter 16.174 (note). [OE *grīn*]

gripes *n. pl.* griffins 10.36. [OF *grip*, ML *grȳpa*]

gripeth *imper. pl.* take hold of, grasp, seize 4.309. *pa. t. sg.* **grop** 4.203, 298. *pl.* **gripen** 4.217. [OE *grīpan, grāp, gripon*]

grisle *n.* horror 19.148, *ham to* ~ to their horror 108 (see **to**). [cf. next and **agrise**]

grislich(e) *adj.* horrible, ghastly 1.180, 10.36, 18.31, 19.104. *comp.* **grisluker** 19.111. [OE *grislic*]

griþ, grið *n.* protection 6.267; peace 18.221; **yriþþ** 13.111 (note), 246. [OE *griþ* from ON]

griþbruche *n.* breach of the peace 1.692. [OE *griþbryce*]

grom *n.* boy 4.58. *pl.* **gromes** 1.603. [cf. MDu *grom* fry, young, and OF *gromet* servant]

grome. See **grame.**

grone *pr. 1 sg.* groan 8D.4. [OE *grānian*]

gronge *n.* farmhouse 4.32. [AN *graunge*]

grop. See **gripeth.**

grounde *n.* bottom (of a stream, well, &c.) 3.41, 5.74, 91; ground 3.47, 7.51, 11.16, *to* ~ to the ground 7.52, 11.45, 99. **grund(e)** 12.165, 19.94, 1.214, 4.286; **grvnde** 8w.38; **grunden** (*obl.*) 10.24. [OE *grúnd*]

groue *v.* grow 14.126. *pr. 3 sg.* **groweþ** 8A.3. [OE *grōwan*] ᵹrucchinᵹ *n.* grumbling 1.301. [from next]

ᵹruchchede *pa. t. pl.* grumbled, complained 17.195. [OF *gruchier*]

ᵹruldepa. *t. subj. sg.* were twanging 1.98. [cf. OE *griellan* provoke]

ᵹrund(e), ᵹrvnde. See ᵹrounde.

ᵹrure *n.* terror 19.108. [OE *gryre*]

ᵹrureful(e) *adj.* terrible 18.32, 19.139. [from prec.]

ᵹuldene *adj.* golden 10.37, 19.193. [OE *gylden*]

ᵹult. See ᵹylt.

ᵹulteð *pr. 3 sg.* sins, offends 19.20. [OE *gyltan*]

ᵹun(ne); ᵹuod(e); ᵹuodnesse. See ᵹinneþ; ᵹod(e); ᵹodnes(se).

ᵹurdel *n.* girdle 8E.61, 18.590; ᵹurdul 80.1; ᵹirdil 8x.5. [OE *gyrdel*]

ᵹuðhede *n.* youth 12.3. [ᵹuheðe +-hede]

ᵹæn *prep.* towards, with respect to 13.25. [OE *on-gēan*; see aᵹein]

ᵹaf(f); ᵹare. See ᵹeue; ᵹore.

ᵹare *adj.* ready, prepared 1.171; ᵹarow, ᵹaru 18.556, 10.203. *pl.* ᵹare 1.520; ᵹarewe, ᵹarowe 10.117, 19.293; ᵹere 8H.21. [OE *gearu, gearw-*]

ᵹat(e), ᵹatte *n.* gate 5.20, 7.259, 11.110, 14.150, 157; yate 14.109, 128. *pl.* ᵹates 11.116. [OE *geat*, A *gæt*; pl. *gatu*] See ᵹate.¹

ᵹe *adv.* yes 5.176, 207, 6.232, 19.88; ya 4.315; (emphatic) ᵹeoi 18.525; yai 14.110. *interj.* indeed 1.690, 18.625, 19.180. [OE *gēa, geā*, A *gē*] Cf. ᵹus.

ᵹe(e) *pron. 2 pl.* you 2.38, 8F.17 (men in general), 13.79, 14.85, 18.21; ᵹhe 3.271; (with suffixed pron.) ᵹét 13.98; ye(e) 4.205,

308, 14.162, 17.22, 185; ᵹe 12.37. *acc., dat.* ᵹou *refl.* 3.269 (for yourselves); you 4.210, 226; ᵹuw 13.83; yu, yw 17.96, 152; eou 10.92; eu 1.751; ou 5.214, 8E.79, G.39, H.36; ov 7.40; ow 1.641, 18.10, 19.158. *poss. adj.* ᵹoure your 3.272; ᵹure 9.185, 13.86; yure 17.71; or 8F.17; ower 1.643, 657, 18.22. *gen. (part.)* ower of you 18.252. Used as polite form to one person: ᵹe, ye 2.73, 4.186; ᵹou, you 2.72, 142, 4.176; ᵹoure 2.71. [OE ᵹē, ēow, ēower] See þou.

ᵹeden(n). See eode.

ᵹeep *adj.* lively, fresh 8G.36. [OE *gēap*]

ᵹef *conj.* if 1.263, 5.98, 204, 8F.6, H. 15, 18.21, 19.135; ᵹef 12.144; yef 17.26, 76; ᵹif 1.51, 2.54, 3.15, 5.134, 7.19, 10.56; ᵹiff 13.11; ᵹeif 6.443; ᵹif 16.30, 195; if 6.32, 85; hif 15.16; to see, try, if 1.536, 3.126, 7.182, 201; even if 19.351; whether 2.224, 6.242, 17.262, 18.671. ~ þat, þet 1.439, 6.52, 59, 19.154; ~ hit be so þat if, on condition that 6.228. [ONb (rare) *gef*, OE *gif*]

ᵹef(e); ᵹehatenn. See ᵹeue; hote(n).

ᵹeiᵹeð *pr. 3 sg.* cries 18.559. *pl.* ᵹeieð 19.152. *subj. sg.* ᵹeᵹe 8N.35. *pa. t. subj. sg.* ᵹeide 18.42. [OE *gēgan*]

ᵹeyn-char *n.* turning back 8H.35. [cf. OE *gēancyrr* and *gegn-*]

ᵹein-cume *n.* return 18.562. [OE *gēancyme, gegn-*]

ᵹelde(n) *n.* yield, surrender 11.31, 19.432; pay (with dir. obj. of payment and dat. of thing paid for) 19.339. *pr. 1 sg.* ᵹelde yield 2.50. *pl.* ᵹelde 2.100; ᵹeldeð return 19.239. *subj. sg.* ᵹelde reward 4.71. *imper. sg.* yeld pay for 17.189. *pa. t. pl.* ᵹulden gave back 2.116. *subj.*

sg. ȝolde 11.27. *pp.* ȝolden restored 2.181; iȝolde paid 3.116. [OE *géldan, gúldon, gólden*]

ȝelle *v.* scream 3.49 (but app. an error for *welle* boil). [OA *gellan*]

ȝelpe *v.* boast 6.227. *pr. 2 sg.* ȝeolpest 1.567; ȝulpest 1.599, 608. *3 sg.* ȝelpeð 19.212. [OE *gylpan*, A *gelpan*]

ȝeme *n.* heed (regularly obj. of nim) 1.473, 7.157, 18.122, 208, 19.167. [OA *ȝéme(n)*]

ȝeme *v.* heed, care about 19.201. [OA *ȝéman*]

ȝemeles *n.* negligence 19.407. [OA *ȝémelē(a)st*]

ȝemeles(e) *adj.* careless, negligent 19.19, 64. [OA *ȝémelēas*]

ȝene *v.* counter, answer 1.505. [cf. ONb *gigegnian* from *gegn* against; see aȝein]

ȝeode; ȝeoi; ȝeolpest. See eode; ȝe; ȝelpe.

ȝeond *prep.* through, over 10.35, 187. [OE *geónd*]

ȝeonge; ȝeongen. See ȝong(e); gange(n).

ȝeoniende *pr. p.* gaping 18.41. [OA *geonian*]

ȝeorde *n.* rod, staff 7.89, 93. *pl.* ȝerden sticks 18.194. [OA *ȝérd*, pl. *-a, -e*]

ȝeorne. See ȝerne *adv.*

ȝeornliche *adv.* assiduously, attentively 18.361, 19.245, 394; eagerly 19.172. [OE *geornlíce*]

ȝeot. See ȝet(e).

ȝeoue *n.* gift 18.454, grace 73. [OM *geofu*]

ȝeoue(n). See ȝeue.

ȝephede *n.* astuteness 1.429. [ȝeep+-hede]

ȝer(e) *n.* year 3.22, 7.5, 8M.5, 9.170, 11.105; yere 14.132, 17.72; gear, gær(e) 16.1, 118, 123. *gen.* (adv.) ȝeares, gæres in [this] year 16.66, 7. *pl.* ȝer(e) 6.67, 10.244; after numeral 7.8, 15, 115, 9.179, yere 14.101,

yeir 14.273; ȝeres in ~ *ant dahes*, pl. of 'a year and a day' 18.555. [OE *gēar*, LWS and A *gēr*]

ȝerden; ȝere. See ȝeorde; ȝare.

ȝerne *v.* desire, covet 8F.27. *pr. 1 sg.* ȝirne 18.642, 655. *3 sg.* yhernes likes 14.1. *subj. sg.* ȝirne 6.45. *pa. t. sg.* iærnde asked for 16.34. [OA *ȝérnan*, WS *ȝírnan*]

ȝerne *adv.* earnestly, eagerly 3.109, 5.93, 6.13; carefully 5.15; ȝeorne 18.139, 201, 19.227; ȝorne 1.346, 407; yerne 4.146, 191, 8R.5. [OE *géorne*]

ȝet(e) *adv.* 1.225, 5.153, 6.111, 8K.11, 10.320, 18.129; ȝĕt 13.159; get 12.26, 16.91; gæt 16.190; yet 17.129; iett 16.61; ȝite 9.101; ȝeot 7.95, 164; ȝuyt 7.252, 277; ȝut 1.349, 425; ȝette 1.575 (rhyming *lę́te*), 18.619. yet, up to now (with neg. or interrog.) 1.349, 353, 5.153, 16.61, strengthening *never* 8K.11, 16.190; still, to this or that time 6.111, 7.95, 252, 10.320, 12.26, 16.145, 17.129, 18.459; at some (future) time 10.327; even 6.404, 18.279, 460, 561, 19.371; further 1.225, 425, 12.143, 13.159; ~ *anes* see **anes**; nevertheless 18.129; ~ *mo, mare* still more 9.101, 18.619; *þe* ~ still, none the less 10.61. [OE *ȝíet(a), ȝȳt*, A *ȝét(a)*; *þā ȝét, ȝét þā*, &c.]

ȝĕt 13.98 = *ȝe it*; see ȝe(e), hit.

ȝetten *adv.* yet, still 18.600. [ȝet(e)+þen, see þan(ne)]

ȝetteð *pr. 3 sg.* grants 19.278. *subj. sg.* ȝetti 18.78. *imper. sg.* ȝette 18.642. *pa. t. sg.* iætte 16.36. [ON *játta* assim. to OE *ȝē* yes; cf. OE *ȝēatan*]

ȝeue *v.* give, grant 6.191, 8G.33; ȝefe 1.668; yeue 4.189, 17 187; ȝeoue(n) 10.141, 18.609;

ȝiue(n)1.650,3.127,7.24, 9.116;
ȝif 3.179, 260; ȝifenn 13.254;
ȝyuen 16.184, ~ *up* surrender
114; iiuen (*up*) 16.267, 284.
infl. infin. to ȝeouene to be
given 18.613, cf. forte ȝeouen
601. *pr. 1 sg.* ȝeue 6.271; ȝiue
1.644. *2 sg.* ȝeuest 6.287. *3 sg.*
ȝeueð18.450,19.100;yefþ,yeft
17.257, 38. *pl.* ȝeueþ 1.734;
ȝeoueð 18.78; ȝiueþ 1.731.
subj. sg. ȝeue 5.34, 6.442,
8H.20,U.7,19.419;ȝeoue 18.312;
yeue, yef 17.79, 170. *imper. sg.*
ȝif 3.119; hyef, hyf 8w.42,
grant 55. *pl.* yeueþ 4.177.*pa. t.
sg.* ȝaf 1.55, 2.155, 3.200 (see
bene *n.*¹), 7.77; ȝaff 13.170;
yaf 17.192; iaf 16.115, 249;
ȝef 18.145, 19.30; ȝæf, ȝeaf
16.7, 22. *pl.* ȝaf 3.188, yaf
4.325; iauen, iafen 16.289,
152;ȝeuen 4.272. *subj. sg.* ȝæfe
13.12; ȝeue 18.411; ȝeoue 7.
155. *pp.* ȝifen 16.40; iȝeuen
18.463, 517; iȝiue 1.359, 7.25.
[OE *gifan,* A *gefan,* M *-geofan;
geaf, gæf; gēafon, gēfon* (cf. ON
gáfu); *gifen, gefen*]
ȝeueðe *adj.* allotted, in store 10.
175. [OE *gifeþe* infl. by ȝeue]
ȝhe *pron. 3 sg. fem. nom.* she
3.197, 264, 291; ȝe 12.68, 72;
ȝho 13.48, 53, 150.(with suffixed
pron.) ȝet 12.89; ȝhõt 13.151.
[OE *hēo,* M *hīe,* with shift of
stress] See heo, sche.
ȝhe. See ȝe(e).
ȝhõt 13.151 = *ȝho it*; see ȝhe, hit.
ȝif(f), ȝifenn. See ȝef, ȝeue.
ȝimmes *n. pl.* jewels 19.275.
[OE *gimm*]
ȝirne; ȝite; ȝiue(n); ȝode;
ȝoȝelinge. See ȝerne *v.*;
ȝet(e); ȝeue; eode; ȝulinge.
Ȝol *n.* Yule, Christmas 6.116.
[OE *geōl*; cf. ON *jól* (pl.)]
ȝolde(n). See ȝelde(n).
ȝollest *pr. 2 sg.* yell, hoot 1.179.
[imit.]

ȝomere *adv.* mournfully 1.293.
[OE *geõmore*] See yemer(e).
ȝong(e), ȝongue *adj.* young 6.
361, 7.9, 24; ȝeonge 10.5;
yong 14.282; ȝung(ue) 9.121,
7.15; iunge 16.308. inclusive
phr. ~ *and old* all 9.63, *þa* ~ *and
þa alde* 10.227. *comp.* ȝongere
2.286. [OE *geóng*]
ȝonge. See gange(n).
ȝore *adv.* for a long time, long
8F.27, M.8; ȝare 5.169; long
ago 18.9. [OE *geāra*]
ȝorne; ȝou, ȝoure. See ȝerne
adv.; ȝe(e).
ȝuheðe *n.* youth 19.431; youth
8R.3. [OE *geoguþ*]
ȝuyt; ȝulden. See ȝet(e);
ȝelde(n).
ȝulinge *n.* yowling, wailing 1.
601; ȝoȝelinge 1.40. [imit.]
ȝulpest; ȝung(ue); ȝure. See
ȝelpe; ȝong(e); ȝe(e).
ȝurnen *pa. t. pl.* ran 10.184.
[OE *ge-úrnon* from *-írnan*; see
erne]
ȝurstendai *adv.* yesterday 6.73.
[OE *gyrstan dæg*]
ȝus *adv.* yes 6.294. [OE *gȳse*]
Cf. ȝe.

ȝut; ȝuw; ȝwane; ȝwanne;
ȝware; ȝwat; ȝweþur; ȝwi,
ȝwy; ȝwiȝt, ȝwiit, ȝwite;
ȝwile, ȝwyle. See ȝet(e);
ȝe(e); whan; whonene;
wher(e); what; hweðer;
whi; whit(e); while.

ha. See he; heo; hi(i).
habbe(n) *v.* 1.194, 3.230, 7.22,
10.251, 11.59, 16.31, 17.83,
18.73; habbenn 13.113; hab
9.169; haue(n) 2.110, 3.103,
6.196, 8E.56, 12.137, 16.17;
hafen 16.11; haf 15.30, 54;
han 5.87; ha 8N.9. have, possess 1.109, 2.110, 3.103, 6.91,
7.22, 9.169, 11.59, 18.73; *to
hauen* to be had 12.76; *hiþte* ~
be in haste 8N.11; take 6.270,

327, 10.25; feel 1.309, 3.219, 7.17, 8D.18, 14.31; (with infin.) have as a duty, be obliged 17. 211. *auxil.* (forming perf.) 2.42, 4.72, 5.45, 6.51, 8R.3, 10.10; (forming perf. infin.) 4.230, 5.87, 8N.9, 15.30, 18.515, 525; (forming pluperf.) 1.172, 2.8, 3.245, 4.38, 5.68, 10.57. *pr. 1 sg.* habbe 1.130, 5.200, 6.67, 17.73, 18.97; habe 6.91; abbe 8R.3, 9; haue, have 3.282, 4.313, 5.45, 8D.29, 14.70, 5.40; haf 14.73; (with prefixed pron.) Ichaue 8D.28; (with suffixed pron.) haui 6.267; haw (-*y* joined in MS.) 15.46. *2 sg.* hauest 1.109, 8D.8, 10.10, 18. 84, 19.87; hast(e) 2.40, 42; (with suffixed pron.) hauestu, hastu 1.626, 15.12; hafs 15.66; has 14.219; hest 17.110. *3 sg.* haueþ, -ð, -th 1. 123, 671, 5. 122, 6.112, 12.33, 18.87, 105, 19.39, 4.72; hafeð, hafueð 10. 73, 81, 109; hafeþþ 13.125; haued, -t 8W.34, 40, T.42; haþ, hath 2.94, 3.141, 8E.37, N.11, 7.68, 17.53; has 14.31, 58. *pl.* habbeþ, -ð 1.309, 639, 17. 109, 18.37, 19.152; habbeth, -t, -tþ 17.22, 69, 198; habbez (= -þ) 7.255; habbeoð 10.305; habeþ 17.242; haueþ 1.633, 5. 256, 6.310; haue(n) 4.213, 316, 12.69, 14.92; haf 15.29; han 2.118, 3.288, 8K.57; as 15.83. *subj. sg.* habbe 8H.32, 18.285, 313; haue 3.76, 226, 4.69 (but see note), 6.51, 202; (with suffixed pron.) haui may I have 6.267; haf 14.65; *pl.* habbe(n) 18.89, 162; haue 8F.17; han 8D.18. *imper. sg.* haue 6.145, 270, 8D.14, 10.25, 18.427. *pl.* habbeþ 2.146. *pa. t. 1, 3 sg.* had(de) 1.172, 2.8, 3.245, 5.24, 7.16, 14.101, 16.145; hade 14.200; adde 11.33, 16.236; hauede 4.38, 128 (see 58 note),

8V.13; hafd(e) 10.57 (? *subj.*), 145, 241, 16.17; hedde 5.285, 16.304, 17.105; hede 5.288; heuede 5.68, 6.9, 184; hefde 16.260, 19.284; hæfde 10.122, 16.9; heafde 16.69. *pl.* hadde(n) 2.212, 3.219, 7.221, 16.155; adde 11.63; haueden 4.167; haffdenn 13.135; hedde(n) 17.11, 44; hefden 16.161, 18.205, 19.288; hæfden 16.296; heafdon 16.94. *subj. 1, 3 sg.* had(de) should have 2.65, would have 7.284, had 1.102, 2.250, 3.270, ~ *ben* (in dependent clause) was 3.193; hedde 5.135; heuede 5.134, 6.381, would have 8E.84; hefde 19. 129, 131. *2 sg.* heuedest 5.177, 6.250; hefdest 18.309. *pl.* hefden 18.310. *pp.* iheed 17.230. [OE *habban*; *hæfþ, hafaþ*; *hæfde*] See nabbe.

hac. See ac(c).

had *n.* person 13.180. [OE *hād*] -had *suff.* forming nouns denoting condition, as spus-, þreo-, widewe-. [OE *-hād*] Cf. -hede.

had(-), hæfde(n); hæfod. See habbe(n); heued.

hæfedd-peninng *n.* poll-tax 13. 24. [heued+OE *pening*, see peni]

hælden *v. intr.* collapse, fall 10.24. *pr. pl.*, *tr.* healdeð pour 18.80. *pa. t. sg.*, *intr.* hæld fell 10.24; heolde advanced 10.221, 266. *pl.* halden 10.275. [OA *hældan*]

hælennde *n.* healer, redeemer 13.86. [OE *hælend*; cf. helen v.²]

hæleðe *n. pl. gen.* of men 10.221. [OE *hæleþ*]

hær; hærme; hærnes; hæse; hæþene; hæued; haf(-); hafd, hafued; haзeþorn. See euer(e); harm(e); hernes *n.*¹; heste; heþen; heued;

habbe(n); heued; hawe-
þorne.

hay *interj.* alas! 15.18. [cf. OF *hé*]

haiward, hay-, haywart *n.*
hedge-keeper 5.26, 8N.24, 27.
[OE *hæg-weard*]

hak *n.* mattock, hoe 14.103. [cf.
MDu *hak*]

hal *adj.* whole, entire, sound, unharmed 10.310, 18.265, 19.106;
hol 3.118. [OE *hāl*]

hald(-); halden. See holde(n);
hælden.

hale *n.* corner, nook 1.2. [OA
halh, dat. *hale*]

halechede; halechen. See
halheð; halhen.

haleð *pr. 3 sg.* drags 12.77. [OF
haler]

haleweiȝe *adj.* healing 10.310.
[see halwei]

half *n.* half 11.105; side 19.162,
181, 267; *a þis* ~ (as *prep.*) before 18.339; halue 18.168, behalf 2.194; *o Ꝿodess hallf* in
God's name 13.77. *pl.* half
directions, points of compass, in
a fowr ~ on all sides 18.383, *a
feouwer* ~ (quasi-*prep.*) into all
parts of 10.138. [OA *half*, obl.
halfe] Cf. æsthallf, norðhalf,
souþhalf, westhalf.

half *adj.* half 5.8, 7.252, 10.99,
16.205. [OA *half*]

half *adv.* half 5.4, 7.155, 8G.37,
19.371. [prec.]

halhen *n. pl.* saints 18.36, 119,
19.313; halechen 16.201. gen.
halwen 11.155. [OE *hālga*]

halheð *pr. 3 sg.* sanctifies 18.581.
pa. t. sg. halechede consecrated
16.135. *pp.* hallȝhedd 13.264.
[OE *hālgian*]

hali(e), -y. See holi(e).

halidom *n.* sacred relics 16.96,
283. [OE *hāligdōm*]

haliliche *adv.* in sanctity 19.300.
[OE *hāliglīce*]

halines *n.* sanctity 14.286. [OE
hālignes]

halle *n.* hall 2.279, 6.22, 9.11,
10.14. *gen.* 10.23. *pl.* halles
9.53. [OA *hall*]

halle; hallȝhe; hallȝhedd;
halp. See al *adj.*; holi(e);
halheð; help(e).

hals *n.* neck 16.177. [OA]

halse *imper. sg.* implore 18.397.
[OA *halsian*]

halsinde *pr. p. adj.* imploring
18.381. [from prec.]

halt; halue. See holde(n);
half.

halwei *n.* healing water, medi-
cinal drink or lotion 9.84;
healewi 18.298. [OE *hālewǣg*,
hǣle-; cf. ON *heilivágr* balm]
See haleweiȝe.

halwen; ham; ham(e). See
halhen; am, hi(i), hom;
hom(e).

hamer *n.* hammer 4.304. *pl.*
homeres 18.335. [OE *hamor*,
homer]

hamseolf. See hemself.

hamward *adv.* towards home
7.152. [OE *hāmweard*]

han; hand; hand(e). See
habbe(n); and; hond(e).

handbare *adj.* empty-handed
4.34. [hond(e)+bare]

handlen, handli *v.* touch, take
into the hands 3.192, 214. [OE
handlian]

hantit; har(e). See hauntest;
hi(i).

harace *n.* horse-breeding estab-
lishment, stud 9.35. [OF
haras]

hard(e) *adj.* hard 1.382; strong,
brave 10.147; heavy, severe
1.652, 11.14, 12.96; heard 19.
131, harsh 146. as *n.* difficult
circumstances 1.449; hardship,
suffering 8w.16, 18.414, 19.189,
heart 19.187. *gen.* heardes
(part.) *na þing* ~ nothing hard
19.185, (irregularly retained
after *of*) 195. *sup.* heardest
18.448. [OE *héard*]

N n

harde *adv.* hard 6.204; heavily 5.195; harshly, cruelly 7.128; severely 12.99; **hearde** 18.327. [OE *héarde*]

hardeliche. See **hardliche.**

hardi, hardy *adj.* bold, brave 2.79, 307; rash 2.20; resolute 18.3, 109; confident 18.113. [OF *hardi*]

hardilike *adv.* boldly, vigorously 12.70. [**hardi**+northerly form of -**liche**]

hardliche *adv.* vigorously 10.20; **hardeliche** bravely 1.280. [OE *heardlíce*]

harlede *pa. t. sg.* dragged 11.68. *pl.* 11.17, 63. [obscure]

harm(e) *n.* harm, injury, damage 1.691, 2.106, 11.88, 14.260; **hearm** 19.133, *mare* ~ *is* more is the pity 18.204; **hærme** in *for Arðures* ~ to do injury to Arthur 10.148. *pl.* **harmes** troubles 8F.10; **hearmes** kinds of harm 18.61. [OE *hearm*]

harpe *n.* harp 1.22, 98. [OE *hearpe*]

has, hast(e), hastu. See **es** *pron.*; **habbe(n).**

hasteliche *adv.* quickly 17.102. [OF *haste*+-**liche**]

hat(e); hat(te). See **hot(e); hote(n).**

hatie *v.* hate 17.80. *pr. 1 sg.* hate 8L.1. *2 sg.* hates 15.20. *3 sg.* **hateþ, -dh** 17.264, 80; **hatiet** 1.186; **heateð** 18.210, 19.124. *pl.* hatied 17.264; **heatieð** 19.126. *pp.* hated 8F.34. [OE *hatian*, M **heatian*]

hattren *n. pl.* clothes 8N.6. [OE *hæteru* pl.]

haþ, hath, haue(-), have(-); haudes. See **habbe(n); heued.**

hauk *n.* hawk 9.123; **hauec(k)** 1.223, 219. *gen.* **hauekes** 1.207. [OE *hafoc*, ON *hauk-r*]

hauntest *pr. 2 sg.* practise, pursue 2.45. *3 sg.* **hantit** 8x.18;

hauntes attends 15.41. [AN *ha(u)nter*]

hauene *n.* harbour 10.161, 221. [OE *hæfen*]

haw. See **habbe(n).**

haweþorne, hawȝþorn *n.* hawthorn 7.188; *attrib.* 7.111; **haȝeþorn** 7.introd. [OE *haguþorn*]

hawle *n.* hail 9.39. [OE *hagol*]

haxst. See **heiȝe.**

he *pron. 3 sg. masc.* he 2.13, 3.12, 4.5, 5.3; it 1.21, 252, 568, 11.37, 14.36; (in reduced stress) **ha** 17.21, 68, a 232, 248. *acc.* **hine** him 1.707, 5.123, 10.10, 18.175; it 1.426, 10.93; **hyne, hin** 17.9, 29; *refl.* 1.329, (with **self**) 10.253. *acc., dat.* **him, hym** (to, for) him 1.150, 2.6, 27, 3.5, 4.126, 5.2, 6.82, 7.10; **himm** 13.10; it 16.121; *refl.* (for) himself 2.29, 93, 123, 3.23, 4.6, 29, 7.74, 8K.19, 9.162, 11.49, 13.23, 18.124; pleonastic, with vb. of motion 5.31, with **be** 1.167, 5.261, with other vbs. 9.133, 10.105, 156. *poss. adj.* **his, hys** his 2.8, (postponed) 306, 3.10, 4.36, 8w.25; **hiss** 13.6; (in reduced stress) **is, ys** 4.3, 7.3, 8H.22, P.2, T.15, 9.134, 11.32, 17.209, 18.294; **hise** *sg.* 4.6, 38, 95, *pl.* 4.30, 48, 12.5, 27, 16.152, 17.15; **ise** 17.227. *pron.* **his, hys** his 3.107, 8D.39; his men 11.37; his possessions 18.462; **is** 11.50. *gen.* of him 4.320 (note), 18.294, (obj.) 18.424, 652. [OE *hē, hine, him, his*] See **himself.**

he; heafde. See **eȝe, heo, hi(i); habbe(n).**

heafedmenn *n. pl.* important men 16.86. [OE *héafodmann*]

heald; healdeð; heale; healen; healewi; heard, -t; hearde. See **holde(n); hælden; hele; helen** *v.²*; **halwei; hard(e); harde.**

heard-iheortet *adj.* hard-

hearted 18.480, 644. [hard(e)
+hert(e); see feol-iheortet
and cf. OE *heardheort*]
heardschipes *n. pl.* sufferings
18.401. [hard(e)+-schipe]
hearm. See harm(e).
hearmin *v. intr.* do harm 19.
326; *tr.* injure 18.248. *pr. pl.*
hearmið 18.337. [OE *hear-
mian*]
heast; heate. See heste; hete.
heatel *adj.* hostile, cruel 18.638,
19.146. [OM **heatol* = WS
hatol]
heateð, -ieð; heaued. See
hatie; heued.
heaued-luuen *n. pl.* chief kinds
of love 18.541. [heued+loue;
cf. next]
heaued-sunne *n.* mortal sin
18.555. [OE *hēafodsynn*]
heaued-þeawes, heued- *n. pl.*
cardinal virtues 19.40, 415.
[heued+þeaw; cf. prec.]
hechelunge *n.* gnashing 19.114.
[? rel. to ME *hechele*, OE **hecel*,
a tool for combing flax]
hed; hedde(n). See heued;
habbe(n).
heddre *n.* blood in a vein 5.43.
[see eddre-blod]
hede *n.* heed: *taken* ~ notice
8E.42. [from OE *hēdan* v.]
-hede *suff.* forming nouns denoting condition, as child-, godd-,
guð-, wrecce-. [OE **-hǣdu*
rel. to -had]
hede; hef; hefde(n); hefed;
hefennlike; hefenn-, heff-
ne(ss). See eode, habbe(n);
heouen; habbe(n); heued;
heouenlich(e); heuen(-).
hegge *n.* hedge 1.17, 59, 8N.8.
[OE *hecge*]
heght *n.* height 14.203, 244; *of a
nellen* ~ an ell high 14.283. [OA
hēhþu]
heglice; hehte(n); heȝe,
heien. See heiȝliche; hote(n);
eȝe.

heie-renning *n.* running of the
eyes 6.283. [eȝe+vbl. n. from
renne]
heiȝ(e) *adj.* 2.29, 129, 7.100,
9.125; heȝe 8E.21, H.14; heh(e)
8N.17, 18.30, 240; hehȝe 10.
287; hei, hey 11.45, 38, 5.31,
15.79; heþ (= *heh*) 8N.35. high
2.29, 7.100, 248, 8E.21, 15.79,
18.233; solemn, splendid 7.196;
exalted 8H.14; noble 18.479; inclusive phr. ~ *and lowe* all 10.
287; ~ *of mode* high-spirited 9.
125; chief, principal 18.240; ~
waie highway 2.327. *an, on
vpon* ~ high 11.38, 45, 18.372,
650, high up 5.31, above 7.175,
19.253, up above 8N.17, aloud
35; *bend on* ~ high-arched 8E.25.
dat. fem. heȝere great 10.202.
comp. herre 18.315. *sup.* hest(e)
8K.36, 18.315, 605; þ'exte =
þe hexte 7.47, hexst noblest 10.
98; heȝhesst 13.240; *on hest* in
the highest seat 19.54. [OE
hē(a)h, late *hēag-*; A comp. *hērra*,
sup. *hē(h)st*] See alrehecst.
heiȝe *adv.* high 2.312; hehe 18.
534; heie, hey 1.604, 15.80.
sup. haxst 10.112. [LOE *hēage*
and *hēh*, sup. adj. *hēahst*]
heiȝliche *adv.* with great ceremony 7.196; heglice 16.231.
[heiȝ(e)+-liche; cf. OE *hēa-
līce*]
heiȝtte. See hote(n).
heil *adj.* healthy, well, in phr.
~ *and sund* 12.23, 125. [ON
heil-l]
heiman *n.* nobleman 11.106.
[heiȝ(e)+man]
heyse *n.* ease: *at* ~ comfortable
8N.28. [OF *eise*]
heyte; heke; held(en). See
hote(n); ek(e); holde(n).
helde *n.* favour, kindness 8F.9.
[LOE *hélde*]
hele *n.* health, cure 8K.72; heale
vigour 18.634; salvation 19.272,
408. [OE *hǣlu*]

hele(n) v.¹ conceal, keep secret 3.272; (absol.) keep silent 6.241, 253. *imper. sg.* **hele** 2.198; **hel** (with dat. of person) 15.40. *pp.* **iheoled** covered 7.253. [OE *helan, helian*]

helen v.² heal 4.263; **healen** 18. 575. *pp.* **ihealet** 18.572. [OE *hælan*]

helere n. saviour 17.163. [prec. +OE *-ere*; cf. **hælennde**]

heles n. *pl.* heels 4.164. [OE *hēla*]

hell(e) n. hell 8G.35, 12.196, 14. 211, 19.5. *gen.* **helle** 18.15, 19. 408. [OE *hell*]

helle-dogge n. hell-hound 18. 383. [prec.+**dogge**]

helle-ware n. *pl.* inhabitants of hell 18.48. [OE *hell-ware*]

helle-wurmes n. *pl.* reptiles of hell 19.109. [**hell(e)**+**worme**]

helmen n. *pl.* (*dat.*) helmets 10. 276. [OE *helm*]

help(e) n. help 3.76, 6.164, 11. 40, 15.54, 16.103; *him on* ~ as a help to him 19.229, *ow on* ~ a help to you 19.253. [OE *help*]

help(e), helpen v. help 1.677 (with dat.), 2.54, 3.140, 6.188, 10.142, 12.135. *pr. 1 sg.* **helpe** 1.342, 386 (with *to*, towards, with). *3 sg.* **helpeþ, -ð** 8L.4, 12.77; *impers.* 8L.8, **helpþ** 1.127; **helpit** 8Y.5; **helps** 14.72. *pl.* **helpen** 6.211, 12.123; **helpeð** 18.436. *subj. sg.* **help(e)** 6.210, 228, 15.61, 17.160. *imper. sg.* **help(e)** 2.62, 6.221. *pa. t. sg.* **halp** 5.84. *subj. pl.* **heolpen** 10.202. *pp.* **holpen** in ~ *him doun with* helped him to take down 4.167; **iholpen** 18.37. [OE *helpan, h(e)alp, hulpon, holpen*]

hem(m). See **hi(i)**.

hemp n. hemp 4.50. [OE *henep*]

hemself pron. *pl.* themselves: *of* ~ from their own number 16. 82; **hamseolf** 18.171, 418;

hamseoluen 18.437. [*hem, ham* (see **hi(i)**)+**self**]

hen n. hen 1.291, 5.7. *pl.* **hennen** 5.28, 32, 40 (*dat.*, see **lete(n)**). [OE *henn*, pl. *henna*]

hend(e) adj. gracious, courteous 6.119, 154, 8T.41, 9.183, 11.123; *as* ~ courteously 6.61; graceful, beautiful 10.38, 15.50. as *n.* fair one 8K.55, 66; *pl.* people of good breeding 8E.42. *sup.* **hendest** 8F.9, 10.90, 18.606. [OE *gehénde* at hand, convenient]

hende *prep.* near: *com hem* ~ approached them 2.186. [OE *ge-hénde*]

hende. See **end(e)**.

heng v. hang. *intr.* 15.80. *tr.*, *pa. t. sg.* **henged** 16.165, 166. *pp.* **henged** 15.82. [ON *hengja*] Cf. **hongi**.

hengen *pa. t. pl.* hung 16.167; **hanged** 16.228. [OE *hēngon*, *pa. t. pl.* of *hōn*] Cf. prec. and **hongi**.

henyng n. insult, dishonourable proposal 8F.8. [from OA *hēnan* humiliate]

henne *adv.* hence, away from here 4.111, 207; **heonne, honne** 1.631, 66; from this life 1.524, 8W.59. [OE *heonan(e)*]

hennefugeles n. *pl.* hens 16.71. [OE *hennfugol*]

hente v. take, seize 8K.71. *pa. t. sg.* **hent** underwent, suffered 11.92. *pl.* **hente** seized 11.16. *pp.* **hent** 8K.55. [OE *hentan*]

heo pron. *3 sg. fem.* she 1.619, 7.12, 8E.8, K.45, 10.23, 75, 18. 488, 19.48; **ho** 1.19, 102; **hoe** 6.20, 341; **hue** 8D.31, K.28; **ha** 6.362, 18.73, 261, 19.44, 62; **he** 1.97, 3.64, 8E.32, L.7, V.14, 20; **hi(i)** 1.10, 141, 3.47, 52, 211, 17.94; **hye** 17.95; **yo** 15.47. it 1.258, 7.94, 178, 253, 18.277, 611, 17.28. *acc.* **heo** her 10.31; **hi** 1.29, 32; *refl.* 1.155. *acc., dat.* **hir(e), hyre** (to, for) her 1.104,

2.138, 3.50, 6.10, 8E.83, 10.43
(*dat.*), 16.308, 17.93, 18.5; *refl.*
(for) herself 6.406, 7.23, 124,
12.71, 18.580; pleonastic, with
vbs. of motion 6.299, 10.40,
other vb. 3.205. it 7.93, 18.532,
613, 19.8, 193, that 18.611. here
3.67, 14.18, *what* ~ *were* what
was the matter with her 3.203.
poss. adj. hir(e), hyr(e) her 1.26,
2.136, 3.211, 7.13, 8E.16, 14.74,
its 18.18, 19.407; her(e) 2.139,
3.48, 8G.30, 17.92; (with force
of objective gen.) of her 1.324,
3.152, 8K.77. *pron. disjunct.*
hiren hers 18.452. [OE *hēo*
(*heō*), M *hīe*; acc. *hī*(*e*); gen., dat.
hire, heore, &c.] See 3he, sche.
heo, heom, heore ; heold(e) ;
heoldon ; heolpen. See hi(i) ;
hælden, holde(n) ; help(e).
heoneward *adv.* away from here
18.133. [henne+OE -*weard*]
heonne ; heorte ; heortes. See
henne ; hert(e) ; hert.
heorteliche *adv.* gladly 18.496.
[cf. OE *ge-heortlīce*, sense un-
certain]
heou. See hou.
heouen *v.* raise, lift: *to* ~ (as *n.*)
lifting 18.393. *imper. sg.* hef
18.394. *pa. t. sg.* hof 10.14.
pl. heuen 10.275. [OE *hebban*,
re-formed on analogy of 3eouen
(see 3eue); pa. t. *hōf, -on*]
heouene ; heoueriche. See
heuen(e) ; heuenriche.
heouene-ware *n. pl.* inhabitants
of heaven 18.48. [OE *heofon-
ware*]
heouenlich(e) *adj.* heavenly 19.
273, 306; hefennlike from
heaven 13.62; euelike spiritual
12.106. [OE *heofonlic*]
heowe *n.* household 8F.33. [OE
hīwen]
heowede *pa. t. sg.* coloured 18.
532. [OE *hīwian, hēowian*]
hepe *n.* group, company 3.202;
on ~ together 10.151. [OE *hēap*]

her(e) *n.* hair 1.306, 18.630;
(single) hair 19.66, 149. [OE
hǣr, A *hēr*]
her(e) *adv.* here 1.426, 2.178,
5.39, 6.68, 8N.21, 12.83; (indicating generally something present) 6.270, 327; here is 18.563;
~ *is* there is 1.752; in this world
8E.84, 19.296; in this (matter)
6.194; ~ *and þere* in various
places 2.97. Prefixed to adv.:
~in(ne) in here 5.104, 18.367;
in, inside 6.321; in this house
6.25, 193; 19.395. ~-onnfasst
near here 13.89. ~ut out of here
18.367. Representing neut.
pron., it, this: ~among in this
matter 1.490. ~bifore(n) before this 5.222, 8v.17. ~efter
after this 16.123, 18.503. ~of
of, about this 2.68, 11.23, 12.
140; for this 19.357. ~to to
this 1.411, 18.473. ~þurh because of this 19.130. [OE *hēr*]
her(e). See er(e) ; heo ; hi(i).
herand-bere *n.* messenger, go-
between 15.56. [erand+agent-
noun from ber, cf. OE -*bora*]
herberg *v.* shelter, receive 15.
9. *pp.* herborwed sheltered,
housed 4.10. [from next]
herboru *n.* lodging 4.10. [OE
herebeorg]
hercni(ð). See herknen.
here *n.* army, raiding force 1.660,
748; hēre host 13.101. [OE
here]
here(n) *v.*¹ hear, listen to 8F.8,
14.1, 25, 19.139. *pr. 1 sg.* here
5.128, 14.12. *3 sg.* hereþ, -ð
8N.33, 18.256, 19.226. *subj. pl.*
here 19.24. *imper. sg.* her 15.
26. *pl.* hereð 12.9. *pa. t. sg.*
herd(e) 3.155, 4.135, 152, 5.
170, 6.2, 14.167; herrde 13.
104. *pl.* herd 14.162; herdon
16.50. *subj. 2 sg.* herdest 18.
43, 45. *pp.* herd 14.92, 16.59;
herrd 13.141. [OA *hēran*] See
ihere(n).

here v.² hire, recruit, engage 17.179. *pa. t. sg.* **herde** 17.186. [OK *hēran* = WS *hȳran*]

heredmen n. pl. retainers 10. 287. [OE *hīredmann, hēorod*; see **hird**]

here-kempen n. pl. warriors 10. 147. [here+kempe]

here-marken n. pl. standards 10.275. [here+mearke]

hereword n. fame 18.633. [OE *hereword*; cf. next]

herien v.¹ praise 19.360. *pr. 1 sg.* **herie** 8H.11. *pl.* **herieð**, -th 7.109, 19.357. *pp.* **ihered** 8v. 23; **yheryed** 8K.36. [OE *herian*]

herien v.² drag, pull 12.123. [OE *hergian*]

hering n. herring 4.26. [OA *hēring*]

heritage n. inheritance 7.20. [OF]

herknen v. listen 6.50. *pr. pl.* **herkne3** (= -þ) expect to hear 3.70. *subj. sg.* **hercni** listen to, attend to 19.394. *imper. pl.* **herkneþ** 8G.39; **hercniŏ** 19. 245. [OA *hercnian*]

herles; **hernde**. See **eorl**; **erand**.

herneys n. armour, gear 2.28, 210. [OF *herneis*]

hernes n.¹ pl. brains 4.235; **hærnes** 16.169. [ON *hjarni,* earlier **hearn-*]

hernes n.² pl. ears 4.344. [ON *heyrn* hearing; see note]

hernest n. serious intention, real meaning 6.230. [OE *éornost*]

herrd(e); **herre**. See **here(n)**; **hei3(e).**

hers n. rump 15.10. [OE *ears* (but see *N & Q* ccviii (1963), 248)]

hersumnesse n. obedience, submission 16.85. [OA *hērsum-nes(se)*]

hert n. hart, stag 4.299. *gen.* **heortes** 18.631. *pl.* **hertes** 12.110, *gen.* 129. [OE *heor(o)t*]

hert(e) n. heart 2.146, 6.10, 356,

8G.3, 14.43; **herrte** 13.114; **heorte** 7.162, 10.172, 18.6, 19. 185; **horte** 1.43, spirit, courage 37, 416; **huerte** 8K.56. *swete* ~ darling 7.66; *great* ~ anger, resentment 18.277. *gen.* **herte, heorte, huerte** 8K.72, u.2, 5, (or first element of compound) ~ *blod* lifeblood 2.310, 4.246, 18.528. *pl.* **heorten** 18.166. [OE *heorte*]

herth; **hertou**. See **erþe**; **art, þou.**

herunge n. hearing 19.17. [from here(n)]

heruest n. autumn 12.70, 16.73. [OE *hærfest, herfest*]

hest; **hest(e)**. See **habbe(n)**; **hei3(e).**

heste n. command, decree: *makede is* ~ decreed 7.195; **heast** 18.65; *as in* ~ as a command 18.255; **hæse** 13.268. *pl.* **heastes** 18.446. [OE *hæs* with developed -*t*] Cf. **biheste.**

het(e); **hete(n)**. See **hote(n)**; **et.**

hete n.¹ heat 12.20, 17.198, 251; **heate** 19.115. [OE *hætu*]

hete n.² hatred 1.123. [OE]

heterliche adv. sternly 18.370. [cf. OE *hetelīce,* modified perh. after biter(e); see *Iuliene* pp. 155-6]

heteueste adv. with relentless firmness 18.65. [hete²+faste]

heþ. See **hei3(e).**

heþe v. mock 8F.10 (I bring no troubles to mock you). [ON *hæða*]

heþen adv. hence, (away) from here 4.113, 6.295. [ON *héðan*]

heþen, hethen, heðene adj. heathen 17.219, 16.190, 10.147; **hæþene** 13.169. [OE *hæþen*]

heþenesse n. heathendom, heathen lands 17.7, 38. [OE *hæþennes(se)*]

heued n. head 1.74, 2.251, 4.333, 6.335; **hefed, hæued** 16.167,

168; eved 8w.25; hafd, hafued 10.29, 79; hed 8E.13, 14.170; heaued 18.84, 19.67, chief, leader 19.36, *coll.* important men 16.3; **hæfod** important person 16.37. *gen.* **haudes** 7.introd. *pl.* **heuedes** 4.334. [OE *hēafod, hĕafd-*]

heuede;   heued-þeawes; heuen.   See   habbe(n); heaued-þeawes; heouen.

heuen(e) *n.* heaven 6.325, 7.6, 8E.84, 12.15, 15.27; *ðe* ∼ 12.13; **heouene** 1.548, 7.54, 8E.21, sky 16.63; **houene** 1.474, 18.99; *vnder* ∼ on earth 9.23. *gen.* **heouene** 18.449; **heffness** 13. 67, 109. *dat.* **heffne** 13.102, 276; **efne** 15.25. [OE *heofon(e)*]

heuen-blys, heuene-blisse *n.* the joy of heaven 14.72, 5.233. [prec.+**blis(s)**, after compounds such as next—prob. orig. gen. phr.]

heuene-king, -kyng *n.* king of heaven 6.31, 89, 8T.30, H.14; **houen-kinġe** 1.522. [OE *heofoncyninġe*]

heuene-lyht *n.* light of heaven 8w.50; **houene-liȝte** 1.478. [OE *heofonlēoht*]

heuenriche *n.* the kingdom of heaven, heaven 12.137; *vnder* ∼ on earth 9.3; **houeneriche** 1.463; **heueriche** 17.83; **heoueriche** 18.623. *gen.* **heueriche** 17.234, 239 (or perh. in compound) **hefennrichess** 13.220; **heoueriches** 18.15. [OE *heofonrīce*]

heuer(e); heuereuchon. See **euer(e); euerechon.**

heui *adj.* heavy 4.76, 5.278. [OE *hefiġ*]

hewe *n.* complexion, colour 3.247; appearance 8H.37; shape, form 13.68; **hou, howe** colour 1.399, 108. [OE *hīw, hēow*]

hewene *v., infl. infin.* **to** ∼ to cut

10.20. *pp.* **hewe** 8N.23. [OE *hēawan,* pp. *hēawen*]

hexst. See **hei3(e).**

hi(i), hy *pron. 3 pl.* they 1.12, 215, 9.15, 10.164, 16.53, 17.7, 2.23, 11.5, 5.41; people 16.201, the people 293; **hie** 17.185; **i** 17.231; **he** 4.9, 45 (2nd), 84, 261, 12.112, 152, 16.156; **heo** 1.574, 620, 7.159, 8H.16, 10.33, 18.236; **hoe** 5.264; **ho** 1.66, 483; **huy** 7.38, 77; **ha** 18.26, 58, 19.107, 115; **a** 10.114. *acc.* **hi(i)** them 1.224, 503, 17.181, 229; **heo** 1.558. *acc., dat.* **hem** (to, for) them, those 2.83, 3.178, 4.154, 5.45, 8H.9; **hemm** 13. 103; **em** 3.189; **heom** 1.723, 7.232, 10.64, 305, 16.57, 18.171; **hom** 1.62, 94, 11.28, 98; **ham** 9.127, 18.24, 59, 19.14, 26; *refl.* (for) themselves 1.722, 3.54, 7.76, 9.156, 11.39, 13.120, 17. 155. *poss. adj.* **her(e)** their 1.485, 2.89, 4.10, 5.43, 16.34; **hire** 3.183, 251, 17.30; **heore** 1.733, 7.16, 10.199, 16.256; **hoere** 5.272; **hor(e)** 1.216, 6.210, 7.238, 11.1; **huere** 8H. 16; **hure** 8v.1; **har(e)** 9.69, 99, 18.54, 305, 19.24. *pron.* theirs 2.107, 19.57. *gen.* of them (part.) 16.279, 17.194, 19.19. [OE *hī(e), hēo; him, heom; hira, heora*] See **þai, es, hemself.**

Hi, Hy, Hic, Hyc; hi(i), hye; hybovt; hybrovt; hyd. See **Ich; heo; bugġen; brynġ(e); huden.**

hider(e), hyder *adv.* here, hither 1.629, 4.136, 6.180, 10.148, 15.53; ∼ *ne þider* (neither) this way nor that 18.67. [OE *hider*]

hiderward, -wart *adv.* to this place, here 1.648, 6.255, 19.157. [prec.+OE -*weard*]

hides *n. pl.* skins 4.184. [OE *hỹd*]

hidut. See **dutten.**

hye *v.* hasten, hurry 8N.35. *pr. 1 sg.* **hihi** 18.21. [OE *hīġian*]

hie; hyef, hyf; hif; hifunde;
hight, hiȝth. See hi(i); ȝeue;
ȝef; find(e); hote(n).
hiȝte n. joy 1.208. [OE hyht, hiht]
hiȝteþ pr. 3 sg. is glad 1.314.
[OE hyhtan]
hihi; hyht. See hye; hote(n).
hihðe n. haste: al on ~ in great
haste 18.64; hiþte (= hihte)
8N.11. [OE hīgþ]
hiil n. haste: in ~ quickly 14.139.
[from OE hīgian; see hye]
hiis. See is.
hyl n. heap 4.158. pl. hulles hills
7.100. [OE hyll]
him(m), hym. See he.
himself, hym- pron. himself
5.126, 12.29, 2.217; him-
selue(n), hym- 17.125, 134,
2.305; himmsellf, -sellfenn
13.5, 272; himseolf, -seolue(n)
18.106, 340, 19.312, 125, 10.
181; himsilf 9.172. as nom.
(emphasizing) 2.217, 305, 10.
181, 18.287, 19.312; He Himself 17.162. refl. obj. of vb.
5.126, 18.462, 19.125; obj. of
prep. 13.5, 272, 17.134, 18.340,
Him 18.106, itself 17.125; dat.
(to) himself 9.172, 12.29. [OE
him (see he)+self; cf. hemself]
hin(e), hyne. See he.
hinen n. pl. lads, fellows 11.139;
servants 19.15. [formed on OE
hīna, gen. pl. of hīgan, hīwan; cf.
heowe]
hir(e), hyre. See heo; hi(i).
hird, hyrd n. household, family
19.13, 50, 8F.34; court 16.1;
company 19.74; army 18.479;
hirede retinue, entourage 10.
155, court 263. [OE hīred,
hīrd-]
hirde-flocc n. company of shepherds 13.103. [OE hirde+floc]
hirdess n. pl. shepherds 13.69,
119. [OE hirde]
hire n. pay, wages 4.174. [OE
hȳr]
hirede; hiren. See hird; heo.

hireseolf, -seoluen pron. herself. nom. (emphasizing) 10.246.
refl., obj. of vb. 18.275, 451;
after prep. 19.205. [OE hire
(see heo)+self; cf. himself]
hyrne n. corner 16.90; hurne
1.14. [OE hȳrne]
his; his(s), hys, hise. See es
pron., is, hit; he.
hit pron. 3 sg. neut., nom. and acc.
it 1.28, 3.26, 5.46, 6.60, 18.27;
hyt 8w.7; it 2.14, 4.4, 7.42,
8B.1, 12.2, 16.242 (acc. of reference); itt 13.97; id (before be)
8v.11; suffixed to vb. calleth
4.13 (note), suget 8v.12, to
pron. ȝet 12.89, ȝēt, ȝhōt 13.
98, 151. refl. 1.313. as dat. 9.4.
With pl. concord, they 7.186,
263, 273, 19.14; with be, identifying complement 3.22, 5.115,
128; introductory, in ~ is, es
there is 1.538, 14.175, ~ nas non
ende there was no end (i.e. their
thirst was limitless) 7.249; sim.
with other vbs. 10.263, 12.149;
pleonastic, repeating subject or
obj. 1.186, 4.70, 5.59, 8v.11;
as impers. subject: anticipating
clause (of happening, &c.) 1.52,
7.138, 10.56; antic. complement
4.67; of indef. pass. ~ was iseid
17.19; of general reference,
'things' 1.716, 3.159, 10.6, 19.
23; indef. 1.569, 7.75, 8B.1, H.1,
10.82, (of a book) 12.83, of time,
&c. 1.41, 5.263, 7.152, 12.161;
subject of impers. vbs. 1.181,
19.29. poss. adj. his its 1.267,
399. [OE hit, him, his]
hiþte. See hihðe.
hiue n. (dat.) hive 16.43. [OE
hȳf, dat. hȳfe]
hiwel; ho. See iuel; heo, hi(i),
on.
hode n. hood 8K.18, 9.126, 168.
[OE hōd]
hoe; hoeld; hoere; hof. See
heo, hi(i); holde(n); hi(i);
heouen, of.

hofþurst *pp. adj.* thirsty 5.273. [OE *ofþyrst*] Cf. aþurst.

hoȝe *n.* care, mind 1.447; how anxiety 9.18. [OE *hogu*]

hoȝfule, hohful *adj.* anxious 1.345, 560. [OE *hohful*]

hok *n.* hook 4.20. [OE *hōc*]

hoked *adj.* hooked 1.79. [OE *hōced*]

hoker *n.* contempt: *to ~ ant to scarne* in contempt and scorn of him (see to) 18.385; disdain 18.488. *pl.* hokeres insults, abuse 19.140. [OE *hocor*]

hol; holde. See hal; old(e).

holde(n) *v.* 1.3, 6.71, 8E.56, F.23; halden 10.62, 16.266, 18.244; helden 3.163. (1) hold, keep 1.100, 2.294, 4.321, 8K.25, 13.151, 18.185; imprison 8L.20; possess, rule 10.62, 13.251, 16.203; support 18.176; maintain 10.305; contain 19.386; preserve 18.611; reserve 17.110; follow 5.5, 10.220, 19.193; conduct, hold (court, &c.) 1.3, 12, 11.9, 90, 16.1; *~ roune* converse privately 6.71; *refl.* stand 18.163, 247; stay, live 1.59, 2.93; conduct oneself 18.244; keep, remain 19.64, 231; *intr.* avail 18.488; *~ mid* adhere to, take the side of 1.638, 10.89, 16.266; *~ wiþ* 11.71, *~ to* 17.215. (2) observe 7.196; honour, abide by 16.156, 317, 18.342, *~ of* 8F.23, *~ to* 1.649. (3) consider, regard as 1.32, 3.66, 6.115, 14.51, *~ for* 7.190, 9.128, 16.314, 19.220; *refl.* think oneself 18.118, 19.204. *pr. 1 sg.* halde 18.638. *2 sg.* oldest 6.115; heldest 2.294. *3 sg.* holt 9.128; halt 1.32, 3.66, 17.269, 18.118; haldes 14.75; heldeþ 2.93. *pl.* holdez (= -þ) 7.196; haldeð 18.163, 19.193. *subj. sg.* holde 15.9; halde 18.185, 19.386. *pl.* halden 19.64. *imper. sg.* hald 10.305, 18.342. *pa. t. sg.* held 3.

199, 4.321, 11.90, 13.151, 16.93; heald 16.1; heold 10.220, 16.203, 18.488; hoeld 5.5; hold 1.100; huld 11.9. *pl.* helden 16.139, 17.215; heolden, -on 10.21, 16.156, 266; holde 1.12; hulde 11.71. *subj. sg.* helde 16.314; holde 1.51. *pp.* halden 14.51; iholde 1.681, 7.190; ihialde 17.110. [OA *hāldan*, WS *héaldan*; *héold, -on*; *hálden*, *héalden*]

hole *n.* hole 12.77; socket (of eye) 4.240. [OE *hol*]

holi(e), holy *adj.* holy, sacred 1.467, 6.254, 7.101, 105, 8X.10, 17.74; hali(e), haly 10.241, 14.255, 290, 16.230, 18.2, 9; hallȝhe 13.255; devout, pious 6.205, 7.2, 18.62; aly 15.84. [OE *hālig, hǎlg-*] See churche, ȝost.

holinesse *n.* holiness 1.532. [OE *hālignes(se)*]

holpen, hom. See help(e) *v.*; hi(1).

hom *adv.* home 3.165, 4.34, 5.34, 8N.25; ham 13.21, 16.73, 18.556. [OE *hām*]

hom(e) *n.* home 1.709; *at ~* 4.57, 90; *from ~* away from home 6.97; ham(e) 13.281, 19.27, 146; *at(t) ~* 13.274, 15.4. [OE *hām*]

hom-come *n.* home-coming 6.108, 293. [prec.+come]

homeres; hon. See hamer; on.

hond(e) *n.* hand 3.83, 4.229, 5.102, 7.178, 10.17; hand(e) 4.197, 15.64, 16.6; (as symbol of pledge) 3.138; possession 2.42, 8K.55, 10.58, 16.9; power, disposal 2.50, 11.80; actions 1.715; strength, vengeance 2.296; side 3.183. *next his ~* very close 14.62; *an ~* in his hand 10.17, opposite 3.184 (note); *em on ~* into their hands (distrib. *sg.*) 3.189; *gest an ~* surrender to 1.609; *haue on ~* bring about

8D.14; *take an* ~ undertake
8F.23; *on* ~ *Ich wil hym take*
I will take responsibility for him
2.153; *of* ~ in action 14.7; *of
myne* ~ at my hands 2.304;
sweren .. to hande (with dat.)
take an oath to bring into the
possession of 16.6; *wiþ word
on* ~ with your pledged word
6.240 (see *N & Q* ccviii (1963),
127). *pl.* honde 3.48; onde
8w.23; honden 10.23, 18.186,
19.58; hondes 2.265. [OE
hánd, hónd; pl. *hónda*]
honddful *n.* handful 18.194.
[OE]
hondred; hone; honger. See
hundred; one *adj.*; hunger.
hongi *v. intr.* hang 5.88, 232.
tr., pr. 3 sg. hongeð 18.534.
[OE *hóngian* intr., *hón* (pp.
hóngen) tr.] Cf. heng, hengen.
hongren. See hungren.
honi, hony *n.* honey 9.46,14.76.
[OE *hunig*]
honne. See henne.
honour(e) *n.* honour, veneration
7.204, 279; credit 2.74, honoures (*sg.*—see note) 140; *vor* ~
of out of respect for 11.56;
onour ceremony 11.93; honur
3.64, creditable thing 228. *pl.*
honour lordships 2.126. [AN
(h)on(o)ur(s)]
honouri *v.* honour 7.150. *pr.
subj. sg.* honoure 8K.20. [AN
hon(o)urer]
hontingue *n.* hunting 7.74. [cf.
OE *huntung*]
hoot. See hote(n).
hope *n.* hope 12.52, 18.352, 19.
122; *for* ~ in hope 8N.14;
hoppe 9.175. [OE *hopa*]
hopieþ *pr. pl.* hope 17.239. *pa.
t. sg.* hopede 5.79. [OE *hopian*]
hor(e). See hi(i).
hord *n.* treasure 8K.71; store, in
leide an ~ stored up 1.325. [OE]
hordere *n.* steward 16.99. [OE,
from prec.]

horderwycan *n.* (*dat.*) office of
steward 16.215. [prec.+wike
n.²]
hore *n.*¹ whore, adulteress 6.99,
18.392, 640. [OE *hóre*]
hore *n.*² stain, defilement 8v.5;
horwȝ dirt, filth 9.34. [OE
horh, horg, horw-]
hore *pr. 1 sg.* grow grey 8F.23.
[OE *hárian*]
horn(e) *n.* horn (instrument)
1.234; corner, point (of a roll of
bread) 4.47. *pl.* horn 16.56.
[OE *hórn*, pl. *-as*]
horn-blaweres *n. pl.* men blowing horns 16.58. [prec.+OE
bláwere]
hors *n.* horse 8L.12, 9.32, 18.29
(*dat.*); *on* ~ on horseback 2.86,
167. *pl.* hors 11.19, 117, 16.53;
horses 2.187. *dat.* horsen 10.
113. [OE *hors*, sg. and pl.]
horte; horwȝ. See hert(e);
hore *n.*²
hosede *adj.* wearing hose 8N.37.
[next+adj. suff. OE *-ede*]
hosen *n. pl.* hose, leg-coverings,
(long) stockings 4.128. [OE
hosa, hose]
hoso. See whose.
hot(e) *adj.* hot 8G.41, 9.104, 17.
125; hat(e) 18.85; fervent 18.
378. *comp.* hattre 18.662. See
alþerhotestd. [OE *hát*, comp.
hát(t)ra]
hote(n) *v. Act.* (1) command,
decree 7.129. *pr. 1 sg.* hote 5.36.
3 sg. ho(o)t 17.82, 96; hateð
19.52; hat 19.67. *imper. sg.* hat
order 18.369. *pa. t. sg.* hehte
10.159, 198; hehten 10.251;
het 17.32. *subj. sg.* hete 10.261.
(2) promise: *pa. t. sg.* hight
14.166. *pp.* hight 14.140, 224;
hyht 8D.29. (3) call, name:
pr. 3 sg. hat 19.51. *pp.* ihote(n),
y- 9.2, 10.introd., 2.135; ȝehe-
ten 16.8, 116; ȝehatenn 13.2;
ihate(n) 10.325, 19.11, 41.
Pass. be called 1.192. *pr. 1, 3 sg.*

hat 14.280, 15.47; hatte 16.232, 19.70; hei3tte 6.177. *2 sg.* hattest 1.191. *pa. t. sg.* hatte 10.269; hehte 10.299; heyte 5.271; hi3th 2.281. [OE *hātan*; *hēt, heht*; *hāten*, pass. *hātte*; hei3tte blends pa. t. forms with pass.]

hou, how *adv. interrog.* how 2.63, 3.26, 6.14, 4.301, 14.18; ou 5.230; heou 10.128; hu 1.46, 12.4, 13.10; hw 4.95; wu 12.3. [OE *hū*]

hou; houle. See hewe; hule.

hounbinde *pr. subj. sg.* set free, deliver (from sin or damnation) 6.315. [OE *unbindan*]

houncurteis *adj.* discourteous 6.46. [OE *un-*+curteis]

hounderstod, -stonde. See understonde.

houndes *n. pl.* houndes 5.290; hundes 16.52. [OE *húnd*]

houne; hounger. See owen(e); hunger.

hounlawe *n.* wrong 6.60. [OE *unlagu*; cf. ON *úlög*]

hounsele *n.* unhappiness, misery 6.175. [OE *unsǣl*]

houpbringe *v.* bring up 5.126. [up+bryng(e)]

houre, hous. See we.

hous(e) *n.* house 5.11, 6.273, 9.38; *to ~* home 6.92; hus(e) 1.337, 4.8, 15.9; religious house 7.222, 16.207, 18.236; household 19.11. [OE *hūs*]

houssebonde, hosse- *n.* husband 6.137, 341; hus(e)bonde head of the house, householder 19.38, 43, 226. [OE *húsbonda* from ON *húsbóndi*]

houssewif *n.* mistress of a household 6.361; husewif 19.22, 230. [hous(e)+wif]

houssong(e) *n.* matins 5.265, 274. [OE *ūhtsáng*]

houen(-). See heuen(-).

houeð *pr. 3 sg.* hovers, stays

12.17, 167. *pl.* houen linger 12.153. [obscure]

how; howe. See ho3e, hou; hewe.

howgate *adv.* how 14.114. [hou +gate n.²]

hu. See hou.

huden *v.* hide *refl.* 18.400. *pr. 1 sg. refl.* hude 1.201. *imper. sg.* hud 1.120. *pp.* hyd 8G.55. [OE *hȳdan*]

hue; huere; huerte; huy; huld(e). See heo; hi(i); hert(e); hi(i); holde(n).

hule *n.*¹ owl 1.4, 143, 173; houle 1.620, 743; vle 1.26. *gen.* hule 1.28. [OE *ūle*]

hule *n.*² hut, shelter 12.81. [OE *hulu* husk]

hvnderfonge; hundes. See underuon; houndes.

hundred *n.* and *adj.* hundred 10.151, 12.128, 16.70; hundret 7.8, 14.101, 18.630, 19.111; hondred 3.117, 6.104; oundred 5.8; hundred-court 11.92. [OE *hundred*, n. with gen. pl.]

hunger *n.* hunger, starvation 4.109, 12.96; hungær 16.179, 188; honger 5.112; hounger 5.13, 68, 6.310. [OE *hungor*]

hungren *v.* feel hungry 12.185; hongren go hungry 8F.33. *pr. 3 sg. impers.* (with dat.) hungreð: *him ~* he is hungry 12.148. [from prec.; cf. OE *hyngran*]

hunke. See unker².

hunten *v.* hunt 16.51. [OE *huntian*]

huntes *n. pl.* hunters 16.50, 51. [OE *hunta*]

hup. See up.

huppe *v.* leap, jump 11.45. *pr. subj. sg.* huppe 8F.42. *imper. sg.* hupe 8N.37. *pa. t. sg.* hupte 11.46, *pl.* 116. [OE **hyppan*; cf. *hoppian*]

hure *adv.* at any rate, even 16.90;

in particular 19.141; ~ an ~
especially 1.11, 339. [OE *huru*]
hure; hurne. See hi(i), we;
hyrne.
hurtes *n. pl.* injuries, wounds
18.299. [OF *hurte* blow]
hus(e); hvs; hus(e)bonde.
See hous(e); we; housse-
bonde.
husberners *n. pl.* burners of
houses 17.121. [hous(e)+
agent noun from barne]
huselauerd *n.* master of the
house 19.10, 19. [OE *hūs-
hlāford*]
husewif; hut; hw; hwa,
hwam; hwan; hwar(e);
hwa(m)se; hwat. See
houssewif; out(e); hou;
who; whan; wher(e);
whose; what, quaþ.
hwatliche *adv.* promptly 1.666.
[OE *hwætlīce*]
hweat. See what *pron.*
hwel *n.* some species of whale
4.23 (note). [OE **hwele*, cf.
whal]
hwen(ne); hweonene; hwer;
hwet. See whan; whonene;
wher(e); what.
hweðer *pron. interrog.* which (of
two) 18.323, 19.116; weþer
1.107. *gen.* hweðeres 18.322.
indef. ʒweþur whichever 7.235;
~ *se* (see so) 18.116. [OE
hwæþer, hweþer]
hwi; hwider; hwile; hwilem,
-en. See whi; whider;
while; whilen.
hwilʒat *adv.* how: ~ þat 4.104.
[OE *hwilc* (see hwuch(e))+gate
n.[2]]
hwilinde *adj.* transitory 19.154.
[modification of OE *hwīl(w)ende*
from while+wend]
hwit; hwo; hwon. See
white(e); who; what.
hwuch(e) *adj. interrog.* of what
kind 1.632, 18.147; what 19.7;
whuch 8H.42; wucche 1.587.

pl. hwucche 18.18, 19.15.
indef. wich whichever 3.51.
rel. wyche which 17.122. *qualifying* hwuch such 18.626 (all
other MSS. *swuch*, &c.). [OE
hwilc, hwylc interrog.]
hwuch *pron. indef.*: ~ *se* whoever
19.82 (see so); wuch whichever
8E.3; wich (*so*) 3.63. *rel.*
whiche which 2.126; quilk in
þe ~ 14.231. [as prec.]

I, i, y. See Ich; in(e); hi(i).
i- *pref.* [OE *ge-*]
iæde; iærnde; iætte; iaf(en);
ialde. See eode; ʒerne *v.*;
ʒetteð; ʒeue; old(e).
i-armed, y- *pp.* armed 11.10,
98, 2.249. [OF *armer*]
iauen. See ʒeue.
ibanned *pp.* summoned 1.626.
[OE *bannan*]
ibe *pr. subj. sg.* be 8v.23. [i-+
be(n)]
ibe(n), ibeo(n); ibede,
ybeden; ybend. See be(n);
bidde(n); bende.
ibere *n.* outcry, clamour 1.178;
iberen 10.86. [OE *gebǣru*] See
bere *n.*[2]
ibye; ibet; iblescede, -et. See
be(n); bete *v.*[2]; blesse.
iblessi *pr. subj. sg.* bless 6.161.
[OE *geblētsian*; see blesse]
iblisset; iblowe. See blissin;
bloweþ.
iboen *pp. adj.* prepared, ready
6.434. [i-+ODan *bóin*, pp. of
bóa prepare]
iboht. See buggen.
ibolwe *pp. adj.* swollen, dis-
tended (with rage) 1.101. [OE
gebolgen from *belgan*; see
abolʒe]
ibonden; ibore(n), y-. See
bynde; ber.
iborhen *pp.* saved 19.312. [OE
geborgen from *beorgan*]
ybounde. See bynde.

ybrad *pp.* (?) tortured (as by fire) 8G.11. [OE *gebrǣdd* from *brǣdan* roast; but perh. from *brǣdan* stretch]

ibred; ibrocht. See bredeþ; bryng(e).

ibroded *pp. adj.* widespread 1. 580. [OE *brādian*; cf. brod(e)]

ibro(u)ȝt(e), ybroht, -brout, -browt; ibunden; ibured. See bryng(e); bynde; burede.

iburst *adj.* bristling, angry 19. 171. [OE *gebyrst*]

ycayred *pp.* driven 8F.35. [ON *keyra*]

ycauȝth *pp.* caught 2.246; ikaut 5.86, 103. [OF *cachier*, pp. modelled on OE *lǣht*, *lāht* from *lǣccan*]

Ich *pron. 1 sg.* I 1.1, 2.50, 3.75, 6.2, 7.1, 8B.6, 18.21; Ych 8H.6, K.54; prefixed to vb., Ichaue, Icholde, Ichot, see habbe(n), wil(e), wite(n), cf. chulle see wil(e); suffixed to vb. kepich 1.110. Ic 8T.5, V.12, 12.2; Icc 13.81; Hic, Hyc 6.237, 8R.3, 15. 39, 44; Ihc 5.159, 6.148; Ih, Yh 8W.52, 1. I, Y 2.51, 3.77, 6.1, 12.1, 4.64; Hi, Hy 8Q.3, 15. 14, 17; Yi 15.34; suffixed to vb., haui 6.267, mihti 8F.33, mosti E.1, moti Q.2, nauy F.10, neddi 5.99, willi 8x.1. *acc., dat.* me (to, for) me 1.34, 39, 2.52, 6.34, 8N.39, 19.149 (*dat.* twice); *refl.* (for) myself 1.56, 2.50, 4.117, 8x.7, 15.77; ~ *se(o)lf* 19.214, emphasizing subject 14.124, see self. *poss. adj.* min(e), myn(e) my (usu. before vowel or *h*) 1.37, 14.118, 18.642, 2.178, 8G.18; see on(e); (before cons.) 8R.3, 10; wrongly divided in *my nayct* 15.58; *obl.* and *pl.* mine, myne 1.314, 2.257, 302, 4.84, 6.311, 10.12, 18.10, 19.186, *gen.* 8K.72; mi, my (before cons.) 1.37, 6.30, 18.286, 2.59; (with

force of objective gen.) of me 8L.34, 18.659. *acc. masc.* minne 10.98, 115. *dat.* mire 10. 28, 100. *pron.* myn mine 8G.29, K.28, L.36, P.2. [OE *ic, mē, mīn*]

ychaunged. See chaunge.

Ichaue, Icholde, Ichot; icleped, -cleoped; icloþed, y-. See Ich and habbe(n), wil(e), wite(n); clepen; cloþed.

icnawen *v.* recognize 18.149. *pr. subj. sg.* icnawe 18.253; icnowe should take account of 1.335. *imper. pl.* yknaweȝ (= -þ) understand 3.26. *pa. t. sg.* ikneu recognized 5.123. *pp.* iknowe in *ben ~ of* confess 5.182. [OE *gecnāwan*; see knowe] Cf. aknowe.

icom(e); icomen, y-. See com.

yconquered *pp.* won, regained 2.127. [OF *conquerre*]

icoren(e), -cornee. See cheosen.

icroked *adj.* curved 1.634. [OE *gecrōcod*; see croked(e)]

icrope; icrunet; icud; icume(n). See crepen; cruneð; kyþe; com.

icundur *adj. comp.* (with *dat.*) more natural, fitting 1.85 (note). [from OE *gecýnde*]

icunnet *adj.* of family, born 18. 605. [i-+OE *cynn* and suff. *-ed*; cf. feol-iheortet, &c., and see kinn]

icwede. See quaþ.

icweme *adj.* pleasing 18.234, 19.391. [OE *gecwēme*]

icweme(n) *v.* please, satisfy 1.742, 19.430. [OE *gecwēman*] See cwemen.

icwiddet *pp.* said, prophesied 19.289. [OE *cwiddian*]

id. See hit.

idel, ydel *adj.* idle 17.184, 1.549; *on ~* fruitlessly 1.552. [OE *īdel*]

idelnesse *n.* emptiness 17.226. [OE *ídelnes(se)*]

idiȝt, **idihte**; **ido**, **ydon**, **idon(e)**; **ydrawe**. See **diht**; **do(n)**; **draᵹen**.

ydres *n. pl.* water-vessels 17.98, 99. [OF *ydre* from L *hydria*]

idrunke; **ieden**. See **drink**; **eode**.

i-entred *pp.* entered 17.236. [OF *entrer*]

i-ete; **iett**; **if**. See **et**; **ᵹet(e)**; **ᵹef**.

ifaie *adv.* gladly 5.199. [OE *gefægen* adj.]

ifare(n); **ifed**, **y-**; **yfel**. See **fare(n)**; **fede(n)**; **euel** *n.*

ifere *n.* companion, comrade, friend 5.172, 185. *pl.* **iferen** 18.542; **iueren** 10.213. [OE *geféra*]

ifere *adv.* together 3.208. [from predic. use of prec.]

ifilet *pp.* filed 18.326. [OE *fílian*]

ifinden *v.* find 18.609; phr. *fondin ant* ~ find out, discover 19.252, 378. *pr. 3 sg.* **ifindeð** 19.178; **ifind** 18.541, 599; **ifint** 18.674. *pa. t. sg.* **ifond** 18.677. [OE *gefíndan*] See **find(e)**.

ifon; **ifoð**; **ifonden**, **-founde**, **-funde**; **ifullet**. See **fon**; **iuo**; **find(e)**; **fille(n)**.

ifurn *adv.* long ago 1.574. [OE *gefýrn*]

iᵹiuen; **iᵹleadet**; **iᵹo(n)**; **iᵹodet**. See **ᵹeue**; **ᵹleadien**; **ᵹo(n)**; **ᵹoded**.

iᵹrap *pa. t. sg.* grasped 10.28. [OE *gegráp*; see **ᵹripeth**]

iᵹrede *n.* crying 1.601. [rel. to **ᵹrede(n)**]

yᵹreiþed; **iᵹret**. See **ᵹreiðede**; **ᵹrete**.

iȝarcket *pp.* prepared 19.382. [OE *gearcian*]

iȝeuen, **-ȝiue**; **iȝolde**; **Ih, Yh.** See **ᵹeue**; **ᵹelde(n)**; **Ich.**

ihal *adj.* whole 19.104. [OE *gehál*]

ihate(n); **Ihc**; **ihealet**; **iheed.** See **hote(n)**; **Ich**; **helen** *v.*²; **habbe(n)**.

ihende *adv.* near 17.60. [OE *gehénde*; see **hende** prep.]

iheoled; **iheord(en)**, **-herd.** See **hele(n)** *v.*¹; **ihere(n)**.

iherde, **-herede**, **-hierde** *pa. t. sg.* hired, recruited 17.208, 212, 216. *pp.* **iherd** 17.229. [cf. OE *gehýran*; see **here** *v.*²]

ihere(n), **y-** *v.* hear 1.180, 352, 2.38, 3.134, 10.86; listen to 6.368, 8H.47; **ihire** 1.228. *pr. 1 sg.* **ihere** 3.229, 5.119. *3 sg.* **ihereð** 19.313. *pl.* **ihereþ** 1.178. *imper. sg..* **yhere** 8F.9. *pl.* **ihereþ** 17.116, 204; **ihiereth** 17.46. *pa. t. sg.* **iherde** 1.3, 5.113, 10.126, 17.14. *pl.* **iherden** 10.189; **iheorden** 7.184. *pp.* **iherd** 1.585, 17.69, 18.663, 19.403; **ihert** 1.721; **iheord** 7.63. [OA *gehéran*; see **here(n)** *v.*¹, to which some pps. may belong]

ihered, **yheryed**; **yhernes**; **ihialde**; **ihierde.** See **herien** *v.*¹; **ᵹerne** *v.*; **holde(n)**; **iherde.**

ihoded *pp.* ordained 1.579. [OE *hádian*]

ihoked *adj.* hooked 1.633. [cf. **hoked**]

ihold *n.* stronghold, shelter 1.401. [OA *geháld*]

iholde; **iholpen**; **ihote(n)**, **y-**; **iiuen**; **ikaut.** See **holde(n)**; **help(e)** *v.*; **hote(n)**; **ᵹeue**; **ycauȝth.**

ihwer *adv.* everywhere 18.288. [OE *gehwǽr*]

ikennen *v.* recognize, distinguish 10.281. [OE *gecennan* make known; see **kenne**]

ikepe *pr. subj. sg.* support 18.360. [OE *gecépan*; see **kepe**]

yknaweȝ, **ikneu**, **iknowe.** See **icnawen.**

iknede *pp.* kneaded 5.256. [OE *cnedan*]

il; iladde; ilast; ilc(e), ilche; ileanet; ilei(i)d; ilek(e); ileosed. See ilk(e)²; led(e); ileste; ilk(e)¹; leneþ¹; legge; ilk(e)¹; leosen.

iler *adj.* empty 11.162. [OE *gelǣr*]

ileste *v.* last, continue 1.257. *pr. 3 sg.* **ilast** 8B.1, 10.269; **ilesteþ** 1.263; **ilest** 1.511. [OE *gelǣstan*; see **leste(n)**]

ilete *n.* appearance, bearing 1.281, 673. [OE *gelǣte*]

yleue *v.* believe 2.257. *pr. pl.* **ileueð** 10.320. *imper. sg.* **yleue** 2.235. [OA *gelēfan*; see **leue(n)** v.³]

ilich(e) *adj.* (with **dat.**) like 1.232, 9.4, 18.29, 19.111, 331. *sup.* **ilikest** (with *towart*) 19. 304. [OE *gelīc*, sup. *gelīcost*]

iliche *adv.* equally, alike 19.316; *eure, e(a)uer* ~ constantly, unchangingly 1.398, 464, 19.358; **ilik(e)** 14.75, *ay* ~ 74. [OE *gelīce*]

ilihtet *pp.* cheered 19.240. [OE *(ge)līhtan*]

ilike *n. pl.* equals: *þine* ~ those like you 1.113. [OE *gelīca*] See **ilich(e).**

ilimet *pp.* stuck 18.193, joined 219. [OE *gelīman*]

ilk(e) *adj.*¹ same, very (after *þe, þat, þis*; sometimes without much force) 1.488, 3.115, 5.99, 14.148, 18.5; **illke** 13.27; **ilc(e)** 16.7, 12, 123; **ilche** 3.16, 94; **ilek(e)** 17.66, 81. *gen.* **ilces** 16.66. as *pron., þat, þet* ~ the same thing 5.47, 19.120; *þe* ~ those (men) 18.163. [OE *ilca* masc., *ilce* fem., neut.]

ilk(e) *adj.*² each, every 3.3, 4.89, 288, 6.307, 12.45; **illc** 13.12, ~ **an** every 17; **ilka** = *ilk a* 14.34; **il** in ~ *del* 4.86 (cf. 14. 228), see **del(e).** [OA *ylc*] Cf. **ech(e).**

ilkan *pron.* each one 4.197;

illcan 13.185, 192; **ilkon** 4.269, everyone 14.25. [prec.+**on(e)**]

ilkines *adj.* of every kind 12.73. [**ilk(e)**²+gen. of **kinn**, q.v. for similar forms] Cf. **alkyn.**

ill(e) *adj.* bad 12.168, 14.42, 46. as *n.* evil-disposed (man) 1.299. [ON *ill-r*]

iloȝe; **iloke**; **iloked.** See **lie**; **lukeð**; **lok.**

ilome *adv.* often 1.49, 11.103, 19.20, 88 (note). [OE *gelōme*]

ilomp *pa. t. sg.* happened 10.156. *pp.* **ilumpe** 10.56. [OE *gelomp*, *gelumpen* from *gelimpan*; see **limpet**]

ylong *adj.* dependent (with *on*) 8M.21, W.10. [OE *geláng*] Cf. **long** *adj.*¹

ilore, yloren; **ilorned**; **iloued, y-**; **ilumpe**; **imad.** See **leosen**; **lerne**; **loue** v.; **ilomp**; **mak.**

imæn *adv.* in company, together 13.107. [OE *gemǣne* adj.; see **imeane**]

imætte, imette *pa. t. impers.* (with acc. of person) dreamt 10. 13, 14. [OE *gemǣtan*] See **matte.**

ymage *n.* statue 2.234. [OF *image*]

ymageoure *n.* sculptor 2.237. [AN *imageur*]

imaked. See **mak.**

imartred *pp.* martyred 7.90, 112. [OE *gemart(y)rian*] See **martyr.**

imealt *pp.* melted 18.330. [OM *gemǣltan*] Cf. **formealte.**

imeane *adj.* common, shared 18.230, 232, 19.317. [OE *gemǣne*] Cf. **meane, ymone.**

imeind, -menged; **imette.** See **mengeþ**; **imætte.**

imette *pa. t. sg.* met 6.157. [OE *gemētan*]

imilked *pp.* milked 7.156. [OE *milcian*]

ymone *n.* intercourse 8v.16. [OE *gemāna*]

imong. See **among(e).**

imunt *pp.* intended: *wat hauest þou* ~ what have you in mind? 5.244. [OE *myntan*]

imurŏret *pp.* murdered 18.53. [OE (*a*-)*myrþrian*]

in(ne) *n.* lodging 3.165; house 6.19, 299. [OE *inn*]

in *adv.* in, inside 2.104, 4.199, 5.25, 8A.1, 11.114, 19.47; intensifying *toward* 10.94. [OE *inn*]

in(e) *prep.* 1.1, 3.4, 4.1, 1.266, 5.138, 17.18; **yn** 8E.70; **inn** 13.52; **i, y** 10.41, 13.26, 18.5, 8N.18, 15.9. (of place) in 1.1, 2.122, 3.10; into 2.261, 4.212, 8K.59, (following infin.) 12.80; to 3.183; on 1.712, 3.7, 8H.2, X.14, 9.153, 19.274, see **erþe**; at 7.171. (of a journey, &c.) on 2.90, 7.120, 17.63. (of dress) in 4.194. (of manner) in 2.37, 6.15, 11.1. (of condition) in 18.98; into 6.306, 8D.13, 9.120; with 8G.49; see **hil.** (of time) in 8H.1; on 11.9, 19.293; at 2.326, 10.1, 17.101; during 5.111; (forming conj.) ~ *þatt tatt* at the time that, when 13.213. (with n. or vb. of believing) in 17.53, 82. [OE *in*] See **inne, into, þer(e) adv.**

ynayled *pp.* nailed 8w.20. [OE *næglian*]

incker *pron. 2 dual gen.* of you two 19.392. [OE *incer*]

inempnet. See **nemme(n).**

ingang *n.* entrance, beginning 16.60; **inȝeong** entry 10.190; **inȝong** 19.36, 46, 166. [OE *ingáng*, and cf. Nb *geong*; see **gange(n)**]

Inglis. See **Englische.**

inmiddes *prep.* in the middle of 14.178. [var. of **amid(de)**, with adv. *-es* as **aȝeines**, &c.]

inne *adv.* in, inside 4.75, 5.23. [OE *inne, innan*]

inne *prep.* in 3.1, 10.91; (following infin.) 4.30, 13.258; (postponed in rel. cl.) 4.123, 5.71,

13.22, 237, **ine** (rhyming *time*) 5.264; see **þer(e) adv., conj.** [OE *inne adv., innan*]. Cf. prec. and **in(e).**

innsihht. See **insiȝt.**

inntill *prep.* into 13.33, 235. [in adv.+**til(l)** prep.]

innwarrdlike. See **inwardliche.**

inogh *n.* enough, a great deal 14.96; **inoȝ** 9.61, 112; **inoh** 1.587; **onoh** 16.175; **inou, inow** 5.79, 4.177. [OE *genōg, genōh, genōg*-]

inogh *adv.* enough 14.92, 268; **inouȝ, inovȝ** greatly 7.11; (following adj., adv.) very 7.23, 43, completely 71, 236; **ynoh** 8E.16; **inou** 5.278, 7.119, 11.11, abundantly 5.83, 259; **ynow** 4.170, 222. [as prec.]

inoh *adj.* (following word qualified) enough, great 10.226; **inouȝ, inovȝ** 7.281, 36; **inou** 5.24, 11.42, abundant, lavish 5.92, 6.93. *pl.* **inoȝe** many 1.16; **inowe, y-** 5.288, 11.97, enough 2.65. [see **inogh** *n.*]

inome, y-. See **nim.**

inre *adj.* inward 18.580. [OE *in(n)ra*]

insiȝt *n.* (object of vbs. **conne, (i)wite(n)**) understanding 7.179; knowledge, skill 1.151; **innsihht** 13.165. [in adv.+**siȝt(e)**]

into *prep.* into 1.106, 3.198, 7.48, 10.144, 18.428; **int** 17.232; to 3.165, 19.362; over, throughout 7.129, 11.68; as far 1.716, 8H.12, N.38. [OE *intɔ*]

inume. See **nim.**

inward *adv.* in, towards the inside 11.35, 18.368; **inwar** 14.170. [OE *inweard*]

inwarde *adj.* inner 19.81; deeply felt, earnest 18.3, 56, 82. [OE *inweard*]

inwardliche *adv.* sincerely, earnestly 18.303, 539, 19.277;

innwarrdlike 13.139. [OE *inweardlice*]

inwiぐ *adv.* inside 19.9, 21. [in adv.+wiþ]

inwiぐ *prep.* within, in 18.125, 475. [as prec.]

i-offred ; i-openet. See offri ; openin.

i-ordret *pp.* arranged, organized 19.283. [OF *ordrĕer*]

ipeint *pp.* painted 1.76. [from OF *peint* pp. of *peindre*]

ypleiede ; yplyht ; ired. See plai ; pliȝtte ; red(e) *v.*

iredi *adj.* ready, fit 7.254. [OE *gerǣde*+*-ig*] Cf. redi.

iren *n.* iron 16.176; irn 18.327. [OE *īren*]

Irish *adj.* Irish 1.238. [from OE *Íras* the Irish]

irobbet. See robbeぐ.

irostid *pp.* roasted 9.102. [OF *rostir*]

irotet *pp.* rooted 18.446. [from verb formed on rote]

is, ys *pr. 3 sg.* is 1.34, 2.17, 3.13, 8k.45, e.7; exists 14.56; iss 13. 87; his 6.28 (see wil), 8r.6, t.41, 17.133; hiis 5.106. *auxil.*(forming pass.) 2.15 (impers.), 52, 5. 106, 8r.6; (forming perf. of intr. vbs.) 8a.1, m.3, 10.108, 13.83. *subj. sg.* si 13.109. [OE *is*, subj. *sī(e)*] See es, nis ; be(n) and other parts.

is(e) ; isæh ; isæid ; isæt ; isah, -sai(ȝ), -say ; isauued ; ischawed ; ischent. See he ; ise ; sai ; set ; ise ; saues ; schawin ; schende.

ischrined *pp.* enshrined, placed in a shrine 7.204, 222. [from vb. formed on OE *scrīn*]

ise, ysee *v.* see 7.278, 9.187; meet 2.13, perceive, understand 273; ysene 2.138; iseo(n) 7. 89, 116, 19.137. *pr. 1 sg.* ysee 8w.22; iseo 19.170, 234; iso 1.243. *2 sg.* isiist 5.232. *3 sg.* iseeþ 9.133; isiþ 1.285; isoþ

1.302. *pl.* iseeþ 9.139; iseoぐ 19.108. *subj. sg.* iseo 1.597; iso 1.420. *pa. t. sg.* isæh 10.41, 196; isah 10.36; iseȝ 1.29; iseh 10. 22, 19.134, 249; isaiȝ 7.15, 157; iseiȝ 7.48; isai, isay 7.27, 172, 11.10; isey 5.280. *pl.* iseiȝe(n) 7.243, 276. *subj. sg.* iseȝe 1.303; isehe 19.134; iseie 5.218. *pp.* iseghe 17.154; isehen 19.87, 156; iseiȝe 7.46, 114; isene 1. 122, 211. [OE *gesēon*; see se]

isealet *pp.* sealed, closed 18.470. [OF *seeler*]

iseche *v.* come to, attain 1.487. [OE *gesēcan*]

ised, -sei(i)d, yseide ; iseghe, -seȝ(e), -seh(e), -sey, -sei-ȝ(en) ; isend, ysent ; isene, -seo(n) ; iserued ; iset(te) ; ysette ; ishend. See sai ; ise ; send ; ise ; serue(n) ; set ; schende.

ishoed *pp. adj.* shod, wearing shoes (of specified quality) 6.320. [OE *gesc(e)ōd*, pp. of (*ge*)*scōgan*]

ishote ; isiist, -siþ ; islaȝe(n), yslawe, -slawȝe, islein ; islide. See ssete ; ise ; sle(n) ; sliden.

isliked *pp.* made plausible 1.501. [OE *-slicod* pp. of *slician]

ismered *pp.* anointed 17.60. [OE *smerian, smyr-*]

ismiten; iso. See smite(n) ; ise.

isome, y- *adj.* assembled, together 10.150; at peace 1.693; peaceable 1.136. [OE *gesōm*]

isomned. See sammnenn.

isoぐet *pp.* proved true 19.289. [OE *sōþian*]

isouȝt ; isped, y- ; ispeke(n) ; ispillet ; ispread ; isriue ; issend. See seche(n) ; spede ; speke(n) ; spille ; sprede ; sriue ; schende.

istelet *adj.* steel-bound 19.142. [from stel(e) with adj.-forming pref. and suff.]

istihen. See steo.

istirret *pp.* studded (as if with stars) 19.275. [OA **gestirred* formed on sterre]

istonden; istounʒe; istrahte; istrengþed. See stonde(n); istunʒe; strek; strengþen.

istreonet *pp.* bred, sprung 18.236. [OA *strēonan*]

istunʒe *pp.* pierced, stabbed 8w.19; istounʒe 5.292. [OE *gestúngen*, pp. of *stíngan*]

isulet. See suleð.

isunde *adj.* healthy: *makien ~* heal 10.309. [OE *gesúnd*]

isundrede, -et *pp.* separated 18.183, 167. [OE *syndrian, sun-drian*]

isunken. See sinke(n).

isuolʒe *pp.* swallowed 1.102. [OE *geswolgen* from *swe(o)lgan*; see forswalʒe]

isuore. See sweren.

iswipt *pp.* carried swiftly 18.183. [OE *swippan* whip]

iswonge *pp.* beaten, scourged 5.291; yswnge 8w.18. [OE *geswúngen*, pp. of *swíngan*]

it(t); itaht; itake, y-; italde; itawt. See hit; teche; tak; tel; teche.

iteiet *pp.* tied 18.206. [OA **tēgan* = WS *tīgan*]

iteilede *adj.* tailed 19.103. [formed on teil; cf. istelet]

itide *v.* betide, come upon 1.691. [OE *getīdan*; see tiden]

itimbred *pp.* caused, brought about 10.109. [OE *(ge)tim-br(i)an* build]

itimed *pp.* happened, come about 10.230. [OE *getīmian*]

itoʒen; itold; itrauailed; ituht; ituket; iturned, -turnt; itweamet. See te; tel; trauailest; tuhten; tukest; turn(e); tweamen.

iþenche *v.* conceive, imagine 17.268. *pr. subj. sg.* remember 1.469. [OE *þencan*; see þenchen]

yþerled; iþoled; iþoht, -þouʒt, -þout. See þurlin; þole(n); þenchen.

iþraste *v.* thrust 10.292. [OE *geþrǽstan*]

iþrunge; iþurlet; iunge; iuaren. See þringet; þurlin; ʒong(e); fare(n).

iuel *pa. t. sg.* befell, happened 17.91; hiwel fell, came 17.188. [OE *gefēoll* from *gefeallan*; see falle(n) v.[1]]

yuel(e); iueng; iueren. See euel(e); iuo *v.*; ifere *n.*

iui *n.* ivy 1.27. [OE *ifig*]

iuis. See iwis.

iuo *n.* enemy 1.674. [OE *gefá*; see fo]

iuo *v.* catch 1.392. *pr. pl.* ifoð 1.603. *pa. t. sg.* iueng seized 10.39. [OE *gefōn, gefēng*; see fon]

yuory *n.* ivory 2.215. [AN *ivorie*]

iuorþe *v.* carry out, perform 10.103. [OE *gefórþian*]

iwakien *v. intr.* awake 10.46. [cf. OE *wacian* and awake]

iwar *adj.* aware 1.103, 11.154. [OE *gewær*]

iweallet; iweddet. See welle *v.*; wedded.

iweiet *pp.* weighed out, exactly measured 18.631. [OE *wegan*]

iwend(e). See wene; wend.

iwende *v.* go 7.69, 121; iwiende 286. *pa. t. sg.* iwende 10.42, 238. [OE *gewéndan*; see wend]

iwent, y-; iweorret. See wend; uuerrien.

iwepnen *n. pl. (dat.)* weapons 10.199. [OE *gewǽpnu*]

iwhillc *adj.* every 13.19, 113. [OE *gehwilc*]

iwil(le) *n.* will, desire, what one wishes 17.124, 161, 201. [OE *gewill*]

iwipet *pp.* wiped away 19.301. [OE *wipian*]

iwis, iwiss(e), ywis(se) *adv.*

certainly, indeed 1.35, 3.42, 6.43, 9.23, 18.200; **iuis** 8v.16; often a mere tag of little force, esp. in rhyme: 3.5, 246, 6.143, 7.208, 267, 8G.25, 11.39. quasi-*n.* in *mid iwisse, y-* certainly, for certain 5.234, 293, 8U.3, W.8, *to iwisse* 10.49. [OE *gewiss*]

iwist. See **iwite** *v.*²

iwite *v.*¹ learn of, hear about 7.131, discover 161, 201, reach 179; **iwitte** understand 9.180. [OE *gewitan*; see **wite(n)** *v.*¹]

iwite *v.*² guard, protect, keep 3.291. *pp.* **iwist** 19.26; **iwust** 7.189. [OE *gewitan*; see **wite(n)** *v.*²]

iwone, iwune *n.* custom, what is usual 1.333, 588. [OE *gewuna*]

ywonne; iworþe; iwounded, -wundet; iwraht, y-, ywroht, iwrowt; iwreken; iwrite(n); iwunet. See **winne(n); wurðen; wundest; wirche; wreoke; writenn; wonen.**

iwurðen be 19.28 (see **lete(n)**), 335; become 18.551. *pr. 3 sg.* **iwurðeð** becomes 18.326. *pl.* 19.106. [OE *gewurþan*; see **wurðen**]

iwurðen; iwust. See **wurðen; iwite** *v.*²

jay *n.* jay 8K.39. [OF]

iambleué *n.* (?) a dance step 9.166. [QF *jambe* leg + *levée* raised]

jaspe *n.* jasper 9.70. [OF]

ioi(e), ioy, joie, joye *n.* joy, pleasure 2.190, 7.6, 54, 9.9, 14.177; *made* ~ rejoiced 3.278. *pl.* **ioies** 5.166. [OF *joie*]

iolyf *adj.* lively, gay 8K.39. [OF *jolif*]

ioupe *n.* loose jacket, tunic 4.194. [OF *jupe*]

Iudeus *n. pl.* Jews 16.225. [L *Iūdēus* sg.]

Iudicum *n.* (the Book of) Judges 18.206. [L, gen. pl.]

Iudisskenn *adj.* Jewish 13.92, 144. [cf. OE *Iūdēisc*]

iugement, jugge- *n.* judgement, sentence 6.246; punishment 7.98. [OF *jugement*]

iuperti *n.* venture, exploit 6.276. [AN *ju parti* divided game]

iustise *n.* justice: ~ *dide* inflicted punishment 16.154, administered justice 16.323–4. [OF]

k-. See also **c-.**

kalde; Kalldewisshe; kam; kan. See **calle(n); Calldewisshe; com; conne.**

kanunes *n. pl.* canons 1.475. [AN *canun*]

kare. See **car(e).**

karefullest *adj. sup.* most miserable 10.242. [from OA *carful*; see **car(e)**]

kaseress. See **caseres.**

kaserr-kinɡ *n.* emperor 13.1, 25. [OE *cāsere* + **kinɡ(e)**)]

kaske *adj.* active, vigorous 4.268. [ON *karsk-r*]

kearf *pa. t. sg.* cut 18.630. *subj. sg.* **kurue** 18.416. [OE *cearf, curfe* from *ceorfan*] See **keoruinde.**

ke33seress. See **caiser.**

keyen *n. pl.* keys 11.120. [OE *cǣg(e)*]

keis *n. pl.* servants, henchmen 19.37. [MW *ceis*; see note]

keiseres. See **caiser.**

kelde *n.* cold, misery 8F.11. [OA *cǽldu = WS *cýldu*] Cf. **cold(e).**

kelinɡ *n.* cod 4.25. [obscure; cf. ON *keila*]

kempe *n.* warrior, soldier 10.125, 281. *pl. gen.* **kempen** 10.180. [OE *cempa*]

kene *adj.* brave, bold, eager 1.663, 4.259, 18.509; fierce 1.212; sharp 8M.3, N.6; keen, acute 1.427, 18.159. [OE *cēne*]

kenede *pa. t. sg.* gave birth to 8F.5. [OE *cennan,* rel. to **kinn**]

kenne v. teach 6.264. *pa. t. sg.*
kend directed 15.53. [OE
cennan, rel. to **conne**, and ON
kenna]
keoruinde *pr. p. adj.* cutting,
sharp 18.159. [OE *ceorfende*;
see **kearf**]
kepe v. observe, watch 8E.46.
pr. 1 sg. **kep** (*-i* joined in MS.)
care, wish (with infin.) 15.9,
care for 28; (with suffixed pron.)
kepich (with *þat* cl.) 1.110.
pa. t. sg. **kepte** watched for
4.145; wished 8F.8. *pl.* **kepten**
watched 16.57. *subj. sg.* **kepte**
would wish 18.128, 417, 553,
would take account 451. [OE
cēpan]
kest(en); **keste**; **kiddenn**;
kimeð; **kync.** See **caste(n)**;
kis(se); **kyþe**; **com**; **king(e)**.
kinde n. kinsfolk, family 13.32;
nature, innate character or
qualities 12.1, 110, 13.180;
kynd 14.36; **cunde, kunde**
1.209, 19.306, 18.329, 502;
kuynde 7.142. *pl.* (in sg. sense)
cunde 1.88. [OE (*ge*)*cýnd(e)*]
kindlen v. kindle 4.181. [cf. ON
kynda kindle, *kyndill* torch]
kinedom(e), kyne- n. kingdom
10.140, 13.11, 252, 18.486;
reign 7.5. *pl.* **kinedomes** 18.
621. [OE *cynedōm*]
kineliche adj. royal 10.58. [OE
cynelic]
kinelond(e) n. kingdom 10.100,
258. [OE *cyne-* as in prec.+
lond(e)]
kineriche n. kingdom 10.303. *pl.*
kineriches 10.289. [OE *cyne-*
rice]
king(e); kyng n. king 1.686, 2.3,
3.264, 7.1, 10.2 (*dat.*), 11.2, 32
(*dat.*), 16.12, 135, 18.467; as
title 14.9, 16.1, after name 105;
cyng 16.41; **kink, kync** 17.41,
15.78. *gen.* **kinges, kynges**
2.22, 3.151, 8v.6, 16.224, 18.
476; **kingess** 13.39; **kyngues**
7.187. *pl.* **kinges, kynges**
8v.4, 9.60, 14.22, 17.6; **kingess**
13.175. *gen.* **kinge** 10.65, 255,
18.604; **kingen** 10.224. [OE
cyning, cyng]
kingriche n. kingdom 17.16.
[OE *cyningrice*] Cf. **kineriche**.
kinn, kynne n. family, stock,
kindred, relatives 13.46, 8L.18;
cun(ne), kun(ne) 1.207, 733,
10.98, 19.132, 1.460, 5.54 (*dat.*),
8L.35; relative 5.123. kind, sort,
in *gen.* **kines** 4.129, **cunnes,
kunnes** elsewhere: *alles* ~ of
every kind, all kinds of 18.637,
19.103; *ani* ~ any sort of 6.15
(note); *none, nones* ~ of no kind,
no sort of 4.129, 5.294; *non
oþer* ~ no other kind of 5.146;
euch oþeres ~ every other kind
of 5.224; *of uueles* ~ *kunde* of a
wicked kind of nature 18.502.
pl. gen. **cunne** 18.37; in *on alle*
~ *wise* in all kinds of ways 18.
453; *fe(o)le, uele* ~ of many kinds
1.20, 5.166, 10.87. [OE *cynn*]
See **alkyn, ilkines, serekin**.
kinnessmenn n. *pl.* family,
descendants 13.39, relatives 229.
[OE *cynnes* gen. of *cynn* (see
prec.)+*menn*]
kippe v. take hold of, seize 4.160.
[cf. ON *kippa* snatch, MDu
kippen catch]
kirke n. church 12.41; **kirrke**
13.262. [ON *kirkja*]
kirnels n. *pl.* seeds 14.249. [OE
cýrnel, dim. of **corn**]
kis(se) v. kiss *intr.* 3.277. *tr.*
3.262; **cusse** 8F.38, G.27. *pa.
t. 1 pl. recip.* (with obj. *vs* each
other) 8L.23. *intr. 3 pl.* **keste**
3.250. [OE *cyssan*, K *cessan*]
kyþe, kiðen v. make known,
show 8L.21, 12.1; **kiþenn** 13.
82; **cuðen** 19.270. *pr. 1 sg.*
cuðe manifest, offer (of feelings)
18.498. *2 sg.* **cuþest** 1.90. *3 sg.*
kiþeþþ relates 13.8, 40; **cuþ**
shows 1 note to 95. *pa. t. pl.*

kiddenn 13.143. *pp.* icud 18. 617. [OE *cȳpan, cÿdde*]
klene; knau, knaw. See clene *adj.*; knowe *v.*
knaue *n.* young man 6.201; cnaue 10.297. [OE *cnafa*]
kneleþ *pr. 3 sg.* kneels 2.34. [cf. OE *cnēowlian*]
kneowe. See knowe *v.*
knes *n. pl.* knees 4.329; knewes 2.33; cneon 18.382. *dat.* knowe: *on* ~ *hym sett* knelt 2.123. [OE *cnēo(w)*, pl. *cnēo(w)*, *cnēowu*]
kneu, knew(e). See knowe *v.*
knif, cnif *n.* knife 4.298, 18.307; chnief 15.20. *pl.* kniues 4.196. [LOE *cnīf* prob. from ON *knīf-r*]
kniȝt(h) *n.* knight 11.2, 2.12, 180; cniht 10.5, 10. *gen.* cnihtes 18.533. *pl.* kniȝttes 2.46, 63; knyhtes 8K.57; knythes 14.11; cnihtes 10.91, 139, 18.508; cnihte 10.206. *dat.* cnihten 10.240. [OE *cniht* boy, servant]
knowe, cnowe *v.* know 6.122; make known, show 8E.65; knaw recognize 14.46; cnawen(n) know 13.215, 18.424, 19.329. *pr. 1 sg.* knau 14.142. *2 sg.* (with suffixed pron.) knouestou 3.256. *pl.* cnaweð 19.62. *pa. t. sg.* kneowe 8F.35; kneu 5.114; knew(e) 2.327, 3.248. [OE *cnāwan, cnēow*]
knowe *n.* See knes.
kok *n.*[1] cook 4.140, 146. [OE *cōc*]
kok *n.*[2]; kome(n); kor(e)n. See coc; com; corn.
kors *n.* curse 5.201. [OE *curs*; see curseð]
kou, kov *n.* cow 7.146, 143; kowe 9.32; cu 8A.7. *pl.* kuyn 7.147. [OE *cū*, pl. *cȳ*]
kouþe. See conne.
kradel-barnes *n. pl.* children in the cradle, babies 4.339. [OE *cradol*+barn]

krake(n), crake *v. tr.* crack, split 4.180. *intr.* 4.284, 335. [OE *cracian* resound]
kuyn;   kuynde;   kume; kume(ð); kun(ne); kunde; kunne. See kou; kinde; cume; com; kinn; kinde; conne.
kunrede *n.* kindred, relatives 1.635. *pl.* cunreadnes families 19.294. [kinn+-rede(n)]
kurue; kuþe. See kearf; conne.

la *interj.* indeed, to be sure 9.34; lo see, look 18.62, 131. [OE *lā*, sense infl. by lok]
laas *n.* noose, snare 2.247. [OF *laz*]
lac, lakke *n.*[1] lack, shortage 9.29, 78. [MDu *lac*]
lac *n.*[2] gift 13.185. *pl.* lakess 13.192. [OE *lāc*]
-lac *suff.* forming nouns (often expressing activity), as fear-, fiht-, ræf-, schend-, tei-. [OE *-lāc* app. related to *lācan* play; cf. ON *-leik-r*, ME *-lec* in feier-, freo-, god-, &c.]
lad(de). See led(e).
ladde *n.* fellow (of low birth), serving-man 4.194, 213, 8N.36. *pl.* laddes 4.156, 268. [origin obscure]
lade *n.* way, journey: *o* ~ on the way 13.186. [OE *lād*]
lady. See lefdi.
ladlechin *v.* make ugly, disfigure 18.265. [OE *lāþ* (see loþ)+ factitive suff. *-lǣcan*; cf. cnaw-lechunge. For *-in* see *Iuliene* p. 238.]
ladlice. See lodlich.
læc *pa. t. sg.* moved quickly, flowed 10.263. [OE *lēc* from *lācan*]
læd;   læfe;   læi;   læide(n); lært ;   lærenn;   læt(en); læuede. See led(e); leue *n.*[1],

n.[2]; **ligge(n)**; **legge**; **lered**; **lere(n)**; **lete(n)**; **leue(n)** *v*.[1]
læuued, **læwed** *adj.* lay 16.3, 45. [OE *læwede*]
laferrd; **laffdiȝ**. See **louerd(e)**; **lefdi**.
lage *adj.* weak 12.189; **lah(e)** low, base 18.231, 463; of little worth 19.218; humble 19.291; **lawe** in *o* ~ down 8N.36; **lowe** of low rank 10.287. [ON *lág-r* low]
lage *n.* law 12.105, 139; *ðe olde* ~ the old, Mosaic, dispensation, *ðe newe* the gospel dispensation 12.103; **laghe** 17.42 (*ialde*), scripture 17; **laȝe** 10.113, jurisdiction 201; **lahe** 18.444, uses, ways 19.305; **lawe** in *with* ~ lawfully 7.20. *pl.* **laȝen** 10.305. [OE *lagu* from ON; pl. *laga*]
lahfulnesse *n.* law-abiding nature 1.699. [from OE *lah-*, combining form of *lagu* (see prec.), +-**ful**+-*nes(se)*]
lahheð, **-inde**. See **lawe** *v.*
lahte *pa. t. sg.* took, got 8H.45; **laute** 4.12. [OE *læhte*, *lāhte* from *læccan*]
lay *n.*[1] song 8D.27. [OF *lai*]
lai *n.*[2] law 14.292. [OF *lei*]
lai, **lay**; **layt**; **lakess**; **lakke**. See **ligge(n)**; **legge**; **lac** *n.*[2]; **lac** *n.*[1]
lam *n.* earth, clay 14.236. [OE *lām*]
lam(e) *adj.* lame, crippled, infirm 1.690, 6.199, 15.67. [OE *lama*]
Lammasse *n.* Lammas, 1 August 16.118. [OE *hlāfmæsse*]
land(e). See **lond(e)**.
lane *n.* loan 19.227; *to* ~ as a loan 18.132 (see **to**). [ON *lán*]
lang(e). See **long(e)**.
lanhure *adv.* at least 18.498. [cf. **la** and **hure**]
lare. See **lore**.
large *adj.* ample 14.93; generous 17.132, 18.606. [OF]

largesse *n.* generosity 8K.49. [OF]
lasse; **last**. See **lesse** *adj.*; **late**, **leatere**.
laste *n.* fault, vice 8F.15. *pl.* **lastes** sinful conduct 8H.17. [ON *lǫst-r*, gen. *lastar*]
laste *adj.*, *v.* See **leatere**, **lesse**; **leste(n)**.
lasteles *adj.* faultless, flawless 8K.33. [from **laste**]
lat(-). See **lete(n)**.
late *adv.* late, in phr. *to* ~ 4.113, 5.81, 8H.35; ~ *and raþe* at all times 2.272. *sup.* **last** last 17. 190, 194. [OE *late*, sup. *latost*]
Latin, **Latyn** *n.* Latin 7.108, 272. [OF *latin*]
Latine *adj.* Latin 14.24. [as prec.]
lað *n.* hostility 19.173. [OE *lāþ* injury] See **loþ**.
lað(e), **lath**. See **loþ**.
laumpes *n. pl.* lamps 7.45. [AN *laumpe*]
laumprei *n.* lamprey 4.39. *pl.* **laumprees** 4.163. [AN *laumpreie*, cf. OF *lamproie*]
launterne *n.* lantern 8K.22. [AN]
laute. See **lahte**.
laue *n.* remainder: *to* ~ remaining 10.293 (see **to**). [OE *lāf*, obl. *lāfe*]
laue; **lauedi**. See **leue(n)** *v.*[1]; **lefdi**.
lauercok *n.* lark 8G.52. *pl.* **leuerokes** 9.107. [OE *lāferce*, *læwerce* infl. by **coc**]
lauerd. See **louerd(e)**.
lawe *v.* laugh, smile 6.401. *imper. pl.* **lahheð** 18.117 (see **bismere**). *pr. p.* **leyende**, **leiȝande**, **-ende** 3.223, 241, 255; **lahhinde** smiling 19.239. *pa. t. sg.* **loȝh** 14.266; **loh** (with *on*) 8E.17; **lou**, **low** 5.23, 148, 4.169 (*on*). [OA *hlæhan*, *hlehhan*; *hlōh*, *hlōg*, *hlōgon*]
lawe. See **lage** *n.*, *adj.*

GLOSSARY
519

lax *n.* salmon 4.22. *pl.* laxes
4.162. [OA *læx*]
leaden; leafde(n); leafdi. See
led(e); leue(n) *v.*¹; lefdi.
lealté *n.* loyalty, faithfulness
8K.52; leuté good faith 6.229.
[OF *lealté*, AN *leuté*]
leane *adj.* lean 19.65. [OE
hlǣne]
lear(-); leasse; least(e). See
lere(n); lesse; leatere, lesse.
leatere *adj. comp.* later 19.117;
latter 18.428. *sup.* last(e) latest,
last 7.267, 17.196, 202; leaste
18.139; *at þe* ~ in the end, after
all 6.141, 7.71, 138, *atte* ~ at
last, finally 11.35, 107. [OM
leatra; OE *læt(e)st* adj., *latost*
adv., M *leatost*]
leattres; leaue. See lettre;
leue *n.*¹, leue(n) *v.*¹
leche *n.* physician 4.263; medicine 8M.12. [OE *lǣce*]
lecherie *n.* lechery, sensuality
8x.8, 17.120; licherie 8x.18.
[OF *lecherie*, *licherie*]
lechur *n.* lecher, libertine 17.132;
lichur 14.31. [AN *lechur*, *lichur*]
led *n.* pot (orig. of lead) 4.190.
[OE *lēad*]
led(e) *v.* 1.642, 6.211, 11.114, 15.
44; ledenn 13.196; leaden 19.
410. (1) lead, conduct 1.216,
2.209, 11.21, 19.74; ~ *hemm þe
weȝȝe* lead them on the way
13.196. (2) bring, carry 7.270,
11.114. (3) accompany 8D.1,
K.67. (4) pass, go through (life)
6.174, 304, 8E.27, 15.42, 18.448,
19.306. (5) *refl.* conduct oneself,
behave 4.53, 19.410. *pr. 1 sg.*
led(e) 6.174, 15.68; ledh 15.44;
lydy 15.42. *2 sg.* ledest 1.630.
3 sg. ledes 8E.27. *pl.* ledeþ
1.216, 6.304; leadeð 18.448,
19.306. *subj. sg.* leade 19.74.
pa. t. sg. ladde 2.170, 175, 7.98;
led(de) 2.209, 228, 13.200. *pl.*
ladde 7.270, 11.21, 45; læd
16.257; ledden 16.272. *pp.* lad

8D.1; ledd 14.65; iladde 1.276.
[OE *lædan*, *lǣdde*]
ledene *n.* language 18.381, 409.
pl. ledenes nations 19.294.
[OE *lǣden, leden*, orig. Latin]
ledy. See lefdi.
lef *n.* leaf (of tree) 8H.3, L.3, M.2;
leue 14.186. *pl.* leues (of book)
1.594. [OE *lēaf, lēaf-*]
lef *adj.* dear, beloved 8E.50;
pleasing (*me is* ~ I like, wish)
6.33, 12.170; leof 18.139; lof
1.159, 187, 217; luef 8F.48;
with irreg. *to* 1.389 (note). as *n.*
dear one, beloved 3.283, 8L.16,
M.11, Q.1, 18.564; leif 14.17;
gen. leoues 18.509, 652. *wk.*,
often voc.: lefe 13.233; leue 2.
141, 3.77, 4.175, (without *n.*)
315, 6.30; leof(u)e 10.28, 98,
dat. leofen 80; leoue 18.261,
510, *pl.* 10, 142. *comp.* leuer(e)
in *him were* ~ he would rather
5.7, sim. 6.382, 8E.46, 15.43, 14.
275 (perh. pers.); leouere 18.
151, 271. *sup.* leof(u)est(e) 10.
22, 97, 214; leouest(e) 10.67,
215, 18.46, 50. [OE *lēof, lēofa*,
&c.]
lefdi, lefdy *n.* lady, mistress 19.
401, 2.100; leafdi 18.35, 468;
leuedi, -y 8D.7, 11, L.1, R.1,
17.89; ledy 8H.44, K.33, sove-
reign 52; laffdiȝ 13.149; lauedi
7.126, 17.5; lady 2.288; *ure* ~
13.149, 17.5, 89, sim. 8T.6,
18.35. *gen.* lefdyes 2.275. *pl.*
leuedis 8H.34, 17.34; ledies
8H.8. [OE *hlǣfdige*]
lefly *adj.* lovely, beautiful 8E.31,
38; leofly E.78; leflich(e) K.13,
20; beloved, dear K.53. [OE
lēoflic]
lefly *adv.* pleasantly, well 8G.19;
leuely willingly, graciously H.
47; leofliche beautifully 19.
235. [OE *lēoflice*]
lefman -mon *n.* loved one,
beloved 8W.33, 41; leofmon
18.465; mistress, sweetheart

6.376; **leuemon** 6.418; **lemman, -mon** 2.94, 14.81, 8L.16,
8, M.6, 6.127 [lef+man]
left adj. left 3.183; **leoft** 10.28;
luft 19.211. [OE lyft, K left]
legat n. legate 16.16. [OF]
legge v. lay, place, put, impose;
(of a wager) 3.122; ~ o(n) lay
(blows) on, strike, beat upon
4.334, 10.276, 18.396. 3 sg.
leigeð 12.120; **leið** 18.545.
subj. sg. **legge** 1.164. imper. sg.
lei 18.396. pa. t. sg. **leide** 1.325,
7.174, 18.148; **leȝȝde** 13.52;
læide 16.302. pl. **leiden, leyden** 10.276, 4.334; **læiden** 16.
182. pp. **leȝȝd** 13.97; **layt,
leyit** 15.66, 83; **ileid** 17.147,
18.447; **ileiid** in up ~ put away
9.118. [OE lecgan, pr. 3 sg.
legeþ, legþ; lægde]
legges n. pl. legs 8K.31. [ON
legg-r]
legheþ; **leȝe**; **leȝȝd(e)**. See
lie; **lie, ligge(n)**; **legge**.
leȝȝtenn v. search for 13.188.
[ON leita]
ley n. falsehood 15.83. [OE lyge,
prob. modified after **lie**]
lei(de), leyden, leigeð, leið;
lei(ȝ)en; **leyende, leiȝande,
-ende**; **leif**; **Leinte**. See
legge; **ligge(n)**; **lawe** v.; **lef**
adj.; **Lente(n)**.
lele adj. true 8E.38, 14.75. [AN
leel]
leme; **lemman, -mon**. See
leome; **lefman**.
lendbon n. haunch 12.121. [OE
lenden-bān]
lende v. land, reach shore 4.1.
[OE léndan; cf. lond(e)]
leneþ[1] pr. 3 sg. gives, sends forth
8E.20. subj. sg. **lene** grant 12.
108. pl. **lend** 2.73. imper. sg.
lene grant 8w.45. pp. **ileanet**
lent 19.39, 228. [OE lǽnan]
leneþ[2] pr. 3 sg. intr. leans 8N.19.
pa. t. sg. refl. **lened** (him) 14.105.
[OA hleonian]

leng(-). See **long(e)** adj.[2], adv.
lenge n. ling 4.100. [cf. early
mod. Du linghe]
lenge v. remain, live 14.275.
[OE lengan]
Lengten. See **Lente(n)**.
lengþe, -ðe n. length 1.130, 19.
318; on ~ at length, in the end
12.194. [OE lengþu]
Lente(n) n. Lent 11.151; **Leinte**
11.128; **Lengten** 16.242. [OE
lencten]
Lenten-tid n. season of Lent
16.60. [OE lencten-tīd]
leo n. lioness 10.37. [OE from L]
Cf. **liun**.
leoden n. pl. people (of a country) 10.introd., 62. [OE léode]
leof(-); **leofly**; **leofliche**; **leofmon**; **leoft**. See **lef** adj.;
lefly adj.; **lefly** adv.; **lefman**;
left.
leome n. glow, brightness 19.
242; **leme** 13.72. [OE léoma]
leomeþ pr. 3 sg. shines 8E.8;
lumes K.21. [from prec.]
leor n. face 19.66, 259; **lere**
cheek 8E.78; **lure** complexion,
beauty 8K.21. [OE hléor]
leorneden. See **lerne**.
leosen v. lose, be deprived of
18.637 (see þurh); waste (time)
18.91; **losen** 1.267; **liese** 17.16.
pr. 2 sg. **lesest** 6.134. 3 sg.
leseþ misses, fails to attain 6.
141. pl. **lesis** 14.6; **liesed** 17.
124. pa. t. sg. **lest** 14.141. pp.
ilore, yloren 11.135, 8N.16;
ileosed 10.174. [OE léosan, K
līosan; léas; loren]
leote; **leoue(-)**. See **lete(n)**;
lef adj.
lepe v. run 3.201. pr. pl. **lepiþ**
jump 9.157. imper. sg. **lep**
5.234. pa. t. sg. **lep** ran, rushed
4.157, 204; jumped, leapt 5.22,
237; **lop** 5.78. pl. **lepe** ran
3.249; **lopen** 4.323. [OE hléa-
pan, hléop, hléopon]
lere. See **leor**.

lere(n) *v.* teach 5.231; learn 4.65, 91, 12.63. *pr. 3 sg.* **lereð** learns 12.49, 53; teaches 12.105, **lereð** 19.200. *pl.* **lærenn** teach 13.223; **lereð** instruct 19.411. *subj. sg.* **leare** 19.50. *pa. t. pl.* **lerden** 19.403. [OE *lǣran* teach] *lǣran* teach]

lered *pp. adj.* learned, in orders, clerical 16.197; **læred** 16.3, 45. [OE *lǣred*; see prec.]

lerne *v.* learn 3.95, 6.48. *pa. t. subj. sg.* **lernede** 6.98. *pl.* **leorneden** 18.203. *pp.* **ilorned** 1.172. [OE *léornian*]

les *imper. sg.* set free 8D.12. *pa. t. sg.* **lesed** released, delivered 8V.24. *pp.* **lesit** 15.34. [OA *lēsan*]

les-. See **leosen**.

lesceunes *n. gen.* of [this] lesson 18.203. [AN *lecun*]

lese *n.* falsehood 10.80. [OE *lēas*]

lesing *n.* falsehood 1.508; lie, lying tale 6.203, 282. [cf. OE *léasung*]

less(e) *adj. comp.* less, smaller, shorter 4.257, 14.186; **leasse** 18.279, 524; **lasse** lower in rank 1.340 (see **more** adj.). as *n.* **lasse** less 7.156. *double comp.* **lessere** of less importance 19.390. *sup.* **leaste** smallest 19.131; **laste** 4.322, 10.292. [OE *lǣssa*, *lǣst*] See **litel**.

lesse *adv. comp.* less 14.79; **leasse** 18.353, 441. *sup.* least 19.77. [OE *lǣs*, *lǣst*]

lest(e) *conj.* lest 6.202, 8F.7, N.4, 18.86, 19.61. [OE *þȳ lǣs þe*]

leste(n) *v.* last, continue, endure 8D.30, 19.202. *pr. 3 sg.* **lastes** 14.84; **lesteþ** 1.249. *subj. sg.* **laste** 8L.6. *pa. t. sg.* **laste** 3.251; **lastede** 16.181. [OE *lǣstan*]

lete *n.* appearance 1.35. [OE *ge-lǣte*] Cf. **ilete**.

lete(n) *v.* 5.51, 8D.20, 16.276; **late** 11.114; **leote** 18.618. (1) let,

allow, leave 1.224, 3.190, 4.142, 5.88, 8L.16; let go (*in, out, down, &c.*) 1.8, 3.258, 4.199, 19.44; ~ *blod* (orig. with dat.) 5.40, 51; ~ *be(o)* leave alone, give up, stop 3.220, 1.657, 693, ~ *iwurðen* 19.28. (2) leave, give up 16.13, 19.32; cease, abandon, forsake 8D.20, W.55, 12.119, 17.80, 18. 556, ~ *awei* 1.133; neglect 1.729. (3) cause to, make (with infin. in active sense, as ~ *fleye*) 4.218, 254, 6.29, 10.165, 16.4. (4) cause, have (with active infin. corresp. to modern pass., cf. **do**) 3.172, 7.125, 181, 10.205, 11.92, 16. 208. (5) think (highly, &c.) of: *leteþ lihtliche of* set little value on 1.732, sim. 3.108, 18.618; ~ *for* consider as 8L.19. *pr. 3 sg.* **let** 1.551, 19.238; **lateð** 12.119; **lat** 1.224. *pl.* **leteþ** 1. 729; (with fut. sense) **lete** 8L.19. *subj. sg.* **lete** 6.196; **leote** 19.44. *1 pl.* **lete** 1.133; **late** 4.310. *imper. sg.* **let(e)** 3.108, 5.174, 6.29, 8L.16; **lat** 1.194, 4.199. *pl.* **leteþ** 1.657; **lateþ** 1.687. *pa. t. 3 sg.* **let** 1.8, 4.142, 11.92, 16.4; **læt** 16.208; **liet** 7.120; **lette** 10.205, 217, 18.399, 19.32. *2 sg.* **lete** 1.576. *pl.* **let(en)** 3.220, 190; **letten** 10.165. *pp.* **leten** 5.40; **læten** 16.13. [OE *lǣtan*, *lēt*, -*on*, *lǣten*; forms with *a* perh. partly from shortening, partly ON *láta*; for *leote*, *lette* see *Iuliene* pp. 247–8]

lettre *n.* letter (missive) 7.178, 200. *pl.* **leattres** 18.470, 471; (letters of the alphabet, characters) 19.80; **lettres** 7.176. [OF *lettre*]

lettunge *n.* hindrance 19.363. [cf. OE *letting*]

leth *n.* hatred 14.31. [OE *lǣþþ(u)*]

leðer *n.* leather 18.530. [OE *leþer-*]

leun ; leuté. See **liun ; lealté.**

leue *n.*[1] permission 3.17, **5.**25, 6.58, 16.14; **læfe** 16.79; **leaue** 18.248; permission to go, leave, in ~ *tak, took, had* 14.229, 2.322, 325. [OE *lēaf*, obl. *lēafe*]

leue *n.*[2] faith, belief 12.189, 192; **læfe** 13.138, 172. [OE *(ge)lēafa*]

leue(-). See **lef** *adj.*

leue(n) *v.*[1] *tr.* leave (behind) 6.153. *intr.* remain, stay 19.388; **laue** 2.252. *pr. 1 sg.* **leaue** leave 18.144. *imper. sg.* **leue** 3.106. *pa. t. sg.* **leafde** 18.141, 145; **læuede** left untouched 16.46. *pl.* **leafden** abandoned 18.515. [OE *lǣfan*] See **bileue**.

leue *v.*[2] *pr. subj. sg.* grant, in wishes: *Louerd,* &c., ~ 6.147, 212, 18.244. [OA *lēfan*]

leue(n) *v.*[3] believe (with *on,* in) 8F.25; *to* ~ to be trusted 8H.19. *pr. 1 sg.* **leue** 18.301. *3 sg.* **leues** 4.208; **leueð** 12.48 (both with *on*). *subj. sg.* **leue** 18.252, 274. *imper. sg.* **leue** (with *vpon*) 8D.27. [OA *(ge)lēfan*] See **beleue**.

leuedi, -y; **leuely**; **leuemon**; **leuer(e)**; **leuerokes**; **leues.** See **lefdi**; **lefly** *adv.*; **lefman**; **lef** *adj.*; **lauercok**; **lef** *n.*

leui *v.* put out leaves 7.94. *pr. 3 sg.* **leued** 8v.2. [from **lef** n.]

lhouþ *pr. 3 sg.* lows 8A.7. [OE *hlōwan*]

lhude; **li**, **ly.** See **lude**; **ligge(n).**

libben *v.* live 3.32, 19.311; **libe** 5.42; **liuie** 5.165; **liue(n)**, **lyue** 12.170, 14.164, 16.215, 8L.16; live to see, experience 8L.10; life in *wel to* ~ well off 15.5 (note). *pr. 1 sg.* **liue** 6.333; **liuie** 8Q.3. *3 sg.* **liueþ, -ð, lyueþ** 6.313, 12.160, 8H.45. *pl.* **liuieð** 19.323. *pr. p.* **libbinde** 19.305. *pa. t. sg.* **liued(e)** 14.273, 16.314. *pl.* **liueden** 19.299. *pp.* **liued** 14.132. [OE *libban*, LWS *lifian*]

lic *n.* body 16.127. [OE *līc*]

licham *n.* body 12.107; **likam** 9.174; **licome** 18.511, 532. [OE *līc-hama, -homa*]

liche *adj.* like (with pron. obj.) 2.232, 241; **like** 14.10. *comp.* **lickre** (with *to*) 18.26. [OE *(ge)līc*] See **ilich(e).**

-liche *suff.* forming advs., as aperte-, bisi-, haste-, stedefast- ; northerly variant **-like** as hardi-. [OE *-līce*]

licherie, -ur; **licht**; **lickre**; **licome.** See **lecherie, -ur**; **lihte**; **liche**; **licham.**

licomlich(e) *adj.* bodily 18.4, 404, 19.196. [OE *līchamlīc*]

licunge *n.* satisfaction, pleasure 18.386, 19.190. [OE *licung*; see **like(n)**]

licwurðe *adj.* pleasant, agreeable 19.391. [OE *līc-wyrþe*]

lydy. See **led(e).**

lie *v.*[1] lie, tell lies; *tr.* speak falsely 5.132; *intr.* **liȝe** 1.513; **leȝe** 8L.28. *pr. 3 sg.* **legheþ** deceives 17.260. *subj. sg.* **liȝe** in *þat þu ne* ~ if you tell the truth 1.379. *imper. sg.* **liȝ** 6.229. *pp.* **iloȝe** 1.507. [OE *lēogan,* pp. *logen*]

lien *v.*[2]; **liese(d)**; **liet.** See **ligge(n)**; **leosen**; **lete(n).**

lif, lyf *n.* life 6.82, 19.32, 3.24, 8D.10; **liif** 5.187, 14.6, 50 (distrib. sg.). *dat.* life 10.103, 13.286; **liue, lyue** 5.227, 14.274, 18.47, 4.232. way of life 5.178; lifetime 5.211, 15.59; creature 15.50; beloved 8K.20, *mi leue* ~ my dear 6.30. *gen.* **liues, lyues** 7.70, 8K.67, 12.100, 19.246; **lifess** 13.265, ~ *boc* 18.105, 13.287; as *adv.* alive 4.346, 18.499. *pl.* **liues** 6.304. *gen.* **life** 13.212. *on life, liue* alive 10.237, 4.61, see **aliue**; *brouȝth of lyf, duden of lyue* see **bryng(e), do(n)**; *a to mine liue* (*þines lifes*) as long as I (you) live 10.50, 304. [OE *lif,* dat. *līfe*]

lif-daie *n.* term of life, life 5.200. *pl.* **lif-dayes** life 5.49. *dat.* **lif-, life-daȝe** 10.284, 170; **liif-dawe** 7.19; see **do(n), bryng(e)**. [OE *lif-dæg, -dagas*; see **dai(e)**]

life. See **libben**.

liflade *n.* conduct of life, living 18.228. [OE *lif-lād*; see **lade**]

lif-siðe *n.* lifetime 19.84. [**lif+siþ(e)**]

lift *imper. sg.* lift 15.64. *pa. t. sg.* **lifte** 4.233. [OSw *lyfta*, cf. OI *lypta*]

lifte *n.* air 9.124; **lufte** 18.63; **lifft(e)** sky 13.161, 174. [OE *lyft*]

lif-wile *n.* lifetime: *his ~* during his life 6.103. [**lif+while**]

ligge(n) *v.* lie 4.142, 7.120; lie down (with infin. *slepe*) 7.234; be idle 4.70; **lien** 16.178; **leȝe** 8E.83. *pr. 3 sg.* **liþ, lið** 1.308, 18.194; **li(i)th** 7.introd., 188; **liht** 8H.44. *pl.* **lien** pertain 16.214; **lys** 15.76. *subj. sg.* **ly** 15.10. *imper. sg.* **li** 18.365. *pa. t. sg.* **lai, lay** 7.79, 106, 10.5, 16.119; **læi** 10.12; stayed 4.57, 90, 10.153; stayed in bed 4.80; was sleeping 7.55; stayed the night 11.131; remained, was 10.218; led 10.220; *læi abiden* stayed waiting 10.123. *pl.* **lay** 4.236; **leien** 10.294; **leiȝen** in *~ slepe* lay sleeping 7.237. *pp.* **leien** in *~ bi* lain with 6.383. [OE *licgan,* pr. 3 sg. *liþ; læg; lægon, lēgon; legen*; in 4 perh. ON *liggja* in pr.]

light. See **liȝt(e)**.

ligten *v.* relieve 12.134. [OE *lihtan*; cf. **liȝt** *adj.*²]

liȝ(e). See **lie**.

liȝt, liht(e) *adj.*¹ full of light 9.65; bright, radiant 8E.8, 19.361. [OE *lĕ(o)ht*]

liȝt, liht, lyht *adj.*² light 8H.3; slight, poor 18.386, 619; easy

5.236; frivolous, foolish 11.139. [OE *lĕ(o)ht*]

liȝt *v.*¹ alight, come down 9.130, 138. *pr. 3 sg.* **lihteð** 19.78. *pl.* **liȝtiþ** 9.108, 131. *pa. t. sg.* **lihte** 18.280, went down 130. *pp.* **liht, lyht** settled 8D.22, F.26. [OE *lĭhtan*]

liȝt(e) *n.* light 1.119, 9.116; **liht, lyht(e)** 19.100, 8L.2, E.20, *in ~* plainly K.68; **lihht** 13.72; **liȝht** 14.152; **lith** 4.316. [OE *lĕ(o)ht, lĭht*]

liȝte *adv.* bright 7.45; **liht** 8K.21. [OE *lĕ(o)hte*]

liȝtliche, liht- *adv.* lightly, slightly 1.732; cheaply 18.527; easily, readily 1.514, 18.195, 525. [OE *lĕ(o)htlice*] See **liȝt** *adj.*², **lihtlich**.

lihht; liht(e); lyht(e). See **liȝt(e); ligge(n), liȝt(e), liȝt** *adj.*¹, *adj.*², *v.*, **liȝte; liȝt(e).**

lihte *v.*² *intr.* grow light, dawn 10.162. *pr. 3 sg.* **licht** shines 17.50. *pa. t. sg. tr.* **lihtede** lighted 16.243. [OE *lĭhtan*]

lihtlich *adj.* easy 1.717. [OE *lĕohtlic*; see **liȝt** *adj.*²]

lihtschipe *n.* swiftness 19.319. [**liȝt** *adj.*²+**-schipe**]

liif, liif-dawe; liith; likam; like. See **lif; lif-daie; ligge(n); licham; liche.**

like(n) *v.* please 3.225, 6.82, 257; **liki** 1.258. *pr. 3 sg.* **likes** 14.54; **likeð** 19.314, (*impers.*) 18.356. *pl.* **likes** 14.26. [OE *lician*]

likful *adj.* pleasing, delightful 9.72. *sup.* **likfullist** 9.56. [prec. +**-ful**]

lilie *n.* lily 1.317, 8K.49; *coll.* lilies 9.80. [OE from L *lilium*]

lylie-leor *adj.* as *n.* fair (-faced) lady 8H.46. [prec.+**leor**]

lylie-lossom *adj.* beautiful as a lily 8E.10. [**lilie**+**lossom**]

lylie-white, whyt *adj.* lily-white 8E.50, D.31. [**lilie**+**whit(e)**]

limes *n. gen.* of [each] limb,

member 19.18. *pl.* **limes** 6.311, 12.5, 16.173; **limen** 19.410. [OE *lim*, pl. *limu*]

lime *n.* (F) file 18.325.

limpet, -ð *pr. 3 sg.* belongs 19.175; *efter þet him ~ to* as far as concerns him 19.402. [OE *limpan*; see **ilomp**]

lyn *n.* linen: *in ~* dressed in linen (tag; cf. **bis, gore**) 8H.46. [OE *līn*]

linde, lynde *n.* lime-tree 1.708, 8H.3. [OE *lind(e)*]

lines *n. pl.* lines 4.50. [OE *line* and OF *ligne*]

linnunge *n.* ceasing 19.268. [from OE *linnan*] Cf. **blynne**.

lippes *n. pl.* lips 8E.38. [OE *lippa*]

lys. See **ligge(n)**.

lisse *n.* peace, rest 8U.2. [OE *liss*]

list *n.* desire 12.186. [from OE *lystan*; see **lust** v.¹]

list. See **lust** v.¹

liste *n.* cunning 1.128. [OE *list*]

listen *v.* listen (to) 12.37. *pr. 3 sg.* **listneð** 12.193; **lustneð** 19.401. *subj. pl.* **lustnin** 19.244. *imper. sg.* **lystne** 8G.38. *pl.* **lustnið** 19.70. *pa. t. sg.* **lustnede** 8K.69. [OE **hlysnian* (Nb *lysna*) infl. by *hlystan*; see **lust** v.²]

lit *n.* colour 8E.78. [ON *lit-r*]

lite. See **lut(e)**.

litel *adj.* little, small, short 3.108, 4.5, 300, 12.58; **litle** 1.734, 17.152; **litell** 12.93, 189; **litell** as *n.* in adv. phr. *a ~* 13.198; **lutel** 1.369, 18.125, 19.192; **lutle** 1.671, 19.264, as *n.* 369. [OE *lȳtel, lȳtl-*, ON *lítill*] Cf. **lut(e)** and see **lesse**.

litel *adv.* 3.257, 16.142; **lutel** 1.543, 18.528, 19.201; **luitel** 5.260, 6.362. a little 1.577, 3.257; little 1.543, 5.260, 6.362, 16.300. [from prec.]

lith. See **li3t(e)**.

litunge *n.* colouring 18.531. [from **lit**]

liþ, lið, lith. See **ligge(n)**.

liðe *adj.* merciful 10.introd. [OE *līþe*]

liðe(n) *v.* (often pleonastic with *come*) go, come 10.37, 322, sail 314; *tr.* take, carry 10.317. [OE *līþan*]

liðeliche *adv.* courteously 19.244. [OE *līþelīce*]

liðere *imper. sg.* let fly, strike 18.370. [v. based on OE *līþere* n., sling]

liun *n.* lion 18.170, 19.171; **leun** 4.294. [AN *liun*] Cf. **leo**.

liue(-), lyue(-). See **lif**; **libben**.

liueneð *n.* sustenance, provisions 18.479, 676; **liuenoðe** 12.93. [ON *lifnaðr* conduct of life]

liuie(ð); lo. See **libben**; **la**.

lockes, lokkes *n. pl.* (locks of) hair 8E.31, K.13. [OE *locc*]

lodlich *adj.* loathsome, horrible 1.32, 71; **ladlice** repulsive, hideous 16.51. [OE *lāþlic*]

lof *n.* headband, fillet 16.174 (note). [OE]

lof. See **lef** *adj.*

lofenn *v.* praise 13.140, 216. [OE *lofian*]

loff *n.* praise 13.110. *dat.* **lofe** in *to ~ annd wurrþe* in praise and worship 13.106 (see to). [OE *lof*]

loft-song *n.* singing, song, of praise 19.319. *pl.* **-songes** 19.358. [prec.+**song(e)**]

logh, loh. See **lawe** *v.*

lok *v.* look 14.202; **lokenn** look at, see 13.14; **loki(n)** 18.365, 19.261, keep, guard, protect 1.384, 11.30. *pr. 2 sg.* **lokest** 18.360. *3 sg.* **lokes** 14.183; **loket** protects 17.65. *pl.* **lokieð** look forward to the time 10.322. *subj. sg.* **loke** 17.134; **loki** 18.280, watch 19.44, protect 1.56. *1 pl.* **loke** (*we*) 13.123. *imper. sg.* **loke** 6.357; see to it, make sure 1.122, 6.398, 8M.15; with refl. dat. *þe* 18.256. *pl.* **lokeþ** 17.262; **lokið** 18.28, 147, 19.76. *pa. t. sg.* **loked(e)** 7.260, 14.197, (with *on*) 10.300. *pp.* **loked** 14. 173; **iloked** ordained, decreed 7.221. [OE *lōcian*]

lokkes. See **lockes.**

lomb *n.* lamb 8A.6. [OE]

lomen *n. pl.* tools 18.415. [OE *lōma*]

lonc *adj.* lank, spare 19.65. [OE *hlanc*, *hlonc]

lond(e) *n.* land, country 2.41, 3.96, 5.101, 7.16; dry land 4.4, 10.44, 12.125; earth, ground 9.138; estates 10.251; **lont** 19. 147, 287; **land(e)** 13.20, 14.178, 15.14, soil 16.186. *dat.* **londen** 10.54. *a*, *in*, *o(n)* ∼ in the country, among men, anywhere 1. 581, 6.266, 8E.50, H.19, K.12, L.14, 10.259, 12.150, 15.46; *to* ∼ to us 1.298; *upe*, *vp o* ∼ in country districts 1.479, 4.31 (note); (*ut*) *of* ∼ abroad 1.572, 16.115. *pl.* **lond** lands 10.16; **londes** countries 17.33; lands, estates 7.124; **landes** 16.120, 125, income from lands 208. *dat.* **londe** 8D.11. [OE *lánd*, *lónd*, sg. and pl.]

long *adj.*¹ dependent (with *on*) 4.69 (note), 8D.10. [OE *ge-láng*; see **ylong**]

long(e) *adj.*² long (of space and time) 1.96, 3.170, 4.196, 216 (see **oȝt** n.), 8B.5, E.31; tall 8E.10, in inclusive phr. ∼ *ne lite* tall or short 4.282; long-lasting 12.93; ∼ *hwile* for a long time 19.285; *hom þoȝte* ∼ *er* it seemed to them (too) long until (they could escape), they were impatient 11.161; *alle* ∼ *niȝt* all night long 1.247, 10.5, sim. **longue** 7.149; **lang** 9.66, 16.227 (see **Fridæi**). *comp.* **lengore** 8E.44. [OE *láng*, *lóng*, comp. *lengra*]

long(e) *adv.* long 1.45, 2.84, 294,

4.63, 8D.26, 18.91; ∼ *bið æuere* as long as ever is 10.66 (note); *so* ∼ *þat* until 5.280; **longue** 7.137; **lang(e)** 16.17, 113. *comp.* **leng** 1.42, 6.148, 16.215; **lenger(e)** 3.124, 4.77, 19.388; **lengre** 18.21, 19.279; **lengore** 8F.26, L.6; **lengour** 5.42; **langar**, **-er** 14.164, 276. [OE *lánge*, *lónge*, comp. *léng*; cf. prec.]

longyng, **-inge** *n.* longing, yearning 8D.1, W.3, 43. [cf. OE *lóngung*]

lont; **loop**; **lop(en)**; **lord.** See **lond(e)**; **loþ**; **lepe**; **louerd(e).**

lordinges *n. pl.* (in address) sirs, gentlemen 9.183, 17.34, 69 [OE *hláfording*]

lore *n.* learning 1.596, 6.4, 8L.29; lesson 6.264; teaching 8F.25, 12.49; **lare** 18.204, 19.401. *pl.* **lores** advice 8H.47. [OE *lār*]

losen. See **leosen.**

losyt *pp.* wasted 15.12. [cf. OE *losian* be lost, perish]

lossom, lussom, lussum *adj.* lovely 8K.17, 33; pleasant, delightful 8E.27. as *n.* lovely creature 8E.17. *comp.* **lussomore** 8K.12. [OE *lufsum*]

lostlase *adj.* listless, surly 8N.36. [**lust**+OE *-lēas*]

lote *imper. sg.* bend down, forward 14.169. [app. misspelling for *loute* (cf. rhyme) from OE *lūtan*]

loþ, loð *adj.* hateful, loathsome (usu. with dat. of person) 1.65, 72, 5.219, 12.170; **lað(e)** 18.656, 19.109; repugnant, displeasing, in phr. *were me loþ* I should be unwilling 6.42; sim. 5.6, 8F.25, **looþ** 2.149, **lath** 14.29. *sup.* **laðest** 18.396, 19.147. [OE *lāþ*]

lou; **loude.** See **lawe** *v.*; **lud(e).**

loupe *v.* run 4.228. [ON *hlaupa*]

loue *n.* love 2.175, 3.59, 6.367, 8D.22; Love (personified) 8K.53, 61; loved one 6.144; **luue, lvue**

8w.5, 29, 16.228, 18.142, 19.25, (personified) 247; luf 14.65, 15. 25; lover 15.24; (with objective gen.) *for wommans* ~ for the love of woman 2.263, sim. 5.193, 7.250, and with pron. 1.324, 8к.77, &c., L.15, 15.22. phr. *for* ~ *ne golde* 2.240, *for* ~ *ne for fere* 7.130. *pl.* luuen 18.599. [OE *lufu*]

loue *v.* love 3.133, 6.136, 8D.19, H.17, make love to 6.87; louie(n) 6.7, 265, 8u.8, 17.224; luue(n) 12.131, 14.52; lufe 15.8; luuie(n) 17.81, 18.467, 611; *to* ~ to be loved 18.98, 664. *pr. 1 sg.* loue 6.144; luf 15.15. *2 sg.* louest 2.47, 8м.14; luuest 18.299. *3 sg.* loueþ 3.24, 6.94, 8G.43; luueþ, -ð 1.186, 17.264, 18.209, 19.339; lufeþþ 13.243; luued 17.81; loues 14.81. *pl.* luue 14.53; luuieþ, -ð 17.264, 18.441, 19.337. *subj. sg.* louie 8м.19; luuie 17.225, 18.275. *pl.* luuien 18.435. *imper. sg.* luue 18.294. *pa. t. sg.* louede 6.343, 7.11; luuede 18.399, 19. 271. *pl.* luuede(n) 16.223, 323, 19.126. *subj. sg.* luuede 18.270, 306. *pp.* loued 8м.5; iloued, y- 6.67, 8R.5. [OE *lufian*]

loue-bene *n.* love-favour 8м.13. [loue n. + OE *bēn*; see benen]

loue-drurye *n.* love-token 2.159. [loue + druri]

loueliche *adj.* beautiful 8к.30. [OE *luflic*]

louerd(e) *n.* lord, master 4.297, 6.17, 11.99, husband 6.70, 119; lord(e) 2.89, 295; lauerd 10. 10, 218, 16.256, 313, 19.6; Lord 2.264, 3.280, 4.208, 6.31, 303 (*interj.*), 7.7, 8т.21, v.7, 17.4, 103, 18.34, 19.4; the Lord 6. 195; laferrd 13.209. *gen.* louerdes 7.26, 193, 12.139; lordes 17.35, 191; lauerdes 18.141, 19.355. [OE *hláford*]

loue-werc *n.* love-making 6.374. [loue + werk]

low; lowe. See lawe *v.*; lage *adj.*

lowse *n.* louse 9.37. [OE *lūs*]

lud(e) *adj.* loud 1.6, 230; loude 3.204. [OE *hlūd*]

lude *adv.* loud, loudly 1.97, 18. 70, 117; lhude 8A.2. *comp.* luddre 18.378. [OE *hlūde*, and *hlŭddre* comp. of *hlūd*; see prec.]

luef; luf(e); luft; lufte. See lef *adj.*; loue *n.*, *v.*; left; lifte.

lugre *n.* ligure, a precious stone 9.91. [from L *ligurius*]

luyte; luitel. See lut(e); litel *adv.*

luken *pa. t. pl.* drew 10.276. [OE *lūcan²*]

lukeð *pr. 3 sg.* closes, shuts 12. 155. *pp.* iloke 5.20. [OE *lūcan¹*, pp. *gelocen*]

lumes. See leomeþ.

Lundenis(s)ce *adj.* of London 16.133, 261. [OE *lundenisc*]

lure. See leor.

luring *n.* frowning, scowling 1.301. [origin obscure]

lussom(-), lussum. See lossom.

lust *n.¹* desire 18.386; pleasure 19.411; appetite 5.96, 100. *pl.* lustes pleasures 19.183. [OE *lust*; cf. list]

lust *n.²* hearing, attention 19.69. [OE *hlyst*]

lust *v.¹* *impers. pr. 3 sg.* wish, desire (with dat. of pers.): *him ne* ~ he does not wish 1.169; sim. 8Q.2; usu. fold. by plain infin., but *to* + infin. 1.393, *to* + n. 168. *pers. pr. 2 sg.* list 3.124. *impers. subj. sg.* luste 18.8, 394; *me* ~ *bet* I would rather 1.39. *pa. t.* luste 7.233. [OE *lystan*; cf. lust n.¹]

lust *v.²* *imper. sg.* listen 1.199, 203. *pl.* lusteþ 1.687. *pa. t. sg.* luste 1.99, 189. [OE *hlystan*] Cf. listen.

lusti *adj.* taking pleasure 19.358. [from lust n.¹]

lustnin. See listen.
lut(e) *adj*. little, small 18.92, 264;
(without art.) 11.63, 168; few
11.33, *ane* ~ a few 18.95; luyte
7.53, 174, short (of time) 94;
lite short (of height) 4.282. as
n. little 11.150; in adv. phr. *a* ~
7.103, 3.226. [OE *lȳt* adv., adj.,
n., ON *lít-t*] Cf. litel.
lut *pron.* few 8H.19, 19.211.[prec.]
lutel, lutle. See litel.
lutli(n) *v*. lessen, decrease *tr.*
1.348, *intr*. 19.369. [OE *lȳtlian*]
luþer(e), luðer *adj*. wicked, evil
7.27, 38, 11.103, 18.250; noxious
7.25. [OE *lȳþre*]
luðerliche *adv*. fiercely 18.370.
[OE *lȳþerlice*]
luue; luue(n), luuie(n). See
loue *n*., *v*.
luueful(e) *adj*. loving 18.217,
290. [loue+-ful]
luue-gleames *n*. *pl*. rays of love
18.651. [loue+OE *glǣm*]
luue-gretunge *n*. loving greeting 18.472. [loue+greting]
luueliche *adv*. lovingly, affec-
tionately 18.261, 273; luuelike
12.139. [OE *luflice*]
luue-salue *n*. loving remedy 18.
266. [loue+salue]
luuewurðe *adj*. worthy of love
18.507. [loue+wurþe]

ma; mac(-). See mo, fai; mak.
macche *n*. husband 13.130. [OE
(*ge*)*mæcca*] Cf. mak(e).
maces *n*. *pl*. mace 9.75. [OF
macis sg., understood as pl.]
macis *n*. *pl*. maces 11.13. [OF
mace]
mad *adj*. mad 8D.2. [OE *ge-
mǣdd*, pp.]
mad(-). See mak.
ma dame *n*. (as address)
madam, my lady 2.177, 293.
[OF] See dame.
madenes. See maid(e).
mæi(e) *n*. kinsman, relative 10.
67, 98, 102 (*dat*.), 16.21. [OE *mæg*]

mære *adj*. famous 10.232; mern
(*dat*.) excellent 10.introd. [OE
mǣre]
mæste; mæssedæi; magt;
magti; maȝȝdenn; maȝȝþ-
hadess; mahe(n), maht(-);
maht(e). See more; masse-;
miȝt(e); mihti; maid(e);
meiðhad; mai; miȝt(e).
may *n*.[1] maiden, girl 8M.18, 15.6.
[OE *mæg* kinswoman and ON
mey acc. of *mæ-r* girl]
May *n*.[1] May 8H.1. [OF *mai*]
mai, may *pr*. *1*, *3 sg*. am/is able
to, can, may 1.141, 2.253, 3.9,
4.71, 12.72; mei, mey 18.91,
19.10, 92, 8F.44; maiȝ 12.28;
can do 8L.32, 19.172, 174. *2 sg*.
miȝt(t) 1.64, 3.139, 6.34, 7.90;
miȝth 2.257; mist (= *miht*) 1.
78; maht 8L.20, 18.492; mait,
mayt 6.49, 4.113; maiȝt 6.258;
maut 6.221. *pl*. mai, may 2.
54, 3.54, 9.15, 15.80; mahe(n)
19.24, 309; moue 17.79; mo-
we(n) 2.38, 8E.42, 60, 17.58;
muee 17.36; muȝe 1.62, 138;
muȝhenn 13.98; muhe(n) 18.
122, 164. *subj. sg*. mahe 18.649,
19.326; moue 6.370; muge 12.
81; muhe 18.257. *pa. t. 1, 3 sg*.
could miȝt(e) 1.42, 3.73, 11.32;
miȝtte 5.112, 6.156; mihte,
myhte 16.11, 177; micthe,
mithe 4.104, 326; mahte 10.
239, 18.67, 19.260; moȝht 14.
126; mouthe 4.97. *pl*. miȝte(n)
7.116, 11.39; miȝtten 2.104;
mihte 10.139; muhten 16.270.
(with infin. of motion understood) could go, turn 2.104,
16.177, 18.67. *subj*. could,
might, would be able to *1, 3 sg*.
miȝt(t)e 1.271, 3.4, 5.58, 87, 6.
83, 7.19; mihte myhte 8E.32, 82,
M.12; (with suffixed pron.) mihti,
myhti 8F.33, 40; mihhte 13.15;
micht(e) 15.16, 17.26; mithe
15.6; mitte 8v.20; mahte
18.410, 19.96; moute 6.14. *2 sg*.

miȝtest 1.192; mihtes, myhtes 8M.11, 16.185; mihtest
10.61; mithest 4.123; michtis
15.30. *pl.* miȝtte(n) 2.64, 5.42;
mihte 1.707; mahten 18.484.
phr. ~ *over* have power over 1.
64 (see ouermyhte); *wel* ~
have reason 1.184; *ful wel* ~
well might be 1.560. [OE *mæg*;
miht, *meaht* (A *mæht*); *magon*,
late *mugon*; *mihte*, late *muhte*]
See conne.

maid(e) *n.* maiden, girl 3.195,
8D.3, 9.140; maiden(e), mayden 3.46, 15.15, 17.217; maidin
9.135; virgin 8F.47, 14.79, and
mayde 8T.35, maȝȝdenn 13.
242, meiden 18.566, 19.274.
gen. maidenes 3.173; meidenes
18.125. *pl.* maidenes 3.28, 53,
madenes 221, maidens 8;
meidnes 19.304. *gen.* maidenes 3.2; maidene 10.307.
[OE *mægden*]

maine *n.* strength, might 5.279.
[OE *mægen*]

maister *n.* master, (as address)
sir 5.206; *attrib.* (as title) 1.147
(note), 704, maistre 736, head
5.272; teacher, tutor 7.29, 84;
meistre 18.255; chief 19.49.
[OF *maistre* and OE *mægester*]

maistri(e), -y, maystry *n.*
masterly deed, feat 6.277; force
8K.64; *for þe* ~ in the highest
degree, exceedingly 8N.28; *lute*
~ no great achievement 11.168.
pl. meistries feats 18.485.
[OF *maistrie*, and phr. *pour
la* ~]

mak, mac, make(n) *v.* make,
do, perform 14.87, 15.57, 3.96,
4.8, 6.142, 8F.19, N.15; cause
(with n. obj.) 3.56; cause to,
make (with obj.+infin., with or
without *to*) 4.182, 7.226, 9.138;
makie(n) 7.125, 10.309, 17.37,
18.135; makeȝe 10.104. For
phrs. see blis(s), chere, del,
heste, ioi(e), mournyng,

murþe, new(e), siker(e). *pr.*
1 sg. mak(e) 6.344, 8K.83. *2 sg.*
makest 1.255, 8L.25, 18.295.
3 sg. makeþ,-ð 2.19, 5.29, 12.19,
19.49; maked 17.131; maket
16.231, 17.133; makið 19.44.
pl. makieð 18.171, 19.287;
makiez (= -þ) 7.196; makeð,
-iþ 1.606, 9.156; maket 8v.1;
mas 14.182. *subj. 2 sg. refl.*
make (*þe*) become 6.39. *3 sg.*
makie 18.262. *imper. sg.* make
6.240, ~ *þe* be 6.328. *pa. t. 1,
3 sg.* maked(e) 3.204, 7.195,
10.38, 16.129, professed 220;
macod held 16.149; made 4.5,
7.118, 17.112, ~ *hym* made himself out, pretended to be 2.29.
2 sg. madest 3.280. *pl.* makeden 16.317; made(n) 2.88,
4.335, 11.6, 17.70, set, shut 11.
130. *pp.* maked 4.122, 6.200,
17.130; macod 16.175; mad(e)
2.220, 8E.5, 14.94; imaked
5.72, composed 7.268, held 17.
87; imaket 18.282; imad 7.10,
17.180. [OE *macian*]

mak(e) *n.* mate, wife 2.59; lover
6.107; peer, equal 14.100, 244.
[OE (*ge*)*maca*] Cf. macche.

makeles *adj.* peerless, incomparable 8v.3. [prec.+OE -*lēas*]

makerel *n.* mackerel 4.26. [OF]

malisoun *n.* curse 3.188. [AN
maleisun]

man *n.* man 2.2, 3.3 (*dat.*), 15,
4.68, 7.2, 9.30; mann 13.12;
mon 5.285, 6.71, 8G.42, N.1,
10.1, 18.50; (generic, without
art., &c.) 1.462, 4.208, 12.36,
14.190, 17.122; person 7.136,
217, *þe* ~ a person 1.417; adult
17.249; liegeman, retainer 3.
136, 10.77; servant 8L.13; ~
iboren born into the world 10.
177. *gen.* mannes 16.177;
monnes 1.254, 18.254, 19.9,
248, with a man 8v.16; monne
18.66, 308 (or *pl.*). *dat.* manne
in *borenn to* ~ born as a man,

incarnate 13.64 (see to); men 16.
129, 17.244. *pl.* men 2.128, 3.27,
7.181; people (in general) 1.302,
5.6, 7.116, 164, 8E.69; subjects
7.128; **manne** 2.47. *gen.*
manne 1.384, *on ~ gemynd* in
living memory 16.67; **monne**
1.333, 18.409; **monnen** 10.149;
monnes 10.131; men 6.207.
dat. men 1.542, 16.180, 18.342;
menn 13.254; manne 1.571;
monne 1.371; monnen 10.145.
[OE *man(n)*, *mon(n)*, and *manna*;
pl. and dat. sg. *men(n)*]

man *pron. indef.* one 3.35, 7.131,
9.56, 12.88, 14.1, 16.49; **mann**
13.273; **mon** 8E.9, K.26, 10.14,
244; **men** 3.32, 4.166, 5.211,
7.34, 8M.14, 14.46, 15.53 (some
of these perh. intended as n. pl.);
me 1.32, 5.75, 6.76 (1st), 8H.17,
N.11, 10.53, 241, 11.144, 16.147,
165, 19.187. *gen.* manis 9.12,
108. [OE *man*, further reduced
in wk. stress]

maner(e) *n.*[1] manner, way 2.37,
6.367, 7.12, 11.1, 14.2, 18.228;
conduct, bearing 2.180; way of
life 18.230; kind 17.168; kind
of, in *eche ~ men* 7.181, *mani ~
frute* 9.49. *pl.* **maneres** conduct 7.13. [AN *manere*]

maneres *n.*[2] *pl.* manors 7.124.
[AN *maneir*]

mani(e), many *adj. pl.* many
3.180, 4.148, 7.210, 16.178;
moni(e), mony 1.72, 6.67,
10.122; (with sg. n.) many a 1.
591, 2.277, 3.287, 8L.24, 9.25,
14.177, 18.160, 19.21, **mani3**
13.166; *~ a(n)* 2.251, 3.286, 6.
224, 14.132; *~ on* many a
one 11.13, (with pl. vb.) 74.
predic. with sg. 2.41. [OE *manig,
monig*]

mani(e) *pron. pl.* many 7.218,
11.101, 102, 16.173; **monie** 10.
267, 18.204. *sg.* **moni** many a
one 19.188. *gen.* **monies** 18.
512. [as prec.]

manifældlice *adj.* of many
kinds 16.232. [OE *manigfeald-
lic*]

mannkinn *n.* mankind, the
human race 13.4, men 14;
manken(ne) 1.683, 17.45;
monkinne 8v.7; **moncun(ne)**
(body of) men 10.89, 226, race,
people 150. *gen.* **mannkinne**
13.228; **moncunnes** 19.272.
dat. **mankunne** 1.509. [OE
manncynn]

manred(e) *n.* homage 3.137,
16.320; *him ~ maked* done
homage to him 16.155; *nam hire
~* received the homage due to
her 7.127. [OE *manrǣden*; cf.
-reden]

mansing *n.* excommunication,
anathema 1.580; **mansingue**
7.268. [OE *a-mānsumung*]

manslechtes *n. pl.* murders 17.
121. [OE (nWS) *mansleht*]

mantles *n. pl.* mantles, cloaks
2.221, 11.115. [OF *mantel*]

mar. See **mor(e).**

marcatte *n.* market-place 17.
183. [cf. OHG and OS *marcat*
from L *mercatus*, and LOE
-*markett*; see *MLR* xlvii (1952),
152–5]

marchaundise *n.* trade, business 6.18. [AN]

mare. See **mor(e), more.**

mark *n.* mark (of money, two-
thirds of a pound) 6.224. *pl.*
mark (after numeral) 3.104,
markes 119. [LOE *marc* prob.
from ML]

marreþ *pr. 3 sg.* injures, harms
8D.3. *pp.* **marred** afflicted
8G.20. [OA *merran*]

martyr *n.* martyr 16.230. *pl.*
martyrs 7.109, 16.164, 19.295.
[OE *martyr* from L]

mas. See **mak.**

masoun *n.* mason 3.84. [AN
mascun, OF *maçon*]

masse *n.* mass 5.252, 7.171, 9.
113; **messe** feast-day: *Sancte*

Petres ~ 16.74 (note; see next and cf. Candelmasse, Cristesmasse, Lammasse).   *pl.* masses 9.117. [OE *mæsse*, M and K *messe*; OF *messe*]

massedæi, mæsse-, messe-, messedei *n.* feast-day (of a saint, &c.) 16.124, 210, 82, 116. *Sancte Andreas* ~ 30 Nov.; *Sancte Iohannis* ~ St. John the Baptist's Day, 24 June; *Sancte Petres* ~ 29 June. [prec.+ dai(e)]

mast. See more.

mater *n.* material (for composition), subject-matter 14.85, 93. [AN *matere*]

matte *pa. t. sg.* dreamt 7.40. [OE *mætan*] See imætte.

maugré *prep.* (with gen.) in spite of: ~ *þin* in spite of you 4.216. [OF *maugré*]

maut. See mai.

mawe *n.* stomach: *into þe* ~ *to* your very vitals 8N.38. [OE *maga*]

me *conj.* but 18.455, 524. [reduced form of AN *mes*; see note on 455]

me. See Ich; man *pron.*

meadlese *adj.* unlimited, continual 18.3, 36, 57. [OE *mæþlēas*; see meþ and cf. meaðful]

meadlese *adv.* continually 18.38. [from prec.]

mealles *n. pl.* clubs 19.142. [prob. OM *mælle* from L *malleus*; see *Iuliene* pp. 183–4]

meallið *pr. pl.* beat 19.102. [from prec.]

meane *adj.* common 19.316. [OE *(ge)mǣne*] See imeane.

meanen. See mene *v.*[2]

meapeð *pr. 3 sg.* wanders, strays 18.241 (note). [app. OE *mēapian* rel. to mod. *mope*]

mearci. See merci.

mearke *n.* mark 18.148, 591, sign 369. [OA *mærc*]

meast(e); Meað. See mor(e), more; meþ.

meaðen *n. pl.* maggots 19.113. [OM *meaða* = WS *maþa*]

meaðful *adj.* moderate 19.222. [from meþ; cf. meadlese]

med(e) *n.*[1] meadow 1.316, 3.172, 8A.3. [OE *mǣd*, A *mēd*]

mede *n.*[2] reward 6.166, 322, 7.36, 12.47, 15.62, 17.177. *pl.* meden 18.18. [OE *mēd*, pl. *mēda*]

medicen *n.* medicine 14.242. [OF *medicine*]

meding *n.* reward 6.271. [from verb based on mede]

meditatiuns *n. pl.* meditations 18.2. [AN *meditaciun* assim. to L]

meel; mei, mey; meiden. See mel; mai; maid(e).

meidenhad *n.* virginity 18.612. [OE *mægdenhād*] Cf. meiðhad.

meinde. See mengeþ.

meiné, meyné *n.* household 4.95, 102. [OF *mai(s)nee, meyné*]

meistre; meistries. See maister; maistri(e).

meistrin *v.* master, overcome 18.302. *pr. 3 sg.* meistreð leads, commands 19.37. [OF *meistrier*]

meiðhad *n.* virginity 18.570. *gen.* maჳჳþhadess 13.239. [OE *mægþhād*] Cf. meidenhad.

mek *adj.* meek, humble 9.64; meoke 19.223. [ON *mjúk-r*, earlier *meuk-*]

meklich *adv.* obediently, submissively 9.144; mikelik kindly 14.168. [prec.+-liche]

mel, meel *n.* meal (food) 5.173, 247. [OE *mæl*, A *mēl*]

mele *n.* meal, flour 4.48. [OE *melu*]

mele *v.* speak 8E.37. [OE *mælan*]

melk; men(n). See milk(e); man *n., pron.*

mend *imper. sg.* soften 15.26.
[shortened from **amende**]
mene *v.*[1] *pr. 1 sg.* mean 12.191,
15.48; ~ *hit bi* refer to 1.92.
[OE *mǣnan*[1]]
mene *v.*[2] complain 8F.20;
meanen 18.319. *refl. (me)*
mene 8L.4. [OE *mǣnan*[2]]
mengeþ *pr. 3 sg. intr.* mingles,
is mixed 8E.53. *pa. t. sg. tr.*
meinde in ~ *hire þout* was perplexed 8v.14. *pp.* **imenged**
confused 10.282; **imeind** 1.18,
306 (note). [OE *mengan, mengde*]
menis *n. pl.* in *maken* ~ enlist
support 6.142 (note). [OF *men*
intermediary]
menske *n.* honour 6.93, 8F.22.
[ON *mennska* humanity, kindness]
menske *v.* honour, adore 8D.23.
[from prec.]
menskful *adj.* noble 8K.7; graceful K.29. [**menske** + **-ful**]
menur *adj.* Minor 8x.7 (see
frer(e)]. [AN]
meoke; meoster; meosure.
See **mek; mester; mesure.**
mer *n.* hindrance 14.67. [from
verb, see **marreþ**]
merci *n.* mercy 3.263, 14.140,
17.161; **mearci** 18.555; *in þe* ~
ido amerced, fined 11.96. as
interj. have pity! 6.127. [OF]
mere *n.* mayor 11.146, 167. [OF
maire]
mern. See **mære.**
mershe *n.* marsh 1.220. [OE
mersc]
mesauenter *n.* misfortune 6.
202. [OF *mesaventure*]
meshe *v.* crush 1.84. [OE
*mǣscan]
message *n.* message, errand
2.299 (see **to**). [OF]
messager(e) *n.* messenger 2.12,
158. *pl.* **messagers** 7.198, 18.
506. [OF *messager*]
messe(-); mest. See
masse(-); mor(e), more.
mester *n.* trade, occupation 4.

91; office 2.29; **meoster** duty,
function 1.556, 19.213, 284;
mister in *what* ~ *man* a man
of what occupation, what sort
of man 3.88 (note). [AN *mester*]
mesure *n.* measure, moderation
19.197; **meosure** 19.51. [OF
mesure]
met(e) *n.*[1] food 1.377, 2.207,
4.57, 5.14, 9.10; provisions 4.
143; fodder 7.144; dinner 11.
140, 157, *atte* ~ at table 152.
[OE *mete*]
met(e) *n.*[2] measure, moderation
18.362, 19.50; *wiðute* ~ beyond
measure 19.94, 319. [OE *ge-met*]
mete(n) *v. tr.* meet, encounter
5.6, 7; (fold. by *wiþ*) 6.394. *pr.
pl. intr.* **meten** 6.358. *pa. t. sg.
tr.* **mette** 4.237, 5.242, 8E.44.
pl. **mette** (*wiþ*) 11.159; *refl.* met
each other 7.229. [OE *mētan*]
mete *adj.* well-proportioned 8E.
73. [OE *ge-mǣte*]
meteles *adj.* without food 7.160.
[**mete** + OE *-lēas*]
metinge, -gue, metyngue *n.*
dream 17.31, 7.62, 71. [OE
mǣting]
mette *pp.* allotted 14.68. [OE
metan]
meþ *n.* moderation 5.97; **Meað**
(personified) Temperance 19.42,
49; **Með** 19.415. [OE *mǣþ*]
mi, my; miccle. See **Ich;**
mikel *adj.*
michel, mychel *adj.* great, large
4.96, 8B.6; much 2.218;
micel(e), mycel(e) 16.13, 146,
89, 207; **mochel(e)** 3.38, 278;
mochil 9.24; **muchel(e)** 1.719,
6.153, 8E.19, 10.256, 18.97, 19.
338; **moch** 9.128; **much(e)**
7.26, 8N.3, 10.23, 11.88, 18.92,
19.236, many 7.172; **mulch**
8c.4. *dat. fem.* **muchel(e)re**
10.194, 219, **muclere** 129. as
n., much: **mic(h)el** 4.83, 16.
239; **moche(l)** 3.36, 125;
muchel 5.98, 6.305, 18.324,

19.12. [OE *micel, mycel*] See **mikel, more**.

michel, mychel *adv.* much, greatly 3.210, 17.15, 2.142; **mochel** 3.133; **muchel(e)** 1. 507, 538, 6.140, 8E.23, 18.70; **much(e)** 1.728, 7.60. [as prec.] See **mikel, mor(e)**.

micht(-), micthe. See **mai**.

mid, myd *prep.* with (of association) 1.18, 5.55, 6.444, 10.18, 18.368–9, 2.168; **mið** 5.30, 89; (before *þ-*) **mit** 1.396, 6.289, (with suffixed pron.) **mitte** with you 3.103 (cf. **tome**). (forming adv. phrs.) 1.138–42, 6.93, 16. 25, 111, 17.161; ~ *hom* in themselves 1.344; ~ *Drihtenes wille* by God's will 10.111; ~ *alle* see **al(le)**; with *sup.*, among, of 10.212. (of means) 5.14, 6.159, 8N.15, 10.23, 11.19; ~ *here migt* with all their strength 12.174. (of agent) by 18.474. *wat* ~ what with, in view of 5.89. **mide** with (postponed) 1.726; (without expressed obj.) thereupon 12.21, with (him) 12.123, with (it) 17.60. [OE *mid*, A (rare) *miþ*; *mið* perh. due to blending with **wiþ**; *mide* extended on analogy of **inne**]

middæi, -dai, -day *n.* midday 16.121, 17.182, 249. [OE *middæg*]

middel, myddel *n.* waist 8E.62, 73, K.29, **midle** 10.39; mean 19.51, **midel** 197. [OE *middel*]

middel *adj.* middle 19.193, 210. [OE]

middelhard *n.* the world 3.30; **middellærd** 13.163, 227. *gen.* **middelærdes** 10.108. [OE *middan-géard* re-formed on **middel** and **ærd(e)**]

mid(d)elniȝte *n.* midnight 1. 241, 477. [OE *middelniht*]

Midewintre Dæi *n.* Midwinter Day, i.e. Christmas Day 16.135. [OE *middewinter*+**dai(e)**]

midle. See **middel**.

Midsumer Dæi *n.* Midsummer Day, 24 June 16.81. [OE *midsumor*+**dai(e)**]

mie *pr. pl. intr.* grate, grind 8N. 39. [OF *mier* crumble]

mielch *adj.* rich in milk 7.154. [OE *milce from *meolc*; cf. **milk(e)**]

miȝt(e) *n.* strength, power 1.344, 628, 7.26, 9.99; **miȝtte** 6.253; **miht(e), myht** 18.103, 8D.21, K.7; **migt** 12.174; **might** 14. 171; **myþt** (= *-ȝt*) 8w.42; **maht(e)** 8E.19, 10.193; **magt** 12.183. *at þi* ~ as well as you can 14.171 (see **at**); *bi mi(ne)* ~ see **bi**. [OE *miht*, A *mæht*]

miȝt(-), mih(h)t(-), myht(-). See **mai**.

mihti *adj.* strong, powerful 18. 475; **magti** 12.68. [OE *mihtig*, A *mæhtig*]

mikel, mykel *adj.* great, grave 6.194, 12.140, 14.153, 15.42, 8L.15; **mikell** 13.66, much 10, long 203, *wk.* **miccle** 6. *pl.* **mikle** 12.190. as *n.* much, a great deal 4.18, 15.36. [OE *micel, micl-*, ON *mikil-l*] See **michel**.

mikel *adv.* much, far 4.320, 6.265; hard 12.68. [as prec.]

mikelik. See **meklich**.

milce *n.* mercy 16.109, 18.563, 19.339, 419. [OE *milts*]

mild(e), mylde *adj.* gentle, kind 6.159, 16.153, 8T.14, X.4, w.48; merciful 18.289. *comp.* **mildre** 1.733. [OE *milde*]

mildelich(e) *adv.* meekly, gently 3.92, 7.104. [OE *mildelice*]

mildherrtnesse *n.* mercy 13. 112. [OE *mildheortnes(se)*]

mile *n.* mile 4.258, 7.252, 80.2; the time taken to walk a mile 3.251. *pl.* (after numeral, sometimes orig. gen.) **mile** 6.104, 11.91, 16.27; (in attrib. phr.) *fif* ~ *wei* five miles' distance 7.242. [OE *mil*]

milk(e) *n.* milk 7.59, 113, 9.149;
melk 9.46. [OE *me(o)lc*, A
milc]
min, mynne *v.* remember 14.
191, 8F.20; munne tell of 19.
342. *imper. pl.* munneð remember 18.17. [ON *minna* and
OE **mynnan*; see *Iuliene* p. 163]
min(e), myn(e). See Ich.
minde *adj.* (with dat. of person)
in mind, present to the thoughts
12.111. [OE *ge-mýnde* mindful]
minstre, mynstre *n.* monastery 16.20, 80. [OE *mynster*]
mint. See munte.
miracle *n.* miracle 7.212, 17.34,
18.50. *pl.* miracles 16.232,
17.111. [OF]
mire *n.* ant 12.68, 92. [perh.
OE; cf. MDu *miere*]
mire. See Ich.
miri(e) *adj.* merry, joyful, gay,
delightful 3.31, 8B.1, 9.5;
muri(e), mury 1.261, 19.319,
389, 8E.37, pleasant 18.484. *sup.*
murgest 8K.41. [OE *myrge*]
miri *adv.* gaily, joyfully 9.100;
murie 8A.9. [OE *myrge*]
mirke *adj.* dark, sightless 12.43.
[ON *myrk-r*]
mirre *n.* myrrh 17.10, 30. [OE
myrra, -e]
mis(se) *v.* be without, lack 3.
237, 6.144, 8U.4. [OE *missan*,
ON *missa*]
misdede, misse- *n.* evil-doing,
crime 1.187; misbehaviour 15.
72. *pl.* misdede sins 5.182.
[OE *misdæd*; see ded(e)]
misdo(n) *v.* act unjustly (*wið*,
towards) 16.129; *tr.* ill-treat
17.68. *pr. 3 sg.* misdeð 18.325.
pl. misdoð 1.728. [OE *misdōn*;
see do(n)]
miself, my- *pron.* myself. as
nom. (emphasizing) 2.311, 8W.
21; miseolf 10.34, 112. *refl.*
obj. of prep. or vb. 3.270, 6.184;
miselue 6.183. [OE *mīn* (see
Ich)+self]

misericorde *n.* pity, compassion 18.271. [OF]
misferde *pa. t. sg.* in ∼ *with* ill-
used, assaulted 4.296. *2 sg.* misferdest misconducted yourself
5.212. [OE *misfēran*]
mysgilt *n.* misbehaviour 15.21.
[OE *mis-*+gylt]
mislich(e) *adj.* various 19.22,
144. [OE *mislic*]
misliche *adv.* wrongly 1.731.
[OE *mislīce* variously, modified
by usual sense of *mis-*]
mislikeþ *pr. 3 sg.* displeases
1.260. [OE *mislīcian*]
misnimeð *pr. 3 sg.* does wrongly
18.261. [OE *mis-*+nim]
misraddest *pa. t. 2 sg.* advised
wrongly 1.116. [OE *misrædan*]
misreke *v.* go astray 1.421. [OE
mis-+recan go]
misrempe *pr. 1 sg.* go wrong
1.745. [OE *mis-*+rempan rush]
missedede. See misdede.
misseið *pr. 3 sg.* speaks ill of
18.324. *pl.* misseggeð 18.336.
[OE *mis-*+sai]
Misselmasse *n.* Michaelmas,
29 September 11.173. [from
St. Michel+masse]
misstorte *v.* come out wrongly
1.423. [OE *mis-*+styrtan; see
sterteþ]
mist *n.* mist, dimness of sight
12.50. [OE]
mist; mister; mit, mið. See
mai; mester; mid.
mythe *v.* conceal, hide 8L.24.
[OE *mīþan*]
mithe(-); mitte; myþt. See
mai; mid; mi3t(e).
mo *adj. comp.* more (in number)
4.273, 5.204, 8K.61, 11.150;
further, additional 11.57; *no* ∼
no other 9.16; ma 10.271, 18.
223. as *pron.* more (people) 19.
189. as *n.* more (in quantity)
9.101. [OE *mā*, adv.] See
more, namo.
mo *adv.* more; besides 8E.66;

neauer þe ~ no more because of
it 1.598; *neuere* .. ~ at no
future time 3.161, sim. *neure
ma* 16.265, see **neuermo**. [as
prec.]

moch, moche(l), mochil. See
michel.

mod(e) *n.* mind, heart, state of
mind 1.407, 8T.14, 10.11, 18.17;
in phrs. (*a*)*mend, torn, wend* (*þi,*
&c.) ~ 6.109, 113, 181, 8L.21,
15.26, 51; feeling 1.8; *Drery* ~
(personified) Sad Heart 8L.5.
heiȝ of ~ high-spirited 9.125;
him on ~ into his mind 10.
introd.; *off one* ~ of one mind
12.112. [OE *mōd*]

moder *n.* mother 2.134, 4.340,
7.7, 19.132; *attrib.* 18.236;
moderr 13.156; **modur** 14.78.
gen. **moders** 14.118. [OE
mōdor]

modi *adj.* high-spirited, proud
6.3, 348. [OE *mōdig*]

moght. See **mai.**

molde *n.* earth 9.87; *on* ~ on
earth, in the world (tag) 8D.2.
[OE *mólde, on móldan*]

mome *n.* (as address) aunt 15.37,
39. [cf. MHG *muome*]

mon *pr. 1 sg.* must 6.182, 8C.3.
pl. **mone** 4.108. [ON *munu*]

mon(-); moncun(ne), -kinne.
See **man, mannkinn.**

mone *n.*[1] moon 4.316, 8E.19,
N.1, 16.121. [OE *mōna*]

mone *n.*[2] opinion 4.84. [OE
*mān; cf. **mene**[1]]

moné *n.* money 3.120. [OF
moneie]

mone; monekes. See **munen;
monke.**

Monenday *n.* Monday 11.9.
[OE *mōnandæg*]

Moneniht *n.* Sunday night 16.
62. [OE *mōnanniht*]

mong *n.* mixture 18.423; change,
alternation 19.117. [OE *ge-
móng*]

monge *v.* move, indulge in 8E.32

(note); stir, in ~ *wiþ murþes*
cheer 8K.15 (note). [from prec.]

monglunge *n.* mixture, con-
tamination 18.422. [from a frequentative vb. based on **mong**]

moni(e), mony. See **mani(e).**

monifalden *v.* multiply 18.675.
[OA *monigfáldan*]

monke *n.* monk 9.162; **munec**
16.19, 222. *pl.* **monekes** 7.255;
monkes 9.52; **muneces,
munekes** 16.56, 194, 1.475.
[OE *munuc*]

mon-weorede *n.* body of men
10.256. [OE *mon-weorod*]

mordaunt *n.* tag (of a pendant)
80.3. [AN]

mor(e) *adv. comp.* more 1.347,
2.144, 4.293, 15.15, 17.37; any
more, in future, again 2.308,
no ~ 8x.1; (intensifying adj.)
worse (*þan*) 8x.17; **mar(e)** 15.
19, 16.258, 18.285, 19.118. *sup.*
mest most 7.32; **meast** 18.447.
[adv. use of next; OE sup. *mǽst*]
See **alremest; michel, mikel,
mo** *advs.*; **namore; neuermore.**

more *adj. comp.* greater, bigger
1.436, .2.200, 3.6, 7.57, 12.88;
more (in quantity) 5.67, 7.18,
9.116; **mare** 14.186, 16.190,
18.204; ~ *of age* older 2.202;
inclusive phr. ~ *an lasse* the
higher and the lower (in rank),
all 1.340. as *n.* more, a greater
or additional amount 2.227,
4.6o, 5.206, 8L.32, 10.324, 16.
250; a longer time 4.55, 14.273.
sup. **moste** biggest 12.142;
mast very large 14.249; **mest**
greatest, highest 1.512, 3.66;
meast(e) 18.224, 19.131;
mæste in *mid þan* ~ of the
greatest 10.212. [OE *mǽre,
mǽst,* Nb *mǽst*] See **michel,
mikel, nam(m)or(e).**

more *n.* root 1.596 (see **top**),
8v.6. [OE *moru*]

moreghen, morghen *n.* morning 17.179, 193; **morn** 14.278; **morwen** morrow, next day 4.79. [OE *morgen*, dat. *morne*; A *margen*]

more3eninge *n.* morning 1.676. [from prec.]

moren *n. dat.* (? *pl.*) moor 10.35. [OE *mōr*]

moren-mylk *n.* morning milk 8E.77. [next+milk(e)]

morn. See **moreghen.**

morð *n.* destruction 10.109. [OE]

morwen. See **moreghen.**

mose *n.* titmouse 1.69. [OE *māse*]

most(e). See **more**; **mot** *v.*

mot *n.* argument 1.326. [OE *ge-mōt*]

mot *pr. 1, 3 sg.* may 3.136, (expressing wish) 8V.11, (subj. equiv. in clause of purpose) 18.649; must 1.329, 415, 6.233, 8N.15, 9.178, 10.50; **mote** 8K.15 (note), 9.180; (with suffixed pron.) **moti** 8Q.2. *2 sg.* **most** must 1.572, note to 132, 5.207, 6.437, 14.107; **moste** 1.570. *pl.* **moten** must 12.103. *subj. sg.* **mote** may (dependent cl. of wish) 1.52, (expressing wish) 6.116, 8G.49, 9.189. *pl.* **mot** 9.184; **mote(n)** 1.487, 7.286, 8T.17, 9.187; must 1.517. *pa. t. sg.* **most** must 2.274; **moste** could, might 7.169, 11.59, 16. 96; must go (infin. understood) 5.85. *pl.* **moste** were allowed to 7.137. *subj.* **moste** would have to 3.259; ~ *liuen* might have lived 16.214; (with suffixed pron.) **mosti** if I could 8E.1. [OE *mōt*, 2 *sg. mōst*; pa. t. *mōste*]

moue; mouht. See **mai; mouþ(e).**

mourne *v.* be sad, feel sorrow 8E.23. *pr. 1 sg.* **murne** long, yearn 8B.7. *subj. sg.* **mourne** 6.148. [OE *múrnan*]

mournyng *n.* sorrow 2.325, 8G.20; *make* ~ grieve 8K.83. [from prec.]

mous *n.* mouse 8N.31. *pl.* **mus** 1.87, 387, *dat.* **muse** 390. [OE *mūs*, pl. *mӯs*]

mout(h)e. See **mai.**

mouþ(e), mouth *n.* 3.72, 5.56, 8K.41, G.27; **mouht** 8E.37; **muþ(e), muð(e)** 1.444, 9.108, 12.59, 18.352; **mudh** 17.123. mouth 1.419, 9.108, 12.59, 18. 242, 19.57; lips 8G.27; words, speech 1.444, 5.56, 18.352, *wi3* ~ (tag) 3.72; voice, singing 8K. 41; appetite 5.100. [OE *mūþ*]

moveth *imper. pl.* go 17.104. [AN *mover*]

mowe *v.* mow 4.279. [OE *māwan*]

mowe(n). See **mai.**

muchedeale *adv.* a great deal 19.120. [michel+del(e)]

much(e), muchel(e), muclere; mudh; muee, muge, mugh-, mu3-, muh-. See **michel; mouþ(e); mai.**

muynde *n.* memory, recollection 7.141. [OE *ge-mӯnd*]

mulch. See **michel** *adj.*

mulne *n.* mill 1.86. [OE *mylen*]

mund *n.* guardian 10.108. [OE]

munec. See **monke.**

munechene *n.* nun 10.242. [OE *mynecen*]

munegunge reminder 19.71, 246; *in ure* ~ to remind him of us 18.592; *of þi* ~ at the recollection of you 19.150; **mungunge** *n.* memory 18.534. [OE *myndgung, mynegung*]

munekes. See **monke.**

munen *v.* remember, bear in mind 12.129; **mone** (*on*) tell (of) 8M.20. *pr. 3 sg.* **muneð** reminds, admonishes 12.92. [ON *muna* remember]

munne. See **min.**

munnyng *n.* remembrance 8F. 21. [from **min**]

munte *imper. sg.* think 8F.21.
pa. t. sg. **mint** intended 16.215.
[OE *myntan*]
murgeþ *pr. 3 sg.* is pleasant
8H.1. [OE *myrgan*; cf. **miri(e)**]
murgest, muri(e), -y; murne.
See **miri(e), miri ; mourne**.
murþe *n.* pleasure, joy, delight
8G.28; **murȝþe** 1.257, 464;
murhðe 19.284, 344; *makieð*
~ rejoice 19.287. *gen.* (personified) **Murðes, Murhðes** 19.
246, 257. *pl.* **murþes** 8E.32
(note), K.15; pleasant sounds,
melodies 8K.44. [OE *myrgþ*]
mus(e). See **mous.**
mustard, -t *n.* mustard 6.287,
280. [OF *moustarde*]
mutli *pr. subj. sg.* increase 18.
223. [OE *myclian*; see note]
muþ(e), muð(e). See **mouþ(e).**

na ; naam. See **no** *adj. adv.*[1];
nim.
nabbe *pr. 1 sg.* have not (full vb.
and auxil., usu. supported by
another neg.) 5.39, 6.68, 10.51;
(with suffixed pron.) **nauy** 8F.
10. *2 sg.* **nauest** 18.316; (with
suffixed pron.) **nauestu,**
neuestu 1.628, 530. *3 sg.*
naueþ, -ð 1.718, 18.188, 310;
naþ 8N.22. *pl.* **nabbe** (before
ȝe) 18.68; **nabbeð** 1.344. *subj.*
sg. **nabbe** 18.334. *pa. t. sg.*
nadde 7.131; **nedde** 5.169;
neuede 6.11. *pl.* **nedden** 17.
223. *subj. 1 sg.* **neddi** I should
not have had 5.99; **nefde** 18.
411; **neuede** 5.98. *3 sg.* **nadde**
1.666; **nedde** 5.100. [OE *nab-
ban, næfde*; see **ne, habbe(n)**]
nacht; **n'adoun**; **nadres**;
næfre; **næs**; **næt**; **næu(e)re**;
nahhi; **nahht**; **naht**. See
noȝt *adv.*; **ne, adoun**; **neddur**; **neuer(e)**; **nas**; **neth**;
neuer(e); **negh**; **niȝt(e)**;
niȝt(e), noȝt.

nai, nay *adv.* no 1.202, 351, 2.
76, 5.188, 6.43, 18.317; *seiz me* ~
of denies me 6.179; *as n.* in tag
witouten ~ assuredly 14.147.
[ON *nei*] Cf. **no** *adv.*[2]
nai ; nayct. See **no** *adj.*;
ahte.
nayl *n.* nail, peg 4.125. *pl.*
neyles 8w.24. [OE *nægl*]
naked, nakid *adj.* naked, bare
4.121, 12.56; *makiþ ham* ~ un-
dress 9.156. [OE *nacod*]
nalde. See **nyl.**
nam *pr. 1 sg.* am not 1.702, 8L.36,
18.604. [OA *n(e)am*; see **ne,**
am]
nam(en) ; namare. See **nim ;**
namore, nam(m)or(e).
namcuðlice *adv.* by name, in
particular 16.35. [OE *nam-
cūþlice*]
name *n.* name 2.156, 4.12, 7.61;
nome 1.720, 5.36, 6.195. [OE
nama, noma]
nameliche *adv.* especially, in
particular 11.50; **nomeliche**
18.1, 37. [from prec.; cf. MDu
namelike]
namo *adj.* no more, no other
1.372, 376. [OE *nā* (see **no**
adv.[1])+**mo**]
namore *adv.* no more, no longer
1.169, 5.65, 8M.5, 11.173;
namare 14.265. [OE *nā* (see
no)+**mor(e)**]
nam(m)or(e) *n.* nothing more,
nothing else 1.751, 3.269, 8G.8,
16.111, 17.94; **nomore** 4.187;
nummore 12.101; **namare**
18.108, no more (people) 10.293.
[as prec.]
nan(e). See **no** *adj.*; **non** *pron.*
nanesweis *adv.* in no way 18.
492, 19.356. [OE **nānes weges*,
adv. gen.] See **no, wai(e).**
nareu *adj.* narrow 16.171;
nearow 18.512. [OE *nearu*]
narewe *adv.* closely 1.68. [OE
nearwe]
nart *pr. 2 sg.* art not, are not

1.285, 367; (with suffixed pron.)
nartou 2.307, **nartu** 1.598.
[OE *neart*; see **art, nam**]
nas *pa. t. 1, 3 sg.* was not (usu.
with another neg.) 2.230, 7.13,
8v.19, 11.4; **nes** 5.3, 8F.4, 18.
462, 19.389; **næs** 10.233. *pl.*
neren 3.208, 6.274. *subj. sg.*
nere were not, was not 1.22,
2.249, 19.137; should not be
7.119; would not be 1.357,
8H.38, 18.501; had not been
19.155, **neore** 10.186. *pl.* **nere**
8H.15. [OE *næs*, KM *nes*, pl.
næron, *nēron*; see **was, nis**]
nat. See **not.**
nature *n.* natural power 17.250.
[OF]
naturel(l)iche *adv.* by nature
17.118, 125. [OF *naturel* +
-*liche*]
naþ. See **nabbe.**
naþeles *adv.* nevertheless, all the
same 3.161, 9.129; **noþeles**
1.105, 279, **neoþeles** 565, 582;
noðele 18.260. [OE *nā þē lǣs*;
cf. next]
naðema *adv.* none the more, not
16.16. [**no** + **þe** + **mo** advs.; cf.
prec.]
**naþing; nauȝth; nausine;
naue-, nauy-; nauer(e);
nawiht, nawt.** See **noþing;
noȝt** *adv.;* **nowcin; nabbe;
neuer(e); noȝt.**
ne *adv.* not (preceding vb.) 1.47,
2.20, 3.80, 13.53; ~ *were* if . .
were not 12.25; redundant 18.
518; (usu. strengthened by another neg. following the vb., esp.
not) 1.540, 2.13, 3.102, 4.38,
132, 5.5; coalescing with auxil.
and other common vbs., see
**nabbe, nam, nas, nyl, nis,
not;** with other vbs., see **n'imette,
n'iso,** see **imette, ise;** with
adv., see **adoun;** with pron., see
nich. no (with comp. adv.) 16.
270. *conj.* nor, (in neg. contexts)
or 1.540, 2.104, 3.14, 6.401–2,

11.55; (introducing sentence)
4.99; (fold. by another neg.) and
5.65, 17.71, 268, 18.78; correl.,
see **neiþer, nouþer;** ~ .. ~
and neither .. nor 11.31. [OE *ne*]
neah; nearow. See **neȝ; nareu.**
nease *n.* nose 19.127. [OM
*neasu = WS *nasu*] Cf. **neose.**
nease-gristles *n. pl.* gristles of
the nose 19.110. [cf. prec. and
OE *næs-gristle*]
neauele *n.* navel 19.112. [OM
*neafela = WS *nafela*]
neauer(e). See **neuer(e).**
neb *n.* face 18.205, 209; **nebbe**
in ~ *to* ~ face to face 19.332. *pl.*
nebbes 18.210, 19.139. [OE
neb(b)]
necheð. See **negh.**
necke *n.* neck 4.249; **nekk** 11.
100. [OE *hnecca*]
ned(e) *n.* need, necessity 5.225,
6.163, 12.140, 14.70; what is
lacking 12.63; **neod(e)** 1.538,
10.254, 18.185, compulsion 39;
nyede 17.159; *at* ~ in distress,
difficulty 12.115, sim. 10.219,
at .. **neoden** 202; *(h)is him* ~
is necessary for him, he must
6.142, sim. 13.205, 17.159. *dat.*
as *adv.* of necessity 13.introd.
pl. **neoden** 18.98; **niedes** 17.
160. [OE (nWS) *nēd, nēod*] See
nedes.
nedd-. See **nabbe.**
neddur *n.* adder 14.200. *pl.*
nadres 16.169; **neddren** 19.
110. [OE *nǣd(d)re*, A *nēdre*]
nedes *adv.* needs, of necessity
2.274, 16.88. [OA *nēdes*, adv.
gen. of **ned(e)**]
nefde. See **nabbe.**
nefe *n.* nephew 16.112. *pl.*
neues 16.152. [OE *nefa*]
negh *v.* come near, approach 14.
257; **newhen** 4.293; **nahhi** 18.
624. *pr. 3 sg.* **necheð** 8B.3.
[from next. ONb *ge-nēhwia*;
nah- app. infl. by ON *ná*, earlier
*náha]

neȝ, neh *adj.* near, close together
3.207, 8E.26. [as next]

neh *adv.* 10.196, 19.370; neah 16.
28; neiȝ 7.32; nei, ney 6.310,
5.32. near, close 7.248, 258,
of ~ from close at hand 18.159.
nearly 6.310, 19.370. *prep.* (with
dat.) 5.32, 261, 7.32, 8E.83, 10.
196. [OE *nē(a)h*] See ner(e),
welneȝ.

neiȝebore *n.* neighbour 5.115.
pl. neiȝebores 11.84. [OE
nēhgebūr]

neyles. See nayl.

neilond, *a* ~ = *an* eilond *n.*
island 12.145, 172. [OA *ēglond*]

neiþer, neyþer *adv.* neither: ~
.. *ne* neither .. nor 3.11, 4.32,
100. [ne+aiþer] Cf. nouþer.

nekk; nel(-). See necke; nyl.

nelde *n.*[1] (as address) old woman,
'gammer' 6.173, 217, &c. [prob.
false division of *min elde,* abbrev.
of *eld(e)moder* grandmother, OE
ealdemōdor; but see note]

nelde *n.*[2] needle 18.635. [OA
nēdl]

nellen. See elne.

nemme(n) *v.* name, mention
7.130, 168. *pr. 1 sg.* nempne
8E.79. *imper. sg.* nempne 18.
397, 619. *pp.* nemmnedd
called 13.30, 122; inempnet
19.274; mentioned 18.178. [OE
nemnan]

nempnunge *n.* naming (sc. of
Christ) 18.368. [from prec.]

nend; nenne; neod(-). See on
prep., end(e); no *adj.*; ned(e).

neodde *pa. t. sg.* compelled,
forced 10.223. [OA *nēdan* infl.
by n. *nēod*; see ned(e)]

neodful *adj.* eager 18.651. [OE
nēodful]

neoleachunge *n.* approach 18.
567. [from OA *ge-nēolǣcan*]

neome(n); neor(re); neore.
See nim; ner(e); nas.

neose *n.* nose 8E.28. [origin obscure; cf. nease and OE *nosu*]

neoþeles; neowcins; neowe.
See naþeles; nowcin; new(e).

nep *n.* cup 18.331. [OM **hnepp*
= WS *hnæpp*]

ner(e) *adv. comp.* nearer 8M.7;
neorre 18.481. as *pos.* near, in
comen ~ approach 2.157, 3.97,
5.38, sim. 14.28; neor in *feor
an* ~ 1.555, sim. 615, *ver and* ~
11.90. *sup.* nest 19.47; nexte
2.17; nexst in ~ *his hand* very
near at hand 14.62. [OE *nēar,*
A *nēor*; *nēxt*] See neh,
alrenecst.

ner; nere(n); nes. See
neuer(e); nas; nas, nis.

nesche *adj.* soft 19.183, 191; as *n.*
softness, ease 19.190; *gen.* (part.)
nesches 19.195. [OE *hnesce*]

nest *adj. sup.* nearest 18.315;
nexte closest 7.50. [OA *nēst,*
nēxt(a)] See neȝ, ner(e).

nest. See ner(e).

neste *n.* nest 1.92, 218. [OE *nest*]

nestes *pr. 2 sg.* (fut. sense) live in
the nest, survive 5.48. [from
prec.; cf. OE *nist(i)an*]

net(h) *n.*[1] net 4.318, 20. *pl.*
netes 4.51. [OE *nett*]

neth *n.*[2] ox 4.76. *gen.* netes 4.49.
pl. næt cattle 16.67. [OE *nēat*]

neu, neuuæ; neue-. See
new(e); nabbe.

neulic, -ly *adv.* quickly 15.33,
52. [OE *nīwlīce*]

neuer(e), never *adv.* never 3.5,
4.34, 5.3, 7.34, 8K.11, 6.118;
nauer(e) 8A.12, 10.6, 53;
neauer(e) 1.539, 18.58, 302;
næu(e)re 10.233, 16.164;
neure 1.165, 16.186; næfre
16.65; ner 8F.4, N.11. not at all
1.60, 4.77, 8M.7, 10.323 (2nd);
~ *þe lesse* no less for that, nevertheless 14.79, cf. naþeles; ~ *a
day* (with neg.) on any day 8L.27;
ne bo þe song ~ *so murie* no
matter how gay the song may be
1.261, sim. 18.58, 564. [OE
næfre]

neuermo *adv.* never again, no
more 5.145; neure ma 16.265.
[prec.+mo adv.]

neuermore *adv.* never again,
never at any time 2.296, 6.103,
9.188; neauermare 19.121,
369; neure mare 16.288. [as
prec., with mor(e)]

neuerte *adv.* never 17.230.
[neuer(e)+to] Cf. æuert.

neues *n.*¹ *pl.* fists 4.344. [ON
hnefi]

neues *n.*²; neure. See nefe;
neuer(e).

new(e) *adj.* new 3.23, 8w.5,
13.178, 14.74; neu 14.145;
neuuæ 16.209; neowe 18.565;
rejuvenated, renewed 12.24, 57;
makest ∼ renew 8L.25. as *n.*
someone new 8F.31. [OE *nīwe,
nēowe*]

newborn *adj.* newborn 14.206.
[OE *nīwe* adv. + *boren*, see
ber]

neweð *pr. 3 sg.* renews, rejuven-
ates 12.3, 9. [OE *nīwian*]

newhen; nexst, nexte. See
negh; ner(e), nest.

nich *adv.* not I, no 1.202. [ne+
Ich]

nyede, niedes; ny3e, nihe(ne).
See ned(e); nine.

ni3t(e) *n.* night 1.252, 5.111, 6.
150, 9.26; ni3th 2.277; niht(e),
nyht 10.5, 18.311, 8D.40; nihht
13.69; nicht 8B.5, 15.17, 17.
30; nigt 12.11; nith 8T.24;
nahht 13.157. *bi* ∼ 3.11, 12.11,
on ∼ by night 16.292. (adv.) ∼
and dai 1.341, 6.150, 7.21,
8M.4, 15.17; (with neg.) ∼ *ne
dai* 1.252; see dai(e). *gen.*
(adv.) nihtes, nyhtes by night
18.249, 8E.83, *be* ∼ 16.162. *pl.*
nihtes 16.56; (as measure of
time, uninflected after numeral)
ni3th, niht in *fourtene* ∼ two
weeks 2.119, 10.123, and in phr.
thre ∼ *ald* 16.121; naht in *ny3e*
∼ (conventional expression of

a short time, as 'nine days'
wonder') 8F.32. [OE *niht, neaht,
A næht*]

ni3tegale, nyhte- *n.* nightingale 1.669, 8M.1; ni3tingale
1.4, 13, 9.96. [OE *nihtegale,*
from prec.+*galan* sing]

nyl *pr. 1 sg.* will not 2.157. *1, 3
sg.* nel(le) 3.56, 5.132, 188,
17.60; nul(e) 6.314, 8D.19,
18.107, 620, will not come 8N.
40, does not want G.17; null(e)
6.295, 8M.10, nulle = *nul he*
N.35. *2 sg.* nult 18.618; (with
suffixed pron.) nelt(o)u 1.106,
5.189; nultu 1.537. *pl.* nulleþ,
-ð 1.722, 10.70. *subj. sg.* nulle
10.56 (note). *pa. t. 1, 3 sg.*
nolde would not 1.115, 6.350,
7.101, 11.31; nalde 18.525;
nulde 10.6. *2 sg.* nolde 2.239;
noldest 3.257; naldest 18.
499. *pl.* nolde 11.5, 148. *subj.
sg.* (condit.) nolde would not
wish 1.700, 5.161; would not
8F.28; nalde 18.270, 634, 19.8.
[OE *nyllan, nellan; nólde,* M
nálde; see ne, wil(e)]

nim, nime(n) *v.* take, seize,
capture 3.112, 1.387, 722 (see
red(e) n.), 7.204, 11.28; neo-
me(n) 18.344, 494, partake of
278; *intr.,* ∼ *in* enter 19.357.
pr. 3 sg. nimeð takes 18.284,
19.353, undertakes 19.56; makes
his way, goes 12.41. *subj. sg.*
nime 1.473 (see 3eme n.);
neome 18.245. *pl.* neome (before *we*) 19.167. *imper. sg.* nim
3.83, 18.368. *pl.* neomeð 18.
121, 19.350. *pa. t. sg.* nam 4.
166, 7.93, 127, 14.231, 16.150;
naam assumed 17.217; nom
5.78, 10.127, 11.49. *pl.* namen
16.126, 161; nome(n) 2.172,
7.157, 223, 10.316, made 7.231,
11.139. *pp.* nomen taken 5.250
(by death); inome, y- 7.132,
10.181, 11.43, raised 2.36;
inume 10.57, cornered 1.349.

[OE *niman*, M *nioman*; *nam*, *nōmon*; *numen*]
n'imette. See ne, imette.
nine, nyne *adj.* nine 14.101, 273, 4.139; ny3e 8F.32; nihe 19.282; nihene 18.198. [OE *nigon*]
nyntene *adj.* nineteen 7.8. [OA *nigontēne*]
ninteoþe *adj.* nineteenth 7.271. [OE *nigontēoþa*]
nis, nys *pr. 3 sg.* is not 1.229, 3.14, 9.3, 18.189; there is not 2.137, 5.145, 8G.36, 10.75, 19. 19; it is not 19.385; (in clause dependent on neg.) is 18.341; nes 8G.5. [OE *nis*; see ne, is, es, was]
n'iso; niste; nith. See ne and ise; not; ni3t(e).
niþe *n.* malice, spite 1.295. [OE *nīþ*]
niþinge *n.* miser, niggard 17.132. [OE *niþing* from ON]
no *adj.* no, (with neg.) any 1.146, 2.40, 3.14, 7.28, 9.13; na 1.533, 14.16, 15.8, 16.46, 18.256; nai 14.102. non(e) (before vowel or *h*) 1.168, 2.146, 8F.10, esp. in ~ *oþer* 1.367, 4.101, 176, 5.146, 6.136; (separated from n.) 7.34, 8M.18, 10.281; (at end of line) 3.131; (after n.) 7.180, (rhyming) 4.333, 6.11, 129, 11.5, with pleonastic *a* 8K.11; (before cons.) 6.65, 88, 8E.20, 12.28; noon 17. 200, 268; nan 14.54, 19.369, (before cons.) 16.128. *acc. masc.* nenne 10.281. *gen.* nones 5. 294 see kinn. *obl. and pl.* none 1.344, 5.3, 6.245, 12.29; nane 10.70, 18.164. [OE *nān*] See non, noman, noþing.
no *adv.*[1] not, no (often qualifying comp.) 1.42, 3.124, 4.293, 9.16; not at all 10.64, 15.8; ~ *þe worse* no worse on that account, none the worse 7.26, sim. ~ *þe lasse* 156; na 14.164, 18.26, 19.388. *conj.* (n)or 9.11, 10.69, 14.186, 15.9; ~ .. ~ neither .. nor

16.93. [OE *nā, nō*] See namo, nam(m)or(e), naþeles, naðema.
no *adv.*[2] no 1.109, 4.227. [as prec.] Cf. nai.
noble *adj.* noble 2.180, 18.505; splendid, excellent 7.43, 280. *comp.* noblere 7.194. *sup.* nobleste 7.191. [OF *noble*]
nobleye *n.* splendour 2.226; nobleys in *of* ~ magnificent 2.209. [OF *nobleie* blended with *noblece*]
nobleliche *adv.* splendidly 7. 189. [noble+-liche]
noen. See non *n.*
no3t *n.* nothing 1.256; noht 19. 168; noth 15.40; nou3t(h) 2.198, 7.27; nowi3t 7.258; nout(h), novt 4.105, 5.39, 6.47, 8v.16, w.26; naht 16.131; na-wiht 1.592, 19.177; nawt 18. 193, 607, 19.174; ~ *wurð* worth nothing 19.177, sim. 1.256; *was him* ~ *of* he cared nothing about 4.105, sim. 16.198. [OE *nā-(wi)ht, nō-(wi)ht*; see wi3t]
no3t *adv.* not at all, not 1.58, 9. 62; noht 8D.19, H.31, 16.61; nohht 13.26; nocht 17.25; nogt 12.158; noght 14.64; nou3t(h) 2.13, 7.13, 11.148; nouct 15.21; nohut 5.220; noui3t 6.56; nout(h), nowt(h) 4.63, 69 (but see note), 5.153, 6.68, 8N.35, 3.197, 12.86; naht 16.280; nacht 17.72; nau3th 2.245; nawt 1.698, 18.29, 19.24. Usu. strengthening *ne, nyl,* &c., but alone in 1.698, 2.75, 3.264, 4.310, 6.38, 8E.79, 9.62, 12.158, 15.21, 16.113. [as prec.]
nohwer *adv.* nowhere, in no particular 19.69, 53; nower 19.370. [OE *nāhwǣr, nōhwǣr*]
nok *n.* corner, fragment: *a fer-þinges* ~ a fraction of a farthing 4.88. [origin obscure, prob. Scand]
nolde; nom. See nyl; nim.

noman *n.* nobody 1.210, 2.253, 7.31, 227, 17.257. [no+man]

nome ; nomeliche ; nomen. See **nim, name ; nameliche ; nim.**

non *n.* the ninth hour of the day, 3 p.m. 6.324; **noen** 6.433; **noon** noon 8E.14; **none** midday meal 9.20. [OE *nōn* from L *nōna hōra*]

non *pron.* none, no one (of persons) 1.663, 2.20, 4.134, 5.160, 8D.20; (of things) 2.230, 7.53; with pl. vb. 17.229; **nan** 14.77, 16.187, 18.121, 19.20; *hi* ~ none of them (pl. vb.) 16.155. *pl.* **nane** 10.64. [OE *nān*; see **no** adj.]

non *adv.* (with comp.) no 5.42. [adv. use of prec.] Cf. **no** *adv.*[1]

non(e). See **no** *adj.*

nones in *for þe* ~ for the occasion 2.220 (but usu. an almost meaningless tag). [for *for þen ones*, extended by adv. gen. ending *-es* from *for þen one*, concerning that one (thing); see **þe** def. art.]

non-tid *n.* noon 16.243. [OE *nōn-tīd*]

noon. See **non** *n.*, **no** *adj.*

norice *n.* nurse 7.59. [OF]

norþ *n.* north: *by* ~ (in the) north 8K.42. [from **norþ** adv.]

north *adj.* northern 4.2. [from next]

norþ, norð *adv.* (to the) north 1.553, 12.62. [OE *norþ*]

norþerne, northerne *adj.* north 8K.3, 1. [OE *norþerne*]

norðhalf *n.* north 16.63. [OE *norþh(e)alf*] See **half.**

not *pr. 1, 3 sg.* do/does not know 2.80, 8H.7, 5.160, 6.305; **nout** 8v.16; **nat** 18.341, 19.75. *pl.* **nute(n)** 18.162, 19.115. *pa. t. 1, 3 sg.* **nuste** 7.57, 179, 8K.11, 10.33; **niste** 17.106. *2 sg.* **nustest** 1.568. *pl.* **nuste(n)**

1.709, 7.166, 10.243. [OE *nāt, nyton; nyste*; see **ne, wite(n)**]

note *n.* duty 1.246, profit, use 365; *wormes to* ~ (be) good (only) for worms 8y.4 (see **to**). [OE *notu*]

noth ; noþeles, noðele ; noþer, noðres. See **noȝt** *n.*; **naþeles ; nouþer** *pron.*

noþer *conj.* nor 9.27, 35. [OE *nōþer* from *nōhwæþer*]

noþerward *adv.* downwards 1.100. [OA *neoþorweard*]

noþing *n.* nothing 1.404, 2.144, 5.111, 6.44, 7.161, 9.47, no creature 5.183; **naþing** 18.450. [OE *nān þing*, late *nāþing*]

noþing *adv.* not at all 1.370, 396. [prec.]

noþir-gat *adv.* in no other way 15.31. [ne+oþer(e)+gate[2]]

nou, now *adv.* now 3.1, 5, 4.58, 191, 5.106, 8F.9, 14.51; **nov** 7.285; **nu** 1.46, 8A.4, 10.93, 13.85, 17.46; **nv** 8w.1. ~ *þenne* accordingly 19.350. [OE *nū*]

nou, now *conj.* now that 6.58, 8s.1, 3.237. [as prec.]

nouct, nouȝt(h), nouiȝt, nout(h), novt ; nout. See **noȝt** *n., adv.*; **not.**

nouþe *adv.* now 3.71, 5.55, 7.40; **nuðe** 18.223, 19.287. [OE *nū þā*; see **nou, þo(o)**]

nouþer, nouther, nowðer *adv.* neither; (after neg.) either 18. 365, 19.381; ~ .. *ne* neither .. nor 1.690, 5.5, 6.308, 16.191, 18.661, 19.165. [OE *nāhwæþer, nō-, nāwþer*] Cf. **neiþer, owðer.**

nouþer *pron.* neither 16.279; **noþer** 15.4. *gen.* **noðres** 19. 392. [as prec.]

now. See **nou.**

nowcin *n.* hardship, distress 19. 185, 221; **nausine** 6.306 (note). *pl.* **neowcins** 19.297. [ON *nauðsyn*; cf. MDu *nootsin* (*c = ts*)] nower. See nohwer.

nowiderwardes *adv.* in no direction 16.177. [OE *nōhwider +-weardes*]

nowi3t, nowt(h); nowðer; nu, nv; nul(-); nummore. See no3t *n., adv.*; nouþer; nou *adv.*; nyl; nam(m)or(e).

nunan *adv.* now, already 18.234. [nou+anon]

nunnerie *n.* nunnery 9.148. [prob. AN *nonnerie*]

nunnes *n. pl.* nuns 9.152. [OE *nunne*]

nurð *n.* noise, disturbance 19.24. [origin obscure; see note]

nuste(n), nute(n); nuðe. See not; nouþe.

O *interj.* O! 2.243, 248. [prob. from L; not OE]

o. See a *adv.*; of *prep.*; on; on(e) *adj.*

oc, ok *adv.* also 12.19, 4.145, 244. [ON *auk*]

oc; oder. See ac(c); oþer *conj.*

odur *n.* scent 9.76. [AN]

of *adv.* off 2.210, 6.335, 7.111, 10.29, 18.630 (1st), 19.127; away 12.95. [OE *of*]

of *prep.*, general except off 12.67, 112, 13.4, 6, &c.; hof 5.295, 6.2; o 14.5, 7, &c., a 231. (of motion) from 1.24, 2.187, 3.27, 4.277, 8K.74, 9.184, 12.177, 16.29 (2nd), off 4.125, out of 2.151, 7.19; (of change of state) 1.286; (of origin) 7.209, belonging to 13.11, ~ *þe world* alive 5.150. (of substance) made of 2.213–15, 3.41, 4.306, 17.99 (2nd), 18.572, *to maken ~ lines* to make lines of 4.50. (of means) by, through, with 1.569, 2.65, 4.10, 5.56, 9.87, 17.99 (1st), ~ *us seoluen* through ourselves 18.115. (of cause) for, because of 1.40, 10.45, 16.188. (of agent) by 2.128, 17.78, 18.169. (of

concern) about, concerning, for 1.9, 3.120, 4.96, 6.356, 8T.10, 10.243; in (the matter of) 6.131, 7.36, 8G.8, 9.4; ~ *heardes* where hardship is concerned 19.195; ~ *bote* see bot(e) n. (dependent on various adjs., nouns, vbs.) see ful(le), pité, praie, recche v.¹, reowe, sad, þannkenn. In functions of *gen.*: (of possession, &c.) 1.14, 4.336, 5.26, 7.5, into 5.233, typical of, symbolizing 8K.45; (of rule and title) 2.3, 13.4, 16.7, 29 (1st); (specifying) 13.32, 16.8 (1st); (in descriptive phrs.) of 1.108, 2.119, 3.8, 8M.9, 12.112, 14.203, ~ *seue 3er* seven years old 7.15; (defining adjs.) in 2.202, 3.233, 6.4, 8G.38, L.26, ~ *heuene* in heaven 15.79; (partitive) 3.30, 4.210, 6.305, 8H.11, (without defining word) some, part, of 1.724, 8N.29, 10.141, 11.147, 13.39, 15.58, ~ *þin* some of your goods 3.100, after *serve* 17.95; (objective gen.) 5.295, 8D.9. ~ *þatt* of the fact that 13.9. offe (at end of rel. clause) from 13.202. [OE *of*; *offe* modelled on inne, cf. mid]

ofdrad *pp. adj.* afraid (*of*) 1.702; ofdred 16.122, 17.16 (with *forto*+infin. = of+-ing), 19.165(*for*); offdredde 13.74. [OE *ofdrǣdd*, *-drêdd*, pp. of *ofdrǣdan*, &c.; see adrad(de)]

ofdrahen *v.* draw out, attract, win 18.529, 540. *pr. 3 sg.* ofdraheð 18.284, 454. [of+dragen]

ofearneð *pr. 3 sg.* earns 19.153. [of+OE *éarnian*]

ofer; offdredde; offe. See ouer; ofdrad; of *prep.*

offearen *v.* terrify, alarm 18.247, 19.63, 185. *pp.* oferd 1.277; offæred 16.64; offearet 19.61, 237. [of+OE *fǣran*; cf. afere]

offrendes *n. pl.* offerings 17.11,
30. [OF *ofrende*]
offri *v.* offer 17.9. *pr. 3 sg.*
offreth 17.53. *subj. pl.* **offre**
(before *we*) 17.47. *imper. pl.*
offreth 17.72. *pa. t. sg.* **offrede**
17.42 (2nd). *pl.* 17.29, 42. *pp.*
i-offred 17.71. [OE *offrian* and
OF *offrir*]
offrinke *n.* offering 17.37. *pl.*
offringes 17.69. [OE *offring*]
offruhte *pp. adj.* frightened 19.
249. [of + OE *fyrhtan*]
ofgan *v.* win, gain 18.497. *pr. 3
sg.* **ofgeað** 18.284. *pp.* **ofgan**
earned 18.453. [OE *ofgān*; see
go(n)]
ofsei *pa. t. sg.* caught sight of 5.
10. [OE *ofseh* from *-sēon*; see **se**]
ofseruet, **-eth** *pr. 3 sg.* deserves,
earns 17.77, 122. *pl.* **ofserueþ**
17.267. [of + *serve*, see **seruest**]
ofsloh *pa. t. sg.* killed 10.226.
pp. **ofslaӡe** 10.284. [OE *ofslōh*,
-slagen from *-slēan*; see **sle(n)**]
oft *adv.* often 1.36, 2.124; **ofte**
4.24, 5.35, 8R.4, W.43, 11.88,
18.14. *phr.* ~ *ant ilome* 19.88
(note). [OE *oft*, extended after
advs. in *-e*]
oftake *v.* overtake 7.244. *pa. t.
pl.* **oftoken** 18.66. [of + **tak**]
oftoned *pp.* irritated, annoyed
1.190. [of + OE *tēonian*]
ofþinkeþ *pr. 3 sg.* causes regret
or repentance: *hit me* ~ I repent
of it 5.205; **ofþuncheþ** displeases 8F.47. *pa. t. sg. impers.*
ofþuӡte *hire* ~ she regretted
1.275. [OE *ofþyncan*; see
þinche and cf. **forþingketh**]
of-urn *n.* greater speed in running: *straf wið heortes* ~ strove
to run faster than the stag
18.631. [of + OM *ýrn*; see
erne]
ofuundred, **-wundred** *pp. adj.*
astonished 16.122, 245. [OE
ofwundrian]

og(en); **oghe**. See **ah**;
owen(e).
oght *adv.* at all, in any way 14.
253; **ohht** 13.147; **ouӡt** 3.105,
256. [see **oӡt**]
oӡe; **oӡene**. See **ah**; **owen(e)**.
oӡt *n.* anything 1.408; **ouӡt(h)**
2.309, 3.107; **outh** in *or* ~ *longe*
before (any) long (time), very
soon 4.216. [OE *ō(wi)ht*]
oht(e) *adj.* brave, valiant 10.1,
178; good, sound 10.222, fit 260.
[attrib. use of prec.]
ohwider *adv.* anywhere 19.27.
[OE *āhwider*, **ō-*]
oile *n.* oil 9.46, 14.140, 166.
[OF]
oiþer *conj.* or 2.10, 11, 12.
[blend of **oþer** *conj.* and OE
ǣgþer, see **aiþer**]
ok. See **ac(c)**, **oc**.
old(e) *adj.* old 1.25, 6.199, 9.63,
12.103, (with determining num.)
7.115; former 1.163; as *n.* in *of
olde* long ago 1.431; **holde** 6.
303, 331; **ald(e)** 10.227, 15.67,
18.117, (with phr. forming
quasi-compd.) 16.121; **eald** 16.
32; **ialde** 17.42. [OE *éald*, A
ǎld] See **ӡong(e)**.
oldest. See **holde(n)**.
olhnin *v.* cajole, wheedle 18.116.
[reduced from **oluhtnin* from
OE *ōlyht* cajolery]
olhnunge *n.* persuasion, blan-
dishment 18.77. [from prec.]
on *adv.* on 4.127 (see **do(n)**), 8F.
13; *telle* ~ begin to tell of 2.53;
taken ~ see **tak**; **an** 10.133.
[OE *on*]
on *prep.*, general except **one**
1.393, 12.146, 178; **onn** 13.4,
&c.; **hon** 6.18; **o** (before cons.)
8N.13, 10.276, 12.2, 13.13, 14.
286, 16.187, 18.16, 152, 19.61,
&c.; **ho** 15.46; (postponed)
6.10, 8G.44, 10.300 (1st), 15.83.
(of place) on 1.131, 2.25, 3.35,
6.358, 8H.3, N.2, 12.121; ~ *þe se*
at sea 4.99; (without expressed

obj.) on it 12.175; in 1.51, 7.93, 178, 8E.64, 10.12, 12.94, 14.286, 16.3, 54, (of a book) 2.321, 12.2; at 16.2. (of time) on 4.79, 12.99, 13.157; in 4.300, 16.118, 129; ~ a(n) day one day 2.1, 6.16; ~ life, liue see **lif**. (of regard) fixed on 4.106, 6.10, 8G.3. (of concern) of, about 6.47, 206, 8M.8, 21, 13.168. (of opposition) at, against 4.265, 14.32; over 11.19, 18.114. (with *manere*, *wise*) in 6.367, 14.2, 10.253, 13.160, 18.23. (specifying) in 2.201, 8F.4; in the person, case, of 1.94, 211; ~ *me* from my appearance 8L.2. ~ *Englis(ch)* in English 7.180, 185. ~ *himseoluen* on his own account 18.339. *whet him ys* ~ what is the matter with him 8G.44. (dependent on various vbs.) in, on, at: see **beleue, leue(n)³, cri, lawe, lok, reowe**. In many phrs. with n. or adj., see **auenture, eke, end(e), erand, fir(e), flod(e), fluht(e), help(e), hepe, hihŏe, hond(e), idel, lade, laȝe** *adj.*, **lengþe, se(e), slep(e), two, uore, writ(e)**. [OE *on*] See **a** *prep.*, **upon**.

on(e) *adj.* one 4.29, 5.7, 132, 17.196, *sixti and* ~ 4.345; a single 1.355, 8M.9; the same 1.137, 2.112, 7.37, 160, 12.112; o 1.459, 3.176, 8D.40; (opposed to 'other') 8N.10; same 1.249. **an** 13.180, 16.88, 18.218, 228, united 18.230 (1st); **a** 14.249, 18.21, 218, 632 (2nd), 668. **on(e)** a certain, merging into *art. indef.* a: 1.1, 2, 2.233, 285, 3.29, 273, 5.11, 213, 618, 7.33, (postponed) 15.84; o 5.266, 17.14. *dat. fem.* **ore** 1.17, 708. [OE *ān*] See **a(n)**.

on(e) *pron.* one (person) 4.227, 7.50, 240, 8D.36, H.11, T.1; a certain person, someone 6.2,

11.41; one (thing) 1.82, 458, 5.198, 7.191; in *bote* ~ *þat* see **bot(e)** *conj.*; *on and on* one and all 5.197, 269. **an** 13.100, 16.69, 18.173; *þe* ~ the one (opposed to 'the other') 18.251 (*dat.*), 19.283; *þat* ~ the one 3.4; *in* ~ in the same state 14.293, together 18.247. *gen.* **anes** 19.351. [as prec.]

onan; **onde**. See **anon**; **hond(e)**.

onde *n.* envy 1.297, 7.17, 18.250; malice, enmity 8D.18; breath 12.149, 187. *gen.* **ondes** for envy 18.291. [OE *ánda*, *ónda* malice, ON *andi* breath]

onder(-). See **under(-)**.

ondergo *v.* (with *of*) occupy oneself with, investigate 7.200. [OE *undergān*, meaning only 'undermine']

ondo; **ondswer-**. See **undo**; **answeren**.

one *adj.* alone, only 7.150; *al* ~ alone 2.217, 7.147, *al* **hone** 5.275; **ane** 10.295, 18.49, 188, 633; *him* ~ by himself 4.83, 18.173, alone 19.225; *hire* ~ 18.241; *myn* ~ by myself 8G.9. [OE *āna* adv.] See **ane** *adv*.

onecles *n. pl.* onyxes 3.44. [OF *onicle*]

onfest *prep.* close by 10.introd. [**on** *prep.*+**faste** adv.] Cf. **her-**, **þær-onnfasst**.

ongel. See **angel**.

onix *n.* onyx 9.92. [L *onyx*]

onlepi *adj.* only, sole 17.53; **anlepi** single, individual 19.352; **alpi** 5.132. [OE (nWS) *ǎnlēpig*]

onlepiliche *adv.* only, solely 17.72. [prec.+**-liche**]

onne *prep.* on (their shoulders) 16.175. [OE *on* extended after **inne**] Cf. **ane**.

onneþe; **onnȝæn**; **onoh**; **onon(-)**. See **vnneþe**; **aȝein**; **inogh**; **anon(-)**.

onont *prep.* as regards, as far as

concerns 19.59; ~ *hireseoluen* in herself 19.205. [OE *on emn* beside]

ono**þ**er; onour. See ano**þ**er *pron.*; honour(e).

onsene *n.* appearance, look 1.664. [OE *onsēon*]

onsih**ð**e *n.* sight 19.241 (note), 285; *his* ~ the sight of him. [on+si**ʒ**t(e)]

ontende(n) *v.* kindle, inspire 18.652, 670. *pr. 3 sg.* ontent 19.418. [OE *onténdan*]

ontendunge *n.* kindling 18.666. [from prec.]

ontful(e) *adj.* envious 18.126, 128. [from onde]

ontswere**ð**; onuri. See answeren; anuri.

onwar *adj.* wary, on one's guard 8H.34. [expanded variant of iwar]

onwis. See vnwis.

onwold *v.* control 6.311. [OA *ge-onwáldian*]

op. See up.

opdrowe *pa. t. pl.* pulled up 5.287. [up+dragen]

ope *adj.* plain, apparent 1.124; open 5.27; open(e) 4.209, 18.400. [OE *open*]

ope *prep.* See uppen.

opeliche *adv.* openly 1.513; openlice 16.201; openliche 18.539; plainly 18.40. [ope+-liche]

openin *v. tr.* open 18.538; explain, expound 19.321. *pp.* i-openet explained 18.20; as *adj.* open, 'patent' 18.471 (note). *pr. 3 sg. intr.* opene**ð** opens 19.362. [OE *openian*]

op(p)on; opward. See upon; upward.

opwinde *v.* wind up 5.75. [up+ OE *windan*]

or *n.* metal 18.325. [cf. OE *ōra*]

or *conj.*[1] or 3.162, 4.36; or else 4.200; ~ .. ~ either .. or 14.44, 68. [reduced from o**þ**er *conj.*]

811493

or *conj.*[2] before 12.39. [as next]

or *prep.* before 4.216 (see o**ʒ**t). [ONb *ār*; cf. er(e)]

or. See **ʒ**e(e).

orchard *n.* orchard, garden 3.29. [OE *ort-géard, orceard*]

orde *n.* point 1.670; beginning 1.743 (see end(e)). [OE *ord*]

ordre *n.* (religious) order 18.232. *pl.* ordres 18.443. [OF]

ore *n.*[1] grace, mercy: of God 2.143, 199; of a mistress 8M.6; *þin* ~ have pity! 5.189; are 13.126. [OE *ār*[1]]

ore *n.*[2] oar 4.298, 313. *pl.* oris 9.154. [OE *ār*[2]]

ore. See on(e) *adj.*; we.

oreisun *n.* prayer 9.165; urisun 17.74. [AN *oreisun, orisun*]

orfcwalm *n.* livestock plague 16.66. [OE *orf-cwealm*]

orgeilus *adj.* proud 17.131. [AN]

ormete *adj.* immense 16.234. [OE *ormǽte*]

orn(e). See erne.

ortreweden *pa. t. pl.* suspected 7.212. [OE *ge-ortréowan* distrust]

ost *n.* host, force 11.108. [OF *(h)ost*]

otwinne *adv.* in two 12.89, 104. [on+ON *tvinn-r*; cf. twinnin]

o**þ**(e) *n.* oath 8F.43, 11.30; a**ð** 16.37. *pl.* o**þ**es 8H.24; a**ð**es, athas, -es 16.96, 265, 155. [OE *āþ*]

o**þ**er(e), o**ð**er *adj.* other, another 1.394, 537, 2.110, 3.80, 4.101, 12.85; o**þ**err 13.160; o**þ**ir 15.70; o**þ**ur(e) 7.13, 108; (after *þat*) to**þ**er 14.84; second 19.41, 221; next 16.81, *ð*at, *þet* ~ the next 16.119, 4.145; *þis* ~ last year 2.239; *fram ende to* ~ from end to end 11.166. *gen.* o**þ**eres 5.224. *dat.* o**þ**re 5.58. *pl.* often uninfl., as 1.160, 4.29, 9.98, but o**þ**re, othre 16.110, 316, 18.36, 44, &c. [OE *ōþer*] See ano**þ**er.

oþer, oðer, other *pron.* other,
the other, someone else 1.7, 2.
106, 11.78, 12.115, 16.126, 280,
19.124; oþur 7.101. þat, þet ~
the second 5.74, 18.69, 579; the
rest 18.129; *non* ~ no one else
3.238, 6.136. *aiþer of* ~ *counseil
þai wiste* each knew the other's
secrets 3.209. *gen.* oþeres 1.9;
oþres, oðres 18.4, 127, 12.121,
19.124. *dat.* (*þe*) oðre 19.283.
pl. oþere 7.242, 11.168; oþre,
oðre, othre 5.217, 17.188, 18.7,
19.58, 12.117, 16.139, 19.280,
16.249 (*dat.*), 316. *gen.* oðres
19.350. [as prec.]

oþer, oðer, other *conj.* or 4.55,
6.133, 8G.52, 10.252, 18.79, 19.
217, 16.166; or else (failing that)
1.412, 572, 5.52, 8N.16, 11.28;
~ .. ~ either .. or 1.244, 5.
14, 18.613–14, 19.20–21 (oder).
[prob. modification of OE *oþþe*,
infl. by *ōhwæþer, ā(w)þer*, &c.] See
or *conj.*[1], oðþe, owðer, aiþer.

oðerweis *adv.* in another way,
otherwise 18.264, 272. [oþer(e)
+wai(e) with adv. gen. *-s*]

oðerwhile *adv.* sometimes 19.
105. [oþer(e)+while]

oðþe *conj.* or 16.70. [OE *oþþe*]

oþwe; ou, ov; ouene; ouer;
ouȝt(h), ouȝte; ounder; ounderfonge, -fost; oundred;
ounseli; ounwi(i)s; oup;
our(e), ovr, ous; ouris.
See owen(e); ȝe(e), hou;
owen(e); we; oȝht, oȝt, ah;
under; underuon; hundred;
unseli; vnwis; up; we; ure.

ouself *pron.* (for) yourselves 8E.
60. [OE *ēow* (see ȝe(e))+self]
Cf. hemself and other prons.

out(e) *adv.* out 2.104, 7.260, 11.
8, 58; away from home 6.345,
houte 79; ut, vt 1.8, 4.229, 221,
19.45, 16.288, 292, ute 290
(note). [OE *ūt, ūte*]

out(e) of *prep.* out of, from
3.246, 5.1, 6.347, 8D.12, 14.180;

ut, vt .. 10.165, 12.4, 16.87,
1.53, 4.240, outside 17.220; ŭt
.. 13.102; hut 8T.26, v.8, w.39,
17.265; *ut of þe seoluen* out of
your mind 18.319. [OE *ūt of*]

outh. See oȝt.

out-ouer *prep.* beyond 14.183.
[out(e)+ouer prep.]

outrage *n.* violence, offence
2.300; act of violence, assault
7.21. [OF]

ouer *adv.* over 5.22; through
18.380. [OE *ofer*]

ouer, over *prep.* over 10.37,
11.113, 12.114, 16.46 (see se(e)),
18.240, 17.28; across 8K.70;
along 8N.26; above 18.7, 19.
347; upon 18.392; ofer throughout 16.48, 67. [as prec.]

oueral *adv.* everywhere 5.19, 69,
11.67, 18.651, 19.13; all the way
5.9. [OA *ofer all*]

ouercumen *v. tr.* overcome, de-
feat 18.394; *intr.* be victorious
1, note to 132. *pr. 3 sg.* ouerkimeð exceeds 18.599. *pl.*
ouercumeð 19.306. *pa. t. pl.*
ouercomen 18.120. *subj. sg.*
ouerkome 1.701. *pp.* ouercome 1.620, surmounted 3.282;
-cume(n) 1.350, 18.490. [OE
ofercuman]

ouerdede *n.* overdoing, excess
1.268. [ouer+ded(e); cf. next]

ouerdon *v.* overdo, do to excess
18.362. [OE *oferdōn*]

ouergeað *pr. 3 sg. tr.* exceeds
18.544. *pl.* ouergað overpower
19.305. *pa. t. sg. intr.* ouer-
hede passed off, disappeared
5.90. *pp.* ouergo finished 1.375.
[OE *ofergān*; see go(n), eode]

ouerhardi *adj.* too bold 19.63.
[ouer+hardi]

ouer-hede; ouerkome. See
ouergeað; ouercumen.

ouermyhte *pa. t. sg.* was more
powerful 16.195. [OE *ofermæg*;
see mai]

ouer-rennes *pr. 3 sg.* runs over,

reviews 14.introd. [ouer+
renne]

ouersah *pa. t. sg.* looked over,
surveyed 10.16; **ouerseȝ** 1.30.
[OE *ofersæh, -seh* from *-sēon*;
see **se**]

ouersithon *adv.* (?) too often
16.191 (note). [ouer+OE *sī-
þum* dat. pl. of **siþ(e)**]

ouertake *v.* overtake, catch 4.
283. *pa. t. sg.* **ouertok** 4.243.
[ouer+tak]

ouerþinne *adj.* too thin, weak
1.416. [ouer+þynne]

ouerwaden *v.* wade through
18.182. [OE *oferwadan*]

ouerweieð *pr. 3 sg.* outweighs
18.449. [ouer+OE *wegan*]

ow; ower. See **ȝe(e)**.

owel *n.* hook 1.80. *pl* eawles 19.
143 [OE *āwul, *ǣwel*]

owen(e) *adj.* own 2.229, 3.113,
7.274; **ouene** 6.421; **houne**
6.390; **oghe** 17.123; **oȝe(ne)**
1.195, 608, 610; **oþwe** (= *oȝwe*)
8w.14; **aȝen** 16.80; **aȝen** 10.77,
176; **aȝhenn** 13.255; **ahne**
18.16, 296, 19.344. *dat. fem.*
aȝere 10.58, 74. [OE *āgen*]

owðer *pron.* either 18.348. [OE
ōhwæþer, ōwþer]

ox *n.* ox 9.32. [OE *oxa*]

pades *n. pl.* toads 16.170. [OE
pad(d)e]

paens *n. pl.* heathens 17.227.
[OF *paien*]

pagne *n.* page 18.360. [OF
pagene]

paieð *pr. 3 sg.* pleases 18.76.
pa. t. sg. **paide** paid (person) 17.
192, (price) 18.389. [OF *payer*]

painime *n.* heathendom 17.78.
[OF *pai(e)nime*]

pais, pays *n.* peace 16.129, 320,
7.241, 231; **peis** 2.118; *churche*
~ security due to a church,
sanctuary 11.59 (note); **pes**
1.688, 18.78; (*interj.*) be quiet,
enough! 2.297; **Pees** Peace (of

mind, personified) 8K.60. [OF
pais, AN *pees*]

palays, paleys *n.* palace 2.113,
172. [OF *palais*]

palle *n.* coverlet: *vnder* ~ in bed
2.282; robe (of rich cloth) 3.20,
6.23. [OE *pæll*]

panier *n.* basket 4.81. *pl.*
paniers 4.28, 73. [OF]

pans; pape(s). See **peni**; **pope**.

par *prep.* (in French phrases) by
6.436, 19.422, 426. See **charité**,
fai, **par amour**.

parage *n.* noble lineage, rank
3.8, 28. [OF]

par amour *adv.* as a favour (to
tell) 2.223; **par amours** pas-
sionately, with all (one's) heart
8L.26; **par amurs** 14.52. [OF
par amur(s), amour(s) by way of
love] See **amour(e)**.

paramour *n.* loved one 14.69.
[from prec.]

part *n.* part 3.260. [OF]

paruenke *n.* periwinkle 8K.50.
[AN *parvenke*]

passeð *pr. 3 sg.* surpasses, exceeds 18.544, 599. *pp.* **pasid**
passed 14.101. [OF *passer*]

passiun *n.* suffering 18.410. *gen.*
passiunes of [His] passion
18.397. [AN]

pasteiis *n. pl.* pasties, pies 9.54.
[OF *pastee*]

paternoster *n.* the Lord's prayer
6.209, 12.61, 15.71, 19.422. [L]

patriarches *n. pl.* patriarchs
17.209, 18.469, 19.286. [OF]

pauylouns *n. pl.* canopies 2.221.
[AN *pavilun*]

pece *n.* length of cloth 18.265.
[OF]

Pees. See **pais**.

peintunge *n.* painting 18.33.
[from *peint* v., prob. from OF
peint pp. of *peindre*; cf. **depeint**]

peinture *n.* picture 18.31. [OF]

peis. See **pais**.

pelle *v.* hasten, hurry 4.78. [ob-
scure]

pelrimage *n.* pilgrimage 17.63. *pl.* **pilgrimages** 2.56. [OF *pelrimage*; cf. OHG (from F) *piligrīm*]

penance *n.* penance 9.178. [OF *pen(e)ance*]

peni, peny *n.* penny 17.234, 180, 2.242; **peninng, pening** 13.12, 18, 272. *pl.* **penies** 4.44; **pones** 6.274; **pans** pence, money 3.102, 119. [OE *pening, penig, pænig*, late *panig*]

pepins *n. pl.* seeds 14.230, 237, **pipins** 281. [OF *pepin*]

pepir *n.* pepper 6.279. [OE *pipor, *peopor*]

pere *n.* peer, equal 2.40; quasi-*adj.* 9.22. [OF *per*]

peres *n. pl.* pears 14.37. [OE *pere*]

peril *n.* peril 17.159. [OF]

perisset *pr. pl.* perish 17.150. *subj. pl.* **perissi** 17.169. [OF *periss-*, pr. stem of *perir*]

person *n.* person 2.22 (note). [OF *persone*]

per-tre *n.* pear-tree 14.37. [OE *pere*+**tre(e)**]

pes; **pett.** See **pais**; **putte.**

pycchynde *pr. p.* setting up 8N.13. [obscure; app. OE *piccan*]

pich *n.* pitch 19.118. [OE *pic*]

pye *n.* magpie 8N.37. [OF *pie*]

piement, pye- *n.* spiced and sweetened wine 9.85, 2.130. [OF *piment*]

pikes *n. pl.* pikes 5.62, 284. [OE *pīc*]

pilche *n.* fur or skin coat 6.225. [OE *pylece*]

pilche-clut *n.* cloth, rag 19.144. [prec.+**clut**]

pilers *n. pl.* pillars 9.67. [OF *piler*]

pilgrimages. See **pelrimage.**

pine, pyne *n.*[1] suffering, pain 3.287, 5.142, 6.305, 8w.27, 15.34, 18.336; torture 19.108, 124. *pl.* **pinen** sufferings 18.24; tortures 19.103, 296; **pines** 16.180. [OE *pīn*]

pine *n.*[2] pine 14.241. [OE *pīn* (-*bēam*), OF *pin*]

pined *pa. t. pl.* tortured 16.163; **pineden** 16.226. *pp.* **pined** 16.165, 227. [OE *pīnian*]

pining *n.* torture 16.164, 226. [cf. OE *pīnung*]

pinnes, pynnes *n. pl.* pegs, nails 9.59, 2.215. [OE *pinn*]

pinsunges *n. pl.* mortifications 18.402. [uncertain; app. rel. to **pining** as *cleanse* to *clean*, implying OE **pinsian*]

pipe *n.* pipe 1.22, 235. [OE *pīpe*]

piping(e) *n.* piping 1.232, 375. [from OE *pīpian*]

pipins. See **pepins.**

pité, pyté *n.* pity, compassion 2.101, 11.63; matter for regret (with *of*) 11.170; *wit* ~ compassionately 14.226. [OF *pité*]

place *n.* place 4.11, 7.78, 95; **plas** open space 2.173. [OF *place*]

play, plaie *n.* amusement, pleasure 2.278; play, gaming, in *legge to* ~ stake 3.122. *pl.* **plawes** games, gambols 8H.2. [OE *plega*, A *plæga*, **plaga*]

plai, plaie(n) *v.* 9.122, 3.110, 98; **plei(e), pleye** 9.156, 11. 138, 136; **plei3en** 7.74. play 3.110, (*at* a game) 98; amuse oneself 1.169, 9.122, 156, *refl.* 7.74; go for amusement 11.136; make love 2.283, 6.438. *imper. sg.* **plai** 3.102. *pp.* **ypleiede** 2.283. [OE *pleg(i)an*]

playces *n. pl.* plaice 4.162. [OF *plaïs*]

plaid, plait *n.* suit (at law), debate 1.695, 5. *gen.* **plaites** 1.330. [OF *plaid, plait*]

plaidi *v.* plead (a case), debate 1.140. [OF *plaidier*]

plaiding *n.* debate 1.12. [from prec.]

plait. See **plaid.**

plantede *pa. t. sg.* planted 16. 220. [OE *plantian*]

plas; plawes; plei(e), pleye,
plei3en. See place; play;
plai.

pleynte *n.* complaint, charge (of
wrongdoing) 2.37. *pl.* pleyntes
8κ.61. [OF *plainte*]

plenté *n.* abundance 9.150; *gret*
~ in great abundance 9.105;
plente3 (= -*þ*) fullness 14.223.
[OF *plenté, plented* (= -*ð*)]

pli3tte *pr. 1 sg.* pledge 6.252.
pp. plyht 8D.28; yplyht H.22.
[OE *plihtan*]

plodde *n.* puddle 11.18. [obscure]

ploges *n. pl.* ploughs 16.68.
[LOE *plôh,* **plôg-,* ON *plôg-r;*
app. of Celtic origin]

podinges *n. pl.* puddings, sausages 9.59. [prob. OF *bo(u)din*]

poer. See power.

poysun *n.* poison 7.23, 25. [AN
poisun]

poke *n.* bag 4.37. *pl.* pokes
4.48. [ONF *pogue, poke* (= OF
poche); cf. ONb *pocca*]

pond; pones. See pound;
peni.

pope *n.* pope 1.492, 7.171, 177,
8E.47; pape 16.212, 18.51. *gen.*
papes 16.14. [OE *pāpa*]

porchas *n.* plunder 11.86. [OF
por-, purchas]

porter *n.* porter, gatekeeper 3.19,
86. *pl.* porters 11.113, 119.
[AN, = OF *portier*]

portereues *n. gen.* of the portreeve, bailiff 11.164. *pl.* portreuen 11.146 (note). [OE
port-gerēfa]

porueide *pa. t. sg.* procured 7.23.
[AN *purveier*]

postes *n. pl.* pillars 10.21. [OE
post]

pound *n.* pound 6.224. *pl.*
pond (after numeral) 3.117.
[OE *púnd* sg. and pl.]

poure *adj.* poor, humble 6.306,
18.125, 468, 19.291; pouere
11.103. poure as *n. pl.* poor

people, (the) poor 1.340, 17.63,
18.411 (*dat.*). [OF *pov(e)re,* AN
poure] See rich(e).

pourueance *n.* provision, ordinance 11.5. [OF *po(u)r-
veance*]

pouerte *n.* poverty, want 6.304.
[OF *poverte*]

power *n.* power 7.18; poer
8κ.60; authority 11.89; office
11.8; strength 11.81; a force of
armed men 11.11, 26, 121. [AN
poёr]

praer *n.* meadow 9.71. [OF
pra(i)ere]

praie *v.* pray, beg 3.109, 121;
preye invite 8N.27. *pr. 1 sg.*
preye 8M.9; pre3e (with *of,* for)
8M.13, 19. *subj. pl.* prey (before
we) 9.189. *imper. sg.* prai
14.135; preye 8T.6. [OF *preier*]

prassiune *n.* prasine, a green
precious stone 9.91. [adapted,
with AN ending, from LL
prasina]

prechur *n.* preacher 17.231.
[AN]

preciouse *adj.* precious 2.219,
3.41; preciuse 9.88. [OF
preci(o)us]

prede; pre3e, prey(e). See
pride; praie.

prei *n.* prey, capture 9.163. [AN
preie]

prelates *n. pl.* prelates 14.22.
[OF *prelat*]

preost(-). See prest.

preoue *n.* proof 18.62. [OF
prueve]

preouin *v.* convict 19.82. [OF
pruev-, accented stem of *pro-
ver*]

prest *n.* priest 1.238, 4.256, 5.52,
17.43; preost 1.534, 579, 10.
introd. *gen.* prestes 1.574,
12.49; preostes 16.194. *pl.*
prestes 6.248; prostes 1.479;
preoste (*dat.*) 1.545. [OE
prēost]

prest *adj.* eager 14.25. [OF]

pride *n.* pride, arrogance 14.30;
prede 17.167; **prude** 6.125,
18.123, 288, 19.224; splendour
8D.35; **pruyte** 7.167; **proude**
1.643. [LOE *prȳde, prȳte*] Cf.
proud.

prikieð *pr. pl.* pierce, sting 18.
77. [OE *prician*]

prynce *n.* prince 2.7, 11. *pl.*
princes, -ʒ 9.60, 14.22. [OF
prince]

prior *n.* prior 16.19, 98; **priur**
18.240. [LOE *prior* from L;
AN *priur*]

pris *n.* value, worth 3.108 (see
lete(n)), 18.390; excellence, in
of ~ excellent 3.39, 66, 6.120;
price 6.446, 18.465; prize 8D.35,
T.32. [OF]

prison *n.* prison 11.22, 147;
prisoun 2.244, 252; **prisun**
16.152, 163. [OF *prison*, AN
pris(o)un]

priur. See **prior.**

priué *adj.* secret, remote 7.99.
[OF *privé*]

priueliche *adv.* in confidence
7.62. [prec.+-**liche**]

priuilegies *n. pl.* privileges,
special rights 16.213. [adapted
from L *privilēgium*]

priuité *n.* privacy: *in* ~ in private 6.84. [OF *privité*]

procession(e) *n.* procession 7.
224, 9.146; **processionem** (L
acc.) 16.83. [OF *procession*]

profetes. See **prophete.**

progeni *n.* progeny, descendants
14.225. [OF *progenie*]

prophete *n.* prophet 17.230,
18.667. *pl.* **prophetes** 17.213,
18.469, 19.286; **profetes** 17.19.
[OF *prophete*, L *prophēta*]

prostes. See **prest.**

proud *adj.* proud, arrogant 3.19,
6.3; as *n.* **prude** proud man
18.124. [LOE *prūd*] Cf. **pride.**

proude. See **pride.**

prouesse *n.* excellence 8K.50.
[OF]

prude; pruyte. See **pride,
proud; pride.**

pruuien *v.* give proof of 18.506.
[?OE *prōfian* infl. by OF *prueve*]
Cf. **preoue, preouin.**

pudrid *pp.* sprinkled, seasoned
9.110. [OF *poudrer*]

puf *n.* puff 18.193. [imit.; cf.
OE *pyffan*]

puyr *adv.* entirely 7.185. [adv.
use of **pur** adj.]

pulte *pa. t. sg.* thrust 11.8.
[app. OE **pyltan*]

pur *adj.* pure 3.128. [OF]

pur *prep.* (OF) for; see **charité.**

put(te) *n.* well 5.71, 113, 117;
pit 7.82, 118, 8T.44, 10.31; grave
8Y.2; *to* ~ *bringe* bury 11.144.
[OE *pytt*]

putte *pa. t. sg.* put forward,
made 8K.61. *pl.* **putten** thrust
4.271. *pp.* **put** driven 14.122;
pett stuffed 2.44. [prob. OE
pȳtan]

qu-. See also **wh-.**

qua(m); quad; quakien. See
who; quaþ; cwakien.

qual *n.* some kind of fish 4.21.
[cf. Du *kwal*; see note]

quare-. See **wher(e).**

quarel *n.* quarrel, crossbow bolt
11.41. [OF]

quarterne *n.* prison, dungeon
16.169. [OE *cweartern*]

quasa; quat. See **whose;
what.**

quaþ *pa. t. sg.* said (quoting
direct speech) 1.143, 3.145,
5.37; **cwaþ, cwað** 1.709, 697;
quoþ, quoð, quoth 2.53, 18.
149, 19.160, 4.175; **quodh** 4.
227; **quad** 5.33, 207; **quod**
5.53, 6.27; **hwat** 4.305. *pp.*
icwede spoken 1.611. [OE
cwæþ, gecweden, parts of *cwepan*]

qued *adj.* wicked 5.200. [adj.
use of next]

qued(e) *n.* evil 5.210, 224, 7.14.
[OE *cwēad* filth]

quedir, -ur. See whaðer.
queynt adj. cunning, crafty
2.165. [AN queinte]
quelle v. kill 6.183, 7.39, 68.
[OE cwellan]
queme. See cwemen.
quen(e) n. queen 2.61, 127, 3.64,
7.20, 8т.33, 10.30; queene 3.24;
quiene 7.125, 265; cuen 16.
268, 307; cwen 18.487. gen.
quiene 7.136. [OE cwēn]
quen. See whan.
quench v. quench 9.12. [OE
-cwencan; see aquenche]
quic adj. living, alive 10.259, 262;
cwic 19.97, 133; ~ eiʒte livestock 11.49. [OE cwic]
quiclich, quyklich adv. quickly,
speedily 2.26, 86; cwicliche
18.99. [OE cwiclīce]
quide n. saying 1.431. pl.
quiðes 10.326. [OE cwide infl.
by cwepan]
quiene. See quen(e).
quyk adv. quickly 2.33, 114, 167.
[adv. use of quic]
quil; quilk; quilum. See
while; hwuch; whilen.
quyne n. woman 15.67. [OE
cwene, rarely cwyne]
quiðes; quod, quodh, quoþ,
quoð, quoth. See quide;
quaþ.

rachenteges. See raketehe.
rad(e) adj. ready, at hand 1.301;
hasty 8н.16. comp. raddere
more inclined 1.484. [OE hræd,
comp. hræd(d)ra]
rad, radde(n). See red(e) v.
radlice adv. soon 16.48. [OE
hrædlīce]
ræd(e). See red(e) n., v.
ræflac n. robbery 16.136. [OE
rēaflāc; see reue]
ræuede(n). See reue.
ræueres n. pl. robbers 16.197.
[OE rēafere; see reue]

rages pr. pl. live wantonly 14.48.
[OF rager]
raght pa. t. sg. stretched, extended tr. 14.205, intr. 211.
[OE ræhte, rǎhte from rǣcan]
raidd adj. afraid 14.156. [ON
hrædd-r]
raketehe n. chain 19.80. pl.
rachenteges 16.174. [OE
racen-tēah, obl. -tēage]
ran. See renne.
randun n. in in o ~ with a rush,
headlong 9.132. [OF en un
randon, AN randun]
rapes n. pl. ropes 16.292. [OE
rāp]
rapelike adv. hurriedly, in haste
12.71. [ON hrapaliga]
rarunge n. screaming 19.139.
[OE rārung]
ras. See rise.
raþe adv. early 2.272 (see late);
quickly, soon 1.658, 6.236;
raðe 10.185; also raþe immediately 17.153. comp. raþer before 5.68, 9.120; reaðere sooner
18.420. [OE hraþe; comp.
hraþor, M *hreaðor]
read- ; reaðere ; reau-. See
red(e) n., v., adj.; raþe ; reue.
recche v.¹ pr. 1 sg. care 1.60,
(with of) 5.228; reche 1.58.
subj. sg. recke 4.341. pa. t. sg.
route 5.260. subj. sg. roʒte
1.305. [OE reccan, pa. t.
rǒhte]
recche v.² go 5.268. [OE reccan
(pa. t. re(a)hte)]
reccnenn v. pay 13.24, 271;
rikenin calculate 19.98. pp.
reccnedd paid 13.18. [OE ge-
recenian]
rechelese adj. careless 19.14.
[OE recce-, rēcelēas]
recke. See recche.
recordin v. repeat 18.262. [OF
recorder]
red(e) n. plan, course of action,
way 1.223, 2.112, 3.80, 4.94,
6.378, 8н.16; good sense 1.274,

448; advice 3.76, 5.50, 6.328, 16.282; reed 5.192, 8F.29; ræd 16.14, 281. *pl.* reades designs 19.333. *at one* ~ agreed 7.37; *a* ~ *taken, nome* make, made, a plan 4.260, 11.139; *nimen heom to* ~ decide 1.722, 7.226; *her is to* ~ here is help 1.426; *what to* ~ what could be done 3.171; *ut of* ~ at her wits' end 1.406. [OE *rǣd*, A *rēd*]

red(e), reden *v.* (1) advise, counsel 1.520, 655, 2.72, 5.130, 6.375, 19.200; present (a case) 1.740; take thought (for) 16.102; treat 8D.8, 24, F.28. (2) read 1.266, 7.274, 8E.39, 14.2, 18. 353; understand 14.42; *iheorden it* ~ heard it read 7.184; *fynd . . to* ~ find something to read 14. 98. *pr. 1 sg.* rede 1.520, 2.72, 12.2. *3 sg.* readeð 19.200; redeð 18.69; redis 14.42. *pl.* redeð, -th 17.3, 18.74. *subj. sg.* ræde 16.102; reade 19.161; rede 5.130. *imper. sg.* red 8D. 24. *pa. t. 3 sg.* radde 6.152, 185, 7.269. *2 sg.* raddest 1.115. *pl.* radden 7.185. *pp.* rad 8D.8; ired 19.424. [OE *rǣdan*, A *rēdan*; pa. t. *rǣdde*]

red(e) *adj.* red 3.50, 8E.38, 9.70; read(e) 18.532, 589. *comp.* redder ruddier 2.201. [OE *rēad*]

-rede(n) *suff.* forming nouns denoting esp. condition, as fer-, frende-, kun-, man-, sib-. [OE *-rǣden*]

redes *pr. 3 sg.* is red 8E.36. [OE *rēadian*]

redi, redy *adj.* ready 2.177, 208, 3.103, 6.434. [OE *(ge)rǣde+ -ig*] Cf. iredi.

redles *adj.* without a plan, at a loss 1.437. [OE *rǣdlēas*]

red-purs *n.* wallet of wisdom 1.440. [red(e)+LOE *purs*]

redunge *n.* reading 18.4, 352. [cf. OE *rǣding*]

reed. See red(e) *n.*

refen *v.* roof 16.209. [OE *hrē-fan*]

reȝel *n.* clothing, covering 1.370. [OE *hrægl*]

reilþein *n.* keeper of the wardrobe 16.99. [prec.+OE *þegn*]

rein *n.* rain 9.41, 10.156, 18.93. [OE *regn*]

reisun, resun *n.* reason 18.533, 587. *pl.* reisuns 18.609. [AN *re(i)sun*]

religiun *n.* religious observance 17.101; religious life 18.231. *pl.* religiuns religious professions 18.443. [AN]

relike *n.* relic 7.190. [OF *relique*]

remunge *n.* crying, wailing 19. 114. [from OA *hrēman*]

rene *n.* watercourse, stream 3.54. [OE *ryne*, K **rene*]

renne *v.* run 4.258, 331; rene (of eyes) 6.281. *pr. 3 sg.* renneð 12.71. *pa. t. sg.* ran 4.277, 8X.15. *pl.* 14.180. [ON *renna*] See erne.

renoun *n.* renown, fame 2.243. [AN *ren(o)un*]

rent(e) *n.* income, living 1.725; profit 9.86. *pl.* rentes revenues 16.208. [OF *rente*]

reodien *v.* make an effort, strive 19.93. [OA *a-reodian* adapt, effect]

reowe *v.* 8F.29; reu 14.146; rewen 12.194. (1) cause sorrow to, grieve 6.235, 8M.7, S.2, 12.99. (2) have pity (*on* or *of*) 6.114, 8D.24, 14.146, 15.23; *tr.* take pity on 8D.7. *pr. 3 sg.* reweþ, -th 6.235, 8S.2, 4. *subj. sg.* rewe 12.99. *imper. sg.* reu 15.23; rew(e) 6.114, 8D.7, 24, L.13, 32. [OE *hrēowan*, pers. and impers.]

reowðe. See reut.

reowðful *adj.* pitiful 19.136. [reut+-ful]

rerde *n.* voice 5.114; rorde 1. 227. [OE *réord*]

rest(e) *n.* rest, peace 1.217, 6.11, 8D.17, T.12, 9.174; (of the setting sun) 10.169. [OE *rest*]

resteð *pr. 3 sg. refl.* rests 12.71, remains 18.153. *imper. sg.* **reste** (= *rest þe*) in ∼ *wel*, a form of greeting 15.1. *pa. t. sg. refl.* **reste** remained, hung 8K.19. *pl.* **resten** rested 7.238, 248. [OE *restan*]

resting *n.* peace of mind 8D.14. [from prec.]

resun ; reu. See **reisun ; reowe.**

reuliche *adv.* piteously 5.107, 6.302 (see **biginne**). [OE *hrēowlīce*]

reut *n.* pity 14.99; **reuþe** matter for pity, pitiful sight 3.239, 11.22; *haue* ∼ *of* pity 6.318; **roupe** sorrow, grief 18.392; **roupe** in *to* ∼ pitiably 8D.8. [reowe + OE noun suff. -*þ(u)*]

reue *n.* bailiff 5.26. [OE *ge-rēfa*]

reue *v.* rob, steal from 3.18; **reauin** 18.350; *to* ∼ to be stolen 18.602. *pr. 3 sg.* **reueþ** (with dat. of pers.) 8D.33; **reaueð** 18.348. *pa. t. sg.* **reuede, ræuede** 16.302, 126. *pl.* **ræueden** 16.184. [OE *rēafian*]

reuestede *pa. t. sg. refl.* put on his vestments 11.55. [OF *revestir*]

rew, rewe(n). See **reowe.**

ribe *n.* rib 5.41. *pl.* **ribbes** 4.327. [OE *ribb*]

rich(e) *adj.* of high rank, noble, powerful, great 1.728, 2.39, 7.17, 10.32; **rice** 16.110, 137; **rike** 14.9; rich, prosperous 2.41; as *n. pl.* in inclusive phr. ∼ *an poure* everyone 1.340; costly, precious 2.214, 6.166, 19.227; splendid 3.1, 132, 6.21, 7.44, 8E.11; excellent 9.55. *sup.* **ricchest(e)** mightiest 10.54, 173; **richest** 18.604. [OE *rīce* and OF *riche*; ON *rik-r*]

riche *n.* kingdom 1.515, 10.141,

13.6; *dat.* **richen** 10.68; **rice** earldom 16.307. [OE *rīce*]

richt, ricthe. See **ri3t(e)** *adj.*

riclic *adv.* richly 15.62. [OE *rīclīce*]

ride(n), ryde(n) *v.* ride *intr.* 10.1, 15, 8E.1, 47; ∼ *or go* ride or walk, i.e. move 3.162; *tr.* 8L.12. *pr. 3 sg. tr.* **rideþ** rides over 2.91. *pr. p.* **ridend** 16.196; **ridinde** 10.264. *pa. t. pl.* **ride** 11.112; **ridone** 16.53. [OE *rīdan*; pa. t. pl. *ridon*]

rifte *n.* veil 10.241. [OE *rift*]

rig *n.* back 4.202; **rug** 1, n. to 132. [OE *hrycg*, ON *hrygg-r*]

rightly *adv.* correctly 14.42. [OE *rihtlīce*]

rigolage *n.* loose living 14.49. [OF]

rigten. See **riht.**

ri3t *adv.* 1.76, 5.274, 7.41; **ri3th** 2.120; **riht, ryht** 1.694, 8D.24, 16.42, 19.247; **rihht** 13.207; **rigt** 12.16; **right** 14.128; **rith** 4.2. straight, directly 2.120, 7.54, 19.247; at once 1.694; straight in front 12.16; rightly, correctly 8D.24, F.28, L.17, 18. 191; just, right, exactly 1.76, 4.2, 139, 5.274, 7.114, 13.207, 16.42; ∼ *ase, so* just as 7.107, 1.80, as if 1.222; fully, all the way 4.332, 14.128; very 7.23. [OE *rihte*]

ri3t(e) *n.* 1.120, 144, 9.62; **riht(e)** 16.11, 18.342, 19.209; **right** 14.29. right, justice 1.414, 14.29, 16.11, 18.342; what is right 1.120, 153, 19.209; deserts 19.56; administering justice 18.338; just judgement 1.144, 19.213. *be gode* ∼ justly 16.300; *mid* ∼ fittingly 1.140, 328, fairly 1.350, justly 16.25; *þour3* ∼ deservedly 3.156; *þro3, wiþ* ∼ by right 9.171, 62. *pl.* **ri3te** deserts, what is proper 1.88; **ri3ttes** just actions 2.45. [OE *riht*]

 riȝt(e) *adj.* 1.170, 7.8, 9.86;
riht(e) 10.25, 18.200, 19.210;
rihht(e) 13.138, 199; richt
17.187; ricthe 4.114; rigte
12.34; rithe 4.40. (1) right
(opposed to left) 4.239, 10.25,
19.210. (2) direct 1.170, 4.40,
13.199; straight 12.34. (3) right,
proper, fitting 1.135, 7.75, 9.86;
correct, true 7.8, 12.192, 13.138;
just 1.200, 19.225; mere 1.212.
[OE *riht*]
riht *v.* aim at, strike 4.253 (note);
rigten straighten 12.65. *pr.
subj. sg.* rihte correct 19.15;
instruct 19.161. [OE *rihtan*; cf.
MDu *rechten* aim]
ryhtfulnesse *n.* virtue 8K.46.
[from OE *rihtful*]
rihtwise *adj.* righteous, just
19.217. [OE *rihtwīs*]
Rihtwis(s)nesse *n.* (personified)
Righteousness, Justice 19.42,
198; rihht- just conduct 13.284.
[OE *rihtwīsnes(se)*]
rike; rikenin. See rich(e);
reccnenn.
rim *n.* hoar-frost 10.264. [OE
hrīm]
rim(e), ryme *n.* rhyme 14.23,
7.186; poem 14.87. *pl.* rimes
poems 14.1, 86. [OF *rime*]
rind(e) *n.* bark 1.382, 9.76. [OE
rind]
rine *v.* rain, fall 10.156. [OE
rīnan]
ringe *v.* ring, toll 5.251. *pa. t. sg.*
rong 11.156. *pl.* ringden 16.
84. [OE *hringan* wk.]
riot *n.* debauchery 14.48. [OF
riote]
ripe *adj.* mature 1.167. [OE
rīpe]
rippe *n.* basket 4.159. [ON
hrip]
ris(e), rys *n.* branch, leafy spray
1.19, 53, 8v.2, 9.8; stem 8D.
32. *pl. (dat.)* rise 1.622. [OE
hrīs]
rise *v.* rise 4.287; arise, come

about 4.93. *pr. p.* risindde
17.7 (note). *pa. t. sg.* ras rose
14.289. *pl.* ras sprang 14.282;
risen rebelled 16.136. [OE
rīsan, rās, rison]
rith; rithe. See riȝt; riȝt(e).
riuer *n.* river 9.149. *pl.* riuers
9.45. [AN *rivere*]
riwle *n.* rule 18.225. [OF *riule*]
rixan *v.* reign 16.305. [OE
rīcsian]
rixleoð *pr. 3 sg.* rules, has power
10.54; rixleð 18.121, 19.267,
420. [OE *rīxlian*; cf. prec.]
rixlunge *n.* rule, power 18.120.
[from prec.]
ro *n.*[1] quiet, rest, peace 6.291,
8F.30. [ON *ró*]
ro *n.*[2] roe 8D.17. [OE *rā*]
robbeð *pr. 3 sg.* robs 18.348.
pa. t. sg. robbed carried off
2.59. *pl.* robbede robbed 11.
69. *pp.* irobbet 19.29. [OF
rob(b)er]
rob(b)erie *n.* plunder: *dude al
to ~* plundered everything 11.
166; robbery 17.120. [OF
roberie]
robes *n. pl.* robes, gowns 2.221,
8F.16. [OF *robe*]
roc *n.* distaff 15.69. [Cf. ON
rokk-r]
rodde *n.* pole 1.604. [OE *rodd*]
rode *n.*[1] rood, the Cross 6.323,
8K.19, x.14, 16.227, 18.16, 19.
266; roed in oath *bi þe holi ~*
6.254. [OE *rōd*]
rode *n.*[2] rosy colouring, pink
cheeks 8E.11; as *adj.* rosy 8E.
35; complexion 8D.32; face
8s.2; rude colour 1.321. [OE
rudu]
rode-steaf *n.* crucifix 18.368,
371. [rode[1]+staf]
rode-tacen *n.* sign of the Cross
18.384. [OE *rōde-tācen*]
rof *n.* roof 10.23. [OE *hrōf*]
roȝte. See recche[1].
Romanisshe *adj.* Roman 13.1.
[OE *rōmānisc*]

romans *n. pl.* romances, verse tales 14.2; romaunz 8E.39. [OF *romans*, AN *romaunz*]

Romescott *n.* Peter's pence, an annual tax paid to the papal see 16.16. [Cf. OE *Rōm-gesceot*]

ronde; rong. See round; ringe.

ropes *n. pl.* ropes 4.51. [OE *rāp*]

rorde. See rerde.

rose *n.* rose 1.321, 8D.32; rose-colour 8E.11. *pl.* rosis 9.79. [OE *rose* from L *rosa*]

roser *n.* rose-bush 8E.36. [AN *roser* = OF *rosier*]

rote *n.* root 8U.10, 9.73, 14.36; rotte 14.210. [LOE *rōt* from ON *rót*]

rotfest *adj.* firmly rooted 16.30. [ON *rótfast-r* adj., *-festa* v.]

roum *adv.* amply, fully 3.276. [OE *rūme*]

round *adj.* round, plump 7.153; Ronde round (table) 14.14. [AN *rund-*, OF *rōonde* (fem.)]

roune *n.* private conversation 6.71; *pl.* runes private counsels 19.333. [OE *rūn* counsel]

rouned *pa. t. sg.* whispered, talked privately 2.163. [OE *rūnian*]

rounyng *n.* private consultation 2.165. [from prec.]

route *n.* company, crowd 9.135; troop of followers, men 11.83, 106. [OF]

route; rouþe. See recche[1], reut.

rowe *n.* row 8E.64. [prob. OE *rāw*]

rowte *v.* roar, howl 4.338. [ON *rauta*]

rubie *n.* ruby 8K.46. *pl.* rubies 8E.64. [OF *rubi*]

rude. See rode[2].

rueð *pr. 3 sg.* stands on end 19.149. [obscure]

rug. See rig.

ruhre *adj. comp.* rougher 18.326. [from OE *rūh*]

rumde *pa. t. sg.* cleared 10.166. *pl.* rumede 11.14. [OE *rȳman*]

runes. See roune.

rung *imper. sg.* rise 18.371. [obscure]

russin *n.* light meal between dinner and supper 9.20. [Ir *ruisín*]

rusteð *pr. 3 sg.* rusts 18.326. [from OE *rust* n.]

sa. See so.

sacrefise *n.* sacrifice 17.43. [OF *sacrifice*]

sad *adj.* sated, weary (*of*) 14.104, 134; (with obj. infin.) 8D.5. [OE *sæd*]

sad; sæ; sæde(n), sægen; sægon, sæ3henn; sæhte; sæhtleden; sæide, sæin; sær3est, særi. See schede; se(e), so *conj.*; sai; se *v.*; sahte *n.*, *adj.*; sahtlede; sai; sori.

særinæsse *n.* sadness, sympathy 10.83. [OE *sārignes(se)*; see sori]

sæt; sagh, sahh; saght; sahe(n). See site; se *v.*; sahte *n.*; sawe.

sahte *n.* settlement 16.313; reconciliation 18.284; peace, agreement, concord 18.135, 156, 281; sæhte 16.315; saght 14.16. [LOE *seaht*, *sæht* from early ON *saht*; cf. OI *sátt*]

sahte *adj.* reconciled 8H.48; sæhte 16.142; saut in agreement 6.222; sayct 15.57. [LOE *sæht* from early ON *saht-r*; cf. OI *sátt-r*]

sahtlede *pa. t. pl.* came to terms 16.276; sathleden 16.278; sæhtleden 16.288. [formed on sahte; cf. rixleoð]

sahtnesse *n.* peace 18.138, 143; sahhtnesse reconciliation 13.246. [Cf. OE *sehtnes(se)* and sahte]

sai, say(en), saie(n) v. 3.93,
15.18, 8E.82, 3.90, 6.2; **sei(en)**
12.143, 16.130; **sægen** 16.224;
sæin 16.202; **segge(n)** 1.142,
18.52; **seggon** 16.61; **sigge(n)**
3.111, 17.135; **sugge(n)** 5.265,
10.6; **sugen** 10.324. say 3.90,
15.18; tell (of) 6.49, 14.55; mention 12.85; ∼ *on me* lay on me
6.198; *herde* ∼ heard tell, said
6.2, 16.290; *beo to* ∼ means 18.
208. *pr. 1 sg.* say, saie 14.47,
6.143; **seye** 4.322; **segge** 1.
202; **sigge** 9.21; **sugge** 10.72;
(with suffixed pron. obj.) **suget**
say it 8v.12. *2 sg.* **seis** 2.
255; **seist** 1.50; (with suffixed
pron.) **saystu** 15.63, **seistou**
2.68. *3 sg.* **seiþ, seið, seith,**
seyth 1.132, 18.92, 7.34, 17.
177; **seiz** (= -þ) 6.179; **seid**
17.258; **seit** 7.273; **sais, says**
14.257, 8M.14. *pl.* **seggen** 16.
47; **siggen** 2.31. *subj. sg.* **saie**
6.55; **segge** 1.60. *1 pl.* **sigge**
17.169. *imper. sg.* **sai, say**
3.131, 5.121; **sei(e)** 1.173,
5.229. *pa.t.sg.* **said(e)** 3.75,
14.107; **seid(e), seyde** 1.9,
4.107, 17.123; **sæide** 10.200;
seȝȝde 13.77; **sede** 1.33, 5.129;
sæde 16.266. *pl.* **seiden,**
seyde(n) 2.107, 8E.72, 17.185;
seidon 16.10; **sæidon** 16.57;
sede(n) 11.44, 17.210; **sæden**
16.122. *subj. sg.* **sede** 1.564.
pp. **said** 6.268; **seid** 4.213;
seȝȝd 13.99; **sehid** 5.210;
iseid, yseide 7.110, 2.284;
iseiid 9.117; **isæid** 10.79; **ised**
1.273. [OE *secgan; sægþ, seg(e)þ;*
sægde, sæde]
say, saiȝ; sayct; sayl; Saynt.
See **se** v.; **sahte** *adj.*; **seyl;**
Seint(e).
saisi v. seize: ∼ *to hire* take into
her hands 7.124. [OF *saisir*]
sake n. in *for* [gen.] ∼ for the
sake of 5.44. [OE *sacu*; cf. ON
fyrir sakir (with gen.) because of]

sakeð; sal(e); salde. See
shake; schal; selle.
salm n. psalm 18.380; **saume**
7.105, 267. [OA *salm*, OF *salme,*
saume]
salmwruhte n. psalmist 18.267,
648. [OA *salmwyrhta*]
saltou, saltu. See **schal.**
saluz n. greeting 18.472. [OF]
saluatiun n. salvation 18.46.
[AN assim. to L]
salue n. healing ointment 4.262,
18.298; medicine, remedy 18.
291. *pl.* **saluen** 18.2. [OA
salf(e)]
same. See **scham(e).**
samenn *adv.* together 13.34.
[OE *samen*]
sammnenn v. gather, collect
13.16. *pa. t. sg.* **somnede** 10.
247. *pp.* **isomned** 10.145, 270.
[OE *samnian, som-*; cf. prec.]
San. See **Seint(e).**
Sancte *adj.* Saint 16.74, 81,
115. [OE *sanct*] See **Seint(e).**
sandes; sang(-); Sannte,
Sant. See **sonde; song(e);**
Seint(e).
saphir n. sapphire 9.89. *pl.*
saphires 3.43. [OF]
sar(e). See **sor(e), sore.**
Sarazins n. pl. Saracens, Mos-
lems 14.16. [OF *Sar(r)azin*]
sardoines n. pl. sardonyxes 3.43.
[OF *sardoine*]
sari. See **sori.**
sarlic *adj.* sorrowful 10.233.
[OE *sārlic*]
sat; sau. See **site; se** v.
sauf *adj.* safe 7.236. [OF]
saul(e) n. soul 10.171, 14.213,
16.147; **sawle** 13.256, 18.505,
19.431; **soule** 5.252, 6.213,
7.70. *gen.* **sawle** 13.224, 18.81,
299, 460, 19.407; **soule** 8U.9;
sawles 19.1; **sowles** 12.66.
pl. **saulen** 17.171; **sawlen** 18.
55. [OE *sāwol*, pl. *sāwla*]
saume. See **salm.**
saumpul n. illustration 14.47.

[AN *essaumple*] See **ensample.**

saut. See **sahte** *adj.*

saute *v.* bring to terms, reconcile 6.220. [cf. LOE *sehtan*, OI *sætta*; see **sahte**]

sauter *n.* psalter 7.266, 276. [AN]

sauueur *n.* Saviour 14.246. [AN]

saues *pr. 3 sg.* saves, delivers 14.71. *imper. sg.* **saue** 17.150; **sauue** 17.169. *pp.* **isauued** 17.171. [AN *sa(u)ver*]

sauur *n.* scent 14.245. [AN]

saw. See **se** *v.*

sawe *n.* something said, words, tale 6.57; **sahe** 18.251. *pl.* **sahen** 19.226. [OE *sagu*, pl. *saga*]

sawle; scæ; scærp(e). See **saul(e); sche; scharp(e).**

scaftes *n. pl.* spears, lances 10.278. [OE *sceaft*]

scal; scam. See **schal; scham(e).**

scaldinde *pr. p. adj.* scalding 18.80. [from ONF *escalder*]

scanen *v. tr.* break 10.278. [OE *scǣnan*]

scantiloun *n.* gauge (for measuring thickness) 3.83. [AN *escantilun = OF *eschantillon*]

scarne *n.* scorn 18.385. [AN *escarn*]

scarniꝺ. See **scorne.**

scatered *pa. t. sg.* squandered 16.146. [app. OE *scaterian; cf. MDu *schaderen* squander, shed]

scaþe; scau, scawe; sceldes; sce(o)ne; sceort; sceouen; scerpe; sceu. See **skaþe; schawin; scheld(e); schen(e); short; shof; scharp(e); schawin.**

schad *n.* discrimination 19.199. [OE *ge-sceād*]

schadewe *n.* shadow 18.25 (note), 27, 19.168, 260; image 18.33. [OE *sceadu*, obl. *scead(u)we*]

schal *pr. 1, 3 sg.* 1.143, 3.26, 7.88, 14.35; **shal(l)** 1.355, 4.77, 6.50, 13.113; **scal** 8x.5, 10.231; **sal** 12.47, 14.67, 15.58, 17.37. *auxil.* must, have to 1.352, 3.26, 5.229, 6.144, 7.66; shall, will (forming fut.) 1.355, 4.74, 5.187, 6.50, 7.88, (*be* understood) 8Y.4; shall go (infin. understood) 1.470. *2 sg.* **schal** 7.89, 19.396; **schalt** 3.91, 14.60, 18.361; **shalt** 1.352, 2.203, 6.118; **sal(e)** 8v.12, 14.116; **salt** 15.56; (with suffixed pron.) **schaltu** 1.165; **shalt(o)u** 1.495, 2.271; **salt(o)u** 8R.1, 15.60. *pl.* **schal** 14.46; **shal** 8L.35; **sal** 14.172; **scholle** 3.27; **shole** 4.215; **solle(n)** 17.177, 254; **schule(n)** 1.631, 18.140, 19.202; **shule(n)** 4.15, 8H.18; **shulenn** 13.95; **shulle(n)** 1.516, 2.96; **scullen** 10.104; **sulen** 12.96; **ssulen** 8Y.4; **sulle** 17.202. *subj. sg.* **schille** 1.641; **shol** 4.209; **schul(l)e** 1.705, 18.619; **shul(l)e** 1.320, 13.277. *pa. t.* (1) owed (attendance) 11.95. (2) *auxil.* had to, ought to 5.267, 16.87; were to 4.193; intended (infin. of motion understood) 18.64; (*indic.* and *subj.*) should, would (forming condit. and indirect fut.) 1.54, 10.136, 11.96, 14.265, 16.185; (subj. equivalent) 2.32, 4.95, 5.75 (indef.), 7.17, 65, 16.112; (of uncertified report) 7.273, 17.14, 18. *1, 3 sg.* **scholde** 1.686, 7.17; **sscholde** 3.292; **sholde** 4.95; **shollde** 13.17; **scolde** 10.142, 16.78; **solde** 17.14; **ssolde** 11.95; **schulde** 18.64; **shuld(e)** 2.32, 5.163; **sculde** 10.53, 16.112; **suld** 14.163. *2 sg.* **sholdest** 1.54, 5.136; **shuldest** 6.432; **sculdest** 16.185. *pl.* **scholde(n)** 1.649, 7.234; **sscholden** 3.212; **sholde** 4.193; **sholldenn** 13.187; **scolden** 16.85; **solden** 17.231; **schulde(n)** 18.514, 19.

179; **shulden** 2.23, 5.264; **suld**
14.85. [OE *sceal, scealt, sculon*
(*scylon*), *scólde*]
schald. See **cold(e).**
scham(e) *n.* 1.50, 6.126;
sham(e) 4.67, 6.251, 8L.15;
scam 15.29; **same** 6.55, 12.87;
ssame 11.106; **schome** 1.123;
shome 5.35, 6.196; **scheome**
18.335, 19.133. shame 1.123,
4.67, 6.196, 8L.15; dishonour
5.99, 6.126, 15.29; insult 1.50,
18.338; shameful thing 6.55,
12.87, 15.65; injury 5.35, 58,
8L.11, 11.106. *a* ~ (with dat.) in
contempt of 1.623; *þis* ~ *me*
haueþ speken has made this
shameful charge against me
6.216. *gen.* **scheome** shameful
18.493. [OE *sceamu, sceomu*]
schamie *pr. subj. 3 sg. impers.*
cause shame to: ~ *þe* shame on
you 1.117. [OE *sceamian*]
schape *n. pl.* shapes, forms 19.
138. [OE *ge-sceap*]
scharp(e) *adj.* sharp 1.79, 109;
scærp(e) 16.172, 176; **scerpe**
10.165. [OE *scearp*]
scharpe *adv.* high 1.97. [OE
scearpe]
schawere *n.* mirror 19.262. [OE
sceáwere]
schawin *v.* 18.24, 115; **scau**
14.215; **schewen** 7.232; **schewi**
7.96; **shæwenn** 13.61; **shewe**
4.280; **sceu** 14.226; **sewi** 1.107;
schowe 6.69. (1) see 4.280;
~ *fore* ordain 16.61. (2) show
1.107, 2.234, 17.41 (it showed),
18.137, 19.270; ~ *forð* exhibit
18.25, 115; reveal, declare
6.69, 7.96, 14.172, 18.24, 19.
290; tell 14.215; *intr.* appear
17.218. *pr. 3 sg.* **schaweð**
18.25, 19.270; **seaweth** 17.176.
subj. sg. **scawe** 16.61. *pa. t. sg.*
schaw(e)de 18.137, 482, 19.
298; **shewed** 2.234; **sceud**
14.194; **seau(e)de, seawede**
17.41, 218, 231. *pp.* **sceud**

14.172; **ischawed** 19.290. [OE
sceáwian, sceáwian; scawe fore
from OE *fore-sceáwian*]
schawles *n.* scarecrow 1.606.
[app. OE **scíewels* (from *scéoh*
shy, cf. MLG *schûwelse* scarer)
re-formed on *sceáwian*]
sche *pron. 3 sg. fem.* she 3.241;
she 2.61, 135; **scæ** 16.262, 292;
scho 14.60, 78; **sco** 14.75.
[prob. OE *hīe, hēo*] See **ȝhe,**
heo.
schede *v.* distinguish 1.153. *pa.*
t. sg. **sad** shed 8T.15. [OE
sceádan, scēadan, pa. t. scéad]
scheker *n.* chess 3.98; chessboard 3.101. [AN *escheker*]
schekeð. See **shake.**
scheld(e) *n.* shield 1.671, 18.171,
19.180. *pl.* **sceldes** 10.278.
[OA *scéld*]
schen(e) *adj.* 15.45, 18.629;
shene 8L.1, 13.162; **scene**
14.193; **sceone** 10.308. beautiful, fair 8L.1, 10.308, 15.45,
18.629, 19.303; bright, shining
13.162, 14.193, 19.262. *comp.*
schenre 19.323; *predic.,* as
adv. 18.93, 95. [OA *scēne*]
schende *v.* reproach 1.210. *pa.*
t. pl. **ssende** destroyed 11.35.
pp. **ischent** put to shame 18.
118; **shend** 6.346; **ishend** destroyed 6.213; **issend** killed
11.40, 158. [OE *scéndan* shame]
schendlac *n.* shame, disgrace
19.141. [prec.+-lac]
schentfulliche *adv.* shamefully
18.640. [from **schende**]
scheome; **scheot.** See
scham(e); ssete.
schep(e) *n.* sheep 9.33, 18.241.
gen. **shepes** 4.49. *pl.* **shep**
5.167; **sep** 6.272. [OA *scēp*,
sg. and pl.]
schewen, -i; schil. See **scha-**
win; skil.
schild(e) *v.* shelter, protect
1.57, 14.260; *intr.* protect oneself 1.62. *pr. 3 sg.* **schilt** 18.519.

imper. sg. **schild** cover, hide 1.119. *pa. t. sg.* **schilde** 19.262. [OE *scildan*]

schille *adj.* shrill, piercing 1.98, 366. [OE *scyl*]

schille *adv.* shrilly 1.614. [from prec.]

schille. See **schal.**

schimmeð *pr. 3 sg.* gleams 19.241. [OE *scimian*]

schineð *pr. 3 sg.* shines, gleams 18.93, 19.241. *pl.* 19.300. *pa. t. sg.* **schon** 7.43, 176; **shon** 8G.2. [OE *scīnan, scān*]

schingles *n. pl.* shingles 9.57. [app. through AN from L *scindula*; cf. MDu *schindel(e)*]

-schipe *suff.* forming nouns denoting esp. condition or quality, as **bisi-, cniht-, frommard-, glad-.** [OE *-scipe*]

schir *adj.* pure 18.103, 405; **shir** (*predic.*, as *adv.*) bright 4.182. [OE *scīr*]

schire *n.* shire, county 7.228; **ssire** shire-court 11.9, 12. *pl.* **schirene** companies of inhabitants of counties 7.229, 237; **schires** 7.235. [OE *scīr*, pl. *scīra*]

schireð *pr. 3 sg.* purifies 18.403. [OE *scīran*]

schirme *v.* fight 1.222. [OF *eschirmir* from Gmc]

schirnesse *n.* purity 18.442. [OE *scīrnes(se)*]

scho; scholde(n), scholle; schome; schon. See **sche; schal; scham(e); schineð.**

schonde *n.* disgrace, ruin 1.610, 691; **sonde** 12.188. [OE *scónd*]

schoten; schowe. See **ssete; schawin.**

schrewe *adj.* ill-disposed, wicked 7.126. [app. OE *scréawa* shrewmouse]

schrewedenesse *n.* wickedness 7.281. [from prec. + adj. ending *-ed*]

s(s)chrichen *v.* scream 3.196,

218. *pr. 2 sg.* **schrichest** 1.179. [imit.]

schrift(e) *n.* confession 19.84; absolution after confession 4.256; **srift** 5.186, 196. [OE *scrift*] Cf. **sriue.**

schrine *n.* shrine 7.280. [OE *scrīn*]

schul-. See **schal.**

schulle *n.* plaice 4.27. [MDu *schulle*]

schuncheð *pr. 3 sg.* starts aside, shies 18.29. [obscure; cf. *Iuliene* p. 164] See **ashunche.**

schunien *v.* shun, avoid 19.200, 392; **sunen** 12.103, 130. *pr. 3 sg.* **schuniet** 1.185; **suneð** 12.87. [OE *scunian*]

schute. See **ssete.**

scilwis *adj.* discerning; as *n. pl.* perceptive men 14.33. [ON *skilvíss*; see **skil**]

scynnes; scip(-). See **sin(ne); ship.**

scipmen *n. pl.* sailors 10.159. [OE *scipmann*]

scyrte *pa. t. sg.* ran short 16.71. [OE *scyrtan*]

sckile; sclæn; sco; scolde(n). See **skil; sle(n); sche; schal.**

scole *n.* school, university 8L.29, 15.28, 41. [OE *scōl*]

scorne *v.* mock, deride 3.228. *imper. pl.* **scarnið** 18.117. [AN *escarnir*; *-o-* unexplained] See **scarne.**

scort. See **short.**

Scotte *n. pl. gen.* of Scots 16.2. [OE *Scotta* from *Scottas*]

scripen *v.* go, fly 10.165. [OE *scrīþan*]

scrowe *n.* scroll 18.308. [AN *escrowe*]

scul-. See **schal.**

scureð *pr. 3 sg.* scours 18.327. [prob. MDu *schuren* from OF *escurer*]

se *pron. 3 sg. masc.* he, the one 17.104, 159. [OE *sē*] See **þe** *pron.*

se *pron. rel.* who 16.9. [OE *se*]
See **þe** *def. art.*

se. See **so**; **þe** *art.*

se, see(n), sen(e), *v.* see, look
at 6.165, 8D.6, 11.22, 2.308,
204, 206, 3.35, 134; **seo(n)** 7.52,
8E.60, 19.329; ~ *þine herte blood*
kill you 2.310. *pr. 1 sg.* **se** 3.77,
4.307, 6.319; **she** 8w.1; **so** 1.34.
3 sg. **seeþ** 2.92, 9.127; **seð** 12.
13; **syþt** (= *syȝt*) 8N.11. *pl.*
seeþ 9.159; **sen** 12.171; **seoð**
18.192, 19.288, 331. *subj. sg.*
seo 18.536. *imper. sg.* **se** 3.242,
~ *to* look (with favour) upon
8T.5. *pa. t. sg.* **sagh** 14.153;
sahh 13.103; **seghȝ** 3.197; **seh**
19.371; **saiȝ** 7.84; **seiȝ** 2.218;
say 4.147; **sei, sey** 5.216,
281, 11.59, 14.209; **sau** 14.216;
saw 4.220, 275. *pl.* **sægon**
16.50, 64; **sæȝhenn** 13.73;
seghe(n) 17.27 (note), 114, 193;
seȝen 8E.72; **seiȝ** 2.105;
seie(n), seye 7.159, 11.158, 38.
subj. sg. **seȝe** 8E.15, 82 (watched
over), L.27; **sehe** 18.40, 45, 19.
256; **soȝe** 12.144. *pp.* **sægon**
16.59; **segon** 16.54; **seȝhenn**
13.66; **sen(e)** 3.226, 12.69, 14.
92; **syen** 15.46; see also **ise.**
[OE *sēon*; *sihþ*; *se(a)h, sæh*;
sāwon, sēgon; *segen*; adj. *ge-sēne*,
see **sene**]

se(e) *n.* sea 1.712, 4.99, 8G.35,
10.313, 12.162, 17.153; the
ocean 9.1; *on* ~ at sea 12.169;
sæ 10.40; *ouer* ~ abroad 16.46,
76; **sea** 18.28, 461. *gen.* **sees**
12.165. [OE *sǣ*]

sea-dingle *n.* deep of the sea-
bed 19.334. [se(e)+*dingle* of
obscure origin; see *OED*]

seau-, seaw-. See **schawin.**

seauinge *n.* sign, token 17.6;
seywinge 17.35. [cf. OE *scēa-
wung*]

sec; secc. See **sukeð;
swich(e).**

seche(n) *v.* seek, look for, search

(for) 1.717, 7.201, 202, 8M.10,
17.39, 18.130, 19.35; **sekenn**
13.188; **secen** go to, visit 16.97.
pr. 3 sg. **sekeð** 12.10. *pl.*
secheþ, -ð, -z try to reach (with
to) 1.346; aim at 18.495; visit
7.256. *subj. sg.* **seche** 19.68. *1 pl.*
seke 12.100. *pr. p.* **sechinde**
19.172. *imper. pl.* **secheȝ** 17.22.
pa. t. sg. **sohvte** 5.69; **soþte**
(= *soȝte*) 8w.15. *pl.* **souȝten**
7.220. *pp.* **sout** 6.423; **soht**
attacked 8K.57; **isouȝt** visited
7.217. [OE *sēcan, sŏhte*]

sed *n.* seed 8A.3, 12.73. [OE *sǣd*]

sede(n). See **sai.**

sedwale *n.* zedoary, an aromatic
plant 9.74. [AN *zedewale* from
Arab *zedwār*]

segge *n.* sedge 1.18. [OE *secg*]

segge(n), -on. See **sai.**

segges *n. pl.* cuttlefish 4.162.
[OF *sèche*]

seghe(n), seghȝ, segon. See
se *v.*

se-grund *n.* bottom of the sea
12.159. [se(e)+**grounde**]

**seȝe(n), seȝhenn, seh(e);
seȝȝd(e), sehid, seid(-),
seyde(n); sei, seie(n), seye;
seiȝ, seiz.** See **se** *v.*; **sai**; **se,
sai.**

seyl, sayl *n.* 4.122, 126. [OE
segl]

Seint(e) *adj.* (prefixed to names)
Saint 4.200, 7.3, 96, 11.156,
17.5, 18.69, 112; **Saynt** 15.2, 7;
Sein 18.70, 110; **Sannte** 13.28,
129; **Sant** 15.13; **San** 15.38.
seinte (F) holy 19.422 (see
charité). [OF *saint*] See
sancte.

**seis(t), seistou, seiþ, seit(h);
seywinge.** See **sai**; **seauinge.**

sek(e) *adj.* sick, ill 5.41, 6.199,
18.574; **seoc** 10.9, 45. as *n. pl.*
sike (the) sick 17.63. [OE *sēoc*]

seke(-). See **seche(n).**

seknesse *n.* sickness 6.200. [OE
sēocnes(se)]

sel(e) *adj.* good 10.introd., 83.
pl. gen. selere 10.180. [back-
formation from OE *sēlra, sēlest*
comp., sup.]
selcut *n.* wonder 14.102. [next]
selcuth *adj.* various, different
14.23. [OE *seldcūþ* rare]
selden *adv.* seldom 3.208, 8D.5;
seldum 12.71. [OE *séldan*]
sele *n.* seal 4.23. [OE *se(o)lh,
sēol-*]
self *adj.* 3.115, 14.124; selua, -e
16.55, 54; seolf(e) 1.637, 19.9;
seolue(n) 10.42, 18.115, 19.5;
sulfe, sulue 1.492, 69. same,
selfsame 3.115, 16.20, 55; very
1.69, 492, 637, 16.54; (emphasizing a n.) himself: ~ *þe mon* man
himself 19.9, *Godd* ~ 19.256;
(emphasizing a pron., *me, þe, us*)
10.42, 78, 18.309, 19.133; (refl.
with pron.) 10.253, 19.5, 214;
see out(e) of. as *n.* in *þi* ~ your
body 14.170. See also hemself,
himself, hireseolf, miself.
[OE *self(a), selfan, -um,* nWS
seolf-]
selhðe *n.* happiness 18.626, 637;
selþe in *wiþ* ~ happily 8H.48.
[OE *sǽlþ; -h-* after *murhðe,* see
murþe]
seli *adj.* unfortunate, poor 6.315,
337; as *n. pl.* (the) blessed 19.
315. [OE *ge-sǽlig*]
selk(e). See swich(e).
selle *v.* sell 4.31; sulle(n) 18.
615; *to* ~ to be sold 18.602, 616.
pr. 3 sg. suleð 18.614. *imper. sg.*
sule 18.390. *pa. t. sg.* salde
18.629; solde 4.85. *pp.* sold
3.150, 4.43. [OE *sellan,* LWS
syllan; pa. t. A *sálde*]
sellice; selþe; selua, -e;
seluer, selure. See seolliche;
selhðe; self; siluer.
semblant *n.* looks, demeanour
18.217, 19.21. [OF]
sembli. See semly.
seme *v.* arbitrate between 1.143.
[OE *sēman*]

semest *pr. 2 sg.* seem 8L.33. *3 sg.*
semeþ suits, is becoming 8E.28.
[ON *sóma* befit, pa. t. subj.
sœmdi, infl. by *sœma* honour and
next]
semly *adj.* fair, beautiful 8K.6;
as *n.* beautiful creature 8D.6;
sembli 9.66. [ON *sœmiligr* be-
coming]
send, sende(n) *v.* send 8H.43,
14.163, 2.159, 10.138; ~ *affter,
efter* send for 6.412, 10.134,
16.108. *pr. 1 sg.* sende 8W.52.
3 sg. sent 17.247, 18.107, 250,
19.62. *subj. sg.* send(e) 6.236,
7.285, 10.93, 14.135, 15.33,
18.273. *imper. sg.* sent 8D.15,
K.2. *pl.* sendeð 18.98. *pa. t. sg.*
sende 7.123, 170, 10.127, 16.45;
sent a message 11.29; sente
17.209; senden 10.118. *pl.*
sende(n) 11.27, 16.134. *pp.*
send 6.214, 14.160; sennd
13.81; isend 11.11; ysent
2.313. [OE *séndan*]
sendal *n.* a kind of fine silk 3.274.
[OF *cendal*]
senden *pr. pl.* are 12.27; sunden
10.117. [OE *sindon,* nWS *seon-
don*] Cf. ar(e), be(n), and other
parts.
sene *adj.* apparent, evident 8L.2,
M.15. [OA *ge-sēne*]. See se.
senid *pa. t. sg. refl.* crossed himself 14.155. [OE *sĕ(g)nian*]
senne; sent(e); seo; seoc;
seolf(e), seolue(n). See
sin(ne); send; se; sek(e);
self.
seolliche *adj.* rare, wonderfu
1.567; as *n.* sellice wonderful
thing 16.47. [OE *sel(d)lic,
syllic*]
seoluer; seon, seoð; seoðe(n),
seoððe(n); seouene. See
siluer; se, soþ(e); siþ;
seuene.
seouenfald *adj.* sevenfold 19.
317. [OA *seofonfáld*]
seoueniht *n.* a week 16.28.

[seuene+niȝt(e); cf. OE *seofon-nihte* adj.]

seoueðe. See seuenþe.

seoueuald *adv.* seven times 18.623, 19.323. [as seouenfald]

sep. See schep(e).

sere *adj.* various, diverse 14.2, 12. [ON *sér*, pron. dat. sg., for or by oneself, separately]

serekin *adj.* of various kinds, diverse 14.21. [prec.+kinn; cf. alkyn]

sereue, serewe(s). See soru.

sergant *n.* servant 17.189; seriaunt 3.9. *pl.* serganz 17.95; seriaunts 3.7. [OF *serja(u)nt*]

serpent *n.* snake 9.31. [OF]

serue(n) *v.* attend upon 3.8; assist at mass 8x.10; serui, servi serve 17.82, 224 (note), 8w.44. *pr. 3 sg.* serueð 18.460; seruiþ serves (a purpose) 9.47. *pl.* seruið 18.461, 19.278. *subj. sg.* serue 2.303; serui 17.225. *pa. t. sg.* seruede 3.289. *pl.* seruede(n) 17.210, 241; (with *of*) dispensed 17.95. *pp.* iserued 17.105. [OF *servir*]

seruest *pr. 2 sg.* (with *affter*) deserve 6.197. *pa. t. pl.* seruede 4.341. [shortened from OF *deservir*] Cf. ofseruet.

seruise *n.* service 17.176, 205. [OF]

se-sond *n.* sand of the sea 12.146. [se(e)+sond]

set, sette(n) *v.* set, place, put 9.168, 6.62 (see spel); bestow 14.89; instal 16.98; settenn establish 13.246; set down 13.274; ∼ *a, on, fyre* set on fire, see fir(e); ∼ *upp* draw up 13.13. *pr. 3 sg.* sett *refl.* in *on knowe hym* ∼ kneels 2.123. *subj. sg.* sette plant 8u.10. *imper. sg.* sete put 8n.26, 18.620. *pa. t. sg.* sette 2.27, 10.31, 13.161, 14.159 (see spel); planted 7.93; applied 16.208; *intr.* in ∼ *to*

fleme took to flight 10.32; (with suffixed pron., see es) setes set them 4.52. *pl.* sette(n) 2.101, 3.187, 16.84; *refl.* lay 3.275; ∼ *togadere* agreed 7.230; settenn agreed 13.184. *pp.* set(te), sett 4.344, 8e.28; seated 2.122; decreed 13.19, 267; *wel* ∼ well spent 4.173; isæt 10.58; iset(te), ysette 18.215, 2.129; appointed 18.338, 339; settled, appeased 18.277. [OE *settan*]

sete(n); sethþe. See site; siþ.

setnesse *n.* order, class 19.315. [OE (*ge*)*setnes(se*)]

settle *n.* seat 16.84. [OE *setl*]

seuene *adj.* seven 12.14; seue 7.15, 9.179; seouene 18.122. [OE *seofon*]

seuenþe *adj.* seventh 4.252, 7.9; seoueðe 18.191, 19.320. [OE *seofoða*, partly re-formed on seuene]

se-weres *n. pl.* enclosures for catching fish 4.52 (note). [se(e)+OE wer weir; OE once *sǣ-wær*]

sewi; sexe. See schawin; sixe.

Sexisne *adj. acc. masc.* Saxon 10.171. [OE *Se(a)xisc*]

sh-. See also sch-.

shæwenn. See schawin.

shake *v. intr.* move, go 8n.11. *pr. 3 sg.* sakeð 12.87; schekeð trembles 19.149. [OE *sc(e)acan*]

shal(l); sham(e). See schal; scham(e).

shankes *n. pl.* shins, legs 4.330. [OE *scanca*]

shap-; she. See shop; sche, se *v.*

shenche *v.* pour out 2.130. [OE *scencan*]

shend; shene; shep(es). See schende; schen(e); schep(e).

sheres *n. pl.* shears 4.125. [OE *scēar* (sg.)]

shereþ *pr. 3 sg.* swerves 8n.4. [obscure]

shewe. See schawin.

shides *n. pl.* split pieces of wood, billets 4.183. [OE *scīd*]

shiling *n. pl.* (uninflected after numeral) shillings 6.270. [OE *scilling*]

ship *n.* ship 4.3; scip(e) in *in* ~ 16.119, *to* ~ 10.158 aboard ship; ssipe 17.145. *pl.* sipes 12.169; scipen 10.122, 165. [OE *scip*, pl. *scipu*]

shir. See schir.

shirte *n.* shirt 4.36. [OE *scyrte*]

shoddreþ *pr. 3 sg.* trembles 8N.4. [cf. MDu *schûderen*]

shof *pa. t. sg.* shoved, pushed 4.138, 158. *pp.* sceouen moved forward 10.314. [OE *sceāf*, *scofen* from *scūfan*]

shol(e), shol(l)de(nn). See schal.

sholdres *n. pl.* shoulders 4.245; shuldre 8K.26. [OE *sculdor*, pl. *sculdru*]

shome; shon. See scham(e); schineð.

shon *n. pl.* shoes 4.128, 6.225. [OE *scō(h)*, pl. *scōs*, gen. *scōna*]

shop *pa. t. sg.* made, turned (into) 6.354; shup created 8H.14. *pp.* shapenn created 13.282; shaped ordained 8F.44. [OE *scōp*, *scapen* from *sc(i)eppan*]

short *adj.* short 1.73; scort 16. 171; sceort small 10.314. [OE *sc(e)ort*]

shoten; shul- ; shuldre ; shup. See ssete ; schal ; sholdres ; shop.

shupping *n.* decree 8F.45. [from OE (LWS) *scyppan* create, destine; cf. shop]

si. See is ; þe *art.*

sib *n.* peace 16.315; sibbe family, stock 13.46. [OE *sibb* kinship, peace]

sibreden *n.* consanguinity 16.39. [prec.+-rede(n)]

syc, siche; siche. See sike(n); swich(e).

sicles *n. pl.* shekels 18.630. [OF *sicle* ult. from Heb]

side *n.* side 7.260; (of the body) 4.271, 8E.76, X.15, 18.538; part 1.307. *pl.* sides 4.277, 327; siden 18.513, 515. [OE *sīde*]

syde *adj.* long, flowing 8F.16. [OE *sīd*]

syen; sigge(n). See se *v.*; sai.

signefiance *n.* meaning 17.69, 116. [OF]

signefieth *pr. 3 sg.* signifies 17.44; signefied, -et 17.54, 123, 61. [OF *signifier*]

siȝt(e) *n.* 9.82, 11.119; syht 8K.6; sigte 12.55; sight 14.151, sihðe 18.421, 19.17, 136; sihhþe 13.118. sense of sight, vision 14.172, 19.17, 290; power of seeing 12.55, 13.118; view 14.151, 204, 18.424; what one sees 19.373; sight, thing seen 9.25, 11.119, 14.195, 19.136; appearance 9.6, 18.421; *Godes* ~ the sight of God 19.328. *on, to* ~ to look at 8K.6, 9.48. [OE *ge-siht*, *(ge)sihþ*]

syk(e) *n.* sighing 8G.48, (personified) L.5; sigh 8M.6. *pl.* sikes 18.311. [OE *sice* infl. by next]

sike(n) *v.* sigh 5.195, 6.260; siche 7.64; syc 8W.30. *pa. t. sg.* siȝt(e) 1.559, 3.74. *pp.* siked 8M.6. [OE *sīcan* str., re-formed on *tǣcan*, &c.]

sike. See sek(e).

siker(e) *adj.* sure, assured, confident 5.58, 19.122, 367; secure, safe 12.100, 18.172; trustworthy 18.260; ~ *to deye* certain to die 3.266; *make me* ~ give me assurance 6.240; ~ *of* confident with respect to 19.203. [OE *sicor*]

sikerliche *adv.* confidently 17. 166; safely, securely 19.193; certainly, assuredly 18.85, 673, 19.312; sikerlike 12.54. [LOE *sicorlīce*]

sikernesse *n.* confidence 19.212; security 19.319. [LOE *sicornes(se)*]

Sykyng *n.* Sighing (personified) 8K.58, 62. [from **sike(n)**]

silk, sylk *n.* silk 3.274, 8E.76, 9.150. [OE *seol(o)c*, adj. *silcen*]

silk. See **swich(e)**.

siluer, syluer *n.* silver 2.219, 16.147; **sylure** 16.130; **seluer** 3.132; **selure** 17.71; **seoluer** 10.252, 18.327, 631; money 4.86. [OE *seolfor, silofr*, &c.]

simenels *n. pl.* a kind of loaves or buns 4.47. [OF *simenel*]

sin(ne), syn(ne) *n.* sin 12.105, 14.125, 71, 15.65, 8F.16; **sunne** 1.523, 5.165, 6.334, 8v.5, 18.121, 19.82; **senne** 17.67, 166; *þou hauest mikel* ~ you sin gravely 6.194. *pl.* **sinnes** 12.38, 16.203; **sinness** 13.86; **scynnes** 15.74; **sennes** 8w.56; **sunnen** 1.518, 5.177, 18.14, 19.79. [OE *synn*, pl. *synna*]

sinful *adj.* sinful 12.45, 186; **sunful** 7.284. [OE *synnful*]

sing, syng, singe(n) *v.* sing 9.100, 8G.19, 1.39, 455, 5.252, 6.401, 8v.3; **singin** 1.542. *pr. 1 sg.* **singe, synge** 1.229, 8w.11. *2 sg.* **singes** 8A.11; **singest, singist, singst** 1.247, 175, 531. *3 sg.* **syngeþ** 2.174; **singet** 1.152; **singað** 16.49; **singuth** 7.105; **singþ** 1.467; **singes** 8M.1. *pl.* **singeþ, -eð** 1.341, 548, 19.282; **singet** 8v.1. *subj. sg.* **singe** 1.182, 534. *pl.* 1.521. *pr. p.* **singinde** 1.515. *imper. sg.* **sing** 8A.2. *pa. t. sg.* **song** 1.20, 680. *pl.* **sungen** 1.621, 16.83; **sunnŋenn** 13.104. [OE *singan, sáng, súngon*]

singularité *n.* individual distinction 18.230; separate way 18.239. [OF]

sinke(n), synke *v.* sink *intr.* go down 5.80, 239; fall 8F.16; *doð hem* ~ submerges them 12.180.

pp. tr. **isunken** 10.246. [OE *sincan, gesuncen*]

synt *conj.* since 15.31. [contracted from *sin* (= *siðen*) *that*]

siouns *n. pl.* shoots 9.74. [AN *ciun*]

sipes. See **ship**.

sir(e) *n.* lord, master 6.75; father 15.3; (as address) sir, sire 2.55, 133, 14.110, 15.2; *leue* ~ 2.141, 4.175; (prefixed to name) 2.95, 5.37. [OF *sire*]

site *n.* sorrow, grief 14.274. [ON **sýt* var. of *sút*; cf. *sýta* grieve]

site, sitte(n) *v.* sit 6.308, 1.218, 5.281, 6.50, 7.149, 19.274. *pr. 2 sg.* **sittest** 1.89. *3 sg.* **sit, syt** 1.86, 8N.7, 19.54; ~ *uuele* goes badly 18.430. *pl.* **sitteþ** 1.640. *pr. p.* **sittende** seated 19.313; living 16.186. *imper. sg.* **sit(e)** 4.188, 6.28, 18.365. *pl.* **sitteð** 10.91. *pa. t. sg.* **sat** 1.15, 2.279, 5.30, 10.9; (of a court) 11.12; lay (of a ship) 4.3; **sæt** remained 10.82. *pl.* **seten** 4.193, 5.32. *subj. sg.* **sete** 7.161, 12. 146. [OE *sittan; sæt; sæton*, A *séton*]

siþ(e), sith, syth *n.* time, occasion 1.241, 6.258, 14.202; lifetime, in *his* ~ in his life 14.264. *pl.* **sithes** times 3.71; **siþe, syþe, sioe** orig. *gen.* in *fele* ~ 4.46, *fyfty* ~ 8L.23, *hundret, þusent,* ~ 19.111, 156. [OE *siþ*]

siþ, siþe(n), siðen, sythen *adv.* afterwards, then 9.143, 4.237, 241, 12.34, 16.193; **siððan, siðþen, siððon** 16.19, 79, 19; **seoðe(n)** 10.311, 19.239; **seoððe(n)** 10.31, 103, 18.330; **sethþe** 7.95, 281; **soþþe** 1.240; **suþþe** 11.18; since 14.120, 145. [OE *siþþan, seoþþan*; ON *síðan*]

siðen *conj.* after, when 12.5, 6; **sothent** 8v.18. [as prec.; *sothent* = *seothen that*]

syþt. See **se** *v.*

siweden *pa. t. pl.* followed, pur-

sued 7.244. *pp.* siwed 8K.62.
[AN *suer, siwer,* = *sivre, siu-*]
siwte *n.* attendance at court 11.
95. [AN *siute*]
sixe *adj., n.* six 4.251; sexe in ~
and seuene 12.14 (note). [OE
six, nWS *sex*]
sixte *adj.* sixth 4.247. [OE *sixta*]
sixtene *adj.* sixteen 4.156. [OE
sixtēne]
sixti *adj.* 4.195, 10.146, 180.
[OE *sixtig*]
skapeþ *pr. 3 sg.* (with fut. sense)
will escape 2.296. [shortened
from ascape]
skaþe *n.* harm, injury 2.271;
scaþe suffering 6.235. [ON
skaði]
skentinge *n.* entertainment 1.
324, pleasure 393. [from ON
skemta amuse]
skere *v.* clear (of a charge) 1.570.
[rel. to ON *skær-r* clean]
sky *n.* sky 14.205. *pl.* skies
clouds 12.14 (note). [ON *ský*
cloud]
skil *n.* something reasonable 6.
52; sckile discrimination, reason 1.142; schil reasoning 14.
191. [ON *skil* distinction]
skinbon *n.* shin-bone 12.120.
[OE *scinbān* adapted to dialects
with *sk-* for *sc-*; cf. NFris *sken-*.
But app. an error for *chin-*;
see note]
slade *n.* valley 14.123. *pl.*
slades 10.187. [OE *slæd*]
slæn, slain; slæp. See sle(n);
slep(e).
slake *pr. 1 sg.* grow weak 8K.81.
[OE *slacian*]
slawe. See sle(n).
slawðe *n.* sloth 18.178, 394.
[OE *slǣwþ* re-formed on *slāw*]
sle(n) *v.* kill 7.24, 28; slæn 10.
64, 95; slo(n) 6.184, 8K.63,
L.20, 17.26. *pr. 3 sg.* sleað
kills 18.168. *subj. sg.* slo
8D.16. *pa. t. sg.* slogh 14.214;
sloh 10.167, 18.632, struck 10.

283; slou 11.41; slow 4.234.
pl. sloghen 16.238; slouȝen
2.115; slowe in *to grounde* ~
struck (men) down 11.99. *subj.
sg.* slowe 8F.40. *pp.* slain 6.
310; slawe 4.230; islaȝe(n)
10.176, 285; yslaw(ȝ)e 2.290,
295; islein 18.53, 500, 19.132.
[OE *slēan,* ONb *slā,* ON *slá*;
OE *slōg, slōh*; *slōgon*; *slagen,
slegen*]
sley, sleie *adj.* crafty, shrewd
5.262, 6.159. [ON *slœg-r*]
sleilich *adv.* skilfully 9.158.
[from prec.]
slep(e) *n.* sleep 5.267, 8K.81,
10.12, 17.31, 18.360; *an* ~ asleep
16.119, *o* ~ 19.61; *to* ~ 17.147;
slæp in *æt þe forme* ~ when
people had just gone to sleep
16.63. [OE *slǣp,* A *slēp*]
slepe(n) *v.* sleep 7.78, 234,
8Q.2, 16.178. *pr. 3 sg.* slepiþ
9.173. *subj. sg.* slepe 19.27.
pr. p. slepinde sleepily 18.366.
pa. t. sg. slep 16.201. [OE
slǣpan, A *slēpan*; *slēp*]
slete *n.* sleet 9.39. [prob. OA
slēt rel. to MLG *slôte*]
slete *v.* bait (with dogs) 5.289.
[OE *slǣtan*]
sleuis *n. pl.* sleeves 9.126. [OA
slēfe]
sli *adj.* such 14.66. [ON *slík-r*]
Cf. swich(e).
sliddrunge *n.* slipping 18.176.
[from OE *slidrian*]
sliden *v.* slip, fall 18.175. *pr. 3 sg.*
slit, slyt 18.173, 8N.3. *pp.*
islide 1.432. [OE *slīdan, sliden*]
slitte *n.* opening of a pocket:
vnder þi ~ in your pocket 3.104.
[OE *slite*]
slo *n.* sloe; *ne is me nouth a* ~
I don't care a fig 4.117. [OE
slā(h)]
slo(n), slogh(en), sloh. See
sle(n).
slogh, slogth *n.* track 14.118,
127, 149. [ON *slóð*]

slong *pa. t. sg.* threw, flung 7.283, 11.18. [ON *slǫng* from *slyngva*]

slou(ʒen), slow(e). See **sle(n).**

sloweste *adj. sup.* slowest 8N.12. [OE *slāw*]

slubbri *adj.* slippery 18.173. [cf. LG *slibberig*]

smæt. See **smite(n).**

smakke *n.* flavour 9.77. [OE *smæc*]

smal(e) *adj.* small, little 1.64, 213, 5.155, 248, 12.157; **smeale** 19.80; weak 1.678; slender 1.160, 8E.62, 73, K.29; thin 1.73, 236. [OE *smæl, smal-*]

smaragde *n.* emerald 9.91. [OF]

smart *adj.* painful 14.58. [OE *smeart*]

smeal; smeale. See **smell; smal(e).**

smeallunge *n.* (sense of) smell 19.18. [prob. from OE **smellan*]

smech *n.* smoke, vapour, fume 17.55, 58. *pl. gen.* **smeche** 19.101. [OA *smēc*]

smechunge *n.* taste 19.17. [from OA *ge-smeccan*]

smell *n.* smell, scent 14.176; **smeal** 19.310. [rel. to **smeallunge**, not in OE]

smeortliche *adv.* quickly 18.381. [from developed sense of **smart**, but vowel from *smeortan* v. (see **smerte**); +**-liche**]

smeoðien *v.* forge 18.334. [OA *smeoþian*; cf. **smith**]

smere *adv.* derisively 5.23. [OE *-smǽre* in *gāl-smǽre* frivolous]

smerte *v.* feel pain, suffer 8w.29. [OE *smeortan* be painful]

smirieð *pr. pl.* anoint 18.77. [OM *smirian*]

smite(n) *v.* strike 1.78, 4.281. *pr. 3 sg.* **smit** *intr.* rush 12.149. *subj. sg.* **smite** hit 4.314. *imper. sg.* **smit** 18.381. *pa. t. sg.* **smot** 4.250, 270; cut 7.51, 111 (*of, off*); **smæt** in ~ *of* struck off from 10.29. *subj. sg.* **smite**

6.335. *pp.* **ismiten** (*of*) 7.132. [OE *smitan, smāt, smiten*]

smith *n.* smith 4.303. [OE *smiþ*]

smiððe *n.* smithy 18.334. [OE *smiþþe*]

smok *n.* a woman's undergarment, shift 8G.54. [OE *smoc*]

smoke *n.* smoke 16.166, 19.101. [OE *smoca*]

smoked *pa. t. sg.* smoked 16.165. [OE *smocian*]

smorðrinde *pr. p. adj.* suffocating 19.101. [from *smorðer-* v., extended from OE *smorian* smother]

smot; snailes. See **smite(n); snawile.**

snakerinde *pr. p.* sneaking 18.364. [from *snaker-* v., prob. extended from ON *snaka* snuff about; see note]

snakes *n. pl.* snakes 16.169. [OE *snaca*]

snawi *adj.* snowy, icy 19.114. [OE *snāwig*]

snawile *n.* snail 9.40. *pl.* **snailes** 1.87. [OE **snagel, snæg(e)l*]

snel(le) *adj.* bold 10.286; swift 1.550. [OE *snell*]

snellich *adv.* quickly 9.163. [OE *snellīce*]

snepe *adj.* foolish; as *n. pl. (dat.)* 1.181 (see **wis(e)**). [OE **snǽp*, cf. ON *snáp-r*]

snikeð *pr. pl.* creep 19.110. [OE *snīcan*]

sniuþ *pr. 3 sg.* snows 1.400. [OE *snīwan*]

snov *n.* snow 1.308, 7.173; **snowe** 1.291. [OE *snāw*]

so *adv. demons.* so, in this way 1.264, 2.274, 3.51, 6.192; in the same sense 7.108; ~ *hit bitide* see **bitide**; *bifel it* ~ it so happened that 4.92; so (in adjurations) 2.76, 303, 5.130, 6.26, 116, 15.61; then 4.194, 17.184; in such a way, to such a degree 1.43, 2.20, 3.3, 4.238, 5.2; **se** 8G.36, 18.59, 19.126, 227; **sa**

(intensifying adj.) 14.217. ~ ..
as, so as .. as 1.97, 250, 3.50;
also .. ~ just as .. so 17.66,
119, *so as* .. ~ 242–3; ~ *þat*
with the result that 4.242, 11.25,
15.59; until 5.10. [OE *swā*] See
swa, also, as(e).
so *adv. rel., conj.* as 1.80, 112,
4.137, 8H.6; se 13.99, 267. such
as 12.184; when 17.193; and
17.149, 183; as .. as (without
correl.) 7.113; *(al)so* .. ~ see
also and prec.; when .. then
17.146. (giving indef. sense to
relatives, &c., q.v.) soever 3.63,
12.118; **sæ** 16.199, se 16.301,
18.116; see **whose**. as if (with
subj.) 1.77, 4.204, 12.87. *se* ..
mare the more 18.326, *eauer se*
.. *mare* 19.125. [OE *swā*] See
son(e) *adv.*
so. See **se** *v.*
socour(e), socure *n.* succour,
help 2.73, 125; *dos* ~ gives help
14.70; **sucurs** 18.57, 478. [AN
sucurs understood as pl.] See
sucuri.
soffteliche *adv.* comfortably 7.
79. [next+-**liche**]
soft(e) *adj.* soft 8E.76; gentle
18.77, 94, 19.327; mild 12.69;
good-tempered 16.154; quiet
1.6. [OE *sōfte*]
soft(e) *adv.* comfortably 3.275,
14.58; gently 10.317, 18.274.
[OE *sōfte*]
softeð *pr. 3 sg.* mollifies 18.76.
[from the adj.]
soge; soht, sohvte. See **se** *v.*;
seche(n).
soiour *n.* space, delay 2.119.
[AN *sojur*]
solas, solace *n.* pleasure, delight 2.266 (see **to**), 9.50, 172;
entertainment, recreation 11.
135. [OF *solas*]
sold(e), solden. See **selle**;
schal.
soler *n.* upper room 7.260. [OE
solor and AN *soler*]

solidos *n. pl.* shillings 16.219.
[L]
sollen. See **schal.**
solsecle *n.* marigold 8K.51. [OF]
som(e). See **sum.**
somed *adv.* together 10.207;
somet 18.199; towards each
other 18.217. [OE *somod*]
someni *v.* summon, call together
11.92; **somoni** 17.17. [OF
somon-, pr. stem of *somo(u)ndre*]
somer. See **sumer(e).**
somer-driuen *pp.* driven on a
packhorse 6.247. [AN *sumer*
packhorse+*driuen* from **driu-
e(n)**]
somet. See **somed.**
sometreadliche *adv.* unani-
mously 19.23. [from **somed**+
red(e); cf. next]
sometreadnesse *n.* agreement,
concord 18.199, 224. [from
somed+**red(e)**; cf. prec.]
somnede; somoni. See **sammnenn; someni.**
son(e) *n.* son 2.3, 10, 3.151,
4.107, 7.3, 8s.4, 10.302; (as
familiar address) 6.167, 171,
15.38, 63; **sun(e)** 8v.20, 10.3,
14.88, 16.126, 17.89, 18.504;
sunu 16.38; *þe* ~ Christ 14.247,
17.52, 19.263, 420. *pl.* **sones**
4.30. [OE *sunu*, pl. *suna*]
son(e) *adv.* at once, immediately
2.36, 5.199, 6.376, 7.104, 8E.32,
11.34, 14.151; **sona** 16.137;
sune 14.252; ~ *anan* immediately 13.63; soon 2.1, 3.248,
7.83, 239, 8F.31, 11.128; early
8L.27; quickly, easily 1.421;
so ~ *so* as soon as 3.221, ~ *se*
13.173, 18.363, 565, ~ *anan se*
13.99. *comp.* **sonere, sonore**
more readily, earlier 7.31, 235;
sonre 18.55. *sup.* **sonest** 18.
536. [OE *sōna*] See **sone** *conj.*
sond *n.* sand, shore 4.3. [OE
sánd, sónd]
sond. See **sund.**
sonde *n.*[1] message 7.170, 8D.15;

messenger, envoy 18.99, 19.62, 234. *gen.* sondes 19.390. *pl.* sonde 10.134, 138; sonden 18.468, 19.403; sandes 16.141. [OE *sánd, sónd,* pl. *sánda*]
sonde *n.*² See schonde.
sondesmon *n.* messenger, emissary 18.253, 260. [from sonde¹]
sone *conj.* as soon as 3.73. [as son(e); OE usu. *sóna swā*]
song(e) *n.* song, singing 1.11, 36, 3.31, 8B.2, 19.308; song 8M.20, W.52; sang, sang 13.105, 14.87. *pl.* songes 1.468; sanges 14.23. *dat.* songe 1.82. [OE *sáng, sóng*]
song; sonne. See sing; sunne.
sonnebe(e)m *n.* sunbeam 8E.7, 14. [OE *sunn(e)bēam;* see sunne, beom]
sooþ. See soþ(e).
sopper *n.* supper 9.20. [OF *so(u)per*]
sor(e) *adj.* painful, severe 4.244, 8L.30; sar 19.170. [OE *sār*]
sor(e) *adv.* bitterly, grievously, painfully, exceedingly 3.74, 217, 4.56, 281, 5.66, 7.64, 8M.7; with difficulty 7.233; sare 18.530. [OE *sāre*]
sore *n.* pain, sorrow 1.348, 435; sar 18.14. [OE *sār*]
sore. See sweren.
soregh *pr. 1 sg.* grieve, feel sad 8B.7; sorw 15.17. [OE *sorgian*]
sorew(h)e. See soru.
Sorewyng *n.* Sorrow, Grief (personified) 8K.58; soruuing sorrow 14.133. [from prec.]
sorghen, sorȝe(n), sorhe. See soru.
sorhful(le), -fule *adj.* sorrowful, grieved 10.172, 301, 18.39, 52. [OE *sorgful*]
sorhfulliche *adv.* painfully 18.640. [prec.+-liche]
sori, sory *adj.* sorrowful, sad 6.338, 8L.22, W.30; sorry, repentant 15.74; distressed 7.265; sari 10.13, 18.305, 594; særi

10.171. *sup.* særȝest 10.234. [OE *sārig,* sense infl. by soru]
soru, sorw(e) *n.* sorrow, grief 14.145, 8C.4, 15.36; painful sight 4.307; sorewe 8G.48, L.21, (personified) L.5; sorewhe 8W.35; sorȝe 1.309, sorȝen 10.226; sorhe 19.97; sereue, serewe 6.186, 5.89, 6.182, (personified) 8K.65. *pl.* sorȝen 10.45, 53 (note), 175; sorghen 17.164; serewes 8L.24. [OE *sorg,* pl. *sorga;* -e- from vb. with mutated vowel]
soruuing; sorw; soster. See Sorewyng; soregh; suster.
sote *n.* fool 14.18. [OE *sott,* OF *sot*]
sotlice *adv.* foolishly 16.146. [prec.+-liche]
sotscipe *n.* foolishness 16.95. [OE]
soþ(e), soð(e) *n.* (the) truth (mostly obj. of sai) 1.173, 5.121, 7.197, 10.6, 72, 16.47, 19.202; sooþ 2.255; *to* ~ in truth 10.76, for a fact 10.244, 13.88, 18.262; *i þe* ~ in the right 18.259; seoð in *i* ~ truly 19.257. See forsoþ. [OE *sōþ*]
soþ(e), soð(e), soth *adj.* true (veracious) 1.229, 5.129, 10.326, 18.92, 19.251, 7.116; (genuine) 13.179, 18.289; truthful 1.444; *bicam* ~ came true 7.71. *comp.* soðð̄ere very true 10.235. [OE *sōþ*]
sothent. See siðen.
sothfast *adj.* true, genuine 17.41; soðfeste truthful, trustworthy 16.57. [OE *sōþfæst*]
soþfasstnessess *n. gen.* of truth 13.281. [OE *sōþfæstnes(se)*]
soþliche *adv.* truly 6.391. [OE *sōþlīce*]
soþþe; soþte, souȝten; soule. See siþ; seche(n); saul(e).
soule-cnul *n.* death-knell 5.251. [saul(e)+OE *cnyll*]
soum. See sum.

soupe *v.* have supper 4.193. OF *so(u)per*]

sout. See seche(n).

souþ *n.* south: *by* ~ (in the) south 8K.42. [from next]

souþ *adv.* (to the) south 1.553; suð 12.62. [OE *sūþ*]

souþhalf *n.* southern part 11.165. [OE *sūþh(e)alf*] See half.

sowel *n.* any food eaten with bread 4.35. [OE *sufel*]

sowles; spac, spak. See saul(e); speke(n).

spaclyche *adv.* quickly 8F.29. [from *spak* adj., cf. ON *spark-r*, *spræk-r* lively, +-liche]

spad *n.* spade 14.103. [OE *spadu*]

spæche. See spech(e).

spale *n.* rest 1.194. [cf. OE *spala* substitute]

spare *pr. subj. sg.* spare 6.443. *pa. t. sg.* sparede in ~ *neyþer tos ne heles* ran at full speed 4.164. *pp.* spared 4.333. [OE *sparian*]

sparke *n.* spark 4.137. [OE *spearca*]

spealie *v.* describe 19.342. *pr. 3 sg.* spealeð means 18.665. [OF *espeler* blended with OE *spelian* represent; cf. spell]

spech(e) *n.* speech, talk, speaking, words 1.338, 3.249, 5.223, 8E.30, 17.36, 19.342; spæche 13.78; word 8M.9; suit, case 1.13, 276, 353. *nis no* ~ *of* nothing is said about 9.111. [OE *sp(r)æc*, A *sprēc*]

speciale *adj.* special 2.158. [OF *especial*]

sped *n.* success 6.141. [OE *spēd*]

spede *v.* succeed, prosper, have one's way 3.126, 6.364, 449, 15.61;(with *of*, in) 6.131; *impers.* (with dat.) go well (with someone) 6.212. *pr. pl.* spedeð 18.227. *pa. t. 3 sg.* spedde 2.166, 4.24, 16.300. *2 sg.* (with

suffixed pron.) speddestu 1.125. *pl.* spedde 1.750. *pp.* sped 6.410, 14.253; ysped 8N.22; isped caused to prosper 19.425. [OE *spēdan*]

speke(n) *v.* speak, tell, 1.197, 2.5, 3.72, 5.170, 6.81; spekenn 13.120; speoke(n) 18.5, 19.69. *infl. infin.* (for)to spekene, speokene 19.397, 392. *pr. 1 sg.* speke 6.355, 14.39. *2 sg.* spekest 8L.33. *3 sg.* spekeþ, -ð 17.175, 18.254, 19.9. *pl.* speken 4.14. *pa. t. 1, 3 sg.* spac, spak 1.274, 3.169, 5.65, 6.331; spec 18.207, 483; spreac 16.76. *2 sg.* speke 1.362. *pl.* speken 17.12, 19.50. *pp.* speken 6.216; ispeke(n) 1.561, 19.377. [OE *sp(r)ecan*; *sp(r)æc*; *sp(r)æcon*, A *sp(r)ēcon*; *sp(r)ecen*]

spel, spell(e) *n.* story 1.752; *setten* ~ *on ende* tell the whole story in order 6.62 (but see note), 14.159; circumlocution 1.200. *pl.* spelles 10.92. *dat.* spellen 10.87. [OE *spell*, sg. and pl.]

spell *v.* tell 14.95. [OE *spellian*; cf. spealie]

spend *pr. pl.* spend, pass 14.50. [OE *-spéndan*]

spene *v.* use, practise 1.121. [app. alteration of prec.]

speoke(n). See speke(n).

speowe *v.* spew, vomit 18.662. *pr. pl.* speoweð 19.105. *pa. t. sg.* speu 4.246. [OE *spīwan*, *spēowan*, pa. t. *spāw* re-formed on cl. VII]

spere *n.* spear 8M.3, W.19. *gen.* speres 1.670. *pl.* speres 5.292; speren 10.277. [OE *spere*, pl. *speru*]

speten *v.* spit 1.39. [OE *spǣtan*; cf. spite]

speu. See speowe.

spicerie *n.* spice store 11.165. [OF *espicerie*]

spices *n. pl.* spices 8E.30. [OF *espice*]

spille v. destroy, ruin 6.233, 432, 7.35; waste 7.87. *pp.* **spilt** 15.22; **ispillet** 18.412. [OE *spillan*]

spire n. *coll.* reeds 1.18. [OE *spir*]

spite *imper. sg.* spit 18.384. [OE *spittan*; cf. **speten**]

spitelsteaf n. spade 18.416. [OE *spitel-* spade+**staf**]

spitel-uuel n. leprosy: *o þe ~* leprous 18.152. [shortening, with changed ending, of OF *hospital*, +**euel**]

spitte n. spit 9.102. [OE *spitu*]

splen n. spleen 5.47. [OF *esplen*, L *splēn*]

sponne n. span 8E.44. [OE *sponn*]

spouse n. spouse, wife or husband 2.287, 6.91; **spuse** 18.391, 554. [OF (*e*)*spus*(*e*)]

spreac. See **speke(n).**

sprede v. spread, expand; open 1.315; **spreaden** 18.235, 651. *pr. 3 sg.* **spredes** 8E.30. *pa. t. sg.* **spradde** 7.42. *pp.* **ispread** stretched 18.511. [OE *sprædan*]

sprengen v. fly, leap 10.277. [OE *sprengan* tr.]

spring n. spring 14.178. [OE]

springe, sprynge v. spring, flower 1.315, 8w.1; grow 8u.12. *pr. 3 sg.* **springeþ, -ð** (of day) breaks 1.480; wells up 1.550, 12.10; **springe3** (= *-þ*) 3.37; **springet** 8T.26; **springþ** puts out shoots 8A.4; **springes** sprouts 8M.2. *pa. t. sg.* **sprong** 7.214; leapt 8w.4. *pl.* **sprongen** 4.137. [OE *springan, spróng, sprúngon*]

spusbreche n. adultery 17.120. [**spouse** in sense 'marriage'+ OE *bryce* as in *ǣw-bryce* adultery]

spuse. See **spouse.**

spus-had n. marriage 18.612. [**spouse**+**-had**]

squier n. squire 11.20, 41. [OF *esquier*]

squir n. builder's square 3.83. [OF *esquire*]

srift. See **schrift(e).**

sriue v. shrive, absolve after confession 5.184. *pp.* **isriue** 5.176. [OE *scrīfan, scrifen*] Cf. **schrift(e).**

sroud n. garment, clothing 6.6. [OE *scrūd*]

srud *pp. adj.* dressed 6.23. [OE *scrȳd*(*d*)]

ssame; sscholde(n); sschrichen; ssende. See **scham(e); schal; schrichen; schende.**

sserreue n. sheriff 11.2, 6. [OE *scīr-gerēfa*]

ssete v. shoot 11.159. *pr. 3 sg.* **scheot** shoots 18.158; *intr.* leaps 19.362. *pa. t. sg.* **sset** fired 11.43. *pl.* **schoten** shot 4.291; **ssote** 11.35; **shoten** *intr.* rushed 4.265. *subj. sg.* **schute** shot 19.182. *pp.* **ishote** sent out 1.23. [OE *scēotan, scēat, scuton, scoten*]

ssipe. See **ship.**

ssipede *pa. t. sg.* rewarded 11.86. [from OE *scipe* n. reward]

ssire; ssolde. See **schire; schal.**

ssoppe n. shop 11.163. [OE *sceoppa*]

ssote. See **ssete.**

ssrewen n. *pl.* evil-disposed men, villains 11.57. [see **schrewe**]

ssulen. See **schal.**

ssute n. shot 11.44. [OE *scyte*]

stabell *adj.* as n. *pl.* sturdy, strong (knights) 14.13. [OF (*e*)*stable*]

stac n. stack 4.82. [ON *stakk-r*]

stad *pp.* placed, set 14.133. [ON *stadd-r*, pp. of *steðja*]

stæl, stal *pa. t. sg.* stole 16.253, 292. *pl.* **stalen** 16.270. [OE *stæl, stǣlon* from *stelan*]

staf n. staff, stick 4.317. *pl.* **staues** 5.62, 284. [OE *stæf*, pl. *stafas*, M **steaf-*]

stage *n.* platform, raised floor 2.233; upper floor 3.7, 27; period, time 14.50. [OF *(e)stage*]

stake *n. pl.* stakes 8N.13. [OE *staca*]

stal(en). See stæl.

stale *n.* stealth 19.76. [OE *stalu* stealing; cf. stæl]

stalun *n.* stallion 9.167. [AN]

stalworþe *adj.* sturdy, strong 4.170. *sup.* stalwardeste 11.85. [OE *stælwyrþe*]

standed *adj.* stone-dead 4.242. [ston(e)+ded]

stand, stant; stanes. See stonde(n); ston(e).

starc, -k *adj.* hard, fierce 1.5; large 6.223. [OE *stearc*]

starest *pr. 2 sg.* glare 1.77. [OE *starian*]

state *n.* state, condition 9.120. [OF *estat*]

staþe *n.* bank, shore 10.introd. [OE *stæþ*]

staues; steah. See staf; steo.

steal *n.* place: *in a* ~ placed 19.325. [OE *stæl*]

stede *n.*¹ place 2.122, 228, 4.12, 16.103, 17.129; stude 1.612, 7.81, 99, 10.269, 18.156, 19.52. *pl.* stedes 4.273; studen 19.269; (orig. *gen.*) stude 1.725. [OE *stede, styde*]

stede *n.*² steed: *vpon* ~ among riders, on earth 8E.48. [OE *stēda*]

stedefast *adj.* steadfast, true 12.133, 191. [OE *stedefæst*]

stedefastliche *adv.* firmly 17.52. [prec.+-liche]

stefne *n.* voice 1.230, 10.116; sound of voices 10.85; steuene 1.530, 547, 15.26, 18.50, 19.150; teaching 1.473. [OE *stefn*]

steire *n.* degree 18.316. *pl.* steiren 18.315. [OE *stæger* staircase]

stel(e) *n.* steel 6.95, 12.177, 18.327, 19.129; steel 2.250. [OA *stēle*]

stench *n.* stench 19.96. [OE *stenc*]

steo *v.* ascend; fly up 7.174. *pa. t. sg.* steah 18.141, 148. *pp.* istihen 18.650. [OE *stīgan, stāh*, re-formed after *wrēon, wrāh/wrēah; stigen*]

steormen *n. pl.* steersmen 10.223. [OE *stēormann*]

steorre(n). See sterre.

steppes *n. pl.* footprints 14.189. [OE *stepe*]

stere *n.* rudder 9.154. [OE *stēor* steering]

sterne *adj.* fierce 9.64; stuyrne harsh, cruel 7.128. [OE *styrne*]

sterre *n.* star 17.5, 8. *pl.* sterres 16.121; steorren(e) 19.300, 7.42; steorre, storre 1.597, 589. [OE *steorra*] See next.

sterrne *n.* star 13.161, 195. *pl.* sternes 4.236; sterrnesse 13.166. [ON *stjarna*, earlier **stearn-*]

sterrne-lem *n.* light of a star 13.173. [prec.+leome]

stert *n.* short time, moment 4.300. [from next]

sterteþ *pr. 3 sg.* leaps 8A.8. *pa. t. sg.* stirt(e) leapt, hastened, rushed 2.292, 3.198, 4.80, 140. [OE *styrtan*]

sterue *v.* die 2.304. *pa. t. 2 sg.* storue 5.151. *pl.* sturuen 16.188. [OE *steorfan, sturfe, -on*]

steuene. See stefne.

steuenyng *n.* assignation 8H.33. [from OE *stefnan* arrange]

sti, sty *n.* path, road 19.210, 8N.26. [OE *stīg*]

stickes *n. pl.* sticks 4.180. [OE *sticca*]

stif *adj.* hard 1.79, 205, stern 5. [OE *stīf*]

stille *adj.* still, without moving 1.218, 5.88, 7.135, 237, 8L.35, 12.167; stil(l) 14.284, 287; calm 17.153; quiet 3.55, 10.82, 19.60; low, subdued 2.19; silent (without speaking) 1.197, 5.36, 6.50, 8L.17. [OE]

stille *adv.* quietly, silently 8R.7,

10.91; softly 8L.33; secretly, privately 2.276, 3.290, 6.86; always 7.160. [OE]

stinkinde *pr. p. adj.* stinking 18. 364. *pa. t. sg.* **stonk** stank 5.94. [OE *stincan; stanc, stonc*]

stinteþ *pr. pl.* stop 9.99. [OE *styntan* blunt]

styred, stireð; **stirt(e)**. See **sturien; sterteþ**.

stith *n.* anvil 4.304. [ON *steði* infl. by **smith**]

styþest *adj. sup.* most powerful 8E.48. [OE *stíþ*]

stiward *n.* steward, controller of a household 18.449. [LOE *stíweard*]

stoc *n.* stump 1.25. [OE *stocc*]

stod(e). See **stonde(n)**.

stode *n.* stud 9.35. [OE *stód*]

stodmere *n.* (= brood mare) villain 2.285. [prec.+OA *mere*]

ston(e) *n.* stone 4.270, 12.30, 17.99; flint 12.177; *freo* ~ 7.253, see **freo**; precious stone, jewel 3.34, 8E.68. *pl.* **stones** 2.219, 5.62; **stonis** 9.88; **stanes** 10. 184, 16.172; uninflected (or representing older dat.) **ston(e)** 3.41, 5.284. [OE *stán*]

stonde(n) *v.* stand 3.190, 18.40, 514; **stand** 14.61, 184. *pr. 1 sg.* **stond** 8w.21. *3 sg.* **stant** 3.57, 7.95; **stont** 1.398, 8E.68, 19.47; *impers.* in *hire* ~ *stronge* it goes hard with her 18.5; **stond** 8N.1. *subj. pl.* **stond** in ~ *to ȝure cheance* risk your luck 9.185. *imper. sg.* **stond** 1.746 (see **aȝein**). *pl.* **stondeð** 18.113. *pa. t. sg.* **stod** 1.25, 3.194, 4.169, 245, 5.257; blew steadily 10.157. *pl.* **stod(e)** 4.155, 324, 8L.23; were in force 10.306; stayed 14. 284. *pp.* **istonden** 10.305. [OE *stándan, stóndan; stód, stódon; gestánden*]

stonden *pa. t. pl.* stoned 4.290. [from **ston(e)**]

stonk. See **stinkinde**.

stopen *pa. t. pl.* strode: ~ *togadere* met in battle, engaged 10. 209. [OE *stópon* from *steppan*]

stor *n.* incense 17.10, 30. [OE *stór*]

story *n.* story 2.211. *pl.* **storis** 14.21. [AN (*e*)*storie*]

storm(e) *n.* storm 9.41, 12.162. [OE *storm*]

storre. See **sterre**.

storre-wis *adj.* learned in astrology 1.586. [**sterre**+**wis(e)**]

storue: stounde. See **sterue; stund(e)**.

stout(e) *adj.* stately, splendid 8K.38; (the) proud, as *n. pl.* in (imperfect) inclusive phr. ~ *and sterne* 9.64. [OF (*e*)*stout*]

straf *pa. t. sg.* strove, competed 18.631. [from OF *estriver* (cf. **strif**), pa. t. after *drive*, &c.]

strang(e); **stream**. See **strong(e); strem**.

strek *pr. subj. sg.* stretch (out), extend, spread 6.441. *pa. t. sg.* **strehte** 10.8. *pp.* **istrahte** outstretched 18.512. [OE *streccan, strehte*, A *stræhte*]

strem *n.* stream 3.40; **stream** current 18.185. *pl.* **stremmes** rivers 14.180. [OE *stréam*]

stremis *pr. 3 sg.* is drenched 9.87. [from prec.]

strengere. See **strong(e)**.

strenges *n. pl.* cords 16.168. [OE *streng*]

strengþe, -ðe, -the *n.* strength 2.245, 8U.7, 17.251, 18.112, 19. 174; force 11.58, 16.216, 18.350; power 18.114; army 16.292; (personified) Fortitude 19.41, 175; *doð him* ~ put pressure upon, constrain 18.76; *in a* ~ strong enough 19.324; **strencþe, -ðe** 1.671, 19.415; **strenþe, -ðe** 1.632, 19.387; **strenghte** 8w.42. *pl.* **strengðen** powers 19.186. [OE *strengþ(u)*]

strengþen *v. refl.* apply oneself,

endeavour 6.170. *tr.* strengthen: *pp.* istrengþed 17.115. [from prec.]

stret(e) *n.* road, street 5.5, 6.395, 11.18. *pl.* stretes 11.162. [OE strǣt, A strēt]

strif *n.* dispute 8G.10; strife 9.27; striif 14.5, 133; force 2.7. [OF (e)strif]

strit *pr. 3 sg.* strides 8N.1. *imper. sg.* stryd 8N.26. [OE strīdan]

stroc *n.* stroke, blow 11.14, 17. [OE *strāc rel. to strīcan]

strok *pa. t. sg.* went 5.9. [OE strāc from strīcan]

stronde *n.* shore 10.164. [OE stránd, strónd]

strong(e) *adj.* strong 1.111, 2.79, 4.97, 6.12, 7.23; strang(e) 2.175, fierce 14.5. big 5.62, 10.19; severe, intense 1.5, 12, 3.287, 4.92, 8w.36; rough 8B.4; gross, flagrant 7.30; difficult 1.413; *ful* ~ too much, deplorable 4.70. *comp.* strengere 16.322. [OE stráng, stróng; strengra]

stronge *adv.* exceedingly 1.190, 5.273; deeply 5.195; harshly (see stonde(n)) 18.6. [OE]

strongliche *adv.* thoroughly 18.330. [OE stranglíce]

stroute *v.* quarrel, make trouble 4.206. [OE strūtian (?)struggle]

strunden *n. pl.* streams 18.237. [obscure]

stu *n.* stewpan, cauldron 9.109. [OF estuve]

stucche *n.* piece, fragment: *ane hwile* ~ a short time 18.387. [OE stycce]

stude(n); stuyrne. See stede[1]; sterne.

stund(e) *n.* time, while 4.285, 12.166, 18.5, 19.392; time of trial 1.452; stounde 6.419, 7.94, 8M.19; short time, moment 11.46. *one* ~ once 5.213; *vmbe* ~ at times 8H.33, 10.85; *vmben ane* ~ after a while 19.233. [OE stúnd]

sturgiun *n.* sturgeon 4.21. [OF sturg(i)un]

sturien *v.* stir, move; *intr.* be up and about 10.7. *pr. 3 sg.* stireð *tr.* 12.162, *intr.* 167. *imper. sg.* sture *refl.* bestir (yourself) 18.372. *pa. t. sg.* sturede *refl.* busied (herself) 7.133; *intr.* rose 10.85. *pp.* styred disturbed 16.258. [OE styrian]

sturnliche *adv.* grimly 10.209. [OE styrnlíce; see sterne]

sturuen. See sterue.

stutteð *pr. 3 sg.* stops (fold. by infin. obj.) 19.397. [prob. ON stytta; see Iuliene p. 166]

such. See swich(e).

sucuri *pr. 1 sg.* will succour 17.164 (note). *subj. sg.* 17.159. *pa. t. sg.* sucurede 17.159. [OF sucurre] See socour(e).

sucurs. See socour(e).

suffri *v.* suffer 17.45. *pa. t. pl.* suffreden allowed 2.109. [AN suffrir]

suǵ(ǵ)e(n), suǵet. See sai.

suhinde *pr. p. adj.* painful 18. 251. [obscure; prob. based on a verb imit. of sighing]

sukeð *pr. 3 sg.* sucks 12.156. *pa. t. sg.* sec 8v.22. [OE sūcan, sēac]

suld, sulen; sule(ð). See schal; selle.

sulement *adv.* only 18.294. [AN]

suleð *pr. 3 sg.* soils, stains 18.581. *pp.* isulet 18.574. [OE sylian]

sulfe. See self.

sulh *n.* plough 18.417. [OE]

sulke; sulle(n). See swich(e); schal, selle.

sully *adv.* wonderfully 8K.6. [LOE syllíce] See seolliche.

sulue. See self.

sum *adj.* some, a, one 2.204, 4.65, 7.21, 8N.24, 10.125, 18.24; som(e) 3.140, 153; soum 5.104. *acc. masc.* somne, sommne 5.192, 125. *gen.* summes

19.184 (see **wai(e)**). *pl.* **sume**
1.336, 455; **summe** in ~ *hi, heo*
some of them 10.164, 165. [OE
sum]

sum *pron.* one 4.270; someone
19.61; some (part) 1.348; **som**
5.18. *pl.* **sume** some 16.170,
188; **summe** 1.606, 4.210, 271,
19.16. [OE *sum*]

sum(m) *adv. rel.* as 13.230, 14.
162; forming *conj.* (1) with
forðriht, swa, q.v.; (2) with
advs. as **wher(e)**, giving indef.
sense: see under the advs.
[Scand. *sum, som* rel. to ON
sem]

sum-chearre *adv.* sometimes
18.36. [OA *æt sumum cerre*]

sumdel *adv.* somewhat, rather
2.202, 19.249; in part, to some
extent 14.144, 19.155, 320;
something of 16.224; a good
deal 5.237. [sum+del(e)]

sumer(e), svmer *n.* summer
1.294, 8A.1, B.1, 12.69; **somer**
8L.3, 11.26. *attrib.* summery,
sunny 1.1 (note), or summer
6.294. *gen.* **someris** 9.151. [OE
sumor]

sumhweat *pron.* something 18.
614; **sumhwet** 18.115, 19.256;
something of 19.316. [sum+
what]

sumhwile *adv.* formerly 18.508;
sumwile 16.189; sometimes
1.6. [sum+while]

sumþing *n.* something 7.58;
summþing 13.94. [sum+
þing(e)]

sumwher *adv.* somewhere 8N.
23. [sum+wher(e)]

sumwile. See **sumhwile.**

sun. See **son(e)** *n.*

sund *adj.* sound, fit 12.23, 125;
sond unharmed 3.118. [OE
ge-súnd; cf. **isunde**]

sunden. See **senden.**

sunderlepes *adv.* separately 19.
315, 345. [OE *sundorlípes*, A
*-hlépes]

sunderliche *adv.* separately 19.
283, 347. [OE *sundorlíce*]

sune. See **son(e)** *n., adv.*

sunegin *v.* sin 19.203. [OE *syn-
gian*; see *Iuliene* p. 166]

sunen. See **schunien.**

Sunendæies *n. gen.* (*adv.*) in *þes
~* on the Sunday 16.49. [OE
Sunnandæg]

sunful; **sungen.** See **sinful**;
sing.

sunne *n.* sun 10.169, 12.18, 16.
120, 17.7, 18.93, 19.324; sun's
rays 12.17; **sonne** 8G.35, S.1.
bineoðe þe ~, under ~ on earth
1.544, 18.161. [OE *sunne*]

sunne-gleam *n.* sunlight 19.
259, 361. [prec.+OE *glǽm*]

sunne(n), sunngenn; sunu.
See **sin(ne); sing; son(e)** *n.*

sur *adj.* sour, bitter 1.526. [OE
súr]

sures *n. pl.* showers, storms 12.
96. [OE *scúr*]

suster *n.* sister 16.299, 18.251,
19.48; **soster** 7.11, 13. *gen.*
suster 10.3, 57. *pl.* **sustren**
18.10, 54, 19.228. [OE *s(w)us-
tor, swostor*, LWS pl. *swustru*]

suð; **suþe**; **suþþe.** See **souþ**;
swiþe; **siþ.**

sua. See **swa.**

sval *pa. t. sg.* swelled up, raged
1.7. [OA *swall* from *swellan*]

sueland *pr. p.* crying 14.208.
[= 'squealing', imit.]

suencten *pa. t. pl.* oppressed,
burdened 16.158. [OE *swencan*]

suerd; **suete**; **sueting.** See
swerd; **swet(e)**; **sweting.**

suetly *adj.* lovely 8K.25. [from
swet(e)]

suetnes(se); **suette(r).** See
swetnesse; **swet(e).**

sueþelband *n.* swaddling band
14.207. [OE *sweþel*+ON *band*]

**suich(e); suic-, svikedom;
svikelhede; suikes; suyken;
suilc(e), suilk; suinc; suyre;
suyt(he); suiþe, -the; suo-**

r(en). See swich(e), swilc;
swikedom(e); swikelede;
swyke; swikeþ; swich(e);
swinc; swyre; swet(e);
swiþe; sweren.

swa adv. demons. so, in this way
13.15, 16.17 (1st), 44, 18.74,
19.263; consequently 16.41; so,
as (in adjuration) 10.56; so, in
such a way 13.56, 16.164; quasi-
pron. (resuming preceding
clause) such, that 16.43, 45; in
such a way that 10.6; sua 14.
174, (intensifying adj.) 63; ~
þet, ðat 16.64, 107; swo 1.561,
17.6 (note); correl. with alswo
17.8, with wanne 17.22, then;
be ~ þet provided that 17.247.
[OE swā] See also, so.

swa adv. rel., conj. as 10.254,
16.42; swa swa 16.29, 85; swa
.. ~ as .. as 16.17; ~ summ as
13.8, 40; anæn ~ see anon;
swo and so 17.15 (note); as if
(with subj.) 1.76. [OE swā,
swā swā] See also, so.

swaliches adv. in such a way
18.258. [prec.+-liche +adv.
-es]

swank. See swinken.

swannes n. gen. (as adj.) swan's
8E.43. [OE swan]

swarte adj. black, dark 10.31,
16.51, 19.80. comp. swartre
18.326. [OE sweart]

swein, sweyn n. attendant (of
a knight), servant 2.12, 10.127,
283. pl. sweines retainers 10.
174. [ON svein-n]

sweng imper. sg. swing 18.382.
[OE swengan]

swerd n. sword 2.250, 4.229;
suerd 11.13, 100; sweord 10.
17, 18.159; sweorede 10.30.
pl. swerdes 4.196; sweord
10.276. [OE swéord, sg. and
pl.]

sweren v. swear, take an oath
16.4. infl. infin. to swerene in
swearing 16.37. pr. pl. swerieð

19.23. subj. sg. swere 8H.24.
pa. t. sg. swor 6.421, 16.96;
suor 16.264; sore 8K.65. pl.
sworen 7.227; suoren 16.279.
subj. sg. swore 8F.43. pp.
suoren 16.155; isuore 11.30.
[OE swerian, swōr, swōron,
sworen]

swet(e), suete adj. sweet 1.526,
7.40, 6.195, 14.245; (of persons)
3.193, 6.127, 8G.23, 14.246; as
n. sweet creature 8K.73; ~ heorte
see hert(e); pleasant, delightful
9.25, 82; suette 14.88; suyt(he)
15.23, 50. comp. suetter 14.76.
sup. swetest 8W.13, 18.608;
swetteste 12.150. [OE swēte,
comp. swēt(t)ra]

swete v. sweat 1.674. [OE
swǣtan]

swetelich(e) adv. sweetly, graciously 3.91, 18.260. [cf. OE
swētlīce]

sweting, sueting, -yng n. sweet
creature, darling 6.222, 8K.2, 34.
[from swet(e)]

swetnesse, suetnes(se) n.
sweetness 19.308, 8K.51, 14.247;
kindness 18.202. [OE swēt-
nes(se)]

swetteste. See swet(e).

sweuen(e) n. dream 7.40, 63,
10.13, 48. [OE swefn]

swich(e), swych, suich(e) adj.
such (a) 2.74, 224, 3.130, 17.138,
7.66, 1.134, 11.24; swuch(e),
swucche 1.575, 669, 7.197,
200, 18.51, 242, 19.219, 287;
suilc(e), suilk 15.5, 16.120,
200, 14.77; swillc, swillke 13.
170, 230; secc 6.83; selk(e)
6.101 (note), 245; siche 17.158;
silk 6.198; such 8E.20, F.14,
v.23; sulke 6.264. swich two
twice as much 3.112. pron.
suich such a one 1.283; pl.
swucche such things 1.592.
[OE swelc, swilc, swylc, swulc]

swideð pr. 3 sg. scorches, singes
12.18. [ON svíða]

swifte adj. swift 9.123, 18.182, 19.361. [OE swift]

swiftschipe n. swiftness 18.631. [prec.+-**schipe**]

swyke n.[1] deceiver 8H.25. pl. **swikes, suikes** traitors 16.137, 153. [OE swica]

swike n.[2] deception, treachery 12.154. [OE swice]

swikedom(e) n. treachery 10.60, 77; **svikedom** 1.119, 123; **suicdom** 16.111. [OE swicdōm partly re-formed on prec.]

swikele adj. deceptive, treacherous 5.86, 103. [OE swicol]

swikelede n. deceit 1.498; **svikelhede** 1.118. [prec.+-**hede**]

swikeþ pr. 3 sg. intr. stops 1.252. imper. sg. **swik** 8A.12. pa. t. pl. tr. **suyken** deceived, betrayed 16.256. [OE swīcan, pa. t. pl. swicon, and swician wk.]

swilc conj. (with subj.) as if 16. 63; **swulc** 10.9, 15; **suich** 1. 374. [OE swilce] Cf. **swich(e)**.

swilen v. wash 4.185. [OE swilian]

swillc, swillke. See **swich(e)**.

swimme v. swim 9.158. pr. 3 sg. **swimmeð** 12.116, 118. [OE swimman]

swinc, suinc, swink(e) n. labour, toil 19.324, 16.205, 4.38, 5.144, 6.134, 9.18. pl. **swinkes** 18.4, 402. [OE swinc]

swine n. pig 9.33. gen. **swines** 4.49; **swineis** 9.179. pl. **swin** 6.272, 16.68, 70. [OE swīn, sg. and pl.]

swinken v. labour, work 4.66. pr. 3 sg. **swinkeþ, -ð** 6.140, 12.68. pa. t. sg. **swank** 4.56. [OE swincan, swanc]

swyre, suyre n. neck 8E.43, K.25, 18.563; **swore** 1.73. [OE swēora, A swīra]

swiþe, -ðe, swyþe, suiþe, -the, suyðe, -the adv. strongly, greatly, severely 5.4, 10.46, 296,

16.159, 208, 18.60; closely 19. 65; quickly, fast 2.87, 4.151, 5.9, 6.156, 10.239; very 4.17, 5.12, 6.302, 7.2, 8E.43, 16.113; **suþe** 1.2, 161. comp. **swiðere** more heavily 18.327; more bitterly 19.126. [OE swīþe, LWS swȳþe]

swo; swor(en); swore. See **swa; sweren; swyre.**

swote adj. sweet, gentle 8U.11, 18.142, 217, 19.327; fragrant 19.310. as n. (in phr. with swete) 8K.73. sup. **swotest** (with swetest) 18.608. [OE swōt] See **swet(e).**

swote-iheortet adj. gentle in heart 18.302. [**swote**+ **hert(e)** ; see **feol-iheortet** and cf. **heard-**]

swoteliche adv. kindly, tenderly 18.483. [cf. OE swōtlīce]

swotnesse n. sweetness 19.311. [OE swōtnes(se)]

swouned pa. t. sg. swooned, fainted 3.71. [ME swounen formed on OE geswōgen pp.]

swuc(c)h(e); swulc. See **swich(e); swilc.**

swulten pa. t. pl. died 16.71. [OE swulton from sweltan]

ta. See **þo** adj., **þo(o)** adv.

table n. table 2.279; **Tabell** in þe Ronde ~ 14.14. [OF table]

taburs n. pl. tabors, small drums 9.137. [AN tabur]

tacen; tachte. See t: k; **teche.**

tacneþþ pr. 3 sg. signi es 13.284. [OE tācnian] Cf. bit cnenn.

tadden n. pl. toads 19.109. [LOE tadde]

tæcen; tæchenn; tær; taght, tahte; tah. See **tak; teche; þer(e)** adv.; **teche; þah** adv.

tak, take(n) v. take 14.114, 2.153, 6.106, 7.236, 8F.32; ~ hede 8E.42; catch 4.99; understand (to be signified) 14.243; refl. in *me* ~ make my way 8x.9; **tacen, tæcen** seize 16.44, 240, 262; ~ *on, an* act, behave 2.96, 10. 130, 133. *pr. 1 sg.* take 8F.23 (see **hond(e)**). *3 sg.* takeþ, -ð 9.135, 12.35, 18.348; *refl.* goes 12.46. *pl.* taken 4.260 (see red(e)); takiþ 9.152; tas 14.43. *subj. sg.* take 8F.42. *imper. sg.* tak(e) 9.112, 14.269. *pa. t. sg.* toc, tok(e) took 13.149, 16.290, 4.125, 14.80; took 2.28, 322 (see leue¹); got 4.87; caught 4.19; committed 11.29; rebuked 17. 152; *intr.* succeeded 16.307; ~ *to* proceeded to 16.140. *pl.* toke(n) 2.320, 7.241; **tokenn** proceeded 13.119; tocan in ~ *and helden* proceeded to hold 16.139. *pp.* take(n) 8L.11, N.9, 24; itake, ytake 8N.25; caught 2.244, 8L.19; drawn 5.43; ~ *to* adopted 5.178. [ON *taka, tók, tóku, tekinn*, re-formed on OE cl. VI]

takenn, tákenn *n.* sign, miracle 13.62, 170. [OE *tācn*]

tald(en). See **tel.**

tale *n.* words, something said 1.288, 2.257, 8E.9, 19.390; conversation 2.185; debate 1.3, 146; charge 1.96, 352; story 18.473; number 9.98; account, in *tel no* ~ *of* hold of no account 3.120. *pl.* 1.193. [OE *talu*, often indecl.]

tame *adj.* subdued 6.200. [OE *tam*]

tanne. See **þan(ne)** *conj.*

tapynage *n.* secrecy 2.89. [OF *tapinage*]

targi *v.* delay 17.257. *pa. t. sg.* **targede** 7.103. [OF *targ(i)er*]

tas; tat(t); taute. See **tak; þat** *adj., conj.;* **teche.**

taueleþ *pr. 3 sg.* plays at dice 1.624. [OE *tæflian*]

te *v.* draw; *intr.* go: *to deþe* ~ die 3.78; **teo(n)** 7.113, 10.182. *pr. 3 sg.* teð goes 12.12, 122. *pl.*

ten 12.114; teoð in *alle* ~ *an* all work together 18.225. *pa. t. sg.* **tey** pulled 5.279. *pp.* **ito3en** brought up 1.683. [OE *tēon, tē(a)h, getogen*]

te; teares. See **to** *prep.,* **þe** *art., adv.,* **þou; teres.**

teche *v.* teach, instruct 1.546, 724; **teachen** 19.412; **tæchenn** show 13.199. *pr. 2 sg.* **techest** 1.510. *3 sg.* **teacheð** 18.114, 354, 19.4. *pl.* **techiþ** 9.165. *subj. sg.* **teache** 19.413. *pa. t. sg.* **tachte** 17.231; **taght** instructed 14.162; **taute** directed 6.219. *subj. sg.* **tahte** misled 8H.39. *pp.* **itaht** 18.9; **itawt** 3.142. [OE *tǣcan; tǎhte, tǽhte*]

techinge *n.* teaching, doctrine 17.210. [OE *tǽcing*]

tedai; tegædere; te33(re). See **todai; togadere; þai** *pron.*

teh (= *teþ*) *n. pl.* teeth 8N.39; **teht** 8E.40. *pl. gen.* **toðes** 19.114. [OE *tēþ*, pl. of *tōþ*]

tey. See **te.**

teil *n.* tail 18.206, 213. *pl.* **teiles** 18.206, 212. [OE *tægl*, M **tegl*]

teilac *n.* entanglement 18.241. [OA *tēgan* tie +-**lac**; see note]

teyte *adj.* active, nimble 4.268. [ON *teit-r*]

teke *prep.* besides, forming *conj.*: ~ *þet* besides (the fact) that 18. 60. [OE *tō ē(a)can*; see **to**, **eke**]

tel, tell(e), tellen *v.*¹ (1) tell 14. 218, 175, 1.751, 5.131, 7.1, 8G. 43, 6.63; speak 6.51, 420, 7.186, 19.129; say 10.87; describe 14. 175, 16.179, 17.269, 19.92; expound, express 1.741, 2.37. (2) count 4.44, 10.146, 18.191; account, hold, consider 1.256 (see **wurð** *adj.*), 3.120 (see **tale**), 8D.39, x.17, 18.545; *lute* ~ *of* take little account of 11.150, *lihtliche* ~ *to* 19.296. *pr. 1 sg.* **tel(le)** 6.387, 8x.17; (fut. sense) 1.203, 8G.39. *2 sg.* **tellest** 6.52;

telst 1.226. *3 sg.* telleþ, -ð
2.37, 12.83, 19.393; tellez
(= -þ) 7.110; teleð 18.206, 545;
telþ 1.256, 17.35. *pl.* telleð
18.191; tellen 2.133. *subj. sg.*
telle 18.250, 257. *pl.* tellen
18.255. *imper. sg.* tel 3.120,
5.197, 6.171; tele 19.89, 256;
telle 2.53. *pa. t. sg.* tald(e)
10.132, 14.160, 18.486, 19.250;
tolde 6.76, 7.62, 8к.54. *pl.*
talden 19.296; tolde 11.150.
subj. sg. talde 18.49, 19.129;
tolde (I) should consider 8d. 39.
pp. tald 14.195; told(e) 2.15,
3.149, 4.44, 6.51; italde 10.146;
itold 3.285, 17.73, 201. [OE
tellan, (A) *tálde*]

tellen *v.²* persuade 6.242. [OE
-tyllan, K **tellan*] Cf. tolleð.

tempeste *n.* storm 17.146. [OF]

temptatiun *n.* temptation 18.49.
pl. temptatiuns 18.1, 56. [AN
tentaciun assim. to L]

ten(n) *adj., n.* ten 3.202, 4.138,
5.48, 16.68. [OA *tēn*]

tene *n.* grief, suffering, vexation
6.158, 174, 8м.4; tone insult
1.50. *pl.* tenes injuries 2.64.
[OE *tēona*] See teone.

tenserie *n.* protection money 16.
183. [OF]

tent *imper. sg.* attend, give heed
14.171. [from tent n., shortened
from OF *atente*]

teo(n). See te.

teone *pr. subj. sg. impers.* vex,
make angry: *me ~ wiþ* I am
vexed with 8n.39. [OE *tēonian*]
See tene.

teoþi *adj.* peevish (?) 18.241.
[obscure; see note(spelling þ also
irregular)]

ter. See þer(e).

teres *n. pl.* tears 1.304, 525,
6.358; teares 18.73, 95, 19.301.
[OE *tēar*]

terme *n.* (appointed) period,
time 3.170. [OF]

tes. See þis *adj.*

Testament *n.* Testament 18.
470. [L *testamentum*]

ti, ty. See þou.

tiden *n. dat.* time, occasion 10.1.
pl. tide (canonical) hours 1.26;
seasons 1.455; tides hours 17.
207. [OE *tīd*, pl. *tīda*]

tiden *v.* happen 8v.15. [OE *tīdan*]
Cf. bitide, itide.

tydyng, tidinge *n.* (piece of)
news 2.18, 10.2; tidende 10.
132; tiþing(u)e 7.198, 11.23;
tiþand 14.263. *pl.* tidinges 19.
159, 236. [cf. LOE *tīdung*, prob.
modification of ON *tīðendi*]

tight *pp. refl.* determined 14.165.
[obscure, app. OE]

tiithest *adv. sup.*, sense uncertain
14.61. [ON *tíðast* = most
quickly; but prob. emend to
stiithest most firmly, from OE
stīþe adv., cf. styþest]

til, tyl *conj.* till 4.43, 6.292,
8т.21, 12.15, 16.152; ~ þat, ðat
4.147, 12.13. [as next]

til(l) *prep.* to 4.132, 274, 8т.17,
13.32, 113, 14.45; (postponed)
4.157, 14.130; into 6.354; for
4.29, 30, 13.266; until 6.293,
14.290. [ONb and ON *til*]

tilde *pa. t. sg.* extended, reached
7.42. [OE *ge-tillan*]

tilen *v.* procure, gain 12.28, 66;
tilie till, cultivate 18.415. *pr.*
3 sg. tileð gets 12.82, 101. *subj.*
sg. tille woɪk upon 6.440. *pa. t.*
sg. tilede 16.199. *pp.* tiled
16.186. [OE *tilian*]

tilward *prep.* towards 14.150.
[til prep.+OE *-weard*]

tim(e), tyme *n.* time 6.124,
8v.23, 12.161, 13.27, 14.223;
time of day 1.239, 5.263; proper
time 2.147; occasion 10.156,
14.222; opportunity, leisure 12.
82; reign 16.129; age 17.207. *at*
one ~ at the same time 7.240; *ed*
a ~ at once 18.632; *in ~* soon,
quickly 11.24; *þe ~ þat* when
14.141. [OE *tīma*]

tin(e). See þou.

tintreohen *n. pl.* torments 19.
297. [OE *tintrega*]

tyraunt *n.* absolute ruler 2.57.
pl. **tyranne** tyrants 2.48. [OF
tiran, tyra(u)nt]

tirgen *v.* tire, be fatigued 12.122.
[OE *tyrgan* vex]

tis. See þis.

tyttes *n. pl.* breasts 8E.58. [OE *titt*]

tiþand, tiþing(u)e. See tydyng.

to *n.* toe 4.274, 8E.63. *pl.* tos
4.164 (see **spare**); **ton** 11.118.
fro þe croune til þe to 4.274, *fram
heued to þe ton* 11.118 from head
to foot. [OE *tā*]

to *adv.* too 1.127, 260, 4.113,
5.81, 8E.26, H.16, 10.153, 18.
644; *al* ~ all too 6.343, 7.116; to
(in phr. with verb) see **go(n)**.
[OE *tō*]

to *prep.* (of direction) to 1.522,
2.10, 3.47, 4.4; against 1.216;
up to, as far as 2.102, 8G.35;
~ *þine honde* into your possession 2.42; (postponed) 5.230,
6.366, 9.177, 10.214. (of indirect obj.) 2.21, 51, 3.92, 5.181,
6.186. (of emotion, *onde*) towards 7.17, 8D.18. (of place)
near to 1.38; at 17.89, 190. (of
kinship, acquaintance) to, with
1.85, 2.145, 13.37. (of reference)
in 5.97. (of value) see **wurð** *adj.*
after certain vbs., see **seche(n)**,
trust, þreatin. (of time) at
1.339, 477; until 4.72, 6.324,
8K.67, 16.60; ~ *lifes, liue* see **lif.**
(of purpose) for 1.188, 2.73,
4.51, 9.20; good for 1.367. (of
benefit) for 1.386, 4.6, 18.405
(2nd), 577; ~ *gode* for the good
(of) 1.485, 12.29, ~ *note* for profit
(of) 1.246, 8Y.4. (of persons,
indicating position, status) as,
to be: ~ *wyfe, wyue* 15.6, 2.152,
~ *kinge* 16.135, sim. 8F.2, V.4,
13.242, 18.51, 189; ~ *manne* in
human form 13.64. (of things,

indicating purpose or result) as,
for: ~ *message* on an errand 2.299,
~ *meding* as a reward 6.271;
~ *laue, lofe, red, soþe, welde* see
the nouns; (with dat. of pers.)
þee ~ *solas* so as to please you
2.266, sim. 10.327, 13.106,
18.117, 19.108. introducing infin. 1.217, 2.21, 3.23, 6.7, *infl.*
see **com, do(n), speke(n)**; (of
purpose) 6.69, 10.149; (qualifying adj.) 1.180, 8K.14; (of
obligation) ~ *leue* to be believed
8H.19, sim. 18.419, 602, 19.200;
(of opportunity) see **habbe(n)**.
te (unstressed) 17.6, 20. [OE
tō] See **foren, forto, what.**

to- *pref.* expressing separation,
destruction, &c. [OE *tō-*]

to. See **two; þe** *art.*

toblaweð *pr. 3 sg.* blows up
18.276. [OE *tōblāwan*]

tobreke(n) *v. tr.* break (down),
break to pieces 1.688, 5.63,
10.229, 278; put an end to, resolve 1.695. *pp.* **tobroke** 5.19.
intr. pa. t. sg. **tobrac** broke
10.25. [OE *tōbrecan, -bræc*; see
breke(n)]

toc(an). See **tak.**

tocheoweð *pr. pl.* chew up 19.
106. [OE *tōcēowan*]

tockning(u)e, tokning(ue) *n.*
presage, portent, sign 7.57, 89,
162, 197. [OE *tācnung*] Cf.
bitacnunge.

todai, -day *adv.* today 6.316,
14.56, 17.37, 72; ~ *þe thrid dai*
see **þridde**; **todæi** 10.110;
todaȝȝ 13.85; **tedai, -day** 17.4,
36. [OE *tōdæg*]

todasste *pa. t. pl.* smashed to
pieces 11.141. [to- +ME
daschen, origin obscure]

todealen *v. tr.* separate, divide
19.381. *pa. t. sg.* **todeld(e)** 10.
187; dispersed 16.146; *intr.*
todælde was divorced 16.307.
pp. **todeled** divided 16.286.
[OE *tōdǣlan*]

todraȝe v. pull to pieces 10.113.
pr. subj. sg. todrawe 8N.34.
pa. t. sg. todroh pulled down
10.23. [to- +draȝen]
todriueð pr. 3 sg. drives away,
scatters 18.193. [OE tōdrīfan]
tofore adv. in front 2.176. [next]
tofore(n) prep. before (of time)
16.73; before, in front of 1.492,
2.34; (postponed) 8N.10; tofor
17.12; touore 1.686, 741. [OE
tōforan]
togadere adv. together 7.230
(see set), 10.209 (see stopen);
togedere 5.156, 214; togidere,
-ȝiddre 3.249, 17.104, 12.128;
togædere, te- 16.142, 193.
[OE tōgædere]
togederes adv. together 18.164,
170. [prec.+adv. -es]
toȝain prep. against, towards
3.216. [OE tōgeagn] Cf. aȝein.
toȝeines prep. against 5.95; in
the face of 19.221; (postponed)
to meet 10.266, togænes 16.
236; togeanes contrary to
16.11; tojanes, -yenes towards
17.7, 215. [OE tōgegnes, -gēanes;
see prec.] Cf. aȝeines.
toȝte adj. as n. trying circumstances 1.449. [OE tōh tough,
with inorganic -t]
tohewe pa. t. pl. cut to pieces
11.141. pp. tohauwen 10.294.
[OE tōhēowon, -hēawen from
-hēawan; see hewene]
tohh; tojanes, toyenes;
tok(e), token(n); told(e). See
þoȝ; toȝeines; tak; tel.
tolleð pr. 3 sg. entices, attracts
12.187, 18.367. [OE *tollian,
cf. for-tyllan seduce]
tome = to me (stressed on to) 1.
354, 630. Cf. mitte (under
mid).
tomorewe, -morwen adv. tomorrow 3.81, 4.78; tomoru
14.56; tomærȝe, -marȝen 10.
93, 117. [OE tōmorgen] Cf.
amorȝe, moreghen.

ton; tone; tonge. See to n.;
tene; tung(e).
tonge n. pair of tongs 1.112.
[OE tóng(e)]
tong-rote n. base of the tongue
14.239. [ON tungu-rœtr (pl.)]
toniȝt, -niht adv. tonight 5.191;
last night 10.10, 12. [OE tō-
niht] Cf. niȝt(e).
took. See tak.
top(pe) n. hair of the head 11.16;
top (of a tree or plant) 14.205:
~ ne more top or root, any part
1.596. pl. toppes heads 1.306
(note). [OE topp]
topasiune n. topaz 9.92. [LL
topazion adapted to AN]
torendeð pr. pl. tear to pieces
19.105. [OE tōréndan]
torn(ede). See turn(e).
torof pa. t. sg. intr. burst apart
4.219. [to- +ON rífa with pa. t.
after drive, &c.]
tort n. turd 1.644. [OE tord]
tortle n. turtle-dove 8G.3. [OE
turtle]
tosamenn adv. together 13.153;
tosomne 10.274. [OE tosamne,
-somne; see samenn]
toschakeð pr. pl. shake to pieces
1.605. [OE tōscacan]
toslit pp. cut open (and so
robbed) 1.440. [OE tōsliten
from -slītan]
tosnaðde pa. t. sg. cut to pieces
10.30. [to- +OE *snāþian rel.
to snīþan]
tosomne. See tosamenn.
tospreat pr. 3 sg. stretches wide
18.672. [OE tōsprǣdan]
tosvolle pp. swollen up 1.101.
[OE tōswollen from -swellan; see
sval]
totere v. tear to pieces 4.266.
pr. pl. totereþ 8N.6. [OE
tōteran]
totose v. tear to pieces 1.70.
[to- +OE *tāsian rel. to tǣsan]
toturuen v. skin, strip 4.184.
[to- +OE *turfian, cf. turf]

totweamde *pa. t. sg.* separated 18.595. *pp.* **totwemde** separated (by annulment of marriage) 16.39. [OE *tōtwǣman*] See **tweamen**.

totwichet *pr. pl.* pluck to pieces 1.605. [to-+OE *twiccian*]

toþer; **toðes**. See **þe** *def. art.*, **oþer(e)**; **teh**.

toun(e) *n.* town 2.111, 7.247, 8H.29, 9.38, 11.21; **tun(e)** 13. 21, 121, 16.54, 68. village 1.711, 4.32, 7.146. (without art.) *fram* ~ 7.146, 252, *in* ~ 6.70, *out of* ~ 6.347, *to* ~ 7.160. *gen.* **tounes** *in* ~ *ende* 11.12, 15.49. *pl.* **tounes** *in in* ~ in the world, among men 8G.4; **tunes** 16.182. [OE *tūn*, orig. enclosure]

tour(e) *n.* tower 3.1, 81, 11.38; **tur** 16.291; **tuur** 8Y.1. *pl.* **toures** 2.139. [LOE *tūr*, OF *tour*]

tourne. See **turn(e)**.

toute *n.* buttocks 9.136. [obscure]

touore. See **tofore(n)**.

toward *adv.* to (it), in 16.43; to (her) 18.5. [OE *tōweard*]

toward(e) *prep.* towards, to 7.224, 10.191, 11.128, 14.115, 18.64; (postponed) 8F.42; against 1.361, 362; **touward** 10.220, 221; **towarrd** 13.200; **towart** 18.209, 19.144; ~ *hire* upon herself 18.285. (divided) *to Gode ward* in God 12.52, towards God 17.56. [OE *tōweard, tō .. weard*]

towarpeð *pr. 3 sg.* destroys 18. 232. [OE *tōweorpan*; see **warpeð**]

trace *n.* path, way: *token her* ~ went 2.320. [OF]

traistest *adj. sup.* most secure 14.59. [ON *treyst-r* pp. of *treysta* make firm]

traitour *n.* traitor 11.31. [AN, acc. of *traitre*]

trauail, traueil *n.* labour 17. 190, 14.89. [OF *travail*]

trauailest *pr. 2 sg.* work, labour 7.87. *pp.* **itravailed** 17.196; **itrauailed** travelled 7.233. [OF *travaillier*]

tre(e) *n.* tree 3.57, 9.71, 14.34; **treo** 7.41, 43, 18.196, 668; **tro** 1.316; **trowe** 1, note to 95. gallows 15.82; the Cross 8s.3, w. 20; beam, wooden bar 4.248, 270; wood 11.37, 18.530. *pl.* **tron** trees 1.395; **treon** pieces of wood 18.667, 668. [OE *trēo(w)*, pl. *trēow(u)*]

treie *n.* pain, affliction 6.158. [OE *trega*]

trendli *pr. subj. sg.* roll 1, note to 95. [OE *-trendlian*]

treo(n); **treowe**. See **tre(e)**; **trewe**.

treoweliche *adv.* truly, faithfully 19.89; **treowliche** loyally 19. 232, 405; **truly** 14.81. [OE *trēowlīce*]

tresor *n.* treasure 19.29, 31, 163; royal treasury 16.145; **treosor** 19.416; **tresour(e)** 2.218, 224. [OF *treso(u)r*]

trespas *n.* offence, crime 11.171. [OF]

trest *n.* trust 3.146. [app. OE **tryst* re-formed from **trust* on **trystan* v., rel. to ON *traust* n., *treysta* v.; see **traistest, trust**]

trest *v.* See **trust**.

tresurers *n. pl.* treasurers 19. 382. [AN *tresorer*]

treunesse *n.* fidelity 3.240. [OE *trēownes(se)*]

treuþe, treuthe, trewþe *n.* (plighted) faith 3.138, 240, 8D.28, F.43, 16.156; **trouþe** 6.252, 8H.20; **trowðe** 19.89; *of* ~ faithful 8H.31. *pl.* **treothes, treuthes** covenants, pledges 16.156, 279. [OE *trēowþ*]

treuthede *n.* faithfulness 14.97. [prec.+-**hede**]

trewe *adj.* true, faithful, loyal 6.95, 121, 8G.4, 38, H.20; of loyalty 11.30; **treowe** 19.382; ~ *bileaue* steadfast faith 18.118, 289, 19.178. **comp. trewer** 6. 122. [OE *trēowe*]

triacle *n.* healing ointment 9.84. [OF]

tricherie *n.* deceit, treachery 7.31, 8H.21. [OF]

trichour *n.* cheat, deceiver 7.30, 8H.22. [AN]

trie *adj.* excellent 9.19, 75. [prob. OF *trie* n., choice]

trikeþ *pr. 3 sg.* hangs down 8E.63. [obscure]

trist(e). See **trust**.

triws *n.* truce 18.339, 342. [pl. of OE *trēow* pledge]

tro(n); trof. See **tre(e) ; þer(e).**

trone *n.* throne 19.274. *pl.* **trones** 19.292. [OF]

trous *n.* bundle 8N.15, 25. [OF *trousse*]

trouue *pr. 1 sg.* believe, think 6.369; **trow** 8H.38 (believe there are). *2 sg.* (with suffixed pron.) **troustu** 6.370. *3 sg.* **troweþ** 8N.9. [OE *trēow(i)an, treōw(i)an*]

trouþe, trowðe; trowe. See **treuþe ; tre(e).**

truan *n.* vagabond 15.35. [OF *truant*]

trucode *pa. t. pl.* (? *sg.*) failed 16.89. [OE *trucian*]

truly. See **treoweliche**.

trume *n.* army, ranks 10.181. [OE *truma*]

trust *pr. 3 sg.* trusts 19.208 (with *on*, in; all others with *to*); **trist** 7.32; **trest** 2.71. *pa. t. sg.* **truste** 7.50; **triste** 3.210, 7.61. *pl.* **truste** 11.157. [app. OE **trystan* rel. to ON *treysta*; see **trest** n.]

tu. See **þou**.

tuht *n.* disciplined conduct, good behaviour 19.52. [OE *tyht*]

tuhten *v.* instruct 19.412. *pr. subj. sg.* **tuhte** discipline 19.25. *pa. t. sg.* **tuhte** made her way,

went 10.239. *pl.* **tuhte(n)** drew, came: ~ *togadere, tosomne* engaged 10.268, 274. *pp.* **ituht** corrected, disciplined 19.399. [OE *tyhtan* draw, persuade; for sense 'go' cf. **te**]

tukest *pr. 2 sg.* ill-treat 1.63. *pp.* **ituket** 18.500. [OE *tūcian*]

tumberel *n.* a kind of fish, perhaps porpoise 4.25. [app. rel. to OF *tumber* v.]

tun(e). See **toun(e)**.

tunder *n.* tinder 12.177. [ON *tundr*; cf. OE *tynder*]

tuneð *pr. 3 sg.* closes 19.362. [OE *tȳnan*]

tung(e) *n.* tongue 1.194, 18.254; in phr. *na* ~ *may tell* 14.175, cf. 17.269, 19.92; **tonge** 1.37. *pl.* **tungen** 19.129. [OE *túnge*]

tunscipe *n. coll.* villagers 16.196. [OE]

tur. See **tour(e)**.

turbut *n.* turbot 4.22. [AN]

turn(e), turnen *v. tr.* turn, convert 1, n. to 132, 18.645; **tvrne** 8w.32; *intr.* change 14.236; ~, *aȝe* return 9.188. *pr. 2 sg.* **turnest** *tr.* 18.295. *3 sg.* **turneþ, -ð** *tr.* 17.248, 18.209; **turniþ** *tr.* 9.136, *intr.* 119. *pl.* **turneþ, -ð** *refl.* 19.232; *intr.* 9.115. *subj. sg.* **turne** *tr.* 18.243; **tourne** *intr.* 6.147. *imper. sg.* **torn** *tr.* 6.109, 113. *pa. t. sg.* **tornede** *tr.* 7.14. *pl.* **turned(e)** *intr.* 3.183, 220. *pp.* **turnd** 6.430; **iturnt** 18.226; **iturned** shaped, rounded (on a lathe) 9.68. [OE *túrnian, týrnan*; AN *turner*]

turneiment *n.* tournament 18. 508. [AN]

turnes *n. pl.* stratagems 19.206. [AN *turn*]

turuf *n.* turf, grass 8Y.1. [OE *turf*]

tus(s); tuur. See **þus ; tour(e)**.

tuengst *pr. 2 sg.* pinch 1.112. [OE *twengan*]

tuynklen v. wink 8R.2. [OE twinclian]

tuo, twa. See two.

tweamen v. separate, divide 18.166, 19.379. imper. sg. tweam 18.197. pp. itweamet 18.195. [OE twǣman]

twei(e), tueie, tueye adj. two 3.177, 7.235, 11.112, 114, 2.189; tweiȝe 10.240; tweien 10.295, 19.386. [OE twēgen masc.] See two.

twelf(e) adj. twelve 4.55, 16.68. [OE twelf]

twenti, twenty n., adj. twenty 3.202, 4.273, 6.270, 16.58, 18.223; combined with units (preceding), four and ~, fif and ~ 3.2, 16.88. [OE twentig]

twentiþe adj. twentieth: foure and ~ twenty-fourth 7.5. [OE twentigoþa]

twybyl n. two-edged axe 8N.15. [OE twibill]

twinne adj. twofold, dual 13.180, 212. [OE twinn, ON tvinn-r]

twinnin v. part 18.595. [from prec.]

twinnunge n. separation 18.594. [from prec.]

two n., adj. two 3.112, 4.133, 5.32, 7.4, 9.13; tuo 5.73, 8E.59; to 7.37, 237, 8W.17, 11.91; on ~ in two 4.250; twa 10.292, 13.221, 16.11, 18.61. [OE twā, fem. and neut. of twēgen] See twei(e), atwo.

þ-. See þe art.

þa, ða; þæ; þaem; þæn; þær. See þe, þo, þo(o); þo(o) conj.; þai pron.; þat pron.; þer(e).

þah adv. though, yet, however 1.737, 18.362, 476, 19.189, 394; (after d, t) tah 19.13, 91, 101. [as next]

þah conj. (with subj.) though, even if 1.597, 8D.18, F.40, H.24,

10.273, 18.410, 19.23, 204; as ~ as if 18.228, 19.143; þau 6.45, 55, 104; after 'no wonder' 6.360. [OE þah, orig. unstressed form of þēah] Cf. þei, þoȝ.

þai adj. demons. pl. those 14.287. [as next]

þai, þay pron. 3 pl. they 3.54, 9.81, 15.29, 82; þei, þey 4.260, 264; þeȝȝ 13.34, 69, ðeȝȝ 31, (after t) teȝȝ 38, 45. acc. þam them 14.239; þeȝȝm 13.171. dat. þam 14.26, 54; þaem 14.47; þai 9.87. poss. þare 14.6; þer(e) 14.6, 50; þeȝȝre 13.60, (after d) teȝȝre 195; gen. of them 13.32. [ON þei-r, þeira, þeim (dat.); OE þǣm] Cf. hi(i).

þai. See þei.

þakkeþ pr. pl. pat 9.142. [OE þaccian]

þam; þamerail. See þai; amera(i)l.

þan(ne) adv. then 1.446, 3.27, 8Q.2, 14.67, 16.285; ðanne 12.95; þonne 1.434; þen(ne), þene 5.64, 6.185, 331, 8F.33, 14.230, 18.167, 19.89. [as next]

þan(ne), þane conj. when 1.121, 4.45, 167, 267, 7.139; ðanne 12.41; (after d) tanne 12.109; þenne 10.93, 101. [as next]

þan(ne), þane conj. than 1.24, 39, 2.145, 4.60, 98, 7.18, 16.191; ðanne 12.88; þen 5.8, 6.123, 8E.44, 18.27, 19.390; (introd. clause with subj.) than that 1.22, 4.112; than if 3.270, 4.294. [OE þanne, þænne]

þan; þane; þankes. See þat pron.,þe art.,þo adj.,þo(o) pron.; þat pron., þe art.; þonk(e).

þannes adv. from there 7.80. [þanon+adv. (gen.) -es] Cf. þenne.

þannkenn v. thank 13.140. pr. 1 sg. þanke 13.281. 3 sg. þankeþ 2.191; þonkeð 19.227 (both fold. by of with the occasion of thanks, as usually). subj.

sg. þoncki 18.266. *pl.* þonkin 19.225 (with direct obj. of thing, dat. of person). *pa. t. sg.* þanked 2.125; þonkede 7.177. [OE *þancian, þoncian*]

þanon *adv.* from there 16.42; þenon 16.28. [OE *þanon(e)*] Cf. þenne.

ðar *pr. 2 sg.* need 6.260. *3 sg. impers.* þaref there need 1.146; þerf (with dat. of person): *ne ~ us* we need not 19.194. *pl. pers.* þurue 19.164, 253. *pa. t. subj. sg. impers.* þourt: *~ him neuere* he would never need 3.5. [OE *þearf, þurfon; þorfte*]

þar; þare, thare; þarhon. See þer(e); þai, þe *art.*, þer(e); þer(e).

þarnes *pr. 3 sg.* is deprived of, loses 4.340. [ON *þar(f)na*]

þart; þas. See þou, art; þe *art.*, þis *adj.*

þat *adj. demons.* that 1.5, 2.90, 3.1, 4.11, 5.78, 8L.10; þatt 13.21; ðat 12.22, 16.178; this 1.607; *~ ower* that of yours 1.657; (after *t*) tat 14.111; þet 16.101, 102, 17.22, 18.27, 19. 279, such 429; þut 11.138, 172. [next] See þe *art.*, þo *adj.*

þat *pron. demons.* that 1.82, 2. 164, 3.175, 4.69, 5.29, 6.139, 7.199; þatt 13.88; ðat 12.82; þet 16.14, 25, 17.30, 17.30, 19.92; it 6.16; the man 8G.19; He 12.54; those (with pl. vb. and complement) 17.75, 18.158, 345; quasi-*adv.* about that 6.54 (see bold(e)). *gen.* þes in *anoþer ~* something more 1.494 (note); *~ þe (conj.)* as 16.57. *dat.* or *inst.* (after preps.) þan 3.217, 5.55; þon 1.425; forming advs. and conjs. 1.156, 619–20, 2.1, 5.108, 10.202, 18.310; þane 17.148; þæn 10.84; þen 8K.74: see after, er(e), for, wiþ. *inst.* þi therefore 1.520. [OE *þæt*, M, K *þet*, neut.; *þæs, þæm,*

þon, þy̅; þæs þe, for þæm, þon (þe), &c.] See þo(o).

þat *pron. rel. indecl.* that, which, who(m) 1.10, 78, 2.7, 17, 3.4, 4.14, 5.55; þatt 13.30; (after *t*) tatt 157; ðat 12.81, 16.174; þet 8w.27, 16.3, 13, 17.17, 18.9, 19.31; ðet 12.10; (correl. with *swich*) as 1.284, 2.74; to whom, which 1.187, 3.260, 6.298, 11.52, 13.170; where 3.181; (of time) when, on which 6.125, 8L.10, 13.157, 18.5; in which 19.247; with which 16.226; referring to a clause (prec. or foll.): which 18.277, 279; governed by foll. prep. (separated): *~ .. inne* in which 13.22, *~ .. of* of whom 14.12, *~ hit is* of *schadewe* of which it is the shadow 18.27; supplemented by specifying pers. prons.: *~ hise* whose 4.235, *~ .. of him* of whom 7.136, *~ .. efter hire* after whom 19.11, *~ .. it* which 7.272; elliptical, incorporating antecedent: that which, what 1.115, 3.168, 5.218, 8D.9, F.44, H.45, 10.314, 17.187, 18.178, 19.13, 77; he who, the one who 1.132, 5.259, 8G.27; those who 8E.72, 14.53; anyone who 17.186. [OE *þæt, þet*, as prec., replacing þe]

þat *conj.* that (introd. subject or object clause) 1.34, 2.15, 3.78, 4.305, 5.60; þatt 13.9 (introd. cl. obj. of *off*), (after *t d*) tatt 19, 23; ðat 12.145, 16.161, tat 12.58; that 6.383; þet 18.42, 19.23. (with cl. of result) so that, in such a way that 3.143, 5.42, 6.11, 8M.5, N.39, 11.22, 16.243; esp. after *so*: 1.44, 3.22, 4.94, 5.2; until 1.749, 2.92, 6.51, 7.239, 8R.9, 10.115. (of time) since 5.154, when 10.118; (loosely) because 4.134. with *neg.*, without (-ing): *~ he ne broucte* without bringing 4.35, sim. 284. fold. by subj. after verbs of command, prayer, purpose, 2.20, 6.147, 12.108, 7.22, 10.64, 12.90; after 'seem' 1.21. introd. command or wish 1.318, 379. Forming compd. conjunctions with preps., e.g. **after, for, þurh** ; with conjs. or advs., e.g. **ȝef, þoȝ, whan** ; divided in **siþen** .. ~ 14.120–1; added to rel. pron. *wham* 8M.21. [OE *þæt, þætte*]

þau. See **þah**.

þe *adv.* demons. (by) so much, on that account, the 1.19, 34, 3.126, 5.202, 6.389, 7.26, 8M.7, 18.326, 19.12; *neuer* ~ *lesse* by no means less for that 14.79; correl. *þe .. þe* the .. the 16.250; (after *d*) *te* 18.420. [OE *þȳ, þē* inst. of *þæt*] Cf. **naþeles, naðema**.

þe *conj.* than 1.372; **þa** or 10.246. [OE *þe*]

þe *def. art.* the; usu. *indecl.*: 1.13, 2.13, 3.7, 4.2, 5.1; **ðe** 12.1, 16.63; **the** 14.33, 16.165; (after *s, t, d*) **te** 12.54, 16.107, 18.64, 81, 19.268; **e** 19.420; app. intended by occas. spellings with other vowel-letters: **þa** 16.176, 17.159; **ða** 16.37, 38, **þæ** 10.41, 16.217; **þo** 17.3, 6, **to** 63. **þ**- before vowels, as **þilk(e)**; **þamerail** 3.66, sim. 16.213, 264; before *h* elided in **þ 'exte**, see **heiȝt(e)**. Occas. inflexions: *sg.* **se** *masc.* nom. 16.1, 2, 12, 17. 54, 58, 166; **si** orig. *fem. nom.*, correct in 17.34 (2nd) but with n. masc. in OE 17.5, 11 and n. masc. in F 17.34 (1st); **þat** orig. *neut.*, still mainly with neut. ns. but generalized esp. before vowels, and tending to **þat** *adj. demons.*: 1.10, 120, 7.177, 225, 8v.2, 11.100, 141; **ðat** 16.114; **þet** 16.13, 17.117, 18.531, 19. 36; ~ *a(n)*, *o(n)* the one, one of them 3.4, 176, 5.75, 18.668; ~ *ilche, il(l)ke* the same, that (*adj.*) 3.3, 16, 13.27, 65, (*pron.*) 5.47;

~ *oþer, oðer* the next 4.145, the second 5.74, the other 5.76, 18.69, 668, ~ *toþer* 14.84; **þone** *masc. acc.* 16.7 (with OE neut.), used as *nom.* 16.40; **ðone** 16.16, 31; **þane** 1.729, 17.152; **þene** 5.113, 126 (and regularly in 5 with *vox* and *wolf*), 10.5, 137; **þan** *acc.* 1.488; *dat.* 1.522, 689, 10.2, 83, 17.183; **þen** *dat.* (with *ende*) 1.701, 7.151, *neut.* 6.19, 299, with orig. *fem.* 6.22; **þun** *acc.* 11.27, 30; **þon** *neut. dat.* 1, note to 95. **þas** *gen. masc.* 1.254, 10.155; **þes, ðes** 16.7 (1st), 14, 18.157, *neut.* (*adv.*) 16. 7 (2nd); **þa** *fem. nom.* 10.24, 39, *acc.* 10.15, 21; **þo** *nom.* 1.26, 155; **þare** *gen.* 1.28, 8v.13, *dat.* 1.31, 96, 10.292; **þere** *gen.* 10. 23, 237 (see **while**), *dat.* 10.27, 40, 142; **þer** 18.382. *pl.* **þa, ða** 10.16, 21, 16.3, 5, 10; **to** 16.230, 237; **þan** *dat.* 10.184, 223. [LOE *þe*, fem. *þeo*, replacing *sē̆, sēo* (K *sīo*), *þæt, þet; þone, þæs, þǣm; þā, þǣre;* pl. *þā, þǣm*] See **þat** *adj.*, **þo** *adj.*

þe *pron.* demons. masc. (preceding rel.) he, the one 18.482. *fem.* **þeo** she 18.265, 283; *as* ~ *þe* being one who 19.204. [LOE *þē̆, þēo* replacing *sē̆, sēo*] Cf. **þat** and **þo(o)** *pron.* demons., **þe** *def. art.*

þe *particle* rel. indecl. who 10.135, 176, 16.6, 110, 18.31, 37, 19.20, 100; **ðe** 16.64; **þa** 10.54, 16.68, 69; **þeo** 1.592; to whom 16.236; which, that 12.94, 18.29, 66, 178, 19.104; in which 16.68; (with personal antecedent understood) anyone who 4.341; he who 18.8, 19.153; those who 18.336. [OE *þe*] Cf. **þat** *pron. rel.*

þe ; **þee** ; **þear**. See **þo(o)** *adv.*, **þou** ; **þou** ; **þer(e)**.

þeaw *n.* virtue 19.51, *god* ~ 34; **þewe** propriety 6.72. *pl.*

þeawes virtues, *gode* ~ 18.6; practices, conduct 19.33; þewes good qualities 2.44. [OE *þēaw*]

þed(e) *n.* people 13.144; nation 13.167; þeode country 18.142. *pl.* (*dat.*) þeode countries 1.537. [OE *þēod*]

þef *n.* thief 5.102; þeof 7.98, 19.7. *pl.* þeues 4.207. [OE *þēof*]

þeȝes; þeȝȝ(-), þei, þey. See þes; þai.

þei, þey *conj.* (usu. with subj.) though 3.24 (indic.), 4.75, 7.85, 101; þai 3.128, 130; þeg, þeȝ 1.682, 48, 137; þeiȝ 2.10, 150; *als, ase* ~ as though 3.84, 7.83, 266. [OE *þē(a)h*] Cf. þah, þoȝ, alþei.

þeines *n. pl.* royal servants, thanes, nobles 10.167, 206; ðeines 16.5. [OE *þegn*]

þemperice; þen. See emperice; þe *art.*, þat *pron.*; þan(ne).

þenchen *v.* (with direct obj. or *of*) think (of), consider 7.139, 19.406; be reminded 18.536; imagine 18.626; as *n.* thinking 18.40; þennkenn 13.5, 7; thinc wonder 14.187; plan, intend 5.125, 6.150, 184, 7.68, 263, 10.160, 11.24; plan to go 10.59; hope 1.113, 5.13. *pr. 1 sg.* þink 3.166; þenke 8M.16. *3 sg.* þencheð 18.645. *pl.* þencheð 18.22. *subj. sg.* þenche 1.472; þince 16.47. *imper. sg.* þench (with *on*) 8M.8, (with *of*) 18.14, 15, 337. *pl.* þencheð 18.671, 19.130. *pa. t. 1, 3 sg.* þoȝte 1.270; þohte 10.160; þouȝt(e) 3.175, 7.19; þouȝth 2.227; þohute 5.13; þoute 4.170, 5.125, 6.150; þouþe he thought 4.58 (note); þowthe 4.296. *2 sg.* þoȝtest 1.113; þohtest 10.59. *pl.* þoȝte 11.24; þouȝten 7.263. *pp.* iþoht 10.48; iþouȝt 7.68, iþout 6.184. [OE *þencan, þŏhte*] Cf. þinche.

þenche; þene; þenke. See þinche; þan(ne) *adv.*, þe *art.*; þenchen.

þenne *adv.* from there 1.684, 4.45; þeonne 18.245, 19.380, *from* ~ 157; þeone 10.191. [OE *þanon(e)* app. infl. by henne] Cf. þanon.

þenne; þennkenn; þenon; þeo; þeode; þeof; þeos(e). See þan(ne); þenchen; þanon; þe *pron. demons., rel.*, þo(o) *pron.*; þed(e); þef; þis.

þeoster *n.* darkness 19.276; þuster 1.154, 186. [OE *þēostru, þȳstru*] See þuster.

þeoster-, þosternesse *n.* darkness 19.102, 99. [OE *þēostor-nes(se)*]

þer(e) *adv. demons.* there 2.210, 3.1, 4.10, 5.20, 18.157; ðer(e) 12.100, 166; ther 16.144; (after *t*) ter 18.101; þær 13.23, 16.2; ðær 16.46; þear 18.156, 19.276; (after *d*) tær 13.49; þar(e) 1.470, 5.33, 7.41, 14.112, 16.150; ðar 12.82; thare 16.213; þor(e) 4.9, 188; ðore 12.44; on this 18.101; to that place 1.676; ~ *doune* down there 7.145; *here and* ~ see her(e); (forming *conj.*) ~ *as(e)* where 7.112, 18.85, 19.386, ~ þær where 13.69; (unemphatic and introductory, preceding verb) 3.15, 57, 4.75, 5.27, 7.214, 8K.43, (inverted) 4.282, 333, 10.83, 14.137. Prefixed to prep. or adv.: ~aboute in the neighbourhood 7.283. ~bi near by 9.147. ~biside near by 1.25, 7.143, 211. ~onnfasst near by 13.65. ~oute, -ute outside 4.205, 236, 11.41, 14.197; þrute 19.46. þruppe above (in a text) 18.178, 207, 281. Representing neut. pron., it, that, this: ~after, -æfter, -æftor, -efter after that 1.45, 16.21, 50, 113, 293; þrefter 18.93, accordingly

389. ~aӡeines in comparison with it 19.276. ~among, -amang in the midst of it 3.32, 9.129. ~ate at it 7.260. ~before, biuore before that 17.113, 11.62. ~bi through it 18.536. ~bituene in the meantime 2. 207. ~for(e), -uore for it 4.44, 87; for that 1.210, 595; at this 11.136; on that account, therefore 2.256, 5.202, 6.80, 15.55, 19.170. ~forth by that place 7.254. ~ihende near it 17.66. ~in(ne) in it, in there 1.401, 2.231, 3.9, 4.19, 16.268, 18.329; in them 2.211; into it 5.234, 7.118; ~ .. inne 3.37, 4.119, 16.269, 19.29; þrin(ne) 18.215, 244, 19.36, 90. ~mid with it, them 1.81, 112. ~of of it, that, this 1.570, 3.260, 5.18, 9.61; of them 7.191; about it 1.146, 5.260; at that 3.219, 5.24; in that 6.9; on it 3.108 (see lete(n)); with it 16.148; ~offe of it 4.14, 13.148; þrof 18.273, of them 19.37, (some) of them 18.116; trof 19.373; of ~ 1. 256 (note). ~on on it 12.31, 18.280; ~hon 8w.10; ~ .. on 14.186; þron 18.537, 618 (see lete(n)). ~ouer above it 12.12. ~to to it, that 1.202, 6.170; there 7.163; at it 11.95; of it 18.318; for that 1.530; for the purpose 18.665; in addition 10. 271, 11.78, 18.90; ~ .. to 1.391. ~towart towards that 19.92; to it 19.95; upon it 19.376. ~þoru, -þur(r)h through, by that 6.346, 11.135, 13.177, 16. 300. þruppe about it 19.404. ~wiþ, -wið with it 18.574; in, about that 12.140; in addition 18.411. ~wiþinne in it 8E.68. [OE þǣr, þār(a), and þǣr, þar(a) in reduced stress]

þer(e) conj. where 4.245, 8F.36, H.17, 18.162; ðer 12.72; as 4.71, 10.12; þar(e) 1.254, 7.90; þǣr

when 16.38; þear 18.193. adv. rel. where, in which 1.26, 650, 5.162, 6.23, 7.92, 12.23; ðar 12. 78; correl. with swuch, as 18. 535; ~ .. abute around which 1.16; ~ .. inne in which 6.20, 300, 7.286, 16.169; ~inne into which 7.82; ~ .. on on which 7.216. [as prec.]

þer(e); þerf. See þai, þe; ðar.

þerwhiles conj. while 2.55, 3.162. [þer(e) + while + adv. gen. -es]

þes, thes n. pl. thighs 6.441, 4.330; þeӡes 8к.31. [OE þēoh, A þēh, sg. and pl.]

þes, ðes. See þat; þe; þis.

þestrede pa. t. sg. grew dark 1b. 119, 242. pl. þestreden 16.125. [OE þēostrian] Cf. þeoster.

þet; þeues; þewe. See þat, þe art.; þef; þeaw.

þewwess n. pl. servants 13.266. [OE þēow]

þ'exte = þe hexte. See heiӡ(e).

þi. See þat pron.; þou.

þicke adj. thick, dense 1.17, 396, 19.98; deep 1.308. [OE þicce]

þicke adv. close together 7.45. sup. þickest most thickly 19. 113. [OE þicce]

þider(e) adv. to that place, there 1.465, 2.148, 3.152, 4.118, 5.12, 268; þuder(e) 7.70, 11.84; hider ne ~ see hider(e); ~ þat to the place where 3.181. ~ as (conj.) where 19.376. [OE þider, þyder]

þiderward adv. to that place 10.272; in that direction 18.420; to that 1.99. [OE þiderweard]

þilk(e) adj. that (same), the 6.146, 326, 9.173; this 6.258; ~ dai schal neuer be the time shall never come 3.231, sim. 6.124; þulke the same 7.95, 286; that 11.8, 119. pl. þilke those 5.148. [þe + ilk(e)]

þilke pron. the one 7.32. pl. those 3.53, 61. [as prec.]

þin(e), þyn; þink, thinc, þince. See þou; þenchen.
þinche v. seem 1.262; þenche 17.225. impers. (with dat.) þunche in me wolde ~ it would seem to me, I should think it 6.238. pr. 3 sg. pers. þincþ 1.500, þuncheð 18.31, 19.66, 116; impers. (with subject hit) þincheþ 1.181, (subject unexpressed) þinchez (= -þ) in me ~ I think 7.284, þinkeþ, -ʒ 6.218, 286, 3.129, þincþ 1.349, (with suffixed pron.) þincþe = þincþ þe in hu ~ bi what do you think of 1.46, þing 1.652, þuncheþ 8G.47, þuncþ 1.630, þunch 1.607, 609. pa. t. sg. pers. þuʒte 1.21, þuht 10.153, þouʒte 3.170, 252; impers. þuʒte in ~ wel wl of (with pron. dat. understood) she thought very badly of 1.31 [but perh. rather a confusion of form for þoʒte from þenchen], þuhte 1.619, 16.58, þouʒte 7.41, 50, þoute 5.94, thoght, þoʒte, þohte 14.204, 11.161, 8E.15. [OE þyncan, þūhte] Cf. þenchen.
þing(e), ðing, thyng n. thing 1.225, 6.88, 8H.13, 12.150, 14. 45; þingue 7.200; þink 15.77; event 16.122; anything 18.261; creature 1.185, 589, 6.425, 8G. 23, 18.318; for mine ~ on my account 1.312. pl. þing, ðing, thing 7.126, 8T.28, 10.101, 16. 99, 14.177; þinges, thinges, thynges 3.261, 8H.40, 17.67, 18.198, 14.21, 26; þingues 7. 37; þinkes 17.81, 122. gen. þinge 1.587, 18.604. dat. þinge, þynge 1.730, 8W.13. See aniþing, noþing, sumþing. [OE þing, sg. and pl.]
þynne adj. thin, scanty 8F.18; þunne as n. thin, poor clothing 8F.15. [OE þynne]
þire. See þou.
þis adj. demons. this; usu. indecl.

in sg.: 2.18, 49, 3.36, 4.109, 6.203, 8B.5, X.2, 11.1; þiss 13. 50; ðis 12.85, 16.1; thys 15.66; (after s, t) tis 12.36, 19.29; ~ ilke this (same) 5.99, 8N.17, 14.39; to ~ day until now 4.72; (of a subject already mentioned) 1.41, 5.80, 6.27, 7.35, 11.159, 12.85; (of a subject taken to be familiar) 2.254, 8H.2, 5, V.1, X.3, 11.103, 12.183, 18.163. Occas. inflexions in sg.: þes masc. nom. 1.195, 7.97, 17.204, tes 18.363; as obl. 18.99, 652; þisne acc. 10.77; þissen masc. or neut. dat. 10.99, 127; þise dat., gender various 17.91, 149, 18.504, þisse 5.225, in mid, at ~ worde (perh. pl.) 1.405, 496, 747; þeos fem. nom. 1.625, 7.123, ~ ilke 18.501; as obl. 19.166; þos 1.41, 353; þissere dat. 10.110. pl. þas 10.101, 173, 16.125; þeos 1.611, 7.86, 186, 18.44, 19.15; þeose 18.20; þes 18.163, 427; þis 7. 37, 223, 8H.2, 11.147, 14.182; þise 2.117, 3.261, 4.310, ðise 12.156; þos 1.95, 476, 17.98. [OE þes, þēos, þis; þisne; þissum, þisse, -re; þās]
þis pron. demons. this 1.625, 3. 245, 6.355, 8V.15, 9.82; þiss 13.181; (after t) tis 19.172; this time, now 3.167, 4.16. pl. þeos 18.634; þeose 19.111; þes 6.275; þos 17.187. [as prec.]
þo adj. demons. that 17.101, 251. [obscure variant of þe def. art.]
þo adj. demons. pl. those, the 4.345, 8K.59; ~ ilek(e) the same 17.66, 80, 81 (but perh. here art.; see ilk(e)); þa 13.117, 16.161; (after t) ta 13.193. dat. þan 10.224. [OE þā, dat. þǣm] See þat adj., þe art.
þo(o) pron. demons. pl. those 1.503, 2.168, 8D.20, 17.118, 269 (dat.); ðo 12.189; þa 13.243, 285; þeo 1.573, 629, 18.37, 79,

19.16, 201. *dat.* þan 1.720. [as
prec.]

þo *pron. rel. pl.* whom 17.212; þa
which, that 10.16, 21, 38; ða
who 16.5. [OE *þā,* pl. of *sē, þæt*]
See þat *pron.,* þe *art.*

þo(o) *adv.* then 1.25, 2.132,
3.175, 5.16 (see er(e)), 17.16;
þa 10.1, 13.7, 16.22; ða 16.24;
(after *d*) ta 13.19, 133; þe in
~ ȝet 10.61 see ȝet(e). [OE *þā*]
See next.

þo(o) *conj.* when 1.625, 2.239,
3.197, 7.55, 17.208; ~ þat, þet
when 5.263, 17.183, because
17.223; þæ 10.161; þa 10.254,
19.279. ~ .. þa when .. then
10.7-8, 16.119, 149. [OE *þā*]

þo; þof; thoȝht. See þe *art.*;
þoȝ; þinche.

þoȝ *conj.* (usu. with subj.)
though 1.220 (indic. in co-ord.
cl.), 9.5, 9; ðoȝ 12.27, 128;
(after *d*) tohh þatt 13.55 (indic.);
þof 14.73, 94; þoþ 16.142. [ON
þó, earlier *þoh] Cf. þah, þei,
alþei.

þoȝte *n.* 1.269; þoht 8G.15, L.4,
18.352; þohht 13.151; þohut
5.223; þouȝt(e) 7.14, 56; þout,
þovt 6.113, 8w.32; þouth 4.
106. thought 5.223; mind,
thoughts 1.269, 7.14, 8L.4, 14,
13.151; meditation 18.352; consideration 19.417; concern 4.
106, 7.21; inclination 6.113,
118, 8G.15; intention 7.102;
plan 7.28; pensiveness, anxiety
7.56, 64; (personified) Care,
Grief 8K.58, 63. *with dedes and
with* ~ in both thought and
action 7.60; *to habben* ~ to be
reminded 18.590. *pl.* þohtes
thoughts 18.36, 44, 19.406.
[OE *(ge)þŏht*]

þoȝte. See þenchen; þinche.

þohhtfull *adj.* thoughtful, re-
flective 13.154. [þoȝte+-ful]

þohhwheþþre *adv.* nevertheless
13.60; þoþwethere, þoþwæ-

there 16.207, 311. [þoȝ+
whaðer; cf. OE *þēah-hwæþere*]

þoht(e), þohut(e). See þenchen, þinche, þoȝte.

þohuuethere *prep.* notwithstanding 16.141. [as þohh-]

þole(n), ðolen *v.* 8L.34, 16.270,
33; þolie(n) 3.160, 18.323,
19.8. *tr.* endure 16.33, 19.97;
suffer 3.160, 8L.34, 16.202, 18.
128, 19.295; allow 19.8; submit
to 19.395. *intr.* hold out 16.270;
suffer 18.316, 323. *pr. 2 sg.*
þolest 18.316. *pl.* þolieð 18.
414. *imper. sg.* þole 19.395.
pa. t. sg. þolede 18.128, 522.
pl. þoleden 16.202, 19.295. *pp.*
þoled 8L.30; iþoled 17.198.
[OE *þolian*]

þolemodnesse *n.* patience 18.
314. [OE *þol(e)mōdnes(se)*]

þon; þoncki; þone, ðone. See
þat *pron.,* þe *art.*; þannkenn;
þe *art.*

þonk(e) *n.* thanks, in *Gode* ~
5.158; gratitude 8F.18; thought,
mind 10.introd., 29; þonc intent 19.22. *gen.* þonkes,
þankes, *adv.* in *hire, here* ~
willingly 1.70, 16.295. [OE
þanc, þonc, (adv.) gen. *þances*]

þonkede, -in; þonne; þor(e),
ðore. See þannkenn;
þan(ne); þer(e) *adv.*

þorn(e) *n.* thorn-tree 7.202, 209.
pl. þornes thorns 8N.6, 14.
[OE *þórn*]

þorn(e)bake *n.* ray, skate 4.27,
100. [prec.+bac]

þorne-wode *n.* brier-bushes 1.
322. [þorn(e)+wod(e)]

thoro, þorouȝ. See þurh.

Þorsdai *n.* Thursday 11.151.
[ON *Þórsdag-r* with substitution
of dai(e)]

þoru(ȝ), thoru. See þurh.

þoru-out *prep.* throughout, right
through 11.21; þureþhut (postponed) 8w.4. [OE *þurh-ūt*]

þos; thosand; þosternesse;

þoþ; þoþwæthere, þoþ-
wethere. See þis; þusend(e);
þeoster-;þoȝ; þohhwheþþre.
þou *pron. 2 sg.* thou, you 2.40,
3.78, 4.114, 5.33, 6.34, 8D.7; þu
1.33, 4.111, 8A.11, 10.10, 16.185,
þv 1.331, 8w.42; ðu 12.143;
thu 16.185; (after *t*) tu 18.19,
47; suffixed to vb.: artu, hertou
1.349, 5.120, axestu 1.457,
canstu 1.589, dostu 1.174,
etestu 1.379, hastu, hauestu
15.12, 1.626, knouestou 3.256,
nartu 1.598, nauestu, neuestu
1.628, 530, neltou, -tu, nultu
5.189, 1.106, 537, saystu,
seistou 15.63, 2.68, saltu,
schaltu, shaltou, -tu 15.60,
1.165, 2.271, 1.495, speddestu
1.125, troustu 6.370, wenestu
1.219, 4.214, wiltou, -tu,
woltou, wultu 3.224, 4.171,
5.186, 1.627, wostu 1.462; prefixed to vb.: þart 8N.38. *acc.,
dat.* þe(e) (to, for) you 1.34,
2.247, 3.98; 1.85, 2.51, 4.122
5.34, 6.33, 8F.10, L.12; suffixed
to vb.: þincþe 1.46; (after *d, t,
ȝ = þ*) te 15.37, 18.297, 19.175,
3.129; see mid; *refl.* (for) yourself 1.117, 6.272, 8H.25, 15.64;
~ seolf 18.623 see self. *poss.
adj.* þin(e) your (usu. before
vowel or *h*) 1.74, 2.310, 3.83,
8R.2, 10.77; (before cons.) 1.119,
6.49, 7.87; *obl.* and *pl.* þine 1.35,
2.42, 5.197, 6.190, 10.63, 18.43;
(with force of objective gen.) of
you 1.163; (after *t, s*) tin(e)
18.53, 19.362; þi (before cons.)
1.73, 2.53, 3.96, 5.133, (before
h) 14.170, 15.54; of you 8L.15;
(after *t, d, s*) ti, ty 18.299, 15.54,
3, 24. *gen. neut.* þines 10.304;
fem. þire 10.57, 81. *dat. fem.*
þire 1.307, 546, 8v.11, 10.80.
pron. þin(e), þyn yours 1.235,
3.105, 6.269, 8L.36. [OE *þū,
-tū, þē, þīn*] See ȝe(e).
þouȝt-, þout-, þovt, þowthe;

þourgh, þourȝ, þourh;
þourt; þous; þousande, -ent,
-ynde; þraȝhe; þrat. See
þenchen, þinche, þoȝte;
þurh; ðar; þus; þusend(e);
þroȝe; þreatin.
þre(e) *adj.* three 3.71, 4.234, 320
(note), 8w.17; ðre 16.70; thre
14.237, 16.121; þreo 18.314,
19.264; þrie 17.6, 20; as *n.* 8G.
33, K.59. [OE *þrēo* fem. and
neut., *þrīe* masc.]
þreagendes *n. gen.* of a corrector
18.271. [OE *þrēagan*]
þreatin *v.* threaten, make threats
18.116. *pr. 2 sg.* þretest (with
to) 1.83. *pa. t. sg.* þrat 8K.63.
[OE *þrēatian*]
þrefter. See þer(e).
þrengde *pa. t. pl.* pressed,
crushed 16.172. [OE **þrengan*,
causative of *þringan*; cf. ON
þrøngva; see þringet]
þreo. See þre(e).
þreohad *n.* trinity 19.420.
[þre(e)+-had]
þreouald, þrofald *adj.* threefold 18.281, 611, 135. [OA
þrifáld assim. to *þrēo*]
þrestelcok *n.* cock song-thrush
8G.51. [þrostle+coc,vowel app.
adjusted to OE *þræsce* thrush]
þrete *n.* threatening 1.58. [OE
þrēat]
þretest. See þreatin.
þretnede *pa. t. sg.* threatened
11.150. [OE *þrēatnian*] Cf.
þreatin.
þretningue *n.* threatening,
threats 7.168. [from prec.]
þridde *adj.* third 1.241, 3.117,
4.135, 19.41; thrid 14.202;
þe ~ dai, todai þe ~ dai the day
after tomorrow 3.167, 14.262.
[OE *þridda*]
þrie; þrin(ne). See þre(e);
þer(e).
þringet *pr. 3 sg.* thrusts (through
the earth) 8v.2. *pl.* þrungeð
throng, crowd 18.170. *pp.*

iþrunge brought close 1.38. [OE þringan, perh. infl. by ON þryngva]

þrinne adj. threefold 13.185; three 4.29, 13.192; thrin 14. 230. [LOE þrinna from ON þrinn-r triple]

ðrist. See þurst.

þriste adj. bold 1.127. [OE þrīst(e)]

þrittende adj. thirteenth 13.207. [ON þrettándi, vowel after next]

þritti n., adj. thirty 3.104, 16.58. [OE þrĭt(t)ig]

þryuen adj. beautiful, as n. in ~ and þro 8G.16. [pp. of ME þriuen from ON þrífa-sk]

þro adj. excellent, as n. in þryuen and ~ delightful creature 8G.16. [obscure, in this phrase only]

þrof; þrofald; þro3. See þer(e); þreouald; þurh.

þro3e n. (space of) time, turn 1.196; þra3he while 13.206. pl. (orig. dat.) þrowe occasions 1.336. [OE þrāg]

þron. See þer(e).

þrostle n. song-thrush 1.617; þrostil 9.96. [OE þrostle]

þrote n. throat 1.24, 8Y.3, 18. 242; ðrote 12.149; throte 16.177; voice 1.366. [OE þrote]

þrowe; þruisse. See þro3e; þrusche.

þrumnesse n. trinity 19.263. [OE þrĭ(n)nes(se) infl. by þrymm glory]

þrungeð; þruppe. See þrin-get; þer(e).

þrusche n. thrush 1.617; þruisse 9.96. [OE þrysce]

þrute; þu, þv, ðu; þuder(e). See þer(e); þou; þider(e)

þuften n. maidservant 18.489. [OE þyften]

þu3te, þuht(e); þulke. See þinche; þilk(e).

þulli adj. such 18.645, 19.367. pl. þulliche 18.44, 19.183, 406. [OE þyllic]

þumbes n. pl. thumbs 16.166. [OE þūma]

þun; þunch(-), þuncþ; þunne;þureþhut. See þe art.; þinche; þynne; þoru-out.

þurh prep. 1.715, 10.121, 16.15, 18.64; þurrh 13.44; ðurh 16.14; ður3 12.14; þurch 17.122; þurhc 16.281; þourgh, þour3, þourh 3.68, 69, 68; þoru 4.42, 6.125, 11.2; thoru, thoro 14.119, 259; þoru3 7.89; þorou3 2.6; þro3 9.171. (of motion) through 4.42 (postponed), 10.121, 11.142, 12.14, 14.119. (of means) by, with 1.715, 2.126, 3.68, 7.89, 8E.9; acting on 16.14, 281. (of cause) because of 6.125, 14.125, 17.122. (of agent) by 2.6, 7.101, 11.80, 13.100; appointed by 11.2. ~ alle þing in every way 7.126; ~ nawt to leosen so as to lose nothing 18.636; ~ þatt through the fact that, if 13.17; ~ þæt, þet (conj.) because 16.15, 21. [OE þurh, þorh]

þurhleasten v. continue 19.122. [þurh+leste(n)]

þurles n. pl. holes 18.399. [OE þyr(e)l]

þurlin v. pierce 18.538. pr. 3 sg. þurleð 18.101. pp. iþurlet 18.510, 608; yþerled 8w.23. [OE þyrlian]

þurlunge n. piercing 18.591. [from prec.]

þurrhsekenn v. search through, examine 13.222. [OE þurhsēcan]

þurst n. thirst 5.67, 6.310, 9. 12; ðrist 12.185. [OE þurst, partly infl. by þyrstan v.]

þurue. See ðar.

þus adv. thus, in this way, so 2.117, 4.63, 5.91, 10.60, 18.198; þvs 8w.34; þuss 13.77; ðus 12.55; þous 3.69; (after d) tus 12.40, tuss 13.107; (modifying adv.) so, 8E.23, 16.39. [OE þus]

þusend(e) n. sg. and pl. 10.146,

180; þusent 18.632, 19.79, 129;
þusen 16.178; þousande,
þousynde 2.65, 85; þousent
5.203; thosand 14.6. [OE
þūsend]
þusgat(e) adv. in this way 4.53,
14.106. [þus+gate n.²]
þuster adj. dark 8T.24. [OE
þȳstre] See þeoster.
þut. See þat adj.
þuuele n. bush, thicket 1.214.
[OE *þūfel, var. of þyfel]
þwertouer adv. across, cross-
wise 18.669. [ON þvert+ouer]

vch(e); ufel; vle. See ech(e);
euel; hule.
umbe, vmbe(n) prep. about,
round 8E.62; ~ (ane) stounde,
stunde, see stund(e). [OE
ymbe, with -n after advs. like
aboute(n); also ON umb]
umben adv. in is ~ busies himself 18.249. [prec.]
vmbilaid pp. surrounded 14.200.
[ON umb+OE belegd; see bi-
legge]
umbistode pa. t. pl. stood
round, beset 4.302. [ON umb+
OE bestōdon from -standen; see
stonde(n)]
vmbiyeden pa. t. pl. surrounded
4.269. [ON umb+OE be-ēodon
pa. t. pl. of begān; see eode]
umble adj. humble 17.132. [OF]
vmthoȝt pa. t. sg. thought, bethought himself 14.189. [ON
umb+OE þōhte, see þenchen;
cf. ymbþencan]
umwile adv. from time to time:
æure ~ again and again 16.
183. [ON umb+while] Cf.
stund(e).
un- pref. expressing (1) negation,
(2) reversal or deprivation. [OE
un-]
vnbalde adj. dispirited 10.84.
[OA unbáld]
unbihefre adj. comp. less profitable 19.390. [from OE behēfe]

unblamet pp. adj. without blame
18.259. [from blame]
vnbounde pp. released 3.284.
[OE unbúnden from -bindan; see
bynde]
unclene adj. unclean 1.91. [OE
unclǽne]
uncuð(e), vn-, -kuð adj. unac-
quainted (wið) 12.60; unaware
(of) 12.154; strange 10.92, 18.
142; vncuth unknown 14.111.
[OE uncūþ]
undep adj. shallow 16.172. [OE
undēop]
under, vnder prep. under 1.86,
2.267, 3.62, 4.344, 8K.18; under
the head of 18.177; under the
authority of 19.18; in (of woods)
8L.31; in a state of 18.554; ~
Criste see Crist; ~ bis, gore,
heuen(riche), palle, þi slitte see
the nouns; onder 7.111, 188;
ounder 5.41, 47. [OE under]
underfangen, -feng. See underuon.
vnderfynde pr. 1 sg. perceive,
understand 8H.6. [under+
find(e)]
vnderfo. See underuon.
underȝetest pr. 2 sg. perceive,
notice, understand 18.363. pa.
t. pl. onderȝeten 7.211; undergæton 16.153. pp. under-,
vnderȝete 1.124, 3.292. [OA
undergetan, -gēton, -geten; cf.
biȝeten]
vnderling n. subject 10.72.
[under+OE -ling]
undersete imper. sg. underpin,
prop 18.196. [under+set]
understonde v. understand, perceive, conceive of 17.36; onderstonde 7.182; hounder- 6.263;
to vnderstonden to be understood (as) 19.39; infl. infin. to
understandene 16.12. pr. 1 sg.
under-, vnderstonde 19.320,
2.196, believe 8K.54. 3 sg. understont 18.273. pl. understondeð 18.97, 19.337. imper.

sg. **understont** 18.201. *pl.*
understondeð 18.23, take heed
19.245. *pa. t. sg.* **under-, vnderstod** gave heed to, took
account of 11.62; *refl.* perceived
3.205, kept command of herself
1.565 (note); **hounderstod** 5.
77. *pl.* **unnderrstodenn** 13.
133; **onderstoden** 7.162, 184.
subj. sg. **understode** 1.408, 7.
192. *pp.* **vnderstanden** 14.227.
[OE *understándan*; see **ston-
de(n)**]
under-tid *n.* the third hour of
the day, 9 a.m. 18.650. [OE
undern-tíd; see **undren**]
underþeden *v.* subject 16.107.
[OE *underþéodan*]
underuon *v.* receive, take 19.
351; **ounderfonge** 5.196. *pr.
2 sg.* **ounderfost** undertake 6.
378. *3 sg.* **underueð** receives
18.266. *subj. sg.* **vnderfo** 3.25.
imper. sg. **hvnderfonge** 8w.60.
pa. t. sg. **underfeng** 16.134,
18.479. *pl.* **underuengen** admitted 10.192. *pp.* **underfangen** 16.144, 212; **-fonge** 17.236;
underfon, -uon 19.396, 64.
[OE *underfón*; see **fon**]
undo, vndo *imper. sg.* unfasten,
open 4.198, 199. *pp.* **vndo** 11.
116, 122; **ondo** 7.178. [OE
undón; see **do(n)**]
undren *n.* mid-morning, 9 a.m.
17.182, 211. [OE *undern*]
unendeliche *adv.* infinitely 18.
628. [cf. ON *ú-endiliga*]
uneðe *adj.* distressing, painful
10.11. [OE *unéaþe*] See **vnneþe.**
uneuenlich *adj.* incomparable
19.95. [from OE *efn(i)an* com-
pare; OE *unefenlic* = diverse]
vneuenliche *adv.* incomparably
18.627. [as prec.]
vnfere *adj.* infirm, weak 14.102.
[LOE *unfére* formed on ON
ú-fœr-r]
unfrið *n.* strife, discord 16.136.
[OE *unfriþ*]

811493

vnglad *adj.* sad 8D.4. [OE *un-
glæd*]
unhope *n.* hopelessness 19.121.
[from **hope**]
unimete, vn- *adj.* immeasur-
able, immense 10.18, 263, 19.
141, 291; excess of 10.280. [OE
ungemete]
unimete *adv.* immeasurably,
immensely 18.476, 19.268, 352.
[OE *ungemete*]
unirude *adj.* enormous 19.142.
[OE *ungerýde* rough] See **unride.**
vniune *n.* large pearl 9.89. [AN
from L *ūnión-em*]
unker¹. See **wit** *pron.*
unker² *pron. 2 dual gen.* of you
two 4.309. *dat.* **hunke** to you
two 1.691 (note). [OE *inc(er)*
confused with *unc(er)* (of) us
two; see **wit**]
unkuð. See **uncuð(e).**
vnlahfulliche *adv.* unlawfully
8K.68. [from OE *lah-*, combining form of *lagu*, +-**ful**+
-**liche**; cf. **lahfulnesse**]
unlede *adj.* miserable, unhappy
1.602. [OE *unlǽde*]
unlimin *v.* loosen, separate 18.
249. [from OE *-límian* cement]
vnmeað. See **unmeþe.**
unmeteliche *adv.* immeasurably 18.627. [cf. OE *unmetlíce*
and **unimete**]
unmeþe *n.* immoderation, excess 1.268; **vnmeað** 19.53. [OE
unmǽþ]
unmihti(e) *adj.* without strength
19.205, 216. [OE *unmihtig*]
unmilde *adj.* harsh, cruel 1.61.
[OE *unmílde*]
unmundlunge *adv.* unexpected-
ly 19.77. [OE *unmyndlunga*]
unmurie *adj.* unpleasant, tedious 1.262. [OE *unmyrge*]
unnderrstodenn. See **understonde.**
vnnen *v.* grant, be willing, wish,
desire (as *imper.*) 18.305, 309.

T t

pr. 1 sg. an grant 1.697; **vnne** wish 8G.45. *2 sg.* **anst** grant 1.602; **unnest** are pleased with 18.300. *pl.* **unnen** 10.63. *pa. t. sg.* **úþe** 13.182. [OE *unnan; ann, unnon; úþe*]

vnneþe *adv.* scarcely, hardly 11.101; **onneþe** 7.115. [OE *unéaþe*] See **uneðe.**

unnunge *n.* favour, generosity 18.291. [from **vnnen**]

unorne *adj.* poor 1.233. [OE *unorne* plain]

unrecheles *n.* thoughtlessness; *on ~* thoughtlessly 18.480. [un-(intensive)+OE *receléas* adj. as n.; cf. **rechelese**]

unrede *n.* wicked advice 1.117; ill-advised action, folly 1.168. [OE *unrǽd*]

unride, vn- *adj.* huge, unwieldy 4.222; enormous 12.147; **un-rude** 19.80. [cf. OE *ungerýde*] See **unirude.**

unriȝt, vnriȝth *n.* wrong, injustice 1.121, 2.52; **unricht** 17. 200; **unriht(e)** in *þu hauest ~* you are mistaken 10.52, *mid ~* improperly, irregularly 16.26. *pl.* **unrihte** 16.33. [OE *unriht*]

unrihtfulnesse *n.* injustice 1. 700. [from OE *unrihtful*]

unripe *adj.* immature 1.236. [OE]

unrude. See **unride.**

vnseheliche *adj.* invisible 19.33. [OE *unsegenlic*]

unseli *adj.* unfortunate (as *n.*) 18.172, evil 19.138; **ounseli** wicked 6.98. [OE *unsǽlig*]

unsibbe *n.* contention, discord 16.13. *pl.* 16.34. [OE *unsibb*]

unstrong *n.* feeble 1.369, 12.7. [OE *unstráng*]

untalelich *adj.* indescribable 19. 97. [from **tale**]

untellendlice *adj.* unspeakable 16.164. [from **tel**]

until *prep.* until 14.288. [ON *und* up to+**til(l)**]

vnto *prep.* to 4.225, 14.123, 172.

[app. after prec.; but cf. OS *unto,* perh. also OE though unrecorded]

untodealet *pp. adj.* undivided 19.264. [OE *untódǽled*] See **todealen.**

untohe *adj.* undisciplined, unruly 19.24, 411. *pl.* **untohene** 19.14. [OE *un(ge)togen* untaught; see **te**]

untoheliche *adv.* in an unruly way 19.20. [prec.+**-liche**]

vntrew(e), un- *adj.* unfaithful 3.233, 8H.29, 14.73; out of true, twisted 12.25, 59 (with play on 'unfaithful'). [OE *untréowe*]

unþankes *n. gen.* as *adv.*, with defining gen.: *here ~* against their will 16.295; **vnþonkes** 19.47. [OE *unþances, -þonces*] See **þonk(e).**

unþeu *n.* vice, sin 1.150; **unþeaw** 19.35, 59. *gen.* **unþeawes** 19. 404. *pl.* **unþeawes** 18.177, 422, 19.376. [OE *unþéaw*] See **þeaw.**

unþolelich *adj.* intolerable 19. 96, 116. [from **þole(n)**]

vnþonkes. See **unþankes.**

unwarnede *pp.* unprotected 19. 178. [from OF *warnir;* see **warneþ**]

unwelde *adj.* weak, infirm 12.5. [from OA *wélde* powerful; cf. **welde** n.]

unweotenesse *n.* ignorance 19. 202. [from OE *witnes* knowledge, infl. by M *weotan;* see **witnesse, wite(n)**]

unwerget *pp. adj.* unwearied 19.282, 357. [from OE *wérgian;* see **wergið**]

vnwiȝt *n.* evil creature, miscreant 1.33, 90; **unwiht** devil 19.5, **unwhiht** 171. *gen.* **un-wihtes** 19.203. *pl.* **unwiȝtis** 1.174. [un-+**wiȝt**; cf. ON *úvætt-r* evil spirit]

unwille *n.* displeasure 1.300; *ouer ~* against our wishes 1.263 (note). [OE *unwilla*]

unwine *n.* enemy 19.375. *pl.*
unwines 18.88. [LOE from
ON *úvin-r*]

vnwis *adj.* foolish 14.121; **onwis**
6.218, unskilful 445; **ounwi(i)s**
6.117, ignorant 5.139. [OE
unwis]

unwraste *n.* evil 10.212. [next]

vnwraste *adj.* wicked, sinful,
evil 8F.17; **vnwreste**, **un-**
1.134, 16.91; **unwreast(e)**
feeble, worthless 18.393, evil,
depraved 18.551, 19.33. [OE
unwrǽst(e)]

unwreaste *adv.* wickedly 18.
560; **unwreste** poorly, badly
1.258. [from prec.]

unwrenche *n.* evil trick 1.125.
[OE *unwrenc*]

unwreo *v.* reveal, explain 19.
321. *pp.* **vnwroȝen, unwroȝe**
discovered, revealed 1.118, 508.
[OE *unwrēon, -wrogen*] Cf.
wreah.

unwreste. See **vnwraste, un-**
wreaste.

unwrþ *adj.* valueless, cheap 1.
255. [from **wurð**]

up, vp *adv.* up 1.156, 4.4, 7.204,
8v.2, 9.136, 19.67; **upp** 13.13;
hup 15.64; **op** 7.47, 213; **oup**
5.246; (out of bed) 1.477, 4.80,
10.8; (to one's feet) 2.36, 4.201,
10.105, (vb. omitted) got up
11.157; above, on high 13.109;
ashore 10.160, (vb. omitted in
command) 178, 12.176; open
11.133 (see bryng(e)). phr. ~
and d(o)un 9.166, thoroughly
3.85; ~ *ido, ileiid* see **do(n)**,
legge; *gyuen, iiuen* ~ see **ȝeue**.
[OE *ūp, upp(e)*] See **upon.**

up(e), vp(e) *prep.* See **uppen.**

upbreideð *pr. pl.* blame 19.140.
[OE *upbregdan*]

upon, vpon *prep.* 4.3, 8D.27,
M.16, 18.148; **vpan** (postponed)
3.146; **op(p)on** 6.204, 7.49;
apon 8E.13, 14.105; **upo, vp o**
18.28, 41, 638, 4.31. (of place)

upon, on 4.3, 202, 18.28, 148;
in, see **lond(e)**; ~ *an hyl* in a
heap 4.158; above 18.638; see
heiȝ(e). (of time) on 14.278;
~ *a dai* one day 6.345. (of belief,
trust) in 3.146, 8D.27. (of reference) of, about 8H.16, M.16;
against 6.204. [**up+on**, infl. by
ON *upp á*; see **uppen**]

uppard. See **upward.**

uppen *prep.* 1.641, 10.14, 268;
uppon 1.656; **upponn** 13.111;
uppe 10.274; **upe, vpe** 1.425,
479, 11.45, 112; **ope** 7.127; **up**,
vp 1.15, 9.149. upon, on 1.15,
9.149, 10.14, 274, 11.112, 13.
111; see **lond(e)**; on to 11.45;
over 7.127; against 1.641, 656.
~ *þon* on that subject 1.425 (see
þat *pron.*). [OE *uppan*, and **up**
adv.; see **upon**, from which
the distinction is not always
clear]

vpriȝt, upriht *adv.* (straight) up,
erect 3.194, 18.668. [OE *up-*
rihte]

vptaken *pp.* taken up, raised (to
his feet) 2.128. [**up+pp.** of
tak]

upward *adv.* upwards 17.56;
uppard 18.66; **opward** on the
way up 5.242. [OE *upweard*]

ur(e), vr(e). See **we.**

ure *n.* hour 17.196. *pl.* **ouris** the
canonical hours 8x.11. [AN
ure, (h)oure]

uri *v.* pray 18.353. [AN *urer*]

urisun. See **oreisun.**

vrning *n.* raiding, attack 11.1.
[from OE *ýrnan*; see **erne**]

us(s), vs; ut(e), vt. See **we;**
out(e).

ute (we) *imper. I pl.* let us 1.737.
[OE *uton*]

uten *adv.* exhausted 4.110. [ON
úti; see note]

vtenemes *adj.* extraordinary 14.
179. [**out(e)+ON** *-næm-r* rel.
to **nim**]

utest. See **utheste.**

utewið *adv.* outside 18.198. [out(e)+wiþ]

utgang *n.* exit, departure 16.61. [OE *ūtgang*]

utheste *n.* hue and cry 1.656; **utest** 1.641. [out(e)+OE *hǣs* calling; cf. **heste**]

utlete *n.* outlet, (?)river-mouth 1.712. [from out(e)+lete(n)]

uttre *adj.* outward, external 18. 401, 580. [OE *ȳt(t)ra*, comp. adj. from *ūte* adv.]

úþe. See **vnnen.**

vðen *n. pl.* waves 10.41, 314. [OE *ȳþ*, pl. *ȳþa*]

uutyede *pa. t. sg.* went out 17. 179. [OE *ūtēode*; see **eode**]

uuel; vuel(e), uuele. See **euel; euel(e), euele.**

uuenan *prep.* upon 10.254. [OE *ufenan*]

vachen; uadir. See **fechche; fader.**

uæie *adj.* doomed, fated to die 10.267, 273. [OE *fǣge*]

uæir. See **fair(e).**

uaile *v.* be of service to, assist 6.188. [OF *vaill-,* accented stem of *valoir*] Cf. **auail.**

vaire, uair-; uale. See **fair(e); fele.**

ualeie, valeie, ualeye *n.* valley 7.100, 145, 164. [AN *valey*]

ualle, valle; van. See **falle(n); fo.**

uanité *n.* frivolity 14.53. [OF *vanité*]

uaren; varpeð; uas; vaste. See **fare(n); warpeð; was; faste** *adv.*

uastinge *n.* fasting 17.62. [from OE *fæstan*; see **fast**]

vat; vawe. See **what** *pron.*; **fain.**

veasten *n.* fasting 18.4. [OE *fæsten*] See **fast.**

veiage *n.* journey, expedition 2.90. [AN]

veien *v.* join 18.596. [OE *fēgan*]

uel; velaghes; ueld; uele; vend. See **wel** *adv.*; **felawe; feld(e); fele; wend.**

venie *n.* request for forgiveness 18.283. [AN]

ueol; ueond. See **falle(n); feond.**

ueondliche *adv.* exceedingly, desperately 10.183. [OE *fēondlice*]

ver; uerde; uere; uereden; ueree. See **fer; ferd(e); was; fereden; fir(e).**

verray *adj.* true, real 17.43. [AN *verrai*]

verrayment *adv.* truly, indeed 2.25. [AN *verraiment*]

verrene. See **feorrene.**

uers, vers *n.* verse 18.9, 7.107, 271; **fers** 7.110. [OF *vers*, OE *fers*]

vers; uerste, verste. See **wors(e) *adj.*; first** *adj.*

uerteþ *pr. 3 sg.* breaks wind 8A.8. [OE **feortan*]

uertu, vertu *n.* power 3.42 (note), 17.137; quality 14.34. [OF *vertu*]

ves. See **was.**

vestement *n.* robe, esp. royal or ceremonial 2.26. [OF]

uet; vewe; vicst. See **fot(e); fæu, feaue; fiȝte.**

victory *n.* victory 2.212. [AN *victorie*]

uid; vif. See **wiþ; wif.**

vigoure *n.* form 2.238. [AN *fig(o)ure*]

viȝte; uihte. See **fiȝte** *n., v.*

uilani, v- *n.* dishonour 6.250, 128; **vileinie** infamous conduct 11.24. [AN *vilanie, vile(i)nie*]

vile *adj.* repulsive, disgusting 9.40. [OF *vil(e)*]

uylle; uilleth. See **wil** *n.*[1]; **wil(e).**

villiche *adv.* ignominiously 11. 17, 20. [vile+-liche]

vilté *n.* shameful conduct, meanness 6.47. [OF *vilté*] vind, uinde. See find(e).

viniter *n.* vintner 11.167. [AN]

viniterie *n.* wine-store 11.167. [from prec.]

uint. See find(e).

visaġe *n.* face, complexion 2.201. [OF]

uisiti *v.* visit 17.63. [OF *visiter*]

uit; vytvten; uliȝe; ulode; uo; uode; uolc. See wiþ; wiþout; flei; flod(e); fo; fod(e); folk(e).

uolde *n.*[1] fold (of cloth) 1.442. *pl.* (*dat.*) crevices 1.382. [from OA *fáldan* v.]

volde *n.*[2] *pl.* (*dat.*) respects, ways 1.72. [from division of OA *manig-fáld* adj.]

volf; uolke; uor, vor. See wolf; folk(e); for.

uore *n.* march: *on* ~ on the march 10.129. [OE *fōr*]

uoreward; uorlost; vorre; vort, uorte; vorto; uorþ, v-, uorð; vorþi; uote; vox; vram; vre; vrom. See foreward(e); forlese; feorre(n); fort; forto; forþ; forþi; fot(e); fox; from; freo; from.

uuæren, uuare(n), uueron; uuan; uuard; uuenden; uuerre. See was; winne(n); wurðen; wene; werre.

uuerrien *v. tr.* and *intr.* make war (on), attack 16.140. *pr. 3 sg.* weorreð 18.89, (with *towart*) 19.375; werrais (with *on*) 14.32. *pp.* iweorret 18.491. [cf. AN *werreier*]

uuerse; uuluelden; uuolde; vuolf; uurecce. See wors(e) *adv.*; fulfille; wil(e); wolf; wrecche adj.

uureide *pa. t. sg.* accused 16.106. [OE *wrēgan*]

uurythen *pa. t. pl.* twisted 16.168. [OE *wriþon* from *wrīþan*]

wa. See who; wo.

wac *adj.* weak 18.114, 19.204. *pl.* wake 19.223, as *n.* 178. [OE *wāc*]

wade *v.* wade 9.180. *pr. 3 sg.* wadeð 12.118. [OE *wadan*]

wæ; wæi. See wo; wai(e).

wæi-sið *n.* journey of affliction, painful experience 10.104. [ON *vei* woe+OE *sīþ* journey; see siþ(e)]

wæl; wærd; wære(n), wæron; wærse; wærð; wæs; wæt; wæx. See wel; wurðen; was; wors(e); wurðen; was; what *pron.*; waxe.

wahes *n. pl.* walls 18.43, 19.36. [OE *wāg*]

wai(e), way *n.* 2.172, 6.1, 10.220, 14.114, 15.11; wei(e), wey(e) 1.170, 224, 5.5, 6.395, 7.120, 17.33, 18.173; wæi 10.166; weiȝe 7.75, 99; weȝȝe 13.196, 203. road, highway 5.5, 6.1, 74; path, 14.117, 18.173; way, road, route 1.170, 2.172, 4.40, 7.75, 11.14, 17.33; distance 13.203; journey 13.206. þe ~ *tak*(e) set out 8N.9, 14.114; *out of þe* ~ isolated, remote 7.99; *his* ~ on his way 1.224, sim. *þi* ~ 15.11; *þe* ~ on the way 13.196. *gen.* weis, *adv.* in *summes* ~ to some extent 19.184, for some time 19.265. [OE *weg*] See awai, anes-, nanes-weis.

way, wei, wey *adv.* away 5.53; *do* ~! stop, enough 2.195, 8L.9, 15.7. [shortened from awai]

way *pa. t. sg.* weighed 5.237. [OE *wæg* from *wegan*]

way *interj.* alas! 8w.31. [cf. OE *wā*, ON *vei*, and weila]

waiissing *n.* washing 9.48. [from waschen]

wailawai *interj.* alas! 1.176; wayleuay 15.18; weylawei, -y 8L.13, 25. [OE *weg lā weg*, ON *vei*] Cf. weila, wolawo.

wayle *adj.* as *n.* beautiful creature 8G.1, 50. [from ME *to wale* at choice, ON *val* choice] Cf. **wale**.

wain *n.* diminution 14.294. [OE *wana* lack, infl. by *wanian* wane]

wayte *n.* watchman 2.318. [ONF *waite*]

waite *v.* (watch over) protect 2.253. *pp.* **wayted** spied on 8L.18. [ONF *wait(i)er*]

wake. See **wac**.

wåkemenn *n. pl.* watchmen 13.117. [OE *wacu*+**man**]

waker *adj.* watchful, alert 19.61. *comp.* **wakere** 19.64, 162. [OE *wacor*]

wakese. See **waxe**.

wakie(n) *v.*[1] be awake, keep awake 8Q.2; keep vigil 17.62; be vigilant 19.7; **wake** 8X.11. *pr. 1 sg.* **wake** lie sleepless 8K.82. *3 sg.* **wakeþ** in tag *when heo ~* 8K.40. [OE *wacian*]

wakien *v.*[2] weaken, become disloyal 10.69. [OE *wācian*]

wal, walle[1] *n.* wall 3.33, 5.10, 11, 2.114. *pl.* **walles** 9.54, 10.229, 18.80. [OA *wall*]

wald(e); walden. See **wil(e); welde**.

wale *v.* choose 8E.2. [from ON *val* choice; cf. **wayle**]

waldend *n.* ruler, master 10.107. [OA *wáldend*; with phr. *domes ~* cf. OE *ealles, wuldres*, &c.]

wale *interj.* alas! 10.51. [OE *wā lā*] Cf. **wolawo**.

walke *v.* go, become 8L.6. *pr. 1 sg.* go about, live 8c.4. [OA *walcan* roll]

walle[2]. See **welle** *n.*

wallinde *pr. p. adj.* boiling 18.84. [from OA *wallan*]

wal-spere *n.* deadly spear 10.290. [OE *wæl-spere*]

wam; wan; wan(e); wand. See **who; what** *pron.*, **winne(n), won** *n.*[1]; **whan; winde**.

wandes *n. pl.* shoots, saplings 14.282. [ON *vǫnd-r*, gen. *vand-ar*]

wandreþ; wanene; wanne. See **wondrien; whonene; whan**.

wanunge. See **woning** *n.*[1]

war *adj.* aware, conscious 4.56, 19.220; *wart it ~* became aware of it 16.242; *wurthen ~* learnt (of this) 16.271; prudent, sensible 1.148, 8D.34, 12.97; careful, cautious 1.126, 19.374; *beþ ~* consider carefully 8H.41. *comp.* **warre** 19.162. [OE *wær*]

war *refl., imper. sg.* take care, be on guard (against) 8H.25. *subj. sg.* **warre** (*hym*) let him take care 14.62. [OE *warian*]

war(e); ward. See **was, wher(e); toward(e), wurðen**.

warde *n.* keeping, charge 11.47; custody 11.65; guard, watch 11.110, 19.57, 62; guardianship, protection 19.1. [OE *wéard*]

wardein *n.* guardian 7.29. [ONF]

warden *v.* guard, keep 19.405. *pr. 3 sg.* **ward** 14.109. *subj. sg.* **wardi** 19.160. [OE *wéardian*]

ware *n.* wares, goods for sale 4.33. [OE *waru*]

wareuore. See **wher(e)**.

warien *n. pl. gen.* of criminals 10.112. [OE *wearg*]

warld. See **world(e)**.

warliche, wear- *adv.* carefully, prudently, watchfully 19.44, 201, 5. [OE *wærlīce*]

warm(e) *adj.* warm 1.402, 6.225; as *n.* warmth 1.346. [OE *wearm*]

warmen *pr. pl.* warm 12.179. [OE *wearmian*]

warnden. See **werne(n)**.

warne *v.*[1] warn, put on one's guard (with double object, of person and thing warned against) 2.106; **warni(n)** 19.158, (with *of* of thing) 71, (*of* and *for*) 173;

admonish 18.270. *pr. 1 sg.*
warni 1.246, 485. *2 sg.* **war-nest** 19.393. *subj. sg.* **warni**
18.260, 19.47. *imper. sg.* **warne**
19.176. *pa. t. sg. refl.* **warnede**
(*hine seoluen*) took precautions
10.253. [OE *war(e)nian*]
warneþ, -ð *v.² pr. 3 sg.* protects,
defends 8E.69, 19.38. [ONF
warnir]
warpeð *pr. 3 sg.* throws 18.8,
562. *subj. sg.* **warpe** 19.48.
imper. pl. **warpeð** 18.82; varpeð 19.385. *pa. t. sg.* **weorp**
18.456; **warp** uttered 1.45.
[OE *weorpan*, pa. t. sg. *wearp*;
see *Iuliene* pp. 169–70]
warschipe *n.* caution 18.169;
(personified) Prudence 19.40,
43. *gen.* **Warschipes** 19.47,
-**schipe** 175. [OE *wærscipe*]
warto; **wart, warð, warth.**
See **wher(e)**; **wurðen.**
was *pa. t. 1, 3 sg.* 1.1, 2.35, 3.116,
4.17, 6.345; **uas** 8v.23; **wass**
13.2; **wasse** 9.120; **wes** 5.2,
6.10, 8E.5, 10.3, 16.128; **wes**
5.258, 6.79; **wæs** 10.131, 16.2.
was 1.1, 2.35, 4.17; there was
10.125, 14.100; *auxil.* (forming
pass.) 2.36, 3.116, 8E.5; (forming pluperf. of intr. vbs.) had
2.55, 5.18, 6.345, 13.3, (sim., tr.
vb. with refl. pron.) 17.147. *2 sg.*
were 5.219; **weore** 10.302. *pl.*
were(n) 1.16, 2.213, 3.3, 4.9;
uere 1.574; **uueron** 16.198;
wæren(n) 13.38, 16.268; **uuæ-**
ren 16.164; **wæron** 16.5, 39;
weore(n) 10.84, 222; **war(e)**
14.122, 17.99; **waren** 16.189,
17.193; **uuaren** 16.160. *subj. 3*
sg. **were** 1.21, 2.14, 3.203, 4.
122, 8F.26; **wære** 13.20, 16.63;
weore 10.9, 219; **war(e)** 3.49,
14.111; **uuare** 16.120; **wor(e)**
4.204, 15.5. were, was, should/
might be 1.723, 2.185, 7.10;
would be 1.85 (*impers.*), 5.7,
6.42; would have been 10.185.

2 sg. **were** 1.53, 3.82, 5.60, 176,
8F.22, 18.659. *pl.* **were(n)** 1.
305, 2.140, 4.339; **weoren** 10.
33, 186. [OE *wæs*, M, K *wes*;
wæron, A, K *wēron*; ON *váru*]
See **is, nas, be(n)** and other
parts.
waschen, wassche *v. tr.* wash
3.48; (with refl. pron. obj.)
3.54; **weschen** 18.578. *pa. t. pl.*
wesse 17.100. [OE *wæscan,
waxan*; pa. t. pl. *wēoxon,
wēoscon]
waste *adj.* deserted 1.17. [ONF
wast]
wastel *n.* loaf of fine flour 4.144.
pl. **wastels** 4.47. [ONF *wastel*]
wat. See **what** *pron.,* **wite(n)**
v.¹
wate *adj.* moist 14.182. [ON
vāt-r] Cf. **wet(e).**
water(e) *n.* water 3.49, 4.178,
5.71, 7.218, 10.246; **watir** 9.12,
47; **weater** 18.30, 80. *pl.*
weattres 18.182, 19.114. [OE
wæter, M *weter*]
water-grund *n.* bottom of a
stretch of water 12.124. [prec.+
grounde]
wath. See **what** *pron.*
wax *n.* growth 14.294. [from
next]
waxe *v.* grow; become, go 8c.3;
wakese 6.182. *pr. 1 sg.* **waxe**
8D.2, K.80. *3 sg.* **west** increases
1.435. *pl.* **waxeþ** become 8F.17;
waxen M.1. *subj. sg.* **waxe** ger-
minate, sprout 12.90. *pa. t. sg.*
wax 8E.18; **wex** 14.102; **wæx**
arose 16.247. *pl.* **wex** grew 14.
284. *pp.* **waxen** grown 4.59.
[OE *weaxan, wēox, wēoxon,
weaxen*]
wde. See **wod(e).**
we *pron. 1 pl.* **we** 1.133, 2.206,
4.108, 8L.23; ('editorial') 2.321,
16.47; ('royal') 2.54; (men in
general) 12.94, 19.24, **wue** 8v.8.
acc., dat. **us, vs** (to, for) us
1.143, 4.199, 12.92; 1.296, 2.70,

8F.41, 17.158; *recip.* each other 8L.23; *refl.* ourselves 12.138, 18.400, 19.162; ~ *seoluen* 19.5 see **self**; **uss** 13.125; **hvs** 8w. 40; **ous** 6.90, 112, 8T.15; **hous** 6.220. *poss. adj.* **ur(e)**, **vr(e)** our 1.298, 4.311, 8N.27, 14.43, 246; **hure** 4.110, 17.157; **oure**, **ovr** 2.207, 5.54, 14.41, 43; **ouer** 1.263 (note); **houre** 5.35, 6.31; **ore** 7.7, 26. *pron.* **ure** ours 18. 596. *gen.* **ur** of us 12.130, **hure** 1.141 (part.); *our* 14.118. [OE *wē, ūs, ūre*]

we *interj.* (of surprise, shock) oh! ah! 6.115. [cf. **way**]

wealden; **wealle**. See **welde** *v.*; **welle** *n.*

weane *n.* misery 18.493. [OE *wēa*, gen. pl. *wēana*]

wearliche; **wearnde**; **weater**. See **warliche**; **werne(n)**; **water(e)**.

wecchen *v. intr., infin.* as *n.* to keep vigil, keeping vigil 18.4. [OE *wæccan*, M **weccan*]

wed *n.* weed 12.74; **wode** reed 1.236. [OE *wēod*]

wed(de) *n.* pledge, security 8N.24, 18.545; *beo to* ~ be security 10.79. [OE *wedd*]

wedded *pa. t. subj. sg.* married, should marry 8F.39. *pp.* **wedde**, **wedded** married, wedded (*adj.*) 6.137, 8; **iweddet** 18.551. [OE *ge-weddian*]

wede *n.* clothing, clothes 4.129. *pl.* **wedes**, **-is** 8N.8, x.3. [OE *wǣd, ge-wǣde*]

weder *n.* weather 8B.4, 12.69, 168. *pl.* **wederes** winds 10.124. [OE *weder*]

weder; **wee**; **we33e**, **wei(e)**, **wey(e)**, **wei3e**; **weide**. See **whider**; **whi**; **wai(e)**; **wide**.

weie *n.* balance 18.447. [OA *wēge*]

weila *interj.* alas! 18.237. [OE *weg lā*; see **wailawai**]

weylawei. See **wailawai**.

wel *n.*[1] well-being, good fortune 8G.45; prosperity, wealth 9.4. [OE *wěl* adv., *wela* n.]

wel *n.*[2] skin 8Y.3. [OE *fell*]

wel(l) *n.*[3] See **welle**.

wel *adv.* well 1.103, 2.249, 4.24, 12.178 (note), 15.1; **wæl** 16.212; **wele**, **well** 14.227, 142; **uel** 1. 345; **wol** 4.43 (note). fittingly 2.43, 5.64, 7.192; (of greeting) kindly 14.256; much 1.602; (with *comp.*) far 2.200, 4.273, 7. 57; quite, fully 12.60, 18.87, esp. with numbers as 4.55, 156, 7.242, 11.105; exactly, just 4.9, 13.9; almost 1.172; easily 4.59, 97, 16.58, 185; readily 1.157; indeed, truly 1.516, 4.296, 5.87, 6.231, 8L.33, 19.244; *as* ~ *as* as well as, in addition to 18.294; *predic.* (impers. with dat.) good, fine: ~ *is him* he is fortunate, does well 9.44, 19.373, sim. ~ *were* would be fortunate 3.3, 8E.57, G.15, 15.5, 19.154; very 1.31, 2.4, 3.87, 5.15, 8B.6, 9.51, (following word qualified) 11. 71; ~ *mani* a great many 7.165. [OE *wěl*] See **bet, beter(e)**.

welcome(n) *adj.* welcome 6.167; as *interj.* 6.26, 255, 425; **welcum(e)** 15.2, 38, 18.560, 19.255; **wilcume** 10.3, 302. *comp.* **welcomore** 6.426. [OE *wilcuma* adapted to **wel**]

welcomeþ *imper. pl.* welcome 2.178. *pr. 3 sg.* **wolcumeþ** 1.318. [OE *wilcumian* adapted as prec.]

welde *n.* power, control: *haueþ to* ~ rules over 6.325, 416. [OE *ge-wéald*]

welde *v.* possess, have in one's power 6.83, 8E.3; control, rule 6.146; **walden** 10.62; **wealden** 18.621; win 18.473; *him* ~ (*refl.*) control his own actions, act by his own will 11.32. [OA *wáldan* and causative *-wéldan, -wǽldan*]

welle *n.* well, spring, fountain 3.37, 4.278, 7.214, 8T.26, 12.10; **walle** 3.45; **wealle** 18.236; **wel(l)** 1.549, 14.179. *pl.* **willis** 9.83. [OA *well(a)*, *wælla*, WS *wylla*, *-e*]

welle *pr. 1 sg.* (*intr.*) suffer agony (of mind) 8G.40. *pp.* **iweallet** founded (of metal) 18.330. [OA *wællan*, *wellan* boil]

welle-ǵrund *n.* bottom of a well 12.22. [welle+ǵrounde]

welle-heued *n.* source 3.57. [welle+heued]

welneʒ *adv.* almost, very nearly 1.44, 297; **welneh** 10.181, 16.107. [OE *wel nē(a)h*; see **wel**, **neh**]

welp(e) *n.* puppy 6.287, 372. [OE *hwelp(a)*]

Welsse *adj.* Welsh 11.115. [OE (nWS) *wēlisc*]

welth *n.* abundance 14.174. [OE *wela*+suff. *-þ* as in *hǣlþ*] Cf. **weole**.

welud *pp.* withered 14.190. [OE *wealwian*]

wen(ne). See **whan.**

wench *n.* girl 9.141. [shortened from **wennchell**]

wend *v.* 9.184, 14.136; **wende(n)** 1.594, 6.118, 7.73, 8w.59, 10.40, 11.122; **wendenn** 13.172. (1) *tr.* turn (over) 1.594; turn, change, alter 6.118, 151, 8L.21, 16.221, 17.138; convert 13.172; direct 3.67, 18.205; send back 18.243. (2) *refl.* go 6.19, 11.153, 13.137, 14.147, 17.27. (3) *intr.* go 2.77, 3.81, 4.346, 5.74, 6.17; (with pleonastic dat. pron.) 10.119; depart (this life) 1.524, 8w.59, 17.246; turn 14.64, 17.257; change 10.157; (with *way* as adv. acc.) wend, go 7.241, sim. *slogh .. wendand* 14.118–21. *pr. 3 sg.* **wendeþ** 2.87; **went** 8T.23, 18.139, 172. *pl.* **wendeþ**, **-ð** 17.246, 19.310; **wendiþ** 9.144;

wenden 12.95. *subj. sg.* **wende** 1.524, 18.243. *pr. p.* **wendand** 14.121. *imper. sg.* **wend(e)** 2.77, 3.81, 8L.21. *pa. t. sg.* **wend(e)** 5.74, 6.17, 7.76, 10.119, 16.221; **went(e)** 2.216, 4.346, 6.19, 14.147. *pl.* **wende(n)** 7.77, 10.179, 11.58, 153, 16.294; **wenndenn** 13.117, 137; **went(en)** 2.113, 167, 3.190, 17.27. *pp.* **wend(e)** 2.86, 6.345; **vend** 5.159; **iwend(e)** 7.242, 11.133, 18.205; **iwent, y-** 17.102, 18.217, 2.90. [OE *wéndan*]

wene *n.* expectation 10.75; opinion 18.513; doubt, in phr. *witouten* ∼ 14.220. [OE *wēn(a)*]

wene *v.* hope for (with gen.) 17.259. *pr. 1 sg.* **wene** think 4.108, 5.128, 10.66, 15.47; suppose 1.652; expect 8L.6; hope 1.706, 8M.14; *Y* ∼ (tag) I know 8M.2. *2 sg.* **wenes** think 2.63; **wen(e)st** 1.47, 195; **wenis(t)** 14.59, 1.231; (with suffixed pron.) **wenestu** 1.219, 4.214. *3 sg.* **weneð** 1.533, 12.88; **wenis** 14.61. *pl.* **weneþ**, **-ð** 1.504, 10.76; **wenen** 12.172. *pa. t. sg.* **wend(e)** thought 3.193, 10.4, 14.154; intended 4.230, 247; hoped 5.276, 16.299. *pl.* **wenden** 10.218, 16.161, 17.195; **uuenden** 16.144. *pp.* **iwend** expected 5.134. [OE *wēnan*]

wenǵen *n. pl.* wings 19.162, 384. [ON *væng-r*]

wennchell *n.* child 13.87. [OE *wencel*]

wenne; went(-). See **win; wend.**

weolcne *n.* sky, clouds 18.101; *under* ∼ in the open 1.640, on earth 10.55. [OE *wolcen*, late *weolcne*]

weolde. See **wil(e).**

weole *n.* riches, wealth 18.628, 19.182. [OA *weola*]

weoleful *adj.* joyful 19.275. [prec.+-**ful**]

weolie *adj.* as *n. pl. gen.* of rich men 18.605 (note). [OA *weolig*]

weorde; weore(n); weorkes. See **word(e); were** *v.*[1], **was; werk.**

weorld-monne *n.* (? *pl.*) man in the world 10.70. [**world(e)**+ **man**]

weorp; weorreð. See **warpeð; uuerrien.**

weorrur, *n.* warrior 18.90. [AN *werrour*]

weouede, weuede *n.* altar 7.172, 174. [OE *wēofod*]

wepes *pr. 3 sg. tr.* weeps for, bewails 14.221. *intr. subj. sg.* **wepe** weep 1.182. *pl.* 1.521. *pr. p.* **weping** 3.263. *pa. t. sg.* **wep** 3.74, 169, 5.107. *pl.* **wepe** 3.250. [OE *wēpan, wēop, wēopon*]

wepne *n.* weapon 5.286. *pl.* **wepnen** 10.61, 117, 18.8, 19. 181. [OE *wǣp(e)n* (A *wēp-*), pl. *wǣpn(u)*]

wer *adj. comp.* worse 14.68. [ON *verri*]

wer; werc. See **wher(e); werk.**

were *n.* doubt, in *boute ~* 9.21. [obscure; perh. orig. variant of **werre**]

were, weore *v.*[1] *tr.* wear 8F.15, 14. *pr. 3 sg.* **werep** 8N.8; *intr.* **wereð** 12.50 (note). [OE *werian*[1]]

were *v.*[2] defend 14.14; **werien** 19. 216. *pr. pl.* **werieð** 18.80, 19.163. *subj. sg.* **werie** 19.160. *imper. sg.* **were** 18.641. [OE *werian*[2]]

were(n); werelld. See **was; world(e).**

weress *n. gen.* man's 13.68. [OE *wer*]

werewed *pp.* torn about, mauled 4.342. [OE *wyrgan*] Cf. **awuriet.**

wergið *pr. pl.* grow tired 18.176. [OE *wērgian*]

wergunge *n.* growing tired, flagging 18.177. [from prec.]

weri(e), wery *adj.* weary 7.246, 8T.12, 10.45. [OE *wērig*]

werien. See **were** *v.*[2]

werienesse *n.* weariness 7.238, 249. [OE *wērignes(se)*]

werk *n.* work 4.134, 8N.16; **werc** action 19.83. *pl.* **werkes** deeds, actions, behaviour 6.245, 17.54, 18.35, 19.73; **workes** 8x.13; **weorkes** building works 16.221. [OE *weorc*, A *werc*]

werkmen *n. pl.* labourers 17.179, 184. [OE *weorcmann*]

werld(e); werm; wernches. See **world(e); worme; wrench(e).**

werne(n) *v.* deny, refuse 4.192, 8T.39; reject 1.394. *pa. t. sg.* **wearnde** refused 18.132. *pl.* **warnden** 10.190. [OE *wérnan, wéarnian*]

werrais. See **uuerrien.**

werre *n.* war 2.118; **uuerre** 16. 247. [ONF *werre*]

wers(te), werse; werþ; wes; weschen, wesse. See **wors(e); wurðen; was; waschen.**

west *n.* west 19.362; *bi ~* (in the) west 8D.37, H.10, K.42, as *prep.* west of 9.1. [from **west** adv.]

west *adj.* west 11.113. [from next]

west *adv.* (in the) west 1.555; (to the) west 16.93. [OE *west*]

west; weste. See **waxe; wite(n)** *v.*[1]

westhalf *n.* western part 18.64. [OE *westh(e)alf*] See **west, half.**

wet. See **what** *pron.*

wet(e) *adj.* wet 10.45, 18.90. [OE *wǣt*] Cf. **wate.**

wete *n.*[1] water 12.21. [OE *wǣta*]

wete *n.*[2] wheat 12.84, 102. [OE *hwǣte*]

wetes *pr. 3 sg.* becomes wet, is dipped 8E.70. [OE *wǣtan* tr.]

weþer; weðer; weuede. See **hweðer; whaðer; weouede.**

wex *n.* wax, candles 7.45. [OA *wex*]

wex; wha; whær; whæt. See **waxe; who; wher(e); what.**

whal *n.* whale, walrus 8E.40. *gen.*
whalles 8E.67, G.1. See bon.
[OE *hwæl, hwal-*]
wham. See who.
whan *adv., conj.* when 2.171,
3.25, 9.113; hwan 4.39, 79;
ʒwane 7.82, 141, since 193;
wan(e), wanne 1.298, 308,
8w.21, Q.2, 11.144, 12.144;
won(e), wonne 1.240, 243, 38;
when 3.101, 8D.23; hwen(ne)
18.79, 19.28, 6; quen 14.70;
wen(ne) 5.75, 151, 6.198, 284,
8Y.1, 14.59; ~ *þat* when 8N.31,
14.165. *interrog.* 3.70, 5.151,
6.284, 14.163. *rel.* 2.204. *indef.*
~ *er*, ~ *se* whenever 8N.17,
18.22 (see euer(e), so). [OE
hwanne, hwonne, hwænne]
whar(e); whaswa. See
wher(e); whose.
what *adj.* what *interrog.* 3.88;
ʒwat 7.57, 194, 263 (with pl. n.);
quat 14.34, 89; whæt 10.175;
whet 8L.28, N.8; hwet 18.111.
indef. ~ .. *se* whatever 18.342.
[from next]
what *pron. interrog.* what 2.68,
6.337, 9.7; whatt 13.61; hwat
1.564, 4.213, 342; ʒwat 7.179,
263; wat 1.271, 5.33, 6.29, 16.
224, 17.93; vat 15.63; hweat
18.563, 619; wæt 10.197; whet
8G.44; hwet 18.19, 19.67; wet
17.46; who 4.205, 5.130, 19.67.
dat. or *inst.* wan in *to* ~ to what
end 1.462. *indef.* as *n.* something, thing 12.58; ~ *so, se* whatever 3.164, 19.194 (cf. whose).
inst. hwon in *for* ~ *þat* if on
occasion (with *subj.*) 19.27. *adv.*
(exclam.) what! 1.566, 688; how
8B.5, L.8, Y.5, quat 14.271; why
5.163; as far as 1.342, 481; ~
mið what with 5.89 (see mid).
compound rel. what 1.60, 141,
10.154, 13.104. *conj.* wath until
17.111 (see alwat). [OE *hwæt*,
M *hwet; hwām hwon*, &c.] See
who.

whaðer *conj.* whether *interrog.*
10.245 (with correl. *þa* or);
quedir (*þat*) 14.139; *indef.*
quedur 14.44; weðer *so* 12.
118. [OE *hwæþer*]
when. See whan.
wher(e) *adv., conj.* where 2.93,
8L.14; hwer 18.156, 19.78;
whær 13.53; wer 6.284, 15.3,
17.13; whar 9.16, 150, 10.33;
hwar(e) 1.685, 4.308; ʒware
7.84, 158; quare- 14.212;
war(e) 1.707, 10.243, 11.67.
interrog. 1.707, 6.284, 10.33, 13.
53. *rel.* 2.93, 8L.14, 9.150, 11.67.
indef. wherever 1.64, 685, 8N.13,
18; ~ *sæ, se* 16.199, 301, 18.156,
19.19, ~ *se .. eauer* 19.78; ~
summ 13.20. Prefixed to prep.:
~bi by which 17.79; ~for(e),
-uore wherefore, why 1.203,
14.160, through which 17.76;
~mide with which 5.112; ~of
from what 19.336; ~to to what
end, why 5.137, 6.313, 18.524, 19.
336; ~þourgh through which
3.266; ~vnder under which 14.
212. [OE *hwær, hwār(a)*, and
hwær, hwăr(a) in reduced stress]
whet. See what.
whi, why *adv.* why *interrog.*
1.106, 8F.25, L.13, 10.108; ʒwi,
ʒwy 7.161, 104; hwi 1.541,
19.335, *for* ~ for what reason
18.98, 466; qui in *for* ~ 14.187;
wi 1.204, 6.64, 314; wee 17.
184. *rel.* hwi for which 18.609.
[OE *hwȳ, hwī*]
whiche. See hwuch.
whider *adv.* where (to) *interrog.*
8N.9; wider, wydur 1.470,
14.64; weder 5.244. *indef.*
hwider *se* wherever 19.310.
[OE *hwider*]
whil(e) *conj.* while 8B.1, D.30,
G.6, L.29; hwil 18.195, 19.394;
wile 6.70, 438, 16.181. [OE
þā hwīle þe, from next]
while *n.* while, time 2.163, 3.252;
hwile 4.257, 18.20, 91; ʒwile,

ʒwyle 7.213, 87; quil 14.173; wile 1.155, 12.93, 15.12; wule 11.32; *leosen his* ~ waste his time 18.91, sim. 15.12, 7.87. *ane* ~ for a time 19.243; (forming *conj.*) *þe* ~ (*þat*) while, as long as 6.444, 7.39, 213, 11.32, *þa* ~ 10.114. *gen.* hwile 18.387; while in *wa wes hire þere* ~ she was sorry 10.237. [OE *hwīl*] See whilen, whiles.

whilen, whylen *adv.* formerly, before, at one time 10.318, 8L. 22; hwilen 17.19; hwilem, hwylem 17.240, 128; wylem 17.42; while 10.230, 325; wile 1.158; quilum at times 14.73. [OE *hwīlum* dat. pl.]

whiles *adv.* in *þe* ~ in the meantime 18.342. *conj.* until 3.166; wiles while 12.51, 82. [while +adv. gen. *-es*]

whit(e), whyt(e) *adj.* white 8E.35, 26, 9.136; fair(-skinned) 8G.1, 50; hwit 18.578; ʒwiʒt, ʒwiit, ʒwite 7.113, 176, 143; wite 8Y.3; with 15.45; ~ *monkes* Cistercians 9.52 (see ɡray). *comp.* whittore 8E.77. [OE *hwīt*, comp. *hwīt(t)ra*]

white. See wite(n)¹.

who *pron.* 2.22, 8F.5, H.9; hwo 4.192, 226; wo 1.143, 152, 4.314, 5.122; wha 10.282; hwa 18.124, 188; qua 14.42, 52; wa 1.740. *interrog.* who 1.143, 152, 2.22, 5.122, 8F.5, 10.282, 18.124. *indef.* (some)one 14.52; anyone who 18.188; if anyone 1.426, 8H.9; whoever 4.192, 226, 314. *acc., dat.* (to, for) whom wham 8E.23, L.4; hwam 19.44; quam 14.10, 15.48; whom 2.303; wom 5.181; wam 6.387. *interrog.* 5.181, 8L.4, 15.48. *rel.* 2.303, 6.387, 8E.23, 14.10; *compound rel.* (containing antecedent, cf. what) 19.44, ~ *þat* 8M. 21. *gen.* whas whose *rel* 2.152, 13.156. [OE *hwā, hwām, hwæs*]

whonene *adv.* whence, from where 1, note to 95; wanene 1.568; wonene 10.introd.; hweonene 19.68, 73; ʒwanne in phr. *fram* ~ *þat* 7.192. [OE *hwanon(e), hwonan(e)*; *eo* after *heonan*, see henne]

whose *pron. indef.* whosoever, whoever, if anyone 9.177; woso 12.188, 193, 17.53; wose 6.445, 8G.38; hoso 7.192, 277; hwase 18.73, 262, 19.424; quasa 14.95; whaswa 10.261; wuasua 16.130; ~ *e(a)uer* 6.361, 18.347. *obl.* hwamse 19. 311 (incorrectly). [OE *swā hwā swā*; see who, so]

whuch; wi. See hwuch(e); whi.

wi-ax *n.* battle-axe 10.19 (note). [OE *wīg*+*ax(e)*]

wycche *n.* witch 8F.46. *pl.* witches 12.184. [OE *wicce*]

wicchecrafft, -crefte, wiecchecrafte *n.* witchcraft 6.206, 1.569, 576. [OE *wiccecræft*]

wicci. See wicke.

wich, wyche. See hwuch(e), hwuch.

wiche *v.* practise witchcraft, use sorcery 6.353. [OE *wiccian*]

wicke *adj.* wicked 7.126; wicci 16.281. [app. from OE *wicca* wizard; cf. wycche]

wycked, wiked *adj.* bad, wicked 8L.12, X.1. [prec.+adj. suff. *-ed*]

wicke-tunes *n. pl.* religious houses 1.476 (note). [OE *wīc-tūn* court; cf. wike¹, toun(e)]

wid, wyd. See wiþ.

wid(e), wyde *adj.* wide, broad 4.272, 8M.10, 19.94; widespread 1.308, 8H.28. [OE *wīd*]

wide *adv.* wide(ly) 4.223, 7.42, 12.148, 18.41; far and wide 7.43, 144, 220, 10.35, 86, *for an* ~ 1.456; from a distance 7.256; weide 10.138. [OE *wīde*]

wider, wydur. See whider.

wyderward *adv. interrog.*: ~

þat in what direction 14.110. [whider + OE -*weard*]

wydewe *n.* widow 7.143. *pl. gen.* **widewene** 5.201. [OE *widewe*]

widewe-had *n.* widowhood 18. 611. [OE *widewanhād*]

widuten; wiecchecrafte. See **wiþoute; wicchecrafft.**

wif, wyf *n.* wife 3.23, 4.297, 6.121, 2.181; **wiif** 2.8, 262; woman 6.27, 8G.12, 18.542; **vif** 6.83; (as address) 15.60; *gode* ~ housewife, mistress of a house 6.300. *dat.* **wiue, wyue, wife, wyfe** 5.212, 228, 2.192; *to* ~ as his wife 2.152, 3.230, 15.6, 16.299 (see **to** *prep.*). *pl.* **wiues** 6.303 (*dat.*), 9.170. *gen.* **wife** 10.242. [OE *wif*]

wiȝ. See **wiþ.**

wiȝt *n.* creature, person 1.312, 364; **wiht, wyht** 1.600, 8H.23; **wyþt** 8N.7; *swet(e)* ~ sweetheart 3.193, 206. *pl.* **wiȝte** creatures 1.87, 160, 343; **wiȝtes** 1.309, 378; **wyhtes** animals 8H.5. [OE *wiht*] See **noȝt** *n.*

wiȝth *adj.* valiant 2.79. [ON *vigt*, neut. of *vig-r*]

wiheles *n. pl.* deceptions 19.176. [OE *wigel(e)* divination, infl. by **wil**²]

wiht, wyht; wiis; wiit. See **wiȝt; wis(e); wit(te).**

wike *n.*¹ *pl.* dwellings 1.384. [OE *wīc*, sg. and. pl.]

wike *n.*² *pl.* services 1.383, 385. [OE *wice*]

wil, wyl, will(e) *n.*¹ will, wish, desire, what one wants 6.53, 8F.6, 18.218, 8F.17, 14.129, 2. 275, 3.173, 5.87, 6.29; **uylle** 8R.10; (the will of God) 7.88, 10.111, 13.82, 16.18, 19.22; disposition 13.114; intention 19.83; Will (personified) 19.10, 398; pleasure: *his hit þi* ~ if you please 6.28, *ȝef hire* ~ *were* if she were willing 8F.6; *to* ~ to their

liking, as they wished 3.289, sim. *att hiss* ~ 13.232; *to mi* ~ as I desire 6.234. *gen. adv.* **willes** spontaneously, voluntarily 18. 39, 522; **wils** at (one's) will: *ware þi* ~ *es* where you please 14.270. [OE (*ge*)*will, willa*]

wil *n.*² craft, deceit 12.183. [doubtful: perh. ONF **wile* = OF *guile*, see **ȝile**, blended with OE *wigle*, see **wiheles**; but see *OED*]

wil *adj.* at a loss, bewildered 4.131. [ON *vill-r*]

wil(e), wyl *pr. 1, 3 sg.* 1.141, 2.148, 3.87, 4.64, 8T.39; **will(e)** 1.198, 3.18, 6.35, 14.95, (with suffixed pron.) **willi** 8X.1 (see **Ich**); **wol(e)** 5.175, 7.277, 8G. 21, M.20; **wolle** 7.40, 8K.75; **wul(e)** 8X.4, 18.74, 19.47; **wulle** 1.535, 706, 10.92, (after *Ich*) **chulle** 18.275, 493. *3 sg.* **wl(e)** 1.284, 9.177. wish, desire, be willing 1.141, 571, 4.171, 12.35, 14.27, 15.8, 18.322, 481; want to go, will go (infin. understood) 5.244–6, 10.101; *auxil.* will (forming fut., often implying wish, intention, &c.) 1.198, 2.148, 3.87, 4.64, 5.131, 8X.2; is accustomed to 3.18, 49. *2 sg.* **wilt** 1.121, 3.78; **wolt** 5.244, 6.241, 8L.21; **wult** 1.571, 18. 322, 481; (with suffixed pron.) **wilt(o)u** 3.224, 4.171; **woltou** 5.186; **wultu** 1.627. *pl.* **wilen** 4.186; **wille(n)** 1.222, 16.224; **wol** 9.180; **wulle** 1.688; **uilleth** 17.176; **wulleð** 19.325. *subj. sg.* **wille** 1.77, 144. *pa. t.* wished, planned 2.5, 3.191, 4.91, 6.64, 10.154; wished to go 7.264; used to 7.146, 147; *subj.* would wish 1.303, 4.66, 6.431, 8E.3, 18.203; would require 18. 20; *auxil. (subj.)* should, would (forming condit. and indirect fut.) 1.70, 3.260, 5.46, 10.200, 11.28. *1, 3 sg.* **wold(e)** 2.5, 3.

191, 4.91, 8F.5, 16.17; **wollde**
13.9; **uuolde** 16.107; **wald(e)**
1.668, 14.138; **weolde** 10.200.
2 sg. **woldest** 1.84, 3.260, 8F.31;
waldest 18.40; **wuldes** 12.143.
pl. **wolde(n)** 4.232, 266, 10.88;
wald(e) 1.636, 14.16; **wulde** 12.
37. *subj. sg.* (with prefixed pron.)
Icholde 11.104; *God wolde* O that
it were God's will, would God
8K.28. [OE *willan, wyllan;*
wólde, wálde] See **nyl.**
wilcume. See **welcome(n).**
wilcweme *adj.* pleased 18.294.
[**wil** *n.*[1] + OE (*ge*)*cwēme;* cf. *wel-*
gecwēme pleasing, and **wel-**
come(n)]
wilde, wylde *adj.* wild 8H.5; unruly 11.139; wanton 8E.2. as *n.*
pl. gen. **wildis** wanton men's
8x.3. [OE *wilde*]
wyle *n.* sorceress 8F.46. [OE
*wigele; cf. **wiheles**]
wile; wylem; wiles. See
whil(e), while; whilen;
whiles.
willeliche *adv.* willingly 18.595.
[cf. OE *willīce, willendlīce*]
willen *v.* wish (with *after,* for)
3.6. [OE *willian*]
willesfule *adj.* wilful, headstrong
19.50, 230. [gen. of **wil** *n.*[1] +
-**ful**]
willis. See **welle** *n.*
wilnest *pr. 2 sg.* desire 19.322.
subj. pl. **wilnin** 18.435. [OE
wilnian]
wimman, wymman *n.* woman
16.304, 15.29; **wimmon,**
wymmon 6.8, 8D.34; **wyman**
15.84, 17.94; **wimon** 6.205,
8v.19; **womman** 2.110, 7.34,
9.30, wife 2.116; **wommon**
8D.37; **womon** 6.122; **wum-**
mon 18.250, 349. *gen.* **wom-**
mans 2.263 (see **loue**). *pl.*
wimmen, wymmen 5.8, 10.
315, 16.162, 8E.2, H.10; **wum-**
men 18.304. *gen.* **wymmens**
2.254; **wimmonne(n)** 10.22,

234. [OE *wīfmann, wimman,* pl.
-men(n)]
win *n.* happiness, joy, pleasure
14.174; **wynne** 8F.14; **wenne**
6.26; **wunne** 1.208, 10.312,
18.26, 19.183; **wnne** 8y.6. *pl.*
wunnen 18.15, 25. [OE *wynn*]
win(e), wyn(e) *n.* wine 9.46,
11.169, 2.130, 8E.71, 17.91. *pl.*
wynes vines 2.105. [OE *wīn*]
wind(e), wynd *n.* wind 9.41,
10.157, 17.147, 18.92, 8K.1. *gen.*
windes 8B.3, 10.124, 18.193.
[OE *wind*]
winde *v. intr.* go 5.76. *pa. t. sg.*
wond went 5.22; rolled 10.29.
tr. **wand** wound, wrapped 13.
51. *pp.* **wundenn** wound 13.57,
96. [OE *windan; wánd, wónd;*
wúnden]
wyndou *n.* window 8L.23. *pl.*
wyndewes 2.214. [ON *vind-*
auga]
wine *n.* friend 12.133 (*dat.*).
[OE]
winiærd *n.* vineyard 16.220;
winyard(e), wyn- 17.180, 205,
181. [OE *wingeard*]
winnde-clŭt *n.* swaddling-cloth
13.51. *pl.* -**clutess** 13.96.
[**winde** + **clut**]
winne(n), wyn(ne) *v.* win, gain,
obtain, earn 3.100, 139, 4.120,
14.72; attain 9.182; come by,
meet 8L.20; **winnenn** (with
infin.) succeed (in —ing) 13.219;
winnan conquer 16.235. *pr. pl.*
winnen contend 12.163. *subj.*
sg. **winne** 3.105. *pa t. sg.* **wan,**
uuan 16.217, 310, 218. *pp.*
wonne 6.58; **ywo.ine** 2.42.
[OE (*ge*)*winnan; wann, wunnen*]
wynne. See **win** *n.*
winter(e) *n.* winter 1.290, 293,
11.107, 12.79. *pl.* **winter** (as
measure of time) years 4.55;
wintre, wyntre (prob. representing earlier *gen.* after
numeral) 16.88, 181, 17.250,
[OE *winter,* pl. *winter, -tru*]

wirche *v.* make, form, do, act 1.468; wurche 8x.12; wrchen 1.286 (note). *pr. 3 sg.* wurcheð performs, does 18.294, 418. *pa. t. sg. intr.* wrohte did (building) work 16.207; *tr.* wrohhte 13.50; wraht(t)e 18. 485, 19.83. *pp.* wroht 8g.13; wrohht sent 13.124; wroȝht 14.143; wrouȝt 3.274; wrout 6.112; wrowt 3.38; ywroht 8e.80, h.32; iwrowt 3.141; iwraht, y- 18.625, 8k.32. [OE *wyrcan, wircan*; *worhte* (A *warhte*), *wrohte*]

wirm. See worme.

wis(e), wys(e) *adj.* wise, skilled, learned 1.148, 6.4, 16.275, 312, 17.17, 19.332; discreet, sensible 1.280, 8d.34, wiis 5.105. as *n.*, *þe ~* the wise man 1.132, 19.206; *pl. (dat.)* in inclusive phr. *~ an sneþe* everyone 1.181. *comp.* wisure 1.598. *sup.* wisest 18.605. [OE *wīs*] See alrewiseste.

wisdom(e) *n.* wisdom, learning 1.567, 684, 3.36, 14.27; wise verdict 1.714; what is wise 19. 209. [OE *wisdōm*]

wise *n.* way, manner 4.288, 5.3, 6.15, 13.160; song, tune 1.54, 661. *dat.* wisen 10.253. *pl.* wise songs 1.621, *dat.* ways 20. [OE *wīse*]

wisi *v.* show 1.547; wiss guide, lead 14.149. [OE *wissian*]

wisman *n.* wise man 14.27. [wis(e)+man]

wisse *n.* guide 18. title. [cf. next]

wissunge *n.* guidance, direction 19.35, 399. [OE *wissung*]

wisste, wist(e). See wite(n) *v.*[1]

wit(te) *n.* mind, intelligence, reason, understanding 1.427, 735, 7.142, 19.9, 28; senses 18. 636; (personified) Reason 19.12, 14; wiit 5.70, an idea 124. *gen.* Wittes 19.34, 399. *pl.* wittes senses 19.17. [OE *(ge)witt*]

wit *pron. 1 dual* we two 10.43. *poss. adj.* unker our 1.360, 738, *gen.* of us two 107. [OE *wit, uncer*]

wit, wyt; witches. See wiþ; wycche.

wite *n.* blame, default 13.26. [OE *wīte*]

wyte *pr. 1 sg.* lay blame for (with *dat.* of person blamed) 8g.12. [OE *wītan*]

wite(n), wyte *v.*[1] know, know of 1.587, 631, 6.29, 8f.5; understand 19.155; witenn 13.9; witte in *do ȝow to ~* let you know 9.101. *pr. 1, 3 sg.* wot 1.61, 3.159, 6.284, 7.170, 8n.7, 17.258; has (of mental qualities) 1.151; woth 4.74; wote 9.34, 175; wat 10.49, 6.235, 14.64, 18.151, 19.199; *1 sg.* (with prefixed pron.) Ichot 8k.5, n.22, 34. *2 sg.* wost 15.48, (with suffixed pron.) wostu 1.462; wat 14.112. *pl.* witen 18.184, 19.332. *subj. sg.* wite 1.318. *God (h)it wot(e)* God knows 1.527, 9.34, 103, 175, *wat God* 6.235, and see Goddot; *þat wot Crist* 15.78, distinct from *Godd hit wite* may God know it 18.151. *imper. pl.* wite, white 13.88, 3.271; witeð 18.114. *pa. t. sg.* wist(e) 1.103, 2.226, 3.173, understood 16.110; wisste 13.53; weste 5.238, 6.79; wuste 1.10, 7.58, 10.154, 11.171. *pl.* wiste 3. 209; wisstenn 13.177; wusten 7.183. *subj. sg.* wist(e) 14. 110, 19.6; weste 5.59, 6.237. [OE *witan; wāt, witon; wiste, wyste*]

wite(n) *v.*[2] protect, guard, defend 19.162, 201, 229, 416. *infl. infin.* to witene 19.169; in his protection 19.254; *warde ~* to keep watch 19.57, 404. *pr. 3 sg.* wit keeps guard 19.59. *pl.* witeð 19.163, 382. *subj. sg.* wite 8u.

12. *imper. sg.* **wite** 10.304. *pa. t. sg.* **wuste** 11.109, 158. [OE *witan*; *wiste*, *wyste*] Cf. **biwiten**, **iwite**, **witien**.

wite. See **whit(e)**.

wite3e *n.* prophet 10.232, 325. [OE *witega*]

witer *adj.*[1] wise, prudent 10. 254. [LOE *witter* from ON *vitr*]

witerli *adv.* clearly, certainly, assuredly 3.271, 6.232; **witerrli3** 13.177; **witerliche** 18.48, 301, 19.88, 372. *comp.* **witer-luker** more clearly 19.321. [cf. MSw *vitterliga* clearly]

witerr *adj.*[2] clear, certain 13.94. [from prec.]

with. See **whit(e)**.

witien *v.* guard, look after 7.75. [OE *-witian*] Cf. **wite(n)**[2].

witles *adj.* without understanding 1.438; foolish 18.279; insane 7.266. [OE *witlēas*]

witnesse *n.* evidence, testimony: ~ *to berene* in testifying 16.37. [OE *witnes(se)*]

witneð *pr. 3 sg.* testifies (to) 18. 106, 110, 296. [ON *vitna*]

witouten, **witute(n)**. See **wiþout**.

witti *adj.* sensible, wise 7.139. [OE *wittig*]

wiþ, **wyþ**, **wið**, **with** *prep.* 1.62, 2.4, 6.71, 8w.17, 1.627, 10.42, 18.65, 4.20, 7.20; **wiþþ** 13.28; **wi3**, **wiz** (= *wiþ*) 3.38, 64, 6.162; **wid**, **wyd** 16.238, 264; **uid** 8v.17; (before various cons.) **wit**, **wyt** 1.56, 222, 4.262, 14.16, 15.68, 8R.2, w.24, 14.30, 15.42; **uit** 8v.10. (of association) with 2.4, 4.64, 10.42, 11.11, 18.144; among 6.207, 8E.6, K.36; in addition to 19.223. (of speech) with, to 2.5, 6.71, (postponed) 162, 7.35. (of instrument) with, by 1, note to 132, 4.20, 7.20, 8D.1, 11.41; in 6.23; because of 8B.6. (of agent) by 6.248, 8L.18.

(of direction) against 1.627, 2.150, 8H.25, 16.238, 19.5. (with 'cleanse') of 1.390. towards 1.62, 5.247, 16.129; on 12.159. (forming *conj.*) ~ *þat*, *þet* provided, on condition that (with *subj.*) 6.192, 226, 18.47; ~ *þan þa* 10.202; ~ *þon þet* 18. 310. [OE *wiþ* blended with **mid**; *wiþ þan þe*, &c.]

withal *adv.* besides, in addition 4.22; **wi3alle** 3.19; in this matter 3.269. [cf. OA *mid alle*; see prec.]

wiðer *n.* conflict, fighting 10.282. [OE *wiþre*, and *wiþer* adj.]

withheld *pa. t. sg.* kept back 4.88. [wiþ + holde(n)]

wiþinne *adv.* within, inside 8E.65, 11.33; **wiðinnen** 16.45, 18.79, 19.16. [OE *wiþinnan*]

wiþinne, **wið-**, **with-** *prep.* within, inside 5.11, 16.100, 17. 262; **wi3-** 3.16; (of time) 8F.32. [as prec.]

wiþout, **wiþoute(n)**, **withoute** *prep.* 9.98, 2.101, 5.142, 8G.10, 11.91, 7.142; **wi3-** 3.102; **wiþhoute(n)** 6.36, 8u.6; **wiðute(n)** 12.182, 18.39, 19.94; **with-** 17. 165; **wit-** 1.139, 8v.5, 15.10; **wiþvte** 9.18; **witoten** 14.67; **vytvten** 15.53. (1) outside 11. 91, 131, 15.10. (2) without *all other refs.* See **fayle**, **nai**, **wo3(e)**. [as next]

wiþoute *adv.* outside 11.34; **witoutte** 14.170; **wiþute** externally, on the surface 1. 419; **wiðuten**, **wid-** 16.45, 100, 271; **wiðvten** 19.16. [OE *wiþūtan*]

wiðstode *pa. t. subj. sg.* resisted 18.48. [OE *wiþstōde* from *-stándan*]

wyþt. See **wi3t.**

wiðward *prep.* together with 18. 227. [wiþ + OE *-weard*]

wiue(s), **wyue**; **wl**; **wl(e)**. See **wif**; **ful(l)**; **ful(e)**, **wil(e)**.

wleatien v. feel disgust 18.661.
[OM *wleatian = WS wlatian]
wlech adj. lukewarm 18.656.
[OM *wlec = WS wlæc]
wlite n. appearance, face 1.317,
19.261, 275, 307; beauty 18.
629; splendour 19.301, 323.
[OE]
wnde; wnder. See **wunde;**
wonder n.
wndri pr. 1 sg. wonder (of, at)
1.184. [OE wundrian]
wnienge; wnne. See **woning**
n.²; **win.**
wo n. woe, sorrow, misery 5.53,
67, 6.189, 8D.13, G.40, 15.36;
harm, injury 5.54, 11.52, 103;
misfortune 8E.69, G.45; wa 10.
177, 18.15, 19.98; **wæ** 10.169;
with dat. of person: ~ is me I am
unhappy, grieve 4.121, 10.177,
19.151; þat me is ~ it grieves me
6.379; him wes, is ~ 5.2, 101,
8U.4; ~ beo þe 19.151; ~ is þe
mon 6.140, sim. 6.298, 303, 10.
169, 18.187; hence as adj., sad
8G.18. ~ me as interj. alas!
18.71; ~ worþe a curse on!
5.96. [OE wā]
wo. See **who.**
wod(e) adj. mad 1.374, 3.49,
4.204, 5.258; waxe, walke ~ go
mad 6.182, 8C.3, L.6; reckless
7.129; furious 4.275, 301. [OE
wōd]
wod(e) n.¹ wood, forest 5.1, 7.76,
8s.1; **wude** 1.395, tree 12.74,
firewood 18.664; **wde** 8A.4. gen.
wodes 7.74. pl. **wodes** 2.324,
8M.1; **wudes** 16.55. [OE
wudu]
wode n.² woad 1.76. [OE wād]
wode n.³ See **wed.**
wode-gore n. (strip of) forest
8L.31. [wod(e)+OE gāra; see
gore]
wodwale n. woodwall, probably
the golden oriole 9.97; **wude-**
wale 1.617. [cf. MLG wede-
wale]

811493

wo3(e) n. wrong, evil 1.120, 154;
wou3 7.24; **woh** injury 18.343;
wou 6.96; **wowe** 2.66. wiþ ~
wrongfully 7.24, 9.62; wiþhouten
~ truly 6.96. [OE wōh, wōg-]
wohere n. wooer 18.505, 645.
[OE wōgere]
wohin v. woo, court, make love
(to) 18.472. pr. 3 sg. **woheð**
18.467, 600; **woweþ** 8H.41. pl.
wowes 8H.5. pa. t. sg. **wohede**
18.504. [OE wōgian]
wohlech n. wooing, courtship:
for ~ to woo her 18.477. [stem
of prec. + suff. as in **cnaw-**
lechunge]
wol. See **wel** adv.; **wil(e).**
wolawo interj. woe, alas! 1.290.
[OE wā lā wā] Cf. **wailawai.**
wolcumeþ; wold. See **wel-**
comeþ; wil(e).
wolde n.¹ keeping, control 3.113.
[OA (ge)wáld]
wolde n.² wood, forest 1.682.
dat. **wolden** hill 10.34. [OA
wáld]
wolde(n), wole. See **wil(e).**
wolf n. wolf 5.108, 118, 9.31;
volf, vuolf 5.148, 221; **wulf**
18.170. gen. **wulues** 18.242.
[OE wulf]
wollde, wolle. See **wil(e).**
wolmongers n. pl. wool merchants 11.114. [OE wull+
mangere]
wolpakces n. pl. bales of wool
11.112. [OE wull+MLG pak]
wolt; wom. See **wil(e); who.**
wombe n. womb 8v.11. pl.
wombes bellies 4.338. [OE
wámb, wómb]
womman, wom(m)on. See
wimman.
won n.¹ dwelling, haunt 8H.28;
house 3.132, 6.21; world 8K.9;
wan abode 19.146. [app. from
ON ván, see next, infl. by
wonen; see OED]
won n.² quantity, store 6.132;
in adv. tag ful god ~ with great

U u

force 4.218, 334, in great number 264. [ON ván; see 4.218 note]

won adj.¹ wan, pale 8K.80. [OE wann, wonn]

won adj.² wont, accustomed 14. 248. [OE ge-wun(a)]

won; wond. See whan; winde.

wonde v. hesitate (in neg. phr.) 6.138, 396, 8D.19. [OE wándian, wóndian]

wonder n. wonder, cause for wonder 6.359, 8E.81, N.3; wunder 12.88, 18.488; wnder 8Q.3; marvel 7.157, 18.564; marvellous creature 12.178. dat. wundre in to ~ atrociously 18.500, al to ~ disastrously 19.11 (see diht). pl. wunder atrocities 16.154, 180; wundres wonderful things 18.485. gen. wnder 1.512. [OE wundor]

wonder adj. wonderful, marvellous 3.21, 7.154. [from prec., orig. in compds.]

wonder adv. marvellously 8E.80; wunder ane wonderfully 10. 296. [as prec.; see ane]

wondrien v. wander 10.35. pr. 3 sg. wandreþ strolls 2.173. [OE wandrian, wondrian]

wondryng n. perplexity 8G.40. [from prec., infl. by ON vandrǽði distress]

wone n.¹ custom, habit, practice 2.9, 3.22; wune 12.127, 19.76. [OE (ge)wuna]

wone n.² want, lack 19.185, 188. [OE wana, wona]

wone. See whan.

wonen v. dwell, live 3.4; wunen stay 12.164; wunien 10.312. pr. 2 sg. wunest 1.254. 3 sg. woneþ 8D.37; wuneþ, -ð 1.710, 10.55, 12.159; wonys 15.49. pl. woniþ 9.16; wunieð 19.307; wunen 12.94. subj. sg. wunnien 10.321. pa. t. sg. wonede 6.20, 7.143; wunede,

-ode 16.42, 80. pl. woneden 5.262, 7.225. pp. woned accustomed 5.105; iwunet 18.508, 19.231, 400. [OE wunian]

wonene. See whonene.

woning n.¹ wailing, lamentation 1.227; wanunge 19.145. [OE wānung] Cf. wanst.

woning n.² dwelling 1.718; wununge 18.154, 19.145, 153; wnienge 1.394. [cf. OE wunung]

wonne. See whan, winne(n).

wonte n. lack: hefdest ~ þrof went without it 18.309. [ON vant adj. neut.]

wonti(n) v. be lacking 18.624, 19.153. pt. 3 sg. wonteð 18.292. [ON vanta]

wontreaðes n. pl. distresses 19. 146. [ON vandrǽði]

wonunge n. diminution 19.326. [OE wonung] Cf. wain.

wope n. weeping 1.517. [OE wōp]

wor(e). See was.

word(e) n. word 1.326, 355, 3.149, 5.132, 8K.69, L.7; news, message 13.123, 18.262, esp. in send ~ 10.128, 14.135, 18.273; speech 1.45, 114, 10.71, 179, 19.83; efter þet ~ is as people say 18.226; weorde name 10. 269. pl. word 1.95, 611, 10.106, 173, 18.20; wordes 1.134, 3. 268, 5.148, 6.159, 7.86, 18.35, 19.72; worden 10.235. dat. worde 1.669; worden 10.313. [OE wórd, sg. and pl.]

wordes n. pl. hosts, companies 19.273, orders 282. [OE weorod]

wordl(e). See world(e).

woreð pr. 3 sg.-intr. fails 18.237. tr. disturbs, troubles 18.423. pl. intr. worið 18.237, 238. [OE wōrian intr.]

worhliche; worht. See wurhliche; wurðen.

wori adj. troubled, confused 18. 429. [rel. to woreð]

workes. See werk.

world(e) n. 5.150, 7.48, 8M.10,
9.184, 17.207, 18.24; worlt
18.18, 64; wordl(e) 17.171,
209; werld(e) 2.137, 230, 12.
94, 14.136, 260; werelld 13.50;
warld 14.91. world, earth 7.48,
8M.10, 18.64; in ~ on earth,
among men 8E.57, F.5, H.28;
for al þe ~ for any reward 6.243,
sim. 5.161; this world (distinguished from that to come)
5.150, 8T.19, 9.184, 12.94, 14.
91, 17.171, 18.18, 19.166; ~
(a) buten ende world without
end, eternally 18.596, 640; from
~ into ~ for ever 19.123, 360.
gen. worldes 5.161, 18.28,
worldly, material 8H.42; worldis 8x.2; werldes 3.36; warlds
14.257; worlde 1.334; worilde
8y.6; warld 14.123. pl. wordles
ages, epochs 17.242. [OE w(e)o-
rold, gen. -e]
worldlich adj. earthly, of this
world 19.192; worltliche 18.
24. [OE woroldlic]
worly. See wurhliche; wurðliche.
worme n. worm 9.40; werm
17.60; wirm insect 12.88, 101.
pl. wormes 1.381, (dat.) 8y.4.
[OE wyrm, wurm]
wors(e) adj. comp. worse 1.219,
6.378; wurse 19.116, 156;
wers, vers 14.38; wærse 16.
282. sup. werste 3.34. [OE
wyrsa, sup. wyrsta] See alreworste.
wors(e) adv. comp. worse 5.202,
7.26; wurse 10.282; wrs 1.34;
werse, uuerse 16.190, 182;
wærse 16.250, 285. me is þe ~
it is the worse for me 1.34; no
þe ~ him nas he was none the
worse 7.26; see þe adv. [OE
wyrs]
worþ(-) ; worth ; wose, woso ;
wost(u), wot(e), woth ;
wou(ȝ). See wurðen ; wurð
adj.; whose ; wite(n) ; woȝ(e).

wouing, n. wooing, soliciting
6.125. [cf. OE wōgung] See
wohin.
wound- ; wous. See wunde,
wundest ; fous.
wowe n. misery 1.292. [OE wāwa]
wowe, wowes, -þ ; wox ;
wraht(t)e. See woȝ(e) ;
wohin ; fox ; wirche.
wrake n. injury 2.154; punishment, vengeance 18.344. [OE
wracu]
wrang. See wrong.
wranne n. wren 1.372, 675. [OE
wrænne]
wrat ; wrað(est), wrath. See
writenn ; wroþ(e).
wraþþe n. anger 11.150;
wreaððe 18.134, 249. [OE
wræþþu] See wreth.
wraþþen v. make angry, offend
6.41. [from prec.]
wrchen. See wirche.
wreah pa. t. sg. concealed 18.510.
pp. wrihe covered, with hidden
meaning 18.473. [OE wrēah,
wrigen from wrēon (orig. cl. I
but infl. by II)] Cf. unwreo.
wreaððe. See wraþþe.
wreccehed n. misery 16.190;
wrechhede 7.128. [next+
-hede]
wrecche, wreche n. wretch,
miserable creature 5.253, 6.298,
8F.39, 5.288; outcast 1.582;
villain 1.570, 627, wrechche
7.282. pl. wrecches 18.463.
[OE wrecca]
wrecche, wreche adj. miserable, despicable 1.251, 364;
wrecce, uurecce poor 16.102,
180, 159, 183. [prec.]
wrecchedom n. misery 19.98.
[wrecche n.+-dom]
wreccheliȝ adv. poorly 13.57.
[from wrecche adj.]
wrechhede; wreke. See
wreccehed; wreoke.
wrench(e) n. trick 17.260;
artifice, device 5.84, 7.33,

wrenc 16.91; trickery 1.330. *pl.* wrenches 19.173; wrences 16.24; wernches 19.6. [OE *wrenc*]

wrencheð *pr. pl.* draw out, expel 18.55. [OE *wrencan* twist]

wrengðe *n.* crookedness, distortion 12.33. [OE *wrengðu* from *wrang*, see wrong; cf. ON *rengð*]

wreoke *v.* avenge (a person *on* another) 18.350. *pr. 3 sg.* wrekeð 18.339. *imper. sg.* wreke 2.78. *pp.* wreke 4.311; iwreken 6.215. [OE *wrecan*, M *wreocan*; pp. *wrecen*]

wretched *adj.* miserable 14.123; wrichede wretched, contemptible 17.65. [wrecche+adj. suff. -ed; cf. wycked]

wreth *n.* anger 14.32; wreþe 17.167. [OE *wræþu*] See wraþþe.

wrichede; wrihe. See wretched; wreah.

writ(e) *n.* written message, letter 7.174, 202; (piece of) writing 19.424; write writing 13.274, writt 13, 287, *o* ~ in writing, *onn eche lifess bokess* ~ in writing in the book of eternal life; *Holi, Hali* ~ Scripture 17.258, 18.346. *pl.* writes Scriptures 17.162. [OE *writ*]

writelinge *n.* trilling 1.48, 546. [from frequentative extension of OE *writian* chirp]

writenn *v.* write; write down, record 13.285. *pr. 3 sg.* writ 1.714. *pa. t. sg.* wrat 18.471. *pp.* iwrite(n) 7.108, 180, 18.105, 19.80, 358; recorded 5.204. [OE *writan*, *wrāt*, *gewriten*]

wroggen; wroght, wrohht(e), wroht(e). See frogge; wirche.

wrong(e) *n.* wrong(doing), injustice 2.45, 260, 8B.6, w.57; wrong suffered, injury 2.53; *þou hast* ~ you do wrong 2.293, sim. *heuede* ~ 6.9. [from next]

wrong *adj.* wrong 7.284; crooked, twisted 12.6; wrang as *n.* wicked man (prob. *dat.*, see loþ) 14.29. [LOE *wráng* from ON **wrang-*, OI *rang-r*]

wronge *adv.* badly 1.152. [from prec.]

wrong-wende *adj.* twisted 18.211. [wrong+wend]

wroþ(e) *adj.* angry, resentful (fold. by *with*) 1.600, 3.178, 5.220, 6.39, 9.30, 11.149; ill-tempered 8F.39 (note); wrooþ 2.150, 256; wrað, wrath 18.349, 14.30. *sup.* wraðest fiercest 10.255. [OE *wrāþ*]

wroþe *adv.* fiercely, cruelly 1.63, 5.291; ill-humouredly 1.293. [OE *wrāþe*]

wrouȝt, wrout, wrowt; wrs; wrþ; wrth, wrþe. See wirche; wors(e) *adv.*; wurð *adj.*; wurðen.

wruhte *n. gen.* maker's 18.332. [OE *wyrhta*, *wryhta*]

wu; wuasua; wucche; wuch; wude; wudewale; wue; wul; wule; wulf. See hou; whose; hwuch(e); hwuch; wod(e) *n.*[1]; wodwale; we; wil(e); while, wil(e); wolf.

wullderr *n.* glory 13.110. [OE *wuldor*]

wulle, wult(u); wulues; wummon. See wil(e); wolf; wimman.

wumme *interj.* alas! 19.151. [app. OE *wā mē*; see wo]

wunde *n.* wound 12.182, 18.496. *pl.* wundes 4.272, 325; woundes 8L.30, 34; wunden 10.291, 309, 18.271, 19.270; wnde 8w.17, 36. [OE *wúnd*]

wundenn; wunder. See winde; wonder.

wunderfule *adj.* full of wonder 18.38, 44. [OE *wundorful*]

wunderlice *adj.* wonderful 16.232. [OE *wundorlic*]

wunderliche *adv.* in a strange

fashion 10.315. [OE *wundor-lice*]

wundest *pr. 2 sg.* wound 18.298. *pp.* wounded 8G.25; iwounded 11.160; iwundet 18.8. [OE *wúndian*]

wune ; wunen, -ien. See **wone** *n.*[1]; **wonen.**

wunliche *adj.* pleasant 10.74, 102. [OE *wynlic*]

wunne ; wununge ; wurche ; wurðeð, wurrdenn. See **win** *n.*; **woning** *n.*[2]; **wirche ; wurðen.**

wurhliche, worh- *adj.* splendid, beautiful 8K.9, 40; **worly** 8H.10. [OE *w(e)orþlic, wurþlic*]. See **wurðliche.**

wurrþe. See **wurð** *n.*

wurrþenn *v.* honour, worship 13.216. [OE *wéorþian, wur-*]

wurrþminnt *n.* honour, worship 13.110. [OE *wurþmynt*]

wurscipe ; wurse. See **wurð-schipe ; wors(e).**

wursi(n) *v. tr.* diminish 19.186, *intr.* deteriorate 369. [OE *wyrsian*; see **wors(e)**]

wurtscipe. See **wurðschipe.**

wurð *n.* price 18.386, 389; **wurrþe** honour, worship 13.106. *pl.* **wurþes** values, equivalents 8G.32 (note). [OE *weorþ, wurþ*]

wurð *adj.* worth, of value 18.356, 635; (with expression of value preceding) *noht* ~ 19.177, *muche* ~ of great merit 19.204; (constr. with *to*) 18.405; **wrþ** in *ne telþ* .. *noȝt* ~ accounts of no value 1.256; **worth** deserving of 14.44; **worȝ** worth 3.130. [OE *w(e)orþ, wurþ*]

wurþe, wurðe *adj.* deserving (*of*) 8F.22; worthy (with infin.) 18.489, 19.46, (with *to*+n.) 18.578. [OE *wýrþe*]

wurðen *v.* 12.133; **wurrþenn** 13.18; **wrþe** 1.506. (1) become 1.283, 356, 5.66, 12.23, 13.74,

16.19, 121, 18.662; ~ *to* turn to 8E.71, 19.168. (2) happen 10.108, 128. (3) be 5.96, 10.171, 12.133, 18.278; (pr. in fut. sense) shall, will be 3.75, 5.191, 248, 10.231; ~ *ded* see **ded.** (4) *auxil.* (forming pass.) be 1.506, 6.213, 13.18, 258, 18.65; (forming conditional) would have 1.278 (note). *pr. 1 sg.* **worþe** 5.191; **worht** 3.75. *2 sg.* **wurðest** 10.231. *3 sg.* **worþ** 1.283, 5.248; **worþeþ** 8E.71; **wurðeð** 19.168; **wurdeð** 12.23; **wrth** 1.356. *subj. sg.* **worþe** 5.96, 6.213; **wurðe** 10.171, 18.278, 662. *pa. t. sg.* **warð, warth** 18.65, 16.19, 123; **ward, uuard** 16. 321, 120; **wart** 16.242; **wærd, wærð** 16.305, 20; **werþ** 5.66. *pl.* **wurrdenn** 13.74; **wurþen, wurthen** 16.121, 271; **wurðe** 16.142. *subj. sg.* **wrþe** 1.278. *pp.* **wurrþenn** 13.3, 156; iwurðen 10.108, 128; **iworþe** 1.406. [OE *wéorþan, wurþan; wearþ, wúrdon; wórden*]

wurðliche *adv.* honourably 10. 61; **worly** beautifully 8G.13. [OE *w(e)orþlice, wur-*] See **wurhliche.**

wurðschipe *n.* worship 18.345; **wurscipe, wurtscipe** honour, respectful ceremony 16.117, 210, 320. [OE *wurþscipe*]

wuste. See **wite(n)** *v.*[1] and *v.*[2]

y-. See also **ȝ.**

ya, yai ; yaf ; yare ; yate. See **ȝe** *adv.*; **ȝeue ; earen ; ȝat(e).**

yateward *n.* gatekeeper 14. 256. [OE *geatweard*] See **ȝate-ward.**

ye(e) ; yede(n) ; yef ; yeft, yefþ. See **ȝe(e) ; eode ; ȝef, ȝeue ; ȝeue.**

yeftte *n.* gift 17.41. [OE *gift* (price of a wife) infl. by **ȝeue**]

yeir ; yeld. See **ȝer(e) ; ȝelde(n).**

yemer(e) *adj.* wretched, grievous 17.124. [OE *gēomor*] See ȝomere.

yemernesse *n.* wretchedness, miserable condition 17.61. [OE *gēomornes(se)*]

yere; yerne; yet; yeue(n); yhernes; yo; yong; you, yu,

yw; youth. See ȝer(e); ȝerne *adv.*; ȝet(e); ȝeue; ȝerne *v.*; heo *pron. fem.*; ȝong(e); ȝe(e); ȝuheðe.

yunder *adv.* yonder, over there 4.188. [prob. OE **geonder*; cf. *geond* and MLG *gender*]

yure. See ȝe(e).

LIST OF NAMES

For names of persons containing *of* or *de* see the word following.

Aaron 17.213.

Abell Abel 14.212.

Abygayl Abigail, wife of King David 2.262.

Abraham 14.290.

Absalones *gen.* of Absalom 18.629.

Adam 2.258, 14.101, 232, 277, 18.455. *gen.* 14.192, 288.

Æðelic Adeliza, later called Matilda 16.5.

Ailmer a friar 5.271.

Alamanie Germany 16.260.

Albamar, Willelm eorl of William of Aumale 16.236.

Aldewingle Aldwinkle, Northamptonshire 16.219.

Alexander bishop of Lincoln 16.151.

Alisaunder Alexander the Great 2.5, 9, &c., -ur 14.3. *gen.* 2.179, 194; Alisaunders 2.122; Alixandres 18.633.

Alle Halwen All Saints' Church 11.155. [OA *alra hǎlgena*, gen. pl.]

Alu(e)red King Alfred 1.265, 431, 443.

Amadase Amadas 14.20.

Andreas, Sancte *gen.* St. Andrew's 16.124; see massedæi.

Angel king of Scotland 10.176.

Angeli. See Iohannis, Sancte.

Angou Anjou 16.261; (the count of) Angæu 294, 306, Angeow 39.

Antigon, Antygon alias of Alexander 2.68, 24.

Arderne, Adam of 11.94 (note).

Argante Morgan le Fay 10.308.

Arður King Arthur 10.5, 8, 11; Arthour 14.9. *gen.* Arðures 10.82, 105. *dat.* Arðure 10.2, 3, 132; Arðuren 143.

Asaeles *gen.* of Asahel 18.631.

Askebert tutor of Kenelm 7.30, 35.

Audelé, Sir Gemes de Sir James of Audley 11.77 (note).

Augusstuss Augustus 13.2.

Austin, Seint St. Augustine 4.200, 18.101, 439, 566.

Aualun Avalon 10.307, 321.

Auelok. See Hauelok.

Balun, Sir Ion de 11.111.

Bartholomew, Sein 18.70, 71.

Bassingbourne, Sir Warin of 11.76.

Bec, the Bec, Normandy 16.247.

Beliales *gen.* Belial's 18.68.

Bernard, Beornard, Sein(t) 18.425, 106.

Bernard the sheriff 4.198, 321.

Besencun Besançon 16.24, 30.

Besile, Sir Maci de 11.3 (note), 8, 27.

Bethleem Bethlehem 17.5, 21; Beþþleæm 13.35, 91. *gen.* Beþþleæmess 13.42, 128.

Beumond Beaumont 11.136 (note), 142.

Blais. See **Stephne.**

Blasfame wife of Candulek 2.59.

Blauncheflour 3.70, 116. *gen.* 206; **Blaunchefloures** 184, **-flours** 222.

Borewenild sister of Kenelm 7.4, 11.

Botolfston Boston, Lincolnshire 6.77.

Brye the country of the Bebryces in Asia Minor 2.3, 57.

Bristowe Bristol 16.257. [OE *Brycgstōw*]

Brumefeld, **Brum(e)sfeld** Brimpsfield, Gloucestershire 11. 87, 82, 98.

Brut Brutus, legendary founder of Britain 14.7.

Brut(t)aine (Great) Britain 10. 94, 136. [OF *Bretaigne*, OE *Bryten*]

Brutlond(e) Britain 10.81, 144. [OE *Brytenlond*]

Burch Peterborough 16.8 (note), 42; **Burhc** 35.

Cadores *gen.* of Cador (earl of Cornwall) 10.298, 302.

Cai Kay, Arthur's seneschal 14.13.

Caim Cain 14.214.

Camelford(e) 10.269, 270.

Candace queen of Sheba 2.135, 195. *gen.* **Candaces** 3, 21, 286.

Candidus younger son of Candace 2.285.

Candulek(e) son of Candace 2.2, 16. *gen.* **Canduleke** 94, **-es** 308.

Cane Cana 17.88.

Cantebyri Canterbury 16.303; (the archbishop of) **Cantwarbyri** 246, **Kaunterburi** 7.199. [OE *Cantwaraburg, -byrig*]

Cesares *gen.* of Caesar (Augustus) 18.633.

Charles Charlemagne 14.15.

Chauntecler a cock 5.37, 46.

Cherubin misunderstood as proper name of an angel 14.109, 167.

Chester 18.229; **Cæstre** (earl of) 16.248. [OE *Lega-ceaster*]

Childrich(e) king of the Saxons 10.135, 137, 144. *gen.* **Childriches** 168. *dat.* **-riche** 141.

Clarice friend of Blauncheflour 3.191, 201. *gen.* 185, **Clarisse** 220.

Clent, Klent Clent, Worcestershire 7.introd., 76, 97, 187.

Clifford, Sir Roger de (of) 11.25, 47, 55, 76.

Clunni Cluny, Burgundy 16.15, 19, 77, 92, 98, **Clunie** 107.

Cokaygn(e), Cokaigne 9.2, 6, 17.

Constantin son of Cador 10.299, **Costæntin** 302.

Cornwale(n) Cornwall 10.224, 247, 256; (the earl of) **Cornwaile** 298, **Cornwalie** 4.150. [OE *Cornwēalas*]

Cotingham Cottingham, Northamptonshire 16.218.

Covbache 'Cow Valley' 7.187, 209, **Cubeche** introd., **Koubache, Kov-** 164, 165, 202. [*kou*+OE *bæce, bece*]

Creasuse *gen.* of Croesus 18.628.

Crist Christ 5.34, 226, 6.332, 365, 8E.82, 12.48, 108, 13.145, 155, 14.80, 15.7, 72 (*dat.*), 16.91, 112, 201, 305, 17.18, 18.464, 19.425. *gen.* **Cristes** 1.389, 16.103, 17.206, **Cristess** 13.262, 263; *for ~ loue* for the love of Christ 5.193. *dat.* **Criste** 5.159, 13.138; *under ~* under heaven, on earth 10.33. See **Iesu.**

Curbuil, Willelm William of Corbeil, archbishop of Canterbury 16.134, 245.

Dalida Delilah 2.260.

Darie a burgess of Babylon (i.e. Old Cairo) 3.75, 142.

borough 16.105; **Heanri** 8, 12, 75, 87.

Henri bishop of Winchester, brother of King Stephen 16.263.

Henri, Sir Sir Henry de Montfort, son of Simon 11.123.

Hereforde Hereford 11.51.

Herodes Herod 17.13, 14, 20, 25.

Hirtan, duke 2.57, 93.

Hyrtlingbyri Irthlingborough, Northamptonshire 16.219.

Howel king of Brittany 10.98 (note).

Hubert the man in the moon 8N.37.

Humber the Humber 4.1. *dat.* **Humbre** 10.142.

Huwe Rauen son of Grim 4.295; Hwe 305.

Ydoine 14.20.

Yndare (unidentified) 2.56.

Ynde India 2.323, 8H.12.

Ingland. See **Englond.**

Ioneck Yonec 14.19.

Irlond(e) Ireland 1.539, 8H.12, 10.248. [OE *Írland*]

Ysaie Isaiah 18.584.

Ysambrase Isumbras 14.19.

Ysote Isolde 14.17.

Iame, Sein St. James 18.110.

Ianekyn Johnny (of London) 8P.1.

Ieremie Jeremiah 18.517, 557.

Ierome, Sein St. Jerome18.357.

Ierusalem Jerusalem 2.56, 17. 12, 16, 88; **3errsalæm** 13.33.

Iesu Jesus 8T.30, U.1, 5, W.41, 51, 18.153, 321, 397, 504; ~ **Crist** 7.177, 8W.11, x.9, 12.46, 13.87, 15.32 (*dat.*), 17.77, 18.45, 240, 19.266, 330; ~ **Godd** 18.126; **Iesus Crist** 17.90. *gen.* **Iesu Cristes** 18.201, 320, 536. See **Crist.**

Ihon, Ione, Sant St. John (the Apostle) 15.13, 27.

Iohan John, a scribe 19.422.

Iohannis, Sancte *gen.* of St.

John (the Baptist) 16.81 (see **massedæi**); ~ (*minstre*) **of Angeli** St.-Jean-d'Angély, south-west of Poitiers 16.9, 23, 94.

Iosæp Joseph 13.28, 130.

Iudas Judas 18.321. *gen.* **Iudase** 320.

Iuhan, Sein St. John (author of the Book of Revelation) 18.582, 657.

Iuly Cesar Julius Caesar 14.4.

Iulienes *gen.* of Julian (the Apostate) 18.65.

Karliun Caerleon on Usk 10. 239.

Kaunterburi. See **Cantebyri.**

Kenelm, Seint 7.introd., 3, 9. *gen.* **Kenelmes** 195, 217, 250.

Kenulf king of Mercia 7.2, 6.

Kinges Halle 11.131 (note).

Kingestone, Nicole of Nicholas of Kingston, mayor of Oxford 11.146.

Koubache, Kov-. See **Covbache.**

Leibourne, Sir Roger of Sir Roger Leyburn 11.78 (note).

Leycestre Leicester 8H.30. [OE *Ligera ceaster*]

Leonard (St.) 15.7.

Leouenaðes *gen.* 10.introd.

Lincolne, Lyn- Lincoln 4.41, 115,130, 8M.17; **Lincol** 16.251, (bishop of) 110, 151. [OE *Lindcolne*]

Lincolneschire 6.78.

Lindeseye, Lyn- Lindsey 4.2, 8M.17.

Lounde Lound, Lincolnshire or Nottinghamshire 8H.30, M.17.

Lundene London 10.188, 16.41, 133, 261, 319, 18.229; **Londone** 8P.1. [OE *Lunden-burg*]

Mærlin. See **Merlin.**

Malduit, Willelm 16.217.